Law in a Therapeutic Key

CAROLINA ACADEMIC PRESS
Studies in Law and Psychology

David B. Wexler
Editorial Advisor

The Law of Deprivation of Liberty
Fred Cohen

Law and Psychology
The Broadening of the Discipline
James R.P. Ogloff, Editor

The Jurisprudence of the Insanity Defense
Michael L. Perlin

Mental Health and Law
Research, Policy and Services
Bruce D. Sales and Saleem A. Shah

Guardianship
The Court of Last Resort for the Elderly and Disabled
Winsor C. Schmidt

Therapeutic Jurisprudence
The Law as a Therapeutic Agent
David B. Wexler

Essays in Therapeutic Jurisprudence
David B. Wexler and Bruce J. Winick

Law in a Therapeutic Key
Developments in Therapeutic Jurisprudence
David B. Wexler and Bruce J. Winick

Therapeutic Jurisprudence Applied
Essays on Mental Health Law
Bruce J. Winick

Law in a Therapeutic Key

Developments in Therapeutic Jurisprudence

David B. Wexler

Bruce J. Winick

CAROLINA ACADEMIC PRESS

Durham, North Carolina

ISBN 0-89089-988-6
LCCN 96-85943

Carolina Academic Press
700 Kent Street
Durham, North Carolina 27701

Telephone (919) 489-7486
Fax (919) 493-5668

Printed in the United States of America

Cover design by Jayne Holsinger

To my brother, Jim,
and my little granddaughter,
Mimi "Minnie Mousekovitz" Bolaños
D.B.W.

To my mom, Deborah,
for her 80th birthday
B.J.W.

Contents

II.   Commentary about Therapeutic Jurisprudence

III.   Empirical Explorations

Acknowledgments

It has once again been a great pleasure for us to publish with the Carolina Academic Press. We are delighted to have this volume included in the Carolina Academic Press Collection in Law and Psychology. Our heartfelt thanks to Keith Sipe, president, and to Tim Colton, Greta Strittmatter, Miranda Bailey, and Mabel Winston.

For their encouragement and support of his work in therapeutic jurisprudence, Professor Wexler thanks Dean Joel Seligman of the University of Arizona College of Law, former University of Arizona Deans Tom Sullivan (now Dean at the University of Minnesota Law School) and Paul Marcus (now Haynes Professor of Law at William and Mary), and Dean Antonio Garcia Padilla of the University of Puerto Rico School of Law.

Professor Winick would like to thank former Dean Mary Doyle and Associate Dean Patrick O. Gudridge of the University of Miami School of Law, as well as present Dean Samuel C. Thompson, Jr., and Vice Dean Laurence M. Rose, for their encouragement and support of this work through their grant to him of a University of Miami School of Law Scholar-in-Residence award.

For research assistance in the preparation of this volume, we deeply appreciate the efforts of Mariclare Hannah, Val Schaffer, Kathryn Maxwell, and Todd McKay at the University of Arizona, and of Douglas Stransky and Bill Collins at the University of Miami. For secretarial assistance, we are deeply indebted to Cynthia Lyons at Miami, and to Kay Clark, Norma Kelly, Rebecca Scheibley, and F. Ellen "Granny" Beerdsen at Arizona.

The core of the volume, of course, consists of scholarship in or about therapeutic jurisprudence written by a number of authors. We are most grateful to them and their publishers for enabling us to use the works in this book. In their order of appearance, they are:

Chapter 1 (Tom R. Tyler)—"The Psychological Consequences of Judicial Procedures: Implications for Civil Commitment Hearings," Southern Methodist University Law Review, Volume 46, pp. 433–445, (1992).

Chapter 2 (Bruce J. Winick)—"The Side Effects of Incompetency Labeling and the Implications for Mental Health Law," Psychology, Public Policy, and Law, Volume 1, pp. 6–42. Copyright © 1995 by the American Psychological Association. Reprinted with permission.

Chapter 3 (Michael L. Perlin)—"(How) Can We Make the Incoherent Coherent?" Reprinted from *The Jurisprudence of the Insanity Defense*, Chapter Nine, pp. 417–437, Carolina Academic Press, (1994).

Chapter 4 (Bruce J. Winick)—"Incompetency to Proceed in the Criminal Process: Past, Present, and Future," pp. 310–340. Reprinted from *Law, Mental Health, and Mental Disorder*, edited by B. Sales & D. Shuman. Copyright © 1996 Brooks/Cole Publishing Company, Pacific Grove, CA 93950, a division of International Thomson Publishing Inc.

Chapter 5 (Richard Barnum and Thomas Grisso)—"Competence to Stand

Trial in Juvenile Court in Massachusetts: Issues of Therapeutic Jurisprudence,"
New England Journal on Criminal and Civil Confinement, Volume 20, pp
321–344. © Copyright New England School of Law 1994. All rights reserved.
Reprinted by permission.

Chapter 6 (Jeffrey A. Klotz)—"Sex Offenders and the Law: New Directions," from *Mental Health and Law: Research, Policy, and Services*, pages
257–282, edited by Bruce D. Sales and Saleem A. Shah, Carolina Academic
Press, (1996).

Chapter 7 (David B. Wexler)—"Some Therapeutic Jurisprudence Implications of the Outpatient Civil Commitment of Pregnant Substance Abusers,"
Politics and the Life Sciences, Volume 15, pp. 73–75 (1996).

Chapter 8 (Fred Cohen and Joel A. Dvoskin)—"Therapeutic Jurisprudence
and Corrections: A Glimpse," New York Law School Journal of Human
Rights, Volume 10, pp. 777–804, (1993).

Chapter 9 (David B. Wexler)—"Therapeutic Jurisprudence and the Criminal
Courts," William & Mary Law Review, Volume 35, pp. 279–299, (1993).

Chapter 10 (Keri A. Gould)—"Turning Rat and Doing Time for Uncharged,
Dismissed, or Acquitted Crimes: Do the Federal Sentencing Guidelines Pro-
mote Respect for the Law?" New York Law School Journal of Human Rights,
Volume 10, pp. 835–875, (1993).

Chapter 11 (Judge Robert J. Kane)—"A Sentencing Model for the 21st Century," from Federal Probation, A Journal of Correctional Philosophy and Practice, pp. 10–15, published by the Administrative Office of the United States
Courts, Washington, DC 20544 (September, 1995).

Chapter 12 (Richard P. Wiebe)—"The Mental Health Implications of Crime
Victims' Rights," pp. 414–438. Reprinted from *Law, Mental Health, and Men-
tal Disorder* edited by B. Sales & D. Shuman. Copyright 1996 Brooks/Cole
Publishing Company, Pacific Grove, CA 93950, a division of International
Thomson Publishing Inc.

Chapter 13 (Leonore M. J. Simon)—"A Therapeutic Jurisprudence Approach to the Legal Processing of Domestic Violence Cases," Psychology, Public Policy, and Law, Volume 1, pp. 43–79. Copyright © (1995) by the American Psychological Association. Adapted with permission.

Chapter 14 (Allison R. Shiff and David B. Wexler)—"Teen Court: A Therapeutic Jurisprudence Perspective," Criminal Law Bulletin, Volume 32, pp.
342–357, (1996).

Chapter 15 (Daniel W. Shuman)—"The Duty of the State to Rescue the Vulnerable in the United States," pp. 131–158. Reprinted with permission from
The Duty to Rescue: The Jurisprudence of Aid, edited by Michael A. Menlowe
and Alexander McCall Smith. Copyright 1993, Dartmouth Publishing Company.

Chapter 16 (Murray Levine)—"A Therapeutic Jurisprudence Analysis of
Mandated Reporting of Child Maltreatment by Psychotherapists," New York
Law School Journal of Human Rights, Volume 10, pp. 711–738, (1993).

Chapter 17 (Kay Kavanagh)—"Don't Ask, Don't Tell: Deception Required,
Disclosure Denied," Psychology, Public Policy, and Law, Volume 1, pp.
142–160. Copyright © (1995) by the American Psychological Association.
Adapted with permission.

Chapter 18 (Rose Daly-Rooney)—"Designing Reasonable Accommodations through Co-Worker Participation: Therapeutic Jurisprudence and the Confidentiality Provision of the Americans with Disabilities Act," Journal of Law and Health, Volume 8, pp. 89–104, (1994).

Chapter 19 (Bruce J. Winick)—"Rethinking the Health Care Delivery Crisis: The Need for a Therapeutic Jurisprudence," Journal of Law and Health, Volume 7, pp. 49–54, (1993).

Chapter 20 (Daniel W. Shuman)—"Therapeutic Jurisprudence and Tort Law: A Limited Subjective Standard of Care," Southern Methodist University Law Review, Volume 46, pp.409–432, (1992).

Chapter 21 (Grant H. Morris)—"Requiring Sound Judgments of Unsound Minds: Tort Liability and the Limits of Therapeutic Jurisprudence," Southern Methodist University Law Review, Volume 47, pp. 1837–1860, (1994).

Chapter 22 (Daniel W. Shuman)—"The Psychology of Compensation in Tort Law," University of Kansas Law Review, Volume 43, pp. 39–77, (1994).

Chapter 23 (Jeffrey A. Klotz)—"Limiting the Psychotherapist-Patient Privilege: The Therapeutic Potential," Criminal Law Bulletin, Volume 27, pp. 416–432, (1991).

Chapter 24 (Bruce J. Winick)—"The Psychotherapist-Patient Privilege: A Therapeutic Jurisprudence View," University of Miami Law Review, Volume 50, pp. 249–265, (January, 1996).

Chapter 25 (Roger I. Abrams, Frances E. Abrams, and Dennis R. Nolan)—"Arbitral Therapy," Rutgers Law Review, Volume 46, pp. 1751–1785, (1994).

Chapter 26 (Jeffrey L. Harrison)—"Class, Personality, Contract, and Unconscionability," William & Mary Law Review, Volume 35, pp. 445–501, (1994).

Chapter 27 (Amiram Elwork and G. Andrew H. Benjamin)—"Lawyers in Distress," Journal of Psychology & Law, Volume 23, pp. 205–229 (1995). Reprinted by permission of Federal Legal Publications, Inc.

Chapter 28 (David Finkelman and Thomas Grisso)—"Therapeutic Jurisprudence: From Idea to Application," New England Journal on Criminal and Civil Confinement, Volume 20, pp. 243–257. © Copyright New England School of Law, 1994. All rights reserved. Reprinted by permission.

Chapter 29 (David B. Wexler)—"Therapeutic Jurisprudence and Changing Conceptions of Legal Scholarship," Behavioral Sciences and the Law, Volume 11, pp. 17–29. Reprinted by permission of John Wiley & Sons, Ltd., Copyright © 1993.

Chapter 30 (Mark A. Small)—"Legal Psychology and Therapeutic Jurisprudence," Saint Louis University Law Journal, Volume 37, pp. 675–700, (1993).

Chapter 31 (David Carson and David B. Wexler)—"New Approaches to Mental Health Law: Will the UK Follow the US Lead, Again?" The Journal of Social Welfare and Family Law, Number One, pp. 79–96, (1994). Reprinted by permission of Routledge, International Thomson Publishing Services.

Chapter 32 (Bruce J. Winick)—A slightly different version of "The Jurisprudence of Therapeutic Jurisprudence," Psychology, Public Policy, and Law, Volume 2, (in press, 1996).

Chapter 33 (Joel Haycock)—"Speaking Truth to Power: Rights, Therapeutic Jurisprudence, and Massachusetts Mental Health Law," New England Journal on Criminal and Civil Confinement, Volume 20, pp. 301–320. © Copyright New England School of Law, 1994. All rights reserved. Reprinted by permission.

Chapter 34 (John Petrila)—"Paternalism and the Unrealized Promise of *Essays in Therapeutic Jurisprudence*," New York Law School Journal of Human Rights, Volume 10, pp. 877–905, (1993).

Chapter 35 (David B. Wexler and Bruce J. Winick)—"Patients, Professionals, and the Path of Therapeutic Jurisprudence: A Response to Petrila," New York Law School Journal of Human Rights, Volume 10, pp. 907–914, (1993).

Chapter 36 (David B. Wexler)—"Justice, Mental Health, and Therapeutic Jurisprudence," Cleveland State Law Review, Volume 40, pp. 517–526, (1992).

Chapter 37 (Robert F. Schopp)—"Therapeutic Jurisprudence and Conflicts among Values in Mental Health Law," Behavioral Sciences and the Law, Volume 11, pp. 31–45. Reprinted by permission of John Wiley & Sons, Ltd., Copyright © 1993.

Chapter 38 (Michael L. Perlin, Keri K. Gould, and Deborah A. Dorfman)—"Therapeutic Jurisprudence and the Civil Rights of Institutionalized Mentally Disabled Persons: Hopeless Oxymoron or Path to Redemption?" Psychology, Public Policy, and Law, Volume 1, pp. 80–119. Copyright © 1995 by the American Psychological Association. Adapted with permission.

Chapter 39 (Christopher Slobogin)—"Therapeutic Jurisprudence: Five Dilemmas to Ponder," Psychology, Public Policy, and Law, Volume 1, pp. 193–219. Copyright © 1995 by the American Psychological Association. Adapted with permission.

Chapter 40 (Bruce D. Sales and Daniel W. Shuman)—"The Newly Emerging Mental Health Law," pp. 2–14. Reprinted from *Law, Mental Health, and Mental Disorder* by B. Sales & D. Shuman. Copyright © 1996 Brooks/Cole Publishing Company, Pacific Grove, CA 93950, a division of International Thomson Publishing Inc.

Chapter 41 (David B. Wexler)—"Reflections on the Scope of Therapeutic Jurisprudence," Psychology, Public Policy, and Law, Volume 1, pp. 220–236. Copyright © 1995 by the American Psychological Association. Adapted with permission.

Chapter 42 (David B. Wexler)—"Applying the Law Therapeutically," Applied and Preventive Psychology, Volume 5, (1996). Copyright © 1996 American Association of Applied and Preventive Psychology (AAAPP). Reprinted with the permission of Cambridge University Press.

Chapter 43 (Bruce Feldthusen)—"The Civil Action for Sexual Battery: Therapeutic Jurisprudence?" Ottawa Law Review, Volume 25, pp. 205–234, (1993).

Chapter 44 (Norman G. Poythress and Stanley L. Brodsky)—"In the Wake of a Negligent Release Law Suit: An Investigation of Professional Consequences and Institutional Impact on a State Psychiatric Hospital," Law and Human Behavior, Volume 16, pp. 155–173. Copyright 1992 by Plenum Publishing Corporation.

Chapter 45 (Elizabeth Anderson, Murray Levine, Anupama Sharma, Louise Feretti, Karen Steinberg, Leah Wallach)—"Coercive Uses of Mandatory Reporting in Therapeutic Relationships," Behavioral Sciences and the Law, Volume 11, pp. 335–347. Reprinted by permission of John Wiley & Sons, Ltd., Copyright © 1993.

Chapter 46 (Jack Susman)—"Resolving Hospital Conflicts: A Study on

Therapeutic Jurisprudence," Journal of Psychiatry & Law, Volume 22, pp. 107–133, (1994). Reprinted by permission of Federal Legal Publications, Inc.

Chapter 47 (Alexander Greer, Mary O'Regan, and Amy Traverso)—"Therapeutic Jurisprudence and Patients' Perceptions of Procedural Due Process of Civil Commitment Hearings." This chapter was prepared specifically for this volume. At the time this research was conducted, Alexander Greer, J.D./M.A., was Assistant Professor of Law & Psychiatry in the Department of Psychiatry at the University of Massachusetts Medical Center in Worcester, Massachusetts. He is now Associate Professor of Psychiatry at the University of Toronto and Senior Researcher and Head of the Law and Psychiatry Program at the Clarke Institute of Psychiatry in Toronto, Ontario, Canada. Mary O'Regan, Ph.D., is Assistant Professor of Psychiatry in the Department of Psychiatry at the University of Massachusetts Medical Center. Amy Traverso, B.A., was Research Assistant in the Department of Psychiatry at the University of Massachusetts Medical Center.

Chapter 48 (Julie Magno Zito, Josef Vitrai, and Thomas J. Craig)—"Toward a Therapeutic Jurisprudence Analysis of Medication Refusal in the Court Review Model," Behavioral Sciences and the Law, Volume 11, pp. 151–163. Reprinted by permission of John Wiley & Sons, Ltd., Copyright © 1993.

Chapter 49 (Daniel W. Shuman, Jean A. Hamilton, and Cynthia E. Daley)—"The Health Effects of Jury Service," Law and Psychology Review, Volume 18, pp. 267–307, (1994).

Chapter 50 (Kim A. Kamin and Jeffrey J. Rachlinski)—"Ex Post ≠ Ex Ante: Determining Liability in Hindsight," Law and Human Behavior, Volume 19, pp. 89–103. Copyright 1995 by Plenum Publishing Corporation.

Introduction

This is a book of and about therapeutic jurisprudence. Therapeutic jurisprudence is the study of the role of the law as a therapeutic agent. It is an interdisciplinary enterprise designed to produce scholarship that is particularly useful for law reform. Therapeutic jurisprudence proposes the exploration of ways in which, consistent with principles of justice, the knowledge, theories, and insights of the mental health and related disciplines can help *shape* the development of the law. Slobogin said it well when he defined therapeutic jurisprudence as "the use of social science to study the extent to which a legal rule or practice promotes the psychological or physical well-being of the people it affects" (this volume, p. 775).

The therapeutic jurisprudence heuristic suggests that the law itself can be seen to function as a kind of therapist or therapeutic agent. Legal rules, legal procedures, and the roles of legal actors (such as lawyers and judges) constitute social forces that , like it or not, often produce therapeutic or antitherapeutic consequences. Therapeutic jurisprudence proposes that we be sensitive to those consequences, and that we ask whether the law's antitherapeutic consequences can be reduced, and its therapeutic consequences enhanced, without subordinating due process and other justice values.

Therapeutic jurisprudence does not suggest that therapeutic considerations should trump other considerations. Therapeutic consequences are merely one category of important factors that should be taken into account. Others include individual autonomy, integrity of the fact-finding process, community safety, and efficiency and economy. Therapeutic jurisprudence does not purport to resolve the questions of what should be done when values conflict; instead, it sets the stage for their sharp articulation. In addition, the therapeutic jurisprudence lens enables the identification of questions in need of empirical research. Speculation about the therapeutic consequences of various legal arrangements or law reform proposals can itself be useful, but empirical research is often necessary to determine whether the law actually operates in the way that theory assumes.

Although it uses the tools of the mental health disciplines, as a field of inquiry therapeutic jurisprudence is by no means confined narrowly to mental health law. Nor is it a law/psychology or a law/mental health smorgasbord. Rather, therapeutic jurisprudence is a conceptual framework that brings together a number of topics that have not generally been recognized as related: how the criminal justice system might traumatize victims of sexual battery (chapter 43), how workers' compensation laws might create the moral hazard of prolonging work-related injury[1], how a fault-based (rather than a no-fault) tort compensation scheme might enhance recovery from personal injury (chapter 22), and how the current law of contracts might operate to reinforce the low self-esteem of disadvantaged contracting parties (chapter 26).

---

1. William E. Wilkinson, Therapeutic Jurisprudence and Workers' Compensation, Arizona Attorney, April, 1994, at 28.

Many developments have occurred in the area of therapeutic jurisprudence in the five short years since we published *Essays in Therapeutic Jurisprudence* (Carolina Academic Press 1991). First, many scholars—more than seventy—have now contributed to the growing body of therapeutic jurisprudence literature. These scholars come not only from the fields of law and psychology (where the great bulk of the work has been done), but also from psychiatry,[2] criminology,[3] and philosophy.[4] Therapeutic jurisprudence work has proliferated in law reviews and interdisciplinary journals, and has been the subject of several conferences and special issues of law journals.[5] Second, therapeutic jurisprudence has developed from a lens for examining mental health law[6] to a therapeutic approach to the law as a whole, as we had anticipated and hoped for in *Essays* (p. x):

> It seems only natural (at least to those of us who specialize in mental health law) that initial forays into therapeutic jurisprudence take place within the core content areas of mental health law. Obviously, however, therapeutic jurisprudence will also have applications in forensic psychiatry generally, in health law, in a variety of allied legal fields (criminal law, juvenile law, family law), and probably across the entire legal spectrum.

Third, the original work has provoked a second generation of therapeutic jurisprudence scholarship—commentary *about* therapeutic jurisprudence itself: explanations, assessments, proposals for development, and critiques. Fourth, the difficult empirical work that is an essential feature of the therapeutic jurisprudence project has began to occur. Fifth, therapeutic jurisprudence has struck a responsive chord with certain members of the judiciary.[7] Finally, therapeutic jurisprudence is beginning to attract the attention of scholars and professionals in other countries,[8] and this emerging comparative law approach, suggested by us in *Essays* (p.320), will surely enrich the field.

---

2. This volume, chapter 5. See also Robert L. Sadoff, Therapeutic Jurisprudence: A View from a Forensic Psychiatrist, 10 New York Law School Journal of Human Rights 825 (1993); Douglas Mossman, Veterans Affairs Disability Compensation: A Case Study in Countertherapeutic Jurisprudence, 24 Bulletin of the American Academy of Psychiatry and Law 27 (1996).

3. This volume, chapter 46.

4. This volume, chapter 37. See also Deborah Mathieu, Mandating Treatment for Pregnant Substance Abusers: A Compromise, 14 Politics and the Life Sciences 199 (1995).

5. Special Theme: Therapeutic Jurisprudence, 1 Psychology, Public Policy, and Law (March 1995); Symposium, Therapeutic Jurisprudence: Bridging the Gap From Theory to Practice, 20 New England Journal on Criminal and Civil Confinement (Summer 1994); Symposium, Therapeutic Jurisprudence: Restructuring Mental Disability Law, 10 New York Law School Journal of Human Rights (No. 3 1993). See also Special Section, Mental Health Law and Mental Health Care, 64 American Journal of Orthopsychiatry (April 1994).

6. For a therapeutic jurisprudence analysis of the field of mental health law, see Bruce J. Winick, Therapeutic Jurisprudence Applied: Essays on Mental Health Law (Carolina Academic Press) (in press).

7. This volume, chapter 11. See also Judge Jack Lehman, The Movement Toward Therapeutic Jurisprudence: An Inside Look at the Origin and Operation of America's First Drug Courts, 10 NJC Alumni 13 (Spring 1995).

8. This volume, chapters 31 and 43. See also David Carson, Therapeutic Jurisprudence for the United Kingdom?, 6 Journal of Forensic Psychiatry 433 (1995).

The present effort is designed to capture and consolidate these developments in a single volume. The book contains theoretical and empirical pieces across a wide substantive law spectrum, and includes the contributions of academics and professionals (including the judiciary) from many different disciplines. Moreover, although the overwhelming majority of contributors are American, specialists in British (chapter 31) and Canadian (chapter 43) law are also represented.

The expanding legal breadth of therapeutic jurisprudence is the topic of Part One of this volume—The Wide-Angle Lens of Therapeutic Jurisprudence. Therapeutic jurisprudence was originally developed within the "core" content areas of mental health law. Accordingly, much therapeutic jurisprudence writing related to—and continues to relate to—matters such as the civil commitment of the mentally ill, the insanity defense, and incompetency in both civil and criminal contexts. The first five selections in Part One track those civil and criminal mental health law themes.

The remainder of Part One, however, consists of therapeutic jurisprudence scholarship that has rippled out from mental health law to other fields of law. These selections should give the reader an appreciation of how therapeutic jurisprudence has developed into a therapeutic perspective on the law in general.

Thus, following the chapters relating to conventional mental health law, we proceed with two pieces on "quasi" mental health law: one relating to the commitment of so-called "sexual psychopaths," and the other relating to the outpatient civil commitment of drug abusers. Following that, the readings turn to correctional law, and then to criminal law and procedure, including the law of sentencing, which is viewed from the perspectives of a trial judge (chapter 11) and of a defense lawyer turned clinical law professor (chapter 10). The criminal law portion ends with a chapter on the rights of crime victims.

After that, there is a chapter on domestic violence, which in many respects is a substantive transition between criminal law and family law. Following that essay are three chapters in the family and juvenile law area. We then include chapters relating to sexual orientation law, disability law, health law, and personal injury and tort law (looking at the therapeutic impact of the law both on injured plaintiffs as well as on actual or potential tort defendants). Following two chapters on the law of evidence, the Part closes with three selections that are among the broadest extensions to date of the therapeutic jurisprudence perspective.[9] One of them relates to therapeutic aspects of labor arbitration law, and one relates to contracts and commercial law, and the final one deals with how the law itself may contribute to the stress suffered by many menbers of the legal profession.

Part Two, Commentary About Therapeutic Jurisprudence, consists not of essays *in* therapeutic jurisprudence (which was the province of Part One), but instead of essays *on* or *about* therapeutic jurisprudence. We believe this "scholarship about scholarship" is useful in giving us a better understanding of what therapeutic jurisprudence is, where it came from, what problems it must confront, and where it might or should lead. The Part begins with an overview of

---

9. See also Patricia Monroe Wisnom, Probate Law and Mediation: A Therapeutic Perspective, 37 Arizona Law Review 1345 (1995).

therapeutic jurisprudence and its development, including an assessment of its potential in the United Kingdom. Then, several selections deal with the crucial justice/rights questions faced by therapeutic jurisprudence. Following what is in our view the best assessment and critique of therapeutic jurisprudence to date—the chapter by Slobogin—the Part closes with a discussion of some newly developing therapeutic jurisprudence issues and avenues, such as the field's growing emphasis on the therapeutic application of existing law.

Finally, in Part Three, Empirical Explorations, the volume includes the empirical work that has been performed to date relating to therapeutic jurisprudence. Comparing Part One with Part Three will provide the reader with an immediate understanding of the wide gap between therapeutic jurisprudence theorizing and the empirical testing of the assumptions underlying such theorizing. The chapters in this Part are more or less organized along a continuum that goes from more exploratory pieces to ones employing more complex methodologies. We hope this Part will give readers a glimpse of what has been done and will encourage them to begin more extensive empirical investigation. This Part may also be used to introduce students in law and in the behavioral sciences to social science methodology and to the trials and tribulations of social science research.

By illustrating the potential that therapeutic jurisprudence holds as a research tool, we hope that this Part also will encourage graduate students in the social and behavioral sciences to see the legal system as a natural laboratory for empirical research. In this way, this volume may help graduate students focus their research agendas, and it may provide grist for the mill of dissertation topics.

Indeed, we hope the book as a whole will suggest many issues that may be tested empirically, and will provide jumping off points for future research and scholarship. The book is addressed to academics, practitioners, and students in a number of disciplines, among them law, psychology, psychiatry, social work, criminal justice and corrections, and public health. We hope it will stimulate thought, further scholarship, and needed law reform.

I.
The Wide-Angle Lens
of Therapeutic
Jurisprudence

Chapter 1

The Psychological Consequences of Judicial Procedures: Implications for Civil Commitment Hearings

Tom R. Tyler

A key Supreme Court decision regarding involuntary civil commitment hearings is *Parham v. J.R.*[1] In *Parham,* the Supreme Court ruled that minors are not entitled to a hearing prior to involuntary admission into a state mental hospital because state psychiatrists, those otherwise responsible for making the admissions decision, could act as a "neutral factfinder."[2]

The identification of "neutral factfinding" as the criterion against which to evaluate the adequacy of judicial hearings is consistent with the legal literature on procedures. That literature typically focuses on issues such as bias, honesty, and expertise.[3] These aspects are regarded as important because they are believed to influence the ability of a procedure to reach an objectively correct outcome.[4]

An important question in determining the balance of authority in commitment hearings is whether the procedural safeguards can assure neutral factfinding.[5] In commitment hearings authority can be given to professional and/or to judicial decision-makers. Professional authority refers to the discretion given to psychiatrists or psychologists to determine mental competence, usually based on tests and interviews with the person whose competence is in question.[6] Judicial authority refers to similar discretion given to judges, typically exercised through some form of judical hearing.[7]

If the key concern in devising commitment procedures is determining the true mental state of the person in order to make the best decision about com-

---

1. 442 U.S. 584 (1979). *Parham* was not the first case to consider the therapeutic consequences of commitment hearings for juveniles. For a review of the history of laws governing the parental commitment of minors, see J.W. Ellis, Volunteering Children: Parental Commitment of Minors to Mental Institutions, 62 Cal. L. Rev. 840–916 (1974).

2. *Parham,* 442 U.S. at 606–07.

3. See Tom R. Tyler, Why People Obey the Law 6–7 (1990).

4. Id.

5. Donald N. Bersoff, Judicial Deference to Nonlegal Decisionmakers: Imposing Simplistic Solutions on Problems of Cognitive Complexity in Mental Disability Law, 46 SMU L. Rev. 329 (1992).

6. Id.

7. Id. One important difference between these two procedures is that judicial hearings involve due process rights, while professional evaluations do not.

mitment, then this balance of authority should be shaped by evaluations of the capabilities of professional and judicial decision-makers.[8] Recent research has documented many errors in clinical decision-making, suggesting that judicial decision-making might be beneficial.[9] If future studies that directly compare the relative error rates in clinical and judicial decision-making suggest that judicial hearings are more accurate, or lead to more desirable errors,[10] those findings would support the use of judicial hearings.

It is also possible to draw potential criteria for evaluating commitment procedures from a different set of criteria used for evaluating legal procedures. These alternative criteria have been articulated by the Supreme Court. In *Goldberg v. Kelley*[11] the Supreme Court argued that welfare recipients are entitled to a hearing of a particular type before their welfare benefits are terminated.[12] Although primarily concerned with issues of accuracy, the Court also recognized that termination without a hearing could be psychologically harmful, potentially damaging feelings of security, dignity, and self-worth.[13] In other cases dealing with the due process rights of students and prisoners, the Court similarly identified the possible psychological harm of experiencing unfair procedures as a reason for granting rights to a hearing.[14]

The potential consequences of the psychological harm of experiencing unfair hearings is articulated most clearly in *Morrissey v. Brewer*.[15] In *Morrissey* the Court indicated that prisoners should be given judicial hearings because denying them due process could cause them psychological harm (i.e. would be antitherapeutic) and thus undermine their rehabilitation.[16]

These decisions are important because the courts recognize the importance of considering the psychological impact of judicial procedures on those experiencing the procedures. This impact is distinct from the desire for a neutral, fact-finding expert, such as a judge or a psychiatrist, who is expected to reach accurate decisions.[17] When conceptualized this way, due process involves giving people judicial procedures that they will perceive as fair.

---

8. Id.

9. See John Monahan & Laurens Walker, Social Science in Law: Cases and Materials (1st ed. 1985).

10. It is important to recognize that the total amount of error in a procedure is not the only criteria for its evaluation. The legal system deems some types of error to be more unacceptable than others. For example, falsely committing a sane peson might be viewed as a more serious error than falsely releasing an insane person.

11. 397 U.S. 254 (1970).

12. Id. at 264.

13. Id. at 264–66.

14. See, e.g., Morrissey v. Brewer, 408 U.S. 471, 472 (1972) (addressing whether the "Due Process Clause of the Fourteenth Amendment requires that a State afford an individual some opportunity to be heard prior to revoking his parole").

15. 408 U.S. 471 (1972).

16. Id. at 484. Some state courts have also recognized similar interests of individuals. For example, the California Supreme Court discussed those interests in People v. Ramirez, 599 P.2d 622 (Cal. 1979).

17. See Parham v. J.R., 442 U.S. 584, 606 (1979).

The law concerning the use of civil commitment hearings to determine mental competence has varied greatly in the degree that it has suggested that people are entitled to judicial hearings. In the past, such hearings, like those involving prisoners, welfare recipients, and students, were often conducted with minimal attention to issues of due process.[18] The introduction of what David Wexler labelled "libertarian commitment codes" has heightened concerns about the due process rights of those involved in involuntary commitment procedures.[19] Protection of those rights requires some form of judicial determination prior to commitment.[20]

Discussions about the appropriate degree of judicial due process that should be involved in commitment procedures raise the question of whether attention to due process rights is wise. Attention to these rights increases judicial authority at the expense of professional authority. Addressing this question involves attention to both the objective quality of professional and judicial commitment procedures and to their psychological consequences. This discussion will focus on the psychological consequences of commitment hearings—i.e. on the therapeutic effects of the commitment process.[21] One potential benefit of judicial hearings is that they result in objectively better outcomes. In addition, they may be psychologically beneficial to the person whose conduct is under review.

I. How People Are Affected by Judicial Hearings

The first issue to be addressed is whether the type of judicial process that people experience influences them independently of the outcome of those procedures. In other words, are there things about a commitment hearing that affect people psychologically but are unrelated to the outcome of the procedure? Does the process itself have therapeutic implications? Legal psychologists have studied a wide variety of decision-making procedures, including jury trials, mediation hearings, arbitration hearings, settlement conferences, informal police-citizen interactions, and plea bargaining hearings, in an effort to understand what determines how people react to their dealings with legal authorities.[22] Unfortunately, there are currently no direct examinations of commitment hearings. Nonetheless, the findings of these other studies have important implications for such hearings.

---

18. See David Wexler, Therapeutic Jurisprudence: The Law as a Therapeutic Agent (1990).

19. Id. at 165–87.

20. Id.

21. There is a large body of psychological literature dealing with the objective quality of the decisions reached through varying legal procedures, in particular the use of different types of juries. That literature will not be addressed in this paper. See Bersoff, supra note 5; John Monahan & Laurens Walker, Social Science in Law: Cases and Materials 79 (2d ed. 1990).

22. See E. Allan Lind & Tom R. Tyler, The Social Psychology of Procedural Justice (1988).

The psychological perspective on judicial hearings builds on the classic research of psychologist John Thibaut and attorney Laurens Walker.[23] Their studies examined how people evaluated the adversary and the inquisitorial trial procedures.[24] Their research focused on procedural preferences, specifically the types of trial procedures that people wanted to use to settle their disputes.[25]

The work of Thibaut and Walker stimulated a number of studies on the psychological consequences of personal experiences with legal authorities.[26] Of particular relevance are studies on the psychological consequences of participating in various aspects of the judicial system.[27] This body of work examines how people react to legal procedures after they have experienced them.[28] It differs from the work of Thibaut and Walker in its reactive character. Instead of choosing a procedure prior to experiencing it (i.e. expressing a preference), people react to a procedure that they have already experienced. Thus, they indicate their degree of satisfaction with the procedure used to deal with their problem.

Subsequent studies also differ from the work of Thibaut and Walker by placing greater weight on the study of real disputes.[29] The original Thibaut and Walker research utilized laboratory experimentation methods that were heavily criticized by the legal community.[30] The studies that will be examined here involve either surveys of people reporting on their personal experiences with judicial procedures or field studies of variations in legal procedures. Field studies of this type also involve an examination of people who have actually experienced different types of judicial proceedings.

The first important finding of studies of people's reactions to judicial procedures is that people are not primarily influenced by the outcome of their experience, i.e. by whether they win or lose their case, whether they go to jail or go free, or whether they pay a large fine or nothing.[31] Further, studies suggest very little impact from the time it takes to resolve a case or the amount of money expended in the effort.[32] The objective characteristics of the case disposition experience have very little psychological impact.[33] An example of these findings is the study by E. Allan Lind comparing bilateral negotiation, mediation,

---

23. John Thibaut & Laurens Walker, Procedural Justice: A Psychological Analysis (1975).

24. Id.

25. Id. Thibaut and Walker also dealt with the objective quality of the decisions reached using different types of legal procedure. Id. However, their research on that topic will not be discussed in this article.

26. Lind & Tyler, supra note 22, at 13.

27. Tom R. Tyler, The Role of Perceived Injustice in Defendants' Evaluation of Their Courtroom Experience, 18 Law & Soc'y Rev. 51 (1984) [hereinafter, Tyler, Role of Perceived Injustice].

28. See, e.g., Tyler, supra note 3 (evaluating how people react to their personal experiences with legal authorities).

29. See Lind & Tyler, supra note 22, at 13–40.

30. Id.

31. See E. Allan Lind et al., In the Eye of the Beholder: Tort Litigants' Evaluations of Their Experiences in the Civil Justice System, 24 Law & Soc'y Rev. 953, 968–71 (1990).

32. Id. at 974.

33. Id. at 968–71, 975.

settlement conferences, and trials.[34] That study found that the amount of money won or lost, the duration of the case disposition process, and the costs of the process to the litigant were all largely unrelated to judgments of fairness and satisfaction.[35]

What does influence people is their assessment of the fairness of the case disposition process. People are most strongly affected by their evaluations of the procedure by which the outcomes are reached—i.e., by their evaluations of the judicial process itself.[36] In other words, people are affected by the way in which decisions are made, irrespective of what those decisions are. People are also influenced by judgments about the fairness of the outcome itself.[37]

The relative importance of receiving a fair outcome or experiencing a fair procedure depends on the types of psychological consequence with which we are concerned. If we are concerned about personal reactions, reaction to the experience or the willingness to voluntarily accept judicial decisions, then people are affected by both the fairness of the outcome and, independently, by the fairness of the procedure.[38]

Studies suggest that if the socializing influence of experience is the issue of concern (i.e., the impact of participating in a judicial hearing on a person's respect for the law and legal authorities), then the primary influence is the person's evaluation of the fairness of the judicial procedure itself, not their evaluations of the outcome.[39] Such respect is important because it has been found to influence everyday behavior toward the law.[40] When people believe that legal authorities are less legitimate, they are less likely to be law-abiding citizens in their everyday lives.[41]

Many of the studies alluded to deal with informal police-citizen interactions,[42] and citizen experiences in small claims courts.[43] These studies focus on the experiences of ordinary citizens, whose primary interactions with the legal system typically involve informal contacts with the police and the courts.[44]

Other studies have focused more directly on judicial hearings. The first is a recent study of felony criminal case disposition.[45] That study examined the im-

---

34. See id. at 953–86.

35. Id. at 980–84.

36. See Lind & Tyler, supra note 22.

37. Id.

38. Id.

39. Tyler, supra note 3, at 94–112. See Tom R. Tyler et al., Maintaining Allegiance Toward Political Authorities: The Role of Prior Attitudes and the Use of Fair Procedures, 33 Am. J. of Pol. Sci. 629 (1989) (examining "the impact of experience with the criminal justice system on defendant attitudes toward legal authorities, law, and government) [hereinafter, Tyler, Maintaining Allegiance].

40. Tyler, supra note 3, at 4–5.

41. Id.

42. Id.; Tom R. Tyler & Robert Folger, Distributional and Procedural Aspects of Satisfaction With Citizen-Police Encounter, Basic & Applied Soc. Psychol. 281–92 (1980).

43. Tyler, Role of Perceived Injustice, supra note 27.

44. See Tyler, supra note 3; Tyler & Folger, supra note 42, at 281; Tyler, Role of Perceived Injustice, supra note 27.

45. See Jonathan Casper et al., Procedural Justice in Felony Cases, 22 Law & Soc'y Rev. 483 (1988).

pact of the case disposition process on both satisfaction with the case disposition process itself and on attitudes toward law and legal authorities.[46]

Although those defendants received outcomes varying from a suspended sentence to twenty years in prison, the objective severity of the outcomes received was not found to influence overall reactions to the case-disposition experiences. Reactions to the case-disposition experience were influenced by: 1) the fairness of the sentence and 2) evaluations of the fairness of the case-disposition process. The impact of the case-disposition process on attitudes toward the legal system was found to be responsive only to evaluations of the fairness of the case-disposition process and not to judgments of distributive justice or to the objective severity of the outcome.[47]

These findings about the felony case disposition process are important for several reasons. First, the deprivation of personal liberty involved is quite substantial. Second, the people involved are marginal members of society: poor, poorly educated, minority, unemployed; those who might be expected to care the least about questions of due process and the most about the favorability of the outcomes they have received.

A second set of findings are from a series of studies of civil tort case hearings conducted by the Rand corporation.[48] These studies examine the resolution of tort cases in settlement conference hearings, mediation/arbitration hearings, and formal trial hearings.[49] The findings of Lind et al., on arbitration in the federal courts are especially striking.[50] All of the cases they studied involved lawsuits over at least $50,000 and some lawsuits involved amounts up to $2,000,000.[51] Yet they found that people's willingness to accept mediation decisions, instead of going on to have a formal trial, were affected by their evaluations of the fairness of the mediation session.[52] Similar findings were obtained by Rand studies that examined the acceptance of arbitration claims in lawsuits over automobile injuries in New Jersey.[53] These findings suggest that civil, like criminal, proceedings are strongly influenced by people's evaluations of procedures.

The findings of the studies I have outlined are very supportive of the speculations of the Supreme Court in the cases I have already noted, *Goldberg v. Kelley*[54] and *Morrissey v. Brewer*.[55] Experiencing judicial procedures that are evaluated as unfair does influence people's respect for legal authorities and for

---

46. Casper, supra note 45, at 483–507; Tyler, Maintaining Allegiance, supra note 39, at 629–52.

47. Casper, supra note 45, at 483–507; Tyler, Maintaining Allegiance, supra note 39, at 629–52.

48. E. Allan Lind et al., Outcome and Process Concerns in Organizational Dispute Resolution, Am. B. Found. Working Paper # 9109 (1991); Robert J. MacCoun et al., Rand Institute for Civil Justice, Alternative Adjudication: An Evaluation of the New Jersey Automobile Arbitration Program (1988).

49. See Lind, supra note 48; MacCoun, supra note 48.

50. Lind, supra note 48.

51. Id. at 1.

52. Id. at 29.

53. MacCoun, supra note 48, at 56–57.

54. 397 U.S. 254 (1970).

55. 408 U.S. 471 (1972).

the law. Further, it shapes people's behavior. People who have experienced a procedure that they judge to be unfair are not only less respectful of the law and legal authorities, they are less likely to accept judicial decisions and less likely to obey the law in the future. These findings point to the possibility of developing exactly the type of social malaise that the Supreme Court speculated might result from experiencing an "arbitrary" (i.e. unfair) procedure.[56]

In their original discussion of procedural justice, Thibaut and Walker suggested that conducting a judicial proceeding using procedures that all parties to a dispute would regard as fair facilitates efforts to "resolve conflicts in such a way as to bind up the social fabric and encourage the continuation of productive exchange between individuals."[57] Similar concerns underlie the therapeutic jurisprudence movement. If people leave commitment hearings with favorable views about the legitimacy of legal authorities, such views are likely to facilitate the subsequent therapeutic process.

A. Subjective Neutrality

It is possible that people care about procedural justice but define it in terms of neutrality such as lack of bias, honesty, the use of expertise, and factual decision-making. If so, they share the concern with factors shaping the objective decision-making quality that has influenced judicial holdings such as *Parham v. J.R.*[58]

Studies indicate that people focus on lack of bias, honesty, and factual decision-making.[59] Each of these aspects of a judicial procedure has some influence on judgments of the procedure's fairness.[60] In addition, people are more likely to indicate that a procedure is fair if it yields them a favorable outcome.

What is interesting is not that the neutrality of a judicial procedure matters—neutrality is after all a core element of procedure that forms the central concept in most textbooks on legal procedure. What is interesting is that there are other aspects of procedures that are more important determinants of people's judgments about procedural fairness. Three such elements will be considered: participation, dignity, and trust.

1. Participation

Studies of people's reactions to judicial procedures consistently find that people regard procedures in which they are allowed to participate as fairer.[61] Participation can involve the presentation of evidence and one's own views (voice or process control), shared decision-making (decision control), or

---

56. *Goldberg*, 397 U.S. at 265.

57. See Thibaut & Walker, supra note 23.

58. 442 U.S. 584 (1979).

59. See Tyler, supra note 3, at 6–7.

60. See Tom R. Tyler & E. Allan Lind, A Rational Model of Authority in Groups, in 25 Advances in Experimental Social Psychology 115, 137–66 (Mark P. Zanna ed., 1992) (discussing existing research on characteristics that make procedures appear fair and addressing features that affect procedural justice judgments).

61. See Lind & Tyler, supra note 22.

both.[62] Studies suggest that either form of participation enhances feelings of fair treatment.[63]

It is not particularly surprising that people value shared control over decisions. Such shared control gives them influence over the outcome of the procedure. It is also not surprising that people value the opportunity to present evidence and express their views. They no doubt feel that this opportunity to present evidence allows them to influence indirectly judicial decisions through persuading the mediator or judge of the validity of their perspective.

What is interesting is that people value the opportunity to present their arguments and state their views even when they indicate that what they say is having little or no influence over the third-party authority.[64] The most striking example of this effect is found in studies allowing people to present their evidence after a decision has been made.[65]

Imagine that you are invited to visit another university because you are being considered for a job. When you arrive your host says that he or she has good news and bad news. The bad news is that someone else has already been hired to fill the job. The good news is that you can still demonstrate how good you would be for the job by giving a job talk. Would you think that you were being more fairly treated than you would if you were simply told that the job had been filled? Interestingly, the answer is yes. In fact, people do place a value on the opportunity to present evidence that is not linked to the influence of that evidence on decisions.

Obviously this example is extreme. Typically the message people receive from authorities is much less straightforward. But the extremity of the example makes the point clear; people do not want to state their opinions simply because they believe that their arguments will influence third-party decisions. Presenting arguments to a third-party has value in and of itself.

2. Dignity

A second important finding of psychological research on people's reactions to their dealings with legal authorities is that people care how they are treated by legal authorities.[66] In other words, they respond to whether they are treated with respect, politeness, and dignity, and whether their rights as citizens are acknowledged.[67] People value the affirmation of their status by legal authorities as competent, equal, citizens and human beings, and they regard procedures as unfair if they are not consistent with that affirmation.[68] To understand the effects of dignity, it is important to recognize that government has an important

---

62. Id.

63. Id.

64. Id.

65. E. Allan Lind et al., Voice, Control, and Procedural Justice: Instrumental and Noninstrumental Concerns in Fairness Judgments, 59 J. Personality & Soc. Psychol. 952, 952–59 (1990).

66. See Tyler, supra note 3; Tyler & Folger, supra note 42; Tyler & Lind, supra note 60.

67. See Lind, supra note 31; Tyler, supra note 3; Tyler & Folger, supra note 42; Tyler & Lind, supra note 60.

68. See Tyler & Lind, supra note 60, at 139–43.

role in defining people's views about their value in society. Such a self evaluation shapes one's feelings of security and self-respect.[69]

3. Trust

Finally, people value evidence that the authorities with whom they are dealing are concerned about their welfare and want to treat them fairly.[70] Trust is the most important quality, but also the most elusive, because it involves a motive attribution.[71] In other words, people must infer whether an authority is or is not motivated to treat them fairly based on that authority's actions.

What influences whether people regard authorities as trustworthy? One factor is participation. People regard authorities who allow them to present evidence as more trustworthy.[72] Similarly, people regard authorities who treat them with dignity and respect as more trustworthy.[73] Finally, the efforts of authorities to explain or account for decisions heighten judgments of trustworthiness.[74]

Concerns about trustworthiness reflect a desire to understand the future actions of authorities.[75] Since people typically believe that motives are stable and unchanging over time, knowledge of the motivations of authorities allows the authorities' future actions to be predicted.[76] If people infer a benevolent disposition in some authority, they can trust that, in the long-run, an authority will behave in ways that serve their interests.[77] For this reason trust is a key component of legitimacy.[78]

The importance of trustworthiness helps to explain an important limitation to the participation effects that have been outlined. People generally feel more fairly treated if they can present evidence, even when they think their evidence does not affect the decisions made by the third party. However, this effect does not occur if people do not believe that their evidence was considered by the third party. Without considering their arguments, people believe that the authority cannot be acting benevolently, and no effect occurs.

The role of trustworthiness also leads to another important conclusion of the study of procedures. Structural features of procedures, such as the provision of a right to appeal, may or may not shape people's feelings about authorities. The key issue to those affected by procedures is whether the authority involved is attempting to be fair in the implementation of rules.[79] Without such a belief the simple existence of structures associated with fairness does

---

69. Robert Lane, Procedural Goods in a Democracy: How One is Treated v. What One Gets, 2 Soc. Just. Res. 177–92 (1988).

70. See Tyler & Lind, supra note 60, at 139–43.

71. Id.

72. Id.

73. Id.

74. Id.

75. Id.

76. Id.

77. Id.

78. Bernard Barber, The Logic and Limits of Trust (1983).

79. Tom R. Tyler & Robert Bies, Interpersonal Aspects of Procedural Justice, in Applied Social Psychology in Business Settings (J.S. Carroll ed., 1990).

not enhance perceived fairness.[80] On the other hand, people can experience "unfair treatment" such as sexism or racism without reporting that the procedures involved were unfair if they infer that the authorities involved are motivated to treat them fairly.[81]

B. Summary

People's evaluations of the fairness of judicial hearings are affected by the opportunities which those procedures provide for people to participate, by the degree to which people judge that they are treated with dignity and respect, and by judgments about the trustworthiness of authorities. Each of these three factors has more influence on judgments of procedural justice than do either evaluations of neutrality or evaluations of the favorableness of the outcome of the hearing.

II. The Psychology of Judicial Hearings

Why do those who experience judicial hearings react to issues of participation, dignity, and trustworthiness? The answer lies in recognizing the important role that legal and political authorities play in defining peoples' feelings of self-esteem, self-worth, and their sense of personal security.

In a study of the citizens of Chicago, people were found to recognize a widespread occurrence of injustice when citizens dealt with the police and courts.[82] Yet the same people almost universally indicated that they believed the authorities would treat them fairly if they personally dealt with them.[83] Tyler and Lind label this belief the "illusion of personal justice" because it reflects a strong belief in one's own invulnerability to unfair treatment.[84] Faye Crosby identified a similar unwillingness to recognize that one is a victim of discrimination, which she labels "comfortable ignorance."[85] In each case, people resist the belief that they are vulnerable, instead seeing themselves as linked to personally benevolent authorities.[86] When people deal with authorities, they open these beliefs to possible disconfirmation.[87]

The importance of self-respect and self-worth is indicated by the centrality of those issues to people's reactions to their experiences with authorities. People may initially approach authorities instrumentally, but they react to their

---

80. See Tyler & Lind, supra note 60, at 139–43.

81. See Tyler, supra note 3, at 91–92.

82. See Tyler & Lind, supra note 60, at 144–58.

83. Id.

84. Id. at 155.

85. Faye Crosby, Relative Deprivation in Organizational Settings, in 6 Research in Organizational Behavior (L.L. Cummings & Barry M. Staw eds., 1984); see also Faye Crosby, The Denial of Personal Discrimination, in American Behavioral Scientist 371; Faye Crosby & Donna Nagata, Denying Personal Advantage (paper presented at the annual meeting of the International Society of Political Psychology, Washington, D.C.) (1990).

86. Tyler & Lind, supra note 60, at 155.

87. Id. at 155 n.19.

experiences by focusing on their implications for the social bond linking people to authorities.[88]

The legal system is one aspect of the larger society, so legal authorities provide people with information about their standing both in the eyes of the law and in society more generally. Research shows that people care about their status and react to their experiences in terms of their implications concerning that status.[89] In contrast, people's concerns about traditional issues such as lack of bias, honesty, factual decision-making, and obtaining favorable outcomes, while important, have less influence on people's judgments regarding the fairness of their experiences.[90]

A. Commitment Hearings

I have discussed a number of studies examining the psychology underlying people's reactions to their dealings with legal authorities. None of these studies directly examines commitment hearings. However, they do examine a variety of legal procedures, including mediation/arbitration hearings, trials, and plea bargaining, which share many basic characteristics with commitment hearings.

The key question is what implications can be drawn from this literature regarding the therapeutic consequences of personal experiences with legal authorities. One implication is that people respond to how decisions are made—a response that is not simply linked to what decisions are. Hence, the psychological arena defined by the Supreme Court in cases such as *Goldberg v. Kelly*[91] and *Morrissey v. Brewer*[92] clearly exists.

Failure to receive due process has a number of negative consequences for people who have personal experiences with legal authorities, including reluctance to accept decisions, diminished respect for the judge, mediator, or other third party, diminished respect for the courts and the legal system, and a diminished willingness to follow legal rules.[93] These effects are completely consistent with the suggestion that experiencing arbitrary procedures leads to social malaise and decreases people's willingness to be integrated into the polity, accepting its authorities and following its rules.

Of particular relevance to the question of therapeutic implications is the issue of behavior. Enhancing respect for authorities, the willingness to voluntarily accept the decisions of authorities, and the willingness to follow social rules are core objectives of any therapeutic program. Hence, it seems likely that future studies of the therapeutic consequences of judicial hearings will demonstrate that commitment hearings experienced as unfair by those potentially being committed will have strongly antitherapeutic consequences.

The findings of studies about fair process have especially important implications for the study of commitment hearings. Judicial hearings in general are

---

88. See William Felstiner et al., The Emergence and Transformation of Disputes: Naming, Blaming, Claiming...., 15 Law & Soc'y Rev. 631 (1973).

89. See Tyler & Lind, supra note 60, at 144–66.

90. Id.

91. 397 U.S. 254 (1970).

92. 408 U.S. 471 (1972).

93. See Tyler, supra note 3.

clearly used by people to gain information about their status as members of society. Perhaps no type of hearing more directly threatens a person's belief that they are an equal member of society than a mental commitment hearing. Given the stigma attached to "insanism,"[94] the label "mentally incompetent" is truly a threat to individuals' ability to define themselves as an equal member of society.[95] Many groups affected by judicial and administrative hearings, welfare recipients, prisoners, and students are socially marginal in some respects. For those and other groups the issue of mental competence is central to issues of self-respect and security in society.

B. Professional vs. Judicial Decision-Making

The psychological perspective that has been outlined highlights the importance of conducting judicial hearings in ways that will have positive psychological consequences on those who undergo commitment hearings. In other words, it is clearly beneficial for personal experiences with judicial authorities to contribute to developing psychological and behavioral characteristics that enhance the therapeutic process. The enhancement of such attitudes and behaviors will, of course, be beneficial irrespective of the disposition of the case (i.e., whether the person involved is or is not committed to a mental institution).

It is also important to note, however, that the characteristics of a hearing that are associated with fairness can be enacted by either judicial or professional decision-makers. In other words, the psychological research reviewed suggests that people will benefit from hearings in which they can participate, in which they are treated with dignity, and in which they believe that they are dealing with trustworthy authorities who are motivated to be fair to them. It seems possible to design either judicial or professional decision-making procedures, or both, so that they will have the characteristics of "fair" decision-making procedures.

The findings outlined are consistent with the suggestion of the therapeutic jurisprudence literature that hearings which lack the characteristics which people associate with due process are likely to be experienced as unfair.[96] Such unfairness, in turn, is likely to have negative consequences for the subsequent therapeutic process. However, it does not point to judicial hearings as the only possible source of procedures that people will experience as unfair. It is also possible that professionals could develop procedures containing some of the elements that have been outlined. If they did so, then professional decision-making procedures might also be therapeutic. It is an empirical question, as yet unanswered, whether mental health professionals could conduct commitment proceedings in ways that would lead people to feel that their views were being considered, that they were being treated with dignity and respect, and that they were dealing with trustworthy authorities.

---

94. See Michael L. Perlin, On "Sanism", 46 SMU L. Rev. 373 (1992).
95. Id.
96. See Wexler, supra note 18.

C. Objective and Psychological Criteria for Procedural Evaluation

There are two distinct issues that need to be considered in evaluating civil commitment procedures. The first is the ability of a procedure to make accurate decisions. Bersoff has outlined the problems, including bias, with professional decision-making in great detail.[97] If future studies indicate that professional decision-making is more subject to such biases and consequently less accurate than judicial decision-making, then accuracy concerns would favor judicial decision-making.

Distinct from accuracy issues are concerns about the psychological impact of procedures, in particular their potential impact on future therapeutic processes. If people become estranged from authority, distrusting others; believing that they are vulnerable, and hence feeling insecure; and lacking in feelings of self-worth, these consequences are disadvantageous and preferably could be avoided. Historically, many of these negative psychological consequences have occurred in the context of professional commitment hearings. Judicial hearings, which have been more sensitive to issues of due process, may have more positive psychological consequences. Ultimately, decisions about the desirability of different judicial procedures need to be responsive to both the objective quality of the decisions made and to the psychological consequences of varying types of decision-making procedure.

---

97. Bersoff, supra note 5.

Chapter 2

The Side Effects of Incompetency Labeling and the Implications for Mental Health Law

Bruce J. Winick

I. Introduction

As with drugs,[1] legal rules designed to produce certain beneficial consequences sometimes create unintended adverse side effects. It is appropriate to
identify these negative effects so that they may be factored into legal policy
analysis and minimized whenever possible. These effects may take many
forms. Sometimes, for example, laws produce negative economic or environmental consequences. Indeed, a body of law and a form of interdisciplinary
scholarship have developed that seek to identify and analyze the economic[2] or
environmental[3] impact of proposed legal rules or policies. Legal rules may

---

1. See, e.g., Riggins v. Nevada, 112 S. Ct. 1810, 1816 (1992) (discussing side effects of
antipsychotic medication); id. at 1818–20 (Kennedy, J., concurring) (discussing adverse side
effects of antipsychotic medication on a criminal defendant's functioning at trial); Washington v. Harper, 494 U.S. 210, 229–30 (1990) (discussing adverse side effects of antipsychotic
medication); Bruce J. Winick, Psychotropic Medication and Competence to Stand Trial,
1977 Am. B. Found. Res. J. 769, 782–83, 786–89 (discussing adverse side effects of antipsychotic, antidepressant, antimanic, and antianxiety drugs).

2. See, e.g., Exec. Order No. 12,291, 3 C.F.R. 127 (1971) (requiring economic impact
statements for certain administrative Policies); Gary Becker & William M. Landes, Essays in
the Economics of Criminal Punishment (1974); Richard Posner, Economic Analysis of Law
(1973); Robert W. Hahn & John A. Hird, The Costs and Benefits of Regulation: Review and
Synthesis, 8 Yale J. on Reg. 233 (1991).

3. See, e.g., National Environmental Policy Act, 42 U.S.C. s 4321 (1989) (requiring environmental impact statements); Environmental Quality: The Twentieth Annual Report of the
Council on Environmental Control (1992); Robert Glicksman & Christopher H. Schroeder,
EPA and the Courts: Twenty Years of Law and Politics (Assessing the Environmental Protec-
tion Agency After Twenty Years: Law, Politics, and Economics), 54 L. & Contemp. Prob.
249 (1991); Ralph A. Luken & Lyman H. Clark, How Efficient Are EPA's Regulations?, 20
Envtl. L. Rep. 10419 (1990); Daniel R. Mandelker, NEPA Alive and Well: The Supreme
Court Takes Two, 19 Envtl. L. Rev. 10385 (1989); William H. Rodgers, Benefits, Costs, and
Risks: Oversight of Health and Environmental Decisionmaking, 4 Harv. Envtl. L. Rev. 191
(1980); Antonio Rossmann, NEPA: Not So Well At Twenty, 20 Envtl. L. Rev. 10174 (1990).

produce negative psychological or behavioral consequences.[4] The effort to assess the negative psychological and behavioral effects of legal rules and to suggest ways in which they may be minimized can be seen as an exercise in therapeutic jurisprudence.[5]

The law sometimes labels people as incompetent in order to achieve certain consequences considered to be desirable. Thus, criminal defendants who because of mental illness are unable to understand the nature of the criminal proceedings or to communicate with counsel are adjudicated incompetent to stand trial.[6] This adjudication suspends the criminal proceedings until treatment can

---

4. See, e.g., Plessy v. Ferguson, 163 U.S. 537 (1896) (adopting separate but equal doctrine that perpetuated racism and racial subjugation), overruled by Brown v. Board of Educ., 347 U.S. 483, 494 (1954) (invalidating school segregation in part because of its negative impact on the "hearts and minds" of those affected); Swift v. Tyson, 41 U.S. 1 (1842) (authorizing federal courts to apply federal common law in diversity cases), overruled by Erie R.R. Co. v. Tompkins, 304 U.S. 64, 74–75 (1938) (noting that Swift had produced unpredictability in the planning of everyday affairs as a result of uncertainty as to the rule of law that would be applied to conflicts over them, producing psychological distress and inhibiting interstate economic transactions); see Henry M. Hart, Jr., The Relation Between State and Federal Law, 54 Colum. L. Rev. 489, 497 (1954) ("People repeatedly subjected, like Pavlov's dogs, to two or more inconsistent sets of directions, without means of resolving the inconsistencies, could not fail in the end to react as the dogs did. The society, collectively, would suffer a nervous breakdown.") (commenting on the effects of Swift). See also David B. Wexler, Therapeutic Jurisprudence: The Law as a Therapeutic Agent 5 (1990) (discussing "law related psychological dysfunction"); Bruce J. Winick, Competency to be Executed: A Therapeutic Jurisprudence Perspective, 10 Behav. Sci. & L. 317, 336 (1992) (same).

5. The theory of therapeutic jurisprudence suggests the need for study of the therapeutic implications of various legal rules and practices. The law can be seen to function as a therapeutic agent, producing therapeutic or antitherapeutic consequences. Therapeutic jurisprudence accordingly seeks to focus attention on an often neglected ingredient in the calculus necessary for performing a sensible policy analysis of law—the therapeutic dimension—and calls for its systematic empirical examination. See generally David B. Wexler & Bruce J. Winick, Essays in Therapeutic Jurisprudence (1992); Michael L. Perlin, What is Therapeutic Jurisprudence?, 10 N.Y.L. Sch. J. Hum. Rts. 623 (1993); David B. Wexler, Therapeutic Jurisprudence and Changing Concepts of Legal Scholarship, 11 Behav. Sci. & L. 17 (1993); David B. Wexler & Bruce J. Winick, The Potential of Therapeutic Jurisprudence: A New Approach to Psychology and the Law, in Law and Psychology: The Broadening of the Discipline 211 (James R. P. Ogloff ed., 1992); David B. Wexler & Bruce J. Winick, Therapeutic Jurisprudence as a New Approach to Mental Health Law Policy Analysis and Research, 45 U. Miami L. Rev. 979 (1991) [hereinafter Therapeutic Jurisprudence as a New Approach]; David B. Wexler & Bruce J. Winick, Therapeutic Jurisprudence and Criminal Justice Mental Health Issues, 16 Mental & Physical Dis. L. Rep. 225 (1992). To identify the therapeutic dimension as a significant factor is not, of course, to suggest that it should trump other considerations. Countervailing normative considerations may often justify a legal rule or practice found to produce antitherapeutic consequences, and therapeutic jurisprudence does not purport to be a method of determining which factor should predominate in decision making. See David B. Wexler, Justice, Mental Health, and Therapeutic Jurisprudence, 40 Clev. St. L. Rev. 27 (1992). Its mission is merely to raise questions that call for a more complete analysis of the relevant considerations, and to use insights from the social and behavioral sciences to attempt to reshape the law so that it can more effectively serve therapeutic ends.

6. See Pate v. Robinson, 383 U.S. 375 (1966); ABA Standing Comm. on Association Standards for Criminal Justice, Criminal Justice Mental Health Standards s 7-4.1 (1989) [here-

improve the defendants' condition so that they may participate more effectively in the proceedings. Use of the incompetent-to-stand-trial label thus is justified on grounds of paternalism, fairness, and increased accuracy in criminal adjudication.[7] Similarly, individuals suffering from mental illness are sometimes determined to be incompetent to make treatment[8] or hospitalization[9] decisions, to manage property,[10] to enter into contracts,[11] to make a will,[12] to marry,[13] or to vote.[14] The legal rules producing these incompetency adjudications sometimes are defended on paternalistic grounds and sometimes are based on the desire to benefit society or protect others.

These determinations are preceded by a clinical evaluation of the individual by one or more psychiatrists or psychologists and often are made publicly, typically following a formal judicial or administrative proceeding at which the individual is called on to testify or at least to observe. The incompetency label is formally applied, often by a judge who, in black robes and sitting atop an elevated platform, is likely to be perceived by the individual as an authority figure possessed of great wisdom and power. Others known to the individual, including friends, family, employer, and co-workers, soon learn of this adjudication, which usually is made a matter of public record.

Incompetency labeling often imposes negative legal effects on the individuals so labeled—depriving them of their liberty to engage in the relevant activ-

---

inafter ABA Standards]; Bruce J. Winick, Incompetency to Stand Trial: Developments in the Law, in Mentally Disordered Offenders: Perspectives from Law and Social Science 3 (John Monahan & Henry J. Steadman eds., 1983) [hereinafter Incompetency to Stand Trial]; Bruce J. Winick, Restructuring Competency to Stand Trial, 32 UCLA L. Rev. 921 (1985) [hereinafter Winick, Restructuring Competency to Stand Trial].

7. Winick, Restructuring Competency to Stand Trial, supra note 6, at 952–59; Note, Incompetency to Stand Trial, 81 Harv. L. Rev. 454, 454 (1967).

8. See Paul S. Applebaum et al., Informed Consent: Legal Theory and Clinical Practice (1987); Samuel Jan Brakel et al., The Mentally Disabled and the Law 341 (3d ed., 1985); Restatement (Second) of Torts s 892 (1979); Alan Meisel et al., Toward a Model of the Legal Doctrine of Informed Consent, 134 Am. J. Psychiatry 285, 287 (1977); Loren Roth et al., Tests of Incompetency to Consent to Treatment, 134 Am. J. Psychiatry 279 (1977); Charles L. Sprung & Bruce J. Winick, Informed Consent in Theory and Practice: Legal and Medical Perspectives on the Informed Consent Doctrine and a Proposed Reconceptualization, 17 Critical Care Med. 1346 (1989); Bruce J. Winick, Competency to Consent to Treatment: The Distinction Between Assent and Objection, 28 Hous. L. Rev. 15 (1991).

9. See Zinermon v. Burch, 494 U.S. 113 (1990); Bruce J. Winick, Competency to Consent to Voluntary Hospitalization: A Therapeutic Jurisprudence Analysis of Zinermon v. Burch, 14 Int'l J. L. & Psychiatry 169 (1991).

10. See Richard C. Allen et al., Mental Impairment and Legal Incompetency 228–29, 253–54 (1968); Brakel et al., supra note 8, at 438–39.

11. See authorities cited in supra note 10.

12. See Allen et al., supra note 10, at 254; Thomas E. Atkinson, Handbook of the Law of Wills 232–33 (2d ed., 1952); Brakel et al., supra note 8, at 439–41; Bruce D. Sales et al., Disabled Persons and the Law 54–55 (1982); Milton D. Green, Public Policies Underlying the Law of Mental Incompetency, 38 Mich. L. Rev. 1189, 1203–1204 (1940).

13. See Allen et al., supra note 10, at 255–56; Brakel et al., supra note 8, at 507; Sales et al., supra note 12, at 13–14.

14. See Allen et al., supra note 10, at 258; Brakel et al., supra note 8, at 445–46; Sales et al., supra note 12, at 99.

ity or exercise the right with respect to which they have been found to be incompetent. Aside from these legal consequences, when the law applies an incompetency label to individuals it brands them in ways that often impose serious social disadvantages, adversely affecting the way others regard and treat them. In addition, this brand and the way individuals perceive it can harm them psychologically in ways that may be serious and long lasting. Not only may they be stigmatized and discredited in the eyes of others, but also their own self-esteem and self-concept may be affected in ways that have a major impact on motivation and functioning. Moreover, the label may significantly diminish their sense of well-being and produce a form of clinical depression.

These consequences have been inadequately analyzed, however. This article examines the negative social and psychological effects of incompetency labeling and comments on the implications of these adverse side effects for mental health law. A number of proposals are offered to eliminate or minimize these adverse effects. The law should rely more on voluntary approaches, reducing the use of coercion and incompetency labeling. Incompetency should be narrowly defined, and competency should be presumed, even for those who have mental illness. Legal labels and procedures should be redesigned to minimize the potential that their use will foster self-attributions by the individuals labeled that perpetuate their social and health problems.

II. The Adverse Effects of Incompetency Labeling

A. Deviance Labeling and Social Stigma

Primitive societies did not engage in deviancy labeling.[15] Small tribes of hunters and gatherers, agrarian villages, and peasant societies were relatively homogeneous and interdependent. They needed each member of the community and generally could not afford the social costs of ostracizing any of them.[16] Moreover, in simple societies, the social unit tended to be small and was characterized by a number of cross-cutting interpersonal networks, promoting a considerable degree of personal interaction.[17] The high degree of social familiarity in such societies rendered unnecessary the use of labels, which tend to communicate through simple and one-dimensional social stereotypes. The significant kinship and other interpersonal linkages between members of such societies also made deviancy labeling, with its resulting social ostracism, socially costly. Not only would such labeling diminish or preclude the contributions of the individual to the community, but it also would increase the risk of social fragmentation and social conflict.[18]

---

15. See Douglas Raybeck, Anthropology and Labeling Theory: A Constructive Critique, 16 Ethos 371 (Dec. 1988).

16. See id. at 378–87 (discussing anthropological studies of the practices of primitive societies).

17. Id. at 376.

18. See id. at 376.

As societies grew in size and complexity, however, individuals became more expendable. As societies became more heterogeneous, deviancy labeling became more widespread as a means of facilitating communication[19] and of increasing the solidarity of other members of the social order.[20] Instead of reconciling the offender to the group, social ostracism became easier. Social and cultural heterogeneity made reconciliation more difficult and more threatening to those in control.[21] Those perceived as troublemakers thus became expendable and were ritualistically ostracized by deviancy labeling.[22] Deviancy labeling serves to marginalize those labeled, [23] causing them to internalize a deviant self-image, and sometimes as a result, to engage in acts of secondary deviance.[24]

A traditional type of deviancy labeling has been application of the label of mental illness.[25] Thomas Scheff and others have criticized the use of the mental illness label on the basis of the severe social disadvantages it poses for those so labeled.[26] Under this view, the mental illness labels lock the individuals into behavior patterns that result from the way others perceive and respond to them and the way the label alters their view of themselves. According to Scheff, the mental illness label causes individuals to adopt a self-conception reflecting a stereotyped image of insanity that has the effect of limiting their capacity for self-control. Individuals' damaged self-concept perpetuates their deviant behavior and launches them on a career of chronic mental disability. In this way, labeling individuals as mentally ill can produce a self-fulfilling prophecy.[27]

---

19. Id. at 391.

20. See Emile Durkheim, The Rules of the Sociological Method (1938); Kai Erikson, A Study in the Sociology of Deviance (1966).

21. See Steven Pfohl, Labeling Criminals, in Law and Deviance (H. Laurence Ross ed., 1981).

22. Raybeck, supra note 15, at 375.

23. See Marshall B. Cornard, Sociology of Deviant Behavior (1974); Edwin M. Lemert, Human Deviance, Social Problems, and Social Control (2d ed., 1972); Raybeck, supra note 15, at 372.

24. See Howard Becker, Studies in the Sociology of Deviance (1963); Thomas J. Scheff, Being Mentally Ill: A Sociological Theory (1966); Edwin M. Schur, Labeling Deviant Behavior: Its Sociological Implication (1971); Judith A. Howard & Randy Levinson, The Overdue Courtship of Attribution and Labeling, 48 Soc. Psychol. Q. 191 (1985); Raybeck, supra note 15, at 372.

25. See Scheff, supra note 24; Thomas J. Scheff, The Labeling Theory of Mental Illness, 39 Am. Soc. Rev. 444 (1974) [hereinafter Scheff, Labeling Theory]; Thomas J. Scheff, The Role of the Mentally Ill and the Dynamics of Mental Disorder: A Research Framework, 26 Sociometry 436 (1963).

26. Scheff, supra note 24; Thomas J. Scheff, Schizophrenia as Ideology, in Labeling Madness (Thomas J. Scheff ed., 1975); William A. Rushing, Individual Resources, Societal Reaction, and Hospital Commitment, 77 Am. J. Soc. 511 (1971); William A. Rushing, Status Resources, Societal Reactions, and Type of Mental Hospital Admission, 43 Am. Soc. Rev. 521 (1978); Scheff, Labeling Theory, supra note 25.

27. See infra notes 33–38 and accompanying text.

Labeling individuals as deviant—such as by characterizing them as mentally ill—may thus produce a lasting stigma that strongly colors the way others regard and interact with them and the way they conceive of themselves. *Stigma* has been defined as "an attribute that is deeply discrediting."[28] Stigmatizing people often causes others to view them as being unable to participate in life normally.[29] The stigmatizing label thus discredits individuals, often pushing them to the periphery of any social situation in which they are involved.[30] Stigmatization frequently results in excluding individuals from social activities and opportunities.[31] "It is as though society, in an effort to prove the correctness of its label, proceeds to narrow the life chances of the stigmatized person to the preconceived notions connected with the stigma."[32]

Social psychologists use the concept of the "self-fulfilling prophecy effect" to describe this phenomenon.[33] This concept posits that the belief of an individual applying a deviance label ("the marker") to another ("the marked") leads the marker to behave in a manner that serves to elicit behavior from the person marked that tends to confirm the belief or prophecy of the marker.[34] For example, a teacher believing that certain pupils are poor students or are troublemakers may tend to treat them in ways that produce behavior by those students that confirms the teacher's original views, even if those views were erroneous.[35] An understanding of this phenomenon has led to a rejection of the former practice followed in some school systems of "tracking." [36] Under this approach, students were grouped in accordance with perceived or demonstrated ability in a particular area, such as reading, and were made aware of their teachers' assessments of their abilities by the label affixed to the group,

---

28. Erving Goffman, Stigma: Notes on the Management of Spoiled Identity 3 (1963). See also Gregory C. Elliott et al., Understanding Stigma: Dimensions of Deviance and Coping, 3 Deviant Beh: An Interdisciplinary J. 275 (1982).

29. Michael S. Sorgen, Labeling and Classification, in The Mentally Retarded Citizen and the Law 215, 221 (Michael Kindred et al. eds., 1976).

30. Id.

31. Id. at 220.

32. Id. at 221.

33. See, e.g., Edward E. Jones et al., Social Stigma: The Psychology of Marked Relationships 177–78 (1984); Mark Snyder, On the Self-Perpetuating Nature of Social Stereotypes, in Cognitive Processes in Stereotyping and Intergroup Behavior 183 (David L. Hamilton ed., 1981).

34. Jones et al., supra note 33, at 177.

35. See Robert Rosenthal & Lenore Jacobson, Pygmalion in the Classroom: Future Expectation and People's Intellectual Development 54–55, 116–18 (1968). See also Goss v. Lopez, 419 U.S. 565 (1975) (notation of school suspension in student's record held to constitute a deprivation of liberty in part because of its impact on how future teachers would regard and treat the student).

36. See generally Jeannie Oakes, Keeping Track: How Schools Structure Inequality (1985); Caroline H. Persell, Education and Inequality: A Theoretical and Empirical Synthesis (1977); James E. Rosenbaum, Making Inequality: The Hidden Curriculum of High School (1976); Walter E. Schafer & Carol Olexa, Tracking and Opportunity: The Locking-out Process and Beyond (1971); Anne Wheelock, Crossing the Tracks: How "Untracking" Can Save America's Schools 9–10 (1992); Karl L. Alexander et al., Curriculum Tracking and Educational Stratification: Some Further Evidence, 43 Am. Soc. Rev. 47 (1978); Barbara Heyns, Selection and Stratification Within Schools, 79 Am. J. Soc. 1434 (1974).

such as Group 1 or Group 6. As a result, many students subsequently behaved in ways that confirmed the expectancies engendered by such grouping; consequently, the tracking process itself altered performance.[37] Similarly, labeling adolescents *juvenile delinquents* may set in motion forces that lead them to behave in ways that fulfill the assigned deviant image.[38]

Application of a deviance label thus sometimes produces a potent and lasting stigma. The notion of the self-fulfilling prophecy explains these adverse effects by showing how the markers sometimes engage in actions that confirm their expectations about labeled individuals by restricting their behavioral opportunities. Thus, the marker's belief that people with mental disabilities cannot perform certain tasks may lead him or her to deny them any opportunity to engage in or learn those tasks.[39] Even if not mentally ill, people so marked may be denied opportunities to engage in certain life activities and thereby may come to function in ways that resemble the stereotyped image of a mentally ill person.

Labeling an individual as mentally ill or mentally retarded can thus be extremely stigmatizing in ways that are likely to produce a self-fulfilling prophecy effect. The mental illness label often produces social ostracism and difficulties in obtaining employment and housing.[40] Moreover, the responses of others to an individual who has been stigmatized in this highly discrediting way are also likely to damage the individual's self-concept. "When and how pervasively the self-concept will reflect the negativity produced by a stigma depends on the nature of the stigma and on the reactions of others in the social environment."[41] Labeling people as mentally retarded imposes a "shattering stigma," impairing their educational and occupational opportunities and dominating every aspect of their lives.[42] The severe social disadvantages of labeling people as mentally ill or mentally retarded are augmented when the individual also is labeled *incompetent*, thereby confirming general stereotypes about mental disability and providing a further rationalization for the deprivation of social, occupational, and educational opportunities.

---

37. Oakes, supra note 36, at 8–9, 129–33, 143–44, 173–77.

38. See Jill Leslie Rosenbaum & Lorraine Prinsky, The Presumption of Influence: Recent Responses to Popular Music Subcultures, 37 Crime & Delinq. 528, 534 (1991). See also Howard S. Becker, Outsiders (1963); Lemert, supra note 23; Frank Tannenbaum, Crime and the Community (1951).

39. Jones et al., supra note 33, at 178.

40. Judi Chamberlin, The Ex-Patients' Movement: Where We've Been and Where We're Going, 11 J. Mind & Behav. 323, 324–25 (1990); Report of the Task Panel on Public Attitudes and Use of Media for Promotion of Mental Health, in IV Task Panel Reports Submitted to the President's Commission on Mental Health 1864, 1870 (1978). For a discussion of the stigmatizing effects of being labeled mentally ill based on a survey of former patients, see Deborah E. Reidy, "Stigma is Social Death": Mental Health Consumers/Survivors Talk About Stigma in Their Lives (Feb. 1993) (unpublished manuscript, on file with author). For first-hand accounts by former patients, see Judi Chamberlin, On Our Own 107–11 (1978); Betty Blaska, First Person Account: What It Is Like To Be Treated Like a CMI, 17 Schizophrenia Bull. 173 (1991).

41. Jones et al., supra note 33, at 113.

42. Sorgen, supra note 29, at 220; see Robert Edgerton, The Cloak of Competence: Stigma in the Lives of the Mentally Retarded 204–208 (1967).

The labeling theory of mental illness associated with Scheff has been controversial. The critics have questioned the extent to which mental illness labeling produces a form of secondary deviance in response to the reactions of others and have argued that it is artificial to view mental illness primarily in this way.[43] They have suggested that mental illness (at least in some of its forms) is legitimately thought of as illness and that the patient's insight that he or she suffers from such illness may be a precondition to improvement. In this view, application of the mental illness label, where appropriate, can be therapeutic in ways that may outweigh its social disadvantages.

The law, however, does not stop at labeling an individual mentally ill. In addition, it often labels those suffering from mental illness as incompetent. The incompetency label has a strongly undesirable global connotation and implies that the individual's incompetency is a personal characteristic, not merely a legal status. Although the patient's insight that he or she suffers from mental illness may be therapeutically essential in some psychiatric conditions, the process of labeling the individual incompetent, as well as the label itself, may be therapeutically detrimental. A patient's acceptance of the mental illness label may be a beneficial prerequisite to taking advantage of therapeutic opportunities[44] only when the patient has a strong internal locus of control.[45] However, an incompetency label may erode the individual's sense of internal control in ways that make a positive outcome in therapy difficult to achieve.[46] Application of an incompetency label usually produces an actual and obvious loss of control. The label is likely also to cause individuals to perceive that they are incompetent, not merely that they have a condition that temporarily

---

43. See, e.g., John S. Strauss & William T. Carpenter, Schizophrenia 128–29 (1981); Otto A. Will, Schizophrenia: Psychological Treatment, in 2 Comprehensive Textbook of Psychiatry 1217 (Harold I. Kaplan et al. eds., 3d ed., 1980); Robert L. Chauncey, Comment on "The Labeling Theory of Mental Illness," 40 Am. Soc. Rev. 248 (1975); Walter R. Gove, Labeling and Mental Illness: A Critique in The Labeling of Deviance 53 (Walter R. Gove ed., 1980); Walter R. Gove, The Labeling Theory of Mental Illness: A Reply to Scheff, 40 Am. Soc. Rev. 242 (1975); Walter R. Gove, Societal Reactions as an Explanation of Mental Illness: An Evaluation, 35 Am. Soc. Rev. 873 (1970); Walter R. Gove & Terry Fain, The Stigma of Mental Hospitalization, 28 Arch. Gen. Psychiatry 494 (1973); Marvin D. Krohn & Marvin L. Akers, An Alternative View of the Labeling Versus Psychiatric Perspective on a Societal Reaction to Mental Illness, 56 Soc. Forces 341 (1977); Charles R. Tittle, Deterrence or Labeling, 53 Soc. Forces 399 (1975); Richard Warner et al., Acceptance of the Mental Illness Label by Psychotic Patients: Effects on Functioning, 59 Am. J. Orthopsychiatry, 398, 399 (1989); Raymond M. Weinstein, Labeling Theory and the Attitudes of Mental Patients: A Review, 24 J. Health & Soc. Behav. 70 (1983).

44. Strauss & Carpenter, supra note 43, at 128–29; Will, supra note 43, at 1232–34.

45. Warner et al., supra note 43, at 399 ("Clinical experience suggests, however, that more than acceptance of illness is required for good outcome. The patient must also have some sense of control over the course of the illness and of being able to use treatment to good effect.") See also Silvano Arieti, Interpretation of Schizophrenia 615 (1974); Alan Breier & John S. Strauss, Self Control in Psychotic Disorders, 40 Am. J. Psychiatry 1141 (1983); Thomas H. McGlashan et al., Does Attitude Toward Psychosis Relate To Outcome?, 138 Am. J. Psychiatry 797 (1981); authorities cited in infra note 107.

46. Warner, supra note 43, at 399.

interferes with effective functioning. The combined effect may be debilitating, reinforcing and prolonging their mental illness.

B. The Psychological Effects of Incompetency Labeling on the Individual

Early work on stigma dealt with the impact of deviancy labeling on how others view and react to the individual—examining what came to be known as the "halo" and "demon" effects[47] and attribution theory generally.[48] Later work on the effects of labeling focused on the impact on individuals who received the label and on their own self-attributions and sense of self-efficacy.[49] Actual or presumed stigmatization by others often is converted into self-stigmatization. At some level, stigmatized individuals will come to accept the

---

47. More than 70 years ago, Edward Thorndike showed that a rater's overall attitude about a subject produced error in evaluating the subject's performance of a specific task. When the rater's overall impression of the subject was favorable, he was rated more highly than his performance objectively would merit. Thorndike called this the "halo" effect. When the rater's overall impression of the subject was negative, the subject was rated less highly than his performance objectively would merit. Thorndike called this the "demon" effect. See Edward L. Thorndike, A Constant Error in Psychological Ratings, 4 J. Experimental Psychol. 25 (1920); see Gerald D. Gibb, Influence of "Halo" and "Demon" Effects in Subjective Grading, 56 Perceptual & Motor Skills 67 (1983); Sheldon J. Lachman & Alan R. Bass, A Direct Study of Halo Effect, 119 J. Psychol. 535, 536 (1985); Brian G. Moritsch & W. Newton Suter, Correlates of Halo Error in Teacher Evaluation, 12 Educ. Res. Q. 29 (1988).

48. Fritz Heider refined Thorndike's concept of the "halo" and "demon" effects into a general theory of attribution under which people tend to causally link an individual's success or failure in the performance of a particular task to his general impression of the individual's overall ability or effort. Accordingly, failure is attributed to, for example, the individual's stupidity, incompetency, or lack of motivation, whereas success is attributed to his genius or determination. See Fritz Heider, The Psychology of Interpersonal Relations (1958). For general discussion of attribution theory, see, e.g., John H. Harvey et al., New Directions in Attribution Research (1976); Sandra Graham, A Review of Attribution Theory in Achievement Contexts, 3 Educ. Psychol. Rev. 5 (1991).

49. See, e.g., Attribution: Basic Issues and Applications (John H. Harvey & Gifford Weary eds., 1985); Integrations of Clinical and Social Psychology (Gifford Weary & Herbert Mirels eds., 1982); Albert Bandura, Recycling Misconceptions of Perceived Self-Efficacy, 8 Cognitive Therapy & Res. 231, 242 (1984); Albert Bandura & Daniel Cervone, Self-Evaluative and Self-Efficacy Mechanisms Governing the Motivational Effects of Goal Systems, 45 J. Personality & Soc. Psychol. (1983); Irvin Brown, Jr. & Dillon K. Inouye, Learned Helplessness Through Modeling: The Role of Perceived Similarity in Competence, 36 J. Personality & Soc. Psychol. 900 (1978); Edwin A. Locke et al., The Effect of Self-Efficacy, Goals, and Task Strategies on Task Performance, 69 J. Applied Psychol. 241 (1984); Dale H. Schunk, Modeling and Attributional Effects on Children's Achievement: A Self-Efficacy Analysis, 73 J. Educ. Psychol. 93 (1981). Self-efficacy theory shows how a person's perception concerning his own skills influences his behavior. Those who regard themselves as highly efficacious challenge themselves to set and meet higher standards of performance while those who see themselves as ineffective have lower aspirations, perform poorly, and give up readily. See Sandra Graham, A Review of Attribution Theory in Achievement Contexts, 3 Educ. Psychol. Q. 5 (1991).

negative message conveyed by the label and discredit themselves.[50] Perhaps even more debilitating than the reactions of others produced by a deviancy label are the effects of the label on individuals' self-concept and self-esteem and their resulting impact on subsequent behavior.

⌐ Labeling individuals as incompetent usually has the effect of removing their ability to make decisions for themselves, at least in the particular area in which their capacity is thought to be lacking. Individuals considered to be incompetent find that their choices and preferences are ignored and that others make choices for them. They often are treated as objects, rather than as people. As a result, events in their lives are perceived to be outside of their control. They are treated as children, subject to the authority, even if benevolently intended, of others. However, unlike biological or adoptive parents, their surrogate decision makers will likely be impersonal state officials or employees whose paternalism is not based on love and is rarely nurturing.

What are the consequences of this loss of control to people's mental health and to their motivation and ability to function? The answer will depend on the individuals and how they define their identity. The concept of the self is largely socially determined, the product of a social process in which others play an essential role in individuals' acquisition of self-knowledge and in the interpretation and evaluation of life experiences.[51] Individuals' construction of self-identity is largely dependent on the effect of reactions that are received from others.[52] Whether a potentially stigmatizing label will damage the individual's self-concept will depend on the importance attached to the quality or trait in question in organizing and interpreting social experiences.[53] If individuals link the label received to a central aspect of identity, the stigmatizing process will begin.[54] This process is illustrated by Marcia Millman's work on the psychology of obesity.[55] The strongly negative reactions that obese people often encounter in public affect self-concept differently, dependent on the individual's evaluation of the importance of weight and appearance in organizing and interpreting his or her life. Women for whom appearance was central to self-image were found to be more damaged by the negative reactions of others to their obesity, whereas many men, whose self-concept was more centrally related to other qualities, remained largely unaffected by such negative reactions.[56] Thus, some individuals will attend closely to a potentially stigmatizing label and to the reactions that it produces in others, suffering a damaged self-image as a result, whereas others will deemphasize or even ignore the label, suffering few adverse effects.[57] Potentially stigmatizing labels thus are processed differently with differential impact depending on the individual's social environment and patterns of social comparison, as well as existing self-concept. If individuals link the stigmatizing label to a central aspect of identity

---

50. Id. Jones et al., supra note 33, at 297.
51. Jones et al., supra note 33, at 111–16.
52. Id. at 111.
53. Id. at 116.
54. Id.
55. Marcia Millman, Such a Pretty Face: Being Fat in America (1980).
56. Jones et al., supra note 33, at 112 (discussing Millman).
57. Id. at 115.

or dispositional make-up, the label and the reactions of others that it generates can have strongly negative effects on self-concept and subsequent behavior.[58] Although being considered overweight or incompetent at tennis or dancing may not damage the self-concept of individuals for whom these attributes are peripheral to self-image, labeling them as incompetent to play an important social or legal role is more likely to be damaging to their self-concept.

 1. *Learned helplessness and other inhibitory effects on performance.* Psychological theory suggests that labeling an individual incompetent may produce a number of adverse effects. Particularly when combined with the actual loss of control that usually accompanies incompetency adjudication, application of the incompetency label may cause depression and decrease motivation. Moreover, it may set up expectancies of failure in the individual that themselves undermine commitment and diminish subsequent performance.

Perhaps the most serious consequence, combining all of these effects, is a syndrome that experimental psychologist Martin Seligman termed *learned helplessness*.[59] As originally conceived, learned helplessness referred to the finding that animals exposed to uncontrollable and inescapable aversive stimuli in a laboratory setting developed "helpless" behavior in other settings. The animals, learning that escape was impossible in the laboratory, would not even attempt escape in the second setting, though escape may have been possible. In his early experimental work, Seligman subjected laboratory dogs to inescapable electric shocks on a noncontingent basis (i.e., unrelated to their actions).[60] The dogs initially attempted to escape the shocks through a variety of voluntary movements. When nothing they could do enabled avoidance of the shocks, the dogs ceased all activity and became compliant, passive, and submissive. Moreover, the ability of the dogs to learn to avoid the shocks was found to decrease.

 Seligman's subsequent experiments demonstrated that organisms quickly learn to generalize from their feelings of powerlessness in the experimental context to other contexts, developing a global sense of powerlessness that de-

---

58. Id. at 116.

59. Martin E. P. Seligman, Helplessness: On Depression, Development, and Death (1975) [hereinafter Helplessness]; Martin E. P. Seligman, Human Helplessness: Theory and Applications (1980) [hereinafter Seligman, Human Helplessness]; Lyn Y. Abramson et al., Learned Helplessness In Humans: An Attributional Analysis, in Human Helplessness: Theory and Applications (Judy Garber & Martin E. P. Seligman eds., 1980); Lyn Y. Abramson et al., Learned Helplessness in Humans: Critique and Reformulation, 87 J. Abnormal Psychol. 49 (1978); Martin E. P. Seligman, Learned Helplessness, 23 Ann. Rev. Med. 407 (1972); Steven F. Maier & Martin E. P. Seligman, Learned Helplessness: Theory and Evidence, 105 J. Experimental Psychol. 33 (1976); J. Bruce Overmier & Martin E. P. Seligman, Effects of Inescapable Shock Upon Subsequent Escape and Avoidance Responding, 63 J. Comp. & Physiological Psychol. 28 (1967). See also Sharon S. Brehm & Jack W. Brehm, Psychological Reactance: A Theory of Freedom and Control 378 (1981); Lenore Walker, The Battered Woman 42–54 (1979) (applying learned helplessness to the battered woman syndrome); Christopher Peterson & Lisa M. Bossio, Learned Helplessness, in Self-defeating Behaviors: Experimental Research, Clinical Impressions, and Practical Implications 235 (Rebecca C. Curtis ed., 1989); Jerry W. Thornton & Paul D. Jacobs, Learned Helplessness in Human Subjects, 87 J. Experimental Psychol. 367 (1971).

60. Overmier & Seligman, supra note 59.

bilitates functioning.[61] In these studies, experimenters held newborn rats in their hands until the rats ceased all voluntary escape movements. After this procedure was repeated several times, the rats were placed in a vat of water. Although rats in a control group not subjected to the holding procedure were able to swim for up to 60 hr. before drowning, those in the experimental group, which had experienced inability to escape from the experimenter's hand, drowned within 30 min. Indeed, many of them made no attempt to swim and sank immediately. Their sense of powerlessness to escape from the hand-holding procedure by squirming had generalized into a powerlessness to avoid drowning by swimming. Feelings of helplessness, in short, tend to spread quickly from one aversive situation to others.

Learned helplessness in animals has become the subject of continued empirical research, much of which has focused on the effects of uncontrollability on animal physiology. Thus, helpless rats were found to be analgesic; their capacity for feeling pain as readily or as deeply as nonhelpless rats was diminished as a result of their increased endorphin levels.[62] In addition, helpless rats were found to experience immunosuppression, fighting off disease less effectively than normal rats.[63]

Seligman's experimental work with animals and then with human subjects led him to generate a theory of learned helplessness that has become a fixture of modern psychology.[64] Learned helplessness posits that subjecting individuals to noncontingent negative (or even positive) consequences can produce generalized feelings of helplessness and hopelessness. Seligman showed that the symptoms produced by this feeling of noncontrollability mirror those of major affective depression.[65] Individuals display retarded initiation of response that parallels the passivity, psychomotor retardation, and social impairment found in depression.[66] They acquire a generalized belief that their actions are doomed to failure.[67] Their self-attribution of failure produces such negative effects as self-blame, guilt, feelings of incompetence, and lowered self-esteem.[68] They develop a generalized apathy, resignation, and lowered intrinsic motivation. Their ability to solve problems is diminished, and their mood is depressed. In

---

61. Martin E. P. Seligman et al., Learned Helplessness in the Rat: Reversibility, Time Course, and Immunization, 88 J. Comp. & Physiological Psychol. 542 (1975).

62. Steven F. Maier & Raymond L. Jackson, Learned Helplessness: All of Us Were Right (and Wrong): Inescapable Shock Has Multiple Effects, in 13 The Psychology of Learning and Motivation 155 (Gordon H. Bowerd ed., 1979); Peterson & Bossio, supra note 59, at 236–37.

63. Mark L. Laudenslager et al., Coping and Immunosuppression: Inescapable But Not Escapable Shock Suppresses Lymphocyte Proliferation, 221 Sci. 568 (1983); Lawrence S. Sklar & Hymie Anisman, Stress and Coping Factors Influence Tumor Growth, 205 Sci. 513 (1979); Madelon A. Visintainer et al., Tumor Rejection in Rats after Inescapable Versus Escapable Shock, 216 Sci. 437 (1982).

64. Peterson & Bossio, supra note 59, at 235.

65. Id. at 243. See infra notes 94–101 and accompanying text.

66. Peterson & Bossio, supra note 59, at 243.

67. Id.

68. Id.

summary, they experience the symptoms of clinical depression and a loss of self-confidence that is itself debilitating.[69]

Because Seligman's essentially behavioral explanation of human depression did not seem wholly satisfactory, he reformulated the doctrine of learned helplessness as applied to human subjects.[70] Using various insights derived from cognitive psychology, particularly expectancy and attribution theory, Seligman reconceptualized learned helplessness to take into account the importance of cognitive factors. Under the revised model, a perceived noncontingent relationship between their actions and the outcomes they experience leads people to believe that events are outside their control. Beliefs about prior noncontingent relationships between actions and outcomes carry over and foster generalized expectations of lack of control. Seligman postulated that the perceived noncontingency between actions and outcomes, particularly if ascribed to personal limitations that are seen as immutable, causes individuals to question their abilities and to attribute their failures to internal deficits or incapacities.[71] The individual's perceptions of noncontrol become linked with low expectancies concerning success, fostering feelings of helplessness and hopelessness. Seligman concluded that these feelings are heightened when individuals attribute their helplessness to three factors.[72] The first is attribution of uncontrollability to internal causes (such as lack of intelligence or physical strength) rather than external causes (such as other people or societal conditions). This leads them to accept personal responsibility for failure. The second is attribution of failure to global deficits ("I am bad at problem-solving") rather than to limited difficulties ("It was a difficult problem"). The third is a perception that the causes

---

69. Friedman and Lackey document the relationship between self-confidence and an individual's capacity for control over events in his life:

> Self-confident people are more able to tolerate delay in achieving control, are more able to take calculated risks, and are more persistent in pursuing control, all of which make it more probable that they will improve their scope, degree, and reliability of control. Self-confident people tend to be dogged and venturesome in their pursuit of control and don't lose heart when obstacles delay their progress. Their confidence leads them to believe that sooner or later they will be successful in improving their control. In contrast, lack of self-confidence is an impediment to control because people who lack self-confidence expect to fail in their efforts to improve their control. They tend to consider struggling for control a waste of time. Their past failures in improving their control have taught them that there is little they can do to insure their success.

Myles I. Friedman & George H. Lackey, The Psychology of Human Control: A General Theory of Purposeful Behavior 73 (1991). People who acquire learned helplessness lose confidence in their future ability to control events in their lives.

> When they consider improving their control, the only outcome they can predict with any confidence is failure, so they usually predict failure in completing all but the most routine tasks that they have mastered. And to exhibit some vestige of control when faced with new contingencies, they arrange to fail, often by not trying to succeed. (Id.)

70. Abramson et al., supra note 59; see also Peterson & Bossio, supra note 59, at 237–38.

71. Seligman, Human Helplessness, supra note 59, at 154–55.

72. Id.

of failure are stable ("It runs in my family"; "I have permanent brain damage") rather than unstable or changeable ("I was tired that day"), so that improvement seems unlikely.

The attributional reformulation of learned helplessness theory posits that objective uncontrollability alone is not debilitating; rather, it is the individual's cognitive perception that uncontrollability is causally related to an internal deficit that leads to generalized expectations of helplessness that carry over into other situations.[73] The insights of this reformulation suggest that learned helplessness may be a likely consequence of incompetency labeling. Learned helplessness may be especially likely to occur when the incompetency label applied suggests general incompetence and is followed by imposed uncontrollability. An incompetency label causes individuals to perceive and attribute the lack of control they experience to internal and relatively stable factors. Such a label will reinforce their perception and belief that events are truly uncontrollable. Whereas individuals who find themselves not in control of their environment generally may not attribute such uncontrollability to themselves, the application of an incompetency label will substantially increase the likelihood that they will attribute causality to internal inability. In summary, an incompetency label makes salient the individual's helplessness and responsibility for it, preventing the person from attributing the problem to other causes.

Attribution theory suggests that even when individuals who experience failure or lack of control have not been labeled incompetent, they may posit the existence of an internal deficit that is responsible for their problems. Psychologists Edward Jones and Steven Berglas have used the term *self-handicapping* to describe this phenomenon.[74] Under this conception, individuals may seek or create reasons for inhibiting future performance in order to avoid potential failure and to reduce a threat to their self-esteem. "The self-handicapper... reaches out for impediments, exaggerates handicaps, and embraces any factor reducing personal responsibility for mediocrity..."[75] Individuals thus tend to discount the role of their own ability in producing failure, attributing it instead to their real or imagined handicap.[76] Self-handicapping serves to mitigate the

---

73. See Peterson & Bossio, supra note 59, at 241.

74. Edward E. Jones & Steven Berglas, Control of Attributions About the Self Through Self-Handicapping Strategies: The Appeal of Alcohol and the Role of Underachievement, 4 Personality & Soc. Psychol. Bull. 200 (1978). See also Robert N. Arkin & Ann Hudson Baumgardner, Self-Handicapping in Attribution: Basic Issues and Applications 169 (John H. Harvey & Gifford Weary eds., 1985); C.R. Snyder & Timothy W. Smith, Symptoms as Self-Handicapping Strategies: The Virtues of Old Wine in a New Bottle, in Integrations of Clinical and Social Psychology 104 (Gifford Weary & Herbert Mirels eds., 1982).

75. Arkin & Baumgardner, supra note 74, at 202. See also Jones & Berglas, supra note 74, at 201 ("By finding or creating impediments that make good performance less likely, the strategist nicely protects his sense of self-competence.").

76. Jones & Berglas, supra note 74, at 201 ("If the person does poorly, the source of the failure is externalized in the impediment."). See Harold H. Kelly, Attribution in Social Interaction, in Attribution: Perceiving the Causes of Behavior 1 (Edward E. Jones et al. eds., 1971); see also Arkin & Baumgardner, supra note 74, at 171 (analyzing this phenomenon as an application of Kelly's discounting principle).

impact of failure feedback and allows them to avoid viewing their failure as a reflection of low ability or lack of general competence.[77]

If this performance-inhibiting phenomenon occurs even when individuals are not labeled incompetent, such labeling, particularly when performed by an authority figure such as a judge or psychiatrist, should increase the tendency for individuals to perceive themselves to be handicapped in the area in question. Even more than a self-handicap attribution, application of an incompetency label causes individuals to inhibit future attempted performance in order to preserve self-esteem. The tendency of self-handicapping to produce failure by inhibiting performance would be magnified by application of an incompetency label that in effect communicates to individuals that attempted performance will be useless. Why, after all, should they attempt a task that they have been told they are incompetent to perform?

Individuals who consider themselves to be handicapped sometimes exert prodigious efforts in order to "overcome their handicap." However, they know that even their prodigious efforts will not overcome incompetency. Individuals who understand their failure to be a function of an internal handicap may not attempt performance, at least during the period in which they think their handicap persists, but may at least maintain a general sense of self-competence. "I could succeed," they may think, "but for my handicap." When their failure is clearly and unambiguously attributed to a lasting lack of ability, however, as it often is when they are labeled incompetent, the likelihood that they will internalize the incompetency attribution is increased. This perception can have debilitating effects on their self-esteem and may produce the "paralytic and painful results of having to give up hope."[78] Whereas self-handicapping may thus preserve their public esteem and illusion of control,[79] application of an incompetency label would be devastating to both self-esteem and the sense of self-control.

People suffering from mental illness often have a history of poor performance in social, occupational, and educational contexts and an already impaired sense of self-esteem and self-efficacy. Labeling them as mentally ill may further their tendency to self-handicap and may inhibit future performance in areas in which they expect that their condition will produce failure. If such mental illness labeling occurs in a context in which they are extended therapeutic opportunities that they are motivated to accept, the illness label may provide the insight needed to engage in a course of therapy that will have beneficial effects. The addition of an incompetency label, however, may destroy this opportunity by making them feel that improvement is unlikely. A student who performs poorly in reading or arithmetic may self-handicap and attempt to avoid future opportunities to engage in these activities. Labeling the student as *learning disabled* may further this tendency, but an individual who truly has a learning disability may learn strategies and techniques to mitigate or overcome this disability. If the student is labeled as incompetent at reading or arith-

---

77. Arkin & Baumgardner, supra note 74, at 170.
78. Arkin & Baumgardner, supra note 74, at 185.
79. Id.

metic, however, he or she may never again attempt these activities with the degree of commitment and energy required to master them.

By reinforcing expectancies of failure and producing generalized expectancies of incompetence, the incompetency label when applied to those with mental illness will predictably frustrate what presumably are the goals of mental health intervention. Any sensible system of mental hospitalization and treatment must be designed to restore patients to the greatest possible degree of functional normality. By having choices made for them, patients labeled as incompetent are deprived of the opportunity to engage in decision making and to exercise skills and may experience further loss of functional capacity as a result.[80] Indeed, this is one explanation for why some patients develop an institutional personality syndrome, finding it difficult to exist outside an institution that makes all important decisions for patients and in which they bear little or no responsibility for decision making.[81]

Labeling mentally ill individuals as incompetent may thus be devastating, diminishing self-esteem and inhibiting future performance. Even more than labeling such persons as mentally ill, labeling them as incompetent may produce or perpetuate learned helplessness. Because an incompetency adjudication produces consequences that individuals often perceive as negative and unrelated to their choices or actions, they may develop generalized feelings of uncontrollability, helplessness, and hopelessness. They may respond with passivity, resig-

---

80. See Bruce D. Sales & Lynn R. Kahle, Law and Attitudes Toward the Mentally Ill, 3 Int'l J. L. & Psychiatry 391, 392 (1980) ("Apart from the potential stigma of not being able to make one's own decisions, there are also the potential problems of diminishing self-esteem caused by the outcome of the adjudication and the actual disuse of decision-making powers, which may lead to degeneration of existing capabilities and behaviors.").

81. See Erving Goffman, Asylums: Essays on the Social Situations of Mental Patients and Other Inmates 3–74 (1962) (discussing the phenomenon of institutional dependence); Charles A. Kiesler & Amy E. Sibulkin, Mental Hospitalization: Myths and Facts about a National Crisis 148 (1987); Michael L. Perlin, 2 Mental Disability Law: Civil and Criminal 1–438 (1989) (hospitalization has frequently caused harm or retarded recovery); Robert F. DeVellis, Learned Helplessness in Institutions, 15 Mental Retardation 10 (Oct. 1977); Richard Cole, Patients' Rights vs. Doctors' Rights: Which Should Take Precedence?, in Refusing Treatment in Mental Institutions: Values in Conflict 59 (A. Edward Doudera & Judith P. Swazey eds., 1982); Edmund G. Doherty, Labeling Effects in Psychiatric Hospitalization: A Study of Diverging Patterns of Inpatient Self-Labeling Process, 32 Arch. Gen. Psychiatry 562 (1975). In addition to breeding learned helplessness, such total institutions condition passivity and helplessness by reinforcing it and by discouraging assertiveness and autonomous behavior. Conditioned helplessness, however, should be distinguished from learned helplessness. It may be that individuals subjected to situations of uncontrollability learn passivity and helplessness as a matter of operant conditioning, i.e., these behavior patterns are reinforced by environmental consequences. This is not, however, learned helplessness. Learned helplessness posits not that an individual learns a particular behavior pattern, but that he or she acquires a generalized expectation of helplessness. This expectation that outcomes and responses will be independent in the future brings about helpless behavior. For an alternative view of helplessness phenomena, hypothesizing that passivity in a situation that is marked by uncontrollability relates to the individual's ego-need to save face, see Arthur Frankel & Melvin L. Snyder, Poor Performance Following Unsolvable Problems: Learned Helplessness Or Egotism?, 36 J. Personality & Soc. Psychol. 1415 (197); Peterson & Bossio, supra note 59, at 240.

nation, and lowered self-esteem. Moreover, the incompetency label causes individuals to attribute their failures to themselves, as due to internal shortcomings that are relatively unchangeable, rather than to universal difficulties or temporary deficits. Not everyone, the individual may reason, is incompetent, not even all patients with mental illness. The incompetency label predictably produces depression and withdrawal and saps motivation. In summary, incompetency labeling may be highly antitherapeutic.

2. *Effects on motivation.* Psychologist Edward Deci's influential work on motivation and behavior has distinguished three different types of motivational subsystems: intrinsic motivational, extrinsic motivational, and amotivational.[82] Intrinsic motivation is based in the need for competence and self-determination. It involves self-determined behavior, an internal perceived locus of causality, feelings of self-determination, and a high degree of perceived competence and self-esteem.

Extrinsic motivation involves greater responsivity to external as opposed to internal cues and arises in contexts in which the behaviors and the rewards are separable. In contrast to the intrinsic subsystem, where rewards are the feelings accompanying self-determined, competent behavior, rewards in the extrinsic subsystem, such as praise or money, are separable from the behavior and its accompanying feelings. The perceived locus of causality for the extrinsic subsystem is external and is experienced as less self-determining. Behaviors are perceived as being controlled by reward contingencies rather than by internal choices, and self-esteem tends to be somewhat lower.

The amotivational subsystem is characterized by an absence of activity. Individuals perceive that there is no relationship between behaviors and rewards or outcomes. Perceived competence, self-determination, and self-esteem tend to be extremely low. People who are amotivational feel helpless, incompetent, and out of control.

Deci's description of the amotivational subsystem parallels Seligman's concept of learned helplessness. According to Deci, with the amotivational subsystem, causality is perceived to be impersonal and behavior and outcomes to be independent. "[S]uch people believe that they cannot attain desired outcomes—so there tends to be no voluntary behavior."[83]

Deci considered intrinsic motivation or the need to be self-determining as a basic human need.[84] This inherent human need to be competent and self-determining parallels what Heinz Hartmann called *independent ego energy*[85] and what Robert White called *effectance motivation*.[86] Deci cited a variety of stud-

---

82. Edward L. Deci, Intrinsic Motivation 61–62 (1975) [hereinafter Deci, Intrinsic Motivation]; Edward L. Deci, The Psychology of Self-determination 41 (1980) [hereinafter Deci, Self-determination].

83. Deci, Intrinsic Motivation, supra note 82, at 67.

84. Id. at 208.

85. See Heinz Hartmann, Ego Psychology and the Problem of Adaptation (1958).

86. Robert W. White, Motivation Reconsidered: The Concept of Competence, 66 Psychol. Rev. 297 (1959). See also Andras Angyal, Foundations for a Science of Personality (1941) (describing the inherent human tendency toward self-determination); Richard De Charms, Personal Causation: The Internal Affective Determinants of Behavior (1968) (human beings strive for personal causation); Kenneth Goldstein, The Organism (1939)

ies providing empirical verification for the importance of self-determination as a motivational propensity.[87] These studies, Deci argued, demonstrate that "the opportunity to be self-determining is intrinsically motivating and the denial of the opportunity to be self-determining undermines people's motivation, learning, and general sense of organismic well-being."[88] Deci concluded that intrinsic motivation is a basic need of the central nervous system.[89] Indeed, in extreme cases, "anecdotal and survey data suggest that the stress of losing the opportunity to be self-determining may cause severe somatic malfunctions and even death."[90]

When people are labeled incompetent and their decision-making control is removed, they are explicitly reminded that they lack an internal locus of control.[91] Such people function on the basis of neither intrinsic nor extrinsic motivation; rather, what Deci called the amotivational subsystem is operative. In this state, the individual experiences "a minimum of behavior, will feel helpless, hopeless, and self-critical, and will not behave because he can see no use in behaving."[92] Such people experience a lack of motivation, initiating behavior less frequently and exhibiting less persistence in goal attainment.[93]

Deci's work suggests that making decisions for oneself is a basic human need, the frustration of which diminishes intrinsic motivation and produces dysfunctional behavior, withdrawal, passivity, and lack of response. When people are allowed to be self-determining, they function more effectively and with greater satisfaction. For example, children in classrooms that stress autonomy have been shown to have higher intrinsic motivation and higher self-esteem than those in control-oriented classrooms.[94] Labeling people as incompetent deprives them of the opportunity for self-determining behavior. Having

---

(human need for self-actualization); Abraham H. Maslow, Motivation and Personality (1954) (self-actualization); Jerome Kagan, Motives and Development, 22 J. Personality & Soc. Psychol. 51 (1972) (suggesting that humans have a "motive for mastery"); Abraham H. Maslow, A Theory of Human Motivation, 50 Psychol. Rev. 370 (1943) (self-actualization).

87. Deci, Intrinsic Motivation, supra note 82, at 209.

88. Id. at 209.

89. Id. at 62.

90. Id.

91. See id. at 212 ("When salient elements of the environment convey information that one is incompetent, it will leave one helpless and amotivational.").

92. Id. at 210.

93. Craig A. Anderson & Lynn H. Arnoult, Attributional Style and Everyday Problems in Living: Depression, Loneliness, and Shyness, 3 Soc. Cognition 16 (1985).

94. See Edward L. Deci et al., Characteristics of the Rewarder and Intrinsic Motivation of the Rewardee, 40 J. Personality & Soc. Psychol. 1 (1981). Deci also demonstrated this relationship between choice and intrinsic motivation in other experimental settings. Edward L. Deci and Richard M. Ryan, The Empirical Exploration of Intrinsic Motivational Processes, 13 Advances in Experimental Soc. Psychol. 39, 59 (1980). Giving people choice may produce a degree of commitment that mobilizes the self-evaluative and self-reinforcing mechanisms that facilitate goal achievement. See Albert Bandura, Social Foundations of Thought and Action: A Social Cognitive Theory 338, 368, 468, 478–80 (1986) (discussing relationship between individual choice and goal attainment); Brehm & Brehm, supra note 59, at 301.

[others make decisions for them produces amotivational behaviors, low self-esteem, passivity, and feelings of inadequacy and incompetency.]

3. Effects on mood. Seligman's observation that conditions of uncontrollability produce the symptoms of clinical depression,[95] and Deci's description of the emotional component of the amotivational subsystem,[96] point to another adverse effect of incompetency labeling.[Such labeling may produce and reinforce depression and other alterations of mood.]Under this analysis, individuals become depressed when highly desired outcomes are believed improbable and highly aversive consequences are believed likely, and they conclude that their behavioral repertoire is incapable of altering these likely outcomes.[97] The intensity and duration of their depression will depend on how general they perceive the deficit to be, on whether it is thought to be stable or irreversible, and on the degree of the trait's internality or relationship to the individuals' self-identity.[98]

The perception and expectation of uncontrollability may produce four differing components of depression: "depressed affect, lower motivation, cognitive deficits (e.g., inability to learn response contingencies), and lower self-esteem."[99] These symptoms of depression, by impairing the individual's concept of self-efficacy, will in turn have a further debilitating effect on motivation and performance.[100] Because an incompetency label strongly communicates to individuals that they are globally impaired, that their impairment is unlikely to change, and that the deficit is internally caused, depression would seem to be a predictable side effect of such labeling.

Empirical studies have shown that for some people, feelings of depression, loneliness, and shyness may be related to a maladaptive attributional style.[101] Such people may explain their successes and failures in a self-defeating way, thereby fostering expectations of poor performance, which in turn dampen motivation, promote rigidity of behavior, and bring about failure and depression.[102] A maladaptive attributional style would tend to be reinforced when in-

---

95. See supra notes 64–69 and accompanying text.

96. See supra notes 82–93 and accompanying text.

97. Abramson et al., supra note 59, at 60.

98. Id.

99. Arkin & Baumgardner, supra note 74, at 249. "The generality of the depression is influenced by the globality of the attributions. The chronicity (or duration) is influenced by the stability of the attributions. The self-esteem component is influenced by the locus of the attributions." Id.

100. Bandura, supra note 94, at 408 ("The impact of mood on self-percepts of efficacy is widespread, rather than confined to the particular domain of functioning in which happiness or sadness was experienced.... [D]espondency can thus lower self-percepts of efficacy that give rise to ineffectual performance, breeding even deeper despondency.").

101. Anderson & Arnoult, supra note 93, at 17. See also Craig A. Anderson, The Causal Structure of Situations: The Generation of Plausible Causal Attributions as a Function of Type of Event Situation, 19 J. Experimental Soc. Psychol. 185 (1983); Martin E. Seligman et al., Depressive Attributional Style, 88 J. Abnormal Psychol. 242 (1979); Hedwig Teglasi & Mary Ann Hoffman, Causal Attributions of Shy Subjects, 16 J. Res. In Personality 376 (1982).

102. Anderson & Arnoult, supra note 93, at 17.

dividuals receive an incompetency label. ⌈Applying such a label to individuals with existing problems may therefore perpetuate depression and related difficulties. ⌉

People who have been labeled incompetent are deprived of their ability to satisfy the basic human need to be self-determining and self-actualizing.[103] Whether it is an innate need or a conditioned desire, a degree of control over important events in their lives seems essential to people's sense of well-being. Happy and well-adjusted people seek to function effectively in life, behaving in ways that generally maximize pleasure and minimize pain. Some degree of actual control and a perception of self-control are essential if this is to be accomplished. Individuals must have some measure of personal control over their actions and the environment in order to function effectively,[104] and belief in one's own efficacy appears essential to effective functioning.[105] Without such a belief individuals are unlikely to initiate potentially rewarding actions or to continue such actions to completion.[106]

Using the concept of "locus of control,"[107] psychologists have demonstrated a relationship between perceptions of control and mood and feelings of psychological well-being. Under this analysis, individuals who perceive themselves as having an internal locus of control are vital, lively, and essentially happy. On the other hand, those who have an external locus of control lose feelings of mastery and a sense of effectiveness and become demoralized and depressed.[108] Seligman showed that perceptions of inability to control consequences produce depression not only when those consequences are aversive, but even when they are positive.[109] By depriving individuals of control over the decision in question and by explicitly labeling them as unable to exercise self-control, an incompetency adjudication predictably will foster feelings of depression and worthlessness. Labeling individuals incompetent therefore places a cloud over their sense of psychological well-being and depresses mood in ways that are strongly unpleasant and that may be debilitating.

III. The Implications for Mental Health Law

Both Deci's work on motivation and Seligman's work on learned helplessness thus suggest that allowing people to be self-determining generally is es-

---

103. See supra notes 84–90 and accompanying text.

104. Arkin & Baumgardner, supra note 74, at 184.

105. Id.

106. See Deci, Self-Determination, supra note 82, at 208–210; Arkin & Baumgardner, supra note 74, at 184; Albert Bandura, Self-Efficacy: Toward a Unifying Theory of Behavioral Change, 84 Psychol. Rev. 191 (1977).

107. Heider, supra note 48; Herbert M. Lefcourt, Locus of Control: Current Trends in Theory and Research (2d ed. 1982); Herbert M. Lefcourt, Perceiving the Self as an Effective Agent, in Perception of Self in Emotional Disorder and Psychotherapy 37 (Lorne M. Hartman & Kirk R. Blankstein eds., 1986).

108. See, e.g., Deci, Self-Determination, supra note 82, at 41; Lefcourt, supra note 107, at 37; Julian B. Rotter, Generalized Expectancies for Internal vs. External Control of Reinforcement, 80 Psychol. Monographs 1 (1966).

109. See Seligman, Human Helplessness, supra note 59, at 154–55.

sential to their psychological well-being and effective functioning. By contrast, labeling them as incompetent and thereby depriving them of the opportunity for self-determining behavior induces feelings of helplessness, hopelessness, depression, and low self-esteem. These feelings and the self-attribution of incompetency that an incompetency adjudication may produce will predictably undermine motivation and effective performance. Overuse of the incompetency label may therefore produce what in therapeutic jurisprudence terms is described as "law-related psychological dysfunction."[110]

This analysis does not necessarily suggest that the concept of incompetency should never be used. There undoubtedly are cases in which an individual's functioning is so impaired by mental illness that the individual is unable either to make decisions or to make them with any degree of rationality. In such cases, the individual's problems are quite real and are not merely an artifact of being labeled incompetent. An understanding of the negative effects of incompetency labeling, however, suggests the need for a careful cost-benefit analysis of the law's use of the label. What benefits are achieved by adjudicating people to be incompetent in the various legal contexts in which this occurs, and do these benefits exceed the individual and social costs that such labeling may impose?

The legal concept of competency is ambiguous and artificial in a number of respects. First, the law treats competency as a dichotomous inquiry in which people are either competent or incompetent. This dichotomous approach is artificial, however. It is more appropriate to understand that there are degrees of competency falling along a continuum and that competency is almost always in flux. It also is inappropriate to regard competency as a descriptive concept. Competency is more a normative than a descriptive notion, reflecting a variety of political and moral judgments. In addition, because the incompetency label is used in a variety of legal contexts, there is a tendency to regard people as either competent or incompetent for all purposes. Competency, however, is a contextualized inquiry. People may be incompetent for one purpose yet be competent for others. Finally, the justifications for using the concept of competency vary with the legal context. Because the concept of competence is rarely defined, however, the tendency is to regard the concept as meaning essentially the same thing in each context. The vagueness of the concept and its use in so many different contexts tend to mask the often different social policies that are implicated. It is necessary to identify clearly the social policies involved in each context in which the concept of competence is used, to determine for each whether these policies justify the adverse effects of incompetency labeling, and to specify standards for applying the concept that reflect the relevant social policies operating in these differing areas.[111]

When the issue is competency to engage in rational decision making, a large number of individuals with mental illness are neither clearly competent nor

---

110. Wexler, supra note 4, at 5; Wexler & Winick, supra note 5, at 313; Wexler & Winick, The Potential of Therapeutic Jurisprudence, supra note 5, at 211, 226; Wexler & Winick, Therapeutic Jurisprudence as a New Approach, supra note 5, at 979, 994; Winick, supra note 4, at 336.

111. Winick, supra note 8, at 22–24; Winick, Restructuring Competency to Stand Trial, supra note 6, at 921.

clearly incompetent. Rather, they properly can be placed in the middle ranges of the competency continuum. Their decision-making capacity may be impaired by mental illness, but they nonetheless are able clearly to express choice and exercise some degree of autonomy and rationality. For these individuals, the use of the incompetency label may be countertherapeutic, defeating the putatively benevolent purposes of the law. Analysis is needed concerning each legal context in which the concept of competence is used to determine when these costs of incompetency labeling outweigh the assumed benefits. In such contexts the law should reconsider the continued use of the incompetency concept. At a minimum, the law in these contexts should recognize a presumption against use of the incompetency label and should define the concept of incompetency narrowly in a way that allows marginal cases to be deemed competent. Even when incompetency labeling is thought justified, a number of steps can be taken to avoid or minimize the harmful effects of such labeling.

The adverse effects of incompetency labeling are sufficiently serious that in many contexts application of the label should be regarded as a deprivation of liberty within the meaning of the Constitution. As a result, in such contexts the state's ability to use its *parens patriae* power, which requires labeling an individual incompetent, should be limited. In these contexts constitutional considerations suggest that incompetency should be defined more narrowly, that competency should be presumed, and that the burden of persuasion should be placed on the party that asserts incompetency. In addition, a number of approaches can be suggested that would avoid incompetency labeling. Even in cases in which such labeling is considered necessary, it may be possible to recharacterize incompetency labels and reshape the labeling process in ways that can minimize adverse effects.

A. Incompetency Labeling as a Deprivation of Constitutional Liberty

The stigma produced by incompetency labeling can be serious and long-lasting. Both the strong social disadvantages suffered by those to whom the law attaches this label, and the effects on the individual's own cognition, motivation, performance, and mood, can be debilitating. Once the existence and extent of this double-edged stigma are recognized, application of an incompetency label can be seen as imposing a deprivation of liberty within the meaning of the Due Process Clause even apart from the associated deprivations that the incompetency label often brings.[112] This is not simply an injury to reputation alone. Without more, such an injury to reputation will not invade constitutionally protected liberty.[113] Incompetency labeling not only damages individuals' reputation in the eyes of the community, but profoundly affects their own self-concept in ways that can be debilitating. Branding individuals as incompe-

---

112. See, e.g., Vitek v. Jones, 445 U.S. 480, 492 (1980) (stigmatization of transfer of prisoner to mental hospital constituted a deprivation of liberty); Goss v. Lopez, 419 U.S. 565, 574 (1975) (stigmatization of students by noting school suspension on their permanent records constituted a deprivation of liberty).

113. Paul v. Davis, 424 U.S. 693 (1976) (distribution by police chief of flyer containing names and photographs of "known shoplifters" held not to infringe a liberty interest, and therefore to require a hearing, absent additional deprivations resulting therefrom).

tent is a trespass and an assault on their psyche in ways that can leave a lasting imprint.[114]

Moreover, when courts apply an incompetency label, it almost always has the legal effect of depriving individuals of associated liberties. An adjudication that a criminal defendant is incompetent to stand trial, for example, justifies deprivation of what otherwise would be the defendant's Sixth Amendment right to speedy trial.[115] A defendant seeking to be found incompetent may not be thought of as being "deprived" of this right, but the label sometimes is applied over objection to defendants asserting their interest in the speedy resolution of their charges.[116] Individuals found incompetent to vote are thereby deprived of exercising the prerogatives of citizens to participate in the democratic process.[117] When individuals are found incompetent to manage their property, to contract or make a conveyance, to give a gift, or to make a will, they lose the right to enjoy or to dispose of their property as they see fit, an interference with both liberty and property. People who are found incompetent to make treatment decisions will be deprived of authority over their bodily integrity[118] and of the liberty to control personal health.[119] Individuals committed to a

---

114. Cf. Brown v. Board of Educ., 347 U.S. 483, 494 (1954). ("To separate them from others of similar age and qualifications solely because of their race generates a feeling of inferiority as to their status in the community that may affect their hearts and minds in a way unlikely ever to be undone.")

115. U.S. Const. amend. VI; see, e.g., Jackson v. Indian, 406 U.S. 715, 740 (1972); Williams v. United States, 250 F.2d 19 (D.C. Cir. 1957); United States v. Pardue, 354 F. Supp. 1377 (D. Conn. 1973); Winick, supra note 1, at 802–805 (discussing speedy trial problems arising in the context of defendants found incompetent to stand trial).

116. Winick, Restructuring Competency to Stand Trial, supra note 6, at 951.

117. See Dunn v. Blumstein, 405 U.S. 330 (1972); Kramer v. Union Free School Dist. Number 15, 395 U.S. 621 (1969).

118. See Cruzan v. Director, Missouri Dep't of Health, 497 U.S. 261 (1990) (liberty interest in making personal health decisions); Ingraham v. Wright, 430 U.S. 651, 673 (1977) (noting that "among the historic liberties so protected was a right to be free from . . . unjustified intrusions on personal security"); Union Pac. Ry. Co. v. Botsford, 141 U.S. 250, 252 (1891) (holding that court may not order plaintiff to submit to pretrial surgical examination); cf. Winston v. Lee, 470 U.S. 753 (1985) (holding that nonconsensual surgical removal of bullet would violate Fourth Amendment's ban on unreasonable searches and seizures). Lower courts have frequently found that patients have a right to refuse treatment grounded in a liberty interest in "bodily integrity, personal security and personal dignity." E.g., Johnson v. Silvers, 742 F.2d 823, 825 (4th Cir. 1984); Lojak v. Quandt, 706 F.2d 1456, 1465 (7th Cir. 1983), cert. denied, 476 U.S. 1067 (1986); Rogers v. Okin, 634 F.2d 650, 652 (1st Cir. 1980), vacated sub nom. Mills v. Rogers, 452 U.S. 291 (1982); Scott v. Plante 532 F.2d 939, 946 n.9 (3d Cir. 1976), vacated, 458 U.S. 1101 (1982); Osgood v. District of Columbia, 567 F. Supp. 1026, 1032 (D.D.C. 1983); Project Release v. Prevost, 551 F. Supp. 1298, 1309 (E.D.N.Y. 1982), aff'd, 722 F.2d 960 (2nd Cir. 1983); Davis v. Hubbard, 506 F. Supp. 915, 930 (N.D. Ohio 1980); Rennie v. Klein, 462 F. Supp. 1131, 1144 (D.N.J. 1978); Large v. Superior Court, 714 P.2d 399, 406 (Ariz. 1986); Rogers v. Commissioner, 458 N.E.2d 308 (Mass. 1983); Opinion of the Justices, 465 A.2d 484, 488 (N.H. 1983); In re K.K.B., 609 P.2d 747, 749 (Okla. 1980). See Bruce J. Winick, On Autonomy: Legal and Psychological Perspectives, 37 Vill. L. Rev. 1705, 1732–35 (1993).

119. Riggins v. Nevada, 112 S. Ct. 1810 (1992) (concluding that Due Process Clause protects criminal defendant's interest in avoiding involuntary administration of antipsychotic

psychiatric facility on the basis of a determination of incompetency thereby lose the basic right to be freed from external restraint.[120] Individuals found to be incompetent to marry may not exercise the fundamental right to participate in marriage and family life.[121] An incompetency label thus frequently results in the deprivation of fundamental liberty and property interests within the protection of the Due Process Clause.

Deprivations this serious should not be imposed unnecessarily. Conventional substantive due process and equal protection analysis require strict judicial scrutiny of governmental action producing such deprivations of liberty.[122] Moreover, the imposition of stigma together with associated deprivations has been recognized to trigger the need for the protection of procedural due process.[123] Yet, the strongly negative impact on an individual's life, liberty, and property of labeling them incompetent has been underappreciated. Constitutional principles should be construed to prevent an incompetency label from being applied unnecessarily. When alternative means exist for accomplishing the government's stated interests without the necessity of imposing an incompetency label, the Constitution should prohibit such labeling.

B. Reconsidering Assertions of the State's *Parens Patriae* Power

The limitations on liberty and on the use of property that often accompany application of an incompetency label are usually justified as exercises of the

drugs); *Cruzan,* 497 at 277–78 (1990) (concluding that a competent person has a constitutionally protected interest in refusing unwanted medical treatment); Washington v. Harper, 494 U.S. 210, 221–22 (1990) (liberty interest in freedom from unwanted antipsychotic medication); Doe v. Bolton, 410 U.S. 179, 192 (1973) (Douglas, J., concurring) (referring to "the freedom to care for one's health and person" as being a fundamental right protected by the Due Process Clause of the Fourteenth Amendment).

120. Foucha v. Louisiana, 112 S. Ct. 1780 (1992); Zinermon v. Burch, 494 U.S. 113 (1990).

121. See, e.g., Turner v. Safley, 482 U.S. 78 (1987); Zablocki v. Redhail, 434 U.S. 374 (1978); Boddie v. Connecticut, 401 U.S. 371 (1971); Shapiro v. Thompson, 394 U.S. 618 (1969); Loving v. Virginia, 388 U.S. 1 (1967); Meyer v. Nebraska, 262 U.S. 390, 399 (1923) (dicta).

122. See, e.g., Foucha v. Louisiana, 112 S. Ct. 1780 (1992) (commitment of an insanity acquittee to a mental hospital held to violate substantive due process where the patient, although thought to be dangerous, was no longer mentally ill); Riggins v. Nevada, 112 S. Ct. 1810 (1992) (involuntary administration of antipsychotic medication during criminal pretrial and trial process would violate substantive due process unless such medication was medically appropriate and constituted the least intrusive means either of protecting the safety of other jail inmates or staff or of maintaining defendant's competency to stand trial) (dicta); Turner v. Safley, 482 U.S. 78 (1987) (right to marry); Kramer v. Union Free School Dist. Number 15, 395 U.S. 621 (1969) (right to vote).

123. E.g., Vitek v. Jones, 445 U.S. 480 (1980) (stigma of mental hospitalization); Owen v. City of Independence, 445 U.S. 622 (1980) (stigma of wrongful dismissal from employment); Goss v. Lopez, 419 U.S. 565 (1975) (stigma of school suspension); Wisconsin v. Constantineau, 400 U.S. 433 (1971) (stigma of "posting"—the listing of the names of individuals who have been publicly intoxicated, which has the effect of preventing them from purchasing alcoholic beverages).

state's *parens patriae* power.[124] This power, grounded in principles of beneficence,[125] authorizes government to engage in decision making in the best interest of persons who by reason of age or disability are incapable of making such
decisions for themselves.[126] Incompetency has therefore historically been
viewed as a limitation on exercise of the *parens patriae* power,[127] a limitation
recognized by a number of courts.[128] Because a finding of incompetency is thus

---

124. See Mills v. Rogers, 457 U.S. 291, 296 (1982); Joel Feinberg, Harm to Self 6 (1986)
(analyzing *parens patriae* power); Winick, supra note 8, at 16 & n.3 (examining government's *parens patriae* power to make decisions for those who are unable to make decisions
for themselves); Note, Developments in the Law—Civil Commitment of the Mentally Ill, 87
Harv. L. Rev. 1190, 1207–45 (1974) (discussing commitment under *parens patriae* power of
state).

125. Winick, supra note 8, at 18.

126. Bruce J. Winick, Legal Limitations on Correctional Therapy and Research, 65 MINN.
L. Rev. 331, 375 (1981) (noting historical derivations of *parens patriae* power); Winick,
supra note 118, at 1772 (discussing relationship between principles favoring individual autonomy and the *parens patriae* power); Note, supra note 124, at 1207–12 (discussing historical roots of *parens patriae* power of state); see, e.g., Addington v. Texas, 441 U.S. 418, 426
(1979) (dicta) (discussing *parens patriae* power of government); O'Connor v. Donaldson,
422 U.S. 563, 583 (1975) (Burger, C.J., concurring) (noting historical roots of *parens patriae*
power).

127. Winick, supra note 8, at 16 & n.3; Winick, supra note 125, at 375; Winick, supra
note 118, at 1772–73; Note, supra note 124, at 1207–12.

128. Some of the cases have recognized this limitation in the context of civil commitment.
E.g., In re Ballay, 482 F.2d 648, 659–60 (D.C. Cir. 1973); Lessard v. Schmidt, 349 F. Supp.
1078, 1094 (E.D. Wis. 1972) (three judge court) (dictum), vacated and remanded on other
grounds, 414 U.S. 473 (1973). Most of the cases, however, have involved assertion of a right
to refuse antipsychotic medication. See, e.g., Bee v. Greaves, 744 F.2d 1387, 1395 (10th Cir.
1984), cert. denied, 469 U.S. 1214 (1985); Rennie v. Klein, 653 F.2d 836, 846–47 & n.12
(3d Cir. 1981) (en banc), vacated and remanded, 458 U.S. 119 (1982); Rogers v. Okin, 634
F.2d 650, 657–59 (1st Cir. 1980) (requiring individual to be incompetent to make a decision
concerning mental health treatment before state can justify use of its *parens patriae* power),
vacated and remanded sub nom. Mills v. Rogers, 457 U.S. 291 (1982); Winters v. Miller, 446
F.2d 65, 68–71 (2nd Cir. 1971) (holding that a woman stated a cause of action on which relief could be granted when she alleged that a hospital rendered involuntary care without first
having her found legally incompetent), cert. denied sub nom., 404 U.S. 985 (1971); Davis v.
Hubbard, 506 F. Supp. 915, 935–36 (N.D. Ohio 1980) (holding that a patient being declared mentally ill does not in itself justify the use of *parens patriae* power to forcibly administer psychotropic drugs when patient is still competent to make decision); People v.
Medina, 705 P.2d 961, 973 (Colo. 1985) (en banc) (specifying limits on involuntary administration of antipsychotic drugs); In re Boyd, 403 A.2d 744, 747 n.5 (D.C. 1979) (holding
that commitment of an individual alone is not sufficient to justify overriding individual's
treatment decisions); Gundy v. Pauley, 619 S.W.2d 730, 731 (Ky. Ct. App. 1981) (refusing to
allow electroconvulsive treatment of patient who was not declared legally incompetent to
consent); Rogers v. Commissioner of the Dep't of Mental Health, 458 N.E.2d 308, 322
(Mass. 1983) (limiting use of state's *parens patriae* power to "rare circumstances"); Opinion
of the Justices, 465 A.2d 484, 489–90 (N.H. 1983) (holding that power to administer
forcible medical treatment does not automatically follow exercise of power to involuntarily
hospitalize patient, but rather requires showing that individual is incapable of making informed decision); Rivers v. Katz, 495 N.E.2d 337, 342–43 (N.Y. 1986) (holding that to impose involuntary antipsychotic medication, state must show that patient is incompetent and

a prerequisite for governmental assertions of the *parens patriae* power that intrude on constitutionally protected liberty interests, procedural due process requires a hearing on the competency question and a fairly formal determination of incompetency.[129] Such a hearing and determination traditionally had been thought unnecessary in cases in which the individual voluntarily sought to waive the right to a hearing and to accept the intrusion or status that the government wished to impose. However, the U.S. Supreme Court's 1990 decision in *Zinermon v. Burch*,[130] if read broadly, may require a determination of competency in all cases involving waiver.

Zinermon's mandate of an "inquiry" into competency when a mentally ill individual seeks voluntary admission to a mental hospital may be construed to require an assessment of competency whenever an individual with mental illness assents to a waiver of rights. Although patients seeking voluntary hospitalization or treatment previously could have obtained it without the necessity of an inquiry into their competency,[131] *Zinermon* seems to suggest that competency must first be assessed.[132] Because some individuals who previously would have been permitted to accept the proposed intervention or status voluntarily and without an assessment of competency now will be found incompetent to do so, *Zinermon* may dramatically increase the use of incompetency labeling. As a result, incompetency labeling, and the adverse side effects it imposes, may increasingly become an unavoidable consequence of assertions of the *parens patriae* power. To the extent that a formal hearing is deemed to be required and is followed by an official finding of incompetency by a judicial or administrative decision maker, these adverse consequences will only increase.

An understanding of the extent of these negative consequences calls for a broad reconsideration of the wisdom of state assertions of the *parens patriae* power. Such paternalism frustrates the political value that society has traditionally placed on autonomy and self-determination[133] but does so on the ground of beneficence. The justification traditionally has been thought to be that the injury caused by denying the individual's autonomy would be exceeded by the harm produced by honoring the choices of those who are incompetent.[134] The added psychological harm of incompetency labeling, how-

---

the existence of a compelling state interest); In re K.K.B., 609 P.2d 747, 750–52 (Okla. 1980) (denying hospital right to administer psychotropic drugs against mentally ill patient's will); Winick, supra note 8, at 16–17 & n.3.

129. Rennie v. Klein, 653 F.2d 836, 847 & n.12 (3d Cir. 1981) (en banc), vacated & remanded, 458 U.S. 1119 (1982); Rogers v. Okin, 634 F.2d 650, 657–59 (1st Cir. 1980), vacated & remanded sub nom. Mills v. Rogers, 457 U.S. 291 (1982); Winters v. Miller, 446 F.2d 65, 71 (2d Cir. 1971), cert. denied sub nom., 404 U.S. 985 (1971); Davis v. Hubbard, 506 F. Supp. 915, 935–36 (N.D. Ohio 1980); People v. Medina, 705 P.2d 961, 973 (Colo. 1985) (en banc). See Bruce J. Winick, The Right to Refuse Psychotropic Medication: Current State of the Law and Beyond, in The Right to Refuse Antipsychotic Medication 7, 17–18 (David Rapoport & John Perry eds., 1986).

130. 494 U.S. 113, 133 & n.18 (1990); see Winick, supra note 9.

131. See Winick, supra note 8, at 29; Winick, supra note 9, at 178–79.

132. *Zinermon,* 494 U.S. at 117.

133. See Winick, supra note 8, at 36–37; Winick, supra note 118, at 1707–55 (analyzing autonomy in legal and political theory).

134. See Winick, supra note 8, at 18.

ever, may call this conclusion into question, at least in many cases. The net harm done to individuals by labeling them incompetent and by intruding on their liberty and autonomy may in fact exceed the harm of honoring at least some incompetent choices.

Striking an appropriate balance will vary, of course, with the harmfulness to individuals of honoring their possibly incompetent choices. If individuals whose decision-making abilities are significantly impaired by mental illness seek to give away all of their worldly possessions[135] or to elect experimental and dangerous treatment such as psychosurgery,[136] the harm to be avoided by not deferring to their choice may far exceed the damage of labeling them incompetent. However, when the harm to be avoided is relatively insignificant— the expenditure or gift of a modest sum, or the election of conventional and nonrisky treatment, for example—it may be better to permit an incompetent choice than to label individuals incompetent.

At least when there is some independent assurance that the individual's assertedly incompetent choice is not unreasonable or exceedingly injurious, it may be preferable to treat the choice as competent and to allow it to be acted on. For example, if a criminal defendant of doubtful competence expresses the choice to plead guilty or stand trial and counsel agrees that this election would be in the defendant's best interests, the defendant should be permitted to make the choice.[137] Similarly, if a patient of doubtful competency seeks to assent to conventional treatment or voluntary hospitalization recommended by a therapist as being in the patient's best interests, the patient should be permitted to do so.[138] In situations like these, the recommendation or approval of professionals with a fiduciary duty to the individual provides reasonable assurance that the choices the mentally ill person seeks to make are not unreasonable and are probably beneficial. In contrast, vetoing that choice

---

135. See Legislative and Social Issues Comm. of the Am. Ass'n on Mental Deficiency, Consent Handbook 7–8 (1977) ("[T]he 'situational capacity' principle might result in the same person being found competent to enter into a contract for the purchase of a shirt but not one for the sale of all his assets (where they may be of great value) for a nominal sum.").

136. Winick, supra note 8, at 41. See, e.g., Kaimowitz v. Michigan Dep't of Mental Health, Civ. No. 73-19434-AW (Mich. Cir. Ct. [Wayne County] July 10, 1973), reprinted in 1 Mental Disability L. Rep. 147 (1973) (holding that psychosurgery which has a high-risk, low-benefit ratio should not be forced on committed persons); Price v. Sheppard, 239 N.W. 2d 905, 912–13 (Minn. 1976) (imposing stringent procedural requirements for psychosurgery); National Comm'n, Psychosurgery 64–66 (DHEW Pub. No. (OS) 77-0001) (1977) (Recommendation 3) (high-risk procedures like psychosurgery require a strong showing of patient competency); Bruce J. Winick, The Right to Refuse Mental Health Treatment: A First Amendment Perspective, 44 U. Miami L. Rev. 1, 64–66 (1989) (patient with a low level of mental competency should not be allowed to consent to dangerous procedures that offer little hope of benefit).

137. Bruce J. Winick, Incompetency to Stand Trial: An Assessment of Costs and Benefits and a Proposal for Reform, 39 Rutgers L. Rev. 243 (1987); Winick, Restructuring Competency to Stand Trial, supra note 6. When counsel disagrees with the wisdom of his possibly incompetent client's election, however, or when the defendant seeks to discharge counsel and enter a plea to a charge carrying serious consequences, the balance should be struck differently, and the defendant's competency should become the subject of inquiry.

138. Winick, supra note 8; Winick, supra note 9.

on the grounds that it is incompetent and adjudicating the patient incompetent may be injurious.

The harm produced by incompetency labeling, as well as the constitutional preference for individual autonomy, accordingly should restrict government *parens patriae* interventions to situations in which they are clearly warranted by the need to avoid serious harm. The law should avoid doing harm in the process of attempting to do good. We should heed Justice Brandeis' admonition to be suspicious of good intentions, particularly when invoked to justify governmental interference with individual choice.[139] Paternalism seems so acceptable because it is part of the human condition and is so deeply rooted in the social biology of our species. Unlike that of many other species, our 9-month gestation period results in birth at a time when infants are unable to care for themselves.[140] Without parental care and nurturing, infants could not long survive. Because such parental paternalism has been necessary for human survival, we tend to accept too readily the metaphor of state paternalism embodied in the *parens patriae* doctrine. Parental paternalism rarely involves incompetency labeling, however, whereas governmental paternalism often does. Moreover, paternalism on the basis of parental love and a knowledge of the child's interest rooted in actual familiarity is much more likely to be beneficial than that engaged in by impersonal state actors who lack an ongoing relationship with the individual. The law therefore should be more hesitant than it has been to justify paternalism by the state.

C. Defining Incompetency Narrowly

Even for applications of governmental paternalism that continue to be regarded as appropriate, an understanding of the adverse side effects of incompetency labeling argues for a narrow definition of incompetency. Legal standards of incompetency often are broad and vague, permitting clinical evaluators relied on by the courts, who typically are paternalistically oriented, to classify marginally competent people with mental disabilities as incompetent.[141] For example, a typical formulation of the standard for competency to stand trial, approved by the U.S. Supreme Court as the standard to be used in federal cases, is whether the defendant "has sufficient present ability to consult with his lawyer with a reasonable degree of rational understanding—and whether he has a rational as well as factual understanding of the proceedings against him."[142] Under this standard, many criminal defendants who wish to

---

139. Olmstead v. United States, 277 U.S. 438, 479 (1928) (Brandeis, J., dissenting) ("Experience should teach us to be most on our guard to protect liberty when the Government's purposes are beneficent. Men born to freedom are naturally alert to repel invasion of their liberty by evil-minded rulers. The greatest dangers to liberty lurk in insidious encroachment by men of zeal, well-meaning but without understanding.").

140. See Willard Gaylin, In the Beginning: Helpless and Dependent, in Doing Good: The Limits of Benevolence 39 (Willard Gaylin et al. eds., 1978).

141. See Winick, Restructuring Competency to Stand Trial, supra note 6, at 982–83.

142. Dusky v. United States, 362 U.S. 402, 402 (1960). Dusky is followed in substance by all jurisdictions, although statutory terminology varies widely. Winick, Restructuring Competency to Stand Trial, supra note 6, at 923 & n.4.

stand trial or plead guilty, and whose interests would be furthered by permitting them to do so, instead are found incompetent and subjected to an enforced delay in the exercise of their right to speedy trial, and to the numerous disadvantages—sometimes including unnecessary detention, hospitalization, and treatment[143]—that follow an incompetency adjudication.

Other examples of broad and vague standards of incompetency occur in the context of informed consent to treatment and hospitalization. In its discussion of competency to consent to voluntary hospitalization in *Zinermon v. Burch*, the U.S. Supreme Court seemed to contemplate that the patient be able "to understand any proffered 'explanation and disclosure of the subject matter' of the [voluntary admission] forms that person is asked to sign, and... 'to make a knowing and willful decision' whether to consent to admission."[144] No general agreement exists concerning the appropriate standard for determining competency to provide informed consent to treatment.[145] The influential President's Commission report on health care decision making defines competency to make treatment decisions as requiring a patient to possess a set of values and goals and to be able to communicate with others, understand information, and reason and deliberate.[146] The breadth and vagueness of these standards of competency ensure a significant degree of variability among clinicians and courts in their application.[147] Moreover, clinicians may apply an artificially high standard of competency, overdiagnosing incompetency in order to bring about what to them seems a more paternalistic result.[148]

Many psychiatric evaluators may regard a competency assessment as an ex-

---

143. See Winick, Incompetency to Stand Trial, supra note 6, at 257–58; Winick, Restructuring Competency to Stand Trial, supra note 6, at 947–48.

144. *Zinermon,* 494 U.S. at 133 (quoting Fla. Stat. s 394.455(22) 1981).

145. Paul S. Appelbaum et al., supra note 8, at 83; Ruth Faden & Tom L. Beauchamp, A History and a Theory of Informed Consent 291 (1986); Thomas Grisso, Evaluating Competencies: Forensic Assessments and Instruments 314–315 (1986); Harold I. Schwartz & Loren H. Roth, Informed Consent and Competency in Psychiatric Practice, 8 Am. Psychiatry Press Rev. of Psychiatry 412, 415 (Allan Tasman et al. eds., 1989); Allan M. Tepper & Amiram Elwork, Competence to Consent to Treatment as a Psycholegal Construct, 8 L. & Hum. Behav. 205, 208 (1984); Jon R. Waltz & Thomas W. Scheuneman, Informed Consent to Therapy, 64 NW. U.L. Rev. 628, 636–37 (1969); Winick, supra note 8, at 24; Note, Informed Consent and the Dying Patient, 83 Yale L.J. 1632, 1653 (1974).

146. 1 President's Comm'n for the Study of Ethical Probs. in Med & Biomed. & Behav. Res., Making Health Care Decisions: A Report on the Ethical and Legal Implications of Informed Consent in the Patient-Practitioner Relationship 57 (1982) [hereinafter President's Comm'n Report]. For other definitions, see Paul S. Appelbaum et al., supra note 8, at 88; Grisso, supra note 145, at 1636; Paul S. Appelbaum & Loren H. Roth, Competency to Consent to Research, 39 Arch. Gen. Psychiatry 951, 951 (1982); James F. Drane, The Many Faces of Competency, 15 Hastings Center Rep. 17 (1985); Loren H. Roth et al., supra note 8, at 279; Schwartz & Roth, supra note 145, at 415; Sprung & Winick, supra note 8, at 1350–51; Tepper & Elwork, supra note 145, at 208–210, 214–16. See also Rivers v. Katz, 495 N.E. 2d 337, 343–44 & n.7 (N.Y. 1986) (eight-factor test).

147. See Winick, supra note 8, at 24–25; Winick, Restructuring Competency to Stand Trial, supra note 6, at 982–83.

148. See Winick, supra note 9, at 208 & n.180.

ercise in clinical description.[149] A competency evaluation, however, inevitably involves subjective cultural, social, political, and legal judgments that are essentially normative in nature.[150] The decision regarding which standard of competency should be used turns on moral, political, and legal judgments concerning the appropriate level of ability that individuals must possess to exercise a variety of liberty and property interests. Recognizing the essentially normative nature of the concept of competency calls for courts and legislatures to clarify the often vague notion of competency to be used in a particular context. Moreover, recognizing that competency is more a legal than a clinical question allows greater flexibility in defining the concept. Thus, we can and should define it more narrowly in order to minimize the adverse side effects of incompetency labeling and more effectively achieve the social policies underlying use of the incompetency concept in its varying contexts.

Tests of competency that require a high level of ability to understand information, rationally manipulate it, and appreciate the implications and consequences of alternative options seem artificially stringent and unrealistic, at least in the absence of extraordinary circumstances. Many "normal" people do not posses these abilities. Many nonmentally ill people frequently lose contact with reality and lack the capacity to think straight, pay attention, process information, and perform at least some key social tasks.[151] Many "normal" criminal defendants, as well as many patients with medical but not mental illness, have linguistic, educational, and social problems that severely impair their ability to function competently in making difficult decisions, particularly during the stress of a criminal trial[152] or a serious ill-

---

149. George J. Annas & Joan E. Densberger, Competency to Refuse Medical Treatment: Autonomy or Paternalism, 15 U. Tol. L. Rev. 561, 574–75 (1984); Winick, supra note 8, at 25.

150. Faden & Beauchamp, supra note 145, at 290; Grisso, supra note 145, at 30; 1 President's Comm'n Report, supra note 146, at 172 (" 'Decisionmaking incapacity' is not a medical or a psychiatric diagnostic category. . . ."); Annas & Densberger, supra note 149, at 575; Paul S. Appelbaum & Thomas Grisso, Assessing Patients' Capacities to Consent to Treatment, 319 New Eng. J. Med. 1635, 1637 (1988); Roth et al., supra note 8, at 279; Winick, supra note 8, at 25–26; Winick, Restructuring Competency to Stand Trial, supra note 6, at 966. See also Winick, supra note 136, at 46–52 (analyzing the nature of psychiatric diagnosis generally).

151. Stephen J. Morse, A Preference for Liberty: The Case Against Involuntary Commitment of the Mentally Disordered, 70 Calif. L. Rev. 54, 64–65 (1982); Stephen J. Morse, Crazy Behavior, Morals and Science: An Analysis of Mental Health Law, 51 S. Cal. L. Rev. 527, 574, 633–35 (1978) [hereinafter Crazy Behavior]; Winick, supra note 8, at 37–38; Winick, Restructuring Competency to Stand Trial, supra note 6, at 970. Appelbaum and Roth, in discussing competency to consent to research, make a similar point, suggesting that

> [Decisions made about research, even by] people of dubious competence, may not differ from the decisions that all of us make in everyday life, such as when buying a used car or choosing a brand of shampoo. . . . [T]he increasing technical complexity of our society makes it likely that many decisions in everyday life are made without appreciation of their consequences, without the ability to manipulate in a rational manner the information that is provided, and probably without full knowledge of the relevant details.

Appelbaum & Roth, supra note 146, at 957.

152. Winick, Restructuring Competency to Stand Trial, supra note 6, at 970–71. See Note, supra note 7, at 459 ("Many defendants lack the intelligence or the legal sophistica-

ness.[153] Although their decision-making competency is sometimes seriously impaired, people who have mental illness are not categorically or inherently more incompetent than nonmentally ill people.[154] More realistic standards of competency are therefore needed that require a lower threshold of decision-making ability. The law should not apply to the mentally ill artificially high standards for decision-making competence that many "normal" people are unable to satisfy.[155]

tion to participate actively in the conduct of their defense."). This conclusion receives empirical support from Grisso's studies of the abilities of both offender and nonoffender adults to understand the Miranda warnings. See generally Grisso, supra note 145. On the basis of several experimental measures of "Miranda comprehension," at least one-quarter of the adults sampled failed to meet an absolute standard for legally adequate understanding of the Miranda warnings and their implications. Id. at 145.

153. Winick, supra note 8, at 39–40; see Robert Burt, Taking Care of Strangers: The Rule of Law in Doctor-Patient Relations 142 (1979); Barrie R. Cassileth et al., Informed Consent—Why Are Its Goals Imperfectly Realized?, 302 New Eng. J. Med. 896, 899 (1980); Carl H. Fellner & John R. Marshall, Kidney Donors—The Myth of Informed Consent, 126 Am. J. Psychiatry 1245, 1250 (1970); F. J. Ingelfinger, Informed (But Uneducated) Consent, 287 New Eng. J. Med. 465, 466 (1972); see also Paul S. Appelbaum et al., Empirical Assessment of Competency to Consent to Psychiatric Hospitalization, 138 Am. J. Psychiatry 1170 (1981) (reviewing empirical studies showing poor recall and understanding of patients in a variety of situations who provided informed consent to medical treatment or research); Sprung & Winick, supra note 8, at 1351 (discussing studies showing deficiencies in recall and understanding of informed consent on the part of nonmentally ill patients).

154. Winick, supra note 9, at 190 & n.112. See Lisa Grossman & Frank Summers, A Study of the Capacity of Schizophrenic Patients to Give Informed Consent, 31 Hosp. & Community Psychiatry 205 (1980) (finding comprehension of consent information in groups of mental patients and medical patients to be fairly equal); Karen McKinnon et al., Clinicians' Assessments of Patients' Decision Making Capacity, 40 Hosp. & Community Psychiatry 1159 (1989) ("Clinical evidence suggests that despite alterations in thinking and mood, psychiatric patients are not automatically less capable than others of making health care decisions."); David A. Soskis, Schizophrenic and Medical Inpatients as Informed Drug Consumers, 35 Arch. Gen. Psychiatry 645 (1978) (patients with schizophrenia found to be more aware of risks and side effects of their medications than medical patients, but medical patients to be more informed about the name and dose of their medication and of their diagnosis); David A. Soskis & Richard L. Jaffe, Communicating with Patients about Antipsychotic Drugs, 20 Comprehensive Psychiatry 126 (1979) (understanding in both groups equal); Barbara Stanley, Informed Consent in Treatment and Research, in Handbook of Forensic Psychology 63, 72–74 (Irving B. Weiner & Allen K. Hess eds., 1987) (reviewing studies finding little difference between psychiatric and medical patients' comprehension of consent information); Barbara Stanley et al., Preliminary Findings on Psychiatric Patients as Research Participants: A Population at Risk?, 138 Am. J. Psychiatry 669 (1981) (no differences found between group of mental and medical patients studied).

155. See Winick, Restructuring Competency to Stand Trial, supra note 6, at 970–75 (criticizing this practice in the context of competency to stand trial). Michael Perlin's concept of sanism may help to explain this unfortunate tendency. Perlin defines sanism as "irrational, unconscious, bias-driven stereotypes and prejudices," similar to those exhibited in cases involving racist, sexist, and other bigoted decision making. Michael L. Perlin, Competency, Deinstitutionalization, and Homelessness: A Story of Marginalization, 28 Hous. L. Rev. 63, 91–93 (1991). See also Michael L. Perlin, On "Sanism," 46 SMU L. Rev. 373 (1992); Michael L. Perlin, Pretexts and Mental Disability Law: The Case of Competency, 47 U. Miami L. Rev. 625 (1993); Michael L. Perlin & Deborah A. Dorfman, Sanism, Social Sci-

D. Presuming Competency

In addition to redefining competency standards more narrowly, recognition of the adverse side effects of incompetency labeling supports application of a strong presumption in favor of competency. Such a presumption in favor of competency has been recognized by case law in a number of jurisdictions[156] and has received broad scholarly support.[157] However, the presumption recently was questioned by the U.S. Supreme Court's broad dicta in *Zinermon v. Burch*.[158] In analyzing the need for a procedural determination of the competency of a person seeking voluntary admission to a psychiatric hospital, the Court in *Zinermon* noted that even if a request for admission to a hospital for medical treatment might justifiably be taken at face value, "a state may not be justified in doing so, without further inquiry, as to a mentally ill person's request for admission and treatment at a mental hospital."[159] This language seems to disapprove of the presumption in favor of the competency of people who are mentally ill and to call for an "inquiry" into the question whenever a mentally ill person seeks hospital admission, and by implication, whenever such a person seeks to exercise any right. If interpreted this way, *Zinermon* may present unintended antitherapeutic consequences.[160] If *Zinermon* is read

---

ence, and the Development of Mental Disability Law Jurisprudence, 11 Behav. Sci. & L. 47 (1993).

156. See, e.g., Lotman v. Security Mut. Life Ins. Co., 478 F.2d 868, 873 (3d Cir. 1973) ("there is a legal presumption that everyone is sane"); Winters v. Miller, 446 F.2d at 68 (holding that a court finding that a patient was mentally ill does not create a presumption that he is incompetent to make decisions); Rogers v. Okin, 478 F. Supp. 1342, 1361, 1363–64 (D. Mass. 1979) ("[A]lthough committed, a mental patient is nonetheless presumed competent to manage his affairs, dispose of property, carry on a licensed profession, and even to vote,"), aff'd in part, reversed in part on other grounds, 634 F.2d 650 (1st Cir. 1980), vacated sub nom. Mills v. Rogers, 457 U.S. 291 (1982); Child v. Wainwright, 148 So. 2d 526, 527 (Fla. 1963) (noting that a criminal defendant is presumed sane); Howe v. Howe, 99 Mass. 88, 98 (1868) (noting presumption of sanity of grantor wishing to void deed for reason of insanity); Lane v. Candura, 376 N.E.2d 1232, 1235 (Mass. App. Ct. 1978) (noting that there is a presumption of competency when determining whether an adult needs guardian appointed by court to make medical decisions); Grannum v. Berard, 422 P.2d 812, 814 (Wash. 1967) (noting that an individual is presumed sane for purpose of consenting to surgery).

157. See, e.g., Brakel et al., supra note 8, at 341 n.167, 375; 1 President's Comm'n Report, supra note 146, at 3, 56 (discussing informed consent and presumption of competency); Grisso, supra note 145, at 314–15 (recognizing the presumption in favor of competency and defining standards of competency); Annas & Densberger, supra note 149, at 575 ("The legal rule is that competence is presumed."); Winick, supra note 8, at 22–23 & n.19 ("The law presumes that people are competent to make decisions unless they have been adjudicated incompetent.").

158. 494 U.S. 113, 133 n.18 (1990).

159. Id. For an analysis of why this statement was dicta and a criticism of its implications, see Winick, supra note 9.

160. See id. at 192–99 (analyzing potential antitherapeutic consequences of a broad reading of Zinermon).

broadly to require a hearing into competency whenever a mentally ill individual engages in decision making, it will dramatically increase the extent of incompetency labeling and of its significant adverse side effects.

The *Zinermon* dicta also runs counter to one of the most significant developments in modern mental health law. Under the approach that once had prevailed in American law, an adjudication of incompetency rendered an individual generally incompetent.[161] The notion of general incompetency, however, has been rejected in favor of an approach requiring adjudication of specific incompetency.[162] Under the modern view, competency is regarded as a contextualized inquiry.[163] An individual's competency is the subject of inquiry only in regard to the specific capacity in question. As a result, under the modern approach, an individual will be determined to be incompetent to perform only particular tasks or roles, for example, to stand trial, make treatment decisions, or manage property.[164] An adjudication of specific incompetency does not render the individual legally incompetent to perform other tasks or play other roles. This trend recognizes that mental illness should not be equated with incompetency, that many individuals suffering from mental illness retain full decision-making capacity, and that even when such illness impairs capacity in one area, it may leave capacity unimpaired in others.[165] As a result, in the con-

---

161. See, e.g., Appelbaum et al., supra note 8, at 82; Brackel et al., supra note 8, at 185, 258, 438–39; David B. Wexler, Mental Health Law: Major Issues 40 (1981); Tepper & Elwork, supra note 145, at 207; Winick, supra note 9, at 207; Winick, supra note 8, at 22–23.

162. E.g., State ex rel. Jones v. Gerhardstein, 416 N.W.2d 883, 895 (Wis. 1987); Appelbaum et al., supra note 8, at 82–83; Brackel et al., supra note 8, at 185, 405–407 (table 7.2, col. 1); Faden & Beauchamp, supra note 144, at 289; Tepper & Elwork, supra note 145, at 207; Winick, supra note 8, at 23.

163. ABA Criminal Justice Mental Health Standards s 7-4.1 commentary at 175 (1986) ("A determination of competence or incompetence is functional in nature, context dependent and pragmatic in orientation."); Ronald Roesch & Stephen L. Golding, Competency to Stand Trial 10–13 (1980); Richard J. Bonnie, The Competence of Criminal Defendants: Beyond Dusky and Drope, 47 U. Miami L. Rev. 539, 549 (1993).

164. See, e.g., Appelbaum et al., supra note 8, at 82–83; Brakel et al., supra note 8, at 175 & n.73; Grisso, supra note 145, at 314; Tepper & Elwork, supra note 145, at 207–208; Winick, supra note 9, at 186.

165. See Am. Psychiatric Ass'n Task Force on DSM-IV, DSM-IV Draft Criteria A:9 (1993):

> In determining whether an individual meets a specified legal standard (e.g., for competence, criminal responsibility, or disability) additional information is usually required beyond that contained in the DSM-IV diagnosis. This might include information about the individual's functional impairments, and how these impairments affect the particular abilities in question. It is precisely because impairments, abilities and disabilities vary widely within each diagnostic category that assignment of a particular diagnosis does not imply a specific level of impairment or disability.

Paul S. Appelbaum & Thomas G. Gutheil, Clinical Handbook of Psychiatry and the Law 218, 220 (1991) ("The mere presence of psychosis, dementia, mental retardation, or some other form of mental illness or disability is insufficient in itself to constitute incompetence."); McKinnon et al., supra note 154, at 1159; Morse, Crazy Behavior, supra note 151, at 573, 588; Winick, supra note 8, at 17–18; Winick, supra note 9, at 188–90.

text of cases raising a constitutional right to refuse antipsychotic medication, courts have begun to recognize that the presumption in favor of competency applies to mentally ill as well as to medically ill people, even to those who have been involuntarily committed under the state's *parens patriae* power on the basis that they are incompetent to make the hospitalization decision for themselves.[166]

The *Zinermon* dicta—with its broad implications that competency should be the subject of inquiry whenever a mentally ill person seeks to exercise choice—should therefore be rethought.[167] Indeed, the serious adverse side effects of incompetency labeling documented in this article make such rethinking especially appropriate. In contexts in which individuals seek voluntarily to make a choice, their choices should rarely be disturbed. If the government seeks to question such choices on the basis that the individuals are incompetent, it should bear a heavy burden of demonstrating incompetency. Competency should be the subject of inquiry only in special cases, rather than in every case involving individuals who are or seem to be mentally ill. The presumption in favor of competency should preclude inquiry into the question in the absence of special factors suggesting that the choice made is the product of mental illness. Because mental illness often does not impair decision-making capacity, its existence alone should not require a competency inquiry.

Although the broad implications of the *Zinermon* dicta are highly questionable, the actual holding in the case—that some "inquiry" should have been made into the competency of the patient involved—seems plainly correct and illustrates the kind of case in which the presumption of competency should be considered to have been rebutted. The patient in *Zinermon* was able to express a preference in favor of hospitalization but appeared confused and delusional, was unable to state the reasons for his choice, and was hallucinating in ways that bore directly on his decision.[168] Indeed, he apparently deliberated under the delusion that the mental hospital he was entering was "heaven."[169] These facts suggest the need for an inquiry into competency and should rebut the presumption of competency that otherwise should apply. When an expression of choice seems to be based on reasons that appear clearly irrelevant, on beliefs that seem clearly irrational, or on outright delusions or hallucinations, further inquiry into the competency question is justified.[170] In the absence of

---

166. See, e.g., Rennie v. Klein, 653 F.2d 836, 847 & n.12 (3d Cir. 1981) (en banc), vacated and remanded, 458 U.S. 1119 (1982); *Okin*, 634 F.2d at 657–59; *Winters*, 446 F.2d at 71; Davis v. Hubbard, 506 F. Supp. 915, 935–36 (N.D. Ohio 1980); *Stickney*, 344 F. Supp. at 379; Anderson v. State, 663 P.2d 570, 571 (Ariz. Ct. App. 1982); People v. Medina, 705 P.2d 961, 973 (Col. 1985) (en banc); In re Boyd, 403 A.2d 744, 747 n.5 (D.C. 1979); Gundy v. Pauley, 619 S.W.2d 730, 731 (Ky. Ct. App. 1981); Rogers v. Commissioner of the Dep't of Mental Health, 390 Mass. 489, 497–98, 458 N.E.2d 308, 314 (1983); Rivers v. Katz, 67 N.Y.2d 485, 493–95, 495 N.E.2d 337, 341–42, 504 N.Y.S.2d 74, 79 (1986); In re K.K.B., 609 P.2d 747, 749 (Okla. 1980); State ex rel. Jones v. Gerhardstein, 141 Wis. 2d 710, 727–731, 736–743, 416 N.W.2d 883, 890–91, 894–96 (1987).

167. See Winick, supra note 9.

168. *Zinermon*, 494 U.S. at 118–20.

169. Id.

170. Winick, supra note 9, at 184 & n.91; see Jeffrey Murphy, Incompetency and Paternalism, 60 Arch. für Rechts-und Sozialphilosophie 465, 473–74 (1974); Tepper & Elwork,

such evidence, however, competency should be presumed and no further inquiry into the subject should be required.

The U.S. Supreme Court's more recent decision in *Medina v. California*[171] is more consistent with the trend of modern mental health law. The Court in *Medina* upheld the constitutionality of a state statute containing a presumption in favor of the competency of a criminal defendant to stand trial and placing the burden of proving incompetency by a preponderance of the evidence on the party raising the competency issue. The issues presented in *Medina* were considerably different from those presented in *Zinermon*. The Court's more recent decision in *Medina*, however, stands as an endorsement of the presumption in favor of competency, in contrast to its earlier questioning of the presumption in *Zinermon*. The Court's decision in *Medina* involved only a question of constitutionality—whether the statutory presumption of competency violated due process by placing on the defendant the burden of proving his own incompetency—rather than a question of the wisdom of the statutory scheme. However, recognition of the adverse side effects of incompetency labeling, which were not considered in *Zinermon*, provides strong support both for the *Medina* decision and the underlying policy judgment made by the California legislature. Whereas *Zinermon* seemed to be a step in the wrong direction, *Medina* sets a truer course.

An understanding of the adverse effects of incompetency labeling thus calls for new legal approaches to minimize application of such labels. In addition to narrowing the definition of incompetency, creating presumptions in favor of

---

supra note 145, at 216–18; Winick, Restructuring Competency to Stand Trial, supra note 6, at 967; see, e.g., Dep't of Human Services v. Northern, 563 S.W.2d 197 (Tenn. App. 1978) (delusional denial by gangrenous patient that she could live without amputation found to render her incompetent to refuse recommended surgery). Where the patient is delusional, but her delusions are not the primary reason for her treatment decision, however, she should not be found incompetent. E.g., In re Maida Yetter, 62 Pa. D. & C.2d 619 (1973). In applying the criteria of "clearly irrational," care should be given to avoid equating the quality of the decisionmaking process with the reasonableness of the result reached. See 1 President's Comm'n Report, supra note 146, at 61; Annas & Densberger, supra note 149, at 571 & n.39 ("the 'outcome approach' trap"); Roth et al., supra note 8, at 281. In the context of consent to voluntary hospitalization or conventional treatment, the potential for this problem is reduced because clinical evaluators will presumably find an assent to hospitalization or treatment (as opposed to an objection thereto) to be a reasonable result. Thus, only in cases in which the assent to admission or treatment is grounded in plainly irrational reasons (such as "God wants me to do it" or "Hospitalization will make me a famous movie star"), or on delusions ("Let me into the hospital so the CIA won't get me") or hallucinations ("The voice told me to have this treatment"), should the presumption of competency be rebutted, justifying further inquiry. See Also Nat'l Inst. Mental Health, Draft Act Governing Hospitalization of the Mentally Ill (1952) (commentary) (analyzing incompetency to consent to hospitalization as loss of "the power to make choices" or confusion that precludes the ability to "make a decision having any relation to the factors bearing on his hospitalization"), cited in Note, supra note 124, at 1217.

171. 112 S. Ct. 2572 (1992); see Bruce J. Winick, Presumptions and Burdens of Proof in Determining Competency to Stand Trial: An Analysis of Medina v. California and of the Supreme Court's New Due Process Methodology in Criminal Cases, 47 U. Miami L. Rev. 817 (1993).

competency, and placing burdens of persuasion on those questioning competency, law scholars should rethink the law's reliance on paternalistic approaches and coercion in this area.

E. Avoiding Incompetency Labeling

Incompetency labeling should be avoided whenever possible through the use of voluntary rather than coercive approaches in mental health law. An incompetency label should never be a precondition for the receipt of services desired by the individual on a voluntary basis. In appropriate circumstances, incompetency may be a condition for the imposition of involuntary hospitalization or coercive treatment when the state invokes *parens patriae* grounds to override an individual's objection to these interventions. However, an individual who requests services should be entitled to receive them solely on the basis of need and availability.[172] Requiring application of an incompetency label as a condition for the receipt of services that are sought on a voluntary basis is gratuitously stigmatizing and potentially antitherapeutic.

Indeed, in contexts in which the individual voluntarily seeks services, using the mental illness label (apart from the incompetency label) itself may often be damaging to the individual. The requirements of insurance reimbursement and governmental funding that often require a mental illness diagnosis accordingly should be rethought. Preventive services for mental illness often are not subject to reimbursement or funding. It is frequently only when the individual's condition is exacerbated to the point that hospitalization is required that reimbursement or governmentally funded services become available. Society should reimburse and provide funding for services designed to help people to avoid or to cope with crises that often necessitate hospitalization. Instead, a clinician typically is unable to receive reimbursement for providing such services without first affixing a diagnosis of mental illness. Although people's crises may be the product of a pathological social situation, they and not the situation receive the diagnosis—a label that in effect announces that they have a mental or emotional "disorder." The new emphasis on general preventive approaches in medicine reflects recognition that it is both more conducive to patient health and less costly to society to prevent problems rather than to treat them. Yet this emphasis on prevention seems absent in the area of the delivery of mental health services. The refusal to permit people with mental health problems to seek help unless they first are diagnosed as "disordered," when that label may be damaging and may exacerbate their problems, imposes serious social, health, and economic costs. The law does not require a diagnostic label as a condition for immunization, nutritional counseling, or certain diagnostic testing, like pap smears or mammography for women of certain ages. Rather, such preventive services are encouraged in order to avoid illness or to detect it at an early point when interventions can be more effective and less expensive. It is time to adopt similar preventive approaches in the mental health area and to offer services to those who would benefit from and who desire them without

---

172. See Winick, supra note 8 (suggesting that the law should distinguish patients who assent to treatment from those who object thereto).

the necessity of branding them with diagnostic labels that may themselves be psychologically dysfunctional.

When the individual does not volunteer for services that the state considers necessary, it should attempt to convince the individual of the desirability of such services or to induce their acceptance through the provision of incentives.[173] When the state believes that an individual's best interests would be furthered by accepting hospitalization, treatment, or some other intervention or status, it should seek to persuade the individual of the merits of this course rather than compelling him or her to accept it and attempting to apply an incompetency label in case of refusal. Rather than formally labeling a criminal defendant incompetent to stand trial, for example, the court should offer the defendant the possibility of a continuance of the trial contingent on obtaining appropriate treatment designed to improve functioning at trial.[174] Instead of subjecting individuals with mental illness to involuntary commitment proceedings and labeling them as incompetent, the state should attempt to persuade them that voluntary or informal admission would be in their best interest.[175] More use should be made of creative inducement approaches and of negotiation and persuasion, and less reliance should be placed on coercion and the attribution of incompetency. The negotiation process itself is empowering, humanizing, and therapeutic. Compulsion and incompetency labeling should be used as a last resort, if at all.

Even when compulsion appears necessary, the law should seek ways of avoiding the use of an incompetency label whenever possible. There probably will remain cases in which a hearing concerning competency is found to be required—for example, when someone persists in an activity that is clearly and seriously detrimental or refuses an intervention that seems to be unquestionably beneficial, and the individual's action seems to be the product of mental illness. Even in such cases, however, individuals should be given repeated opportunities to change their minds before being adjudicated to be incompetent. Individuals in such a situation may be willing to share decision-making power with an appointed guardian, particularly if the guardian is a family member or friend. Such a restricted guardianship arrangement may be seen as an attractive alternative to a determination of incompetency that may totally divest individuals of decision-making power. Instead of finding individuals incompetent to manage their property, for example, the state should encourage appointment of guardians who would have the more limited power to oversee decisions by the individuals, perhaps including the authority to veto major decisions but not necessarily to make them unilaterally.[176] Individuals might resist an adjudication of incompetency and the appointment of a guardian to exer-

---

173. See Bruce J. Winick, Harnessing the Power of the Bet: Wagering with the Government as a Means of Individual and Social Change, 45 U. Miami L. Rev. 737 (1991) (suggesting that, as an alternative to compulsion, government should offer to enter into contingency contracts with individuals in order to induce certain desired behavior).

174. See Wexler & Winick, Therapeutic Jurisprudence as a New Approach, supra note 5, at 998; Winick, Restructuring Competency to Stand Trial, supra note 6, at 979–80.

175. See Winick, supra note 9, at 192–99 (analyzing the therapeutic value of voluntary hospitalization).

176. See Sales & Kahle, supra note 80, at 392.

cise full power over the individual's property but might be willing to accept such a partial guardianship arrangement. Similarly, individuals might resist an involuntary commitment or treatment order coupled with a finding of incompetency but be willing to accept appointment of a restricted guardian able to make or assist in such decisions.[177]

Even when other approaches prove unsuccessful and the intervention sought by the state is thought to be essential, incompetency labeling may be avoidable. Just as a court has broad equitable powers to fashion provisional relief in order to avoid irreparable harm pending a permanent disposition of a matter in litigation,[178] judicial and administrative decision making concerning those suffering from mental illness should include the use of flexible provisional remedies. For example, on the basis of a preliminary evidentiary showing, a temporary period of hospitalization or treatment could be ordered, a temporary restraint on the transfer of property pending treatment could be issued, or a temporary continuance pending treatment could be granted in a criminal case, thereby avoiding for the time being the necessity of adjudicating the individual incompetent. Individuals faced with such a provisional remedy may agree to enter into negotiations concerning the conditions under which they voluntarily would accept the intervention sought by the state, thereby, it is hoped, rendering compulsion and the use of an incompetency label ultimately unnecessary.

Incompetency labeling also can be avoided by encouraging individuals to make greater use of advance directive instruments and health care proxies. These arrangements allow individuals to anticipate the possibility of a future period in which their decision-making capacity will be impaired and to execute a formal instrument directing how decisions will be made on their behalf or selecting a proxy, such as a trusted relative or friend, to make the decision. A living will is an example of such an advance directive instrument by which patients can express the wish, for example, to discontinue life-support services or nourishment should they be in a persistent vegetative state.[179] Living will-type instruments and durable powers of attorney can be used by mentally ill individuals whose illness is in remission or under control to direct how future hospitalization or treatment decisions should be made in the event that their condition renders them incompetent in the future.[180] They similarly can be used by

177. See Charles M. Culver & Bernard Gert, The Morality of Involuntary Hospitalization, in The Law-Medicine Relation: A Philosophical Exploration 151, 179 (Stuart F. Spicker et al., eds., 1981) (discussing possibility of allowing manic patient to appoint "guardianship committee" that could sanction future detention and treatment decisions).

178. See, e.g., Fed. R. Civ. P. 65 (authorizing entry of temporary restraining order or preliminary injunction).

179. See Cruzan v. Director, Missouri Dep't of Health, 497 U.S. 261 (1990) (suggesting the general enforceability of such advance directives when the patient's future wishes have clearly been expressed).

180. See Lester J. Perling, Health Care Advance Directives: Implications for Florida Mental Health Patients, 48 U. Miami L. Rev. 193 (1993) (summarizing the use of mental health advance directives and the right of mentally ill persons to direct their psychiatric care and concluding that the law seems to support furthering self-determination by expanding the use of advance directives in a mental health context); Gary N. Sales, The Health Care Proxy for Mental Illness: Can it Work and Should We Want it To? 21 Bull. Am. Acad. Psychiatry & L.

persons in the early stages of Alzheimer's disease or some other form of dementia or organic mental disorder to engage in advance planning concerning residential care and management of property. Such advance planning avoids the need for state coercion and incompetency adjudication with its accompanying labeling effects while preserving the individual's sense of dignity and autonomy.

F. Recharacterizing Incompetency Labels and Reshaping the Labeling Process

Even when an incompetency label is found to be necessary, the law should seek ways of minimizing the potential adverse effects. The language used to label legal statuses should be revised to minimize the potential for negative self-attributions by the individual affected. Instead of finding a criminal defendant incompetent to stand trial, for example, the court could determine the need for what could be called a *treatment continuance* and in appropriate cases order treatment designed to increase trial functioning.[181] Instead of being adjudicated incompetent to manage their property, individuals could be found *temporarily impaired* in this area, a label that suggests hope rather than hopelessness and encourages them to view their "temporary" problem as one that can be resolved through appropriate treatment. Even finding criminal defendants or civilly committed patients to be *temporarily incapacitated* rather than *incompetent* may limit their perception that their impairment is permanent and outside their control, an attribution that would increase the adverse effects of an incompetency label.[182]

For the same reasons, to the extent that application of an incompetency label is deemed necessary, that label should be narrowly tailored to the individual's specific impairment. Thus, individuals who are deemed incompetent to enter into a contract for the sale of a house or a business should be labeled (if at all) *temporarily impaired to sell* a business or a house, rather than generally incompetent to manage property. This more specific and limited label would not necessarily preclude them, without the approval of a guardian, from entering into other, less significant contractual arrangements, such as buying clothes, hiring or discharging a secretary, or selling or giving away a painting. Limited and context-specific incompetency labels of this kind are more consistent with the trend in modern mental health law in favor of specific rather

---

161 (1992) (discussing the difficulties of applying advance directives and health care proxies in a mental health context).

181. See Sales & Kahle, supra note 80, at 394:

> For example, the term "incompetent to stand trial" implies a trait-like permanent malady when, in fact, the concept it should convey legally is really a temporary one. An incompetent person is one whom we would expect to stay that way. The term "unable to stand trial" is less laden with unnecessary trait-like and permanent implications because unable people often later become able. Attribution theories of attitude change would predict that trait-like attributions should carry more negative connotations than terms that imply more ephemeral phenomena.

182. See supra notes 71–73 and accompanying text.

than general incompetency[183] and would tend to limit the risk that individuals will interpret the impairment as global and relatively stable, an attribution that would increase the likelihood of learned helplessness and other inhibitory patterns that will interfere with their regaining competency in the future.[184] Similarly, a form of a nolo contendere or "no contest" plea to a "temporary impairment" status or even to incompetency in various contexts could be encouraged. Although such a plea in the criminal area, at least in some circumstances, may be antitherapeutic and decrease the potential for rehabilitation,[185] allowing individuals to participate in plea negotiations and make choices in various mental health contexts can be positive. To the extent that mentally ill individuals engage in consultation with their counsel and decide that such a "plea" would be more in their interests than being determined to be incompetent, the process alone could have important therapeutic advantages.

The role of counsel can be therapeutic in other respects as well. Criminal defendants who face a determination that they are incompetent to stand trial may be told certain things by counsel about that determination that can mitigate its potential adverse effects. For example, counsel can tell them that such a finding is largely a vehicle for obtaining an advantageous postponement in their trials and that it will give them the opportunity to obtain needed treatment that will increase their functioning and relieve their suffering. In addition, counsel can point out that their ability to participate in the trial that ultimately will be held will be enhanced as a result of the incompetency postponement, as will the potential for a more favorable outcome.[186] This is not a suggestion that counsels relax their advocacy role on behalf of their clients in pursuing their clients' interests as the clients articulate them. However, if the counsels foresee the inevitability of an incompetency adjudication, attempting to persuade their clients to negotiate a more favorable settlement or explaining the outcome in ways that will minimize the likelihood of self-attributions by the clients that ultimately would be more damaging, may be little different from the role that counsels in criminal cases often play in the plea bargaining and sentencing process. Real therapeutic potential in the relationship between counsel and client in these contexts may be underappreciated and unrealized. Even when an incompetency label is applied, how counsel interprets it to the client may help to mitigate the potentially serious adverse side effects that otherwise are possible.

---

183. See supra notes 162–63 and accompanying text.

184. See supra notes 71–73 and accompanying text.

185. See Wexler & Winick, Therapeutic Jurisprudence and Criminal Justice Mental Health Issues, supra note 5, at 229–30. See also Jeffrey A. Klotz et al., Cognitive Restructuring Through Law: A Therapeutic Jurisprudence Approach to Sex Offenders and the Plea Process, 15 U. Puget Sound L. Rev. 529 (1992).

186. See Keri A. Gould, Therapeutic Jurisprudence and the Arraignment Process; The Defense Attorney's Dilemma: Whether to Request a Competency Evaluation, in Mental Health Law and Practice Through the Life Cycle 67 (Simon Verdun-Jones & Monique Layton eds., 1994).

IV. Conclusion

Incompetency labeling can produce serious adverse consequences for those labeled. They are stigmatized in the eyes of the community in a manner that influences the way others perceive and treat them. Moreover, they may come to view themselves in ways that can reinforce and even worsen their impairment. Labeling them incompetent may cause them to inhibit performance or to avoid it altogether in the area in which they previously have performed poorly. Their motivation to attempt future behavior in the area in question may be altered in ways that prevent future success, and they may experience serious depression and a damaged sense of psychological well-being. Their sense of self-esteem and self-efficacy may be impaired in ways that are debilitating. They may experience learned helplessness, becoming withdrawn, unresponsive, passive, submissive, helpless, and hopeless. In summary, incompetency labeling may itself be psychologically damaging and even disabling. It may set up a self-fulfilling prophecy that serves to increase and perpetuate the individual's social and mental health problems.

An understanding of the serious adverse consequences of incompetency labeling should sensitize legal decision makers to redesign legal standards, procedures, and the roles of counsel, judges, and other legal actors in ways that are calculated to avoid or minimize these damaging effects. The law should rely less on compulsion and paternalism. Instead, it should encourage voluntariness, providing incentives for individuals to act in desired ways rather than requiring them to do so.[187] In some cases it may be preferable to allow individuals to make their own choices, even if unwise.

Incompetency should be narrowly defined, and competency should be presumed. An inquiry into competency should be required only when specific behavior calls an individual's behavior into question. Mental illness alone should not justify such an inquiry, and when a determination of competency is required, the burden of proof should be on the party asserting that individuals are incompetent.

When coercive interventions are deemed necessary, creative approaches should be used to avoid or minimize the potential that individuals will respond with a self-attribution of general and permanent incompetency. At a minimum, the terminology of incompetency labels should be redesigned to reflect the limited and context-specific nature of individuals' impairment. The message that the label conveys to individuals need not suggest a permanent impairment of an essential ability to function. Instead, it should allow them to see their condition as a difficulty that can be overcome if they seek treatment and are highly committed to it. Moreover, the message that the label conveys can be powerfully influenced by the lawyers and judges involved in the process. How they communicate to individuals in the labeling process can help individuals to interpret the message of the label in a positive rather than a negative manner, as suggesting hope, not hopelessness. In areas where the

---

187. See Winick, supra note 173 (suggesting the use of behavioral contracts as an alternative to government coercion in certain contexts).

law, like medicine, seeks to do good, it too needs to heed the admonition that it avoid doing harm.[188]

---

188. The Hippocratic Oath, which is at the core of medical ethics, imposes a duty of benevolence and nonmalevolence on the physician. The Oath provides:

> I swear by Apollo the physician, by Aesculapius, Hygeia, and Panacea, and I take to witness all the gods, all the goddesses, to keep according to my ability and my judgment the following Oath: [I] will prescribe regimen for the good of my patients according to my ability and my judgment and never do harm to anyone. To please no one will I prescribe a deadly drug, nor give advice which may cause his death....I will preserve the purity of my life and my art....In every house where I come I will enter only for the good of my patients, keeping myself far from all intentional ill-doing....

State v. Perry, 610 So. 2d 746, 751–52 (La. 1992) (quoting Hippocrates c. 460–400 B.C., Stedman's Medical Dictionary 647 (4th Unabridged Lawyer's ed., 1976); see Winick, supra note 4, at 332.

Chapter 3

The Jurisprudence of the Insanity Defense

Michael L. Perlin

[This selection is drawn from the final chapter of Professor Perlin's award-winning book, recipient of the American Psychiatric Association's Manfred S. Guttmacher Award in Forensic Psychiatry.]

A. Introduction

I began this book by stating that our insanity defense jurisprudence was incoherent and that this incoherence mattered. I have sought to demonstrate the depth of that incoherence, the roots of the incoherence, and the way that our biases, prejudices and cognitive distortions perpetuate the incoherence. In this final chapter, I will first assess recent developments in the field of therapeutic jurisprudence, in an effort to determine what insights can be brought to bear on this inquiry. After that, I will offer some proscriptions and prescriptions that, I believe, will help lead us to a reconstructed insanity defense jurisprudence.

B. The Promise of Therapeutic Jurisprudence

1. Introduction[1]

"Therapeutic jurisprudence" studies the role of the law as a therapeutic agent.[2] This perspective recognizes that substantive rules, legal procedures and lawyers' roles may have either therapeutic or antitherapeutic consequences, and questions whether such rules, procedures and roles can or should be re-

---

1. The material infra notes 2–9 is generally adapted from Perlin & Dorfman, Sanism, Social Science, and the Development of Mental Disability Law Jurisprudence, 11 Behav. Sci. & L. 47, 63–64 (1993).

2. See Therapeutic Jurisprudence: The Law as a Therapeutic Agent (D. Wexler ed. 1990) (Therapeutic Jurisprudence); Essays in Therapeutic Jurisprudence (D. Wexler & B. Winick eds. 1991); Wexler, Putting Mental Health Into Mental Health Law: Therapeutic Jurisprudence, 16 Law & Hum. Behav. 27 (1992) (Wexler, Putting); Wexler & Winick, Therapeutic Jurisprudence and Criminal Justice Mental Health Issues, 16 Ment. & Phys. Dis. L. Rptr. 225 (1992) (Wexler & Winick, Criminal Justice); Wexler, Therapeutic Jurisprudence and Changing Conceptions of Legal Scholarship, 11 Behav. Sci. & L. 17 (1993) (Wexler, Changing); Wexler & Winick, Therapeutic Jurisprudence as a New Approach to Mental Health Law Policy Analysis and Research, 45 U. Miami L. Rev. 979 (1991) (Wexler & Winick, New Approach); Klotz et al, Cognitive Restructuring Through Law: A Therapeutic Jurisprudence Approach to Sex Offenders at the Plea Process, 15 U. Puget Sound L. Rev. 529 (1992).

shaped so as to enhance their therapeutic potential, while not subordinating due process principles.[3]

While an impressive body of literature has been produced,[4] there has not yet been a systematic investigation into the reasons *why* some courts decide cases "therapeutically" and others "anti-therapeutically." I believe that the answer can be found, in significant part, in sanism. Sanism is such a dominant psychological force that it (1) distorts "rational" decisionmaking, (2) encourages (albeit on at least a partially-unconscious level) pretextuality *and* teleology, and (3) prevents decisionmakers from intelligently and coherently focusing on questions that are meaningful to therapeutic jurisprudential inquiries.[5]

The types of sanist decisions that I have already discussed operate in an ostensibly *a*therapeutic world; although some decisions may be, in fact, therapeutic and others may be, in fact, antitherapeutic,[6] these outcomes seem to arise almost in spite of themselves.[7] In short, we cannot make any lasting progress in "putting mental health into mental health law"[8] until we confront the system's sanist biases and the ways that these sanist biases blunt our ability to intelligently weigh and assess social science data in the creation of a mental disability law jurisprudence.

2. Therapeutic Jurisprudence and the Insanity Defense

Application of therapeutic jurisprudence principles to the insanity defense reveals many "pressure points" that bear on any jurisprudential reconstruction. In order to make our insanity defense system coherent, we need to weigh

---

3. Wexler, Health Care Compliance Principles and the Insanity Acquittee Conditional Release Process, in Essays, supra note 2, at 199, 199–200 n. 5; see generally, Wexler, Putting, supra note 2.

4. See Wexler & Winick, New Approach, supra note 2, at 981 n. 9.

5. See M. Perlin, "Law as a Therapeutic and Antitherapeutic Agent," paper presented at the Massachusetts Department of Mental Health's Division of Forensic Mental Health's annual conference, Auburn, MA (May 1992) (suggesting that influence of sanism must be considered in therapeutic jurisprudence investigations); Perlin, What Is Therapeutic Jurisprudence? 10 N.Y.L. Sch. J. Hum. Rts. __ (1993) (in press).

6. E.g., I believe that the decision in State v. Krol, 68 N.J. 236, 344 A. 2d 289 (expanding procedural due process protection rights at the post-insanity acquittal commitment hearing) is therapeutic and the decision in Jones v. United States, 463 U.S. 354 (1983) (restricting such rights) is anti-therapeutic. See supra chapter 4 E 2 d.

7. See e.g., discussions in Wexler & Winick, New Approach, supra note 2, at 990–92 (right to refuse treatment), 992–97 (treatment of incompetent death row inmates), and 997–1001 (treatment of incompetency to stand trial); Wexler & Winick, Criminal Justice, supra note 2, at 229–30 (sex offender guilty pleas); see also, Perlin, *Tarasoff* and the Dilemma of the Dangerous Patient: New Directions for the 1990s, 16 Law & Psychol. Rev. 29, 54–62 (1992) (duty to protect in tort law); Perlin, Reading the Supreme Court's Tea Leaves: Predicting Judicial Behavior in Civil and Criminal Right to Refuse Treatment Cases, 12 Am. J. Forens. Psychiatry 37, 54 (1991) (Perlin Tea Leaves) (right to refuse treatment); Perlin, Hospitalized Patients and the Right to Sexual Interaction: Beyond the Last Frontier? 21 NYU Rev. L. & Soc'l Change __ (1993) (in press) (right of institutionalized patients to sexual autonomy); see generally, 1 M.L. Perlin, Mental Disability Law: Civil and Criminal (1989), § 1.05A, at 5–8, and sources cited (1992 pocket part).

8. See Wexler, Putting, supra note 2.

the therapeutic potential of the different policy choices that are presented at each of these points. If we do this, we may uncover a strategy that will enable us to combat the sanism and pretextuality that currently drives the insanity defense system. At the same time, this strategy should serve as an effective counterweight to the teleological ways that courts have traditionally weighed social science evidence in insanity defense cases.[9]

a. Is a non-responsibility verdict therapeutic?   Given the "rivers of ink, mountains of printers' lead [and] forests of paper" that have been spilled over every aspect of the insanity defense,[10] it is astonishing that this question has been so rarely asked (and even more rarely answered). Insanity defense adherents often couch their support with reference to our traditional disapproval of punishment without responsibility.[11] Opponents (mostly) raise fraudulent arguments about the ways that the insanity defense contributes to crime waves and allows "factually guilty" persons to evade punishment; other opponents construct principled arguments that look to other aspects of the criminal justice system to mediate against the punishment of mentally disabled criminal defendants.[12] Rarely are therapeutic jurisprudence issues raised anywhere in the debate.

There are, though, some exceptions. One undercurrent of the abolition movement is an insinuation of volition on the part of insanity defense pleaders: that certain defendants "indulge" in certain behaviors to "make themselves" not responsible. Thus, a popular sanist myth is:

> Mentally disabled individuals simply don't try hard enough. They give in too easily to their basest instincts, and do not exercise appropriate self-restraint.[13]

---

9. See Wexler, Insanity Issues After Hinckley: Time for a Change, 35 Contemp. Psychol. 1068, 1069 (1990) (explicitly calling for therapeutic jurisprudence inquiries into insanity defense cases).

10. See Morris, Psychiatry and the Dangerous Criminal, 41 S. Cal. L. Rev. 514, 516 (1968).

11. See e.g., United States v. Lyons, 739 F. 2d 994, 995 (5th Cir. 1984) (Rubin, J., dissenting) (insanity defense reflects "fundamental moral principles of our criminal law" and rests on "assumptions that are older than our Republic"); Bonnie & Slobogin, The Role of Mental Health Professionals in the Criminal Process: The Case for Informed Speculation, 66 Va. L. Rev. 427, 448 (1980) (insanity defense rests on "beliefs about human rationality, deterrability and free will"); Livermore & Meehl, The Virtues of M'Naghten, 51 Minn. L. Rev. 789, 797 (1967) (insanity defense is bulwark of law's "moorings of condemnation for moral failure").

12. Compare e.g., The Insanity Defense Hearings Before the Senate Comm. on the Judiciary, 97th Cong., 2d Sess. 27 (1982) (comments of then-Attorney General William French Smith) (insanity defense is major stumbling block in the restoration of the "effectiveness of Federal law enforcement," and tilts the balance between the forces of law and the forces of lawlessness"), to supra chapter 6 D 6 a (1) (discussing work of Dr. Abraham Halpern).

13. Perlin, On "Sanism," 46 SMU L. Rev. 373, 396 (1992). See e.g., State v. Duckworth, 496 So. 2d 624, 635 (La. App. 1986) (juror who felt defendant would be responsible for actions as long as he "wanted to do them" not excused for cause) (no error); Balkin, The Rhetoric of Responsibility, 76 Va. L. Rev. 197, 238 (1990) (Hinckley prosecutor suggested to jurors "if Hinckley had emotional problems, they were largely his own fault").

These arguments, of course, are never buttressed by any empirical support. Prosecutors or jurors make assertions as if they were "givens", and rebuttals are rarely offered. Sanism underlies these allegations, and, as currently formulated, they can be dismissed out of hand in any therapeutic jurisprudence analysis.[14]

There are other approaches, however, that might illuminate the underlying issues. Labeling theory, for example, might appear to lend support to a finding that the insanity defense is antitherapeutic.[15] Labeling theory is the study of the process by which a label is, correctly or incorrectly, placed on a particular individual, as well as society's perception of and reaction to that label (and to the labeled person), and the labeled person's eventual fulfillment of society's expectations concerning that label.[16] Labels are more readily accepted by the community if a high-ranking person does the initial characterization.[17]

Labeling theorists believe that the potential negative consequences of stigmatizing offenders outweigh any benefits. Specifically, they argue that, by labeling an offender "deviant," the state may produce "secondary deviance," or other antisocial acts that are a result of the labeling.[18] On the other hand, critics of labeling theory have responded that no empirical data prove that secondary deviance is, in fact, a result of the labeling.[19] These critics also see positive outcomes as flowing from labeling, such as isolation, incapacitation and general deterrence, and, perhaps, "channeling [the labeled individual] toward appropriate rehabilitative services (specific deterrence and rehabilitation)."[20]

Labels accompany stereotypes. These labels stigmatize, assign negative associations to an outsider, "complicate any effort to resist the designation implied by difference,"[21] and allow the labeler to fail to imagine the perspective of the

---

14. If empirical support were to be offered in support of any of these propositions, it would, of course, be appropriate to re-evaluate them in that context.

15. But compare Weisberg, Criminal Law, Criminology, and the Small World of Legal Scholarship, 63 U. Colo. L. Rev. 521, 527 (1992) ("The history of American sociological criminology has yielded largely a plethora of schemes—from deviance theory to strain theory to control theory to labeling theory to subcultural differential association to reintegrative shaming theories—that almost all criminal law scholars ignore out of a predisposed disdain for the intellectual power of sociology").

16. Lynn, Unconstitutional Inhibitions: "Political Propaganda" and the Foreign Agents Registration Act, 33 N.Y.L. Sch. L. Rev. 345, 368 n.153 (1988), citing, inter alia, F. Cullen, Toward a Paradigm of Labelling Theory 30 (1978).

17. Lynn, supra note 16, at 368, citing E. Rubington & M. Weinberg, Deviance, the Interactionist Perspective 6 (4th ed. 1981).

18. Massaro, Shame, Culture, and American Criminal Law, 89 Mich. L. Rev. 1880, 1919 (1991), discussing, inter alia, R. Trojanowicz & M. Morash, Juvenile Delinquency: Concepts and Control 59–61 (4th ed. 1987); Gove, The Labelling Perspective: An Overview, in The Labeling of Deviance 9 (W. Gove ed., 2d ed. 1980).

19. Massaro, supra note 18, at 1920, citing, inter alia, Gove, supra note 18, at 13–15 (collecting empirical work).

20. Massaro, supra note 18 at 1920, citing Gove, supra note 18, at 18.

21. Minow, 1984 Forward: Justice Engendered, 101 Harv. L. Rev. 10, 38 (1987); S. Gilman, Difference and Pathology: Stereotypes of Sexuality, Race and Madness 12, 18–35 (1985).

outsider.[22] Labels are especially pernicious, for they frequently lead labeled individuals to internalize negative expectations and social practices that majoritarian society identifies as characteristically endemic to the labeled group.[23] From these labels, "categorizations assume a life of their own."[24] In turn, any act that fails to follow standards set by a dominant group becomes a deviation.[25]

Labeling must be considered through the special filter of mental disability. There is, for example, a growing body of psychological research that the stigma attached to the label of mental illness can affect a person's self-perception and interpersonal relations, as well as the response of society in general.[26] Society's attitudes toward the mentally ill have a demonstrable effect on how patients see themselves and how adequately they adjust, and the public is more tolerant of deviance when it is not described by a mental disability label.[27]

What impact should this have on the insanity defense? The phrase "insanity acquittee" is clearly a pejorative label. Does that labeling affect the individual's self-perception?[28] If he were, instead, labeled "criminal," would that be a better or worse alternative? What other negative attributions does society make about such a person? Would society still make these attributions if there were

---

22. Minow, supra note 21, at 51 n. 201. See generally, Final Report: Task Force on Stigma and Discrimination (NY State Office of Mental Health, Mar. 6, 1990), at 1–2.

23. Note, Teaching Inequality: The Problem of Public School Tracking, 102 Harv. L. Rev. 1318, 1333 (1989); Glassner, Labeling Theory, in The Sociology of Deviance 71 (M. Rosenberg, R. Stebbins & A. Turowitz eds. 1982); L. Tempey, American Delinquency: Its Meaning and Construction 341–68 (1978); see generally, Weithorn, Mental Hospitalization of Troublesome Youth: An Analysis of Skyrocketing Admission Rates, 40 Stan. L. Rev. 773, 805–07, 820–26 (1988); Sweet, Deinstitutionalization of Status Offenders: In Perspective, 18 Pepperdine L. Rev. 389 (1991).

24. Delgado et al, Fairness and Formality: Minimizing the Role of Prejudice in Alternative Dispute Resolution, 1985 Wis. L. Rev. 1359, 1381: "What enables people to reject members of other races is the supportive (unconscious and automatic) bias elicited by categorization," quoting Larsen, Social Categorization and Attitude Change, 111 J. Soc'l Psychology 113, 114 (1980).

25. Chester, Perceived Relative Deprivation as a Cause of Property Crime, 22 Crime & Delinq. 17, 22 (1976), as quoted in Wilson, Urban Homesteading: A Compromise Between Squatters and the Law, 35 N.Y.L. Sch. L. Rev. 709, 714–15 n. 38 (1990).

26. Splane, Tort Liability of the Mentally Ill in Negligence Actions, 93 Yale L.J. 153, 167 n. 75 (1983), citing, inter alia, Farina et al, Mental Illness and the Impact of Believing Others Know About It, 77 J. Abnormal Psychology 1 (1971) (believing others to be aware of their status as mentally ill caused persons to feel less appreciated, appear more tense, and to find performance tasks more difficult); Farina, Holland & Ring, Role of Stigma and Set in Interpersonal Interaction, 71 J. Abnormal Psychology 421 (1966) (mentally ill persons described as less desirable as friends and neighbors than criminals).

27. Johannsen, Attitudes Toward Mental Patients: A Review of Empirical Research, 53 Mental Hygiene 218, 222–23 (1969); Sarbin & Mancuso, Failure of a Moral Enterprise: Attitudes of the Public Toward Mental Illness, 35 J. Consult. & Clin. Psychology 159, 159 (1970).

28. On the impact of sex offender labeling, see Walsh, Twice Labeled: The Effect of Psychiatric Labels on the Sentencing of Sex Offenders, 37 Soc'l Probs. 375, 385–86 (1990) (both probation officers and judges "are consistently and powerfully influenced" by labels).

no insanity defense? Do insanity acquittees act in certain ways to conform their behavior to public perceptions?

Several scholars have discussed the question of whether defendants could be denied the use of the insanity defense if they were found to have been "culpable" in causing the conditions that led to the use of the defense.[29] On the other hand, as Professor Wexler has pointed out, a schizophrenic patient who fails to take antipsychotic medication may not be culpable if his impaired mental state led to that refusal.[30] In such an instance, Professor Finkel argues, "When we recognize…that we are in danger of coming apart at the psychic seams, so to speak…then we should get ourselves help;…the alternative course, to do nothing, is unacceptable and inexcusable…"[31]

Taking a slightly different tack, Robert Fein claims that the insanity defense encourages NGRI acquittees to absolve themselves of responsibility for their actions and retards their treatment progress.[32] His thesis is this: for the NGRI verdict to work, insanity acquittees must "accept emotional responsibility for actions committed during periods of gross mental disorder"; operationally, the fact of acquittal serves to retard the acceptance of this responsibility.[33]

He gives several examples to illustrate his thesis (drawn from his experiences at Bridgewater State Hospital in Massachusetts). In one case, a patient to whom he refers as H.B. stated, "The judge said I was not guilty; I shouldn't be here. I am no longer sick." The same patient complained further that it was "unfair" that he was institutionalized since he had not committed a crime. In addition, the patient refused to participate in psychotherapy and "was granted his wish to stop taking his medicine."[34] A second insanity acquittee (A.L.),

---

29. See e.g., Wexler, Inducing Therapeutic Compliance through the Criminal Law, in Essays, supra note 3, at 187, 196, quoting, inter alia, Robinson, Causing the Conditions of One's Own Defense: A Study of the Limits of Theory in Criminal Law Doctrine, 71 Va. L. Rev. 1, 23–25 (1985); see e.g., Wash. Rev. Code Ann. § 10.77.010 (7) (1990) ("No condition of the mind proximately induced by the voluntary act of a person charged with crime shall constitute 'insanity'"); see also, e.g., Slodov, Criminal Responsibility and the Noncompliant Psychiatric Offender: Risking Madness, 40 Case W. Res. L. Rev. 271 (1989); Tiffany, The Drunk, the Insane, and the Criminal Courts: Deciding What to Make of Self-Induced Insanity, 69 Wash. U. L.Q. 221 (1991).

30. Wexler, supra note 29, at 195; see generally, Slodov, supra note 28. This issue is addressed, albeit elliptically, in People v. Smith, 124 Ill. App. 3d 805, 465 N.E. 2d 101, 103 (1984) (antipsychotic medication had been prescribed for defendant which he took only one time; "One week later, the defendant fatally stabbed the victim in the instant case"). * * * Other questions are raised if an individual asserts a constitutional right to refuse medication, see Perlin, Tea Leaves, supra note 7, and then commits a criminal act, or if he commits a criminal act while under the influence of a prescribed antipsychotic drug, see People v. Caulley, 197 Mich. App. 177, 494 N.W. 2d 853 (1992) (reversing conviction; defendant could establish viable insanity defense if he could demonstrate that the "involuntary use," via medical prescription, of drugs created a state of mind equivalent to insanity).

31. N. Finkel, Insanity on Trial 288 (1988). This argument assumes a fact not necessarily in evidence: that such "help" is available to all individuals who might seek it.

32. Fein, How the Insanity Acquittal Retards Treatment, in Therapeutic Jurisprudence, supra note 2, at 49.

33. Id. at 52.

34. Id. at 53.

when asked by the judge at his recommitment hearing to describe how he felt about having injured his victims, replied, "The judge said I was not guilty. I'm sorry I did it but I think I've done enough time...I haven't gotten in any fights here."[35]

According to Fein, the fact that the insanity defense implies "that violent behavior is caused by 'illness' and is not committed by persons with thoughts and feelings...appears to decrease the possibility that mentally disordered persons will be able to utilize treatment services," and that the NGRI verdict thus "may work against the needs of the defendants labeled by the courts as 'sick.'"[36] The verdict, he concludes, "provides a convenient way for the offender to avoid thinking about his violent behavior and its meaning."[37]

Fein's arguments are provocative, but, to my mind, fail to prove his point.[38] First, H.B.'s perceptions of the verdict are simply wrong; a finding of NGRI does not mean that a defendant is "no longer sick" or that he "shouldn't be [in the hospital." On the other hand, this misunderstanding may be an indicia of the degree of severity of his illness; he may be *so* seriously mentally disabled that he cannot frame the type of thought process that would lead him to understand the limits of his responsibility. Second, his refusal to participate in psychotherapy and his decision to exercise his right to refuse the involuntary imposition of medication may raise therapeutic jurisprudence questions about the right to refuse treatment[39] but not about the underlying substantive insanity verdict.[40]

On the other hand, H.B.'s complaint that it was "unfair" to not know when he would be discharged may raise a serious issue but not necessarily one that goes to Fein's central thesis. This uncertainty *may* be anti-therapeutic. However, if it is, it would seem to call into question post-commitment retention schemes such as the one upheld by the Supreme Court in *Jones v. United States*[41] under which a defendant can be held in a forensic hospital beyond the maximum term to which he could have been sentenced had he been convicted

---

35. Id. at 54.

36. Id. at 58.

37. Id. at 55.

38. First, both of his NGRI examples are exceptional cases. H.B. was a former police officer and marine whose victim was a bar bouncer who had attacked the defendant a year prior to the murder that led to his insanity acquittal. Id. at 52–53. As I have discussed, such verdicts are disproportionately entered in cases where law enforcement officials are defendants; the additional fact that the victim was a non-stranger/former aggressor might make the verdict even more understandable. See supra chapter 4 D 4. A.L., a quiet, withdrawn man who attacked several strangers (leaving one permanently disfigured), was visited daily in the forensic hospital by his family who referred to the series of attacks as "Al's accident." Fein, supra note 31, at 54. Certainly, this constant exculpatory "support" by his family could have served as a powerful incentive leading him to deny responsibility for his actions.

39. See e.g., Perlin, Tea Leaves, supra note 7; Winick, Competency to Consent to Treatment: The Distinction Between Assent and Objection, in Essays, supra note 2, at 41.

40. There has also been virtually no litigation on the question of a "right to refuse psychotherapy," and what little has been attempted has been unsuccessful. See 2 M.L. Perlin, supra note 7, § 5.56, at 398–99 (discussing United States v. Stine, 675 F. 2d 69, 71–72 (3d Cir. 1982)).

41. 463 U.S. 354 (1983).

of the underlying crime. This does not challenge the therapeutic potential of the insanity defense, but of a commitment system that insures lengthier stays in hospitals for insanity acquittees.

What about Fein's conclusions? Does failure to assign responsibility lessen an insanity acquittee's initiative to get better? Does this question imply some quantum of blame; that the patient could get better "if he really wanted to"?[42] Is there any responsibility on institutional staff here? Should they be held accountable to try to deal with the type of behavior exhibited in the H.B. and A.L. cases?

What about his conclusion that the verdict implies that violent behavior is "caused" by mental illness? This use of causation sounds like the *Durham* product test,[43] a formulation that was abandoned in the District of Columbia in 1972. Neither the *M'Naghten* nor the ALI tests are couched in causal language; to make this link here is to set up an ultimate straw man.

Also, the implication that the insanity verdict suggests that the behavior in question is not that of individuals with "thoughts and feelings" falls wide of the mark. The insanity defense is usually pled only by people with the most disordered thoughts; when the verdict is successful, it is often the reflection of jurors' conclusions that the underlying crime was a response to the power of those strong thoughts.

In short, although I find Fein's piece thoughtful, I do not believe that it makes the case that the insanity defense is anti-therapeutic. It appears that no one in the facility ever explained to the two acquittees the actual meaning of the jury's verdict nor, apparently, did anyone ever counsel A.L.'s family that their reinforcement of his denial was most likely antitherapeutic.[44] He provides no evidence that his criticism would be valid if such explanations had been offered. It is not the fact of the nonresponsibility verdict that is antitherapeutic, but the way that the verdict is processed by the defendant after the insanity acquittal. It would seem that some measure of cognitive restructuring as to the defense's meaning[45] and its likely consequences for the defendant would eliminate almost all of Fein's criticisms.

What about the other side? May a non-responsibility defense be "therapeutic"? I believe that it may be. The standard explanation as to why the defense is therapeutic is articulated best by Judge Bazelon: "By declaring a small number not responsible, we emphasize the responsibility of all others who commit crimes."[46] In other words, the existence of the insanity defense gives coherence to the entire fabric of criminal sentencing. We punish responsible defendants for a variety of reasons: to incapacitate them, to deter others, to educate others, (perhaps) to rehabilitate them.[47] By punishing non-responsible defendants,

---

42. See supra chapter 8, note 43, discussing State v. Duckworth, 496 So. 2d 624, 635 (La. App. 1986), and Balkin, supra note 13, at 238.

43. See supra chapter 3 A 1 c (2).

44. Of course, if the individuals' mental states were so impaired that they could not understand the meaning of the insanity acquittal, it is unlikely that *any* explanation would have been therapeutic or antitherapeutic.

45. Compare Klotz et al, supra note 2.

46. D. Bazelon, Questioning Authority: Justice and Criminal Law 2 (1988).

47. See supra chapter 2 C.

we diminish all the rationales for punishment of the others whom we believe to be responsible for their crimes.

However, this argument may simply be a retrospective rationalization and not a therapeutic justification at all. It may be that we allow the insanity defense to survive precisely because so few criminal defendants come within its scope.[48] This allows us to isolate those few without endangering the overall administration of the criminal justice system.[49] This may also explain why Judge Bazelon's consideration of "rotten social background" as potentially providing a basis for an insanity defense (on the theory that it significantly impaired the defendant's ability to exercise free choice)[50] never attracted more positive public support.[51] Recognition and/or acceptance of this position would imperil the legal system's "tensile strength,"[52] by calling into question literally thousands of criminal convictions entered each year. In other words, this argument in support of the insanity defense is an important instrumental one, but may not normatively provide a therapeutic basis for the defense.

On the other hand, the insanity defense system recognizes that certain individuals—because of mental disability—are to be diverted from the criminal justice system.[53] If such defendants receive constitutionally meaningful treatment in psychiatric hospitals, then this diversion will be therapeutic.[54] More importantly, if these defendants are spared prison—where mentally disabled prisoners are often institutionalized in facilities bereft of even minimal mental health services, and are often treated more harshly than other inmates[55]—then there may

---

48. See supra chapter 3 B 1 b (1).

49. This may actually be a sanist justification for the insanity defense, since it enables us to say that these few defendants are so sufficiently not "like us" that we can treat them safely as an outgroup. Not coincidentally, such individuals are often treated in facilities in areas at a significant distance from major population centers.

50. United States v. Alexander, 471 F. 2d 923, 957–65 (D.C. Cir. 1972) (Bazelon, J., concurring in part & dissenting in part).

51. For a sampling of the academic debate, see e.g., Bazelon, The Morality of the Criminal Law, 49 S. Cal. L. Rev. 385 (1976); Morse, The Twilight of Welfare Criminology: A Reply to Judge Bazelon, 49 S. Cal. L. Rev. 1247 (1976); Delgado, "Rotten Social Background": Should the Criminal Law Recognize a Defense of Severe Environmental Deprivation? 3 Law & Inequal. 9 (1985).

52. See supra chapter 8 A.

53. Compare Halpern, The Insanity Defense in the 21st Century, 35 Int'l J. Offender Ther. & Compar. Criminol. 188, 188 (1991) (arguing that insanity defense draws resources of forensic hospitals "while individuals with clear-cut psychiatric illnesses...are left to deteriorate in prison without a modicum of therapy"). On the recent increase in the number of mentally ill pre-trial jail detainees, see Palermo, Gumz & Liska, Mental Illness and Criminal Behavior Revisited, 36 Int'l J. Offender Ther. & Compar. Criminol. 53 (1992).

54. In the "pecking order" of prisoners, the mentally ill have always been plagued by an exceptionally low status. See Halleck, The Criminal's Problem With Psychiatry, in Readings in Law and Psychiatry 51 (R. Allen et al eds. 1975).

55. See e.g., Tillery v. Owens, 907 F. 2d 418, 424–25 (3d Cir. 1990) (mentally ill inmates often double-celled with inmates in administrative custody, a practice characterized by an expert witness as "putting the chickens in the fox's lair"); Baskin, Sommers & Steadman, Assessing the Impact of Psychiatric Impairment on Prison Violence, 19 J. Crim. Just. 271, 272 (1991) (psychiatrically impaired inmates more likely to be victimized by other prisoners due

be an additional therapeutic impact.[56] If, in a prison context, we are likely to cognitively resolve the "logical dissonance of classifying mad/bad persons as bad persons,"[57] then the separation of severely mentally disabled individuals from the prison population will have yet an extra therapeutic outcome.[58]

A therapeutic jurisprudence analysis also underscores the banality and vacuity of the guilty but mentally ill (GBMI) plea.[59] Jurors are deceived into entering the GBMI verdict as a compromise, either as a means of expressing their position that the defendant's mental illness should be seen as somehow contributory to his criminal behavior, or as an aspiration that the defendant receive treatment while serving his sentence. The statistics reveal that this hope is an illusion; GBMI defendants receive no treatment, and are subject to life-plus sentences (or the death penalty). Further, the reality that the GBMI verdict is nothing more than a label is hidden from jurors who are denied information by the court as to the verdict's operational meaning.

I suggest that this analysis is a starting point for a more comprehensive investigation of the question posed. As I will argue in my concluding section, unless scholars and insanity defense decisionmakers confront the importance of this inquiry, our endless tinkering with the procedural and substantive contours of the defense will have little ultimate meaning.

b. Does the substantive standard matter?[60] The much-ballyhooed Insanity Defense Reform Act eliminated the volitional prong from the insanity defense

---

to displays of bizarre or inappropriate behavior). On the multiple roots of homicide defendants' post-detention psychotic reactions, see Arboleda-Florez, Post-Homicide Psychotic Reaction, 25 Int'l J. Offender Ther. & Compar. Criminol. 47 (1981). On the relationship between prison violence and mental illness, see Baskin, Sommers & Steadman, supra. * * * Proponents of abolishing involuntary civil commitment have conceded that this might result in more mentally disabled persons being imprisoned. See C. Warren, The Court of Last Resort: Mental Illness and the Law 100–101 (1982) (section written by Stephen J. Morse). Responds Andrew Scull: "While Morse may not balk at the prospect of sending the mentally ill to prison, a...system of justice built around the concept of criminal responsibility almost certainly will." Scull, The Theory and Practice of Civil Commitment, 82 Mich. L. Rev. 793, 803 (1984).

56. On the way that progressive conditional release of NGRI acquittees is therapeutically beneficial, see McGreevey, Steadman, Dvoskin & Dollard, New York State's System of Managing Insanity Acquittees in the Community, 42 Hosp. & Commun. Psychiatry 512 (1991). On the other side of this coin, if severely mentally disabled persons are diverted from prisons, it may serve to make those facilities safer for non-mentally disabled prisoners as well.

57. Hayman, Beyond Penry: The Remedial Use of the Mentally Retarded Label in Death Penalty Sentencing, 59 UMKC L. Rev. 17, 47 n. 161 (1990) (quoting H. Toch & K. Adams, The Disturbed Violent Offender 18–19 (1989)).

58. See generally, H. Toch & K. Adams, Coping: Maladaptation in Prisons (1989); H. Toch. Mosaic of Despair: Human Breakdown in Prison (rev. ed. 1992). On the other hand, if adequate treatment is not offered in forensic mental health facilities, the ensuing institutionalization in such environments may also be antitherapeutic.

59. See supra chapter 3 A 1 c (4).

60. For the purposes of this section, I will assume that the choice of standard has at least a symbolic value. See e.g., Homant & Kennedy, Subjective Factors in Clinicians' Judgments of Insanity: Comparison of a Hypothetical Case and an Actual Case, 18 Prof'l Psychol.: Res. & Prac. 439, 455 (1987): "[I]nsanity defense trials...will continue to play an important

in federal courts because of the fear that this was not "measurable" (as cognition presumably was), and that this reduction would lead to an elimination of verdicts that had been termed "moral mistakes."[61] Yet, the best available empirical studies suggest that volition may be accurately measurable, in some instances even more accurately than cognition.[62]

This same evidence offers an important therapeutic jurisprudence insight. The very individuals who meet the volitional standard (but not the cognitive test) may be exactly those individuals who would be the most problematic prison inmates and whose mental disabilities might be most treatable in a controlled forensic hospital setting.[63] Here, it appears that our political cant and rhetoric has blunted any efforts to inform ourselves of the therapeutic potential of substantive insanity formulations less restrictive than the *M'Naghten* test.

c. Do procedural rules matter?   The allocation of proof to the state or the defendant may be a critical decision in the formulation of an insanity defense standard.[64] The placement of the burden on the defendant (especially where it involves a clear and convincing quantum of evidence) will make it more likely that insanity defenses offered by severely mentally disabled criminal defendants will be rejected.[65] This, in turn, may increase the number of imprisoned seriously mentally disabled prisoners, an outcome that is self-evidently antitherapeutic for the unsuccessful insanity pleaders and may also be potentially hazardous for prison staff and other prisoners.[66]

---

symbolic role. They will underline the fact that reasons for criminal behavior are indeed important, and that a principled and effective response to offenders must follow from an understanding of the individuals." * * * At the least, the choice of standard conveys a parameters, see supra chapter 6, text at notes 191–92, to jurors as to the legislature's feelings about the role of the insanity defense in a criminal justice system. This is an area that has seen significant empirical inquiry. See supra chapter 6 D 5 b and chapter 6 D 6 a, discussing, inter alia, the work of Professor Norman Finkel and his colleagues.

61. See supra chapter 5, text at note 55.

62. See Silver & Spodak, Dissection of the Prongs of ALI: Retrospective Assessment of Criminal Responsibility by the Psychiatric Staff of the Clifton T. Perkins Hospital Center, 11 Bull. Am. Acad. Psychiatry & L. 383, 390 (1983) (contemporaneous empirical research has shown some evidence that the elimination of this prong from the insanity defense "may systematically exclude...that class of psychotic patients [patients with manic disorders] whose illness is clearest in symptomatology, must likely biologic in origin, most eminently treatable, and potentially most disruptive in penal detention"); see also, Rogers, Assessment of Criminal Responsibility: Empirical Advances and Unanswered Questions, 15 J. Psychiatry & L. 73, 78 (1987) (arguments that volitional non-responsibility cannot be measured are "an intellectual charade played for the benefit of an uninformed public"). See supra chapter 6, note 239.

63. See Silver & Spodak, supra note 62.

64. See supra chapter 3 A 2.

65. For a pointed case example, see State v. Zmich, 160 Ariz. 108, 770 P.2d 776 (1989), discussed supra chapter 3, note 123.

66. By saying this, I am *not* suggesting that mentally disabled criminal defendants are, as a class, more dangerous than other criminal defendants. I am arguing rather that the placement of such individuals into a general prison population (supervised by a prison staff that may have no training or experience in the identification and/or treatment of such disabilities) may create hazardous and harmful conditions for all involved.

Other procedural issues call out for further study as well. Courts are hopelessly split on informing insanity jurors about the meaning of the insanity verdict, and about whether or not counsel can comment on such verdict outcomes in summations.[67] If we learn that jurors are misinformed about the ultimate outcome of a successful insanity plea [68] and that jurors may over-convict "legitimate" insanity defendants (because of a false fear that they will be quickly released from all custodial restraints, a fear often exacerbated by inflammatory prosecutorial summations),[69] then decisions that deprive them of this empirical information (and allow for the dissemination of inaccurate information) are anti-therapeutic.[70]

In *Ake v. Oklahoma*, the Supreme Court ruled that if a criminal defendant were to make an "ex parte threshold showing...that his sanity was likely to be a significant factor in his defense," the state must assure him access to a "competent psychiatrist...[to] assist in the evaluation, preparation, and presentation of the defense."[71] Most post-*Ake* decisions have read that holding tepidly,[72] and defendants are frequently deprived of adequate expert assistance.[73] Again, in those few cases where insanity is contested, this may lead to legitimately non-responsible defendants being improperly convicted.

In *Barefoot v. Estelle*, the Supreme Court approved of expert testimony on future dangerousness, even where the expert had not examined the defendant in question.[74] This uniformly-criticized decision[75] "flies in the face of...relevant scientific literature,...is inconsistent with the development of evidence law doctrine, and...makes a mockery of earlier Supreme Court decisions cau-

---

67. See generally, 3 M.L. Perlin, supra note 7, § 15.16, at 336–39 (categorizing cases).

68. See e.g., Price v. State, 274 Ind. 479, 412 N.E. 2d 783, 788 (1980) (De Bruler, J., concurring in result) (explaining that, as a result of his "success," the insanity acquittee "is placed on a separate track towards confinement under the auspices of attendants and doctors rather than on a track toward confinement under the auspices of guards and wardens").

69. See supra chapter 3 B 1 b (1).

70. For perhaps the most incomprehensible decision dealing with judicial instructions, see supra chapter 7, text accompanying notes 133–35, discussing Geschwendt v. Ryan, 967 F. 2d 877 (3d Cir. 1992) (en banc), and id. at 891 (Aldisert, J., dissenting).

71. 470 U.S. 68, 82–83 (1985).

72. See 3 M.L. Perlin, supra note 7, § 17.17, at 549–53, and id., n. 404.1 at 215–26 (1992 pocket part) (listing cases).

73. See e.g., Brown v. State, 743 P. 2d 133 (Okla. Crim. App. 1987); State v. Bearthes, 329 N.C. 149, 405 S.E. 2d 170 (1991); Henderson v. Dugger, 925 F. 2d 1309 (9th Cir. 1991). But see, De Freece v. State, 848 S.W. 2d 150, 1993 WL 44429 (Tex. Cr. App. 1993) (*Ake* requires more than a disinterested witness; expert must be able to assist in developing favorable testimony, supply bases on which to cross-examine state's expert and, if necessary, testify on behalf of the defendant).

74. 463 U.S. 880 (1983); see supra chapter 4 E 2 f (1).

75. See 3 M.L. Perlin, supra note 7, § 17.14, at 536–40; see e.g., Risinger, Denbeaux & Saks, Exorcism of Ignorance as a Proxy for Rational Knowledge: The Lessons of Handwriting Identification "Expertise", 137 U. Pa. L. Rev. 731, 780–81 n. 215 (1989) ("We have yet to find a single word of praise for, or in defense of, *Barefoot* in the literature of either science or law").

tioning that *extra* reliability is needed in capital cases."[76] Again, it heightens the likelihood of inappropriate convictions in insanity cases—an anti-therapeutic outcome.

This leads to another set of inquiries. What impact do examiners' pre-existing political attitudes have on insanity case dispositions? A body of research literature has developed that demonstrates that various sorts of political biases affect mental health professionals' judgments of insanity in particular cases,[77] and that the primary predictor of an expert witness's view on a particular case is his pre-existing feelings about the defense.[78] Other research shows that most expert witnesses do not know the actual substantive insanity standard used in their jurisdiction.[79] If improper or inaccurate verdicts in insanity cases are entered because of these biases or lack of knowledge, this would clearly also affect any therapeutic effect that the defense might have.

d. Should post-acquittal commitment procedures track the traditional involuntary civil commitment model, or is a separate, more restrictive means of determining commitment appropriate?

Few contrasts in insanity defense jurisprudence are more stark than the difference between post-acquittal commitments in states that follow the model of the New Jersey Supreme Court in *State v. Krol*[80] and those that adhere to the system found to be constitutional by the United States Supreme Court in *Jones v. United States*.[81] *Krol* finds the distinction between criminal and civil commitment a meaningless one; *Jones*, on the other hand, sees the prior commission of a criminal act (even a *de minimis* one) as a sufficient predicate for an entirely different set of procedural and substantive rules.

Self-evidently, the *Krol* system should lead to fewer defendants being institutionalized, and shorter terms of confinement; the *Jones* scheme just the opposite. Is it therapeutic for defendants to be released from custody more quickly, or is it more therapeutic for insanity pleaders to be institutionalized for longer periods of time (longer, perhaps, than had they been sentenced to the maximum for the underlying crime)?[82]

In addition, the *Krol/Jones* split has a symbolic value that may also mask therapeutic content. If we say (as did the *Krol* court) that there is no difference

---

76. Perlin, The Supreme Court, the Mentally Disabled Criminal Defendant, Psychiatric Testimony in Death Penalty Cases, and the Power of Symbolism: Dulling the Ake in Barefoot's Achilles Heel, 3 N.Y.L. Sch. Hum. Rts. Ann. 91, 111 (1985) (emphasis in original).

77. See e.g., Homant et al, Ideology as a Determinant of Views on the Insanity Defense, 14 J. Crim. Just. 37, 57 (1986).

78. Homant & Kennedy, Judgment of Legal Insanity as a Function of Attitude Toward the Insanity Defense, 8 Int'l J. L. & Psychiatry 67 (1986).

79. Rogers & Turner, Understanding of Insanity: A National Survey of Forensic Psychologists and Psychiatrists, 7 Health L. Canada 71 (1987).

80. 68 N.J. 236, 344 A. 2d 289 (1975); see supra chapter 4 E 2 d.

81. 463 U.S. 354 (1983); see supra chapter 4 E 2 d.

82. Michael Jones, the appellant in the Supreme Court case, had been arrested and charged with attempted petit larceny in 1975, was still institutionalized at the time of the Supreme Court decision in 1983, and remains institutionalized today.

between criminal and civil commitment, then we are minimizing the criminal component of the insanity defense finding, and maximizing the mental disability component. On the other hand, if we say that a defendant's original criminal act (no matter how minor) colors all subsequent aspects of the criminal process, then we are saying that *any* involvement in that process serves as a "trump" over any other individual facet of the case. The resolution of this symbolic split is likely to be longer terms of post-acquittal hospitalization in *Jones* jurisdictions and shorter in *Krol* jurisdictions. Again, therapeutic jurisprudence questions are raised by this inquiry.

In a careful analysis of the collateral issue of how the release hearing should be structured, Professor Wexler has examined the work of Donald Meichenbaum and Dennis Turk[83] that was written to help medical professionals increase patient treatment adherence.[84] Meichenbaum and Turk's research led them to conclude that such adherence is likely to be increased when a patient is given choice and participation in the selection of treatment alternatives and goals.[85]

Placing this work in the context of the release hearing, Wexler looks for ways that courts might employ these compliance principles to increase a patient's adherence behavior once released.[86] Such strategies as the use of behavioral contracts, the creation of procedures that track plea bargain approval hearings,[87] and the involvement of the acquittee in the hearing itself ("to test the patient's understanding of the regimen and to insure that the patient agrees with it and had input into its design")[88] would assure a greater level of patient compliance. Under this model, "the court is itself an HCP [health care professional]," and Wexler recommends behaviors to the judge to enhance patient adherence.[89]

Importantly, Wexler acknowledges that courts may resist these behaviors for many of the same reasons that health care professionals may resist, among them that the procedures are complicated, enhancement strategies are a "frill," the strategies will not work with the population in question.[90] Notwithstanding these potential (and likely) complaints, Wexler concludes that this approach is one that deserves experimental implementation. "[L]ike it or not,"

---

83. D. Meichenbaum & D. Turk, Facilitating Treatment Adherence: A Practitioner's Guidebook (1987) (Facilitating).

84. Wexler, supra note 3, at 199.

85. Winick, Harnessing the Power of the Bet: Wagering with the Government as a Mechanism for Social and Individual Change, in Essays, supra note 2, at 245 n. 93, citing Facilitating, supra note 83, at 157, 159, 175.

86. Wexler, supra note 3, at 209.

87. See Fed. R. Crim. Proc. 11.

88. Wexler, supra note 3, at 210.

89. Id. at 212. See also id.: "For instance, the judge can make sure to introduce himself or herself to the patient, can be attentive, can avoid using legal or medical jargon, can allow the patient to tell his or her story without undue interruption, can make sure the patient understands the precise treatment regimen, and can even sit at the same level and at the same conference table as the patient—perhaps in a mental health facility conference room rather than in a courtroom."

90. Id. at 217.

he concludes, it is probable that "the behavior of courts play a critical role in the adherence behavior of conditionally released insanity acquittees."[91] The simple recognition by courts that their decisions and actions have a therapeutic or anti-therapeutic consequence should be a critical factor in this sort of decisionmaking.[92]

Wexler's arguments here are compelling ones, and offer a blueprint for scholars and other insanity defense decisionmakers. As of yet, there has been little reaction to his suggestions among other legal scholars.[93] On the other hand, as the face of mental disability law scholarship changes,[94] we can hope that researchers turn their attention to this important question.

e. Once institutionalized, how are insanity acquittees to be treated?   Little academic attention has been paid to the question of the institutional treatment rights of insanity acquittees. Although a smattering of caselaw finds that both the right to treatment and the right to refuse treatment apply,[95] there has been little systemic consideration of this question since Anne Singer and June German's groundbreaking analysis in 1976.[96]

On the question of a right to refuse treatment, several questions are raised from a therapeutic jurisprudence perspective. If refusal of treatment serves autonomy values (by allowing institutionalized patients to make individual health care decisions that they could freely make in the community), is it therapeutic to expand this right for this population? On the other hand, if refusal of medication leads to more florid symptomatology (and an exacerbation of delusions and hallucinations), is that anti-therapeutic *in se*? If drugs merely mask symptoms, resulting in damaging neurological side-effects? Now that Justice Kennedy has taken a bold and expansive pro-refusal position in his autonomy-privileging concurrence in *Riggins v. Nevada*,[97] can we expect that further attention will be paid to this issue? Until rigorous therapeutic jurisprudence analyses are applied here, arguments as to whether insanity acquittees should have the same rights, fewer rights, or more rights than civil patients in these areas will likely remain unresolved.

---

91. Id. at 218.

92. Id. at 218 n. 147, citing Wexler & Schopp, Therapeutic Jurisprudence: A New Approach to Mental Health Law, in Handbook of Psychology and Law (D. Kagehiro & W. Laufer eds.) (in press).

93. The only citation to the article is in Wexler & Winick, Therapeutic Jurisprudence as a New Approach to Mental Health Law Policy Analysis and Research, 45 U. Miami L. Rev. 979, 981 (1991).

94. See Wexler, Changing, supra note 2; M. Perlin & D. Dorfman, "The Invisible Renaissance of Mental Disability Law Scholarship: A Case Study in Subordination" (manuscript in progress).

95. See supra; see Perlin, Tea Leaves, supra note 7.

96. German & Singer, Punishing the Not Guilty: Hospitalization of Persons Found Not Guilty By Reason of Insanity, 29 Rutgers L. Rev. 1011, 1017–35 (1976). A recent case has expanded the right of access to a law library and to legal research materials—previously held to apply to prisoners, pretrial detainees and persons committed following a finding of incompetency to stand trial—to patients institutionalized after an NGRI verdict. See Hatch v. Yamauchi, 809 F. Supp. 59 (E.D. Ark. 1992).

97. 112 S. Ct. 1810, 1817 (1992); see supra chapter 4 E 2 f (2).

f. How should insanity acquittees be monitored in community settings?   The paradox here should be self-evident. Insanity acquittees are the most despised group of individuals in society. Most commentators agree that one of the reasons our insanity defense jurisprudence is so repressive is to make it as difficult as possible for insanity acquittees to ever reenter society;[98] the thought that such individuals are ever to be released fills much of the public with dread and/or consternation.[99] On the other hand, most research studies show that individuals who are subject to gradual lessening of restraints are better reintegrated into the community upon release.[100] Some sort of monitoring appears to be appropriate, but little attention has been paid in the legal literature to this question from a therapeutic jurisprudence perspective.[101]

g. Other therapeutic jurisprudence issues.   In addition to these questions, there remains a whole menu of other issues that need to be considered from a therapeutic jurisprudence perspective: the procedural due process requirements needed at the recommitment process,[102] the right of defendants to refuse to enter an insanity plea,[103] the impact of a failed insanity plea on a subsequent sentence,[104] the impact of a successful plea on other legal statuses,[105] and the

---

98. See supra chapter 4 E 2 d.

99. See e.g., Ellis, The Consequences of the Insanity Defense: Proposals to Reform Post-Acquittal Commitment Laws, 35 Cath. U. L. Rev. 961, 962 (1986) ("the public's concern is less with whether blame properly can be assigned to a particular defendant than with determining when he will get out").

100. See e.g., McGreevey, Steadman, Dvoskin & Dollard, supra note 56; Wexler, supra note 3, at 213–14.

101. For a parallel inquiry, see Renaud, R. v. Fuller: Time to Brush Aside the Rule Prohibiting Therapeutic Remands? 35 Crim. L. Q. 91 (1992) (Part I), and id., 35 Crim. L. Q. 156 (1993) (Part II).

102. On the procedural due process protections required in civil cases following a conditional release, see 1 M.L. Perlin, supra note 7, § 3.54 at 363–68. The case law that has developed around conditional release generally calls for procedural due process protections much like those at initial involuntary civil commitment hearings. As of yet, there has been virtually no case law dealing with this specific question as it applies to the population of insanity acquittees. * * * Some questions that must be addressed here include the following: Is a hearing with full procedural due process protections therapeutically valuable for individuals facing recommitment? Or, is the possibility that such protections might result in fewer recommitments antitherapeutic? Does the Supreme Court's decision in Foucha v. Louisiana, 112 S. Ct. 1780 (1992) (declaring unconstitutional a state law that provided for the continued insanity commitment of an NGRI acquittee who was no longer mentally ill apply in this context?

103. See generally, 3 M.L. Perlin, supra note 7, § 15.34, at 384–88.

104. Statistics seem to indicate that defendants who are unsuccessful in their NGRI pleas are frequently given lengthier sentences than like defendants who do not raise a non-responsibility defense. See supra chapter 3 B 1 b (1). If we assume that a significant percentage of these defendants are mentally ill, this finding suggests that the plea is even a riskier gambit than has generally been thought.

105. See e.g., Salton, Mental Capacity and Liability Insurance Clauses: The Effect of Insanity Upon Intent, 78 Calif. L. Rev. 1027 (1990). When a defendant is found NGRI, there are potential effects on other legal interactions. Can an NGRI defendant be prosecuted for "criminal" acts that take place in forensic hospitals or other mental institutions? Can he be disciplined for violating institutional rules? Can he be civilly liable for his tortious acts?

systemic ways that counsel is assigned to potential insanity pleaders[106] are all questions that can and should be considered in therapeutic jurisprudence analyses.

3. Conclusion

As I have sought to demonstrate, the therapeutic jurisprudence inquiry is a critical one to the future development of the insanity defense. I believe that, if we are to make any headway as a society in eliminating the sanism that affects all of mental disability jurisprudence (but that especially contaminates insanity defense law), we must carefully consider each of these therapeutic jurisprudence questions.

* * *

Compare Koehler v. State, 830 S.W. 2d 665 (Tex. App. 1992), rev. den. (1992) (determination of incompetence to manage one's own affairs not a prima facie showing of incompetency to stand trial).

106. Counsel made available to mentally disabled criminal defendants is often substandard. See Perlin, Fatal Assumption: A Critical Evaluation of the Role of Counsel in Mental Disability Cases, 16 Law & Hum. Behav. 39 (1992). Lawyers representing such persons often ignore potential mental status defenses, or, in some cases, contradictorily, seek to have the insanity defense imposed on their client over his objection. Such lawyers often succumb to sanist stereotypes and are compliant co-conspirators in pretextual court decisions. See Perlin, supra note 13, at 404–06.

Chapter 4

Incompetency to Proceed in the Criminal Process: Past, Present, and Future

Bruce J. Winick

If, at any time in the criminal proceedings, a defendant appears to have a mental illness, the issue of his or her competence to proceed may be raised. This may occur when the defendant seeks to plead guilty or to stand trial. It may occur when the defendant seeks to waive certain constitutional rights, such as the right to counsel or to a jury trial. Even after conviction, the issue may be raised at a sentencing hearing, or when the government attempts to administer punishment, including capital punishment. The issue usually is raised by defense counsel, but also may be raised by the prosecution or the court itself, even over the opposition of the defendant, who may prefer to proceed despite his or her mental illness.

When the competency issue is raised, a court typically will appoint several clinical evaluators to conduct a formal assessment of the defendant's competency. These clinical evaluators examine the defendant and then submit written reports to the court. The court then decides the issue, sometimes following a hearing at which the examiners testify and are subject to cross-examination. If the court finds the defendant incompetent, the criminal proceedings are suspended and the defendant is ordered into treatment, typically on an inpatient basis. Treatment is designed not to cure the defendant but to restore competence. If such restoration is thought to have been achieved, a new round of evaluations and hearings will occur, and if the court is satisfied concerning the defendant's competence, the criminal proceedings will be resumed.

This chapter examines the competency process, analyzing the legal framework that has evolved for competency determination and the disposition of those found incompetent to proceed. It discusses the origins of the competency process, the purposes the doctrine is designed to accomplish, and the costs and burdens that existing practices impose. It criticizes existing practices as costly, burdensome to defendants, and often inconsistent with the stated justifications for the doctrine. The various rules and procedures used in this area are analyzed from a therapeutic jurisprudence perspective (see generally "Bibliography," 1993; Perlin, 1993a; Wexler, 1993; Wexler & Winick, 1991a, 1991b, 1992a, 1992b). Not only do these rules and procedures often impose heavy burdens on criminal defendants with mental illness whom they are designed to protect, but they also frequently produce antitherapeutic consequences for those found incompetent and divert limited clinical resources from treatment to evaluation.

Substantial reforms thus are needed. Ten years ago, I proposed a radical restructuring of the incompetency doctrine (Winick, 1985). In this chapter I review that proposal and offer several refinements growing out of my more recent work in therapeutic jurisprudence. I suggest changes in the way competency should be defined and evaluated and attempt to reshape the existing doctrine in order to eliminate its most objectionable features.

This chapter analyzes problems of incompetency to stand trial resulting from mental illness. Sometimes defendants are found incompetent as a result of mental retardation. The issues raised by mental retardation are considerably different from those raised by mental illness. Unlike mental illness, mental retardation is congenital, untreatable, and unchangeable. Moreover, individuals with mental retardation are always of subaverage intelligence and are often extremely vulnerable to suggestive influences, making waiver issues always problematic. For these and other reasons, the discussion in this chapter is limited to incompetency produced by mental illness, and its suggestions are not intended to apply to those with the distinct problems caused by mental retardation (Ellis, 1992; Ellis & Luckasson, 1985).

Incompetency in the Criminal Process: Past and Present

Historical Origins of the Incompetency Doctrine

The common law origins of the incompetency doctrine have been traced to mid-17th-century England (Group for the Advancement of Psychiatry, 1974; Hale, 1736; Winick, 1983, 1985). Blackstone (1783/1979) wrote that a defendant who becomes "mad" after the commission of an offense should not be arraigned "because he is not able to plead...with the advice and caution that he ought," and should not be tried, for "how can he make his defense?" The ban on trial of an incompetent defendant has been traced to the common law prohibition on trials in absentia (trials held in defendant's absence), and to the difficulties encountered by the English courts when a defendant frustrated the ritual of the common law trial by remaining mute instead of pleading to the charges (Foote, 1960; Gobert, 1973; Group for the Advancement of Psychiatry, 1974; Winick, 1983; see for example, *Frith's Case*, 1790; *Kinloch's Case*, 1746). Without a plea the trial could not go forward. In such cases, English courts were obliged to determine whether the defendant was "mute by visitation of God" or "mute of malice." If "mute of malice" the defendant was subjected to a form of medieval torture, the *peine forte et dure*, in which increasingly heavier weights were placed on the defendant's chest in an effort to compel a plea. If "mute by visitation of God," the defendant was spared this painful ritual. The category "mute by visitation of God" originally encompassed the "deaf and dumb," but its scope gradually expanded to include "lunatics." At the discretion of the Chancellor, a jury could be empaneled to conduct an inquiry into the defendant's competency.

At this early stage of the development of the incompetency doctrine in England, self-representation rather than representation by counsel was the common practice (*Faretta v. California*, 1975; Winick, 1989). Indeed, in serious criminal cases, counsel was prohibited, and the defendant was required to "appear before the court in his own person and conduct his own defense in his own words" (*Faretta v. California*, 1975, p. 823, quoting Pollock & Maitland, 1898/1968). The prohibition against the assistance of counsel continued for centuries in felony and treason cases (Pollock & Maitland, 1898/1968; Stephen, 1883/1964). Thus, during the formative period of the incompetency doctrine, in many cases the defendant stood alone before the court and trial was merely "a long argument between the prisoner and the counsel for the Crown" (*Faretta v. California*, 1975, pp. 823–824, citing Stephen, 1883/1964). During the time when the incompetency doctrine was shaped, it was imperative that the defendant be competent because he or she was required to conduct his or her own defense.

The common law rationale for the incompetency doctrine has now largely become obsolete (Gobert, 1973; "Incompetency to Stand Trial," 1967; Winick, 1983, 1987). Today the assistance of counsel is available as a matter of constitutional right (*Argersinger v. Hamlin*, 1972; *Gideon v. Wainwright*, 1963; U.S. Constitution, amendment 6, 1791; Winick, 1989). As a result, in the modern criminal case, it is counsel who must be competent, and the competence of the defendant, although still required, takes on secondary importance.

Modern Justifications for the Incompetency Doctrine

Although the historical justifications for the doctrine have largely been eclipsed, a number of justifications for the modern doctrine remain. In part, the doctrine is justified based on *parens patriae* (protectionist) considerations—the desire to prevent unfairness to the defendant and to prevent a potentially erroneous conviction that could result from requiring the defendant to stand trial while significantly impaired by mental illness. Even though many of the strategic decisions in the modern criminal trial process are made by counsel, the defendant, if impaired, may be unable or unwilling to communicate facts that might be critical to counsel or the court (Bonnie, 1993; Weihofen, 1954). This concern has led the Supreme Court to deem the bar against trying an incompetent defendant "fundamental to an adversary system of justice" (*Drope v. Missouri*, 1975). Avoiding inaccuracy in criminal adjudication serves not only the individual's interests in avoiding unjust conviction, but also the societal interest in the reliability of the criminal process (Bonnie, 1993; Winick, 1985).

The incompetency doctrine also may be defended as necessary for preserving the moral dignity of the criminal process. This process would be threatened by trying defendants who lack a meaningful understanding of the nature of the criminal proceedings (Bonnie, 1993). This justification relates to the need to ensure public respect and confidence in the criminal process—considerations basic to the legitimacy of the criminal justice system (Winick, 1983, 1985).

The competency doctrine also protects the criminal defendant's interest in autonomous decision making concerning his or her defense (Winick, 1992). Although many issues of strategy and tactics are decided by counsel, certain key decisions must be made by the defendant (Bonnie, 1993). In our system, the defendant must make the decisions whether to plead guilty, to waive jury trial, to be present during trial, and to testify (see generally American Bar Association, 1992b; for example, *Adams v. United States ex rel. McCann,* 1942; *Brookhart v. Janus,* 1966; *Jones v. Barnes,* 1983; O'Neil, 1990; *Rock v. Arkansas,* 1987; *Wainwright v. Sykes,* 1977; Winick, 1985). As a result, the defendant must be competent to make these decisions.

A final justification for the incompetency doctrine is the need to preserve the decorum of the courtroom and the resulting dignity of the trial process, which could be threatened by permitting the trial of a mentally impaired defendant unable to control his or her courtroom conduct ("Incompetency to Stand Trial," 1967; Winick, 1985). However, in light of alternative measures for dealing with this problem, it alone should not justify barring the trial of an otherwise competent defendant (Bonnie, 1993; Winick, 1985).

The Modern Practice

Under the modern practice applicable in all American jurisdictions, a criminal defendant is deemed incompetent to stand trial if, as a result of mental illness, he or she is unable to understand the nature of the proceedings or to assist counsel in making a defense (see generally American Bar Association, 1989; Roesch & Golding, 1980; Steadman, 1979; Winick, 1991d). Virtually all criminal defendants who appear to have mental illness at any time in the criminal trial process are ordered by the court to be evaluated for competency (*Drope v. Missouri,* 1975; Winick, 1985). The competency issue usually is raised by motion of defense counsel requesting a competency evaluation. The prosecution may also raise the issue by motion. In addition, the judge may, on his or her own motion, request a competency evaluation when the evidence presents a bona fide doubt as to the defendant's competency (*Drope v. Missouri,* 1975). Failure of a court to order a competency evaluation when reasonable grounds exist to question the defendant's competency will violate the defendant's right to due process,[1] requiring reversal of any conviction obtained (*Drope v. Missouri,* 1975; *Pate v. Robinson,* 1966). As a result, courts typically order a formal competency evaluation in virtually every case in which doubt about the defendant's competency is raised, necessitating an evaluation by two to three court-appointed clinicians, who then submit written reports to the court (Roesch & Golding, 1980; Winick, 1985). Several studies have concluded that the vast majority of defendants are referred inappropriately for competency evaluations and have suggested that the competency process is often invoked for strategic purposes (Winick, 1985; see, for example, American Bar Association, 1983; Chernoff & Schaffer, 1972; Cooke, Johnston, & Pogany, 1973; Ennis & Emery, 1978; Golding, Roesch, & Schreiber, 1984; Halpern, 1975; McGarry, 1969; Roesch & Golding, 1979, 1980; Shah, 1981; Steadman &

---

1. The Fourteenth Amendendent to the U.S. Constitution imposes the requirement that the states not deprive a person of liberty without "due process of law." This requires that the states use fair procedures in the criminal process, including a prohibition on proceediing against an individual who is incompetent to stand trial.

Braff, 1978; Steadman & Hartstone, 1983; Stone, 1978; Wexler & Scoville, 1971).[2]

It is estimated that 25,000 defendants are evaluated for competency in America each year, and that the number is increasing (Steadman & Hartstone, 1983). Perhaps because the threshold for requiring a competency hearing is so low, a large percentage of defendants evaluated are found competent—as many as 96% or more in some jurisdictions, and probably no less than 75% in most (Winick, 1993a). Nearly all of those found incompetent are hospitalized for treatment (Roesch & Golding, 1979; Winick, 1985). These defendants are treated, usually with psychotropic drugs (Winick, 1993b), and most will be returned to court within several months as having been restored to competency (Winick, 1985). Some are hospitalized for longer periods, and some are never restored to competency (Winick, 1985).[3]

The Costs and Burdens of the Incompetency Process

The existing competency process imposes serious burdens on defendants and is extremely costly. Virtually all criminal defendants exhibiting symptoms of mental illness are subjected to a formal evaluation for competency; yet a considerable number of defendants may not require formal evaluation (Winick, 1985).

Empirical research on the costs of competency evaluation and treatment is almost nonexistent. However, data from a study I conducted 10 years ago of costs in Dade County, Florida, are useful as a rough basis for projecting costs nationally (Winick, 1985). Evaluation costs for an initial competency assessment averaged $2327, excluding court costs and the expense of additional defense attorney, prosecutor, and judge time. These costs were based on outpatient evaluation. Inpatient evaluation for competency, still used in some jurisdictions, could easily double and even quadruple these costs (Winick, 1985). If a defendant is found incompetent at this initial stage, he or she is hospitalized for several months of treatment, at an added average cost of $20,351, excluding several thousand dollars in court costs attributable to attorney time and hearings (Winick, 1985). Total cost for the typical defendant found incompetent in Dade County thus exceeded $22,678, excluding attorney and court costs. Costs for some cases ran considerably higher (Winick, 1985).[4]

---

2. The incompetency process may be invoked by both sides to obtain delay, by prosecutors to avoid bail or an insanity acquittal or to effect hospitalization that might not otherwise be possible under the state's civil commitment statute, or by defense attorneys to obtain mental health recommendations for use in making an insanity defense, in plea bargaining, or in a sentencing.

3. Those who are permanently incompetent or are unlikely to be restored to competency within a reasonable period must either be civilly committed or released (see *Jackson v. Indiana*, 1972). Their criminal charges, however, must remain unresolved, and they may be prosecuted in the future should they then become competent.

4. Dade County uses a relatively inexpensive system of outpatient evaluations. Expensive inpatient evaluations are used more frequently in some jurisdictions.

Using these Dade County figures, which I assume to be low and which are based on costs prevailing 10 years ago, it can be estimated that in excess of $185 million is spent annually on competency evaluation and treatment in America (Winick, 1985). The actual costs today may be two to three times as high. With attorney and court costs included, the costs of the incompetency process nationally may well exceed $1 billion per year. Moreover, formal competency evaluations occur in many cases in which less formal screening could suffice. Therefore, the competency determination results in a diversion of limited clinical resources to evaluation that otherwise could be used for treatment.

The incompetency process also frequently imposes serious burdens on defendants. Prior to the Supreme Court's 1972 decision in *Jackson v. Indiana*, defendants hospitalized for incompetency to stand trial received what amounted to an indeterminate sentence of confinement in a mental hospital, typically for many years, often exceeding the maximum sentence for the crime charged, and sometimes lasting a lifetime (Winick, 1985). In *Jackson,* the Court recognized a constitutional limit on the duration of incompetency commitment, holding that a defendant committed solely based on trial incompetency "cannot be held more than a reasonable period of time necessary to determine whether there is a substantial probability that he will attain that capacity in the foreseeable future" (p. 738). Any continued confinement, the Court held, must be based on the probability that the defendant will be returned to competency within the foreseeable future. If the treatment provided does not succeed in advancing the defendant toward that goal, then the state either must institute customary civil commitment proceedings, if it wishes to detain the defendant, or must release him or her (*Jackson v. Indiana,* 1972; Winick, 1985). Although *Jackson* marked an end to the most egregious cases of indefinite incompetency commitment, many states have responded insufficiently to the Court's decision and abuses persist (Melton, Weithorn, & Slobogin, 1985; Winick, 1985).

Lengthy incompetency commitment is particularly burdensome for defendants charged with misdemeanors, perhaps a majority of those found incompetent (Winick, 1985). Many of these defendants would pay a small fine or receive a period of probation were they convicted. Instead, they might spend many months and even years confined as incompetent. Many of the hospitals in which the defendants are confined are maximum security institutions that are poorly funded and staffed (Winick, 1985). Although many states now authorize outpatient treatment for trial incompetency, most defendants found incompetent are still hospitalized (Winick, 1985). Such hospitalization is frequently unnecessarily restrictive of defendant's liberty and unnecessarily stigmatizing (Winick, 1985). In some jurisdictions, a short-term commitment based on incompetency to stand trial is used as an alternative to ordinary civil commitment. In misdemeanor cases, these defendants often will be released after several months with their charges dismissed. However, even this period of hospital confinement may be unnecessary, may not satisfy state commitment criteria, and will be more restrictive and less therapeutic than typical civil hospitalization.

Even for those not ultimately found incompetent, a court-ordered competency evaluation often prevents the setting of bail, ensuring that the defendant is held in custody, separated from family, friends, and other community ties for a lengthy period (Winick, 1985). Moreover, this period of confinement for evaluation or treatment often is not credited against a sentence later received (Winick, 1985). As a result, defendants who are evaluated are potentially confined for longer than they would have been had they been permitted to waive their incompetency and either plead guilty or stand trial at the outset.

These delays undermine the Sixth Amendment's guarantee to a speedy trial. While an incompetency determination is being made witnesses may die or disappear, memories may fade, and evidence may become lost or unavailable. These difficulties can burden both the defense and the prosecution, and may significantly impede a just and reliable determination of the charges. In addition, lengthy delays may compromise the basic purposes of the criminal law. If the defendant is guilty, delay in the trial process diminishes the possibilities for rehabilitation. Delayed punishment may also weaken the deterrent effect of the criminal sanction and frustrate the interests of victims in seeing that justice is done. Undue delay will be especially prejudicial if the defendant is innocent (Winick, 1993a).

The incompetency determination also imposes a serious stigma on defendants labeled incompetent to stand trial. Even though these defendants already bear the stigma of criminal accusation, the added stigma of being labeled incompetent may be considerably worse than being accused of a crime (American Bar Association, 1983). Moreover, these defendants are further stigmatized by their being associated with the often notorious institutions to which they are committed—high-security mental health correction facilities like Dannamoura, Bridgewater, or Ionia—that evoke in the public mind an image of the dangerously mad (Burt, 1974; Winick, 1977, 1985).

In addition to its impact on how others may perceive the defendant, an incompetency label may also impose serious negative psychological effects on the individual so labeled (see generally Sales & Kahle, 1980; Winick, 1995). The label "incompetent" has an unfortunate general connotation that may make people feel not only that they are unfit to stand trial, but that they are broadly incompetent to do anything. Moreover, the "incompetent" label suggests a permanent deficit, rather than a temporary impairment. Individuals so labeled may, therefore, come to think that their difficulties cannot be helped. This can impede successful treatment. Imposition of an incompetency label can thus be seriously debilitating to the individual. Many criminal defendants already have serious problems that they may feel are outside their control. Labeling them incompetent, particularly against their will, can foster what Martin Seligman (1975) called "learned helplessness," a syndrome characterized by generalized feelings of helplessness, hopelessness, depression, and lack of motivation (Abramson, Garber, & Seligman, 1980; Abramson, Seligman, & Teasdale, 1978; Maier & Seligman, 1976; Seligman & Garber, 1980) that mirrors the symptoms of clinical depression (Peterson & Bossio, 1989).

In practice, the incompetency doctrine thus raises significant problems and imposes serious burdens on defendants and high costs on states. Although designed for their protection, the burdens it places on defendants are so substantial that the American Bar Association (ABA) committee that developed the ABA's *Criminal Justice Mental Health Standards* (1983) suggested that defense counsel may conclude that it is in their clients' best interests not to raise the issue.

Restructuring the Incompetency Process
Distinguishing Assent from Objection

The ABA committee has indicated that if the severe problems associated with the competency doctrine continue, "perhaps we should address more clearly the concept of possible waiver on the part of a defendant" (§ 7.162). Under existing practices, a defendant deemed incompetent may not stand trial or plead guilty even if he or she wishes to do so (American Bar Association, 1983; *Drope v. Missouri,* 1975; see, for example, *Hamm v. Jabe,* 1983; *Medina v. California,* 1992). Indeed, existing practices require the defense attorney to raise the competency question with the court whenever a genuine doubt about competency arises, even if counsel believes that raising the issue will not be in the defendant's best interests (American Bar Association, 1989).

In my previous article (Winick, 1985), I suggested that waiver might be possible in limited circumstances for defendants impaired by mental illness who, with the concurrence of counsel, clearly and voluntarily express the desire to stand trial or plead guilty notwithstanding their mental impairment. I suggested that the incompetency process be restructured to distinguish two different types of cases. The first is when defendants assert their own incompetency as a ground for temporarily halting the criminal proceedings. The second is when the defendant wishes to proceed notwithstanding his or her impairment, but the incompetency status is sought either by motion of the prosecution or by action of the court itself. In the former case, a system of trial continuances should be substituted for the existing formal competency process. In the latter, waiver could be considered, with appropriate safeguards, when the defendant clearly and voluntarily expresses a preference for trial or a guilty plea and counsel concurs. In the alternative, even if the defendant is deemed incompetent to waive the supposed benefits of the incompetency doctrine, counsel should be permitted to do so on behalf of the defendant, on the basis that the defense lawyer, as a fiduciary (a person in a position of trust), should be permitted to substitute his or her judgment for that of an incompetent client.

This proposal for restructuring the incompetency-to-stand-trial doctrine was controversial. It challenged thinking that regarded competency as an essential prerequisite for waiver of rights in the criminal process, and seemed inconsistent with the Supreme Court's jurisprudence in this area. I argued, however, that allowing a defendant of doubtful competence to waive the "benefits" of the incompetency doctrine would not violate the purposes of the doctrine as long as safeguards, including the advice and agreement of counsel, were required (Winick, 1985). I also argued that the Supreme Court's language in *Pate v. Robinson* (1966), suggesting that incompetent defendants could not waive the incompetency status, was dicta (not essential to the decision in that case), and could easily be discarded (Winick, 1985). I discussed legal and clinical practices, both in the criminal area and elsewhere, that accept waiver in many situations in which the individual whose rights are waived never participates in the decision or is of doubtful competence (Winick, 1985). These practices support a distinction between assent and objection. That distinction should justify the application of differential standards of waiver in the incompetency-to-stand-trial context based on whether the defendant seeks to accept trial or a guilty plea or to object to trial on the basis of his or her mental illness. I suggested that our conceptions of competency in the criminal process were artificial and were based on myth and unrealistic models of the criminal process and of the differences between criminal defendants with mental illness and "normal" defendants (Winick, 1985).

In the 10 years since advancing my original proposals for restructuring the incompetency process, I have developed further some of the ideas on which my proposals were based. More specifically, my work in therapeutic jurisprudence explored in greater detail the distinction between assent and objection and its implications for defining competency (Wexler & Winick, 1991a, 1991b). I have analyzed the use of this distinction in two noncriminal areas—competency to consent to treatment (Winick, 1991a) and competency to consent to voluntary hospitalization (Winick, 1991b). Further, I have analyzed the value of autonomy and its role in mental health law (Winick, 1992), and explored the psychological value of allowing individuals to exercise choice (Winick, 1992, 1994a) and the corresponding disadvantages of denying them the opportunity to be self-determining (Winick, 1994b). In addition, I have analyzed the various procedural modes for determining competency (Winick, 1991b), including the role of presumptions and burdens of proof in this process (Winick, 1993a). This further thinking in the last 10 years on restructuring competency to stand trial has led to several refinements in the argument and additional proposals. In what follows in this section, I set forth an expanded proposal for how the incompetency process can be reformed.

Waiver and the Purposes of the Incompetency Doctrine

Can defendants who may be incompetent waive the "benefits" of the incompetency status? The incompetency doctrine is not designed solely to protect the defendant's interests, but also serves societal interests in preserving the moral dignity of the criminal process and in avoiding erroneous convictions, both of which might be compromised by permitting trial of an incompetent defendant (Winick, 1993a). In my original article I acknowledged these and other societal interests that are thought to justify the incompetency doctrine (Winick, 1985), but questioned "whether in practice the competency doctrine actually accomplishes these asserted benefits" (p. 950). We can speculate that some of these benefits of the incompetency doctrine are present for defendants who assert their incompetency as a basis for postponing the trial ("objectors" to trial), and that these benefits outweigh the burdens the doctrine would impose on the defendant (Bonnie, 1993). But for defendants who prefer trial or a guilty plea in accordance with the advice of counsel, or at least with the approval of counsel ("assenters"), these benefits may be more theoretical than real, and may fall far short of outweighing the burdens imposed.

My proposal assumes that the defendant has the ability clearly and voluntarily to articulate a preference either for trial or a guilty plea. It also assumes that defense counsel, after careful consideration, concurs in the judgment that this preference seems reasonable in the circumstances and that the client's assent is not basically irrational. This requirement is consistent with the role of the defense lawyer. After the defense lawyer receives sufficient information from the defendant and investigates the facts and the law, he or she typically will select an appropriate defense strategy (Winick, 1985). When the defendant assents to this strategy, and counsel thinks the defendant has a basic understanding of the choice made, counsel's judgment is entitled to great weight. In most cases it will be counsel's recommendation to go to trial or to enter a guilty plea to which the defendant assents. In some cases, however, the choice will originate with the defendant and counsel will approve or at least acquiesce in that choice. Counsel's agreement with the client's choice provides an assurance by a person who has a professional fiduciary relationship with the defendant that proceeding to trial or entering a guilty plea is in the defendant's best interests. In such cases, deference both to the autonomy of the defendant and to the professional expertise of counsel makes it appropriate to erect a presumption in favor of competency, that is, a rule that assumes that defendants are competent until proven otherwise. Counsel's acquiescence to the client's decision provides reasonable assurance that accuracy in adjudication will not be frustrated. A defense attorney concerned that allowing a guilty plea or proceeding to trial with an impaired defendant might result in an unjust conviction, because either the client lacks a basic understanding of the choice made, or the choice made seems clearly inconsistent with the defendant's interests, should not and presumably would not provide the concurrence that my proposal requires.

Allowing a trial that both the defendant and his or her counsel wish to proceed with is a provisional decision that the trial judge can rescind if, as the case unfolds, concerns for accuracy arise. Moreover, if defense counsel, during trial, realizes that the defendant's impairment is more significant than earlier thought, and that the client's inabilities seem likely to produce an inaccurate result, then counsel can seek a determination of incompetency based on this new information. Because competency is a fluctuating state and a defendant's condition may change during the course of a trial, the trial judge has a continuing duty to reconsider the issue of competency at any time when reasonable doubt about the defendant's competency is raised (*Drope v. Missouri*, 1975; Winick, 1993a). At best, a pretrial competency determination constitutes a prediction about how the defendant will perform at a future trial. If during trial, defense counsel, contrary to an initial assessment, concludes that the defendant's impairment is materially interfering with the ability to communicate or provide essential assistance, the attorney then can bring concrete examples of such incapacities to the court's attention and seek a mistrial. The court possesses broad discretion concerning the grant of a mistrial (Federal Rules of Criminal Procedure, Rule 43(b)-(c), 1986; *Illinois v. Allen*, 1970; *Snyder v. Massachusetts*, 1934; see, for example, *Hamm v. Jabe*, 1983), and can at that point order a clinical evaluation of competency to assist in determining the issue.

The risk of inaccuracy in adjudication also may be minimized through use of the trial court's power to set aside verdicts in the interest of justice (for example, Federal Rules of Criminal Procedure, Rule 33, 1986), or to allow a new trial if additional evidence affecting the verdict later materializes that would have been available but for the defendant's incompetency (Burt & Morris, 1972). Thus, a number of safety valves prevent truly incompetent defendants from subjecting themselves to trials.

Let us consider the concern for accuracy in adjudication in perspective. Waivers are customarily accepted in other criminal contexts, even though allowing such waivers might affect accuracy. First, the Supreme Court has held that a defendant may waive the right to counsel and represent himself or herself (*Faretta v. California,* 1975). Thus, the Court recognizes that respect for individual autonomy may override the societal concern for accuracy in adjudication (Winick, 1985). Second, a defendant may plead guilty (and thereby waive all trial-related constitutional rights) even if unwilling to concede commission of a crime (*North Carolina v. Alford,* 1970; *White Hawk v. Solem,* 1982, 1983; see also American Law Institute, 1972), and even in the absence of a factual basis to believe that he or she has done so (Barkai, 1977; Goldstein, 1981; Halberstam, 1982; see, for example, Federal Rules of Criminal Procedure, Rule 11(f), 1986). Even though acceptance of such a plea may lead to an erroneous conviction, the desire to let the accused resolve the charges together with society's interest in facilitating negotiated settlements outweigh the concern for accuracy. These waiver-of-counsel and guilty-plea cases arose in contexts in which the defendant's competency was not questioned, and therefore may not be as persuasive in contexts in which competency is in issue. However, they demonstrate that deference to autonomy sometimes trumps reliability concerns.

Finally, an incompetent defendant whose "free will" is impaired by mental illness may confess to a crime (*Colorado v. Connelly,* 1986). These confessions are given great weight by juries, and if inaccurate, can produce unjust convictions. If a defendant without counsel may confess to a crime and thereby waive Fifth Amendment and *Miranda* rights, notwithstanding his or her substantial mental impairment, why should a mentally impaired defendant who wishes to accept counsel's recommendation not be able to waive the due process right to avoid trial while incompetent?

In addition to the societal concern for accuracy in adjudication, the incompetency doctrine serves other significant societal interests. For example, the doctrine may be essential to preserving the moral dignity of the criminal process. Does this interest justify barring conviction of defendants who can be said to lack a meaningful moral understanding of wrongdoing and punishment or the nature of criminal prosecution (Bonnie, 1993)? Would concern for the moral dignity of the criminal process be frustrated by permitting a mentally impaired defendant to be tried in accordance with his or her wish to follow defense counsel's recommendation? Would this concern be frustrated if the choice for trial was the defendant's and counsel acquiesced in that choice as reasonable in the circumstances?

Two types of cases seem plainly not to justify a bar on trial. First, a defendant lacking any meaningful understanding of wrongdoing might qualify for the insanity defense, and if so, would be neither convicted nor punished. A defendant who otherwise possesses sufficient abilities to make an insanity defense thus should not be disqualified from doing so by a lack of moral understanding of his or her wrongdoing. Second, it can be conceded that a defendant lacking a meaningful understanding of punishment should not be punished (Winick, 1985). However, such a lack of understanding can be taken into account at sentencing, or at the time of administration of punishment, or such punishment can be deferred (Winick, 1985). This concern therefore should not be used as a justification for putting off a trial desired by the defendant and his or her lawyer.

The concern with avoiding trial for a defendant lacking a meaningful understanding of the nature of criminal prosecution is more serious. But how much understanding should be required before a defendant's trial would threaten the moral dignity of the criminal process? We should be careful not to set this standard too high lest we disqualify not only defendants with mental illness from facing their charges, but also many "normal" defendants. Indeed, many criminal defendants who do not have a mental illness may lack a meaningful understanding of the nature of criminal prosecution (Winick, 1985). Defendants generally are willing to defer to their attorneys, just as most medical patients are willing to defer to their doctors concerning appropriate medical treatment (Winick, 1985). Many defendants do not comprehend the nature of their choices and are willing to delegate decision making to a professional in whom they place their trust.

Moreover, a complete understanding of the nature of criminal prosecution is unnecessary in the overwhelming number of cases in which the charges are resolved through a guilty plea (Winick, 1985). Defendants who plead guilty do not need to possess a high level of understanding concerning the trial process because they will not participate in it. These defendants need to possess sufficient skills to help counsel reconstruct the alleged crime and evaluate possible defenses in order to allow counsel to assess the strength of the prosecution's case. However, we should not ignore the fact that in a substantial number of cases the defendant with mental illness, like defendants generally, probably has committed the crime with which he or she is charged and lacks a credible defense. For these defendants, a guilty plea is almost always the best option. The plea negotiation process is conducted exclusively by counsel, with little need for the client's assistance. Therefore, when the negotiation produces a plea that the defendant finds more desirable than an incompetency adjudication (which will only postpone trial or a guilty plea to a later date), the defendant should be permitted to accept the plea, provided he or she possesses a rudimentary understanding of the consequences (that is, the sentence to be imposed and that he or she forgoes trial and various trial-related rights). A more complete understanding of the nature of a criminal prosecution thus may be only rarely required. Its absence therefore should not disqualify a defendant with mental illness who has a basic understanding of the nature of a guilty plea from being able to accept such a plea.

In *Godinez v. Moran* (1993), the Supreme Court rejected the contention that competency to plead guilty should require a higher standard than competency to stand trial. Therefore, the Court suggested that the general standard for competency to stand trial should apply as well to other competency issues arising in the criminal process. The Court did not consider, however, whether in an appropriate case the test of competency to plead guilty might be a lower standard than for competency to stand trial. In fact, the notion of competency is best understood in the context of the decisions presented (American Bar Association, 1989; Bonnie, 1993; Roesch & Golding, 1979). To the extent that *Godinez* holds that the same standard of competency must be applied across the board, regardless of the particular issue or the nature of the case, it is open to serious criticism.

We should not insist on an abstract notion of competency based on a model of the criminal case as involving a full-blown trial in which the defendant will testify and must have considerable skills in order to participate with counsel in complicated strategic decision making. Rather, we should apply a flexible standard of competency that requires only that the defendant possess the abilities that will be necessary in the particular case. This is particularly true in misdemeanor cases, where an overwhelming majority of defendants plead guilty. In the past 20 years, tightening civil commitment standards and the practice of deinstitutionalization have had the effect of funneling many former civil patients who commit minor nuisances into the criminal process, with the result that a majority of defendants evaluated for competency are charged only with minor misdemeanors (see Bonovitz & Guy, 1979; Dickey, 1980; Geller & Lister, 1978; Shah, 1981; Teplin, 1983; Wexler, 1983; Winick, 1985, 1987). A defendant arrested for a petty offense such as disorderly conduct or shoplifting usually will be able to plead guilty and pay a small fine. If the defendant is incompetent to stand trial, however, he or she may face many months of incarceration in a jail and in a maximum security mental hospital that resembles one. If the defendant then is restored to competency and returned to court, he or she probably will accept the same plea bargain at that point. When acceptance of a guilty plea imposes such nominal consequences on the defendant, the degree of competency required to accept a plea that is clearly and voluntarily sought by the defendant, with the advice and concurrence of counsel, should be relatively modest. When the consequences are substantial—a felony conviction carrying a lengthy prison sentence, for example—the degree of competency required to plead guilty can be higher. And in cases in which the defendant seeks to plead guilty to a capital offense, thereby being exposed to a possible death sentence, a relatively high degree of competency and understanding should be required (*Beck v. Alabama*, 1980; *Coker v. Georgia*, 1977; *Eddings v. Oklahoma*, 1982; *Enmund v. Florida*, 1982; *Furman v. Georgia*, 1972; *Gardner v. Florida*, 1977; *Gregg v. Georgia*, 1976; *Lockett v. Ohio*, 1978; *Solem v. Helm*, 1983; Winick, 1982; *Woodson v. North Carolina*, 1976).

Such a sliding-scale approach to defining competency is reasonable and consistent with the desire to protect the accuracy and moral dignity of the criminal process. Indeed, basic principles of criminal procedure reflect such a sliding-scale approach by requiring less procedural protections in the trial of petty offenses than in more serious cases. For example, the U.S. Supreme Court has recognized a petty-offense exception to the Sixth Amendment right to trial by jury (*Baldwin v. New York*, 1970; *Bloom v. Illinois*, 1968). Under this exception, jury trial is unavailable in cases in which the authorized penalty does not exceed six months imprisonment (see *Duncan v. Louisiana*, 1968; *Singer v. United States*, 1965). Similarly, although the right to counsel is an essential feature of our adversary system (see *Faretta v. California*, 1975; *Powell v. Alabama*, 1932), indigent defendants are not entitled to the appointment of counsel in misdemeanor cases in which the defendant does not receive a sentence of imprisonment (see *Argersinger v. Hamlin*, 1972; *Scott v. Illinois*, 1980), and thus must face a professional prosecutor without assistance. When the stakes are relatively low, as they are in misdemeanor cases in which a prison sentence is either ruled out or will not exceed six months, important procedural safeguards are dispensed with.

A similar distinction between petty offenses and more serious cases could be applied in the incompetency-to-stand-trial context. To the extent that concerns with accuracy and the moral dignity of the criminal process make us reluctant to permit guilty pleas or trials for assenting defendants whose competency is in question, we should have considerably less reluctance when the defendant seeks to plead guilty or stand trial for a petty misdemeanor. Imposing the burdens of an incompetency adjudication on an unwilling defendant who would prefer to plead guilty in accordance with counsel's advice or with counsel's acquiescence seems unjustified unless the defendant is grossly incompetent. When competence is more marginal, the societal concerns for accuracy and the moral dignity of the criminal process should not be deemed to outweigh the defendant's desire to have an expeditious resolution of the charges.

Even if we continue generally to bar guilty pleas by defendants when there is doubt about their competence, a petty-offense (or even a misdemeanor) exception to the incompetency doctrine should be recognized. This exception should apply in cases in which the defendant clearly and voluntarily expresses assent to counsel's recommendation or expresses a desire to plead with which counsel approves. Because such a high percentage of incompetency cases arise in the misdemeanor context, such a rule would eliminate many of the high costs and burdens of the incompetency process. Limitations on civil commitment and the deinstitutionalization process have had the unintended effect of funneling into the criminal process many thousands of individuals who previously would have been committed civilly. The incompetency process has become a sort of "backdoor" commitment route. In effect, these misdemeanor incompetency-to-stand-trial commitments are short-term alternatives to civil commitment, and not truly criminal dispositions. Following a brief period of incompetency hospitalization, these defendants typically are released and their criminal charges are dismissed. Many of these individuals do not belong in the criminal process, and most do not belong in the hospital. They belong in the community but require continued services. Instead of spending millions of dollars in the criminal system on the processing of these misdemeanor incompetency cases, this money should be spent on services in the community to meet the continued medical and social needs of these individuals. By adopting the petty-offense misdemeanor exception proposed, we could effectuate such savings and reallocate the funds to the community services that are needed. Such an exception would be easy to adopt legislatively. An amendment to state incompetency-to-stand-trial statutes or court rules could provide that in all misdemeanor cases (or in all misdemeanor cases in which a prison sentence is ruled out), a defendant clearly and voluntarily electing to plead guilty or *nolo contendere* (no contest) with the approval of counsel will be presumed to be competent to do so.

Many defendants, of course, whether charged with a misdemeanor or a felony, will wish to stand trial rather than to plead guilty. Even when the defendant does not elect to plead guilty, but wishes to face the charges and to put the prosecution to its proof, the concerns for accuracy and for preserving the moral dignity of the criminal process will not necessarily be compromised by applying a low standard of competency for defendants assenting to the recommendation of counsel. These concerns assume that in our adversary system the truth determination process will be unfairly skewed in favor of the prosecution whenever the defendant's ability to understand the nature of the proceeding and participate fully in the defense is impaired. Yet there are some cases in which the defense strategy does not require the defendant's participation or understanding, and other cases in which the defendant's participation would not help significantly (see American Bar Association, 1983; Chernoff & Schaffer, 1972; Winick, 1985). Indeed, in cases in which the insanity defense is raised—which it will be in many cases involving defendants whose competency is in question—defense counsel may find it more advantageous to present the defendant to the trier of facts in his or her existing condition, rather than after having been restored to competency and returned to court on what may be a high dose of psychotropic medication that may affect the jury's assessment of the person's credibility (see American Bar Association, 1983; *Commonwealth v. Louraine,* 1983; *In re Pray,* 1975; *Riggins v. Nevada,* 1992; *State v. Jojola,* 1976; *State v. Murphy,* 1960; Winick, 1985). In addition, there are many cases in which defense counsel will raise a legal defense that does not require the defendant's participation, and that may be determined based on a pretrial motion. These include cases involving a motion to dismiss the indictment for lack of a speedy trial or for violation of the ban on double jeopardy. These also include cases involving a motion to suppress critical evidence obtained in violation of the defendant's Fourth, Fifth, or Sixth Amendment rights, or some other legal attack on the indictment or on the admissibility of key evidence. In addition, they include cases in which counsel raises police or prosecutorial misconduct. Deferring consideration of these legal challenges to the prosecution until after the defendant has received what might be a lengthy period of confinement for incompetency treatment seems questionable in cases in which counsel wishes to proceed and the defendant clearly and voluntarily agrees (*Jackson v. Indiana,* 1972). Requiring an incompetency delay in such cases cannot reasonably be justified based on concerns for accuracy or for preserving the dignity of the criminal process.

Instead of a rigid bar on the trial of a defendant of questionable competency, we should adopt a more flexible sliding-scale approach. We should use standards that reflect the highly contextualized nature of competency and that seek to determine it based on the precise degree of ability that a defendant will require in the case in question. Especially when the consequences to the defendant are relatively minor and the defense strategy in the case requires little assistance and participation by the defendant, we should be more willing to defer to the autonomy of a defendant who is clearly able to agree to the trial strategy recommended by counsel, even if his or her autonomy is reduced by mental illness. In many cases, respecting such autonomy, and permitting the case to proceed, at least provisionally, will produce just, fair, and accurate results that do not compromise the moral dignity of the criminal process.

A Presumption in Favor of Competency

Even if the protections of the incompetency doctrine should be deemed waivable, what procedures should be used to ensure the validity of waiver in individual cases? When fundamental rights like the right to counsel or to a trial are involved, expression of a preference to waive the right alone cannot suffice to create a valid waiver. To waive such rights, "the waiver must 'be knowing and intelligent' and the court must assure, on the record that these criteria have been satisfied" (Bonnie, 1993, p. 944). Absent any understanding of the nature and consequences of the decision, the ability to express a preference cannot itself resolve the competency question.

Although the mere expression of a preference cannot alone meet the requirements for competency to waive at least certain fundamental constitutional rights, my proposal does not suggest that expression of preference alone should be an acceptable definition of competency. Rather, defendants whose competency is in question should be permitted to waive these rights when they clearly and voluntarily express a preference to do so, provided certain other conditions are satisfied, including the concurrence of counsel. I do not equate the ability to express such a preference with competency or suggest that incompetent defendants should be permitted to waive these rights: "[T]he high value attached to the principle of individual autonomy does not mean that incompetent expressions of autonomy are or should be accepted" (Winick, 1985, p. 966).

Determining whether an expression of preference is competent, however, is often difficult, and a large percentage of cases could be decided either way. It is difficult to ascertain an individual's ability to process information and engage in rational decision making. Moreover, evaluators may tend to confuse the quality of the decision-making process with the reasonableness of the result reached. As a result, an approach to determining competency that presumed the competency of an individual able to articulate a preference should be used in cases in which counsel concurred with the choice made (Winick, 1985). Many cases will involve marginal defendants on the borderline of competence. To prevent excessive paternalism we should presume that individuals who are able to express a choice are competent. Moreover, existing practices in both criminal and noncriminal contexts support such a presumption (Winick, 1985).

How would a presumption of this type work? A presumption in favor of competency in cases in which the defendant can clearly and voluntarily express a preference is not the same as adopting the ability to express a preference as a substantive definition of competency. In my original article I recognized that when the defendant's expressed preference is based on "irrelevant reasons ('I will plead guilty because I am an insect'), irrational beliefs ('I will stand trial and thereby become a movie star'), or outright delusions ('I am an extraterrestrial and will return to my planet')," that expression of choice does not represent a sufficient degree of autonomy to be worthy of respect (Winick, 1985, p. 967). However, "[a]n individual able to express a choice is exercising at least some autonomy, and our respect for the principle of autonomy makes it appropriate to utilize a presumption of competency to guide the decision-maker in such a case" (p. 967). The presumption of competency would not shield clearly incompetent expressions of choice. Such a presumption "does not always decide a case; it is a rebuttable presumption" (p. 967; see also Winick, 1992, p. 1776; 1993a, p. 862).

As a result, a presumption in favor of competency is not a substantive test of competency to waive rights, but is a procedural rule concerning how such competency should be ascertained. There are elements of both a substantive and a procedural rule encompassed in my proposal. In my initial article, I suggested that the law "should apply only a relatively low standard of competency and minimal scrutiny when the defendant, with the concurrence of his attorney, expresses the wish to stand trial, and a higher standard and more intense scrutiny when the state asserts that the defendant should be tried over his objection that he is incompetent" (Winick, 1985, p. 968). Clearly expressed choice by the defendant in favor of resolving the charges speedily, either by trial or a guilty plea, is entitled to a degree of respect that permits only limited scrutiny of that choice by the courts. A high degree of scrutiny is appropriate, however, when the state seeks to prevent the defendant from invoking incompetency as a shield to an immediate trial, asserting a desire for treatment designed to improve his or her final functioning. Other than suggesting a low standard of competency for assent and a higher standard for objection, my proposal did not set forth a substantive definition of competency. It did, however, offer a procedural tool to be used in making competency determinations.

For the presumption in favor of competency to apply, I would require both the defendant's voluntary expression of choice and counsel's concurrence. By requiring the concurrence of counsel, my proposal would leave the matter of whether the defendant possesses sufficient competence largely to the judgment of counsel. A lower threshold of competence would be used for decisions that assent to counsel's recommendation than for those that object. When the defendant objects to counsel's recommendation concerning a matter for which the law requires a personal decision by the defendant—such as waiver of jury trial or the decision to testify or to decline to do so—the client's preference should be honored unless he or she is highly incompetent. If counsel believes the client to be competent, counsel must defer to the defendant's expression of preference with regard to at least one of these issues that the law leaves to the defendant, and probably also should do so for many other issues. If, on the other hand, counsel believes the client to be incompetent in this regard, counsel should raise the competency issue and the court would then conduct an inquiry into the matter. When there is assent, however, if the defendant is able clearly and voluntarily to express a decision, counsel's concurrence would constitute an implicit representation that the client is sufficiently competent to make the decision.

Unless the prosecution could produce evidence suggesting a lack of competence to engage in decision making concerning one of these crucial issues, or unless the court's own contact with the defendant produces statements by the defendant suggesting a lack of decisional competence in this regard, no further inquiry should occur. With regard to decisions that are not among the limited number requiring a defendant's personal decision—the myriad tactical and evidentiary decisions arising at the pretrial and trial stages—I would allow counsel to act on behalf of a client even when competence to engage in rational decision making is in doubt.

My proposal thus has the effect of moving much of the competency determination process from the formal judicial arena to the attorney-client relationship. Rather than having extensive clinical evaluation of competence followed by judicial determination, the bulk of the determinations of competence would be subsumed within the professional relationship. Counsel would always remain free to obtain a clinical consultation if needed, as part of the defendant's Sixth Amendment right to effective assistance of counsel (see *Ake v. Oklahoma*, 1985), or could always obtain consultation from another attorney to help in the decision-making process. However, leaving the bulk of competency assessment within the attorney-client relationship should produce fair decisions that do not conflict with the societal purposes underlying the competency doctrine. The ability of the prosecutor to obtain specific evidence of incompetency when it is available, or of the court to conduct its own inquiry of the defendant in court, provides additional assurance that leaving much of the decision making in this area to the attorney-client relationship will not undermine the moral dignity of the criminal process or the concern for accuracy in adjudication.

My original proposal drew heavily on an analogy between the attorney-client relationship and the doctor-patient relationship (Winick, 1985). In the context of competency to make treatment and hospitalization decisions, clinicians typically are trusted to make their own assessments of their patients, at least in cases of patient assent to interventions recommended by the physician (Winick, 1991a, 1991b). Attorneys, like physicians, have a fiduciary relationship with their clients. Both attorneys and physicians are charged with a professional duty to promote and protect the best interests of their clients. Moreover, like physicians, attorneys are best situated to understand the specific aspects of their clients' cases and to assess competence.

Competence to stand trial is fundamentally a legal question. The skills needed to participate in the criminal process are skills that a lawyer is better able to assess than would be a clinical evaluator. Moreover, the lawyer is in the best position to understand the skill that will be needed in the context of the particular case. The special constitutional obligation that the Sixth Amendment places on attorneys to provide effective assistance of counsel to their clients "entails a wide sphere of discretion to define and implement the strategic objectives of the defense" (Bonnie, 1993, p. 565). The Sixth Amendment policies also justify insulating the attorney-client relationship from undue prosecutorial or judicial inquiry (Bonnie, 1993).

In my initial article, as an alternative to allowing a defendant of questionable competency to waive the protections of the incompetency doctrine, I proposed that counsel should be able to "waive" the doctrine on the defendant's behalf as long as the client assents (Winick, 1985). I have now concluded that the concept of "waiver" seems awkward in this context. Counsel may waive a variety of trial-related rights through action or inaction, thereby binding the client whether or not the client has participated in the decision (Winick, 1985). However, there are several critical constitutional rights that, under existing constitutional and ethical theory, require the client's own voluntary and knowing waiver, including the right to plead guilty, the decision whether to have a jury trial, and the decision whether to testify (Bonnie, 1993; Winick, 1985). Because permitting an attorney to waive these rights would conflict with deeply ingrained principles, an across-the-board waiver theory would go too far. However, surrogate decision making by the attorney would be possible with regard at least to certain issues in cases that involve trials (Bonnie, 1993). In the case of at least certain fundamental rights, permitting waiver by counsel would be inconsistent with accepted doctrine. But these instances aside, counsel may waive virtually all the rights and strategic options that a defendant enjoys in our criminal system.

I strongly disagree with the current requirement that attorneys and courts initiate an inquiry into competency whenever they harbor a genuine doubt about the defendant's competence, even when counsel believes that raising the issue is not in the client's best interests (American Bar Association, 1989; Bonnie, 1993; Chernoff & Schaffer, 1972; Uphoff, 1988). In my view, this judgment should be left largely in the hands of defense counsel. The current requirement imposes a responsibility on defense counsel that is basically inconsistent with counsel's obligations to protect and promote the best interests of the client. Such a conflict seriously burdens the professional relationship. It erodes client trust and confidence in counsel and impairs the ability of counsel to function effectively. Placing counsel in such an untenable position undermines the Sixth Amendment right to counsel and should be deemed constitutionally suspect (see American Bar Association, 1980; *Polk County v. Dodson*, 1981).

My original proposal talked about waiver in this context, arguing that counsel should be permitted not to raise the competency question when both counsel and client conclude that resolution of the criminal charges would be more in the defendant's interests than an incompetency adjudication (Winick, 1985). Because the attorney is in the best position to decide whether an inquiry into competency should be undertaken, in the context of most rights and strategic options, waiver or surrogate decision making by counsel should be permitted. In addition, the requirement that counsel initiate a formal competency inquiry whenever doubt is raised about the defendant's competency should be relaxed. With the exception of the waiver of certain fundamental rights, the judgment should be left to the attorney-client relationship.

By leaving such a large measure of discretion in the hands of counsel, my proposal might be subject to three criticisms. First, given the inconsistent quality of the criminal defense bar, can counsel be counted on to perform this role effectively? Second, will adoption of the proposal produce excessive appellate or habeas corpus litigation challenging guilty verdicts or guilty pleas on the ground that the defendant was incompetent? Third, will counsel abuse the authority delegated under the proposal to attempt to gain strategic advantage? Although these concerns are legitimate, none is so serious as to make the presumption proposal unfeasible.

First, placing the bulk of competency decision making in the hands of defense counsel assumes an attorney who is competent and will zealously safeguard the defendant's interests. The Sixth Amendment guarantees the effective assistance of counsel. However, it must be conceded that the quality of the criminal defense bar is varied, and that in some areas, the promise of the Sixth Amendment remains unfulfilled. Many criminal attorneys are talented, energetic advocates who effectively represent their clients' interests. Sadly, however, some are not. Some suffer under caseloads too heavy to devote sufficient time to a particular case. Some are incompetent, and some even are unethical.

Leaving incompetency decision making largely in the hands of counsel thus raises certain risks. These risks increase in cases involving defendants with mental disabilities because such clients are particularly vulnerable to malpractice by counsel. Notwithstanding these risks, in designing legal rules it seems sensible in general to make the assumption that defense attorneys are competent and will vigorously represent their clients' interests. To minimize this risk, a trial court should be particularly sensitive to the possibility of ineffectiveness of counsel, and when appropriate, should question counsel to ensure that the defendant's interests are properly represented. Counsel for an impaired client bears a special degree of professional responsibility (see American Bar Association, 1992a). A court must be especially alert to the potential breakdown in the adversary system when defense counsel is ineffective in representing a defendant with mental illness (Winick, 1993a). Although in general, under the proposal outlined here, the trial court should leave the competency question to counsel, when the court has concerns in this area, it would be appropriate to inquire of counsel whether the defendant's mental condition has been fully considered by counsel, and whether counsel has had the opportunity to consult with a defense clinician concerning the question (Bonnie, 1993). There is "a problem of quality assurance" in this area, but "[if] attention to 'competence' should be enhanced in this context, it should be directed toward the competence of counsel, not the competence of the defendant" (pp. 567, 578). To the extent that some attorneys fail effectively to perform the role my proposal would assign them, the possibility of a collateral attack on any resulting conviction based on ineffective assistance of counsel would be available.

Second, will my proposal produce extensive appellate or habeas corpus litigation by defendants allowed to stand trial or plead guilty? The use of an informal process utilizing a presumption in favor of competency should not have the effect of promoting extensive appellate litigation by defendants who are convicted or collateral attacks on their guilty pleas. In cases in which the presumption of competence is not rebutted, the discussion between the trial judge and the defendant suggested above should create an adequate record that would insulate the case from appeal or collateral attacks questioning competence. Insulation from subsequent attack could be further ensured if the court required counsel to make a statement on the record that the defendant's decision has been made after consultation with counsel, that it seems to the attorney to be reasonable and to be in the client's best interests, and that counsel believes that the defendant possesses sufficient competence to make the decision. Such a statement by counsel would not necessarily preclude counsel from later raising the question of competency if, as the trial unfolded, counsel became convinced that the defendant's condition had changed, or that counsel's original assessment of competency was in error. Should counsel become convinced during trial that, contrary to his or her initial conclusion, the defendant actually was incompetent, counsel's motion, together with a detailed recitation of the circumstances giving rise to this change of view, should create enough doubt to require the trial court to hold a new inquiry (Burt & Morris, 1972; *Drope v. Missouri*, 1975; *Illinois v. Allen*, 1970; *Snyder v. Massachusetts*, 1934; Winick, 1993a).

Third, will adoption of my proposal invite defense counsel to use the presumption process to gain discovery concerning the prosecution's case? Will defense counsel be tempted to abuse the process by opting for a trial to test the strength of the prosecution's evidence, but preserving the ability to bail out if the case appears to be going poorly? This concern underestimates the professional ethics of the defense bar and the ability of trial judges to police counsel appearing in their courts to prevent attorney abuse. When counsel certifies that the client seems competent and that the choice to go forward seems to be in his or her best interests, we should be willing to assume that counsel is acting in good faith, and that any subsequent representation to the court by counsel that counsel now has come to the belief that the client is incompetent also is made in good faith. Few attorneys will wish to risk even a trial judge's suspicion that they are attempting to perpetuate a fraud on the court.

These three concerns, therefore, do not justify rejection of the proposal. If adopted, the proposal made here would avoid many unnecessary formal judicial determinations of competency. It also would avoid much unnecessary clinical evaluation, thereby allowing a reallocation of scarce clinical resources from evaluation to treatment. Furthermore, it would reduce many of the costs and burdens of existing practices. When a defendant of questionable competency is willing voluntarily to assent to counsel's recommendation concerning a defense strategy that seems more in the defendant's interests than an incompetency adjudication, the defendant's wishes should generally be respected. Both allowing a measure of surrogate decision making or waiver by counsel and substituting a presumption in favor of competency in cases of assent for the present practice of requiring a formal competency determination whenever doubt about competency is raised would do much to reform the law in this area. The proposed restructuring would provide greater deference to the autonomy both of the individual and of the attorney-client relationship consistent with the protective objectives and societal concerns underlying the incompetency doctrine.

But would adoption of the proposal be constitutional? My argument that we should allow defendants of questionable competency to waive the "benefits" of the incompetency doctrine must contend with the dilemma that, under *Pate v. Robinson* (1966), incompetent defendants could not waive their rights. To avoid this dilemma, I propose use of a presumption that would avoid further inquiry into whether a mentally impaired defendant actually was incompetent in cases in which the defendant was able to assent to a recommendation of counsel in favor of trial or a guilty plea. In such cases, a formal competency evaluation and determination would be avoided. Use of a procedural presumption would not violate *Pate v. Robinson*'s holding that a fair procedural determination of the competency issue should occur whenever a reasonable doubt about the question is raised. Although a conclusive or irrebuttable presumption is really a substantive rule, a rebuttable presumption such as the one contemplated is a procedural device that determines how a substantive issue will be decided. A presumption allocates (and sometimes reallocates) a burden of proof. The party challenging a presumption has the burden of demonstrating its falsity. Moreover, a presumption requires the party challenging the presumption to present some evidence tending to negate it. In the absence of such a showing, further inquiry usually is considered unnecessary, the presumption is deemed unrebutted, and the truth of the issue that is the subject of the presumption is treated as having been established.

When reasonable doubt about competency is raised in a criminal case, due process requires a fair determination of the issue. This is actually the holding of *Pate v. Robinson* and *Drope v. Missouri,* two leading Supreme Court competency-to-stand-trial cases that often are construed to place a total bar on trying an incompetent defendant. My proposal suggests the use of a presumption in favor of competency in cases in which the defendant, with the advice and agreement of counsel, clearly and voluntarily expressed a preference in favor of trial or a guilty plea. This presumption would not be destroyed by the existence of reasonable doubt about the defendant's competency (Winick, 1993a). Even when doubt about competency triggers an inquiry under *Pate* and

Drope, the presumption in favor of competency would continue to inform the adjudication of the issue by placing the burden of proving incompetency on the party challenging the presumption, which in this context would be the prosecution (Winick, 1993a).

If the prosecution fails to produce specific evidence of the defendant's incompetency, the presumption remains unrebutted, and the criminal proceeding then may continue (Winick, 1993a). To rebut the presumption, the prosecution would need to produce some evidence suggesting that the defendant's express choice was the product of his or her mental illness. This production burden could be carried by adducing evidence that suggested, for example, that the defendant's choice was the product of pathological delusions or hallucinations, was based on beliefs that were intrinsically irrational or on reasons that were clearly irrelevant, or was the result of a mood disorder that impaired the defendant's judgment or motivation to act self-interestedly (see Winick, 1985, 1991a; see also Murphy, 1974; Tepper & Elwork, 1984). In addition, the trial judge would always be free to engage in a short exchange with the defendant of the kind that typically occurs in connection with the acceptance of a guilty plea (see, for example, Federal Rules of Criminal Procedure, Rule 11, 1986), and would be required to do so when the defendant seeks to plead guilty or waive certain fundamental rights, like the right to counsel. The judge's questioning would provide additional assurance that the defendant's expressed preference is indeed voluntary, that the defendant has at least a rudimentary understanding of the nature of the right sought to be waived, and that the defendant's responses do not suggest that the decision is the product of cognitive impairment or a mood disorder.

In the absence of such evidence produced by the prosecution or responses by the defendant that themselves raise such questions, the presumption in favor of competency would remain unrebutted, and no further inquiry would occur. As previously mentioned, in the case of a defendant wishing to stand trial, a decision at the outset honoring the defendant's choice can be regarded as provisional, and may be reconsidered as the trial unfolds if the defendant's conduct or demeanor suggests incompetency or if defense counsel decides to raise the issue. If at the initial competency inquiry, the prosecution comes forward with evidence suggesting that the defendant's choice of a trial or a guilty plea is incompetent, or if the defendant's responses to the trial judge's inquiries raise a serious question of competency, the court can always then order a more formal competency evaluation and hold a further hearing on the issue. In many cases, however, applying a procedural presumption of competency and placing the burden of proof on the party challenging competency can succeed in avoiding the formal clinical evaluation of competency that now typically (and often unnecessarily) occurs.

This procedure should satisfy the due process requirement of conducting an inquiry into competency when reasonable doubt is raised about the issue. *Pate v. Robinson* imposes a constitutional obligation on the trial judge to raise the competency issue and hold a hearing to appraise a defendant's competency whenever sufficient evidence of incompetency comes to his or her attention. *Pate* does not, however, specify the nature of the hearing required. Due process is a flexible notion and does not always require a formal trial-type hearing. Even if the defendant appears to have mental illness or has a history of mental illness, an informal inquiry into competency using the presumption proposed here should meet the requirement of due process. That presumption, it should be emphasized, applies only in cases in which the defendant, with the advice and concurrence of counsel, clearly expresses a preference for trial or a guilty plea. A more elaborate hearing can always be held should the presumption of competency be rebutted, if the court finds this to be necessary.

Although under *Pate*, the existence of mental illness might trigger the need for an inquiry into the competency question, an informal inquiry into the issue using a presumption in favor of competency in cases in which the defendant, with the concurrence of counsel, wishes to go forward should suffice. A more formal inquiry could be held if the presumption is rebutted. Although it may trigger the need for some inquiry under *Pate*, mental illness alone—even one of the major mental illnesses like schizophrenia, major depression, or bipolar disorder—would not be sufficient to rebut the presumption of competency that I argue should exist when a defendant can clearly express a preference that counsel concurs in. Mental illness should not be equated with incompetency. Many individuals suffering from even serious mental illness retain full decision-making capacity, and even when such illness impairs capacity in one area of functioning, it may leave capacity unimpaired in others (American Psychiatric Association, 1993b; Appelbaum & Gutheil, 1991; McKinnon, Cournos, & Stanley, 1989; Morse, 1978; Winick, 1991a, 1991b). More than mental illness alone thus should be required to rebut the presumption of competency; specific evidence suggesting that the defendant's decision is the product of mental illness would be needed.

The Supreme Court's decision in *Medina v. California* (1992) clearly supports the constitutionality of the use of the presumption of competence suggested here (see Winick, 1993a). *Medina* upheld the constitutionality of a statutory presumption in favor of the competency of a criminal defendant and the placement of the burden of proof in an adjudication of the issue on the party challenging competency. The Court's rejection of the challenge to the statutory presumption involved there, raised by a defendant who asserted that it was constitutionally unfair to place the burden on him of establishing his own incompetency, constitutes an endorsement of the constitutionality of the use of presumptions in the competency-to-stand-trial area. The use of a presumption in favor of competency will prevent full inquiry into the matter in some cases, and therefore may produce a risk of error. But *Medina* shows that such a risk of error in the determination of competency will not violate *Pate* (Winick, 1993a). As a result, although the presumption procedure outlined here might result in permitting waiver by at least some defendants presumed competent who actually are incompetent, *Medina* demonstrates that a procedural rule governing the determination of criminal competency is not unconstitutional because it fails to eliminate the possibility of error in the application of the incompetency test.

Medina's endorsement of the constitutionality of presumptions in favor of competency stands in sharp contrast to the Supreme Court's decision two years earlier in *Zinermon v. Burch* (1990; see also Winick, 1991b). In the course of discussing the necessity of a procedural determination of the competency of a mental patient seeking voluntary admission to a psychiatric hospital, the Court in *Zinermon* noted that even if a request for admission to a hospital for medical treatment might justifiably be taken at face value, "a state may not be justified in doing so without further inquiry as to a mentally ill person's request for admission and treatment at a mental hospital" (Winick, 1991b, p. 133 n. 18). This language seems to disapprove of the presumption in favor of the competency of mentally ill persons that has been the trend of modern mental health law, and to call for an "inquiry" into the issue whenever a person with mental illness seeks hospitalization. Construed broadly, the *Zinermon* language could also suggest the need for such an inquiry whenever a person with mental illness seeks to exercise any rights, including the assertion or waiver of rights in the criminal process. This language, however, was dicta, and if taken literally, would seriously undermine the institution of voluntary hospitalization and impose unintended antitherapeutic consequences on patients and serious fiscal costs on the states (Winick, 1991b).

The presumption in favor of the competency of persons with mental illness, which the *Zinermon* dicta seems to question, has been a significant recent development in mental health law (Winick, 1991a). The presumption in favor of competency constitutes a recognition that mental illness does not necessarily produce incompetency, and frequently does not do so (American Psychiatric Association, 1993b; Appelbaum & Gutheil, 1991; Winick, 1991b). Moreover, it reflects a preference in favor of individual autonomy grounded in both political and legal theory and psychological principles (Winick, 1992).

Although the implication of the *Zinermon* dicta are questionable (Winick, 1991b), the holding of the case—that some "inquiry" into competency should have been made when the patient involved in that case sought admission to a mental hospital—seems clearly correct and can be used to illustrate the kind of case in which a presumption in favor of competency should be considered to have been rebutted. The patient in *Zinermon* was able to express a preference for hospitalization but appeared confused and delusional at the time, was unable to state the reasons for his choice, and was hallucinating in ways that related directly to his decision (Winick, 1991b). In fact, he apparently believed that the psychiatric hospital he was entering was "heaven" (*Zinermon v. Burch,* 1990, pp. 118–120; Winick, 1991b). These facts certainly suggest the need for an inquiry into competency and would rebut any presumption in favor of competency that would apply in this and other cases. However, in the absence of facts such as these suggesting that the individual's expressed choice is the product of mental illness, competency should be presumed, and a formal inquiry into the competency question should be unnecessary (American Psychiatric Association, 1993a; Winick, 1994a).

Although the issues presented in *Medina v. California* were quite different from those presented in *Zinermon,* the *Medina* decision seemed to endorse a presumption in favor of competency, whereas the *Zinermon* decision had challenged it (Winick, 1993a). California's statutory presumption in favor of competency examined in *Medina* represents "the enlightened approach of modern mental health law" (Winick, 1993a, p. 863). *Medina* upheld the constitutionality of the California statute, and hence in no way affects the Court's earlier holding in *Zinermon.* But the Court's endorsement of the presumption in favor of competency in *Medina* is a welcome step away from the questionable implications of *Zinermon's* broad dicta.

Medina paves the way for adoption of the proposal made here—that a presumption of competency should exist when a defendant, with the advice and concurrence of counsel, can clearly and voluntarily express a preference for trial or a guilty plea, and that unless the prosecution can produce specific evidence showing that the defendant's expressed preference is incompetent, or this conclusion is suggested by the defendant's own statements in a discussion with the trial judge, the defendant's waiver should be accepted. By upholding the constitutionality of a statutory presumption in favor of competency and assigning the burden of proof on the issue to the party asserting incompetency, *Medina* suggests that the proposal advanced here also would meet constitutional requirements. Once it is recognized that the use of the procedural presumption of competency suggested here would be constitutionally permissible, the reasons for adopting it become compelling. Such a procedure would further the value deeply ingrained in our American constitutional heritage of protecting and promoting individual autonomy (for example, *Faretta v. California*, 1975; see generally, Winick, 1992). In addition, it would have the effect of reducing some of the unnecessary costs of the existing incompetency process as well as the serious burdens it imposes on defendants. Moreover, as suggested earlier, the use of the procedural presumption proposed here could further these interests without sacrificing the concern for fairness and accuracy in adjudication and without undermining the moral dignity of the criminal process.

Substituting "Treatment Continuances" for the Formal Incompetency Process

In view of the constitutional questions that this waiver proposal raises, further scholarly work may be necessary before legal changes are likely to occur. However, there should be no constitutional impediment to adoption of one aspect of this initial proposal—the suggestion that much of the competency evaluation process should be replaced with a system of trial continuances. Cases in which a defendant seeks to waive the incompetency doctrine and stand trial or plead guilty over an objection by the prosecution that he or she is incompetent probably represent only a very small percentage of total cases. In the overwhelming majority of cases, it is the defendant through his or her counsel who raises the incompetency doctrine as a bar to trial. Under existing practices, the defendant's request triggers a formal competency evaluation. In my initial proposal, I suggested that rather than invoking the formal evaluation process in such cases, a continuance of reasonable duration could be granted to the defendant based on a written certification of counsel that, in counsel's view, the defendant is incompetent (Burt & Morris, 1972; Szasz, 1971; Winick, 1985).

Under this proposal, counsel could be required to certify that the continuance is sought in good faith and on reasonable grounds, and to set forth the specific observations and statements of the defendant that form the basis for the request. Once such a continuance has been granted, a request for a further continuance would need to be supported by a statement from a clinician certifying that the defendant is incompetent, stating that the defendant is receiving appropriate treatment, and predicting a restoration of the defendant's competence within a reasonable period (Winick, 1985). The clinician's statement could also be required to include a specific treatment plan, detailing the kinds of treatment attempted and proposed. The defendant would be permitted substantial choice in electing the type of treatment desired to improve his or her trial functioning. The place of treatment, of course, will depend on the defendant's bail status. If the defendant is in custody, such treatment will occur either in a jail or in a security mental health facility; if released, in the community as an outpatient or voluntary inpatient. The defendant would bear the cost of treatment if not in custody unless he or she is indigent.

In addition to avoiding the cost of unnecessary clinical evaluation and formal judicial determination of the defendant's competency, this proposal could have considerable therapeutic advantages for the defendant. Based on the literature on the psychology of choice (see Winick, 1991a, 1991b, 1992, 1994b), it can be hypothesized that the potential for successful treatment of defendants who are incompetent to stand trial is increased when the defendant accepts treatment voluntarily rather than when the defendant is forced to enter a forensic facility (Wexler & Winick, 1991a; Winick, 1985; see generally Wexler, 1991; Winick, 1992, 1994a). Placing the burden on the defendant (and his or her counsel) to arrange for treatment with a provider of choice as a condition for receiving the requested continuance can thus be justified not only as efficient, but also as therapeutic. With active treatment, particularly treatment the defendant seeks to obtain, the great majority of mentally impaired defendants can be expected to gain sufficient competency to participate in trial within several weeks or months (Winick, 1985).

Whereas, under existing practice, an incompetency determination suspends the criminal proceedings, the treatment continuance proposed need not do so. During the continuance the defense attorney may be required to file any pretrial motions that can be resolved without the client's assistance (see *Jackson v. Indiana,* 1972). Although the grant of a treatment continuance would suspend the defendant's right to a speedy trial, defense counsel, at any time, would be permitted to file a notice with the court that the defendant has become competent, and proceedings should thereafter resume, with speedy trial periods again running.

Requiring certificates from counsel and from a clinician as conditions for the grant or renewal of a continuance, coupled with judicial supervision, should prevent abuse of the treatment continuance process as a means of obtaining delay. The trial judge maintains wide discretion over whether to grant or deny requested continuances (see *Morris v. Slappy,* 1983; Winick, 1985), and the judge could condition granting of a treatment continuance on receipt of weekly or monthly reports from the defendant's attorney or the treating clinician. The court would always be able to order an independent clinical evaluation and court-supervised treatment if deemed necessary. The process, of course, also would be monitored by the prosecutor, who could always move for a formal competency evaluation if abuse of the continuance process was suspected (Winick, 1985).

The proposal that a defendant voluntarily accept treatment as a condition for the grant of a trial continuance also could be joined with a form of "wagering" or behavioral contracting (Wexler, 1991; Wexler & Winick, 1991a; Winick, 1991c). Under this proposal, to further increase the efficacy of treatment, the defendant and the trial court could enter into a contingency contract under which the defendant would receive the continuance sought in exchange for an agreement to participate in an appropriate treatment program and for making periodic progress toward the goal of restoration to competency. A schedule of target goals and dates could be included, culminating in a restoration to competency within a period specified in the contract. The incentive to perform effectively in treatment could be increased in jurisdictions in which the defendant does not automatically receive credit against any ultimate sentence received for time spent in incompetency commitment (Winick, 1985). In such jurisdictions, a credit against sentence may be used as a reinforcer in the contingency contract to provide an additional inducement for an expeditious restoration to competency (Wexler & Winick, 1991a).

Substituting a system of trial continuances for the existing formal incompetency process also would have the salutary effect of avoiding unnecessary incompetency labeling. As previously indicated, the term *incompetency to stand trial* has an unfortunate connotation, implying a traitlike immutable impairment rather than a temporary difficulty that in most cases can easily be remedied (Sales & Kahle, 1980; Winick, 1995). The negative psychological effects of using an incompetency label in this area can be avoided by granting what can be called a *treatment continuance,* a label that has no similar negative connotations. Even when it is necessary to make a formal incompetency determination—for example, when the defendant seeks to waive a right that he or she is determined to be incompetent to waive—the defendant could be found *temporarily impaired* or *temporarily unable to waive* the right in question (Sales & Kahle, 1980; Winick, 1995). Such a label suggests hope rather than hopelessness, and encourages the individual to view his or her "temporary" problem as one that can be resolved through appropriate treatment. Such a redesigned label will be less stigmatizing to defendants and will have the effect of limiting the risk that the individual will interpret the impairment as global and relatively stable, an attribution that would increase the likelihood of learned helplessness and other inhibitory patterns that will interfere with competency in the future (Bonnie, 1992; Gould, in press; Winick, 1995).

Defining and Evaluating Competency in the Criminal Process

The Supreme Court's classic formulation of the standard for incompetency in the criminal process was adopted in the 1960 case of *Dusky v. United States* (see Winick, 1985). The Court held that a court was required to determine whether the defendant "has sufficient present ability to consult with his lawyer with a reasonable degree of rational understanding and whether he has a rational as well as factual understanding of the proceedings against him" (*Dusky v. United States,* 1960, p. 402). Although some courts had applied a more demanding standard of competency when a defendant attempted to plead guilty or waive counsel (requiring the ability to make a reasoned choice), in *Godinez v. Moran* (1993) the Supreme Court rejected such a higher standard. Instead, the Court found that the *Dusky* formulation was the appropriate test of competency throughout the criminal process. The *Dusky* standard emphasizes the ability to understand and consult, not necessarily the ability to engage in rational decision making. In *Godinez,* the Court distinguished between competency and the knowledge and voluntariness required for the waiver of certain fundamental rights. A competency inquiry, the Court noted, focuses on the defendant's "mental capacity; the question is whether he has the *ability* to understanding the proceedings" (*Godinez v. Moran,* 1993, p. 2687 n. 12). By contrast, the Court noted, the inquiry into "knowing and voluntary...is to determine whether the defendant actually *does* understand the significance and consequences of a particular decision and whether the decision is uncoerced" (p. 2687 n. 12).

Although the Court thus clarified that its competency standard was not as broad as some courts had thought, the standard still is broad, open-textured, and vague, permitting clinical evaluators substantial latitude in interpreting and applying the test (Bonnie, 1993; Winick, 1985). The clinical instruments available for competency assessment compound the problem (Grisso, 1986). These instruments typically list the many potentially relevant capacities that a defendant might need without prescribing scoring criteria for how these capacities should be rated (Bonnie, 1993). Moreover, because clinical evaluators rarely consult with counsel to ascertain the particular skills the defendant will need to have to function effectively in the particular case, the assessment instruments encourage clinical evaluators to apply a generalized, abstract standard of competency, rather than following a more appropriate contextualized approach to competency assessment (American Bar Association, 1989; Grisso, 1986; Melton et al., 1985; Roesch & Golding, 1980). By simply relying on clinical judgment based on all the circumstances, these instruments make competency assessment a highly discretionary exercise in clinical judgment (Bonnie, 1993). Many clinical evaluators are paternalistically oriented, and without more concrete guidance tend to classify marginally competent mental patients as incompetent (Winick, 1985). The literature documents the tendency of clinical evaluations in the criminal courts to misunderstand the legal issues involved in incompetency, frequently confusing it with legal insanity or with the clinical definition of psychosis (Winick, 1985). Some clinicians overdiagnose incompetency to bring about what to them seems a more humane disposition of the case or to secure mental health treatment because they assume it will be helpful (Winick, 1985). The discretion vested in clinical evaluators is both increased and made more troubling by the fact that appellate courts rarely review and almost never reverse trial court competency determinations (Bonnie, 1993), and that trial judges almost always defer to clinical evaluators (Bonnie, 1993; Golding, Roesch, & Schreiber, 1984; Hart & Hare, 1992; Reich & Tookey, 1986).

Decision making in this area thus is effectively delegated to clinical evaluators making low-visibility and essentially unreviewed decisions pursuant to a vague, abstract standard. This situation tends to obscure the distinction between the clinical and legal components of incompetency in the criminal process and allows clinicians to regard a competency assessment as largely an exercise in clinical description. Assessing competency, however, inevitably involves cultural, social, political, and legal judgments that are more normative in nature than clinical (Grisso, 1986; Winick, 1985, 1991a). Recognizing the essentially legal nature of the concept of competency in the criminal process calls for courts and legislatures to define competency with greater precision. Moreover, recognition of the high costs and burdens imposed by the incompetency-to-stand-trial process argues for a narrow definition of competency that results in classifying marginally competent defendants as competent rather than as incompetent (Winick, 1993a). In defining competency to stand trial, the law should not apply to defendants suffering from mental illness artifically high standards for decision-making capacity that many "normal" criminal defendants are unable to satisfy (Perlin, 1991, 1992, 1993a; Perlin & Dorfman, 1993; Winick, 1985). For this reason, Bonnie's efforts to delineate in detail the various components of competency to stand trial is to be applauded (Bonnie, 1993). Moreover, his efforts and those of his co-researchers in the MacArthur Network on Mental Health and the Law to develop more detailed assessment instruments and to conduct empirical research on the decision-making abilities of both "normal" and mentally ill defendants will be most useful.

As previously suggested, the definition of competency should vary depending on whether the defendant assents to a recommendation made by counsel or objects to it. Assent to counsel's recommendation provides an assurance that the choice made by the defendant is reasonable and likely to be in the defendant's best interests. Erring on the side of finding a marginally competent assenting defendant to be competent therefore will not undermine the societal interests in accuracy and the moral dignity of the criminal process. When the defendant objects to counsel's recommendation, this assurance that the defendant's choice is reasonable is not present, and these societal concerns justify a higher degree of scrutiny of the defendant's competency.

Bonnie's analysis of incompetency decision making in the context of decisions whether to raise an insanity defense has demonstrated that existing practice reflects a distinction in the way defendants are dealt with depending on whether they assent or object to the recommendations of counsel (Bonnie, 1992, 1993). Bonnie found that when the defendant pleads insanity in accordance with counsel's recommendation, the courts in practice used a "basic understanding" test of competency in which capacity to understand the nature and consequences of the decision sufficed. When defendants refused a recommended insanity plea, however, and the defense attorney raised doubts about competency, a higher test of competency was applied, requiring an appreciation of the reasons for the decision.

Agreeing with my proposal, Bonnie has recommended a two-level test for decisional competence based on whether the defendant assents or objects to counsel's advice. In general, he suggests that a basic understanding test of competency is all that should be required for decisions, including those waiving constitutional rights, when the defendant assents to counsel's recommendation. Under this low-level test, only the ability to express a choice and to understand its nature and consequences would be required, and deficits or impairments bearing on the defendant's reasons for accepting counsel's recommendation would not be the subject of inquiry. When, however, the defendant insists on acting contrary to counsel's advice in a manner that raises doubts about competency, Bonnie suggests that the test should require ability to make a reasoned choice. This is a more stringent test that requires appreciation and the ability to engage in rational decision making.

While my proposal for a lower standard of competency in cases of assent to counsel's recommendation and a higher standard in cases of objection did not attempt to define those differing standards, Bonnie's approach attempts to do so. The results of his further work with the MacArthur Network on Mental Health and the Law to operationalize these standards in assessment instruments and to test their administration are eagerly awaited. Although the

Supreme Court in *Godinez* refused to depart from the unitary standard of competency associated with the *Dusky* formulation, it declined to do so on constitutional grounds. Thus, the states must accept the *Dusky* standard as a constitutional minimum, but they are free to go beyond it and fashion differing tests of competency for different contexts, including recognizing a distinction between assent and objection.

Conclusion

I have recommended a restructured incompetency process that recognizes a distinction between assent and objection, and that presumes competency in cases in which the defendant assents to counsel's recommendation or in which counsel approves the defendant's choice. I have further recommended the use of certifications by counsel, both in cases in which such a presumption is applied and in those in which the defendant seeks to raise his or her mental impairment as a bar to trial and counsel seeks what I would call a *treatment continuance*. These recommendations will have the effect of subsuming the bulk of the competency determination process within the attorney-client relationship. This would be preferable to the present process, in which almost all determinations are made through a formal judicial process that relies heavily on often unnecessary clinical evaluations. Under this proposal, many decisions about competency will be left to counsel, a professional with a duty to act in the defendant's best interests and who is best situated to ascertain the client's deficits and their impact on the skills needed to participate in the criminal case at hand. When necessary, of course, counsel will have access to clinical assistance in making these decisions, but in most cases, the decision will be left to counsel.

Moving competency determinations from clinicians to defense attorneys should increase the accuracy of competency decision making, particularly in light of the tendency of clinical evaluators to misunderstand the incompetency standard and to overdiagnose incompetency (Winick, 1985). Moreover, it would recognize that competency in the criminal process is more a legal than a clinical question, involving legal and normative judgments and not merely clinical ones. In addition, it would avoid a serious conflict of interest for counsel that can undermine the attorney-client relationship and threaten the values underlying the Sixth Amendment right to counsel. Finally, subsuming the bulk of competency determination under the attorney-client relationship would avoid an unnecessary drain on scarce clinical time, allowing a reallocation of clinical resources from evaluation to treatment. This reallocation can increase the quality of the incompetency treatment process and limit existing delays, allowing defendants impaired by mental illness to improve more rapidly and to obtain a more expeditious disposition of their criminal charges.

If implemented, these recommendations thus can transform the existing way we define and evaluate competency in the criminal process, and the way we deal with defendants whose abilities to assume the role of criminal defendants are impaired by mental illness. The most seriously impaired would still be able to claim the protections of the existing doctrine, although most would receive treatment continuances rather than being labeled incompetent. Those whose impairment is marginal would be able either to obtain treatment, which they themselves arrange and choose as a condition for receiving a brief continuance, or if they prefer, would be permitted to plead guilty or face their charges. Most defendants assenting to counsel's recommendations would be able to have their choices honored. Only those whose assent seems clearly to be a product of mental illness would have their choices interfered with. The result can be a restructured competency doctrine that fulfills its protective purposes in a way that is more sensitive to individual autonomy, and that avoids many unnecessary costs and many of the burdens of delay, stigma, and unnecessary hospitalization that existing practices too often impose.

References

Abramson, L.Y., Garber, J., & Seligman, M.E.P. (1980). Learned helplessness in humans: An attributional analysis. In J. Garber & M.E.P. Seligman (Eds.), Human helplessness: Theory and applications (pp. 3–34). New York: Academic Press.

Abramson, L.Y., Seligman, M.E.P., & Teasdale, J. (1978). Learned helplessness in humans: Critique and reformulation. Journal of Abnormal Psychology, 87, 49–74.

Adams v. United States *ex rel.* McCann, 317 U.S. 269 (1942).

Ake v. Oklahoma, 470 U.S. 68 (1985).

American Bar Association. (1980). Standards for criminal justice (2nd ed.). Boston: Little, Brown.

American Bar Association. (1983). First tentative draft: Criminal justice mental health standards. Washington, DC: American Bar Association.

American Bar Association. (1989). Criminal justice mental health standards. Washington, DC: American Bar Association.

American Bar Association. (1992a). Model Rules of Professional Conduct. Chicago: Center for Professional Responsibility.

American Bar Association. (1992b). Standards for criminal justice: Providing defense service (3rd ed.). Washington, DC: American Bar Association.

American Law Institute. (1972). Model code of pre-arraignment procedures (tentative draft No. 5). Philadelphia: American Law Institute.

American Psychiatric Association, Task Force on Consent to Voluntary Hospitalization. (1993a). Consent to voluntary hospitalization (Task Force Report No. 34). Washington, DC: American Psychiatric Institute.

American Psychiatric Association, Task Force on DSM-IV. (1993b). DSM-IV Draft Criteria. Washington, DC: American Psychiatric Association.

Appelbaum, P.S., & Gutheil, T.G. (1991). Clinical handbook of psychiatry and the law (2nd ed.). Baltimore, MD: Williams & Wilkins.

Argersinger v. Hamlin, 407 U.S. 25 (1972).

Baldwin v. New York, 399 U.S. 66 (1970).

Barkai, J.L. (1977). Accuracy inquiries for all felony and misdemeanor pleas: Voluntary pleas but innocent defendants. University of Pennsylvania Law Review, 126, 88–146.

Beck v. Alabama, 447 U.S. 625 (1980).

Bibliography of therapeutic jurisprudence. (1993). New York Law School Journal of Human Rights, 10, 915–926.

Blackstone, W. (1979). Commentaries on the laws of England. Chicago: University of Chicago Press. (Original work published 1783)

Bloom v. Illinois, 391 U.S. 194 (1968).

Bonnie, R.J. (1992). The competence of criminal defendants: A theoretical reformulation. Behavioral Sciences and the Law, 10, 291–316.

Bonnie, R.J. (1993). The competence of criminal defendants: Beyond Dusky and Drope. University of Miami Law Review, 47, 539–601.

Bonovitz, J.C., & Guy, E.B. (1979). Impact of restrictive civil commitment procedures on a prison psychiatric service. American Journal of Psychiatry, 136, 1045–1048.

Brookhart v. Janus, 384 U.S. 1 (1966).

Burt, R.A. (1974). Of mad dogs and scientists: The perils of the "criminal-insane." University of Pennsylvania Law Review, 123, 258–296.

Burt, R.A., & Morris, N. (1972). A proposal for the abolition of the incompetency plea. University of Chicago Law Review, 40, 66–95.

Chernoff, P.A., & Schaffer, W.G. (1972). Defending the mentally ill: Ethical quicksand. American Criminal Law Review, 10, 505–531.

Coker v. Georgia, 433 U.S. 584 (1977).

Colorado v. Connelly, 479 U.S. 157 (1986).

Commonwealth v. Louraine, 453 N.E.2d 437 (Mass. 1983).

Cooke, G., Johnston, N., & Pogany, E. (1973). Factors affecting referral to determine competency to stand trial. American Journal of Psychiatry, 130, 870–875.

Dickey, W. (1980). Incompetency and the non-dangerous mentally ill client. Criminal Law Bulletin, 16, 22–40.

Drope v. Missouri, 420 U.S. 162 (1975).

Duncan v. Louisiana, 391 U.S. 145 (1968).

Dusky v. United States, 362 U.S. 402 (1960).

Eddings v. Oklahoma, 455 U.S. 104 (1982).

Ellis, J.W. (1992). Decisions by and for people with mental retardation: Balancing considerations of autonomy and protection. Villanova Law Review, 37, 1779–1809.

Ellis, J.W., & Luckasson, R.A. (1985). Mentally retarded criminal defendants. George Washington Law Review, 53, 414–493.

Enmund v. Florida, 458 U.S. 782 (1982).

Ennis, B.J., & Emery, R.D. (1978). The rights of mental patients: The revised edition of the basic ACLU guide to a mental patient's rights. New York: Avon Books.

Faretta v. California, 422 U.S. 806 (1975).

Federal Rules of Criminal Procedure, 18 U.S.C. (1986).

Foote, C. (1960). A comment on pre-trial commitment of criminal defendants. University of Pennsylvania Law Review, 108, 832–846.

Frith's Case, 22 How. St. Tr. 307 (1790).

Furman v. Georgia, 408 U.S. 238 (1972).

Gardner v. Florida, 430 U.S. 349 (1977).

Geller, J.L., & Lister, E.D. (1978). The process of criminal commitment for pretrial psychiatric examination: An evaluation. American Journal of Psychiatry, 135, 53–60.

Gideon v. Wainwright, 372 U.S. 335 (1963).

Gobert, J.J. (1973). Competency to stand trial: A pre- and post-Jackson analysis. Tennessee Law Review, 40, 659–688.

Godinez v. Moran, 113 S. Ct. 2680 (1993).

Golding, S.L., Roesch, R., & Schreiber, J. (1984). Assessment and conceptualization of competency to stand trial: Preliminary data on the interdisciplinary fitness interview. Law and Human Behavior, 8, 321–334.

Goldstein, A.S. (1981). The passive judiciary: Prosecutorial discretion and the guilty plea. Baton Rouge: Louisiana State University Press.

Gould, K.A. (in press). Therapeutic jurisprudence and the arraignment process: The defense attorney's dilemma: Whether to request a competency evaluation. In S. Verdun-Jones & M. Layton (Eds.), Mental health law and practice through the life cycle.

Gregg v. Georgia, 428 U.S. 153 (1976).

Grisso, T. (1986). Evaluating competencies: Forensic assessment and instruments. New York: Plenum.

Group for the Advancement of Psychiatry. (1974). Misuse of psychiatry in the criminal courts: Competency to stand trial. New York: Group for the Advancement of Psychiatry.

Halberstam, M. (1982). Towards neutral principles in the administration of criminal justice: A critique of Supreme Court decisions sanctioning the plea bargaining process. Journal of Criminal Law and Criminology, 73, 1–49.

Hale, M. (1736). The history of the pleas of the crown. London: E. and R. Nutt and R. Gosling.

Halpern, A.L. (1975). Use and misuse of psychiatry in competency examinations of criminal defendants. Psychiatric Annals, 5, 123–150.

Hamm v. Jabe, 706 F.2d 765 (6th Cir. 1983).

Hart, S.D., & Hare, R.D. (1992). Predicting fitness to stand trial: The relative power of demographic, criminal, and clinical variables. Forensic Reports, 5, 53–59.

Illinois v. Allen, 397 U.S. 337 (1970).

Incompetency to stand trial. (1967). Harvard Law Review, 81, 454–473.

Jackson v. Indiana, 406 U.S. 715 (1972).

Jones v. Barnes, 463 U.S. 745 (1983).

Kinloch's Case, 18 How. St. Tr. 395 (1746).

Lockett v. Ohio, 438 U.S. 586 (1978).

Maier, S.F., & Seligman, M.E.P. (1976). Learned helplessness: Theory and evidence. Journal of Experimental Psychology: General, 105, 33–46.

McGarry, L.A. (1969). Demonstration and research in competency for trial and mental illness: Review and preview. Boston University Law Review, 49, 46–61.

McKinnon, K., Cournos, F., & Stanley, B. (1989). Rivers in practice: Clinicians' assessments of patients' decision making capacity. Hospital and Community Psychiatry, 40, 1159–1162.

Medina v. California, 112 S. Ct. 2572 (1992).

Melton, G.B., Weithorn, L.A., & Slobogin, C. (1985). Community mental health centers and the courts: An evaluation of community-based forensic services. Lincoln: University of Nebraska Press.

Morris v. Slappy, 461 U.S. 1 (1983).

Morse, S.J. (1978). Crazy behavior, morals, and science: An analysis of mental health law. Southern California Law Review, 51, 527–654.

Murphy, J. (1974). Incompetency and paternalism. Archiv für Rechts-und Sozialphilosophie, 60, 465–474.

North Carolina v. Alford, 400 U.S. 25 (1970).

O'Neil, T.P. (1990). Vindicating the defendant's constitutional right to testify at a criminal trial: The need for an on-the-record waiver. University of Pittsburgh Law Review, 51, 809–839.

Pate v. Robinson, 383 U.S. 375 (1966).

Perlin, M.L. (1991). Competency, deinstitutionalization, and homelessness: A story of marginalization. Houston Law Review, 28, 63–142.

Perlin, M.L. (1992). On "sanism." SMU Law Review, 46, 373–407.

Perlin, M.L. (1993a). Pretexts and mental disability law: The case of competency. University of Miami Law Review, 47, 625–688.

Perlin, M.L. (1993b). What is therapeutic jurisprudence? New York Law School Journal of Human Rights, 10, 623–636.

Perlin, M.L., & Dorfman, D.A. (1993). Sanism, social science, and the development of mental disability law jurisprudence. Behavioral Sciences and the Law, 11, 47–66.

Peterson, C., & Bossio, L.M. (1989). Learned helplessness. In R.C. Curtis (Ed.), Self-defeating behaviors: Experimental research, clinical impressions, and practical implications (pp. 235–236). New York: Plenum.

Polk County v. Dodson, 454 U.S. 312 (1981).

Pollock, F., & Maitland, F.W. (1968). The history of English law before the time of Edward I (2nd ed.). London: Cambridge University Press. (Original work published 1898)

Powell v. Alabama, 287 U.S. 45 (1932).

In re Pray, 336 A.2d 174 (Vt. 1975).

Reich, J.H., & Tookey, L. (1986). Disagreements between court and psychiatrist on competency to stand trial. Journal of Clinical Psychiatry, 47, 29–30.

Riggins v. Nevada, 112 S. Ct. 1810 (1992).

Rock v. Arkansas, 483 U.S. 44 (1987).

Roesch, R.J., & Golding, S.L. (1979). Treatment and disposition of defendants found incompetent to stand trial: A review and a proposal. International Journal of Law and Psychiatry, 2, 349–370.

Roesch, R.J., & Golding, S.L. (1980). Competency to stand trial. Urbana: University of Illinois Press.

Sales, B.D., & Kahle, L.R. (1980). Law and attitudes toward the mentally ill. International Journal of Law and Psychiatry, 3, 391–403.

Scott v. Illinois, 440 U.S. 367 (1980).

Seligman, M.E.P. (1975). Helplessness: On depression, development, and death. San Francisco: Freeman.

Seligman, M.E.P., & Garber, J. (Eds.). (1980). Human helplessness: Theory and applications. New York: Academic Press.

Shah, S.A. (1981). Legal and mental health system interactions: Major developments and research needs. International Journal of Law and Psychiatry, 4, 219–270.

Singer v. United States, 380 U.S. 24 (1965).

Snyder v. Massachusetts, 291 U.S. 97 (1934).

Solem v. Helm, 463 U.S. 277 (1983).

State v. Jojola, 553 P.2d 1296 (N.M. Ct. App. 1976).

State v. Murphy, 355 P.2d 323 (Wash. 1960).

Steadman, H.J. (1979). Beating a rap? Defendants found incompetent to stand trial. Chicago: University of Chicago Press.

Steadman, H.J., & Braff, J. (1978). Crimes of violence and incompetency diversion. Journal of Criminal Law and Criminology, 66, 73–78.

Steadman, H.J., & Hartstone, E. (1983). Defendants incompetent to stand trial. In J. Monahan & H.J. Steadman (Eds.), Mentally disordered offenders: Perspectives from law and social science. New York: Plenum.

Stephen, J.F. (1964). A history of the criminal law of England. New York: B. Franklin. (Original work published 1883)

Stone, A.A. (1978). Comment. American Journal of Psychiatry, 135, 61–63.

Symposium—Therapeutic jurisprudence: Restructuring mental disability law. (1993). New York Law School Journal of Human Rights, 10, 623–926.

Szasz, T.S. (1971). Psychiatric justice. New York: Collier.

Teplin, L.A. (1983). The criminalization of the mentally ill: Speculation in search of data. Psychological Bulletin, 94, 54–67.

Tepper, A.M., & Elwork, A. (1984). Competence to consent to treatment as a psycholegal construct. Law and Human Behavior, 8, 205–223.

Uphoff, R.J. (1988). The role of the criminal defense lawyer in representing the mentally impaired defendant: Zealous advocate or officer of the court? Wisconsin Law Review, 1988, 65–109.

Wainwright v. Sykes, 433 U.S. 72 (1977).

Weihofen, H. (1954). Mental disorder as a criminal defense. Buffalo, NY: Dennis.

Wexler, D.B. (1983). The structure of civil commitment: Patterns, pressures, and interactions in mental health legislation. Law and Human Behavior, 7, 1–30.

Wexler, D.B. (1991). Health care compliance principles and the insanity acquitee conditional release process. Criminal Law Bulletin, 27, 18–41.

Wexler, D.B. (1992). Justice, mental health, and therapeutic jurisprudence. Cleveland State Law Review, 40, 517–526.

Wexler, D.B. (1993). Therapeutic jurisprudence and changing concepts of legal scholarship. Behavioral Sciences and the Law, 11, 17–29.

Wexler, D.B., & Scoville, S.E. (1971). Special project—The administration of psychiatric justice: Theory and practice in Arizona. Arizona Law Review, 13, 1–259.

Wexler, D.B., & Winick, B.J. (1991a). Essays in therapeutic jurisprudence. Durham, NC: Carolina Academic Press.

Wexler, D.B., & Winick, B.J. (1991b). Therapeutic jurisprudence as a new approach to mental health law policy analysis and research. University of Miami Law Review, 45, 979–1004.

Wexler, D.B., & Winick, B.J. (1992a). The potential of therapeutic jurisprudence: A new approach to psychology and the law. In J.R.P. Ogloff (Ed.), Law and psychology: The broadening of the discipline (pp. 211–239). Durham, NC: Carolina Academic Press.

Wexler, D.B., & Winick, B.J. (1992b). Therapeutic jurisprudence and criminal justice mental health issues. Mental and Physical Disability Law Reporter, 16, 225–231.

White Hawk v. Solem, 693 F.2d 825 (8th Cir. 1982), *cert. denied*, 460 U.S. 1054 (1983).

Winick, B.J. (1977). Psychotropic medication and competency to stand trial. American Bar Foundation Research Journal, 81, 769–816.

Winick, B.J. (1982). Prosecutorial peremptory challenge practices in capital cases: An empirical study and a constitutional analysis. Michigan Law Review, 81, 1–98.

Winick, B.J. (1983). Incompetency to stand trial: Developments in the law. In J. Monahan & H.J. Steadman (Eds.), Mentally disordered offenders: Perspectives from law and social science (pp. 3–38). New York: Plenum.

Winick, B.J. (1985). Restructuring competency to stand trial. UCLA Law Review, 32, 921–985.

Winick, B.J. (1987). Incompetency to stand trial: An assessment of costs and benefits, and a proposal for reform. Rutgers Law Review, 39, 243–287.

Winick, B.J. (1989). Forfeiture of attorney's fees under RICO and CCE and the right to counsel of choice: The constitutional dilemma and how to avoid it. University of Miami Law Review, 43, 765–869.

Winick, B.J. (1991a). Competency to consent to treatment: The distinction between assent and objection. Houston Law Review, 28, 15–61.

Winick, B.J. (1991b). Competency to consent to voluntary hospitalization: A therapeutic jurisprudence analysis of Zinermon v. Burch. International Journal of Law and Psychiatry, 14, 169–214.

Winick, B.J. (1991c). Harnessing the power of the bet: Wagering with the government as a mechanism for social and individual change. University of Miami Law Review, 45, 737–816.

Winick, B.J. (1991d). The mentally disordered defendant in Florida. In Florida Criminal Rules and Practice (Part 2, §§ 7.1–7.95). Tallahassee, FL: Continuing Legal Education.

Winick, B.J. (1992). On autonomy: Legal and psychological perspectives. Villanova Law Review, 37, 1705–1777.

Winick, B.J. (1993a). Presumptions and burdens of proof in determining competency to stand trial: An analysis of Medina v. California and the Supreme Court's new due process methodology in criminal cases. University of Miami Law Review, 47, 817–866.

Winick, B.J. (1993b). Psychotropic medication in the criminal trial process: The constitutional and therapeutic implications of Riggins v. Nevada. New York Law School Journal of Human Rights, 10, 637–709.

Winick, B.J. (1994a). How to handle voluntary hospitalization after Zinerman v. Burch. Administration and Policy in Mental Health, 21, 395–406.

Winick, B.J. (1994b). The right to refuse mental health treatment: A therapeutic jurisprudence analysis. International Journal of Law and Psychiatry, 17, 99–117.

Winick, B.J. (1995). The side effects of incompetency labeling and the implications for mental health law. Psychology, Public Policy, and Law, 1(1), 6–42.

Woodson v. North Carolina, 428 U.S. 280 (1976).

Zinermon v. Burch, 494 U.S. 113 (1990).

Chapter 5

Competence to Stand Trial in Juvenile Court in Massachusetts: Issues of Therapeutic Jurisprudence

Richard Barnum
Thomas Grisso

I. Introduction

Therapeutic jurisprudence is the name given by David B. Wexler to a perspective he suggests using to analyze interactions between law and mental health.[1] Traditional scholarship in mental health law has focused on analysis of statutes and cases from the point of view of their contributions to the developing rights of the mentally ill. Wexler's approach asks us to focus less one-sidedly on issues of rights as provided by doctrinal analysis of the law itself, by considering in addition certain issues of process within the legal system involving the mentally ill. The therapeutic jurisprudence perspective directs us to examine how the law works either to support or to subvert efforts at providing mental health care, and the effects of participation in the legal process upon the defendant or patient who experiences that process. The issue of competence to stand trial in juvenile court is interesting to examine from this perspective.

Competence to stand trial is a fundamental concept in criminal law, but its application to juvenile court is less clear. Because of its legal ambiguity, competence to stand trial in juvenile court attracts attention from the traditional "rights" perspective, as well as from the therapeutic jurisprudence perspective. Examining the issue from both perspectives can help illustrate the concepts of therapeutic jurisprudence, and help determine its potential usefulness as an approach to understanding interactions between law and mental health.

We will look briefly at the statute regarding competence to stand trial as a juvenile in Massachusetts,[2] review some commentary on the issues involved and then examine in greater detail some impressions about the law in practice, looking for indications of how the law is actually used. We will then examine the potential impact on mental health care for juvenile defendants, as well as the potential positive and negative effects of legal attention to a juvenile's competence to stand trial. The focus of this article is limited to juvenile offenses

---

1. See David B. Wexler, Putting Mental Health into Mental Health Law, 16 Law & Hum. Behav. 27, 27–38 (1992) [hereinafter Mental Health Law]; Essays in Therapeutic Jurisprudence (David B. Wexler & Bruce J. Winick eds., 1991) [hereinafter Essays].

2. See Mass. Gen. L. ch. 123, §§ 15–17 (1992).

that do not lead to the possibility of transfer to criminal court. Both the stakes and the interests involved in the transfer hearing situation are different from those involved in routine delinquency proceedings; therefore, the issues involving competence to stand trial in a transfer hearing are also different. They deserve their own exploration, which is beyond the scope of the present article.

II. Legal Analysis

A. The Law

In Massachusetts, the statute that covers mental health law also sets out the judicial and mental health system procedures for dealing with issues of competence to stand trial and criminal responsibility in criminal proceedings.[3] This statute provides that at any point in a criminal proceeding, questions regarding the defendant's competence to take part in the proceeding may arise, and the court may order an evaluation of the defendant by a designated psychologist or psychiatrist regarding this issue.[4]

Initial evaluation usually takes place at the courthouse.[5] If the results of this screening evaluation indicate that hospitalization for further evaluation of the issue is called for, the court may commit the defendant to a mental health facility for this purpose, for a period of up to forty days.[6] Following the evaluation, the defendant returns to court with a report of clinical findings relevant to the issue of competence to stand trial;[7] this report will also include recommendations as to the defendant's need for further care and treatment in the mental health system.[8] The law provides that the court will then hold a hearing on the issue of competence to stand trial.[9] If the court finds the defendant competent, the trial proceeds; if the court finds the defendant not competent, the trial is continued until either the defendant becomes competent or the case is dismissed.[10] The law provides that an incompetent defendant may be committed for further evaluations of his present competence or, if still found incompetent, the likelihood of his restoration to competence.[11]

The Massachusetts General Laws do not refer explicitly to the issue of competence to stand trial in juvenile court; however, chapter 123 of Massachusetts General Law, section 15(f) has been read to address this issue obliquely.[12] It says: "In like manner to the proceedings under paragraphs (a), (b), (c), and (e) of this section, a court may order a psychiatric or psychological examination

---

3. See id.
4. Id.
5. Mass. Gen. L. ch. 123, § 15(a) (1992).
6. Id. § 15(b).
7. Id. § 15(c).
8. Id.
9. Id. § 15(d).
10. Id.
11. Id. § 16.
12. Id. § 15(f).

or a period of observation for an alleged delinquent in a facility to aid the court in its disposition. Such period shall not exceed forty days."[13]

According to this reading, the term "in like manner"[14] in this section means that the issue of competence to stand trial[15] is as relevant to juvenile proceedings as it is to criminal proceedings, and will be handled by the courts in the same manner. The section is, however, ambiguous in the following ways.

First, section 15(f) does not say that section 15(d) is as applicable to juvenile proceedings as it is to adult proceedings; the section is silent on this point.[16] Section 15(d) provides for hearings and determinations on the issue of competence, and reads as follows:

> If...the court is satisfied that the defendant is competent to stand trial, the case shall continue according to the usual course of criminal proceedings; otherwise the court shall hold a hearing on whether the defendant is competent to stand trial....If the defendant is found incompetent to stand trial, trial...shall be stayed until...the defendant becomes competent to stand trial, unless the case is dismissed.[17]

The fact that section 15(f)[18] does not refer to section 15(d)[19] suggests that the legislature may have intended either (1) that juveniles could be evaluated regarding competence to stand trial, but that courts could not make determinations on the issue; or (2) that juveniles could be evaluated only regarding the issue of criminal responsibility per sections 15(a)–(c),[20] but not regarding competence to stand trial; or (3) that the omission of section 15(d)[21] was an oversight; or (4) that section 15(f)[22] does not in fact refer to the application of competence to stand trial to juvenile court, but instead to something else entirely.

According to the Chief Justice of the Juvenile Court Department, section 15(f) does not in fact intend to address competence or criminal responsibility in juvenile court.[23] According to this view, the legislature took for granted that these concepts applied to juvenile delinquency proceedings, and saw no need to address the issues explicitly. Therefore, the phrase "in like manner to the proceedings under paragraphs (a), (b), (c), and (e) of this section" does not refer to the concepts in those paragraphs; instead, it simply extends the evaluation procedures described in those paragraphs to delinquency proceedings.[24] Furthermore, it states that those evaluation procedures may be used to evalu-

13. Id.

14. Id.

15. See id. § 15(a)–(c).

16. Mass. Gen. L. ch. 123, § 15(f) (1992).

17. Id. § 15(d).

18. Id. § 15(f).

19. Id. § 15(d).

20. Id. § 15(a)–(c).

21. Id. § 15(d).

22. Id. § 15(f).

23. Interview with Francis G. Poitrast, C.J., Juvenile Ct. Dep't of the Trial Ct. of the Commonwealth of Massachusetts in Boston, MA (June 15, 1992).

24. See Mass. Gen. L. ch. 123, § 15(a)–(e) (1992).

ate an unadjudicated delinquency defendant regarding disposition, a process for which the criminal law does not provide.[25]

Chapter 123 of Massachusetts General Law, section 16 describes the procedures for further hospitalization, evaluation and treatment after an initial finding of incompetence to stand trial.[26] This section refers to criminal trials and defendants and does not make specific reference to its application in juvenile delinquency proceedings.[27] It provides limits on the time that a case against an incompetent defendant may be held open, which relate to the maximum criminal sentence possible for the specific charges.[28] It does not make any reference to the application of this formula to the less determinate periods of commitment to a youth service agency that might result from a finding of juvenile delinquency.[29]

In summary, the explicit Massachusetts law regarding the issue of competence to stand trial in juvenile court is incomplete and somewhat ambiguous.[30] It refers to extending the criminal court evaluations of competence and criminal responsibility to the juvenile court, but is inexplicit regarding whether it intends to apply the actual concepts to delinquency proceedings. It makes no explicit statement regarding whether juvenile defendants have a right to be competent to stand trial in a delinquency matter, or about what might happen to them in the event that they are found incompetent. Though courts in other states have addressed these issues, no published cases in Massachusetts are available to clarify these issues.[31]

B. The Law in Principle

The usual approach when commenting on legal questions in juvenile court is to note the alleged traditional differences between juvenile and criminal courts. This is accomplished by exploring the statutes and decisions that define or restrict those differences and proposing specific ways that a juvenile court could deal procedurally with this ambiguous jurisdiction that is neither criminal nor civil. For example, in a critique of the juvenile court, Gary B. Melton reviewed the legal decisions which establish due process protections in juvenile court.[32] He noted that the juvenile court system has not succeeded in providing care and treatment for children and adolescents.[33] Melton suggested that the juvenile court should differ from the criminal court not by having less due

---

25. See id.

26. Mass. Gen. L. ch. 123, § 16 (1992).

27. Id.

28. Id.

29. Id.

30. See id. §§ 15–17.

31. Thomas Grisso et al., Competency to Stand Trial in Juvenile Court, 10 Int'l J. L. & Psychiatry 1, 16–19 (1987).

32. Gary B. Melton, Taking Gault Seriously: Toward a New Juvenile Court, 68 Neb. L. Rev. 146, 147–50 (1989).

33. Id. at 158–64.

process and procedural protection, but by offering more due process and procedural protections than the criminal court.[34] He argued that children need extra protections from the cumbersome authority of the state by virtue of their youth and special vulnerability.[35] Melton did not specifically address the issue of competence to stand trial in juvenile court.[36]

In an extensive exploration of the issue of criminal responsibility in juvenile delinquency proceedings, James C. Weissman offered a somewhat different suggestion.[37] He agreed that children are different from adults and therefore need special protections in the context of legal proceedings against them.[38] Weissman did not suppose, however, that the law could provide these protections simply by adding new protections to the same ones afforded adults. Instead, he offered the concept of "substituted protections."[39] This concept involves understanding the role of due process rights and protections in the adult criminal system, and taking account of the developmental differences between adults and children in such matters as time sense, understanding, and independence. Weissman proposed to design specific procedures that would afford the same protections for children within the context of juvenile proceedings as adults in criminal proceedings.[40]

These procedures might require different practices than those involved in providing the same protections in adult criminal court. Weissman's thesis offers an approach to understanding competence to stand trial in juvenile court, but his discussion did not pursue this specific issue.[41] Thomas Grisso and his colleagues provided a detailed exploration of a variety of issues involving competence to stand trial in juvenile court.[42] Like others, they explored the basic principles involved in transposing this issue into the juvenile court. They began by asking what purposes are served by raising the issue of competence to stand trial in a juvenile proceeding.[43] They also reviewed the features of children's psychological capacities that courts have considered in determining issues of juveniles' competence to stand trial.[44] Grisso and his colleagues considered empirical data about the general knowledge and reasoning capacities of children and adolescents that would seem to be relevant to the issue of competence to stand trial.[45] Their research noted that a finding of incompetence may lead to different outcomes in different legal jurisdictions, and recommended that research attend to actual observation of juvenile defendants' functioning in col-

---

34. Id. at 164–66.

35. Id.

36. Id. at 157–58.

37. James C. Weissman, Toward an Integrated Theory of Delinquency Responsibility, 60 Denver L.J. 485, 513 (1982–1983).

38. Id. at 511.

39. Id.

40. Id. at 513.

41. Id.

42. See generally Grisso et al., supra note 31.

43. Id. at 2–8.

44. Id. at 8–10.

45. Id. at 10–16.

laboration with attorneys, to learn what psychological features may be relevant to the issue of their competence to stand trial.[46]

What would be required in order to pursue further the traditional approach to understanding and implementing competence to stand trial as a right in juvenile court? One would need to consider in detail the nature of this right in criminal court, the concrete differences between criminal and juvenile court and how to apply the right to juvenile court in light of those differences.

The fundamental basis for the right to avoid trial when incompetent is to avoid unfairly exposing a person to criminal liability and sanctions in the person's absence. If a person is not mentally present and able to defend oneself, then it is not fair to proceed against him or her. There is no similar right in civil proceedings, such as those involving civil commitment, despite the fact that these proceedings may actually have liberty stakes that are higher than those of many criminal trials. One would ask whether, in this light, a juvenile delinquency proceeding is more like a civil commitment hearing or more like a criminal trial regarding the interests and stakes at issue. More specifically, one should explore the possible range of juvenile delinquency proceedings, to determine in what situations the same sorts of rights to competence enjoyed by adult defendants should be accorded to juveniles. This is accomplished by exploring the circumstances under which the right to be competent to stand trial might be waived, and by whom, as well as the related questions of whether there is a right to remain incompetent and to avoid criminal liability on that basis.

Finally, one would explore which functional capacities of a juvenile shall be considered under specific circumstances to determine the juvenile's competence to take appropriate part in the proceedings.[47] To the extent that treatment is a likely outcome of a delinquency adjudication, one might need to attend to a youth's appreciation of this potential outcome, in addition to the usual capacities related more specifically to the trial process. This appreciation would include such matters as the indications for treatment, its potential benefits and risks and its expected time course. If there were doubts as to the juvenile's competence in any of these areas, then it would be important to attend to the role of the juvenile's family because, in other potentially related circumstances (e.g., competence to consent to treatment), the juvenile's parent routinely stands-in for the incompetent juvenile. Similarly, one would need to attend to the possible roles of guardians ad litem or other special advocates in establishing the competence to stand trial of a juvenile defendant.[48]

Such an exploration would be valuable for articulating principles at work in the interactions between mental health and law in the juvenile area. Given the ambiguity of the law itself in the specific area of competence to stand trial in juvenile court, it could conceivably have an impact on clarifying legal practice. This sort of exploration, however, amounts to the type of "doctrinal analysis" that scholars claim is of diminishing value in moving forward our critical

---

46. Id. at 16–19.
47. Id. at 10–15.
48. Id. at 18–19.

thinking about mental health law.[49] If the experience in adult mental health law is any indication, the usefulness of this line of exploration in terms of fostering real improvements in either mental health or legal practice is likely to be limited.

Wexler's notion of therapeutic jurisprudence recommends a different approach to this exploration.[50] His approach focuses less on the articulation of abstract rights and more on the characterization of realities.[51] It seeks opportunities to improve practice by applying what we know about psychological processes to specific situations in the legal system where mental health issues arise.[52] To follow this approach, we must set aside the temptation to follow the path towards articulating what should be involved in addressing competence to stand trial in juvenile court. Instead, we must look first at what really happens when this issue is raised, and focus on the impact of this process on the mental health of juveniles.

C. The Law in Practice

We can gain some general impressions of how courts practically address the question of competence to stand trial in juvenile court by looking first at some features of the forensic mental health system in Massachusetts, and then at some competence evaluations in juvenile court.

1. The System

Delinquency jurisdiction in Massachusetts extends from ages seven to seventeen. Youths accused of crimes occurring before their seventeenth birthday are brought before either a juvenile court or the juvenile session of a district court. As of this writing there are only four juvenile courts in the state;[53] everywhere else (including most neighborhoods in Boston), district courts have jurisdiction over delinquency matters. The laws and procedural rules governing delinquency cases in both courts are identical, but there are important informal functional and organizational differences between them. In late 1992, legislation was passed to expand the Juvenile Court Department and remove jurisdiction over juvenile matters from District Courts' Juvenile Sessions. The analysis offered here of the law in practice is based on the workings of the system prior to the implementation of that change.

Juvenile courts deal only with juvenile matters: delinquency, status offenses, and child abuse and neglect. Juvenile courts are better staffed than are district courts, with both judges and probation officers, so that the time given to individual cases is greater. Each juvenile court has its own court clinic to provide mental health evaluations of children and families involved with the court.

49. See generally Ingo Keilitz & Ronald Roesch, Improving Justice and Mental Health Systems Interactions: In Search of a New Paradigm, 16 Law & Hum. Behav., 5, 5–26 (1992); John Petrila, Redefining Mental Health Law: Thoughts on a New Agenda, 16 Law & Hum. Behav. 89 (1992).

50. See Essays, supra note 1.

51. Essays, supra note 1, at 17–19.

52. Id. at 19–37.

53. The Juvenile Courts are located in Boston, Worcester, Springfield, and Bristol County.

These clinics specialize in juvenile matters; for the most part they are staffed by clinicians experienced in child and adolescent mental health problems, but not certified as Designated Forensic Professionals.[54]

District courts are the local courts of initial jurisdiction for minor criminal and civil matters, and generally do not focus on juvenile matters. Almost every district court has access to forensic mental health services on site, although most district courts do not have their own clinics and need to share services with other courts. These services focus primarily on explicit forensic evaluations of competence and criminal responsibility. Most district courts do not have access to juvenile specialists, and so juvenile evaluations for these courts are conducted by clinicians whose primary experience is in performing forensic evaluations of adults.

Adolescents in Massachusetts who need inpatient mental health care may enter either private psychiatric hospitals or specialized inpatient adolescent units operated with the support of the Department of Mental Health (DMH). In the past five years, the development of specialized adolescent units and increased participation by private hospitals in the Medicaid program have led to a major increase in the availability of inpatient beds for adolescents.

2. Competence Evaluations in Juvenile Court

Although juvenile courts and district courts are governed by the same laws and have the same fundamental relationships with the mental health system, there are important differences in how they respond to mental health issues involving juvenile defendants. One such difference is in the area of inpatient commitments of juvenile defendants for evaluation of competence to stand trial. Although it is difficult to obtain exact data on this issue, observers agree that inpatient section 15(b) commitments of juveniles for evaluation of competence to stand trial come disproportionately from district courts, rather than from juvenile courts.[55]

In the adult criminal justice system, it appears that defendants are frequently referred for evaluation of competence to stand trial for a variety of reasons that appear to relate less to the question of competence, than to a desire to gather general clinical information about them, or to effect involuntary treatment without having to meet civil commitment criteria.[56] One might wonder whether inpatient evaluation of juveniles regarding competence may also serve apparently extraneous purposes.

To examine this question, we reviewed the clinical records of all juveniles who were committed for evaluation of competence to stand trial to the DMH adolescent inpatient unit that receives most of these cases, for a four-month period spanning 1991 and 1992.[57] Seven juveniles were committed for evaluation of competence to stand trial during this period, and the clinical data in their records did not give us reason to believe that these seven cases were not

---

54. Robert A. Fein et al., The Designated Forensic Professional Program: A State Government-University Partnership to Improve Forensic Mental Health Services, 18 J. Mental Health Admin. 223 (1991).

55. Mass. Gen. L. ch. 123, § 15(b) (1992).

56. See generally Gary B. Melton et al., Psychological Evaluations for the Court: A Handbook for Mental Health Professionals 70 (1987).

57. Mass. Gen. L. ch. 123, § 15(b) (1992).

representative of the general population of section 15(b) commitments of juvenile defendants in Massachusetts.[58]

Each of these seven consecutive commitments from district courts had undergone the appropriate outpatient screening evaluation, addressing the need for hospitalization for the purpose of conducting the evaluation. The clinician in one of these commitments suggested that hospitalization was not needed, but the judge overruled this opinion and ordered the commitment. In the other six cases, inpatient evaluation was recommended by the screening evaluation. No screening evaluation report made a strong case to support the need for inpatient forensic evaluation. One of the reports alluded to a history of mental illness and current indications of depression and suicidal tendency, but did not clarify the relevance of these concerns to any forensic agenda. Two other screening reports described significant histories of emotional disturbance for which a marginal case might be made for elective inpatient clinical evaluation, but did not establish any significant forensic evaluation question. The remaining three screening reports made no substantial case either for inpatient clinical evaluation or for forensic evaluation. Since all these cases were hospitalized without clinical forensic indications, we conclude that these committments were for the most part made for reasons other than a need for forensic evaluations.[59]

Finally, DMH inpatient admission statistics indicate that virtually no juvenile defendants are committed to hospitals under section 16 of Massachusetts General Laws chapter 123.[60] This suggests that unlike adult criminal courts, both juvenile and district courts do not commit juvenile defendants to hospitals after finding them incompetent to stand trial. Common practice appears to be that when courts do find juvenile defendants incompetent to stand trial, they tend to dismiss delinquency charges and to proceed with civil commitment or some other civil disposition aimed at providing further care and treatment.

These impressions suggest that for juveniles, forensic mental health evaluation of competence to stand trial tends to be used not for explicit forensic evaluation purposes, but rather for the broader purpose of obtaining generic clinical evaluation and treatment. Cases are committed on this basis more often by district courts; this may be because their court clinic services are less well prepared to conduct clinical evaluations of juveniles than are the clinics of juvenile courts. The screening reports supporting a need for inpatient commitment often verify some clinical disturbance which the courts want contained and evaluated; but generally they do not make a clear case for impairments in any specific capacities relevant to competence to stand trial as a juvenile, whatever these capacities may be. The proportion of juveniles who are actually found legally incompetent on the basis of these evaluations appears to be small.

The law, in practice, seems not to be seriously concerned with understanding the impact of juvenile defendants' developmental or psychological impair-

---

58. These seven cases are not published legal cases, but instead are seven individual clinical examples of § 15(b) commitments. For reasons of confidentiality, the names of the cases will not be provided.

59. See generally Melton et al., supra note 56, at 70.

60. Mass. Gen. L. ch. 123, § 16 (1992).

ments on their abilities to understand and take appropriate part in their delinquency hearings. Instead, the legal system appears to be more concerned with obtaining general inpatient mental health evaluation, to contribute to its understanding of the needs of the juveniles involved and to its planning for disposition of these cases.

III. Implications for Juveniles' Welfare

Given this interpretation of the legal system's application of competence to stand trial in juvenile court, we are stimulated by the therapeutic jurisprudence perspective to examine the implications of this legal process and mechanism for juveniles themselves. First, if Massachusetts' courts use the issue of competence to stand trial primarily to commit youth in order to obtain general clinical information and treatment, is this mechanism likely to achieve therapeutic objectives? Or does the mechanism present a risk of negative consequences for mental health care? Second, in cases where courts truly are concerned about juveniles' competence to stand trial, how might juveniles, as participants in the legal process, be affected by legal procedures associated with this right?

A. Obtaining Effective Mental Health Care

Using forensic commitment for evaluation of competence to stand trial may be a creative way for courts to obtain clinical information about juvenile defendants. This information, which would have been hard to obtain otherwise, might be useful in crafting helpful responses. Youths who are emotionally and behaviorally unstable and who also have antisocial problems may not be appealing candidates for routine outpatient mental health evaluation services. They may resist involvement in voluntary evaluation, and they may not meet the usual standards for involuntary civil commitment to obtain inpatient evaluation. Using the legal question of competence to stand trial as a route to inpatient evaluation might open doors for these youth to appropriate mental health care which both the law and the mental health system would otherwise tend to keep closed.

On the other hand, using inpatient forensic commitment in this manner is potentially a problem for clinical care in a variety of ways. Such commitment may foster confusion about the real reason for the hospitalization. The commitment may be disruptive to the youth, the youth's family and the hospital program as well. This confusion and disruption may lead to an inferior evaluation, which specifically misinforms both the court and potential mental health providers about the youth's problems and capacities in the following ways.

Confusion regarding the true *purpose* of the commitment can lead to an evaluation that does not tell the court what it wants to know. If examiners believe that the juvenile is being referred for an evaluation of competence, they will focus their evaluation on the juvenile's ability to participate in a trial. If the court actually wants to learn something else about the juvenile, it may be disappointed.

Furthermore, disruptions inherent in the use of the hospital setting itself may contribute to *misinforming* the court about the youth's condition and needs. These disruptions are of two types.

First, the hospitals conducting these evaluations tend to be at a significant distance from the youth's home. As a result, inpatient commitment tends to disrupt whatever community investments a youth may have in such areas as family, school, church, and work. In addition, families often find it difficult to be involved in the evaluation process. Hospital staff may therefore find it difficult to evaluate the nature and strength of the youth's investments in the community. This difficulty can lead to the evaluation misinforming the court, by not including adequate attention either to significant community strengths or to important problems in the youth's dealings with the community.

Second, these commitments tend to be disruptive to the hospitals themselves. The forensic commitment process does not require that a youth meet the usual standard of medical necessity for psychiatric hospitalization. As a result, some youths committed on this basis do not manifest the sort of severe symptoms of mental illness that most adolescent inpatients do, especially after an initial brief period of stabilization. As a result, inpatient clinical staff may soon conclude that these youths were inappropriately admitted to the hospital. These same youths may show aggressive, exploitive, disruptive, or manipulative behavior in the hospital setting. When they do, staff may react with anger at having to manage difficult behavior in youths who have no clinical need for hospital treatment.

These two kinds of disruption may combine to contribute to a distorted view of the youth's problems. With inadequate information about the youth's functioning in the community, and with a sense of frustration with the apparent inappropriateness of the hospitalization, the inpatient forensic examiner may tend to minimize the nature and degree of psychopathology in the youth. This minimization may increase the likelihood that the court will respond to the youth's offenses in a more retributive and less service-oriented manner than might be appropriate for the case.

In summary, the potential benefit of using inpatient commitment for evaluation of competence to stand trial with juvenile defendants is that it allows youths who might not otherwise be hospitalized to be exposed to detailed inpatient evaluation of their mental health status and needs. A potential problem with this practice is its disruptiveness for the youths themselves, their families and the hospitals dealing with them. Another problem is the possibility that by focusing solely on the issue of competence, evaluation undertaken in this manner may fail to provide to the court useful or accurate information about the youth's overall mental health needs.

We are not able to offer impressions as to how these potential costs and benefits may balance in usual practice in various types of cases. We suspect that the benefits may outweigh the costs when a forensic examiner has been made aware that the court would like to have information about the youth's general mental health status and treatment needs, in addition to information about the youth's competence. In such a situation, the examiner may attend carefully to both issues. Such a multiple evaluation may be inefficient or wasteful if the court is not genuinely concerned about competence to stand trial, but it is not likely to be harmful to the youth if it is done well.

Under what circumstances it may prove to be helpful to a juvenile defendant to involve him in inpatient evaluation of competence to stand trial is a question for empirical research. It would be important to learn what type of evaluation would be more likely to lead the youth to clinically appropriate and successful mental health care. In concert with juvenile court involvement, these types of evaluations include: those focusing on competence, those focusing on the assessment of their treatment needs, and those focusing on both competence and treatment needs.

B. Providing a Right to be Competent to Stand Trial

As noted earlier, in most situations in which the issue of the competence of a juvenile defendant to stand trial arises, the court may be less concerned with the substantive issue of protecting the youth's right to be competent, and more concerned with gaining psychological information about the youth which may be helpful in the disposition of the case. But in some situations the court may be genuinely concerned about the real issue of competence. What might be the impact of the court's attention to this question on the youth and his care, for good or for ill?

1. Therapeutic Effects

Possible therapeutic effects of attending seriously to this question might include the development of a clearer understanding of a juvenile defendant's functional capacities, associated not only with standing trial, but also relevant to successful treatment. In situations where a youth was indeed mentally ill and not able to understand the charges or to cooperate in a defense, identification of and remediation for this incapacity prior to adjudicating the offense could have significant benefits for the youth's participation both in the delinquency adjudication and in any subsequent treatment.

Insisting that such a juvenile offender be competent in order to stand trial would enable the offender to be involved in the adjudication. The offender would be less able to deny or avoid the specific implications of a delinquency finding (i.e., that something was done wrong) in response to which the juvenile needs to change. Adjudicating the case when the offender does not understand what is going on will not provide a firm foundation on which to base efforts aimed at helping the defendant take responsibility and develop his or her own motivation for treatment; nor will failing to adjudicate the case at all, and simply trying to provide treatment on a civil basis.

Insisting that a juvenile offender be competent in order to stand trial might support efforts at treatment by improving the youth's accountability. An offender is more likely to have a positive response to treatment when he or she is able to take responsibility for the behavior that the treatment aims to change.[61] If a mental disability prevents the offender from appreciating what was alleged to have occurred or from taking a reasonable role in establishing the facts of the matter, it is difficult to expect the offender to become an ally in treatment.

---

61. Richard Barnum, The Development of Responsibility: Implications for Juvenile Justice, in From Children to Citizens: The Role of the Juvenile Court (Francis Hartmann ed., 1987); Stephen Bengis, A Comprehensive Service Delivery and a Continuum of Care for Adolescent Offenders (1986); National Adolescent Perpetrator Network, Preliminary Report from National Task Force (1988).

Insisting that a juvenile defendant be competent to stand trial might encourage mental health providers to attend more carefully to other areas of competence, more specifically related to consenting to treatment. In addition to fostering understanding of the indications for treatment by ensuring that the youth understands the charge, this attention would extend to other areas relevant to treatment. Evaluation would address whether the youth could understand the mechanisms of treatment approaches, their expected time course and what to expect by way of adverse effects, such as increases in dysphoria or changes in family or other significant relationships. Paying careful attention to a youth's appreciation for these dispositional issues would be relevant to the evaluation of competence to stand trial, and would improve the process of contracting for treatment in the event that the youth was adjudicated delinquent and treatment was ordered as part of a disposition.

2. Antitherapeutic Effects

Possible antitherapeutic effects associated with analyzing competence to stand trial for juveniles generally stem from the introduction of more formal legal requirements to the juvenile court. These requirements may lead to further delays in processing cases, and to a reduction in the personal impact on the defendant of the juvenile court process.

Delay is especially antitherapeutic to juvenile matters in a number of ways. First, to the extent that juvenile adjudication will actually lead to treatment, it is likely that delaying adjudication will delay treatment. This not only means that the onset of treatment benefits is delayed and a disturbance may have more time to develop, but also that the total time available for treatment may be reduced because the end of juvenile jurisdiction will usually mean the end of supervised treatment. Second, delays increase disruption and discontinuity in community life for youth who will be returning to the community after the court process.

Increases in formality of juvenile processing may also reduce the impact of the process for the juvenile defendant. Formal process removes the court even further from the realm of routine family and community interactions which are likely to be familiar and to have some implicit legitimacy in the eyes of a juvenile defendant. This removal may create more confusion in the mind of a defendant regarding the process, the issues at stake, and its significance for him, and this confusion may further compromise the youth's understanding of the process. In this way, formal protections for a confused defendant may breed further confusion and lead to a significant reduction in the court's capacity to reach an adjudication, especially for defendants who have the types of mental disabilities that would raise questions as to their competence to stand trial.

In summary, the potential therapeutic and antitherapeutic effects of providing a right to be competent to stand trial in juvenile court are congruent with the legal costs and benefits. Insisting on the right requires greater clarity in the juvenile adjudication process, with the promise of a result that is both purer legally and more effective therapeutically. The potential costs of this requirement, however, include the establishment of a degree of formality that could delay proceedings and undermine the immediacy and even the jurisdiction of the juvenile delinquency process.

C. Case Example

The extent to which attention to the issue of competence to stand trial in juvenile delinquency proceedings in Massachusetts actually tends to have either therapeutic or antitherapeutic effects is difficult to determine. Certainly in individual cases these effects, and no doubt others as well, will have varying impacts that will result in different individual balances of cost and benefit. There are very few juvenile cases in Massachusetts in which the issue of competence to stand trial is a focus of serious legal attention. Therefore, we can offer no overall impressions concerning whether or how raising the issue is likely either to harm or to benefit a juvenile's mental health care. We offer the following case example, however, as an illustration of some of the clinical problems and clinical-legal interactions that may arise in such cases.

> This fourteen-year-old boy was brought to the juvenile session of a local district court on a charge of rape, accused of molesting a younger boy. The facts of the case suggested that he had himself been a victim of sexual abuse by older unrelated men, who had also had some part to play in instigating his abuse of the younger boy. This district court was one of the few with access to specialized juvenile court clinic services, and he was referred to the juvenile program of the court clinic for out-patient evaluation and support. Psychological evaluation found him to show cognitive functioning bordering on mild mental retardation.[62] Because of the unstable nature of his family situation, it was recommended that he be held in detention for further clinical evaluation. When he arrived at the detention center, he made a suicide attempt that he later characterized as only manipulative, but which had a high level of potential lethality. He was hospitalized on an emergency basis, where he was further evaluated, characterized as depressed, and begun on antidepressant medication.
>
> At the conclusion of his hospital stay, he was returned to court, where he was found delinquent on the rape charge. The case was immediately appealed to be heard as a jury trial at the juvenile court. There he was willing to admit to having molested the younger boy, but he indicated that the older men had made him do it. The juvenile court requested clinical evaluation regarding dispositional planning, under the provisions of a section of the delinquency law[63] which allows such evaluations to be ordered[64] based on the expectation that he would plead delinquent. The court clinic provided this evaluation, but noted that in light of the uncertainties about what had really transpired in this sexual offense, it was difficult to offer firm recommendations regarding specific placement and treatment. The court then became sufficiently concerned about the issues of fairness involved in potentially finding him delinquent on the basis of behavior that had been coerced, and about the apparent simplicity of his manner of speaking in attempting to plead, that it ordered further clinical evaluation of his competence to stand trial under the provisions of Chapter 123, section 15(a).[65]
>
> We should note here that the court was not intending to generate generic mental health or dispositional information by this referral; ample clinical data

---

62. Tests showed a verbal I.Q. of 65, and a full scale I.Q. of 72.

63. Mass. Gen. L. ch. 119, § 68A (1992).

64. Evaluations may be ordered with the consent of the parent and the agency conducting the evaluation.

65. Mass. Gen. L. ch. 123, § 15(a) (1992).

was already available from the previous hospitalization and the two previous court clinic evaluations. The court was quite explicitly concerned about issues of competence to stand trial, specifically the boy's capacity to plead delinquent and his capacity to waive his right to a jury trial.

Further detailed clinical evaluation of these capacities determined that his overall psychological functioning was in the mentally retarded range, and that he suffered from intermittently high levels of anxiety that contributed to depression and to impulsive suicidal behavior. His language functioning was in the mentally retarded range, with receptive language worse than expressive; a likely example of this discrepancy was his confusing the words "jury" and "attorney" in his first interview, leading to considerable confusion regarding his understanding of the functions of these two players in the legal system. When he was told that "jury" and "lawyer" were not the same thing, he recognized the mistake, and was able to be clearer about the respective roles of attorneys and juries. However, on repeat examination after a few weeks, he did not appear to retain any of this information. He never was able to demonstrate a clear understanding of his own role in deciding whether the case would be decided by a judge or by a jury, or what the relationship might be between his pleading delinquent and his desire that the judge might exonerate him because he had been forced to do what he did. He was consistent in understanding that, if he were to plead delinquent, the case would take less time, he would need to return to court less often, and he would be able to enter a program sooner.

Because his case had not been adjudicated, clinical evaluation regarding the potential for further sexual aggression was not pursued in detail. This decision was based both on ethical considerations about pursuing potentially self-incriminating admissions prior to the adjudication of the matter, and also on concerns about the clinical validity of such admissions as he might make, in the absence of legal determinations of the facts of the case.[66] As a result, it was not possible to offer a firm opinion on the issue of likelihood of future harm to others on this basis.

On the basis of these clinical evaluation findings, the court ruled that the defendant was competent to stand trial, but not competent to plead delinquent or to waive his right to a jury trial. The case was continued for an additional two months pending jury trial. During this period the defendant remained in detention on bail status, showed some further emotional instability and made another suicide gesture. He was hospitalized again. He was not seen as suffering from a major affective disorder, but was seen as trying to manipulate discharge from detention. When the date for the jury trial arrived, the family of the victim indicated that they could not accept the victim's testifying to his victimization before a jury. The case was then continued without a finding, and the court placed the boy on pretrial probation for an extended period.

As part of his probation, he was referred for residential treatment to the Department of Social Services (DSS), the state agency serving abused and neglected children, as well as status offenders. While awaiting long-term placement, he was placed in a shelter, where he raped another adolescent resident. He was subsequently placed in a long-term residential school by DSS. Although this program included specific sexual offender treatment, he continued to be resistant to identifying himself as an offender, and his progress was slow. When

---

66. See generally Elizabeth B. Saunders & George A. Awad, Assessment, Management, and Treatment Planning for Male Adolescent Sexual Offenders, 58 Am. J. Orthopsychiatry 571 (1988).

he came to trial in the district court for the second rape, he was adjudicated delinquent, and given a suspended commitment to the Department of Youth Services (DYS), the youth corrections agency. Following this adjudication, he began to show more willingness to see himself as a perpetrator as well as a victim, and his treatment progress improved.[67]

This case illustrates one fundamental dilemma in establishing a right to be competent to stand trial in a juvenile process where the stakes of the adjudication include both treatment and prevention of further violent offending. This youth's inability to understand what was required of him in order to waive a jury trial and plead delinquent led to his being involved in a more formal adjudicatory proceeding, taking part in which was beyond the capacity of the victim/witness. As a result, it was not possible to adjudicate the case, and the court could not complete efforts at specific evaluation of his risk of further sexual perpetration. He was initially placed in a program that did not offer any specific treatment, where he offended again. His confusion over his degree of responsibility for the rapes apparently slowed his subsequent course of treatment, and it appeared that his subsequent adjudication for the second rape helped clear up this confusion and improve the effectiveness of his treatment.

In this case, it was clear that the court was seriously and legitimately concerned about the defendant's capacity to understand the complexity of the legal process in which he found himself. The court in fact arrived at a legally elegant compromise, finding him competent to stand trial but not to plead or to waive a jury trial. This compromise protected the youth from incriminating himself incompetently and thereby exposing himself unfairly to state intrusion and loss of liberty, but it also aimed to adjudicate the case appropriately and allow treatment to proceed on a rational basis. The compromise was not fully successful, and the case could not be adjudicated. The court's careful attention to the defendant's competence to stand trial does not appear to have improved his sense of the fairness and appropriateness of his participation in the judicial process. Instead, it appears likely to have added to his confusion, and that of those charged with his treatment, regarding the degree of risk he presented and the extent of his responsibility for it.

IV. Conclusion

Massachusetts statutes appear to establish a right to be competent to stand trial in juvenile court, though not without some ambiguity.[68] The use of the law in this area suggests that courts commonly have little specific concern about the impact of mental disorders on abilities that may be relevant to competence to be adjudicated a juvenile delinquent—whatever those abilities may be. Courts instead appear most often to use the occasion of evaluating a juve-

---

67. The case example is not a published legal case, but rather a clinical vignette. It is not a hypothetical case; thus, for reasons of confidentiality identifying information is not provided.

68. Mass. Gen. L. ch. 123, §§ 15–17 (1992).

nile defendant's competence to stand trial as a means to gain general information about the youth's mental condition and treatment needs.

When the issue of a juvenile's competence to stand trial is addressed in a substantive way, challenging questions arise as to what capacities in a youth are relevant to this issue, in what ways they may differ from analogous capacities in adults and how they should be addressed and measured in clinical evaluation. These are matters first for legal theorizing. In addressing these questions, as well as in providing for both the legal and clinical needs of juvenile defendants, it would be useful to have a clearer understanding of the impact of raising the issue on delinquency proceedings and the participants in them. The therapeutic jurisprudence approach encourages us to explore this impact, asking whether this use of the law is of benefit to juvenile defendants by increasing the likelihood of successful treatment through the delinquency process.

The clinical importance of accountability in treating juvenile offenders increases the importance of a formal adjudication process as a foundation for effective treatment. To be meaningful clinically as well as legally, this adjudication must presumably in some way involve the defendant as a competent participant. It is not clear whether addressing competence to stand trial in juvenile court in a manner analogous to the adult criminal process succeeds generally in engaging defendants in this meaningful process. Alternatively, it may confuse them, or even engender contempt in them for a legal process that seems fraught with technicalities and may appear to be reluctant to adjudicate them. This is a matter for further research.

This analysis does not allow us to offer any comprehensive recommendations about how to deal with the issue of competence to stand trial when it arises in juvenile court. We do, however, make the following suggestions for clinical-legal practice. Just as in the adult criminal context, when the question of a juvenile defendant's competence to stand trial arises, it is important for legal and mental health professionals alike to seek clarification concerning the basis for raising the issue. Clinicians should be aware that even though the ultimate determination of competence is a matter for the court, in reality the issues involved in juvenile court competence are obscure and difficult. As a result, legal professionals will likely be eager for help, and perhaps more likely to be swayed in defining a clinical evaluation agenda than in adult matters where the issues and stakes appear clearer.

In addressing requests for consultation about juveniles regarding competence to stand trial initially, it is important to clarify what functional deficits the juvenile appears to have. Do these deficits appear likely to interfere with the ability to take an appropriate part in the delinquency hearing process, or is the purpose of raising the issue simply to find a way to obtain general clinical services such as hospital containment or a general diagnostic evaluation? If a youth appears to have a genuine deficit that may affect his or her competence to take part in the proceedings, it is important then to pay attention to the nature of the proceedings, and to the youth's real involvement in them.

In matters involving more serious charges, especially those involving potential transfer to criminal court, the impact of an incompetence finding can be very significant in determining the course of a legal process with major impact on the juvenile.[69] In minor delinquency matters, it is likely to matter less one way or the other.

It is important to attend to the nature of the offense with which the youth is charged, and consider what the impact of a formal adjudication of this offense is likely to be with regard to placement options and treatment involvement for the juvenile. It may be difficult to find an appropriate balance between proceeding with less formality—and perhaps less definitiveness—and proceeding with greater formality, with more caution to provide protection, but perhaps with less potential for ultimately resolving the case. When treatment is expected to be the ultimate result of a juvenile adjudication, it may help to remember that when treatment is the issue at stake, courts have found there is less need for formal procedural protections.[70]

When the purpose for raising the competence to stand trial issue appears to be more clinical than legal, the consultant should search for ways to meet these clinical needs directly and appropriately. This would include the use of detailed outpatient evaluation with access to family and community. Whether the goals for the evaluation are primarily clinical or forensic, hospitalization should not be recommended unless it is clinically necessary. Both forensic and clinical goals can be met perfectly well, and possibly better, when addressed on an outpatient basis, than when pursued by an inpatient evaluation under the guise of a request for a competence to stand trial evaluation.

---

69. See Richard Barnum, Clinical Evaluation of Juvenile Delinquents Facing Transfer to Adult Courts, 26 J. Am. Acad. Child & Adolescent Psychiatry 922 (1987); Elissa P. Benedek, Waiver of Juveniles to Adult Court (1985).

70. See Richard Barnum et al., Patient Warnings in Court-Ordered Evaluations of Children and Families, 15 Bull. Am. Acad. of Psychiatry & L. 283 (1987); Commonwealth v. Lamb, 311 N.E.2d 47 (Mass. 1974).

Chapter 6

Sex Offenders and the Law: New Directions

Jeffrey A. Klotz

The increase in reported crimes of a sexual nature has resulted in a heightened awareness and concern among the public about the potential dangers that sex offenders pose to society. In response to public outcry for protection from sex offenders who are perceived to be both mentally ill and dangerous, legislatures have enacted laws intended to both protect the public and provide treatment for those persons who, by virtue of their behaviors, ostensibly are in need of therapeutic intervention. At the same time, social scientists and mental health professionals have been trying to develop treatments for sex offenders in hopes of reducing the likelihood that the harmful behaviors will persist.

Instead of providing a comprehensive review of the ways in which the legal system handles sex offenders or a full review of the clinical literature regarding the nature and treatment of sexually deviant behaviors,[1] this chapter will illustrate how analyzing legal and clinical issues through the perspective of therapeutic jurisprudence can generate a variety of empirical issues relating to the concerns of both the mental health and legal communities in regard to the legal handling of alleged and adjudicated sex offenders. This chapter will begin by describing how the law has dealt with sex offenders through special dispositional statutes known as "sexual psychopath laws." Next, these laws will be examined through the perspective of therapeutic jurisprudence, followed by other examples of how the therapeutic jurisprudence approach can be applied to psycholegal issues relating to sex offenders and the law.

Special Processing of Sex Offenders under the Law

Legislatures have implemented a variety of programs to deal with sex offenders. The set of such laws which has received the most attention are the so-called "sexual psychopath" statutes.[2] In general, sexual psychopath laws "treat sex offenders as a separate category subject to procedures different from those

---

1. For reviews of the clinical treatment literature see Marshall & Pithers (1994); Brooks (1992); Furby, Weinrott, & Blackshaw (1989); Lockhart, Saunders & Cleveland (1988); Grossman (1985); and Monahan & Davis (1983).

2. Although different states have different names for these statutes, such as "sexually dangerous persons acts" and "mentally disordered sex offenders acts," the term "sexual psychopath" will be used in this chapter to collectively refer to these laws.

followed in either the criminal justice or the civil commitment process" (Brakel, Parry, & Weiner, 1985, p. 740). The typical sexual psychopath law endeavors to serve both public protection and therapeutic functions by providing for both indefinite, involuntarily commitment, and special dispositions, including treatment, to dangerous sex offenders (C. Veneziano & L. Veneziano, 1987; Brakel, et al., 1985; Sullivan, 1976). How the laws are structured to achieve these objectives, however, differs from state to state in several respects, including: (1) to whom the laws apply; (2) by whom the proceedings are initiated; (3) the timing of the proceedings (pre-conviction, post-conviction/presentence, or post-conviction/ post-sentence); (4) whether the person is entitled to a hearing, a jury, and/or representation by counsel; (5) the duration of the commitment period; and (6) the nature of release proceedings (see generally, Brakel et al., 1985).

Under Washington State's controversial Sexually Violent Predators (SVP) law [Wash. Rev. Code §§ 71.09.010–.902 (1992 & Supp. 1995)][3] for example, the state has the power to indefinitely commit individuals who are found to be "sexually violent predators." A commitment action under the Washington law commences when a prosecuting attorney or attorney general files a petition alleging an individual is a "sexually violent predator" [Wash. Rev. Code § 71.09.030 (1992 & Supp. 1995)], defined as:

> any person who has been convicted of or charged with a crime of sexual violence and who suffers from a mental abnormality or personality disorder which makes the person likely to engage in predatory acts of sexual violence [Wash.Rev.Code § 71.09.020(1) (1992 & Supp. 1995)].

After the petition has been filed, the action is brought to trial. Any individual adjudicated to be a sexually violent predator is then indefinitely committed to the state department of social and health services (DSHS) special commitment center for care and treatment [Wash. Rev. Code. § 71.09.060 (1992)]. The offender may only be released if DSHS determines he or she is no longer dangerous, or if the offender directly petitions the court for release [Wash. Rev. Code § 71.09.090 (1992 & Supp. 1995)].

Two features of the Washington law distinguish it from prior sexual psychopath legislation. First, commitment under the law comes only *after* the offender has served his full prison term. Thus, treatment is in addition to, and not in lieu of, punishment. Second, the prosecutor does not have to allege or prove a recent overt act of violence to invoke the law against an incarcerated individual (LaFond, 1992a; *In re* Young, 1993). Once the offender is released into the community after being confined for a sex offense, however, the state must provide evidence of a recent overt act in its petition to initiate sexual predator proceedings (*In re* Young, 1993).

A fundamental assumption of most sexual psychopath legislation is that the propensity to commit sexually violent crimes results from specific mental disorders (Small, 1992). These laws also assume that mental health professionals are

---

3. Because the Washington law has generated a great deal of controversy, particular attention will be paid in this chapter to the SVP law. For a full discussion of issues relating to Washington's SVP law, see "Predators and Politics" (1992), a symposium issue dedicated to the Washington statute.

able to make accurate predictions about an offender's future behavior, and that large numbers of offenders with qualifying disorders are treatable (see Wettstein, 1992). In fact, it was this therapeutic ideal that prompted the state of Michigan to adopt the first sexual psychopath law in 1937 (Brakel et al., 1985). Other states followed suit, and by 1970, 29 states and the District of Columbia had sexual psychopath statutes in some form on their books (Brakel et al., 1985).

After the height of the sexual psychopath legislation movement, however, the assumption that sex offenders were both mentally ill and treatable was challenged by the psychiatric and legal communities (Fujimoto, 1992; Small, 1992; R.D. Miller, Stava, & R.K. Miller, 1988). Organizations such as the Group for the Advancement of Psychiatry (1977) and the American Bar Association Criminal Justice Standards Committee (American Bar Association, 1989) advocated the repeal of sexual psychopath legislation because of the dubious theoretical and empirical relationship between a specific mental disability and sexually violent tendencies (see also, Reardon, 1992). Moreover, the ability of mental health professionals to predict dangerousness has been plagued by serious debate (see Brooks, 1992; LaFond, 1992b). Because of these and other criticisms, sexual psychopath legislation fell into disfavor, and many states began to repeal their sexual psychopath laws (Brakel et al., 1985. See also, Small, 1992; C. Veneziano & L. Veneziano, 1987). In 1990, however, Washington State broke from this trend by revamping and resurrecting its sex offender involuntary commitment system. Whether this has signalled a reversal of the abolitionist trend remains to be seen, since current sex offender involuntary commitment statutes are actively employed in only a handful of states (Fujimoto, 1992).

Along with the retreat from sexual psychopath legislation has been an increased emphasis on the successful prosecution and punishment of sex offenders, while increasing services, such as treatment and advocacy programs, to assist victims of sex crimes (LaFond, 1992a; C. Veneziano & L. Veneziano, 1987). Despite this trend, a majority of states still offer treatment to sex offenders through their mental health or correctional agencies (Small, 1992).

Empirical Research

Very little research has been conducted which specifically looks at the processing of sex offenders under sexual psychopath laws (C. Veneziano & L. Veneziano, 1987). The research which has been done in this area, such as that done by Dix (1976), Forst, (1978), Konecni, Mulcahy, & Ebbesen, (1980), Sturgeon & Taylor (1980), Pacht & Cowden, (1974), and Steadman, Monahan, Harstone, Davis & Robbins, (1982), has tended to focus on issues related to the treatment, diagnosis and classification of sex offenders committed under the laws. This is not inappropriate because a principal empirical issue raised by sexual psychopath legislation is whether the treatment programs provided for by the laws have a significant impact on the recidivism of the sex offenders who participate in the programs. Such research is necessary to evaluate the value of the programs established by the laws (Small, 1992).

Unfortunately, this research has been, for the most part, atheoretical and plagued by methodological weaknesses (Small, 1992; C. Veneziano & L. Veneziano, 1987). Because of the limitations in the existing data, none of the treatment programs offered under these laws have been established as effective (Furby, 1989; C. Veneziano & L. Veneziano, 1987). Consequently, little is known about our ability to reduce the recidivism of sex offenders through such therapeutic interventions.

Further weakening the viability of the sex offender laws is the fact that the assumption that those who commit sex offenses are necessarily mentally disordered and dangerous has never been empirically validated (see generally, Reardon, 1992; LaFond, 1992b; C. Veneziano & L. Veneziano, 1987). The same can be said about the dubious ability of clinicians to predict future violence (see Brooks, 1992; LaFond, 1992b). It may even be that, in general, the perceived need of lawmakers and mental health professionals to distinguish sex offenders from other offenders when prescribing treatment and/or punishment, may be empirically unfounded (see Scheingold, Olson & Pershing, 1992).

Clearly, sound research into these issues would provide valuable insight into important issues relating to the disposition and processing of sex offenders though the legal system. As currently framed, however, these clinical questions can only yield clinical answers. Asking whether a particular *treatment* promotes therapeutic outcomes will not tell us whether the *law itself* promotes therapeutic outcomes. Inquiring into whether the law itself produces therapeutic or antitherapeutic consequences is the explicit task of "therapeutic jurisprudence," the study of the role of the law as a therapeutic agent (Wexler & Winick, 1991a; Wexler, 1990; Wexler, 1993b; Wexler, 1995). How therapeutic jurisprudence as an analytical tool can give rise to an interesting set of clinical and legal issues in regard to the legal processing of sex offenders will be the focus of the balance of this chapter.

The Law as Independent Variable: Therapeutic Jurisprudence

Therapeutic jurisprudence is a refreshing and highly interdisciplinary enterprise whose task is "to identify—and ultimately to examine empirically—relationships between legal arrangements and therapeutic outcomes" (Wexler, 1992b, p.32). Specifically, the therapeutic jurisprudence method examines the extent to which the law may have therapeutic or antitherapeutic significance.[4] Used in this way, the therapeutic jurisprudence heuristic is a powerful research tool which gives rise to a whole host of new and innovative empirical questions.

In methodological terms, therapeutic jurisprudence treats "the law" as an independent variable. In therapeutic jurisprudence scholarship and research, "the law" includes legal rules, procedures, the behavior of legal actors, such as judges and lawyers, and the operation of the legal system (Wexler, 1990;

---

4. This approach does not argue that therapeutic concerns should supersede other considerations, but only that empirical information from the social sciences can inform legal decision-making (Schopp, 1993; Wexler, 1992a; Wexler & Winick, 1991b).

Wexler & Winick, 1991a; see also Sales, 1983). For instance, as we shall see, sexual psychopath legislation (rules), the criminal plea process (procedures), and the behavior of judges and lawyers (legal actors) might all operate in a therapeutic or antitherapeutic manner. Moreover, the therapeutic jurisprudence quest is not limited to specific substantive areas of the law. Although it began as an offshoot of traditional mental health, therapeutic jurisprudence as a research tool has expanded into many other areas of the law, including criminal law, juvenile and family law, tort law and the law of evidence, to name a few (Wexler, 1995; Wexler 1993a)

The dependent variables in therapeutic jurisprudence always consist of what will be referred to collectively in this chapter as "therapeutic outcomes," and may include any number of psychological, behavioral or social measures. For instance, the therapeutic outcome of interest may be the extent to which an offender's *behavior* (e.g., acts of sexual deviance), *cognitive* processes (e.g., cognitive distortions), or receptivity to or success in treatment are affected by a given legal arrangement.

Therapeutic jurisprudence also leaves unrestricted the identity of the "subjects" whose mental, behavioral, or social health might be influenced by the legal scheme of interest. Indeed, the subject pool is not limited to criminal defendants or mental health patients, but may also include judges, psychotherapists, crime victims, families, or jurors, to name a few (Wexler, 1995).

Although the notion of treating the law as an independent variable and therapeutic outcomes as dependent variables is not a new one, therapeutic jurisprudence's unique spin is to combine these two sets of variables in the search for measurable links between the law and therapeutic outcomes.[5] Thus, the therapeutic jurisprudence heuristic can be a useful means of generating otherwise unexplored policy and research questions.

When discussing the operation of therapeutic jurisprudence, it may prove helpful to keep in mind that the law may produce therapeutic or antitherapeutic consequences in either of two ways: it may do so *deliberately*, or it may do so *inadvertently*. An example of a deliberate attempt to achieve therapeutic objectives is provided by the sexual psychopath legislation discussed earlier, which sets up specific treatment programs for sex offenders or otherwise provides for rehabilitative dispositions for these offenders.[6]

---

5. The "newness" of therapeutic jurisprudence has been questioned by scholars such as Petrila (1993). However, therapeutic jurisprudence is not heralded by its scholars as completely new. Professors Wexler and Winick (1993) themselves question the newness of therapeutic jurisprudence, and view it as:

> ...merely a sharper conceptualization of and focus on work that a number of us ...had been engaging in earlier...This sharpened focus, we believe, helped generate much scholarship that otherwise would likely have gone unwritten, and,.. .has created a community of therapeutic jurisprudence scholars interested in law/mental health issues in *many* fields of law, not simply conventional mental health law. In that sense, we hope therapeutic jurisprudence has helped invigorate and restructure the law/mental health field (p. 909, n.9).

6. Another example can be found in the area of driving under the influence statutes. For example, Arizona's D.U.I. laws provide for mandatory alcohol and/or substance abuse evaluations, treatment and education for convicted impaired drivers [Arizona Revised Statutes §

The "success" of these deliberate attempts to achieve therapeutic goals through legal intervention is typically judged by whether the explicit therapeutic objectives have been achieved. Once the theoretical links between the law and therapeutic outcomes have been identified, the task of therapeutic jurisprudence is to empirically examine the extent to which the previously identified aspect of the law is related to previously identified therapeutic outcomes.

In addition to *deliberately* acting as a therapeutic agent, the law may also *inadvertently* act in a therapeutic or antitherapeutic fashion. It is these less obvious connections between the law and therapeutic outcomes which have been of particular interest to therapeutic jurisprudence scholars, perhaps because identifying these relationships, which later may become the focus of empirical research, may be the most challenging and exciting aspect of therapeutic jurisprudence scholarship. The balance of this chapter will be devoted to illustrating how a therapeutic jurisprudence inquiry can flesh out otherwise "hidden" empirical links between the mental health and behavior of sex offenders and various legal apparatuses.

Therapeutic Jurisprudence and Sex Offenders

In the area of sex offenders and the law, therapeutic jurisprudence asks this general question: to what extent does the law affect therapeutically relevant variables relating to sex offenders?[7] The discussion of this issue will begin with an exploration of sexual psychopath legislation and the ways in which such laws might operate to inadvertently produce therapeutic or antitherapeutic results. ***

Sexual Psychopath Laws and Therapeutic Jurisprudence

Several aspects of sexual psychopath legislation might influence therapeutic outcomes, including the structure levels of the treatment programs, the gatekeeping procedures, the assessment and screening processes, and the plea process. In addition, the laws might produce incentives related to treatment and behavior. Each of these will be discussed in turn.

Structure Levels

Small (1992) described how sex offender treatment options provided for by sexual psychopath legislation differ in terms of the degree of structure provided by the legislature. According to Small, the various treatment programs can be characterized along a continuum as being either "structured," "loosely structured," or "ad hoc." Structured programs are those whose procedures are specifically controlled by the legislature. For instance, legislatures in these jurisdictions might spell out in detail which offenses render a person eligible for

---

28-694 (Supp.1994)]. Only if a defendant completes the screening and treatment (if necessary) may the judge suspend a portion of the mandatory jail term.

7. In a similar vein, Small (1992) has suggested that researchers and policymakers examine how the "legal context" affects sex offender treatment programs, and vice versa.

processing under the program, or who screens the offenders and decides which ones are entitled to treatment. Legislative control over whether and under what conditions an offender is eligible for release from the programs is another characteristic of structured programs (Small, 1992).

Loosely structured treatment programs, on the other hand, exist in states which have either modified or abolished sexual psychopath legislation, yet retain specialized sex offender treatment programs. In these systems, treatment is provided through alternative procedures or less detailed sexual psychopath procedures. In California, for example, although the sexual psychopath legislation was repealed, other statutes were enacted which provide for treatment of sex offenders at state hospitals as an option during the latter part of a prison term (Small, 1992, p.136–38).

Finally, ad hoc programs exist in jurisdictions which have repealed their sexual psychopath legislation, and thus offer treatment to sex offenders only through programs available in the criminal justice system. Because such programs lack any meaningful legislative structure for dealing specifically with sex offenders, convicted sex offenders in these states might receive treatment in prison, might be civilly committed, or might receive no treatment at all (Small, 1992, p.138).

It is not unlikely that the legislatures in the different states adopted the programs they did, at least in part, based upon an articulated belief in the therapeutic value of a given structure level. But even if a program's structure is merely a product of fiscal and political pressures rather than therapeutic considerations, the structure of the program itself could still produce unexpected therapeutic or antitherapeutic consequences.

One way to assess the therapeutic value, either intended or unintended, of the different program structures would be to conduct cross-jurisdictional research comparing treatment outcome variables of the offenders in these different programs. If, for instance, research suggested that the ad hoc or loosely structured programs outperform the structured programs on therapeutic measures, the trend to repeal sexual psychopath legislation might ironically have done more to protect the public than would the enactment of rigid, well-structured laws aimed at accomplishing these same objectives. Research into such issues might thus provide counter-intuitive insight into the therapeutic or antitherapeutic worth of these different legislative structures.

Gatekeeping

The methods employed to include or exclude offenders from the treatment programs under sexual psychopath legislation are also of interest to therapeutic jurisprudence. According to Small (1992), states differ on who determines whether an offender is entitled to treatment under the laws. This screening function may rest with either a judge, a panel of independent examiners, or the clinical staff responsible for the treatment and care of the offender once admitted to the program (Small, 1992). Small (1992) suggests that when someone other than the clinical staff performs this gatekeeping function, treatment facilities become overcrowded, and treatable offenders are denied treatment while untreatable offenders may receive it. Small argues that it would be preferable, therefore, to shift the screening authority to the clinicians who have the apparent ability to assess amenability to treatment. This would apparently help ensure that those who would benefit from treatment will get it, and those who would not benefit do not deplete the program's valuable resources.

One conclusion to be reached from these observations is that the laws which provide for non-clinical gatekeepers might be antitherapeutic. On the other hand, granting clinicians exclusive control over the gatekeeping function might be therapeutically detrimental if the clinicians over-admit offenders to the programs by implementing overly-inclusive admission standards, leading to over-crowed programs and diluted treatment. This might happen if the program's funding or budget depended upon the number of participants treated. Similarly, antitherapeutic consequences might result if clinicians excluded certain treatable patients from the programs because they are viewed as particularly difficult or problematic. These patients who are otherwise treatable but nevertheless have poor prognoses might be excluded not only to avoid having to deal with them, but also so that the "success rate" of the program might stay artificially high due to the pre-selected "treatable" sample, perhaps leading to enhanced or continued budgetary allocations from the legislature.

The extent to which different procedures for processing sex offenders into treatment programs have therapeutic or antitherapeutic consequences, as well as whether and for what reasons clinical gatekeepers include or exclude candidates from sex offender treatment programs, are empirical questions. Eventually, research could be done which addresses whether one set of screening procedures is preferable to the others from a therapeutic perspective, all else being equal.

Assessment

Other therapeutic jurisprudence questions relate to the process by which offenders are initially assessed regarding their amenability to treatment under the programs. A potentially antitherapeutic result of this process is that the offender is exposed to a potent labeling effect (Walsh, 1990). Ironically, being labeled as "treatable" can negatively influence sentencing judges, who tend to incarcerate these offenders for longer periods than had they never been assessed (Small, 1992).

Under these assessment schemes, offenders are given an incentive to avoid being labelled as a treatable sex offender. An offender who is able to somehow avoid assessment or the paradoxically damning "treatable" label would likely spend less total time incarcerated than would his counterpart who was labelled "treatable." If in fact some treatment is therapeutically preferable to no treatment, then the assessment process under sexual psychopath legislation might be inadvertently antitherapeutic.

Treatment Incentives

Although there may be situations in which a person might be required to undergo treatment out of some sort of a court-ordered or statutory obligation, those in need of psychological treatment must at some point and on some level agree to participate in treatment. As with any other decision-making process, factors exist which can influence a person's decision to forego or participate in sex offense treatment. Arguably, any set of laws which explicitly or implicitly influences treatment-seeking decisions should, preferably, provide incentives for potential patients to *seek* rather than to *forego* treatment.

A therapeutic jurisprudence inquiry might ask whether sexual psychopath laws offer incentives or disincentives to offenders to seek out or participate in treatment. For example, does Washington's SVP law, which provides for indefinite post-incarceration civil commitment of sexually violent predators, operate to encourage incarcerated sex offenders to *avoid* treatment in prison for fear of being identified as possible candidates for such commitment under the special law (see LaFond, 1992b)? Conversely, might the existence of the special law lead sex offenders in Washington to *seek out* treatment in prison—in the hope that successful treatment will *lessen* the chances of being processed under the law? According to one Washington State Attorney General (Tweten, 1991), sex offenders who seek treatment in prison might indeed reduce their risk of being considered as a candidate for SVP processing:

> If [sex offenders] have had sex offender treatment in prison, that is something we review and assess prior to filing.... In some of these cases that have been reviewed, they have not been filed because the experts have determined (psychologists, psychiatrists in the prison system) that indeed the person has benefitted from the sexual deviancy treatment, and those people we have not found enough of a basis upon which to file.

Another issue relating to treatment under the Washington law involves the question of whether the law actually (and ironically) targets the *least* treatable sex offenders and discourages or obstructs treatment of a larger sex offender population (see Wettstein, 1992). Since those offenders committed as sexual predators are probably those who never participated in or benefitted from earlier attempts at treatment, those committed under the sexual predator law are probably the least treatable offenders (Wettstein, 1992). If so, the *ordinary* prison population might house a more treatable universe than would the civil treatment facility where the predators are ultimately committed. This becomes problematic if resources for treatment are limited and those "ordinary" offenders who are the most treatable go without because available resources have been expended on a less treatable population. In addition, to the extent that the law focuses on disposition of sexual predators and ignores treatment of "ordinary" sex offenders, this more treatable group might go untreated. Finally, those "ordinary" sex offenders may avoid treatment so as not to be identified as candidates for commitment under the SVP law.

Thus, a law that confines and attempts to treat a tiny number of perhaps untreatable persons may ultimately discourage treatment of or deny treatment to a much larger group of more treatable persons. If that is the case, the Washington law may prove to be antitherapeutic, a result that would not occur if sex offenders were processed under the criminal code without the disincentive of indefinite incarceration provided by the SVP statute.

Plea Bargaining

The Washington law might also inadvertently foster deleterious cognitive processes in sex offenders. Because the law is triggered by a criminal conviction for a qualifying sexual offense, the prospect of indefinite commitment under the law might discourage guilty defendants from pleading guilty to such potentially qualifying sexual offenses. Instead, sex offenders might seek to "charge bargain" to a non-qualifying offense, or even opt to go to trial to avoid being processed under the statute. In this way, the Washington law might operate antitherapeutically by encouraging guilty defendants to deny and minimize their guilt [a strong tendency already attributed to sex offenders (Perkins, 1991)], through the plea or trial process, thereby reinforcing these "cognitive distortions" (Pollock & Hashmall, 1991; Gudjonsson, 1990; Abel, Gore, Holland, Camp, Becker & Rathner, 1989; Abel, Becker & Cunningham-Rathner, 1984) and impeding treatment (Perkins, 1991).

If research were to confirm the therapeutically injurious impact of this procedure, prosecutors might in certain circumstances agree, in exchange for a guilty plea to a qualifying offense, not to use the particular offense pled to as a trigger for commitment under the statute.[8] In this way, the law could be used as an incentive for the guilty offender to plead guilty and to admit guilt to the charged offense, an arguably therapeutic result. Additionally, with the fear of being identified as predators having been removed, some offenders might be more inclined to seek treatment in prison in hopes of preventing future offenses that could again expose them to potential commitment under the statute, another arguably therapeutically preferential result. This discussion illustrates how the therapeutic capacity of a law can come not only from the *use* of the law as foreseen by the enacting legislature, but also from the promised *non-use* of the law by the actors within the system.

Moreover, to the extent that the sexual psychopath laws, such as the Washington statute, provide an incentive for guilty sex offenders to protest their innocence and proceed to trial in an effort to avoid indefinite incarceration, the period of denial might be extended through the trial process. If such defendants are nonetheless convicted, the trial and their trial testimony could serve to strengthen their cognitive distortions and their resistance to therapy. Further, a conviction at trial stands a reasonable chance of being appealed. The pendency of the appellate process will provide still another disincentive to admit the commission of the underlying acts (see State v. Imlay, 1991).

Behavioral Incentives

Still other issues exist relating to the incentives Washington's law might produce. For instance, the Office of the Washington State Attorney General (1990) adopted standards for deciding when and under what circumstances SVP commitment petitions should be filed. One of the Standards specifies that a petition should be filed only if

> [t]he offender has a provable pattern of prior predatory acts; i.e. acts directed toward either (a) strangers or (b) individuals with whom a relationship has been established or promoted for the primary purpose of victimization.

Restricting the law's commitment power to predators in this fashion seems to make the law unavailable to prosecutors who want to seek commitment of offenders who have acted against certain family members.

---

8. There is some evidence that prosecutors do use the threat of civil commitment under the statutes as a bargaining chip in plea bargaining (C. Veneziano & L. Veneziano, 1987; Oliver, 1983).

A therapeutic jurisprudence scholar might ask whether attempting to deter those who offend against strangers with such long-term losses of liberty might induce those offenders to reduce predation of *strangers*, but then to focus their sexual attentions on younger *family* members. Another unfortunate result might be that some offenders would become more likely to kill their victims to decrease the chances of detection, apprehension, and identification as a sexual predator subject to indefinite civil commitment under the Washington law. Again, these are empirical questions which could be addressed by social scientists interested in the relationship between the law and human behavior.

We can see that sexual psychopath statutes can have a number of therapeutically-relevant consequences in areas beyond the statutes themselves. Applying the therapeutic jurisprudence approach helps to shed light on such matters and provides fertile ground for empirical inquiry.

*   *   *

Conclusion

This chapter was intended to introduce social scientists and legal and mental health professionals to a useful analytical tool which can be used to examine a variety of clinical and legal issues relating to sex offenders. If that objective has been achieved, social scientists will generate more research employing the law as an independent variable with potentially therapeutic or antitherapeutic consequences. Similarly, lawmakers, practicing attorneys and legal scholars will begin to consider the therapeutic implications of their policies, practices, and academic endeavors. Mental health professionals' practices might also be influenced to the extent that legal procedures affect psychological states of patients. As interdisciplinary interest in therapeutic jurisprudence continues to grow, researchers will provide themselves with a rich research agenda, mental health professionals might emphasize different issues in treatment, and legal professionals might begin to look to the social sciences as a source of valuable information when evaluating proposed or existing legislation, procedures, or practices.

References

Abel, G. G., Becker, J. V., Cunningham-Rathner, J. (1984). Complications, consent, and cognitions in sex between children and adults, International Journal of Law and Psychiatry, 7, 89–103.

Abel, G. G., Gore, D. K., Holland, C. L., Camp, N., Becker, J. V., & Rathner, J. (1989). The measurement of cognitive distortions of child molesters. Annals of Sex Research, 2, 135–152.

American Bar Association. (1989). ABA Criminal Justice Mental Health Standards. Washington, D.C.: Author.

Arizona Revised Statutes § 28-694 (Supp.1994).

Brakel, S., Parry, J., & Weiner, B. (1985). The mentally disabled and the law (3rd ed.). Chicago: American Bar Foundation.

Brooks, A. D. (1992). The constitutionality and morality of civilly committing violent sexual predators. University of Puget Sound Law Review, 15, 709–754.

Dix, G. E. (1976). Differential processing of abnormal sex offenders: Utilization of California's mentally disordered sex offender program. Journal of Criminal Law & Criminology, 67, 233–243.

Forst, M. L. (1978). Civil commitment and social control. Lexington, Mass.: Lexington Books.

Fujimoto, B. K. (1992). Sexual violence, sanity, and safety: Constitutional parameters for involuntary civil commitment of sex offenders. University of Puget Sound Law Review, 15, 879–911.

Furby, L., Weinrott, M. R., & Blackshaw, L. (1989). Sex offender recidivism: A review. Psychological Bulletin, 105, 3–30.

Grossman, L. S. (1985). Research directions in the evaluation and treatment of sex offenders: An analysis. Behavioral Sciences & the Law, 3, 421–440.

Group for the Advancement of Psychiatry. (1977). Psychiatry and sex psychopath legislation: The 30s to the 80s. New York: Author.

Gudjonsson, G. H. (1990). Cognitive distortions and blame attribution among paedophiles. Sexual & Marital Therapy, 5, 183–185.

In Re Young, 857 P.2d 989 (Wash.1993).

Klotz, J. A., Wexler, D. B., Sales, B. D., & Becker, J.V. (1992). Cognitive restructuring through law: A therapeutic jurisprudence approach to sex offenders and the plea process. University of Puget Sound Law Review, 15, 579–595.

Konecni, V., Mulcahy, E., & Ebbesen, E. (1980). Prison or mental hospital: Factors affecting the processing of persons suspected of being "mentally disordered sex offenders." In P.D. Lipsett & B.D. Sales (Eds.), New directions in psycholegal research (pp.87–124). New York: Van Nostrand Reinhold.

LaFond, J. Q. (1992a). Washington's sexually violent predator law: A deliberate misuse of the therapeutic state for social control. University of Puget Sound Law Review, 15, 655–708.

LaFond, J. Q. (1992b). Washington's sexually violent predators statute: Law or lottery? A response to Professor Brooks. University of Puget Sound Law Review, 15, 755–779.

Lockhart, L. L., Saunders, B. E., & Cleveland, P. (1988). Adult male sex offenders: An overview of treatment techniques. Journal of Social Work and Human Sexuality, 7(2), 1–32.

Marshall, W. L., & Pithers. W. D. (1994). A reconsideration of treatment outcome with sex offenders. Criminal Justice and Behavior, 21, 10–27.

Miller, R. D., Stava, L. J., & Miller, R. K. (1988). The insanity defense for sex offenders: Jury decisions after repeal of Wisconsin's sex crimes laws. Hospital & Community Psychiatry, 39, 186–189.

Monahan, J., & Davis, S, (1983). Mentally disordered sex offenders. In J. Monahan and H. Steadman (Eds.), Mentally disordered sex offenders: Perspectives from law and social science (pp.191–204). New York: Plenum Press.

Office of the Washington State Attorney General (Dec. 18, 1990). Sexually Violent Predator Filing Standards, Final Draft.

Oliver, A. D. (1983). The mentally disordered sex offender: Facts and fictions. The American Journal of Forensic Psychiatry, 3, 87–99.

Pacht, A. R., & Cowden, J. E. (1974). An exploratory study of five-hundred sex offenders. Criminal Justice and Behavior, 1, 13–20.

Perkins, D. (1991). Clinical work with sex offenders in secure settings. In C. R. Hollin & K. Howells (Eds.), Clinical approaches to sex offenders and their victims (pp. 151 ff.). New York: Wiley.

Petrila, J. (1993). Paternalism and the unrealized promise of "Essays in Therapeutic Jurisprudence" [Review of Essays in therapeutic jurisprudence]. New York Law School Journal of Human Rights, 10, 877–905.

Pollock, N. L., & Hashmall, J. M., (1991). The excuses of child molesters. Behavioral Sciences & the Law, 9, 53–59.

Predators and politics: A symposium on Washington's sexually violent predators statute (1992). University of Puget Sound Law Review 15(3).

Reardon, J. D. (1992). Sexual predators: Mental illness or abnormality? A psychiatrist's perspective. University of Puget Sound Law Review, 15, 849–853.

Sales, B. D. (1983). The legal regulation of psychology: Professional and scientific interactions. In C. J. Scheirer & B. L. Hammonds (Eds.), The master lecture series, volume II: Psychology and the law (pp. 9–35). Washington, D.C.: American Psychological Association.

Scheingold, S., Olson, T., & Pershing, J. (1992). The politics of sexual psychopathy: Washington state's sexual predator legislation. University of Puget Sound Law Review, 15, 809–820.

Schopp, R. F. (1993). Therapeutic jurisprudence and conflicts among values in mental health law. Behavioral Sciences & the Law, 11, 31–45.

Small, M. A. (1992). The legal context of mentally disordered sex offender (MDSO) treatment programs. Criminal Justice and Behavior, 19, 127–142.

Steadman, H., Monahan, J., Harstone, E., Davis, S. K., & Robbins, P. C., (1982). Mentally disordered offenders: A national survey of patients and facilities. Law and Human Behavior, 6, 31–38.

Sturgeon, V. H., & Taylor, J. (1980). Report of a five-year follow-up study of mentally disordered sex offenders released from Atascadero State Hospital in 1973. Criminal Justice Journal, 4, 31–63.

Sullivan, P. (1976). Commitment of sexual psychopaths and the requirements of procedural due process. Fordham Law Review, 44, 923–949.

Tweten, J. (1991) [speaker]. Circle of Fear (PBS television broadcast, November 12, 1991)

Veneziano C., & Veneziano, L. (1987). The legal trends in the disposition of sex crimes: Implications for theory, research, and policy. The Journal of Psychiatry & Law, Summer, 205–227.

Walsh, A. (1990). Twice labeled: The effect of psychiatric labeling on the sentencing of sex offenders. Social Problems, 37, 375–389.

Washington Revised Code §§ 71.09.010–.902 (1992 & Supp. 1995).

Washington Revised Code § 71.09.020(1) (1992 & Supp. 1995).

Washington Revised Code § 71.09.030 (1992 & Supp. 1995).

Washington Revised Code § 71.09.060 (1992).

Washington Revised Code § 71.09.090 (1992 & Supp. 1995).

Wettstein, R. M. (1992). A psychiatric perspective on Washington's sexually violent predators statute. University of Puget Sound Law Review, 15, 597–633.

Wexler, D. B. (1990). Thereapeutic jurisprudence. Durham, NC: Carolina Academic Press.

Wexler, D. B. (1992a). Justice, mental health, and therapeutic jurisprudence. Cleveland State Law Review, 40, 517–526.

Wexler, D. B. (1992b). Putting mental health into mental health law: Therapeutic jurisprudence. Law and Human Behavior, 16, 27–38.

Wexler, D. B. (1993a). New directions in therapeutic jurisprudence: Breaking the bounds of conventional mental health law scholarship. New York Law School Journal of Human Rights, 10, 759–776.

Wexler, D. B., (1993b). Therapeutic jurisprudence and changing conceptions of legal scholarship. Behavioral Sciences & the Law, 11, 17–29.

Wexler, D. B. (1995). Reflections on the scope of therapeutic jurisprudence. Psychology, Public Policy, and Law, 1, 220–236.

Wexler, D. B., & Winick, B. J. (1991a). Essays in therapeutic jurisprudence. Durham, NC: Carolina Academic Press.

Wexler, D. B., & Winick, B. J. (1991b). Therapeutic jurisprudence as a new approach to mental health law policy analysis and research. University of Miami Law Review, 45, 979–1004.

Wexler, D. B., & Winick, B. J. (1993). Patients, professionals, and the path of therapeutic jurisprudence: A response to Petrila. New York Law School Journal of Human Rights, 10, 907–914.

Chapter 7

Some Therapeutic Jurisprudence Implications of the Outpatient Civil Commitment of Pregnant Substance Abusers

David B. Wexler

[This selection comments on a proposal, not reproduced here, by Professor Deborah Mathieu, advocating the outpatient civil commitment of pregnant drug abusers.]

In crafting her compromise proposal advocating the outpatient civil commitment of pregnant substance abusers, Deborah Mathieu (1995) makes use of the therapeutic jurisprudence perspective (Wexler, 1994; see also Wexler and Winick, 1991). She especially notes how treatment compliance can be enhanced if one makes a "public" commitment to comply, and how rehabilitation can be furthered if one acknowledges, rather than denies, behavioral wrongdoing (see Wexler, 1993).

Other commentators will no doubt react to several aspects of Mathieu's important and controversial proposal. I will confine my remarks to some of the therapeutic jurisprudence implications of her suggested reform.

Therapeutic jurisprudence, as Mathieu notes, looks at the law itself as a potential therapist or therapeutic agent, and asks us to examine the therapeutic and antitherapeutic consequences of legal rules, legal procedures, and of the roles of legal actors. By looking at the law in this way, therapeutic jurisprudence typically generates a rich set of empirical and normative questions (Perlin, 1993; Slobogin, 1995; Wexler, 1995). The important issue of how the legal system should respond to pregnant substance abusers is a highly appropriate topic for a therapeutic jurisprudence inquiry, and no such inquiry has yet been conducted.

Mathieu is correct in noting that certain psychological principles relating to health care compliance can probably be employed in a legal context to facilitate the treatment adherence of pregnant substance abusers:

> The psychological principles suggest that when one signs a behavioral contract, one is more likely to comply than if one does not make such an agreement. Also, one who makes a "public" commitment to comply—a commitment to persons above and beyond the medical provider—is more likely to comply than one who does not make such public commitment. Further, if family members are involved and aware of a patient's agreement, the patient is more likely to comply with the conditions than if family members are uninvolved in the process (Wexler, 1994:260).

Moreover, Mathieu is on solid ground in asserting that many law-violators deny or minimize their wrongdoing, and is likely correct in asserting that "requiring a pregnant substance abuser to formally acknowledge the harm she is causing to her future child and to avow publicly to cease the harmful activity may indeed go a long way in helping her to do so—especially if regular therapeutic support is available" (1995:204).

The problem, as I see it, is that Mathieu's legal scheme does not fit neatly with these psychological principles. As I understand Mathieu's proposal, a pregnant substance abuser could, after a due process hearing, be civilly committed to a community-based outpatient program. Full-fledged commitment to a residential drug treatment program would be occasioned only upon the respondent's failure to participate—or presumably to participate adequately—in the community-based outpatient program.

But if a respondent is, after a judicial hearing, ordered to participate in a community program, where does behavioral contracting between the respondent and the government occur? What induces the respondent to "acknowledge the harm she is causing to her future child"? What motivates her "to avow publicly to cease the harmful activity"?

The psychological principles invoked by Mathieu fit better into a legal format that allows a court, in its discretion, to impose either an outpatient or an inpatient disposition. In such a legal context, a respondent, seeking to avoid an inpatient disposition, might acknowledge her drug abuse problem and might, with her lawyer, affirmatively propose an outpatient arrangement acceptable to her. She might eagerly embody the proposed or agreed-to treatment terms and conditions in a behavioral contract, might have agreed-upon family members present at the judicial hearing called to consider the outpatient treatment plan, and could, at the hearing, be asked to make the desired public commitment to comply (Wexler, 1993).

I in no way suggest that Mathieu, to exploit these psychological principles, modify her purely outpatient commitment proposal to one that would permit either an outpatient or an inpatient disposition. Therapeutic jurisprudence calls upon us to be sensitive to the therapeutic consequences of legal arrangements, but it in no way suggests that therapeutic considerations should trump other considerations—such as those relating to justice (Schopp, 1993). And Mathieu has taken pains to argue, on justice grounds, against the confinement (penal or civil) of pregnant drug abusers, at least as an initial disposition.

Interestingly, even therapeutic considerations alone might not call for a commitment scheme that would authorize inpatient as well as outpatient treatment. Defending her purely outpatient commitment proposal, Mathieu notes that "using the coercive force of the state to back the policy puts pregnant substance abusers on notice that society abhors the harm they cause," and she argues that "this may lead some women to seek help voluntarily who otherwise would not" (1995:205).

While Mathieu may be correct about that empirical assertion, it is important to recognize that the more encompassing and intrusive a coercive scheme is, the more it may dissuade some treatment candidates from voluntarily seeking treatment. Thus, "even if coerced treatment benefits those on whom it is imposed, other prospective patients, it is argued, may be deterred from seeking treatment voluntarily for fear that they, too, will be committed" (Monahan et al., 1995:249; see also Campbell and Schraiber, 1989). A civil commitment law that authorized not only outpatient commitment but also the possible residential confinement of pregnant drug abusers might, therefore, operate to frighten some pregnant drug abusing women away from seeking treatment for drug problems or even from seeking advice on prenatal care.

Although it is of course ultimately an empirical question, it may well be that Mathieu's "compromise" proposal of outpatient commitment will satisfy justice concerns and, at the same time, strike an appropriate therapeutic balance of giving pregnant substance abusers, in her terms, "a push in the right direction" without being so onerous as to discourage an appreciable number of women from voluntarily availing themselves of needed services.[1] Moreover, Mathieu's proposal, if ultimately accepted, could be implemented in a manner sensitive to considerations of therapeutic jurisprudence (Wexler, 1995).

In that regard, Mathieu's insistence on due process guarantees is likely to promote therapeutic as well as justice objectives. Behavioral scientists have recently emphasized the therapeutic significance of according patients "voice" in legal and administrative proceedings (Tyler, 1992; Susman, 1994). Finally, recent preliminary empirical work on perceived coercion and on the process of mental hospital admission could bear heavily on the implementation of Mathieu's law reform measure:

> Patients believe that they should be included as much as they wish to be in the process of determining whether they will be admitted to the hospital. They believe that those involved in the admission process should be motivated by an appropriate degree of concern for their well-being, and they evaluate the legitimacy of involved persons' actions in light of the motivations they attribute to them. Finally, patients believe that others should act toward them in good faith. The others should be personally or professionally qualified to participate in the admission process, should act without deceit, and should treat the patient with equality and respect.
>
> When the admission process violates these moral norms—when the patient is excluded from participation in the decision about whether he or she should be hospitalized, when the actions of others appear to be selfishly motivated, or when others lack the personal or professional qualifications to intervene, or lie to or disrespect the patient—coercion may be more likely to be perceived, and resented. When these moral norms are adhered to, many apparently coercive acts seem to be accepted by the patient as morally legitimate (Bennett et al., 1993:304).

Mathieu has provided some interesting food for thought for those interested in politics, law, medicine, criminology, and psychology. I hope the therapeutic jurisprudence perspective can enrich—as well as it will surely be enriched by—the overall discussion.

---

1. A key component in striking an appropriate balance may relate to whether the outpatient program demands abstinence or whether it merely involves counseling, education, and encouragement in the direction of abstinence. If abstinence is required, backed by the threat of residential confinement in the event of relapse or noncompliance, many women may be discouraged from voluntarily seeking treatment. Alternatively, the law might encourage pregnant addicts to seek services voluntarily at certain well-publicized "safe" treatment sites "where, by law, professionals may be relieved of the duty and even the right of instituting commitment proceedings" (Wexler, 1995:234).

References

Bennett, N.S., C.W. Lidz, J. Monahan, E. Mulvey, S.K. Hoge, L.H. Roth, and W. Gardner (1993)." Inclusion, Motivation, and Good Faith: The Morality of Coercion in Mental Hospital Admission." Behavioral Sciences and the Law 11:295–306.

Campbell, J. and R. Schraiber (1989). In Pursuit of Wellness: The Well-Being Project. Vol. 6. Sacramento: California Department of Mental Health.

Mathieu, D. (1995). "Mandating Treatment for Pregnant Substance Abusers: A Compromise." Politics and the Life Sciences 14:199–208.

Monahan, J., S.K. Hoge, C. Lidz, L.H. Roth, N. Bennett, W. Gardner, and E. Mulvey (1995). "Coercion and Commitment: Understanding Involuntary Mental Hospital Admission." International Journal of Law and Psychiatry 18:249–63.

Perlin, M.L. (1993). "What is Therapeutic Jurisprudence?" New York Law School Journal of Human Rights 10:623–36.

Schopp, R.F. (1993). "Therapeutic Jurisprudence and Conflicts Among Values in Mental Health Law." Behavioral Sciences and the Law 11:31–45.

Slobogin, C. (1995). "Therapeutic Jurisprudence: Five Dilemmas to Ponder." Psychology, Public Policy, and Law 1:193–219.

Susman, J. (1994). "Resolving Hospital Conflicts: A Study on Therapeutic Jurisprudence." Journal of Psychiatry and Law 22:107–33.

Tyler, T.R. (1992). "The Psychological Consequences of Judicial Procedures: Implications for Civil Commitment Hearings." Southern Methodist University Law Review 46:433–45.

Wexler, D.B. (1993). "Therapeutic Jurisprudence and the Criminal Courts." William and Mary Law Review 35:279–99.

Wexler, D.B. (1994). "An Orientation to Therapeutic Jurisprudence." New England Journal on Criminal and Civil Confinement 20:259–64.

Wexler, D.B. (1995). "Reflections on the Scope of Therapeutic Jurisprudence." Psychology, Public Policy, and Law 1:220–36.

Wexler, D.B. and B.J. Winick (1991). Essays in Therapeutic Jurisprudence: Durham, N.C.: Carolina Academic Press.

Chapter 8

Therapeutic Jurisprudence and Corrections: A Glimpse

Fred Cohen
Joel A. Dvoskin

* * *

Custodial Suicide: An Exercise in Therapeutic Jurisprudence

We concede what the reader will recognize; it is something of a stretch from our initial grappling with the meaning of therapeutic jurisprudence and its implications to looking at corrections through the eyes of therapeutic jurisprudence to the present topic: custodial suicide. This no-frills section represents our effort to more specifically apply therapeutic jurisprudence analysis to a concrete, emotionally charged subject within corrections.

We are amateurs at this and, in effect, are displaying our early notes albeit with a bit of polish. Thus, we approach therapeutic jurisprudence and custodial suicide without a clear blueprint and with some uncertainty. We did learn that the manipulation of legal doctrine needs to be joined with our earlier "on the ground" approach and we do give that a run.

When a captive takes his or her own life—and this happens about 400 times a year in jails and at least 100 times a year in prisons[67]—what are the legal issues involved surrounding liability? And where might a therapeutic jurisprudence perspective be of some value? Clearly, no rational person will view such a suicide as therapeutic, particularly since so many are accomplished while the victim is under the influence of some drug and experiencing the initial terror of confinement.

In a recent article, Cohen summarized the applicable federal case law as follows:

> 1. Custodians—whether they be police at a lockup, sheriffs at a jail or correctional officials at a prison—are not insurers of the life and safety of those in

---

67. See Bureau of Justice, *supra* note 38, at 669 (134 suicides in state and federal correctional facilities in 1990). However, the National Center on Institutions and Alternatives (NCIA) conducted a survey which determined the number of jail suicides in 1985 and 1986 to be 453 and 401 respectively. Lindsay M. Hayes, *National Study of Jail Suicides: Seven Years Later,* 60 Psychiatric Q. 7, 15 (1989).

their charge. While there clearly are constitutional duties to preserve life and to provide medical or mental health care, these duties will not translate into some guarantee of safety, health, or the continuity of life.

2. The standard for liability in the federal courts is deliberate (sometimes referred to as reckless) indifference which, at a minimum, means culpability beyond mere negligence. The defendants must be shown either to have had knowledge of a particular vulnerability to suicide or be required to have known; this knowledge must create a strong likelihood, as opposed to the possibility, of suicide; and this "strong likelihood" must be so obvious that a lay person would easily recognize the need for some preventive action. Parenthetically, the courts seem to be unaware of the fact that they are borrowing the "obvious to a layman" phrase from prison and jail mental health cases which state that a mental illness or medical need is serious if it would be obvious to a lay person that treatment was needed. A custodial suicide *per se* is *not* conclusive proof of deliberate indifference. If it were then custodians would in fact be required to provide suicide-proof institutions.

3. The general right of detainees to receive basic medical or mental health care does *not* place upon jail officials the responsibility to screen every detainee for suicidal tendencies. A high percentage of detainees arrive at a lockup or jail under the influence of alcohol or some other drug and judicial decisions now hold that being "under the influence" *alone* does not enhance the custodian's duty to screen or to take extraordinary suicide preventive measures.[68]

The issue of special relevance to therapeutic jurisprudence we wish to explore relates to the requirement that one "knew or should have known" of the risk and the suggestion that where there is no legally imposed duty to develop suicide-relevant information, the federal courts place a premium on ignorance. This plainly discourages the wider adoption and use of reasonably easy to use and accurate suicide screening and assessment instruments and even encourages the manipulation of records to avoid use of the term "suicide risk."

In *Cruzan v. Director, Missouri Dep't of Health*,[69] the Supreme Court reaffirmed the right of a competent, unconfined person to refuse forced administration of life saving interventions.[70] The Court accepted the power of the state to impose procedural hurdles in safeguarding decisions by incompetents as to the continuity of life.[71] When a person is in custody, these issues are quite different. The custodian has an unequivocal duty to preserve life which clearly extends to preventing suicides.[72] Thus, while the general, preventive duty is clear, it is the scope and implementation of the duty which raise problems.

Absent a present, credible threat to commit suicide or actual knowledge that the individual has in fact attempted suicide, the federal courts are extremely

---

68. Fred Cohen, Liability for Custodial Suicide: The Information Base Requirements, Jail Suicide Update, Summer 1992 at 1, 2 (footnotes omitted).

69. 497 U.S. 261 (1990).

70. Id. at 278.

71. Id. at 280–81.

72. See Martinez v. Turner, 977 F.2d 421, 423 (8th Cir. 1992) (permitting the force feeding of inmate when life or health is in danger). But see Thor v. Superior Court, 855 P.2d 375 (Cal. 1993) (denying a doctor's petition to surgically implant feeding and medication tubes into a mentally competent quadriplegic prisoner who refused life-sustaining treatment).

reluctant to impose liability. In *Edwards v. Gilbert*,[73] the court stated flatly, "[i]n the absence of a previous threat or an earlier attempt at suicide, we know of no federal court in the nation or any other court within this circuit that has concluded that official conduct in failing to prevent a suicide constitutes deliberate indifference."[74]

For our purposes we may put aside the many questions related to the appropriate measures to be taken when there is reason to take seriously a suicide threat; measures ranging from close to intensive observation, special cell placement, removal of items of clothing which may be used to cause death, avoidance of single-celling, and the like. The anterior question is when should (or must) those precautions be taken? We certainly would not argue that such precautions are necessary for every detainee or for every inmate. If all captives were ordered to be placed under close, illuminated observation, twenty-four hours a day, *and if those orders were effectively carried out*, then presumably custodial suicides could be eliminated. This blunderbuss approach would sacrifice the already minimal claims to freedom and privacy enjoyed by captives, and doubtlessly would create a needless array of severe management and personnel allocation problems. Thus, a plainly desirable—even therapeutic—outcome is outweighed by the considerable loss associated with the means required.

The issue, then, lies somewhere between all and none; between taking all captives' privacy and dignity and attempting to locate and reasonably protect the "at risk" population.

The goal of preserving the life of captives seems to be so clearly a dominant value as to need no debate.[75] To reiterate, the general duty of custodians to preserve life is clear; the trick is to determine the trigger for, and the dimensions of, that duty.[76] More particularly, should it include a duty to develop suicide relevant information, a duty to share such information, and a further training-type duty to know how to interpret certain behavior or signs as creating a suicide threat? We would answer yes to all three questions and assert further that use of therapeutic jurisprudence analysis dictates that answer.

Therapeutic jurisprudence analysis, with its emphasis on outcomes, cannot entirely eschew doctrinal analysis. In the case of custodial suicide, where the fatal act is carried out by the victim, one must think through the basic components of culpable omissions. Thus, before we take on each of these questions, we will display our doctrinal note pad on omissions.

With the legal duty defined here as preventive, liability analysis always will involve the question of a culpable omission. Since a section 1983 claim[77]—either to treatment or safety—requires that the defendant act, or fail to act, with

---

73. 867 F.2d 1271 (11th Cir. 1989).

74. Id. at 1275 (footnote omitted).

75. See, e.g., Simmons v. City of Philadelphia, 947 F.2d 1042, 1067–68 (3d Cir. 1991) (holding that a municipality has a constitutional duty to provide persons in custody some quantum of care and protection).

76. E.g., McLauglin v. Sullivan, 461 A.2d 123, 125 (N.H. 1983). See Fred Cohen & Joel Dvoskin, Inmates With Mental Disorders: A Guide to Law and Practice, 16 Mental & Physical Disability L. Rep. 339, 345 n.12 (1992).

77. 42 U.S.C. § 1983 (1988).

deliberate indifference,[78] we must somehow fit these omissions into the domain of deliberate indifference.

An omission is defined by a specific act or acts which if done would have satisfied the actor's obligation.[79] Failure to obtain relevant information will not by itself impose liability, except perhaps as a violation of local law requiring this activity.[80]

Our concern is not with employer-employee consequences. Rather, it is with the failure to seek information which, if obtained, would likely have alerted the custodian and would be causally related to a preventable suicide. If legal causation is an important policy question, as an assignment of blame, then given the custodian's relationship in time and space to the captive, given the general duty of care and *de facto* dependance by the captive on the custodian, doctrinal manipulation on the causation issue is relatively easy.[81]

We expand duty to encompass enlarged notions of liability. Enlarged notions of liability may create inducements to prevent the tragedy of custodial suicide.

We have not read about a fellow captive being sued or criminally charged with failure to prevent a suicide or to interrupt one in process. The issue here is not only the likelihood of a captive being judgment proof; it is probably because we never thought about it and, more importantly, because suicide prevention is the legal obligation of the custodian and only the moral obligation of the fellow captive.

It is not difficult to establish that it is negligence for a jailor to fail to check a jail's easily obtainable master files for evidence of prior suicide attempts, for an earlier shift with knowledge of suicide threats to overlook sharing this information with the incoming shift, or for an arresting officer to fail to inform the booking officers of his knowledge of the arrestee's suicide attempts. However, to establish section 1983 liability, the trick is to characterize such omissions as deliberate indifference.[82]

Deliberate indifference is the constitutionally mandated mental element for liability in prisoner health care litigation as well as a "duty to protect." *Estelle v. Gamble* established this culpability requirement, although a search of all Supreme Court decisions reveals no prior reference to deliberate indifference or to any close variation of the phrase.[83] Given the novelty of the phrase one

---

78. *Estelle,* 429 U.S. at 106 ("[P]risoner must allege acts or omissions sufficiently harmful to evidence deliberate indifference."); *Simmons,* 947 F.2d at 1064 (requiring a § 1983 claimant to show "policymakers" deliberately chose or acquiesced to long standing policy of inaction).

79. See, e.g., Model Penal Code § 2.01(3)(b) (1985) (stating the liability for the commission of an offense may not be based on an omission unaccompanied by action unless a duty to perform the omitted act is otherwise imposed by law).

80. E.g., N.Y. Penal Law § 15.10 (McKinney 1987).

81. Cf. Bishop v. Stoneman, 508 F.2d 1224, 1226 (2d Cir. 1974) (holding that a series of incidents that are closely related in time may disclose a pattern of conduct amounting to deliberate indifference by prison officials). See generally Charles M. Holt, Sheriff's Liability for Prisoner Suicide: Hemly v. Bebber, 64 N.C. L. Rev. 1520 (1986) (analyzing the criteria reviewed when determining custodial liability for prisoner suicides).

82. See generally City of Canton v. Harris, 489 U.S. 378 (1989) (discussing level of inadequate training needed to establish municipal liability for failure to train police).

83. Search of Westlaw S.Ct. and S.Ct. Old databases (Nov. 11, 1993).

might have expected some effort at definition. Instead, the *Estelle* decision labored only to explain what deliberate indifference was not.

> [A]n inadvertent failure to provide adequate medical care cannot be said to constitute "an unnecessary and wanton infliction of pain" or to be "repugnant to the conscience of mankind." Thus, a complaint that a physician has been negligent in diagnosing or treating a medical condition does not state a valid claim of medical mistreatment under the Eighth Amendment. Medical malpractice does not become a constitutional violation merely because the victim is a prisoner.[84]

The avoidance of needless pain or death is at the core of deliberate indifference and the necessary bridge to the harm requirement.

One of the most intriguing discussions of deliberate indifference, which culminates in the most defense-oriented definitions, is by Judge Richard Posner in *Duckworth v. Franzen.*[85] After marking off negligence, recklessness, and deliberateness as the three traditional mental elements to be consulted in order to determine deliberate indifference, Judge Posner states:

> If the word "punishment" in cases of prisoner mistreatment is to retain a link with normal usage, the infliction of suffering on prisoners can be found to violate the Eighth Amendment only if that infliction is either deliberate, or reckless in the criminal law sense. Gross negligence is not enough. Unlike criminal recklessness it does not import danger so great that knowledge of the danger can be inferred; and we remind that the "indifference" to the prisoner's welfare must be "deliberate" implying such knowledge.[86]

More recent decisions from the Seventh Circuit support the *Duckworth* formulation and, indeed, actually may increase the burden for plaintiffs. For example, in *Salazar v. City of Chicago*[87] the court reiterated the "reckless in a criminal sense" formulation emphasizing the need for "'complete indifference to risk—when the actor does not care whether the other person lives or dies, despite knowing there is a significant risk of death.'"[88]

In *Langley v. Coughlin,*[89] a prison mental health case, the federal magistrate took a bit more expansive view of deliberate indifference, stating:

> [A]n isolated and inadvertent error in treating even a serious medical need would not constitute a violation since the Eighth Amendment does not constitutionalize the law of medical malpractice. On the other hand, a serious failure to provide needed medical attention when the defendants are fully aware of that need could well constitute deliberate indifference, even if they did not act with a punitive intent.
>
> ...[W]hile one isolated failure to treat, without more, is ordinarily not actionable, it may in fact rise to the level of a constitutional violation if the surrounding circumstances suggest a degree of deliberateness, rather than inadvertence, in the failure to render meaningful treatment. Moreover, the inference of

---

84. Estelle v. Gamble, 429 U.S. at 105–06.
85. 780 F.2d 645 (7th Cir. 1985).
86. Id. at 652–53 (citations omitted).
87. 940 F.2d 233 (7th Cir. 1991).
88. Id. at 238 (quoting Archie v. City of Racine, 847 F.2d 1211, 1219 (7th Cir. 1988)).
89. 715 F. Supp. 522 (S.D.N.Y. 1989).

such indifference may be based upon proof of a series of individual failures by the prison to provide adequate medical care even if each such failure—viewed in isolation—might amount only to simple negligence.[90]

"Two key points may be discerned from the above excerpt. First, deliberate indifference may be shown by a series of negligent acts or omissions which then may cumulate to become a constitutional violation. No single act or omission need attain deliberate indifference...."[91]

Where a jail has experienced a number of suicides (as in the Upper Darby, PA cases[92] and the recently reported forty-seven Mississippi jail suicides[93]) then clearly there is notice that a problem exists. Whether that problem is a failure to screen, failure to take minimal precautions, or even design failure is not clear.

This, of course, is not the same type of notice as that provided by a captive's shouts of wanting to die. But it is plain enough to construct at least the duty to screen for suicide risk. When the general screening produces a history of mental hospitalization or prior suicide attempts, a custodian should have the duty to go further, discover more facts through a detailed history, and perhaps institute precautions. Beyond the individual scream and a history of successful custodial suicides, there is data that allows construction of an "at risk" profile.

The best data on jail suicides comes from the Nation Center on Institutions and Alternatives (NCIA) located in Alexandria, VA. NCIA's 1986 study replicated a study it conducted seven years earlier[94] and the key indicators were virtually the same: fifty percent of jail suicides are completed within the first twenty-four hours of confinement; twenty-seven percent in the first three hours.[95]

Two of every three victims were in isolation and ninety-four percent died by hanging.[96] Ninety percent were detainees and sixty percent were intoxicated when confined.[97] In police holding facilities, sixty-four percent died within three hours of confinement.[98] In jails, eighty-nine percent of the victims were not screened for suicidal behavior, while in lock-ups, ninety-seven percent were not.[99] The average age of a suicide victim is thirty and the detention is almost always for a non-violent crime.[100]

---

90. Id. at 536 (citations and footnotes omitted).

91. Cohen & Dvoskin, supra note 76, at 343.

92. Colburn v. Upper Darby, 838 F.2d 663, 672 (3d Cir. 1988) (reversing dismissal of complaint because allegation that local officials inadequately monitored jails stated sufficient cause of action where three suicides occurred in police custody in three years), cert. denied, 489 U.S. 1065 (1989).

93. Michael Isikoff, Reno Orders Probe of Hangings in Mississippi Jails, Wash. Post, Apr. 15, 1993, at A3.

94. See Hayes, supra note 67, at 7.

95. Id. at 20.

96. Id. at 20, 19.

97. Id. at 12, 19.

98. Id. at 20.

99. See Hayes, supra note 67, at 21.

100. Id. at 18. Space does not permit a more complete summary of NCIA's data. However, there are some interesting anomalies: black inmates account for 41% of jail population,

The data scream at us: the relatively young, intoxicated or drugged, isolated, white, non-violent inmate in the initial hours of confinement commits suicide by hanging. He hasn't been screened and, obviously, has not been watched closely enough.

A more recent, albeit small scale, study argues that there may indeed be more than one suicide profile.

> Thus, in all likelihood, there is not one profile but rather a variety of suicide profiles. One is probably composed of first-time arrestees who are intoxicated at the time of arrest, who are overwhelmed by the stress of the jail environment, and who attempt shortly after incarceration. Recently, several studies have been published which indicate a much higher prevalence of panic disorders and attacks in the general population, as well as indicate a link between panic attacks and suicide attempts. Given the stress of the jail environment, this may have specific application to this particular subgroup, whose existence is well documented in the two NCIA studies.
>
> An additional profile encompasses the inmate who is vulnerable to any changes in his support system and who attempts suicide. Another is the inmate arrested for more serious charges and who attempts after several months, usually in relation to a court date. Undoubtedly others will also be identified. While other studies have postulated or identified these groups, the present study has accumulated further evidence to support their existence and added insight into an important variable—the presence of significant mental disorders and a chronic history of both suicide attempts and mental illness which make these two groups more vulnerable and at risk.[101]

This data does suggest that the risk—and the profile—changes somewhat as time in confinement is extended. For the earliest stages of confinement the remedy is plain and inexpensive: intake screening and suicide prevention training of officers.

Every set of standards and accreditation procedures of which we are aware calls for policy and procedure mandating screening and subsequent evaluation when indicated.[102] Some thirty-six states have adopted jail standards but "most states lack even the basic criteria for suicide prevention."[103] Only eight states' jail standards specify suicidal behavior inquiry on their intake screening.[104]

The presence or absence of standards does not correlate with constitutional mandates. With the results so tragic, with the number of deaths sufficiently high and with prevention so easy and inexpensive, the case for deliberate indifference when there is no screening/evaluation seems clear. However, when the federal

---

but only 16% of all suicides. Id. at 13, 18. Most victims are single and the hours between midnight and 3 a.m. are the most dangerous. Id. at 18, 19.

101. Larry D. LeBrun, Characteristics of Male Suicide Attempts in the Sacramento County Jail, 1985–87, Jail Suicide Update, Fall 1989 at 1, 3.

102. See, e.g., National Standards of Jail Suicide Prevention, Jail Suicide Update, Summer 1989 at 1, 1 (discussing the need for standard of suicide prevention in jails).

103. State Standards and Suicide Prevention: A Report Card, Jail Suicide Update, Summer 1989 at 4, 4.

104. Id.

courts require actual knowledge of risk there is a powerful disincentive to acquire relevant, preventive information.

Most civil suicide cases are settled but, of course, that still expends public money and personal tragedy remains, including the trauma often experienced by staff.[105] Despite the stereotype of correctional officers as unfeeling or cynical, it has been our consistent experience that "successful" suicides in correctional settings have a devastating emotional effect on the staff involved.[106] In part, this may be due to the incident review, investigation, and possible sanctions for failing to perform their duty to keep each inmate alive. But to an equal or greater extent, one hears about feelings of guilt ("he died on my watch; I was supposed to be there"), loss, sadness, and even anger that sound eerily similar to what surviving family members express in similar situations.

Conclusion

Finally, one's diagnosis on the cause of suicide will dictate the nature of the legal obligation. However, in the earliest stages of custodial obligation— certainly the first forty-eight hours—the initial obligation is preventive and if the initial crisis passes and the episode seems situational and not linked with mental illness, that may be the end of the obligation. If the diagnosis is that the suicidal captive is seriously mentally ill then, along with a preventive obligation, there is a treatment obligation. The longer the confinement the more likely the preventive obligation will merge into the treatment obligation.

We have walked the halls of many prisons and jails and one of us bears heavy oversight responsibility for captives whose suicide potential is a constant concern. Thus, this exercise is, in fact, one that flows from the library as well as the real world walk we earlier recommended.

Custodial suicide initially seemed like a good candidate for a therapeutic jurisprudence exercise because we were bedeviled by the federal courts' narrow and seemingly insensitive approach to the deliberate indifference standards for section 1983 liability. The "know or should have known" part of the equation has been resolved essentially in favor of an actual knowledge requirement whereas a more generous view of "should have known" would have expanded liability potential but also likely stimulated ameliorative measures.

Plainly, if the reduction of custodial suicides is a therapeutic end to pursue, to the extent that the federal courts are seen as the focus for this objective— and, of course, that is open to reasonable debate—then "should have known" must be pried open and new content poured in. This new content must discourage willful or reckless ignorance and encourage reasonable efforts to identify and then react to the at-risk captive population.

---

105. Cf. Lewis L. Laska, Medical Malpractice Cases Not to File, 20 Mem. St. U. L. Rev. 27, 59 (1989) (verdict in suicide/medical malpractice case is rare).

106. See Paul J. Heald, Retroactivity, Capital Sentencing, and the Jurisdictional Contours of Habeas Corpus, 42 Ala. L. Rev. 1273, 1331 (1991) (discussing the stress of being a correctional officer as a mitigating factor in death penalty cases).

Chapter 9

Therapeutic Jurisprudence and the Criminal Courts

David B. Wexler

I. Introduction

Speaking recently at the Teaching Conference on Criminal Law and Criminal Procedure sponsored by the Association of American Law Schools, Professor George Fletcher was of the opinion that the behavioral sciences unfortunately seem to offer little to the criminal law:

> [T]he elite schools in the east are still dominated by two schools of criminal law that I would call Dead School #1 [emphasizing the Model Penal Code] and Dead School #2.... Dead School #2 is most clearly reflected at Yale, and that is the school of social science and the criminal law, and I think my attitude toward Dead School #2 is one more of regret than of sarcasm. I wish it were the case that the social sciences had something to offer us in the study of criminal law, but frankly I haven't seen anything come out in this school for a long time...[M]aybe some of you will...[know of] an important article that's been published suggesting, clarifying, social science, psychoanalytic, or sociological perspectives on the criminal law. I have not seen anything in a long time, and yet the old insights of times gone by still prevail in significant quarters of the field.[1]

This Essay, however, will show how the therapeutic jurisprudence perspective may enable the criminal law to profit from some of the insights that the behavioral sciences provide.

* * *

---

1. Professor George Fletcher, A Critical Appraisal of Criminal Law and Procedure, Address at the Teaching Conference on Criminal Law and Criminal Procedure sponsored by the Association of American Law Schools (May 16–21, 1987) (audiotape available from Audio Archives International, Inc., Falls Church, Virginia). My thanks to Michael Perlin for calling my attention to these remarks. See Michael L. Perlin & Deborah A. Dorfman, The Invisible Renaissance of Mental Disability Law Scholarship: A Case Study of Subordination (unpublished manuscript, on file with the author).

Of course, the approach will likely comport better with the criminal law if re-habilitation, though certainly not a legitimate reason for incarceration,[4] is at least regarded without hostility.[5]

* * *

Cross-pollination with criminal law and procedure is especially appropri-ate because many mental health law scholars are themselves "crossovers" from the criminal law and procedure field.[10] Indeed, mental health law largely grew from the work of advocates and scholars who emphasized the massive deprivation of liberty inherent in civil commitment and argued that constitu-tional criminal procedure protections ought to be extended to the mental health system.[11]

One apparent reason for the development of therapeutic jurisprudence is that, with the crumbling of its constitutional criminal procedure foundation, mental health law is hungry for new approaches.[12] The same can be said, a fortiori, of criminal law and procedure.

Therapeutic jurisprudence promises criminal law much more than merely a new twist on the topics that overlap between mental health law and criminal law—incompetence to stand trial and the insanity defense. To be sure, thera-peutic jurisprudence has something to say about these and related issues, but the purpose of this Essay is to show the less obvious potential influence of therapeutic jurisprudence.

Substantively, this Essay will stray from core mental health law issues in order to indicate the potential reach of therapeutic jurisprudence in the crimi-nal law area. Moreover, instead of focusing on more obvious and traditional types of law, legal scholarship, and law reform—matters such as codes, cases, and constitutional precedents—this Essay will focus on the role of the judge. The focus will demonstrate precisely how broad the conception of law is to therapeutic jurisprudence.[14]

This Essay will use as illustrations work that has been performed in thera-peutic jurisprudence in two relevant areas: (1) sex offenders and the plea process, and (2) the conditional release process and the psychology of com-pliance.

---

4. Norval Morris, The Future of Imprisonment 13–20 (1974).

5. Id.; see also Gilles Renaud, R. v. Fuller: Time to Brush Aside the Rule Prohibiting Therapeutic Remands?, 35 Crim.L.Q. 91 (1992) (discussing Canadian and British Common-wealth law regarding the appropriateness of pre-sentence remand to craft individualized sen-tences). On the value of rehabilitation in the penal system, see Francis T. Cullen & Karen E. Gilbert, Reaffirming Rehabilitation (1982); Ted Palmer, The Re-Emergence of Correctional Intervention (1992); Edgardo Rotman, Beyond Punishment: A New View on the Rehabilita-tion of Criminal Offenders (1990).

10. David B. Wexler, Putting Mental Health into Mental Health Law: Therapeutic Ju-risprudence, 16 Law & Hum.Behav. 27, 28 n. 4 (1992).

11. Id. at 28–29.

12. Daniel W. Shuman, Overview, 46 SMU L.Rev. 323 (1992) (introducing a symposium on changes in mental disability law scholarship).

14. See David B. Wexler, Therapeutic Jurisprudence and Changing Conceptions of Legal Scholarship, 11 Behav. Sci. & L. 17 (1993).

II. Sex Offenders and the Plea Process[15]

One of the most striking features of sex offenders, particularly child molesters, is their heavy "denial and minimization"[16] of their behavior. Clinicians have studied and classified these "cognitive distortions,"[17] which are evidenced by statements such as "nothing happened," "something happened but it wasn't my idea," or "something happened and it was my idea but it wasn't sexual."[18] Moreover, mental health professionals believe that "the key issues...of offender denial, motivation to change and cooperation in the process of treatment...are all aspects of the offender's functioning which are just as amenable to analysis and modification as the sex offending behavior itself."[19] In fact, manuals exist for the treatment of child molesters which cover such matters as "cognitive restructuring."[20] One approach to cognitive restructuring uses the technique of role-reversal: "the therapist role-plays being a child molester who uses the various...cognitive distortions, [and] the patients are asked to take the role of a probation officer, a policeman, a family member, or anyone who might interact with a child molester, and attempt to confront the beliefs role-played by the therapist."[21] The role-reversal process is used to lead the offenders to "rethink their own cognitions."[22]

A therapeutic jurisprudence approach to the sex offense area might ask whether the law, including the rules, procedures, and roles of lawyers and judges, operates therapeutically or antitherapeutically upon sex offenders. For example, does the law in this area promote cognitive restructuring? Or does it instead promote cognitive distortion, and thus perhaps contribute to psychological dysfunction and criminality? It may well be, as one British psychologist has observed, that "many aspects of the justice system are inadvertently geared towards fostering offender denial."[23] In that connection, the therapeutic jurisprudence approach applied to sex offenders produces the following suggestions.

Sex offenders usually are extremely unwilling to admit guilt, even when the state's evidence is impressive, and therefore, they often seek to plead "no contest," or nolo contendere.[24] A nolo plea permits the sex offender to accept the conse-

---

15. For a further discussion of therapeutic jurisprudence in this area, see Jeffrey A. Klotz, David B. Wexler, Bruce D. Sales, & Judith V. Becker, Cognitive Restructuring Through Law: A Therapeutic Jurisprudence Approach to Sex Offenders and the Plea Process, 15 U. Puget Sound L.Rev. 579 (1992).

16. Derek Perkins, Clinical Work with Sex Offenders in Secure Settings, in Clinical Approaches to Sex Offenders and Their Victims 151, 168 (Clive R. Hollin & Kevin Howells eds., 1991).

17. Nathan L. Pollock & Judith M. Hashmall, The Excuses of Child Molesters, 9 Behav.Sci. & L. 53, 54 (1991); see also Gene G. Abel et al., Complications, Consent, and Cognitions in Sex Between Children and Adults, 7 Int'l J.L. & Psychiatry 89 (1984).

18. Pollock & Hashmall, supra note 17, at 57.

19. Perkins, supra note 16, at 152.

20. Gene G. Abel et al., Treatment Manual for Child Molesters (unpublished manuscript, on file with the author).

21. Id.

22. Id.

23. Perkins, supra note 16, at 152.

24. See, e.g., In re Guilty Plea Cases, 235 N.W.2d 132, 147 (Mich.1975) (holding that a

quences of a conviction without going to trial and without admitting guilt.[25] Indeed, some offenders will seek to enter a so-called Alford plea which permits the defendant to plead guilty while at the same time protesting his innocence.[26]

Courts may and often do accept such pleas, although generally they have no obligation to do so.[27] The acceptance of *nolo* and *Alford* pleas from sex offenders, however, may reinforce cognitive distortions and denial. This frame of mind may lead the offenders to reject offers of treatment directed at decreasing their deviant sexual arousal and increasing their nondeviant sexual arousal and social/sexual skills.[28] Alternatively, the mindset may undermine the potential success of such treatment even if the offender is persuaded or required to participate in it.[29]

Moreover, judicial willingness to accept *nolo* and *Alford* pleas may make it easy, perhaps too easy, for defense attorneys to arrange plea bargains acceptable to their clients. If judges were reluctant to accept pleas in sex offender cases unaccompanied by an admission of guilt, defense lawyers would need to coax more actively those clients who lack plausible defenses to admit guilt and accept the bargain. Professor Alschuler's written remarks in a somewhat different context are relevant:

> It may often be a lawyer's duty to emphasize in harsh terms the force of the prosecution's evidence: "What about this fact? Is it going to go away? How the hell would you vote if you were a juror in your case?" It may sometimes be a lawyer's duty to say bluntly, "I cannot possibly beat this case. You are going to spend a long time in jail, and the only question is how long."[30]

Thus, if jurisdictions refused to recognize *nolo* and *Alford* pleas, or if judges were reluctant to accept them in sex offender cases, the law would induce defense lawyers to engage their clients in an exercise of "cognitive restructuring," including role-reversal. For example, the defense attorney may ask the sex offender how he would vote as a juror in the case. In therapeutic jurisprudence terms, the result would be a revised legal arrangement that would restructure the role of the defense lawyer in a way that would promote therapeutic values.

---

court which accepts a nolo plea must give justifying reasons and that the reluctance to admit a sordid crime, such as sexual assault on a child, appears to be such a reason), cert. denied, 429 U.S. 1108 (1977).

25. North Carolina v. Alford, 400 U.S. 25, 35 (1970).

26. Id. at 37–39; see Albert W. Alschuler, The Defense Attorney's Role in Plea Bargaining, 84 Yale L.J. 1179, 1280, 1286 n. 290 (1975) (discussing plea arrangements in sex offender cases); Curtis J. Shipley, Note, The Alford Plea: A Necessary but Unpredictable Tool for the Criminal Defendant, 72 Iowa L.Rev. 1063 (1987) (addressing the lack of uniformity in the acceptance of *Alford* pleas).

27. 400 U.S. at 38 n. 11. An occasional case suggests that trial courts ordinarily must accept such pleas. See United States v. Gaskins, 485 F.2d 1046 (D.C.Cir.1973).

28. Perkins, supra note 16, at 161–67 (discussing treatment techniques for sex offenders).

29. See infra note 45 and accompanying text.

30. Alschuler, supra note 26, at 1309.

The therapeutic potential of the role of the judge also could be enhanced in guilty plea cases if the court engaged in detailed questioning of the defendant about the factual basis of the plea.[31] Specifically, the judge could address, on the record, some of the matters typically subject to cognitive distortion by sex offenders. In his classic study of guilty pleas, Donald Newman describes one metropolitan court's procedure that may be particularly pertinent for our purposes: a post-plea-of-guilty hearing in which, "[a]fter receiving...a guilty plea from a defendant...the court requires the defendant to take the stand, under oath, and state that he did commit the crime and exactly how he committed it."[32] Judges could buttress the effect of pleas with full admissions of guilt by means of a judicial sentencing policy particularly unsympathetic to sex offenders who stand trial and offer a defense that the jury rejected and that the judge independently found perjurious.[33]

A plea procedure that encourages a sex offender to make a detailed admission of guilt should work, therefore, against denial and cognitive distortion and toward cognitive restructuring.[34] Moreover, should the offender vacillate

---

31. See H. Richard Uviller, Pleading Guilty: A Critique of Four Models, 41 Law & Contemp. Prob. 102, 121 (1977) (asserting that the form and extent of the inquiry is a matter left "largely to the discretion of the judge") (citation omitted). Pursuant to some select authority, judges already have an obligation to probe the factual basis of the plea. See, e.g., Fed.R.Crim.P. 11(f); Standards for Criminal Justice § 14-1.6 (Am. Bar Ass'n 1986). But see State v. Brooks, 586 P.2d 1270 (Ariz.1978) (upholding the guilty plea in a child molestation case despite the absence of an explicit statement by the defendant that the acts were motivated by an abnormal sexual interest in children).

32. Donald J. Newman, Conviction: The Determination of Guilt or Innocence Without Trial 19–20 (1966); see also Albert W. Alschuler, The Trial Judge's Role in Plea Bargaining, Part I, 76 Colum.L.Rev. 1059 (1976) (contending that the bargaining process can operate in a better manner when judges take an active part); Abraham S. Goldstein & Martin Marcus, The Myth of Judicial Supervision in Three "Inquisitorial" Systems: France, Italy and Germany, 87 Yale L.J. 240, 268–69 (1977) (stating that if the judge plays an active role in the plea process, the plea acceptance procedure might resemble the routine trial of uncontested cases in the Continental system).

33. See United States v. Dunnigan, 113 S.Ct. 1111 (1993) (upholding sentence enhancement under the "obstruction of justice" section of the U.S. Sentencing Guidelines because of the defendant's trial perjury); United States v. Grayson, 438 U.S. 41 (1978) (holding that it is proper for the court when imposing sentences to consider perjury committed during the defense of a criminal case); see also United States v. Saunders, 973 F.2d 1354 (7th Cir.1992) (finding that the federal sentencing guidelines sentence reduction for "acceptance of responsibility" does not unconstitutionally burden the right to trial), cert. denied, 113 S.Ct. 1026 (1993). For a therapeutic jurisprudence inquiry into the treatment of sex offenders under the Washington Sexually Violent Predator Statute, see Klotz et al., supra note 15, at 592–95; John Q. La Fond, Washington's Sexually Violent Predator Law: A Deliberate Misuse of the Therapeutic State for Social Control, 15 U. Puget Sound L.Rev. 655, 700 (1992).

34. See United States v. Miller, 910 F.2d 1321 (6th Cir.1990) (discouraging full acceptance of responsibility by increasing the sentence under U.S. Sentencing Guidelines for admitting other relevant conduct in an interview with a probation officer), cert. denied, 111 S.Ct. 980 (1991). But see United States v. Faulkner, 934 F.2d 190, 192–94 (9th Cir.1991) (holding that the court cannot increase the sentence by taking into account matters dismissed

and deny his guilt when in a correctional institution or community treatment program, an "adequate record with which to confront the person" may induce him again to accept responsibility,[35] and perhaps "to participate in institutional therapy programs"[36] or to participate more meaningfully in such programs.[37]

This new therapeutic jurisprudence approach to sex offenders and the plea process is, of course, merely suggestive. Ultimately, the question whether cognitive distortions are impacted by judicial behavior in accepting a guilty plea is an empirical one. If therapeutic jurisprudence has an influence on criminal law scholarship, part of that influence will be in encouraging empirical studies.[38]

Many of the matters seem readily testable. For instance, there are existing methods of measuring cognitive distortions of pedophiles.[39] Moreover, legal anthropologist Susan Philips of the University of Arizona has observed change of plea hearings and has concluded that judges do indeed have different styles of ascertaining the factual basis of a plea:

> Some judges described the events that led to the defendant being charged, or had either the prosecution or defense lawyer describe them, and then asked the defendant if he agreed with the description. Other judges tried to get the defendant himself to describe those events. The latter strategy...requires more involvement from the defendant and a more confessional mode of admission and met with more resistance from defendants.[40]

---

or uncharged pursuant to a plea agreement); In re D.M.B., 481 N.W.2d 905 (Neb.1992) (deciding that, in a parental rights termination case, the court cannot order a parent to comply with a rehabilitation plan that relates to sexual abuse therapy when the sexual abuse charge was dismissed upon the parent's admission of neglect).

35. Newman, supra note 32, at 222.

36. Id.

37. A final factor which may be relevant to "cognitive restructuring through law" relates to the type of plea bargain offered a sex offender. An offender might be charged with the actual crime the state believes he committed, and might receive a sentence concession for an "on-the-nose" plea to that charge. Uviller, supra note 31, at 109. Alternatively, he may be charged with the actual crime, but be allowed to plead to a reduced charge. Id. at 108; see also Newman, supra note 32, at 105–08, 119 (discussing lesser pleas in sex offender cases). "Charge" bargaining, rather than "sentence" bargaining, is particularly prevalent in jurisdictions in which mandatory sentencing has shifted discretion from the courts (in sentencing) to the prosecution (in charging). Albert W. Alschuler, Sentencing Reform and Prosecutorial Power: A Critique of Recent Proposals for "Fixed" and "Presumptive" Sentencing, 126 U.Pa.L.Rev. 550 (1978). An interesting and generally unasked question regarding the wisdom of alternative sentencing and bargaining schemes is whether "charge" bargaining feeds into cognitive distortion more so than does "sentence" bargaining.

38. Such studies are underway at the University of Arizona. See Klotz et al., supra note 15, at 580.

39. See id. at 581 nn. 7–9.

40. Susan U. Philips, Criminal Defendant's Resistance to Confession in the Guilty Plea 4, Paper Presented at Law and Society Association Meetings, Berkeley, California (May 31–June 3, 1990) (on file with the author). Because the law prescribes no precise formula for the factual basis inquiry even in jurisdictions where a factual basis must be found prior to entering judgment on a plea, that judges do not follow a uniform path in making the factual basis determination is no surprise. Compare Fed.R.Crim.P. 11(f) ("[T]he court should not enter a judgment upon such plea without making such inquiry as shall satisfy it that there is

Philips categorizes the judges as either "Procedure Oriented" or "Record Oriented."[41] The Procedure Oriented judges emphasize the personal involvement of the defendant, while the Record Oriented judges minimize that involvement and view their role as making a neat record invulnerable to collateral or appellate attack.[42] From wide-ranging interviews with the judges in her study, Philips concludes that the Procedure Oriented judges are politically liberal and the Record Oriented judges are politically conservative.[43] The irony is that, if the therapeutic jurisprudence speculation holds true upon empirical examination, the liberal judges may be performing a greater crime control function than their conservative counterparts.[44]

In any event, it would be feasible to undertake a post-plea study to determine whether defendants in sex cases who, presumably through a process of random assignment, appear and plead before Procedure Oriented judges retain fewer cognitive distortions than those who plead before Record Oriented judges. Alternatively, one might study the issue of cognitive distortion through a more indirect, policy-oriented approach. That is, one might investigate whether sex case defendants pleading before Procedure Oriented judges are more willing than the control group defendants to participate in therapy sessions which are later offered to them. If the results of such studies are promising, a further therapeutic jurisprudence undertaking could develop "model" colloquies for establishing the factual basis of pleas to various sex offenses and other offenses, and eventually subject those colloquies to empirical study.[45]

We know, especially from therapists' reports, that denial, minimization, and cognitive distortions are particularly pronounced among sex offenders and child molesters.[46] What we do not yet seem to know is whether sex offenders

---

a factual basis for the plea.") with Standards for Criminal Justice § 14-1.6(b) (Am. Bar Ass'n 1986) ("Generally, in determining the accuracy of a plea of guilty, the court may require the defendant to make a detailed statement in the defendant's own words concerning the commission of the offense to which the defendant is pleading.").

41. Philips, supra note 40.

42. Id.

43. Interview with Susan U. Philips, Professor of Anthropology, University of Arizona (Oct. 14, 1992) (discussing Professor Philips' research that will form the basis of a book, now in preparation, tentatively entitled Ideological Diversity in Courtroom Discourse: Due Process Judicial Discretion in the Guilty Plea).

44. The crime control function served by defendant admissions in the plea process officially was recognized when, on July 28, 1980, Attorney General Benjamin Civiletti released and published, for the first time in a single source, the U.S. Department of Justice Principles of Federal Prosecution. See James E. Bond, Plea Bargaining and Guilty Pleas app. D-1 (2d ed. 1983) (publishing excerpt relating to the role of the federal prosecutor in entering into plea agreements). In determining whether to enter into a plea agreement, the government attorney was cautioned to consider all relevant factors, including "the defendant's remorse or contrition and his willingness to assume responsibility for his conduct." Id. at app. D-4. The commentary to the standards notes that "[t]hese are factors that bear upon the likelihood of his repetition of the conduct involved." Id. at app. D-6.

45. See Mary Kay Wheeler, Comment, Guilty Plea Colloquies: Let the Record Show..., 45 Mont.L.Rev. 295 (1984) (arguing that some form of standard guilty plea colloquy should be adopted by the courts).

46. See Klotz et al., supra note 15, at 581 nn. 7 & 9.

are unique in their harboring of strong cognitive distortions, or whether other types of offenders—or perhaps offenders in general—are as prone to cognitive distortions.[47]

Reports exist from clinicians who treat sex offenders, but reports do not exist on the extent to which offenders such as carjackers cognitively distort, claiming that "I didn't do it," "I did it but it wasn't my idea," or "I did it, and it was my idea, but I was only kidding around." If rehabilitation reclaims a legitimate role in the criminal justice system, the potential role of the judge in cognitive restructuring for purposes of corrections and rehabilitation may become important well beyond the area of sex offenders.[48]

Several current issues in the general law of sentencing also may appear somewhat different if looked at through the therapeutic jurisprudence "lens." For example, would rehabilitation be advanced if sentencing courts, or sentencing guidelines, formulated sentences based upon such factors as a defendant's "acceptance of responsibility,"[49] or a defendant's "obstruction of justice" for committing perjury during his or her trial?[50] Would it be normatively appropriate to take such matters into account?[51]

----

47. See Bruce v. United States, 379 F.2d 113, 120 n. 19 (D.C.Cir.1967) (noting the tendency of criminal defendants "to deny or gloss over their involvement"); Gresham M. Sykes & David Matza, Techniques of Neutralization: A Theory of Delinquency, 22 Am.Soc.Rev. 664 (1957); Philips, supra note 40.

48. See supra notes 4–5 and accompanying text. In Montana v. Imlay, 113 S.Ct. 444 (1992), the United States Supreme Court granted certiorari in a child molestation case to consider whether the Fifth Amendment self-incrimination clause bars a state from conditioning probation on the probationer's successful completion of a therapy program in which the probationer would be required to admit having committed the crime. The Court, however, later dismissed certiorari as improvidently granted, apparently because the procedural posture of the case called upon it to render an advisory opinion. See also Murray Levine & Eric Doherty, The Fifth Amendment and Therapeutic Requirements to Admit Abuse, 18 Crim. Just. & Behav. 98 (1991).

If rehabilitative efforts, either during imprisonment or during probation, are undertaken seriously with other types of offenders and with persons with grave substance abuse problems, the Fifth Amendment problem posed in *Imlay* is likely to arise outside the current context of sex offense cases. The *Imlay* problem might be avoided in probation settings, however, if courts take the view that an offender's denial might properly be used in "determining whether a particular defendant is an appropriate candidate for probation in the first instance." Gilfillen v. State, 582 N.E.2d 821, 824 (Ind.1991); see also Self-Incrimination Rights Conflicts with Treatment, Home Release Programs, 4 Correctional L.Rep. 1 (1992) (discussing the Fifth Amendment issue in a broader correctional context).

49. United States v. Valencia, 957 F.2d 153 (5th Cir.1992) (holding that the court must be convinced the defendant has accepted responsibility in order to reduce the sentence on this basis).

50. See supra note 33 and accompanying text. For an interesting state court decision regarding the impropriety of classifying trial perjury as an aggravating circumstance, see State v. Houf, 841 P.2d 42 (Wash.1992).

51. The sentencing process raises many other normative and therapeutic issues. For discussion of the relationship among the defendant's actual behavior, the behavior with which the defendant has been charged, the defendant's acknowledgment of what occurred, and the sentence imposed, see Newman, supra note 32, at 222. See also United States v. Galloway, 976 F.2d 414 (8th Cir.), cert. denied, 113 S.Ct. 429 (1992); Michael H. Tonry, Real Offense

III. The Conditional Release Process and the Psychology of Compliance

The medical profession has long known that patients often fail to comply with prescribed treatment regimens.[52] Increasingly, the health care compliance problem has attracted the attention of psychologists interested in understanding, explaining, and improving patient compliance.[53] Meichenbaum and Turk present a set of principles designed to help the medical profession increase patient treatment adherence.[54]

Their book does not discuss the legal system at all. Nonetheless, the book served as the basis for a therapeutic jurisprudence exercise in how insanity acquittee conditional release hearings might be restructured—and how the judicial role in such hearings might be altered—to enhance the probability of medication and treatment adherence of insanity acquittees eventually granted conditional release.[55] In this section, the Essay will examine the principles Meichenbaum and Turk present and suggest how criminal courts may apply these principles in the context of probationary sentencing.

A. The Principles

One of the most important reasons for nonadherence is the failure of the health care professional ("HCP") to instruct the patient adequately about the treatment regimen.[56] Indeed, although physicians commonly seem not to acknowledge it, "the behavior of the HCP plays a critical role in the adherence process."[57] Nonadherence is promoted when the HCP is distant, looks and acts busy, reads case notes during the interview, uses jargon, asks patients questions calling for "yes or no" answers, cuts off the patient, does not permit patients to tell their stories in their own words, fails to state the exact treatment regimen or states it in unclear or technical terms, adopts a moralizing, high-powered stance, and terminates the interview abruptly.[58] HCPs are advised, by contrast, to introduce themselves, avoid unexplained jargon, and elicit patient suggestions and preferences.[59]

The patient's active involvement in negotiating and designing the treatment program is of tremendous importance to adherence and favorable outcome.[60]

Sentencing: The Model Sentencing and Corrections Act, 72 J.Crim.L. & Criminology 1550 (1981).

52. Donald Meichenbaum & Dennis C. Turk, Facilitating Treatment Adherence: A Practitioner's Guidebook 21–31 (1987).

53. Id.

54. Id. at 71–229.

55. See David B. Wexler, Health Care Compliance Principles and the Insanity Acquittee Conditional Release Process, 27 Crim.L.Bull. 18 (1991).

56. Meichenbaum & Turk, supra note 52, at 67; see also Wexler, supra note 55, at 24.

57. Meichenbaum & Turk, supra note 52, at 63 (emphasis omitted).

58. Id. at 78.

59. Id. at 81.

60. Id. at 81, 171.

Even giving a patient a choice over some of the more minor details can have salutary effects.[61] To promote patient adherence, the HCP should linguistically cast the treatment program in a manner that capitalizes on the patient's involvement and agreement.[62] For example, directive terminology such as, "[w]hat you are to do is...," should be replaced by a softer, more bilateral statement, such as, "[s]o what you have agreed to try is...."[63] Adherence will be nurtured further if the HCP has high prestige and is perceived to be competent, attentive, practical, and motivated by the best interests of the client.[64]

A particularly profitable avenue of HCP questioning relates to the patient's past compliance efforts: "What kinds of things in the past have you tried that were unsuccessful? How is what you have agreed to do now different?"[65] It is also profitable for the HCP to raise mild counterarguments about the patient's prospective compliance.[66] When the HCP indicates to the patient certain obstacles and drawbacks to compliance, the patient will have an opportunity to minimize and counter the HCP's arguments, thus "fostering the patient's sense of control, commitment, and degree of hope."[67] A patient presented with mild counterarguments to compliance who nonetheless announces to a prestigious HCP his intention to comply will be "anchored" to the compliance decision by anticipated disapproval from the HCP and by anticipated self-disapproval.[68]

Involving significant others, such as family members, in the treatment process is also likely to enhance patient adherence.[69] Family members aware of the treatment regimen can encourage, remind, and prod the patient, and can help the HCP assess patient compliance.[70] One suggested technique for involving significant others is for the HCP to bring in agreed-upon family members and to have the patient personally explain to them the nature of the illness and the proposed treatment.[71] When an HCP has a patient explain his or her medical problem and agreed-on course of treatment to family members, the active patient participation provides an opportunity to "assess her comprehension, to elicit a public commitment, and to strengthen her adherence-related attitudes."[72]

One reason the presence of significant others enhances patient compliance is that "[p]ublic commitment leads to greater adherence than does private commitment."[73] In addition to the motivational power of anticipated self-disapproval and the anticipated social disapproval of the HCP, a patient who has previously made a commitment to significant others will be anchored to com-

---

61. Id. at 171.
62. Id. at 79.
63. Id.
64. Id. at 172.
65. Id. at 175.
66. Id.
67. Id. at 176.
68. Id.
69. Id. at 124.
70. Id.
71. Id.
72. Id.
73. Id. at 174.

pliance by their anticipated disapproval as well.[74] Thus, "insofar as patients can be encouraged to inform one or more people (in addition to the HCP) of their intentions to follow the treatment regimen, there is an increased likelihood of adherence."[75]

When negotiating a course of treatment with a patient, HCPs can profit from the behavior modification literature regarding "behavioral contracting."[76] Such "behavioral" or "contingency" contracting "capitalizes on the patient-HCP relationship by actively involving the patient in the therapeutic decision-making process and by providing...incentives (rewards) for achievement of treatment objectives."[77]

The relevant literature seems to suggest that behavioral contracting works best when the contract is individually tailored to the particular needs and desires of a given patient,[78] when it defines the target behavior expected of the patient with specificity,[79] when it spells out the positive and aversive consequences that will attach, respectively, to compliance and to noncompliance,[80] and when it includes the "specific dates for contract initiation, termination, and renewal."[81]

B. The Application to Probation

In *Health Care Compliance Principles and the Insanity Acquittee Conditional Release Process*,[82] I suggested how the psychological principles discussed above might be incorporated into insanity acquittee conditional release hearings and how we might then conduct empirical research to see if those reforms actually work to increase patient compliance with court-ordered conditional release conditions, such as the taking of antipsychotic medication.[83] It is not at all difficult to transfer the principles to the criminal court setting, with the objective of increasing a probationer's compliance with the conditions of supervised release.[84]

In the criminal context, the relevant stages would be those culminating in a judicial proceeding at which a probationary sentence is to be imposed, whether following a trial or the acceptance of a plea agreement.[85] For example, such a hearing can actively involve the defendant in order to test the defendant's understanding of the conditions, to ensure that he or she agrees to

---

74. Toni M. Massaro, Shame, Culture, and American Criminal Law, 89 Mich.L.Rev. 1880 (1991).

75. Meichenbaum & Turk, supra note 52, at 174.

76. Id. at 164–73.

77. Id. at 164–65.

78. Id. at 168.

79. Id. at 174.

80. Id. at 168.

81. Id. at 170.

82. Wexler, supra note 55.

83. Id. at 19, 40–41.

84. Id. at 19.

85. Id. at 20–21.

them and, ideally, to allow the defendant some input into the design of the conditions.

The court can structure and shape the hearing so as to invoke a number of other important health care compliance principles. For example, the hearing could serve as a forum for the defendant to make a "public commitment" to comply with the probation conditions.[86] That way, the commitment would be made to a high-status judicial official and to any significant others, such as family members, whose presence at the hearing the court deemed appropriate.[87]

The hearing can also provide an excellent opportunity for the court to discuss with the defendant past unsuccessful compliance efforts and the extent to which the current plan differs from any earlier, unsuccessful ones.[88] The hearing is an ideal forum for presenting the patient with "mild counterarguments" to compliance, enabling the patient to counter those arguments and to accordingly become "anchored" to the compliance decision.[89]

As a result of matters aired at the hearing, a plan of probation resembling a behavioral contract may be approved by the court. When the agreement is approved finally, the court will have solicited the patient's commitment, perhaps both orally and in writing, and will have attended to the other important behavioral contracting principles, such as individual tailoring, specification of expected termination dates, specification of expected patient behavior and positive and aversive consequences.[90] A court is free to conceptualize and frame the conditional release as an agreement between the court and the defendant, rather than as an order.[91]

Indeed, because the court would shape and approve the release conditions, the court itself would function somewhat like an HCP, and the judge should, therefore, attend to the HCP behavioral factors thought to enhance patient adherence.[92] For example, the judge could introduce himself or herself to the defendant, be attentive, avoid using jargon, and allow the defendant to tell his or her story without undue interruption.[93]

By exploiting the psychological compliance principles, the judiciary would in essence transform the probationary process into one that is far more individually tailored to the defendant and into one that seeks the input of the would-be probationer far more than does the traditional system. Indeed, the employment of the psychological principles may also be suited to the use of the emerging "intermediate" sanctions, such as intensive probation supervision, community service, day reporting centers, and home confinement.[94] So

---

86. Id.
87. Id.
88. Id.
89. Id. at 32–33.
90. Id.
91. Id. at 34.
92. Id.
93. Id.
94. For a description and analysis of these and other "intermediate" sanctions, see Norval Morris & Michael Tonry, Between Prison and Probation: Intermediate Punishments in a Rational Sentencing System (1990); Smart Sentencing: The Emergence of Intermediate Sanctions (James M. Burne et al. eds., 1992).

long as the sentencing scheme permits "interchangeability," or "substitutability"[95] of intermediate sanctions, so that the sentencing judge may select among them, a judge inclined to use the psychological principles noted in this Essay could allow the defendant to have substantial input into the sanction selection process.[96]

Will judges be willing and able to bring these psychological principles into play in the criminal courtroom? Interestingly, psychologists Meichenbaum and Turk had similar concerns about whether HCPs would "adhere" to the recommendations set forth in their book.[97] The factors underlying HCP reluctance are likely to apply with equal force to judicial actors. HCPs are likely to voice the following reservations about using the recommended compliance principles: patients *should* take HCP advice or simply suffer the consequences of noncompliance;[98] the principles simply will not work with *their* particular patient populations;[99] the recommended procedures are too complicated and numerous;[100] there is simply no time in day-to-day practice to implement the procedures;[101] the system does not support frills like adherence counseling;[102] and, finally, HCPs cannot make use of the principles because most HCPs are not mental health professionals and, accordingly, have not been trained in psychological techniques of adherence.[103]

Meichenbaum and Turk provide powerful counterarguments to the anticipated HCP reluctance, and those counterarguments can likewise apply to anticipated judicial reluctance. Although the procedures may seem a bit complicated initially, they will soon require less attention[104] and will, in the long run, improve the quality of service.[105] At the early stages, one can use checklists as

---

95. On the issue of "interchangeability" or "substitutability" of intermediate sanctions, see the discussion and sources cited in Principled Sentencing 329–32 (Andrew von Hirsch & Andrew Ashworth eds., 1992).

96. This Essay focuses on the role of the criminal court. It should be noted, however, that the psychological principles discussed in the text could also be used by prosecutors in arranging for pretrial diversion. See id. at 396–99 (discussing the relationship between sentencing theory and prosecutorial processes). Whether at sentencing or as a pretrial exercise of prosecutorial discretion, it is possible to arrange matters so that the offender or defendant is given the opportunity to provide input into the process and the decision. The victim, too, may be brought into the process, perhaps for fairness or for therapeutic purposes. Id. at 399, 402. The psychological literature on "procedural justice," tying the litigants' perceptions of fairness and compliance with legal requirements to the "voice" and other input they are given in legal proceedings, plainly can relate to the therapeutic jurisprudence approach, both with respect to offenders and to victims. For a discussion blending the two perspectives, see Tom R. Tyler, The Psychological Consequences of Judicial Procedures: Implications for Civil Commitment Hearings, 46 SMU L.Rev. 433 (1992).

97. Meichenbaum & Turk, supra note 52, at 253–57.

98. Id. at 257.

99. Id.

100. Id.

101. Id.

102. Id.

103. Id.

104. Id. at 262.

105. Id. at 263–64.

memory prompts.[106] Finally, on the subject of clinical skill, "[n]o great amount of specialized training"[107] is required to use the recommended enhancement techniques.[108]

Judges *should* take an interest in compliance with their orders and in better serving society. Some surely will. Moreover, today's law students are exposed to interdisciplinary insights far more than were past generations of law students. When today's students ascend to the bench, they should feel fairly comfortable integrating behavioral science into the legal system.

IV. Conclusion

Just as the courts, at least those of tomorrow, may be persuaded to comply with the conditional release recommendations advanced above, the courts may also be convinced to conduct change of plea hearings and to otherwise behave in a manner likely to promote rehabilitation without frustrating the goals of the justice system.[109] Urging criminal courts to become more aware of the therapeutic and rehabilitative consequences of their behavior, however, may evoke criticisms of therapeutic jurisprudence, such as that made by Gary Melton, that "experience with the juvenile court has shown that judges make lousy social workers."[110] Actually, I agree with Melton that our experience with juvenile courts of the past has shown that judges make lousy social workers. Therapeutic jurisprudence, however, teaches that judges function as social workers regardless of whether they know it or like it. Either judges will be reluctant to accept no contest pleas from sex offenders or they will not be reluctant; either judges will engage guilt-pleading defendants in a detailed colloquy regarding the crime or they will not do so; either they will expect a would-be probationer to sign a behavioral contract and to make a public commitment to comply or they will not do these things. Because judges presumably are affecting therapeutic and rehabilitative consequences anyway, a therapeutic jurisprudence approach would suggest that, while they remain fully cognizant of their obligation to dispense justice according to principles of due process of law, judges should indeed try to become less lousy in their inescapable role as social worker.

---

106. Id. at 262.

107. Id. at 261.

108. Id.

109. Ted Rubin, Now to Make the Criminal Courts More Like the Juvenile Courts, 13 Santa Clara L.Rev. 104 (1972).

110. Gary B. Melton, The Law Is a Good Thing (Psychology Is, Too): Human Rights in Psychological Jurisprudence, 16 Law & Hum.Behav. 381, 386 (1992).

Chapter 10

Turning Rat and Doing Time for Uncharged, Dismissed, or Acquitted Crimes: Do the Federal Sentencing Guidelines Promote Respect for the Law?

Keri A. Gould

I. Introduction

The impetus for this article was a lunch I had with an attorney-friend who primarily represents indigent federal defendants. En route to the restaurant, my friend bitterly complained about the institutional injustices suffered by his clients, most of whom have been arrested on federal drug-related charges.[1] "In particular," he decried, "the government makes all of its cases by 'turning rats'[2]—by shaking down the small-time criminals[3] so that they inform on

---

1. Nationally, over ⅓ of the combined state and federal new inmates are drug offenders. Over 60% of those in federal prisons have been convicted of drug offenses. Jack B. Weinstein, The War On Drugs Is Self-Defeating, N.Y. Times, July 8, 1993 at A19. In 1981, drug defendants numbered about 7,500, comprising close to 18% of the federal criminal caseload. By 1990, federal drug offenders numbered more than 20,000 or about one third of the caseload. Nationally, more than 64% of the federal criminal caseload increase over the past decade is due to drug cases. Terrence Dunworth & Charles D. Weisselberg, Felony Cases and the Federal Courts: the Guidelines Experience, 66 S. Cal. L. Rev. 99, 124 (1992).

2. "Rats," "snitches," "stoolies," "finks," or persons who "turn" or "twist" are all terms which refer to informants. Popular imagery of such people is particularly negative. James W. Marquart & Julian B. Roebuck, Prison Guards and "Snitches", 25 British J. Crim. 217, 217 (1985); Evan Haglund, Note, Impeaching the Underworld Informant, 63 S. Cal. L. Rev. 1405, 1408–9 (1990) (a "twist" or immunized informant trades information for leniency on his charges).

3. Henry J. Reske, Senior Judge Declines Drug Cases, 79 A.B.A. J., 22, 22 (July 1993). Disproportionately severe sentences for low level drug offenders continue to sustain widespread judicial criticism. Deborah Young, Rethinking the Commission's Drug Guidelines: Courier Cases Where Quantity Overstates Culpability, 3 Fed. Sentencing Rep. 63 (1990). Most recently, Judge John S. Martin (S.D.N.Y.) has written, "sending street level dealers..to jail for ten years will have no impact on the drug problem in this country. It does, however, reflect poorly on our system of justice." U.S. v. Genao, 831 F. Supp. 246, 254 (S.D.N.Y. 1993). See Edward Adams, Federal Judge Scores Mandatory Sentences for Dealing Drugs, N.Y.L.J., Aug. 26, 1993, at A1. The use of lengthy imprisonment to dissipate the drug war was found to be inadequate at the state level as well. Assemblyman Daniel L. Feldman of

friends and family."[4] Having practiced in the New York State system, where "turning"[5] defendants is less common, I inquired about how federal prosecutors are able to turn rats with such ease and with such a high rate of success.[6] My friend replied that Assistant United States Attorneys are able to compel compliance from defendants because the United States Sentencing Guidelines permit departures from the applicable guideline sentencing ranges[7] or mandatory minimum sentences[8] only when the prosecutor makes a motion to decrease the sentence due to the defendant's substantial assistance in the investigation or prosecution of another person.[9]

Brooklyn, a past criminal justice chairman of the National Conference of State Legislators, believes that the problem with crime crackdown is that it focuses on the lower levels of the drug culture, packing the prisons with easy long-term convictions. Francis X. Clines, Prisons Run Out of Cells, Money and Choices, N.Y. Times, May 28, 1993, at B7.

4. The federal government has increasingly used the defendant's former cohorts, other criminals acting as informants, and even family members coerced into informing on relatives, as the source of such witness testimony. Steven S. Nemerson, Coercive Sentencing, 64 Minn. L. Rev. 669, 679 (1980).

5. "Turning" occurs when a defendant is turned into a witness for the prosecution, for which he or she generally receives a more favorable sentence. Selwyn Raab, The Care And Feeding of a Mafia Turncoat, N.Y.Times, Mar. 8, 1992, § 4, at 16.

6. Success is measured here by the number of convictions sustained on the basis of "rat" testimony. No information is available on the number of cases which result in convictions based upon "rat" testimony. However, such information is available with regard to the number of informants used by law enforcement agencies. In one year the FBI reported using 2,800 informants and in the previous year, paying nearly 1.5 million dollars to informants, resulting in 2,600 arrests. Haglund, supra note 2, at 1411.

7. To sentence a person convicted of a federal crime which does not carry a statutory minimum (or maximum), judges must use the essentially mathematical calculation delineated in the United States Sentencing Guidelines Manual. See infra, notes 59–71 and accompanying text. Judges may depart downward from the presumptive range pursuant to the guidelines of rendering substantial assistance to the government resulting in a fruitful investigation or conviction upon the motion of the prosecutor. 18 U.S.C.A. app. 4 § 5K1.1 (West Supp. 1993). See also Wade v. United States, 112 S.Ct. 1840, 1843–44 (1992) (courts may only review prosecutor's refusal to file a motion for downward departure based upon defendant's substantial assistance if refusal is based on an unconstitutional motive). In 1989, six percent of all federal cases involved a substantial assistance motion for downward departure. Ilene H. Nagel & Steven J. Schulhofer, A Tale of Three Cities: An Empirical Study of Charging and Bargaining Practices Under the Federal Sentencing Guidelines, 66 S. Cal. L. Rev. 501, 553 (1992).

8. There are a significant number of federal offenses which require statutory minimum periods of incarceration. Approximately 100 separate federal mandatory minimum provisions are currently codified. Only four of those statutes, relating to firearm and drug offenses, account for the majority of mandatory minimum sentences. Dunworth & Weisselberg, supra note 1, at 111. Judges may depart below the set minimum sentence pursuant to 18 U.S.C. § 3553(e) (1993), for rendering substantial assistance, which also requires a government motion.

9. See 18 U.S.C.A. app. 4 § 5K1.1 (West Supp. 1993) and 18 U.S.C. § 3553(e) (1988). "The guidelines provide only one way to avoid prison: the accused must 'cooperate' and furnish 'substantial assistance' to the government." John Lewis, Cooperation Under the Guidelines, N.Y.L.J., Apr. 30, 1993, at 2. However, this is not the only way to depart from the guideline minimum sentences. 18 U.S.C. § 3553(b) (1992) and 18 U.S.C.A. app. 4 § 5K2.0 (West Supp. 1993) allow judges to deviate in the "atypical case" where "mitigating circum-

"It is no secret," my friend went on, "that federal sentences are excessive and overly harsh, particularly in relation to drug cases,[10] which make up the large bulk of a Federal Criminal Justice Act[11] attorney's caseload. When faced with the prospect of extraordinarily long incarceration, many defendants see no other option than to do or say whatever it is which will spare them from greater prison time."[12]

---

stances exist which have not adequately been taken into consideration by the Sentencing Commission in formulating the guidelines that should result in a sentence different from that described." The district court must state the "specific reason" for such a departure. 18 U.S.C.A. § 3553(c)(2) (West Supp. 1993). Any such departure may be reviewed by an appellate court. 18 U.S.C. § 3742(f) (1993). An upward departure is subject to appeal from the defendant and a downward departure is subject to appeal from the prosecutor. Under 18 U.S.C.A. app. 4 § 5K2.0 (West Supp. 1993), the guidelines allow judges to depart downward based upon the victim's conduct, 18 U.S.C.A. app. 4 § 5K2.10 (West Supp. 1993); lesser harm, 18 U.S.C.A. app. 4 § 5K2.11 (West Supp. 1993); coercion and duress, 18 U.S.C.A. app. 4 § 5K2.12 (West Supp. 1993); or diminished capacity, 18 U.S.C.A. app. 4 § 5K2.13 (West Supp. 1993). For instance, diminished capacity may be cause for a downward departure where "the defendant committed a non-violent offense while suffering from significantly reduced mental capacity not resulting from voluntary use of drugs and other intoxicants." 18 U.S.C.A. app. 4 § 5K2.13 (West Supp. 1993).

In practice, district courts have infrequently departed from guideline ranges and such departures have frequently been overturned by the appellate courts. Cf. Williams v. United States, 112 S. Ct. 1112, 1120 (1992) (adopting a two-part departure analysis where the reviewing court must first determine if there was an incorrect application of the guidelines under 18 U.S.C. 3742(f) (1993) and second, if the resulting sentence is an unreasonably high or low departure from the relevant guideline range); United States v. Restrepo, 999 F.2d 640, 644 (2nd Cir. 1993) (alien status may warrant leniency in an extraordinary case, but impending deportation of defendant is not enough to trigger downward departure); United States v. Denardi, 892 F.2d 269 (3rd Cir. 1989) (defendant's cooperation with government, absence of prior criminal record, exemplary work history, lifetime of love and devotion to family and friends, and extreme hardship suffered by defendant's family as a result of sentence are not mitigating factors so as to allow departure from guideline range); United States v. Desormeaux, 952 F.2d 182, 185 (8th Cir. 1991) (district court's downward departure overturned despite defendant's history of abuse and resulting emotional trauma, positive post-arrest conduct, and victim's wrongful conduct). The extent to which courts have allowed the use of individual characteristics to depart under 18 U.S.C.A. app. 4 § 5K2.0 has varied. Karin Bornstein, *5K2.0 Departures for 5H Individual Characteristics: A Backdoor Out of the Federal Sentencing Guidelines*, 24 Col. Hum. Rts. L. Rev. 135, 146 (1992–93) (arguing that the variance reflects different judges' own preferences for different theories of punishment and that some judges have departed in order to further the goal of rehabilitation). Overall, in 1990, federal courts cumulatively departed 15.7% of the time and sentenced within the guidelines 83.4% of the time. These figures do not distinguish the basis upon which the departure was made. Id. at 160. However, the reasons most often listed for § 5K2.0 departures are substantial assistance, terms of plea bargain agreement, acceptance of responsibility, family ties, adequacy of decreased sentence to meet the purposes of sentencing, physical condition, age, maintaining the defendant's sentence on par with co-defendant's sentences, and rehabilitation. Id.

10. See Young, supra note 3, at 63.

11. 18 U.S.C.A. § 3006A (West Supp. 1993) (The CJA panel provides a plan for furnishing representation for any person financially unable to obtain adequate representation).

12. "The prosecutor now has so much discretion and power in charging and in recommending departures from the guidelines and even minimum sentences that very few defen-

"As if that wasn't bad enough," he went on, "during the sentencing phase of the trial, the judges can consider evidence of uncharged crimes, dismissed counts, and even charges for which the defendant has been acquitted."[13] "Think of it," he exclaimed, "even if your client was acquitted of a crime, or the charges were dismissed pursuant to plea negotiations, those alleged crimes can still legitimately impact your client's sentence."[14]

---

dants can withstand pressure to 'cooperate'." Jack B. Weinstein, A Trial Judge's Reflections on Departures From the Federal Sentencing Guidelines, 5 Fed. Sentencing Rep. 6, 7 (1992). Professor Alan Dershowitz believes that the Racketeer Influenced and Corrupt Organizations law (RICO) "almost forces cooperation because people who are threatened with the RICO statute have no choice but to cooperate... Once people become cooperators, they become cooperators with a vengeance. I've seen my clients try to make up stories." Mark Curriden, No Honor Among Thieves, A.B.A. J., June 1989, at 52, 56 (1989).

13. A person may be sentenced to prison on the basis of conduct of which a jury has acquitted him, or on the basis of charges that did not result in conviction. Daniel J. Freed, Federal Sentencing in Wake of Guidelines: Unacceptable Limits on the Discretion of Sentencers, 101 Yale L.J. 1681, 1714 (1992). The argument, of course, is that the uncharged, dismissed, or acquitted crimes are related conduct which should be taken into consideration to apply a "just" sentence. William W. Wilkens & John R. Steer, Relevant Conduct: The Cornerstone of the Federal Sentencing Guidelines, 41 S.C. L. Rev. 495, 514 (1990). A decision was made by the United States Sentencing Commission ("Commission") to use a hybrid "real offense" sentencing system rather than a "conviction based" system. 18 U.S.C.A. app. 4 § 1B1.2 (1993). See generally Stephen Breyer, The Federal Sentencing Guidelines and the Key Compromises Upon Which They Rest, 17 Hofstra L. Rev. 1 (1988) (discussing compromises made in order to use this system). A "real offense" system allows the judge to consider factual information about the crime which was not brought out in the trial as well as other allegations against the offender which have never been "acknowledged by the defendant nor proven in court beyond a reasonable doubt." Freed, supra at 1712. See also United States v. Rodriguez-Gonzalez, 899 F.2d 177, 181–82 (2d Cir. 1990) (double jeopardy and due process are not violated when defendant's sentence is enhanced on basis of conduct which resulted in an acquittal of those charges), cert. denied, 498 U.S. 844 (1990). Contrary to the federal system, the Minnesota guidelines reject real offense sentencing (as did every other sentencing commission convened in the United States) with the rationale that due process is offended when the government or court allows the use of unadjudicated crime information to enhance guideline sentences. Freed, supra at 1713 n.168.

14. 18 U.S.C.A. app. 4 § 1B1.3 (West Supp. 1993). The guidelines seek to punish offenders for "the actual conduct..engaged [in] regardless of the charges for which [the defendant] was indicted or convicted." United States v. Galloway, 943 F.2d 897, 900 (8th Cir. 1991). Under 18 U.S.C.A. app. 4 § 1B1.4 (West Supp. 1993), the court may consider "without limitation, any information concerning background, character and conduct of the defendant, unless otherwise prohibited by law." See 18 U.S.C. § 3661 (1992) (distinguishing between factors that determine the applicable guideline sentencing range and information a court may consider in imposing sentence within that range). The court may take into consideration uncharged, dismissed, or acquitted crimes. United States v. Wood, 924 F.2d 399 (1st Cir. 1991) (allowing evidence of uncharged drug transactions, which allegedly took place months before, to be admitted in setting base offense level). One survey indicated that in half of all cases uncharged conduct increases the offender's sentence. Gerald W. Heaney, The Reality in Guideline Sentencing, 28 Am. Crim. L. Rev. 161, 209 (1991). Additionally, under 18 U.S.C.A. app. 4 § 6A1.3 (West Supp. 1993), the sentencing judge may consider hearsay evidence of defendant's criminal history and activities if such evidence bears sufficient indicia of reliability to support its probable accuracy. See United States v. Marshall, 519 F. Supp. 751

My friend believes that the system is fundamentally unfair, and is supported and promoted by legislative rules and prosecutorial procedures which oppose fundamental values established in our society.[15] He finds it reprehensible that clients are forced to make impossible decisions between inordinately long periods of incarceration or "ratting" and placing themselves and their families at risk.[16]

My friend, a seasoned defense attorney, feels so ethically maligned by the system that he questions whether the federal sentencing guidelines, or the actions of those empowered under the guidelines, square with society's ideals of morality and fairness. It stands to reason that the same consternation is felt by federal defendants and inmates.[17] This pervasive sense of injustice is worrisome and emphasizes the need and importance of analyzing the guidelines through a therapeutic jurisprudence perspective.[18] In other words, essential to a policy-oriented assessment of whether the guidelines can and do fulfill their legislative goals is an investigation into the effects the guidelines have on those

---

(D.C. Wis. 1981), aff'd, 719 F.2d 887 (7th Cir. 1983); United States v. Fatico, 579 F.2d 707 (2d Cir. 1978). The Commission believes that the preponderance of the evidence standard is appropriate to resolve factual disputes. 18 U.S.C.A. app. 4 §6A1.3 (1993); Federal Sentencing Guidelines Manual 339 (West 1993) (commentary). The Ninth Circuit defines preponderance of the evidence in sentencing as "a sufficient weight of evidence to convince a reasonable person of the probable existence of the enhancing factor." United States v. Restrepo, 903 F.2d 648, 654–5 (9th Cir. 1989); reh'g granted, 912 F.2d 1568 (1990), withdrawn in part on other grounds, 946 F.2d 654 (1991). Judges also rely heavily upon the hearsay information contained in the presentence report when determining the applicable sentence range. Probation officers conduct in-depth investigations and write the reports. Fed. R. Crim. P. rule 32(C). See also United States v. Chaikin, 960 F.2d 171, 174 (D.C. Cir. 1992) (sentencing court may consider defendant's background and criminal history outside convicted counts and including charges in indictment dismissed by prosecutors). In addition, judges may consider evidence excluded from trial based upon Fourth Amendment violations when determining sentencing range. United States v. Lynch, 934 F.2d 1226 (11th Cir. 1991), cert. denied, 112 S.Ct. 885 (1992).

15. There is a long tradition of judicial leniency for informant testimony, but the Federal Sentencing Guidelines present the first time that the Supreme Court has sanctioned the codification of such behavior. See infra note 46 and accompanying text.

16. Jack B. Weinstein, The Informer: Hero or Villain?—Ethical and Legal Problems, N.Y.L.J., Nov. 8, 1992, at 1; Lewis, supra note 9, at 2 ("Cooperating is dangerous. Of the 13,000 people enrolled in the Federal Witness Protection Program, more than one half are at risk merely because they are related to actual witnesses.").

17. There is evidence that the basis of most inmate complaints is the manner in which they are treated. When inmates perceive that they are dealt with capriciously by the correctional administration or individual officers, psychological stress is created—even in the most humane of prisons. James Bonta & Paul Gendreau, Reexamining the Cruel and Unusual Punishment of Prison Life, 14 Law & Hum. Behav. 347, 361 (1990). One of the few studies of inmate perception of indeterminate sentencing found a disturbing theme wherein twenty percent of those interviewed (the majority of whom were serving time for serious crimes) believed that switching to a system of determinate sentencing would result in a "likely increase of violence both in and outside of prison." Calvin J. Larson & Bruce B. Berg, Inmates Perceptions of Determinate and Indeterminate Sentences, 7 Behavioral Sci. & L. 127, 132 (1989). For a definition of "indeterminate" sentencing, see infra note 111.

18. For a definition and discussion of therapeutic jurisprudence, see infra notes 22–47 and accompanying text.

accused and/or convicted of federal crimes.[19] This article begins such an inquiry by looking at particular guidelines provisions in relation to the specific goal of promoting respect for the law.

This article questions the practices of coercing defendants to "rat" in return for lesser sentences and using evidence of uncharged, dismissed or acquitted crimes to boost sentences. Specifically, this article questions whether these practices significantly contribute to the federal defendants' and inmates' perceptions of the system as immoral such that there is a measurable effect on trial behavior, correctional facility misbehavior, or on recidivism rates. In doing so, this article hopes to encourage behavioral scientists and members of the legal community to empirically study the following issues:

• Do federal defendants have the perception that the law does not support a commitment to "moral" norms?

• If so, which defendants are most likely to hold such beliefs and how, if at all, does this impact the federal criminal justice system?

• Do certain provisions of the Federal Sentencing Guidelines produce antitherapeutic effects on inmates? Should this have an effect on federal sentencing policy?

A discussion of these issues, examined with a therapeutic jurisprudence perspective, may enlighten us as to the faulty functioning of the federal criminal system and uncover issues to be investigated and resolved by interdisciplinary methodology.[20]

This article proceeds in the following manner: Part II discusses therapeutic jurisprudence and its application to criminology; Part III gives a brief history and structural synopsis of the Federal Sentencing Guidelines; Part IV details the sentencing departure provisions; Part V relates those provisions to the general goals of sentencing and one specific guideline goal—promoting respect for the law; Part VI details the demographics of the federal inmate population and illustrates the way sentencing departure provisions provoke perjurious testimony at trial, correctional institution management problems, and perhaps increased recidivism rates; Part VII concludes by suggesting that if an empirical study can link the occurrence of those behaviors with inmate reaction to cer-

---

19. Another aspect of this therapeutic jurisprudence perspective, although beyond the scope of this article, is the impact a defense attorney's frustration or ambivalence with adhering to certain criminal procedure provisions has on the system as a whole and on the individual client. How often, and in what manner are such frustrations communicated to clients and how do such explicit or implicit communications impact on the attorney-client relationship and case strategy? See Keri A. Gould, Therapeutic Jurisprudence and the Arraignment Process: The Defense Attorney's Dilemma—Whether to Request a Competency Examination, 16 Int. J. L. & Psychiatry (forthcoming 1994) (therapeutic jurisprudence analysis of the attorney-client relationship during the arraignment process with regard to requesting a competency examination).

20. "Many such questions require analysis by economists, scientists, law enforcement specialists, sociologists, ethnicists, religious leaders and others." Weinstein, supra note 1, at A19. A multitude of difficult questions are raised in the effort to devise a more effective drug strategy. See David B. Wexler, Therapeutic Jurisprudence and Changing Conceptions of Legal Scholarship, 11 Behavioral Sci. & L. 17 (1993).

tain guideline provisions, then the guidelines are not promoting respect for the law as mandated by the legislature.

II. *Therapeutic Jurisprudence*

Therapeutic jurisprudence is an interdisciplinary approach to formulating investigative quests aimed at resolving some of the most difficult social science issues confronted by modern lawmakers. The development of this scholarly approach followed a shift within legal writings toward expanding the boundaries of interdisciplinary research, thereby promoting policy arguments to resolve social dilemmas. This shift follows a new concept of law which recognizes that legislatures and administrators, as much as judges, are primary lawmakers.[21] In today's hands-on legal world, the analysis of a law's direct impact on a particular social problem or set of social problems is heralded over less efficient appellate case analysis.[22] A law is deemed successful if its results satisfactorily tackle the immediate social dilemma.[23] This new legal scholarship often offers recommendations or reformulated areas of inquiry which instruct legislatures and other administrative bodies on how to achieve such law reform.[24] This approach is particularly relevant when examining the federal policy on criminal justice sentencing. The federal sentencing policies were formulated by the legislature which in turn entrusted the United States Sentencing Commission to achieve its goals through the promulgation of the Federal Sentencing Guidelines.[25]

Therapeutic jurisprudence is the study of the role of the law as a therapeutic agent, exploring the extent to which substantive rules, legal procedures, and the roles of judges and lawyers produce therapeutic or antitherapeutic consequences.[26] It promotes an interdisciplinary approach to assessing policy

---

21. Wexler, supra note 20, at 18.

22. Id. at 19.

23. Id. at 18.

24. Id. at 19.

25. See generally 28 U.S.C. § 991 (1984) (establishing the United States Sentencing Commission and directing it to establish sentencing policies and practices). The courts have granted the Commission broad discretion in interpreting the validity of individual guidelines, Mistretta v. United States, 488 U.S. 361 (1989), policy statements, Williams v. United States, 112 S. Ct. 1112 (1992), and commentary, Stinson v. United States, 113 S. Ct. 1913 (1993).

26. See generally Therapeutic Jurisprudence: The Law as a Therapeutic Agent (David B. Wexler ed., 1990) [hereinafter Law as Agent]; Essays in Therapeutic Jurisprudence (David B. Wexler & Bruce J. Winick eds., 1991) [hereinafter Essays]; Wexler, supra note 20, at 17; David B. Wexler & Bruce J. Winick, Therapeutic Jurisprudence and Criminal Justice Mental Health Issues, 16 Mental & Physical Disability L. Rep. 225, 225 (1992) [hereinafter Wexler & Winick, Criminal Mental Health]; David B. Wexler & Bruce J. Winick, Therapeutic Jurisprudence as a New Approach to Mental Health Law Policy Analysis and Research, 45 U. Miami L. Rev. 979, 981 (1991) [hereinafter Wexler & Winick, New Approach]; Michael Perlin & Deborah A. Dorfman, Sanism, Social Science, and the Development of Mental Disability Law Jurisprudence, 11 Behavioral Sci. & L. 47 (1993).

considerations in legal practice where the prescriptive focus is on the therapeutic value of the process,[27] within the boundaries set by principles of justice.[28] However, such methodology does not suggest that clinical concerns predominate all others, nor does it presume to trump civil liberties.[29]

Therapeutic jurisprudence is primarily concerned with legal issues and proscribes deference to clinical expertise.[30] Overall, therapeutic jurisprudence assumes a hypothesis-generating role which typically calls for further multi-disciplinary research.[31]

Therapeutic jurisprudence was originally envisioned as an alternative to traditional constitutional doctrinal analysis of mental health law. Increasingly, however, there has been significant "spill-over" into other substantive fields

---

27. Healthcare professionals may define the term therapeutic in its prototypical manner, such that its use as an analytically descriptive term is disputed:

I am troubled by the use of the term therapeutic and I am concerned that the good intentions [of those advocating therapeutic jurisprudence research] may be thwarted. Let me explain why:

(1) The term therapeutic applies to an individual person usually. In that context it is easier (although it is still hard) to define what a therapeutic outcome should be. The use of the term as it applies to more than one person, such as with regard to the outcome of a criminal case where the impact of the process on the victim is as important as the impact on the defendant, becomes much more complicated. Almost all legal decisions are a balance of complex interests, and I don't know if we can denote that by using the term therapeutic.

(2) Even when dealing with the individual case, even in a clinical sense, it can be very difficult to decide what is therapeutic and what is not, and we [psychiatrists] go through a trial and error process trying to find that out. Wisely, the medical community has come to the notion of "above all, do no harm." This is a much modest mandate than saying we have to be therapeutic.

(3) Since we are all informed by our own training and philosophies, there is a danger that we inadvertently imbue those terms with our own meaning and I have heard therapeutic equated with civil liberties. It may be so in some cases that the greatest democracy may be the most therapeutic, but that is definitely not true in all cases. As lawyers you may be more prone to subscribe to that bias and then use the term therapeutic in a way which obviates or makes less clear where you are coming from.

Dr. Renata Wack, Kirby Forensic Psychiatric Center, Remarks at the Symposium on Therapeutic Jurisprudence: Restructuring Mental Disability Law, at The New York Law School (April 23, 1993) [hereinafter Remarks of Wack] (video tape on file with author). Legal doctrines from the therapeutic jurisprudence perspective sometimes constrain the manner in which the mental health system can pursue its therapeutic mission, but in other circumstances legal protection and the therapeutic mission of the mental health system converge. Robert F. Schopp, Therapeutic Jurisprudence and Conflicts Among Values in Mental Health Law, 11 Behavioral Sci. & L. 31, 31 (1993).

28. Wexler, supra note 20, at 17.

29. Id.; Wexler & Winick, New Approach, supra note 26, at 982.

30. Wexler & Winick, New Approach, supra note 26, at 983. See Remarks of Wack, supra note 27.

31. Wexler, supra note 20, at 21.

including tort law,[32] attorney-client relationships,[33] criminal law,[34] criminal procedure law,[35] and juvenile law.[36] This article seeks to apply the premises of therapeutic jurisprudence to generate empirical data so as to better understand the questions raised by the implementation of the Federal Sentencing Guidelines. Therapeutic jurisprudence can help to demystify the application of social science in law.[37] Thus, this article raises questions whether the effects of the perceived (or misperceived) injustices resulting from the downward departure provision for informants and the practice by which judges may consider uncharged, dismissed or acquitted crimes in determining presumptive sentence ranges, influence federal defendants and inmates in an antitherapeutic manner.

Despite voluminous materials on the public's normative judgment of appropriate federal sentencing,[38] prosecutorial reaction to the guidelines,[39] defense attorney opinion on the topic, and the federal judges' reactions,[40] empirical ev-

---

32. Daniel W. Shuman, Therapeutic Jurisprudence and Tort Law: A Limited Subjective Standard of Care, 46 SMU L. Rev. 409, 410 (1992); Robert F. Schopp, The Psychotherapist's Duty to Protect the Public: The Appropriate Standard and the Foundation in Legal Theory and Empirical Premises, 70 Neb. L. Rev. 327, 329 (1991); Robert F. Schopp & David B. Wexler, Shooting Yourself in the Foot with Due Care: Psychotherapists and Crystallized Standards of Tort Liability, 17 J. Psychiatry & L. 163, 164 (1989); Bruce Feldthusen, Sexual Battery as Therapeutic Jurisprudence, (Feb. 2, 1993) (unpublished manuscript, on file with author).

33. Gould, supra note 19 (applying tenets of therapeutic jurisprudence to the lawyering skill of counseling criminal clients during the arraignment process with regard to the request of a competency examination).

34. See David B. Wexler, Inducing Therapeutic Compliance Through the Criminal Law, 14 Law & Psychol. Rev. 43, 49–50 (1990); David B. Wexler, Insanity Issues After Hinckley: Time for a Change, 35 Contemp. Psychol. 1068 (1990).

35. Wexler & Winick, Criminal Mental Health, supra note 26, at 226; Jeffrey A. Klotz & David B. Wexler, et al., Cognitive Restructuring Through Law: A Therapeutic Jurisprudence Approach to Sex Offenders and the Plea Process, 15 U. Puget Sound L. Rev. 579, 581–83 (1992); David B. Wexler, Health Care Compliance Principles and the Insanity Acquitee Conditional Release Process, 27 Crim. L. Bull. 18, 29–34 (1991) [hereinafter Wexler, Healthcare Compliance].

36. Murray Levine, A Therapeutic Jurisprudence Analysis of Mandated Reporting of Child Maltreatment by Psychotherapists, 10 N.Y.L. Sch. J. Hum. Rts. 711 (1993) (this issue).

37. See Laurens Walker & John Monahan, Social Facts: Scientific Methodology as Legal Precedent, 76 Cal. L. Rev. 877, 879 (1988) (stating court's reliance upon social science research should have precedential value only to the extent that it determines whether the methodology used is a legally acceptable way to prove a claim. The particular application in a single research effort would not be accorded precedential force.); John Monahan & Laurens Walker, Judicial Use of Social Science Research, 15 Law & Hum. Behav. 571, 571 (1991) (increasingly courts have sought out research data on their own when the parties have not provided it).

38. Ilene H. Nagel, Structuring Sentencing Discretion: The New Federal Sentencing Guidelines, 80 J. Crim. L. & Criminology 883, 884 (1990).

39. The U.S. Attorney's Office in the Eastern District of New York has also acknowledged the excessive harshness of the required sentences for federal drug laws in certain circumstances. To get around the excessive sentences, charges against accused drug couriers of "mules" caught at Kennedy Airport are routinely "bumped down" to the next lowest level, a charge which does not carry a statutory minimum sentence. Daniel Wise, Procedure Allows Drug Couriers To Receive Lighter Sentences, N.Y.L.J., June 4, 1993, at 1.

40. In April 1993, Senior U.S. District Judge Jack Weinstein, of the Eastern District of New York, announced in a speech given at Benjamin N. Cardozo School of Law, that he was

idence on the effects of the guidelines as interpreted by criminal defendants and offenders is very limited.[41] This exemplifies the criminal justice system's condoned marginalization of criminal defendants. Unfortunately, because the courts and legislatures ignore or minimize "consumer" views and opinions on sentencing reform risks, they have "fail[ed] to obtain invaluable information from those in a position to offer unique and unanticipated insights."[42]

The disparate treatment of criminal defendants is also shown in Michael Perlin's work on sanism,[43] in which he describes the discriminatory, pretextual reasoning used by courts and the legal system against people with mental disabilities. Perlin persuasively argues that due to sanism, courts teleologically process social science information to ensure that the courts' preordained, pre-

---

taking his "name out of the wheel for drug cases" because "I simply cannot sentence another impoverished person whose destruction has no discernable effect on the drug trade." At this same time, Senior U.S. District Judge Whitman Knapp of the Southern District of New York announced that he would preside over drug trials, but would refer the cases to other judges for sentencing. Both judges made these declarations based upon their belief that the government's emphasis on long imprisonment without treatment, rehabilitation or prevention was a failure. Henry J. Reske, Senior Judge Declines Drug Cases, A.B.A. J., July 1993 at 22. Judge J. Lawrence Irving resigned from the federal bench because he believed that the sentencing guidelines and the increasing number of mandatory minimum sentences were too harsh and were "dehumanizing the sentencing process." Criticizing Sentencing Rules, U.S. Judge Resigns, N.Y. Times, Sept. 30, 1990 at 22.

State court judges have also joined in voicing dissatisfaction with excessive drug sentences which disproportionately affect low-level drug users. E.g., People v. Perez, 599 N.Y.S.2d 269, 270–71 (1993) (Carro, J., concurring) (defendant's sentence for drug offense modified downward in the interests of justice):

> In considering this sentencing issue I cannot help but question whether the hemorrhage of taxpayer funds used to warehouse thousands of low-level drug users and sellers for long periods of time in our dangerously overcrowded prisons, at a cost $35,000 per year per inmate in addition to the capital expenditure of $180,000 per prison cell, could not be more productively and humanely directed toward prevention, through education, and treatment of drug addiction. The increasingly unavoidable conclusion that with the passage of time is becoming more widely recognized and articulated by respected representatives of our criminal justice system, is that the primary method currently utilized to deal with the drug epidemic, essentially an effort to eliminate the availability of drugs on our streets, while increasing inordinately the length of prison terms for low-level drug offenders, has failed.

Id. (citations omitted).

41. One notable exception is Larson & Berg, supra note 17, at 132 (finding that more inmates in a Massachusetts maximum security prison were opposed to or undecided about, rather than in favor of, determinate sentencing. It is worth noting that at the time of the study Massachusetts had an indeterminate sentencing system, but that there was growing support for a bill seeking to implement a presumptive sentencing system which had been before the state legislature since 1884).

42. Larson & Berg, supra note 17, at 128.

43. Michael L. Perlin, On "Sanism", 46 SMU L. Rev. 373, 398–406 (1992) [hereinafter Perlin, Sanism]; Perlin & Dorfman, Sanism and Social Science, supra note 26, at 52–53; Michael L. Perlin, Competency, Deinstitutionalization and Homelessness: A Story of Marginalization, 28 Hous. L. Rev. 63, 92 (1991).

textual result occurs.[44] Similarly, I opine that certain provisions of the guidelines, promulgated by the Commission and upheld by the courts, serve to marginalize defendants and inmates, ignore differing perceptions of fairness in the law, dismiss the psychological trauma of "ratting," and, in opposition to an express goal of the guidelines, breed contempt rather than respect for the legal process.

Is this simply "old law" methodology which needs to be infused with "new law" scholarship? Certainly there have been traditional constitutional challenges to aspects of the Federal Sentencing Guidelines[45] as well as innovative theories advanced.[46] But perhaps, as in mental health law, it is time to use an interdisciplinary approach to promote law reform in this area.[47]

III. The Federal Sentencing Guidelines

Before considering the relationship between defendants or inmates most offended by the guideline provisions and the legislature's failure to attain its goal of promoting respect for the law, it is useful to briefly look at legislative history. The Sentencing Reform Act of 1984[48] was passed on October 12, 1984, to promote honesty in sentencing and reduce sentence disparity.[49] The most far-reaching provision of the 1984 Act provided for the creation of an independent commission in the judicial branch of the United States, known as the United States Sentencing Commission.[50] In October 1985, President Reagan appointed seven persons to serve as the first members of the Commission.[51] Congress entrusted the Commission with a mandate to promulgate binding "guidelines,"[52] general

---

44. Perlin, Sanism, supra note 43, at 400–04.

45. See Mistretta v. United States, 488 U.S. 361, 361 (1989) (finding the Federal Sentencing Guidelines to be constitutional); David A. Hoffman, The Federal Sentencing Guidelines and Confrontation Rights, 42 Duke L. J. 382, 384 (1992) (arguing that there will be additional constitutional challenges to the guidelines based upon confrontation issues); Mark V. Tushnet, The Sentencing Commission and Constitutional Theory: Bowls and Plateaus in Separation of Powers Theory, 66 S. Cal. L. Rev. 581, 581 (1992) (arguing there is no difference between the functional and formal approach to questions of separation of powers).

46. See, e.g., Susan N. Herman, The Tail That Wagged the Dog: Bifurcated Fact-Finding Under the Federal Sentencing Guidelines and the Limits of Due Process, 66 S. Cal. L. Rev. 289, 293 (1992) (arguing for trial-type procedural protections to determine offense-related facts to be used at sentencing).

47. "In the meantime, real people in the real world face the consequences of the 'mathematization' of the criminal justice process wherein judges, lawyers, the accused and the system itself are reduced to integers in a pseudo-objective attempt to make sense out of human frailty which by definition makes none." United States v. Boshell, 728 F. Supp. 632, 642 (E.D. Wash. 1990).

48. Pub. L. No. 98-473, 98 Stat. 1987 (1984), amended by 28 U.S.C. §§ 991–8 (1988).

49. Nagel, supra note 38, at 883 (author was the first Commissioner appointed to the Sentencing Commission); Breyer, supra note 13, at 4.

50. 28 U.S.C. § 991(a) (1993).

51. Nagel, supra note 38, at 884.

52. 28 U.S.C. § 944(a)(1) (1988). See Mistretta v. United States, 488 U.S. at 361, 391 (holding that the guidelines bind judges and courts in the exercise of their uncontested responsibility to pass sentence in criminal cases).

"policy statements,"[53] and commentary,[54] to be known collectively as the Federal Sentencing Guidelines. These guidelines are contained in the United States Sentencing Guidelines Manual ("Manual"),[55] and were meant to ensure a more just and effective sentencing system.[56] In addition to promulgating the guidelines, the Commission also was charged with developing a way to assess the effectiveness of the guidelines in meeting the Congressionally defined goals of sentencing.[57]

After several years of discussion, investigation and preliminary drafts, the controversial Federal Sentencing Guidelines became law in November 1987. The guidelines were greeted with an extraordinary amount of criticism[58] and a plethora of conflicting court decisions which resulted in the guidelines' patchwork implementation.[59] It was not until 1989, when the Supreme Court ruled

---

53. 28 U.S.C. § 944(a)(2) (1988). See Williams v. United States, 112 S. Ct. 1112, 1115 (1992) (holding policy statement to be an authoritative guide to the meaning of the applicable guideline).

54. The Sentencing Reform Act does not specifically authorize commentary, but the Act does refer to it: "the court shall consider only the sentencing guidelines, policy statements, and official commentary of the Sentencing Commission [when determining whether to depart from guideline range]." 18 U.S.C.A. § 3553(b) (West Supp. 1993). See Stinson v. United States, 113 S. Ct. 1913, 1915 (1993) (commentary which interprets or explains a guideline is authoritative unless it violates the Constitution or a federal statute, or is inconsistent with or is a plainly erroneous reading of that guideline).

55. Federal Sentencing Guidelines Manual 1 (West 1993).

56. See 28 U.S.C. § 991(b)(1)(B) (1988).

57. The purposes of the Commission are to:
(1) establish sentencing policies and practices for the Federal criminal justice system that—
(A) assure the meeting of the purposes of sentencing as set forth in section 3553(a)(2) of title 18, United States Code;
(B) provide certainty and fairness in meeting the purposes of sentencing, avoiding unwarranted sentencing disparities among defendants with similar records who have been found guilty of similar criminal conduct while maintaining sufficient flexibility to permit individualized sentences when warranted by mitigating or aggravating factors not taken into account in the establishment of general sentencing practices; and
(C) reflect, to the extent practicable, advancement in knowledge of human behavior as it relates to the criminal justice process; and
(2) *develop means of measuring the degree to which the sentencing, penal, and correctional practices are effective in meeting the purposes of sentencing* as set forth in sections 3553(a)(2) of Title 18, United States Code.
28 U.S.C. § 991(b)(1) (1988) (emphasis supplied).

58. Dunworth & Weisselberg, supra note 1, at 100–6; See Kenneth R. Feinberg, The Federal Guidelines and the Underlying Purposes of Sentencing, 3 Fed. Sentencing Rep. 326 (1990) (stating that any meaningful discussion of the purposes to be served by the sentence are lost in the application of the guidelines).

59. Theresa W. Karle & Thomas Sager, Are the Federal Sentencing Guidelines Meeting Congressional Goals?: An Empirical and Case Law Analysis, 40 Emory L. J. 393, 402 (1991); Nagel, supra note 38, at 906; Marvin E. Frankel & Leonard Orland, A Conversation About Sentencing Commissions and Guidelines, 64 U. Colo. L. Rev. 655, 664 (1993) ("with good reason, the judgments of the Federal Commission have been quite harsh").

in *Mistretta v. United States*[60] that the guidelines were constitutional, that they were fully implemented in all jurisdictions.[61]

The sentencing structure set up under the guidelines uses a mathematical calculation to arrive at the presumptive sentence. Under its scheme, the judge first uses a correlation table to match the statute under which the defendant has been convicted to the specific guideline which addresses that particular crime.[62] The guideline chosen assigns a value, or base offense level, to the crime on a forty-three point scale. Then the judge adjusts the base level to account for "special offense characteristics" associated with the charges for which the defendant has been convicted.[63] Included at this stage are considerations such as whether a dangerous weapon was used in the commission of the offense.[64] The subtotal is then adjusted for special victim circumstances,[65] such as the defendant's role in the offense, whether there has been an obstruction of justice, whether the defendant was convicted of multiple counts,[66] and whether the defendant has accepted personal responsibility for the offense.[67] The resultant value equals the "total offense level."[68]

Next the judge considers the defendant's criminal history and arrives at one of six criminal history categories.[69] Each category has a range of two to three criminal history points, which are determined by the length of the prior sentences.[70] The judge then plots the offense level and criminal history value on a sentencing chart made up of two hundred and fifty-eight sentence boxes on a two dimensional matrix.[71] The intersection of the two axes frames the permissible sentencing range.[72]

In reality, it is generally the probation officer, within the Pre-Sentence Investigation Report (PSI) who performs the technical calculations on behalf of the

---

60. 488 U.S. 361 (1989) (holding Congress did not excessively delegate its legislative power and the creation of the Commission did not violate separation of powers).

61. This is not to say, however, that departure policies are the same in every jurisdiction. In fact, at least one study has shown that there are significant differences between districts. Nagel & Schulhofer, supra note 7, at 553.

62. 18 U.S.C.A. app. 4 § 1B1.2 (West Supp. 1993).

63. 18 U.S.C.A. app. 4 § 1B1.1(b) (West Supp. 1993).

64. See United States v. Heldberg, 907 F.2d 91 (9th Cir. 1990); United States v. Medred, 905 F.2d 935 (6th Cir. 1990). See also 18 U.S.C.A. app 4 § 1B1.4 (West Supp. 1993).

65. 18 U.S.C.A. app. 4 §§ 1B1.1(c), 3A1.1-.3, 3B1.1-.4 and 3C1.1-.2 (West Supp. 1993).

66. 18 U.S.C.A. app. 4 §§ 1B1.1(d) and 3D1.1-.5 (West Supp. 1993).

67. 18 U.S.C.A. app. 4 §§ 1B1.1(e) and 3E1.1 (West Supp. 1993). This section allows for a two-point decrease in offense level.

68. See 18 U.S.C.A. app. 4 §§ 1B1.1(A)-1B1.1(I) (West Supp. 1993).

69. 18 U.S.C.A. app. 4 §§ 1B1.1(f) and 4A1.1 (1993).

70. Each prior sentence of more than 13 months is assigned three points. 18 U.S.C.A. app. 4 § 4A1.1(a) (West Supp. 1993).

71. Jonathan D. Lupkin, Note, 5K1.1 and Substantial Assistance Departure: The Illusory Carrot of the Federal Sentencing Guidelines, 91 Colum. L. Rev. 1519, 1522 (1991).

72. 18 U.S.C.A. app. 4 § 1B1.1(g) (West Supp. 1972). Most state guideline systems use sentencing grids with 12 or less levels as opposed to the 46 in the Federal Sentencing Guidelines. Donald P. Lay, Rethinking the Guidelines: A Call for Cooperation, 101 Yale L.J. 1755, 1770 (1992). Cf. Marc Miller, True Grid: Revealing Sentencing Policy, 25 U.C. Davis L. Rev. 587, 612 (1992) (suggesting an alternative simplified sentencing grid).

judge.[73] At least one judge has voiced concern because "Probation reports are no longer designed to find out good as well as bad things about defendants. They merely mechanically describe what the guidelines consider relevant so that the judge often will not be aware that there is a basis for departure."[74] In the vast majority of cases, judges simply accept the facts and calculations set forth in the PSIs.[75]

Within the permissible sentencing range, the judge must determine an appropriate sentence, consistent with the concerns and purposes of the Act. These include the nature and circumstances of the offense, the history and characteristics of the defendant, the need to achieve the recognized purposes of sentencing, the kinds of sentences available, pertinent policy statements, the need to avoid unwarranted disparities among similarly situated defendants, the need to provide restitution to any victims of the offense, and the establishment of the sentence in the guidelines.[76] The judge may consider any relevant information regarding the defendant's background, character, and conduct.[77] In practice, the phrase "relevant information," as used within the guidelines, has a particular, rigid meaning and application.[78] Judges generally are not free to use such information to fashion a sentence outside the boundaries set by the mathematical sentencing equation.

IV. Sentencing Departures

A. Downward Departures for Substantial Government Assistance

The guidelines that allow for judicial departure from the presumptive guideline ranges fall under two exception provisions. The first exception addresses "atypical cases" not "adequately addressed" in the guidelines, but which may warrant departure from them.[79] The Commission promulgated a non-exhaustive series of policy statements which suggest such atypical factors.[80]

---

73. Fed. R. Crim. P. 32(c) Rule 12.8.3 states:
    The PSI must contain: (1) the history and characteristics of the defendant, including prior criminal record and any circumstances affecting the defendant's behavior that might be helpful in sentencing; (2) the guideline categories, types of sentences and the sentencing range that the probation officer believes apply to the particular case, and an explanation of any factors that might warrant departure; (3) pertinent policy statements issued by the Sentencing Commission; (4) the impact of the crime on the victim; (5) the nature and extent of non prison programs available to the defendant; and (6) any other information that may be required by the court in sentencing.
Criminal Procedure Project, 81 Geo. L.J. 1423, 1446–7 (1993).
74. Weinstein, supra note 12, at 8.
75. Dunworth & Weisselberg, supra note 1, at 108 (sentencing courts calculated different guidelines ranges from probation officers in only 10% of cases).
76. 18 U.S.C. § 3553(a)(1)-(7) (1988).
77. 18 U.S.C. § 3661 (1988).
78. 18 U.S.C.A. app. 4 § 1B1.3 (West Supp. 1993).
79. 18 U.S.C. § 3553(b) (1988).
80. 18 U.S.C.A. app. 4 §§ 5k2.0–.16 (West Supp. 1993).

The second departure exception is provided by Policy Statement § 5K1.1, termed "Substantial Assistance to Authorities." The § 5K1.1 departure provision does not derive its authority from §3553(b), as in the case of the 5K2.0 departures, but was promulgated pursuant to 28 U.S.C. §994(n), in a provision added as part of the Anti-Drug Abuse Act of 1986,[81] and was expressly designed to function with the guidelines and the 1984 Act.[82] In the 1986 Act, Congress also enacted mandatory minimum penalties for certain drug and weapons offenses.[83] The number of congressionally mandated offenses with mandatory minimum sentences has increased steadily since that time.[84]

The Sentencing Commission issued Policy Statement § 5K1.1, effective on November 1, 1987. At that time, § 5K1.1 provided: "Upon motion of the government stating that the defendant has made *a good faith effort to provide* substantial assistance in the investigation or prosecution of another person who has committed an offense, the court may depart from the guidelines."[85] However, amendments effective two years later, replaced "made a good faith effort to provide" with "provided."[86] The Commission explained the amendment as a clarification of its intent that "departures under this policy statement [must] be based upon the provision of substantial assistance," not merely a willingness to provide such assistance.[87] This amendment gave federal prosecutors even greater power to "squeeze" defendants than they previously had. Now, even those who may want to "rat" may not be able to meet the high burden of providing information which results in the conviction of another. This allows prosecutors to demand even more dangerous levels of defendant criminal involvement such as wearing a "wire" or infiltrating protected conversations[88] in order to qualify for the government motion for a departure below the guideline sentence or the minimum mandatory sentences.[89]

---

81. Anti-Drug Abuse Act of 1986, Pub. L. No. 99-570, § 1008, 100 Stat. 3207, 3207–08. See Jonathan D. Lupkin, Note, 5K1.1 and Substantial Assistance Departure: The Illusory Carrot of the Federal Sentencing Guidelines, 91 Colum. L. Rev. 1519, 1523–24 (1991); William W. Wilkins, Jr., Plea Negotiations, Acceptance of Responsibility, Role of the Offender, and Departures: Policy Decisions in the Promulgation of the Federal Sentencing Guidelines, 23 Wake Forest L. Rev. 181, 196–202 (1988).

82. Pub. L. No. 99-570 at § 1009.

83. Drug Possession Penalty Act of 1986, Pub. L. No. 99-570 §§ 1051–52, 100 Stat. 3207-8 (codified at 21 U.S.C. § 951 (1986)); Ballistic Knife Prohibition Act of 1986, Pub. L. No. 99-570 §§ 10001–04, 100 Stat. 3207-166 (codified at 15 U.S.C. §§ 1241, 1245 (1986)).

84. Karle & Sager, supra note 59, at 418.

85. 18 U.S.C.A. app. 4 § 5K1.1 (West Supp. 1989) (emphasis supplied).

86. United States Sentencing Commission, Guidelines Manual, app. C 133 at 290 (West 1990).

87. Bradford C. Mank, Rewarding Defendant Cooperation Under the Federal Sentencing Guidelines: Judge vs. Prosecutors, 1990 Crim. L. Bull. 399, 406 (1990).

88. Cf. Nagel & Schulhofer, supra note 7, at 556 (AUSAs manipulate 5K1.1 departures for sympathetic informants).

89. 18 U.S.C. § 3553(e) (1988) (necessitating a motion by the prosecutor).

B. Sentencing on the Basis of Uncharged, Dismissed or Acquitted Crimes

During its deliberations, the Commission debated the merits of a system where guideline range is determined entirely from the offenses resulting in conviction or from all alleged offense behavior.[90] The Commission ultimately settled on a somewhat hybrid system. The guidelines use the conviction offense to determine the base-level offense[91] and then, in the process of adjusting the base level offense, allow the court to consider all alleged criminal conduct of the defendant.[92] Such information need only be established by a preponderance of the evidence.[93] However, there have been several courts which, under certain circumstances, have required a heightened standard.[94]

---

90. Wilkens & Steer, supra note 13, at 497; Breyer, supra note 13, at 8–9. See United States v. Lghodaro, 967 F.2d 1028, 1030 (5th Cir. 1992) (PSIs form factual basis for judge's sentencing determinations); United States v. Boatner, 966 F.2d 1575, 1578 (11th Cir. 1992) (PSI forms factual and legal basis for judge's sentencing determination); United States v. Helmsley, 941 F.2d 71, 98 (2d Cir. 1991), cert. denied, 112 S. Ct. 1162 (1992) (PSIs provide objective and factual information); United States v. Terry, 916 F.2d 157, 160 (4th Cir. 1990) (PSI forms factual basis for judge's sentencing determinations); United States v. Jackson, 886 F.2d 838, 842 (7th Cir. 1989) (court may rely upon information contained in the presentence report).

91. 18 U.S.C.A. app. 4 § 1B1.2(a) (1993) (An exception to this provision states that "in the case of a plea agreement containing a stipulation that specifically establishes a more serious offense than the offense of conviction, determine the offense guideline section in Chapter Two most applicable to the stipulated offense.").

92. The parameters of the base level adjustments may be found in 18 U.S.C.A. app. 4 § 1B1.3 (West Supp. 1993).

93. United States v. Ross, 905 F.2d 1050, 1054 (7th Cir. 1990), cert. denied, 498 U.S. 863 (1990); United States v. Avila, 905 F.2d 295, 297 (9th Cir. 1990); United States v. Byrd, 898 F.2d 450, 452 (5th Cir. 1990); United States v. Frederick, 897 F.2d 490, 491–92 (10th Cir. 1990), cert. denied, 498 U.S. 863 (1990); United States v. Alston, 895 F.2d 1362, 1373 (11th Cir. 1990); United States v. Gooden, 892 F.2d 725, 728 (8th Cir. 1989), cert. denied, 110 U.S. 908 (1990); United States v. Silverman, 889 F.2d 1531, 1535 (6th Cir. 1989); United States v. Guerra, 888 F.2d 247, 251 (2d Cir. 1989); United States v. Williams, 880 F.2d 804, 806 (4th Cir. 1989); United States v. Urrego-Linares, 879 F.2d 1234, 1239 (4th Cir. 1989), cert. denied, 493 U.S. 943 (1989); United States v. Wright, 873 F.2d 437, 441 (1st Cir. 1989).

94. See Conference on the Federal Sentencing Guidelines: Summary of Proceedings, 101 Yale L.J. 2053, 2055 (1992) [hereinafter Yale Summary] "When the sentencing hearing is the tail that wags the dog of the substantive offense, perhaps due process requires more than a minimum indicium of reliability, and a higher standard of proof, such as clear and convincing evidence, should be applied." Id. at 2055. "In every area of the law, the greater the sanction that might be imposed, the greater the burden of proof we require. This sliding scale should apply to sentencing. If a given fact is going to ratchet a sentence up many levels, the required burden of proof should be greater than the standard of proof for a fact with little effect on a sentence." Id. at 2065. See also United States v. Townley, 929 F.2d 365 (8th Cir. 1991) (holding that due process may require facts supporting an 18-level increase based upon uncharged relevant conduct to be established by clear and convincing evidence); United States v. Restrepo, 946 F.2d 661, 661 (9th Cir. 1991) (Tang, J., concurring) ("[T]he severity of penal consequences associated with a sentencing factor may in some cases tip the balance toward requiring heightened procedural protection in determining the applicability of that factor."); Joseph P. Sargent, Comment, The Standard of Proof Under the Federal Sentencing

Not only can the judge use hearsay information contained in the pre-sentence report to increase the sentence, but, he or she can also use conduct for which the defendant was acquitted at trial to adjust the sentence upwards.[95] Pursuant to the "relevant conduct" provision,[96] the judge must consider all conduct involved with the charged offense.[97] Relevant conduct may include acts which were neither charged as a separate offense, nor elements of the offense of conviction.[98] For instance, if the defendant was charged with possession of a firearm and possession of a certain amount of drugs, but was only convicted of possession of a lesser amount of drugs, the judge, despite a jury acquittal on the other two counts, could find by a preponderance of the evidence, that the defendant had a gun and the larger weight of contraband, and sentence him or her accordingly.

Unfortunately, this anomaly has lead to abuses of the system by government agents. For instance, drug enforcement agents who are knowledgeable about the guidelines, may negotiate with the defendants to buy a larger amount of drugs than originally bargained for, so as to expose the defendant to an increased sentence[99] or they may arrange for the deal to go down in a location, such as near a school, which will lead to increased sentences under mandatory minimum laws.[100] Unscrupulous prosecutors can then rely on judges to use this information to increase sentences even if they are unable to build a strong enough case to prove the defendant's guilt beyond a reasonable doubt on the most severe charges at trial. Reliance upon unproven allegations increases the leverage available to prosecutors in plea-bargaining and specifically in inducing recalcitrant defendants to "rat."

Thus far, these practices have stood up to constitutional challenge.[101] Prior to the imposition of the Federal Sentencing Guidelines, judges had great latitude in sentence determinations.[102] The Court was loathe to inhibit a judge's assessment of an offender's rehabilitation potential by precluding the judge from using so-called "related information" which was subject to the evidentiary procedures required at trial.[103] This has remained the rule despite the fact

---

Guidelines: Raising the Standard to Beyond a Reasonable Doubt, 28 Wake Forest L. Rev. 463, 466 (1993) (increasing standard of proof needed when sentencing judge sought to impose an upward departure from 30 months to 30 years based upon uncharged relevant conduct offered at sentencing).

95. See Sargent, supra note 94, at 476; Yale Summary, supra note 94, at 2073 ("The Guideline's approach to measuring relevant conduct is seriously flawed. It measures all relevant conduct against the same scale, whether or not the defendant has been tried and convicted for the conduct. This is bad penology and bad morality.").

96. See Wilkens & Steer, supra note 13, at 497; Sargent, supra note 94, at 469.

97. 18 U.S.C.A. app. 4 § 1B1.3(a)(1) (West Supp. 1993).

98. Id.

99. See Yale Summary, supra note 94, at 2059. See also Kinder v. United States, 946 F.2d 362, 365 (5th Cir. 1991), cert. denied, 112 S.Ct. 2290 (1992) (on the question of burden of proof as to sentencing).

100. Yale Summary, supra note 94, at 2074.

101. *Kinder*, 946 F.2d at 362.

102. See, e.g., Williams v. New York, 337 U.S. 241 (1949).

103. Id. at 247.

that under the guidelines, the judge's discretion in fashioning an appropriate sentence has been severely curtailed.

V. The Goals of Sentencing

It is generally accepted that there are four purposes of sentencing: retribution, deterrence, incapacitation, and rehabilitation.[104] Throughout history, one or the other of these purposes has dominated sentencing theory and practice.[105] At the heart of each new sentencing philosophy is a series of goals which embrace the current favored purpose. At different times, the legislature,[106] the sentencing judge,[107] or various other administrative groups[108] have been entrusted with the primary responsibility of fulfilling sentencing goals.

The Sentencing Commission began its work at a time when enthusiasm for rehabilitation theory was waning.[109] Several studies indicated that criminal rehabilitation was a dead-end goal.[110] Public outcry about increased violence and crime placed the pressure on law-makers to move away from indeterminate sentencing,[111] which was believed to produce disparate sentences, and move

---

104. Nagel, supra note 38, at 887.

105. See generally id. (reviewing sentencing theory from Moses to the present).

106. Congress has met this responsibility by creating the Federal Sentencing Commission and by passing legislation which delineates mandatory minimum sentences for certain crimes.

107. Federal district judges were the prime arbiters of divining sentences under the indeterminate sentencing system in effect prior to the implementation of the Federal Sentencing Guidelines. Sentences, as long as they were within the broad ranges set down by statute, were essentially unreviewable by the appellate courts. United States v. Schneider, 502 F.2d 897, 898 (8th Cir. 1974); see United States v. DeBright, 710 F.2d 1404, 1405 (9th Cir. 1982) (limited appellate review to determine if district court properly exercised discretion); United States v. Barbara, 683 F.2d 164, 166 (6th Cir. 1982).

108. Under the present indeterminate sentencing system, the Commission, and perhaps the United States Attorneys, fulfill this role. Under an indeterminate sentencing system, the parole boards function in this way by determining when an inmate is ready to be released from the correctional institution.

109. Karle & Sager, supra note 59, at 394; Karen Bornstein, 5K2.0 Departures for 5H Individual Characteristics: A Backdoor Out of the Federal Sentencing Guidelines, 24 Colum. Hum. Rts. L. Rev. 135, 138–39 (1992–3); Nagel, supra note 38, at 884, 895–7.

110. Douglas S. Lipton et al., The Effectiveness of Correctional Treatment: A Survey of Treatment Evaluation Studies (1975) (promoting the "Nothing Works" theory). Later, Martinson renounced his views of probation as a rehabilitative method, Robert Martinson & Judith Wilks, Save Parole Supervision, 41 Federal Probation 23, 23 n.3 (1977), and two years later he found "startling examples" of rehabilitative treatment programs, Robert Martinson, New Findings, New Views: A Note of Caution Regarding Sentencing Reform, 7 Hofstra L. Rev. 242, 255 (1979).

111. In indeterminate sentencing, an offender is sentenced to a "flexible sentence"; that is, the length of actual incarceration is handed down by the sentencing judge in terms of a minimum-maximum range. The actual amount of time served is determined by both conditional "good time" early releases (approved by the correctional facility administration) and periodic evaluations of the prisoner's overall rehabilitation (as determined by the parole board). Marc Miller, Purposes at Sentencing, 66 S. Cal. L. Rev. 413, 435 n. 94 (1992).

toward a "just desserts" sentencing rationale.[112] The "just deserts" sentencing theory imputes a ranking of criminal behaviors by severity and applies a similarly ranked order of punishments.[113] Thus, in theory, the just desserts system of sentencing advocates a system which punishes individuals who violate the rights of others in accordance with their individual level of blameworthiness[114] and satisfies the public hunger for the expression of communal blame upon the culpable.[115] In this way, the criminal conduct is punished without regard to individual characteristics or circumstances.

Much has been written on the purposes of sentencing under the Federal Sentencing Guidelines.[116] Rather than deconstructing the layers of political rhetoric contained in the legislative history,[117] this article proposes a therapeutic jurisprudence paradigm which draws upon some of the statutory purpose language of promoting respect for the law[118] and the language of the enabling act which directs the Commission to develop a means of measuring the effectiveness of the guidelines in meeting its goals.[119]

The Sentencing Reform Act of 1984 directed Congress to create a Commission[120] and also provided instructions for federal judges.[121] Congress directed the Sentencing Commission to establish guidelines which would serve the multiple goals and purposes of federal sentencing as established by Congress.[122] The express statutory purposes are to promote respect for the law, to deter criminal behavior, to protect the public, and to rehabilitate criminals.[123]

In turn, the Commission promulgated guidelines to aid the sentencing judge in adhering to the same goals of criminal punishment established by the en-

---

112. Breyer, supra note 13, at 15.

113. Id.

114. Nagel, supra note 38, at 898.

115. Jennifer Moore, Corporate Culpability Under the Federal Sentencing Guidelines, 34 Ariz. L. Rev. 743, 748 (1992).

116. Miller, supra note 111, at 417; Leonard J. Long, Millers Algebra of Purposes at Sentencing, 66 S. Cal. L. Rev. 483, 483–84 (1992) (responding to Miller's Purposes at Sentencing); Breyer, supra note 13, at 4 (Congress's purposes were to put "honesty in sentencing" and to reduce "unjustifiably wide sentencing disparity"); Karle & Sager, supra note 59, at 397; Nagel & Schulberger, supra note 7, at 501. According to some writers, the purposes of Congress and of the Commission are not always one and the same. Professor Miller argues that there should be a match between offenders, sentence purpose, and the sentence, to be determined at the time of sentencing and that sentences should have a clearly articulated purpose or purposes, but that purpose may be different at different points in the criminal justice process. Miller, supra note 111, at 415.

117. Kate Stith & Steve Y. Koh, The Politics of Sentencing Reform: The Legislative History of the Federal Sentencing Guidelines, 28 Wake Forest L. Rev. 223 (1993) (for an exhaustive review of pertinent legislative history beginning in 1975 when Senator Edward M. Kennedy originally introduced legislation to establish the United States Sentencing Commission).

118. 18 U.S.C. § 3553 (1988).

119. 28 U.S.C. § 991(b)(1)(B) (1988).

120. Pub. L. No. 98-473, § 217, 98 Stat. 2017 (1984) (The Sentencing Reform Act of 1984).

121. 18 U.S.C. § 3553 (1984).

122. The statutory list of sentencing purposes appears at 18 U.S.C. §3553(a)(2) (1988).

123. Id.

abling legislation so that the sentencing ranges in the guidelines were to be consistent with all of the provisions of Title 18 of the United States Code.[124]

In reviewing the statutory sentencing purposes, the most intriguing purpose is the stated goal of "promoting respect for the law."[125] What little authority there is seems to indicate that promoting respect for the law is a retributive goal,[126] at least in as far as it is linked with the phrases "need to reflect the seriousness of the offense" and "provide just punishment." Promoting respect for the law is apparently aimed at the public's perception of the law rather than that of the individual offender. However, this author opines that it makes more sense to extract this goal from its retributive neighbor-phrases and investigate the internalization of a defendant's moral respect and compliance with the legal system. In turn, such an analysis could buttress the public's understanding and respect for the law,[127] which may be the intent of Congress's retributive characterization of this goal. Presumably, laws which modify behavior or attitudes in a socially acceptable way should receive greater respect from society than laws which merely satisfy a sense of retribution without the concomitant behavioral adaptation.

In either paradigm, a relevant field of inquiry is whether it is possible to legislate attitudinal change within the correctional system. In other contexts, most notably the recently passed Americans With Disabilities Act, such attitudinal change has been attempted.[128]

---

124. 28 U.S.C. § 994(a) (1988).

125. 18 U.S.C. § 3553(a)(2)(B) (1988).

126. See United States v. Mercedes, No. § 90 Cr. 0450 (RWS), 1991 WL 210945 (S.D.N.Y. Oct. 4, 1991) (Sweet, J., sentencing opinion):

> A departure upward is appropriate is [sic] Mercedes's case. *Respect for the law* will be furthered by imposing a longer sentence here. Mercedes was a fugitive from a prior New York City arrest when most of the activities these charges were based on occurred. This arrest apparently did not give him pause to consider the legality of his actions, in fact, he ignored it.

Id. at *2 (emphasis added).

127. I suspect that this phrase was included as a response to the public's outcry against indeterminate sentences. This perception was inflamed by the belief that sentences did not accurately reflect the amount of time the defendant remained incarcerated. "[T]he recent 100 years or so of indeterminate sentencing—meaning largely unmeasured and uncontrolled judicial discretion in fixing sentences—was the era that could properly be characterized as one of 'lawlessness'." Marvin E. Frankel & Leonard Orland, A Conversation About Sentencing Commissions and Guidelines, 64 U. Colo. L. Rev. 655, 658 (1993).

128. The Americans with Disabilities Act, 42 U.S.C. § 12101 et seq. (1990), has been hailed as the most significant civil rights law since the 1960's. Peter Susser, The ADA: Dramatically Expanded Federal Rights for Disabled Americans, 16 Employee Rel. L.J. 157, 157 (1990); Lowell Weicker, Historical Background of the Americans With Disabilities Act, 64 Temp. L. Rev. 387, 387 (1991) (stating that the ADA expresses a national goal of assuring equal opportunity, full participation, independent living and economic self-sufficiency, and eradication of continuing unfair and unnecessary discrimination and prejudice against those having or perceived as having mental and physical disabilities).

VI. The Federal Offender Population

A. Significant Numbers of Federal Inmates Have Mental Disabilities

Surprisingly, there is very little literature on the psychological makeup of prisoners in general, and even less on those serving time in federal correctional facilities.[129] In fact, if there is evidence that a significant percentage of inmates maintain a perception of unfairness with regard to their treatment under the Federal Sentencing Guidelines,[130] can we make demographic predictions about how certain prisoners will respond? Research in this area may provide us with increased insight into prison populations and the connection between sentencing practices, correctional programming, and recidivism.

In the mean time, we know that the prison population is growing by leaps and bounds.[131] The federal inmate population which was thought to be 53,347 at the end of 1989, has in 1992, approached 66,000 inmates housed in sixty-eight institutions.[132] In 1992 the institutions were being operated at one hundred and forty-five percent of design capacity.[133] The number of federal prisoners continues to grow much faster than the rate of growth in the state systems. In 1993, federal inmates numbered 80,259, an increase of over twelve percent from the year before.[134] With every increase, correctional efficiency must continue to focus on the provision of appropriate services, including mental health services to prisoners and the safety concerns of inmates and employees. Therefore, any information which could shed proactive light on potentially volatile situations could be a great service.

It seems likely that inmates with mental disorders may express anger, fear and disillusionment in maladaptive ways. Most researchers agree that a signif-

---

129. Henry J. Steadman et al., A Survey of Mental Disability Among State Prison Inmates, 38 Hosp. & Community Psychiatry 1086, 1086 (1987) (stating that there is a paucity of empirical studies on the occurrence of mental disorder in prisons); Edward Zamble & Frank Porporino, Coping, Imprisonment, and Rehabilitation, 17 Crim. Just. & Behav. 53, 54 (1990) (stating that there is a dearth of methodologically rigorous psychological research on the effects of imprisonment); Richard J. Bonnie, The Competence of Criminal Defendants With Mental Retardation to Participate in Their Own Defense, 81 J. Crim. L. & Criminology 419, 421 (1990) (stating that empirical data on "under-identification" theory, which purports that the mentally retarded evade accurate identification within the criminal justice system, is sparse).

130. Edgardo Rotman, Beyond Punishment 15, 16 (1990) ("Unfairness is essentially a disproportion between offense and punitive reaction. An unfair sentence is bound to generate antisocial reactions. A fair sentence favors the process of reconciliation between the lawbreaker and the community.").

131. Peter Kerr, The Detoxing of Prisoner 88A0802, N.Y.Times MAG., June 27, 1993, at 23, 26 (the present number of prisoners in the United States is expected to rise from 1.3 million to more than 2 million people by the year 2000).

132. Yale Summary, supra note 94, at 2063.

133. Id.

134. Prison Jam Hits Record Drug Arrests Cited in Crush, N.Y. Newsday, May 10, 1993, at 19.

icant proportion of inmates have some degree of diminished self-esteem and marginal maladjustment to societal concerns which may be reflective of underlying personality disorders or emotional distress.[135] One study found that upon entering prison, inmates reported a higher incidence of psychiatric disorders than a control sample from the surrounding area.[136] Often disorders are not diagnosed even with the most diligent of screening efforts because the symptoms are subtle or easily hidden by the inmate.[137] The disorder may also remain in remission until a time later in the prisoner's continued retention.[138] The same is true for mentally retarded prisoners, whose disabilities are often unrecognized by attorneys, courts and prison administrators.[139] Empirical evidence has consistently shown that diagnosed mental retardation is found in about ten percent of the correctional population.[140]

Studies show that prisons have a large, relatively predictable number of inmates with severe mental illness.[141] These numbers may include relatively large numbers of persons diagnosed as psychopaths.[142] Consequently, in one study, "fifteen to thirty percent of a sample of federal inmates met the 'commonly used research criterion for the diagnosis of psychopathology,' depending on the security level of the correctional institution."[143]

A study of the New York State prison population found that eight percent of the state's inmates have severe psychiatric or functional disabilities that clearly warrant some type of mental health intervention and another sixteen percent have significant mental disabilities which require periodic services.[144] "[S]ubstantial impairments to functioning in the general prison population"

---

135. J.P. Prestelli, Maximum-Security Hospital Ward, 32 Med. Sci. & L. 337 (1992) (stating that personality disorders are more prevalent in prisoners than in the general population); Donald G. Dutton & Stephen D. Hart, Risk Markers for Family Violence in a Federally Incarcerated Population, 15 Int. J. L. & Psychiatry 101, 110 (1992) (finding a high prevalence rate for personality disorders in Canada's federal system, with narcissism and borderline personalities over-represented). See Zamble & Porporino, supra note 129, at 58 (finding very strong evidence that offenders were unable to cope adequately with ordinary life situations. Seven percent of the inmates had at least a mild level of depression, and almost 1 in 10 had scores indicating they were severely depressed. 53% had ranges of high anxiety as defined by another standardized test). Id. at 64. However, the authors found that over the course of the next few months of incarceration, the combined total of those who were either depressed or highly anxious fell by almost one-third to 37%. After another year, the total dropped to about 21%, indicating that at least some inmates can satisfactorily adjust to the prison setting. Id.

136. Bonta & Gendreau, supra note 17, at 356.

137. Fred Cohen & Joel Dvoskin, Inmates with Mental Disorders: A Guide to Law and Practice, 16 Mental & Physical Disability L. Rep. 462, 465 (1992).

138. Id.

139. Bonnie, supra note 129, at 420–21.

140. Id. at 421.

141. Cohen & Dvoskin, supra note 137, at 463.

142. Grant Harris et al., Psychopathology and Violent Recidivism, 15 Law & Hum. Behav. 625, 625 (1991).

143. Id.

144. Steadman, supra note 129, at 1089.

were found in nearly one-quarter of the New York state prison population.[145] However, the specific nature and extent of those disabilities was not assessed.

B. Empirical Methodology Must Devise an Instrument to Measure Inmate Morals

It seems reasonable to suspect that the system cannot instill respect for the law where the law is perceived to be incompatible with personal or group values.[146] Respect in this context is important because it influences everyday behavior toward the law.[147] In the correctional context, everyday behavior is measured in terms of compliance with facility rules. Thus, the psychological constructs with which an inmate enters the facility may have implications for behavior within the correctional institution as well as future behavior when the inmate is released from incarceration.

When devising an empirical instrument which can accurately reflect inmate morals, one difficulty which may be encountered is the identification of individual values. This may be a particularly pernicious problem if the inmate is from a subculture which embraces some values not held by the larger or dominant society.[148] Thus, any empirical methodology used should take into account an understanding of social and cultural factors in order to avoid an ineffective and offensive ethnocentric approach.[149] For instance, at least one study has found that persons involved in felony cases, who may be unfaily characterized as marginal adherents to society's value system (the poor, the poorly educated, minorities, or the unemployed) are most influenced by procedural fairness rather than the leniency of the sentence they receive.[150] Similar findings hold true across a spectrum of research participants. Studies conducted on non-incarcerated people, who have experienced a legal procedure that they judged to be unfair, found that those persons had less respect for the law and legal authorities and are less likely to accept judicial decisions.[151] This

---

145. Id. An older, less extensive study of prisoners in Oklahoma found that 10% were severely or acutely disturbed and 35% required some mental health treatment. Id. at 1086 (citing J.F. James et al., Psychiatric Morbidity in Prisons, 11 Hosp. & Community Psychiatry 674 (1980)).

146. Studies suggest that when assessing the impact of participation in the legal process on a person's respect for the law and legal authorities, the primary influence is the person's evaluation of the fairness of the judicial procedure itself, not the evaluation of the legal outcome. Tom R. Tyler, The Psychological Consequences of Judicial Procedures: Implications for Civil Commitment Hearings, 46 SMU L. Rev. 433, 437 (1992) [hereinafter Tyler, Psychological Consequences]; Tom R. Tyler, Why People Obey the Law, 94–112 (1990) [hereinafter Tyler, People Obey].

147. Tyler, People Obey, supra note 146, at 94–95.

148. Edgardo Rotman, Beyond Punishment: A New View on the Rehabilitation of Criminal Offenders 7 (1990).

149. Id.

150. Tyler, Psychological Consequences, supra note 146, at 438.

151. Daniel W. Shuman & Jean A. Hamilton, Jury Service—It May Change Your Mind: Perceptions of Fairness of Jurors and Nonjurors, 46 SMU L. Rev. 449, 451 (1992); Tyler, Psychological Consequences, supra note 146, at 439.

can lead to a "gradual erosion of obedience to the law."[152] The recognition of the relation between fair legal procedures and the development of a participant's sense of justice has not been lost on the judiciary. The Supreme Court relied on the psychological impact of the judicial process in establishing the right to judicial hearings in several contexts.[153]

C. The Morality of "Ratting"

Despite the myriad of moral and ethical differences held by a multicultural prison population, the societal ban against informing spans many cultures and religions and has persisted since ancient times.[154] Even the words we use to describe an informant indicate that it is something bad.[155] Prison studies have offered little systematic research on "snitches"[156] or the "sociology of treachery."[157] What little work has been done simply declares that the role of the "rat" exists and is negatively valued.[158]

> From the schoolyard 'tattletale' to the police officer's 'confidential informant' to the Pentagon 'whistle blower,' our society is deeply ambivalent toward those who report the wrongdoing of others to the authorities. On one hand, society values informers.... On the other hand, society scorns informers as betrayers of confidence. Even one who violates an antisocial pact such as the police officer's code of silence is viewed as having breached a trust. Such breaches leave all of us less secure in our reliance on the confidence of others.[159]

Citizens generally have no legal duty to report criminal activity of which they may be aware.[160] However, the law deviates from this general rule to make distinctions based upon the degree of harm presented to some classes of particularly vulnerable victims. For instance, certain classes of people may be legally obligated to report certain kinds of actual and suspected activity, in-

---

152. Shuman & Hamilton, supra note 151, at 451.

153. Goldberg v. Kelly, 397 U.S. 254, 264–66 (1970) (terminating welfare benefits without a hearing could be psychologically harmful); Morrissey v. Brewer, 408 U.S. 471, 484 (1972) (holding revocation of parole without judicial hearing could cause prisoners psychological harm); Tyler, Psychological Consequences, supra note 146.

154. Weinstein, supra note 16, at 4 (relating orthodox jewish law's disdain of informers back to Roman times). Informing is also an unforgivable sin to the Irish, and understandably so in a country where the government and the police were for centuries the enemy of the people. Id.

155. Id. at 3.

156. Marquart & Roebuck, supra note 2, at 218.

157. See Malin Akerstrom, The Social Construction of Snitches, 9 Deviant Behav. 155 (1988).

158. Id.

159. Gerard E. Lynch, The Lawyer As Informer, 1986 Duke L. J. 491, 491 (1986).

160. Failure to report a felony was the misdemeanor "misprision" at common law. The crime evidently still exists in England and in South Carolina (State v. Carson, 262 S.E. 2d 918 (S.C. 1980)) but it has been historically criticized from the beginnings of our system of modern justice: "It may be the duty of a citizen to accuse every offender, and to proclaim every offense which comes to his knowledge; but the law which would punish him in every case, for not performing this duty, is too harsh for man." Marbury v. Brooks, 20 U.S. (7 Wheat.) 556, 575–76 (1822).

cluding physicians, teachers and other childcare professionals who are obligated by statute to report all suspected instances of child abuse.[161] Even without statutory obligation or sanction, most people acknowledge a prevailing moral duty to protect their subjectively-defined community from harm. Generally, if citizens have information about an intended or completed heinous crime, it is expected that they will give such information to the law enforcement authorities, absent an overwhelming fear of personal or familial harm.[162] Of course, the decision about what criminal activity tips the balance so as to compel a person to go to the authorities is a subjective call which balances the harm to self or community and the ambivalence of informing.

Because society's ambivalence toward informing is rooted in the complex interplay of moral values, it deserves the respect of our justice system,[163] at least insofar as to recognize its impact on legal rules and practices. For instance, informing in a criminal case has the presumptive social benefit of aiding in the conviction of an offender. That presumptive societal benefit, however, must be weighed against the moral costs to the informer.[164]

According to Professor Lynch, the most important factors to be weighed in balancing the risks to the defendant with the attendant risks imposed upon the criminal justice system are "the connection between the potential witness and the crime, the relationship between the witness and the perpetrator, and the seriousness of the crime."[165] These relationships are most influential in the case of a non-victim witness-informer. It is in this situation that the "rat" is most likely to be negatively perceived as the betrayer of confidences.

"Ratting" means that you are informing on someone who has a legitimate claim on your silence. The relationship between the informant and offender is a key ingredient in determining the morality of informing, both in the eyes of the public and from the perspective of the informant. Public condemnation of "ratting" typically forms the opinions supporting a moral obligation of silence. Where there has been an explicit promise not to reveal certain information, the informant has a moral duty not to reveal the information. Likewise, where the structure of a personal bond contains an implied promise of loyalty to a relationship, such as family membership or ethnic ties, there is an expectation of silence.[166] This moral commitment may also be grounded in a social or professional relationship. Some of these relationships are so prized in our society that they are accorded protection through evidentiary privileges.[167] In

---

161. See Levine, supra note 36.

162. Despite the seduction of fulfilling a moral imperative, most people find the idea of reporting another's less heinous legal transgressions to be morally reprehensible. The subjective nature of drawing such a line results in an inexact determination of moral conviction. For example, in the early 1980s there were several news stories about high school students who learned of the killing of a classmate by someone they knew. No students came forward to the authorities, and when later questioned about their actions, the students persisted in their belief that it was wrong to "tell." Weinstein, supra note 16, at 4.

163. Lynch, supra note 159, at 492.

164. Id. at 522.

165. Id. at 523.

166. Id. at 528.

167. See Lynch, supra note 159, at 530.

such cases, even where the need for such information is great, the law "has determined that the social benefits of preserving some relationships outweigh the need for information."[168]

When can a person justify subordinating larger loyalties in favor of self-preservation? The propriety of informing seems to vary with the gravity of the offense in question. Under any consequencialist moral system, the harm that the informer seeks to prevent must be weighed against the wrong that will result from the betrayal of friends and associates. "It is anomalous but I think true, that destroying these ties [between parent and child, spouses, extended family and tribe through the overuse of informers] creates grave problems for a society that can lose all sense of humanity because its members lose much of their feelings for those near to them."[169]

VII. Conclusion

The bottom line is do we care? Or should we care? Are the inmates who are presumably most at risk, the young,[170] those jaded by excessive sentences,[171] racial and ethnic minorities,[172] and at least twenty-five percent of the prison population which are believed to have mental disabilities,[173] a group significant enough to impact on policy considerations? Because of the dramatic effect their behavioral reactions may have on the system as a whole, they are significant.

---

168. Lynch, supra note 159, at 529. For example, a person is not required to testify against his or her spouse because they share a close confidential relationship. The marital relationship is protected because of its social benefit and because it is intrinsically valuable to the parties involved. "To impose on such a fundamental relationship would be to violate human dignity." Id. at 530. Other relationships are not as fundamental, but nevertheless are of enormous value, both to society and to the individual. Family relationships, professional associations, religious affiliations, friendships, and even the vague ties of acquaintance and fellowship that bind neighbors or people from the same hometown are all relations essential to both social and individual well-being. Id. Professor Lynch goes on to make the point that even the bonds which unite criminals joined in a common venture have moral value as an expression of human solidarity. However, the potential danger posed by criminals increasing the scope and efficiency of their criminal activities by banding together may outweigh any benefit that results from the relationship. Id.

169. Weinstein, supra note 16, at 4.

170. R. Barry Ruback & Timothy S. Carr, Prison Crowding Over Time: The Relationship of Density and Changes in Density to Infraction Rates, 20 Crim. Just. & Behav. 131, 141 (1993).

171. One study found that longer sentences were associated with greater levels of recidivism than shorter sentences. See Paul B. Paulus & Mary T. Dzindolet, The Effects of Prison Confinement, in Psychology and Social Policy 327 (Peter Suedfeld & Philip E. Tetlock eds., 1992).

172. "Most alarming, however, is the disproportionate number of minority offenders in our state and federal prisons. We incarcerate African American males at four times the rate of South Africa." Debra L. Dailey, Prison and Race in Minnesota, 64 U. Col. L. Rev. 761, 761 (1993).

173. Henry J. Steadman et al., A Survey of Mental Disability Among State Prison Inmates, 38 Hosp. & Community Psychiatry 1086 (1987).

Development of this hypothesis must begin with the query, do accused and/or convicted federal offenders perceive the Federal Sentencing Guidelines provisions as unjust?[174] Second, are federal defendants and inmates sophisticated enough to differentiate between their overall feelings of disempowerment within the system and their specific response to treatment under Guideline provisions?[175] Third, can an empirical instrument be designed to test such an inquiry?[176] Fourth, once we have this information, can the offending legal provisions be modified to increase the defendant-inmates' perception of fairness and promote cooperation and compliance with socially desirable goals?[177]

If we assume that there is a significant proportion of defendants and inmates who can articulate a specific resentment from their perceived unjust treatment under the guidelines and that an instrument can be devised to measure such responses, then social scientists should be able to correlate these feelings of unfairness with empirical evidence of behavioral trends within the trial system, the correctional facility, and possibly with trends in recidivism. These correlations could be used to initiate policy considerations in future amendments to, or applications of, particular provisions of the Federal Sentencing Guidelines.

One conclusion which may be substantiated by such research is that persons forced to "rat"[178] against others have a greater propensity to give perjured testimony,[179] thereby throwing the trial process into chaos. The probative value

---

174. An important finding by studies of people's reactions to judicial procedures is that people are not primarily influenced by the outcome of their experience but by their assessment of the fairness of the case disposition process and the fairness of the sentence. Jonathan Casper et al., Procedural Justice in Felony Cases, 22 Law & Soc'y Rev. 483, 485 (1988); Tyler, Psychological Consequences, supra note 146, at 436–37.

175. On a management level, some have observed decreased incentives for good behavior from inmates because of the reduced amount of sentence reduction time available for forfeiture in the disciplinary process. On the other hand, the reduced sentence disparity and increased certainty of release dates tended to lessen a source of frustration in the inmate population. Yale Summary, supra note 94, at 2063 (comments of Harlen W. Penn).

176. Laurens Walker & John Monahan, Social Facts: Scientific Methodology as Legal Precedent, 76 Cal. L. Rev. 877, 877 (1988); John Monahan & Laurens Walker, Judicial Use of Social Science Research, 15 Law & Hum. Behav. 571, 571 (1991).

177. See Wexler, Health Care Compliance, supra note 35, at 27–28 (stating judges at conditional release hearings could use principles of health care compliance such as behavioral contracts); Bruce J. Winick, Harnessing the Power of the Bet: Wagering with the Government as a Mechanism for Social and Individual Change, in Essays, supra note 26, at 219, 239 (stating that when criminal sanctions have not succeeded in deterring socially harmful behavior, we need to devise new approaches to supplement criminal sanctions).

178. The term "rat" is used here to distinguish between the coerced testimony of some witnesses from the volitional desire of others to testify against another.

179. Haglund, supra note 2, at 1416 (Jailhouse informants are remarkably unreliable and intuition suggests that they are cut from the same cloth as other informants so that the ingenuity of jailhouse informants' lies illustrate the potential for perjury committed by others. When an informant does not have any or enough information to bargain for leniency, he or she may be tempted to fabricate information.). "It is difficult to imagine a greater motivation to lie than the inducement of a reduced sentence." United States v. Cervantes-Pacheco, 826 F.2d 310, 315 (5th Cir. 1987).

of any potentially coerced testimony is suspect;[180] courts have recognized the power of emotional coercion as well as physical intimidation.[181] Unfortunately, there is a history of "jailhouse rats"[182] who use the system both to manipulate the government into lenient sentences and as a means to continue criminal enterprises.[183] There is always a danger in using informants to make cases[184] because the "rats," due to emotional lability, greed, or sociopathic personality, may have no compunction about using perjured testimony to achieve an objective.

Generating data on the cognitive responses of "turned" inmates may lead to important insights in predicting the occurrence of related administrative concerns within correctional management. When "ratting" is seen as the only means of decreasing draconian sentences, the potential for racing to the prosecutor is inevitable. This leads to disparity in sentencing, depending upon which criminal actor reaches the prosecutor's ear first.[185] Persons known to be informers are often obliged to remain in protective custody for the duration of their sentence, at a significantly increased cost to the government. For example, the state of Arizona implemented a determinate sentencing system in July of 1978.[186] During that year, the state correctional complex housed thirty peo-

---

180. Arizona v. Fulminante, 499 U.S. 279, 287–88, 292–93 (1991) (holding that prisoner's confession to undercover jailhouse informant was involuntary and violated the 14th Amendment).

181. As interrogators have turned to more subtle forms of psychological persuasion, courts have found the mental condition of the defendant to be a more significant factor. *Fulminante*, 499 U.S. at 286 n.2.

182. "Jailhouse informant" describes a person who informs law enforcement officers of "confessions" made by cellmates. Elizabeth A. Ganong, Note, Involuntary Confessions and the Jailhouse Informant: An Examination of Arizona v. Fulminante, 19 Hastings Const. L.Q. 911, 912 n.16 (1992).

183. Over the last 10 years the Los Angeles District Attorney used jailhouse informants to obtain convictions in more than 120 cases. Jana Winograde, Note, Jailhouse Informants and the Need for Judicial Use Immunity in Habeas Corpus Proceeding, 78 Cal. L. Rev. 755, 756 (1990). However, a scandal broke in 1988 involving jailhouse snitch Leslie White. White testified in three unrelated murder cases and one burglary case within a span of 36 days. He was released from jail three weeks later, several months ahead of his scheduled release. "Every time I come here," White boasted, "I inform and get back out." A Snitch's Story, Time Mag., Dec. 12, 1988, at 32. White said that he and other informants commit perjury "because we have learned that the reward, the privileges, the favors and the freedom offered by the district attorney for jailhouse informant testimony far outweighs any reward for the truth." Ted Rohrlich, Jail Inmate Says He Lied in Role as Informant, L.A. Times, Dec. 1, 1988, at 1.

184. Nonetheless, informant testimony is used in a huge number of cases. See Haglund, supra note 2, at 1412.

185. "It was quite common that the lookout would get 20 years, the triggerman three years, because the triggerman got to the prosecutor first." Joel Dvoskin, Address at New York Law School Journal of Human Rights Symposium, Therapeutic Jurisprudence: Restructuring Mental Disability Law (Apr. 23, 1993) (regarding correctional observations in the wake of implementing the Arizona State determinate sentencing system) (video tape on file with author). See Yale Summary, supra note 94, at 2058 (Joe B. Brown, former U.S. Attorney, Nashville, Tennessee, urges the rejection of a proposal to allow judges to depart).

186. Ariz. Rev. Stat. Ann. §§ 13-101 (1994).

ple in protective custody beds. Three years later, the number of inmates requiring protective custody increased to three hundred and thirty, a jump of 1100 percent. This increase has been attributed to the vast numbers of criminal defendants seeking sentencing leniency by informing on others, thereby requiring specialized treatment in state facilities.[187]

Of course, not all defendants possess the right kind or quality of information to qualify for the assistance reduction. This is often true of so-called "skells,"[188] who typically face extraordinarily long prison terms even when charged with the distribution of small quantities of drugs.[189] Even if the government does not offer the "skell" a deal, potential leaks as to the identity of the informant often oblige the government to provide protection to such persons in the interests of safety within the institution.

Another area ripe for inquiry is whether inmates who are demoralized by a system they find to be at odds with their own moral code and who believe that the system is merely a charade of justice are the same people who will have difficulty conforming their behavior to that mandated by the correctional institution.[190] Research in this area is sparse as well. However, some research regarding certain inmate groups may be found. For example, persons with untreated mental disabilities are more likely to be involved in disciplinary incidents,[191] young prisoners cause the most institutional disruption,[192] and incidents related to racial discord may explain increased disciplinary infractions.[193] Are these the inmates who find the system the most unfair? A research strategy is needed to answer these questions.

It may be possible to gain some insight by looking at studies on motivation and to apply those findings to the situations encountered by prisoners sentenced under the Federal Sentencing Guidelines. The work of Edward Deci is particularly instructive. Deci has distinguished three types of motivational systems: intrinsic, extrinsic and amotivational.[194] The amotivational system takes

---

187. Dvoskin, supra note 185.

188. Stephen J. Schulhofer & Ilene H. Nagel, Negotiated Pleas Under the Federal Sentencing Guidelines: The First Fifteen Months, 27 Am. Crim. L. Rev. 231, 270 (1989) (explaining that "skells" are addicted sellers who deal in small quantities of drugs to support their own habits).

189. Id. at 270 n.136 (stating that a defendant who is charged with distributing less than five grams of crack, has two similar prior convictions, and is over 18 years old is looking at a guideline range of roughly 22 to 27 years imprisonment if convicted).

190. Larson & Berg, supra note 17, at 136 (Inmates interviewed for purpose of study expressed the contention that determinate sentencing is irrational and vindictive. It was "obvious" to these inmates that the same crime may be committed in different ways and for different reasons.).

191. Cohen & Dvoskin, supra note 137, at 463 (stating untreated mentally ill inmates are more likely to be involved in serious disciplinary infractions including assaults on staff and other inmates, as well as being victimized themselves by predatory inmates).

192. Ruback & Carr, supra note 170, at 131 (stating that disciplinary infraction rates and assault rates are primarily a function of an increasing proportion of young inmates in the prison population).

193. Id. at 135.

194. See Edward L. Deci, Intrinsic Motivation(1975); Edward L. Deci, The Psychology of Self-Determination 140 (1980).

over when a person perceives "that there is no relationship between behaviors and rewards on outcomes. Perceived competence, self-determination and self-esteem tend to be extremely low. People who are amotivational feel helpless, incompetent and out-of-control."[195] If inmates feel demoralized by the procedural injustice they experience under the guidelines, and continue to feel this way upon entering the correctional institution, then subsequent maladaptive behavior and the inability to follow correctional directives may be expected pursuant to the operation of the inmate's amotivational response system.[196]

A third issue to consider is that of recidivism. Can we make the claim that the same inmates who are most likely to give perjured testimony or cause disciplinary problems within the institution, are those with recurrent recidivism statistics? There is support for the proposition that inmates who participate in correctional programs, those who see the system as working in a rational way, may continue to use the system in an acceptable way once they get out, therefore maintaining a reduction in criminal recidivism.[197] A variety of current behavioral or cognitive measures were related to recidivism. Prisoners who had little respect for the system were the most likely to become recidivists.[198] However, there is little evidence that psychiatric programs in prison have any direct relationship on recidivism rates outside prison.[199]

By Congressional mandate, the guidelines seek to promote respect for the law. This goal, in a therapeutic jurisprudence formulation, should be aggressively pursued. In keeping with the Congressional mandate, the Commission is to develop a "means of measuring the degree to which the sentencing ... practices are effective in meeting the ... purposes set forth."[200] The therapeutic jurisprudence formulation offers an interdisciplinary paradigm for assessing the therapeutic effect of certain provisions of the guidelines on federal offenders. Unfortunately, the guidelines have not decreased criminal activity.[201] Even

---

195. See Bruce Winick, The Side Effects of Incompetency Labeling and the Implications of Mental Health Law 26 (1993) (unpublished manuscript on file with author).

196. Id. at 29.

197. Paul Gendreau & Robert R. Ross, Revivification of Rehabilitation: Evidence from the 1980's, 4 Just. Q. 349, 350–51 (1987) (stating that reduction in criminal recidivism may be possible through correctional rehabilitation). The notion of prison "therapeutic communities" is based upon similar concepts, where participants are resocialized and eventually forced to embrace responsibility, honesty and caring for others. Researchers have been cautiously optimistic about the success of therapeutic communities in lowering recidivism rates. Id.; Harry K. Wexler et al., Outcome Evaluation of a Prison Therapeutic Community for Substance Abuse Treatment, 17 Crim. Just. & Behav. 71, 89 (1990) (convincing evidence that prison-based treatment can produce significant reductions in recidivism rates). Likewise, the "bootcamp" approach focuses youths on changing their attitudes toward themselves and toward criminal behavior. Paulus & Dzindolet, supra note 171, at 333.

198. Zamble & Porporino, supra note 129, at 59.

199. Cohen & Dvoskin, supra note 137, at 464. Contra Zamble & Porporino, supra note 128, at 53 ("It has become increasingly clear that appropriate application of contemporary behavioral and cognitive treatments can change offender's behavior, even when judged by the bottom-line criterion of recidivism rate.") (citations omitted).

200. 28 U.S.C. § 991(b) (1988).

201. Weinstein, supra note 12, at 8.

though the guidelines receive overwhelmingly negative reviews,[202] they appear to be a fixed part of our federal criminal procedure. Despite the ever-increasing explosion of articles on all aspects of the guidelines, there are few normative or empirical studies which assess the guidelines provisions from the perspective of the defendant or inmate. This article suggests a research agenda which challenges others to generate empirical data to decrease that gap.

I suspect that such empirical data will show that the offender's consternation, anguish, and rebellion cannot be relieved over carrot soup and salad in a trendy Tribeca lunch spot. However, we must begin to acknowledge the offender's emotional and behavioral responses from trial through incarceration, and consider the role these responses may play in recidivism rates.

---

202. Only four out of hundreds who testified before the Federal Courts Study Committee supported the guidelines. Those four were the Attorney General Richard Thornburgh and three members of the commission. Michael Tonry, The Success of Judge Frankel's Sentencing Commission, 64 U. Colo. L. Rev. 713, 715 (1993).

Chapter 11

A Sentencing Model for the 21st Century

Judge Robert J. Kane

Introduction

For a quarter of a century Massachusetts has followed the national example of responding to the crime problem through the same indiscriminate use of power that defined our Vietnam policies. Our crime strategy has been to indiscriminately incarcerate offenders under the theory that this massive use of power would frighten criminals into submission. Like the Vietnamese who saw our bombs and napalm as reasons to escalate their resistance, the alienated youth of America see our mandatory disparities and punitive mistakes as justifications for their senseless and violent expressions of personal power. They sit in our courtrooms and witness the careless manner of our judgments, and these impressions strengthen their rageful feelings of how corrupt and shameless the law is. Their complaints of sentencing incoherency are equally voiced by victims who witness career criminals' sentences discounted under unconscionable plea bargains.

We are now approaching the 21st century when we expect that larger teenage populations will dramatically increase crime rates. Conservative forecasters of these crime trends are already arguing for policies that will enlarge incapacitation strategies[1] and weaken privacy rights.[2] Before Massachusetts follows this stale advice, the leadership of this state ought to carefully review the accumulated evidence of what incarceration policies have actually produced.[3] This review of incarceration policies' poor results can help us recreate sentencing into a strategic use of power for the purposes of increasing incarceration rates and sentences of intractable and dangerous offenders while providing treatment opportunities for offenders engaged in the ageless struggle of defining their identities. Massachusetts' new Sentencing Commission offers opportunities for examining sentencing practices and outcomes and for designing a new sentencing architecture that allows for the tactical use of punishment and prevention powers. This article's purpose is to explore alternative sentencing approaches to Massachusetts' indiscriminate sentencing perspectives and practices.

This article focuses its attention on ideas for modernizing sentencing practices in Massachusetts' 68 district courts. These district courts presently possess broad criminal jurisdiction that incorporates all misdemeanors and

---

1. John J. DiIulio, "The Question of Black Crime," The Public Interest, Fall 1994, p. 15.
2. James Q. Wilson, "What to Do about Crime," Commentary, September 1995, p. 28.
3. Empirical evidence does not establish any deterrence effect from incapacitation policies. John J. DiIulio, "Does Prison Pay," The Brookings Review, Fall 1991, p. 31.

many felonies including narcotic sales, indecent assaults, and aggravated batteries. The judges of these courts process over one-quarter million criminal cases representing over 90 percent of the state's criminal business. Generally, district court judges are empowered to exercise broad discretion in determining sentences, and this discretion is mainly restricted by statutory penalty ceilings. Notwithstanding the availability of discretion, the prevailing sentencing pattern is judicial approval of plea bargains which are considered servicable to the courts' case management interests.

Massachusetts Sentencing Commission

The Massachusetts Sentencing Commission is now responsible for redesigning sentencing powers through the development of sentencing guidelines that will provide sentencing ranges for offenses and permit flexibility for individualized sentencing of defendants. The enabling statute also authorizes the Commission to recommend other sentencing changes necessary for accomplishing the goals of sentencing credibility and justice which, respectively, incorporate the principles of proportionate and enforceable punishments. Accomplishing these sentencing goals will require the enactment of not only sentencing guidelines but also adjunct sentencing information systems capable of: discriminating hard- and soft-core defendants; placing soft-core offenders into effective and accessible treatment slots; and enforcing treatment contracts.

Commission recommendations for accessing and processing information on dangerousness, recidivism, and treatment potential are necessary corollaries for sentencing guideline applications and exemptions since the guidelines will leave to the court the choice of a sentence within the sentencing range and the judgment of whether special circumstances warrant sentences above or below the range. If sentencing guideline legislation fails to structure the processing of sentencing choices, the negotiation capacities and sentencing perspectives of two lawyers will continue to largely determine what happens to defendants. Following plea bargain recommendations will continue to produce errors in sorting hard- and soft-core offenders.

For purposes of illustrating how irrational plea bargaining is, a cross- referencing of professional used car sales transactions is useful. A fair used car price is a function of an experienced seller and a sophiscated buyer who negotiate from objective price information (Blue Book) and subjective factors that cause an upward or downward price shift. This commercial transaction model is not the pattern for plea bargaining in the district court where plea bargaining often functions through inexperienced parties or unevenly skilled parties who negotiate on incomplete information of offenders' subjective histories and partial or no information on offenders' dangerousness, recidivism risk, or suitability for treatment interventions. This combination of uneven and inexperienced negotiators and incomplete information produces irrational and unequal sentencing outcomes. Where, for example, an inexperienced defender negotiates with an equally inexperienced but aggressive prosecutor over a school zone sale by an addict whose record is negligible and who is treatable, the negotiated settlement may well produce a jail sentence in exchange for a cancellation of the school zone mandatory penalty. Conversely, a negotiation involving an inexperienced and timid prosecutor and a skilled and aggressive defense counsel over a sale by a chronic drug seller may result in minimal or no imprisonment. This negotiation process obviously produces unreliable determinations on what offenders warrant incapacitation.

Furthermore, plea negotiations over defendants' liberty commonly result in probation compromises; and these sentences, structured by lawyers, usually uninformed and often uninterested in behavioral management, are generally silent on the sentence's objectives and approach. Such general lack of thoughtful reflection creates a meaningless and purposeless probation. The court is left without any organized, articulate expression about whether the probation contract is for the purpose of control, treatment, or restitution. The court, in other words, finds itself with an empty voice on what means are necessary for achieving desired outcomes.

Restructuring Sentencing Choices

While plea bargaining is a practical necessity for managing criminal caseloads, we can lessen the impact of the lawyers' subjective thinking on sentencing by centering plea and sentencing discussions on objective information. We can accomplish this by defining what criteria such as an offender's risk will determine where the offender fits within a sentencing range and by supplying the plea and sentencing process with diagnostic and prognostic information on the offender. Similar to negotiations of damages in a civil liability case, the lawyers would use, instead of medical bills and doctor reports, the offender's biographical, attitudinal, and clinical information to discuss the risk and management of the risk. And, just as a doctor forecasts an injury's progression and longevity, a probation analyst, using risk assessment methods, could forecast the recidivism potential of the offender. This probation analyst, like a doctor, could for defendants considered treatable produce treatment recommendations. The information analyst, using a treatment classification system, could construct a prevention plan that matches the offender's treatment profile with a compatible and accessible program.

The sentencing hearing would then function as a mechanism for considering counter arguments on the incapacitation and prevention analysis. Where the court elects a prevention strategy, the judicial professional would follow a medical model of explaining the plan, listening to compliance problems, and clarifying consequences for noncompliance.

Implementing information systems necessary for reliably sorting offenders requires redefining probation's mission from micro case management responsibilities to classification/program management functions. Reorganized probation services would incorporate: (1) redefinition of probation job responsibilities and development of salary incentive programs based on performance measurements; (2) creation of court-based purchase of accounts and establishment of purchase of service allocation formulas incorporating performance-based criteria; (3) development of sentencing classification systems.

Under this reorganization, the probation service would be modernized into an agency driven by information. The operating unit for creating and using this information would be a probation team. Probation teams would consist of interchangeable specialists for: data collection/analysis; program development/management; and treatment compliance. This functional specialization would sponsor professional development and performance through rotational assignments and team dynamism. Probation team performance would be competitively driven by the use of salary incentives indexed by outcome criteria relating to performance levels of probation clients. Client performance criteria would incorporate such indicia as rearrests, program stay, employment productivity, and the quality of offenders' family relationships.

Under this model the probation central office would become responsible for developing and operationalizing sentencing classification systems that would provide markers for sorting hard-core offenders and criteria for matching probation clients with treatment modalities. This classification capacity for more precisely identifying probationers' dangerousness, recidivism risk, and rehabilitative potential would be largely developed through the accumulation and analysis of: (1) social science studies on offenders' risk; (2) other jurisdictions' classification systems; and (3) Massachusetts data on offenders' recidivism. The programmers could then identify data, such as school behavior, employment history, residential stability, family and peer relationships, and criminogenic attitudes for use as recidivism markers.

The other function of this classification system would be the development of treatment models for discrete offender populations. These treatment population profiles indicating what works for whom would be based on criminal justice and social science research. The treatment information system would also inform the decisionmaker of length of stay, cost, support services, and success criteria. Data on client performance would inform probation of treatment violations and providers' performance.

Operationally, probation officers would construct classification reports on offenders whose offense or record indicated that a conviction would probably result in intensive probation or imprisonment. Within 21 days of arraignment, probation would develop for the court a report structured around certain information categories, such as school performance and family relationships, helpful in assessing dangerousness, recidivism, and treatment suitability. This information would be computerized within a categorically defined database designed to incorporate supplementary informational entries. The computerized database would be designed for collection of hard data such as domestic abuse information, care and protection files, and Registry of Motor Vehicle information. Soft data on persons' lifestyles and attitudes could be collected through interviews by probation officers trained in accessing information. All oral data entries would be verifiable through either documentary or secondary sources.

This sentencing report, integrated into recidivism, dangerousness, and treatment analyses, would function as the information base for decisions on incapacitation and probation. Using these analyses for sentencing decisions, judges could: discriminate hard- and soft-core defendants; increase incapacitation rates for intractable offenders; and channel soft-core offenders into effective treatment programs.

Probation promises would be enforced by the mutual self-interest of the probation team and treatment providers in either adjusting a probation contract or incapacitating offenders whose behaviors were symptomatic of criminal propensities or behaviors. Team decisionmaking would insure that compliance specialists were not functioning in an excessively punitive manner. For purposes of ensuring probation enforcement reviews, sentencing legislation could require periodic probation review sessions.

This sentence model's complexity may seem oversized for the district courts' resource base. The model may appear to overstress probation resources by requiring services for: (1) collecting, processing, and analyzing offender histories; (2) allocating and auditing purchase-of-service monies; and (3) reviewing and enforcing probation contracts. In reality this amounts to modest resource costs. Informational and programmatic functions would replace probation hours largely dedicated to office reviews. This functional reallocation is sensible as research studies indicate questionable outcomes through probation supervision models. Furthermore, this informational and programmatic function for probation would largely eliminate the need for time-intensive probation courtroom services, and any residual record retrieval duties under the new model could be efficiently allocated to clerical personnel.

A second apparent resource problem is this model's requirements for greater judicial involvement in sentencing offenders. More judicial sentencing time would only be required where a case involves either incapacitation or supervised probation. Secondly, this sentencing process would involve reports that could be read before taking the bench; and sentencing bench time would replace the significant judicial time spent in unstructured lobby and courtroom conversations on possible pleas.

A third apparent problem with this model is its negative effects on plea bargaining through the model's potential production of high offender risk estimates that would harden prosecutors' sentencing recommendations. This apparent plea bargaining problem is of marginal importance as plea bargaining is largely a function of estimates of trial outcomes.[4] Analysis that may reveal an offender's high risk may well promote plea bargaining by increasing defense counsel's awareness of a severe sentencing outcome after trial. Defense counsel's willingness to enter into meaningful plea negotiations with the prosecution may be agreeable to prosecutors who see degrees of risk in going to trial. Pleas can be further promoted under this sentencing model if the model follows Federal sentencing rules in allowing for favorable consideration of timely case resolutions.

Management problems with this model lessen through illustration of the model's applications. For purposes of illustration, let's consider the model's application in the hypothetical case of William James, age 17, who appears on June 1 in the New Bedford District Court on a complaint charging assault and battery by means of a dangerous weapon. On June 1, Mr. James, like any defendant, provides basic biographical data and supplementary data on schooling, family, and employment relationships to a trained probation analyst. The analyst creates for Mr. James a sentencing information file. The file integrates into a computerized information system generally divided into risk and treatment sections and discretely broken down into the following categories: (1) school information indexed by suspensions, academic performance, and intel-

4. Charles Silberman, Criminal Violence, Criminal Justice. New York: Random House, 1978, p. 272.

ligence testing; (2) familial relationships including incidents of sexual and physical abuse; (3) employment information broken down into skills, work periods, and reasons for job changes and unemployment. The analyst, after interviewing the defendant, then through a series of protocols, collects and analyzes institutional data on school, family, and employment. The analyst also interviews two or more informed and reliable parties for the purpose of supplementing and verifying offender oral histories.

Using standardized risk assessment methods, the analyst would assess such risk indicators as: (1) cognitive capacity; (2) chronicity of school misbehaviors; (3) family relationships; (4) onset of criminal behaviors; (5) addictive history; (6) criminogenic attitudes. Using these risk markers, the analyst would then provide a risk score to the offender. Where the risk score was moderate or below, the analyst would assess treatment potential and where an affirmative analysis occurred, develop a treatment profile broken down into: (1) learning style; (2) treatment needs; (3) treatment deficits, i.e., ability to pay. This part of the assessment would conclude with specific recommendations on: (1) treatment providers; (2) length of stay; (3) special conditions; (4) payment method.

In a busy urban court, this collection system would initially apply to approximately 60 defendants each week.[5] If only six probation officers were assigned to the function, each probation officer would be required to conduct only two risk interviews a day. This two-a-day number is misleading as once files were created the only new work for an arrestee would be supplementing the file. Going back to Mr. James, his risk analysis created in 21 days was a moderate-to-high risk on the basis of the following information: (1) chronic misbehavior resulting in multiple suspensions; (2) early onset (age 12) of criminal activities; (3) escalating use of narcotic substances; (4) normal intelligence; (5) positive treatment attitudes revealed by a self-initiated detoxification stay; (6) enabling parents. This information package, including the average sentence for this offense and offender; the offender's risk; the described harmed; and, where applicable, treatment recommendations, centers the attorneys' thinking and interactions on an appropriate sentence. Using the average sentence and the risk score as departure points and relying on the probation analyst as an interpreter of the underlying information, the attorneys, at a plea conference, can select a sentence on the basis of facts and rational analysis. This rational processing of information through the filters of the normative sentence, the subjective harm, the offender's individualized risk, and, where applicable, treatment eligibility, would convey to the defendant and the victim a fair and intelligible process for the judicial choice of an appropriate sentence.

Promoting Public Safety Interests

Serious consideration of this proposed sentencing model requires an examination of the article's assumption that substantial public benefits from enacting these changes justify the costs of undertaking them. This examination of

---

5. This assumes that 3,000 of the 8,000 defendants who are likely to appear in the New Bedford District Court qualify for an offender risk assessment.

the benefits of this sentencing model begins with a consideration of what crime reduction benefits could be achieved by changing our sentencing system from the present to the proposed approach.

The district courts, over the course of a year, sentence approximately 15,000 defendants to houses of correction.[6] While these offenders are imprisoned, their crime rate is obviously zero. That crime rate, however, reportedly jumps to over 60 percent within 1 year of their release.[7] Over the course of a year, the district courts also place over 8,000 defendants on intensive probation.[8] Within 1 year, approximately 40 percent of those probationers recidivate.[9] For this sentencing proposal to make sense as a crime prevention policy, it must persuasively prove that the costs of implementing this proposal will result in a significantly lower amount of serious crimes being committed by these two groups. These sentencing changes can achieve these lower crime rates only if the proposed sorting method is substantially better than present methods in: (1) increasing the incarceration rates of those who cannot be safely managed in the community; (2) lengthening prison terms of those offenders who are extremely likely after release to reoffend; (3) using treatment programs that lower the recidivism rates of treatable offenders who are presently being incarcerated or placed on probation.

To illustrate this sentencing model's crime reduction potential, reasonably assume that of the 60 percent of the house of correction population who recidivate within 1 year 70 percent are hard-core offenders. It then follows that a 50 percent change in increasing sentences by 1 year for this group will prevent thousands of crimes.[10] Secondly, assume that of the 8,000 who are placed on highly structured probation this new system identifies 2,000 as presenting a high risk of committing crimes. Using a 50 percent influence factor on sentencing decisions, 1,000 of these offenders would either go to jail or be placed on strict monitoring systems that would either eliminate or lower their crime rates. Even if the latter group were not controlled, proposed changes in probation would increase the likelihood of a probation revocation taking place.

The second part of this proposal's thesis is that it will outperform incapacitation and traditional probation in achieving lower recidivism rates for offenders who are treatable. Of the prison population who reenter society, approximately 40 percent of those within 1 year do not recidivate. As there is little evidence that prison deterred their behaviors, then these offenders either haven't been caught or didn't require jail. The latter group would have obviously performed as well on probation at less expense. Of the group who continue to recidivate and who are either reapprehended or undetected, there is,

6. Court Commitments to Massachusetts County Facilities During 1992. Boston, MA: Massachusetts Department of Corrections.

7. Based on numerous conversations with county corrections officials.

8. Massachusetts Department of Probation Research Division Reports for 1995. Boston, MA: Office of the Commissioner of Probation.

9. The Classification of Male and Female Offenders by the Massachusetts Probation System. Boston, MA: Center for Applied Social Research, Northeastern University, February 1991.

10. An extremely conservative estimate of a hard-core offender's average crime rate is 10 crimes a year. John J. DiIulio, "Does Prison Pay," pp. 31, 32.

besides a hard-core population, a substantial number who could have been safely and effectively managed through community or residential treatment rather than jail. This claim is supported by a common sense understanding that offenders who are in residential treatment or intensively participating in community treatment services are not likely to be committing crimes. Of course, where offenders who are offered treatment do not satisfy treatment rules under this sentencing model, they would quickly return to court for revocation proceedings.

Thirdly, this proposed sentencing model would structure the treatment plan so as to take advantage of proven methods for increasing positive treatment outcomes. One such method is classifying offenders' learning styles, cognitive capacities, and treatment needs and placing them in programs that can handle those aptitudes and needs.[11] Also, this proposal would structure the processing of the decision so to enable an offender to appreciate the reasons for the sentence and to understand what treatment goals, obligations, and consequences apply.

For two reasons, this processing model would be better than current sentencing methods in securing offender follow through on treatment plans. Firstly, common sense indicates that impacted parties are more ready to accept and support decisions where effective communication of the reasons for the decision and opportunities for dialogue occur. Where, for example, a principal, without talking to the students or teachers or reviewing all school records, allows only certain students to be promoted, those left behind are not likely to follow the principal's remedial recommendations. Where, on the other hand, the principal, upon reviewing the student's performance and listening to the teacher and the failing student, crafts a promotional plan especially designed for the student's problems and aptitudes, that student's motivation for following that plan substantially increases.

Therapeutic jurisprudence scholarship also supports this claim that judicial attention to probation decisions can promote positive outcomes. This scholarship compares judicial sentencing practices to health care providers' practices in securing client compliance with health care treatment plans. Using studies on health care compliance outcomes, this therapeutic scholarship reveals health care compliance problems where the health care professional adopts distant, distracted, and abrupt styles for explaining client treatment requirements.[12] Positive compliance outcomes are associated by this health care research with health care professionals who are "perceived to be competent, attentive, practical, and motivated by the best interests of the client."[13] These analogous studies certainly provide support for the conclusion that judicial thoughtfulness in processing the probation choice and care in explaining that treatment plan, obligations, and consequences, both positive and negative, will increase the likelihood that the probationer will comply with the probation contract.

---

11. Paul Gendreau and Robert Ross, "Reverification of Rehabilitation Evidence from the 1980's," Justice Quarterly, September 1987, pp. 370–75.

12. David B. Wexler, Therapeutic Jurisprudence and the Criminal Courts. Williamsburg, VA: William and Mary Law School, Fall 1993.

13. David B. Wexler, Therapeutic Jurisprudence and the Criminal Courts. Williamsburg, VA: William and Mary Law School, Fall 1993.

Nevertheless, the critical assumption for achieving these significant reductions in criminal behaviors is the claim that the proposed processing of sentences will more effectively sort hard- and soft-core offenders than the present sentencing process. Conservative and liberal scholars strongly agree that mandatory incapacitation measures capture a substantial numbers of soft-core offenders[14] and that traditional sentencing systems, like Massachusetts', are poor sorters of which offenders warrant jail. Mandatory measures like Massachusetts' required 2-year on-and-after requirement for school zone drug offenses are extremely overinclusive in their applications.

Besides applying overinclusive mandatory jail penalties, judges in Massachusetts district courts send offenders to jail based on the quality of thinking involved in plea recommendations. As previously discussed, these recommendations, leveraged by the dynamics of plea brokers' perspectives, personalities, and relationships, obviously generate errors in under and over incapacitating offenders. Functioning in an environment without substantial information or predictive standards on an offender's risk, this process rather arbitrarily arrives at its compromised settlements of who goes to jail and for how long.

In contrast, this proposed process would supplement the present information base consisting of an adult record and police report with information that illuminates the offender's risk potential. As recently reiterated by John Laub, offender's risk can be more fully considered by courts that collect and analyze accessible information on the offender's school and family experiences.[15] These school records; CHINS files, care and protection records, domestic violence reports, and juvenile histories can inform the court of the persistency and intensity of the offender's violation of social controls. These records and supplementary interviews can also provide the court with information on the offender's capacity for cognitively restructuring his thinking and his willingness to do so. A summary and explanation of this information, through an easily readable probation risk report, could provide accessible information for framing the issues at both the plea conference and sentencing hearing. Where the plea negotiation incorporates consideration of information disclosing patterns of criminal behavior and the offender's aptitude and will for changing that pattern, the incapacitation decision will be more reliable.

Enacting This Sentencing Model

These ideas for reorganizing sentencing may appeal to political leaders who have recently expressed support for providing funds for treating offenders. These leaders may find in these proposals assurances that treatment monies will go to treatment programs that work. By implementing the model proposed in this article, the right choices could be made on what offenders to treat, what treatment services to offer, and what treatment providers ought to be given funding. Of course, for all this to happen, "courts will have to change; they will have to become models of fairness... living demonstrations

---

14. James Q. Wilson, "Prisons in a Free Society," The Public Interest, Fall 1994, p. 38.

15. John H. Laub and Janet Lauritson, "The Precursors of Criminal Offending Across the Life Course," Federal Probation, September 1994, p. 52.

that justice is possible, that human beings can be treated with decency and concern."[16]

---

16. Charles Silberman, Criminal Violence, Criminal Justice. New York: Random House, 1978, p. 257.

Chapter 12

The Mental Health Implications of Crime Victims' Rights

Richard P. Wiebe

U.S. citizens expect their federal, state, and local governments to provide the police, court, and correctional services necessary to enforce the criminal law. This public responsibility evolved over several centuries from a system of dispute resolution that was predominantly private. In England and Europe following the fall of the Roman Empire, around the fifth century A.D., the family of a victim seeking redress could declare a "blood feud" against the person, property, and family of the wrongdoer, seeking both payment and vengeance (Henderson, 1992). English law, from which U.S. jurisprudence evolved, began to limit the extent of the blood feud in the 11th century, permitting it only where the injured party had demanded and been refused reasonable payment for the injury from the offender (Henderson, 1992); soon, the offender became responsible for the payment of a fine to the king as well (Schafer, 1968). At first, some crimes—such as killing by stealth, arson, treason, housebreaking, and open theft—required the death or mutilation of the offender; the offender could not merely pay compensation to the victim or the victim's family (Greenburg, 1984). Eventually, the transition to public enforcement of criminal law was complete. Current U.S. criminal law views crimes as offenses against the state, not against the victims (Elias, 1986).

In the interests of public order, and in the face of centralized criminal justice, rights of criminal defendants were easily ignored. The U.S. Constitution's Bill of Rights, however, contains some protections for specific defendants. Enacted after the original Constitution, the Bill of Rights contains the following provisions governing the rights of persons suspected, accused, or convicted of committing a crime:

> AMENDMENT IV: The right of the people to be secure in their persons, houses, papers, and effects, against unreasonable searches and seizures, shall not be violated, and no warrants shall issue but upon probable cause, supported by oath or affirmation, and particularly describing the place to be searched, and the persons or things to be seized.

> AMENDMENT V: No person shall be held to answer for a capital, or otherwise infamous crime, unless on a presentment or indictment of a grand jury, except in cases arising in the land or naval forces, or in the militia, when in actual service in time of war or public danger; nor shall any person be subject to the same offense to be twice put in jeopardy of life or limb; nor shall be compelled in any criminal case to be a witness against himself; nor be deprived of life, liberty or property, without due process of law; nor shall private property be taken for public use without just compensation.

> AMENDMENT VI: In all criminal prosecutions, the accused shall enjoy the right to a speedy and public trial, by an impartial jury of the State and district

wherein the crime shall have been committed, which district shall have previously ascertained by law, and to be informed of the nature and cause of the accusation; to be confronted with the witnesses against him; to have compulsory process for obtaining witnesses in his favor; and to have the assistance of counsel for his defense.

AMENDMENT VIII: Excessive bail shall not be required, or cruel and unusual punishments inflicted.

Initially, these rights applied only to persons accused of federal crimes, but they were applied to state defendants through the post-Civil War Supreme Court's interpretation of the Civil Rights Amendments (*Yick Wo v. Hopkins*, 1886). However, it was not until the 1950s that rights of criminals began to assume paramount importance in the criminal justice system. Defendants received "Miranda warnings" and court-appointed lawyers. The exclusionary rule, allowing only evidence obtained legally to be used against the accused (*Weeks v. United States*, 1913), was applied. Prison conditions were scrutinized; prisoners received counseling, employment training, schooling, medical care, and libraries, because their absence could be construed as "cruel and unusual punishment" under the Eighth Amendment (Karmen, 1984).

During this period of emphasis on defendants' rights, neither the Supreme Court nor state or national legislatures focused on the needs of crime victims. Although the right to protect individuals from the government was constitutionally compelling, the focus on the rights of defendants without talk of the rights of those they injured was not politically persuasive. Thus, in the aftermath of defendants' rights, a picture began to emerge of the "forgotten victim," victimized twice: first by the criminal, then by the system (Karmen, 1984; President's Task Force on Victims of Crime, 1982). In response, legislatures began to enact laws establishing rights for victims, at first focusing on government-funded victim compensation to crime victims. California passed the first such statute in 1965, followed by New York in 1966, Hawaii in 1967, and Massachusetts in 1968 (Roberts, 1990). Other victims' rights began to populate statute books and state constitutions; currently, there may be up to 30,000 different state and federal victims' rights laws (S. S. Howley, personal communication, December 30, 1993). Public interest peaked during the early Reagan years, with the establishment of the President's Task Force on Victims of Crime and the release of its final report in 1982. Many of the recommendations of the Task Force have been enacted (see, for example, U.S. Department of Justice, Office of Justice Programs, 1986), but nowhere have they and other victim-oriented measures been systematically evaluated for their effects on the psychological recovery of victims themselves. An evaluation of this type may help guide the future of victims' rights, so that victims may avoid being victimized a third time.

The goals of this chapter are to survey the scope and purposes of victims' rights provisions; to discuss, from current psychological research, the effects of those provisions on the mental health of victims; to compare these effects with those intended by lawmakers and advocates—that is, whether intended goals have been attained, and whether the laws resulted in unintended consequences; and to suggest possible directions for victims' rights that would better serve victims' mental health. The analysis fits the framework of *therapeutic jurisprudence*, which attempts to determine the extent to which legal processes benefit or harm the people involved (Wexler & Winick, 1991). However, it would be naive to assert that therapeutic jurisprudence alone can, or should, dictate the agenda of victims' rights. Laws are enacted within the context of the existing social structure, and other political and moral considerations may prevail over therapeutic outcomes (Sales & Shuman, 1994).

Before going forward, one caveat is in order. Crimes can be placed, with overlap and exceptions, into three broad categories. The first, so-called victimless crimes, such as vandalism of a public place, drunken driving, prostitution, drug use, insider trading, and desertion from the armed forces, lack specific victims (although they can clearly result in harm). Other crimes, like illegal dumping of toxic waste and espionage, may have specific victims, but their consequences may be delayed and the identity of the victims and extent of harm may not be readily apparent. The third broad category, including "street crimes" such as assault, homicide, robbery, rape, and burglary, together with fraud against individuals, involves specific, readily ascertainable victims; victims' rights provisions tend to focus on these crimes. Thus, the rest of this chapter focuses on this third category.

The Scope and Purposes of Victims' Rights

The word *victim* stems from the Latin *victima*, a person or animal sacrificed during a religious ceremony. The word has since acquired more connotations—for example, there are victims of floods, cancer, accidents, prejudice, and crime (Karmen, 1984). Unlike the sacrificial victim, a crime victim suffers consequences unintended by society and may have certain rights under law that accrue after victimization. Aside from the quest for justice, a topic beyond the scope of this chapter, the proliferation of victims' rights has stemmed from the desire to ease victims' psychological suffering. The next section outlines the details of that suffering.

The Experience of the Victim

Criminal victimization can leave psychological scars that endure as long as or longer than any physical or financial damage (Fischer, 1984; Frank, 1988; Henderson, 1992). Criminal victimization may result in anxiety disorders, depression, drug and alcohol abuse, fear, flashbacks, lowered self-esteem, sexual dysfunction, somatic complaints, suicidal ideation, suspiciousness, and a sense of social isolation (Fischer, 1984; Keane, 1989; Lurigio & Resick, 1990). In some cases victims may suffer from posttraumatic stress disorder (PTSD) (American Psychiatric Association, 1994).[1]

Although much of the research on the impact of crime has focused on rape, victims of other crimes may suffer qualitatively similar consequences (Resick, 1987). Other factors being equal, like level of violence and victim's perception

---

1. Victims of other kinds of trauma, such as serious accidents and illnesses, war, and technological and natural disasters, often develop the same mental health problems as crime victims (Frieze, Hymer, & Greenberg, 1987; Keane, 1989).

of danger, rape may harm the victim's mental health more than do other violent crimes (Kilpatrick, 1989; Kilpatrick et al., 1985), but this issue is not settled (Resick, 1987; Riggs, Kilpatrick, & Resnick, 1992). Significant psychological injuries have been reported among victims of many other crimes, including assault (Lurigio & Resick, 1990; Riggs et al., 1992; Shepherd, 1990; Steinmetz, 1984; Wirtz & Harrell, 1987), attempted rape (Becker, Skinner, Abel, Howell, & Bruce, 1982), bank fraud (Ganzini, McFarland, & Cutler, 1990), burglary (Brown & Harris, 1989), child abuse (Cavaiola & Schiff, 1988), kidnapping (Terr, 1983), and robbery (Kilpatrick et al., 1985). In addition, families of crime victims in general (Riggs & Kilpatrick, 1990) and of rape (Mio, 1991; Orzek, 1983) and homicide (Amick-McMullen, Kilpatrick, & Resnick, 1991; McCune, 1989) victims in particular often develop psychological symptoms as a result of the crime. Finally, community residents may suffer as a result of public vandalism, a crime with no specific victim (Reiss, 1986).

The consequences of victimization are not necessarily intuitively obvious. Although crime victims indeed experience more mental health problems than do other persons (Ganzini, McFarland, & Cutler, 1990; Kilpatrick et al., 1985; Riggs et al., 1992; Santiago, McCall-Perez, Gorcey, & Beigel, 1985), the severity of the crime does not necessarily predict the severity of the symptoms. For example, Becker et al. (1982) found that victims of attempted rape and rape did not significantly differ in their short- and long-term responses to the assault; Ganzini et al. (1990) found significant levels of depression in victims of the relatively placid crime of bank fraud. Furthermore, though it is clear that support from family members and friends can assist a victim's recovery (Janoff-Bulman & Frieze, 1983), those persons do not always understand the extent of psychological trauma and may think the victim should have recovered earlier than is reasonable to expect (Mio, 1991; Riggs & Kilpatrick, 1990; Sales, Baum, & Shore, 1984). In addition, not all crime victims will react the same way to similar victimizations (Lurigio & Resick, 1990; Shapland, 1986).

Similarly, the duration of symptoms is difficult to predict. Symptoms can begin immediately after the attack and persist over a lifetime (Santiago et al., 1985). Fifty-seven percent of rape victims in a community survey reported having suffered PTSD symptoms at some point in their lives, with 16% reporting current PTSD symptoms, an average of 17 years after the rape (Kilpatrick, Saunders, Vernonen, Best, & Von, 1987).

Cognitive and behavioral psychologists have attempted to explain this persistence of symptoms through several mechanisms. Through classical conditioning, a crime victim may unconsciously associate an aversive event, the crime itself, with a previously neutral stimulus, such as the street on which the crime occurred (Wirtz & Harrell, 1987). The victim would then respond with fear and anxiety to the street itself, even when it appears objectively to be safe. These responses may be extremely resistant to extinction (Kilpatrick et al., 1987; Veronen, Kilpatrick, & Resick, 1979). In addition, depression may result from learned helplessness, where a victim has been traumatized as a result of an experience over which he or she had no control (Peterson & Seligman, 1983). Persistence of symptoms may also be associated with an enduring modification of beliefs. Studies have shown that violent crime can alter victims' beliefs regarding their safety, self-esteem, and trust, whereas property crimes affect victims' beliefs concerning safety; these beliefs, in turn, affect psychological distress (Janoff-Belman & Frieze, 1983; Norris & Kaniasty, 1991).

Symptoms may also endure because, left to themselves, crime victims may select inefficacious techniques for recovery. Research focusing on victims' coping strategies outside a therapeutic relationship found that some victims' methods, such as changing phone numbers, staying at home, moving, not going out alone, installing new locks, bolting locks more, owning or carrying a weapon, changing jobs, and generally exercising more caution, failed to facilitate their recovery significantly. In fact, changing phone numbers and staying home more correlated with *higher* psychological distress levels both one and six months after the crime (Wirtz & Harrell, 1987; see also Cohen, 1987). Similarly, remaining at home and withdrawing from others correlates with poor postrape adjustment (Meyer & Taylor, 1986). Without assistance, then, many crime victims will continue to experience significant adverse psychological symptoms.

The Framework of Victims' Rights

Despite their suffering, recognition and establishment of a societal obligation to crime victims has been long delayed. The constitutional framework of American criminal procedure seeks to limit governmental power over individuals. The constitution does not obligate the government to provide services or benefits to individuals. This framework implicitly assumes that crime victims benefit from just prosecution of the perpetrator. Thus, in the absence of affirmative statutory recognition of crime victims' rights, the American criminal justice system grants the victim no special stature within it other than as a complaining witness, and it assumes no obligation to the crime victim as an individual, such as by according the victim a right to compensation or services. In the absence of victims' rights and victim assistance programs, crime victims must provide their own transportation to and from court and must assist the prosecution, over whose conduct they have no control, by identifying witnesses, attending the trial, and subjecting themselves to intrusive cross-examination by the defendant's attorney. They also must pay their own medical and counseling bills (Sales, Rich, & Reich, 1987). Because many crimes go unreported, most reported crimes fail to result in an arrest, and most arrests do not lead to a trial. Thus, whatever benefits crime victims enjoy from criminal prosecution will not be available to most crime victims.

Victims' rights attempt to address these problems of victims through various means. The first broad category of victims' rights contains measures aimed at benefiting victims through increasing penalties for, and decreasing the liberties of, accused and convicted criminals. Thus, the provisions recommended under this rubric of victims' rights address the accused directly and the victim indirectly. "Getting tough" on criminals by, for example, increasing sentences, limiting bail, and abolishing the exclusionary rule, focuses directly on the criminal. The desired result of more convictions, longer sentences, and a safer society benefits crime victims by decreasing their chances of being revictimized (President's Task Force on Victims of Crime, 1982) and may satisfy victims' desire for revenge (Henderson, 1992). This orientation has been dubbed the "crime control" model of victims' rights (see, for example, McShane & Williams, 1992).

A second category of provisions and services, compatible with the crime control perspective, affects victims directly within the criminal justice system. Some, such as victim or witness assistance programs, help victims negotiate the criminal justice system by, for example, providing transportation to and from court, court escorts, and referrals to other community agencies. Others, such as statutes requiring victim impact statements at sentencing, provide a significant role for the victim in the proceedings themselves. These statements include testimony from or on behalf of the victim regarding the effects the crime had on the victim, whether physical, economic, psychological, or social. This category of provisions may also affect offenders: for example, with support from a victim or witness assistance program, a crime victim may become a better and more cooperative witness, resulting in a greater probability of conviction.

A third category provides alternatives to traditional criminal justice procedures and outcomes. Examples include mediation between offenders and victims, restitution from offenders to victims, and civil rights suits by victims against offenders. These procedures can address individual aspects of victimization more easily than conventional criminal court and are more amenable to victim control.

The final category bestows direct benefits on victims, including victim compensation and mental health services. Provisions in the third and fourth categories can also be encompassed by the crime control model (President's Task Force on Victims of Crime, 1982), but radical victimologists are more concerned with the possibility that, in the implementation of provisions within the first two categories, crime control can be emphasized and victims ignored (Elias, 1993; McShane & Williams, 1992).

Although concern for the victim began to emerge in the 1960s, many of these provisions, both victim- and crime-oriented, have only recently become law. Several protections for victims of federal crimes appeared in the Federal Victim and Witness Assistance Act in 1982 (the Victim/Witness Act). This act protected the privacy of victims of federal crimes and gave them a presumptive right to restitution from offenders. The Victim/Witness Act also mandated that evidence concerning the impact of the crime on the victim, or "victim impact statements," be accepted in federal trials (U.S. Department of Justice, Office of Justice Programs, 1986). The laws of most of the states as well now require these statements (National Victim Center, 1993).

Two years later, Congress passed the Victims of Crime Act (VOCA) (Public Law 98-473), whose most significant provision established the Crime Victims Fund. This fund provides up to $100,000,000 annually to state and local victim compensation and victim/witness assistance programs (Roberts, 1990). Currently, every state, as well as the federal government and the District of Columbia, has a victim compensation program (National Association of Victim Compensation Boards, 1993b) and provides some services to crime victims (National Victim Center, 1993). Furthermore, 17 states have so-called Victims' Bills of Rights; 9 appear in state constitutions (Reske, 1992). Finally, mandatory sentencing guidelines have been enacted on the federal level and in many states (National Victim Center, 1993).

Let us consider these four categories in greater detail.

Crime Control: Increased Sanctions

Where convictions are not obtained or tough sentences not imposed, many crime victims believe the system has failed. Victims often believe that the scales of justice have tilted in favor of criminals and that the current system "has proven itself incapable of dealing with crime" (Harrington, 1982, p. vi). They may therefore feel neglected and vulnerable, exacerbating the consequences of their victimization. In response, much of what has been enacted as victims' rights limit the rights of accused and convicted criminals in the hope of making convictions easier and detention longer (Dittenhoffer & Ericson, 1992). Cross-examination has been curtailed, hearsay permitted at preliminary hearings, preventive detention authorized, mandatory minimum and "true" life sentences imposed, concurrent sentences reduced, and the exclusionary rule limited (Viano, 1987). The constitutionality of such victims' rights initiatives is the subject of current debate, with courts nationwide having disagreed on their constitutionality, but it appears that many will survive judicial scrutiny (Carrington & Nicholson, 1989).

No Right to Safety The most important victims' right would be a right not to be a victim. However, a specific person generally has no right to safety unless the government has accepted some special duty to protect that particular person, such as when a witness is under police protection (see *American Law Reports,* 1985). A person cannot successfully claim that his or her rights have been violated simply because he or she was victimized, for example, in a town that maintained regular police patrols at or near the crime scene. The criminal justice system represents an attempt to maintain public safety; it does not provide a guarantee.

Crime Control: Crime Victims and the Criminal Trial

Believing that their special status is not acknowledged, crime victims have long complained of being ignored and used by the criminal justice system. Provisions to address these concerns fall into two main types: those guaranteeing the victim a "voice" in criminal proceedings, and those governing out-of-court interactions between the victim and the system.

Granting Victims a "Voice" Although the Bill of Rights applies to all U.S. citizens, the Constitution grants victims of crime no rights comparable to those protecting the accused (Goddu, 1993). This omission has created what many have perceived as a system that favors the accused at the expense of the victim (President's Task Force on Victims of Crime, 1982). For example, whereas criminal defendants have the absolute right to confront the witnesses against them, victims do not have the reciprocal right to confront the accused; in criminal proceedings, the prosecutor, not the victim, decides whether the victim will be a witness.

More broadly, the victim has little or no control over whether, or to what extent, the accused will be prosecuted. Though, in many jurisdictions, a victim may hire an attorney to assist with the prosecution (Sales et al., 1987), this is not practical for many crime victims: violent crimes strike members of poor households more often than persons of higher income (Bastian, 1993).

To increase victim involvement in the system, the President's Task Force proposed adding victims' rights to the Sixth Amendment of the U.S. Constitution. The Task Force suggested that "the victim in every criminal prosecution shall have the right to be present and to be heard at all critical stages of judicial proceedings" (President's Task Force on Victims of Crime, 1982). This does not specify the extent to which the trier of fact (the jury in a jury trial, the judge in a nonjury trial) shall consider the victim's statements, and does not specify what a "critical" stage might be; it might not give victims the right to participate, for example, in plea bargaining negotiations, but only to attend court when the plea is accepted by the judge. For instance, the Washington State Constitution grants victims the rights to be informed of and attend court proceedings and to make statements at sentencing and any other stage, such as a parole hearing, where the defendant's release is being considered, but does not address plea bargaining (Washington State Constitution, 1989).

Other, narrower statutes permit or require statements regarding the impact of the crime on the victim and the victim's family to be introduced when the case is being tried, when the defendant is being sentenced, or both. Victim impact statements have been challenged by defendants who claim that the character or eloquence of the victim or the victim's family should have no bearing on the defendant's sentence. However, the U.S. Supreme Court recently permitted such evidence to be introduced in capital cases (*Payne v. Tennessee*, 1991, overruling *Booth v. Maryland*, 1989).

Relations with the System A victims' bill of rights, or similar scheme, seeks to compel the criminal justice system to treat the crime victim with respect. Some of the common statutes grant victims the right:

1. To be informed of the final disposition of the case;
2. To be notified if any court proceeding for which they have received a subpoena will not occur as scheduled;
3. To receive protection from victim intimidation and to be provided with information as to the level of protection available;
4. To be informed of the procedure for receiving witness fees;
5. To be provided, wherever practical, with a secure waiting area away from defendants;
6. To have personal property in the possession of law enforcement agencies returned as expeditiously as possible, where feasible, photographing the property and returning it to the owner within ten days of being taken; and
7. To be provided with appropriate employer intercession so that loss of pay and other benefits resulting from court appearances will be minimized. (Goddu, 1993, p. 251)

None of these provisions has a direct impact on the conduct of the trial itself; rather, each indirectly affects the outcome by facilitating the victim's participation as a witness against the defendant.

In addition, some states require that victims be notified of the offender's status at all stages of the proceedings, through sentence completion. The victim, and, under some statutes, the community, would be told when the defendant has been released for any reason, including parole, work release, furlough, or completion of the full term of the sentence. They would also be informed if the prisoner escapes (National Victim Center, 1993).

Alternatives to Traditional Justice

A criminal who completes a prison sentence is considered to have satisfied his or her debt to society. However, the debt to the victim may not have been addressed at all. For a victim who still suffers from the effects of the crime, alternatives to this traditional paradigm, including restitution, mediation, and civil litigation, can reestablish the connection between the criminal and the victim that was broken when the state took over the prosecution and can compel the criminal to take responsibility for the consequences of the crime.

Restitution Theoretically, restitution affords the victim a chance to be fully compensated for losses or injuries by the person responsible, the perpetrator. Restitution comprises a judicially ordered payment from offender to victim, either after trial or as part of a plea agreement. It is often made a condition of probation to encourage compliance. Restitution is available in most states and in federal court. Under the Victim/Witness Act (1982), a judge in a federal case must order restitution or expressly state reasons for not so doing. Restitution may also be ordered as part of a mediated agreement between the offender and the victim (Dittenhoffer & Ericson, 1992).

Mediation Victim-offender mediation (VOM), or reconciliation, takes advantage of the "potential for activity, for participation" inherent in conflicts between victims and offenders (Christie, 1977, p. 7). Through VOM, an agreement between the offender and the victim replaces a judicial determination. The agreement can require the offender to make payments or provide services directly to the victim, to perform community service, or to fulfill a combination of these obligations (Umbreit, 1989).

VOM attempts to grant crime victims some control over criminal justice, with the extent of control dependent on the program design. In some designs, the judge refers a case to mediation only after conviction with the instruction that the victim and offender agree on the amount of restitution, often not to exceed a limit set by the judge (Dittenhoffer & Ericson, 1992). Other designs require that both victim and offender opt out of the criminal trial process voluntarily and allow a full range of possible outcomes, as described above (Umbreit, 1989).

Civil Courts and Crime Victims Concurrent with the takeover of criminal justice by the state, separate civil tort systems evolved where victims could sue offenders for money damages in the civil courts. However, this remedy, still theoretically available to all crime victims, can be used successfully in only a minority of cases (Roberts, 1990).

For a tort action to succeed, a *tortfeasor*—an entity responsible for the harm—must be identified and found to have breached a legal duty to the injured party. For the injured party to attain complete relief, the tortfeasor must have assets or insurance to pay the judgment. These requirements limit the feasibility of torts for most crime victims. Even if identified, the offender may be a family member or acquaintance whom the victim does not wish to sue, or the evidence in the case may be weak. Moreover, not all criminals have easily identifiable assets, if they have assets at all. If the offender is a family member, the assets may be identical to those of the victim. In addition, insurance policies generally do not insure persons against the consequences of their own intentional criminal actions. Finally, it is very difficult for an incarcerated offender to earn enough money to pay a civil judgment.

A poor offender may occasion a search for "deep pockets," an entity other than the primary offender that may be held responsible for the victimization. Deep pockets can be found, for example, in landlords who have undertaken the duty of providing security services but whose services are provided negligently (*American Law Reports*, 1975).

Victims may also bring suit seeking money damages from the government for a denial of constitutional rights. For example, in *DeShaney v. Winnebago County Department of Social Services* (1989), the family of a child left brain damaged by his father sued—albeit unsuccessfully—the local social services agency, claiming that the agency had deprived the child of his life, liberty, or property without due process of law under the Fourteenth Amendment to the U.S. Constitution because it failed to take appropriate actions to protect the child despite reports of previous abuse. Although the Court held that the Constitution recognized no such claim, it acknowledged the possibility of a state law tort claim in such a case.

Direct Benefits to Victim: Compensation, Services

Other programs exist for crime victims whose needs the various court systems cannot address fully. Victim compensation programs make government payments directly to eligible crime victims, partly in response to the inadequacies of restitution. Most require that the victim apply for an award; awards generally extend to compensation for physical injuries and "necessary" personal property only, such as wheelchairs and eyeglasses (Geis, 1990). Victim compensation can also pay for therapy of the victim's choice, subject, in most states, to time or money limitations (National Association of Victim Compensation Boards, 1993b). These programs exist in all 50 states, the District of Columbia, and the federal government (National Association of Victim Compensation Boards, 1993a).

Victims may also be assisted by victim service agencies, which are often nonprofit and exist at least in part on government grants (Roberts, 1990). These services emerged to overcome limitations placed on victims by the criminal justice system. Although this system provides many avenues for victims to seek recompense and recovery, victims must participate in the system to gain access to these rights. Unfortunately, low reporting rates for many of the most serious crimes hinder the reach of many victim rights' provisions, especially those based solely in the courts. A community survey conducted by Kilpatrick et al. (1987) revealed that almost 25% of the sample of women had been victims of a completed rape during their lifetime, but only 15% of these rapes had ever been reported to the police. In addition, restrictions on victim compensation can further inhibit what victims recover.

Victim service programs grew out of grassroots organizations of the 1970s dedicated to, and often founded by, victims of particular crimes, like sexual assault or drunk driving. Funding under the Victims of Crimes Act and various state initiatives has encouraged the establishment of these programs, with

Table 20-1   Services Provided by Programs

Type of Service	Number of Programs	Percentage
Explain court process	131	71
Make referrals	126	69
Provide court escort	120	65
Help with victim compensation applications	118	64
Public education	112	61
Assist with employers	111	60
Provide transportation to court	109	59
Provide crisis intervention	99	54
Provide child care	69	38
Provide emergency money	45	25
Repair locks	22	12

Source: Roberts (1990, p. 47).

their number currently exceeding 5000 (Davis & Henley, 1990). These agencies generally assist victims of any crime. In a survey of 184 local victim service programs, summarized in Table 20.1, Roberts (1990) found they most commonly provided explanations of the court process and referrals to other agencies, and less commonly provided lock repair and emergency money. In addition, crime victims may take advantage of other public services that are open to all, like county mental health departments and public hospitals.

The Mental Health Consequences of Victims' Rights

The past 15 years have seen victims' rights and services proliferate. What remains to be established, however, is which of these provisions and programs actually benefit victims, where *benefit* is not simply defined within the terms of the theory that generated the right. For example, an advocate of the crime control model may be concerned with convictions and sentence length, whereas a radical victimologist may applaud any victim-oriented measure that does not result in harsher punishment for the criminal.

Evaluation of rights and services may be approached by combining examinations of the actual, not theoretical, effects of crime on victims (for example, Kilpatrick et al., 1985) and the efficacy of various therapies (Frank, 1988; Kilpatrick and Calhoun, 1988). Under this perspective, laws should seek to deliver the proper therapies to the proper victims. This assumes, however, that the only necessary treatment for the consequences of victimization happens in the clinic, and it ignores the role of the rest of the victim's environmental context.

A broader approach is illustrated by two trends in social science research that seek explicitly to determine the effects of laws and legal processes on the people they affect. The first, *procedural justice,* studies user satisfaction with courts and other adjudicative processes (Thibaut & Walker, 1975). This research shows that, regardless of the outcome of their case, persons who believe that they have been heard, taken seriously, and treated with respect are more likely to be satisfied with their court experience than those who believe otherwise (Fischer, 1984). The procedural justice research suggests that citizens are more likely to accept a system if they believe the authorities will listen to their concerns (Tyler, 1987). A procedure is "just" when people affected thereby are satisfied with it.

Unlike procedural justice, the second law and social science perspective, *therapeutic jurisprudence,* does not limit itself to a single dependent variable. Therapeutic jurisprudence seeks to assist the law to achieve its potential to advance therapeutic outcomes (Sales & Shuman, 1994). This norm need not conflict with other views on victims' rights that also aim to help crime victims. From the perspective of therapeutic jurisprudence, then, an analysis of victims' rights should seek to discover the effects of laws and legal processes on the recovery of previctimization psychological functioning of victims. Some research does attempt to make procedural justice part of therapeutic jurisprudence. However, it appears to assume that its outcome measures, such as satisfaction with the court process, belief in the fairness of the procedure, and trust in the system, benefit the consumers of the system without empirically confirming this benefit (see, for example, Tyler, 1992).

Evaluation of Increased Criminal Sanctions

The crime control model of victims' rights, designed to benefit victims primarily by incarcerating criminals, has been criticized by radical victimologists (Elias, 1983a; Fattah, 1992; Goddu, 1993; Henderson, 1992; Karmen, 1984; McShane & Williams, 1992). These critics do not accept the "common assumptions about crime victims—that they are all 'outraged' and want revenge and tougher law enforcement" (Henderson, 1992, p. 111). Radical victimology argues that this is only incidentally a victim-oriented perspective. Furthermore, some have accused conservative political groups of using the rhetoric of "victims' rights" to advance their "law and order" agenda (Elias, 1986, 1993; McShane & Williams, 1992).

Research has not yet demonstrated a link between conviction or harsh punishment of offenders and victims' recovery (Halleck, 1989; Umbreit, 1989). However, victims may benefit from the satisfaction of their desires for safety or vengeance.

Safety

The interjection of victims' rights initiatives into American jurisdictions has occurred as public fear of crime, specifically street crime, has escalated, while the crime rate generally has leveled out. In fact, according to the U.S. Department of Justice, the total number of criminal victimizations in America actually *declined* slightly between 1972 and 1992, with per capita rates of personal theft, household larceny, and burglary sinking significantly during that period. Assault, robbery, and rape rates have remained about the same, which means (with population growth) that the total number of such violent crimes has risen slightly (Bastian, 1993).

The proposition that incarceration following a serious crime will prevent future crime has been questioned. Because the crime rate declines sharply with age irrespective of incarceration or apprehension rates, serious offenders should be incarcerated *before* they begin to commit serious offenses if we are to prevent crime (Gottfredson & Hirschi, 1990). Problems, of course, arise: predictions are not necessarily accurate, and concerns for the civil liberties of both children and parents mitigate against intrusive programs for at-risk youth.

Thus, it is not clear that victims do, or should, feel safer today as a consequence of these victims' rights initiatives. Ironically, measures aimed at increasing sentences and convictions, which are partially aimed at incapacitation of the criminal and safety of society, could actually increase the tendencies of the victim to withdraw by making the world appear to be an even harsher place than it is (Elias, 1993). Unfortunately, there has been very little research on this subject.

Vengeance

Aside from a desire for safety, a desire for justice or vengeance may motivate victims, and this desire may interfere with recovery if left unresolved. Victimization appears to lead to a loss of the sense of control over one's life. Recovery occurs only after the victim assumes responsibility for dealing with the traumatic experience, instead of attempting to shut it out of consciousness (Henderson, 1992). Past and future victimization can be distinguished: coping strategies may represent the attempt to deal with past victimization by preventing future victimization. Yet, if the existential perspective has some weight, recovery will not occur until the victim makes the past victimization part of his or her life (Henderson, 1992). Indeed, cognitive and behavioral therapies aim to allow the victims to return to normal, previctimization functioning in the world, instead of withdrawing from it (Foa, 1991; Frank, 1988). To achieve previctimization functioning, it may be necessary to abandon vengeance to recover precrime mental health (Halleck, 1989). And if it is important to help restore the victim's belief system (Kennedy, 1983; Norris & Kaniasty, 1991), victims may need to abandon vengeance. Victims who retain their anger or who attempt to avoid situations that resemble the conditions of the earlier victimization, for example by refusing ever to walk outside after dark, can become phobic and never approach any situation, no matter how harmless, that resembles the crime conditions.

Anger may be important in initiating the recovery process; anger has been positively correlated with longer life among cancer patients (Wortman, 1983), though, by itself, it increases the risks of heart disease and hypertension. Perhaps anger connected with a desire for vengeance can benefit crime victims, as long as that anger is resolved; as discussed below, successful recovery has been reported for torture victims who testify publicly about their experiences (Pope & Garcia-Peltoniemi, 1991).

In sum, it is not clear whether provisions that simply increase penalties for offenders have any salutary effects on the psychological recovery of victims. However, measures requiring the active participation of victims, like victim impact statements, could satisfy victims as well as crime control advocates.

Victims in the Justice System: Consequences of Provisions

Provisions designed either to give victims a voice in or to smooth their relations with the criminal justice system can affect victims' mental health either directly or indirectly. If, for example, a victim's postcrime anxiety diminishes as a result of testifying to the impact of the crime on his or her life, the testimony has had a direct effect. If, however, the victim's improvement is due to satisfaction at the long sentence the judge imposed after hearing the victim impact statement, the testimony had an indirect effect.

Three major questions arise concerning the relationships between (1) criminal sanctions and victim psychological functioning, (2) victim participation in the trial and sanctions, and (3) the victim's dealings with the criminal justice system and victim mental health. As discussed above, little research exists to illuminate the first question.

With regard to the second, some evidence suggests that victim impact statements in capital trials increase the likelihood that the jury will impose the death sentence (Burkhead, Luginbuhl, & Wrenn, 1994), but this question is not settled. Indeed, a simple answer to the second question has proved elusive; most research in this area has focused on the decision making of the judge and jury without specifically testing the victims' role as a predictor. The third question has been studied more extensively. However, there has been no consensus on the criteria used to evaluate effects, which may reflect an underlying clash of goals. Although therapeutic jurisprudence measures the benefit to victims of laws and legal processes, procedural justice measures the more specific variable of satisfaction with such processes and assumes that satisfaction, besides being therapeutic, benefits society (Tyler, 1992). If not satisfied with the justice system, crime victims add their voice to the democratic cacophony of competing desires and may lose respect for, and even disobey, the law themselves (see Tyler, 1992). Therefore, satisfaction of consumers becomes a legitimate and sometimes overriding goal of the system, and procedural justice an important perspective.

It is important, however, to retain sight of crime victims' long-term psychological outlook and not focus only on their immediate satisfaction with court procedures. As satisfied customers, victims may assume they have received the limit of the system's assistance and may cease their quest for full recovery. To explore the relationship between procedural justice and recovery, victims' satisfaction with court procedures could be used as an *independent* variable, or predicator, of subsequent mental health functioning. Other variables, such as the outcome of the trial, the seriousness of the harm, and the treatment of the victim outside the justice system, may also be important predictors; this area remains largely unexplored. Although legislatures have enacted a plethora of statutes attempting to ease the victim's experience with the court system, research does not yet support the contention that the quality of this experience significantly aids the victim's eventual psychological recovery (see, for example, Cluss, Boughton, Frank, Stewart, & West, 1983; Lurigio & Resick. 1990).

Maximizing procedural justice, however, most likely does no harm. It is difficult to see how provisions that seek respectful treatment of victims in court could interfere with their recovery, and such provisions may be of significant benefit (Resick, 1987). Furthermore, because a victim's perception of control has been shown to be important to recovery (Kelly, 1990), and persons who believe they have had a voice in court proceedings are generally more satisfied with those proceedings than those who do not so believe, it is possible that the notions of "voice" and "control" represent the same underlying psychological process. If so, victim participation in the court process may be therapeutic, including at plea bargaining and other stages generally closed to the public.

Effects of Granting Victims a "Voice"

As already noted, because a major concern of victims seems to be their alienation from and lack of involvement in criminal proceedings, allowing victims to make a statement at sentencing and other stages of the criminal process could benefit victims psychologically (Fischer, 1984). However, the mere fact that victims have been heard does not guarantee that their wishes will be followed. For example, in a study of sexual assault cases in Ohio, the expressed wishes of victims regarding sentencing options were not followed to any significant degree by the judge (Walsh, 1992). Research is needed to determine the psychological effects on victims of having their wishes ignored, even though Tyler (1987) suggests that being heard may be sufficient.

Testimony and Oral Histories It is possible that testifying in court, and especially informing the court about the personal impact of the crime, benefits the victim (see Sahjpaul & Renner, 1988). Support for the idea that public disclosure can help victims recover is found in the success of testimonial and oral history therapy for victims of torture (C. Bouwkamp, personal communication, July 13, 1994). Such persons can, with the assistance of a therapist, either prepare oral histories to be shared with other victims and their families (Herbst, 1992), prepare a written document from tape-recorded testimony in a therapeutic setting (Cienfuegos & Monelli, 1983), or publicly denounce their tormentors (Pope & Garcia-Peltoniemi, 1991). Consistent with research on victim involvement in sentencing, however, torture victims may suffer negative consequences when their testimony is ignored (Pope & Garcia-Peltoniemi, 1991). The same may be true regarding the overall responsiveness of the criminal justice system. Furthermore, testimony may not be appropriate for everybody, as the popularity of laws protecting the privacy of sexual assault victims attests.

Victims' Rights: Rights without Remedies

Although victims' rights—to privacy, notification of the status of the victim, to have personal property used at trial returned expeditiously, and so forth—may be couched in the rhetoric of "rights" (as in "victims' bills of rights"), they differ significantly from criminals' rights: they generally are not enforceable (Goddu, 1993). Sanctions for a failure to honor the rights of the accused differ starkly from those available to a victim whose rights are violated. The best known of the sanctions for violations of the rights of the accused is the "exclusionary rule."

The Exclusionary Rule The exclusionary rule excludes evidence gathered in violation of a defendant's Fourth Amendment rights under the U.S. Constitution. The decision to exclude illegally obtained evidence is unrelated to the probative value of the evidence or the consequence of exclusion to a conviction or acquittal (*Weeks v. United States,* 1913). No equivalent rule exists under current victim rights' schemes: sanctions against the government for failing to observe and protect the rights of victims do not exist (Eikenberry, 1989; Polito, 1990; Roland, 1989), unless, in some cases, the government breached a special duty and the victim was injured as a result of the breach (*American Law Reports,* 1986). Furthermore, it would probably be inappropriate to punish the *accused* for the government's failure to follow the letter of victims' rights. For example, under the Washington State Constitution the victim has the right to attend all court proceedings. If the consequence of a denial of this right were easier conviction of the defendant, this would violate the defendant's well-established right to be judged only on evidence actually presented in the courtroom. However, the fact that many victims' rights are unenforceable may harm victims.

Notification of the Status of the Offender One victim right deserves special mention because it may operate to harm the victim if enforced. Where a statute requires notification of the status of the convicted and imprisoned offender, victims who are not so notified but who are not harmed by that particular offender will have no recourse (*American Law Reports*, 1985, 1986). On the other hand, notification may not benefit victims. Although no definitive research could be found addressing this issue, it is possible that this could actually harm victims by causing them to lead a fearful, socially restricted lifestyle (C. Bouwkamp, personal communication, July 13, 1994), at least in the absence of other effective supports.

The Effects of Alternative Criminal Justice

The victims' rights discussed above involve the traditional criminal justice system, where the state, not the victim, plays the role of the injured party. Alternatives, including restitution, mediation, and civil torts, still cast the victim as victim, and still within a government context. On the other hand, the amount of control ceded to victims varies among individual programs, ranging from restitution ordered without consulting the victim to face-to-face mediation between the victim and the offender.

Evaluating Restitution

Aside from the obvious monetary benefit to victims, successful restitution can have a salutary effect on the victim's satisfaction with the court process (Rosen & Harland, 1990). It can also increase the offender's chances of rehabilitation by fostering a fruitful relationship between the offender and the probation officer (Galaway, 1988), which may itself benefit the victim. Restitution can be made part of any reasonable model of corrections, either as punishment, equity, recompense, or rehabilitation (Matthews, 1981). When made part of an agreement between the victim and the offender, it can help the victim achieve closure of the criminal experience and enhance recovery (Henderson, 1992; Umbreit, 1989).

Although theoretically restitution could fully compensate victims for their losses, practically it cannot be relied on to do so. Despite the fact that advocacy for its implementation came primarily from the victims' rights movement (Rosen & Harland, 1990), restitution serves primarily the aims of the system, and only tangentially the needs of the victim. For example, an American Bar Association study revealed victim dissatisfaction with attempts made to collect from offenders, as well as with the failure of restitution programs both to consult with victims regarding the amounts of awards and to keep them apprised of the progress of collections (Hillenbrand, 1990). Probation officers often cease attempting to collect from an offender who has not made full payment but is leading a stable family life because the probation officer's main interest is in the offender, not the victim (Zapf & Cole, 1985). Furthermore, restitution orders generally seek to compensate victims only for economic losses, such as lost or destroyed property, medical bills, and lost wages; offenders need not pay victims to compensate for the pain and suffering caused by the crime (Rosen & Harland, 1990).

Inadequacies of restitution for victims is not surprising, as justice to the victim is not the primary goal of restitution orders. The U.S. Supreme Court has made it clear that restitution does not operate strictly to assist victims:

> Although restitution does resemble a judgment "for the benefit of" the victim, the context in which it is imposed undermines that conclusion. The victim has no control over the amount of restitution awarded or over the decision to award restitution. Moreover, the decision to impose restitution generally does not turn on the victim's injury, but on the penal goals of the State and the situation of the defendant.... Because criminal proceedings focus on the State's interests in rehabilitation and punishment, rather than on the victim's desire for compensation, we conclude that restitution orders... operate "for the benefit of" the State. (*Kelly v. Robinson,* 1986, pp. 362–363)

This means that a restitution order that operates unfairly toward the victim will nonetheless be acceptable to the courts if it advances a correctional purpose. The victim's irrelevance is also illustrated by orders that restitution be paid to third parties, such as insurance companies (see, for example, *Hagler v. State,* 1993).

A further difficulty with restitution lies in the uneven distribution of resources among criminals. As in 11th-century England, restitution could allow the successful modern criminal to buy his or her way out of an offense (Geis, 1990). This could actually lead to more crime because money, not prison time, would be the cost of getting caught. Such a system could harm both actual and potential crime victims.

Evaluation of Mediation

The major failure of restitution surfaces when it is imposed by a court and administered without regard to the victim's needs. Mediation, or reconciliation, can integrate the victim into the restitution process as well as offer a return to the "golden age of the victim," when criminal justice "served only [the victim's] private interests. No other aspects of crime could compete with this concept in this privately administered criminal law" (Schafer, 1968, pp. 7, 20). Further, it is consistent with a characterization of criminal justice as essentially a private matter that has been usurped by the state (Christie, 1977) and with the theory that no victim will recover from a crime until he or she finds meaning in the experience, to reassert control over his or her life (Henderson, 1992). Programs seeking to mediate agreements between the victim and offender in face-to-face meetings offer victims hope for control.

Victim-offender mediation, currently limited mainly to family disputes and juvenile property crimes (Menard & Salius, 1990), has not been exhaustively researched. It could, however, afford certain crime victims the chance to reinstitute their precrime equilibrium by, among other things, allowing them to confront both the offender and the crime. A strictly voluntary program has the additional advantage of allowing the victim complete autonomy of choice, hence retention of control.

Reservations exist regarding mediation's potential, however. For example, some believe that domestic violence victims should never meet face to face with the offender, as the underlying dynamics of the relationship will prevent the victim from achieving a satisfactory resolution (Geffner, 1992; Menard & Salius, 1990). In fact, mediation may be inappropriate in all cases of extreme violence (Geffner, 1992).[2] Nevertheless, because of its potential for personal resolution of the victimization experience, mediation offers many crime victims hope of real procedural justice and the possibility that their alienation from the system may be substantially reduced.

Evaluation of Civil Courts and Victims

A final alternative to the criminal trial may be found in the civil courts, where the burden of proof is lower and the reparation from the defendant potentially unlimited. Whomever the defendant may be, a civil trial can provide an opportunity to a crime victim to receive full compensation for any and all financial, psychological, and physical injuries suffered as a result of the crime (minus legal fees, which can be substantial). However, some legislatures limit the damages that may be awarded in such suits (Sales et al., 1987). Because economic security appears to be associated with psychological recovery (Lurigio & Resick, 1990), successful suits can facilitate victims' recovery; however, research is needed to determine the extent to which these suits are used by crime victims, and whether awards actually help victims to recover (Sales et al., 1987).

When the defendant is indigent, suit may be brought against a third party, usually a government entity. However, unless the agency has breached a specific duty resulting in injury, the suit will not succeed. The case of *Martinez v. California* (1980) helps illuminate the boundaries of the responsibility of the criminal justice system. Here, the family of a woman killed by an ex-convict five months after he was released sued the state on the basis of the alleged gross negligence of penal authorities. The Court unanimously held that the act resulting in the death was that of the murderer, not the state, and that the woman had been in no unique danger relative to the general populace. It is not likely that these boundaries of state responsibility will be extended by the courts in the near future. In their analysis of victim-related decisions of the Reagan-era Court, Carrington and Nicholson (1989) concluded that "while the conservative majority of the Court are willing to protect society from the criminals themselves, they are not willing to extend that protection to those endangered by the negligence of the bureaucrats" (p. 11; see also McShane & Williams, 1992).

Finally, it may matter against whom a victim is successful. Suits against third parties, though potentially lucrative, do not allow the victim to deal directly with the offender. For example, in the case of *DeShaney v. Winnebago*

---

2. With regard to its impact on corrections as well, it is possible that mediation may promise more, such as a substantial reduction in imprisonment, than it can deliver. A Canadian study suggested that judges may view mediation not as an alternative to incarceration, but as a supplement to probation or other nonprison sanctions (Dittenhoffer & Ericson, 1992).

County Department of Social Services (1989), brought as a constitutional claim rather than a tort claim, the 11-year-old plaintiff was left brain-damaged after an assault by his father, following months of repeated complaints by third parties to the local child protective agency. The agency had intervened earlier but later returned the child to the father and subsequently chose to take no action in the face of new complaints. The Court held that, because the agency had not then taken custody of the boy, it had assumed no duty to him, though in dissent, Justice Blackmun pointed out that, under the law, the agency had sole jurisdiction over the child's case and provided the only legal alternative to the father's care. Even if the suit had succeeded, however, the boy may have benefited more psychologically from a settlement with, or award from, his father instead of a third party (Shuman, 1994).

Evaluation of Victim Compensation

Victim compensation schemes represent a more clinical perspective than do interactive solutions to victimization. Instead of the result of an interaction between two persons, criminal victimization is considered a disorder to be treated physically, financially, and psychologically. Under this perspective, if fully funded and liberally distributed, victim compensation could represent the best hope for many crime victims' psychological recovery because it could pay for all the therapy a victim needs. However, many victim compensation programs are restrictive in their reach and miserly in their execution. A study of an Ohio state program, for example, revealed that less than $6 million of the $18 million allocated by the state legislature was actually awarded in 1988, and 52% of the applicants for awards in 1987 were denied (Roberts, 1990). Similar results had earlier been obtained in New York and New Jersey (Elias, 1983b). In addition, the programs do not necessarily reach deep into the pool of potential claimants: Elias estimated in 1983 that only 1% to 2% of New York and New Jersey crime victims sought compensation, and a 1989 study revealed that only 8% of eligible New Jersey crime victims filed claims (Roberts, 1990). Instead of making all crime victims eligible for awards, states limit them in various ways, including setting maximum awards, denying awards to persons victimized by members of their own households, making poverty a prerequisite for an award, granting awards only where there was physical injury, and not compensating for pain and suffering (Roland, 1989).

These limits may be necessary because the total costs of crime are staggering. By using jury awards as a measurement, one investigator has estimated the annual cost of crime, including pain and suffering, at over $90 billion (Cohen, 1988). In contrast, the total amount awarded by state victim compensation programs was approximately $200 million in 1992, or about one-fifth of 1% of the total cost of crime. California alone accounted for $75 million (National Association of Victim Compensation Boards, 1993b). Obviously, without full funding, some limitations on awards will be necessary, and many have been justified on public policy grounds. However, by placing the burden of proof for eligibility on the victim (Sales et al., 1987), compensation programs may harm even successful applicants. One study demonstrated significant dissatisfaction with the criminal justice process among successful and unsuccessful applicants who were required to show financial need to receive compensation (Elias, 1983b).

Many states also place significant limitations on compensation to fund psychological services but do not similarly limit the use of monies for other medical expenses (National Association of Victim Compensation Boards, 1993a). An examination of limitations placed on postvictimization counseling by various state compensation boards reveals that, of 46 states surveyed, 14 do not pay for counseling for family members of homicide victims, 28 do not pay for counseling for the families of rape victims, and 3 others assist parents or caretakers only—not children. Furthermore, though many states place no limits on the extent of counseling or require a treatment plan if the counseling extends past a certain point, other states severely restrict payment: South Carolina limits coverage to the greater of 15 sessions or 90 days, and Montana places a $500-per-person cap on counseling expenses (National Association of Victim Compensation Boards, 1993b). Such limitations do not appear empirically justified, because symptoms can persist for years and extend to family members (for example, Kilpatrick et al., 1987; Amick-McMullen et al., 1991). In addition, victims of unreported crimes have no access to victim compensation but still represent a major public health concern.

Finally, limitations on awards and severe scrutiny of applications may also cause ineligible victims or unsuccessful applicants to blame themselves for their victimization. Until compensation and services are available to victims of all crimes—including but not limited to crimes within the family, white-collar, and environmental crimes—victims of noncovered crimes may suffer additionally because society has not acknowledged their victimization. Self-blame has been associated with poor recovery (Meyer & Taylor, 1986). But even if acknowledged, because victim compensation comes from a third party, it broadens the gulf between the criminal and the victim. Thus it eliminates the hope inherent in mediation, for example, for reconciliation with and restitution from the offender.

Consequences of Victim Services

It is beyond the scope of this chapter to evaluate individual victim service agencies. The great number of them ensures that they will range in quality. However, an understanding of the experience and needs of the crime victim assists any specific evaluation. Governments, whether by establishing public programs or funding nonprofit agencies, should attempt to provide victims with the right to access to victim services in accordance with current research and should provide for ongoing evaluation of the effectiveness of these programs (Salasin, 1981). Particular attention should be paid to the choice of criteria used in the evaluations. Agency bureaucracies should not be permitted to dictate research and evaluation agendas because their first loyalties will tend to be to the institution (Chelimsky, 1981). Concern for victims' long-term functioning should underlie any evaluation, and evaluations should be conducted such that they are comparable to each other. In this way, public dollars can be directed to achieve maximum benefits to victims.

Because the entire court process can be stressful to crime victims, they should receive some sort of counseling, not only for the effects of the crime but also to prepare them for court itself, especially for the experience of testifying (Resick, 1987). Such counseling, as well as other services provided by victim service agencies, should take into account the following knowledge about victims, their symptoms, and their recovery.

Victim Characteristics: Gender and Age Responses to criminal victimization vary across victims and crimes. Specific responses to trauma are difficult to predict simply from victim characteristics, even when characteristics of the crime are also considered (Resnick, Kilpatrick, & Lipovsky, 1991). However, trauma seems less severe in younger, male, higher-socioeconomic-status persons whose precrime psychological adjustment was strong and who have been relatively free from previous victimization (Lurigio & Resick, 1990). In addition, research on "resilient" adults, who function well despite severely traumatic childhoods, reveals that they share several characteristics: they are intelligent, creative, economically successful, socially and politically active, and have maintained close ties to others throughout their lives (Higgins, 1994, p. 20). Instead of being inherent, many of these characteristics probably developed after victimization; as such, they would provide goals for therapy.

Although many of these characteristics seem to require little explanation, the fact that men may react less severely to crime is more problematic. It may be that the difference is due to measurement error: men may underreport assault-related trauma because of the cultural dictates of masculinity (Stanko & Hobdell, 1993). If the differences are real, it may be that women's coping strategies fail more often than men's, because women generally take fewer risks than men due to both internal and external domestic social controls. The same controls that reduce their vulnerability to crime also lead to their reluctance to abandon their roles within the family following victimization, and prevent their search for "exits" from family structures that may have become harmful (Hagen, 1990). Finally, distress from sexual assault, because of women's evolved psychology, may be responsible for the difference. If rape is maladaptive from an evolutionary perspective, because it robs women of their ability to be sexually selective in order to control their reproduction, women of reproductive age should suffer more psychological pain following rape than girls or older women because it is more important, genetically, for them to avoid it. Significant psychological pain resulting from rape would be adaptive, because women of reproductive age would be motivated by the threat of such pain to avoid rape more than would other women. In support of this hypothesis, research has found psychological pain following rape to be greatest during the reproductive years (Thornhill & Thornhill, 1990; see also Buss, 1994, p. 165).

Therapy Researchers have directed much attention to the diagnosis and treatment of mental health problems resulting from crime, with work concentrated on rape victims. Success has been reported for general cognitive behavioral therapy, including systematic desensitization (Frank, 1988; but see Kilpatrick & Calhoun, 1988), the cognitive-behavioral techniques of stress inoculation and prolonged exposure (Foa, 1991), and group therapy (Yassen & Glass, 1984), among other interventions. However, there seems to be no consensus as to the single best treatment to use (Foa, 1991). Furthermore, improvements have not consistently been measured against base rates: victims seem to improve over time even with no formal treatment (Shapland, 1986).

These observations comport with the general findings of clinical psychology that, overall, different psychotherapies generate similar outcomes (Stiles, Shapiro, & Elliot, 1986). However, most clinical research has not examined treatment by subject interactions. As victims vary in their responses to crime, they may vary in their responses to therapy. Where specific treatments can be matched with particular subjects, the possibility for successful therapy increases (Shoham & Rohrbaugh, 1993).

Social Support Finally, victim service agencies should take into account the amount, quality, and victim's perception of social support, which can affect recovery (Kaniasty & Norris, 1992). However, families of victims, especially rape victims, go through their own victimization and may not be able to give adequate support (Mio, 1991; Riggs & Kilpatrick, 1990). Therefore, families should be involved in counseling to aid in the recovery of the victim and for themselves (Mio, 1991; Orzek, 1983; Sales et al., 1984). Families do not always have realistic expectations regarding the victim's progress, and their impatience could be detrimental (Riggs & Kilpatrick, 1990). It is interesting to note that the victim's perception of the quality and quantity of social support may be more important than the amount actually received (Kaniasty & Norris, 1992).

The Future of Victims' Rights

It is important to utilize empirical evidence when deciding to implement or retain specific victims' rights. Specific victims' rights provisions should be examined to determine the extent to which they facilitate the victim's psychological functioning and should not be lauded merely because they are called "victims' rights." However, if no psychological benefit to victims is found for a particular right, political realities or cultural norms may still require its retention (Sales & Shuman, 1994).

Under the current structure of American law, it would be a mistake to assume that all the psychological needs of victims can be addressed through the traditional criminal justice system. Pre-Norman England, characterized by private justice, may indeed have been the "golden age of the victim" (Schafer, 1968), or it may have been that the status of the victim, especially one of low social standing, was enhanced only after the king took over the burdens of prosecution (Greenburg, 1984). However, it does not seem to be either the effect or intent for victims' rights to return to the ninth century, when victims had sole responsibility for resolving conflicts with offenders. Modern victims' rights generally have not diminished the power of the state by returning control to the victims. Instead, they involve the victim more extensively in the state's campaign against criminals and create new bureaucracies to serve and assist victims (see, for example, Elias, 1993). Restitution, for instance, in old England belonged to the victim; in modern America, it is another tool of corrections (*Kelly v. Robinson,* 1986). Unless victims gain real control over criminal justice proceedings, society, not the individual victim, will remain the injured party in the eyes of the court, and the government, not the victim, will be the prosecutor's client. Because the criminal justice system will retain its present form for the foreseeable future, and because harm to victims can persist long after a criminal case is completed, meaningful victim participation in the criminal courts—including, in some cases, the opportunity to resolve disputes directly with offenders—should be combined with services geared toward the victim's psychological needs.

The reliance on large government entities such as victim compensation agencies and the courts to address victims' concerns clashes with the perspective that conceptualizes crime as a form of conflict belonging to the parties involved (Christie, 1977). Theoretically, the harm resulting from crimes against specific persons could be handled privately (Greenburg, 1984). However, because crimes are considered offenses against the state or against its citizens as a whole, the prosecution and incarceration of a criminal is generally the sole responsibility of the government entity: a victim cannot privately imprison or execute his or her offender and has only a limited right to assist with the prosecution (Sales et al., 1987). It can be argued that the government that prosecutes takes property—specifically, the debt, monetary or moral, owed by the offender—from the victim (Christie, 1977). The modern victims' rights movement stems from the perception that crime victims have not received enough in return.

On the other hand, where bureaucracies exist, they should respond to the needs of the victim in light of their purposes. For example, a victim who is entitled to compensation should not have to jump through procedural hoops to obtain that award. Rather, eligibility for compensation should routinely be made part of every criminal investigation and a determination mailed to the victim as a matter of course; part of the determination would include the amount of insurance available to the victim, and as part of the award, the compensation board could authorize future medical or psychological services, if insurance were unavailable. The victim would either accept or appeal the determination; if accepted, the award could be in the victim's hands within a month of the crime. Information gathered would also be useful for the determination of restitution at later stages of the proceedings as well as in plea bargaining negotiations. This would require funding of victim compensation beyond current levels.

Control over the process seems to be important to crime victims (Henderson, 1992; Kelly, 1990; Resick, 1987; but see Tyler, 1987), and this should be also factored into victims' rights laws. Plea bargaining, currently the exclusive domain of the prosecution, might provide an avenue for victims to gain some control over the process. The process of plea bargaining, when a prosecutor and a defendant negotiate a plea to an offense, generally occurs without the victim's approval.

Only the defendant, not the victim, has a right to a trial. A necessary concomitant of plea bargaining is the defendant's waiver of this right, but the victim cannot insist the case be brought to trial. Some states, including Washington, have amended their constitutions to guarantee some victim involvement in the trial and sentencing. However, these generally do not cede control of the trial to the victim (see, for example, Eikenberry, 1989).

Even the quest for vengeance could accommodate victims' desires for control. Active vengeance may be gained by confronting a surrogate for the offender; for example, rape victims may benefit from confronting convicted rapists, even if not their own (Warshaw, 1988). More directly, researchers should seek to determine whether vengeance is compatible with victim-involving procedures like mediation, and compare results with the effects of other judicial actions that seem to encompass vengeance, such as mandatory prison sentences and routine denial of bail.

Finally, because many victims fall outside the reach of victims' rights, these laws should be reevaluated. Currently, victims' rights laws cover those who typically fit a societally accepted view of the "ideal victim"; the victim most easily accepted as blameless by society is a physically weak person, engaged in a respectable activity in a place they could not be blamed for being, victimized by a stronger person unknown to him or her (Christie, 1977). An actual victim can vary in several ways from this profile. For example, it is possible to view drug addicts as victims of the crime of drug selling. Drug treatment would then be provided as a right, in a nonjudgmental atmosphere, not, for example, as a condition of probation. Society's attraction to protecting and avenging the "ideal victim" ignores the prevalence of crime within socioeconomic class or within the family, the reality of white-collar, environmental, and corporate crime, the relationship between victim and criminal in date and acquaintance rape, and official negligence or wrongdoing (McShane & Williams, 1992; Warshaw, 1988, see, for example, *DeShaney v. Winnebago County Department of Social Services*, 1989).

Conclusion

Victims need to feel in control and safe, able to live normal lives. If crime control provisions control crime, they may someday be all that are needed. Until then, there will be victims and the need for victims' rights. Victims' rights should be oriented toward the psychological recovery of victims, focusing on the needs of specific victims. This means taking into account the variability and persistence of symptoms and accepting that victims must participate in their own recovery (Higgins, 1994).

References

American Law Reports 3rd, 66, 202 (1975).

American Law Reports 4th, 38, 1194 (1985).

American Law Reports 4th, 46, 948 (1986).

American Psychiatric Association. (1994). Diagnostic and statistical manual of mental disorders (4th ed.). Washington, DC: Author.

Amick-McMullen, A., Kilpatrick, D.G., & Resnick, H.S. (1991). Homicide as risk factor for PTSD among surviving family members [Special issue: Environmental risk factors in the development of psychopathology]. Behavior Modification, 15(4), 545–559.

Bastian, L.D. (1993). Criminal victimization 1992: A national crime victimization survey report. Washington, DC: U.S. Department of Justice, Bureau of Justice Statistics.

Becker, J., Skinner, L.J., Abel, G.G., Howell, J., & Bruce, J. (1982). The effects of sexual assault on rape and attempted rape victims. Victimology, 7(1–4), 106–113.

Booth v. Maryland, 482 U.S. 496 (1989).

Brown, B.B., & Harris, P.B. (1989). Residential burglary victimization: Reactions to the invasion of a primary territory. Journal of Environmental Psychology, 9(2), 119–132.

Burkhead, M.L., Luginbuhl, J.S., & Wrenn. (1994, March). Victim impact evidence in capital trials: What are its effects? Paper presented at the meeting of the American Psychology-Law Society, North Carolina State University, Raleigh.

Buss, D.B. (1994). The evolution of desire: Strategies of human mating. New York: Basic Books.

Carrington, F., & Nicholson, G. (1989). Victims' rights: An idea whose time has come—Five years later: The maturing of an idea. Pepperdine Law Review: Follow-Up Issue on Victims' Rights, 17(1), 1–18.

Cavaiola, A.A., & Schiff, M. (1988). Behavioral sequelae of physical and/or sexual abuse. Child Abuse and Neglect, 12(2), 181–188.

Chelimsky, E. (1981). Serving victims: Agency incentives and individual needs. In S.E. Salasin (Ed.), Evaluating victim services (pp. 21–37). Newbury Park, CA: Sage.

Christie, N. (1977). Conflicts as property. British Journal of Criminology, 17(1), 1–15.

Cienfuegos, A.J., & Monelli, C. (1983). The testimony of political repression as a therapeutic instrument. American Journal of Orthopsychiatry, 53(1), 43–51.

Cluss, P.A., Boughton, J., Frank, E., Stewart, B.D., & West, D. (1983). The rape victim: Psychological correlates of participation in the legal process. Criminal Justice and Behavior, 10(3), 342–357.

Cohen, L.J. (1987). The psychological aftermath of rate: Long-term effects and individual differences in recovery. Journal of Social and Clinical Psychology, 5(4), 525–534.

Cohen, M.A. (1988). Pain, suffering, and jury awards: A study of the cost of crime to victims. Law and Society Review, 22(3), 537–555.

Davis, R.C., & Henley, M. (1990). Victim service programs. In A.J. Lurigio, W.G. Skogan, & R.C. Davis (Eds.), Victims of crime: Problems, policies, and programs (Sage Criminal Justice System Annals No. 25, pp. 50–68). Newbury Park, CA: Sage.

DeShaney v. Winnebago County Department of Social Services, 109 S.Ct. 998 (1989).

Dittenhoffer, T., & Ericson, R.V. (1992). The victim/offender reconciliation programme: A message to the correctional reformers. In E.A. Fattah (Ed.), Towards a critical victimology (pp. 311–346). New York: St. Martin's Press.

Eikenberry, K. (1989). The elevation of victims' rights in Washington State: Constitutional status. Pepperdine Law Review: Follow-Up Issue on Victims' Rights, 17(1), 19–33.

Elias, R. (1983a). The symbolic politics of victim compensation. Victimology, 8(1–2), 213–224.

Elias, R. (1983b). Victims of the system: Crime victims and compensation in American politics and criminal justice. New Brunswick, NJ: Transaction Books.

Elias, R. (1986). The politics of victimization: Victims, victimology, and human rights. New York: Oxford University Press.

Elias, R. (1993). Victims still: The political manipulation of crime victims. Newbury Park, CA: Sage.

Fattah, E.A. (1992). The need for a critical victimology. In E.A. Fattah (Ed.), Towards a critical victimology. New York: St. Martin's Press.

Fischer, C.T. (1984). Being criminally victimized: An illustrated structure. American Behavioral Scientist, 27(6), 723–738.

Foa, E.B. (1991). Treatment of posttraumatic stress disorder in rape victims: A comparison between cognitive-behavioral procedures and counseling. Journal of Consulting and Clinical Psychology, 59(5), 715–723.

Frank, E. (1988, August). Immediate and delayed treatment of rape victims. Conference of the New York Academy of Sciences: Human sexual aggression: Current perspectives. Annals of the New York Academy of Sciences, 528, 296–309.

Frieze, I.H., Hymer, S., & Greenberg, M.S. (1987). Describing the crime victim: Psychological reactions to victimization. Professional Psychology: Research and Practice, 18(4), 299–315.

Galaway, B. (1988). Crime victim and offender mediation as a social work strategy. Social Service Review, 62(4), 668–683.

Ganzini, L., McFarland, B.H., & Cutler, D. (1990). Prevalence of mental disorders after catastrophic financial loss. Journal of Nervous and Mental Disease, 178(11), 680–685.

Geffner, R. (1992). Guidelines for using mediation with abusive couples. Psychotherapy in Private Practice, 10(1–2), 77–92.

Geis, G. (1990). Crime victims: Practices and prospects. In A.J. Lurigio, W.G. Skogan, & R.C. Davis (Eds.), Victims of crime: Problems, policies, and programs (Sage Criminal Justice System Annals No. 25, pp. 50–68). Newbury Park, CA: Sage.

Goddu, C.R. (1993). Victims' "rights" or a fair trial wronged. Buffalo Law Review, 41(1), 244–272.

Gottfredson, M.R., & Hirschi, T. (1990). A general theory of crime. Stanford: Stanford University Press.

Greenburg, J. (1984). The victim in historical perspective: Some aspects of the English experience. Journal of Social Issues, 40(1), 77–102.

Hagen, J. (1990). The structuration of gender and deviance: A power-control theory of vulnerability to crime and the search for deviant role exits. Canadian Review of Sociology and Anthropology, 27(2), 137–156.

Hagler v. State, 625 So.2nd. 1190 (Ala. 1993).

Halleck, S.L. (1989). Vengeance and victimization. Victimology, 5(2–4), 99–109.

Harrington, L.H. (1982). Statement of the Chairman. In President's Task Force on Victims of Crime, Final report. Washington, DC: Author.

Henderson, L.N. (1992). The wrongs of victims' rights. In E.A. Fattah (Ed.), Towards a critical victimology (pp. 100–192). New York: St. Martin's Press.

Herbst, P.R. (1992). From helpless victim to empowered survivor: Oral history as a treatment for survivors of torture [Special issue: Refugee women and their mental health: I. Shattered societies, shattered lives]. Women and Therapy, 13(1–2), 141–154.

Higgins, G.O. (1994). Resilient adults: Overcoming a cruel past. San Francisco: Jossey-Bass.

Hillenbrand, S. (1990). Restitution and victim rights in the 1980's. In A.J. Lurigio, W.G. Skogan, & R.C. Davis (Eds.), Victims of crime: Problems, policies, and programs (Sage Criminal Justice System Annals No. 25, pp. 188–204). Newbury Park, CA: Sage.

Janoff-Bulman, R., & Frieze, I.H. (1983). A theoretical perspective for understanding reactions to victimization. Journal of Social Issues, 39(2), 1–17.

Kaniasty, K., & Norris, F.H. (1992). Social support and victims of crime: Matching event, support, and outcome. American Journal of Community Psychology, 20(2), 211–241.

Karmen, A. (1984). Crime victims: an introduction to victimology. Pacific Grove, CA: Brooks/Cole.

Keane, T.M. (1989). Post-traumatic stress disorder: Current status and future directions. Behavior Therapy, 20, 149–153.

Kelly, D. (1990). Victim participation in the criminal justice system. In A.J. Lurigio, W.G. Skogan, & R.C. Davis (Eds.), Victims of crime: Problems, policies and programs (Sage Criminal Justice System Annals No. 25, pp. 172–187). Newbury Park, CA: Sage.

Kelly v. Robinson, 479 U.S. 36 (1986).

Kennedy, D.B. (1983). Implications of the victimization syndrome for clinical intervention with crime victims. Personnel and Guidance Journal, 62(4), 219–222.

Kilpatrick, D.G. (1989). Victim and crime factors associated with the development of crime-related post-traumatic stress disorder. Behavior Therapy, 20(2), 199–214.

Kilpatrick, D.G., Best, C.L., Veronen, L.J., Amick, A.E., Villeponteaux, L.A., & Ruff, G.A. (1985). Mental health correlates of crime victimization: A community survey. Journal of Consulting and Clinical Psychology, 53(6), 866–873.

Kilpatrick, D.G., & Calhoun, K.S. (1988). Early behavioral treatment for rape trauma: Efficacy or artifact? Behavior Therapy, 19(3), 421–427.

Kilpatrick, D.G., Saunders, B.E., Veronen, L.G., Best, C.L., & Von, J.M. (1987). Criminal victimization: Lifetime prevalence, reporting to police, and psychological impact. Crime and Delinquency, 33(4), 479–489.

Lurigio, A.J., & Resick, P.A. (1990). Healing the psychological wounds of criminal victimization: Predicting postcrime distress and recovery. In A.J. Lurigio, W.G. Skogan, & R.C. Davis (Eds.), Victims of crime: Problems, policies, and programs (Sage Criminal Justice System Annals No. 25, pp. 50–68). Newbury Park, CA: Sage.

Martinez v. California, 444 U.S. 27 (1980).

Matthews, W.G. (1981). Restitution: The chameleon of corrections. Journal of Offender Counseling, Services, and Rehabilitation, 5(3–4), 77–92.

McCune, N. (1989). Children surviving parental murder. British Journal of Psychiatry, 154, 889.

McShane, M.D., & Williams, F.P. (1992). Radical victimology: A critique of the concept of victim in traditional victimology. Crime and Delinquency, 38(2), 258–271.

Menard, A.E., & Salius, A.J. (1990). Judicial response to family violence: The importance of message. Mediation Quarterly, 7(4), 293–302.

Meyer, C.B., & Taylor, S.E. (1986). Adjustment to rape. Journal of Personality and Social Psychology, 50(6), 1226–1234.

Mio, J.S. (1991). The effects of rape upon victims and families: Implications for a comprehensive family therapy. American Journal of Family Therapy, 19(2), 147–159.

National Association of Victim Compensation Boards. (1993a). Counseling expense comparison, 1989–1992. Washington, DC: Author.

National Association of Victim Compensation Boards. (1993b). State mental health cost control rules. Washington, DC: Author.

National Victim Center. (1993). Database on victims' rights. Alexandria, VA: Author.

Norris, F.H., & Kaniasty, K. (1991). The psychological experience of crime: A test of the mediating role of beliefs in explaining the distress of crime. Journal of Social and Clinical Psychology, 10(3), 239–261.

Orzek, A.M. (1983). Sexual assault: The female victim, her male partner, and their relationship. Personnel and Guidance Journal, 62(3), 143–146.

Payne v. Tennessee, 111 S.Ct. 2597 (1991).

Peterson, C.S., & Seligman, M.E.P. (1983). Learned helplessness and victimization. Journal of Social Issues, 39(2), 103–116.

Polito, K.E. (1990). The rights of crime victims in the criminal justice system: Is justice blind to the victims of crime? New England Journal on Criminal and Civil Confinement, 16, 241–269.

Pope, K.S., & Garcia-Peltoniemi, R.E. (1991). Responding to victims of torture: Clinical issues, professional responsibilities, and useful resources. Professional Psychology: Research and Practice, 22(4), 269–276.

President's Task Force on Victims of Crime. (1982). Final report. Washington, DC: Author.

Reiss, A.J. (1986). Policy implications of crime victim surveys. In E.A. Fattah (Ed.), From crime policy to victim policy: Reorienting the justice system (pp. 246–260). London: Macmillan.

Resick, P.A. (1987). Psychological effects of victimization: Implications for the criminal justice system. Crime and Delinquency, 33(4), 468–478.

Resick, P.A. (1990). Victims of sexual assault. In A.J. Lurigio, W.G. Skogan, & R.C. Davis (Eds.), Victims of crime: Problems, policies and programs (Sage Criminal Justice System Annals No. 25, pp. 69–86). Newbury Park, CA: Sage.

Reske, H.J. (1992). Helping crime's casualties. American Bar Association Journal, 78, 34–38.

Resnick, H.S., Kilpatrick, D.G., & Lipovsky, J.A. (1991). Assessment of rape-related posttraumatic stress disorder: Stressor and symptom dimensions [Special section: Issues and methods in assessment of posttraumatic stress disorder]. Psychological Assessment, 3(4), 561–572.

Riggs, D.S., & Kilpatrick, D.G. (1990). Families and friends: Indirect victimization by crime. In A.J. Lurigio, W.G. Skogan, & R.C. Davis (Eds.), Victims of crime: Problems, policies, and programs (Sage Criminal Justice System Annals No. 25, pp. 120–138). Newbury Park, CA: Sage.

Riggs, D.S., Kilpatrick, D.G., & Resnick, H.S. (1992). Long-term psychological distress associated with marital rape and aggravated assault: A comparison to other crime victims. Journal of Family Violence, 7(4), 283–296.

Roberts, A.R. (1990). Helping crime victims: Research, policy, and practice. Newbury Park, CA: Sage.

Roland, D.L. (1989). Progress in the Victim Reform Movement: No longer the "forgotten victim." Pepperdine Law Review: Follow-Up Issue on Victims' Rights, 17(1), 35–58.

Rosen, C.J., & Harland, A.T. (1990). Restitution to crime victims as a presumptive requirement in criminal case dispositions. In A.R. Roberts (Ed.), Helping crime victims: Research, policy, and practice (pp. 233–248). Newbury Park, CA: Sage.

Sahjpaul, S., & Renner, K.E. (1988). The new sexual assault law: The victim's experience in court. American Journal of Community Psychology, 16(4), 503–513.

Salasin, S.E. (1981). Services to victims: Needs assessment. In S.E. Salasin (Ed.), Evaluating victim services (pp. 21–37). Newbury Park, CA: Sage.

Sales, B., Rich, R.F., & Reich, J. (1987). Victimization policy research. Professional Psychology: Research and Practice, 18(4), 326–337.

Sales, B.D., & Shuman, D.W. (1994). Mental health law and mental health care. American Journal of Orthopsychiatry, 64, 172–179.

Sales, E., Baum, M., & Shore, B. (1984). Victim readjustment following assault. Journal of Social Issues, 40(1), 117–136.

Santiago, J.M., McCall-Perez, F., Gorcey, M., & Beigel, A. (1985). Long-term psychological effects of rape in 35 rape victims. American Journal of Psychiatry, 142(11), 1338–1340.

Schafer, S. (1968). The victim and his criminal: A study in functional responsibility. New York: Random House.

Shapland, J. (1986). Victim assistance and the criminal justice system: The victim's perspective. In E.A. Fattah (Ed.), From crime policy to victim policy: Reorienting the justice system (pp. 218–233). Hong Kong: Macmillan.

Shepherd, J. (1990). Victims of personal violence: The relevance of Symonds' model of psychological response and loss-theory. British Journal of Social Work, 20(4), 309–332.

Shoham, V., & Rohrbaugh, M. (1993). Aptitude x treatment interaction (ATI) research: Sharpening the focus, widening the lens. In M. Aveline & D.A. Shapiro (Eds.), Research foundations for psychotherapy. New York: Wiley.

Shuman, D.W. (1994). The psychology of compensation in tort law. Kansas Law Review, 43, 39–77.

Stanko, E., & Hobdell, K. (1993). Assault on men: Masculinity and male victimization. British Journal of Criminology, 33(3), 400–415.

Steinmetz, C.H. (1984). Coping with serious crime: Self-help and outside help. Victimology, 9(3–4), 324–343.

Stiles, W.B., Shapiro, D.A., & Elliot, R. (1986). Are all psychotherapies equivalent? American Psychologist, 41(2), 165–180.

Terr, L.C. (1983). Chowchilla revisited: The effects of psychic trauma four years after a school-bus kidnapping. American Journal of Psychiatry, 140(12), 1543–1550.

Thibaut, J., & Walker, L. (1975). Procedural justice: A psychological analysis. Hillsdale, NJ: Erlbaum.

Thornhill, N.W., & Thornhill, R. (1990). An evolutionary analysis of psychological pain following rape: III. Effects of force and violence. Aggressive Behavior, 16(5), 297–330.

Tyler, T.R. (1987). Conditions leading to value-expressive effects in judgments of procedural justice: A test of four models. Journal of Personality and Social Psychology, 52(2), 333–344.

Tyler, T.R. (1992). The psychological consequences of judicial procedures: Implications for civil commitment hearings. Southern Methodist University Law Review, 46, 433–445.

Umbreit, M.S. (1989). Crime victims seeking fairness, not revenge: Toward restorative justice. Federal Probation, 53(3), 52–57.

U.S. Department of Justice, Office of Justice Programs. (1986). Four years later: A report of the President's Task Force on Victims of Crime. Washington, DC: Government Printing Office.

Veronen, L.G., Kilpatrick, D.G., & Resick, P.A. (1979). Treating fear and anxiety in rape victims: Implications for the criminal justice system. In W.H. Parsonage (Ed.), Perspectives in victimology. Newbury Park, CA: Sage.

Viano, E. (1987). Victim's rights and the Constitution: Reflections on a Bicentennial. Crime and Delinquency, 33(4), 438–451.

Victims of Crimes Act (1984). Public Law 98-473.

Walsh, A. (1992). Placebo justice: Victim recommendations and offender sentences in sexual assault cases. In E.A. Fattah (Ed.), Towards a critical victimology (pp. 294–310). New York: St. Martin's Press.

Warshaw, R. (1988). I never called it rape. New York: HarperCollins.

Washington State Constitution 8200, 51st sess. (1989).

Weeks v. United States, 232 U.S. 883 (1913).

Wexler, D.B., & Winick, B.J. (1991). Essays in therapeutic jurisprudence. Durham, NC: Carolina Academic Press.

Wirtz, P.W., & Harrell, A.V. (1987). Effects of postassault exposure to attack-similar stimuli on long-term recovery of victims. Journal of Consulting and Clinical Psychology, 55(1), 10–16.

Wortman, C.B. (1983). Coping with victimization: Conclusions and implications for future research. Journal of Social Issues, 39(2), 195–221.

Yassen, J., & Glass, L. (1984). Sexual assault survivors groups: A feminist practice perspective. Social Work, 29(3), 252–257.

Yick Wo v. Hopkins, 118 U.S. 356 (1886).

Zapf, M.K., & Cole, B. (1985). Yukon restitution study. Canadian Journal of Criminology, 27(4), 477–490.

A Therapeutic Jurisprudence Approach to the Legal Processing of Domestic Violence Cases

Leonore M.J. Simon

Recent media coverage of the trial of O.J. Simpson has focused public attention on the legal system's chronic failure to respond more effectively to cases of domestic violence.[1] For example, a recent study by the Justice Department found that slightly more than half (51%) of the defendants in spouse killings had been previously arrested.[2] The legal response to domestic violence cases has been so weak that offenders seem to walk away from a legal encounter believing that they can batter their intimate partner or ex–partner with impunity.

The term domestic violence carries different meanings across the literature. In this article, the term is used to refer to violence between spouses, ex-spouses, intimates, and ex-intimates. Although both men and women are vic-

---

1. See Linda Gordon, Heroes of Their Own Lives: The Politics and History of Family Violence (1989); Elizabeth Pleck, Domestic Tyranny: The Making of Social Policy Against Family Violence from Colonial Times to the Present (1987); The Police Found., Domestic Violence and the Police: Studies in Detroit and Kansas City (1977); U.S. Comm'n on Civ. Rts., Under the Rule of Thumb: Battered Women and the Administration of Justice (1982); Richard A. Berk et al., Bringing the Cops Back In: A Study of Efforts to Make the Criminal Justice System More Responsive to Incidents of Family Violence, 9 Soc. Sci. Res. 193, 194–198 (1980); Eve S. Buzawa & Carl G. Buzawa, Introduction to Domestic Violence: The Changing Criminal Justice Response at xv (Eve S. Buzawa & Carl G. Buzawa eds., 1992) (hereinafter Changing Response); Robert E. Emery, Family Violence, 44 Am. Psychol. 321, 326 (1989); Delbert S. Elliott, Criminal Justice Procedures, in 11 Family Violence: Crime and Justice: An Annual Review of the Research 428 (Lloyd Ohlin & Michael Tonry eds., 1989) (hereinafter Family Violence); Jeffrey Fagan and Angela Browne, Violence Between Spouses and Intimates: Physical Aggression Between Women and Men in Intimate Relationships, in 3 Understanding and Preventing Violence: Social Influences 115, 122–27 (Albert J. Reiss, Jr. & Jeffrey A. Roth eds., 1993); David A. Ford, Wife Battery and Criminal Justice: A Study of Victim Decision-Making, 32 Fam. Rel. 463, 465–469, 472–474 (1983); Michele Ingrasia & Melinda Beck, Patterns of Abuse, Newsweek, July 4, 1994, at 26, 28; Tamar Lewin, Case Might Fit Pattern of Abuse, Experts Say, N.Y. Times, June 19, 1994, at A20.

2. John M. Dawson & Patrick A. Langan, U.S. Dep't of Justice, Murder in Families 2, 5 (1994). It cannot be determined from this study for what types of offenses those defendants had previously been arrested. It is interesting that the study indicates that 35% of the victims in spouse killings also had a prior criminal record. Note that this study's definition of spouse includes spouses and common-law spouses. It appears that other intimate killings involving couples who were not living together are included in the "other" family category.

timized by partners, injuries and lethal injuries from such partner violence fall disproportionately on women.[3] The focus of this article is on violent acts committed by men against women that would be considered a violent crime if it were committed against a stranger. These violent acts include physical assault, sexual assault, and homicide committed, threatened, or attempted by intimate partners.

Although our legal system has become less accepting of the physical assault of wives, especially in severe cases, a husband's assault on his wife continues to carry fewer legal sanctions than a similar assault of a stranger.[4] Only in the last two decades have laws and policies about domestic violence undergone major changes, with their implementation varying widely among jurisdictions.[5]

The legal system's failure to respond more consistently and effectively to such cases has alarming implications for battered women and their children. For instance, when a spouse kills a spouse, wives are the victims in nearly two thirds of the cases.[6] The escalation of violence against women can, and all too frequently does, result in their deaths.[7] Compared with victims of violence by

---

3. See e.g., Murray A. Straus, Conceptualization and Measurement of Battering: Implications for Public Policy, in Woman Battering: Policy Responses 19, 24–32 (Michael Steinman ed., 1991) (estimating that the number of women who are battered annually ranges between 3 and 6 million). Murray A. Straus & Richard J. Gelles, Societal Change in Family Violence from 1975 to 1985 as Revealed by Two National Surveys, 48 J. Marriage & Fam. 465, 470 (1986) (indicating that a minimum of 2 million women are severely assaulted annually by their male partners). But see Dawson & Langan, supra note 2, at 1, 3 (indicating that the predominance of husbands as defendants varied by race). Dawson and Langan found that, overall, husbands comprised about 60% of the defendants; in Black killings, wives were about as likely as husbands to be charged with killing their spouses.

4. E.g., Ford, supra note 1, at 472–474.

5. National Council Juvenile & Family Court Judges, Family Violence: State-of-the-Art Court Programs 5 (1992); Family Violence: A Model St. Code s 201 (National Council Juvenile & Family Court Judges 1994) (hereinafter Model St. Code); Elliott, supra note 1; Nancy K. D. Lemon, Criminal Cases Concerning Domestic Violence, 25 Juv. & Fam. L. Dig. 345 (1993); Robert G. Spector, Marital Tort Cases Concerning Domestic Violence, 25 Juv. & Fam. L. Dig. 399 (1993); Joan Zorza, Civil Cases Concerning Domestic Violence, 25 Juv. & Fam. L. Dig. 375 (1993).

6. See Dawson & Langan, supra note 2, at 3. See also Angela Browne & Kirk R. Williams, Exploring the Effect of Resource Availability and the Likelihood of Female-Perpetrated Homicides, 23 Law & Soc'y Rev. 75, 76, 86 (1989) (indicating that male-perpetrated homicide primarily involves acquaintances and strangers; female-perpetrated homicide primarily involves an intimate male partner); Margo I. Wilson & Martin Daly, Who Kills Whom in Spouse Killings? On the Exceptional Sex Ratio of Spousal Homicides in the United States, 30 Criminology 189, 206 (1992) (comparing men and women who kill spouses and finding that a large proportion of spouse killings perpetrated by wives, but almost none of those perpetrated by husbands, are acts of self-defense).

7. Daniel G. Saunders & Angela Browne, Domestic Homicide, in Case Studies in Family Violence 379, 380–81 (Robert T. Ammerman & Michel Hersen eds., 1990); Margaret A. Zahn, Homicide in the Twentieth Century: Trends, Types, and Causes, in 1 Violence in America: The History of Violence, at 126 (Ted Robert Gurr ed., 1989) (indicating that more than half the women murdered in the United States are killed by male partners or ex-partners). Patrick A. Langan & Christopher A. Innes, U.S. Dep't of Justice, Preventing Domestic Violence Against Women 3 (1986) (indicating that although most incidents of domestic violence

strangers, victims of domestic violence are at far greater risk of recurring victimization.[8] Even in cases where the battered woman leaves the relationship, evidence suggests that the greatest risk of domestic violence is faced by separated and divorced women.[9] In addition, men who abuse their wives are more likely to be abusive toward their children.[10] Some investigators believe that as many as 80% of men who batter women also batter a child.[11] The more severely the mother is abused, the worse the child is abused.[12]

In general, criticisms leveled at the legal system have emphasized the comparative lack of serious consequences accorded acts of domestic violence.[13]

---

are labeled as misdemeanors, many of these assaults are actually relatively serious: "[I]n terms of actual bodily injury, as many as half of all incidents of domestic violence that police would classify as misdemeanors are as serious as or more serious than 90% of all violent crimes that police would classify as felonies." Consequently, the tendency to classify domestic violence offenses as misdemeanors belies the seriousness of these events).

8. Langan & Innes, supra note 7, at 3.

9. E.g., Gwynn Nettler, Killing One Another 108–20 (1982); Brian Wiersema & Colin Loftin, Estimates of Assault by Intimates from the National Crime Survey (1994); Desmond Ellis, Post-Separation Woman Abuse: The Contribution of Lawyers as "Barracudas," and "Counsellors," 10 Intl. J. L. & Psychiatry 403, 408 (1987); Leslie W. Kennedy & Donald G. Dutton, The Incidence of Wife Assault in Alberta, 21 Canad. J. Behav. Sci. 40, 49 (1989) (finding extremely high rates of domestic violence after the breakup of a relationship); Martha Mahoney, Legal Images of Battered Women: Redefining the Issue of Separation, 90 Mich. L. Rev. 1, 5–6, 64–68 (1991) (offering a theory of separation assault to explain spouse battering as a way in which the batterer uses violence to prevent a woman from seeking autonomy from the relationship).

10. Angela Browne, When Battered Women Kill (1987); Barbara J. Hart, National Council Juvenile & Family Court Judges, State Codes on Domestic Violence: Analysis, Commentary, and Recommendations 79 (1992); Gerald T. Hotaling & Murray A. Straus, Intrafamily Violence, and Crime and Violence Outside the Family, in Family Violence, supra note 1; Murray A. Straus, Ordinary Violence, Child Abuse, and Wife Beating: What Do They Have in Common? in The Dark Side of Families: Current Family Violence Research 213 (David Finkelhor et al. eds., 1983); C. F. Telch & C. U. Lindquist, Violent vs. Nonviolent Couples: A Comparison of Patterns, 21 Psychotherapy 242 (1984).

11. Peter G. Jaffe et al., Children of Battered Women 20 (1990) (estimating that 30%–40% of men who batter their wives also abuse their children); Meredith Hofford & Richard J. Gable, Significant Intervention: Coordinated Strategies to Deter Family Violence, in Families in Court 89 (Meredith Hofford ed., 1989); Jean Giles-Sims, A Longitudinal Study of Battered Children of Battered Wives, 34 Fam. Rel. 205, 207 (1985) (finding that battered women are also prone to abuse their children).

12. Lee H. Bowker et al., On the Relationship Between Wife Beating and Child Abuse, in Feminist Perspectives on Wife Abuse 133 (Kersti Yllo & Michele Bograd eds., 1988).

13. But see Elliott, supra note 1, at 428, 462 (suggesting that the limited empirical evidence available does not necessarily support the idea that different factors are involved in the legal processing of violent domestic and violent nondomestic offenders); Dawson & Langan, supra note 2, at 7 (suggesting that their study demonstrates that "in several important respects, the criminal justice outcomes of family murder defendants were about the same overall as those of other murder defendants"). In reaching this broad conclusion, Dawson and Langan overlook the disparities in legal outcomes of some of their own data; much of these data are displayed in tables but not addressed directly. For example, they state that compared to other murder defendants, those in family murder cases are as likely to be convicted of murder. In the same table that they refer to (Table 12, at 7), one can clearly see that spouse

Similar criminal behavior against strangers incurs severe sanctions.[14] The hesitancy to invoke legal sanctions in cases of spouse abuse has historically been linked to the view that such incidents are family affairs and not the true business of the legal system.[15] Traditionally, police have not responded to battered woman calls,[16] and prosecutors and judges have treated domestic violence as a

---

killers are less likely than nonfamily killers to be convicted of murder, and more likely to be convicted of manslaughter.

14. Attorney General's Task Force on Family Violence: Final Report, 11–12 (1984) (noting that assaults on strangers tend to be prosecuted, whereas assaults against family members are viewed as noncriminal, family matters). Dawson & Langan, supra note 2, at 7 (Table 12 indicates that spouse killers are more likely to be convicted of lesser categories of homicides such as manslaughter than nonfamily killers; they are also more likely to receive probation or a shorter prison sentence than nonfamily killers); Stephen B. Herrell & Meredith Hofford, Family Violence Project, National Council Juvenile & Family Court Judges, Family Violence: Improving Court Practice 25 (1990).

15. Louise Armstrong, The Home Front: Notes from the Family War Zone (1983); Commonwealth Secreteriat, Women & Development Programme, Confronting Violence: A Manual for Commonwealth Action (1987); Gail A. Goolkasian, U.S. Dep't of Justice, Confronting Domestic Violence: a Guide for Criminal Justice Agencies 3 (1992); Gordon, supra, note 1; National Advisory Comm'n on Crim. Just. Standards & Goals, Courts (1973); Pleck, supra, note 1; C. E. Silberman, Criminal Violence, Criminal Justice (1978); Barbara E. Smith, U.S. Dep't of Justice, Non-stranger Violence: The Criminal Court's Response (1983); U.S. Comm'n on Civ. Rts., supra note 1; Nanette J. Davis, Battered Women: Implications for Social Control, 12 Contemp. Crises 345, 348 (1988); R. Emerson Dobash & Russell P. Dobash, Wives: The 'Appropriate' Victims of Marital Violence, 2 Victimology: An Int'l J. 426 (1977); Elliott, supra, note 1; Margaret May, Violence and the Family: An Historical Perspective, in Violence and the Family (J. P. Martin ed., 1978); K. McCann, Battered Women and the Law: The Limits of Legislation, in Women in Law: Explorations in Law, Family, and Sexuality (Julie Brophy & Carol Smart eds., 1985); Joanne L. Miller et al., Felony Punishments: A Factorial Survey of Perceived Justice in Criminal Sentencing, 82 J. Crim. L. & Criminology 396, 409–410 (1991); Elizabeth Pleck, Criminal Approaches to Family Violence, 1640–1980, in Family Violence 19, supra note 1, at 20–21, 53; Marc Riedel, Stranger Violence: Perspectives, Issues, and Problems, 78 J. Crim. L. & Criminology 223 (1987); Jocelynne A. Scutt, Going Backwards: Law 'Reform' and Women Bashing, 9 Women's Stud. Int. F. 49, 50 (1986) (contending that the term domestic violence is a euphemism for criminal assaults occurring in the home); David B. Wexler, An Offense-Victim Approach to Insanity Defense Reform, 26 Ariz. L. Rev. 17, 21 (1984) (suggesting that public objection to use of the insanity defense can be dissipated, if, through legislation, the defense is made unavailable to homicide defendants who are strangers to the victim); David B. Wexler, Redefining the Insanity Problem, 53 Geo. Wash. L. Rev. 528, 552 (noting that the public is more sympathetic to use of the insanity defense in family homicides than in stranger homicides (1985); Franklin E. Zimring, Toward a Jurisprudence of Family Violence, in Family Violence 547, 548 supra, note 1; Private Violence, Time, September 5, 1983, at 18–19.

16. E.g., R. Emerson Dobash & Russell P. Dobash, Violence Against Wives: A Case Against the Patriarchy (1979); Roger Langley & Richard C. Levy, Wife Beating: The Silent Crisis (1977); Lenore E. Walker, The Battered Woman (1979); D. H. Bayley, The Tactical Choices of Patrol Officers, 14 J. Crim. Just. 329 (1986); Sarah Fenstermaker Berk & Donileen R. Loseke, Handling Family Violence: Situational Determinants of Police Arrest in Domestic Disturbances, 15 Law & Soc'y Rev. 317, 319 (1980–1981); Lee H. Bowker, Police Services to Battered Women—Bad or Not So Bad?, 9 Crim. Just. & Behav. 476 (1982); Buzawa & Buzawa, supra note 1; Raymond Parnas, The Police Response to Domestic Dis-

noncriminal event.[17] The low sanction severity traditionally associated with domestic violence cases may actually reinforce the underlying causes of marital violence.[18] Batterers tend to deny or minimize their violent behavior,[19] a perception that is fueled both by police annoyance with victims[20] and by prosecution and judicial indifference.[21]

This insensitivity to domestic violence victims has not been the domain solely of the criminal justice system.[22] The civil justice system has presented its own obstacles to these victims.[23] Historically, civil remedies such as restraining

---

turbance, 2 Wis. L. Rev. 914, 949 (1967); Douglas A. Smith & Jody R. Klein, Police Control of Interpersonal Disputes, 31 Soc. Probs. 468, 478 (1984) (finding that arrest is likely to be effected when the complainant is female in both domestic and nondomestic disputes). But see Eve S. Buzawa & Thomas Austin, Determining Police Response to Domestic Violence Victims: The Role of Victim Preference, 36 Am. Behav. Sci. 610, 613 (1993) (finding that the presence of bystanders during the violence increased the chances that an arrest would be made).

17. See Lisa G. Lerman, Center for Women Policy Studies, Prosecution of Spouse Abuse: Innovations in Criminal Justice Response (1983); Elizabeth A. Stanko, Intimate Intrusions: Women's Experience of Male Violence (1985); Vera Inst. Of Justice, Felony Arrests: Their Prosecution & Disposition in New York City's Courts (1977); Jane W. Ellis, Prosecutorial Discretion to Charge in Cases of Spousal Assault: A Dialogue, 75 J. Crim. L. & Criminology 56 (1984); Martha H. Field & Henry F. Field, Marital Violence and the Criminal Justice Process: Neither Justice Nor Peace, 47 Soc. Serv. Rev. 221, 232, 235 (1973); M. D. A. Freeman, Violence Against Women: Does the Legal System Provide Solutions or Itself Constitute the Problem?, 7 Brit. J. of L. & Soc'y 215, 238–240 (1980) (illustrating how judges have perpetuated the idea of a husband's right to chastise his wife); Raymond I. Parnas, The Judicial Response to Intra-Family Violence, 54 Minn. L. Rev. 585, 643 (1970); Lynn Hecht Schafran, Documenting Gender Bias in the Courts: The Task Force Approach, 70 Judicature 280, 283–284 (1987) (finding that although state domestic violence legislation provides adequate statutory protections for the battered woman, judicial enforcement is lax due to stereotypes about the victims). Schafran notes that judges tend to minimize domestic violence offenses and often adhere to the view that they are not criminal matters. See also Dobash & Dobash, supra note 15, at 426; Janell Schmidt & Ellen Hochstedler Steury, Prosecutorial Discretion in Filing Charges in Domestic Violence Cases, 27 Criminology 487 (1989); Elizabeth A. Stanko, Would You Believe This Woman?, in Judge, Lawyer, Victim, and Thief (Nicole Hahn Rafter & Elizabeth A. Stanko eds., 1982).

18. E.g., Elliott, supra note 1, at 427, 428, 446–47; Fagan & Browne, supra note 1, at 225, 227.

19. See discussion infra part I.A.

20. E.g., Kathleen J. Ferraro, Policing Battered Women, 36 Soc. Probs. 61, 68–69 (1989) (finding that after adoption of a presumptive arrest policy in Phoenix, Arizona, police officers did not implement it in a uniform manner). Ferraro found that police held stereotypes about battered women, blamed them for their own victimization, and expressed disdain for the victims. She indicates that one officer expressed the view that a man should be allowed to do whatever he wants in his own home, and that he himself had recently punched a hole in his living room wall during an argument with his wife. Although no research has been done on this issue, one wonders what the prevalence of spouse abuse is among police officers and how their own marital problems influence their enforcement of domestic violence laws.

21. E.g., Buzawa & Buzawa, supra note 1.

22. Irene Frieze & Angela Browne, Violence in Marriage, in Family Violence, supra note 1, at 163.

23. See generally Natalie Loder Clark, Marital Privacy: New Remedies for Old Wrongs,

orders have been unavailable to the majority of victims of domestic violence,[24] and when issued have not been enforced by legal officials.[25] Consequently, when civil remedies such as restraining orders have been used to avert further violence, they have provided victims with a false sense of security. In the case of restraining orders, this is due to the legal system's failure to sanction violators as well as the increased risk of harm to victims who separate from or divorce abusers.[26] Another thorny issue, the issuance of mutual restraining orders by the courts, has further compromised the safety of victims by sending mixed messages to the perpetrators and to the police about the seriousness of the batterer's actions.[27]

The less severe legal sanctions include treatment programs available to domestic violence offenders that are not available to offenders in stranger crimes. The current trend in the legal processing of domestic violence offenders emphasizes mental health treatment in lieu of punishment.[28] This treatment policy toward do-

---

16 Cumb. L. Rev. 229 (1986) (pointing out that recognizing interspousal tort immunities continues to bar recovery for victims of domestic violence); Andree G. Gagnon, Ending Mandatory Divorce Mediation for Battered Women, 15 Harv. Women's L. J. 272 (1992) (examining mediation practices and why they are inappropriate in divorce cases where there is a history of domestic violence); Elizabeth Topliffe, Why Civil Protection Orders Are Effective Remedies for Domestic Violence but Mutual Protection Orders Are Not, 67 Ind. L. J. 1039 (Fall 1992) (exploring use of mutual protection orders against both the batterer and victim and discussing why mutual protective orders harm women who are victims of domestic violence).

The legal system is not alone in ignoring domestic violence. There is evidence that physicians treating physical injuries sustained by domestic violence victims are not interested in addressing the cause of the injuries because they compartmentalize their role as healer. In addition, there is evidence that physicians and nurses are disdainful of battered women, blaming them for their victimization. Because medical professionals are frequently the only or the first professionals to come in contact with battered women, these findings suggest that changes in medical practices are warranted. See Mildred Daley Pagelow, Adult Victims of Domestic Violence: Battered Women, 7 J. Interpersonal Violence 87, 89–92 (1992) (indicating that as many as 25% of women using emergency rooms are battered and that medical professionals frequently are insensitive to these women); Teri Randall, Domestic Violence Begets Other Problems of Which Physicians Must Be Aware to Be Effective, 264 JAMA 940 (1990) (indicating that many physicians rationalize their lack of interest by insisting that they are not social workers).

24. Hart, supra note 10, at 23; Molly Chaudhuri & Kathleen Daly, Do Restraining Orders Help?, in Changing Responses, supra note 1, at 227, 230 (pointing out the historical requirement that battered women had to initiate divorce proceedings prior to requesting a restraining order).

25. Adele Harrell et al., The Urban Inst., Court Processing and the Effects of Restraining Orders for Domestic Violence Victims 74 (1993) (establishing empirically that the majority of offenders in two Colorado cities violated restraining orders, and that police were unlikely to arrest offenders for violations when called by the victims).

26. E.g., Browne, supra note 10; Hart, supra note 10.

27. Peter Finn & Sarah Colson, U.S. Dep't of Justice, Civil Protection Orders: Legislation, Current Court Practice, and Enforcement (1990); Herrell & Hofford, supra note 14.

28. E.g., Adelle Harrell, The Urban Inst., Evaluation of Court-ordered Treatment for Domestic Violence Offenders 1 (1991) (noting that batterer treatment programs exist in all states as a sentencing alternative); Ellen Pence & Michael Paymar, Education Groups for

mestic violence offenders contrasts sharply with the denial of rehabilitation programs to general criminal offenders on the basis of skepticism about the effectiveness of offender treatment.[29] Hundreds of domestic violence offender treatment programs later, outcome evaluations have yielded mixed and unpromising results.[30] In contrast, application of criminal sanctions in domestic violence cases has a consistent small effect on the likelihood of reducing repeat violence under certain circumstances.[31] For example, men who batter are best deterred from fur-

---

Men Who Batter: The Duluth Model (1993) (describing one of the oldest treatment programs for batterers that focuses on confronting the men's cognitive patterns and sexist attitudes); Nanci Burns & Colin Meredith, Evaluation of the Effectiveness of Group Treatment For Men Who Batter, in Evaluating Justice 241, 242, 260, 262 (Joe Hudson & Julian Roberts eds., 1993) (indicating that as a form of diversion from treatment, the number of treatment groups for men who batter has grown into the hundreds, despite their questionable effectiveness. They also note that despite discouraging outcome results, victims consistently report feeling safer with their partner in treatment, and in many cases, choose to remain in the relationship because of the treatment.)

29. Generally, there is a discrepancy in the literature about the effectiveness of offender treatment programs. Although earlier research casts doubt on the success of such programs, more recent studies indicate that treatment programs can be successful when they are theoretically sound and they are applied under the right conditions. See, e.g., Peter Greenwood, Rand Corp., The Role of Planned Interventions in Studying the Desistance of Criminal Behavior in a Longitudinal Study 3–4 (1988) (noting the existence of strong and positive effects for some new forms of programming that appear to combine many of the most promising approaches of the past two decades); Ted Palmer, The Re-Emergence of Correctional Intervention (1992) (indicating that research in the last three decades shows that many programs work); D. A. Andrews et al., Does Correctional Treatment Work? A Clinically Relevant and Psychologically Informed Meta-Analysis, 28 Criminology 369 (1990) (finding that correctional services can be effective under the right conditions); Rhena L. Izzo & Robert R. Ross, Meta-Analysis of Rehabilitation Programs for Juvenile Delinquents: A Brief Report, 17 Crim. Just. & Behav. 134, 141 (1990) (indicating that the effectiveness of rehabilitation program may depend as much on how it is applied as on the theoretical soundness of the approach used); Steven P. Lab & John T. Whitehead, From "Nothing Works" to "the Appropriate" Works: The Latest Stop on the Search for the Secular Grail, 28 Criminology 405 (1990) (noting that most of the evidence on correctional programs does not suggest widespread success, although some interventions are found to be effective).

30. E.g., Harrell, supra note 25, at 65; Hart, supra note 10, at 57; Burns & Meredith, supra note 28, at 262; Donald G. Dutton, The Outcome of Court-Mandated Treatment for Wife Assault: A Quasi-Experimental Evaluation, 1 Violence & Victims 163 (1986); Jeffrey L. Edleson & Roger J. Grusznski, Treating Men Who Batter: Four Years of Outcome Data, 12 J. Soc. Serv. Res. 3 (1988); L. Kevin Hamberger & James E. Hastings, Recidivism Following Spouse Abuse Abatement Counseling, 5 Violence & Victims 157, 163–166 (1990) (finding recidivists were more personality disordered and reported higher levels of substance abuse both before and after treatment); Daniel G. Saunders & Sandra T. Azar, Treatment Programs for Family Violence, in Family Violence, supra note 1, at 481, 520.

31. E.g., Jeffrey L. Edleson & M. Syers, Domestic Abuse Project, The Relative Long-term Effects of Group Treatments for Men Who Batter 23 (1990) (indicating that "over a long period of time the possibility of new court involvement becomes the strongest deterrent to further violence"); Harrell, supra note 25, at 24; Jeffrey Edleson & M. Myers, The Relative Effectiveness of Group Treatments for Men Who Batter, 26 Soc. Work Res. & Abstracts 10 (1990); Peter G. Jaffe et al., The Impact of Police Laying Charges in Cases of Wife Assault, 1 J. Fam. Violence 37; R. M. Tolman & L. W. Bennett, A Review of Quantitative Research on

ther violence if they believe that the penalties for recidivism are both certain and severe.[32]

Men Who Batter, 5 J. Interpersonal Violence 87 (1990); See also Richard A. Berk & Phyllis J. Newton, Does Arrest Really Deter Wife Battery? An Effort to Replicate the Findings of the Minneapolis Spouse Abuse Experiment, 50 Am. Soc. Rev. 253 (1985) (finding that arrests substantially decrease the number of new incidents of spouse abuse); Lawrence W. Sherman & Richard A. Berk, The Specific Deterrent Effects of Arrest For Domestic Assault, 49 Am. Soc. Rev. 261, 265–268 (1984) (concluding that arrest was more effective in reducing subsequent violence in misdemeanor wife assault cases than other police responses). But see contradictory results from replications of Sherman & Berk's study, Franklyn W. Dunford et al., The Omaha Domestic Violence Police Experiments. Final Report (1989) (failing to detect a deterrent impact for a warrantless arrest; however, finding that when a suspect fled the scene before the police arrived, but was arrested later under a police-initiated warrant, he was significantly less likely to batter the same victim within a 1-year follow-up period); Franklyn W. Dunford et al., The Role of Arrest in Domestic Assault: The Omaha Police Experiment, 28 Criminology 183 (1990); J. David Hirschel & I. W. Hutchinson, III, Female Spouse Abuse and the Police Response, 83 J. Crim. L. & Criminology 73 (1992); J. David Hirschel et al., Charlotte Spouse Assault Replication Project: Final Report, Nat'l Inst. Just. (1991); J. David Hirschel et al., The Failure of Arrest to Deter Spouse Abuse, 29 J. Res. Crime & Delinq. 7 (1992).

In both the Omaha and Charlotte replications, arrest was not found to significantly reduce recidivism; moreover, the incidence of recidivism in Charlotte was highest for the arrest group. It is interesting that the researchers who have studied the specific deterrent effects of arrest on domestic violence offenders have become almost fixated on this legal remedy without seeming to realize that, as an intervention alone without other criminal justice follow-up such as prosecution, conviction, and sentencing, it is not a very strong intervention. This appears to be the only type of violent crime that is supposedly deterred by mere arrest and possible incarceration for a few hours.

This line of research on the deterrent effects of arrest on domestic violence offenders has extended to examining how informal sanctions may mediate the effects of arrest. For example, arrest has been found to deter future violence among employed offenders, whereas it has been found to increase the likelihood of future violence among unemployed offenders. Although prior violence with the same victim was included as an independent variable, other variables that might be more explanatory (such as overall past criminal record) were not. These studies also fail to measure future violence with different victims. Unfortunately, such results tend to be used to rationalize the differential legal treatment of offenders in lieu of having a uniform mandatory arrest policy. See Richard A. Berk et al., The Deterrent Effect of Arrest in Incidents of Domestic Violence: A Bayesian Analysis of Four Field Experiments, 57 Am. Soc. Rev. 698, 706 (1992); Anthony M. Pate & Edwin E. Hamilton, Formal and Informal Deterrents to Domestic Violence: The Dade County Spouse Assault Experiment, 57 Am. Soc. Rev. 691, 695 (1992).

32. Harrell et al., supra note 25, at 36 (finding that the majority of batterers predicted serious legal consequences if they violated the restraining order); Diane C. Carmody & Kirk R. Williams, Wife Assault and Perceptions of Sanctions, 2 Violence & Victims (1987) (finding that assaultive men perceived arrest as more certain and social condemnation as more likely and more severe than nonassaultive men; repeat offenders were less likely to perceive arrest as a severe sanction than one-time offenders); Michael Steinman, Coordinated Criminal Justice Interventions and Recidivism Among Batterers, in Woman Battering, supra note 3, at 221 (arguing that coordinating arrest with other criminal justice sanctions decreased the probability of recidivism).

Due to the intersection of therapeutic and legal concerns in domestic violence cases,[33] this article uses the framework of therapeutic jurisprudence to address ways in which the legal system advances or impedes therapeutic goals.[34] The schema of therapeutic jurisprudence suggests that the law can act as a therapeutic agent,[35] whereby legal rules, legal procedures, and the roles of legal actors (such as police, lawyers, and judges) can constitute social forces that often produce therapeutic or antitherapeutic results.[36] "Therapeutic ju-

---

33. See, e.g., Mildred Daley Pagelow, Family Violence (1984); Browne, supra note 8; Browne & Fagan, supra note 1, at 211; Gerald T. Hotaling & David B. Sugarman, An Analysis of Risk Markers in Husband to Wife Violence: The Current State of the Knowledge, 1 Violence & Victims 101, 106, 111 (1986) (finding that witnessing parental violence is a risk marker for involvement in a violent relationship as an adult among both women and men); Alan J. Tomkins et al., The Plight of Children Who Witness Woman Battering: Psychological Knowledge and Policy Implications, 18 L. & Psychol. Rev. 137, 139 (noting the lack of attention devoted to children who witness domestic violence); Bonnie E. Carlson, Children's Observations of Interparental Violence, in Battered Women and Their Families: Intervention Strategies and Treatment Programs 147, 159–160 (Albert R. Roberts ed., 1984) (estimating that about 3 million children witness their mothers being physically or sexually assaulted each year).

Although the children of violent couples are obviously victims, the literature on domestic violence neglects this area. For purposes of this article, the term victim will be limited to the battered woman. Future research is needed, however, to address antitherapeutic and therapeutic effects of legal action or inaction on the children of assaultive couples.

34. Michael L. Perlin, What is Therapeutic Jurisprudence?, 10 N.Y.L. Sch. J. Hum. Rts. 623 (1993).

35. Therapeutic Jurisprudence: The Law as a Therapeutic Agent (David B. Wexler ed., 1990); Essays in Therapeutic Jurisprudence (David B. Wexler & Bruce J. Winick eds., 1991); David B. Wexler, New Directions in Therapeutic Jurisprudence: Breaking the Bounds of Conventional Mental Health Law Scholarship, 10 N.Y.L. Sch. J. Hum. Rts. 759 (1993).

36. See David B. Wexler, Health Care Compliance Principles and the Insanity Acquittee Conditional Release Process, 27 Crim. L. Bull. 18, 40 (1991) (applying psychological principles of achieving patient compliance with treatment regimens to insanity acquittee conditional release hearings); David B. Wexler, Therapeutic Jurisprudence and the Criminal Courts, 35 Wm. & Mary L. Rev. 279, 295–298 (1993) (applying psychological principles of achieving patient compliance with treatment regimens to increase a probationer's compliance with the conditions of his supervised release).

In addition to achieving therapeutic outcomes, judges may be called on to engage in other therapeutic roles or activities. For example, judges are relying on their own social judgments about competency rather than medical or psychological opinions. On the basis of these judicial assessments of competency, judges make legal decisions that could be construed as treatments (using the term broadly). See Edward Felsenthal, Judges Find Themselves Acting as Doctors in Alzheimer's Cases, Wall St. J., May 21, 1994, at B1 (noting that judges are increasingly being asked to evaluate the evidence of individual competency). This article reinforces David Wexler's observation that judges are doing social work or therapy whether they realize it or not.

The legal provision of certain defenses for charged defendants may also facilitate avoidance of responsibility, producing antitherapeutic effects. See Margot Slade, At the Bar: In a Number of Cases Defendants Are Portraying Themselves as Victims, N.Y. Times, May 20, 1994, at B20 (describing examples of current cases, including a domestic violence killing committed by the batterer, where defendants use defenses that depict them as victims, result-

risprudence proposes that we be sensitive to such consequences, rather than ignore them, and that we ask whether the law's antitherapeutic consequences
can be reduced, and its therapeutic consequences enhanced, without subordinating due process and justice values."[37] Consequently, therapeutic jurisprudence attempts "to identify—and ultimately examine empirically—relationships between legal arrangements and therapeutic outcomes."[38] The
therapeutic jurisprudence schema does not advocate that therapeutic concerns
supplant other factors, but only that legal decisionmaking can and should benefit from the insights of the mental health and related disciplines.[39] Within the
limits set by principles of justice, therapeutic jurisprudence suggests that the
law should be designed to serve more effectively as a therapeutic agent.[40] The

ing in reduction of charges or hung juries).

37. Wexler, 1993, supra note 35, at 762.

38. See David B. Wexler, Putting Mental Health into Mental Health Law: Therapeutic Jurisprudence, 16 L. & Hum. Behav. 27, 32 (1992).

39. Wexler, 1993, supra note 35, at 763; See also David B. Wexler & Bruce J. Winick,
Therapeutic Jurisprudence as a New Approach to Mental Health Law Policy Analysis and
Research, 45 U. Miami L. Rev. 979 (1991) (describing how the therapeutic "lens" can gen-
erate a new set of research inquiries).

40. See, e.g., Jeffrey A. Klotz et al., Cognitive Restructuring Through Law: A Therapeutic
Jurisprudence Approach to Sex Offenders and the Plea Process, 15 Univ. Puget Sound L. Rev.
579 (1992) (suggesting that certain aspects of the plea process, such as a guilty plea or no
contest plea, can operate antitherapeutically to reinforce sex offenders' cognitive distortions
or be used therapeutically by promoting cognitive restructuring of such dysfunctional thinking processes); Daniel W. Shuman et al., The Health Effects of Jury Service, 18 L. & Psychol.
Rev. 267 (1994) (finding that jurors serving on traumatic trials can develop serious mental
health problems such as depression). Shuman et al. recommend ways in which the judicial
system can protect jurors from the negative health effects of service on traumatic trials. See
also Bruce J. Winick, Harnessing the Power of the Bet: Wagering with the Government as a
Mechanism for Social and Individual Change, 45 U. Miami L. Rev., 737 (1991) (applying
the behavioral, social, and cognitive therapy literature to negotiate difficult social problems
such as drug addiction). Winick suggests that government can wager with individuals by entering into a form of contingency contract in which the agreement provides for a positive reinforcer on completion of the goal, but requires application of an aversive consequence or
penalty should the goal not be reached. With the social problem of drug addition, Winick
suggests that a government wager with an addict can be used to restructure the behavioral
contingencies of drug use, providing social rewards for entering and successfully completing
treatment and social punishment negotiated in advance for failure to meet program goals.

A current example of therapeutic jurisprudence at work in felony drug cases is the Miami
Drug Court in effect since 1989. It has transformed the traditional punitive criminal justice
approach to drug offenses into a schema that emphasizes a court-based approach to the
treatment of felony drug defendants. The outpatient drug treatment counselors, the judge,
the prosecutor, and the defense attorney provide a mental-health team approach to the treatment of less serious drug offenders, who, if successful, are diverted from the criminal justice
system. See John S. Goldkamp & Doris Weiland, U.S. Dep't of Justice, Assessing the Impact
of Dade County's Felony Drug Court 10 (1993); John S. Goldkamp & Doris Weiland, Crime
& Justice Research Inst., Assessing the Impact of Dade County's Felony Drug Court: Executive Summary 41–42 (1993) (indicating that the Miami Drug Court shows promising outcome results in terms of recidivism compared to drug and nondrug offenders not processed
through the program); John S. Goldkamp & Doris Weiland, Crime & Justice Research Institute, Assessing the Impact of Dade County's Felony Drug Court: Final Report (1993) (sug-

emphasis incorporating research from varied disciplines facilitates a new perspective on an old problem.[41]

Using the therapeutic jurisprudence perspective, I examine the psychology of offenders who commit domestic violence crimes in Part I. In Part II, I explore the psychology of domestic violence victims. The impact of the arrest and prosecution stages of the criminal justice system is discussed in Part III. In Part IV, I explore trials, plea bargains, and sentencing issues, and in Part V, I examine the use of restraining orders. The discussion of these issues and the therapeutic jurisprudence perspective presented in this article can inform law reform efforts, criminal justice policy, and mental health policy.

I. Psychology of Domestic Violence Offenders

A. Characteristics of Domestic Violence Offenders

Little is known about the psychological characteristics of batterers or about men who kill current or ex-wives or girlfriends.[42] Most of the knowledge we have is based on interviews with female victims.[43] A comprehensive review published by the National Academy of Sciences[44] indicates that "the few studies of violent men have been limited to small samples of repeatedly assaultive participants in treatment programs,[45] voluntary or self-selected samples,[46] or assailants identified by the criminal justice system who also frequently are violent."[47]

---

gesting that the new therapeutic role of the drug court necessitates a more interactive working relationship between the court and the treatment agencies); John S. Goldkamp & Doris Weiland, Crime & Justice Research Inst., Justice & Treatment Innovation: The Drug Court Movement 27–28 (1993) (suggesting that the role of the prosecutor necessarily becomes transformed as he or she is asked to play a therapeutic role); John S. Goldkamp, Miami's Treatment Drug Court for Felony Defendants: Some Implications of Assessment Findings, 74 Prison J. 110, 113–17 (1994).

41. See e.g., Pleck, supra note 1; Buzawa & Buzawa, supra note 1; Elliott, supra note 1; Gordon, supra note 1.

42. Fagan & Browne, supra note 1, at 185.

43. Fagan & Browne, supra note 1, at 185; Frieze & Browne, supra note 22.

44. Fagan & Browne, supra note 1, at 185.

45. Daniel J. Sonkin, Domestic Violence on Trial: Psychological and Legal Dimensions of Family Violence (1987); Ronald D. Maiuro et al., Assertiveness Deficits and Hostility in Domestically Violent Men, 1 Violence & Victims 279 (1986), cited in Fagan & Browne, supra note 1, at 185.

46. Alan Rosenbaum & K. Daniel O'Leary, Marital Violence: Characteristics of Abusive Couples, 49 J. Consult. & Clin. Psychol. 63 (1981), cited in Fagan & Browne, supra note 1, at 185; Nancy Shields et al., Patterns of Family and Non-Family Violence: Violent Husbands and Violent Men, 3 Violence & Victims 83 (1988), cited in Fagan & Browne, supra note 1, at 185.

47. Donald G. Dutton & Catherine Strachan, Motivational Needs For Power and Spouse Specific Assertiveness in Assaultive and Non-Assaultive Men, 2 Violence & Victims 145 (1987), cited in Fagan & Browne, supra note 1, at 185; Jeffrey L. Edelson & Mary Pat Brygger, Gender Differences in Reporting of Battering Incidences, 35 Fam. Rel. 377 (1986), cited in Fagan & Browne, supra note 1, at 185; Kevin L. Hamberger & James E. Hastings, Char-

Characteristics of domestic violence offenders that can be gleaned from the various studies indicate that men tend to neutralize[48] their violent behavior by rationalization or externalization of blame.[49] They are likely to underreport their violence,[50] minimize its harm and severity,[51] and even deny their behavior.[52] They tend to attribute more involvement to the victim than is justified by either witness or police reports[53] or blame their violent behavior on alcohol.[54] While blaming the vic-

---

acteristics of Male Spouse Abusers Consistent with Personality Disorders, 39 Hosp. & Community Psychiatry 763 (1988), cited in Fagan & Browne, supra note 1, at 185.

48. Albert Bandura, The Social Learning Perspective: Mechanisms of Aggression, in Psychology of Crime and Criminal Justices (Hans Toch ed., 1979) (theorizing that aggressive individuals minimize and rationalize through a process of neutralization of punishment, whereby ordinary self-punishment processes are suspended or diminished); Gresham M. Sykes & David Matza, Techniques of Neutralization: A Theory of Delinquency, 22 Am. Soc. Rev. 667 (1957) (asserting that denial of responsibility is one of several techniques of neutralization that individuals generally use to justify criminal behavior); Donald G. Dutton, Wife Assaulter's Explanations for Assault: The Neutralization of Self-Punishment, 18 Canad. J. Behav. Sci. 380, 385 (1986) (finding that court-mandated subjects were less likely to take responsibility for their violence than were men who were self-referred subjects).

49. Fagan & Browne, supra note 1, at 217; James Ptacek, Why Do Men Batter Their Wives?, in Feminist Perspectives on Wife Abuse, supra note 12, at 155 (suggesting that batterer rationalizations and excuses are reinforced by legal responses to battering).

50. James Browning & Donald Dutton, Assessment of Wife Assault With the Conflict Tactics Scale: Using Couple Data to Quantify the Differential Reporting Effect, 48 J. Marriage & Fam. 375 (1986); Edleson & Brygger, supra note 47; E. N. Jouriles & K. D. O'Leary, Interpersonal Reliability of Reports of Marital Violence, 53 J. Consult. & Clin. Psychol. 419 (1985); Maximiliane E. Szinovacz, Using Couple Data as a Methodological Tool: The Case of Marital Violence, 45 J. Marriage & Fam. 633 (1983).

51. Those offenders who attribute their behavior to their wives are more likely to minimize the severity of their actions.

52. K. Daniel O'Leary & Ileana Arias, Assessing Agreement of Reports of Spouse Abuse, in Family Abuse and its Consequences: New Directions for Research 218 (Gerald T. Hotaling et al. eds., 1988); Szinovacz, supra note 50.

53. Daniel J. Sonkin & M. Durphy, Learning to Live Without Violence: A Handbook for Men (1985).

54. Dawson & Langan, supra note 2, at 3–4 (indicating that 54% of defendants and 50% of victims consumed alcoholic drinks prior to the homicide); Morton Bard & Joseph Zacker, Assaultiveness and Alcohol Use in Family Disputes, 12 Criminology 281, 291 (1974) (finding that family disputes are not usually influenced by alcohol use); Daniel J. Sonkin et al., The Male Batterer: A Treatment Approach (1985); James J. Collins, Jr., Suggested Explanatory Frameworks to Clarify the Alcohol Use/Violence Relationship, 15 Contemp. Drug Probs. 107 (1988) (describing how relaxed standards of accountability under the influence of certain substances are sometimes used to explain the occurrence of certain behaviors during intoxication); Diane Hoshall Coleman & Murray A. Straus, Alcohol Abuse and Family Violence, in Alcohol, Drug Abuse and Aggression, supra at 104; Donald G. Dutton, An Ecologically Nested Theory of Male Violence Toward Intimates, 8 Int'l J. Women's Stud. 404 (1985); Fagan and Browne, supra note 1, at 217; Glenda Kaufman Kantor & Murray A. Straus, The "Drunken Bum" Theory of Wife Beating, 34 Soc. Probs. 213, 225 (1987); Joan McCord, Considerations of Causes in Alcohol-Related Violence, in Res. Monograph No. 24. Alcohol and Interpersonal Violence: Fostering Multidisciplinary Perspectives 71, 72–73, 76 (S. Martin ed., 1993) (exploring the complicated role that alcohol may play in violent behavior); Nancy Shields & Christine R. Hanneke, Battered Wives' Reactions to Marital Rape,

tim, offenders also tend to perceive themselves as the victim.[55] As a result of these characteristics, batterers are not likely to seek treatment voluntarily.[56]

An examination of reported personality characteristics of batterers suggests that they have many psychological problems. These include histories of mental illness,[57] histories of childhood exposure to violence,[58] attachment

in The Dark Side of Families, supra note 10 at 131; Gisela Speiker, What is the Linkage Between Alcohol Abuse and Violence, in Alcohol, Drug Abuse and Aggression 125 (Ed Gotteil et al. eds., 1983) (finding that both offenders and victims blamed alcohol for the violence).

55. E.g., James E. Hastings & L. Kevin Hamberger, Personality Characteristics of Spouse Abusers: A Controlled Comparison, 3 Violence & Victims 31, 44 (1988) (finding that the domestic violence offender is so self-absorbed that true empathy and reciprocity in relationships in impossible); Amy Holtzworth-Munroe & Glenn Hutchinson, Attributing Negative Intent to Wife Behavior: The Attributions of Maritally Violent Versus Nonviolent Men, 102 J. Abnormal Psychol. 206, 209 (1993) (finding that violent husbands are more likely than nondistressed husbands to attribute negative intentions, selfish motivation, and blame to the wife).

56. L. Kevin Hamberger & James E. Hastings, Characteristics of Spouse Abusers: Predictors of Treatment Acceptance, 1 J. Interpersonal Violence 363, 370 (1986) (suggesting that court orders are essential to motivate offenders to pursue treatment).

57. Dawson & Langan, supra note 2, at 3 (indicating that 12% of defendants who kill a spouse have a history of mental illness); Hamberger & Hastings, supra note 47, at 765, 769 (deducing that the generalized antisocial acting out of male spouse abusers is consistent with personality disorder in general and antisocial personality disorder in particular). The implication of the Hamberger and Hastings research is that the majority of domestic violence offenders may be highly treatment-resistant and may not benefit much from the typical short-term offender treatment programs now in vogue. However, there may be some offenders who need and could benefit from pharmacological or other therapeutic services. It is likely, however, that even these mentally ill offenders also suffer from personality disorders, complicating the treatment picture. Future research is needed to assess the prevalence of treatable mental disorders among domestic violence offenders. For example, some of the reported moody and erratic behavior exhibited by domestic violence offenders is consistent with components of a bipolar disorder. See Am. Psychiatric Ass'n, Diagnostic and Statistical Manual of Mental Disorders, Fourth Edition (DSM-IV) 359 (296.89) (1994). Bipolar II Disorder (recurrent major depressive episodes with hypomanic episodes) is characterized as a major mood disorder that includes the occurrence of one or more major depressive episodes accompanied by at least one hypomanic episode. The symptoms cause clinically significant distress or impairment in social, occupational, or other important areas of functioning.

58. Browne, supra note 10; Richard J. Gelles, The Violent Home: A Study of Physical Agression Between Husbands and Wives (1974); Pagelow, supra note 33; P. Lynn Caesar, Exposure to Violence in Families of Origin Among Wife Abusers and Maritally Nonviolent Men, 3 Violence & Victims 49 (1988); Jeffrey A. Fagan et al., Violent Men or Violent Husbands? Background Factors and Situational Correlates, in The Dark Side of Families, supra note 10 at 49; Hotaling & Sugarman, supra note 33, at 111–114; Peter Neidig et al., Attitudinal Characteristics of Males Who Have Engaged in Spouse Abuse, 1 J. Fam. Violence 223 (1986); Rosenbaum & O'Leary, supra note 46; Straus, supra note 10.

Note that most of the studies measure exposure to violence in families of origin retrospectively. A series of ongoing prospective studies on the effects of physical child abuse on development of aggressive behavior and other forms of psychopathology has interesting implications for the development of violent relationships as adults. See Kenneth A. Dodge et al., Mechanisms in the Cycle of Violence, 250 Science 1678, 1681 (1990) (finding that children physically abused prior to entering kindergarten become significantly more aggressive in school than nonabused children). This study also found that physically abused children

deficits,[59] extreme fluctuations in mood,[60] suicidal ideation,[61] alcohol abuse,[62] low self-esteem,[63] chronic hostility or anger,[64] extreme jealousy,[65] need for control,[66] unassertiveness,[67] physical abuse toward children,[68] cognitive distortions of social cues,[69] distortions in information processing and social skills deficits,[70]

---

had more maladaptive social information processing skills than nonabused children: Physically abused children became less attentive to relevant social cues, more biased toward attributing hostile intent, and less likely to generate competent solutions to interpersonal problems. See also Kenneth A. Dodge, Effects of Physical Maltreatment on the Development of Peer Relations, 6 Dev. & Psychopathology 43, 49–52, 52–53 (1994) (following this same sample of children for 5 years, finding that physically abused children are more likely to be disliked, less popular, and more socially withdrawn than nonabused children for every year of the evaluation, with the magnitude of the differences growing over time). The authors suggest that abused children develop problematic interpersonal relationships and acquire violent strategies for solving interpersonal problems.

59. Steven Stosny, Love Without Hurt: Ending Attachment Abuse (unpublished manuscript).

60. Jennifer Baker Fleming, Stopping Wife Abuse, 1979; Walker, supra note 16.

61. Browne, supra note 10.

62. Dawson & Langan, supra note 2, at 3; Lenore E. Walker, The Battered Woman Syndrome (1984); Coleman & Straus, supra note 54; Fagan et al., supra note 58; Edward W. Gondolf, Who Are Those Guys? Toward a Behavioral Typology of Batterers, 3 Violence & Victims 187 (1988); Hotaling & Sugarman, supra note 33, at 111; Kantor & Straus, supra note 54; Glenda K. Kantor & Murray A. Straus, Substance Abuse as a Precipitant of Wife Abuse Victimizations, 15 Am. J. Drug & Alcohol Abuse 173 (1989); Brenda A. Miller et al., Spousal Violence Among Alcoholic Women as Compared to a Random Household Sample of Women, 50 J. on Stud. on Alcoholism 533 (1988); Pleck, supra, note 1; Shields et al., supra note 46.

63. Lewis Okun, Woman Abuse: Facts Replacing Myths 70 (1986) (indicating that jealousy, projection of blame for the violence, and low self-esteem are all closely interrelated); Pagelow, supra note 33; Neidig, supra note 58.

64. Albert Bandura, Aggression: A Social Learning Analysis (1973); Maiuro et al., supra note 45; Raymond Novaco, The Functions and Regulation of the Arousal of Anger, 133 Am. J. Psychiatry 1124 (1976).

65. L. Bowker, Beating Wife-beating (1983); Terry Davidson, Conjugal Crime (1978); Okun, supra note 63, at 68–71; B. J. Rounsaville, Theories in Marital Violence: Evidence From A Study of Battered Women, 3 Victimology 11.

66. Fleming, supra note 60; Okun, supra note 63, at 69; Browning & Dutton, supra note 50; Dutton & Strachan, supra note 47; Margaret Elbow, Theoretical Considerations of Violent Marriages, 58 Soc. Casework 515, 517, 519 (1977).

67. Rosenbaum & O'Leary, supra note 46; Telch & Lindquist, supra note 10.

68. American Humane Ass'n, U.S. Dep't Health & Hum. Serv., National Analysis of Official Child Abuse and Neglect Reporting (1980); Browne, supra note 10; Walker, supra note 14; Hotaling & Straus, supra note 8; Straus, supra note 8; Telch & Lindquist, supra note 10.

69. Bandura, supra note 64; Novaco, supra note 64.

70. Amy Holtzworth-Munroe, Social Skill Deficits in Maritally Violent Men: Interpreting the Data Using a Social Information Processing Model, 12 Clin. Psychol. Rev. 605 (1992) (suggesting that the differing cognitive processing styles of violent men result in social skill deficits); Amy Holtzworth-Munroe & Kimberly Anglin, The Competency of Responses Given by Maritally Violent Versus Nonviolent Men to Problematic Marital Situations, 6 Violence & Victims 259 (1991) (finding that violent men have more difficulty generating competent responses than nonviolent men).

strong sex role stereotypes,[71] and lack of verbal skills.[72] Typologies of offenders that have been developed[73] have been discrepant in their findings, however.[74]

B. Do Domestic Violence Offenders Specialize?

No discussion of the characteristics of domestic violence offenders is complete without addressing whether they victimize only intimate partners or are instead generalists in assaultive behavior and other crime. Most criminological research suggests that general criminal offenders do not specialize in violence.[75] However, the legal and academic treatment of domestic violence as separate from general criminal violence has implied that it is a specialty.[76] The notion of specialization is so entrenched that current research and practice singles out family violence[77] in general and spouse abuse[78] in particular as special and distinct types of violence that are not to be viewed as a subset of violent behavior.[79]

Yet, after years of treating domestic violence as a specialty, researchers are beginning to find that a sizable proportion of domestic violence offenders are also violent outside the home.[80] There is little evidence that the majority of do-

---

71. Gondolf, supra note 62.

72. Browning & Dutton, supra note 50; Dutton & Strachan, supra note 47; Maiuro et al., supra note 45; Novaco, supra note 64; Rosenbaum & O'Leary, supra note 46.

73. Donald G. Dutton, Profiling of Wife Assaulters: Preliminary Evidence for a Trimodal Analysis, 3 Violence & Victims 5 (1988).

74. Caesar, supra note 58; Elbow, supra note 66; Fagan et al., supra note 58; Gondolf, supra note 62; Hamberger & Hastings, supra note 56, at 370; L. Kevin Hamberger & James E. Hastings, Personality Correlates of Men Who Abuse Their Partners: A Cross-Validational Study, 1 J. Fam. Violence 323, 329–331 (1986) (finding that spouse abusers possess personality disorder profiles consistent with borderline, antisocial, and dependent types); Amy Holtzworth-Munroe & Gregory L. Stuart, Typologies of Male Batterers: Three Subtypes and the Differences Among Them, Psychol. Bull. (forthcoming 1995) (proposing a typology of batterers that consists of family only, dysphoric-borderline, and generally violent-antisocial batterers); Hotaling & Straus, supra note 10; Shields et al., supra note 46.

75. Michael Gottfredson & Travis Hirschi, A General Theory of Crime (1990); Michael Gottfredson & Travis Hirschi, The Generality of Deviance (1994); Donna M. Hamparian et al., The Violent Few (1978); Donald J. West & David P. Farrington, The Delinquent Way of Life: Third Report of the Cambridge Study in Delinquent Development (1977); Marvin E. Wolfgang et al., Delinquency in a Birth Cohort (1972); Alfred Blumstein & Jacqueline Cohen, Estimation of Individual Crime Rates From Arrest Records, 70 J. Crim. L. & Criminology 561 (1979); Dean G. Rojek & Maynard L. Erickson, Delinquent Careers: A Test of the Career Escalation Model, 20 Criminology 5 (1982).

76. E.g., Lawrence W. Sherman, Policing Domestic Violence (1992).

77. K. Daniel O'Leary, Through a Psychological Lens: Personality Traits, Personality Disorders, and Levels of Violence, in Current Controversies on Family Violence 7 (Richard J. Gelles & Donileen R. Loseke eds., 1993).

78. E.g., Normand D. Petrik et al., Powerlessness and the Need to Control: The Male Abuser's Dilemma, 9 J. Interpersonal Violence 278 (1994).

79. Dobash & Dobash, supra note 16; Laurie Wardell et al., Science and Violence Against Wives, in The Dark Side of Families, supra note 10, at 69.

80. Walker, supra note 16, at 135 (finding that 20% of batterers were violent with indi-

mestic violence offenders specialize in assaults toward intimates.[81] Instead, the evidence is consistent with the research on general criminal offenders that indicates that they are generalists and commit a variety of offenses.[82] As a result, domestic violence offenders do not need a separate explanation for their violent acts.[83] Singling out domestic violence offenders for special treatment by the legal system not only perpetuates the myth of specialization, but communicates to offenders and victims that offenses are not as serious when committed against an intimate as they are when committed against a stranger.[84]

C. A Cognitive Therapy Approach

In addressing the legal and therapeutic concerns of domestic violence offenders, the legal system can effect therapeutic changes in offenders by applying some of the principles of cognitive therapy used in psychology.[85] Cognitive

---

viduals other than their wives); Fagan et al., in The Dark Side of Families, supra note 58 (noting that 46% of spouse abusers had been arrested before for other violence. The most violent spouse abusers were also violent toward strangers, whereas those less violent at home were not violent toward strangers.). Fagan et al. also found that the longer the duration and the more severe the abuse at home, the more likely were these men to assault strangers. See also John P. Flynn, Recent Findings Related to Wife Abuse, 58 Soc. Casework 13 (1977) (finding that at least one-third of batterers had previous records of other types of criminal assaults; J. J. Gayford, Wife Battering: A Preliminary Study of 100 Cases, 1 British Medical Journal 194, 196 (1975) (finding that 50% of a sample of wife abusers had spent time in prison, and 33% of those prison terms were for violent offenses against strangers); Shields et al., supra note 46 (examining three types of violent men: those violent only toward spouses, those violent only toward persons outside the family, and the overlapping generally violent men). Shields et al. found that generally violent men and men only violent toward nonfamily members were almost indistinguishable in terms of background characteristics, but wife-only abusers were quite different in terms of socioeconomic status, educational attainment, attitudes, and prior conviction rates. Furthermore, 45% of generally violent men began their adult violence by victimizing only nonfamily members. See generally Shields and Hanneke, supra note 54 (finding that generally violent men were more similar to stranger assailants than those violent only within their families); S. O. White & Murray A. Straus, The Implications of Family Violence for Rehabilitation Strategies, in New Directions in the Rehabilitation of Criminal Offenders, at 26 (Susan E. Martin et al. eds., 1981) (indicating that men who are violent toward their wives are arrested or convicted for a property or violent crime against a stranger at almost twice the rate of nonviolent spouses; severely violent husbands are convicted of a property or violent crime against a stranger at almost four times the rate of nonviolent spouses).

81. E.g., Fagan et al., in The Dark Side of Families, supra note 58; Shields et al., supra note 46.

82. Gottfredson & Hirschi, supra note 75, at 91–94; Leonore Simon, The Victim-Offender Relationship, in The Generality of Deviance, supra note 75 at 215, 231–232.

83. Gottfredson & Hirschi, supra note 75, at 140–41, 165–67, 237–39.

84. Simon, supra note 82, at 231–32.

85. See Klotz et al., supra note 40 (applying principles of cognitive therapy to assess how certain aspects of the plea process can be used by the legal system to confront cognitive distortions of sex offenders).

In applying the schema of cognitive therapy to the legal and therapeutic concerns of domestic violence offenders, one might ask: Why choose cognitive therapy over other modalities such as marital therapy or family therapy? As will become clearer in the subsequent dis-

interventions have been effective in the psychological treatment of a broad range of disorders[86] and provide a useful framework for the legal processing of

cussion of domestic violence victims in Section II, infra, the current research and practice climate assigns no responsibility or pathology to the victim. Therefore, it is reasoned, the victim does not need to change, and marital therapy would just reinforce victim self-blame and offender denial. Furthermore, from a more practical vantage point, it is recognized that marital therapy would subject the victim to the coercive manipulations of the offender, further victimizing her. However, given the high likelihood that victims either will remain with or return to the relationship, perhaps marital therapy should not automatically be ruled out. There is also research on battering couples indicating that both parties to the violence can benefit from marital therapy. See Julia C. Babcock et al., Power and Violence: The Relation Between Communication Patterns, Power Discrepancies, and Domestic Violence, 61 J. of Consult. & Clin. Psychol. 40, 48 (1993) (finding that both parties to a battering relationship are poor communicators, and that husbands feel powerless in the relationship); James V. Cordova et al., Negative Reciprocity and Communication in Couples with a Violent Husband, 102 J. Abnormal Psychol. 559, 563 (1993) (indicating that women in battering relationships contribute actively to the conflict); Amy Holtzworth-Munroe et al., The Assessment and Treatment of Marital Violence: An Introduction for the Marital Therapist, in Clinical Handbook of Marital Therapy, 2nd ed., at 40 (Neil S. Jacobson & Alan S. Gurman eds., 1994) (providing a guide of the various assessment and treatment strategies that can be used with violent couples); Amy Holtzworth-Munroe & Glenn Hutchinson, supra note 55 at 209 (1993) (finding that certain situations involving jealousy, rejection, and public embarrassment from the wife are likely to elicit attributions of negative intent from violent husbands); Holtzworth-Munroe & Stuart, supra note 74 (developing a typology of male batterers and suggesting that some subtypes may be more amenable to treatment than others); Neil S. Jacobson et al., Affect, Verbal Content, and Psychophysiology in the Arguments of Couples With a Violent Husband, 62 J. Consult. & Clin. Psychol. 982–988 (1994) (finding that both wives and husbands in battering relationships evidenced more aggression at home and looked angrier in the laboratory than did nonviolent couples); John R. Lutzker & Vincent B. Van Hasselt, Family Violence, in Handbook of Clinical Behavior Therapy 417, 430–31 (Samuel M. Turner et al., eds., 1992) (suggesting the use of couples therapy where the wife is not in danger of physical harm and the couple expresses the desire to improve their relationship). In cases where marital therapy is deemed appropriate, family therapy involving the children as well as the couple might also be effective, particularly for the children. However, no research has directly explored this area. For this article, cognitive therapy was chosen because it can be used successfully in treating distressed couples as well as individuals. See Holtzworth-Munroe et al., 1994, supra.

86. E.g., Aaron T. Beck, Cognitive Therapy and Emotional Disorders (1976); Aaron T. Beck et al., Cognitive Therapy of Depression (1979); Aaron T. Beck, Love Is Never Enough: How Couples Can Overcome Misunderstandings, Resolve Conflicts, and Solve Relationship Problems Through Cognitive Therapy (1988); Aaron T. Beck et al., Cognitive Therapy of Personality Disorders (1990); Arthur Freeman et al., Clinical Applications of Cognitive Therapy (1990); John C. Masters et al., Behavior Therapy: Techniques and Empirical Findings, 3rd ed. (1987); Allen E. Bergin & Sol L. Garfield Eds., Handbook of Psychotherapy and Behavior Change: An Empirical Analysis 2d ed. (1978); Albert Ellis, Reason and Emotion in Psychotherapy (1994); Donald H. Meichenbaum, Cognitive Behavior Modification (1977); Kim Faulkner et al., Cognitive-Behavioral Group Treatment for Male Spouse Abusers, 7 J. Fam. Violence 37 (1992); John R. Lutzker & Vincent B. Van Hasselt, in Handbook of Clinical Behavior Therapy, supra note 85, at 430–431; M. J. Mahoney, Reflections on the Cognitive Learning Trend in Psychotherapy, 32 Am. Psychol. 5 (1977); M. J. Mahoney, Theoretical Developments in the Cognitive Psychotherapies, 61 J. Consult. & Clin. Psychol. 187 (1993); Albert Ellis, Rational-Emotive Therapy and Cognitive Behavior Ther-

domestic violence offenders. On the basis of the idea that thinking plays a role in the etiology and maintenance of at least some disorders, these treatments seek to improve mental health by changing maladaptive beliefs and providing new information processing skills.[87]

Cognitive learning theorists believe that conscious thoughts play a major role in mediating emotional and instrumental behavior in human beings.[88] In particular, Aaron Beck's cognitive therapy[89] approach asserts that individuals with emotional problems possess dysfunctional automatic thoughts that are exaggerated, distorted, mistaken, or unrealistic.[90] These dysfunctional, automatic thoughts, called cognitive distortions,[91] shape the perception and interpretation of events.[92]

---

apy: Similarities and Differences, 4 Cognitive Therapy & Res. 325 (1980).

Note that the term cognitive therapy encompasses cognitive as well as cognitive-behavioral approaches. See Steven D. Hollon & Aaron T. Beck, Cognitive and Cognitive-Behavioral Therapies, in Handbook of Psychotherapy and Behavior Change, supra at 428, 429 (noting that although cognitive and cognitive-behavioral approaches differ in terms of their developmental histories, each approach has borrowed from the other over the years, blurring the distinctions).

87. Aaron T. Beck & Marjorie Weishaar, Cognitive Therapy, in Comprehensive Handbook of Cognitive Therapy 21 (Arthur Freeman et al. eds., 1989); Hollon & Beck, supra note 86, at 428.

An important issue that arises in this discussion of cognitive therapy is whether the therapeutic modality would be effective with offenders who possess low self-control. There is a broad literature detailing how to treat individuals with low self-control such as substance abusers, obese individuals, smokers, and individuals with problems controlling their anger. Self-control therapy can provide clients who engage in self-defeating or injurious behavior with strategies for dealing with problem situations. The cognitive-behavioral approach advocated in this article is a major component of treating individuals with low self-control. See E.g., Aaron T. Beck et al., Cognitive Therapy of Substance Abuse (1993) (applying the cognitive model to conceptualization, assessment, and treatment of substance abuse); Masters et al., supra note 86, at 444 (providing an excellent review of self-control approaches with different behavioral problems); Timothy J. O'Farrell, Treating Alcohol Problems: Marital and Family Interventions (1993) (using more of a marital and family therapy approach to treating alcoholics).

88. Masters et al., supra note 86, at 386.

89. Beck, 1976, supra note 86; Beck et al., 1979, supra note 86. Most of Beck's research has concentrated on using his cognitive approach to assess and treat depression. The minds of depressed individuals are believed to be filled with negative automatic thoughts that influence their moods. Even when these individuals are not depressed, they engage in certain underlying dysfunctional attitudes that put them at risk for future depression.

90. Freeman et al., 1990, supra note 86, at 4; W. Edward Craighead et al., Unipolar Depression, in Handbook of Clinical Behavior Therapy, 2nd ed. 99, 102 (Samuel M. Turner et al. eds., 1992) (indicating that these cognitions are called automatic thoughts because the individual frequently is not aware of them: "They are believed to reflect the operation of underlying cognitive structures or schemata that influence what we attend to, how we encode it, and what we later remember.").

91. "During psychological distress, the shift to a more primitive information-processing system is apparent in systematic errors in reasoning, called cognitive distortions." See Beck & Weishaar, supra note 87, at 23.

92. Rian E. McMullin, Handbook of Cognitive Therapy Techniques (1986); Beck & Weishaar, supra note 87 at 4 (listing commonly observed cognitive distortions).

Much of the therapy involves assisting the client in ferreting out automatic thinking and the underlying dysfunctional assumptions, and then in retraining the individual to think more logically and realistically and to modify fundamental underlying beliefs.[93] The approach relies heavily on the process of empirical disconfirmation; clients are taught to treat their beliefs as hypotheses that can be tested and to gather information and conduct behavioral experiments to test them.[94] In monitoring and evaluating their dysfunctional thoughts, clients are taught to modify self-defeating thinking by countering their automatic thoughts with adaptive responses, a form of cognitive restructuring.[95]

A therapeutic jurisprudence approach to the legal handling of domestic violence offenders can use the principles of cognitive therapy to confront batterers' faulty thinking and promote more adaptive cognitive processing. The various techniques of neutralization used by domestic violence offenders can be categorized into four types of cognitive distortions about the offense[96]: (a) cognitive distortions that morally justify or euphemistically label the violence; (b) cognitive distortions that disavow responsibility; (c) cognitive distortions that minimize the effects of the violence; and (d) cognitive distortions that dehumanize or blame the victim. By challenging these techniques of neutralization in the articulation and enforcement of its laws and policies, the legal system can achieve therapeutic results for the offender and the victim. For example, the police can confront offender denial by taking domestic violence calls seriously, responding quickly, and making arrests where legally appropriate. Prosecutors can challenge offender neutralization by prosecuting these cases fully and granting diversion only in extraordinary cases. The use of plea bargains by the prosecutor in domestic violence cases may not be advisable, particularly the use of charge bargaining, because the offender is allowed to escape responsibility for the actual crime in question. Prosecutors can also confront offender minimization by recommending sentences commensurate with comparable crimes by strangers. Judges can confront offender denial and minimization by taking these cases seriously and by sentencing these offenders in the same way offenders who are strangers are sentenced. As soon as judges enter any type of court order in a domestic violence case, they can confront offender minimization of violations by

---

93. In dealing with severe depression, the initial focus, perhaps over the first several sessions, is largely behavioral. Beck suggests that depressed people typically see themselves as losers, unable to accomplish anything, and the provision of any success experience can have a mood-elevating effect. Graduated tasks or activities are assigned early in treatment to enhance the individual's sense of self-efficacy, highly credible information that they can cope. See Beck et al., 1979, supra note 86; Craighead et al., supra note 90, at 109 (indicating that automatic thoughts are reflective of maladaptive beliefs such as "I'm no good," "I have to be perfect," or "I have to be liked by everyone": After maladaptive beliefs are identified, clients are instructed to test their validity).

94. Craighead et al., supra note 90, at 109.

95. Masters et al., supra note 86, at 422; McMullin, supra note 92, at xv (noting that the therapist helps clients to engage in cognitive restructuring— to change their irrational beliefs and shift their perceptions from those that are unrealistic and harmful to those that are more rational and useful).

96. Fagan & Browne, supra note 1, at 217–18.

monitoring, identifying, and sanctioning them. Judicial development of a means of monitoring compliance is essential in both civil and criminal orders.

II. Psychology of Domestic Violence Victims

Empirical research on domestic violence consists mostly of research on victims.[97] According to the existing literature, "other than their abuse histories and socioeconomic status, there do not appear to be consistent patterns that differentiate victims from nonvictims."[98] A thorough reading of the literature on victims indicates that victims are well-adjusted individuals whose maladaptive symptoms "are sequalae of marital violence rather than antecedents or concurrent factors."[99]

The few victim characteristics that have been isolated include: witnessing family violence as a child or adolescent, age, and alcohol abuse.[100] There is evidence to suggest that victims are more likely to abuse alcohol than are nonvictims,[101] although researchers argue that the causal relationship between alcohol abuse and victimization is not clear. Younger women are at greater risk for victimization than older women.[102] Experiencing abuse as children and witnessing parental violence increases a woman's probability of being abused by her partner.[103]

Research evidence indicates that battered women have difficulty leaving battering relationships, and various reasons are tendered.[104] Such reasons include learned helplessness,[105] "traumatic bonding,"[106] the intensification

---

97. Fagan & Browne, supra note 1.

98. Id at 198; Hotaling & Sugarman, supra note 33, at 106–111.

99. Fagan & Browne, supra note 1, citing Lenore E. Walker, The Battered Woman Syndrome; G. Margolin, Interpersonal and Intrapersonal Factors Associated With Marital Violence, in Family Abuse and its Consequences: New Directions for Research, supra note 52, at 53.

100. Fagan & Browne, supra note 1, at 201.

101. Kantor & Straus, supra note 54, at 179–183; Miller et al., supra note 15.

102. Fagan & Browne, supra note 1, at 201–2.

103. Murray A. Straus et al., Behind Closed Doors: Violence in the American Family (1980); Debra Kalmuss, The Intergenerational Transmission of Marital Aggression, 46 J. Marriage Fam. 11 (1984); Hotaling & Sugarman, supra note 33, at 106.

104. Fagan & Browne, supra note 1, at 219.

105. Lenore Walker describes three distinct phases of the typical battering relationship. A "tension building phase" erupts into an "acute battering incident," which in turn is followed by "loving contrition." The first phase is marked by verbal arguments and increasing tension between the man and woman. This is followed by the second phase in which the man becomes violent toward the woman. The third phase is characterized by the man's remorse and promises never to beat the woman again. Despite the man's promises in the third phase, the cycle eventually begins anew, resulting in further violence. See Walker, supra note 64 at 86–87, 95–96; Walker, supra note 16 at 55–70; Lenore Walker, Terrifying Love (1989).

To explain why a battered woman does not leave the abusive relationship, Walker invokes an adaptation of Martin Seligman's "learned helplessness" theory. Seligman found that laboratory dogs, after being subjected to repeated shocks over which they had no control, "learned" that they were helpless. After initial attempts to escape proved futile, the dogs stopped trying even when presented with opportunities for escape. See also Martin E. P. Seligman et al., Alleviation of Learned Helplessness in the Dog, 73 J. Abnormal Psychol. 256 (1968).

106. Donald G. Dutton & Susan Lee Painter, Traumatic Bonding: The Development of

of violence and threats after the victim leaves or attempts to separate from the abuser,[107] shock reactions of victims to abuse, and practical problems in separating.[108]

Although treatment programs for batterers are quite common,[109] there appears to be an absence of treatment programs for women outside the supportive services found in women's shelters.[110] The absence of meaningful treatment for victims appears to be a combination of a hesitancy to assign any responsibility or blame to the woman and an insistence that any symptoms the victim may have are the effects rather than precursors of battering.[111] Even accepting the argument that the victim's symptoms result from the battering, it is clinically accepted that battered women have many of the symptoms of posttraumatic stress disorder[112] found in other trauma victims and thus desperately

---

Emotional Attachments in Battered Women and Other Relationships of Intermittent Abuse, 6 Victimology: An Int'l J. 139 (1981); Donald G. Dutton & Susan L. Painter, Emotional Attachments in Abusive Relationships: A Test of Traumatic Bonding Theory, 8 Violence & Victims 105 (1993) (developing a concept of "traumatic bonding" that occurs where powerful emotional attachments are seen to develop from two features of abusive relationships: power imbalance and intermittent good-bad treatment). Dutton and Painter suggest that an expert witness can clarify the role of traumatic bonding in contributing, along with other pressures, to the overall difficulty battered women have in leaving abusive relationships.

107. Browne, supra note 10.

108. Id.

109. Janet A. Geller, Breaking Destructive Patterns: Multiple Strategies for Treating Partner Abuse (1992); Donald G. Dutton et al., Arrest and Reduction of Repeat Wife Assault, in Changing Response, supra note 1, at 111.

110. Mary Ann Dutton, Empowering and Healing the Battered Woman: A Model for Assessment & Intervention (1992) (arguing for a comprehensive assessment and treatment approach to battered women).

111. See e.g., Id. (emphasizing that the victim is not responsible for any aspect of her victimization). But see Ronnie Janoff-Bulman, Characterological Versus Behavioral Self-Blame: Inquiries Into Depression and Rape, 37 J. of Personality & Soc. Psychol. 1798, 1808 (1979) (suggesting a therapeutic role for rape victim self-blame if it helps her reestablish a belief in her relative control over life outcomes and identify ways of minimizing future victimization).

112. Posttraumatic stress disorder (PTSD) is classified as an anxiety disorder in which symptoms are developed "following exposure to an extreme traumatic stressor involving direct personal experience of an event that involves actual or threatened death or serious injury, or other threat to one's physical integrity...." See American Psychiatric Association, Diagnostic and Statistical Manual of Mental Disorders, Fourth Edition 424 (309.81) (DSM-IV) (1994); DSM-IV describes posttraumatic stress disorder as characterized by symptoms of intrusive thoughts or memories; avoidance of stimuli associated with the trauma or the feelings associated with the trauma; and heightened autonomic arousal. Dutton, supra note 110 (indicating that although discussions of interventions with battered women often make reference to some of the psychological effects, typically posttraumatic therapies with battered women have not been widely described); Frank M. Ochberg, Post-Traumatic Therapy and Victims of Violence 8–9 (1988) (suggesting that a victim may suffer from a distinct subcategory of traumatic stress that may or may not reach the threshold for posttraumatic stress disorder). Ochberg lists likely victim symptoms that include feelings of denial, fear, generalized anxiety, hypervigilance, depression, intrusive thoughts, shame, self-blame, denigration, defilement, low self-esteem, helplessness, and addictive behaviors. Jennifer C. Jones & David H. Barlow, The Etiology of Posttraumatic

need meaningful treatment. The lack of mental health treatment also increases the likelihood that if a woman leaves a battering relationship, she will enter another violent relationship.[113]

A reading of the relevant literature suggests that the battered woman is likely to indulge in specific dysfunctional thoughts that perpetuate her relationship to the batterer.[114] These include denial or minimization of the abuse and excusing the batterer's behavior. Her cognitive distortions are likely to involve maladaptive beliefs such as "it is better to have an abusive relationship

---

Stress Disorder, 10 Clin. Psychol. Rev. 299 (1990); See also I. Lisa McCann et al., Trauma and Victimization; A Model of Psychological Adaptation, 16 Counseling Psychol. 531 (1988).

Although not viewing victimization from a PTSD schema, Janoff-Bulman proposes that a victim's response is the result of the shattering of basic assumptions about self and the world. When assumptions of invulnerability, the world as meaningful, and positive self-perception are shattered by the experience of victimization, disorientation and stress result. See Ronnie Janoff-Bulman, Criminal vs. Non-criminal Victimization: Victims' Reactions, 10 Victimology: An Int'l J. 498 (1985); Ronnie Janoff-Bulman, Shattered Assumptions (1992); Ronnie Janoff-Bulman, Assumptive Worlds and the Stress of Traumatic Events: Applications of the Schema Construct, 7 Soc. Cognition 113 (1989).

113. Debra Kalmus & Judith Seltzer, Continuity of Marital Behavior in Remarriage: The Case of Spouse Abuse, 48 J. Marriage & Fam. 113 (1986). A failure to adequately research victim issues is pervasive in the research literature. The evidence on the issue of serial victimization appears to be mostly anecdotal. For example, a recent unsolved murder of a 23-year-old victim in New York raised numerous questions about her background because no one reported her as missing or claimed her body until the police accidentally came across her identity. Once her identity was established, it became evident that she had been repeatedly victimized by intimates and strangers beginning in her childhood. Four days prior to her killing, she walked out of a shelter for battered women. She had gone into the shelter after having been beaten by a boyfriend with a criminal record. Earlier in the year, this victim had gotten a restraining order against another abusive boyfriend with a criminal record. In addition to evidence of multiple victimizations at the hands of intimate partners, this young woman had also been raped while out on the street. Clearly, research is needed that examines in detail the relationship of childhood victimization to adult victimization by intimates and nonintimates. See Joseph B. Treaster, Slain Jogger's Long, Painful Trail: Many Contradictions, but Trouble Was Her Constant, N.Y. Times, October 2, 1994, at 33. See also Joan McCord, Deterrence of Domestic Violence: A Critical Review of Research, 29 J. Res. Crime & Delinq. 229, 232–233, 235 (1992) (criticizing the domestic violence research for narrowly defining recidivism in terms of one victim instead of serial victims). McCord points out that offenders who use violence in one relationship are likely to be violent in others. If a legal or therapeutic intervention results in the break-up of one violent relationship, the violence may be re-enacted by either party in a subsequent relationship. McCord also suggests that the current literature fails to assess the effects of legal interventions on different types of victims. For example, the beliefs of victims regarding the legitimacy of using violence may be related to how victims respond to legal intervention. Victims may also react differently to legal interventions depending on the extent of their experience with the legal system in the past.

114. Dutton, supra note 110, at 97; see also Janoff-Bulman, Victimology, supra note 112, at 502–507 (describing how individuals victimized by someone they know and trust are particularly vulnerable to the shattering of basic assumptions about self and the world).

than no relationship at all,"[115] and related beliefs such as "if I don't remain in this relationship, I'm never going to be in another one," or "any cost is worth paying for a relationship."[116] Additional faulty thinking by battered women leads them to the conclusion that they are helpless in escaping the violence.[117] Many of these dysfunctional thoughts are likely to impair the judgment of the battered woman. For example, it is not uncommon for battered women to ignore or minimize signals of danger, not responding in a manner that would potentially increase their safety.[118]

Cognitive restructuring can be used to challenge many of these dysfunctional thoughts. For example, the self-blame commonly seen in battered women can be confronted by reattributing responsibility for the violence to the batterer.[119] The cognitive distortion of helplessness can be confronted by persuading a victim to accept personal responsibility for her safety and her choices.[120]

Much of this cognitive restructuring can be achieved by altering the response of those representing social institutions that are chief among the external barriers to battered women's seeking safety.[121] Assuring that the legal system will protect the battered woman from violence and will arrest, prosecute, convict, and sentence the batterer will facilitate the woman's reattribution of blame for the violence.[122] This intervention requires that legal actors, including police officers, prosecutors, attorneys in general, judges, and probation officers, be sensitive to the problem and dynamics of domestic violence cases. Criminal justice system actors can be educated about the impact of not prosecuting a domestic violence case. Treating each act of domestic violence as a criminal act against the state rather than merely a family matter is essential in challenging the fear and ambivalence many victims feel in cooperating with the batterer's prosecution.[123]

This sensitivity should extend beyond the criminal justice system to civil proceedings that involve battering couples. For example, the legal system has considerable power in determining the level of protection available to a victim through restraining orders, divorce, custody, and visitation decisions.[124]

---

115. Dutton, supra note 110, at 97.

116. Id. at 98.

117. Id. at 110.

118. Id. at 110. Most researchers in the field, including Dutton, argue that this type of behavior is a consequence of coping with the terror of abuse. However, this contention is not empirically validated, and there is the probability that battered women were blind to the batterer's earlier and more subtle pathological characteristics.

119. Id. at 123.

120. Id.

121. Id. at 126.

122. Barbara Hart, Battered Women and the Criminal Justice System, 36 Am. Behav. Sci. 624, 627, 632, 635 (1993).

123. Dutton, supra note 110, at 127.

124. Id.

III. Arrest and Prosecution of Offenders

Having thus far described the psychology of domestic violence offenders and victims, the remainder of the article addresses the different stages of the legal system and how they can be restructured to provide therapeutic processes and outcomes for both parties. As was pointed out in the introduction, the legal system has a history of failing to respond appropriately to domestic violence cases. In addition to reinforcing offender and victim cognitive distortions about their respective roles in the violence, these legal policies have been physically dangerous for the victims and their children. A stage-by-stage analysis of these problems and potential remedies follows.

Prior theory and research suggests that nonstranger offenses are treated more leniently at all stages of the legal proceedings.[125] The closer the relationship between the victim and the offender, the less likely the police are to make an arrest,[126] the less likely the prosecutor is to bring formal charges,[127] the less likely a conviction or prison sentence will result,[128] the shorter prison sentences are

---

125. Donald Black, The Behavior of Law (1976); Michael Gottfredson & Don M. Gottfredson, Decision Making in Criminal Justice: Toward the Rational Exercise of Discretion 72 (1988).

126. Black, supra note 125; A. J. Reiss, Jr., The Police & the Public (1971); U.S. Comm'n on Civ. Rts., supra note 1; Berk & Loseke, supra note 14; Donald J. Black, The Social Organization of Arrest, 23 Stan. L. Rev. 1087, 1097 (1971); Ford, supra note 1; H. Goldstein, Police Policy Formulation: A Proposal for Improving Police Performance, 65 Mich. L. Rev. 1123, 1138 (1967); Raymond I. Parnas, Police Discretion and Diversion of Incidents of Intra-Family Violence, 36 L. & Contemp. Probs. 539 (1971); Elizabeth Truninger, Marital Violence: The Legal Solutions, 23 Hastings L. J. 259 (1971); Robert E. Worden & Alissa A. Pollitz, Police Arrests in Domestic Disturbances: A Further Look, 18 L. & Soc'y Rev. 105, 113 (1984).

127. B. Boland et al., U.S. Dep't of Justice, The Prosecution of Felony Arrests (1983); K. Brosi, Institute for Law & Society Resolution, A Cross-City Comparison of Felony Case Processing (1979); Marjory D. Fields, U.S. Comm'n on Civil Rights, Wife Beating: Government Intervention Policies & Practices, in Battered Women: Issues of Public Policy (1978); Peter W. Greenwood et al., U.S. Dep't of Justice, Prosecution of Adult Felony Defendants in Los Angeles County: A Policy Perspective (1973); H. Lundsgaarde, Murder in Space City: A Cultural Analysis of Houston Homicide Patterns (1977); Del Martin, Battered Wives (1976); Del Martin, U.S. Comm'n on Civil Rights Overview—Scope of The Problem, in Battered Women: Issues of Public Policy (1978); Smith, supra note 15; U.S. Comm'n on Civil Rights, supra note 1; Vera Institute Justice, supra note 17; K. M. Williams, Institute for Social Resolution, The Role of the Victim in the Prosecution of Violent Offenses (1978); R. E. Dobash & R. P. Dobash, supra note 13; Field & Field, supra note 13, at 231–232; Linda G. Lerman, Prosecution of Wife Beaters: Institutional Obstacles and Innovations, in Violence in the Home: Interdisciplinary Perspectives (Mary Lystad ed., 1986); Parnas, supra note 17; David Rauma, Going for Gold: Prosecutorial Decision Making in Cases of Wife Assault, 13 Soc. Sci. Res. 321, 342 (1984).

128. Frank J. Cannavale, Jr. & William D. Falcon, Witness Cooperation: with a Handbook of Witness Management (1976); Lorenne Clark & Debra Lewis, Rape: The Price of Coercive Sexuality (1977); B. Forst et Al., What Happens after Arrest? (1977); Lynda Lytle Holmstrom & Ann Wolbert Burgess, The Victim of Rape: The Institutional Reaction (1978); Gary D. LaFree, Rape & Criminal Justice: The Construction of Sexual Assault (1989); Lundsgaarde, supra note 127; U.S. Comm'n on Civil Rights, supra note 1; Vera Inst. Justice, supra note 17; Edna Erez & Pamela Tontodonato, The Effect of Victim Participation in Sentencing Outcome,

likely to be,[129] and the less likely a sentence of capital punishment will be handed down.[130]

These legal system responses are troubling given that a large number of homicides and aggravated assaults are committed by and against intimate partners.[131] The legal system offers the last and sometimes the only protection available to domestic violence victims who hope to end the violence in their lives.[132] Failure to deal effectively with perpetrators and victims of family violence leads to victimization by the legal system itself as well as certain repetition of violent behavior in the next generation.[133]

The arrest and prosecution phase of the criminal justice system may result in therapeutic or antitherapeutic effects on offenders and victims of domestic violence. Laws, policies, and legal decisions can either reinforce cognitive distortions of offenders and victims or promote more adaptive cognitions. Because the police and prosecutors are gatekeepers for the number and type of domestic violence cases that are criminally pursued,[134] decisions to arrest and prosecute may have mental health implications for the offender and the victim.

A. Arrest

The police have historically failed to intervene effectively in cases of domestic violence.[135] For instance, one study found that the pattern of police re-

---

28 Criminology 451 (1990); Samuel R. Gross & Robert Mauro, Patterns of Death: An Analysis of Racial Disparities in Capital Sentencing and Homicide Victimization, 37 Stan. L. Rev. 27, 58 (1984); Gary D. LaFree, Variables Affecting Guilty Pleas and Convictions in Rape Cases: Toward a Social Theory of Rape Processing, 58 Soc. Forces 833, 842, 847 (1980); Terance D. Miethe, Stereotypical Conceptions and Criminal Processing: The Case of the Victim-Offender Relationship, 4 Just. Q. 571 (1987).

Note that only the U.S. Comm'n on Civil Rights publication specifically addresses the differential treatment of domestic violence cases. Other work generally compares the differential legal treatment of stranger and nonstranger offenses. Most of the work on legal processing of domestic violence offenders has focused on arrest decisions.

129. William M. Rhodes & C. Conly, U.S. Dep't of Justice, Analysis of Federal Sentencing: Final Report (1981); Erez & Tontodonato, supra note 128.

130. Gross & Mauro, supra note 128, at 58.

131. K. Rose & J. Goss, U.S. Dep't of Justice, Domestic Violence Statistics (1989).

132. Herrell & Hofford, supra note 14, at 3.

133. See generally Jaffe et al., supra note 11.

134. Ford, supra note 1, at 464.

135. E.g., Nancy Loving, Police Executive Research Forum, Responding to Spouse Abuse and Wife Beating: A Guide for Police (1980); Lisa R. Beck, Protecting Battered Women: A Proposal for Comprehensive Domestic Violence Legislation in New York, 15 Fordham Urb. L.J. 999, 1001 (1987); Berk & Loseke, supra note 16 at 32; Dobash & Dobash, supra note 15 at 207; Field & Field, supra note 17, at 227–230; Ford, supra note 1, at 465–466; Roger Langley & Richard C. Levy, Wife Abuse and the Police Response, 47 FBI L. Enforcement Bull. 4 (1978); Parnas, supra note 16; Truninger, supra note 126; Carolyn R. Hathaway, Case Comment: Gender Based Discrimination in Police Reluctance to Respond to Domestic Assault Complaints, 75 Geo. L.J. 667, 672 (1986). But see Elliott, supra note 1, at 438–441 (finding that the general belief that police are more lenient in domestic assault than other assaults is neither confirmed nor contradicted by the little research that focuses on that question).

sponse was directly related to the rates of domestic homicide: Police had been repeatedly called to the scenes of most domestic homicides.[136] Other evidence suggests that police intentionally delay their response to domestic violence calls, hoping that the conflict will be resolved by the time they arrive.[137] Generally, the literature suggests that police have traditionally felt more comfortable responding to strangers' crimes such as robbery, due to stereotypes of the participants in domestic violence cases as well as lack of knowledge in how to respond effectively to those cases.[138]

One commentator has characterized police intervention as iatrogenic, meaning that their presence exacerbates conflict.[139] This is understandable. Because the police are typically the first legal actors to be apprised of the incident,[140] the priority they assign to the case can not only have detrimental effects on the victim and her children, but can also continue to legitimize the offender's violence at home.[141] When police respond slowly or not at all to domestic violence cases,[142] offenders are encouraged to deny or minimize their behavior, whereas victims continue to feel helpless and blameworthy. In contrast, police policies can promote therapeutic effects for both offenders and victims by mandating that domestic violence calls receive priority over less serious personal crimes or property crimes.[143]

Once the decision is made to go to the scene of a domestic violence report, police officers are likely to be met by a terrorized and probably injured victim (and her children) and an angry offender who denies his violence and blames the victim. Only a warrantless, probable cause arrest of domestic violence perpetrators committing an assault or any other crime[144] can challenge the entrenched, destructive, and maladaptive thoughts of the offender while empowering and protecting the victim and her children. By taking the offender into

---

136. M. Wilt & J. Bannon, The Police Found., Domestic Violence and the Police: Studies in Detroit and Kansas City (1977).

137. Donald J. Black, The Manners and Customs of the Police 117 (1980); Nan Oppenlander, Coping or Copping Out: Police Service Delivery in Domestic Disputes, 20 Criminology 449, 453 (1982).

138. Ford, supra note 1, at 465–466 (documenting, among other problems with police response, that police dislike being called on to assume the role of counselor, for which they have no professional training).

139. Harvey A. Barocas, Crisis Intervention and Iatrogenic Reactions, 1 Group Analysis 36 (1973). See also McCord, supra note 113, at 234 (suggesting that police officers may hold values that legitimize the use of violence in a relationship, affecting how they behave at the scene of a domestic violence incident).

140. Ford, supra note 1, at 464.

141. Fleming, supra note 60, at 170–171 (1979) (suggesting that internal procedures of police departments assign low priority to domestic violence calls, thus delaying the arrival of patrol units in the field).

142. Ford, supra note 1, at 465–466 (commenting that if the police fail to respond to a battered woman call, she might be left entirely outside the criminal justice system, regardless of her needs or ultimate intent).

143. Herrell & Hofford, supra note 14, at 33.

144. Lisa G. Lerman et al., National Center on Women & Family L., Arrest in Domestic Violence Cases: A State-By-State Summary (1987) (noting that most states have adopted legislation calling for mandatory or presumptive arrest); Hart, supra note 8, at 6.

custody, the police are communicating to him and the victim that he has committed a criminal act and that he is responsible for his violent behavior.[145] By not making an arrest at this time, the police are facilitating offender denial.[146] Moreover, the victim is encouraged to continue to feel helpless, blamed, and worthless.[147]

By taking domestic violence cases seriously and arresting offenders when legally warranted, the police can validate the victim's right to be free from personal violence. Given the likelihood that threats or additional violence will occur unless the offender is arrested, arrest of the offender can at least provide temporary safety from harm for the victim and her children. This is also a timely opportunity for the police to inform the victim of other available services (such as restraining orders) to ensure her safety in the future.[148]

In addition to a formal arrest (or warrant for an arrest if an offender is not found at the scene), the manner in which police deal with domestic violence cases currently has antitherapeutic effects on the victims. It is not uncommon for police to blame the victim or disparage her in some other way.[149] This type of behavior merely reinforces the victim's low self-esteem and feelings of isolation and helplessness. Police training can address this problem so that officers can be more sensitive and helpful to victims. Training could address general aspects of the dynamics of domestic violence, the potential lethality of these cases, services available for battered women and their children, and the legal

---

145. Sherman & Berk, supra note 31, at 262–263.

146. See David B. Wexler & Bruce J. Winick, Therapeutic Jurisprudence and Criminal Justice Mental Health Issues, 16 Mental & Physical Disability L. Rep. 225 (1992).

147. Buzawa & Austin, supra note 16, at 616–618 (finding that victim preference was a major determinant of police decision to arrest, and that this factor resulted in 85% of the victims being highly satisfied with the police response).

148. Herrell & Hofford, supra note 14, at 33 (noting that other services that could be made available to the victim at the time of the incident include transportation to the emergency room or hospital for treatment of injuries; referral or transportation to alternative housing or shelter; protection while gathering necessary belongings; insuring the safety and care of children in the home; and printed information about court processes, whom to contact for information on the case, the badge number and name of the responding officer, and how to obtain additional assistance); Langan & Innes, supra note 7, at 4 (finding that women who called the police were less likely than the women who did not call to become repeat victims); Kathleen O. Beitiks, Violence on the Homefront: A Tiny Step to Alleviate Dangers, Cal. B. J., August 1994 at 1, 6 (describing how the police in Los Angeles typically refer a domestic violence victim to the Domestic Violence Project for free assistance in obtaining immediate restraining orders); Oppenlander, supra note 137, at 461–462 (finding that, although police officers were aware of referral groups that would be appropriate for battered women, it was rare for an officer to refer a victim to a social service agency); Raymond I. Parnas, The Response of Some Relevant Community Resources to Intra-Family Violence, 44 Ind. L.J. 159, 180 (1969) (suggesting that the highest number of referrals would result from the police notifying relevant agencies about the needs of the violent couple).

149. Ferraro, supra note 20, at 68–69; Ford, supra note 1, at 466 (documenting that police perception of the victim influenced the degree of consideration shown for her; rational, nondemanding, and deferential victims are likely to be more supported by the officers); Pam Waaland & Stuart Keeley, Police Decision Making in Wife Abuse: The Impact of Legal and Extralegal Factors, 9 L. & Hum. Behav. 355, 361 (1985) (finding that victim antagonism and alcohol use resulted in her being blamed for the violence).

obligation of the police to provide protection.[150] Receiving training in handling domestic violence cases may enable officers to respond to these calls with more sensitivity and effectiveness.

Not surprisingly, the indifference of police to victims of domestic violence has led to a number of lawsuits.[151] One of the most publicized cases of this kind involved a woman who was brutally assaulted and left paralyzed by her estranged husband after she had repeatedly sought police protection.[152] The $2.3 million award granted to Tracey Thurman in that suit and awards in other lawsuits are believed to have prompted police departments to effect policy changes in domestic violence cases.[153] Another spur to change has been attributed to the results[154] and wide publicity[155] of a pilot study in Minneapolis finding that arrest in misdemeanor domestic violence assaults had a significantly greater effect than other responses by police in reducing future acts of violence by offenders. These factors and others[156] are leading to policy changes of the police role in domestic violence cases.

B. Prosecution

The prosecution of an offense usually occurs in response to a police report.[157] Generally, prosecutors wield a great deal of discretion regarding whom

---

150. Herrell & Hofford, supra note 14 at 34; Eve S. Buzawa, Police Officer Response to Domestic Violence Legislation in Michigan, 10 J. Police Sci. & Admin. 415, 423 (1982) (finding that even modest police training can transform attitudes and behavior of officers); Ferraro, supra note 20, at 70 (finding that even though the Arizona domestic violence statute requires officers to inform victims of resources available to them, officers seldom did so because they felt provision of this information was not part of their job of restoring order).

151. See Marvin Zalman, The Courts' Response to Police Intervention in Domestic Violence, in Changing Response, supra note 1, at 79 (reviewing successful constitutional challenges and tort actions involving egregious cases in which the police clearly abdicated their responsibility to protect victims of domestic violence).

152. Thurman et al. v. City of Torrington, 595 F. Supp. 1521 (Conn. 1984).

153. Buzawa & Buzawa, supra note 1, at XII.

154. Sherman & Berk, supra note 26, at 270 (encouraging the use of the results of their study to alter police practices in domestic violence cases).

155. Arnold Binder & James Meeker, Arrest as a Method to Control Spouse Abuse, in Changing Response, supra note 1, at 129, 133–136 (discussing how the principal investigators of the Minneapolis police arrest study actively sought to sell their study and results to the public, police, and criminal justice officials in order to effect policy changes in police practices; this was done despite methodological problems of the study raising issues of internal and external validity); Richard O. Lempert, From the Editor, 18 L. & Soc'y Rev. 505 (1984) (arguing that the Minneapolis Domestic Violence Experiment results may have been prematurely and unduly publicized); Lawrence W. Sherman & Ellen G. Cohn, The Impact of Research on Legal Policy: The Minneapolis Domestic Violence Experiment, 23 L. & Soc'y Rev. 117 (1989) (defending their efforts to widely publicize the Minneapolis Domestic Violence Experiment in order to improve legal effectiveness and encourage replications in different cities).

156. Binder & Meeker, supra note 155 at 3 (reviewing the evolving response to domestic violence in the context of an overall change in societal attitudes).

157. When the police are not called, or if they are called but do not arrest, a victim may initiate charges on her own by going to the prosecutor's office and swearing out a probable

to charge and what charge to file.[158] Prosecutors use this discretion to screen some suspects out of the criminal justice system altogether, divert others to community programs outside the system, bargain for information and guilty pleas, and prosecute some defendants fully.[159] For example, studies of the screening function indicate that only 25% of cases brought to the attention of 94 U.S. attorneys ended in formal prosecution.[160] This type of day-to-day decisionmaking is conducted by prosecutors who make their decisions relatively free of control, although they may be influenced by the desires and opinions of the public, the police, and other government officials.

Case law accords the prosecutor wide latitude in the discretionary exercise of his/her prosecution powers so long as the decision is not deliberately based on unjustifiable standards such as race, religion, or other arbitrary classifications.[161] Legality of this discretion extends to decisions of whether to charge with a crime or not, to refer the individual elsewhere (e.g., diversion), to drop charges, to negotiate guilty pleas, and to try contested cases.

In general criminal cases, the prosecutor considers various factors in deciding whether to bring formal charges against a suspect, including seriousness of the crime,[162] strength of the evidence and adequacy of witnesses,[163] the suspect's background and characteristics,[164] the costs and benefits of obtaining a conviction,[165] and attitude of the community toward the offense the suspect is believed

---

cause affidavit with her allegation against the man. See Goolkasian, supra note 15, at 3; Lerman, supra note 17 (noting that in the past victims were often required to sign charges in domestic violence cases, unlike in most other cases, to show that they were willing to cooperate with the prosecution); David A. Ford & Mary Jean Regoli, The Preventive Impacts of Policies for Prosecuting Wife Batterers, in Changing Response, supra note 1, at 18; Schmidt & Steury, supra note 17 at 503–504. (finding that prosecutors appear to file charges less often in cases where the victims initiate charges on their own than in cases which enter through police action, even when cases are comparable in seriousness of injuries).

158. Gottfredson & Gottfredson, supra note 125.

159. Id.

160. Richard S. Frase, The Decision to File Federal Criminal Charges: A Quantitative Study of Prosecutorial Discretion, 47 U. Chi. L. Rev. 246 (1980).

161. E.g., Town of Newton et al. v. Rumery, 480 U.S. 386 (1987); Wayte v. United States, 470 U.S. 598 (1985); United States v. Goodwin, 457 U.S. 368 (1982); Bordenkircher v. Hayes, 434 U.S. 357 (1978); Oyler v. Boles, 368 U.S. 448 (1962); United States v. Cox, 342 F.2d 167 (5th Cir. 1965).

162. Brosi, supra note 127; James Eisenstein & Herbert Jacob, Felony Justice (1977); Greenwood, supra note 127; I. Bernstein et al., Charge Reduction: An Intermediary Stage in the Process of Labeling Criminal Defendants, 56 Soc. Forces 363 (1977); B. Forst & K. Brosi, A Theoretical and Empirical Analysis of the Prosecutor, 6 J. Legal Stud. 177 (1977); Frase, supra note 160; J. Kaplan, Prosecutorial Discretion—A Comment, 60 NW. U.L. Rev. 174 (1965).

163. Greenwood et al., supra note 127; Bernstein et al., supra note 162; Brosi, supra note 127; Frase, supra note 161; Forst et al., supra note 128; Forst & Brosi, supra note 163; Kaplan, supra note 162.

164. Bernstein et al., supra note 162; Forst & Brosi, supra note 162; Frase, supra note 160.

165. F. Miller, Prosecution: The Decision to Charge a Suspect with a Crime (1970); Brosi, supra note 127; Frase, supra note 160; Kaplan, supra note 162.

to have committed.[166] In addition, there is evidence that the decision to prosecute is based on characteristics of the victim[167] and the victim-offender relationship.[168]

In domestic violence cases, prosecutors may use the same broad range of tools used in general criminal cases. They have the discretion to effect a variety of policies, ranging from dismissing a case through prosecuting to conviction with harsh punishment.[169] They also can recommend sentences not specifically prescribed by statute but allowed as conditions of probation. For example, offenders may be required to participate in rehabilitative treatment programs as a requirement of probation.[170]

Although a great deal of attention has been paid to investigating the police decision to arrest domestic violence offenders, very little research has examined the decisionmaking by the prosecutor in these cases. In an early thought-provoking study, it was concluded that the prosecution of domestic violence cases had the effect of converting a system thought to function under standard rules into a system whose processes are subject to chance.[171] For example, the manner in which a victim's complaint was processed depended on who was taking complaints on any particular day. In addition, careless handling and errors in processing complaints caused legal inaction in many cases. These and other findings indicated that the victim's efforts to prosecute an offender had little institutional support, and often had the effect of wearing the victim down long before the offender was due to stand trial.

Historically, prosecutors, like other actors in the legal system, have not been very sympathetic to the plight of victims of domestic violence.[172] Prosecutorial

---

166. Miller, supra note 165.

167. Id.; Williams, supra note 127.

168. Brosi, supra note 127; Greenwood et al., supra note 127; Lerman, supra note 17, at 24–29; Raymond Parnas, Prosecutorial and Judicial Handling of Family Violence, 9 Crim. L. Bull. 733, 735 (1973); Vera Inst. Justice, supra note 17; Williams, supra note 127.

169. Ford & Regoli, supra note 158, at 183.

Although not addressing the issue of prosecutorial discretion, Professor Ford describes an interesting application of exchange and power processes theory to the prosecution function in domestic violence cases. He argues that control over prosecution decisions by the domestic violence victim can correct the balance of power in a violent relationship, deterring her partner's violence. See David A. Ford, Prosecution As a Victim Power Resource: A Note on Empowering Women in Violent Conjugal Relationships, 25 L. & Soc'y Rev. 313, 318, 331 (1991) (arguing that in making a significant threat to prosecute by initiating steps to invoke the process, a battered woman is able to exercise power that was previously absent in her relationship).

170. Ford & Regoli, supra note 157, at 183.

171. Ford, supra note 1, at 467, 473 (finding that this chaotic legal processing of cases was true of police, prosecutors, and judges).

172. Naomi R. Cahn, Innovative Approaches to the Prosecution of Domestic Violence Crimes: An Overview, in Changing Response, supra note 1, at 161; Ford, supra note 1, at 472 (finding that prosecutors had a policy of putting a case on hold for a 3-day cooling-off period); Ellis, supra note 17 (exploring the ambivalence that exists regarding the prosecutor's use of discretion in domestic violence cases); Donileen R. Loseke, Evaluation Research and the Practice of Social Services: A Case for Qualitative Methodology, 18 J. Contemp. Ethnography 202, 213, 218 (1989) (finding that a prosecution team was uncomfortable with the fact that to prevent victims from dropping out, they had to provide constant social support throughout the proceedings); Pagelow, supra note 20, at 96–99 (indicating that although ar-

decisions in these cases are often complicated by the common victim behavior of changing her mind and asking that the charges against the offender be dismissed.[173] This sometimes results in prosecutorial policy that places the filing decision on the victim. Such policy typically results in the filing of a comparatively low number of charges.[174] For example, one study of the reasons that prosecutors decided not to charge domestic violence cases found that, in 45% of the cases, the primary reason for the failure to go forward was the victim's wishes.[175] An antitherapeutic effect of following such a policy is that it provides an opportunity for the abuser to intimidate and prevent the victim from pursuing the charges.[176]

That victims frequently change their minds about pressing charges against the batterer, coupled with the common prosecutorial perception that such crimes are trivial,[177] influences many prosecutors to avoid prosecution of domestic violence cases. Prosecutors possess their own stereotypes of battered women. Consequently, prosecutors often rationalize their decisions not to prosecute by blaming the victim and assuming that women provoke the violence against them.[178]

A number of jurisdictions have demonstrated that victims are more helpful if the prosecution goes forward with or without their cooperation.[179] By controlling the criminal process, the prosecutor provides a powerful message that the offender may not avoid criminal sanctions through control over the victim or the victim's refusal to cooperate.[180] Precluding victims from influencing prosecution forces prosecutors to take these cases seriously and establishes that domestic violence is a crime against society. Allowing the victim to take an active part in the prosecution of the offender can also result in feelings of

---

rests appear to have increased in some areas, there has been no correspondingly higher rate of prosecutions and guilty pleas).

173. Ford & Regoli, supra note 157, at 184; Kathleen J. Ferraro & Tascha Boychuk, The Court's Response to Interpersonal Violence: A Comparison of Intimate and Nonintimate Assault, in Domestic Violence, supra note 1, at 213 (noting that victim cooperation is viewed as such a problem in domestic violence cases that prosecutors have established a "cooling off" period, a procedure lacking in nondomestic violence cases); Ford, supra note 1, at 470–471 (describing the various victim motives for initiating prosecution, and commenting that prosecutors' expectation of ulterior motives seemed to generate a disregard for victim needs); Rauma, supra note 127.

174. Cahn, supra note 172, at 161.

175. Schmidt & Steury, supra note 17, at 495.

176. Cahn, supra note 172, at 166.

177. Cahn, supra note 172, at 162.

178. Lerman, supra note 17; U.S. Comm'n on Civil Rights, supra note 1; Ford, supra note 1, at 472 (addressing the stereotypical treatment of domestic violence victims by prosecutors in their policy of putting their cases on hold during a cooling-off period); Schafran, supra note 17, at 283 (noting that judges also hold stereotypes of domestic violence victims, and that they rarely inquire into whether a victim was coerced into withdrawing her complaint).

179. Herrell & Hofford, supra note 14, at 36; Cahn, supra note 172, at 167–168 (noting that as a more drastic measure, some jurisdictions have adopted no-drop policies, which emphasize that the prosecutors control decisionmaking by precluding the victim from deciding to drop charges).

180. Cahn, supra note 172, at 167–68.

empowerment for her that can alter the balance of power in the battering relationship and lower rates of future violence.[181]

Some jurisdictions have found it helpful to implement guidelines on when to file charges in domestic violence cases.[182] Having such guidelines in place increases the filing of domestic violence charges.[183] It is clear that by increasing the filing of domestic violence cases, offenders are less likely to think they can use violence against their wives. The effect on the victims is likely to be less tolerance of violent behavior.

A current prosecutorial trend is to divert these offenders and refer them to a treatment program.[184] Diversion programs are an alternative to traditional

---

181. Ford & Regoli, supra note 157 at 181, 194. It should be noted that far less research has been conducted on the deterrent effects of full prosecution of domestic violence offenders than has been done on the deterrent effects of their arrest; Ford, supra note 1, at 471 (showing that many victims were motivated to prosecute by the desire to demonstrate that they had control over the situation—control that could be used to deter future violence).

182. Prosecutors are encouraged to consider various factors including seriousness of injuries, use of deadly weapon, offender's prior criminal history, offender's past history of violence, and the potential lethality of the situation. See Cahn, supra note 172, at 166–67; Ford, supra note 1, at 467 (discussing how individual discretion can leave a victim's fate to chance).

183. Cahn, supra note 172, at 166–67.

184. If diversion is used, experts suggest that there are basic guidelines on the appropriate type of treatment. Treatment that focuses solely on anger management is discouraged. It is believed to continue the blame of the victim for provoking the batterer while overlooking the root problems of the batterer. Similarly, joint counseling with the victim or mediation suggests that the victim played some role in precipitating the violence, and that she also needs to change her behavior. Instead, there is general agreement that batterer treatment needs to increase the offender's responsibility for his violence, decrease offender dependence on the victim, and teach him how to control his behavior. There is also general agreement that diversion should occur postplea, so that the batterer admits responsibility for his actions. The treatment is believed to be more effective if it is mandatory for a specific period of time. Finally, the offender's attendance should be carefully monitored, with the provision that if he fails to attend, prosecution will continue or a sentence will be imposed. See e.g., Pence & Paymar, supra note 28; David Adams, Treatment Models of Men Who Batter: A Profeminist Analysis, in Feminist Perspectives on Wife Abuse, supra note 12 at 176; A. Ganley, Perpetrators of Domestic Violence: An Overview of Counseling the Court-Mandated Client, in Domestic Violence on Trial: Psychological & Legal Dimensions of Family Violence (David Sonkin ed., 1986); Pagelow, supra note 23, at 98 (concluding that the literature is mixed on the effectiveness of diversion programs).

Granting domestic violence offenders diversion is also problematic in that it implies that domestic violence is different and less serious than stranger violence. Thus far, it is questionable whether diversion and treatment of these offenders has been successful. See e.g., David A. Ford & Mary Jean Regoli, National Institute of Justice, Final Report, The Indianapolis Domestic Violence Prosecution Experiment 70 (1993); David A. Ford & Mary Jean Regoli, The Criminal Prosecution of Wife Assaulters: Process, Problems, and Effects, in Legal Response to Wife Assault 127, 157 (N. Zoe Hilton ed., 1993). Nevertheless, we treat domestic violence offenders differently (arguably preferentially) as a matter of national policy. Nowhere is this more evident than by the specially created domestic violence courts and legal projects. See e.g., National Council Juvenile and Family Court Judges, supra note 5. See also, Jane Gross, Simpson Case Galvanizes U.S. about Domestic Violence, N.Y. Times, July 4, 1994, at 6 (describing innovative programs including a highly acclaimed domestic violence court in Dade County, Florida, where convicted offenders are diverted to a 6-month treat-

criminal prosecution and sentencing through which case processing is suspended while the defendant completes a treatment program.[185] The decision as to whether diversion should occur prior to or after pleading guilty is controversial.[186] Given the batterer's lack of motivation to seek treatment on his own, it makes sense to condition diversion on an admission of guilt and attendant conditions of probation.[187] Otherwise, offenders may believe that they are "getting off" their criminal charges if they do not receive the message that domestic violence is a crime.[188] Diversion also extends the time that a case is held open so that, if there is a violation, the offender can be prosecuted.[189] Having the charges hanging over the offender's head and the threat of prosecution at any misstep will provide the victim with some power over his compliance.

Given the controversy over diversion programs, the National Council of Juvenile and Family Court Judges recommends that diversion be granted only in extraordinary cases, and then only after a guilty plea has been entered.[190] The organization notes that diversion is inappropriate when it is used to weed out cases from the court's calendar; when first offenders are chronic abusers; when the required treatment is only of brief duration and is not monitored; and when the use of diversion is perceived as a less than serious response to the crime.[191]

In summary, there are a variety of prosecutorial functions in domestic violence cases that have an antitherapeutic effect on both offenders and victims. Lenient treatment by the prosecutor communicates to the offender and the victim that the violent behavior is considered trivial. This is likely to feed into the offenders' perceptions that they have done nothing wrong and encourages them to continue to blame the victim. Reform aimed at more vigorous prose-

---

ment program and return to court every 2 months for a year).

185. Two types of diversion programs are used: (a) postcharge but pretrial, so that the batterer is referred to counseling before trial even begins and, if he completes the counseling, the charges are not otherwise prosecuted; and (b) postplea, where the defendant actually enters a guilty plea, but his sentence is stayed if he complies with a counseling program as part of his probation. See Goolkasian, supra note 15, at 6–7; Lerman, supra note 13; Cahn, supra note 172, at 160.

186. Cahn, supra note 172, at 160; Naomi Cahn & Lisa G. Lerman, Prosecuting Woman Abuse, in Woman Battering: Policy Responses 95 (Michael Steinman ed., 1991).

187. Hamberger & Hastings, supra note 56, at 370–71; L. Kevin Hamberger & James E. Hastings, Counseling Male Spouse Abusers: Characteristics of Treatment Completers and Dropouts, 4 Violence & Victims 275, 280, 282 (1989) (finding that court-mandated participants are less likely to drop out of treatment programs than are nonmandated individuals).

188. Cahn, supra note 172, at 173.

189. To prevent abuse of the diversion process, some jurisdictions have developed strict eligibility guidelines for when diversion is appropriate. Factors to be considered are whether the offense is a misdemeanor or felony; past history or convictions for violent offenses; past revocation of probation or parole; prior diversion for domestic violence; seriousness of injury to the victim; victim's consent; and the offender's motivation and agreement with the terms of diversion. See Cahn, supra note 172, at 173; Kathleen Waits, The Criminal Justice System's Response to Battering: Understanding the Problem, Forging the Solutions, 60 Wash. L. Rev. 267 (1985).

190. Herrell & Hofford, supra note 14, at 38.

191. Id.

cution of domestic violence cases can help offenders take responsibility for their hurtful behavior.[192] Consistent prosecution can also empower victims and help them feel that the violence is not their responsibility. Written guidelines can assist prosecutors with decisions about when and whom to charge in these cases. As with the police, prosecutors can be trained to understand the dynamics of domestic violence and the potential dangerousness of the offenders if not sanctioned. Training can also alter prosecutorial stereotypes of battered women, enabling them to respond more sensitively to domestic violence cases.

When diversion programs are used, the National Association of Juvenile and Family Court Judges' eligibility guidelines should be followed. The most important element in the use of diversion appears to be that an offender plea of guilty be entered. Otherwise, offenders can continue to rationalize their violence or think they have escaped liability for their conduct. In addition, active monitoring of the offender's participation in the treatment program with the threat and use of sanctions for noncompliance are critical to combat batterers' cognitive distortions that they have done nothing wrong or illegal.

IV. Trials, Plea Bargains, and Sentencing Issues

Certain aspects of the adjudication and sentencing of domestic violence offenders can have therapeutic and antitherapeutic consequences for the offender and victim. For instance, the decision to go to trial or not, the types of pleas and plea bargains used, and the sentencing decisions can extend the cognitive distortions of both parties or promote more adaptive and functional thinking and behavior.

A. Trials and Plea Bargains

The practice of plea bargaining enters into the prosecutor's decision to charge, and if so, on what charge.[193] Plea bargaining is widespread, typically requiring that the defendant give up his right to go to trial in exchange for a reduction in the charge or sentence (or both).[194] Although there is considerable variation among jurisdictions in guilty plea rates, about 90% of persons adjudicated guilty are guilty as a result of a guilty plea.[195]

---

192. Raymond Parnas, The Relevance of Criminal Law to Interspousal Violence, in Family Violence 190, 191 (J. Eekelaar & S. Katz eds., 1978) (advocating traditional criminal justice sanctions against domestic violence offenders at the first minimal signs of trouble given what we know about the experience of escalation from minimal to aggravated injury).

193. Gottfredson & Gottfredson, supra, note 125.

194. James Eisenstein & Herbert Jacob, Felony Justice (1977); Malcolm Feeley, Court Reform on Trial: Why Simple Solutions Fail (1983); M. Heumann, Plea Bargaining (1978); Lynn Mather, Plea Bargaining on Trial: The Process of Criminal Case Disposition (1979); Arthur Rosett & Donald Cressey, Justice by Consent: Plea-bargains in the American Courthouse (1976); A. Alschuler, The Prosecutor's Role in Plea Bargaining, 36 U. Chi. L. Rev. 50 (1968); J. Casper, Reformers vs. Abolitionists: Some Notes for Further Research on Plea Bargaining, 13 Law & Soc'y Rev. 567 (1979).

195. U.S. Dep't of Justice, The Prevalence of Guilty Pleas (1984).

Controversy exists as to whether defendants who plea bargain and plead guilty get lighter sentences than defendants who exercise their right to trial. Some studies report sentencing differentials favoring those who plead guilty,[196] whereas others indicate that factors such as seriousness of the charge and nature of the offender's prior record may be more important in determining the sentence.[197] In fact, several studies have found an association between offense seriousness and mode of disposition, with more serious cases being more likely to go to trial.[198]

As discussed in the previous section on the prosecution of offenses, many domestic violence cases are diverted prior to or after a plea of guilty. In the latter case, the plea bargaining process is used to encourage offenders to plead guilty in exchange for diversion into a treatment program in lieu of other sanctions. Those offenders who do not qualify for diversion programs may still use plea bargains to avoid the maximum punishment. No research is available on the use of plea bargains in domestic violence cases, making this a fertile ground of inquiry for future studies.[199]

There is also no research on factors that influence a domestic violence offender to forego his right to trial and enter into a plea bargain.[200] Given the cognitive distortions present in most offenders about their violence, one would expect that they are more likely to go to trial because they feel unjustly prosecuted. It is likely, however, that pleading guilty instead of fighting the charges in a full trial may have more therapeutic effects for both the offender and the victim. This would be expected to be more true for offenders who plead guilty as charged and not as true for offenders whose charges are bargained down or who plead no contest.[201] Consequently, any manner of proceeding in court

---

196. David Brereton & Jonathan D. Casper, Does it Pay to Plead Guilty? Differential Sentencing and the Functioning of Criminal Courts, 16 L. & Soc'y Rev. 45, 55–57 (1981–1982); Peter Nardulli, The Courtroom Elite (1978); W. M. Rhodes & C. Conly, U.S. Dep't of Justice, Analysis of Federal Sentencing: Final Report (1981); William D. Rich et al., National Center for State Courts, Sentencing Guidelines: Their Operation and Impact on the Courts (1981); L. Paul Sutton, National Criminal Justice Info. & Stat. Service, Variations in Federal Criminal Sentences: A Statistical Assessment at the National Level (1978); L. Tiffany et al., A Statistical Analysis of Sentencing in Federal Courts: Defendants Convicted After Trial, 1967–1968, 4 J. Legal Stud. 369, 380 (1975); T. Uhlman & N. Walker, He Takes Some of My Time; I Take Some of His: An Analysis of Judicial Sentencing Patterns in Jury Cases, 14 Law & Soc'y Rev. 23 (1980).

197. Eisenstein & Jacob, supra, note 162.

198. Eisenstein & Jacob, Id.; John Hagan, Parameters of Criminal Prosecution: An Application of Path Analysis to a Problem of Criminal Justice, 65 J. Crim. L. & Criminology, 536, 541 (1975).

199. Dawson & Langan, supra note 2, at 7 (indicating that spouse killers are more likely to plead guilty than nonfamily killers, but omits more specific analyses of the plea).

200. Id. (although spouse killers are more likely to plead guilty than nonfamily killers, only 42% did so. Spouse killers were also more likely to be convicted at trial than nonfamily killers).

201. Klotz et al., supra note 40, at 584, 587 (arguing that the type of plea a sex offender enters may affect the individual's cognitive distortions: Both a no contest plea and charge bargaining can have antitherapeutic effects on sex offenders by allowing them to escape an admission of guilt to the actual charged offense).

other than a guilty plea to the offense as charged may reinforce denial and minimization of the violent behavior of the domestic violence offender.[202] When the offender takes responsibility in this way, the victim can desist from self-blame and begin the process of healing. The therapeutic impact of a guilty plea can be reinforced by a judicial sentencing policy that recognizes a guilty plea as a first step in the offender's rehabilitation.[203]

Clearly, research is needed on the effects of various types of guilty pleas and trial postures on the entrenched dysfunctional thoughts of the domestic violence offender. Particularly, does pleading guilty as charged therapeutically alter the cognitive distortions of the offender? Does proceeding to trial further cement the cognitive distortions? When treatment is part of a plea bargain, can the effects of pleading guilty be teased out from the effects of treatment per se? Other research questions involve the role of the prosecuting and defense attorneys in the case.[204] For example, how does zealous, adversarial posturing by the defendant's attorney affect the defendant's thinking about the offense?

B. Sentencing

After a guilty plea or a finding of guilt at trial in a domestic violence case, there are two possibilities for the offender: probation or fine (or both), or imprisonment.[205] Probation generally includes participation in counseling or other diversionary programs. The National Council on Juvenile and Family Court Judges indicates that the primary goals of domestic violence sentencing are to stop the violence, protect the victim and family members, and hold the offender accountable.[206] It suggests that provision be made for formal supervi-

---

202. Wexler & Winick, supra note 146.

Note that critics of therapeutic jurisprudence worry that individual civil rights interests may be forsaken when we emphasize the therapeutic value of pleading guilty to a criminal offense. See, e.g., Joel Haycock, Speaking Truth to Power: Rights, Therapeutic Jurisprudence, and Massachusetts Mental Health Law, 20 New Eng. J. Crim. & Civ. Confinement 301, 304, 315 (1994) (cautioning that the focus on the concept of therapeutic jurisprudence in criminal cases carries the risk that individual civil rights will be ignored in favor of therapeutic concerns). See also John Petrila, Paternalism and the Unrealized Promise: Essays in Therapeutic Jurisprudence, 10 N.Y.L. Sch. J. Hum. Rts. 877, 879, 891–92 (1993) (accusing therapeutic jurisprudence scholars of subordinating individual civil liberties to the interest of obtaining therapeutic outcomes).

203. Wexler & Winick, supra note 146.

204. See Klotz et al., supra note 40, at 586 (discussing the defense attorney's role in engaging the client in cognitive restructuring by confronting him with damaging evidence against him).

205. Cahn, supra note 172, at 175.

206. The National Council of Juvenile and Family Court Judges advocates that the judge at a sentencing hearing be provided with a substantial amount of information and a presentence report regardless of whether the offense is a misdemeanor, felony, or a restraining order violation. Information critical to an informed sentencing decision includes information on the offender's criminal history; impact of the violence on the victim and the victim's recommendation for sentencing; history of abusive behavior that may not be reflected in the offender's criminal record; drug, alcohol, and mental health evaluations; history of prior court contacts by the family; and in-

sion and monitoring of the offender's behavior if he is granted probation.[207]

Although research suggests that stranger offenders fare worse than non-stranger offenders in sentencing outcome,[208] no research examines the sentencing differential between domestic violence offenders and stranger offenders.[209] Clearly, the dearth of research on this matter suggests that future researchers may want to examine sentencing outcome differentials between domestic violence offenders and stranger assault-homicide offenders.[210] We do know, however, the sentencing disposition for batterers is rarely incarceration.[211] Imprisonment is extremely rare even for felonious aggravated assaults.[212]

Prosecutors can request tougher sentences, thereby educating both the abuser and the court about the seriousness of the crime.[213] Some jurisdictions statutorily mandate that prosecutors make all reasonable efforts to persuade the court to impose the most severe authorized sentence on a person convicted of spouse abuse.[214] Other jurisdictions provide judicial and probation guidelines that set out a presumptive sentence recommendation for misdemeanor offenses, beginning with 30 to 60 days in jail, suspended on conditions that protect the victim and rehabilitate the offender.[215] Requiring prosecutors to recommend sentences commensurate with other crimes could have therapeutic effects on offenders and victims by communicating to them that a serious crime has occurred, and that the perpetrator will be punished.[216]

---

formation about children and others living in the home who may be affected by the violence. As to alcohol or drug abuse (or both), the organization recognizes that treatment will not solve the problem but may be a necessary prerequisite to treatment for the violence. It suggests examining prior court contacts by the family because many of these families are highly dysfunctional and have had a variety of interactions with the court. See Herrell & Hofford, supra note 14, at 19.

207. Id.

208. Gottfredson & Gottfredson, supra note 125; Rhodes and Conly, supra note 129; Erez & Tontodonato, supra note 128.

209. But see Dawson & Langan, supra note 2, at 7–8 (finding that spouse killers are more likely to receive probation and incur shorter prison sentences than nonfamily killings). Note that when Dawson and Langan controlled for many offender, victim, and offense characteristics, however, they did not find differences in sentencing severity between family and nonfamily murders. However, their analysis did not examine whether differences in sentencing severity existed between spouse killers and nonfamily killers. Future research may want to re-analyze this rich data set to determine whether such differences exist between spouse and nonfamily killers. See also Goolkasian, supra note 15, at 5 (indicating that sentences for convicted batterers have traditionally been much lighter than for violent crimes involving strangers).

210. The paucity of research on this issue is exemplified by a comprehensive review of the sentencing literature that found that offense seriousness and prior record are consistently the most important determinants of sentence but did not even mention the victim-offender relationship. See Alfred Blumstein et al., Research on Sentencing: The Search for Reform (1983).

211. Waits, supra note 189; but see Dawson & Langan, supra note 2, at 7 (finding that convicted family murder defendants were not significantly less likely to receive a prison sentence).

212. Ferraro & Boychuk, supra note 173, at 221 (indicating that this is true for both domestic violence and nondomestic violence aggravated assaults).

213. Tougher sentences for domestic violence would also help empower victims, who typically feel powerless in such situations.

214. Cahn, supra note 172, at 175.

215. Goolkasian, supra note 15, at 5–6.

216. An argument could even be made that domestic violence offenders should be treated

Judges also can confront offender denial and minimization by sentencing these cases as they would other crimes, and by recognizing that offenders will violate sentencing orders and conditions with impunity if they believe nothing will happen to them.[217] Consistently ordering some sort of additional penalty for those found guilty of past violations of court orders or conditions of sentencing can communicate to offenders that they will be punished for each infraction.[218] As with any form of behavior modification, offenders need to know that they cannot escape liability for single lapses in compliance. To be consistent, courts should develop a means of monitoring compliance with both criminal and civil court orders. The National Council of Juvenile and Family Court Judges suggests that judges may wish to set cases for periodic review, whether or not a violation has been reported.[219]

If judges use diversion or conditions of probation, psychological principles can be used to facilitate offender compliance. For example, David Wexler reviews the psychological literature that sets forth ways of achieving patient compliance with treatment regimens.[220] He then applies those principles to achieving greater compliance with conditions of probation on the part of probationers. Wexler suggests that probationers might be more likely to comply with conditions of their probation if the court order is individually tailored to fit their needs, and if the judge seeks the input and commitment from the defendant.[221] One could apply Wexler's reasoning to fashioning diversion and probation orders for domestic violence offenders. To increase domestic violence offender adherence with conditions, hearings can actively involve the offender in arriving at the conditions, ensure that he understands what is expected of him, and solicit his agreement with and commitment to the conditions.[222] Research is needed to assess the effectiveness of such an approach to the achievement of compliance by domestic violence offenders.[223]

V. Restraining Orders

In addition to the invocation of criminal sanctions against domestic violence offenders, legal reforms over the last 10 years have made it possible for victims to seek help and protection from the civil justice system.[224] Remedies available through civil courts include temporary and permanent restraining orders,[225] di-

---

more harshly than, say, stranger offenders committing comparable crimes because of the greater frequency of their offending and the higher likelihood of their offenses becoming fatal to the victim.

217. Herrell & Hofford, supra note 14, at 21.

218. Id.

219. Id.

220. See Wexler, 1993 supra note 35, at 291–94.

221. Id. at 295–97.

222. Id. at 295.

223. Id. at 769 (suggesting that the area of sentencing, in general, is ripe for therapeutic jurisprudence inquiry).

224. Louis W. McHardy, Introduction, 25 Juv. & Fam. L. Dig., 1 (1993).

225. E.g., Sheila M. Murphy, Orders of Protection and the Battered Woman Syndrome, 23 Loy. U. Chi. L. J. 397 (1992) (discussing the importance of the judiciary in intervening

vorce and child custody proceedings,[226] and suits for compensatory and punitive damages for marital torts.[227] This article focuses on restraining orders because they complement the use of criminal remedies in domestic violence cases. Therapeutic and antitherapeutic effects can result from the accessibility, use, and enforcement of these protective orders.

Civil restraining orders can be an effective remedy for obtaining immediate relief for domestic violence victims.[228] They may be used in conjunction with criminal sanctions or as an exclusive legal remedy[229] and are now available to battered women in every jurisdiction.[230] The order typically offers a domestic violence victim a judicial injunction that directs the offender to cease battering, threatening, or harming both the woman and, where appropriate, other family members such as children.[231] Many state codes authorize the trial court to award the victim an ex parte (i.e., without the defendant being at the hearing) temporary restraining order if imminent danger exists, and a hearing is scheduled on the permanent restraining order within a reasonable period of time.[232]

The forms required to obtain a restraining order, however, may be discouragingly complex for women not represented by an attorney or assisted by someone who is familiar with the forms and the courts.[233] The usefulness of the restraining orders depends on the specificity of relief ordered, enforcement practices of the police and courts, the severity of violence in the year prior to the order, and the level of resistance by the man during the hearing.[234]

The legal system can accomplish therapeutic as well as legal goals by improving the accessibility, issuance, and enforcement of restraining orders in domestic

---

and issuing protection orders against domestic violence).

226. Hart, supra note 10.

227. Robert G. Spector, Marital Tort Cases Concerning Domestic Violence, 25 Juv. & Fam. L. Dig. 399 (1993).

228. Harrell et al., supra note 25, at 1; Peter Finn, Civil Protection Orders: A Flawed Opportunity for Intervention, in Woman Battering, supra note 3, at 155, 180–181 (1991).

229. Harrell et al., supra note 25, at 1; Finn, supra note 228, at 181 (noting that many women in some jurisdictions seem to prefer to seek civil protection orders to prevent being battered than to file criminal complaints).

230. Hart, supra note 10, at 5.

231. Chaudhuri & Daly, Changing Response, supra note 24, at 228.

232. E.g., Harrell et al., supra note 25, at 15 (indicating that Colorado statute requires a hearing within 14 days); Hart, supra note 10 at 12–13; Herrell & Hofford, supra note 12, at 22; Model St. Code, supra note 5, at s 305.

233. Harrell et al., supra note 25, at 23.

234. Hart, supra note 10, at 23; Harrell et al., supra note 25, at 31–32, 36, 59, 63–74 (reporting that violations of restraining orders are reported by over half of the women who obtain them). Harrell et al. found that a large proportion of women failed to seek permanent restraining orders. The most frequently cited reason was that the partner stopped bothering her after issuance of the temporary order. The next most frequently cited reasons were that he could not be located for service of the temporary order, and that he talked her out of obtaining a permanent order. Most men believed that the police or courts would respond if they violated the order and took the order seriously. However, despite provision of criminal sanctions for restraining order violations, men who continued abuse faced low risks of arrest or return to court.

violence cases.[235] For example, judges can facilitate the process of obtaining both temporary and permanent restraining orders by ensuring that women get the legal papers served on the offenders.[236] Accomplishing this objective may necessitate redefining the role of the judge in these proceedings.[237] The judge's role can also be improved by personalizing the orders to fit each victim's needs.[238]

Empirical findings indicate that the majority of offenders violate a restraining order within 1 year of its issuance,[239] and that the severity of pre-order abuse and the intensity of the offender's resistance to the order at the hearing are highly predictive of noncompliance.[240] Consequently, judges are presented with a challenge to insure that their orders are carried out. On the basis of the psychological literature, several suggestions can be made to encourage offenders to comply with the court order.

First, offenders are more likely to comply with restraining orders if they feel that judges are neutral, honest authorities who allow them to state their views and who treat them with dignity.[241] Consequently, if offenders feel respectfully listened to, feel they have greater input into fashioning the order, and view the proceedings as fair, they may be more likely to comply with a court order.

Second, the behavioral psychological technique of contingency contracting[242] may increase compliance by offenders with restraining orders. In a therapeutic setting, this involves the therapist and client entering into a formal agreement wherein they jointly choose the behavioral goals to be achieved and the reinforcement or aversive consequences that the client will receive on

235. The use of permanent restraining orders raises intriguing issues for this area. See Harrell et al., supra note 25, at 41, 76–81 (finding that over 40% of women who obtained a temporary restraining order did not return for a permanent order because they were unable to get the temporary order served on their partners). Due to space limitations, further discussion of permanent restraining orders is omitted here.

236. Id. at 41, 77.

237. Id. at 77 (suggesting that judges could take a leadership role with other agencies and criminal justice players by, for example, encouraging sheriffs to take a more active role in serving these papers). See also, Goldkamp, supra note 40, at 113–14 (describing the modified role of the judge who is part of a treatment team in the Miami Drug Court).

238. Harrell et al., supra note 25, at 78 (noting that typically judges rely on standard forms for all cases with the effect that a large proportion of women feel that the order omits to cover something the victim needs).

239. Id. at 79.

240. Id. at 79; see also Chaudhuri & Daly, in Changing Response, supra note 24, at 227 (showing empirically that a temporary restraining order was less likely to deter offenders with prior criminal records for nonfamily offenses who had substance abuse problems and was unlikely to result in the arrest of the offender when the police were called).

241. See generally E. Allan Lind & Tom R. Tyler, The Social Psychology of Procedural Justice (1988); Tom R. Tyler, Why People Obey the Law (1990) (suggesting that people obey the law because they view it as just and moral; they react to their experiences by evaluating justice or injustice; and in evaluating the justice of their experiences, they consider factors unrelated to outcome, such as whether they have had a chance to state their case and been treated with dignity and respect).

242. See generally Samuel M. Turner et al., Handbook of Clinical Behavior Therapy (1992); John C. Masters, Behavior Therapy (1987); Donald Meichenbaum & Dennis Turk, Facilitating Treatment Adherence: A Practitioner's Guidebook (1987); Winick, supra note 35, at 749.

achievement or nonachievement of those goals.[243] Several conditions increase the effectiveness of these contracts in a therapeutic setting. These include tailoring the agreement to fit individual needs,[244] defining in detail the specific behavior expected of the individual,[245] listing in detail the consequences of compliance or noncompliance,[246] specifying the dates that the contract covers,[247] attaining the individual's commitment to follow the agreement in both oral and written form,[248] and requiring that the individual sign the contract.[249] Such an approach has been suggested for use by judges in order to increase an insanity acquittee's compliance with conditions of release.[250]

Therapeutic jurisprudence principles suggest that judges composing restraining orders might increase compliance by asking offenders to enter into a behavioral contract with the court. The success of this venture would depend on following the guidelines associated with effective agreements. Victims would experience greater feelings of satisfaction with the legal process involved in obtaining the protective order if judges made an effort to tailor each order to fit the needs of the individual victim.[251] In addition to affecting victim satisfaction, specifically tailoring the restraining order can protect women from severe future violence.[252] Judges also need to use clear and unambiguous language in composing restraining orders.[253] Confusion over what is covered by the order can be eliminated by explaining the conditions to the women and specifically tailoring conditions for the men using nonlegal jargon.[254] Finally, judges can benefit from training designed to instill an understanding of the dynamics of domestic violence, the effects of civil orders of protection, and the types of conditions courts may impose in these cases.[255]

---

243. See Wexler, supra note 28, at 199; David B. Wexler, Justice, Mental Health, and Therapeutic Jurisprudence, 40 Clev. St. L. Rev. 517, at 519; Winick, supra note 35, at 749.

244. Meichenbaum & Turk, supra note 242, at 167–68.

245. Id. at 174.

246. Id. at 168.

247. Id. at 170.

248. Id. at 175.

249. Id. at 170.

250. David B. Wexler, Health Care Compliance Principles and the Insanity Acquittee Conditional Release Process, in Essays in Therapeutic Jurisprudence (David B. Wexler & Bruce J. Winick eds., 1991); Wexler, supra note 35, at 199.

251. Harrell et al., supra note 25, at 59, 78 (finding that judges tend to rely on standard restraining order forms in the majority of cases and do not personalize the order).

252. Id. (finding that women are likely to report that the order does not contain all the provisions they want, and that these women are significantly more likely to be at risk for severe violence than women who are satisfied with the order).

253. Harrell et al., supra note 25, at 76 (finding that both men and women report confusion about the content of the order).

254. Harrell et al., supra, note 25, at 78.

255. Judicial abuse in the issuance of mutual restraining orders, even when the batterer has not requested an order, is believed to be a major problem. The argument against the issuance of mutual restraining orders is that doing so perpetuates the historical fallacy that battered women are responsible for the batterer's behavior. Mutual orders of protection are also believed to perpetuate the violence by exonerating the abuser and by giving confusing directions to the police. See Harrell et al., supra note 25, at 80; Schafran, supra note 17, at 284.

Therapeutic objectives can also be accomplished by the police who are called out on restraining order violations. It is recommended that police training and supervision emphasize the importance of arresting offenders who violate valid restraining orders.[256] This training might educate officers about the probable lethal outcomes of their failure to arrest in these cases. Not arresting and prosecuting such offenders encourages them to violate the law in the future and makes a mockery of the legal system. Nonenforcement by the police also can reduce a woman's sense of empowerment and safety that accompanied obtaining the order in the first place. If victims view restraining orders as an exercise in futility, they are less likely to turn to the legal system for help in the future.

VI. Conclusion

Ample research indicates that the laws, policies, and legal actors involved in domestic violence cases can achieve iatrogenic or therapeutic effects on both offenders and victims. This article explored the ways in which the legal system reinforces maladaptive behavior by offenders and victims, and how it can influence changes in such behavior through legal mechanisms. Where empirical research was found to address these issues, it was cited. However, in most cases, empirical research is not being carried out to prove the assertions that were made. This is an area where behavioral scientists can empirically demonstrate ways in which the law can improve the legal processing of domestic violence cases. For example, researchers may want to investigate the role of plea bargains and sentencing dispositions in domestic violence cases because the manner in which a case is disposed of in court can affect the way domestic violence offenders and victims view their roles in the violence. There is an argument that allowing an offender to plead guilty to a lesser charge can reinforce his cognitive distortions about the seriousness of his behavior. Other fertile ground for research is a scientific comparison of the therapeutic effects of legal sanctions and more traditional therapeutic modalities in reducing future domestic violence because there is preliminary evidence that legal sanctions have a consistent effect in reducing future violence in these cases. Future studies would need to measure the probable serial nature of domestic violence and include multiple violent offender-victim dyads. Also of interest would be an examination of how well domestic violence legislation is implemented as well as the responsiveness of the criminal justice system to women who attempt to avail themselves of support services.

Because the article focused on offenders and victims in domestic violence cases, only minimal attention was paid to the consequences for children in these relationships. Future scholarly writing needs to address these issues more fully. Such investigations might examine the effects of legal decisions on children of violent couples—for example, in child custody and visitation matters.[257] Other

---

256. Harrell et al., supra note 25, at 78.

257. See Naomi R. Cahn, Civil Images of Battered Women: The Impact of Domestic Violence on Child Custody Decisions, 44 Vand. L. Rev. 1041, 1082 (1991) (arguing that unless courts consider the impact of parental violence on the child, their custody decisions will not

future research could investigate the effects on children whose mothers are incarcerated for killing a battering spouse. Furthermore, given that battered women have posttraumatic stress disorder symptoms and are likely to abuse their children, the effect of battered woman treatment on the well-being of her children might provide interesting information on the possible prevention of psychopathology and violent behavior among children.

be in the best interest of the child); McCord, supra note 113, at 233 (suggesting that future studies might look at whether legal interventions have contributed to the increase in homeless families: Such assessments could include measures of the family's welfare over a period of at least 1 year); Tomkins et al., supra note 36, at 179–183 (suggesting that a man who batters his wife could be charged with child abuse of the children who witnessed it).

Chapter 14

Teen Court: A Therapeutic Jurisprudence Perspective

Allison R. Shiff
David B. Wexler

Introduction

Youths under 18 currently account for more than 16% of all arrests in this country;[1] since 1989, referrals to Tucson, Arizona's juvenile court have increased by 53%;[2] in Raleigh, North Carolina, more than twice as many juveniles were transferred to adult superior court in 1994 than in 1993.[3] Such devastating statistics reveal the continued allure of drugs, guns, and fast money to the modern American teen. Since the typical offender embarks on his criminal career at age 14 and continues into his early 20s, early intervention is imperative.[4]

To combat this epidemic, teen courts offer an alternative to juvenile courts for teens who commit their first misdemeanors. These courts are intended to serve as effective intervention and prevention programs, with both social and economic objectives: to turn troubled kids around before becoming hardened criminals and to reduce the number of criminals, imprisoned at costs approaching $50,000 a year.[5] The original teen court, the model for more than 70 cities throughout the country, originated in 1983 in Odessa, Texas.[6] There are now approximately 30 courts in Texas and 150 nationwide.[7] While costs of the programs range from $30,000/year in Odessa, Texas, to over $87,000/year in Tucson, Arizona, these figures are still substantially less than the cost of processing the same youths through the juvenile court system.

---

1. CBS Evening News: Las Vegas Teen Crime Being Tried in Teen Courts (CBS television broadcast, Dec. 27, 1994).

2. Edward L. Cook, Volunteers Needed for Teen Court Work, Ariz. Daily Star, Jan. 1, 1995, at B2.

3. Jaleh Hagigh, Record Number of Juveniles Tried as Adults in '94, The News and Observer, Jan. 13, 1995, at B1.

4. Roger Tatarian, In This Court, Teens Truly Face Jury of Peers, Fresno Bee, Feb. 19, 1995, at B5.

5. Tatarian, supra note 4.

6. CBS This Morning: Recap of CBS This Morning's News (CBS television broadcast, Dec. 28, 1994).

7. Carol Masciola, Teen Courts Taking Off on Success in L.A., Texas, The Orange County Register, June 1, 1995; Donnette Dunbar, Kids Face Peers in Teen Court, The Omaha World-Herald 1, March 18, 1996.

Teen courts employ positive peer pressure in an attempt to divert these first-time offenders from becoming career criminals. Teen jurors demand a high level of responsibility from their peers; since jurors know the pressures teens face, they also know that these pressures can be resisted. Judge Pro Tem Karen S. Adam agrees that in Tucson's teen court, "[t]he kids tend to be harder on each other than adults would be...[t]hey really want their peers to be held accountable."[8] This hands-on participation in the legal process can benefit teens by socializing them and aiding in the adaptation of appropriate behaviors.[9]

Teen courts have implemented these goals through a variety of formats. The two most common formats employed are: (1) the typical court format, with a teen prosecutor and a teen defense attorney presenting the case to a teen jury, and (2) the grand jury format, in which a teen presents his own case and is questioned by the jury, typically composed of 6 or 12 teens.[10] In either scenario the only adult present, besides the defendant's parent, is the volunteer judge facilitating the proceedings. A suggested variation, discussed later, might build on these formats by providing a teen attorney to represent the victim.

Teen court's allure is that it teaches juveniles the consequences of breaking the law while keeping their records clear of criminal violations. To prevent abuse of the system, most teen courts are limited to first-time offenses that involve relatively mild transgressions.[11] Typical referrals to the courts include misdemeanors such as vandalism, shoplifting, assault, disorderly conduct, graffiti, and possession and consumption of alcohol.

In addition to limiting participation to first-time offenders, most teen courts require that the offender first admit guilt and agree to accept the judgment. Sentences usually involve community service, but may also require long essays, formal apologies to victims, restitution for damages, traffic survival school, after-school tutoring programs, self-esteem workshops, drug and alcohol counseling, and conflict mediation programs.

Tucson's teen court imposes three mandatory sentences on all offenders: a basic training class (a parent-child program which focuses on self-esteem, communication skills, and decision-making), at least one jury duty service, and at least one letter of apology. The jury determines who receives such letters, but more than one letter is typically required as part of a sentence (i.e., shoplifting may require apology letters to both the store and the defendant's parents). An offender typically has sixty days to complete his sentence.[12] Once completed, the charges are expunged from his record.

---

8. Cook, supra note 2; Brent Trinacty, Teen Court Convenes, Tuscon Citizen, Jan. 28, 1995, at A1.

9. Gary B. Melton, Children as Legal Actors, in D.K. Kagehiro & W.S. Laufer, Handbook of Psychology and Law 275–291 (New York: Springer-Verlag, 1992).

10. Nancy Weil, Teenagers' Court Does Justice to Education, St. Petersburg Times, Feb. 7, 1995, at 5; There are several variations on these models. In Fresno's teen court, the defendant presents his own case and the probation officer presents the state's. Peer jurors then question the defendant and his parents. Tatarian, supra note 4.

11. Mary Doclar, Teen Court Teaches Lessons Early, Ft. Worth Star Telegram, Jan. 2, 1995, at 11.

12. Failure to complete the sentence results in the case's referral back to the juvenile court system.

The Process, the Participants, and Preliminary Results

Teen courts focus on changing future behavior of the primary player, the defendant. The teen jurors and the teen attorneys, however, are equally crucial to the teen court concept.

Defendants

An Illinois court illustrates the typical process for defendants who participate in teen courts: a youth who commits a crime is given the opportunity to attend teen court by the state's attorneys, police, probation, or school officials; the youth must admit guilt prior to attending teen court; the youth appears in front of teen jurors and lawyers with a parent/guardian; jurors hand down a sentence under the supervision of an adult judge; the defendant apologizes to the victim and serves his sentence; after completing the sentence, the youth returns to teen court as a juror; if the defendant rejects or fails to complete the sentence, the case reverts to juvenile court.[13]

Before the teen may participate in the teen court process, a parent must sign an agreement to comply with the rules (such as attendance at parenting classes and, for teens found in possession, attendance at drug and alcohol classes). If the parent fails to follow through with any aspect of the contract, the case is sent back to juvenile court.

Jurors

Juries are composed of both former defendants and teen volunteers, but no specific ratio between the two is required. Certain courts do, however, impose some restrictions. For example, one Los Angeles court requires that jurors not attend the same school as defendants or know the youth they are sentencing.[14]

Former defendants whose sentences include jury duty must select their trial dates at their exit interviews. The rest of the jury slots are then filled with volunteers. Prior to service, jurors must complete a training session, which includes a mock trial observation. Volunteers are attracted through the media and through presentations at local schools.

Attorneys

Students participate in training sessions to become attorneys, learning the basic philosophies and duties of their roles. The judicial system's professionals who run these sessions emphasize the importance of fairness and confidentiality.[15] In addition to these overriding concepts, teens are advised as to practical

12. `Good' Peer Pressure Sought in Proceedings of Teen Court, State Journal-Register (Springfield, Ill.), Jan. 23, 1995, at 18.

14. Andrea Gerlin, Teenage Defendants Get Juries of Their Peers, Wall St. J., June 3, 1994, at B1.

15. Brent Trinacty, supra n.8.

matters: they are taught to project their voices, bring notebooks and pens, spend time preparing prior to court, and to maintain eye contact with the jurors. Practicing attorneys also assist teens in analyzing cases by helping identify aggravating and mitigating circumstances.

Results

While juvenile courts have been in operation for years, teen courts are asserted to be a more effective means of deterring and rehabilitating youths who commit minor crimes. Teen courts boast a long list of benefits over the current juvenile justice system for teens charged with minor offenses: they lighten the juvenile justice system's load, provide community service volunteers, process cases more quickly and cheaply, result in very low rates of recidivism, discourage juvenile delinquency, reduce street crime, and educate teens about the legal system.

Further, the passion exhibited by teens representing other teens cannot be duplicated by adults who have worked in the system for years. One of teen court's primary benefits is that participants take their work seriously; cases that might be overlooked in the regular court system are given thorough attention by teens. A teen lawyer remarked, "I take it very seriously. I pay attention to every single case because there's a kid's life at stake here."[16] The program coordinator added, "They do a lot of research, a lot of calling—school police, Highway Patrol, mothers, sisters, teachers and anybody else—to find out the true story."[17]

Statistics reveal that rates of recidivism from teen courts are impressively low: Las Vegas has not had a single repeat offender from a teen court participant;[18] a teen court in Gila County, Arizona, noted a drop in teen recidivism from 45% to 12%;[19] only 17 out of 107 defendants in Denver have re-offended, mostly involving minor violations;[20] only 3% of juveniles who appeared before teen court in Los Angeles County have been re-arrested;[21] and finally, 30 teen courts in Texas show a recidivism rate below 5%, versus the 30–50% rate in the state's juvenile courts.[22]

---

16. CBS This Morning: Recap of CBS This Morning's News, supra note 6.

17. Id.

18. Id.

19. Trinacty, supra note 8.

20. David J. Chaffee, Note, Teen Court: Empowering Teens to Judge Teens, 22 Colo. Law. 2521 (1993).

21. Teen Court Getting Tough About Crime, Orange County Register, Dec. 27, 1994, at A16.

22. Recidivism statistics touting teen courts must, however, be read with some caution. Teen courts do not get into hard-core cases where correction is less likely. Teen court is limited to defendants who have committed their first minor crimes; these defendants usually participate because they desire to clear their records. This self-selection may be a reason that teen courts have resulted in lower rates of recidivism. Therefore, it is not surprising that these teens who commit their first minor offenses are less likely than juvenile court defendants to re-offend in the future. Comparing rates of recidivism from the two courts may actually be comparing rates for conscientious juveniles committing their first-time misdemeanors with teens embarking on their criminal careers.

Looking Through the Lens of Therapeutic Jurisprudence

This article proposes to use therapeutic jurisprudence to look at teen courts through a somewhat different lens. Therapeutic jurisprudence is a discipline which looks at the therapeutic impact of the law on the various participants involved. Legal rules, legal procedures, and the roles of legal actors constitute social forces that often produce therapeutic or antitherapeutic consequences; therapeutic jurisprudence challenges us to reduce antitherapeutic consequences, and to enhance therapeutic consequences, without subordinating due process and other justice values.[23] Examining teen court through a therapeutic jurisprudence lens may help us to analyze and further develop the use of this decisionmaking body.

In teen courts, the principal player targeted by the process is clearly the defendant. The jurors, teen attorneys, and victims are, however, also likely to be affected by the process.

The Defendants and Defense Attorneys

Defendants who participate in teen courts may be influenced, and perhaps in part rehabilitated, by such peer review. Confronting defendants with a jury of their peers helps promote the acceptance of responsibility; this positive peer pressure seems to work. Falls River, Mass. City Council President Steven Camara explains, "When I was young...if an authority figure rendered a punishment, I always felt resentful. But when my peers caused me discomfort, I felt, 'What can I do to make them accept me?' As a teen, you want to be accepted by your group."[24]

Teen defendants seem more likely to take responsibility for their actions when they feel that the triers of fact understand them. Peer review in this forum provides defense attorneys with the unique opportunity to confront their clients with possible juror perceptions of the facts.[25] In addition, this socially-aware jury is better able to question a teen's motives. Teen juror Claire Skipper, 16, of Saugus, California, commented that teen court has jurors who "can smell a lie...[a] teen-ager can sense when another teen-ager is lying... [t]hey know how real teens are."[26] Therefore, teen courts encourage defendants to put themselves in jurors' shoes, take responsibility for their actions, and understand how society views their crimes.

---

23. David B. Wexler & Bruce J. Winick, Essays in Therapeutic Jurisprudence (Carolina Academic Press, 1991). David B. Wexler & Bruce J. Winick, Therapeutic Jurisprudence as a New Approach to Mental Health Law Policy Analysis and Research, 45 U. Miami L. Rev. 979, 981 (1991).

24. Linda Borg, Teen Court Program Proposed, Providence J. Bull., July 7, 1995, at D01.

25 If regularly employed by defense attorneys, this form of cognitive restructuring by confrontation may help to promote a defendant's acceptance of responsibility.

26. Laurence Darmiento, Teen Court to Start in Newhall, L.A. Daily News, July 31, 1995.

Teen courts engage in individualized sentencing, with rehabilitation as an important objective. Further, including jury duty in an offender's sentence helps emphasize the former offender's membership in law-abiding society, allowing him to view the system from the other side. Teen courts can therefore be effective in preventing the negative effects of a "delinquent" label from channeling a teen towards a criminal career;[27] sentences provide a two-way street which allow offenders to turn back once they have repaid the community.

The role of the defense attorney may also be therapeutic for the defense attorneys themselves. In providing teens with the opportunity to defend their peers, defense attorneys may gain a better understanding of some of the underlying reasons teens may be driven to crime. Many teen defense attorneys incorporate these underlying influences into their oral arguments as mitigating factors.[28] By illustrating the way society views the offenders, this interaction may be therapeutic in "inoculating" the attorneys from their own future entanglement with the law and in rehabilitating former defendants who serve as defense attorneys.

But the defendant/defense attorney interaction also poses potential problems. Teen defense attorneys may misconstrue their role as one in which they must re-characterize the crime to try to achieve the least possible sentence. A defense attorney's effort to minimize the offense, in an attempt to minimize the penalty, may impede a defendant's acceptance of responsibility.

When a defense attorney focuses solely on striving for the least possible sentence—by accepting a defendant's story at face value, by mischaracterizing the crime, or by portraying the defendant as the victim—this approach may conflict with the court's general goal of rehabilitating defendants (and of propelling the teen attorney along a responsible law-abiding and law-respecting path). In seeking to minimize the defendant's sentence, defense attorneys may forego the opportunity to confront their clients with their crimes. Accepting a defendant's statements at face value, without further questioning, may add to the defendant's resistance and inhibit the courts' effectiveness in deterring future criminal behavior.[29] Mischaracterization is also a problem in the courts. One teen defense attorney instructed her client, "You have to look like a perfect angel," emphasizing the importance of appearing innocent, rather than taking responsibility for her actions.

A related problem results when defense attorneys characterize the perpetrators as victims, overemphasizing mitigating circumstances or a less-than-perfect home life. This coincides with the popular trend in today's society of

27. Bruce J. Winick, The Side Effects of Incompetency Labeling and the Implications for Mental Health Law, 1 Psychol., Pub. Pol'y & L. (1995); Chris Patterson, Bay County Bar Forwards Teens Court as Juvenile Sanction Alternative, 69 Oct. Fla. B.J. 95 (1995).

28. In one case, while prosecutors claimed that a teen "should have known better than to succumb to peer pressure," defense attorneys responded that the teen is "a good student with no previous alcohol problems," and is both "ashamed and sorry for her actions." Carmen Duarte, Teen Court Staff Tests Its Judgment, Meting Out Punishment to 'Defendant,' Ariz. Daily Star, Jan. 22, 1995, at B1.

29. David B. Wexler & Robert F. Schopp, Therapeutic Jurisprudence: A New Approach to Mental Health Law, in D.K. Kagehiro & W.S. Laufer, Handbook of Psychology and Law 361–378 (Springer-Verlag, 1992).

shirking responsibility for our actions by claiming to be a victim, rather than seeking out solutions to our problems.[30]

One possible way to avoid the defendant's denial of responsibility is to begin the trial by having the judge and jury ask the defendant to reaffirm his admission of guilt. Such an admission, after all, is a prerequisite to participation in teen court. If the defendant refuses to take full responsibility for his actions in front of the jury, the case may then be sent back to juvenile court.

An additional way to avoid such antitherapeutic results is to modify the role of teen defense attorneys, changing the role of the attorneys to one of affirmatively proposing and justifying acceptable sentences. Having the defendant assist his attorney in proposing an appropriate sentence is an additional method of confronting the defendant with his acts and giving him a sense of voice in designing the appropriate penalty.

People regard the decision-making process as being more fair when they are allowed to participate. Thus, this modified role for attorneys, and for attorney-client interaction, should not only help the defendant take responsibility for his actions, but should also provide him with a more positive view of the system as a whole.[31] Adherence to such sentences should then be heightened by the defendant's active involvement in designing and negotiating his or her own sentence.[32]

The Jury

Teens pass barbecue chips and Goobers around the table while debating the appropriate sentence for a defendant. Having teens as jurors in this setting brings both law-abiding and former law-breaking teens face-to-face with some of the toughest issues in the juvenile crime debate. How much punishment is appropriate for a young boy/girl? How can a teen be turned away from crime?

Participation as a teen juror may benefit both the court and the teen juror. Teen juries, like adult juries, serve several important functions: 1) by placing the verdict in the hands of a group of impartial individuals, the jury system works to enhance accuracy in developing an appropriate sentence;[33] 2) by including community members who are independent of the formal judicial structure, the jury system legitimizes the process and strives to increase offender compliance;[34] and 3) by educating jurors, the jury system informs teens as to

---

30. Martha Minow, Surviving Victim Talk, 40 UCLA L. Rev. 1411 (1993).

31. Tom R. Tyler, Why People Obey the Law (Yale University Press, 1990).

32. David B. Wexler, Therapeutic Jurisprudence and the Criminal Courts, 35 Wm. & Mary L. Rev. 279, 292 (1993). See also David B. Wexler, Some Therapeutic Jurisprudence Implications of the Outpatient Civil Commitment of Pregnant Substance Abusers, Politics and the Life Sciences 24 (February, 1996) (in press); Tom R. Tyler, The Psychological Consequences of Judicial Procedures: Implications for Civil Commitment Hearings, 46 SMU L. Rev. 433 (1992).

33. Glenn Newman, Note, The Summary Jury Trial as a Method of Dispute Resolution in the Federal Courts, 1990 U. Ill. L. Rev. 177, 182 (1990).

34. Herbert Jacob, Justice in America: Courts, Lawyers and the Judicial Process 125–36 (Little, Brown, 3d ed. 1978); Daniel W. Shuman, et al., "The Health Effects of Jury Service," 18 Law & Psychol. Rev. 267, 280 (1994).

the inner-workings of the judicial system and enhances jurors' attitudes of the system's fairness.[35]

Just as allowing defendants input in proposing their own sentences should increase their satisfaction with and respect for the process, allowing teens to participate as jurors may also give them a greater sense of respect for the judicial system.[36] Granting impartial teens a "voice" in teen justice may then increase their perceived fairness of such a system and encourage them to obey the law in the future. The process may therefore operate to rehabilitate former defendants serving as jurors and may, at the same time, "inoculate" others on the jury from committing similar crimes.

Further, allowing teens to serve as jurors instills in them a sense of confidence. In an age when teens constantly feel criticized, positive statements from adults increase teens' self-respect and self-esteem. Teen courts provide positive attention adolescents need. Nik Stanworth, 17, from Santa Ana, California enjoys serving on juries, explaining, "When you are up there you feel older, more mature."[37]

The courts' impact on teen jurors—by discouraging them from committing similar offenses and by educating them about the court system—may be substantial.[38] Educating teens about the legal system can be significant in legal socialization. Citizens' rights mean more to those who understand, experience, and appreciate the entitlement of such freedoms;[39] legal socialization theorists emphasize the impact of experiential variables over didactic instruction of legal concepts.[40] Melton has hypothesized that legal-socializing effects result from participation in legal decisionmaking, especially if a conflict of ideas is involved and if constructs are linked to everyday decisions.[41] Teen courts can teach legal socialization in a practical and useful context. Therefore, teen courts can help teens to better understand their role as future legal decision makers and as law-abiding citizens.

Allowing juries to be composed of both teen volunteers and former defendants (serving as part of their sentences) poses potential problems; these former defendants may be excessively tough on new offenders.[42] However, having the opportunity to be tough on new offenders may, in turn, make teens tougher on themselves when confronted with future challenges. Although some courts require a unanimous verdict, the judge may determine the appropriate sentence if the teens are unable to come to an agreement.

---

35. Daniel W. Shuman, et al., Jury Service Perceptions of Fairness of Jurors and Nonjurors, 46 SMU L. Rev. 449, 468 (1992).

36. Tyler, supra note 31.

37. Leslie Berkman, A Jury of Their Peers, L.A. Times, June 1, 1995, at 1.

38. Jury service promotes positive behavior by allowing teens to understand how society views the perpetrators of crime. Orange County Superior Court Judge James P. Gray expressed that, "We know full well some of the jurors have probably done the same things as the perpetrator, so we are showing them as well that it isn't appropriate." Berkman, supra note 37.

39. Gary B. Melton, The Significance of Law in the Everyday Lives of Children and Families, 22 Ga. L. Rev. 851, 889–890 (1988).

40. Melton, supra note 9 at 285.

41. Melton, supra note 9 at 286.

42. To avoid this possibility, any sentence must be approved by the judge overseeing the proceedings.

While having such control over a peer's future may be positive in empowering teens, jurors often catch a slight case of megalomania. This suggests that, in addition to providing for a more defined composition of former defendants to volunteers, limits should be set on how many times a juror may be allowed to serve.[43]

Prosecuting attorneys

The role of the prosecuting attorney , in emphasizing that teens should be held accountable for their actions regardless of a bad background or other extenuating circumstances, may be therapeutic for both the defendant and the attorney. One student prefers the role of the prosecuting attorney, stating, "I've learned a lot of respect for the system."[44]

The role may inoculate at-risk teen attorneys from committing the same crimes and may be particularly effective in rehabilitating former defendants who serve as prosecuting attorneys. Representing the state in such an area should make these participants more law-abiding and break through teens' possible inclination to minimize the effects of committing criminal acts.

The downside of the role of the prosecuting attorney is that teen attorneys often think they are required to mischaracterize defendants or their crimes. Such a perception may breed a sense of disrespect for the judicial system. It is in this role, especially, that the danger of courtroom dramatics may lead to defendant-badgering in a teen's effort to emulate his television counterparts.[45] To combat this, the importance of truthful representation and "doing justice" must be key points emphasized in legal training.[46]

Victims

Because teen courts are limited to minor crimes, the cases do not typically involve traumatized victims. Nonetheless, the courts currently involve victims in the process through the commonly-used penalties of apologies and restitution to the victim. Such involvement is likely to help defendants and jurors develop empathy for crime victims, and it is likely to have a beneficial effect on victims' mental health.[47]

---

43. For instance, volunteers might be permitted to serve once, former defendants, twice. If teens desire future involvement in the courts, these veteran jurors could serve as victims' attorneys in the proposed structure, discussed later, which includes representation of victims.

44. Angel Hernandez, The Young Arm of the Law, Rocky Mtn. News, Dec. 28, 1994, at A30.

45. One teen stated that "We have to bring out the worst in them, as terrible as it seems." Another added "We are supposed to make them look like a loathsome criminal." Doclar, supra note 11.

46. See Brady v. Maryland, 373 U.S. 83(1963).

47. See Richard P. Wiebe, The Mental Health Implications of Crime Victims' Rights, in Law, Mental Health, and Mental Disorder 414 (B. Sales & D.

Shuman, eds.) (Brooks/Cole, 1996). For more on apology, see Bruce Feldthusen, The Civil Action for Sexual Battery: Therapeutic Jurisprudence?, 25 Ottawa L. Rev. 203 (1993); Daniel W. Shuman, The Psychology of Compensation in Tort Law, 43 U. Kansas L. Rev. 39 (1994).

A Proposal: Victims' Rights and Empathy Training Through Law

Teen court coordinators should consider introducing into teen court some elements of the adult arena's growing victim rights movement. Such reforms basically fall into three areas: victim compensation, victim satisfaction, and victim impact.[48]

Victim compensation reforms are typically designed to provide victims restitution for their harm. This component has already been integrated into the courts by sentences involving monetary restitution and penalties aimed at compensating the harm caused by the defendant. Victim satisfaction reforms typically enable victims to be more comfortable in their interactions with the criminal justice system. Since victims of teen-court crimes are not typically traumatically affected by these misdemeanors, this component need not play as great a role in teen courts. Allowing the victims to participate in the process may nonetheless help victims by indicating to them that the criminal justice system takes care of their needs.

Victim impact reforms, those which allow victims to have a voice in criminal proceedings, can beneficially be introduced into teen courts. An example of such a reform would give victims the right to provide the court with victim impact statements. These statements could include victim testimony regarding the economic, psychological, or social effects the crime has had on the victim. The very preparation and presentation of such statements should be therapeutically beneficial for the victims: a substantial body of psychological research suggests that positive healing effects (in terms of mental and physical health) are derived from writing and speaking about negative emotional events.[49] The victim impact statement should, of course, then be used as a factor in the sentence imposed by the jurors. Moreover, by considering the crime from the vantage point of the victim, which would be part-and-parcel of proposing and setting an appropriate sentence, the defendant, the teen attorneys, and the teen jurors should all learn better to empathize with crime victims—and the conventional wisdom holds that empathy is a crucial component in law-abiding behavior.[50]

---

48. See Wiebe, supra note 47.

49. James W. Pennebaker, Opening Up: The Healing Power of Confiding in Others (William Morrow & Co., 1990).

50. In addition to impact statements, other ways to incorporate this empathy component are to: 1) videotape all victims affected by the defendant's behavior, play these videotapes for the court, and have the defendant's letter of apology include a summary of the crime from the victim's perspective; 2) have victims testify as part of the trial and ask the defendant to address this testimony in his letter of apology; 3) have the victim testify and the defendant explain how and why a crime was committed, along with the defendant's apology; and 4) have defendants examine the list of possible sentences and suggest and justify an appropriate sentence for the crime.

For more on empathy, and on its relation to relapse prevention in sex offenders, see W.L. Marshall, Assessment, Treatment, and Theorizing About Sex Offenders: Developments During the Past Twenty Years and Further Directions, 23 Criminal Justice and Behavior 162, 173 74, 183, 185–86 (1996). Much more work needs to be performed on the development of empathy in adolescents and on its role in turning teens away from delinquent behavior. For a recent review of the rehabilitation literature in general, see Paul Gendreau, Offender

An important role for empathy training in teen courts is suggested by recent victim-empathy work relating to "relapse prevention" treatment.[51] William Pithers, a prison psychologist who developed a "perspective-taking" therapy in the context of working with child molesters, explains, "[E]mpathy with the victim shifts perception so that the denial of pain, even in one's fantasies, is difficult."[52] Teaching a former offender empathy for his victim helps combat his distorted thinking about his crime and its effect on the victim, motivating him to resist the temptation to repeat his crime.

Pithers attempts to convey victim empathy through a variety of processes:

> The offenders read heart-wrenching accounts of crimes like their own, told from the victim's perspective. They also watch videotapes of victims tearfully telling what it was like to be molested. The offenders then write about their own offense from the victim's point of view, imagining what the victim felt. They read this account to a therapy group and try to answer questions about the assault from the victim's perspective. Finally, the offender goes through a simulated reenactment of the crime, this time playing the role of the victim.[53]

While some courts currently focus on developing victim empathy by use of mandatory apology letters and restitution tailored to the crime, we believe the emphasis on empathy can perhaps best be expanded by the appointment of a third teen attorney in the process—a *victim's* attorney. A teen attorney could represent the victim, help prepare a victim impact statement, brief the victim for testifying, or help prepare a videotaped interview and impact statement.

The role of victim's attorney could itself be particularly therapeutic for at-risk teens—and for former *defendants* (who, in addition to being sentenced to serve on a teen jury, might also be sentenced to serve as victim's attorney in the future). Serving in the real-life role of victim attorney would force the teen to identify with the crime victim's perspective—seemingly accomplishing, through the operation of the legal system itself, something closely akin to the "perspective-taking" empathy therapy proposed by Pithers. Since lack of empathy appears to be a major factor in the development of criminal behavior, the use of the legal system to teach empathy to youths may be a particularly fruitful enterprise—perhaps even more fruitful than teaching empathy to adult offenders who lack it.

Conclusion

The teen court concept is interesting and important. Although preliminary recidivism statistics must be read cautiously, teen court may well prove to be a highly therapeutic tool, especially if fine-tuned to increase victim participation and if honed to exploit its potential for teaching empathy.

Rehabilitation: What We Know and What Needs to be Done, 23 Criminal Justice and Behavior 144 (1996).

51. Daniel Goleman, Therapies Offer Hope for Sex Offenders, New York Times, April 14, 1992, at C1. Used with child molesters, such treatment has proved promising, resulting in half as many of its participants reoffending when compared with those not treated with empathy therapy.

52. Daniel Goleman, Emotional Intelligence 107 (Bantam Books, 1995).

53. Id.

In fact, the concept is so intriguing that we ought to explore the possibility of increasing teen involvement—and extensive victim participation—in *ordinary* juvenile court. To be sure, teens could not be the principal participants or decisionmakers in such courts, but that does not prevent the use of teens (including former defendants participating as part of a sentence) as "advisory juries" on adjudication or disposition, or as legal assistants to attorneys representing the state, the defense, or victims.

The teen court model described here seems to share some important features with the Continental criminal justice system, where: a decisionmaking body, composed of a judge and "lay assessors," actively interacts with and questions the defendant; where the defendant is encouraged to accept responsibility; where the victim, as well as the state and the defendant, is represented by an attorney; and where the sentencing structure permits the judge and lay assessors to impose a sentence geared at least in part toward rehabilitation.[54] As therapeutic jurisprudence increases its comparative law focus,[55] we should explicitly explore other legal models and consider whether we might be able to increase our rehabilitative yield by importing certain features of other systems without sacrificing justice-related objectives.[56] (Indeed, such a comparative law focus may result also in other nations considering the feasibility of modifying their own systems to incorporate certain features of American law, such as teen court.) In any event, perhaps we should think creatively about "rejuvenating" juvenile court instead of, as some are proposing, simply throwing in the towel and abolishing it.[57]

54. Myron Moskovitz, The O.J. Inquisition: A United States Encounter with Continental Criminal Justice, 28 Vand. J. Transnational Law 973 (1995).

55. E.g., David Carson, Therapeutic Jurisprudence for the United Kingdom?, 6 J. Forensic Psychiatry 463 (1995).

56. David B. Wexler, Justice, Mental Health, and Therapeutic Jurisprudence, 40 Cleveland State L. Rev. 517 (1992). See generally Symposium: Comparative Criminal Justice Issues in the United States, West Germany, England, and France, 42 Maryland L. Rev. 1 (1983). For a summary of the empirical research regarding accuracy and perceived fairness in adversary, inquisitorial, and hybrid decisionmaking methods, see Mark R. Fondacaro, Toward a Synthesis of Law and Social Science: Due Process and Procedural Justice in the Context of National Health Care Reform, 72 Denver Univ. L. Rev. 303, 325–37 (1995). American behavioral science, as well as American law, needs to transcend its national boundaries. See Gendreau, supra note 50, at 152 ("More blatant examples of ethnocentrism are the fact that American reviews on treatment effectiveness almost never reference the literature from foreign countries where different approaches to the 'crime problem' exist (e.g., less incarceration).")

57. See Martha Minow, What Ever Happened to Children's Rights?, 80 Minn. L. Rev. 267, 291 & n. 138 (1995).

Chapter 15

The Duty of the State to Rescue
the Vulnerable in the United States

Daniel W. Shuman

1 Introduction: The Wrong Question

The debate over the duty to rescue has been eclipsed by concerns about the obligations of private citizens,[1] yet, with the possible exception of privately employed emergency medical personnel, few private citizens regularly encounter people threatened with immediate and substantial harm by disasters of natural or human origin who look to them for rescue. Rather, it is from the state, through its law enforcement, fire fighting and social service agencies, that those in peril regularly seek assistance. Thus any discussion of the duty to come to the aid of another in peril that did not address the duty of the state to rescue vulnerable members of society would be incomplete.

The discussion in Chapters 1 and 2 [of the book from which the present chapter has been drawn] focuses on the arguments that underlie the common law rule on failing to recognise a duty to come to the aid of another in peril. These arguments deal with the problems inherent in defining the extent of a duty to rescue and, in the view of some, render a duty to rescue impracticable. If tort law were concerned only with autonomous individuals it might be justified in recognising a duty to avoid intentionally or negligently injuring others and not recognising a duty to rescue. But our society is comprised of autonomous and non-autonomous individuals and tort law must address both. Whatever force these arguments have against a duty to rescue autonomous individuals they do not adequately address the specific problem of vulnerable and dependent persons who may have a claim on the state, even if they have no claim on other private citizens.

In what follows, I look at the problem of one vulnerable group in society, abused children. Although there is an understandable inclination to recognise a duty to rescue abused children, there are dangers with this. Even if the analysis in Chapters 1 and 2 supported a general duty to rescue, this analysis ignores the therapeutic dimension of the duty to rescue. Rescue proceeds on the assumption that it will be therapeutic; we encourage rescue because we think it will be beneficial to the physical or emotional health of the person rescued. If

---

1. James B. Ames, 'Law and Morals', 22 Harvard Law Review, 97 (1908); Frances Bohlen, 'The Moral Duty to Aid Others as a Basis of Tort Law', 56 University of Pennsylvania Law Review, 217 (1908); Saul Levmore, 'Waiting for Rescue: An Essay on the Evolution and Incentive Structure of the Law of Affirmative Obligations', 72 Virginia Law Review, 879 (1986); Ernest J. Weinrib, 'The Case for a Duty to Rescue', 90 Yale Law Journal, 247 (1980).

legal intervention on behalf of abused children lacks a likely therapeutic outcome, then a duty to rescue may leave children worse off than if no intervention had occurred.

2   *The Traditional Rule*

2.1   The Odds Always Favour the House

It is not particularly surprising that the state which creates the law, albeit
democratically, has not chosen to impose upon itself a duty to come to the aid
of its citizens. The state is, in the final analysis, interested in the perpetuation
of the state. In the United States the state[2] has the right, but not an inherent
duty, to come to the aid of vulnerable populations.

The absence of an inherent duty of the state to come to the aid of vulnerable populations has its roots in the failure to recognise an inherent structural
or constitutional obligation on the part of the state to provide for the health or
economic security of its citizens. The United States Constitution is a written
document that establishes the contours of the relationship between the state
and the individual. It limits the powers of the state over the individual, but imposes no affirmative burden on the state to aid the individual.[3] The state is not
obliged, for example, to provide health care, housing or payments for unemployment, old age or disability. These programmes do exist, but the decision to
provide for them is controlled by democratic politics rather than constitutional
mandate. This results in a patchwork of programmes and services that provide
for people who fit various uncoordinated categorical limitations. For example,
while there is no national health insurance in the United States, there are separate health care programmes for the poor, the elderly, veterans and Native
Americans.[4] The scope and extent of these programmes are a function of the
financial fortunes and largesse of the state at a given time.

The constitutional or structural limitations imposed on these programmes
are proscriptive, not prescriptive. The state need not act to aid its citizens, but

---

2. The term 'state' has multiple meanings in the United States. It may refer to the 50 states
that comprise the United States and it may also refer to the government—federal, state and
local—in its entirety. The unique nature of federalism in the United States involving a sharing of power between the federal and state governments and the distinct roles each plays in
social welfare programmes renders the distinction one of consequence. However, given the
space and scope limitations of this chapter, I have chosen to lump the federal and state governments together in my use of the word 'state' and treatment of the duty to rescue except
where I have explicitly indicated otherwise.

3. Although scholars have challenged this negative view of the constitution, the courts
have maintained its viability. See Susan Bandes, 'The Negative Constitution: A Critique', 88
Michigan Law Review, 2271 (1990). See also Catherine Mackinnon, Feminism Unmodified
(Cambridge, 1987), 207, advancing a feminist critique of the negative constitution.

4. Health Services for the Homeless, 42 U.S.C.A. § 256 (West 1991); Health Services for
Residents of Public Housing, 42 U.S.C.A. § 256a (West 1991); Health Services for Aged and
Disabled, 42 U.S.C.A. §§ 1395–1396ccc (West 1991); Hospital, Nursing Home, Domiciliary,
and Medical Care, 38 U.S.C.A. §§ 1701–1764 (West 1991 & Supp. 1992); Indian Health
Care Improvement Act 25 U.S.C.A. §§ 1601–1682 (West 1983 & Supp. 1992).

if it chooses to do so there are proscriptions that limit its actions. Equal protection and due process considerations largely define the scope of these proscriptions. For example, if the state chooses to provide programmes for dependent populations it may not deny the benefits of those programmes to members of a disfavoured minority.[5] And, although the state need not create a public benefit programme, if it does so it may not withdraw benefits without timely notice and a meaningful opportunity to be heard.[6] State tort law has not recognised a non-constitutionally derived duty to come to the aid of vulnerable citizens, although it has recognised a state's voluntary assumption of a duty to aid its citizens.[7] However, even when a state has voluntarily assumed a duty to aid its citizens, several obstacles stand in the path of a plaintiff seeking recovery for injuries from a breach of that voluntarily assumed duty.

In many states, under the public duty doctrine, whatever duty the state has assumed is construed to be owed to the general public and not to any particular member of the public. This doctrine has been traced to Cooley's 1877 treatise, *Liability of Public Officers*[8] and has been carried forward in his treatise on torts:

> If the duty which the official authority imposes upon an officer is a duty to the public, a failure to perform it, or an inadequate or erroneous performance, must be public, not an individual injury, and must be redressed, if at all, in some form of public prosecution.[9]

The public duty doctrine distinguishes duties owed by a public official to the general public, which can only be enforced by the general public through public prosecution, and duties owed to specific members of the public, which can be enforced by those specific individuals. The public duty doctrine posits a rigid hierarchical distribution of political power; the public may seek redress for public wrongs by public officials only through other public officials. Since statutory duties to provide police and fire protection, for example, are addressed to the public at large, rather than any person in particular, under the public duty doctrine the failure of the police or fire department to provide protection does not give rise to a duty enforceable in tort law by an injured plaintiff.[10] Although the actions of the state may in some instances create a special relationship that narrows the obligation owed to the public to an obligation to a specific individual,[11] other sets of hurdles face a plaintiff seeking recovery for a breach of that duty.

5. Yick Wo v. Hopkins, 118 U.S. 356 (1886).

6. Goldberg v. Kelly, 397 U.S. 254 (1970).

7. W. Page Keeton et al., Prosser and Keeton on the Law of Torts (St. Paul, 5 ed., 1984), § 56.

8. Thomas Cooley, Liability of Public Officers (St. Louis, 1877).

9. Thomas Cooley, A Treatise on the Law of Torts, or the Wrongs Which Arise Independently of Contract (Chicago, 4th ed., 1932), 385.

10. Williams v. State, 34 Cal.3d 18, 664 P.2d 137, 192 Cal. Rptr. 233 (1983); Cuffy v. City of New York, 69 N.Y.2d 255, 505 N.E.2d 937 (1987); Chapman v. Philadelphia, 290 Pa. Super. 281, 434 A.2d 753 (1981).

11. Schuster v. City of New York, 154 N.E.2d 534 (N.Y. 1958).

States may not be sued for their torts without their consent.[12] Although most states have abrogated sovereign immunity, the abrogation is limited to ministerial acts and specifically excludes the exercise of discretionary governmental functions.[13] This limitation is based upon a concern that courts not substitute their own discretion for the government's exercise of discretion under the guise of adjudicating tort claims. Thus, for example, the decision to create a programme in which prisoners are paroled is a discretionary governmental function immune from challenge in a tort action arising out of an injury caused a private citizen by a parolee.[14] Many states have also limited the amount of recovery against the state in any tort action,[15] and many recognise a good faith immunity for official acts.[16]

Although state tort law may support a duty to rescue based upon a special relationship when the state has voluntarily undertaken to engage in a particular activity, the decision to recognise a duty ultimately rests with the state. Because state tort law recognises a duty only when the state voluntarily undertakes an activity, the state can obviate any duty simply by refusing to undertake any effort to rescue.[17] The capacity to decide for whom it should intervene is defined by the state's *parens patriae* power. The right of the state to intervene directly on behalf of the vulnerable and dependent under its *parens patriae* power[18] encompasses the authority to act for the benefit of those who are unable to care for themselves because of age, illness or circumstance. A partial list of these populations includes incapacitated decision makers like Nancy Cruzan[19] and Karen Ann Quinlan,[20] the mentally disabled,[21] unborn

---

12. Both the states and the federal government must compensate owners of property for public takings. Chicago, Burlington & Quincy Ry. Co. v. Chicago, 166 U.S. 226 (1897).

13. Brasel v. Children's Services Div., 56 Or. App. 559, 642 P.2d 696 (1982).

14. State v. Silva, 478 P.2d 591 (Nev. 1970).

15. Or. Rev. Stat. Ann. § 30.270 (1991) ($50,000); Wis. Stat. Ann § 893.80 (West Supp 1989) ($50,000).

16. Mo. Ann. Stat. § 210.135 (Vernon 1983); Ill. Ann. Stat. ch. 23, para. 2059 (Smith-Hurd Supp. 1992); N.Y. Social Services Law § 419 (McKinney Supp. 1992); Fla. Stat. Ann. § 415.511 (West Supp 1992); Minn. Stat. Ann. § 626.536, Subd. 4 (West Supp. 1992): N.C. Gen. Stat. § 7A-550 (1991); N.D. Cent. Code § 50-25.1-09 (1989); S.D. Codified Laws Ann. § 26-8A-14 (1992); Wyo. Stat. § 14-3-209 (1986).

17. See, for example, Indian Towing Co., Inc. v. United States, 350 U.S. 61, 69 (1955) (Coast Guard not obliged to maintain lighthouse service, but if it represents that it maintains a particular lighthouse it is obliged to use due care in maintaining it in good working order).

18. See Hawaii v. Standard Development Co., 405 U.S. 251 (1972); Falkland v. Bertie, 23 Eng. Rep. 815 (Ch. 1696). 'Under this doctrine the sovereign has both the right and the duty to protect the persons and property of those who are unable to care for themselves because of minority or mental illness. In England, the guardianship of those under legal disability was originally intrusted to the feudal lords, but was taken over by the Crown in the 13th century and delegated to the Lord Chancellor. In this country, the royal prerogative was inherited by the individual states and has been held to constitute part of the original jurisdiction of equity courts' (Hugh A. Ross, 'Commitment of the Mentally Ill: Problems in Law and Policy', 57 Michigan Law Review, 945, at 956–7 (1959) (citations omitted)).

19. Cruzan v. Director, Missouri Dept. of Health, 110 S. Ct. 284 (1990).

20. *In re Quinlan*, 335 A.2d 647 (N.J. 1976).

21. Samuel J. Brakel et al., The Mentally Disabled and the Law (Chicago, 1985), 24–5.

foetuses[22] and abused children.[23] I have chosen the case of abused children as a vehicle to examine the state's duty to rescue, for two reasons.

First, abused children clearly do not fit the construct that might be used to justify the no duty to rescue rule. Abused children are not competent adults capable of caring for themselves.[24] The cases of Nancy Cruzan and Karen Ann Quinlan also involve incapacitated decision makers, but are distinguishable. They present the duty of the state *not* to rescue. In those cases the state is an uninvited rescuer; the legal issue presented is the right of the person to refuse to be rescued by the state from the consequences of that person's own decision or lack thereof. In the cases involving abused children the state is an invited rescuer; the legal issue presented is the right of the person to be rescued by the state from the abuse of a third party. What these cases do have in common is the question whether rescue by the state is ultimately therapeutic. Will state intervention be beneficial whether or not it is sought? It is certainly possible to reconstruct the issue presented in cases like *Cruzan* and *Quinlan* to ask whether these individuals have a right to be rescued from themselves or their surrogates, yet this reconstruction so broadens the concept of a duty to rescue as to shift the focus from the issue of rescue to the issue of autonomy. Retaining the focus on the case of abused children avoids the interjection of an interesting but confounding issue in this discussion.

Second, a recent decision of the United States Supreme Court, *DeShaney v. Winnebago County Department of Social Services*,[25] presents a controversial ruling on the duty of the state to rescue abused children in a compelling context.

2.2   DeShaney v. Winnebago County Department of Social Services[26]

DeShaney presented to the United States Supreme Court a civil rights claim of a young boy who was severely beaten by his father following an unsuccessful intervention by the defendant social service agency. Joshua DeShaney's parents were divorced when he was an infant and he was awarded to the custody of his father. Following the divorce, the defendant social service agency received numerous complaints that Joshua was being physically abused by his father. Finally, after Joshua was admitted to a hospital with bruises and abrasions, the agency obtained an order removing Joshua from the home temporarily, but subsequently returned him when an interdisciplinary child protection team concluded that there was insufficient evidence of abuse to retain custody. The agency did, however, obtain an agreement, in conjunction with Joshua's return, that the father would participate in a counselling programme, make changes in family living arrangements and enter Joshua in a pre-school

22. Roe v. Wade, 410 U.S. 113 (1973).

23. Santosky v. Kramer, 455 U.S. 745, 766 (1982); Stanley v. Illinois, 405 U.S. 645 (1972).

24. Robert Burt, 'Forcing Protection on Children and Their Parents: The Impact of Wyman v. James', 69 Michigan Law Review, 1259 (1971).

25. 489 U.S. 189 (1989).

26. Ibid.

programme (Head Start) to monitor his condition. Joshua's father did not fulfil the agreement, the complaints of abuse continued and Joshua made frequent trips to the emergency room for traumatic injuries. The agency made numerous ineffectual inquiries, but did not again seek to remove him from the home. Finally, Joshua's father inflicted injuries on his four-year-old son so severe that Joshua sustained permanent irreversible brain damage requiring life-long care in an institution for the profoundly retarded. Joshua's mother then instituted a federal civil rights claim, as Joshua's guardian, against the social service agency for depriving him of his liberty in violation of the Fourteenth Amendment of the Constitution by failing to protect Joshua.

The Supreme Court affirmed the rulings of the district court and court of appeals rejecting the civil right claim against the county social services agency. It reasoned that Joshua was not constitutionally entitled to protection from the state to prevent abuse by his father. The Court ruled that the Due Process Clause of the Fourteenth Amendment creates no general duty to protect children from parental abuse. The Court rested its doctrinal analysis on the proposition that the constitution guarantees no governmentally insured minimum level of safety or security. Because the physical abuse occurred at the hands of Joshua's father, and the Court characterised the state's role as failing to act to avert that abuse, the majority opinion found no violation of a constitutional duty.

The argument on behalf of Joshua's guardian suggested that there was little dispute, in the abstract, about the existence of an affirmative constitutional obligation to protect children from parental abuse. Joshua's guardian argued that there was an enforceable constitutional duty of protection based upon the existence of a special relationship between the state and Joshua arising out of the state's abortive efforts on Joshua's behalf. In prior opinions involving harm following failed efforts by the state, the provision of medical care to prisoners[27] and involuntarily institutionalised retarded citizens,[28] the Court had recognised a constitutional obligation to provide these persons with a minimum level of care. A number of federal courts of appeal had relied upon these decisions to find a special relationship in circumstances similar to Joshua's triggering a constitutional duty to protect children from abuse in these limited circumstances.[29]

The *DeShaney* majority distinguished the Court's prior decisions and rejected the claim that a special relationship between the state social service agency and Joshua triggered a duty to protect Joshua from abuse by his father. It held that a special relationship between the state agency and the individual triggers a duty to protect the individual only when the state takes a person into custody and holds that person involuntarily. Because the state had released Joshua to his father before the final batterings, Joshua could not meet the custodial requirement imposed by the Court to establish a special relationship. Unnecessary to the holding and therefore not discussed was another hurdle that the plaintiff would have had to overcome even if the Court had recog-

---

27. Estelle v. Gamble, 429 U.S. 97 (1982).

28. Youngberg v. Romeo, 457 U.S. 307 (1982).

29. Benjamin Zipursky, 'DeShaney and the Jurisprudence of Compassion', 65 New York University Law Review, 1101, at 1107 n. 58 (1990).

nised the plaintiff's claim: good faith immunity.[30] The Court was careful to point out that the state's undertaking the abortive rescue might render it liable under state tort law. Because the validity of state tort claims do not fall within the jurisdiction of the Supreme Court, and in any event were not raised in this case, they were not pursued further in this opinion. What the Court was careful not to point out was the likely reason that this claim was brought as a federal civil rights action rather than a state tort claim.

Plaintiffs often choose federally based civil rights claims rather than state tort claims to avoid the immunity, damage cap and limited duty hurdles, noted earlier, that exist under state law. Wisconsin imposed a ceiling of $50,000 per claim in its limited abrogation of sovereign immunity.[31] Wisconsin also retained immunity for discretionary governmental functions. Typical of the claims that might be brought are those involving negligence in the operation of a state-owned motor vehicle, which do not involve the exercise of governmental discretion.[32] Thus it was highly unlikely that in Wisconsin, where this case arose, a state tort claim would be brought. Many states have enacted good faith immunity for all official acts of child protective service workers.[33] Under the public duty doctrine, other states have interpreted the state's duty as owing to the general public but not any particular member of the public.[34] Most importantly, either by resurrection of sovereign immunity or refusing to remain in the child abuse rescue business, the state can prospectively obviate any tort liability for failure to rescue abused children. Federal civil rights claims, however, are grounded on federal constitutional law and may not be rejected as a matter of state law.

Both the facts that gave rise to *DeShaney* and the court's austere response to these facts are troubling. The court's response is a stale formulaic doctrinal analysis based largely upon an action/inaction dichotomy.[35] There is a temptation to respond to this approach and to criticise the decision on its own terms. Most critics of *DeShaney* have not resisted this temptation and have argued that the creation of the child protection agency and response to the complaints of abuse take this case out of the category of inaction or non-feasance.[36] Oth-

---

30. Harlow v. Fitzgerald, 457 U.S. 800 (1982).

31. Wis. Stat. Ann. § 893.80 (West supp. 1989).

32. Wisconsin would render government conduct immune from tort claims unless it involved wilful and wanton conduct or a ministerial act, as contrasted with a discretionary function. C.L. v. Olson, 422 N.W.2d 614 (Wis. 1988); Yotvat v. Roth, 290 N.W.2d 524 (Wis. Ct. App. 1980).

33. See authorities cited supra, n. 16.

34. See, for example, Nelson v. Freeman, 537 F. Supp. 602, 610–11 (W.D. Mo. 1982) (federal court sitting in a diversity action applying Missouri law rejects under Missouri's public duty doctrine a claim that child protective service was liable for failing to investigate a report of sexual abuse of a child).

35. Aviam Soifer, 'Moral Ambition, Formalism, and the "Free World" of DeShaney', 57 George Washington Law Review, 1513 (1989).

36. Jack M. Beerman, 'Administrative Failure and Local Democracy: The Politics of DeShaney', Duke Law Journal, 1078 (1990); Thomas A. Eaton and Michael L. Wells, 'Government Inaction as a Constitutional Tort: DeShaney and Its Aftermath', 66 Washington Law Review, 107 (1991); Laurence Tribe, 'The Curvature of Constitutional Space: What Lawyers Can Learn From Modern Physics', 103 Harvard Law Review, 1 (1989).

ers have pointed to the history surrounding the adoption of the Fourteenth Amendment as an affirmative response to slavery to criticise the Court's interpretation that it constitutes only a negative limitation on the states.[37] It is important to avoid the temptation to be drawn into the debate on these terms for it has not and is not likely to yield any new insights or analysis. The debate is mired in a doctrinal rut. Rediscovering constitutional history or reconceptualising causation distinguishing action and inaction may strengthen criticisms of the Court's reasoning, but seem likely to accomplish little else. This debate devolves into a zero-sum game pitting those who seek to protect child victims of abuse against those who seek to protect the constitutional rights of the accused.[38] A new approach with new insights is needed to re-energise that debate. One approach that offers new insights into this problem is therapeutic jurisprudence.

3   Therapeutic Jurisprudence

3.1   A Therapeutic Once-Over

Therapeutic jurisprudence is a mode of legal analysis that considers the law's potential as a therapeutic agent.[39] It posits that, whenever it is possible to do so without offending other important normative values, legal rules should encourage therapeutic outcomes. Therapeutic jurisprudence calls for a systematic empirical examination of the therapeutic dimension of the law,[40] and, while the inquiry suggested by therapeutic jurisprudence has certainly been undertaken previously without that label, the advantage of therapeutic jurisprudence is that it sharpens the focus of this legal lens.

For an example of this analysis, consider an application of therapeutic jurisprudence to another area in which the state has chosen to exercise its authority to come to the aid of a vulnerable population—civil commitment of the mentally disabled. There is a body of research indicating that voluntary hospitalisation is more effective in treating the mentally disabled than involuntary

---

37. Akhil R. Amar and Daniel Widawsky, 'Child Abuse as Slavery: A Thirteenth Amendment Response to DeShaney', 105 Harvard Law Review, 1359 (1992).

38. Madelyn S. Milchman, 'Professional Controversies in Child Sexual Abuse Assessment', 20 Journal Psychiatry and Law, 45, at 50 (1992).

39. David B. Wexler and Bruce J. Winick, Essays in Therapeutic Jurisprudence (Durham, 1991); David B. Wexler, Therapeutic Jurisprudence: The Law as a Therapeutic Agent (Durham, 1990), vii.

40. Wexler and Winick, op. cit., xi. This inquiry into the therapeutic dimension of law can be analysed from four perspectives. First, the law may play a role in producing psychological dysfunction through discouragement of necessary treatment, encouragement of unnecessary treatment and encouragement of sick behaviour or absence of responsibility; ibid., at 19–24. Second, legal rules may explicitly seek to promote therapeutic consequences as in the case of a right to treatment; ibid., at 24–30. Third, legal procedures may play a therapeutic role in the parties' psychological response to the legal process, as contrasted with the outcome; ibid., at 30–33. Fourth, the roles played by attorneys and judges may have therapeutic consequences for the other actors in the legal process; ibid., at 33–7.

hospitalisation.[41] A therapeutic jurisprudence analysis would suggest that, unless other important normative values would be offended, the state's interest in treatment of the mentally disabled should be advanced by encouraging voluntary treatment and permitting involuntary treatment, if at all, only after efforts to encourage voluntary treatment have failed.[42] It is particularly appropriate to examine the duty of the state to come to the aid of abused children from the perspective of therapeutic jurisprudence. The debate over the duty to rescue has been dominated by doctrinal analysis devoid of empirical inquiry.[43] While the doctrinal analysis is necessary, alone it is not sufficient. The argument in favour of a duty to rescue, specifically in the context of child abuse, is therapeutically driven: it implicitly assumes that the reason for rescuing abused children is a therapeutic outcome—safer and healthier children. Yet it infrequently goes beyond merely assuming that things will improve if we just do something. If a duty to rescue abused children is therapeutically driven, then it is reasonable to rephrase the inquiry to ask when rescue will be therapeutic and only then, if at all, to consider a duty to rescue.

The proponents of a duty to rescue abused children assume an easy and successful rescue. They would have us believe that the existence of abuse is invariably clear, that the goal of intervention is acknowledged by all, and that the result of the process will be safer and healthier children. Remarkably, both the majority and the dissent in *DeShaney* give scant attention to the reality exposed by the facts of that case. The social service agency did not ignore the reports of abuse of Joshua DeShaney. It responded by seizing Joshua and returning him only after an interdisciplinary team concluded, albeit wrongly with the benefit of hindsight, that the evidence did not justify retaining custody. And it responded with a proposal for a counselling programme for Joshua's father, a change in living arrangements at Joshua's home, and a pre-school programme for Joshua to monitor his situation. Whether the social service agency was inaccurate, indifferent or inadequate is unclear from the record. What is clear is that trying is not enough, and that it may make things worse.

3.2   The Harm in Trying

Creating chaos out of order Successful rescue of abused children turns on the satisfaction of two requirements: the ability to identify abuse and the ability to respond appropriately. To rescue an abused child successfully there must first exist the ability to make an accurate determination that abuse has occurred and the ability to make an accurate identification of the source of that abuse—

41. Mary L. Durham and John M. LaFond, 'A Search for the Missing Premise of Involuntary Therapeutic Commitment: Effective Treatment of the Mentally Ill', 40 Rutgers Law Review, 303 (1988); Leonard I. Stein and May Test, 'Alternative to Mental Hospital Treatment: I. Conceptual Model, Treatment Programme, and Clinical Evaluation', 37 Archives of General Psychiatry, 392 (1980); Bruce J. Winick, 'Competency to Consent to Voluntary Hospitalization: A Therapeutic Jurisprudence Analysis of Zinermon v. Burch', in Wexler and Winick, op. cit., 83.

42. Brakel et al., op. cit., 178 n. 10.

43. See articles cited supra, n. 1.

who needs to be rescued and from whom? Determining the existence of abuse and the identity of the abuser in the case of child sexual abuse frequently pits the testimony of a child against the testimony of an adult. When the sexual abuse consists of penetration, the physical evidence of abuse is less demonstrable than lay expectations might suggest.[44] But, when the sexual abuse consists of inappropriate touching, rather than penetration, no physical evidence of abuse may exist and, in any event, the identity of the abuser is not likely to be subject to non-testimonial proof.

The research literature does not reveal accurate tests to identify victims of sexual abuse or sexual abusers. We must proceed cautiously:

> Child abuse research has grown geometrically over the past 2 decades, leading to a major expansion of our knowledge base. However, the quality of research designs and methods has not advanced in proportion to the quantity of the studies. Consequentially, many questionable research findings have found a life of their own and are often treated as 'established facts' despite being based on methodologically inadequate studies.[45]

One popular subject of testimony by some child abuse professionals to aid in identifying children who have been sexually abused is the child sexual abuse accommodation syndrome, a pattern of behaviour thought to be common in children who have been victims of sexual abuse.[46] This pattern of behaviour is thought to include secrecy, helplessness, accommodation, unconvincing and delayed disclosures, and recantation of disruptive disclosures.[47] One problem with the use of this syndrome as a forensic tool to identify children who have been sexually abused is that a critical review of the published research does not reveal that children have common reactions to sexual abuse.[48]

Meta-analysis of the research reveals that children react in diverse ways to sexual abuse, depending upon a number of variables that include the age and developmental level of the child, the frequency of abuse and the time period

---

44. When penetration is alleged to have occurred, the ability to ascertain whether abuse occurred from a physical examination of the hymenal orifice diameter of girls or perianal examination of boys or girls is of questionable validity. Jan E. Paradise, 'Predictive Accuracy and the Diagnosis of Sexual Abuse: A Big Issue About a Little Tissue', 13 Child Abuse & Neglect, 13 (1989); John McCann, 'Perianal Findings in Prepubertal Children Selected for Non Abuse: A Descriptive Study', 13 Child Abuse & Neglect, 179 (1989).

45. Erich Mash and David A. Wolfe, 'Methodological Issues in Research on Physical Child Abuse', 18 (1) Criminal Justice & Behavior, 8 (1991). See also Jeffrey J. Haugaard and Robert E. Emery, 'Methodological Issues in Child Sexual Abuse Research', 13 Child Abuse & Neglect, 89 (1989).

46. David McCord, 'Expert Psychological Testimony About Child Complaints in Sexual Abuse Prosecutions: A Foray into The Admissibility of Novel Psychological Evidence', 77 J. Criminal Law & Criminology, 1, at 9 (1986).

47. Roland C. Summit, 'The Child Abuse Accommodation Syndrome', 7 Child Abuse & Neglect, 177 (1983).

48. In addition, the research that purports to identify this syndrome is plagued by methodological flaws. It often fails to compare matched samples of abused and non-abused children and thus fails to account for differences in socio-economic status or race, for example, that may produce the effects seen. See Mash and Wolf, op. cit., supra, n. 45, at 17.

over which it occurred, the relationship of the abuser to the child, the manipulation or control of the child by the abuser, the reaction of family and friends to the revelation of abuse, and the degree of violence involved.[49] The syndrome does not distinguish the effects of other stressors in the child's life, such as a divorce of parents, change in residence or problems at school.[50] Thus confidence that a child's behaviour is a reliable indicator of sexual abuse is unfounded. Compounding the problem of our limited knowledge about behaviour that identifies sexually abused children is the problem of the reliability of allegations of sexual abuse. For example, 'professionals often believe that allegations [of abuse] that arise in divorce/custody disputes are less likely to be true'.[51] The concern that parents and others may play a role in encouraging children's complaints of abuse raises the question of children's memory and suggestibility that has been a particular concern in cases of sexual abuse. 'How good, in both absolute and relative terms, is the memory of children for eye-witnessed or experienced events? How do the child's memory functions change with age? How is a child's recall of events best facilitated and least contaminated?...Unfortunately, the state of [psychology] is such that we do not answer with one voice.'[52]

The extent of the problem may be best illustrated by a report of researchers whose work most strongly supports children's resistance to suggestion:

> Children do not make up facts often, both studies agree, but...we can conclude that children are especially likely to accept an interviewer's suggestions when they are younger, when they are interrogated after a long delay, when they feel intimidated by the interviewer, when the interviewer's suggestions are strongly stated and frequently repeated, and when more than one interviewer makes the same strong suggestions.[53]

At best, there is much with which to be concerned as adults with their own agenda play a role in asserting, denying and investigating allegations of child abuse. Accordingly, judges and juries are often concerned whether to believe the child who claims to have been abused rather than the adult who denies the

---

49. Lucy Berliner, 'Clinical Work With Sexually Abused Children', in Clive R. Hollin and Kevin Howells (Eds), Clinical Approaches to Sex Offenders and Their Victims (New York, 1991), 211; Angela Browne and David Finkelhor, 'Impact of Child Sexual Abuse: A Review of the Literature', 99 Psychological Bulletin, 66 (1986); Suzanne M. Sgroi, 'Child Sexual Assault: Some Guidelines for Intervention and Assessment', in Ann W. Burgess et al. (Eds), Sexual Assault of Children & Adolescents (Lexington, 1978), 134–5.

50. Mash and Wolf, op. cit., *supra*, n. 45, at 17.

51. Lucy Berliner and Jon R. Conte, 'The Process of Victimization: The Victim's Perspective', 14 Child Abuse & Neglect, 29 (1990). See also Nancy Thoennes and Jessica Pearson, 'A Difficult Dilemma: Responding to Sexual Abuse Allegations in Custody and Visitation Disputes', in Douglas J. Besharov (Ed.), Protecting Children From Abuse and Neglect: Policy and Practice (Springfield, 1988), 93–4.

52. John Doris (Ed.), The Suggestibility of Children's Recollections (Washington, DC, 1991).

53. Gail S. Goodman and Alison Clarke-Stewart, 'Suggestibility in Children's Testimony: Implications for Sexual Abuse Investigations', in John Doris (Ed.), The Suggestibility of Children's Recollections (Washington, DC, 1991), 103.

abuse.[54] Here again some child abuse professionals have offered their expertise on yet another form of syndrome evidence, the battering parent syndrome. The battering parent syndrome is a cluster of traits thought common in adults who physically abuse children.[55] These traits include low self-esteem, a short temper, high blood pressure, social isolation, lack of trust, inadequate child development knowledge and parenting skills, and having been abused as a child.[56] The use of this syndrome in identifying battering parents poses two problems. First, the rules of evidence exclude the use of character evidence when offered to show conformity and have therefore resulted in exclusion of this evidence when offered to identify the defendant as an abuser.[57] Second, there is substantial disagreement in the research literature about these traits thought common in adults who abuse children.[58] One researcher has opined

---

54. Gail S. Goodman et al., 'When a Child Takes the Stand: Jurors' Perceptions of Children's Eyewitness Testimony', 11 Law & Human Behavior, 27 (1987); Michael R. Leippe, 'Children on the Witness Stand: A Communication/Persuasion Analysis of Jurors' Reactions to Child Witnesses', in Stephen J. Ceci et al. (Eds), Children's Eyewitness Memory (New York, 1987). But see David F. Ross et al., 'The Child in the Eyes of the Jury: Assessing Mock Jurors' Perceptions of the Child Witness', 14 Law & Human Behavior, 5 (1990).

55. Thomas Bulleit Jr., 'The Battering Parent Syndrome: Inexpert Testimony as Character Evidence', 17 Journal of Law Reform, 653 (1984).

56. Audrey M. Berger, 'The Child Abusing Family (Pt I)', 8 Am. J. Family Therapy, 53 (1980); William N. Friedrich and Karen K. Wheeler, 'The Abusing Parent Revisited: A Decade of Psychological Research', 170 J. Nervous & Mental Disease, 577 (1982).

57. Daniel W. Shuman, Psychiatric and Psychological Evidence (Colorado Springs, 1986), 314–16. At best this character evidence describes increased behaviour of the type studied in the target group as compared with the general population, but says nothing about the behaviour of a particular person on a particular occasion. Consequentially the use of character evidence to show conformity is generally inadmissible unless the defendant chooses to open the door to this evidence (Fed. R. Evid. 404 (a)). The nature of these data gives clues to their possible misuse. For example, while retrospective studies suggest that many abusive parents were abused as children, prospective studies reveal that most parents who were abused as children do not abuse their children. Mash and Wolf, op. cit., supra, n. 45, at 15. Juries may be insensitive to the risk of false positives in utilising this evidence.

Thus thoughtful researchers who claim to have developed accurate instrments to identify abusers tout their devices as screening tools to identify individuals in need of help and not for forensic use to determine retrospectively that someone abused a particular child on a particular occasion. Joel S. Milner, 'Physical Child Abuse Perpetrator Screening and Evaluations', 18 (1) Criminal Justice & Behavior, 47, at 50 (1991).

58. See for example, William A. Attemeir et al., 'Prediction of Child Abuse: a Prospective Study of Feasibility', 8 Child Abuse & Neglect, 393 (1984). This prospective study used the characteristics of the battering parent syndrome to determine their accuracy in predicting abuse in a population of 1400 expectant mothers at Vanderbilt University Hospital. Using these criteria it was predicted that 273 would abuse their children. In a two-year follow-up using the child abuse reporting registry it was discovered that 6 per cent of 273 predicted to abuse did abuse and that 1 per cent of 1127 predicted to be non-abusers abused. As 2 per cent of the population studied abused, a prediction of non-abuse would be 98 per cent accurate. See also Ben Bursten, 'Detecting Child Abuse by Studying Parents', 13 Bulletin of the American Academy of Psychiatry & Law, 273 (1985).

Even in the case of the Child Abuse Potential Inventory, a psychological test thought to be highly accurate in predicting potential for abuse, prudent researchers have noted that "psychologists using the CAP and similar instruments should be especially careful to ensure that

that 'the ability to separate out a distinct group of parents (or future parents) who will physically abuse or serious [*sic*] neglect one or more of their children will probably never be possible'.[59]

Putting aside the evidentiary limitations on the use of character evidence to show conformity, both the potential inaccuracy and accuracy of this syndrome is troubling. If the battering parent syndrome inaccurately describes child abusers, then it suggests the lack of an accurate basis for determining the identity of abusers. We may be punishing or treating the wrong person. Accordingly, not only is it unlikely that intervention will be therapeutic, but the child may be placed at increased risk owing to the false sense of security that the danger has been abated. If the battering parent syndrome accurately identifies abusers, then it suggests an anti-therapeutic consequence of intervention. The dynamic described by the battering parent syndrome is that of a person with poor impulse control and lack of social support systems who responds to stress with displaced aggression towards a child.[60] An accusation of child abuse directed at a person described by that dynamic can be expected to increase the stress that precipitated the abuse and, correspondingly, increase the risk of inappropriate anger or resentment. The irony is that, if the battering parent syndrome accurately identifies the behaviour of child abusers, the very act of rescue from abuse is likely to increase the risk of abuse for that child or other members of the family unless great skill and effort are utilised.[61]

Yet another syndrome, the battered child syndrome,[62] offers assistance in identifying children who have been physically abused. 'Although the findings are quite variable, the syndrome should be considered in any child exhibiting evidence of possible trauma or neglect (fracture of any bone, subdural

---

legal and social service agencies do not substantiate allegations of abuse merely on the basis of such tests". Gary B. Melton and Susan Limbers, 'Psychologists' Involvement in Cases of Child Maltreatment: Limits of Role and Expertise', 44 American Psychologist, 1225, at 1231 (1989).

59. Ray Helfer, 'Basic Issues Concerning Predictions', in Ray Helfer and C. Henry Kempe (Eds), Child Abuse and Neglect: The Family and the Community (Cambridge, Massachusetts, 1976), 363.

60. This relationship is supported by the research linking life events, stress and lack of social support with abuse. Dorothy C. Howze and Jonathon B. Kotch, 'Disentangling Life Events, Stress and Social Support: Implications for the Primary Prevention of Child Abuse and Neglect', 8 Child Abuse & Neglect, 401 (1984).

61. It might be suggested that Sherman and Berk's research on the effects of arrest for simple domestic violence rebuts this suggestion, but that conclusion is not supported by their research. Lawrence W. Sherman and Richard A. Berk, 'The Specific Deterrent Effect of Arrest for Domestic Assault', 49 American Sociological Review, 261 (1984). Sherman and Berk found that the likelihood of future domestic violence decreased when police arrested the suspect rather than ordered the suspect to leave or offered advice. Even apart from the methodological flaws in this research and the absence of parallel aetiologies for spousal abuse and child abuse, this research reinforces rather than rebuts the suggestion that botched rescues may increase the risk of child abuse. Sherman and Berk's finding is not that intervention, just doing something, necessarily makes things better. Rather it is that there is an appropriate response, and that some responses are much better than others.

62. C. Henry Kempe et al., 'The Battered Child Syndrome', 181 Journal of the American Medical Association, 17 (1962).

hematoma, multiple soft tissue injuries, poor hygiene, or malnutrition) or where there is a marked discrepancy between the clinical findings and the historical data as supplied by the parents.'[63] The breadth of the battered child syndrome suggests that it may be useful as a clinical tool for health care providers in a case like *DeShaney* to identify cases in which further investigation of abuse is appropriate, but that it is not particularly useful as a forensic tool to identify cases in which abuse has occurred. Moreover, abuse can mimic organic and psychosocial diseases and organic and psychosocial diseases can mimic abuse.[64]

Although the use of misinformed myths, referred to by one author as 'ordinary common sense',[65] may lead to the conclusion that the existence and source of abuse will ordinarily be clear, a careful review of the research reveals that confidence in our ability to make accurate determinations of these questions is misplaced. Our facile constructs of what abuse and abusers look like reinforces convenient but erroneous myths. In our desire to simplify and control, we have deluded ourselves into believing that there is an order to the chaos.

What does the dog do after it catches the car it was chasing? The second requirement for successful rescue of abused children by the state is the ability to respond appropriately. Even if we could accurately determine who has been abused by whom, we are faced with the proverbial problem of the dog who chases cars. 'No conflict has caused greater dissention [*sic*] among professionals working on behalf of abused children than the use of criminal prosecutions as a response to child abuse.'[66] There is sharp disagreement amongst professionals within the field between the inconsistent goals of treatment and punishment that is highlighted when the abuser is related to the child victim. The dominance of one approach over the other seems to vary over time.[67]

Those who argue in favour of treatment as the goal of intervention point to the role of family systems and the need to break the intergeneration cycle of abuse.[68] 'In working with the family it is essential to change both interactions

---

63. Ibid., at 24.

64. Katherine K. Christoffel et al., 'Should Child Abuse and Neglect be Considered When a Child Dies Unexpectedly?', 139 Am. J. Dis. Child., 876 (1985); Robert H. Kirschner and Robert J. Stein, 'The Mistaken Diagnosis of Child Abuse: A Form of Medical Abuse', 139 Am. J. Dis. Child., 873 (1985).

65. Michael Perlin, 'Pretextuality, Psychiatry and Law: Of 'Ordinary Common Sense', Heuristic Reasoning, and Cognitive Dissonance', 19 Bulletin American Academy of Psychiatry & Law, 131 (1991).

66. James Peters et al., 'Child Abuse is a Criminal Offense', in Children and the Law (Washington, DC, 1988), 161.

67. Douglas J. Besharov, The Vulnerable Social Workers: Liability for Serving Children and Families (Silver Springs, 1985). Besharov opines that 'most Americans believe that child maltreatment is primarily a social and psychological ill and that treatment and rehabilitation, not punishment and retribution, are the best means of protecting children'. Douglas J. Besharov, "Doing Something" About Child Abuse: The Need to Narrow the Grounds for State Intervention', 8 Harvard Journal of Law & Public Policy, 539, at 553 (1985).

68. Noel Lustig et al., 'Incest: A Family Group Survival Pattern', 14 Archives of General Psychiatry, 31 (1966).

to prevent or ameliorate abuse, and also to understand the specific meanings, beliefs, and realities of the family which connect with the abusive behaviour. Each member carries such realities, whether the family continues together or not, and these also require change.'[69] The familial denial that frequently surrounds abuse may increase and the willingness to participate in treatment may decrease when abuse is categorised as a criminal act. Punishment of the abuser may exacerbate familial tensions, including the financial repercussions of incarceration of the abuser whose support is lost. Even when a parent has sexually abused a child, the child may experience guilt over the parent's confinement,[70] and incarceration may leave the abuser in the criminal justice system without treatment.

Even if there were agreement upon the goal of treatment, however, that would not end the inquiry. There is not a professional consensus on the cause of child abuse.[71] In the case of both physical[72] and sexual abuse[73] of children multiple models or theories exist. Given the disagreement on aetiology, it is hardly surprising that, in general, treatment has not been a panacea.[74] Even the most highly touted programmes reveal a decrease in abuse in only 40 per cent or less of the families treated.[75] Moreover, there is a risk that treatment inappropriately visits responsibility for the abuse on non-abusing members of the family.[76] Those who argue in favour of punishment as the goal of intervention point to the need to protect the child and other vulnerable members of society

---

69. Arnon Bentovim, 'Clinical Work With Families in Which Sexual Abuse Has Occurred', in Clive R. Hollin and Kevin Howells (Eds), Clinical Approaches to Sex Offenders and Their Victims (New York, 1991), 189.

70. Jeffrey J. Haugaard, 'The Use of Theories About the Etiology of Incest as Guidelines for Legal and Therapeutic Interactions', 6 Behavioral Sciences and the Law, 221, at 232 (1988).

71. Sandra T. Azar, 'Models of Child Abuse: A Metatheoretical Analysis', 18 (1) Criminal Justice & Behavior, 30 (1991); Richard I. Lanyon, 'Theories of Sex Offending', in Clive R. Hollin and Kevin Howells (Eds), Clinical Approaches to Sex Offenders and Their Victims (New York, 1991).

72. The theories advanced to explain physical abuse can be grouped according to assumptions regarding defect, deficiency, disruption and mismatch: Azar, op. cit., supra, n. 71, 34. An example of a defect theory is that abuse results from biologically triggered aggression. A deficiency theory views abuse as learned behaviour. Disruption theorists view abuse as responsive to some external stress such as a financial strain. Mismatch theorists suggest a transactional disparity.

73. The theories to explain child sexual abuse include psychodynamic theories (such as Oedipal complex), behavioural theories (such as learned behaviour), and biological theories (for example hormonal or chromosomal make-up): Jon R. Conte, 'The Nature of Sexual Offenses Against Children', in Clive R. Hollin and Kevin, Howells (Eds), op. cit., 37–39.

74. Anne H. Cohn and Deborah Dar, 'Is Treatment Too Late: What Ten Years of Evaluate Research Tell Us', 11 Child Abuse & Neglect, 433, at 440 (1987).

75. Laille Gabinet, 'Child Abuse Treatment Failures Reveal Need for Redefinition of the Problem', 7 Child Abuse & Neglect, 395, at 396 (1983); Gordon Hall and Richard Hirschman, 'Sexual Aggression Against Children: A Conceptual Perspective of Etiology', 19 (1) Criminal Justice & Behavior, 8, at 9 (1992); Keith L. Kaufman and Leslie Rudy, 'Future Directions in the Treatment of Physical Child Abuse', 18 (1) Criminal Justice & Behavior, 82, at 83 (1991).

76. Jan Hindman, Just Before Dawn (Ontario, 1989), 38.

from abuse and to send a strong deterrent message that child abuse will not be tolerated. They challenge a distinction in the punishment of strangers, but not family members who engage in similar acts with children[77] and they argue that children should not be treated differently from other victims of violence. They also point out that punishment vindicates a sense of fairness and serves an educative function.

Yet, at least as a specific deterrent, the benefits of punishment alone are limited: 'Incarcerating the offender, without treatment, is only a temporary solution.'[78] While punishment does not perforce preclude treatment, it has anti-therapeutic consequences. From the perspective of the child, punishment of the offender may require that the child confront the abuser in court and be subjected to rigorous cross-examination.[79] In theory, a child's testifying against an adult abuser has the potential to be an empowering, therapeutic act. In practice, however, critics have charged that abused children are twice victimised, once by the abuser and a second time by the legal system.[80] Consequentially, a large percentage of cases are dropped because of the reluctance of the child to testify.[81]

Other anti-therapeutic consequences of punishment result from certain facets of the criminal justice system that reinforce common cognitive distortions in sex offenders that deny or minimise the inappropriateness of their conduct. Restructuring these cognitive distortions is an important part of the treatment process.[82] Plea bargaining dominates criminal adjudication and the cases of sex offenders are no exception.[83] The plea bargaining process may reinforce sexual offenders' denial or minimisation of their actions by accepting no contest (*nolo contendere*) pleas without an admission of guilt.[84] These cognitive distortions may also be reinforced by the way in which individuals identified as child sexual abusers are treated by fellow prisoners. Moreover, research on the efficacy of prison treatment programmes reveals that, when they are available, they may change behaviour within the institution, but there is

---

77. Scott Harshbargar, 'Prosecution is an Appropriate Response in Child Sexual Abuse Cases', 2 J. Interpersonal Violence, 108 (1987).

78. Reuben Lang et al., 'Treatment of Incest and Pedophilic Offenders: A Pilot Study', 6 Behavioral Sciences & the Law, 239, at 251 (1988).

79. But see Maryland v. Craig, 110 S. Ct. 3157 (1990) (confrontation clause does not impose an absolute requirement of a face-to-face meeting between the defendant and a six-year-old victim of child abuse if the court determines that the child would experience serious emotional trauma such that the child could not reasonably communicate).

80. Eli H. Newberger, 'Prosecution: A Problematic Approach to Child Abuse', 2 J. Interpersonal Violence, 112 (1987).

81. State v. Brevard, 484 A.2d 1330, 1333 (N.J. Super 1984) (one prosecutor's office estimated that 4 per cent of its child abuse cases were dropped for this reason).

82. See infra, notes 92 and 93, and accompanying text.

83. Jeffrey A. Klotz, et al., 'Cognitive Restructuring Through Law: A Therapeutic Jurisprudence Approach to Sex Offenders and the Plea Process', 15 University of Puget Sound Law Review, 601, at 604 (1992).

84. David B. Wexler and Bruce J. Winick, 'Therapeutic Jurisprudence and Criminal Justice Mental Health Issues', 16 Mental Disability Law Reporter, 225, at 229 (1992).

scant evidence that they reduce the rate of recidivism upon release, and they show less promise than community-based treatment programmes.[85]

3.3 Zen and the Art of Rescue

Those who address the duty to rescue abused children often behave as if they were writing the script for an old Hollywood western in which the classification of the good folks and the bad folks is clear and calling in the cavalry guarantees that the good folks will be successfully rescued from the bad folks. The lessons of history should temper that zeal. The classification of the good folks and the bad folks has often changed with an historical perspective, and calling in the cavalry has often done more harm than good.[86]

Proponents of a duty to rescue proceed on the assumption that intervention is generally preferable to non-intervention, yet we know little about the consequences of this choice: 'The impact of intervention has not been measured. There is virtually no longitudinal research measuring the impact of various types of intervention and no research comparing intervention to nonintervention.'[87] We are quick to forget that 'the real purpose of the scientific method is to make sure nature hasn't misled you into thinking you know something that you actually don't know'.[88]

There are numerous known limitations on intervention. Our capacity to identify the abused and the abuser and to agree upon and effectuate the goals of treatment or punishment will often be unsuccessful even with optimal efforts. We operate with imperfect knowledge and, far too often, with inadequate resources. In addition, there are 'several well known and consistently identified barriers to accurate judgment that negatively impinge upon the reliability and validity of human decisionmaking generally and clinician's decisionmaking particularly and [suggest] that judgments of experienced clinicians are in many cases more susceptible to error than those of trainees and sometimes even lay decisionmakers'.[89] The judgmental errors, or heuristics, identified by cognitive psychologists are availability, representativeness and anchoring. Availability refers to the tendency to give undue weight to an event based upon the ease with which it can be recalled. Thus a particularly vivid characteristic of an abused child may be remembered by a child protective service worker to the exclusion of other less vivid but more numerous characteristics when generalising about the characteristics of abused children. Representative-

---

85. Derek Perkins, 'Clinical Work With Sex Offenders in Secure Settings', in Clive R. Hollin and Kevin Howells (Eds), op. cit., 173.

86. Dee A. Brown, Bury My Heart at Wounded Knee: An Indian History of the American West (New York, 1970).

87. Michael S. Wald, 'Thinking About Public Policy Toward Abuse and Neglect of Children: A Review of Before the Best Interests of the Child', 78 Michigan Law Review, 645, at 691 (1980).

88. Robert Pirsig, Zen & the Art of Motorcycle Maintenance (New York, 1975).

89. Donald N. Bersoff, 'Judicial Deference to Nonlegal Decisionmakers: Imposing Simplistic Solutions on Problems of Cognitive Complexity in Mental Health Law', 46 Southern Methodist University Law Review, 329 (1992).

ness refers to erroneous associations with a larger organisational structure that ignore such considerations as base rates and sample size. Thus a child protective service worker who sees a particular characteristic in a large number of abused children may assume that this trait distinguishes abused children from non-abused children, without examining other explanations for these characteristics, such as ethnicity or socio-economic status, or comparing the frequency of that characteristic in a controlled study of large numbers of abused and non-abused children of differing ethnicity and socio-economic status. Anchoring refers to the tendency to make a final decision based upon initial impressions rather than subsequent information. For example, a child protective service worker who meets early in the investigation an alleged abuser who makes a favourable impression is more likely to discount subsequently received evidence pointing to that person as the source of the abuse than if the worker meets that person late in the investigation having received all other available evidence of abuse.

The capacity of child care professionals to make accurate determinations of abuse and abuser is limited.[90] Perhaps more perplexing, however, is the fact that child care professionals, like other professionals, often profess their competence to reach accurate conclusions in the face of overwhelming research to the contrary. In our rush to do good we embrace an omniscience that obscures the complexity of the problem and increases the likelihood of unsuccessful rescue. And unsuccessful rescue of abused children entails more than simply not obtaining the desired positive result. It risks dissuading others from assisting, and also poses numerous anti-therapeutic risks.[91] As noted above, unsuccessful rescue may exacerbate the stress that precipitated the abuse and increase the risk of inappropriate anger or resentment towards the child or other family members. Thus unsuccessful rescue may increase the probability and severity of physical abuse. In addition, unsuccessful rescue risks hardening both the physical and sexual abuser to treatment.

Research on individuals who sexually abuse children reveals a series of cognitive distortions to deny or minimise responsibility for their actions.[92] 'I did not touch the child,' 'It was the child's idea,' or 'It was enjoyable to the child' are typical of child sexual abusers' cognitive distortions.[93] An important part

---

90. Stephanie Ladson et al., 'Do Physicians Recognise Sexual Abuse?', 141 Am. J. Dis. Child., 411–15 (1987).

91. One anti-therapeutic risk I will not explore in detail given the scope of this chapter is the impact of intrusion by the state upon the parent-child relationship. To those who see the importance of an adequate psychological relationship between the child and parent as requiring parental autonomy unbroken by state intrusion, rescue, successful or unsuccessful, is detrimental to the child's development. Joseph Goldstein et al., Before the Best Interests of the Child (New York, 1979), 8–10.

92. Derek Perkins, 'Clinical Work With Sex Offenders in Secure Settings', in Clive R. Hollin and Kevin Howells (Eds), op. cit., 168.

93. Gene G. Abel et al., 'Complications, Consent, and Cognitions in Sex Between Children and Adults', 7 International Journal of Law & Psychiatry, 89, at 98–101 (1984); Nathan Pollock and Judith M. Hashmall, 'The Excuses of Child Molesters', 9 Behaviorial Sciences & Law, 53, at 57 (1991).

of the treatment process is restructuring these cognitive distortions. Research on caregivers who physically abuse children reveals that they often feel justified by children's defiance of their authority.[94] When intervention founders because of insufficient evidence to conclude that abuse occurred or because of insufficient resources to pursue the case it risks reinforcing the abuser's denial, minimisation or justification. *DeShaney* provides a powerful example of this risk. Joshua was temporarily seized by the social service agency and then returned to his father because of insufficient evidence of abuse, although the agency did advance a therapeutic programme. The actions of Joshua's father in continuing to abuse Joshua and in failing to comply with the therapeutic programme raise the troubling question as to whether the return based upon insufficient evidence of abuse reinforced the denial, minimisation or justification of his actions and overshadowed the agency's message that there was a serious problem for which he needed, and the agency offered, help.

Thus, if a duty of the state to rescue abused children should be recognised only when rescue will be therapeutic, it will rarely be possible to justify such a duty. Our knowledge and ability to address child abuse seriously lag behind our humanitarian instincts. Tell the cavalry to stand down. It may be best to assist by not rescuing. 'Judicious non-intervention' has been suggested by Edwin Schur in the context of juvenile delinquency to minimise judicial intervention in specific cases.[95] Rather than intervene in individual cases of delinquency, Schur argues that our efforts should be directed toward voluntary programmes that address the underlying problems that foster delinquency. Notwithstanding the differences between delinquency and abuse, the logic of non-intervention in individual cases can also be advanced in the case of child abuse. If a duty to rescue individual abused children should be recognised only when rescue will be therapeutic, then limits on our knowledge of who, when and how to rescue that thwart therapeutic results should limit recognition of a duty to rescue individual children. It might be argued that, rather than abandon the concept of a duty to rescue abused children, that duty should be reconstructed. Research consistently reveals a correlation between poverty and physical abuse of children.[96] While physical abuse of children exists in rich and poor families, poverty undoubtedly adds to the emotional burden of any family. One commentator explains the dynamic between poverty and abuse as resulting from an 'inability to participate in the economic process of society, their own feelings of inadequacy, and [that] society is reluctant to bear the responsibility for effectively meeting their needs'.[97] At least as a response to physical abuse, broad-based voluntary social programmes designed to address the issues that underlie poverty—employment, health care, education and housing—may maximise the therapeutic consequences for the greatest number

---

94. Dorothee Dietrich et al., 'Some Factors Influencing Abusers' Justifications of their Child Abuse', 14 Child Abuse & Neglect, 337, at 343 (1990).

95. Edwin M. Schur, Radical Nonintervention: Rethinking the Delinquency Problem (Englewood, 1973), 155.

96. US Dept of Health & Human Services, Study of National Incidence and Prevalence of Child Abuse and Neglect, 7-7 (1988).

97. Sanford Katz, When Parents Fail (Boston, 1971), 26–7.

of children and minimise the anti-therapeutic consequences of ineffective intervention in specific cases.[98]

The attractiveness of this solution must, however, ultimately be tempered by the enormity of the task and the political realities. Not only is it difficult to articulate meaningful criteria for a state duty to eradicate poverty, but, at least in the United States, the political trends suggest that such an effort is unlikely to be fruitful in the foreseeable future. Moreover, it is unlikely that efforts directed towards rescuing individual abused children will be abandoned. Thus, while a therapeutic jurisprudence analysis may not support a duty to rescue in specific cases, the certainty that such efforts will continue calls for an analysis of ways in which the anti-therapeutic effects of the existing legal regime might be minimised. Inappropriate termination of attempts to rescue abused children are anti-therapeutic. In addition to terminating the rescue and leaving the child vulnerable to continued abuse, inappropriate termination risks making matters worse than if no rescue was attempted, by exacerbating tensions and reinforcing the abuser's cognitive distortions surrounding abuse. One way that the law can play a therapeutic role in avoiding inappropriate termination of attempts to rescue abused children is by minimising the difference between investigative standards for child abuse and adjudicative standards for termination of parental rights or criminal conviction for abuse.[99]

One investigative statutory duty that applies in all states to those who work with children, and in many states to everyone, is the duty to report child abuse.[100] The difference between investigative standards for mandatory reporting of child abuse and adjudicative standards for prosecution and/or termination of parental rights may play an unrecognised anti-therapeutic role in initiating rescues that will be terminated for failure to satisfy the adjudicative standard. It also floods the system with inappropriate cases so that investigation and prosecution of appropriate cases is frustrated. Society's response to the problem of child abuse, beginning in the mid-1960s, has been to pass increasingly vague and over-broad laws that mandate the reporting of child abuse.[101] Although the adjudicative standard requires proof beyond a reasonable doubt of a past act of abuse in criminal cases and proof by clear and convincing evidence in termination cases, investigative standards often require only reasonable cause to suspect that an undefined harm to a child's health or

---

98. See Leroy H. Peterson, 'Child Abuse and Neglect: The Myth of Classlessness', 48 American Journal of Orthopsychiatry, 608 (1978).

99. Because of the strong concern with perpetuation of the family, termination is permissible only upon a showing of abuse, neglect or abandonment by clear and convincing evidence. Santosky v. Kramer, 455 U.S. 745 (1982). Criminal prosecution of child abuse requires proof beyond a reasonable doubt. *In re Winship*, 397 U.S. 358 (1970). The duty to report abuse, however, is typically triggered by reasonable cause to suspect abuse. 42 U.S.C. §§ 5101–07 (1982).

100. Margaret H. Meriwether, 'Child Abuse Reporting Laws: Time For a Change', 20 Family Law Quarterly, 141 (1986).

101. Douglas J. Besharov, 'The Need to Narrow the Grounds for State Interventions', in Douglas J. Besharov (Ed.), Protecting Children from Abuse and Neglect (Springfield, 1988), 72. Although these statutes were initially narrowly focused, addressing only physicians who were required to report serious physical injury or non-accidental injury, the class of reporters and the kinds of conditions required to be reported has quickly expanded.

welfare is threatened.[102] Moreover, it is far from clear that the vague and over-broad reporting laws have been aimed at the appropriate cases. While common sense might suggest that these laws result in identifying more cases of abuse, the resulting number of false positives and false negatives is alarming: some 60 per cent of reported cases are not substantiated by child protective services and over 60 per cent of abuse remains unreported.[103]

These vague and over-broad reporting requirements have resulted in a geometric increase in the number of reported cases.[104] In practice, however, 'the epidemic of reporting has not been matched by a rise in appropriate services to the child and family'.[105] As reporting rises at an astounding rate, funding for child protective services has not kept pace. The low threshold of reporting has resulted in a system that is inundated with reports of insubstantial or unproven risks and thus is often unable to respond effectively when real danger exists.[106] Twenty-five per cent of child deaths from abuse and neglect occur after reports have been made to child protective service agencies.[107] Good intentions have brought the system to its knees. *DeShaney* stands as a glaring example of this problem. Moreover, child protective service workers are overworked and suffer from low pay and high turnover.[108] In short, the difference in the investigative and adjudicative standards may well be anti-therapeutic and there appears to be good reason to crystallise the standards[109] and narrow the gap by raising the investigative standard for mandatory reporting of child abuse.

---

102. The Federal Child Abuse Prevention and Treatment Act, 42 U.S.C. §§ 5101–07 (1982), currently requires reporting physical or mental injury 'under circumstances which indicate that the child's health or welfare is harmed or threatened thereby'. In addition to the problems of ambiguity concerning what is intended by physical or mental injury, the act is not limited by its terms to serious injury. The sufficiency of evidence to trigger this standard is 'reasonable cause to suspect' abuse.

103. American Association for Protecting Children, Highlights of Official Child Neglect and Abuse Reporting (1985); United States Dept. of Health and Human Services, Study Findings, National Study of the Incidence and Severity of Child Abuse & Neglect (1981); Besharov, op. cit., supra, n. 101.

104. Barbara J. Nelson, Making an Issue of Child Abuse (Chicago, 1984).

105. Holly Watson and Murray Levine, 'Psychotherapy and Mandated Reporting of Child Abuse', 59 American Journal of Orthopsychiatry, 246, at 249 (1989); Select Committee on Children, Youth and Families U.S. House of Representatives, Abused Children in America: Victims of Official Neglect, H.R. Doc. No. 164, 100th Cong., 1st Sess. (1987).

106. Besharov, op. cit., supra, n. 101, at 48.

107. Lorene F. Schaefer, 'Abused Children and State Created Protection Agencies; A Proposed 1983 Standard', 57 University of Cincinnati Law Review, 1419, at 1419 n. 1 (1985); Region VI Resource Center on Child Abuse & Neglect, Child Deaths in Texas, 26 (1981); Mayberry, 'Child Protective Services in New York City: An Analysis of Case Management', 109 (May 1979) (unpublished manuscript).

108. George E. Fyer et al., 'The Child Protective Service Workers: A Profile of Needs, Attitudes and Utilization of Professional Resources', 12 Child Abuse & Neglect, 481 (1988).

109. Murray Levine et al., 'Informing Psychotherapy Clients of the Mandate to Report Suspected Child Maltreatment' paper presented at the American Psychology Law Society, San Diego, California (14 March, 1992); Robert F. Schopp, 'The Psychotherapist's Duty to Protect the Public: The Appropriate Standard and the Foundation in Legal Theory and Empirical Premises', 70 Nebraska Law Review, 327 (1991).

The duty to report child abuse should be crystallised through a practical articulation of the specific types of behaviours required to be reported and those not required to be reported. Reporting of inappropriate cases takes precious time from child protective services and threatens to bring about the anti-therapeutic consequences discussed previously. To crystallise and close the gap between investigative and adjudicative standards requires consideration of the magnitude of the harm required to be reported, its nature (that is, physical, sexual or emotional harm) and the relevant time frame (past or future harm). The greater the harm, the more it is limited to physical and sexual abuse, and the more it is limited to past harm, the narrower becomes the gap between the investigative and adjudicative standards.

Another potential anti-therapeutic consequence of the duty to report child abuse occurs when a patient discloses abuse to a therapist who is then required to report that abuse. Consider the case of a parent in treatment for issues not thought to be related to abuse who tells the therapist about an incident one year ago when the parent lost her temper and used excessive force to discipline her child. It is unlikely that this incident will result in termination of parental rights or criminal prosecution, yet the therapist is probably under an obligation to report the incident to the authorities. Accepting the limitations on the efficacy of therapy noted above,[110] given that the state is likely to offer nothing better than the treatment that the parent has already instituted and may well offer worse, keeping this person in treatment with her current therapist may be the best that we may hope for to reduce the risk of her abusing again. Therefore, when the abuser is already in treatment and termination or prosecution is unlikely, reporting should not be mandatory if it impedes treatment. Therapists often regard mandatory reporting of child abuse as a threat to treatment.[111] Although the effect of the fear of disclosure on treatment is far from clear,[112] therapists often perceive disruption of their ability to help and the poor quality of child protective services as justifying non-reporting.[113] When the abuser is already in treatment there is a compelling reason to consider recognising an exception to the reporting requirement so long as there is no reason to believe that the abuse is continuing and treatment of the child and

---

110. See notes 74 and 75.

111. Fred S. Berlin et al., 'Effects of Statutes Requiring Psychiatrists to Report Suspected Abuse of Children', 148 American Journal of Psychiatry, 449 (1991); Robert Weinstock and Diane Weinstock, 'Child Abuse Reporting Trends: An Unperceived Threat to Confidentiality', 33 J. Forensic Services, 418, at 421 (1988); Gail L. Zellman, 'Linking Schools and Social Services: The Case of Child Abuse Reporting', 12 Education Evaluation & Policy Analysis, 41 (1990). But see Watson and Levine, op. cit., supra, n. 105, 252. Watson and Levine studied the records of 65 cases in which a psychotherapist at a child and adolescent outpatient psychiatric clinic made a report of abuse. In one-quarter of the cases the disclosure had a therapeutic benefit, in one-quarter of the cases the patient left therapy after the report, and in one-half of the cases there was no detectable difference in therapy.

112. Daniel W. Shuman and Myron F. Weiner, The Psychotherapist-Patient Privilege: A Critical Examination (Springfield, 1987).

113. Gail L. Zellman, 'Child Abuse Reporting and Failure to Report Among Mandated Reporters', 5 J. Interpersonal Violence, 3, at 21 (1990).

the family is adequately addressed.[114] There is no evidence that therapists provide a unique fund of evidence of abuse that is not otherwise discoverable, and this exception would have no application to anyone other than the therapist. Therefore, if the abuse is continuing or has risen to a significant level, others who are not excepted from the reporting requirement, such as teachers and primary care physicians, will still be required to report the abuse.

It seems unlikely that child protective service agencies will receive a substantial increase in funding at any time in the near future and it is not clear that funding directed to the reduction of child abuse would best be put to that use in any event. The therapeutic role that the law can play is to reduce overreporting and unsubstantiated cases of abuse that dilute the efforts of child protective services. The law should assist in permitting child protective services to focus maximal effort on serious cases of abuse that are not otherwise being adequately addressed. Perhaps then they will have the capacity to respond appropriately to tomorrow's Joshua DeShaney.

4 Conclusion

Duty is not some magical incantation or a concept 'sacrosanct in itself, but only an expression of the sum total of those considerations of policy which lead the law to say that the particular plaintiff is entitled to protection'.[115] It is difficult to construct a vision of a caring society in which children are not entitled to protection from abuse. Thus there is an understandable desire to recognise a duty of the state to rescue abused children. This desire may affirm our sense of humanity, but it ignores the empirical evidence that intervention in specific cases will not necessarily make things better and may make things worse. Our knowledge of who has abused whom, and when and how to intervene is woefully incomplete. Charging in with good intentions but inadequate skills or resources risks causing significant harm. Viewing the duty of the state to rescue individual abused children through the lens of therapeutic jurisprudence leads to the conclusion that, because the evidence in favour of rescue being therapeutic is not persuasive, a duty of the state to rescue individual children cannot be justified.

Intervention in specific cases of abuse may be the least effective way to realise the vision of a caring society in which children are entitled to protection from abuse. Recasting the duty to rescue abused children as a broadly based duty of the state to eradicate the poverty that precipitates much physical abuse could reduce physical abuse more effectively while minimising the anti-therapeutic consequences of intervention in specific cases. This duty, however, seems impracticable as a specific duty in tort law and as a political reality. Perhaps the most therapeutic change in the duty to rescue that may be achieved to per-

---

114. See Berlin, op. cit., supra, n. 111, at 450, describing an attempt to recognise such an exception in Maryland that was rejected as politically inexpedient after one year of operation.

115. Smith v. Alameda Co. Serv. Agency, 90 Cal. App. 3d 929, 935, 153 Cal. Rptr. 712, 715 (1979) (citation omitted).

mit child protective services to focus limited resources on serious cases of abuse is narrowing and crystallising the requirements for intervention.

The role of the law in changing behaviour also cautions against a duty of the state to rescue abused children in specific cases. The failure of a private citizen to effect an easy rescue in the paradigmatic case of the child drowning in a shallow pool[116] may well turn on the private citizen's motivation. The only barrier to successful rescue in this paradigm is the willingness of the private citizen to act. Thus, if tort law plays a role in the actions of private citizens,[117] recognition of a duty to rescue increases the likelihood of a successful rescue of the drowning child by a private citizen.[118] The failure of the state to rescue an abused child successfully is not similarly an easy rescue whose success turns only on the motivation of the rescuer. The problem cannot similarly be categorised as a function of our not wanting to rescue, rather than not knowing how. Unlike the citizen who walks past the child drowning in the shallow pool, there is evidence in the positive law of every state that it has the motivation to rescue abused children. Every state in the United States has a mandatory child abuse reporting law and child protective service agencies to respond to cases of suspected child abuse. The potential of tort liability for failing to act on a report of abuse would only increase the risk of perfunctory removal with cursory investigation leaving the issue of return to the court, thereby insulating the workers from liability.[119] Rather than motivation, what stands in the way of successful rescue of abused children in specific cases is a multitude of factors that include methodologically sound research on the identification and treatment of abuse, adequate funding and staffing of well trained childcare professionals, and a directed, narrowly focused charge. Recognition of a duty to rescue does not adequately address the considerations that make successful rescue of abused children in specific cases by the state more likely.

---

116. Fowler v. Harper and Fleming James Jr., 3 The Law of Torts (Boston, 2nd ed., 1986), § 18.6, at 718 n. 9.

117. Daniel W. Shuman, 'The Psychology of Deterrence in Tort Law'; forthcoming: 42 Kansas Law Review (1993).

118. See Saul Levmore,'Waiting for Rescue: An Essay on the Evolution & Incentive Structure of Affirmative Obligations', 72 Virginia Law Review, 879 (1986).

119. Besharov, op. cit., supra, n. 101, 83; Peter Schuck, Suing Government: Citizen Remedies for Official Wrongs (New Haven, 1983), 75.

Chapter 16

A Therapeutic Jurisprudence Analysis of Mandated Reporting of Child Maltreatment by Psychotherapists

Murray Levine

I. Introduction

In addition to focusing on the rights, duties, and fairness of procedures in mental health law, therapeutic jurisprudence directs our attention to whether rules of law facilitate or impede therapeutic aims.[1] Rules of law implemented in complex social contexts may have unintended or unanticipated consequences; therapeutic jurisprudence directs us to attend to a specific consequence, namely a therapeutic effect. The deductions of therapeutic consequences from an analysis of the legal rule become hypotheses subject to empirical testing as illustrated in studies grounded in a general psychological jurisprudence.[2]

Therapeutic jurisprudence points us in a direction. However, because we are dealing with a law's therapeutic effects, the law is necessarily implemented in an organized social context. Our social system incorporates patients or clients, therapists and service providers, and parents and relatives of patients or clients, among others. When formal legal activity is involved, the functionaries of the law are also involved. Each functionary performs and interacts within a social organization. Each person performing a role has interests which he or she strives to fulfill. We must assume the actors are not passive but are actively pursuing their interests. They adapt their behavior to available resources, to barriers to obtaining resources, or to threats to their current adaptation.[3]

The system of interest I will focus upon is child protection in New York State. Child protective service (CPS) agencies, the successors to the private So-

---

1. David B. Wexler, An Introduction to Therapeutic Jurisprudence, in Therapeutic Jurisprudence: The Law as a Therapeutic Agent 3, 3–5 (David B. Wexler, ed., 1990); Bruce J. Winick, Competency to Consent to Voluntary Hospitalization: A Therapeutic Jurisprudence Analysis of Zinermon v. Birch, in Essays in Therapeutic Jurisprudence 83, 83 (David B. Wexler & Bruce J. Winick eds., 1991).

2. See David W. Shuman, Overview, 46 SMU L. Rev. 323, 324–25 (1992) (overview of Symposium, Psychological Jurisprudence: Another Perspective). See also David B. Wexler, Therapeutic Jurisprudence and Changing Conceptions of Legal Scholarship, 11 Behavioral Sci. & L. 17, 21 (1993) ("Therapeutic jurisprudence will lead us to raise questions, the answers to which are empirical and normative.")

3. See generally Murray Levine & David Perkins, Principles of Community Psychology 100–125 (1987) (discussing psychological adaptation to environments).

cieties for the Prevention of Cruelty to Children that developed in the 1870s,[4] now embedded within public social services departments, receive so many reports of suspected child maltreatment that the National Advisory Body for the National Center on Child Abuse and Neglect released a report asserting that the system was in crisis and in need of drastic reform.[5] One element subject to reform is the mandate to designated professionals working with children and families to report suspected child maltreatment.[6]

In what follows, I will define the law's therapeutic aim, examine the child protection system as it operates, and examine some of the rules of law that may promote or impede therapeutic aims. In particular, I will concentrate on the impact of the mandate to report suspected child maltreatment on the psychotherapy relationship. I will illustrate the complexities that are introduced when we view a system through a broader therapeutic jurisprudence lens that takes into account the characteristics of the roles played by actors in the system.

Child protection legislation has an impact on the confidential psychotherapy relationship. The law requiring the breach of confidentiality has a clear therapeutic purpose, but so also do provisions for confidential and privileged communications. Professors Shuman and Weiner have argued that the absence of a legal privilege has little or no effect on whether clients choose to enter psychiatric or psychological treatment and that once having entered, their treatment is unaffected by the lack of privilege.[7] In pre-therapeutic jurisprudence days, they were saying that the law of privilege had neither therapeutic nor antitherapeutic effects. That proposition may be true on the very general level at which they examined it. However, Shuman and Weiner did not examine the effects on a psychotherapeutic relationship when a privilege did not exist. Under child protection statutes, privilege is limited for the purpose of making a report to state authorities to protect a child. Will that limitation of privilege have an effect on an ongoing confidential relationship?

II. Note on Method

To illustrate the issues, I will present excerpts from open ended, semi-structured interviews conducted with thirty psychotherapists who had made one or

---

4. Murray Levine & Adeline Levine, Helping Children: a Social History 208–210 (1992).

5. U.S. Advisory Board on Child Abuse and Neglect, Office of Human Development Services, Critical First Steps in a National Emergency 2, 92 (1990).

6. See Margaret H. Meriwether, Child Abuse Reporting Laws: Time for a Change, 20 Fam. L. Q. 141, 145–46, 164 (1986) (discussing the need for all professionals who work with children to report abuse); see also Douglas Besharov, Gaining Control Over Child Abuse Reports, 48 Pub. Welfare 34, 34 (1990) (stating that all states now require a broader category of professionals to report abuse); Elizabeth D. Hutchison, Mandatory Reporting Laws: Child Protective Case Finding Gone Awry? 38 Soc. Work 56, 57 (1993) (the definition of those who are required to report suspected child abuse has been expanded). But see David Finkelhor, Is Child Abuse Overreported?, 48 Pub. Welfare 23, 28–9 (1990) (Finkelhor believes that the reporting system is not out of kilter, but that a certain amount of inefficiency is inevitable).

7. Daniel W. Shuman & Myron F. Weiner, The Privilege Study: An Empirical Examination of the Psychotherapist-Patient Privilege, 60 N.C.L. Rev. 893, 894 (1982).

more reports within the previous year on clients they had in therapy, and with twenty-five CPS workers who had investigated reports coming from mental health sources.[8] The therapists were asked to think of a case they had reported within the past year, and the CPS workers were asked to think of a recent case in which they had received a report from a mental health source. The interviewees were all volunteers who responded to an announcement offering to pay $20 for an interview on this general subject. The psychotherapists came from six agencies in two counties, and the CPS workers from two counties.

The survey was conducted by a group associated with the State University of New York at Buffalo. Three of us have extensive experience as line CPS workers, and the graduate students are advanced trainees in clinical psychology with clinical experience. We reviewed the examples and tested our interpretations against the experience of team members as a means of identifying idiosyncratic and typical examples. We used something like a process of cross-checking to guide our presentation and our conclusions. Our aim is to produce representations that "ring true."[9]

We do not have a systematic sample. Our interest is not in specifying the frequency of occurrence of different events, but rather in identifying essential issues that will be encountered inevitably by those working in similar situations. We assume an organized social world with regularities that occur because social settings tend to be coercive of the behavior they elicit.[10] In the absence of evidence to the contrary, experiences in a given setting are more likely to be typical than atypical. We asked our respondents to tell us whether the events they related were typical of their experiences. Usually, more than one respondent described similar occurrences. Often, we were able to identify complementary phenomena in the transcripts of interviews with therapists and with CPS workers. We also used members of our research group as a social control.

III. The Child Protection System

A. History

The child protection system developed when mid-nineteenth century "child savers"[11] became concerned about the plight of impoverished immigrant families who sometimes abandoned their children, who sometimes exploited them, and who sometimes treated them with great harshness.[12] Child protective ser-

---

8. Murray Levine et al., Mandated Reporting and the Therapeutic Alliance in the Context of the Child Protection System (Baldy Center for Law & Social Policy, SUNY Buffalo, Working Paper Series CL91.02).

9. See generally Murray Levine et al., Learning from Seymour Sarason, 18 Am. J. Community Psychol. 343 (1990) (explaining the value of research work which is insightful, challenging, and makes a "positive contribution" to knowledge).

10. Levine & Perkins, supra note 3, at 107.

11. Anthony M. Platt, The Child Savers: The Invention of Delinquency (1969).

12. Linda Gordon, Heroes of Their Own Lives: The Politics and History of Family Violence 32–37 (1988).

vices were authorized under the state's *parens patriae* and police powers.[13] The intent was to protect children, often by removing them from their parents and placing them in institutions.[14]

One early catalyst in the child protection movement was the well publicized case of Mary Ellen, a child placed by a charitable organization with a foster family who was cruelly abused by that family. A missionary learned of the case, but found that neither she nor any other agency had authority to intervene in an intact family where the child had not been abandoned. Eventually, the American Society for the Prevention of Cruelty to Animals acted.[15] Her case resulted in a criminal trial and the conviction of her caretaker for assault.[16] The trial received a great deal of publicity.[17] In 1875, the attorney Elbridge Gerry organized the New York Society for the Prevention of Cruelty to Children.[18]

Child maltreatment was never high on the public agenda although the child protection movement spread throughout the United States very quickly.[19] In the early twentieth century, child protection became caught up in the struggle to remove welfare functions from the private sector and place them in public agencies. The Social Security Act of 1935 provided the decisive element in reform by conditioning federal reimbursement upon the creation of centralized state welfare authorities and the delivery of services in local communities.[20]

Child abuse was rediscovered after World War II.[21] Pediatric roentgenologists reported unexplained cases of multiple healed fractures in infants and children.[22] The Children's Bureau had been collecting information on child maltreatment and supported some research on the topic.[23] C. Henry Kempe and his co-workers' study of the frequency of serious injury and deaths in emergency rooms, accompanied by an editorial in the Journal of the American Medical Association, and a well publicized symposium at the American Medical Association meetings, pushed the issue to the front burner.[24] A great deal of publicity, and professional acceptance followed.[25] Not long after, almost all

---

13. See New York ex rel. State Board of Charities v. New York Soc'y Prevention of Cruelty to Children, 55 N.E. 1063, 1065 (1900).

14. In re Knowack, 53 N.E. 676, 677 (1899).

15. The legal basis for intervention was not that the child was entitled the legal protection afforded animals; rather it was initiated by a writ de homine replegiando, an English writ of law that removes one person from the custody of another. Mason P. Thomas, Jr., Child Abuse and Neglect, Part I: Historical Overview, Legal Matrix, and Social Perspectives, 50 N.C.L. Rev. 293, 307 (1972).

16. Id. at 310.

17. Stephen Lazoritz, Whatever Happened to Mary Ellen? 14 Child Abuse and Neglect 143, 145–147 (1990).

18. Thomas, supra note 15, at 307–08.

19. R. C. McCrea, The Humane Movement: A Descriptive Survey 389–431 (1910).

20. Levine & Levine, supra note 4, ch. 12.

21. Barbara J. Nelson, Making an Issue of Child Abuse 11–12 (1984).

22. Id.

23. Id. at 45.

24. Id. at 13, 16. See C. Henry Kempe et al., The Battered Child Syndrome, 181 J. Am. Med. Ass'n 17 (1962).

25. Stephen J. Pfohl, The "Discovery" of Child Abuse, 24 Soc. Probs. 310, 310 (1977).

states developed reporting laws, and reports of child maltreatment skyrocketed.[26]

Reporting laws were adopted in order to allow physicians to report without concern about breaching confidentiality.[27] Legislators believed that a reporting law and a state hotline were inexpensive means of expressing concern about children.[28] They badly underestimated the frequency of child maltreatment in the United States.[29] Reports grew from 669,000 in 1976 to 2,086,000 in 1986.[30] The list of those mandated to report grew as well,[31] without regard to the fact that the first laws were really directed to emergency room physicians who generally do not have continuing relationships with patients.[32] The frequency of sex abuse cases has also grown from 3.2% of reports in 1976 to 15.7% in 1986.[33] These figures continue to grow. The number of reports in 1992 will be about 2.7 million, placing the entire system under strain.[34]

B. Therapeutic Aim

The therapeutic purpose of the child protection statutes and the reporting law may be stated simply—to protect children from maltreatment that threatens them physically and psychologically.[35] The intent of the law is to prevent children "from suffering further injury and impairment."[36] The state intends this intervention to "protect children from injury or mistreatment and to help safeguard their physical, mental and emotional well-being."[37] At its best, the law requires the Social Service Department to assist a family in distress by eliminating the maltreatment and to restore family competence. Even if a child is removed from a family, it is considered a temporary action.[38] Social Services has a duty to work to restore the child to a renewed family.[39] Often families

---

26. Nelson, supra note 21, at 13, 16. Abuse was emphasized rather than the far more frequent case of neglect in order to insulate legislation to protect children from association with the then politically unpopular War on Poverty. Id. at 14–15.

27. See Monrad Paulsen et al., Child Abuse Reporting Laws: Some Legislative History, 34 Geo. Wash. L. Rev. 482, 483 (1966); Cf. Pfohl, supra note 25, at 316, 320.

28. Nelson, supra note 21, at 76–77.

29. Id.

30. Bureau of the Census, U.S. Dep't of Commerce, Statistical Abstracts of the United States 186 (1992).

31. Mark A. Small, Policy Review of Child Abuse and Neglect Reporting Statutes, 14 Law & Pol'y 129, 131 (1992).

32. See Pfohl, supra note 25, at 317, 319.

33. Bureau of the Census, supra note 30.

34. U.S. Advisory Board on Child Abuse and Neglect, supra note 5, at 15.

35. See Nelson, supra note 21, at 13–14.

36. N.Y. Soc. Serv. Law § 411 (McKinney 1992).

37. N.Y. Fam. Ct. Act § 1011 (McKinney 1983 & Supp. 1993).

38. N.Y. Fam. Ct. Act § 1055(b)(i) (McKinney Supp. 1993) (initially placements are one year long).

39. See, e.g., N.Y. Soc. Serv. Law § 384-1(a)(iii) (McKinney 1992) ("The state's first obligation is to help the family with services to prevent its break-up or to reunite it if the child has already left home.").

will be referred for counseling or psychotherapy as a consequence of a child protection investigation or an adjudication of abuse or neglect.

C. Due Process Considerations

The therapeutic purpose of protecting the child is so greatly valued that society is willing to intrude on the constitutionally protected privacy of the family in order to protect a child. Society accords a low standard of due process protections to the parent when the state does intrude.[40] An investigation is triggered by a "reasonable cause to suspect,"[41] a relatively low standard of evidence for maltreatment. An investigator has the authority to enter a home in an emergency and to remove a child temporarily.[42] An administrative determination, made by the investigator, requires only "some credible evidence" of maltreatment.[43] The determination is subject to appeal.[44] Moreover, the investigating agency and the investigative worker are granted immunity from prosecution for most errors that might be made in the course of an investigation.[45]

An adjudication in cases that reach a family or juvenile court in a dependency and neglect hearing[46] requires only a "preponderance" of the evidence.[47] The respondent to a neglect or abuse petition has no right to a jury trial, a reduced right to confront witnesses, and a limited Fifth Amendment right against self incrimination.[48] In contrast to a criminal trial, the silence of a respondent in this type of civil proceeding may be used as evidence against the respondent.[49] Moreover, child protection statutes limit privilege so that it is not available in a child protection proceeding.[50] A therapist's records may be subpoenaed and the therapist required to testify. The standard for introducing evidence is not very high. The judge may follow civil law procedure, but has discretion to modify those procedures.[51] In some circumstances, hearsay may

---

40. See generally Santosky v. Kramer, 455 U.S. 745, 769 (1982) (holding clear and convincing evidence as the standard of proof).

41. N.Y. Soc. Serv. Law § 413.1 (McKinney 1992).

42. N.Y. Soc. Serv. Law § 417 (McKinney 1992).

43. N.Y. Soc. Serv. Law § 412.12 (McKinney 1992).

44. N.Y. Soc. Serv. Law § 422.8 (McKinney 1992).

45. See Cheryl A. Nohejl et al., Risk Assessment Implementation and Legal Liability in CPS Practice, 14 Law & Pol'y 185, 189–190 (1992).

46. Such hearings constitute about 15% of "indicated" cases. Douglas J. Besharov, The Need to Narrow the Grounds for State Intervention, in Protecting Children from Abuse and Neglect: Policy and Practice 47, 57 (D. J. Besharov ed. 1988).

47. N.Y. Fam. Ct. Act § 1046(b)(i) (McKinney 1983).

48. Murray Levine & Eric Doherty, Professional Issues: The Fifth Amendment and Therapeutic Requirements to Admit Abuse, 18 Crim. Just. & Behav. 98, 99 (1991).

49. In re Commissioner of Soc. Servs. v. Philip De G., 450 N.E.2d 681, 683 (1983).

50. N.Y. Fam. Ct. Act § 1046(a)(vii) (McKinney 1983).

51. See N.Y. Fam. Ct. Act § 165(a) (McKinney 1983) ("The provisions of the civil practice law and rules shall apply to the extent that they are appropriate to the proceedings involved.").

be used to corroborate hearsay.[52] The adjudication may result in the exercise of the coercive power of the court to implement a treatment plan.[53]

Given the limitations on other rights and the level of due process afforded respondents, we should examine the costs and benefits of reporting legislation carefully.

IV. How the Law Affects Therapists and Therapy

The standards in all states for mandated reporting of suspected child maltreatment include some variant of "reasonable suspicion."[54] This vague standard reflects a policy decision to cast a broad net to identify all cases of maltreatment. The policy insures that there will be a large number of false positives (cases of suspected maltreatment that prove to be unfounded) and assumes that the cost of investigating false positives is less important than the potential for protecting children. The policy also assumes, if not a helpful system, at least a benign one. That assumption is open to question.

A. Participating in the System

Social policy aims, ethical requirements, and legal requirements should be congruent. When they conflict, actors in the system experience stress[55] and tend to feel that aspects of the law are obstructive, irrational, or absurd.[56] Therapists and CPS investigators have different tasks and share overlapping, but different, cultures. Therapists are concerned about their clients and seek to help them through the exercise of particular professional skills. Reporting takes place within a system of investigation and intervention. From the viewpoint of the reporting therapist, the outcomes may be unpredictable. Unpredictability derives, in part, from the application of the vague governing statutory definitions. Also, the investigative process may have emotional effects on the clients who are reported. One of the therapists we interviewed said about reporting:

> It's not pleasant...I feel like I have created a train wreck somewhere. But I know that it's part of the job and I am willing to accept that...It is a yucky feeling. I have done it numerous times and it doesn't get any better. If anything

---

52. Murray Levine & Lori Battistoni, The Corroboration Requirement in Child Sex Abuse Cases, 9 Behavioral Sci. & L. 3, 7 (1991).

53. See N.Y. Fam. Ct. Act § 1057 (McKinney 1983) ("Rules of court shall define permissible terms and conditions of supervision under this section."); N.Y. Fam. Ct. Act §1072(b) (McKinney 1983) (failure to comply with terms and conditions of supervision is punishable by up to six months in jail).

54. Meriwether, supra note 6, at 146.

55. H. Watson, Child Abuse Reporting: Factors Affecting the Decision Process 47 (1991) (unpublished Ph.D. thesis, SUNY Buffalo) (75% of therapists who made a report experienced it as personally stressful).

56. Gail L. Zellman & Stephen Antler, Mandated Reporters and CPS: A Study in Frustration, 48 Pub. Welfare 30, 34–35 (1990).

it gets worse because the more I have to do it, the more I appreciate the impact on the family.[57]

Another therapist compared the experience with involuntarily hospitalizing someone. For him, the experience of reporting suspected child maltreatment was very different:

> The first time I filed a report, I had that same feeling: this is going to be very painful, but they'll [the clients] recognize...how it was necessary and benefitted them...I don't feel that way anymore. I just do it, but I hold my breath while doing it because I don't know what's going to happen...I don't even have the self satisfaction of feeling I prevented something. I don't feel the system works well or benefits clients.[58]

B. Emotional Costs of a Report

In addition to the dollar costs to the state,[59] to say nothing of legal costs to a respondent of an investigation, there are emotional or other costs to the family. Richard Wexler has documented some of the horror stories that have led to adverse publicity and law suits.[60] Our CPS investigators provided us with numerous examples of emotional costs to the subjects of their investigations.[61] CPS investigators are aware that their very appearance raises the specter that children may be removed from the home:

> Oh yeah. They'd go to the door and they were very guarded. They don't want to talk to you because they are afraid you are going to walk out the door with their kids. They are very frightened of child protection. We terrorize people... Just the thought of CPS frightens people.[62]

When the therapist is uncertain or anxious about the therapeutic value of a report, and makes the report just to comply with the law, the therapist is coerced by potential civil and criminal penalties, or by agency policy, to act against his or her professional judgment. Therapists are also concerned about another cost of reporting: the impact on the therapeutic alliance.[63]

---

57. Levine et al., supra note 8, at 11.

58. Id. at 12.

59. The New York Department of Social Services estimates that a hot line screening call costs $6, while an investigation costs $309. Bureau of Management, Planning and Evaluation, N.Y.S. Dep't of Social Services, Unfounded Cps Rep., Interim Rep., Phase I 1 (1991).

60. See generally Richard Wexler, Wounded Innocents: The Real Victims of the War Against Child Abuse (1990).

61. Murray Levine, et al., Child Protection Workers' Views of Mandated Reports of Child Maltreatment Made by Psychotherapists 3–5 (Sept. 30, 1992) (unpublished manuscript, on file with the author).

62. Id. at 3.

63. See generally The Psychotherapeutic Process: A Research Handbook (Leslie S. Greenberg & William Pinsof eds., 1986) (describing a therapeutic alliance as the bond between the therapist and patient that creates a sense that they are in a joint struggle against the patient's problem).

C. Informing the Client of the Mandate to Report

The therapeutic alliance develops with the first encounter between therapist and client. Most therapists feel an ethical responsibility to inform a client of the limits of confidentiality. Informing the client is an act that respects a client's autonomy. Enhancing client autonomy is certainly a therapeutic goal, but the reporting mandate complicates the effort to meet the duty to inform. What should the therapist inform the client about?

What constitutes reportable maltreatment? Our therapists had little hesitancy about reporting incidents involving visible signs of injury and disclosures of sexual abuse when the allegation was clear and the perpetrator was named.[64] The criteria for other types of maltreatment were less clear. One therapist summed up the problem with unintended irony: "The reporting criteria are unambiguous. The incidents that come up are ambiguous."[65]

If the standards for reporting are vague to mandated reporters who receive some training in reporting, what must they be like for clients who, upon entering treatment, might be informed of the psychotherapist's duty to report suspected child maltreatment? Psychotherapists appear reluctant to engage clients in any detailed discussion of the limits of confidentiality when clients enter psychotherapy despite ethical, if not legal, duties to do so.[66] What is a client to understand by the vague terms that are often embedded in an assurance of confidentiality?

We have very little knowledge of common practices in obtaining informed consent for psychotherapy. Only half of the therapists in one survey said they always provided information about confidentiality limits. A little over half provided information orally only.[67] A minority of respondents (36.9%) in another survey said they forewarned their clients of the duty to report suspected maltreatment either orally or by means of a written notice.[68] About 57% gave warnings only when a suspicion was aroused or a disclosure was actually

---

64. The therapists seemed to adopt criteria for reporting that were similar to those described in the literature based on surveys and vignette studies. See Brosig & Kalichman, Clinicians' Reporting of Suspected Child Abuse: A Review of the Empirical Literature, 12 Clinical Psychol. Rev. 155, 163–165 (1992).

65. Levine et al., supra note 8, at 18.

66. See Charles P. Ewing, Mental Health Clinicians and the Law: An Overview of Current Law Governing Professional Practice, in Psychology, Psychiatry, and the Law: A Clinical and Forensic Handbook 527 (Charles P. Ewing ed., 1985); See generally American Association of Counseling and Development, Ethical Standards of the American Association of Counseling and Development (3rd revision), 67 J. Counseling & Dev. 4 (1988); American Association of Marriage and Family Therapists, Code of Ethics, Rule 2.1 (1991); American Psychiatric Association, Principle 5: Confidentiality (amended June 2, 1989); Federation of Societies for Clinical Social Work, Code of Ethics (1988).

67. Katherine M. Nicolai & Norman A. Scott, Psychotherapy's Miranda Warning: Effects of Informing Clients of Confidentiality Limits on Reporting Child Abuse 4 (March 14, 1992) (unpublished manuscript, on file with the author).

68. Wesley B. Crenshaw & James W. Lichtenberg, Child Abuse and the Limits of Confidentiality: Forewarning Practices, 11 Behavioral Sci. & L. 181, 189 (1993).

made.[69] In effect, more than half did not give their clients notice before the duty to report crystallized.[70] One of the agencies where some of our therapists worked had a policy of not informing clients in advance because they dealt with high risk clients and were concerned that clients would not disclose maltreatment.

Assuming the desirability, what should be conveyed to a client at the outset to support an autonomous decision? How much can or should the therapist explain what is meant by child maltreatment? How much should a therapist convey about the consequences of a report of child maltreatment? Should the therapist tell about the limitations of privilege if a report is made[71] and that a child protection investigation could lead to a criminal investigation?[72]

Therapists acknowledge that informing clients in advance is helpful in enhancing the relationship: "It's clear that we respect and acknowledge confidentiality. There's relief on the part of the client because we are clear."[73]

However, in presenting the limitations, our therapists said they emphasize confidentiality and mention limitations:

> It's tricky because you are laying out confidentiality with people and that's important to establish, but there's also the dilemma about whether you emphasize that [reporting mandate] and not get disclosures that...need to be disclosed and discussed and treated. So I don't go crazy emphasizing that.... I don't know if I am violating people's rights in that. It's an ongoing question that's hard to answer, but I do make clear what confidentiality is, especially when you are working with kids.[74]

Anticipating the effect on therapy, the therapist may not always convey the mandate to report:

> Now...in the first few interviews, or one of the first interviews [I try to] say that if anything is ever disclosed to me, I need to do this [report]. There may be times when I may have forgotten to do that. It's not a hundred percent foolproof, but I try to do that.[75]

Note that by emphasizing confidentiality and omitting to tell the clients about the limits, therapists may find themselves in a bind when a client does disclose a reportable episode. A therapist working with an adolescent said: "I felt just horrible, like I had really betrayed her."[76]

Therapists who work with high risk clients may not inform their clients of the mandate to report either because they assume the client knows of the man-

---

69. Id.

70. Robert F. Schopp, The Psychotherapist's Duty to Protect the Public: The Appropriate Standard and the Foundation in Legal Theory and Empirical Premises, 70 Neb. L. Rev. 327, 342 (1991).

71. N.Y. Soc. Serv. Law § 415 (McKinney 1992) (permitting disclosure of "any other information which the commissioner may, by regulation, require, or the person making the report believes might be helpful, in the furtherance of the purposes of this title.").

72. See Levine & Doherty, supra note 48, at 101.

73. Levine et al., supra note 8, at 13.

74. Id. at 14–15.

75. Id. at 15.

76. Id. at 16.

date and doesn't need the warning, or because they are concerned about losing the fragile rapport they have with clients who may not be entering treatment entirely of their own free will.[77]

One hazard of mandated reporting is the exposure to criminal prosecution if a client discloses an episode of abuse. What a client learns about the limits of confidentiality through an informed consent formula can result in a severe drop in disclosures of episodes of abuse if the client does enter treatment, and may act as a deterrent to the voluntary entry into treatment of some pedophiles. Thus, the mandate to report under some conditions may have an antitherapeutic effect both in restricting topics that come up for discussion in treatment and in failing to protect children from further episodes of abuse.

What do clients understand even if warned? Assuming a minimal warning, what does the client understand? Views of what constitutes maltreatment may vary widely among CPS investigators, therapists, and clients. For example, a parent who severely punishes a child by using a belt and leaves marks may view himself as a good parent trying to discipline a wayward child. The parent, in discussing his or her frustration or guilt in disciplining a child, may not understand how the therapist or the CPS investigator will look at those well intended actions. Nor will the client appreciate the nature of the investigation until he or she experiences it:

> The initial reaction [upon being informed] is very matter of fact: "I understand." After that person [CPS worker] comes out, then it really sinks in. "My God, this is going on. I'm furious," and she gets furious at the guy who made the report. So I really wasn't surprised with her reaction [delayed anger] because I have seen it before...I would like to think they really heard what I was saying and take it in, and I am not sure they really did that...So in hindsight, I can see that talking about being a mandated reporter, it just didn't connect with them.[79]

D. Unfounded Reports

The vague statutory standards and the different standards of evidence used by CPS investigators and therapists lead to unfounded reports. Nationally, sixty percent of reports are unfounded.[80] Most of our therapists told the client when they made a report because they felt an ethical obligation and a therapeutic hope that the communication would help preserve trust and the therapeutic alliance. However, about half of the CPS investigators we interviewed would have preferred an unannounced visit. Thus, differing obligations in the two roles leads to conflict between the actors. Statistically speaking, when a therapist makes a report, the odds are against indication by the CPS investigator. That means that therapists are left to deal with clients who were told by the state, implicitly if not explicitly, that the therapist was "wrong" in making

---

77. Mandated reporters are granted either good faith or absolute immunity for reports made pursuant to the mandate. Besharov, supra note 46.

78. Fred S. Berlin et al., Effects of Statutes Requiring Psychiatrists to Report Suspected Sexual Abuse of Children, 148 Am. J. Psychiatry 449, 451 (1991).

79. Levine et al., supra note 8, at 16.

80. Besharov, supra note 6.

the report.[81] If the report was unfounded, the client was subject to an upsetting experience that would confirm that the system was an adversary not a friend:

> When the mother learned of the report, she threatened to pack up the kids and leave the city. She was convinced her children would be taken from her. She was also fearful that welfare authorities would discover she was living with a man and would stop her public assistance.[82]

The report was unfounded. According to the therapist, the CPS worker said: "This isn't any big deal. We don't even know why you reported this. There's no marks on the child."[83]

E. Stale and Inappropriate Reports

We have identified two classes of reports that are likely to be unfounded—stale reports and inappropriate reports. Reporting statutes contain nothing like a "statute of limitations" or a requirement that the suspected maltreatment be ongoing or imminent. Stale reports are made when the therapist takes a literal view of the law's requirements and reports an episode from the client's past.[84] A CPS worker described a report she had investigated:

> She was upset one day, and she slapped her child across the arm and left...supposedly left a red mark. The mother had not had her son since three years ago. So basically that was it. This person called in a report because her client told her that she swatted her son on the shoulder and thought she may have left a red mark and felt bad about doing that.... The mother pulled out of treatment immediately. She was gone.[85]

Our therapists and CPS workers provided a number of other examples of stale reports. They estimate that anywhere from two to twenty percent of reports coming from mental health sources may be in this category.

The second category, inappropriate reports, reflects both a lack of appreciation of the conditions under which CPS can intervene and vague statutory cri-

---

81. Compare Wexler and Winick's concept that the criminal plea process may contribute to cognitive distortion or cognitive restructuring with sex offenders. David B. Wexler & Bruce J. Winick, Therapeutic Jurisprudence and Criminal Justice Mental Health Issues, 16 Mental & Physical Disability L. Rep. 225, 229 (1992). See Jeffrey A. Klotz et al., Cognitive Restructuring Through Law: A Therapeutic Jurisprudence Approach to Sex Offenders and the Plea Process, 15 U. Puget Sound L. Rev. 579 (1992) (discussing the implication of the Alford plea for cognitive restructuring in sex offenders).

82. Levine et al., supra note 8, at 10.

83. Id. at 11.

84. One might expect the state hot line would screen out reports which are stale or inappropriate. However, the comments of CPS investigators in our interviews suggest that in their view, the hot line does not screen out a sufficient number of what one CPS investigator termed "garbage reports." The state believes that the hot line does screen out a significant number of reports that if investigated would be unfounded. Bureau of Mgmt., supra note 59, at 4. The unexpected comments from CPS investigators, along with the comments of experienced therapists who said they had learned to manipulate the hot line, gave us some insight into the dynamics that affect the process of communication from mandated reporter to hot line and then from hot line to CPS investigator. Levine et al., supra note 61, at 19–21.

85. Levine et al., supra note 61, at 5–6.

teria: "We had lots of reports from therapists treating schizophrenics or personality disorders and I think it is because they're worried that these people could do something to their children."[86]

In discussing another case, the CPS investigator pointed out that she could do nothing in the absence of evidence of maltreatment, or specific threatening conduct by the parent:

> We continually have these disagreements and I find that to be fairly common with most therapists who call in. There's going to be trouble, they'll say... there's going to be trouble. We are operating on what's going on right now, this minute, not what may happen next month or next year.[87]

Another problem arises because the reporting mandate increases the power imbalance between therapist and client.[88] Therapists and CPS investigators stated that reports were made and received when a client dropped out of treatment and the therapist wanted CPS to bring the client back into treatment. Sometimes, the CPS investigators felt the reports were made out of pique that the client had rejected the therapist. We have described how the reporting power was used coercively by therapists to shake up a family, to force a course of action on a client, to attack resistance to treatment or to pursue some other objective such as getting a parent to confront past history of abuse.[89] The therapists' judgments may be correct, and the therapeutic ends may be valid. However, if the report is unfounded, the therapeutic aim may well be frustrated. The CPS investigator cannot indicate a report that does not meet legal standards of maltreatment, and the client receives the message that the therapist was wrong.

This type of disagreement leads to conflicts between therapists and CPS investigators. Therapists, who feel their training is superior to that of CPS investigators, may feel that their views deserve more consideration by CPS workers than they sometimes receive. Unfounded cases are sometimes interpreted by the therapist as an insult to the therapist's competence. On the other hand CPS investigators felt that therapists did not know CPS functions or limits, and the investigator considered the therapist's attitudes to be difficult:

---

86. Id. at 12.

87. Levine et al., supra note 61, at 12. See David J. Agatstein, Child Abuse Reporting in New York State: The Dilemma of the Mental Health Profession, 34 N.Y.L. Sch. L. Rev. 115, 154 (1989) (the issue is whether the child is currently abused or neglected). Even though the New York statute does not require injury to the child and permits intervention when some injury threatens, the possibilities for preventive intervention are restricted by due process considerations. N.Y. Fam. Ct. Act § 1012(e)(i) (McKinney 1983 & Supp. 1993) ("[O]r creates a substantial risk of death...."); N.Y. Fam. Ct. Act § 1012(e)(ii) (McKinney 1983 & Supp. 1993) ("[C]reates or allows to be created a substantial risk...."); N.Y. Fam. Ct. Act § 1012 (f)(i) (McKinney 1983 & Supp. 1993) ("[O]r is in imminent danger of becoming impaired...."); N.Y. Fam. Ct. Act § 1012 (f)(i)(B) (McKinney 1983 & Supp. 1993) ("[O]r a substantial risk thereof.").

88. Michael L. Perlin, Power Imbalances in Therapeutic and Forensic Relationships, 9 Behavioral Sci. & L. 111, 115 (1991).

89. Elizabeth Anderson et al., Coercive Uses of Mandatory Reporting in Therapeutic Relationships, 11 Behavioral Sci. & L. 335 (1993).

> They [therapists] may think this is not a good atmosphere or a good environ-
> ment for this child. They will request us to remove the child or make us feel like
> it's, you know that's our number one priority and it's difficult to let these peo-
> ple [therapists] know what the law requires.... They can be very condescending
> at times. [As] mental health professionals, they know from mind and...the
> family dynamics and what's going on in everybody's head so that can be a
> problem for us.[90]

Other communication problems arise because of the different roles and
tasks that therapists and CPS workers have. We will not address this issue
here. Our emphasis on some of the problems should not obscure the fact that
good working relationships develop regularly between therapists and CPS investigators, especially among repeat players.

F. Impact on Treatment

What happens to treatment when a report is made? The available data suggests that about twenty-five percent of psychotherapy clients who are subject
to a mandated report will drop out of treatment shortly after the report is
made.[91] This number does not take into account those who drop out psychologically but are unable to leave therapy physically because they are already
enmeshed with child protection, social services or the criminal justice systems.[92] All of our cases came from agencies. Therefore, we do not know what
the drop out rate might be in private practice settings.

Our therapists reported numerous examples of clients leaving treatment,
and these were confirmed by the observations of CPS investigators. A client on
whom a report has been made often feels angered and betrayed. The following
quotation is from one of the CPS workers who investigated a report coming
from a therapist:

> The mother was very angry that they had called in a report, extremely angry...
> I think that termination with the therapist who called it in was important at
> this point even though they [clinic and therapists] are good treatment providers
> and there was nothing wrong with the treatment they were providing; mother
> perceived it as wrong.[93]

A second example from a therapist illustrates the same point:

> She [the client] was angry, denying, frustrated. I am sure she was hurt. You
> know we had started to develop a rapport in the first session. And here at the
> second session it was almost like I was beating her over the head with [it]....I
> didn't feel comfortable at all in reporting this because I truly believed she
> would not be back...I tried reaching the family, tried reaching the mother to
> ask her if she would like to come in and talk...but I could never reach her.
> There was never any answer.[94]

---

90. Levine et al., supra note 61, at 17.

91. Holly Watson & Murray Levine, Psychotherapy and Mandated Reporting of Child
Abuse, 59 Am. J. Orthopsychiatry 246, 252–253 (1989).

92. Id. at 254.

93. Levine et al., supra note 61, at 14.

94. Levine et al., supra note 8, at 36.

Reports made about third parties not in treatment[95] have less of a negative impact on the therapy relationship.[96] Improvement is more likely to occur when the report is made about a third party not in treatment.[97] A CPS investigator observed, "Mom [who was in treatment] was very receptive, cordial, open, glad I came...Dad, [not in treatment] who really the allegations were against...Dad, well, he wasn't so receptive. He was really defensive, more guarded."[98]

The end result of a report may be an investigation and an adjudication in which the client is ordered back into treatment. For example, a client who voluntarily sought treatment disclosed episodes of intrafamilial sexual abuse, which was reported. The client was ordered by the family court judge to leave the home and to remain in therapy until the therapist and the social services department felt he could return.[99] However, the client was also prosecuted criminally.[100] The CPS investigator commented, "they bargained down and he was put on probation and ordered into therapy which he was already in."[101]

Perhaps there was merit in prosecuting; perhaps the victim felt more secure or empowered. However what was the effect on the subsequent treatment? We have no information in this case whether therapy was now so spoiled for the client that he was unable to make use of it.

G. Resistance Following a Report

If the client remained in treatment, often the damage to the therapeutic alliance was reflected in guardedness, and related to a loss of trust on the part of the client. A therapist noted:

> I felt that she became more superficial with me after the report even though she continued to share with me the incidents of concern....I felt that she learned to set limits with the sharing of too much information. I felt that she was less open, less spontaneous....We had a very good relationship for a long time, at least a year and a half. And I felt that our relationship was damaged.[102]

Children may be subject to pressure after a report is made either to recant, or to refuse to give further information. A therapist working with a child noted:

---

95. A sophisticated client may use the system to make a report about a third party as a tactic in a custody dispute or as a weapon in a relationship. See Roe v. Superior Court, 280 Cal. Rptr. 380, 385–386 (Cal. Ct. App. 1991)

96. Watson & Levine, supra note 91.

97. Id.

98. Murray Levine, Reporting Clients Already in Treatment 9 (July 8, 1992) (unpublished manuscript, on file with the author).

99. Clients ordered into treatment may still protest their innocence, but therapists insist that no improvement can be made until the client admits the abuse. Under some conditions, the therapeutic requirement may raise Fifth Amendment issues. Levine & Doherty, supra note 48, at 98–99; see Montana v. Imlay, 113 S. Ct. 444 (1992) (White, J., dissenting from the dismissal of the writ of certiorari).

100. The district attorney's office is entitled to request all reports for review for consideration of criminal prosecution. N.Y. Soc. Serv. Law § 424.4 (McKinney 1993).

101. Levine, supra note 98, at 5.

102. Levine et al., supra note 8, at 38.

What my hunch is that the family, the parents sat each one of them down and asked them if they told anybody anything and read them the riot act, that they better not tell anybody anything....So I don't think it is going to encourage these kids to open up. That [threats to the child] is one of the risks of doing this kind of reporting.[103]

H. Working Through the Resistance

Our therapists reported that it was sometimes possible to work through resistance and reestablish the therapeutic alliance. Many therapists felt that if the alliance was strong to begin with, the relationship could survive the report. However, some therapists said that it took several weeks of working on the resistance before it dissipated:

The short term effect is that they withdraw, because the anger is so up front, and the relationship is really broken. You spend a lot of time the next few weeks and months and try to rejoin and reengage....So short term the relationship is cut off, it's disrupted, and long term it's maybe rejoined.[104]

In this day and age of managed care and limited insurance payments for psychotherapy, we can ask how fair it is to the client to use limited insurance time to work through resistance that was stimulated by the mandated report.

I. Some Positive Effects on Treatment

Not all reports produce negative results. Watson and Levine found that forty percent of cases that were reported by psychotherapists showed improvement after the report.[105] Harper and Irvin, working in an inpatient pediatric setting with allegations of medical neglect, found that reports improved parent cooperation with medical treatment, and the patients' parents did not flee after a report was made.[106] Some of our therapists also used the reporting power to impress upon reluctant or denying clients the effect of their behavior on their children:

Reporting is a way to acknowledge to parents that your behavior has a very serious impact on how your kids will behave, and there are some things that you have to start taking in a responsible way right now...They are going to have to acknowledge a problem and deal with it instead of denying it.[107]

Some therapists found the report strengthened the therapeutic alliance, or helped the client to focus on abuse issues that had been avoided before:

---

103. Elizabeth Anderson, et al., Consequences and Dilemmas in Therapeutic Relationships with Families Resulting from Mandatory Reporting Legislation, 14 Law & Pol'y 241, 249 (1992).

104. Levine et al., supra note 8, at 38.

105. Watson & Levine, supra note 91.

106. Gordon Harper & Elizabeth Irvin, Alliance Formation with Parents: Limit-Setting and the Effect of Mandated Reporting, 55 Am. J. Orthopsychiatry 550, 553 (1985).

107. Levine et al., supra note 8, at 41.

We finally got down to some real work that needed to be done. When I think about it, that was sort of the last crisis. Actually, we have been able to deal a lot around her own sexual abuse when she was a child and that [report] was sort of a turning point.[108]

Therapists reported that some children felt relieved that the report was made, and that someone was concerned enough to take action. Some therapists believed the child clients may have learned trust, or that they did not have to put up with abuse, or that they could safely reveal their plight to another and be protected.

V. Implications for the Concept of Therapeutic Jurisprudence

The major therapeutic purpose of mandated reporting and child protection legislation is to protect children. In keeping with the therapeutic jurisprudence inquiry, we can ask if the law fulfills its purpose. Sometimes the appropriate criteria are less than obvious.[109] Has the reporting law met its purpose of identifying children at-risk and preventing harm to them?[110] Shuman summarizes studies to the effect that the law has failed to meet its therapeutic objectives.[111] Given present knowledge, and the likelihood of obtaining adequate resources to serve children and families, Shuman argues that the state should not assume a duty to protect children, although he does not call for the abolition of child protection efforts.[112]

Protecting children depends on the availability of resources to serve children and families adequately after a case is identified. Protecting children by removing them from the home is problematic. Critics claim children may be at higher risk of maltreatment if they enter foster homes than if they remain in their own homes.[113] Certainly the foster care system is overloaded.[114] That we cannot consider the impact of the law without considering the treatment resources shows that therapeutic jurisprudence analysis must be extended to

---

108. Id. at 40.

109. David B. Wexler & Bruce J. Winick, Therapeutic Jurisprudence as a New Approach to Mental Health Policy Analysis and Research, 45 U. Miami L. Rev. 979, 985 (1991) ("[T]he conflicting therapeutic consequences...must be identified and defined in ways that can be measured.").

110. One criterion may be whether fatalities are prevented. The claim that child fatalities have decreased since reporting laws have been in effect is in dispute. Some argue the rate of child fatalities has not changed over the years. Hutchison, supra note 6, at 61.

111. Daniel W. Shuman, The Duty of the State to Rescue the Vulnerable in the United States, in The Duty to Rescue: The Jurisprudence of Aid 131 (Michael A. Menlowe & Alexander McCall Smith, eds., 1993).

112. Id.

113. Wexler, supra note 60, at 167–68.

114. See U.S. Advisory Bd. on Child Abuse and Neglect, Office of Human Dev. Serv., supra note 5, at xiv ("[D]espite the heroic efforts of many foster parents, the foster care system is in crisis.").

consider much more of the context within which the particular law operates, especially if "the law should be designed to serve more effectively as a therapeutic agent."[115]

On the assumption that reporting and investigation has a low cost compared to preventing injury to a child, the law guarantees a high proportion of false positives or unfounded reports. These reports have an emotional cost, a dollar cost, and affect therapeutic process and outcomes. Given the low standard triggering reports ("reasonable cause to suspect"),[116] and the level of due process afforded the subjects of investigations and adjudications,[117] some erroneous determinations are made. These determinations may be leading to some backlash among those who claim they have been falsely accused.[118] Additional costs are the impacts on the confidential psychotherapy relationship, on the therapist and on the client. The therapeutic jurisprudence inquiry centering on the client or defendant without considering the social system may be too narrow.

A great many resources go into investigation. Does the investigation fulfill a therapeutic purpose? In addition to the 60% or more of unfounded cases, a substantial number of cases are indicated and closed on the same day.[119] In some cases services are offered to the family even if the case is closed. The subject of the report may have refused services, and the social services department may not believe that the evidence is strong enough, or the danger to the child is not severe enough, to warrant taking the case to court. In some cases the process of investigation itself, even if the report is unfounded, may have some salutary effect on a family, or it may result in some services to the family, although there are many barriers to delivering services to families in need during investigations.[120] The negative impact of investigations have been documented, but we don't have systematic follow up research on how much protection an investigation provides. Research in this field is difficult because under New York State law unfounded cases are expunged.[121] We have very little idea of the rate of re-report in that population. A rule of law designed for one purpose, to protect privacy, acts as a barrier to finding out whether another law is actually accomplishing its purpose.

Whatever the impact of the investigation itself, we are developing evidence that the mandated reporting requirement has both negative and positive conse-

---

115. Klotz et al., supra note 81, at 580.

116. See N.Y. Soc. Serv. Law § 413.1 (McKinney 1992).

117. See Santosky v. Kramer, 455 U.S. 745, 769 (1982) (holding clear and convincing evidence as the standard of proof).

118. See David Hechler, The Battle and the Backlash 111–129 (1988).

119. See Murray Levine & Howard J. Doueck, Research Center for Children and Youth, SUNY Buffalo, Final Report, Child at Risk Field System: Findings from Ontario County 29 (finding 70.9% of indicated cases were closed the same day they were indicated); see also Performance Monitoring and Analysis Unit, N.Y.S. Dep't of Soc. Serv., Monitoring and Analysis Profiles with Selected Data: 1987–1991, at 4, 13 (1992) (stating that in New York City, 44.3% of cases are closed at indication, and in the rest of the state the figure is 67.1%).

120. See Barbara J. Meddin & Ingrid Hansen, The Services Provided During a Child Abuse and/or Neglect Case Investigation and the Barriers that Exist to Service Provision, 9 Child Abuse & Neglect 175, 176 (1985).

121. See N.Y. Soc. Serv. Law § 424 (McKinney 1992).

quences for the psychotherapy relationship. Moreover, the mandate to report interacts with other important ethical, if not legal, requirements such as providing information sufficient for the client to make an autonomous decision. Once again, the therapeutic jurisprudence inquiry may be too narrow. We need a broader lens to help identify variables in the social context that interact and help to determine the eventual therapeutic impact of the law in question. The concept of therapeutic jurisprudence carries us a certain distance, but its tenets need expansion if it is to guide research.

The theoretical approaches that have so far characterized much of the therapeutic jurisprudence literature have been very helpful in alerting us to a way of thinking. However, as the example of child protection and mandated reporting illustrates, the consequences of a law may be far reaching indeed. Those who are affected by it have a myriad of concerns and interests that will influence how a rule of law may affect a therapeutic purpose. If we are to attempt to design laws which have therapeutic purposes, we will have to be alert to the maxim that it is always more complicated than it seems. The law on the books is not the same as the law in action. The law in action is shaped by an elaborate social context and therapeutic jurisprudential analysis needs to take the context into account.

Chapter 17

Don't Ask, Don't Tell: Deception Required, Disclosure Denied

Kay Kavanagh

When President Bill Clinton promised to lift the ban against service in the military by gay, lesbian, and bisexual people, he emphasized, repeatedly, the distinction between status and conduct.[1] Official recognition of the distinction, in fact, was the central goal of President Clinton's efforts to lift the ban. Following a contentious period of negotiation with leaders of the armed forces and Congress, however, the ultimate policy on service in the military by gay, lesbian, and bisexual people bears little resemblance to President Clinton's stated aspirations.

Perhaps because the incubation period of the ultimate policy was longer than the average attention span for public issues, many people remain unaware of the actual provisions of the new policy and its treatment of the status-conduct distinction. The ultimate policy manages to maintain the fiction of a distinction between status and conduct only by continuing to define statements of status as conduct and then prohibiting them.

This article is not about the military; it is about the harmfulness of forced concealment and the benefits of voluntary disclosure. The military policy on gay men, lesbians, and bisexuals serves as a convenient vehicle to explore these topics because of the massive publicity given to the don't ask, don't tell policy and its familiarity (however sketchy) to most readers.

---

1. In various news conferences, President Clinton, beginning almost immediately after taking the oath of office, articulated the distinction. See The President's News Conference, 29 Weekly Comp. Pres. Doc. 108, 109 (Jan. 29, 1993) ("The issue is whether men and women...should be excluded from military service solely on the basis of their status. And I believe they should not."); Session with the Cleveland City Club, 29 Weekly Comp. Pres. Doc 805 (May 10, 1993) ("Here is what this whole debate is about. It is about whether someone should be able to acknowledge, if asked or otherwise, homosexuality and do nothing else, do nothing to violate the code of military conduct and not be kicked out of the service. And my position is yes."); Remarks Announcing the New Policy on Gays and Lesbians in the Military, 29 Weekly Comp. Pres. Doc. 1369, 1370 (July 19, 1993):

> I stated then [while giving a speech at the Kennedy School of Government at Harvard] what I still believe, that I thought there ought to be a presumption that people who wish to do so should be able to serve their country if they are willing to conform to the high standards of the military and that the emphasis should be always on people's conduct, not their status.

To place the concerns explored in this article in the context of therapeutic jurisprudence, particularly in light of David Wexler's article in this issue,[2] I suggest that the old and new policies on gay men, lesbians, and bisexuals in the military are antitherapeutic not only for gay, lesbian, and bisexual servicemembers but for their families (including their unseen partners) as well. Secondarily, but importantly, the old and new policies are antitherapeutic for heterosexual servicemembers as well because they encourage and perpetuate prejudice that is based on ignorance and deter the development of productive relationships. By *antitherapeutic*, I mean that the policies do not "promote...the psychological or physical well-being of the people [they] affect...."[3] Finally, though it has ramifications well beyond the military, the law scrutinized in this article is most definitely "micro"—a policy promulgated by Congress primarily in response to concerns expressed by leaders of the Armed Services, and directives promulgated by the Department of Defense. The legal players, however, are many: commanding officers (gay, lesbian, bisexual, and heterosexual); other officers (gay, lesbian, bisexual, and heterosexual); and enlisted servicemembers (gay, lesbian, bisexual, and heterosexual). Administrative boards and the federal courts enter the scene only after major legal and personal events have occurred.

The old and new policies are antitherapeutic because they force the gay, lesbian, or bisexual servicemember to conceal his or her sexual identity, or be closeted, which in turn results in superficial social interactions and relationships with others. Yet the concealment required in order to be closeted is not only the concealment of the gay, lesbian, or bisexual person's sexual orientation.[4] Rather, the effect of this forced concealment is in large part antitherapeutic because it entails concealment of other details that surround the secret—sexual identity—details that could lead to revelation of the secret.[5]

In this article, I explore some of the therapeutic benefits of allowing gay, lesbian, and bisexual servicemembers to disclose their identity voluntarily and suggest some of the opportunities lost by requiring concealment. I briefly outline the provisions of the old, the new, and the promised policies, highlighting their differences and similarities. A brief review of these policies reveals that neither the old nor the new policy is grounded in concerns about conduct, but in prejudice against persons who identify themselves as gay, lesbian, or bisexual. After considering the opportunities lost by rejection of the original Clinton proposal, I then turn briefly to psychological literature on self-disclosure,

---

2. Reflections on the Scope of Therapeutic Jurisprudence, 1 Psychol. Pub. Pol'y & L., 220–236 (1995).

3. See David Wexler, 1 Psychol. Pub. Pol'y & L. at 224 (quoting Christopher Slobogin, Therapeutic Jurisprudence: Five Dilemmas to Ponder, 1 Psychol. Pub. Pol'y & L., 193–219 (1995)).

4. See n. 58, infra, describing a situation that many heterosexuals have found themselves in or known a close friend to have been in at one time or another.

5. One way to understand the effects of being closeted, with the resulting isolation from others, is to imagine a central aspect of your life, and then avoid saying anything or doing anything that might imply anything about or reasonably allow an inference about that aspect of your life. It is a far more complex task than simply concealing one fact.

the benefits of self-disclosure for persons disclosing, and the role that self-disclosure plays in reducing prejudice.

I. Three Policies: The Old, the Promised, and the New

A. Old Policy

The key assumption underlying the old policy was that "homosexuality is incompatible with military service."[6] Consistent with that assumption, the following practices were effected:

> 1. Applicants to the military services were asked about their sexual orientation before being accepted for service, with statements of gay, lesbian, or bisexual orientation serving as grounds for denial of admission[7];
> 2. Grounds for discharge included a *homosexual act*; a statement by a member that he or she is gay, lesbian, or bisexual; or marriage or attempted marriage to a person of the same gender[8]; and
> 3. Allegations, whether reliable or not, of gay, lesbian, or bisexual sexual conduct *or orientation* resulted in massive "witch hunts," designed to ferret out information about and identities of gay, lesbian, and bisexual servicemembers, followed by separation of large numbers of servicemembers from the Armed Forces.[9]

In other words, no distinction was made between status and conduct; statements of identification as gay, lesbian, or bisexual were grounds for discharge.

B. Promised ("Phantom") Policy

In contrast to the central assumption underlying the old policy (that "homosexuality is incompatible with the military"), a key assumption underlying

---

6. 32 C.F.R. s 41.3(c), App. A, pt. 1, H.1.a. (rev. July 1, 1993).

7. Before the induction physical, prospective servicemembers were asked to indicate whether they had "homosexual tendencies" on Medical History Form 93. In addition, questions about homosexuality were posed during the medical history interviews as well. Military and Veterans, in Sexual Orientation and the Law, s 6.06 [4][h], 6–61, 6–62 (Release #5 10/92, superseded by Release #7, 11/94). See also Watkins v. United States Army, 875 F.2d 699, 701 (9th Cir. 1989) (en banc), cert. denied, 498 U.S. 957 (1990) (describing servicemember's revelation of "homosexual tendencies" at preinduction physical); Allan Berube, Getting In, in Coming Out under Fire: The History of Gay Men and Women in World War Two 8–33 (1990) (describing armed services' screening procedures for gay men and lesbians during World War II).

8. 32 C.F.R. s 41.3(c) App. A., pt. 1, H.1.c.(1)-(3) (rev. July 1, 1993).

9. See generally Berube, supra note 7; Mary Ann Humphrey, My Country, My Right to Serve: Experiences of Gay Men and Women in the Military, World War II to the Present (1990); and Randy Shilts, Conduct Unbecoming: Lesbians and Gays in the U.S. Military, Vietnam to the Persian Gulf (1993).

the promised policy was the significance of the distinction between orientation (or status) and conduct.[10] The promised policy would have looked something like this:

1. *Don't ask.* Questions about sexual orientation would not be asked of applicants for the armed services.

2. *Don't care.* Statements about gay, lesbian, or bisexual orientation would be of no more consequence than statements of heterosexual orientation.

3. *Be fair.* Prohibited sexual conduct would be prosecuted when evidence of such conduct arose in the normal course of events, without "witch hunts," without regard to the actors' sexual orientation, but with regard only to the conduct prohibited under the Uniform Code of Military Justice.[11] Prohibited conduct—heterosexual or homosexual—would be treated (ignored or prosecuted) similarly.[12]

The promised policy, however, remains a phantom, as do most of the benefits that would have resulted from it.

C. New Policy

The new policy has three major components, and its labels, at least, are familiar: "Don't ask," "Don't tell," and, less familiar to some, "Don't pursue."[13]

---

10. The issue is not whether there should be homosexuals in the military. Everyone concedes that there are. The issue is whether men and women, who can and have served with real distinction, should be excluded from military service solely on the basis of their status. And I believe they should not.
The President's News Conference, 29 Weekly Comp. Pres. Doc. 108, 109 (Jan. 29, 1993).

11. Under Articles 120, 125, and 134 of the Uniform Code of Military Justice, 10 U.S.C.A. ss 920, 925, 934 (West Supp. 1994), prohibited conduct includes adultery, indecent assault, wrongful cohabitation, fraternization, indecent language, indecent acts with another, pandering and prostitution, sodomy, and bigamy. See Meinhold v. United States DOD, 34 F.3d 1469, 1478 (9th Cir. 1994) (Court notes under old policy no assumptions made that heterosexuals, because heterosexual, will engage in prohibited conduct under the Uniform Code of Military Justice, yet old policy [like new policy] makes such assumptions about gay, lesbian, and bisexual servicemembers). Id. at 1478 and n. 10.

12. Though beyond the scope of this article, the conduct-status distinction has been criticized as being, ultimately, of limited utility in the quest for gay, lesbian, and bisexual rights, except perhaps in the military context, and then only in limited circumstances. See Patricia A. Cain, Litigating for Lesbian & Gay Rights: A Legal History, 79 Va. L. Rev. 1551, 1621–27 (1993).

13. The new policy is revealed in three separate sources: First, the Secretary of Defense issued Preliminary Policy Guidelines on Homosexuals in the Military, dated July 19, 1993 (hereinafter "Guidelines"); second, Congress enacted its Policy Concerning Homosexuality in the Armed Forces on Nov. 30, 1993, 10 U.S.C.A. s 654 (West Supp. 1994) (hereinafter "Statute"); and third, the Secretary of Defense, on Dec. 22, 1993, issued Directives Implementing the New DOD Policy on Homosexual Conduct in the Armed Forces, designed to take effect Feb. 5, 1994 (hereinafter "Directives"). For a comprehensive listing of the new regulations, including the directives, issued by the Department of Defense as well as the various services, see Military and Veterans, supra note 7, at s 6.03, 6-6 & n. 6, 7 (Release #7, 11/94). The Directives are essentially a detailed guide for application of the new policy, giving examples of when a commanding officer should "not ask"; what a commanding officer should do when someone "tells"; and when a commanding officer should or should not

1. *Don't ask ("accession policy")*. The "don't ask" part of the new policy is as promised; the guidelines provide a clear departure from the armed services practice that had required applicants to reveal whether they are homosexual or bisexual:

> *Accession policy*
> Applicants for military service will no longer be asked or required to reveal if they are homosexual or bisexual, but applicants will be informed of the conduct that is proscribed for members of the armed forces, including homosexual conduct.[14]

The basis for the "don't ask" part of the new policy is apparently that "[s]exual orientation is considered a personal and private matter."[15]

2. *Don't tell ("discharge policy")*. Although it is a definite departure from the *promised* policy, the "don't tell" part of the new policy is essentially indistinguishable from the *old* policy. "Don't tell" requires gay, lesbian, and bisexual servicemembers to refrain from any statements of personal identification as gay, lesbian, or bisexual.

> *Discharge policy*
> Sexual orientation will not be a bar to service unless manifested by homosexual conduct. The military will discharge members who engage in *homosexual conduct*, which is *defined* as a homosexual act, *a statement that the member is homosexual or bisexual*, or a marriage or attempted marriage to someone of the same gender.[16]

The italicized language reveals that the conduct-status distinction of the promised policy did not make its way into the new policy. Nevertheless, the Directives reflect an attempt to bolster the fiction of the conduct-status distinction by providing the following explanation:

"pursue." I will refer to the Guidelines, the Statute, and the Directives in the aggregate as the "new policy." (Copies of Guidelines and Directives on file with the author).

14. Guidelines.

15. Id. I should point out, though, that the Statute provides that it is the "sense of Congress that" the armed forces should continue not to question applicants about homosexuality, but that "the Secretary of Defense may reinstate" such questioning as the secretary "considers appropriate if the Secretary determines that it is necessary...to effectuate the policy set forth" in the statute. Pub. L. No. 103-160, s 571(d) (codified at 10 U.S.C.A. s 654). In other words, the "don't ask" portion of the Statute is actually "don't ask unless you want to."

16. Guidelines (emphasis added). For those who might be confused by the similarity of the old and new policies, the following explanation might be helpful and confirms that in fact the confusion is well grounded:

> Sec. Aspin: "Yes, the [new] policy, Senator, is don't ask/don't tell/don't pursue. We're saying in this policy 'don't tell.' The policy before was 'don't tell.' The 'don't tell' part is not different, the 'don't ask' is different, the 'don't pursue' is different. The 'don't ask' is a policy which is—it will not be part of the forms, it will not be part of the inquisition [sic] here, and the 'don't pursue' is the issue of investigations and witch hunts.

Hearing on Gays in the Military Before the Senate Committee on the Armed Services, 103d Cong., 1st Sess. (July 20, 1993) (hereinafter "Senate Hearings").

> A statement by a member that demonstrates a propensity or intent to engage in homosexual acts is grounds for separation not because it reflects the member's sexual orientation, but because the statement indicates a likelihood that the member engages in or will engage in homosexual acts.[17]

The way a person makes a statement demonstrating such a propensity or intent (whether the person realizes or intends it or not) is to say "I am gay," "I am a lesbian," or "I am bisexual."[18] The new policy provides that such a statement creates a rebuttable presumption that the servicemember intends to engage in homosexual acts.[19] In announcing the Directives on December 22, 1993, Jamie Gorelick, then general counsel for the Department of Defense, stated that the "rebuttable presumption...existed before [but] was (a) hard to find, and (b) hard to understand."[20] The rebuttable presumption may be easier to find but is no easier to understand.

Propensity is not defined in the Statute but is defined in the Directives as "more than an abstract preference or desire to engage in homosexual acts; [propensity] indicates a likelihood that a person engages in or will engage in homosexual acts."[21] The new policy defines *homosexual* as "[a] person, regardless of sex, who engages in, attempts to engage in, has a propensity to engage in, or intends to engage in homosexual acts."[22] In other words, when a person says "I am gay," "I am a lesbian," or "I am bisexual," the new policy says the person is saying "I have a propensity or intent to engage in homosexual acts."

In one opinion that has considered the rebuttable presumption under the new policy, Federal District Judge William Nickerson referred to *Webster's Third New International Dictionary* in attempting to fathom the meaning of *propensity*. He expressed skepticism about how

> one who is [by definition] born with an innate tendency, a "propensity," to commit a homosexual act can prove that he or she does not have such a propensity. To invite someone to prove that he or she does not have an inborn tendency seems like a hollow offer.[23]

---

17. Directives (revising DOD Directive 1332.14, 32 C.F.R. s 41.1 App. A, pt. 1, H.2).

18. See Directives, Guidelines for Fact-Finding Inquiries into Homosexual Conduct, 4-2(5)(b).

19. The new policy provides that a member who makes a statement identifying him- or herself as gay, lesbian, or bisexual may avoid discharge if there is a "further finding, made and approved in accordance with procedures set forth in the regulations, that the member has demonstrated that he or she is not a person who engages in, attempts to engage in, has a propensity to engage in, or intends to engage in homosexual acts." Directives (emphasis added). In effect, a person may avoid discharge if he or she can demonstrate that he or she is not gay, because a person who is gay is, by definition under the new policy, "a person who engages in, attempts to engage in, has a propensity to engage in, or intends to engage in homosexual acts." Directives No. 1332.14, Definitions, Enc. 2.

20. Defense Department Briefing Re: Regulations on Homosexual Conduct in the Military, Federal News Service, Dec. 22, (1993), available in LEXIS, Nexis Library, Fednew file.

21. Directive No. 1332.14, Definitions, Enc. 2.

22. Id.

23. Able v. United States, 847 F. Supp. 1038, 1040 (E.D.N.Y. 1994).

So far, the Department of Defense has not made clear how a person will prove, as a substantive matter, lack of "propensity" or "intent."

In addition to retaining the approach of the old policy that equated statements of sexual orientation with prohibited conduct, but in marked contrast to the old policy, the new policy has an expanded definition of "homosexual act." The Statute defines the term *homosexual act* as follows:

> (A) any bodily contact, actively undertaken or passively permitted, between members of the same sex for the purpose of satisfying sexual desires; and
> *(B) any bodily contact which a reasonable person would understand to demonstrate a propensity or intent to engage in an act described in subparagraph (A).*[24]

Not surprisingly, *reasonable person* is not defined. Suffice it to say that a "reasonable person" is probably not a reasonable gay, lesbian, or bisexual person. The Directives give as examples of the conduct described above in subsection (B) "handholding or kissing, in most circumstances."[25]

In summary, the "don't tell" part of the new policy is virtually indistinguishable from the old policy, except that with the addition of "secondary homosexual acts," it has the potential to be more punitive than the old and leaves more room for disparate enforcement of its regulations against gay men, lesbians, and bisexuals or those perceived to be gay, lesbian, or bisexual.

3. *Don't pursue.*

> *Investigations policy*
> No investigations or inquiries will be conducted solely to determine a servicemember's sexual orientation. Commanders will initiate inquiries or investigations when there is credible information that a basis for discharge or disciplinary action exists. Sexual orientation, absent credible information that a crime has been committed, will not be the subject of a criminal investigation. An allegation or statement by another that a servicemember is a homosexual, alone, is not grounds for either a criminal investigation or a commander's inquiry.[26]

In addition, the Directives specifically provide that the following activities will not be grounds for initiating an investigation: a servicemember's reading of publications for the gay community, participation in gay rallies or marches in civilian clothes, or attendance at gay or lesbian functions, including, for example, gay bars.[27] These provisions, which appear to expand, however slightly, the rights of gay, lesbian, and bisexual servicemembers, nevertheless call for a healthy skepticism. A fascinating and revealing interchange on this aspect of the new policy occurred during the Senate Hearings of the Senate Armed Services Committee:

---

24. 10 U.S.C.A. s 654(f)(3)(A)-(B) (West Supp. 1994) (emphasis added). Subsection (A) is identical to language of the regulations under the old policy. See 32 C.F.R. s 41.3(c) App. A, pt. 1, H.1.b. (3) (rev. July 1, 1993) (definition of homosexual act under the old policy). Subsection B (set forth above) is new.

25. Directive No. 1332.30, Enc. 4, Guidelines for Fact-Finding Inquiries Into Homosexual Conduct, 4-2.

26. Guidelines, 1.

27. Directives, Guidelines for Fact-Finding Inquiries Into Homosexual Conduct, 4-3, 4-4.

Sen. McCain: So—so what you're saying is that in—in—but yet, being in a homosexual parade, marching in a gay rights rally in civilian clothes is not homosexual conduct.

Sec. Aspin: Because *a person might be a heterosexual who's* in favor of gay rights and attends [sic] the gay parade, yes.

Sen. McCain: If that person is dressed in—in a—bizarre clothing and under the banner of—some organization which advocates—

Sen. Aspin: No.

Sen. McCain:—certain things, what does that mean?

Sec. Aspin: It depends under the circumstances. But the point is that a person should not be automatically barred from attending a gay parade if they are—if they're doing it in civilian clothes because a person who goes—attends a gay parade—*does not prove that they are a homosexual just by attending a the* [sic] *parade.*

. . . . .

Gen. Powell: I don't know how we could say to a *heterosexual service member that if they chose to go to a gay rights parade*, either to observe it or to make a statement about their view of it, but they, themselves, are *heterosexual, that we should tell them they can't do that, or that we should take some action against them for doing it.*[28]

The inescapable conclusion here is that because *heterosexuals* might engage in this conduct, it cannot be prohibited.[29] Thus, what might on its face appear to be an expansion of rights of gays, lesbians, and bisexuals, in effect appears intended to protect conduct because *heterosexuals* might wish to engage in it.

In summary, the new policy, if effected in its most benign form, will allow closeted gay, lesbian, and bisexual servicemembers to serve without fear of witch hunts. They may engage in certain activities that formerly would have served as grounds to initiate witch hunts (for instance, they may subscribe to gay or lesbian publications without fear of reprisal). What they may not do, above all, is say that they are gay, lesbian, or bisexual or participate visibly in any conduct from which a "reasonable person" would infer a propensity or intent to engage in a homosexual act.

II. Same Policy: Prejudice at the Core

Despite its substantial similarity to the old policy, the new policy differs in a very significant way from the old: It formally acknowledges, in a way the old policy did not, the presence in the armed services of gay and lesbian people. Moreover, it states that sexual orientation is a personal and private matter. Finally, it articulates quite explicitly, if not convincingly, that conduct, not status, is at issue.

Yet the new policy, like the old policy, continues to be grounded in prejudice against gay, lesbian, and bisexual persons and continues not to be directed to-

---

28. Senate Hearings, July 20, 1993 (emphasis added).

29. The testimony suggests an odd protection of "conduct" because of the "status" of persons who might engage in the conduct—a most unusual approach to the distinction between status and conduct.

ward conduct, but rather toward *persons* "with a propensity"—in other words, it is directed toward status. That this is so is made clear by two provisions that have *not* changed. First, like the old policy, the new policy continues to allow a person who has been proven to have engaged in homosexual acts to remain in the armed services if the determination is further made, among others, that the "member does not have a propensity or intent to engage in homosexual acts"; in other words, if the member is not a "homosexual" as defined in the new policy.[30] Second, and in ironic contrast, a servicemember who has stated, "I am gay," but about whom there is no proof of homosexual acts, shall be discharged, unless the servicemember rebuts the presumption that he or she has the "propensity to engage in, or intends to engage in homosexual acts."[31] In short, despite the rhetoric accompanying the new policy, conduct is "forgivable"; status is not.

Given that prejudice against gay men, lesbians, and bisexuals is at the base of the policy (a conclusion that only the most naive reader of the policy could escape), I then address the real question: How may this prejudice be eliminated?[32] One way of addressing this prejudice would simply be to allow gay,

---

30. The new policy, like the old policy, provides one exception to discharge on the basis of proof of homosexual acts: that the "conduct is a departure from the member's usual and customary behavior"; that it is "unlikely to recur"; that it did not involve "force or coercion"; that the member's "continued presence in the armed forces is consistent with...proper discipline, good order, and morale"; and "the member does not have a propensity or intent to engage in homosexual acts." 10 U.S.C.A. s 654(b)(1)(A)-(E) (West Supp. 1994) (emphasis added). Note that this provision applies to "homosexual acts," not to homosexual conduct. Homosexual acts, under both the old and the new policies, involve bodily contact of some kind, though the definition of homosexual acts under the new policy expands the range of contact to include contact that "a reasonable person would understand to demonstrate a propensity or intent to engage in" bodily contact between members of the same sex to satisfy sexual desires. 10 U.S.C.A. s 654(f)(3)(B) (West Supp. 1994). See also supra, note 24 and accompanying text. For the analog from the old policy, see 32 C.F.R. s 41.1 et seq., App. A., pt. 1.H.1.c. (1)(a)-(e) (rev. July 1, 1993).

31. This reality has not gone unnoticed. In Steffan v. Aspin, 8 F.3d 57 (D.C. Cir. 1993), reh'g granted, 1994 U.S. App. LEXIS 9977 (D.C. Cir. 1994) (en banc), a case decided under the old policy, the original three-judge panel of the D.C. Circuit noted that in two identical situations involving homosexual acts, a heterosexual servicemember would escape discharge, but a gay servicemember would not. Id. at 65. The opinion of the three-judge panel was later vacated by the D.C. Circuit sitting en banc, which issued its decision on the merits at 1994 U.S. App. LEXIS 33045 (Nov. 22, 1994).

See supra, note 19 (discussing rebuttable presumption provisions of new policy).

32. Whether considering the old or the new policy, the basis is the same. To cite only one example, in Cammermeyer v. Aspin, 850 F. Supp 910 (W.D. Wash. 1994), the district court accepted Colonel Margarethe Cammermeyer's argument that the old policy was based on prejudice, despite the government's reliance in part on congressional findings supporting the new policy. Those parts of the old policy the court considered in so ruling are provisions that have survived in substantially the same form in the new policy—that is, that a statement that "I am gay" or "I am a lesbian" or "I am bisexual" is grounds for discharge. The district court concluded, after reviewing extensive submissions on the issue, that "the Government, for its part, has failed to offer any evidence showing that its justifications are based on anything but prejudice. An examination of the record demonstrates that the sole motivation for the exclusion of acknowledged homosexuals from military service is prejudice." Id. at 924.

lesbian, and bisexual persons who choose to do so to reveal their sexual identity. There would be two benefits as a result: the benefits to gay, lesbian, and bisexual servicemembers resulting from self-disclosure, and the benefits to heterosexual servicemembers whose stereotypes about gay and lesbian people could be compared with their actual, informed experience.[33]

Even though the policy on sexual orientation in the military is unlikely to be revisited by Congress or the Department of Defense on a voluntary basis any time soon, it is at least possible that judicial intervention may require it. More important, by scrutinizing the military policy and the overtness of the prejudice that continues to drive it, legal scholars, psychologists, and others who shape policy may glean insights that can be applied in other contexts.

A. Deception Required, Isolation Incurred

By acknowledging the presence in the armed forces of a substantial number of gay and lesbian servicemembers, those crafting the new policy were forced to face a long-standing reality that had previously been denied. The evolution of the policy from the old to the new has shifted from a stance of denial (homosexuality is incompatible with the military) to one of mandated deception. Theoretically, gay men and lesbians had not existed in the military—they were to have been denied admission to the military at the accession stage of the process—and mistakes made at the accession stage were "corrected" later, at the witch hunt stage. Gay men, lesbians, and bisexual women and men gained entry through one of two ways: by answering truthfully the questions posed to them (either because the questions designed to screen for sexual orientation were inartful, nonspecific, or not posed at all,[34] because direct statements of homosexuality were disbelieved or ignored[35]) or by lying.[36] These lies were, of course, not officially sanctioned; to the contrary, a prospective servicemember

---

33. It would be naive at best to suggest that such prejudice could be eliminated simply by removing penalties to gay, lesbian, and bisexual servicemembers for revealing their sexual orientation. However, models for addressing heterosexual prejudice exist, both from obvious parallels relative to the treatment of African American male and female servicemembers in the military as well as from the experiences of other countries who have allowed gay, lesbian, and bisexual persons to serve in the military (Canada, Denmark, Netherlands, Sweden, Israel). See Cammermeyer v. Aspin, 850 F. Supp. at 921–23 (W.D. Wash. 1994) (discussing various studies on effect of homosexuality in the military).

34. See Berube, supra note 7, at 8–33. See generally, Humphrey, supra note 9; Shilts, supra note 9.

35. See e.g., Watkins v. United States Army, 875 F.2d 699, 701–703 (9th Cir. 1989) (en banc), cert. denied, 498 U.S. 957 (1990) (Sgt. Perry Watkins, who was drafted in 1967, repeatedly stated, in response to Army inquiries, that he was homosexual, yet was allowed to remain in the Army until 1981, when the Army recommended discharge on the basis of his statement that he was a homosexual). For a more detailed picture of Sgt. Watkins's experience with the Army, see William N. Eskridge, Jr., Gaylegal Narratives, 46 Stan. L. Rev. 607, 611–19 (1994).

36. Berube, supra note 7, at 8–33.

who lied was exposed to later penalties, including discharge for fraudulent statements.[37]

Now, however, leaders of the armed forces themselves have publicly acknowledged that gay, lesbian, and bisexual servicemembers have served and continue to serve well in the military, but maintain that to allow openly gay and lesbian servicemembers to serve would result in a "breakdown of unit cohesion."[38] Thus, the policy purports to distinguish between sexual status or orientation (which is a personal and private matter and theoretically acceptable) and homosexual conduct (which is theoretically not acceptable).

Because the new policy, like the old, includes in its definition of "homosexual conduct" truthful statements of identity, gay, lesbian, and bisexual servicemembers will inevitably be confronted with situations where the most natural truthful response would result in revealing one's identity or status, and by doing so, the servicemember will engage in conduct that will result in initiation of administrative separation proceedings.

One commentator has described the effect of the new policy as imposing "a duty of deception...within a culture that otherwise demands strict adherence to the ideals of honor and duty."[39] The policy's name itself

> sets the tone for the conspiracy of silence and pretense contemplated by [the] compromise. Additionally, by expecting and demanding that members of sexual minorities deflect inquiries about status to conceal important aspects of their lives, personalities, and identities, the policy creates a duty to participate in officially sanctioned deception. In turn, this institutionalized deception invites the formation of an underground group within military culture defined by dishonesty.[40]

The kinds of deception required, and the effects on servicemembers, may not be fully comprehended by the framers of the new policy and, perhaps more important, may not be realized by those crafting policy for other, less rigidly controlled environments.

The effects of forced nondisclosure are felt by the gay man, lesbian, or bisexual person who is denied the opportunity to share relevant information with others and by those to whom such disclosures are not made—be they gay or straight. For persons who are denied the opportunity to reveal important information about themselves, the effect can be one of distressing and unnecessary isolation. Moreover, lesbians, gay men, and bisexual women and men who engage in efforts to "pass" as heterosexual—which demands constant passive as well as (usually) active deception—can "experience a painful dis-

---

37. Military and Veterans, supra note 7, s 6.02[1], 6-6 & n.11. (Release #6, 10/93, superseded by Release #7, 11/94).

38. See, e.g., Senate Hearings (May 11, 1993) (Testimony of Gen. Norman Schwarzkopf) ("Homosexuals have served in the past and done a great job serving their country, and I feel they can in the future. It is the question of open homosexuality in a unit that causes this breakdown in unit cohesion.") Id.

39. Francisco Valdes, Sexual Minorities in the Military: Charting the Constitutional Frontiers of Status and Conduct, 27 Creighton L. Rev. 384, 472 (1994).

40. Id.

crepancy between their public and private identities."[41] "[G]ay people who are passing may feel inauthentic, that they are living a lie, and that others would not accept them if they knew the truth."[42] As a result of the concealment, gay people "create distance from others in order to avoid revealing their sexual orientation. When contact cannot be avoided, they may keep their interactions at a superficial level as a self-protective strategy."[43]

Ironically, in testimony at the Senate hearings, then-Secretary of Defense Les Aspin stated that

> [u]nder the old policy, a homosexual service member had to lie and actually hide his or her orientation. In other words, they had to work hard to keep off the radar screen. Under the new policy, they will have to work to get onto the radar screen. That's progress.[44]

Secretary Aspin was correct, but only minimally. "Don't ask" is progress. The part he got wrong is that servicemembers will be required to work very hard not to lie and will still have to work very hard to "keep off the radar screen," because concealment requires very hard work.

Another result of "passing" is that it

> impedes development of close personal relationships. The covert gay man [or lesbian or bisexual] fears intimacy because it threatens to reveal his [or her] secret status. Potentially supportive persons sense this reluctance, generally without understanding its source, and become frustrated in their attempts to get "closer." Eventually they withdraw.[45]

As a result of the failure to share important personal information, the scrutinized individual often is isolated not only from heterosexuals but also from other lesbians and gay men, any of whom could provide a possible social community.[46] Finally, the person who must keep his or her sexual identity secret "is thwarted in developing his [or her] social support relationships because he [or she] is unable to reciprocate in the sharing of intimate details of his [or her] emotional life, without threatening his [or her] status. This disclosure is a necessary component to achieving emotional intimacy."[47]

B. Disclosure Denied: Harms Engendered, Benefits Foregone

In contrast to the negative effects of concealment of one's identity, researchers have observed that "[p]sychological adjustment appears to be highest among those who are committed to their lesbian or gay identity and who

---

41. Gregory M. Herek, Myths About Sexual Orientation: A Lawyer's Guide to Social Science Research, 1 Law & Sexuality 133, 146 (1991).

42. Gregory M. Herek, Stigma, Prejudice, and Violence Against Lesbians and Gay Men, in Homosexuality: Research Implications for Public Policy 60, 74 (John C. Gonsiorek & James D. Weinrich eds., 1991).

43. Id.

44. Senate Hearings (July 20, 1993).

45. Raymond M. Berger, Passing and Social Support Among Gay Men, 23 J. of Homosexuality, 85, 89 (1992) (citations omitted).

46. Id.

47. Id. (citing Sidney M. Jourard, The Transparent Self (rev. ed. 1971).

do not attempt to hide their homosexuality from others."[48] A recent study of "passing" among gay men (cited above) confirmed, not surprisingly, the hypothesis "that passing adversely affects the quality of social support."[49] The author suggested that

> the quality of perceived social support will be greatest when there is an honest and trusting relationship between the support giver and the recipient. Honesty and trust flourish best when the recipient feels that he is understood and "known" for his true self. In order to increase the quality of social support available to gay clients, helping professionals may encourage these clients to make themselves fully known to at least some members of their networks, in order to facilitate the availability of high quality social support.[50]

One of the generally held assumptions that makes disclosure of gay, lesbian, or bisexual identity difficult, and that impedes productive discussion of sexual orientation, is the assumption that gay, lesbian, and bisexual persons are *defined* by their sexual orientation in ways that heterosexual persons are not, and that "sexual orientation" refers exclusively to sexual conduct.[51] By considering the concepts included in the term *sexual orientation*, however, this assumption is shown to be seriously misleading:

> Many different aspects of human sexuality are discussed under the rubric of *sexual* orientation. These include: (1) engaging in specific *sexual behaviors* with partners of a particular gender; (2) having a *personal preference* for or ongoing attraction to partners of a particular gender; (3) developing a *private personal* identity as gay, lesbian, heterosexual, or bisexual; (4) establishing a *public iden-*

---

48. Herek, supra note 41, at 145 & n.53.

49. Berger, supra note 45, at 89, 94–95.

50. Id. at 94–95. The author pointed out, however, that "passing may impede social support in a tolerant and supportive environment; but it may be a prerequisite for receiving even minimal levels of support in an environment intolerant or hostile to homosexuality." Id. For a discussion of selective disclosure, see infra n. 63 and accompanying text.

51. Gregory M. Herek, Sexual Orientation and Military Service: A Social Science Perspective, 48, American Psychologist 538, 545 (1993). Herek demonstrates this point with the following observations:

> Some heterosexual personnel, for example, may perceive lesbians or gay men to be flaunting their sexuality when they merely identify themselves as lesbian or gay, or when they display a partner's photograph in a setting in which heterosexuals are allowed to do so. Such perceptions result from the lack of nonsexual social roles and identities for lesbians and gay men comparable to those available to heterosexuals through institutions such as marriage. Consequently, conduct that is regarded as innocuous when performed by a heterosexual (e.g., stating that one is married, greeting a spouse with a kiss) can be perceived as an inappropriate public manifestation of private sexuality when performed by a lesbian or gay man.

Id. at 545 (emphasis added).

See also Cain, supra note 12, at 1625–27 (noting that sexual identity may be attributable to life events and relationships "apart from actual sexual conduct," suggesting, for example, "intense emotional attachments to persons of the same sex" as a "sufficient indicator of sexual identity") (citations omitted).

tity based on sexual orientation; and (5) *identifying with a community* of sexual orientation.[52]

In other words, *sexual orientation* describes a range of concepts, behaviors, and qualities that extends beyond sexual conduct alone. In light of the foregoing description, it should come as no surprise, then, that "[l]esbian and gay male intimate relationships, like their heterosexual counterparts, do not always include an overtly sexual component."[53] Consistent with the broad range of personal aspects incorporated in the concept of sexual orientation, by coming out of the closet a gay, lesbian, or bisexual person may be attempting to communicate information relating to any one or more, but not necessarily all, of these aspects of his or her identity. Thus, even though it may appear on the face of the new policy that the only disclosure that is being prohibited is a disclosure that relates to an individual's sexual conduct, in fact the range of disclosures denied is likely to be far broader.

As mentioned earlier, the "don't care" part of the promised policy would have allowed gay, lesbian, and bisexual servicemembers to come out of the closet. Under the promised policy, the disclosure "I am a lesbian," "I am gay," or "I am bisexual" would have been an unremarkable statement of identity. It is, of course, such a direct disclosure of identity (in no way limited to, nor even necessarily including, discussions about sexual conduct) and one that comes to mind most readily when most people think of someone "coming out of the closet." Unmistakably, however, that is precisely the kind of disclosure that the new policy, like the old, prohibits.

However, for many people, coming out of the closet often does not involve such a direct statement of identity. Rather, it involves making truly unremarkable disclosures, such as *with whom* one goes grocery shopping, shares a checking account, takes a vacation; *to whom* one apologizes for failing to do the dishes (or for failing to do them properly), for squeezing the toothpaste from the top of the tube rather than from the bottom, for leaving various household supplies scattered throughout the house rather than returning them to their appointed places; *from whom* one receives a phone call, a message, or flowers on one's birthday; and *with or without whom* one goes home for the holidays.

Conversely, it can be these pedestrian yet very personal aspects of a life that remain hidden when one is closeted—far less interesting to some, but far more real and pervasive in the lives of most gay, lesbian, and bisexual persons, than revelations about "propensity," "prohibited conduct," or "homosexual acts," with which the leaders of the armed forces and Congress profess to be so concerned and appear, to some, to be so obsessed. Yet by prohibiting disclosure of one's sexual orientation (only, of course, if the "sexual orientation" that is a "personal and private matter" happens to be gay, lesbian, or bisexual, rather than heterosexual), inevitably the disclosures of these everyday but essentially life-defining details will be denied as well. The promised policy would have effected powerful changes in the lives of gay, lesbian, and bisexual servicemembers by allowing disclosures not only about identity, but, possibly more impor-

---

52. Herek, supra note 41, at 134–35 (footnotes omitted) (emphasis in original).
53. Id. at 135 (citations omitted).

tant, about the day-to-day life events that people who work together often share with each other.[54]

The effect would have been dramatic because the most difficult part about being closeted is *not* the requirement that one remain quiet about one's sexual practices. That is the easy and natural part of being closeted—and the part of being closeted that for many (if not most) people would not change with a change of policy. The most difficult part about being closeted, though, is the requirement that one conceal basic life events and facts from those to whom it would be natural to reveal them.

One of my own experiences of "coming out of the closet" in a relatively large law firm may demonstrate the point.[55] After about 6 months there (where, as it turned out, I worked for almost 7 years), I visited my supervising partner in his office in an unsuccessful effort to resign. He closed the door, directed that his calls be held, and talked with me. One thing he had noticed about me, he said, was that I did not seem to socialize much with people at the firm. One reason he enjoyed working there, he said, was because when he came to work he was with his friends. It did not seem to him to be that way for me. I did not seem comfortable to him. I explained that I was a lesbian and did not feel comfortable bringing my partner to the [multitude of] social events the firm had but did not feel comfortable attending them alone either. I really do not remember now whether I had yet mentioned her to anyone at the firm. He told me that I should bring her and not worry about it.

By the end of our meeting I had agreed to hang on for a while longer, we agreed that I would take a week's vacation, and he said he would talk to some of the members of the management committee about my situation. (I told him I did not care what he said to whom, as long as I got my vacation.)

I never did find out exactly what happened, but when I returned from my vacation, I was visited by several of the partners on the firm's management committee. One thing that one of them said to me has stayed with me: "Secrecy is a form of dishonesty. You don't need to live that way."

For the most part, I stopped living that way. One of the most liberating parts of "not living that way" was that I no longer had to carry cash; if I wanted to pledge money for the Bowlathon or buy Girl Scout cookies I could write a check on our joint checking account without worrying about it. Another thing I could do was put my partner's picture in my office. (This, much to my chagrin, was met—and continues to be met—with confused questions. "Is that your daughter?" people ask about the woman who is 10 months my senior; or, my all-time favorite: "Is that a picture of you when you were younger?"[56] So much for being out of the closet.)

---

54. The new policy does not explicitly prohibit the disclosures I identify as so natural and crucial. Nevertheless, the natural result of the requirement that gay men, lesbians, and bisexuals not reveal their sexual orientation is to preclude disclosure of related information in an effort to conceal the prohibited fact. See note 58 and accompanying text, infra.

55. I say "one" of my experiences in coming out of the closet because, as with any hidden trait, one is constantly confronted with whether to reveal one's self to others in a given context.

56. My answer is not always the same, depending on the identity of the person asking the question, the context, and how much time I and the questioner have to spend on the re-

Of course, secrecy is not always a form of dishonesty,[57] but it often is. To protect one secret people often feel that they must conceal other aspects of their lives as well. It is often the concealment of those *other* aspects of their lives, and not concealment of the *secret itself*, that becomes most painful.[58] The isolation that results is one that is not healthy for gay, lesbian, or bisexual persons; their partners; or those who are misled or cut out of their lives for reasons that, by necessity, are not apparent. One can only speculate (and one must) how such isolation could be good for the "unit cohesion" that the military relies on so heavily to justify the new policy, as it did to justify the old.

C. Elimination of Prejudice

Research on prejudice in relation to other minority groups has shown that

> intergroup contact often reduces prejudice in the majority group when the contact meets several conditions: When it is encouraged by the institution in which it occurs, makes shared goals salient, and fosters inter-group cooperation; when the contact is ongoing and intimate rather than brief and superficial; and when members of the two groups are of equal status and share important values. The applicability of this contact hypothesis to antigay prejudice is supported by data showing that heterosexuals with openly gay friends or acquaintances are more likely than others to hold accepting attitudes toward gay people in general.[59]

---

sponse to such a simple question. Often I say it is a picture of the "woman I live with," a response with which I am deeply uncomfortable; other times, the "artist who painted all these pictures on my wall"; other times, "my partner." I have considered "life companion," but I do not feel I am old enough to use that term yet; "soulmate" has a nice ring to it but is not perfect either.

57. See Sissela Bok, Secrets: On the Ethics of Concealment and Revelation (1982) (in-depth treatment of ethical issues arising from the use of secrets in a wide range of contexts).

58. Erving Goffman, Stigma, Notes on the Management of Spoiled Identity (1963), referred to this as suffering "from 'in-deeper-ism,' that is, pressure to elaborate a lie further and further to prevent a given disclosure." Goffman also noted that these "adaptive techniques can themselves give rise to hurt feelings and misunderstandings on the part of others." Id. at 83.

The isolation and painfulness that often results from efforts to conceal one central fact can be easily demonstrated by considering situations that are not unique to gay men and lesbians. Many heterosexuals have, at one time or another, found themselves with information about themselves that they feel restrained from disclosing: a close relationship with a person of a race, religion, or social class that is unacceptable to the person's family, or involvement in an intimate relationship with another person that one wishes not to reveal to one's spouse or other intimate. The range of information that one becomes inhibited from revealing grows, all because small details lead to, or result from, the central, secret fact. As a result of the one secret, more and more information about one's life becomes inaccessible to the other family members, or spouse, or person who cannot be allowed to know the secret. The result, inevitably, is a distancing of the relationship with other family members, or spouse, in large part because of the dearth of information being disclosed and the cautiousness with which the concealing person must approach all interaction. The ultimate result is a superficial and distant relationship. See generally id. at 83–91.

59. Herek, supra note 41, at 171 (footnotes and citations omitted).

Put another way, to facilitate reduction of group prejudice, "interactions should occur under conditions of equal status, common goals, cooperation, and moderate intimacy."[60] In addition,

> common group memberships other than sexual orientation should be made salient (e.g., religious, social, ethnic, and political); contact should occur on a one-to-one basis rather than group-to-group; and the lesbian or gay man should violate some commonly held stereotype or several homosexual persons should be visible so as to demonstrate the diversity of the community.[61]

Although it is not absolutely clear that interpersonal contact with a gay man, lesbian, or bisexual "causes" heterosexuals to develop more positive attitudes toward gay men (and presumably, toward lesbians), there is a positive correlation between positive attitudes toward gay men and friendships or acquaintance with a known gay man or lesbian.[62] Herek and Glunt surmised that this may be the result of "a tendency among lesbians and gay men for selective disclosure," being more likely to disclose sexual orientation to persons from whom they expect a positive response.[63] This may very well be an important component in the decision to disclose, because not every act of disclosure of sexual identity meets with approval. One of the important judgments that gay men, lesbians, and bisexuals must make, routinely, is when and to whom to disclose their sexual orientation. Thus, it should come as no surprise that selective disclosure is the norm and not the exception. Even though this confuses the question of causation with correlation, it is a reality that cannot and should not be ignored.[64] Either way, the correlation is encouraging: Even if it

---

60. Gregory M. Herek, Beyond Homophobia: A Social Psychological Perspective on Attitudes Toward Lesbians and Gay Men, in 10 J. of Homosexuality 1, 14 (John P. DeCecco ed., 1984).

61. Id. (citations omitted).

62. Gregory M. Herek & Eric K. Glunt, Interpersonal Contact and Heterosexuals' Attitudes Toward Gay Men: Results from a National Survey, 30 J. of Sex Res. 239, 242–43 (concluding that personal contact with a gay man or lesbian is a powerful predictor of heterosexuals' attitudes toward gay men, with all categories of respondents with contact experiences expressing less negative attitudes. This was true for all groups except for political conservatives, whose negative attitudes, while less than those of political conservatives without contact with a gay man or lesbian, were not so in a statistically significant amount). Id.

63. Id. at 243.

64. The possibility that this positive correlation could be the result of careful decision making by the gay man, lesbian, or bisexual to disclose to a person likely to be accepting suggests that there may be particular benefits to voluntary, rather than forced, disclosure of sexual orientation.

The potential benefits of voluntary disclosure by persons with disabilities in the context of the Americans with Disabilities Act, 42 U.S.C.A. s 12101 et seq., confidentiality provisions is explored by Rose Daly-Rooney in Designing Reasonable Accommodations Through Co-Worker Participation: Therapeutic Jurisprudence and the Confidentiality Provision of the Americans with Disabilities Act, 8 J. L. & Health (1994). Daly-Rooney proposed that by encouraging limited voluntary disclosure of information that an employer is required to keep confidential, and that a worker has the right to have kept confidential, coworkers might better cooperate both with developing a workable accommodation as well as welcoming the

reflects only selective disclosure, it shows at a minimum more accurate judg-ments than not on the part of the disclosers—judgments that, in light of con-tinuing prejudice against gay men, lesbians, and bisexuals, reflect important survival skills.

Not only does the reduction of prejudice (and formalized discrimination) against them promise obvious benefits for gay men, lesbians, and bisexuals, but heterosexuals would benefit as well:

> [A]ntigay prejudice also has negative consequences for heterosexuals. Because of the stigma attached to homosexuality, many heterosexuals restrict their own behavior in order to avoid being labeled gay....Antigay prejudice also inter-feres with same-sex friendships. Males with strongly antigay attitudes appear to have less intimate nonsexual friendships with other men than do males with tolerant attitudes.[65]

Another benefit to heterosexuals from the reduction of antigay prejudice is that many heterosexuals, whether they know it or not, have close family mem-bers who are gay or lesbian. The pain suffered by observing a close relative suffer from prejudice (or from causes unknown to the observer) would be di-minished by a reduction in prejudice generally. Finally, heterosexuals are often the unwitting recipients of the apparent coldness or detachment of gay and les-bian coworkers of family members who may be spending considerable energy avoiding even moderate intimacy with coworkers or family members in order to avoid detection as gay or lesbian. These efforts not only conceal one's "gay-ness" or "lesbianism"; they often conceal as well one's warmth, humor, ex-pressions of empathy, enthusiasm, and positive energy that could be shared with others and contributed to the work or other relevant community.

It is ironic that the ideal circumstances described above[66] for reduction of prejudice already exist in the military context. Servicemembers share common goals, equal status with those of their own rank, situations of moderate inti-macy, and they have ongoing interactions. Perhaps it is because of this ideal situation for confronting prejudice that the significant steps toward elimina-tion of racism in the military have been possible.

Unfortunately, the new policy (like the old) fails to take advantage of the military's remarkable suitability for interactions that could result in the dis-mantling of prejudice rather than in its encouragement. Rather, the Depart-ment of Defense Directives for implementing the new policy make clear that the ideal circumstances that exist in the military will not be used to enhance self-disclosure and greater understanding. The Department of Defense has made this explicit in its "Teaching Scenarios" to commanding officers for briefing on the DoD Policy on Homosexual Conduct. These scenarios offer a remarkable opportunity to consider what could have been and indeed, what

---

disabled coworker into the work community. Daly-Rooney specifically hypothesized that without such disclosure, the disabled worker might be subject to inaccurate speculation by other workers on the basis of stereotypes and that the disabled worker might, in an effort to conceal the disability, appear to be distant, unfriendly, and strange. Parallels exist to the sit-uation of the closeted person trying to conceal mundane details of his or her life to avoid de-tection as gay, lesbian, or bisexual.

65. Herek, supra note 42, at 75 (citations omitted).

66. See supra notes 59–61 and accompanying text.

still could be, should the courts, the Congress, the President, or the military it-self come to their collective senses on the subject.

DOD Training Guidance for DOD Policy on Homosexual Conduct in the Armed Forces[67]

The briefing plan consists of (among other things) hypothetical Teaching Scenarios. The directions for the Teaching Scenarios are themselves instructive: selected excerpts from the instructions and one of the complete teaching scenarios follow:

Briefer's Guidance Sheet

. . . . .

Realize that effective implementation and compliance with this policy is directly related to the professionalism of your presentation.

—The briefing IS informational, IS a clarification of policy, and IS factual.

—The briefing IS NOT sensitivity training, IS NOT a "gripe" session, and IS NOT intended to discuss personal values or beliefs.

[The introduction to the hypothetical scenarios follows:]
The following hypothetical scenarios are for training purposes only. They are not meant to prescribe "correct" outcomes, but to illustrate how relevant personnel should approach issues that may arise under the DOD policy on homosexual conduct in the Armed Forces. The scenarios do not establish any evidentiary standards or create any substantive or procedural rights.

Scenario 13[68]
   Situation. An officer tells his best friend, another officer, that he has recently come to terms with his sexuality and has decided that he is a homosexual. He says, however, that he has not engaged in any homosexual acts during his six years of military service, and that he will continue to refrain from such acts. Although the officer asks his friend not to tell anyone else about their conversation, the friend tells the commanding officer (CO). Having determined that the friend's account of the officer's statement constitutes credible evidence of homosexual conduct, the CO then asks the officer whether he told his friend that he is a homosexual. The officer answers, "Yes."

At a Board of Inquiry hearing, the Service presents the testimony of the officer's friend and the CO about the officer's statements to them. There is no evidence that the officer engaged in any homosexual acts.

The officer presents testimony from several fellow officers and subordinate enlisted persons, all males. Those individuals testify that the officer has never stated or suggested to them that he is a homosexual and has never made any sexual advances or engaged in sexual innuendo [sic] toward them or anyone they know. They also state that the officer is an outstanding leader, that he is always truthful and conscientious, and that they believe he is fully capable of abiding by all Service regulations, including its restrictions on homosexual con-

---

67. Memorandum (undated) Re: Training Guidance for DOD Policy on Homosexual Conduct in the Armed Forces, from Edwin Dorn to Assistant Secretaries of the Army, Navy, and Air Force: DOD Policy on Homosexual Conduct Training Plan.
68. This hypothetical teaching scenario is taken verbatim from the DOD Policy on Homosexual Conduct Training Plan.

duct. Finally, the officer himself testifies that, although he considers himself a homosexual, he has not engaged in any homosexual acts during his six years of service and that he intends to continue to refrain from such acts during the remainder of his term of service.

Issue. How should the Board consider whether the officer has successfully rebutted the presumption?

Discussion. The officer's statement to his friend that he is a homosexual created a rebuttable presumption that the officer engages in or has the propensity or intent to engage in homosexual acts. The question for the Board is whether the officer's evidence succeeded in rebutting that presumption by demonstrating that the officer in fact does not engage in homosexual acts and is unlikely to do so. In making that determination, the Board could consider, among other things: the evidence that the officer had not engaged in any homosexual acts; the officer's credibility; the testimony from other Service members about the officer's past conduct, character, and credibility; and the nature and circumstances of the officer's statements to his friend and commanding officer. If the Board determines that this evidence demonstrated that the officer did not engage in homosexual acts and was not likely to do so, it would find that the officer had rebutted the presumption and would recommend that he be retained. If, however, in weighing all the evidence, the Board determines that the officer had not rebutted the presumption, it would recommend separation.

Note that the scenario possesses each one of the ideal components of a productive disclosure likely to result in a reduction of prejudice: the participants enjoy equal status, the disclosure was in the context of a one-on-one interaction, the participants had a likelihood of repeated interactions, and the participants shared a common context and goals and values unrelated to the topic of the disclosure. In addition, this scenario is as interesting for what it assumes as it is for what it explicitly expresses:

1. It assumes, probably reasonably, that an officer would tell his or her best friend, another officer, something highly personal and important and that the officer would ask that the disclosure be treated confidentially;

2. It assumes, whether reasonably or not, that the best friend would go to the commanding officer and "report" the friend (perhaps because the "best friend" would be torn between loyalty toward the best friend and a sense of duty to report a "forbidden statement" by a fellow officer);

3. It assumes (apparently realistically) that on the basis of that disclosure, separation proceedings would inexorably follow;

4. It hypothesizes (realistically, on the basis of historical events[69]) that the testimony about the gay officer from fellow officers would be glowing and positive; and

---

69. See the following cases, each involving gay or lesbian servicemembers faced with discharges on the grounds of homosexuality, about whom testimonials were consistently positive: Steffan v. Aspin, 8 F.3d 57, 59 (D.C. Cir. 1993), reh'g (en banc) granted, 1994 U.S. App. LEXIS 9977 (D.C. Cir. 1994) (cadet at U.S. Naval Academy who had received "consistently outstanding marks for his leadership and military performance," who was a "model for his classmates and subordinates") (the D.C. Circuit, sitting en banc, eventually affirmed the District Court's decision denying Steffan any remedy for his discharge from the United States Naval Academy as a result of admitting that he was a homosexual, 1994 U.S. App. LEXIS 33045 (D.C. Cir. Nov. 22, 1994)); Watkins v. United States Army, 875 F.2d 699 (9th Cir.

5. It concludes that the officer might or might not be separated as a result of the testimony outlined, even though all of the testimony is consistent with a finding only that the officer is gay and none of which suggests an "intent" to engage in prohibited conduct.

The scenario itself speaks volumes about the new policy: friendship betrayed, self-discovery interrupted, and personal and institutional energies wasted—all in the futile effort to make predictions about complex and deeply personal events that have no bearing on the mission of the military. The disclosure of sexual orientation by the gay officer results in disruption because the Directives of the new policy so provide. Such disclosures need not be met with such fanfare. They are, ultimately, made far more significant because they are prohibited. Once the novelty of "knowing" what was previously only "suspected" has worn off, the military, like other institutions that have allowed gay and lesbian workers to share information about their lives, will discover that gay men, lesbians, and bisexuals, like heterosexual men and women, spend most of their time and energy focusing on issues that are far more mundane and at the same time far more important than the issues discussed in this article.

In other words, the military would discover what most people already know: Gay men, lesbians, and bisexual women and men, like heterosexual men and women, have lives that are both complex and humdrum, tragedy filled and situation comedylike; dreams that are both too big and too small; desks that are either messy or neat; shoes that are either polished or scuffed; parents who are either supportive or critical; and lives that have a whole lot *less* to do with sexual conduct than most members of either group would be comfortable admitting.

1989) (en banc), cert. denied, 498 U.S. 957 (1990) (detailing a 15-year Army career of meritorious service); Cammermeyer v. Aspin, 850 F. Supp. 910, 912–13 (W.D. Wash. 1994) (detailing Cammermeyer's distinguished service as an Army nurse and citing letter from Washington state's governor, who is commander-in-chief of Washington State National Guard, stating, "if Colonel Cammermeyer's discharge becomes final, this would be both a significant loss to the State of Washington and a senseless end to the career of a distinguished, long-time member of the armed services.") Id. at 913.

Chapter 18

Designing Reasonable Accommodations through Co-Worker Participation: Therapeutic Jurisprudence and the Confidentiality Provision of the Americans with Disabilites Act

Rose A. Daly-Rooney

I. Introduction

Working is a state of being that many people with disabilities cannot take for granted because, as a recent Harris Poll found, over 8 million people with disabilities want to work but cannot find a job.[2] Not only is working an avenue of financial support and independence, it is also a source of self-esteem and an opportunity to make friends and social contacts. Because of prohibitions against discrimination on the basis of disability by most private employers,[3] the Americans with Disabilities Act (ADA) offers the potential for relief from the staggering level of unemployment faced by people with disabilities.

The Americans with Disabilities Act prohibits discrimination on the basis of disability in employment, public accommodations, transportation, communi-

---

2. S. Rep. NO. 116, 101st Cong., 1st Sess. 107 (1989).

3. See 42 U.S.C. §§ 12111–12117 (Supp. V 1993). Employment provisions apply to private employers with 15 or more employees, state and local governments, employment agencies, and labor unions. Id. § 12111(2), (5)(A). Employment discrimination by state and local governments is also prohibited under Title II of the ADA. See 42 U.S.C. §§ 12131–12133 (Supp. V 1993). Although a plain reading of Title II (Non-Discrimination in State and Local Government) does not indicate that Title II includes employment discrimination, the legislative history and the implementing regulations do make clear that employment discrimination is prohibited under Title II. H.R. Rep. No. 485, 101st Cong., 2d Sess. 84 (1990), reprinted in 1990 U.S.C.C.A.N. 367; 28 C.F.R. § 35.140 (1994). See also Ethridge v. Alabama, 860 F. Supp. 808 (M.D. Ala. 1994) (concluding that employment discrimination is prohibited by entities covered under Title II).

Exempted from the requirements of the ADA are the federal government, a corporation wholly owned by the federal government, Indian tribes, and certain bona fide private membership clubs. 42 U.S.C. § 12111(5)(B).

cation, and services provided by state and local government.[4] Title I of the ADA addresses employment discrimination against people with disabilities.[5] Among other things, the ADA prohibits an employer from rejecting an applicant solely because of the need to provide that applicant with a reasonable accommodation.[6] At the same time, the ADA requires that an employer maintain confidentiality about the applicant or employee's medical condition or medical history obtained during acceptable inquiries, including those inquiries needed to design appropriate accommodations.[7]

II. A Therapeutic Jurisprudence Proposal

The ADA's provision that requires an employer to maintain confidentiality of the medical condition and history of the applicant or employee may actually impair the employer's ability to effectively and efficiently integrate applicants and employees with disabilities in the workplace. This article uses a therapeutic jurisprudence approach[8] to suggest that the confidentiality requirement of the ADA should not be implemented in a manner that forecloses active participation by co-workers in designing reasonable accommodations for and with applicants and employees with disabilities. A group including the applicant, co-workers, and the supervisor should engage in a group brainstorming process to design reasonable accommodations which may lead to more therapeutic results in the integration of employees with disabilities in the workforce.

Legally, just as a psychotherapy patient may waive therapist/patient confidentiality and allow a therapist to inform a third party of the patient's condition or communications,[9] an employee with a disability should presumably be

---

4. 42 U.S.C. §§ 12111–12189 (Supp. V 1993); 47 U.S.C. §§ 152, 221, 225, 611 (1988 & Supp. V 1993).

5. 42 U.S.C. §§ 12111–12117.

6. Id. § 12112(b)(5)(B).

7. Id. § 12112(d)(3)(B).

8. Therapeutic jurisprudence is the study of the role of the law (rules, procedures, and legal roles) as a therapeutic agent. David B. Wexler, New Directions in Therapeutic Jurisprudence: Breaking the Bounds of Conventional Mental Health Law Scholarship, 10 N.Y. L. Sch. J. Hum. Rts. 759, 761–62 (1993). The development and implementation of laws have therapeutic and anti-therapeutic consequences. Id. at 762. The doctrine of therapeutic jurisprudence "proposes that we be sensitive to those consequences, rather than iggnore [sic] them, and that we ask whether the law's antitherapeutic consequences can be reduced and its therapeutic consequences enhanced without subordinating due process and justice values." Id.

9. David B. Wexler, Patients, Therapists, and Third Parties: The Victimological Virtures of Tarasoff, in Therapeutic Jurisprudence: The Law as a Therapeutic Agent 201, 232–234, 233 n.192, 234 n.200 (David B. Wexler ed., 1990).

The law offers other examples of protected persons being permitted to waive rights granted by the Constitution, statutes, and common law. For example, a person is permitted to waive the Constitutional requirements of probable cause and a search warrant by consenting to a search. See United States v. Morales, 972 F.2d 1007 (9th Cir. 1992), cert. denied, 113 S. Ct. 1665 (1993). Although husbands and wives enjoy a spousal privilege to prevent adverse testimony in a criminal trial, the spouse who holds the privilege may waive it. See Graham C. Lilly, An Introduction to the Law of Evidence § 9.4 (2d Ed. 1987). Another example which comes from the employment arena is the statutory right to a jury trial in an ac-

able to waive the ADA's confidentiality provision.[10] Such a waiver would allow an employer to discuss with co-workers certain otherwise confidential information relating to the employee's disability.

This proposal to involve co-workers is based on several premises which flow from psychological theory but which deserve empirical study in the disability/employment context. The general theory is that giving a person input or a "voice" in the decisionmaking process substantially increases the likelihood that she will regard the ultimate decision as fair and comply with it.[11] Accordingly, a co-worker may be more willing to implement a plan to accommodate a worker with a disability (and be far less resentful of the accommodation) if she helped design the plan than if she is simply told to implement it. Second, an employee with a disability may not feel as isolated from other employees if they all worked together to design accommodations. In addition, a group brainstorming session may encourage focusing on the job duties instead of the limitations of the employee or applicant with the disability. Finally, a process involving co-workers who actually perform the work may lead to development of more natural and less expensive supports in the workplace to accommodate the employee with the disability.

This article provides three hypothetical cases for consideration, a background on the requirement of reasonable accommodations under the ADA,[12] discussion

---

tion to recover damages for intentional discrimination in the workplace, 42 U.S.C. § 1981a(c)(L) (Supp. V 1993), which, as with any other right to a jury trial, may be waived by the parties. See, e.g., Scharnhorst V. Independent Sch. Dist., 686 F.2d 637 (8th Cir. 1982), cert. denied, 462 U.s. 1109 (1983) (finding that the right to a jury trial in an age discrimination claim may be waived by an untimely demand for a jury, despite the fact that the waiver was unintended or inadvertent).

10. Surely, nothing in the law would prevent the employee from personally informing co-workers about the disability. It seems logical, then, for the law to permit the employee to authorize the employer to disclose certain facts to relevant co-workers. If the law were somehow interpreted not to allow such a waiver, the employee herself could of course make all the necessary disclosures, but in the unlikely event the ADA is so interpreted by the courts, an amendment expressly providing for a waiver of confidentiality would be very much in order.

The use of a waiver keeps the control of whether information is disclosed in the hands of the applicant or employee with the disability. That decision to exercise the right of confidentiality is protected by another provision of the ADA which makes it unlawful for anyone to "coerce, intimidate, threaten, harass or interfere with any individual in the exercise or enjoyment of…any right granted or protected by this part." 29 C.F.R. § 1630.12 (1994).

In the majority of cases the disabled employee should be sufficiently competent to waive the confidentiality provision. A possible scenario involving an employee who might be under legal guardianship and not "competent" to waive her rights would be the situation presented in hypothetical Case #1. See supra p. 92.

11. Tom R. Tyler, The Psychological Consequences of Judicial Procedures: Implications for Civil Commitment Hearings, 46 SMU L. Rev. 433, 439–40 (1992); David B. Wexler, Health Care Compliance Principles and the Insanity Acquittee Conditional Release Process, in Essays in Therapeutic Jurisprudence 199, 203–08 (David B. Wexler & Bruce J. Winick eds., 1991).

12. Section IV of this article, relating to the background of the ADA, is largely drawn from Rose Daly-Rooney, Reconciling Conflicts Between the Americans with Disabilities Act and The National Labor Relations Act to Accommodate People with Disabilities, 6 DePaul Bus. L.J. 387 (1994).

of the confidentiality requirement, and the implication of confidentiality requirements on designing reasonable accommodations by a group process.

III. *Hypothetical Cases*

Consider in the following examples whether the assistance of co-workers might be helpful in designing reasonable accommodations which would permit these applicants to perform the job.

Case 1. Shana is applying for a position as a dishwasher at a restaurant. Dishwashers usually load and unload a large dishwasher, operate the dishwasher and do general cleanup in the kitchen, including sweeping and mopping, taking out garbage and cleaning outside the restaurant in the back parking lot. Shana is a 26 year old woman who is moderately mentally retarded. She can read and write at approximately the third grade level. She has excellent adaptive skills: she lives semi-independently in an apartment in the community, can use city transportation, and can perform most household tasks, such as cleaning. She has some behavioral problems, such as perseverating on certain conversational topics about television shows and, at times, demonstrating inappropriate affect. To learn a new job thoroughly she needs about two weeks of one-on-one training.

Case 2. John applied for a position as a sales clerk in a major department store in the men's department. Sales clerks in this department must assist customers with questions or in locating merchandise, ring up sales and take payment for items purchased in the department, change the merchandise and assist with setting up displays. John is a 21 year old man who uses a wheelchair. He has no use of his legs but has full use of his arms and hands. He has good upper body strength.

Case 3. Jane is applying for a position as an associate at a medium size law firm which specializes in commercial work and personal injury and employment discrimination on behalf of plaintiffs. The firm needs an associate to assist senior partners in personal injury and employment discrimination work. Jane is deaf. She can effectively read lips in one-on-one settings, but uses an interpreter in larger groups, such as meetings and at trial. She needs to use a Telecommunication Device for the Deaf (TDD) or an operator relay system for telephone conversations.

Co-workers could provide an integral role in designing accommodations for these employees. People who perform the job daily are in a better position to provide a detailed description of the job-related functions than are their supervisors. For example, the cook or waitresses may be able to tell, more precisely than the manager or owner, how many times the dishwasher usually has to be loaded/unloaded within a shift and how much time it takes to load and unload the dishwasher. Co-workers also may be able to supply information to help determine those tasks which are essential to the performance of the job. Another sales clerk may be able to tell how often sales racks of merchandise have to be rearranged and if other store employees help with this process. Combined with information about the abilities of the applicant or employee, the co-worker may have valuable ideas about making adaptations. We will return to these matters in greater detail after describing the ADA and some provisions which may impact on the process of co-worker involvement.

IV. Background: The ADA and Reasonable Accommodations

The ADA prohibits employers from inquiring about the nature and severity of a disability, but does permit inquiries about limitations that might interfere with performing the job.[13] This inquiry necessarily includes asking the applicant or employee whether she can perform the job with or without an accommodation. Information about the medical condition or history of the applicant or employee may be given to answer this inquiry. If so, that information must be treated by the employer as a confidential medical record.[14] Therefore, understanding the ADA's provisions regarding reasonable accommodations and confidentiality are essential.

A. Eligibility

The ADA requires numerous individualized determinations by covered employers[15] making employment decisions about people with disabilities. Evaluating whether an individual is disabled is one of the first of these individualized inquiries. Disability is defined as a "physical or mental impairment that substantially limits one or more of the major life activities" of an individual.[16] Working is a major life activity.[17] Generally, there are no categorical determinations.[18] For example, not all people with epilepsy are disabled according to this definition. One person with epilepsy who has seizures that are infrequent and less serious may not have a substantial limitation of a major life activity while another person with epilepsy may have frequent and serious seizures which impair the ability to work or perform other major life activities. Determining whether an individual is substantially limited in a major life activity,[19] and specifically in the major activity

---

13. 42 U.S.C. § 12112(d)(2), (d)(4) (Supp. V 1993).

14. Id. § 12112(d)(3)(B), (d)(4)(C).

15. For an explanation of what constitutes a covered employer, see supra note 3.

16. 42 U.S.C. § 12102(2)(A) (Supp. V 1993). Also included within the definition of disability is a record of a mental or physical impairment which substantially limits a major life activity or being regarded as having such as impairment. Id. § 12102(2)(B)-(C). Since these types of disabilities often do not require consideration of reasonable accommodations, they are not discussed further in the article. However, having a record of such an impairment is an important definition to keep in mind regarding the requirement to keep medical information and history confidential.

17. 29 C.F.R. § 1630.2(i) (1994).

18. There are some conditions which are not covered under the ADA. For example, the term disability does not include "transvestism, transsexualism, pedophilia, exhibitionism, voyeurism, gender identity disorders not resulting from physical impairments, or other sexual behavior disorders;...compulsive gambling, kleptomania, or pyromania; or...psychoactive substance use disorders resulting from current illegal use of drugs." 42 U.S.C. §12211(b) (Supp. V 1993).

19. 29 C.F.R. § 1630.2(j)(2)(i)-(iii). Factors considered in determining whether an individual is substantially limited include: "(i) the nature and severity of the impairment; (ii) the du-

of working, are also individualized inquiries.[20]

Once an individual meets the statutory definition of disabled, she must otherwise be qualified to perform the essential functions of the job either with or without a reasonable accommodation.[21] Designing the accommodation requires (1) distinguishing between the functions that are essential rather than marginal to the job[22] and (2) assessing whether an employee with a disability could perform the essential function with or without a reasonable accommodation.[23]

B. Reasonable Accommodation

The ADA prohibits a covered employer from discriminating against a qualified individual with a disability by not making a reasonable accommodation for the known physical or mental limitation.[24] The ADA envisions that an employer's efforts to make reasonable accommodations for individuals with disabilities may include:

> [m]aking existing facilities used by employees readily accessible to and usable by individuals with disabilities[,]...job restructuring, part-time or modified work schedules, reassignment to a vacant position, acquisition or modification of equipment or devices, appropriate adjustment or modifications of examinations, training materials or policies, the provision of qualified readers or interpreters, and other similar accommodations for individuals with disabilities.[25]

Congress intended that the ADA would level the playing field between employees and applicants with or without disabilities by removing a major obstacle to employment: failure to make accommodations. Under the ADA, reliance by employers on the cost and inconvenience of reasonable accommodations as grounds for not employing otherwise qualified people with disabilities is discriminatory, subject to the defenses noted in the next subsection.

---

ration or expected duration of the impairment; and (iii) the permanent or long term impact of or resulting from the impairment." Id.

20. 29 C.F.R. § 1630.2(j)(3)(ii). Factors which may be considered in determining whether an individual is substantially limited in the life activity of working include:

  (A) The geographical area to which the individual has reasonable access;
  (B) The job from which the individual has been disqualified because of an impairment, and the number and types of jobs utilizing similar training, knowledge, skills or abilities, within that geographical area, from which the individual is also disqualified because of the impairment (class of jobs); and/or
  (C) The job from which the individual has been disqualified because of an impairment, and the number and types of other jobs not utilizing similar training, knowledge, skills or abilities, within that geographical area, from which the individual is also disqualified because of the impairment (broad range of jobs in various classes).

Id.

21. 42 U.S.C. § 12111(8) (Supp. V 1993).
22. 29 C.F.R. app. § 1630.2(o) (1994).
23. Id.
24. 42 U.S.C. § 12112(a), (b)(5)(A).
25. Id. § 12111(9).

C. Employer's Defenses

The defenses of undue hardship and business necessity set boundaries on the lengths an employer must go to accommodate the applicant or employee with a disability. If an employer proves that an accommodation would incur "significant difficulty or expense" in light of a variety of factors set out in the regulations, the employer is not required to provide that accommodation.[26] If, however, the employee offers to pay for part or all of the accommodation or use outside resources, such as services through the state department of vocational rehabilitation, then the employer may not consider those costs in determining reasonableness.[27]

Generally, an employer may defeat a claim of discrimination for using a standard, test, or selection criteria that has an adverse and disparate impact upon people with disabilities if it is proven (1) to be job-related, (2) consistent with business necessity, and (3) *that its performance cannot be accomplished by providing a reasonable accommodation.*[28] However, by definition of this tripartite standard, even if the employer has a standard or policy that is job-related and consistent with business necessity, she may be required to make an exception to or modify the application of the policy for a person with a disability if it would not be burdensome. For example, if a retail employer gives one hour lunch breaks to its employees, but a person with diabetes requires two half-hour breaks during a shift to take medicine and eat, then the employer may have to relax the standard in that case.

D. The Process of Designing the Reasonable Accommodation

Designing a reasonable accommodation is an interactive process between the employer, the employee, and outside resources when necessary.[29] The employer should consider those alternatives preferred by the employee; however, the employer is ultimately free to choose the least costly alternative.[30]

V. Confidentiality Requirement and Designing Reasonable Accommodations

A. Discussion of the Confidentiality Requirement

The ADA prohibits pre-employment medical examinations or inquiries about whether the applicant or employee is disabled and about the nature and severity of the disability[31] and requires confidential treatment of medical information

---

26. 29 C.F.R. app. § 1630.2(p).

27. Id.

28. 29 C.F.R. § 1630.15(b) (1994).

29. Id. at app. § 1630.2(o).

30. 29 C.F.R. app. § 1630.9 (1994).

31. 42 U.S.C. § 12112(d)(2)(A), (d)(4)(A) (Supp. V 1993).

obtained in post-offer examinations.[32] An acceptable inquiry by employers is whether the applicant would be able to perform job-related functions.[33] If an otherwise qualified applicant with a disability can perform the essential functions of a job with or without a reasonable accommodation, she must be considered for the position in the same manner as other qualified applicants are considered. The employer cannot prefer the applicant without a disability solely because the applicant with a disability will need an accommodation unless the accommodation would impose an undue hardship.[34] For example, the managing partner of the law firm who recruits and hires lawyers could ask Jane how she could (with or without a reasonable accommodation) conduct interviews with new clients and hold meetings with existing clients. But she could not ask Jane when she became deaf and the reason for the deafness.

While making acceptable inquiries[35] the employer may learn about the medical information or medical history of the applicant. If so, the employer must treat the information about medical condition or history of the applicant as a confidential medical record.[36]

There are exceptions to the confidentiality requirement of these records.[37] Two express exceptions which relate to the theory of co-worker involvement in the design of reasonable accommodations include disclosure to supervisors and managers[38] and to first aid or safety personnel.[39] Therefore, only certain employees, specifically supervisors and safety personnel, may be informed about the medical condition or disability status of an employee with a disability under these circumstances. There is no express exception for *other* co-workers to be informed about this information.

An article by Christopher Bell, a disability law specialist, suggests that the ADA is likely to be implemented without co-worker participation because of the confidentiality requirement.[40] Without exploring the notion of an employer seeking an employee's waiver of the confidentiality provision in his article, Bell indicates that "[b]ecause an employer is prohibited by the ADA's confidentiality provisions from disclosing the disability status of an employee, an employer

---

32. 29 C.F.R. app. § 1630.14(b) (1994).

33. 42 U.S.C. § 12112(d)(2)(B).

34. 29 C.F.R. app. § 1630.9(b) (1994).

35. Acceptable inquiries, in addition to whether the applicant can perform job-related functions with or without an accommodation, include requests for the applicant (once an offer of employment has been made) or employee to undergo medical examination, but certain conditions must be met. See 42 U.S.C. § 12112(d)(3), (d)(4)(B).

36. Id. § 12112(d)(3)(B).

37. Id. § 12112(d)(3)(B) (excepting certain managers, supervisors, safety personnel and government officials). Additionally, it is not inconsistent with the ADA to require the collection of confidential medical information for compliance with state worker's compensation laws, 29 C.F.R. app. § 1630.14(b), or to satisfy the affirmative action requirements of § 503 of the Rehabilitation Act, 29 C.F.R. app. § 1630.14(a).

38. 42 U.S.C. § 12112(d)(3)(B)(i) (allowing disclosure of information relating to job duty restrictions and necessary accommodations).

39. Id. § 12112(d)(3)(B)(ii) (allowing disclosure if emergency treatment may be required for the disabled employee).

40. Christopher G. Bell, The Americans with Disabilities Act, Mental Disability, and Work, Dec. 2, 1993 (on file with author).

is not in a position to explain that these items [accommodations], perceived by co-workers as special treatment, are mandated by law because of an employee's disability."[41] Certainly, if the confidentiality provision of the ADA is interpreted to preclude the disclosure of information to co-workers to permit them to understand why a particular accommodation for an individual is needed,[42] it would preclude the disclosure of information to allow the co-worker to assist in designing the accommodation in the first place. My thesis, however, is that the ADA may often (though not always) be more effectively implemented if the employee with a disability agrees to waive the confidentiality requirement for the limited purpose of permitting relevant co-workers to be involved in designing reasonable accommodations.

B. Implications for the Design of Reasonable Accommodations

The importance of obtaining information and assistance from other employees in designing reasonable accommodations will vary depending upon the nature of the job, the abilities of the applicant with a disability, the applicant's or employee's familiarity with the job duties, and the importance of interaction among employees for job-related functions. For example, in the hypothetical cases, Shana's mental retardation may result in her contributing somewhat less to the design of the accommodation than might be true in the case of either Jane or John. Similarly, the cooperation of co-workers may play a more significant role for Shana and John than for Jane, who may do more solitary work. However, even though John would be the expert on how to accomplish tasks without being limited by the disability, he may not be very familiar with all of the job duties of a sales clerk. Involvement of co-workers may be beneficial in determining the duties and frequency of those duties on the job.

The employer should not bring in co-workers to discuss reasonable accommodations if the employee and employer alone could work out details of the specific accommodation, the details do not involve the cooperation of other workers, and the accommodation is not likely to be noticed and resented by the co-workers.[43] However, in those cases where either (1) the applicant or employee cannot contribute as effectively to the design of the reasonable accommodation, either due to unfamiliarity with the job functions or to the nature of the disability, or (2) the success of the accommodation depends on cooperation or non-resentment of other employees, the employer should ideally be able to open the discussion to relevant co-workers with the consent of the applicant or employee with the disability.

---

41. Id. at 12.

42. Bell does indicate that an employer may be able to provide general information to the co-workers in the form of training, but cautions that "...training must be presented in such a way as to avoid disclosure of a particular employee's disability...." Bell, supra note 40, at 13.

43. "Relevant co-workers" needs to be defined so that the group is limited to those people who could meaningfully contribute to the process. Also, for a workplace where relevant co-workers included large numbers in the workforce, the group brainstorming process may need to include selected relevant workers to make the process manageable. A group of more than five will probably decrease the efficiency of the group.

C. The Mechanics of the Group Process

Ideally, the group brainstorming process should include the applicant or employee with a disability and relevant co-workers.[44] The covered employer should set the tone that the company wants to accommodate the employee and would like input on how best to arrange the accommodation. This method might discourage people from discussing barriers and instead focus the discussions on the accommodation. The group should work from a job description or, if none is available, should create a list of job duties. From those duties the group should identify the essential job duties. Then, the applicant could address how she could perform those duties with or without a reasonable accommodation. In the case of Jane, other first year associates may be able to identify how much time they spend meeting and talking to clients or opposing attorneys to aid in determining how much time may be needed for interpreter services for Jane.

For duties which the applicant or employee could not perform, the group would generate ideas for making the function feasible for the applicant. Then, following the meeting, the applicant could state her preferences and the employer could consider all of the input in deciding on the most appropriate alternative. If the employee's medical information or history was revealed as a part of that discussion, the employee would be waiving the right to confidentiality of that information within that setting.[45]

Any information not disclosed by the employee or permitted to be disclosed by the employee would still be protected by the confidentiality requirement. An employer might learn about other confidential information from other sources, such as a work-related physical examination or the employment application that is not needed to design the accommodation. The medical information or history that was discovered from other sources but not useful to creating the accommodation would still be subject to the confidentiality requirements. For example, if John had to get a post-employment physical, the physical may include information about the medical history of the paraplegia. This information would not be necessary for designing the accommodation and would not normally come up in the brainstorming process. The employer would need to protect that information as confidential despite the disclosure of other medical information about the nature of John's limitation.

---

44. Whenever an employee wishes to participate in the group brainstorming process she should be informed by the employer that the ADA provides for the private discussion between the employer and employee and protects any confidential medical information that is disclosed. If the employee agrees, the employer may have the employee disclose the confidential information to the group. If any confidential information will be disclosed the employer should obtain a waiver from the employee to permit disclosures that would otherwise be considered confidential information protected by the ADA. To protect both the employee and the employer, the waiver should specifically outline the information that will be disclosed.

In some instances, the employees may not be competent (or may even have a guardian) and be unable to waive this right. The employer may wish to seek permission of the employee and guardian to make the disclosure.

45. Disclosure of confidential information in the group brainstorming process would not automatically permit disclosure of the same information by the employer to other sources. For example, the employer would not be able to disclose the information to a prospective employer simply on the basis of this past disclosure.

Disclosure by the employer of protected medical information arising in the group brainstorming process would be prohibited for purposes other than designing and implementing the reasonable accommodation through co-worker participation. By analogy to the express exceptions to the confidentiality requirement, if disclosure to safety personnel for emergency treatment is warranted, that exception would not warrant disclosure to persons other than safety personnel.

D. Application to the Hypothetical Cases

People usually are more receptive to an idea if they contributed to its development.[46] In the case of Shana, she will probably need intense training for about two weeks, but will then be able to handle the repetitive tasks of her job as a dishwasher. On an ongoing basis she may need reminders or cues from the other staff to stay on task or to stop talking about certain subjects. She may also need assistance in filling out timecards, timesheets, or other incidental paperwork. Shana could give her co-workers guidance on how she would like to be reminded so that the reminders and cues are not demeaning or patronizing.

If the restaurant manager, as a training "program," simply assigns Shana to "shadow" dishwashers on other shifts without enlisting the other dishwashers' cooperation, Shana may not obtain the necessary training and may fail in her duties. However, if the manager was permitted to tell the relevant employees about Shana's limitations in behavior and learning style that would likely impact her training and employment, the manager might be able to ask the other workers how that training could best be provided. Some dishwashers may volunteer to have her "shadow" them. Others might share "shortcuts" they use to remember their job duties or functions, such as a simple checklist. In one study of a small number of work settings employing people with more severe disabilities, researchers observed instances where "mentor" co-workers provided reminders, suggestions, and demonstrations to help their co-workers with disabilities learn the tricks of the trade.[47]

The group brainstorming process might help break down the isolation and barriers that some people with disabilities experience on the job. Whenever a "minority" breaks into unchartered territories, as many people with disabilities will with the onset of the ADA, they may not be readily accepted because people do not understand their disability or may believe that the person was hired or selected because of the disability.

Without disclosure in the group brainstorming process, co-workers may speculate about the worker and the disability. Their imaginations may roam, and the conclusions may be highly inaccurate and based on stereotypes. For example, Shana, who is mentally retarded with some behavioral challenges, may be perceived as mentally ill by her co-workers. Similarly, if Shana lives in a group home, and her retardation is not known to co-workers, she might, to preserve secrecy, decline a co-worker's offer of a ride home on a rainy day, leading the co-

---

46. Cf. Wexler, supra note 9, at 204–05.

47. David C. Hagner, The Social Interactions and Job Supports of Supported Employees, in Natural Supports in School, at Work, and in the Community for People with Severe Disabilities 217, 229–33 (Jan Nisbet ed., 1992) [hereinafter Natural Supports].

worker to feel rebuffed and likely to conclude that Shana is a very strange person. Shana may be better understood if the co-workers learn that her behavior and skill acquisition are affected by mental retardation. Workers with disabilities are more likely to garner co-worker acceptance based on accurate information rather than stereotypes and speculation. Accommodations produced by group effort may build better understanding about the nature of the disability and help co-workers view the individual as a person aside from the disability.

The interactions and teamwork required to develop the accommodation may span the working relationship that follows. The process may encourage accommodations between employees with disabilities and those without disabilities. If accommodations go in both directions the process is likely to increase acceptance of the co-worker with a disability as a team member. For example, suppose John needs to work the day shift because he relied on accessible public transportation that was unavailable after 7 p.m., and that Mary, a co-worker who does not have a disability, agreed to accommodate John by taking some extra night shifts. John might also accommodate Mary by coming in earlier once a week, so that Mary could go to a class. In the study previously mentioned, researchers noted that co-workers without disabilities tended to make accommodations for each other.[48]

If co-workers participate in designing the accommodation and understand the necessity for it, the worker with the disability may be accepted into a natural workplace culture of mutual accommodations. One-directional supports can result in a "benevolence trap" in which people with disabilities always benefit from the good works of others but are not offered the opportunities to provide assistance in return.[49] One-directional accommodations are likely to have the same effect.

The disclosure of necessary information for the accommodation may also produce a collateral benefit of removing barriers to communication with co-workers imposed by the co-worker with a disability. Some people with disabilities may wish to hide or mask the existence of a disability to avoid ridicule. Once co-workers learn about the limitations through participation in the group brainstorming process, the co-worker with a disability may feel more at ease talking to her co-workers without fear of revealing information that will lead the others to learn about the disability. For example, if Shana's co-workers knew of her mental retardation, they would not be shocked to learn that she lives in a group home, she would not be embarrassed to accept a ride home on a rainy day, and the situation of her strangely rebuffing them and refusing a ride on a rainy day would never arise.

A brainstorming session to identify accommodations has the potential to take the focus from disability to ability. Job descriptions are often based on the norm of the employee. For example, in *Prewitt v. United States Postal Service*,[50] a job requirement for a mail sorting position was an ability to raise the arm above the shoulder as a shelf for casing mail was above shoulder height. If

---

48. Id. at 231–32.

49. Michael J. Callahan, Job Site Training and Natural Supports, in Natural Supports, supra note 47, at 257, 273–74.

50. 662 F.2d 292 (5th Cir. 1981). This case involved the Rehabilitation Act of 1973 which has a provision similar to the ADA's provision requiring reasonable accommodations.

the shelf were lowered, however, Mr. Prewitt, who had a physical disability that limited his ability to raise his arm above shoulder level, would be able to case the mail.[51] The court noted that the "requirement" was not really a requirement because it was not necessary for the performance of the job.[52]

If the group concentrates on the job-related functions and how the individual applicant can perform these functions, the group will naturally be addressing abilities rather than limitations. In Shana's case, the brainstorming process would focus on the duties of a dishwasher, such as loading the dishwashing machine, operating the equipment, and handling the various cleaning tasks, and would not focus on Shana's IQ or her grade equivalent for reading skills. An incidental result of this group effort may also lead to the development of job descriptions not based on the norm of the employee without disabilities. Developing job descriptions that do not focus on these differences should have an empowering effect upon workers with disabilities.

In the case of John, who applies for a position as a sales clerk in a men's department at a major department store, the group brainstorming process might expose the ways in which a job description contains Prewitt-like requirements. For example, John can ring up sales if the table holding the cash register is lowered, and he can assist customers if there is enough room between the racks and in the dressing room. He should be able to reach merchandise above arm level with a "reaching device" that is used for items. It may be a physical barrier built into the workplace or included in the job description or the workplace, and not the limitations of a disability, that prevents John from performing a job-related function.

In the supported employment movement,[53] there is a trend to use "natural" rather than "artificial" supports for employees whenever possible.[54] Natural supports are the use of typical people and environments to accommodate the integration of a person with a disability rather than "relying on specialized services and personnel."[55] For example, using a specially trained job coach to train and supervise Shana would be an artificial support because the job coach is not a part of the natural work setting. An example of a natural accommodation would be for Shana to train by "shadowing" another dishwasher to observe the tasks of the job and attempt to gradually take on the tasks herself.

Natural supports have come into favor because they are generally cheaper and enhance the opportunity for more effective inclusion of people with disabilities. In the case of Jane, who applied for an associate's position at a per-

---

51. Prewitt, 662 F.2d at 305.

52. See id. at 309.

53. "Supported employment began as a philosophical commitment to improve the employment outcomes of individuals with severe disabilities. Supported employment is now a major national initiative with its own technology, practical legislation, and funding system. In its simplest form, supported employment provides paid employment in integrated work settings to individuals previously excluded from work. The success of this approach lies in the provision of intense, individual training and support during the initial stages of employment, and of ongoing assistance, enabling an individual to maintain employment for extended periods of time." Paul Wehman, Supported Employment and Opportunities for Integration, in The ADA Mandate for Social Change 69, 70 (Paul Wehman, ed., 1993).

54. Callahan, in Natural Supports, supra note 47, at 257–58.

55. Jan Nisbet, Introduction, in Natural Supports, supra note 47, at 5.

sonal injury law firm, a more natural support may be to hire a secretary or paralegal who knows sign language rather than hiring an interpreter whose only function is to sign for Jane.[56] Obtaining a secretary or paralegal that can sign might cost more than an employee without that skill, but it would be cheaper than hiring two employees. The secretary or paralegal could do other duties for Jane, but could do sign language interpretation for attorney meetings and in court. Therefore, the presence of a paralegal, secretary, or other support personnel would be more natural to the work setting than an interpreter who was waiting on standby.

VI. Conclusion

Designing reasonable accommodations that effectively integrate people with disabilities into the workplace will be essential to the successful implementation of the ADA. Further study of the usefulness of co-worker participation in the group brainstorming process to design accommodations is warranted to determine if it has expected therapeutic benefits for the worker with the disability and the co-workers.

One way to test this theory would be to study integration of disabled workers at two large comparable employers. Applicants and employees with disabilities of one employer could be encouraged to participate in the group process and waive the confidentiality requirement to the extent medical information is discussed in the group process. The second employer could implement the ADA pursuant to a "business as usual" policy and the accommodation would presumably be ordinarily determined privately with the employer only. Disabled applicants and employees and co-workers at the two settings could later be compared using a number of measures to examine integration in the workforce, effectiveness of the accommodation, job performance, turnover and job satisfaction.

If further study confirms that the group process is in fact more effective, as this article speculates it would be, a therapeutic jurisprudence approach would be to keep the confidentiality requirement in the ADA as is, but to allow employers to encourage voluntary disclosure of limited information by employees for the group brainstorming process. In this sense, therapeutic jurisprudence would urge "law reform" not by changing the law itself, but by suggesting that employers, as one type of "implementer" of the law,[57] voluntarily change their behavior and role in order to encourage employees to consider waiving the ADA confidentiality provision for the limited purpose of co-worker participation in the group brainstorming process.

---

56. S. Rep. No. 116, supra note 2, at 108 (citing testimony of Dr. I. King Jordan, President of Gallaudet University, who suggested that interpreters can be hired to do other things as well as interpret and specifically offered the example of secretaries and professional staff).

57. See David B. Wexler, Therapeutic Jurisprudence and Changing Conceptions of Legal Scholarship, 11 Behavioral Sci. & Law 17, 28 (1993) (referring to private therapists as legal "administrators" of the law).

Rethinking the Health Care Delivery Crisis: The Need for a Therapeutic Jurisprudence

Bruce J. Winick

The intense debate over national health policy seems to reflect a new consensus about the need to overhaul our health care delivery system. As the nation moves toward health care reform, we must ensure that we create a system that is fair, that provides incentives both to reduce costs and encourage wellness, and that is sensitive to the delivery system's inevitable impact on patient health.

Health care costs are estimated at $940 billion a year. These costs have escalated so dramatically—approximately ten percent a year—that even many in the middle class must go without adequate health care or obtain it only at great personal sacrifice. This is especially true for increasing numbers of people who cannot afford health insurance. One suggested solution is to require employers in businesses over a specified size to provide a certain level of health insurance for full-time employees. But the cost of insurance has risen so sharply that many employers will respond by hiring certain employees only on a part-time basis in order to avoid this requirement. The demand for a system of national health coverage has thus increased.

In designing a sensible system of national health insurance we need to avoid a repetition of the built-in inflationary pressures that followed the adoption of Medicaid and Medicare. Medicaid and Medicare eligibility encouraged many to increase their use of health care services, in part because they no longer needed to bear the costs (or full costs) of services. This increased demand, exceeding the supply of health care services, predictably produced price hikes. Other factors undoubtedly have contributed to the escalation of health care costs, including the tendency of some doctors to order unnecessary diagnostic tests, over-reliance on high technology, and the general unresponsiveness of medical costs to competitive pressures. But the increased demand produced by Medicaid and Medicare probably played a role. This is simple economics.

Freed of the disincentive of having to pay for, minimize, or avoid unnecessary services, many individuals overused health care, leading to problems of waste and inefficiency. For many customers, going to an "all-you-can-eat" restaurant where a fixed price buys an unlimited quantity of food seems to produce overeating. Similarly, a health care reimbursement scheme that reduces the disincentive to be parsimonious in the utilization of services will predictably produce inappropriate and inefficient use of resources. This is simple psychology.

Moreover, when demand for services is unchecked by considerations of cost, their price remains unchecked by the pressures of competition. In a health care system in which someone else pays the bills—government or an insurance company—and in which providers can increase their profits by selling more, or more expensive, services, there is bound to be a constant escalation in services. Imagine if, in the all-you-can-eat restaurant, the restaurant gets paid by someone other than the customer based on the quantity of food consumed.

Similar problems have haunted health maintenance organizations (HMOs). HMOs are designed to encourage more preventative approaches by placing incentives on providers to keep consumers enrolled in their programs healthy in order to avoid the provision of more expensive treatment services. This is a good idea, placing the emphasis on wellness services, giving the provider an incentive to keep the patient healthy, and avoiding the incentive to provide unnecessary services in order to increase profits. However, these plans probably also have produced excess and inefficient service utilization by consumers, driving up costs to providers and discouraging many from offering services on an HMO basis. Providing valued services without any marginal cost to the consumer predictably will have the effect of reinforcing the *use* of such services, not necessarily their *appropriate use*.

A number of methods of cost containment have been discussed, including utilization review, upper limits on specified services, and price controls. In addition to these, we need to recapture, at least to some extent, the incentive for people to use health care services appropriately and efficiently. When people must pay for services out of their own pockets, they have a greater incentive to use only those services that they really need. Requiring people to pay out of their own pockets, however, is not truly possible for the increasing numbers in our society who lack pockets that are deep enough.

Instead of structuring national health insurance on a Medicaid-type reimbursement basis, we might develop an approach in which a specified level of health care dollars is guaranteed to any individual (or any individual within certain income categories). Any expenditures in excess of this amount would be subject to a co-insurance-type sharing in which the individual would pay a specified percentage of the extra costs, say twenty percent. To discourage consumers from spending the specified amount even if they do not need to do so, we might similarly allow them to receive a percentage of the unspent portion, for example, twenty percent or fifty percent. The proposal would not use a deductible amount, as some insurance schemes do, under which the individual must pay the first several hundred dollars before reimbursement could start. In the health care context, such a deductible may have the unintended effect of discouraging some people from obtaining important diagnostic and preventative services in order to avoid paying the deductible.

Such preventative services, designed to keep people healthy and avoid more expensive treatment, should be encouraged rather than discouraged. The system should be structured so as to remove impediments to preventative approaches, some of which (for example, immunizations and nutritional counseling) could be available at reduced costs in order to encourage their utilization. In addition, services classified as preventative could be exempted from "co-insurance" or cost-sharing, or could be made the subject of cost-sharing at a reduced rate to the consumer. In these ways the health care system can be reconceptualized as a wellness system rather than merely as one designed to respond to and treat illness. By encouraging wellness services and providing the individual with a cash incentive to stay healthy, the system would be employing a form of "wagering" or behavioral contracting with individuals to look after their own health.[1]

To further encourage proper utilization of services, the cost of obtaining a second opinion prior to certain types of surgery or other expensive or hazardous interventions could be exempted from co-insurance or otherwise subsidized. Getting a second opinion would allow patients to avoid unnecessary services, and may produce added confidence in the need for appropriate services, a feeling that may in itself increase their therapeutic value.

The specified annual amount of health care payment guaranteed each individual could be set legislatively, or through use of a flexible administrative process that each year could establish the amount in light of changing circumstances, much the way the New York City Rent Stabilization Board each year specifies permissible limits for increased rent for apartment lease renewals. Such an annual adjustment would also function as a mechanism of health care cost containment, limiting the inflationary spirals that we have had in recent years. The specified annual amount could either be identical for all individuals, or vary with income level in accordance with a principle similar to the one used in the progressive income tax. Above certain income levels, perhaps determined as a matter of adjusted gross income for federal income tax purposes, an individual's or family's health benefits might decrease and be eliminated altogether when income exceeds higher levels.

There are several categories of patients for which the limits on reimbursement and the incentive scheme suggested here could not work or would work imperfectly. Those born with certain conditions, such as Down's syndrome or cerebral palsy, will require more medical care at considerably higher expense, and hence should not be subject to the same reimbursement limits applicable to most people. Similarly, those experiencing catastrophic illnesses or accidents—cancer, AIDS, or an auto accident leaving them paralyzed, for example—cannot control their health needs and will require additional help as a matter of equity. Moreover, veterans who have suffered service-related disabilities, for which under our long-standing tradition they receive free care from Veteran's Administration facilities, have a legitimate entitlement claim to the continuation of such care that should not be disturbed by the restructuring of our health care system applicable to people generally. The elderly similarly should be given special consideration. Advancing age itself produces increased health needs. At least those whose income has fallen below certain limits as a result of retirement or partial retirement should be eligible for a higher degree of eligibility for reimbursement. In addition, some adjustments in eligibility may need to be made for the poor, or at least for those eligible for welfare, who cannot be expected to share in the costs of their medical care.

Caring for the health needs of those with congenital abnormalities or other severe disabilities, those suffering catastrophic illnesses or injuries, veterans who have become injured in the defense of their country, and the poor and the elderly will be expensive. But an emerging social consensus regards the provision of basic health care for those in our community who cannot afford it for

---

1. See Bruce J. Winick, Harnessing the Power of the Bet: Wagering with the Government as a Mechanism for Social and Individual Change, 45 U. Miami L. Rev. 737 (1991).

themselves to be a matter of equity. For others, however, a system employing reimbursement limits, cost-sharing, and incentives toward wellness and appropriate and efficient service utilization seems appropriate.

Paying for the high cost of a new national health care delivery system will require creative approaches. The proposal that a portion of the amounts needed should be raised through a special tax on tobacco and alcohol is a good one. Use of these substances undeniably causes serious health risks and necessitates costly treatment services. Taxing their sale in a way that discourages their use can be defended as a public health measure in addition to providing a source of revenue for paying for the health needs of all. Similarly, a special tax can be considered for certain "junk foods"—those with little nutritional value that pose risks to health. These should not be considered "sin taxes," as some have termed them, but rather as methods of discouraging unhealthy practices and requiring those who persist in being unwise to internalize the costs of their bad habits.

If the new health care system works as intended, it may help to pay for itself through increased productivity. Preventative approaches will lessen employee absenteeism and lengthen the productive lives of workers. Although the added tax revenues thus produced may be difficult to estimate, they could go a long way toward paying for the added cost of ensuring universal health coverage.

The reimbursement scheme could be structured to use a "voucher" system in order to harness the psychological power of choice. Individuals like to make decisions for themselves. Indeed, allowing an individual to choose his or her own health provider or type of service would produce not only greater patient satisfaction, but predictably also would increase the efficacy of treatment.[2] Expectancy theory and other principles of social and cognitive psychology support the prediction that people will respond better in a variety of therapeutic situations, with a higher degree of compliance with treatment recommendations, when they have a measure of choice in regard to both the treatment itself and the selection of the provider of services. For these reasons, the restructured health care system should reject the approaches of some health insurance schemes and managed care proposals that restrict patients to a list of providers or that assign them to particular providers. These approaches ignore the psychological power of choice and may actually reduce the effective provision of services as well as patient satisfaction, compliance, and positive response.

The private market would presumably adjust for varying demands for different kinds of providers and services by providing a wide array of such services that consumers could purchase with their "vouchers." In economic terms, the market would respond to consumer demand by providing differing services to meet different individual demands, and competition for health vouchers would keep prices down and produce an efficient and rational allocation of resources.

There are problems, however, with "voucher" systems. Food stamps are illustrative. A secondary market is often created in the vouchers, which may defeat the purpose of the program. For example, in some cities there exists a

---

2. See Bruce J. Winick, Competency to Consent to Treatment: The Distinction between Assent and Objection, 28 Hous. L. Rev. 15 (1991); Bruce J. Winick, On Autonomy: Legal and Psychological Perspectives, 37 Vill. L. Rev. (forthcoming, 1993).

black market for food stamps in which some individuals barter their stamps for money or other commodities (including illicit drugs or alcohol). In order to avoid such a secondary market, and the high administrative costs of having a bureaucracy involved in the issuance and redemption of vouchers, the program could use some credit card-type arrangement in which individuals would be issued a credit card with which to charge their health services, or perhaps those with existing credit cards could use them. This would decrease the potential for fraud, and because the "voucher" would not be negotiable bearer paper, would make it difficult for the development of a secondary market in vouchers. The use of already existing credit cards, or the provision of incentives for credit card companies to develop and administer the use of a card for this purpose, could minimize the potential bureaucratic inefficiencies of having government itself play the major operational role.

Employers should be encouraged to provide a variety of health insurance and health care packages for their employees which employees can elect as alternatives to the credit card voucher system guaranteeing the specified limits of services described above. Perhaps tax credits could be used to provide an incentive for employers, the way tax incentives have been used to encourage the construction of low-income housing. Providing incentives to employers to participate in solving the health care delivery problem may be preferable to requiring them to do so in ways that might produce unanticipated negative effects, such as reduction of full-time positions.

In redesigning the health care delivery system, we need to be sensitive to the inevitable impact of the system we develop on patient health.[3] We should therefore build in appropriate incentives for the proper utilization of preventative approaches, for patients to assume responsibility for their own health, and for efficient and effective use of services generally. We also need to maximize the opportunities for patient choice and control in matters of health care in order to realize the psychological benefits this can produce, increasing the efficacy of treatment, patients' sense of self-efficacy, and consumer satisfaction. The legal and regulatory structures we adopt can produce positive or negative consequences for individual and public health. In addition to considerations of equity and economy, we should take these therapeutic implications into account in redesigning our health care delivery system.

---

3. See David B. Wexler & Bruce J. Winick, Essays in Therapeutic Jurisprudence (1991); David B. Wexler & Bruce J. Winick, The Potential of Therapeutic Jurisprudence: A New Approach to Law and Psychology, in Law and Psychology: The Broadening of the Discipline 211 (James R.P. Ogloff ed., 1992); David B. Wexler & Bruce J. Winick, Therapeutic Jurisprudence as a New Approach to Mental Health Law Policy Analysis and Research, 45 U. Miami L. Rev. 979 (1991).

Chapter 20

Therapeutic Jurisprudence and Tort Law: A Limited Subjective Standard of Care

Daniel W. Shuman

I. Introduction

Therapeutic jurisprudence is a mode of legal analysis that focuses on the law's potential as a therapeutic agent.[1] Its premise is that legal rules should encourage therapeutic outcomes when it is possible to do so without offending other important normative values.[2] "Therapeutic jurisprudence simply seeks to focus attention on an often neglected ingredient in the calculus necessary for performing a sensible policy analysis of mental health law and practice—the therapeutic dimension—and to call for a systematic empirical examination of this dimension."[3] If, for example, empirical examination reveals that voluntary treatment for mental illness is more effective than involuntary treatment,[4] the law should encourage voluntary treatment and permit involuntary treatment, if at all, only after efforts to encourage voluntary treatment have failed.[5] In

---

1. David B. Wexler & Bruce J. Winick, Essays in Therapeutic Jurisprudence (1991); David B. Wexler, Therapeutic Jurisprudence: The Law as a Therapeutic Agent ix (1990).

2. Wexler & Wincik, supra note 1, at xi.

3. Id. This inquiry into the therapeutic dimension of law can be analyzed from four perspectives. First, the law may play a role in producing psychological dysfunction through discouragement of necessary treatment, encouragement of unnecessary treatment, and encouragement of sick behavior or absence of responsibility. Id. at 19–24. Second, legal rules may explicitly seek to promote therapeutic consequences as in the case of a right to treatment. Id. at 24–30. Third, legal procedures may play a therapeutic role in the parties' psychological response to the legal process, as contrasted with the outcome. Id. at 30–33. Fourth, the roles played by attorneys and judges may have therapeutic consequences for the other actors in the legal process. Id. at 33–37. This proposal falls within the second perspective.

4. See Mary L. Durham & John Q. LaFond, A Search for the Missing Premise of Involuntary Therapeutic Commitment: Effective Treatment of the Mentally Ill, 40 Rutgers L. Rev. 303, 310 (1988); Leonard I. Stein & Mary Ann Test, Alternative to Mental Hospital Treatment: I. Conceptual Model, Treatment Program, and Clinical Evaluation, 37 Archives Gen. Psychiatry 392 (1980); Bruce J. Winick, Competency to Consent to Voluntary Hospitalization: A Therapeutic Jurisprudence Analysis of Zinermon v. Burch, 14 Int'l J.L. & Psychiatry 169 (1991), cited in Wexler & Winick, supra note 1, at 83.

5. Samuel J. Brakel et al., the Mentally Disabled and the Law 178 n.10 (3d ed. 1985)

contrast, if empirical examination reveals that a physician-patient or psychotherapist-patient privilege does not result in more effective psychotherapy, then it cannot be justified on therapeutic jurisprudence grounds.[6]

The insights from therapeutic jurisprudence are particularly relevant to fault based tort law.[7] The goals of fault based tort law are compensation and deterrence.[8] Tort judgments are intended to compensate the injured and to deter potential injurers from engaging in unsafe conduct. Thus, tort law and therapeutic jurisprudence share a common agenda, the reduction of injury and the restoration of the injured. This article will explore the first item of that common agenda, deterring injury-producing conduct.

The goal of deterrence is, however, compromised by a conjunctive requirement of tort law. Only when the two goals of deterrence and compensation coincide in a case are tort sanctions available. Unreasonably unsafe conduct that does not result in injury is not subject to tort sanctions,[9] and dangerous conduct that does not result in significant injury is unlikely to resort in tort sanctions.[10]

The capacity of tort law to shape behavior, even apart from the limitation on deterrence imposed by this conjunctive requirement, is admittedly problematic. Tort law standards are imprecise and uncertain.[11] The mechanism

---

6. Daniel W. Shuman & Myron F. Weiner, The Psychotherapist-Patient Privilege: A Critical Examination 6 (1987). This research concludes that for the vast majority of persons the privilege does not play a role in the decision to seek therapy or to reveal information during therapy. Just because a privilege or other rule cannot be justified on therapeutic jurisprudence grounds does not necessarily yield the conclusion that the rule is not justifiable. A psychotherapist-patient privilege that cannot be justified on the utilitarian grounds that it is necessary for effective therapy might nonetheless be supported by deontological concerns with privacy as an important societal value. For a discussion of the therapeutic potential of Shuman and Weiner's research, see Jeffrey A. Klotz, Limiting the Psychotherapist-Patient Privilege: The Therapeutic Potential, 27 Crim. L. Bull. 416, 417 (1991).

7. In negligence and intentional torts, fault based liability is explicit. In strict products liability, fault is purportedly not a consideration, yet it is not absent from the relevant standards. Plaintiffs must prove that the product was defective, not merely that they were injured. In practice, the test for defective products operates much like the test for negligence. See James A. Henderson & Theodore Eisenberg, The Quiet Revolution in Products Liability: An Empirical Study of Legal Change, 37 UCLA L. Rev. 479, 489 (1990). Therefore, strict liability notwithstanding, it is appropriate to characterize tort law in the United States as a fault-based liability system. Moreover, the goal of removing the requirement of proving fault in strict product liability cases is to enhance its deterrent effect.

8. David G. Owen, Deterrence and Desert in Tort Law: A Comment, 73 Cal. L. Rev. 665, 666 (1985); Richard Pierce Jr., Institutional Aspects of Tort Reform, 73 Cal. L. Rev. 917, 917 n.1 (1985); Daniel W. Shuman, The Psychology of Deterrence in Tort Law 4 (Mar. 20, 1992) (unpublished manuscript on file with the author).

9. See Barnes v. Bovenmyer, 122 N.W.2d 312, 317 (Iowa 1963).

10. See, e.g., Report of the Harvard Medical Practice Study to the State of New York, Patients, Doctors and Lawyers: Medical Injury, Malpractice, and Patient Compensation in New York (1990). This study revealed that fewer than one in eight patients injured by medical negligence instituted a claim for compensation and that most of the cases in which claims were not instituted involved small damage claims. Id. at 12.

11. To operate as an effective deterrent, tort law should articulate a clear standard of appropriate behavior that is then communicated to decisionmakers who can understand this

through which tort law is thought to affect decisionmaking rests on assumptions that lack psychiatric or psychological validation.[12] The deterrence goal of tort law rejects a normative explanation for behavior, in which tort law plays an informative rather than a coercive role. Tort law assumes, without inquiry into the literature of psychiatry or psychology, that people are aware of the potential of tort sanctions and consequently choose safer behavior to avoid these sanctions. Notwithstanding the practical problems of whether the deterrence goal of tort law actually works, and the many calls for adoption of a no fault compensation scheme,[13] fault based tort law remains vital and its demise may be greatly exaggerated.[14] There is a powerful intuitive appeal to the claim that tort law shapes behavior. As long as fault based tort liability remains, its potential as a therapeutic agent should not be ignored.[15]

An exploration of the therapeutic potential of tort law suggests an examination of the relationship between mental or emotional problems and accidents. Do mental or emotional problems play a role in accident causation? If they do, ameliorating mental and emotional problems may reduce the number of accidents and consequential injuries. Thus, if tort law can encourage appropriate[16] utilization of mental health care, if mental health care is effective in

---

standard and modify their conduct to avoid the tort sanctions that will otherwise occur. The corpus of tort law in any jurisdiction consists of settlements, jury verdicts, trials to the court, appellate decisions, statutes, and administrative rules. This body of law rarely articulates a clear standard of appropriate behavior within a single jurisdiction. Moreover, our federal system of government results in fifty state and a federal set of rules that are infrequently the same. Even assuming the ability to predict which set of rules will apply to a multistate transaction, the ability to predict the outcome of a case based upon what a jury will do in applying those rules in a particular case is an art not a science. Thus, tort law is often criticized as increasing rather than decreasing uncertainty about standards of appropriate behavior. Shuman, supra note 8, at 7–8 (footnotes omitted).

12. "Deterrence posits a psychological relationship, so it is strange that most analyses of it have ignored decision makers' emotions, perceptions, and calculations and have instead relied on deductive logic based on the premise that people are highly rational." Robert Jervis, Introduction: Approach and Assumptions, in Psychology and Deterrence 1 (Robert Jervis ed., 1985). (Jervis' observations about deterrence focus on its application to international conflict; however, this observation is equally perceptive concerning the role of deterrence in tort law.)

13. Jeffery O'connell, The Injury Industry and the Remedy of No Fault Insurance 94–105 (1971); Stephen B. Sugerman, Doing Away With Tort Law, 73 Cal. L. Rev. 555, 659–64 (1985).

14. With apologies to Samuel Clemens.

15. The effort to transform fault based tort law into a no fault compensation system has been criticized, among other grounds, on the basis that any possibility of effective deterrence would be lost. Craig Brown, Deterrence in Tort and No-Fault: The New Zealand Experience, 73 Cal. L. Rev. 976, 976–77 (1985); Thomas A. Ford, The Fault With "No Fault", 61 A.B.A.J. 1071, 1072 (1975); Elisabeth M. Landes, Insurance, Liability, and Accidents: A Theoretical and Empirical Investigation of the Effects of No-Fault Insurance, 25 J.L. & Econ. 49, 50, 57–65 (1982).

16. Research on medical care has revealed that one out of every hundred hospitalized patients is injured as the result of negligent medical care. Report Harvard Medical Practice Study to the State of New York, Patients, Doctors, and Lawyers: Medical Injury, Malpractice Litigation, and Patient Compensation in New York (1990). Because diagnosis and treatment

treating mental or emotional problems,[17] and if ameliorating mental or emotional problems can reduce the number of accidents, the accident reduction goals of tort law and therapeutic jurisprudence coalesce to support that result.

II. The Relationship of Accidental Injury and Mental or Emotional Problems

Tort law doctrine and scholarship have largely ignored the psychology of deterrence, why people behave the way they do and how tort law shapes behavior.[18] Instead, economic analysis has dominated the examination of the impact of tort law based upon an unverified assumption that people act rationally and that the object of that rational behavior is the accumulation of wealth.[19] Thus, it is not surprising that the impact of tort law on the mentally ill has also been largely ignored.[20]

There is a developing body of legal scholarship on the impact of tort liability on those who treat the mentally ill.[21] Ironically, the therapeutic consequences of tort liability on the mentally ill have escaped direct scrutiny.[22] This approach sends an implicit message that reinforces a model of learned helplessness for mentally ill persons. It teaches that the locus of control for mentally ill persons is external rather than internal.[23] To address the problems of the clients each profession is intended to serve, the legal profession focuses on

have certain risks associated with them, unnecessary or inappropriate care should not be encouraged.

17. The demand for cost-effective treatments by third party payors has generated substantial outcome research for mental health care. One type of care that has generated a massive amount of research is psychotherapy. See, e.g., Nathan B. Epstein & Louis A. Vlok, Research on the Results of Psychotherapy: A Summary of Evidence, 138 Am. J. Psychiatry 1027 (1981); Perry London & Gerald Klerman, Evaluating Psychotherapy, 139 Am. J. Psychiatry 709 (1982). While significant methodological difficulties plague the research on this question, there seems to be general agreement from this research that psychotherapy may be effective in treating individuals suffering from nonpsychotic depression or moderate anxieties. Beyond that there is a divergence of opinion.

18. Shuman, supra note 8.

19. See, e.g., Guido Calabresi, The Cost of Accidents 24–30 (1970); William Landes & Richard Posner, The Economic Structure of Tort Law (1987); R. H. Coase, The Problem of Social Cost, 3 J.L. & Econ. 1 (1960).

20. James W. Ellis, Tort Responsibility of Mentally Disabled Persons, 1981 Am. B. Found. Res. J. 1079, 1079–81 (1981).

21. See David B. Wexler & Robert F. Schopp, How and When to Correct for Juror Hindsight Bias in Mental Health Malpractice Litigation: Some Preliminary Observations, 7 Behav. Sci. & L. 485 (1989); David B. Wexler & Robert F. Schopp, Shooting Yourself in the Foot with Due Care: Psychotherapists and Crystallized Standards of Tort Liability, 17 J. Psychiatry & L. 13 (1989).

22. Even in articles that do address the therapeutic consequences of tort law, the interests of the client/patient are addressed indirectly, as a function of the law's impact on the mental health professional. See Robert F. Schopp, The Psychotherapist's Duty to Protect the Public: The Appropriate Standard and the Foundation in Legal Theory and Empirical Premises, 70 Neb. L. Rev. 327 (1991).

23. See discussion of attribution theory, infra notes 63–64 and accompanying text.

the problems of the mental health profession, without directly addressing the client/patient's interests.[24] The appropriate inquiry ought to consider the therapeutic consequence of tort liability on the mentally ill. The sensible premise of therapeutic jurisprudence suggests that if mental illness plays a role in accident causation, tort liability rules should, whenever possible to do so without offending other important normative values, encourage and support voluntary, efficacious treatment.[25]

The suggestion that the accident reduction goals of tort law and therapeutic jurisprudence coalesce points to an exploration of the role of mental illness in accidents. It is often assumed, but has less often been the subject of careful investigation, that there is a linkage between mental illness and accidents, particularly automobile accidents.[26] The potential impact of this linkage is significant given the human and economic cost of accidents and the extent of mental illness in our society. The direct and indirect cost of accidents in the United States, one-fifth of which involve motor vehicles, is estimated to be 175.9 billion dollars per year.[27] Current estimates of the level of individuals in the United States who suffer from a mental disorder are at fourteen percent of the population.[28] Additionally, research suggests that certain categories of mentally ill individuals have lower rates of accidents after treatment.[29]

Notwithstanding this assumption, there is good reason to question the linkage between mental illness and accidents. The frequency with which the men-

---

24. Although there are a number of articles that address the tort liability of the mentally ill, they tend to focus on whether it is consistent with fault based tort liability. See James Barr Ames, Law and Morals, 22 Harv. L. Rev. 97, 99–100 (1908); Francis H. Bohlen, Liability in Tort of Infants and Insane Persons, 23 Mich. L. Rev. 9, 31–34 (1924); William B. Hornblower, Insanity and the Law of Negligence, 5 Colum. L. Rev. 278, 278 (1905). These articles are not concerned with the way the mentally ill might behave in light of these rules.

25. See Durham & LaFond, Stein & Test, and Winick, supra note 4.

26. Laura A. Cushman et al., Psychiatric Disorders and Motor Vehicle Accidents, 67 Psychol. Rep. 483, 484 (1990).

27. Deborah F. Hensler et al., Compensation for Accidental Injuries in the United States 1 (Rand 1991).

28. Cushman, supra note 26, at 486–87. Some estimate that at any given time, one in four Americans suffers from depression, anxiety, or other emotional disorders. The President's Commission on Mental Health (1978). The extent of the problem is revealed in the fact that Valium and Librium are the most frequently prescribed drugs throughout the world. L.F. Rittelmeyer, Minor Tranquilizers: Prescribing Practices of Primary Care Physicians, 23 Psychosomatics 223, 226 (1982).

29. Robert C. Eelkmena et al., A Statistical Study on the Relationship Between Mental Illness and Traffic Accidents—A Pilot Study, 60 Am. J. Pub. Health 459, 460 (1970). Although individuals in the study discharged from a state hospital had a higher rate of accidents than a comparable group of individuals in the population who were not diagnosed as mentally ill, the groups labeled as psychotics and psychoneurotic had reduced rates of accidents following treatment. Those labeled as alcoholics and personality disorder sufferers did not respond as favorably. Id. at 461. The finding that accident rates of alcoholics and persons suffering from personality disorders were not reduced after hospitalization corresponds with Gottfredson and Hirschi's findings that criminal behavior and noncriminal behavior such as accidents can be explained as a lack of self-control caused by ineffective child rearing. Michael R. Gottfredson & Travis Hirschi, A General Theory of Crime 91–97 (1990).

tally ill cause accidents, at least as reflected in one crude indicator, appellate caselaw, does not suggest that seriously mentally ill persons account for a disproportionate number of accidents.[30] More directly, recent accident research questions the linkage between mental illness and the rate of automobile accidents.[31] Moreover, mental illness may serve as a screening factor to exclude people from positions of risk creation. Mental illness is a ground to deny or suspend a license to practice law,[32] medicine,[33] and psychology.[34] Additionally, mental illness is a ground to deny or suspend a license to operate a motor vehicle.[35] Mental illness is also a practical disqualifying factor in business. Acting crazy in a working environment quickly excludes one from the business world.

---

30. William J. Curran, Tort Liability of the Mentally Ill and Mentally Deficient, 21 Ohio St. L.J. 52, 64 (1960). Curran's survey of the case law as of 1960 reveals few cases in which a tort "insanity defense" was raised. Accepting the accuracy of this survey, it is far from clear whether this is a valid indicator of the frequency with which the mentally ill cause accidents. It may be that mentally ill people commit torts with lesser frequency than those who are not mentally ill; it may be that mentally ill people commit torts with the same frequency as those who are not mentally ill but have fewer assets or insurance and are therefore sued less often; it may be that mentally ill people commit torts with the same frequency as those who are not mentally ill but that insurance companies settle rather than litigate these cases; or, it may be that mentally ill people who are sued fail to raise their illness as a defense because courts have not been receptive to this argument. Thus, appellate case law is not necessarily a reliable indicator of the nexus between mental illness and accident causation.

31. Cushman, supra note 26, at 487. Cushman's study of accident victims found that the percentage with psychiatric diagnoses was lower than national estimates of the percentage of the population thought subject to these diagnoses; individuals with psychiatric diagnoses were not involved in single-car accidents (where suicide might be a likely explanation) with a greater frequency than those who did not have a psychiatric diagnosis; and, individuals with psychiatric diagnoses were not cited more often for inattention or failure to yield the right of way. Id. at 486–87. See also J. Isherwood et al., Life Event Stress, Psychosocial Factors, Suicide Attempt and Auto-Accident Proclivity, 26 J. Psychosomatic Res. 371 (1982) (study analyzing assocation between life event stress and suicide attempts as well as auto accidents). This research parallels the research addressing another myth about the mentally ill, that they are more dangerous than non-mentally ill persons. See Michael Perlin, On "Sanism", 46 SMU L. Rev. 373, (1992). Although that research focuses on intentional rather than negligent acts, both findings dispel myths that we should be more fearful of harm at the hands of the mentally ill. Linda A. Teplin, The Criminality of the Mentally Ill: A Dangerous Misconception, 142 Am. J. Psychiatry 593, 595 (1985).

32. Tex. Gov't Code Ann. § 82.027(b)(2) (Vernon 1988).

33. Tex. Rev. Civ. Stat. Ann. art. 4495b, § 3.08(16) (Vernon Supp. 1992).

34. Tex. Rev. Civ. Stat. Ann. art. 4512c, § 11(d)(3) (Vernon Supp. 1992).

35. Tex. Rev. Civ. Stat. Ann. art. 6687b, § 4(5) & (7) (Vernon Supp. 1992). Although mental illness or incapacity remains a ground to deny or suspend a driver's license, procedures that do not provide the driver a timely hearing and opportunity to be heard on this issue have been found unconstitutional. Freitag v. Carter, 489 F.2d 1377, 1382 (7th Cir. 1973); Jones v. Penny, 387 F. Supp. 383, 394–95 (M.D.N.C. 1974).

Those mentally ill persons who are involuntarily hospitalized or found incompetent may be automatically denied driving privileges. Brakel, supra note 5, at 493–505. It is not at all clear, however, that the walking wounded, those with minor mental or emotional problems, report these problems to the appropriate state agencies of their own volition or that these problems are reported by their therapists.

Therefore, the therapeutic potential of tort law is likely to be limited if focused exclusively on those who suffer from major mental illness. To achieve a broader impact, concern with the therapeutic impact of tort law should not be limited to those suffering from major mental illness, but should include the walking wounded.[36] All humans confront powerlessness and the inevitability of death, regardless of race, class or gender. Our response to the loss of a job or the death of a loved one may fade with time and escape diagnosis as a major mental illness.[37] Nonetheless, its impact may be profound. At a minimum, it may affect our concentration and responsiveness. Inclusion of the walking wounded in a discussion of the therapeutic impact of tort law is sound both in terms of expanding the therapeutic potential of tort law and in light of the current research on stress.

Research seeking to identify the characteristics of accident-prone drivers initially focused on physical and psychological characteristics viewed as stable.[38] This research suggested a correlation between auto accidents and psychosocial variables such as aggressiveness, depression, and social maladjustment.[39] However, the inability of these variables to explain accident rates for individual drivers over time indicated the limitations of the research that suggested accident proneness was a stable characteristic of certain drivers.[40] In addition, research has dispelled the fiction that removing the mythical five percent of the drivers who cause fifty percent of the accidents would have a significant impact on the total number of automobile accidents.[41]

These findings led to research focusing on the relationship of accident rates to life events (i.e., change in marital status, change in employment status, change in financial status), the degree of adjustment such events require, and the subjective stress experienced from these changes.[42] This research pointed to a significant correlation between life changes, subjective stress, and accident

---

36. Others have referred to what I understand to be the same group as the worried well. See, e.g., Epstein & Vlok, supra note 17, at 1034; James E. Barrett et al., The Prevalence of Psychiatric Disorders in a Primary Care Practice, 45 Archives Gen. Psychiatry 1100 (1988).

37. For example, American Psychiatric Association's Diagnostic and Statistical Manual of Mental Disorders 217 (3d ed. revised 1987) (DSM-III-R) describes the diagnostic criteria for a Major Depressive Episode to include a depressed mood or loss of interest in virtually all activities for at least two weeks. However, the diagnostic criteria excludes individuals who experience normal reactions to losing a loved one. Id. at 218–19. A depressed mood or loss of interest in all activities is considered a normal reaction to such an event and is not considered a mental disorder if, for example, it only lasts for a matter of months. Id. at 360–61.

38. See Fleming James, Jr. & John J. Dickinson, Accident Proneness and Accident Law, 63 Harv. L. Rev. 769, 772–75 (1950).

39. Morris S. Schulzinger, the Accident Syndrome, 14–15 (1956); A.E. Suchman, Cultural and Social Factors in Accident Occurrence and Control, 7 J. Occup. Med. 487, 488 (1965); Stanford G. Wrogg, The Role of Emotions in Industrial Accidents, 3 Archives Env. Health 519 (1961).

40. D.H. Schuster & J.P. Guilford, The Psychometric Prediction of Problem Drivers, 6 Hum. Factors 393 (1964).

41. Department of Transportation Driver-Behavior and Accident Involvement: Implications for Tort Liability 75 (1970).

42. These events are described in Thomas H. Holmes & Richard R. Rahe, The Social

rates.[43] Transient situational stress, which everyone may experience at some point in their lives, is currently regarded as a significant factor in accident cau-

Readjustment Rating Scale, 11 J. Psychosomatic Res. 213, 216 (1967):

Rank	Life Event	Mean Value
1	Death of spouse	100
2	Divorce	73
3	Marital separation	65
4	Jail Term	63
5	Death of close family member	63
6	Personal injury or illness	53
7	Marriage	50
8	Fired at work	47
9	Marital reconciliation	45
10	Retirement	45
11	Change in health of family member	44
12	Pregnancy	40
13	Sex difficulties	39
14	Gain of new family member	39
15	Business readjustment	39
16	Change in financial state	38
17	Death of close friend	37
18	Change to different line of work	36
19	Change in number of arguments with spouse	35
20	Mortgage over $10,000	31
21	Foreclosure of mortgage or loan	30
22	Change in responsibilities at work	29
23	Son or daughter leaving home	29
24	Trouble with in-laws	29
25	Outstanding personal achievement	28
26	Wife begin or stop work	26
27	Begin or end school	26
28	Change in living conditions	25
29	Revision of personal habits	24
30	Trouble with boss	23
31	Change in work hours or conditions	20
32	Change in residence	20
33	Change in schools	20
34	Change in recreation	19
35	Change in church activities	19
36	Change in social activities	18
37	Mortgage or loan less than $10,000	17
38	Change in sleeping habits	16
39	Change in number of family get-togethers	15
40	Change in eating habits	15
41	Vacation	13
42	Christmas	12
43	Minor violations of the law	11

43. L. McMurray, Emotional Stress and Driving Performance: The Effect of Divorce, 1 Behav. Res. in Highway Safety 100 (1970) (accident rates for individuals in divorce proceedings were doubled in the six months preceding and following the date of the divorce); Melvin L. Selzer et al., Fatal Accidents: The Role of Psychopathology, Social Stress, and Acute Disturbance, 124 Am. J. Psychiatry 1028, 1029 (1968) (fifty-two percent of drivers found at

sation. "These studies suggest that recent life events (e.g., birth of a child, divorce, death of a friend or relative, change of job, financial change) that bring about a significant change in an individual's ongoing life pattern may cause psychological turmoil that can exacerbate the risk of accident or illness."[44] From the perspective of therapeutic jurisprudence and the accident reduction goal of tort law, the correlation between stress and accidents points away from an exclusive focus on those who suffer from a major mental illness, such as schizophrenia, and toward inclusion of the walking wounded—individuals whose life changes and subjective response to stress significantly reduce their concentration or responsiveness.[45]

The magnitude of this problem is illustrated by recent research on stress and professions. A level of emotional discomfort seems to be a consequence of professional career choices. In research conducted in the 1980s during the boom market for attorneys, Benjamin, Kaszniak, Sales, and Shanfield found in an Arizona study that prospective law students' levels of depression were comparable to that found in the general population of three to nine percent.[46] By late spring of the first year of law school thirty-two percent of the law students reported that they were depressed, and by the third year forty percent of the students reported that they were depressed.[47] Two years following graduation from law school, seventeen percent reported that they were depressed. A subsequent study of practicing attorneys in the state of Washington by Benjamin, Darling, and Sales found that nineteen percent of the lawyers reported depression.[48] Although major mental illness may exclude people from practicing law, medicine, or psychology, participating in these activities may create a level of stress that is positively correlated with the risk of injury.[49]

---

fault in fatal automobile accidents had previously experienced interpersonal, employment, or financial stresses as contrasted with eighteen percent of the control group); Melvin L. Selzer & Amiram Vinokur, Life Events, Subjective Stress, and Traffic Accidents, 131 Am. J. Psychiatry 903, 904–05 (1974) (demographic and personality variables were not statistically significantly correlated with accident causation as contrasted with life changes and subjective stress, i.e., serious disturbance with spouse of parents, serious pressure on the job or at school, serious financial disturbance).

44. James C. Helmkamp & Craig M. Bone, The Effect of Time in a New Job on Hospitalization Rates for Accidents and Injuries in the U.S. Navy, 1977 through 1983, 29 J. Occupational Med. 653, 658 (1987).

45. See, e.g., David DuBois et al., Accident Reduction Through Stress Management, 1 J. Bus. & Psychol. 5 (1986).

46. G. Andrew H. Benjamin et al., The Role of Legal Education in Producing Psychological Distress Among Law Students, Am. B. Found. Res. J. 225, 225 (1986). See also Lennart Levi, Occupational Stress: Spice of Life or Kiss of Death?, 45 Am. Psychol. 1142, 1142 (1990).

47. Benjamin, supra note 46, at 236.

48. G. Andrew H. Benjamin et al., The Prevalence of Depression, Alcohol, and Cocaine Abuse Among United States Lawyers, 13 Int'l. J. L. and Psychiatry 233, 240 (1990).

49. The effects of professional stress are certainly not limited to the practice of law. One state wide study of admission records of community mental health centers found a disproportion percentage of hospital and health care workers experiencing mental health problems. Michael J. Colligan et al., Occupational Incidence Rates of Mental Health Disorders, 3 J. Hum. Stress 34, 36 (1977).

III. A Limited Subjective Standard of Care

How does tort law respond to this understanding of accident causation? Does tort law ask only that we do the best we can? Is mental illness or transient situational stress factored into the evaluation of a defendant's tort liability? Contract law recognizes mental illness as an exculpatory condition under the label of contractual capacity.[50] Criminal law recognizes mental illness as an exculpatory condition under an insanity defense, negation of intent, or diminished capacity.[51] In contrast, tort law does not recognize mental illness as an exculpatory condition. With a single exception, American jurisdictions refuse to take the defendant's mental illness or other emotional problems into account in formulating the relevant standard of care in tort cases.[52] Holmes' classic exposition of this position is often cited as the justification for the objective standard of care in American tort law.

> The standards of the law are standards of general application. The law takes no account of the infinite varieties of temperament, intellect, and education which make the internal character of a given act so different in different men. It does not attempt to see men as God sees them, for more than one sufficient reason. In the first place, the impossibility of nicely measuring a man's powers and limitations is far clearer than that of ascertaining his knowledge of law, which has been thought to account for what is called the presumption that every man knows the law. But a more satisfactory explanation is, that, when men live in society, a certain average of conduct, a sacrifice of individual peculiarities going beyond a certain point, is necessary to the general welfare. If, for instance, a man is born hasty and awkward, is always having accidents and hurting himself and his neighbors, no doubt his congenital defects will be allowed for in the courts of Heaven, but his slips are no less troublesome to his neighbors than if they sprang from guilty neglect. His neighbors accordingly require him, at his proper peril, to come up to their standard, and the courts which they establish decline to take his personal equation into account.[53]

Holmes justified the objective standard on the grounds of problems of measuring individual capacities and the right to expect a minimal level of care from one's neighbors. Others have noted as reasons advanced in favor of the rule that as between the plaintiff and defendant, the party who caused the loss should be required to compensate for the resulting harm; feared logistical problems of administering a civil insanity defense; encouraging greater care by guardians of the mentally ill; and, the risk of eroding the objective standard of care.[54]

---

50. Daniel W. Shuman, Psychiatric and Psychological Evidence 361 (1986).

51. Id. at 273–78.

52. Hudnall v. Sellner, 800 F.2d 377, 384 (4th Cir. 1986), cert. denied, 479 U.S. 1069 (1987); Restatement (Second) of Torts, s 283(B) (1965). "Unless the actor is a child, his insanity or other mental deficiency does not relieve the actor from liability for conduct which does not conform to the standard of a reasonable man under like circumstances." Id.

53. O.W. Holmes Jr., The Common Law 86–87 (1963).

54. James B. Ellis, Tort Responsibility of Mentally Disabled Persons, 1981 Am. B. Found. Res. J. 1079, 1083–84 (1981). See also William J. Curran, Tort Liability of the Mentally Ill and Deficient, 21 Ohio St. L.J. 52, 54 (1960).

Although tort law takes the physical illness of defendants into account by judging the conduct of physically disabled defendants against other similarly disabled persons, the conduct of mentally ill defendants is judged against those who do not suffer from a similar disability.[55] Interestingly, many of the arguments against a subjective standard of care apply with equal force in the case of physically ill defendants. Specifically, the argument that as between the plaintiff and defendant, the party who caused the loss should be required to compensate for the resulting harm, does not suggest a distinction in the standard of care for physically and mentally incapacitated defendants.[56] Thus, the argument that it is necessary to maintain the dichotomy between a subjective standard for the physically incapacitated and an objective standard for the mentally incapacitated to serve the goal of compensating innocent plaintiffs is unconvincing.

The objective standard of care has been consistently criticized in the academic literature as conceptually unsound in a fault based liability system.[57] Prior to the 19th century, when strict liability dominated tort law and the morally laden concept of fault was largely irrelevant to the determination of liability, it may have been logical to measure the behavior of the mentally ill and non-mentally ill by a single standard. However, in the fault-based system of liability that evolved in the 19th century, the single standard raises a troubling moral quandary.

Recognizing this moral quandary, I nonetheless accept the objective standard of care, with the limitations noted later, although I do not accept the reasons traditionally given for the objective standard.[58] The objective standard of care is a therapeutic agent. It encourages a therapeutic result by stating to the mentally ill and walking wounded that they cannot rely on their mental or emotional problems to avoid responsibility for their behavior or failure to initiate treatment.[59] A response from one psychotherapist, questioned about data

---

55. Warren A. Seavey, Negligence: Subjective or Objective?, 41 Harv. L. Rev. 1, 13–14 (1927).

56. Ultimately the roots of the distinction may be found in society's unfounded myths about the mentally ill. See Perlin, supra note 31.

57. See Ellis, supra note 54; Curran, supra note 54.

58. The argument that a subjective judgment measuring individual capacity is unworkable is a smoke screen. Tort law regularly makes subjective judgments about individual capacity in other contexts. For example, tort law makes subjective judgments about the degree of impairment a plaintiff has suffered and the pain and suffering the plaintiff experienced. The argument that the party who was injured through no fault of his or her own should be compensated is more troubling. One response, which I do not find particularly satisfying, is that there are always tradeoffs in achieving any beneficial result in the law. A more satisfying response to this concern points in the direction of the wisdom implicit in comparative fault that accidents are rarely caused exclusively by one party. Thus, the example of the plaintiff injured without his or her own fault is a chimera. See also George J. Alexander & Thomas S. Szasz, Mental Illness as an Excuse for Civil Wrongs, 43 Notre Dame L. Rev. 24, 33 (1967) (arguing in favor of holding the mentally ill liable for their torts on libertarian grounds).

59. Stephen J. Morse, Crazy Behavior, Moral, and Mental Health Law, 51 S. Cal. L. Rev. 527 (1978); John T. Monahan, Abolish the Insanity Defense?—Not Yet, 26 Rutgers L. Rev. 719 (1973). See also David B. Wexler, Inducing Therapeutic Compliance Through the Criminal Law, 14 L. & Psychol. Rev. 43 (1990) (the author relies on research that has found that

involving mental illness and accidents, explained in vivid terms the therapeutic potential of the objective standard of care: "I hate it when you legal people interfere with the only proven motivator for the mentally ill to seek treatment because they realize that they are people responsible for their actions like everyone else."[60] If the mentally ill and walking wounded behave, as the deterrence theorists of tort law posit, like the normal population behave and rely on the threat of tort sanctions to shape their actions,[61] then the objective standard of care encourages them to behave responsibly and seek treatment.

Research from numerous psychological perspectives supports the conclusion that a person's perception of free choice and responsibility for behavior has a significant impact upon that behavior.[62] One explanation comes from attribution theory which explains that people behave according to their perception and understanding of events. "[A]ttributions affect our feelings about past events and our expectations about future ones, our attitudes toward other persons and our reactions to their behavior, and our conceptions of ourselves and our efforts to improve our fortunes."[63] For example, a student who attributes her failure on an exam to low ability, over which she has no control, is less likely to put substantial effort into the class than a student who attributes her failure to lack of effort, over which she has control.[64] The impact of attribution theory is not limited to normal people. In particular, attribution theory's focus on "learned helpless," attributing success or failure to forces outside of ourselves, has relevance to behavior across diagnostic categories. The import of attribution theory and numerous other psychological perspectives is that not excusing people from tort liability for their mental or emotional problems encourages them to take greater responsibility for their actions. This is revisionist therapeutic jurisprudence at its best. So far, so good.

---

recidivists with known, treatable low serotonin levels are correlated with higher rates of recidivism, to argue that defendants should be subject to enhanced punishment for failure to avail themselves of treatment).

60. Telephone interview with anonymous psychotherapist (Oct. 1991). This response may be explained in alternate ways. It may be that the psychotherapist is simply describing a clinical observation that mentally ill people who have sought treatment with this therapist have mentioned that concern with legal responsibility for their actions is a reason for seeking therapy. Alternatively, it may be that the psychotherapist is expressing a personal concern with malpractice liability that translates as, "do not exculpate the mentally ill; rather, hold them, not their therapists, solely responsible for their conduct and not as the court did in *Tarasoff*." See Tarasoff v. Regents of Univ. of Cal., 551 P.2d 334 (Cal. 1976).

61. Shuman, supra note 8. Beyond the problems that all individuals have in learning about and using tort law in their decisions, the potential impact of mental illness on cognitive and volitional capacity presents a more serious challenge to the deterrent goal of tort law.

62. Monahan, supra note 59, at 721. Monahan discusses research from the locus of control, cognitive dissonance, attribution, achievement motivation, personal causation, reactance, and perceived control theories that support this conclusion. Id. at 721–22.

63. H.H. Kelley & J.L. Michela, Attribution Theory and Research, 31 Ann. Rev. Psychol. 457, 489 (1980).

64. Sandra Graham, Communicating Low Ability in the Classroom: Bad Things Good Teachers Sometimes Do, in Attribution Theory: Applications to Achievement, Mental Health, and Interpersonal Conflict 17 (Sandra Graham & Valerie S. Folkes eds., 1990).

But what of the mentally ill and walking wounded who respond to this therapeutic incentive and seek treatment which has not yet achieved its desired result? How are those who are still in treatment—the uncured—regarded by tort law? Tort law is, at best, indifferent to a defendant's efforts to receive mental health care. Seeking help does not reduce tort law's expectations of the defendant.[65] The mentally ill and walking wounded who are aware of their mental health problems and pursue treatment are held to the same standard as those who are aware of their mental health problems and refuse to pursue treatment. A defendant who has instituted a course of treatment for mental or emotional problems, has complied fully with the prescribed treatment regime, and has become preoccupied with problems raised during psychotherapy resulting in reduced concentration or responsiveness while driving which, in turn, causes an accident, is judged according to the objective standard without regard to the treatment efforts. Tort defendants receive no extra credit for extra effort in seeking treatment.

There are two responses to this criticism. Each response points to therapeutic benefits of the objective standard's indifference to treatment efforts. The first approach is tough love for tortfeasors. "Get better, no excuses accepted," may be a more powerful, albeit less nurturing motivator, than one which leaves the door open to excuses. Tort law takes a "no excuses accepted" approach in strict products liability.[66] The deterrent rationale for strict products liability rejects a good faith defense on the ground that it encourages the highest possible level of care.[67] By analogy, because best efforts at treatment do not count in tort law, people may be encouraged to seek out the most effective mental health treatment and comply fully with prescribed treatment regimes. Only successful outcomes are rewarded, not best efforts.

Another response to this criticism of no extra credit for seeking treatment is that tort law's indifference to treatment efforts may have therapeutic benefits by failing to reinforce learned helplessness. Labeling those who seek treatment as less responsible for their tortious behavior could teach these individuals to behave less responsibly. Both the no excuses accepted and the avoidance of learned helplessness approach are, superficially, plausible revisionist rationales for tort law's indifference to treatment efforts. The problem with these rationales only becomes apparent when mental health treatment is examined more closely.

The failure to factor treatment efforts into the standard of care can be justified on therapeutic jurisprudence grounds only if the patient's good faith participation in treatment is the sine qua non of efficacious treatment. Patient co-

---

65. Seeking help may actually increase tort law's expectations for the defendant. As discussed infra notes 79–80 and accompanying text, knowledge gained through diagnosis or treatment of a mental health problem may increase the defendant's awareness of the risks posed by the illness and require the defendant to act with reference to that increased knowledge.

66. "The rule is one of strict liability, making the seller subject to liability to the user or consumer even though he has exercised all possible care in the preparation and sale of the product." Restatement (Second) of Torts § 402A cmt. a. (1965).

67. See Escola v. Coca Cola Bottling Co., 150 P.2d 436, 440 (1944) (Traynor, J., concurring).

operation in treatment is extremely important, but the failure to factor treatment efforts into the standard of care can be justified only if patient cooperation is not merely a necessary but also a sufficient condition of efficacious treatment. That approach encapsulates the magic pill approach to health care. Health care professionals have a safe, quick, and effective treatment for mental health problems. All a patient need do to be effectively treated is to follow the doctor's orders.

Application of the magic pill construct to the treatment of mental or emotional problems may be based, in part, upon a flawed analogy to the treatment of physical illness. There may be a tendency to think of treatment for mental or emotional problems based on a model of a common available treatment for physical illness that is quick and effective when the patient follows the doctor's orders. To the extent that a magical medical pill for physical illness exists, it is the use of antibiotics to treat acute bacterial infections.[68] The magical medical pill exists; the patient need only take it as prescribed to be effectively treated. The application of this construct to the treatment of mental or emotional problems, however, is flawed for two reasons.

First, the treatment model based on physical illness is itself flawed in that it incorrectly assumes that certain common, available treatments of physical disorders are representative of the universe of treatment for physical disorders. This error corresponds to cognitive psychology's availability heuristic.[69] Although the responsiveness of some treatments for physical illnesses that we call to mind is direct and immediate when the patient follows the doctor's orders, that model is not descriptive of the universe of treatments for physical illness. The use of chemotherapy to treat certain cancers may extend over a significant time period and its long term efficacy is often unclear.[70] The efficacy of organ transplantation may be unclear for an extended period of time.[71] Uncertainty abounds in the treatment of physical illness. HIV is a sobering reminder of the limits of medicine's ability to treat physical illness and of our expectation that medicine should and will develop a magic pill to protect us from the effects of catastrophic illness. Thus, it is inaccurate to characterize the treatment model, even for physical illness, as direct and immediate with its efficacy turning exclusively on patient compliance.

Second, there is a tendency to assume that mental illness does or should respond to treatment in similar fashion to the flawed model of treatment for physical illness. As in the case of physical illness, the benefits of treatment for mental illness are not often direct or immediate and do not turn exclusively on

---

68. The chemicals used to treat specific microorganisms in infectious diseases are often referred to as antibiotics, antimicrobic, and chemotherapeutic agents. Lowell S. Young, Antimicrobial Therapy, in Textbook of Medicine 1596 (James B. Wyngaarden et al. eds., 19th ed. 1991). The greatest success in the use of these agents has occurred in the treatment of acute bacterial infections. Id.

69. Amos Tversky & Daniel Kahneman, Availability: A Heuristic for Judging Frequency and Probability, in Judgment under Uncertainty: Heuristics and Biases (Daniel Kahneman et al. eds., 1982).

70. I Cancer: Principles and Practice of Oncology 278 (Vincent T. DeVita, Jr. et al. eds., 3d ed. 1989).

71. II The Kidney 2344 (Barry M. Brenner & Floyd C. Rector, Jr. eds., 4th ed. 1991).

patient cooperation.[72] Psychotherapy is commonly used to treat mental illness or disorder. Beyond the consensus that psychotherapy is effective for the treatment of nonpsychotic depression or moderate anxieties, however, there is not a consensus about its efficacy.[73]

Even when psychotherapy is an effective treatment, the benefits of therapy are not necessarily linear.[74] Psychotherapy typically entails exploration of painful issues that the patient has repressed. The amount of pain associated with these issues is likely to be positively correlated with the importance of addressing these issues in therapy. Exploration of these repressed issues may result in the patient feeling worse before feeling better. Short term bad feelings induced or exacerbated by psychotherapy are likely to affect concentration or responsiveness. Thus, psychotherapy that is effective in the long term may nonetheless increase the risk of accidental injury in the short term.

Another common treatment for mental illness or disorder is the use of psychopharmacological agents, psychoactive drugs. Treatment of mental illness or disorder with psychopharmacological agents, the treatment of choice for schizophrenic and affective disorders,[75] for example, presents a host of problems that may increase the risk of accidental injuries.[76] Not all individuals treated with psychopharmacological agents for these illnesses respond to these medications. For example, approximately twenty-five percent of schizophrenic patients have significant symptoms on traditional neuroleptic medications.[77] Even for those individuals who do respond to these medications, psychopharmacological treatment often requires an adjustment of medication over time.[78] Indi-

---

72. The argument that treatment of mental illness is or should be immediate may superficially be fueled by Single Session Therapy (SST). See Moshe Talmon, Single-Session Therapy: Maximizing the Effect of the First (and Often Only) Therapeutic Encounter 1–3 (1990). SST is a new approach to psychotherapy that posits that a single session may be as beneficial as multiple sessions for most patients. Apart from the question of long term outcome research for SST, its underlying premise is not that treatment is immediately effective, but rather that given the limited capacity of lengthy therapy to address many psychological problems, one session is no worse that one hundred sessions and patients will often not return for more than the initial session.

73. See Epstein & Vlok, supra note 17; London & Klerman, supra note 17.

74. A psychoanalytic explanation for this phenomenon focuses on resistance. The work of analysis in uncovering repressed pathology is threatening to the patient and is expected to cause the patient to invoke a host of defenses to resist therapeutic progress. Working through the resistance is at the core of the analytic process. Robert L. Stewart, Psychoanalysis and Psychoanalytic Psychotherapy, in II Comprehensive Textbook of Psychiatry/IV 1343 (Harold I. Kaplan & Benjamin J. Sadock eds., 4th ed. 1985).

75. Schizophrenic disorders are typically treated with antipsychotic medications, which do not cure the disorder, but suppress the symptoms. W. Reid, Treatment of the DSM-III Psychiatric Disorders 13 (1983). Affective disorders are typically treated with tricyclic or tetracyclic antidepressants. Id. at 129–35.

76. Gerry Oster et al., Benzodiazepine Tranquilizers and the Risk of Accidental Injury, 80 Am. J. Pub. Health 1467, 1467 (1990).

77. J.M. Davis & Regina Casper, Antipsychotic Drugs: Clinical Pharmacology and Therapeutic Use, 14 Drugs 260 (1977).

78. Philip May, Prediction of Schizophrenic Patients' Response to Pharmacotherapy, in Psychopharmacology: A Generation of Progress (Morris A. Lipton et al. eds., 1977).

viduals respond differently to medication. The recommended dose may be too small and fail to ameliorate the symptoms of the illness, or too large and cause unintended decrease in cognitive function. If tort law is to encourage a therapeutic outcome it must acknowledge and accommodate these consequences of treatment.

The failure to factor treatment efforts into the standard of care cannot be justified on therapeutic jurisprudence grounds. Patients' good faith participation in treatment is a necessary but not a sufficient condition of efficacious treatment. Mental health professionals do not have safe, quick, and effective treatments for all mental health problems. Good faith on the part of the patient will not invariably lead to a beneficial therapeutic outcome and, even when it ultimately does, it may result in a short term increase in the risk of accidental injury. If tort law is to be realistic in its support of patient efforts to receive efficacious treatment it must factor into the legal response a recognition that notwithstanding the patient's complete cooperation, treatment will not invariably make things better and may make things worse.

Those who respond to the objective standard's therapeutic incentive and receive a thorough psychiatric or psychological diagnosis fare even worse under tort law than those who ignore the symptoms of their illness. Tort law imposes a greater burden on those who discover specific knowledge of risks.[79] Increased knowledge of risks triggers a correlatively greater burden to guard against those risks. Thus, an individual who discovers that he suffers from an illness that poses risks to others owes an obligation to guard against those risks that would not exist if the illness had not been discovered. An example from the realm of physical illnesses is illustrative. An individual who is aware that he is HIV positive may be liable in tort for failing to disclose this information to a sexual partner who becomes infected, where an individual who has no reason to believe that he is HIV positive and transmits the disease to a sexual partner would not be.[80] Similarly, an individual who has received a diagnosis of manic-depression is put on notice of the risks of the cyclical nature of this illness. Thus, as contrasted with an undiagnosed manic-depressive, the person who has received the diagnosis owes a duty to guard against the risk of accidental injury to others posed by this illness.

If tort law operates as an incentive for behavior, the objective standard of care's indifference to treatment and harsh response to diagnosis seems unlikely to encourage the diagnosis or treatment of mental or emotional problems for either the seriously mentally ill or the walking wounded. A more precise accommodation of the interests implicated by the tort system requires a distinction in approach for those who sought treatment prior to the injury producing

---

79. "The standard of the reasonable man requires only a minimum of attention, perception, memory, knowledge, intelligence, and judgment in order to recognize the existence of the risk. If the actor has in fact more than the minimum of these qualities, he is required to exercise these superior qualities that he has in a reasonable manner under the circumstances. The standard becomes, in other words, that of a reasonable man with such superior qualities." Restatement (Second) of Torts § 289, cmt m.

80. Richard C. Schoenstein, Note, Standards of Conduct, Multiple Defendants and Full Recovery in Tort Liability for the Transmission of Human Immunodeficiency Virus, 18 Hofstra L. Rev. 37, 42 (1989).

conduct at issue and those who did not. The objective standard encourages the mentally ill and walking wounded to behave responsibly and seek treatment. It should remain as an incentive for those who did not seek treatment prior to the injury-producing conduct at issue. However, for those who have behaved responsibly and sought treatment prior to the injury-producing conduct, the objective standard ignores or frustrates their efforts.

In the case of a defendant who initiated a regime of treatment for a mental or emotional problem *before* the injury-producing conduct at issue, the objective standard of care should be modified in favor of a limited subjective standard of care that evaluates the defendant's conduct in light of the treatment received. If the defendant instituted treatment prior to the injury producing conduct and complied fully with the treatment regime, the defendant should not singularly bear the risk that the treatment has not to date been efficacious. This result seems particularly appropriate in light of the emergence of comparative negligence.[81]

This distinction draws implicit support from the case law. An exception recognized in some jurisdictions to the rule that mental illness is not factored into the standard of care for tort defendants is that sudden and unexpected mental illness that affects the capacity of the defendant to conform to the standards of a reasonable person excuses the defendant from being held to the objective standard of care.[82] Without regard to the psychological reality this rule assumes about the occurrence of sudden and unexpected episodes of mental illness, the rationale for this exception is germane to the modification of the standard of care proposed. When the defendant has no notice of the mental illness, there is nothing that the defendant can do to reduce the risk posed by the mental illness. When the defendant has notice of the mental illness, the defendant can act to reduce the risk. Notice of the illness, therefore, requires action

---

81. Ellis, supra note 54, at 1097. An implicit assumption that underlies comparative negligence is that accidents are seldom caused exclusively by one party. Typically, it is a combination of activities that result in injury-producing behavior. Thus, it is inappropriate to visit responsibility for the injury exclusively on one party. In the sense in which comparative negligence is typically used, fault or negligence is apportioned among the parties whose conduct proximately caused the injury. I use the concept here more broadly when I speak about the patient not singularly bearing the risk that the treatment has not yet been efficacious. I am not suggesting that a third party—the therapist or psychiatric researcher—has proximately contributed to the plaintiff's injury in the way that term is used as a legal term of art. Rather, I am suggesting that the patient who has pursued treatment in good faith which has not yet been effective shares the responsibility, although not necessarily the blame, for that result with the therapist who may not have chosen the best therapy and/or the researchers who may have not discovered a more efficacious therapy. This line of reasoning raises a troubling problem for the limited subjective standard of care. Should individuals for whom no effective treatment is currently known, i.e., personality disorders, benefit from its application?

82. Breunig v. American Family Ins. Co., 173 N.W.2d 619 (Wis. 1970).

    We think the statement that insanity is no defense is too broad when it is applied to a negligence case where the driver is suddenly overcome without forewarning by a mental disability or disorder which incapacitates him from conforming his conduct to the standards of a reasonable man under like circumstances.

Id. at 624. See also Kuhn v. Zabotsky, 224 N.E.2d 137, 141 (1967) (denying insanity defense to a civil cause of action).

to reduce that risk.[83] This action may involve a constellation of responses including avoiding certain behaviors (i.e. driving an automobile) and securing treatment for the mental illness. If obtaining treatment is a reasonable response to notice of the mental illness, then obtaining treatment should be factored into the measurement of the reasonableness of the defendant's conduct.

This distinction also draws implicit support from the use of evidence of mental disability in another context. Evidence of the defendant's mental disability offered in mitigation of the death penalty must be considered by the sentencing authority.[84] Evidence of the defendant's mental disability is more likely to be effective in mitigation of the death penalty when the defendant received mental health care before committing the crime.[85] This is arguably because prior mental health care offers baseline evidence of the defendant's mental illness outside the context of the instant proceeding. Alternatively, it may reflect a common sense construct used by jurors in administration of the insanity defense.[86] Those who sought help before their current legal troubles may be considered less morally blameworthy than those who did not seek help and caused harm. The use of a subjective standard of care for those who sought help before the tortious conduct at issue is supported by a similar common sense construct.

Mentally ill and walking wounded defendants who instituted treatment prior to their injury-producing conduct should be judged on a limited subjective standard of care that takes their efforts at treatment into account and encourages them to use their knowledge of their illness to the greatest effect. Since the proposed rule is designed to encourage treatment to reduce the risk of accidental injury, the first conjunctive element of the test is that the defendant must have instituted treatment in good faith prior to the injury-producing conduct. If the defendant did not initiate treatment prior to the injury-producing conduct, the defendant would not be judged on the modified standard of care but, instead, on the traditional objective standard of care[87]—no therapeu-

---

83. There is, of course, an illogic built into the exception. It assumes that mental illness has no debilitating effect on the capacity of the defendant to seek treatment. The proliferation of a second generation of "in need of treatment" standards for civil commitment address mentally ill individuals who are in need of treatment and who are incapacitated and unable to recognize that need as a result of their illness. Tex. Health & Safety Code Ann. § 574.034 (Vernon 1992); Wash. Rev. Code Ann. § 71.05.020(1) (Wash. Supp. 1989). These statutes assume the existence of a population of mentally ill individuals who are by reason of their illness incapable of ascertaining their need for treatment. Cliff P. Stromberg & Alan A. Stone, A Model State Law on Civil Commitment of the Mentally Ill, 20 Harv. J. on Legis. 275, 301–02 (1983).

84. Penry v. Lynaugh, 492 U.S. 302, 327–28 (1989); Lockett v. United States, 438 U.S. 586, 605–08 (1978).

85. Lawrence White, The Mental Illness Defense in the Capital Penalty Hearing, 5 Behav. Sci. & L. 411, 417 (1987).

86. See Norman J. Finkel, Maligning and Misconstruing Jurors' Insanity Verdicts: A Rebuttal, 1 Forensic Rep. 97, 107 (1988).

87. Even in the case of a defendant who sought treatment by making a timely appointment but was involved in an accident before treatment could begin, I would favor encouraging treatment by application of the modified standard. This situation does admittedly present other problems, such as lack of a baseline from which to gauge the defendant's conduct.

tic efforts, no special therapeutic jurisprudence standard. The date the patient initiated treatment is readily verifiable since records of patient care are required by professional regulation[88] and each patient's treatment results in a paper trail of checks, receipts, and insurance claim forms.

If the defendant initiated treatment but missed therapy sessions or failed to take prescribed medication[89] or otherwise failed to comply fully with the treatment regime, then the defendant should not be judged on the limited subjective standard of care. Although not necessarily sufficient in and of itself, patient cooperation is a necessary condition of efficacious treatment. The limited subjective standard of care is intended to support compliance with prescribed treatment. Only therapeutic good faith justifies application of the modified standard of care.

An illustrative case is *Johnson v. Lambotte*.[90] The defendant, Johnson, was an involuntarily committed patient who had received electro-convulsive treatment and thorazine for her "chronic schizophrenic state of paranoid type." Johnson left the hospital unnoticed by the hospital staff, found a car with the motor running, and drove it into Lambotte's car. Lambotte sued for the resulting damages. The court did not consider Johnson's mental illness relevant under the traditional objective standard of care. Nor should mental illness trigger the limited subjective standard of care, both because she did not initiate treatment voluntarily[91] and because she abandoned treatment prematurely. Since no therapeutic good faith was shown, no special therapeutic jurisprudence standard should be applied.

A more troubling problem is the individual who seeks treatment that is unavailable due to the location or cost. Mental health care for the poor has been largely unavailable.[92] The incidence of increasing unemployment, lack of adequate insurance, and managed care contributes to significant financial limits on access to mental health care. There are cogent social policy reasons for using the same modified standard of care for the person making a good faith effort to obtain treatment that is financially unavailable and for the person who has begun the process of treatment. This extension of the limited subjective standard of care is, however, problematic. It will be more difficult to doc-

---

88. See, e.g., Tex. State Board of Examiners of Psychologists, 22 Tex. Admin. Code § 465.22 (1987) (Record Maintenance) (requirement that psychologists maintain accurate, current, and pertinent records of psychological services).

89. Stuyvesant Assoc. v. Doe, 534 A.2d 448, 450 (N.J. Super. Ct. App. Div. 1987) (defendant-tenant, diagnosed as a schizophrenic, who failed to appear for regular injection of prolixine decanate without providing an explanation, became delusional, damaged rental dwelling, was subject to eviction and liable for property damage).

90. 363 P.2d 165 (Colo. 1961).

91. The distinction between voluntary and involuntary mental health care is admittedly illusory. Janet A. Gilboy and John R. Schmidt, Voluntary Hospitalization of the Mentally Ill, 66 NW. U. L. Rev. 429, 430 (1971). Some voluntary patients seek care only in response to threats of job loss, divorce, or involuntary hospitalization. Some involuntary patients receive care on an involuntary basis because of concerns regarding their capacity to consent to voluntary care or fears that they will seek premature release.

92. Barbara Lerner, Therapy in the Ghetto: Political Impotence and Personal Disintegration 5 (1970); S. Garfield, Research in Client Variable in Psychotherapy, in Handbook of Psychotherapy and Behavior Change 213 (S. Garfield & Allen Bergin eds., 1986).

ument efforts to secure treatment and to judge each person's ability to afford mental care.

Another difficult question is how to decide which treatments should trigger the limited standard of care. A broad array of treatments and mental health professionals exist. Tort law should not be indifferent to the defendant's choice of treatment. Only those treatments that have been proven effective through rigorous scientific studies should trigger the limited standard of care. The unknowns may dominate mental health care. A treatment currently labeled as fringe may one day justify recognition as a safe and effective treatment of choice for certain mental disorders. Yet, if the therapeutic goal of a limited standard of care is efficacious treatment, only resort to treatments that have been shown to be effective in well-designed studies should be supported by the limited subjective standard of care. Unproven treatments are pursued at the risk of forgoing the beneficial application of the limited standard of care. There is a developing literature on outcome research in health care precipitated by cost conscious third party payers—insurance companies and governmental entities.[93] The same concerns with efficacious outcomes are germane to therapeutic jurisprudence and provide a body of research from which consumers of health care and tort law may draw.

If the judge or jury finds that the first element of the test (institution of efficacious treatment prior to the injury producing conduct) has been satisfied, it should then proceed to the second prong of the test and consider the impact of the defendant's mental or emotional problems and treatment on the defendant's conduct. The second prong of the test asks the fact finder to decide whether the defendant performed as well as society is entitled to expect such a person to behave, considering their mental or emotional problem and the treatment obtained. Tort law considers whether a blind defendant behaved as well as society should expect a blind person to behave under the circumstances.[94] Similarly, tort law should consider whether a defendant with a mental or emotional problem behaved as well as society should expect a person to behave given the mental or emotional problems and treatment obtained. If the defendant has performed as well as society should reasonably expect given the defendant's mental and emotional problems and the treatment received, then the defendant has met the modified standard of care.

The limited subjective standard of care should not be misconstrued as a grant of immunity to the mentally ill and walking wounded. Its application will not invariably result in a lowered expectation for the defendant's behavior. Consider the case of a person who has completed a course of therapy for stress management.[95] The goal of stress management is to teach individuals to man-

---

93. See, e.g., Oregon Health Services Commission, The 1991 Prioritization of Health Services.

94. See Restatement (Second) of Torts § 283(c) (1965). "If the actor is ill or otherwise physically disabled, the standard of conduct to which he must conform to avoid being negligent is that of a reasonable man under like disability." Id.

95. I am indebted to Grant Morris for suggesting this problem. For a review of the outcome research on stress management, see Lawrence J. Murphy, Occupational Stress Management: A Review and Appraisal, 57 J. Occup. Med. 1, 7 (1984). The strategies tested include biofeedback, meditation, muscle relaxation, and cognitive restructuring.

age their physiological and psychological reactions to stressful situations. One year later, the person experiences significant stress but does not use the stress management techniques learned. As a consequence, the person fails to concentrate while driving and causes a collision. An evaluation of that person's behavior under the limited subjective standard would ask whether the defendant behaved as well as society should expect given the mental or emotional problem and the treatment received. Here the treatment was directed to identify and deal constructively with stress. Given the defendant's knowledge of stress management techniques, the defendant has not behaved as prudently as should be expected and would not escape liability under the limited subjective standard of care.

The use of a subjective standard of care for those mentally ill and walking wounded who sought treatment prior to the alleged tortious conduct avoids the criticism often leveled at a subjective standard of care. The argument that a uniform, predictable standard will evaporate and yield an infinite number of unworkable, individualized standards is not germane in these circumstances for three reasons: (1) the number of individuals who may invoke this standard is capped; (2) there is a disincentive to invoke the standard; and (3) there are pre-existing standards to measure the behavior of these individuals. The number of individuals who will have sought efficacious mental health care prior to the injury producing conduct is self limited. The floodgates of criticism remain closed. The rule is designed to encourage preaccident treatment to reduce the risk of accidental injury. Only those who instituted efficacious treatment prior to the injury producing conduct could invoke this rule.

The floodgates concern is also ameliorated by a disincentive to invoke this modified standard. Invocation of this modified standard requires public admission of treatment for a mental or emotional problem and public disclosure of confidential therapist-patient communications. People labelled as mentally ill face a broad array of prejudices and immutable stereotypes.[96] Thus a motorist who is sued for negligent driving may be unwilling to engage in a public disclosure of this sort to defend the claim.[97] An attorney or physician who is sued for malpractice may be unwilling to risk the impact of that admission as a cost of defending the claim.

The concern that a modified standard presents insuperable problems of diagnosis and application of an individualized standard is also misplaced. Diagnosis of individuals who invoke the modified standard and assessment of their individual capacities is aided by the requirement that they have received treatment prior to the injury-producing conduct when no secondary gain was present. Again, these individuals are self-defined by the act of seeking mental health care prior to the tortious conduct at issue. Also, there is a professionally determined pre-accident baseline that may be used to measure the defendant's conduct.

---

96. Perlin, supra note 31.

97. There are certainly instances in which plaintiffs appear to have foregone claims for psychological injuries to avoid the disclosure of mental health records. See, e.g., Martin v. Martelli, 554 N.Y.S.2d 787, 789 (1990) (holding that it would be imprudent to order release of all mental health records where there was no relation to accident, but allowing in camera inspection).

The fear that people may seek treatment as a boiler plate defense against tort liability for unplanned future acts of negligence is unjustified. If the person seeking treatment has mental health problems that may benefit from treatment and actually complies with the prescribed treatment, a therapeutic result accrues regardless of the reason. This treatment may reduce the risk of injury and advance the accident reduction goal of tort law and therapeutic jurisprudence. If the person seeking treatment has no mental health problems that may benefit from treatment, a professionally determined baseline exists to defeat application of the limited subjective standard of care.

The fear that individuals may plan to commit a tort and use prior initiation of treatment as a defense is also unjustified for two reasons. First, the treatment may ameliorate the risk of the planned tortious conduct. Treatment may provide a therapeutic outlet for the thoughts or feelings that underlay the planned tort. Second, planned tortious conduct is an intentional tort, not a negligent tort. Although the defendant's mental or emotional problems are irrelevant to the standard of care in negligence actions, they are relevant in the case of intentional torts.[98] The defendant's mental or emotional problems are relevant to evaluate the defendant's intent to bring about a particular result or to be substantially certain that it will result. Thus, people planning tortious conduct who purposefully institute treatment to lay the groundwork for a later defense may be dissuaded from engaging in the planned tortious conduct and gain no legal advantage under the subjective standard.

An individualized standard factoring mental illness into the evaluation of conduct is generally permitted for plaintiffs on the issue of contributory negligence.[99] Contrary to the fears articulated about administering a civil insanity defense, the individualized standard for the contributory negligence of plaintiffs has not been reported to present insuperable problems. This may be relevant evidence that a limited subjective standard for mentally ill and walking wounded defendants who sought treatment prior to the tortious conduct would also not present insuperable problems.

IV. Conclusion

There is much to be said in favor of a limited subjective standard of care for the mentally ill and walking wounded who initiate treatment prior to the in-

---

98. In the case of torts such as battery that have a specific intent requirement, the existence of mental illness is a relevant consideration in the defendant's capacity to form that intent. W. Page Keeton et al., Prosser and Keeton on the Law of Torts § 135, at 1073 (5th ed. 1984).

99. Restatement (Second) of Torts § 464 (1965) ("Unless the actor is a child or insane person, the standard of conduct to which he must conform for his own protection is that of a reasonable person under like circumstances."); W. Page Keeton et al., Prosser and Keeton on the Law of Torts s 32, at 178 n.39 (5th ed. 1984) ("The great majority of courts in the contributory negligence context apply a lower standard of care and consider the plaintiff's incapacity as only one of the 'circumstances' to be considered in judging the quality of his conduct."). See also Curran, supra note 30, at 63 (citing seven pre-Restatement (Second) of Torts cases, five of which apply a subjective standard for contributory negligence and two which do not).

jury-producing conduct. Such a standard offers the potential to implement the accident reduction goal shared by tort law and therapeutic jurisprudence on a grand scale. The limited subjective standard has a limited downside risk since the floodgates are closed as of the date of the injury-producing conduct. And, the limited subjective standard of care has a built in baseline for measuring the defendant's conduct that should make its application easier and provide a disincentive for inappropriate use.

A limited subjective standard of care for the mentally ill and walking wounded who initiated treatment prior to the alleged tortious conduct may be convincing on therapeutic jurisprudence grounds and may deflect the arguments traditionally used to justify the objective standard of care. However, even if one is convinced by these arguments, there may be other reasons to challenge this proposal for a limited subjective standard of care. This proposal, which seeks to implement a modified standard of care to reduce the rate of injury, may be attacked as utilitarian. Utilitarian reasoning is vulnerable both because of its consequentialist approach and its unexplored empirical premises. The consequentialist concern is that utilitarianism is a result oriented approach focused on "maximized happiness"[100] that excludes consideration of other competing values.[101] Some critics have viewed therapeutic jurisprudence as a utilitarian-based reasoning that measures all legal decisions by their therapeutic consequences. Therapeutic jurisprudence has, however, moved quickly to counter this consequentialist criticism by recognizing that therapeutic consequences are not the only important concern in legal decisionmaking, but only one of a competing set of concerns.[102] Whether this pragmatic reformulation will result in a more careful balancing of interests must await future judgment.

A specific example of this consequentialist concern with therapeutic jurisprudence in the case of a therapeutically based standard of care for the mentally ill and walking wounded is the impact of that standard of care on another normative value, compensation. Even if a limited subjective standard of care encourages treatment, it denies compensation to plaintiffs injured through no fault of their own.[103] Thus, even if a limited subjective standard of care encourages a greater level of safety in some cases, that benefit must be balanced against denying compensation to some injured plaintiffs.

---

100. See Jeremy Bentham, An Introduction to the Principles of Morals and Legislation 2 (Athlone P. London 1970) (1789) (discussing the utilitarianism approach).

101. H.L.A. Hart, Between Utility and Rights, 79 Colum. L. Rev. 828, 828 (1979). Hart identifies two politically separate criticisms of utilitarianism. American conservatives criticize utilitarianism for its ignorance of "the moral importance of the separateness or distinctiveness of human persons." Id. See John Rawls, A Theory of Justice 46–53 (1971) (discussing moral theory). American liberals criticize utilitarianism for its denial of the moral title to equal concern and respect. Hart, supra at 828. Leonard G. Ratner, The Utilitarian Imperative: Autonomy, Reciprocity, and Revolution, 12 Hofstra L. Rev. 723, 749–55 (1984).

102. Wexler & Winick, supra note 1.

103. As noted earlier, the argument that any significant number of injuries occur without shared responsibility for the result may be a chimera. Yet, even if in a small number of cases, it is clear that in some instances this may occur. See Alexander & Szasz, supra note 58, and accompanying text.

Compensation is, however, a relativist rather than an absolute concern of tort law. Not all injured plaintiffs are compensated by tort law. Plaintiffs seriously injured by conduct not thought to be in need of deterrence are not offered compensation by tort law. More specifically, the goal of compensation is subserved for plaintiffs injured by physically incapacitated defendants whose conduct is measured against those who are similarly disabled.

Thus, the fact that one consequence of the limited subjective standard of care for the mentally ill and the walking wounded will be to deny compensation to injured plaintiffs should not, by itself, result in a rejection of the rule. The choice necessitates a careful balancing of interests. This balancing should not occur in the abstract. Rather, it requires a precise analysis of the cost of injuries avoided against the cost of injuries not compensated. The posture of this question highlights another flaw in utilitarian based reasoning.

Utilitarian reasoning is vulnerable because it often assumes, without empirical examination, that a legal rule will result in a particular societal consequence. If a rule is based on a consequentialist rationale (i.e., that we should impose stiff criminal sentences on violent criminals to deter violent crime), empirical examination of the consequence of the rule (i.e., the relationship between the severity of punishment and the rate of violent crime) is obligatory. Similarly, the argument for a therapeutic jurisprudence based on the limited subjective standard of care for mentally ill tort defendants turns on a series of empirically verifiable links. These empirically verifiable links include an assumption that tort law influences behavior, that mental or emotional problems play a causative role in tortious conduct, and that safe and effective treatment exists for mental or emotional problems. If any of these empirical premises is false, then therapeutic jurisprudence does not support the application of a limited subjective standard of care for mentally ill and walking wounded tort defendants.

The wisdom of this proposal thus returns to its original premise. Should tort law attempt to deter unsafe behavior? Perhaps it should not. Yet, if it should seek to do so effectively, tort law should not ignore the psychological reality of accident causation and the therapeutic potential of the standard of care.

Chapter 21

Requiring Sound Judgments of Unsound Minds: Tort Liability and the Limits of Therapeutic Jurisprudence

Grant H. Morris

"Insanity is a more difficult matter to deal with...."[1]

I. Introduction

Tort liability is imposed on mentally disordered defendants as if they had no such disorder. If, for example, a person with a diagnosable disorder of paranoid schizophrenia[2] strikes another because of a delusional belief that the other is about to attack, the mentally disordered person will be held liable for the tort of battery.[3] The court asks only whether the defendant acted with the

---

1. O. W. Holmes, Jr., The Common Law 109 (1881).

2. Schizophrenia is a common, major mental disorder. According to the American Psychiatric Association, many large studies have reported a prevalence rate of 0.2% to 2.0%. Typically, the prevalence rate is reported to be between 0.5% and 1.0%. American Psychiatric Ass'n, Diagnostic and Statistical Manual of Mental Disorders (DSM-IV) 282 (4th ed. 1994). According to the 1990 census, the total population in the United States is 248,709,873. 1993 The World Almanac and Book of Facts 387 (Mark S. Hoffman ed., 125th ed. 1992). A 1% prevalence rate for schizophrenia would be approximately 2,500,000 people.

Paranoid schizophrenia is a type of schizophrenia characterized by "the presence of prominent delusions or auditory hallucinations in the context of a relative preservation of cognitive functioning and affect." American Psychiatric Ass'n , supra at 287.

3. See, e.g., McGuire v. Almy, 8 N.E.2d 760 (Mass. 1937). The defendant, characterized by the court as an insane person, struck the plaintiff, her nurse, with a piece of furniture. The jury found that the defendant acted with an intent to strike and injure the plaintiff. The defendant was held liable. The Supreme Judicial Court of Massachusetts summarized the rule as follows:

> [W]here an insane person by his act does intentional damage to the person or property of another he is liable for that damage in the same circumstances in which a normal person would be liable. This means that insofar as a particular intent would be necessary in order to render a normal person liable, the insane person, in order to be liable, must have been capable of entertaining that same intent and must have entertained it in fact. But the law will not inquire further into his peculiar mental condition with a view to excusing him if it should appear that delusion or other consequence of his affliction has caused him to entertain that intent or that a normal person would not have entertained it. Id. at 763.

purpose of making a harmful or offensive contact or with knowledge that such contact was substantially certain to result. The defendant's delusional belief that prompted the tortious action does not excuse tort liability. In essence, the defendant's misinterpretation of reality is treated as a nonexculpating mistake.

In a conventional mistake case, the defendant engages in conduct that injures the plaintiff, and the defendant intends to engage in that conduct and to produce that injury at the time the defendant acts. The defendant claims, however, to have acted under an erroneous, but reasonable, belief that circumstances existed justifying the defendant's behavior. In the absence of any other privilege, a good faith, reasonable mistake will not excuse tort liability.[4] Similarly, if a mentally disordered defendant acts with the intent required to impose tort liability on a nonmentally disordered defendant, the mentally disordered person's good faith, but unreasonable, mistake will not preclude tort liability.[5]

Liability of mentally disordered persons is not limited to intentional torts. If, for example, a mentally disordered motorist fails to control his or her car because of a delusional belief that God is directing the vehicle, the motorist will be held liable in negligence for damages that result.[6] The court asks only whether the defendant's conduct conformed to the standard of the reasonable, prudent person engaged in that activity—an objective standard that measures negligence for both mentally disordered and nonmentally disordered defendants.[7]

---

4. See, e.g., Ranson v. Kitner, 31 Ill. App. 241 (1888). The defendants, hunting for wolves, killed the plaintiff's dog believing it to be a wolf. They were held liable for the value of the dog, notwithstanding their good faith mistake.

5. If a tort requires a specific intent, however, a mentally disordered defendant who acts without such intent has not committed the tort and should not be, but sometimes has been, held liable. Deceit and malicious prosecution are examples of specific intent torts. W. Page Keeton et al., Prosser and Keeton on the Law of Torts § 135, at 1074 (5th ed. 1984). See also Restatement (Second) of Torts § 895J cmt. c (1979). Similarly, punitive damages should not be imposed on a mentally disordered defendant whose intentional tortious conduct was not accompanied by the malicious motive or outrageousness required to justify its imposition. Keeton, supra at 1074.

6. Breunig v. American Family Ins. Co., 173 N.W.2d 619 (Wis. 1970).

7. See, e.g., Johnson v. Lambotte, 363 P.2d 165, 166 (Colo. 1961) (The defendant, a patient being treated for chronic paranoid schizophrenia, left the hospital, drove a car, and collided with the plaintiff's car. The defendant was held liable for negligent operation of the automobile.); Shapiro v. Tchernowitz, 155 N.Y.S.2d 1011, 1016 (N.Y. Sup. Ct. 1956) (In discharging bullets from his gun, the defendant shot and killed the plaintiff's husband. In a wrongful death action, the defendant was held liable for negligence.); Ellis v. Fixico, 50 P.2d 162, 164 (Okla. 1935) (The plaintiff alleged that the defendant, a mentally disordered person, negligently allowed her car to be driven in a reckless manner by her driver, resulting in a collision and injuries to the plaintiff. The Supreme Court of Oklahoma held that a demurrer to the petition should not have been sustained. The court relied on a statute holding a person of unsound mind civilly liable for a wrong "in like manner as any other person."). See infra note 23 for cases decided since 1965.

Throughout the twentieth century, law review commentators have overwhelmingly,[8] although not quite unanimously,[9] criticized the courts' refusal to consider a defendant's mental disorder in assessing tort liability. The articles are remarkably alike. A typical article begins by tracing the principle to *Weaver v. Ward*.[10] In this 1616 King's Bench decision, the court stated in its dictum[11] that "if a lunatic hurt a man, he shall be answerable in trespass...."[12] The statement was not remarkable because, at the time, strict liability was imposed on all defendants who caused harm. The court used the lunatic example merely to distinguish tort law from criminal law which excuses mentally disordered defendants if they lack *mens rea*.

With the development of fault-based liability and societal acceptance of a medical model to explain mental disorder,[13] one would suspect that *Weaver's* "lunatic" dictum would be long forgotten. One's suspicions would be incorrect. *Weaver* has endured due to the court's recognition, also in dictum, that a defendant will not be liable for a purely accidental injury. *Weaver* is the earliest known case to suggest this limitation on strict liability.[14]

---

8. Articles criticizing the imposition of fault-based tort liability on mentally disordered defendants include: Robert M. Ague, Jr., The Liability of Insane Persons in Tort Actions, 60 Dick. L. Rev. 211 (1956); Frances H. Bohlen, Liability in Tort of Infants and Insane Persons, 23 Mich. L. Rev. 9 (1924); W.G.H. Cook, Mental Deficiency in Relation to Tort, 21 Colum. L. Rev. 333 (1921); William J. Curran, Tort Liability of the Mentally Ill and Mentally Deficient, 21 Ohio St. L.J. 52 (1960); James W. Ellis, Tort Responsibility of Mentally Disabled Persons, 1981 Am. B. Found. Res. J. 1079; Wm. B. Hornblower, Insanity and the Law of Negligence, 5 Colum. L. Rev. 278 (1905); David E. Seidelson, Reasonable Expectations and Subjective Standards in Negligence Law: The Minor, the Mentally Impaired, and the Mentally Incompetent, 50 Geo. Wash. L. Rev. 17 (1981); Wm. Justus Wilkinson, Mental Incompetency as a Defense to Tort Liability, 17 Rocky Mtn. L. Rev. 38 (1944).

9. Two articles defend the imposition of fault-based tort liability on mentally disordered defendants. See George J. Alexander & Thomas S. Szasz, Mental Illness as an Excuse for Civil Wrongs, 43 Notre Dame Law. 24 (1967); Stephanie I. Splane, Note, Tort Liability of the Mentally Ill in Negligence Actions, 93 Yale L.J. 153 (1983).

10. 80 Eng. Rep. 284 (K.B. 1616).

11. In *Weaver*, the plaintiff and the defendant were trained soldiers engaged in a military exercise. In discharging his musket, the defendant wounded the plaintiff. The defendant was held liable because the injury did not occur "utterly without his fault." Id. The defendant did not claim that he suffered from a mental disorder that should excuse his conduct.

12. Id.

13. Justice Michael Musmanno reported on the changing societal attitude toward mental disorder:

> Today modern science and society take a view of mental trouble quite different from that which prevailed down through the ages. In the ancient days victims of cerebral disorders were regarded as subhuman; they were assumed to be possessed of the devil and devoid of spirit, feeling, and the sensibilities of man; they were ostracized from community life. But time has opened the eyes of the sensible world and it is now recognized that a malady of the brain, so far as spirit and morals are concerned, is no different from a disease of the liver....

Commonwealth ex rel. Edinger v. Edinger, 98 A.2d 172, 174 (Pa. 1953).

14. William L. Prosser et al. , Cases and Materials on Torts 6 (8th ed. 1988).

Commentators usually note that appellate cases upholding tort liability of mentally disordered defendants are few in number and infrequent in occurrence—especially cases involving negligence. For example, Cook,[15] writing in 1921, and Bohlen,[16] writing in 1924, could find only one case[17] holding a mentally disordered defendant liable for negligence. Curran,[18] writing in 1960, could find only one additional case—and that case was a trial court decision in the same jurisdiction as the first.[19]

This scant authority, however, influenced the American Law Institute in its Restatement of Torts. The first Restatement, published in 1934, contained a caveat in which the Institute expressed no opinion on whether mentally disordered persons are required to conform to the reasonable person standard.[20] The caveat was deleted in the 1948 supplement.[21] The second Restatement, published in 1965, specifically identified mentally disordered defendants as in-

---

15. Cook, supra note 8, at 349.

16. Bohlen, supra note 8, at 23.

17. Williams v. Hays, 38 N.E. 449 (N.Y. 1894), subsequent appeal, 52 N.E. 589 (N.Y. 1899). A ship captain was in a state of exhaustion after working 48 hours to save the ship from a storm. In a dazed condition, he declined the assistance of tugboats offering to tow the disabled vessel. The ship was destroyed. Although the issues in the two appeals differed, in each the New York Court of Appeals recognized that mental disorder was not a defense to a claim of negligence. The New York Court of Appeals decisions in *Williams* are discussed at length in Bohlen, supra note 8, at 23–27. *Williams* is considered the leading American case holding that negligence liability of the mentally disordered is measured by the objective, reasonable person standard. Ague, supra note 8, at 215. The case was even cited as authority in the totally unrelated *Palsgraf* case. Palsgraf v. Long Island R.R., 162 N.E. 99, 102 (N.Y. 1928) (Andrews, J., dissenting).

18. Curran, supra note 8, at 61.

19. Sforza v. Green Bus Lines, Inc., 268 N.Y.S. 446, 448 (N.Y. City Mun. Ct. 1934). (The defendant bus driver suddenly became insane, lost control of the bus, and collided with the plaintiff's parked truck. The defendant was held liable for negligence.).

20. Restatement of Torts § 283 (1934). The first Restatement's position is supported by Hornblower. Writing in 1905, Hornblower asserted that despite the New York Court of Appeals's decisions in *Williams*, the liability of a mentally disordered defendant for negligence remained an open question even in New York state. Hornblower, supra note 8, at 297. Other noted authorities predicted that courts would not impose tort liability on mentally disordered defendants. Ames, writing in 1908, prophesied that American courts "will sooner or later apply to the lunatic the ethical principle of no liability without fault." James Barr Ames, Law and Morals, 22 Harv. L. Rev. 97, 100 (1908). Bohlen, writing in 1924, asserted that the decisions and opinions he discussed in his article "seem logically to imply that insanity is a bar to recovery." Bohlen, supra note 8, at 28. Dean Bohlen served as the Reporter for the first Restatement of Torts.

21. Restatement of Torts § 283 (Supp. 1948). The American Law Institute first considered the question of tort liability of mentally disordered persons at its 1929 annual meeting. The caveat was added at that time. Its deletion in 1948 can hardly be attributed to the one reported case decided between 1929 and 1948 imposing negligence liability on a mentally disordered defendant. Rather, the American Law Institute relied on opinions from several intentional tort cases that contained language broad enough to impose negligence liability in future cases. Id. at 654–58. "Once it is clearly seen that the insane person who intentionally injures another is subjected to tort liability despite his moral innocence...then these decisions become controlling authority for imposing liability for the same harm, unintentionally caused by one who is personally neither more nor less blameworthy." Id. at 658.

dividuals who are subject to liability for conduct that does not conform to the reasonable person standard.[22] The American Law Institute's capitulation provided new authority to help settle a questionable rule.[23] Nevertheless, the continued dearth of negligence cases supporting the rule and the continued academic onslaught challenging the rule suggest that its future is uncertain.[24]

Commentators invariably list the courts' stated reasons for imposing the reasonable person test on the mentally disordered.[25] But the reasons are often

---

22. Restatement (Second) of Torts § 283B (1965); see also id. § 895J (1979) (stating that mentally disordered persons are not immune from tort liability solely because of their disorder).

23. Since 1965, five cases have followed § 283B by imposing negligence liability on mentally disordered defendants for conduct that did not conform to the reasonable person standard. Turner v. Caldwell, 421 A.2d 876, 876 (Conn. Super. Ct. 1980) (The defendant's claim that she was suddenly stricken by mental illness rendering her unable to control her vehicle was not a defense to an action grounded in negligence.); Jolley v. Powell, 299 So. 2d 647, 649 (Fla. Dist. Ct. App. 1974), cert. denied, 309 So. 2d 7 (Fla. 1975) (The defendant shot and killed the deceased but was acquitted of homicide by reason of insanity. In a wrongful death claim, the court construed the defendant's action as unintentional. The court held: "[W]hen the predicate for a wrongful death action is unintentional tort the standard against which such tort is measured is the objective, 'reasonable man standard' and the subjective state of mind of the tortfeasor is irrelevant."); Kuhn v. Zabotsky, 224 N.E.2d 137, 141 (Ohio 1967) (The defendant, claiming to have been suddenly stricken by a mental illness, drove his car into the rear of the plaintiff's car, inflicting personal injury and property damage. The court held the defendant liable for negligence.); Schumann v. Crofoot, 602 P.2d 298, 300 (Or. 1979) (An attorney who suffered from a psychotic disorder was held liable for professional negligence. The court specifically accepted the rule stated in § 283B.); Breunig v. American Family Ins. Co., 173 N.W.2d 619, 624 (Wis. 1970) (The court upheld a jury verdict against a mentally disordered defendant whose delusion affected her ability to operate her vehicle as a reasonable, prudent driver. In this case, evidence was sufficient to enable the jury to find that the defendant could anticipate the occurrence of incapacitating delusions. The court ruled, however, that if a situation arises in which the defendant is suddenly overcome without forewarning by a disabling mental disorder, liability will not be imposed.).

One post-1965 case specifically rejected the position that a mentally disordered person is liable for negligence. Fitzgerald v. Lawhorn, 294 A.2d 338 (Conn. C.P. 1972) (The defendant shot and wounded the plaintiff. The trial court judge found no intent to injure and treated the plaintiff's suit as a claim of negligence. The judge found for the defendant, characterizing the rule imposing tort liability on the mentally disordered as "an outdated point of view." Id. at 339. However, in apparent confusion, the court asserted: "The standard of conduct demanded of an insane person should not be any greater than the standard of conduct which it is reasonable for one to expect of a sane person. A sane individual is only required to exercise the standard of conduct which a reasonably prudent person would exercise under the same circumstances." Id.).

24. Keeton, supra note 5, at 1075 ("[T]he permanent direction of the law may be in doubt even now.").

25. The commentators' lists vary in number from three to six. Bohlen, for example, identifies three reasons for the rule: (1) the *Weaver* dictum, (2) a reappearance of liability without fault, and (3) liability for failure to perform a duty imposed on owners or occupiers of land or on persons engaged in certain trades. Bohlen, supra note 8, at 12. Ellis's list of six is the most comprehensive, although it includes reasons suggested by section 283B of the Restatement Second of Torts and by Prosser, as well as reasons articulated in court opinions. Ellis identifies the following reasons:

presented as straw men who are unable to bear the weight of even the most perfunctory analysis. To the claim that the rule is necessary to assure that innocent plaintiffs receive compensation from those who injure them, the answer has been that liability in negligence is not liability without fault.[26] For torts in which fault is a prerequisite to liability for nonmentally disordered persons, nothing less should be required for liability of the mentally disordered. To the contention that all people living in society, including mentally disordered people, should be held responsible for their torts, the refutation has been that tort liability is dependent upon a finding of tortious behavior. The question of whether a mentally disordered defendant has committed a tort cannot be answered by saying he or she is liable for all torts that he or she commits.[27] To the assertion that imposing liability on mentally disordered persons encourages guardians to control their activities or to obtain their involuntary confinement, the response has been that guardians who inadequately supervise persons under their authority are liable for their own negligence, and thus it is unnecessary to impose tort liability on the mentally disordered persons as well.[28] To

---

1) "[W]here one of two innocent persons must suffer a loss, it should be borne by the one who occasioned it."

2) Liability for negligent acts will encourage those who are responsible for mentally disabled persons (their families or guardians) to look after them and prevent them from doing harm.

3) If mentally disabled people are to live in liberty in society, they should pay for the damage they cause.

4) Mental disability is easily feigned, and defendants might choose such an act of duplicity to avoid liability.

5) It is difficult for courts to distinguish between "true" mental disability and variations in temperament, intellect, and emotional balance, and to allow all such differences to serve as excuses would erode the objective standard in all cases.

6) The insanity defense and the doctrine of diminished capacity have wreaked havoc in the field of criminal law, and this chaos should not be recreated in tort law.

Ellis, supra note 8, at 1083–84 (footnotes omitted).

26. Ague stated that this reason "is nothing more than strict (or absolute) liability dressed up in Sunday-go-to-meetin' garb. In the case of the lunatic let's not drift back into that unmoral abyss once again!" Ague, supra note 8, at 222. Seidelson noted that negligence law generally does not shift the loss from an innocent victim to a nonculpable, innocent actor. Seidelson, supra note 8, at 38.

27. The Second Restatement of Torts clearly separates the standard used to measure whether a mentally disordered person's conduct is negligent from the question of whether mental disorder immunizes a person from liability for conduct that is tortious. Compare Restatement (Second) of Torts § 283B (1965) with § 895J (1979).

28. Clarence Morris & C. Robert Morris, Jr., Morris on Torts 50–51 (2d ed. 1980); Alexander & Szasz, supra note 9, at 35–36. Seidelson declared this reason to be "hardly more than a cynical fabrication to support a rule of law almost facially unfathomable." Seidelson, supra note 8, at 38.

Today, as a result of deinstitutionalization of mental patient populations from large state hospitals, most mentally disordered people live in the community. If they receive treatment for their disorders, treatment occurs in community programs. Even involuntary commitment is typically of short duration and occurs in local facilities. A policy that encourages guardians to seek involuntary commitment of mentally disordered persons in order to avoid

the argument that mental disorder is easily feigned, and that the rule is needed to prevent nonmentally disordered defendants from succeeding with false claims, the rebuttal has been that the stigma and social consequences that accompany the label of mental disorder are a sufficient deterrent to its unwarranted use.[29] To the challenge that the objective standard would be jeopardized by attempts to distinguish mental disorder from nonqualifying peculiarities of temperament and character, the defense has been that abdication of judicial responsibility cannot be countenanced by a preference for easy resolution over proper resolution.[30] Admittedly, requiring an assessment of mental disorder increases the difficulty of decision making.[31] Nevertheless, confronting this difficulty is preferable to blindly imposing tort liability on mentally disordered persons who committed no torts.[32] The objective standard of care has already

---

tort liability is clearly outdated—if not out of touch with reality. See Splane, supra note 9, at 156–57 n.20 and 163 n.58.

29. See, e.g., Ellis, supra note 8, at 1087 (The label of mental illness carries a substantial stigma in our society. Although mentally incompetent people may escape contract obligations, false claims of mental incapacity are rare.); Seidelson, supra note 8, at 39 (Anyone willing to risk an adjudication of mental incompetence "in exchange for the possible evasion of liability in negligence would have to be crazy."). Seidelson also asserted that judges and juries are as competent to distinguish between a real and spurious defense of mental disorder as they are other defenses. Id. at 38.

Diagnostic agreement among psychiatrists and other mental health professionals has improved significantly with the use of specified criteria for each mental disorder contained in succeeding editions of the American Psychiatric Association's Diagnostic and Statistical Manual (DSM). DSM-III, published in 1980, was a marked improvement over previous editions, resulting in greater diagnostic inter-rater reliability. DSM-III-R was published in 1987 and DSM-IV was published in 1994. With each revision of the DSM, diagnosis tends to become more accurate and detection of false claims of mental disorder improves. See Ellis, supra note 8, at 1086–87.

30. Seidelson, supra note 8, at 40.

31. Prosser has often been credited with suggesting that courts have been reluctant to introduce into tort cases "the confusion and unsatisfactory tests attending proof of insanity in criminal cases." William L. Prosser, Handbook of the Law of Torts 1090 (1941). Succeeding editions of the Prosser treatise contain the same statement. See, e.g., Keeton , supra note 5, at 1073. Prosser, however, cites Bohlen's 1924 law review article as the source of the idea. Bohlen, supra note 8, at 36 n.38. Although Bohlen presents the idea, he rejects it on the merits, declaring:

> [I]t seems unworthy of the law, whose purpose it should be to do justice and to perfect its machinery so that justice may be done, to deny immunity to persons so insane as to be incapable of culpability because of the difficulty of evolving a test satisfactory alike to lawyer and alienist [i.e., psychiatrist] by which the precise degree of mental deficiency which precludes culpability may be determined.

Id.

32. Ague, supra note 8, at 224 ("[N]o rule governing [mental disorder] will be infallible; but certainly an imperfect rule is better than no rule at all in such a case....Just because the criminal law rules on insanity fall far short of perfection is no reason why we should throw up our hands and say the same thing will happen in the tort field."); Seidelson, supra note 8, at 40 ("[T]he judicial refusal to define the 'insanity defense' [in tort cases] appears inconsistent with the conduct of courts in criminal cases and unjustified by the difficulty of the task.").

been abandoned for children,[33] when they are engaged in childhood activities, and for physically disabled individuals.[34] If fairness requires its abandonment for the mentally disordered, justice should not be thwarted by appeals to expediency.[35]

After rejecting the various reasons for the rule, commentators complete their typical articles by offering one of two solutions. Some commentators, especially those writing before 1960, would absolve mentally disordered persons from fault-based tort liability.[36] These writers narrowly define "mentally disordered persons" to include only those individuals who lack the capacity to appreciate the possible consequences of their behavior.[37] Because these individuals are unable to conform to the reasonable person standard, injuries caused by their conduct should be considered the result of unavoidable accidents.[38] Motorists who are suddenly and unexpectedly overcome with heart attacks,

---

33. Restatement (Second) of Torts § 283A (1965). The objective standard, however, is applied to children engaged in dangerous activities that require adult qualifications. Id. cmt. c. The objective standard is applied, not to encourage children to exercise greater care when engaging in adult activities, but rather, to discourage them from engaging in adult activities in the first place.

34. Id. § 283C.

35. In other civil and criminal contexts, a person's mental disorder is considered in arriving at a just result. In the civil context, examples include guardianship, civil commitment, and testamentary capacity; in the criminal context, examples include the insanity defense and diminished capacity. No overwhelming difficulty has been encountered in considering mental disorder in those contexts. No overwhelming difficulty is likely to be encountered if mental disorder is considered in determining tort liability. Ellis, supra note 8, at 1089–90.

36. See, e.g., Ague, supra note 8, at 227 ("Can lunatics be said to be at fault simply because they are lunatics and 'know not what they do?' The question would seem to answer itself without further recourse to the scriptures."); Bohlen, supra note 8, at 28 ("[W]here the incapacity is mental, the same mental deficiency which prevents him from performing the duties normally incident to the relation or of conducting himself properly in the activity which he undertakes, would equally preclude his capacity for fault in entering the relation or undertaking the activity."); Cook, supra note 8, at 344 ("[W]here a lunatic is incapable of knowing what he is doing, i.e., where he is not a responsible being at all, he would appear not to be liable: the result in such a case being that the person damaged through the act or omission of the lunatic would be in a position analogous to that of a person who has suffered damage through inevitable accident...."); Hornblower, supra note 8, at 293 ("That a man should be responsible in damages for failing to do what he was physically or mentally unable to do, is certainly shocking to the common-sense of the average individual."); Wilkinson, supra note 8, at 57 ("If fault is the crux of negligence it is, indeed, hard to make a logical case for holding a mentally incompetent person liable for negligence, for where can fault be found?").

37. See, e.g., Bohlen, supra note 8, at 9 ("Insane persons" defined as "incapable of forming a culpable intention, or whose incapacity to realize the probable consequences of their conduct makes it unjust to require them to conform to the standards of conduct legally required of...mentally normal persons."); Hornblower, supra note 8, at 283 ("When we come, however, to the question of a person *non compos mentis*, we have a situation of absolute mental incapacity....").

38. In an unavoidable accident, even though the defendant's conduct injured the plaintiff, the result was not intended by the defendant, and the defendant was not negligent. The defendant is not liable. Keeton, supra note 5, at 162.

strokes, or fainting spells are not held liable for resulting injuries;[39] mentally disordered persons who are unable to control their conduct should be absolved as well.

Other commentators, especially those writing in the early 1980s, would measure fault-based tort liability of mentally disordered persons using a subjective standard of care.[40] Even these writers narrowly define "mentally disordered persons" to include only those individuals who are factually incapable of achieving the level of conduct required of the objective reasonable person.[41] Just as the law does not require the blind person to see, the deaf person to hear, or the young child to act with the maturity and wisdom of an adult, a similar allowance should be made for those mentally disordered defendants who are incapable of conforming to the objective reasonable person standard.[42]

Recently, however, a new perspective has been introduced to the standard of care controversy. Daniel Shuman, filtering his ideas through the prism of therapeutic jurisprudence, has proposed expanding the subjective standard to include persons who have initiated treatment for their mental disorder or for the transient situational stress they are experiencing.[43] Shuman's proposal is original and provocative. Upon reflection, however, I believe that it is flawed and should be rejected. In Part II, I analyze Shuman's proposal.[44] In Part III, I suggest an alternative solution that I believe is preferable.

---

39. Id.

40. Ellis, supra note 8, at 1109 ("Adoption of a subjective standard...may be seen as a modest step toward equitable treatment of the mentally handicapped before the law."); Seidelson, supra note 8, at 44 ("Is it justifiable to frustrate legally a claimant's reasonable expectations by giving the benefit of a subjective standard to an incompetent who is the only potentially viable defendant? I think the answer is yes.").

41. Ellis, supra note 8, at 1108 ("[The subjective standard] does not immunize mentally disabled people from responsibility for their torts, but it does provide them with a defense when they can show that they did their best to avoid the accident and that further preventive measures were beyond their ability."); Seidelson, supra note 8, at 45 ("Under our definition of mental incompetence, the actor suffering from this infirmity cannot possibly act consistently with the reasonable person standard.").

42. For a comprehensive discussion analogizing mentally disordered persons to physically disabled persons and children, see Ellis, supra note 8, at 1098–106. Ellis asserts that although these analogies are "helpful tools," id. at 1106, "neither is perfectly apt." Id. at 1098. He concludes, nevertheless, that mentally disordered defendants should not be "held to a standard that they are definitionally incapable of meeting." Id. at 1108.

43. Daniel W. Shuman, Therapeutic Jurisprudence and Tort Law: A Limited Subjective Standard of Care, 46 SMU L. Rev. 409, 426 (1992).

44. Perhaps "reanalyze" is a more apt word choice. At Professor Shuman's request, I previously critiqued his article while it was in draft stage. In the published article, he graciously acknowledged my "helpful comments" to that draft. Id. at 409; see also, id. at 428 n.95.

II. *Expanding the Subjective Standard: A Critique*

A. The Proposal

In a...book published in 1990, David Wexler used the term "therapeutic jurisprudence" to describe the study of law as a therapeutic agent.[45] Without subordinating other competing values, the therapeutic jurisprudence perspective seeks to enlighten legal decision making in order to enhance therapeutic consequences and diminish antitherapeutic consequences.[46]

Shuman asserts that in their desire to deter injury-producing conduct, fault-based tort law and therapeutic jurisprudence share a common agenda.[47] Tort law's therapeutic potential is advanced by encouraging individuals with mental or emotional problems to undergo effective treatment to ameliorate their conditions and reduce their accident-producing potential.[48] By threatening tort liability for unreasonable behavior, the objective reasonable person standard induces those in need of treatment to obtain it.[49] Thus, Shuman would continue to use that standard for those defendants who did not seek treatment prior to the injury-producing conduct. However, for those defendants who initiated treatment for their mental or emotional problem prior to the injury-producing conduct, Shuman proposes using a subjective standard of care that assesses the defendant's conduct in light of the treatment received.[50] Although use of a subjective standard will not always result in a lowered expectation for the defendant's behavior,[51] in some situations it will. For example, some therapies that are effective in the long term may actually increase the short term risk of accidental injury.[52] In determining whether a person under treatment performed as well as society could reasonably expect, society should be willing to consider the person's willingness to undergo treatment and the effects of that treatment on the person.[53] To maximize the therapeutic potential of tort law, Shuman would not limit his proposal to individuals suffering from major mental illnesses. Rather, he would also include the "walking wounded"[54]—identified as individuals whose life changes have produced transient situational stress.[55]

---

45. David B. Wexler, Therapeutic Jurisprudence: The Law as a Therapeutic Agent (1990). A companion volume was published a year later. David B. Wexler & Bruce J. Winick, Essays in Therapeutic Jurisprudence (1991).

46. Wexler , supra note 45, at 3–20; Wexler & Winick , supra note 45, at x–xii, 17–38. Therapeutic jurisprudence principles have strongly influenced recent mental health law scholarship. David B. Wexler, Therapeutic Jurisprudence and Changing Conceptions of Legal Scholarship, 11 Behavioral Sci. & L. 17 (1993) (discussing sources).

47. Shuman, supra note 43, at 410. Shuman expresses doubt, however, that tort law is capable of deterring injury-producing conduct. See infra notes 83–88 and accompanying text.

48. Shuman, supra note 43, at 411–12.

49. Id. at 424.

50. Id.

51. Id. at 428.

52. Id. at 423.

53. Id. at 428.

54. Id. at 414. Shuman notes that the "walking wounded" have been denominated by others as the "worried well." Id. n.36 (citing sources).

55. Id. at 416.

B. The Proposal Undervalues the Compensation Objective

In the first paragraph of his article, Shuman admits that therapeutic jurisprudence encourages a therapeutic outcome "when it is possible to do so without offending other important normative values."[56] Shuman acknowledges that tort law has two objectives: deterrence of potential injurers from engaging in unsafe conduct and compensation of injured victims.[57] But Shuman fails to consider the importance of the compensation goal to present-day tort law. Nineteenth century barriers to a plaintiff's tort recovery have been demolished by the actions of twentieth century courts:[58] A privity requirement for recovery against manufacturers of defective products has been abandoned;[59] charitable,[60] intra-family,[61] and governmental[62] immunities have been eliminated in whole or in part; a rule imposing no duty to avoid prenatal injuries has been renounced;[63] an impact requirement to recover for negligently inflicted mental injury has been repudiated;[64] rigid classification of trespassers and licensees to reduce or eliminate the duty owed by land occupiers has been rejected;[65] the doctrine of contributory negligence has been replaced with comparative negligence rules.[66] The goal of compensation also has been strengthened by the courts' acceptance of loss distribution principles.[67] In some areas,

---

56. Id. at 409. Even Wexler, the father of therapeutic jurisprudence, admits that therapeutic considerations should not trump other, more important, normative values. See, e.g., David B. Wexler, Therapeutic Jurisprudence and the Criminal Courts, 35 Wm. & Mary L. Rev. 279, 280 (1993); David B. Wexler, Justice, Mental Health, and Therapeutic Jurisprudence, 40 Clev. St. L. Rev. 517, 518 (1992). Therapeutic jurisprudence would restructure the law to better accomplish therapeutic goals only if, in a given context, other things (i.e., normative values) were equal. Therapeutic jurisprudence does not resolve the question of whether those other things are equal. Wexler, Therapeutic Jurisprudence and the Criminal Courts, supra at 280; Wexler & Winick , supra note 45, at xi–xii.

57. Shuman, supra note 43, at 410.

58. Edmund Ursin, Judicial Creativity and Tort Law, 49 Geo. Wash. L. Rev. 229, 301 (1981).

59. See, e.g., MacPherson v. Buick Motor Co., 111 N.E. 1050, 1053 (N.Y. 1916).

60. See, e.g., President of Georgetown College v. Hughes, 130 F.2d 810, 825 (D.C. Cir. 1942).

61. See, e.g., Brown v. Brown, 89 A. 889, 891 (Conn. 1914) (abrogating intraspousal immunity); Goller v. White, 122 N.W.2d 193, 198 (Wis. 1963) (abrogating parent-child immunity).

62. See, e.g., Stone v. Arizona Highway Comm'n, 381 P.2d 107, 109 (Ariz. 1963) (abrogating the immunity of the state government); Hargrove v. Town of Cocoa Beach, 96 So. 2d 130, 133 (Fla. 1957) (abrogating the immunity of municipal corporations).

63. See, e.g., Bonbrest v. Kotz, 65 F. Supp. 138, 142 (D.D.C. 1946) (recovery allowed to viable fetus who was born alive); Turpin v. Sortini, 643 P.2d 954, 966 (Cal. 1982) ("wrongful life" recovery permitted for the cost of extraordinary medical expenses incurred due to infant plaintiff's handicaps); Verkennes v. Corniea, 38 N.W.2d 838, 841 (Minn. 1949) (upheld claim for wrongful death of viable fetus).

64. See, e.g., Battalla v. State, 176 N.E.2d 729, 730 (N.Y. 1961).

65. See, e.g., Rowland v. Christian, 443 P.2d 561, 568 (Cal. 1968).

66. See, e.g., Hoffman v. Jones, 280 So. 2d 431, 438 (Fla. 1973); Li v. Yellow Cab Co., 532 P.2d 1226, 1232 (Cal. 1975).

67. See Ursin, supra note 58, at 301–03.

notably employee injuries,[68] minor automobile accidents,[69] and defective products,[70] fault-based liability has been supplanted by liability without fault, thus enabling injured plaintiffs to obtain compensation without even proving that defendants were blameworthy wrongdoers in need of deterrence.[71]

In determining whether a defendant's negligence should be measured by an objective or a subjective test, the compensation goal cannot be ignored. If a subjective standard of care is employed for persons with mental and emotional problems who are undergoing treatment, then injured innocent victims will be forced to absorb the costs of injuries produced by the increased risk of substandard behavior posed by those defendants. Such a result is antithetical to the compensation objective and to the twentieth century tort law developments that support this objective.[72]

Shuman concedes that his proposal, while encouraging treatment, denies compensation to innocent plaintiffs. He notes, however, that compensation is "a relativist rather than an absolute concern of tort law."[73] Fault-based tort law does not award compensation to an injured plaintiff unless the defendant has been found blameworthy. Thus, when a plaintiff is injured by a physically incapacitated defendant whose conduct is measured by a subjective standard

---

68. N.Y. Work. Comp. Law §§ 1 to 49-hh (McKinney 1993). In 1910, New York was the first state to enact a Workers' Compensation Law. 1910 N.Y. Laws 674 (designated as Article 14-A of the N.Y. Labor Law of 1909). One year later, the statute was declared unconstitutional. Ives v. South Buffalo Ry., 94 N.E. 431, 448 (N.Y. 1911). The New York legislature amended the state constitution to provide for a system of workers' compensation, N.Y. Const. art. 1, § 18, and reenacted the Workers' Compensation Law in 1914. 1914 N.Y. Laws ch. 41. The reenacted law was held constitutional. Jensen v. Southern Pac. Co., 109 N.E. 600, 604 (N.Y. 1915). See also Wis. Stat. Ann. §§ 102.01–.89 (West Supp. 1993). Wisconsin was the second state to enact a Workers' Compensation Law. In 1911, the law, as originally enacted, was held constitutional. Borgnis v. Falk Co., 133 N.W. 209, 222 (Wis. 1911).

69. Mass. Gen. Laws Ann. ch. 90, § 34M (West Supp. 1993). Massachusetts' no fault automobile statute, the nation's first, was held constitutional in Pinnick v. Cleary, 271 N.E.2d 592, 611 (Mass. 1971).

70. Greenman v. Yuba Power Products, Inc., 377 P.2d 897, 901 (Cal. 1963). Strict liability for manufacturing defects seems firmly established. However, definitional difficulties have been encountered in design defect and product warning cases. For those cases, recent proposals seek restoration of negligence as the basis of liability. See, e.g., American Law Institute, 2 Reporters' Study on Enterprise Liability for Personal Injury 16, 39, 81–82 (1991).

71. It should be noted, however, that tort liability accounts for only a small portion of the compensation received for injuries. A recent RAND study found that liability compensation is attempted for only one injury in ten. Deborah R. Hensler et al., Compensation For Accidental Injuries in the United States 110 (1991).

72. See, e.g., Goff v. Taylor, 708 S.W.2d 113, 115 (Ky. Ct. App. 1986):
That the subjective standard would afford fairer treatment of a defendant afflicted with a mental disability cannot be disputed. The question the commentators do not attempt to reach is the fairness to the victim of the wrongful conduct. Is a victim any less entitled to compensation for his loss because of the mental deficiencies of his tortfeasor? We believe the answer is no and the tort law as it stands has long served to accommodate that principle.

73. Shuman, supra note 43, at 431.

that includes this incapacitation, the injured plaintiff may receive no compensation.[74]

Shuman's analogy is not convincing. Admittedly, a subjective standard is used to measure the conduct of a person who is blind, deaf, or otherwise seriously physically challenged.[75] To the extent possible, the law requires physically challenged individuals to undertake appropriate precautions in order to reduce the increased risk from their disability. For example, a blind person venturing out on the city streets may be expected to use a white cane or a seeing-eye dog. Nevertheless, even with this precaution, the blind person is simply unable to achieve the level of safety of a person with sight. Because the condition of blindness can be proven easily and because we are all aware of the effect of that condition on the person's ability to anticipate harm, society is willing to tolerate the increased risk by holding the blind person to the standard of the reasonable blind person.[76]

Although the subjective standard is applied both to physically challenged plaintiffs and defendants, in most cases involving physically challenged persons, the plaintiff was the physically challenged litigant.[77] The subjective standard may have been accepted originally by courts eager to avoid the harsh contributory negligence doctrine and accord physically challenged plaintiffs an opportunity for recovery.[78]

Typically, however, the standard of care is not subjectified for a person who has a physical illness.[79] If, for example, I am suffering from influenza and drive

---

74. Id.

75. Restatement (Second) of Torts § 283C (1965).

76. The Restatement commentary suggests that a subjective standard is used for physical disability but not for mental disability because of "the greater public familiarity with the former, and the comparative ease and certainty with which it can be proved." Id. cmt. b.

77. Fleming James, Jr., The Qualities of the Reasonable Man in Negligence Cases, 16 Mo. L. Rev. 1, 21 (1951). Similarly, in most cases using a relaxed standard of care for children, the plaintiff was the child. Id. at 24.

78. Some writers have urged adoption of an explicit double standard: Physically challenged people and children should be judged by the objective test when they are defendants and by the subjective test when they are plaintiffs. Using a relaxed standard for plaintiffs would enable them to avoid being found contributorily negligent and increase their opportunity to obtain full compensation for their injuries. Fleming James, Jr. & John J. Dickinson, Accident Proneness and Accident Law, 63 Harv. L. Rev. 769, 786–89 (1950). Courts, however, did not adopt the double standard proposal even in jurisdictions that applied the doctrine of contributory negligence. See, e.g., Faith v. Massengill, 121 S.E.2d 657, 660 (Ga. Ct. App. 1961) (expressly applying the same standard to determine a child's negligence and contributory negligence); John S. Irvin, Note, Torts—Negligence—The Standard of Care for Children: A Possible Negligence-Contributory Negligence Double Standard, 38 Or. L. Rev. 268, 275 (1959) (asserting that the double standard proposal has not been supported by case law). With the widespread adoption of comparative negligence, the proposal is even less supportable. Contributorily negligent plaintiffs are able to recover for that portion of their injuries attributable to the defendants' negligence.

79. Although the language of § 283C applies a subjective standard of care to physical illness as well as to physical disability, every case cited as authority for the physical illness category involved heart attack, stroke, epileptic seizure, fainting spell or other loss of con-

my car, I am not held to the standard of the reasonable person with influenza. Even if I obtain treatment for my condition, for example, I ingest a medicine that causes drowsiness, and I fall asleep while driving, I am still held to the objective standard of the reasonable, prudent driver. Shuman's target population, which includes the walking wounded as well as those suffering from major mental illness, is more analogous to the physically ill for whom an objective standard is used, rather than the physically challenged for whom a subjective standard is used.[80]

Additionally, mentally disordered persons are far more likely to be involved in tort litigation as defendants than are physically challenged persons. For example, two-thirds of all tort claims for nonfatal personal injuries involve motor vehicle accidents.[81] Blind people do not drive automobiles,[82] but people with mental or emotional problems often do. Innocent plaintiffs who have been subjected to an unreasonable risk of harm from the activities of mentally disordered defendants have a legitimate claim for compensation.

C. The Proposal's Deterrent Effect Is Unproven and Unnecessary

Tort law assumes that people are aware of potential tort sanctions and alter their behavior to avoid them.[83] Shuman admits, however, that tort law's ability to deter unsafe conduct is problematic.[84] Reporting on extensive research,[85] Shuman recently concluded that none of the mainstream psychiatric and psy-

---

sciousness that was sudden, unforeseeable, and totally incapacitating. Restatement (Second) of Torts § 283C app. (1966). See, e.g., Moore v. Capital Transit Co., 226 F.2d 57 (D.C. Cir. 1955) (convulsive seizure), cert. denied, 350 U.S. 966 (1956); Moore v. Presnell, 379 A.2d 1246 (Md. Ct. Spec. App. 1977) (sudden, unforeseeable loss of consciousness); Weldon Tool Co. v. Kelley, 76 N.E.2d 629 (Ohio Ct. App. 1947) (sudden heart pains); Keller v. Wonn, 87 S.E.2d 453 (W. Va. 1955) (massive cerebral hemorrhage). Arguably, these examples could be classified as unavoidable accidents.

80. After carefully analyzing the analogies of physically disabled persons and children to mentally disordered persons, one writer concluded: "[N]either of the analogies is so perfect that it is self-evident that manifest injustice is done when courts refuse to apply a subjective standard to mentally handicapped adults." Ellis, supra note 8, at 1106.

81. Hensler , supra note 71, at 110.

82. Partially sighted and other physically challenged individuals may drive automobiles and engage in other activities that subject them to tort liability. Typically, however, the extent and permanence of their disability is known before they engage in the activity, and society may obligate them to undertake precautionary measures to minimize the increased risk. Requiring a physically challenged person to obtain a driver's license assures that with precautions in place, the person is capable of meeting minimally acceptable standards of driving. Children who drive automobiles or who engage in other adult activities are held to the objective standard of the reasonable adult. Restatement (Second) of Torts § 283A cmt. c (1965).

83. Shuman, supra note 43, at 411.

84. Id. at 410.

85. Daniel W. Shuman, The Psychology of Deterrence in Tort Law, 42 Kan. L. Rev. 115, 140–64 (1993).

chological theories of human behavior[86] supports the deterrence theory of tort law.[87] Indeed, the claim of tort law's deterrent effect rests on society's intuitive belief that a person's behavior is influenced by potential tort liability.[88] Without empirical verification of the deterrence claim, however, courts should be reluctant to adopt a proposal that sacrifices the compensation objective.

Shuman asserts that if tort law does operate as an incentive for appropriate behavior, people with mental or emotional problems will not be encouraged to seek treatment if an objective standard of care is applied to them regardless of whether they initiate treatment prior to the injury-producing conduct.[89] Shuman favors the promise of a subjective standard as a necessary inducement for treatment. He presents an example of a defendant who initiates treatment, complies fully with the prescribed treatment regime but who experiences reduced concentration or responsiveness while driving because he or she is preoccupied with problems raised during psychotherapy.[90] In judging that person's tort liability, Shuman rejects use of an objective standard that gives the defendant no extra credit for a responsible decision to seek treatment.[91] From Shuman's perspective, a subjective standard should be used because successful treatment will ultimately reduce the risk of injury from defendants who have sought treatment.

Tort law, however, acts much more directly. If deterrence works, it works by imposing tort liability on defendants who engage in unsafe behavior. As applied to Shuman's driving example, the conduct that society wishes to encourage is safe driving, not treatment of a mental or emotional problem that may result in safe driving in the uncertain future. If people are rational enough to seek treatment for their mental problems prior to engaging in dangerous activities, they should be rational enough not to engage in those activities if the treatment they receive exposes potential plaintiffs to unreasonable risks of harm through reduced concentration or responsiveness.

The subjective standard inducement may not even achieve the treatment goal. Just as most people do not calculate their potential tort liability before they act, most people with mental and emotional problems will not choose to obtain treatment relying on the knowledge that they will only be held to a subjective standard if they injure another person while undergoing treatment. People just don't act that way. They will seek treatment if they believe it will benefit them by reducing some disturbing symptoms such as depression or anxiety.

---

86. Shuman grouped the mainstream theories into organic, biological, psychodynamic, behavioral, and cognitive schools. Id. at 140.

87. Id. at 167. Shuman noted that the deterrence goal of tort law could be achieved if the tort system were modified using the social learning theory model of human behavior. The modification would require that more meritorious claims of tortious behavior be brought to increase the likelihood that inappropriate behavior is perceived to be punished. Because of society's desire to reduce, not increase, civil litigation, Shuman opined that an attempt to conform the tort system to social learning theory is not likely to succeed. Id. at 165.

88. Shuman, supra note 43, at 411.

89. Id. at 424.

90. Id. at 420.

91. Id.

That is why people seek treatment, not because of a promise of a relaxed standard of care that may reduce their tort liability.

D. The Proposal's Consequences Are Potentially Antitherapeutic

People who believe they are free and responsible for their actions behave differently from people who believe that they lack choice and responsibility.[92] According to attribution theory, people are less likely to strive for success when they attribute success or failure to outside forces that they are powerless to control.[93] If people are able to avoid tort liability by "blaming" their mental or emotional problems for their substandard conduct, they will behave less responsibly.[94] Thus, by requiring them to conform to the objective standard of conduct applicable to others, the law compels responsible behavior and refuses to reinforce feelings of learned helplessness.[95] In this way, the objective standard is therapeutically beneficial.

Shuman, however, rejects this argument for those individuals who have initiated treatment for their mental or emotional condition. He notes that a person's willingness to undergo treatment "is not merely a necessary but also a sufficient condition of efficacious treatment."[96] For this reason, Shuman asserts that a refusal to factor treatment efforts into the standard of care cannot be justified.[97]

Shuman's reasoning is not persuasive. Admittedly, no magic pill exists for the quick and effective treatment of mental problems. Treatment that may reduce the risk of injury in the long term may not reduce it, and may even increase it, in the short term. But precisely because treatment is not immediately effective, a person with a mental or emotional problem should weigh the risks of engaging in dangerous activities while undergoing the treatment process. Using a subjective standard of care to enable a mentally disturbed defendant to avoid tort liability reinforces the message that a decision to seek treatment is all that society requires of the individual. In essence, reliance on the uncertainties of the treatment process replaces reliance on the mental or emotional condition itself as an excuse for irresponsible behavior. Helplessness is learned, but from a new source.

Additionally, one can question Shuman's assumption that effective treatment pursued to its logical conclusion will ultimately reduce the risk of injury. Some forms of effective treatment have antitherapeutic consequences that in-

---

92. John Monahan, Abolish the Insanity Defense?—Not Yet, 26 Rutgers L. Rev. 719, 721–23 (1973) (discussing empirical research on human behavior).

93. Harold H. Kelley & John L. Michela, Attribution Theory and Research, 31 Ann. Rev. Psychol. 457, 480–89 (1980) (discussing consequences of attributions).

94. Similarly, by failing to assign personal responsibility for criminal conduct, successful insanity defenses may hinder treatment of insanity acquittees. To the extent acquittees believe their crimes were caused by their illnesses, they will be less inclined to undergo a treatment process designed to change their thoughts and actions. Robert A. Fein, How the Insanity Acquittal Retards Treatment, 8 Law & Hum. Behav. 283, 291 (1984).

95. Shuman, supra note 43, at 421.

96. Id.

97. Id.

crease the potential for danger even while reducing or eliminating the patient's symptoms. For example, psychotropic medications are the treatment of choice for schizophrenic and affective disorders.[98] Many patients receive long-term treatment with these medications and experience impaired memory, reasoning ability, and learning capacity on a continuing basis.[99] Before rushing to embrace a state of therapeutic grace, these deleterious consequences must be fully considered—both by individuals in deciding whether to accept treatment, and by society in deciding whether to encourage treatment.

Use of a subjective standard has other antitherapeutic consequences for people with mental or emotional problems. By refusing to hold them accountable as ordinary persons, society denies their status as full-fledged human beings.[100] Their immunity from tort liability compels others to shun them, increasing their isolation.[101] Pressure to institutionalize them, or reinstitutionalize them, is inevitable.[102] In contrast, an objective standard is consistent with current mental health treatment policy that encourages voluntary treatment efforts in the community setting.[103]

Tort law attempts to strike a balance between a plaintiff's claim to protection against injury and a defendant's claim to freedom of action.[104] Thus, in considering whether a subjective standard is therapeutic or antitherapeutic, its effects on the plaintiff must be considered as well as its effects on the defendant. Specifically, does a court judgment imposing tort liability on the defendant have a beneficial restorative effect on the plaintiff? In a recent article, Shuman examined behavioral research on this issue and concluded that it

---

98. Id. at 423.

99. Bruce J. Winick, The Right to Refuse Psychotropic Medication: Current State of the Law and Beyond, in The Right to Refuse Antipsychotic Medication 7, 11 (David Rapoport & John Parry, eds., 1986).

The temporary and permanent adverse affects of medication have been proven in numerous studies and attested to by courts and commentators. See, e.g., Rogers v. Okin, 478 F. Supp. 1342, 1359–60 (D. Mass. 1979), aff'd in part, rev'd in part, 634 F.2d 650 (1st Cir. 1980), vacated sub nom. Mills v. Rogers, 457 U.S. 291 (1982); Rennie v. Klein, 462 F. Supp. 1131, 1137–38 (D.N.J. 1978); Riese v. St. Mary's Hosp., 271 Cal. Rptr. 199, 203–04 (Cal. Ct. App. 1987); Dennis E. Cichon, The Right to "Just Say No": A History and Analysis of the Right to Refuse Antipsychotic Drugs, 53 La. L. Rev. 283, 297–310 (1992) (discussing research on side effects).

100. Alexander & Szasz, supra note 9, at 35; Splane, supra note 9, at 167.

101. Alexander & Szasz, supra note 9, at 36.

102. Id. at 38. "If a person deemed civilly irresponsible is at large, surely he cannot be allowed to continue to commit torts without compensating his victims. A person enjoying the liberties of a sane citizen, but licensed at law to commit tortious acts with impunity, is unthinkable." Id.

The antitherapeutic effects of institutionalization include stigma, dependency, isolation, and degeneration. See Splane, supra note 9, at 161–62, for discussion and sources.

103. Splane, supra note 9, at 160–69. "The objective standard helps minimize the burden on the community from deinstitutionalization, helps foster community acceptance of the mentally ill, and encourages the mentally ill to become self-sufficient, responsible members of the community." Id. at 163–64.

104. Keeton , supra note 5, at 6.

did.[105] In fact, victims are most satisfied when they receive compensation from the person who injured them rather than from a third party.[106] Shuman opined that "the psychological primacy of compensation may not be adequately addressed by sterile payments to an injured person from a third party lacking responsibility for causing the harm to the plaintiff."[107] Obviously, tort law's potential restorative effect is completely lost if, in a fault-based system, a mentally disturbed defendant is absolved from all responsibility. The injured plaintiff recovers from no one.

E. The Proposal Is Overinclusive

If Shuman's subjective standard proposal were limited exclusively to those who suffer from major mental illnesses, the proposal would differ little from earlier proposals.[108] However, because any person's concentration and responsiveness may be profoundly impacted by the death of a loved one, the loss of a job, the experience of obtaining a legal education,[109] or other transient situational stress, Shuman expands the subjective standard shield to include the walking wounded as well.[110]

Such expansion is clearly unwarranted. Shuman cites research finding that 14% of the population, that is, thirty-five million Americans, suffer from a mental disorder.[111] More recent research, based on structured psychiatric interviews with 8,098 men and women who were selected to be representative of the entire population, revealed that 48% had experienced a mental disorder during their lifetimes, and that 29.5% had experienced a mental disorder within the twelve months preceding the interview.[112] Extrapolating these percentages to the entire population suggests that 120 million Americans experience a mental disorder during their lifetimes and that seventy-five million experience a mental disorder within any twelve-month period. Obviously, a

---

105. Daniel W. Shuman, The Psychology of Compensation in Tort Law 62 (January 10, 1994) (unpublished manuscript, on file with the author).

106. Andre deCarufel, Victims' Satisfaction with Compensation: Effects of Initial Disadvantage and Third Party Intervention, 11 J. Applied Soc. Psychol. 445, 452 (1981).

107. Shuman, supra note 105, at 22.

108. See supra notes 40–41 and accompanying text.

109. Shuman, supra note 43, at 417 (discussing reports that 32% of students were depressed by the end of their first year of law school and that 40% were depressed by the third year).

110. Id. at 414–15.

111. Id. at 413 (discussing Laura A. Cushman et al., Psychiatric Disorders and Motor Vehicle Accidents, 67 Psychol. Rep. 483, 486–87 (1990)).

112. Ronald C. Kessler et al., Lifetime and 12-Month Prevalence of DSM-III-R Psychiatric Disorders in the United States: Results from the National Comorbidity Survey, 51 Arch. Gen. Psychiatry 8, 12 (1994). Data was gathered on the prevalence of 14 DSM-III-R psychiatric disorders. The most common were major depressive episode (17.1% lifetime, 10.3% within last 12 months), alcohol dependence (14.1% lifetime, 7.2% within last 12 months), social phobias (13.3% lifetime, 7.9% within last 12 months), and simple phobias (11.3% lifetime, 8.8% within last 12 months). Id. Of those persons with a history of at least one mental disorder, 56% had two or more. Id. at 17.

proposal that may extend the subjective standard to persons experiencing a mental disorder, or even more broadly to persons under stress, has enormous implications for the determination of tort liability.

In the landmark case of *Vaughan v. Menlove*,[113] the court weighed the merits of the objective and subjective standards. Chief Justice Tindal explained that the subjective standard was rejected because liability determined by the good faith judgment of the defendant "would be as variable as the length of the foot of each individual."[114] In fact, because most defendants do make good faith judgments, one commentator even suggested that a subjective standard "would tend to produce nearly universal immunity from liability."[115] In contrast, by requiring the individual to conform to the objective, reasonable person standard, a community level of safety can be uniformly maintained.[116]

As previously discussed, the less demanding subjective standard has supplanted the objective standard for physically challenged individuals and children. The law recognizes that they are incapable of conforming to the objective standard and thus are not at fault when they fail to do so.[117] Can a similar dispensation be claimed by persons with mental or emotional problems? An affirmative response can only be given if their otherwise tortious behavior was caused by the mental condition and not by free choice.[118]

A finding that a defendant is mentally disordered does not, in and of itself, justify a further finding that the defendant's behavior was uncontrollably caused by the mental disorder, or even that the behavior was related to the mental disorder.[119] After reviewing clinical observations of mentally disordered people, empirical research comparing mentally disordered and nonmentally disordered people, and empirical research bearing directly on the rationality and normality of mentally disordered people,[120] Morse concluded that the behavioral differences between mentally disordered and nonmentally disordered people are less pronounced than is usually supposed.[121] In fact, considerable evidence suggests that mentally disordered people "are capable of behaving

---

113. 132 Eng. Rep. 490 (C.P. 1837).

114. Id. at 493. Determining liability by considering whether the defendant acted honestly and to the best of his or her own judgment "would leave so vague a line as to afford no rule at all, the degree of judgment belonging to each individual being infinitely various." Id.

115. Seidelson, supra note 8, at 19.

116. Restatement (Second) of Torts § 283 cmt. c (1965).

117. See supra notes 33–34, 75–82 and accompanying text.

118. Seidelson asserted that a subjective standard is warranted only when a litigant's "subjective characteristic makes it uniquely difficult for the litigant to comply with the reasonable person standard, and if judicial cognizance of that characteristic does not frustrate the other litigant's reasonable expectations." Seidelson, supra note 8, at 20.

119. Stephen J. Morse, Crazy Behavior, Morals, and Science: An Analysis of Mental Health Law, 51 S. Cal. L. Rev. 527, 581 (1978) [hereinafter Morse I]; see also Stephen J. Morse, Treating Crazy People Less Specially, 90 W. Va. L. Rev. 353, 353 (1987) [hereinafter Morse II] "[S]pecial legal treatment results from the assumption that crazy people are not responsible for their behavior, an assumption buttressed by the mistaken and usually unanalyzed notion that mental disorder per se deprives people of responsibility." Id.

120. Morse II, supra note 119, at 362.

121. Id. at 366.

normally and rationally."[122] Especially relevant are studies of the behavior of mentally disordered people in real world contexts, such as driving cars, holding jobs, or managing finances. Mentally disordered people were found to be better able to perform these tasks than is usually assumed, "and their behavior is often indistinguishable from the behavior of normal people."[123] Morse found that, at most, mental disorder slightly predisposes a person to socially unacceptable behavior, but that such behavior is rarely, if ever, irresistible.[124]

In his article, Shuman acknowledges the questionable linkage between mental disorder and conduct that produces accidental injury.[125] Despite this acknowledgement, Shuman does not restrict his subjective test proposal to that small group whose mental disorders render them incapable of controlling their injurious conduct. Incredibly, Shuman concludes that to maximize the therapeutic potential of tort law, the subjective standard should be extended to the walking wounded.[126] Although Shuman correctly observes that stress may affect our concentration and responsiveness, he does not prove that people under stress are incapable of adhering to the objective standard of the reasonable person. Although we may wish to encourage people under stress to obtain treatment, absent such proof we should be unwilling to reward them for getting treatment by using a subjective standard of care to measure their tort liability.

To narrow the target population qualifying for the subjective standard, Shuman imposes treatment obligations. As formulated, however, those obligations generate more questions than answers. For example, Shuman would limit the subjective standard to those defendants who initiated treatment prior to their injury-producing conduct.[127] One may question whether this treatment requirement effectively narrows the target population. The recent massive study

---

122. Morse I, supra note 119, at 576. Morse concluded: "Most people with mental disorders, even severe ones, are not different enough from normal persons to warrant special treatment, and there is little scientific reason to believe that they cannot control themselves." Id. at 653.

123. Morse II, supra note 119, at 369.

124. Morse I, supra note 119, at 571. Some recent research suggests that mental disorder may be related to violent behavior. The increased risk of violence, however, was found only among those mentally disordered persons who were currently experiencing psychotic symptoms. Bruce G. Link et al., The Violent and Illegal Behavior of Mental Patients Reconsidered, 57 Am. Soc. Rev. 275 (1992); Jeffrey W. Swanson et al., Violence and Psychiatric Disorder in the Community: Evidence from the Epidemiologic Catchment Area Surveys, 41 Hosp. & Community Psychiatry 761, 761 (1990). The elevated risk of violence for actively psychotic individuals has been characterized as "modest" and makes only a "trivial contribution" to the total violence in our society. Link, supra, at 290.

125. Shuman, supra note 43, at 413. In another article, Shuman noted that the relationship between the organic abnormality of epilepsy and automobile accidents is not as direct as might be thought. Although drivers with epilepsy have an increased risk of automobile accidents, studies show that only 11% of the accidents in which they are involved are attributable to seizures. The major cause of automobile accidents both for epileptics and the general population is driver error. Shuman, supra note 85, at 142 (discussing Allan Krumholz et al., Driving and Epilepsy: A Review and Reappraisal, 265 JAMA 622, 622 (1991)).

126. Shuman, supra note 43, at 414.

127. Id. at 426.

on the prevalence of mental disorder revealed that professional treatment was obtained by 42% of those who experienced a mental disorder during their lifetimes and 20.9% of those who experienced a mental disorder within the preceding twelve months.[128] Extrapolating these percentages to the entire population suggests that fifty million people would meet the treatment requirement during their lifetimes and fifteen million would do so within a twelve-month period. These large numbers reflecting the prevalence of treatment exist without any subjective tort standard inducement. How much larger will these numbers become if Shuman's proposal is adopted and achieves its therapeutic objective?

Additionally, would the initiation-of-treatment requirement be used inappropriately to exclude mentally disordered people who have been released from involuntary hospitalization on condition that they continue to take postconfinement medications? Should they be denied a subjective test because they did not volunteer for treatment originally? Perhaps compliance with the treatment regimen should be sufficient without an initiation-of-treatment requirement.

For the subjective standard to be applicable, Shuman requires full compliance with the treatment regime.[129] If a patient sometimes forgets to take his or her medication, as we all do on occasion, or if a patient infrequently cancels an appointment with a therapist, is he or she forever branded with an objective standard? If not, then how do we measure the requirement of full compliance? In answering that question, must we consider the significance of that missed medication or canceled appointment on the subsequent accident-producing behavior or is noncompliance with treatment determinative without reference to its causative effect?

Shuman also wrestles with the problem of treatment unavailability.[130] Apparently, he would extend the subjective standard to indigent people who made a good faith effort to obtain treatment that is financially unavailable. He admits, however, that difficulty is likely to be encountered in documenting efforts to obtain treatment and to assess financial incapacity.[131] Should the subjective standard be extended to people living in rural areas for whom treatment is unavailable? How much inconvenience must one endure in making a good faith effort to obtain treatment? Most importantly, what if treatment is unavailable because the person's mental disorder is untreatable? Should that person be excluded because we can not use the tort law incentive to encourage that person to obtain treatment that is nonexistent? If so, how can we justify a distinction between the untreatable and the indigent or the rural dweller?

Finally, Shuman limits use of the subjective standard to situations in which the defendant, prior to the injury-producing conduct, initiated a treatment that has "been proven effective through rigorous scientific studies."[132] Although Shuman's purpose is to eliminate fringe treatments from consideration, he provides no definition of efficacious treatment. In fact, earlier in his article, Shu-

---

128. Kessler, supra note 112, at 14.
129. Shuman, supra note 43, at 426.
130. Id. at 427.
131. Id.
132. Id.

man notes that although psychotherapy is considered to be effective for the treatment of nonpsychotic depression and moderate anxieties, no consensus exists about psychotherapy's efficacy for other mental or emotional problems.[133] Would he exclude even this mainstream psychiatric treatment unless the initiating patient suffered from depression or anxiety?

To prevent unwarranted use of the subjective standard by people with no mental problems, Shuman requires an evaluation by a mental health professional.[134] But such an evaluation is not likely to be an effective barrier. Mental health professionals are trained to make diagnoses. If a person initiates treatment, complaining of sleeplessness, anxiety, depression, or any other symptom, some diagnosis is likely to be made and some treatment prescribed. The diagnosis of unspecified mental disorder (nonpsychotic) is made when enough information has been provided to rule out a psychotic disorder but not enough information is available to make another diagnosis.[135]

In deciding what constitutes an effective treatment, should one consider the qualifications of the therapist? Should distinctions be drawn between various mental health professionals—for example, should therapy by social workers or marriage, family, and child counsellors serve to reduce the standard of care? Should a distinction be drawn between all mental health professionals and priests or other lay-counsellors? For example, if a person suffered depression because of the untimely death of a loved one, should that individual be denied the subjective standard for choosing to interact with a lay-support group rather than a psychologist? Should someone with a significant drinking problem be denied the subjective standard for regularly attending meetings of Alcoholics Anonymous instead of seeing a psychiatrist? What if a psychiatrist or psychologist recommended these lay-support groups at an initial diagnostic session? Have these treatments been proven effective through rigorous scientific studies?

The argument for a subjective standard is weakened by a requirement that treatment effectiveness be proven. If a particular treatment has undergone rigorous scientific studies, then in addition to knowing whether that treatment is effective, we should also know the limitations of and the dangers inherent in that treatment. For example, before prescribing psychotropic medication, the psychiatrist considers not only its potential effectiveness, but its potential side effects such as drowsiness or decreased cognitive function. If the psychiatrist knows that the patient will drive an automobile and then prescribes the medication without informing the patient of these risks, the psychiatrist can be held liable for injuries caused by these side effects. If the psychiatrist informs the patient of these potentially dangerous side effects and the patient with such knowledge decides to drive the automobile anyway, the patient should be held liable for injuries that are produced by the side effects. The patient's duty to exercise reasonable care should not be diminished.

---

133. Id. at 422.
134. Id. at 429.
135. American Psychiatric Ass'n , supra note 2, at 687.

III. Toward a Reasonable Solution

Shuman's attempt to encourage mental health treatment is likely to be endorsed by mental health professionals. After all, it offers them full employment. Almost everyone would benefit from treatment for the stress of everyday living. If a person seeks treatment, under Shuman's proposal he or she is eligible for the subjective standard of care.[136] The proposal is far too expansive to be acceptable. Other, more narrowly crafted, proposals that apply the subjective standard to people with diagnosable mental disorders should also be rejected.[137] Injurious behavior has not been proven to be uncontrollably caused by mental disorder.[138]

But should an objective test be used in each and every case? I think not.

In *The Common Law*, Holmes defended the objective, reasonable person standard.[139] In an often-quoted passage,[140] Holmes asserted that by sacrificing consideration of individual peculiarities and minute differences of character,[141] the objective standard assures that innocent plaintiffs will be protected against a socially unacceptable level of risky behavior. Holmes cautioned, however, that use of the objective standard assumes that potential defendants possess ordinary capacity to avoid harm. Thus, "[w]hen a man has a distinct defect of such a nature that all can recognize it as making certain precautions impossible, he will not be held answerable for not taking them."[142] As examples, Holmes mentioned physically challenged individuals and children. Holmes then noted:

> Insanity is a more difficult matter to deal with, and no general rule can be laid down about it. There is no doubt that in many cases a man may be insane, and yet perfectly capable of taking the precautions, and of being influenced by the motives, which the circumstances demand. But if insanity of a pronounced type exists, manifestly incapacitating the sufferer from complying with the rule which he has broken, good sense would require it to be admitted as an excuse.[143]

With increased understanding of mental disorder, Holmes's solution may be even more appropriate today than when he first suggested it over a hundred years ago. Even Morse, who asserted that mentally disordered people generally are capable of behaving rationally,[144] acknowledged that "[t]he law should interfere and nullify the usual legal significance of a person's actions...if it is satisfied that the individual was incapable, for whatever reason, of meeting the

---

136. See supra notes 108–31 and accompanying text.

137. See Curran, supra note 8, at 74 (discussing whether a subjective test should apply to people with personality disorders).

138. See supra notes 119–24 and accompanying text.

139. Holmes , supra note 1, at 108–09.

140. Keeton , supra note 5, at 176. Shuman quotes Holmes's statement in full. Shuman, supra note 43, at 418.

141. Holmes , supra note 1, at 108.

142. Id. at 109.

143. Id.

144. See supra notes 119–24 and accompanying text.

functional criteria for competence and full legal responsibility."[145] As an example of incapacity, Morse cited a chronically disabled, hallucinating, delusional person wandering the streets in rags and speaking gibberish.[146] Tort cases involving such people occur infrequently, but when they do occur, they should be handled appropriately.

In 1970, the Wisconsin Supreme Court refused to apply the objective standard to every case involving a severely mentally disordered defendant. In *Breunig v. American Family Ins. Co.*,[147] the court held that if a defendant is suddenly overcome without forewarning by a mental disorder that prevents conformance to the reasonable person standard, the defendant will be absolved from liability as if he or she had suffered a sudden incapacitating physical injury such as an unexpected heart attack, epileptic seizure, stroke, or fainting spell.[148] In essence, the defendant is relieved from liability because the sudden, incapacitating mental disorder is treated as an unavoidable accident.

The *Breunig* court's willingness to absolve incapacitated mentally disordered defendants from tort liability is commendable. However, the court's attempt to distinguish sudden mental disorder from other mental disorder has been strongly criticized.[149] Although sudden incapacitation seems an appropriate requirement for cases involving physical disabilities, it is inappropriate for cases involving mental disabilities. Severely mentally disordered individuals may be unable to control their behavior even though their disorder was not of sudden onset. In such cases, fault cannot be found. To paraphrase Holmes, if severe mental disorder has manifestly incapacitated a defendant from complying with the reasonable person standard, the injury was produced by an unavoidable accident, and the defendant should be absolved from responsibility.

Acceptance of Holmes's modest proposal will have little immediate impact on tort liability of mentally disordered persons. Most will continue to be judged by the objective reasonable person standard. But in those few cases in which the disorder manifestly incapacitates the defendant from complying with that standard, liability for negligence will not be imposed.[150] Attempts to broaden this narrow principle of nonliability should be resisted absent proof that the person's mental disorder was casually linked to the tortious behavior.

---

145. Morse I, supra note 119, at 649. See also Ellis, supra note 8, at 1089: "But among those cases in which causation is established, it is likely that the law would demand (as it does in the criminal field) that the disability involved be of sufficient magnitude or of a particular type to warrant exoneration from responsibility for torts."

146. Morse II, supra note 119, at 370.

147. 173 N.W.2d 619 (Wis. 1970).

148. Id. at 624. In *Breunig*, however, the court affirmed a finding of liability, noting that the evidence was sufficient to permit the jury to find that the driver of an automobile had sufficient warning or knowledge that hallucinations would occur and affect her driving. Id. at 625.

149. See, e.g., Ellis, supra note 8, at 1101–02.

150. For intentional tort liability to be imposed on a mentally disordered defendant, the defendant must act with an intent to bring about tortious consequences. "Intent" requires that the defendant desires the consequences or knows that the consequences are substantially certain to result from his or her act. Restatement (Second) of Torts § 8A cmt. b (1965). This requirement provides protection against liability without fault in an intentional tort context.

Chapter 22

The Psychology of Compensation in Tort Law

Daniel W. Shuman

I. Introduction

Scant attention has been paid to the consequences of compensating injured persons with tort dollars. Does the source or system of compensation, as contrasted with the sum of compensation, matter to injured persons? Do plaintiffs who receive compensation from defendants after a determination of fault experience a beneficial restorative effect unlike claimants who receive equivalent dollar compensation through a first-party insurance or no-fault statutory compensation system? Conversely, are tort plaintiffs traumatized by the tort system; does it deter or delay their restoration until the termination of the litigation? From both the vantage point of society and of injured persons, the costs and inefficiencies of tort compensation are difficult to justify unless injured persons are beneficially affected by the compensation source or system, as well as the sum of compensation. The onslaught of attacks on the tort system, claiming that both society and injured persons would be better off with first-party insurance or nofault compensation, compels an examination of the psychology of compensation in tort law.[1]

Modern tort law is rooted in the legal system's search for an alternative to the blood feud.[2] These origins are powerful evidence of a primal need of in-

---

1. See, e.g., Jeffrey O'Connell, The Injury Industry and the Remedy of No-Fault Insurance (1971) (analyzing the auto insurance industry and suggesting no-fault insurance as a remedy to its ills); Stephen D. Sugarman, Doing Away With Tort Law, 73 Cal. L. Rev. 555 (1985) (discussing the status of tort law and tort reform and proposing several schemes to address the alleged failures of the present system). For a critique of both the tort system and its detractors, see Steven D. Smith, The Critics and the "Crisis": A Reassessment of Current Conceptions of Tort Law, 72 Cornell L. Rev. 765 (1987).

The current debate about the need to control medical malpractice costs as an aspect of national health care reform provides yet another reason for scrutinizing the effect of tort law on injured persons. See The President's Health Security Plan: Draft Report 189–91 (Sept. 7, 1993), reprinted in The President's Health Security Plan (Time Books 1993) (proposing reforms for the medical malpractice system).

2. Wex S. Malone, Ruminations on the Role of Fault in the History of the Common Law of Torts, 31 La. L. Rev. 1, 1–3 (1970). Indeed, one noted commentator has suggested that at its outset the legal system "attempted nothing more affirmatively than to furnish the injured person a substitute for revenge." Roscoe Pound, The End of Law as Developed in Legal Rules and Doctrines, 27 Harv. L. Rev. 195, 199 (1914). But see Geoffrey MacCormack, Revenge and Compensation in Early Law, 21 Am. J. Comp. L. 69, 83 (1973) (arguing that nei-

jured persons to seek vindication for their injury beyond mere compensation for the monetary value of their loss. Tort law's civilizing effort evolved, along the way, into a highly individualistic common law system that made possible judgments of responsibility for harm in a social context in which the impact of liability insurance and loss spreading doctrines were minimal.[3] Although perhaps lacking the affective or temporal allure of the blood feud, the early common law tort system may well have been a viable substitute to temper this primal need. It visited both the moral and the financial responsibility for harm directly on wrongdoers.

We have, however, evolved from that highly individualistic common law tort system to a system of loss distribution in which the responsibility for compensation and the responsibility for harm are often independent. Ninety percent of compensation for accidental injuries does not involve tort claims against wrongdoers; instead it is paid by, for example, first-party insurance or government compensation programs.[4] Although the impact of insurance and government compensation is less for intentional torts, which logically should result in a greater likelihood of payment directly by injurers, the linkage between compensation and responsibility for harm is weak there as well. Perhaps because of the reduced role of insurance and government compensation programs in cases involving intentional torts, less than half of the amount awarded by juries for intentional torts is ever paid.[5]

"Even where compensation is paid under tort, it is usually paid by someone other than the person at fault, since the law has departed some way from its fault base in allowing, or rather insisting on, liability insurance and vicarious liability."[6] The remaining vestiges of individual injurer tort responsibility for payment are also under increasing attack.[7] This transformation from a system of individual responsibility for harm and compensation to a loss distribution system in which responsibility for harm and responsibility for compensation are often independent has taken place without adequate consideration of the role of the tort system as an alternative means for injured parties to satisfy their primal needs. The risk in not examining the psychology of compensation in tort law is both the failure to utilize the full restorative po-

---

ther a historical review nor an examination of modern primitive societies supports the theory of an evolution in societies from revenge to compensation).

3. For example, the action of trespass, arising in the 13th century, was a quasi-criminal proceeding and failure to pay the fine levied subjected the defendant to imprisonment. Malone, supra note 2, at 10. Tort liability insurance did not appear on the scene in the United States until 1886, and the debate over whether it was permissible to insure against liability for negligence was not generally resolved until the 20th century. Breeden v. Frankfort Marine, Accident & Plate Glass Ins. Co., 119 S.W. 576, 588–89 (Mo. 1909).

4. Deborah R. Hensler et al., Compensation for Accidental Injuries in the United States 107–08, 175 (1991).

5. Michael G. Shanley & Mark A. Peterson, Posttrial Adjustments to Jury Awards 35–36 (1987).

6. Sally M. Lloyd-Bostock, Common Sense Morality and Accident Compensation, in Psychology, Law and Legal Processes 93, 95 (David F. Farrington et al. eds., 1979).

7. See sources cited supra note 1.

tential of tort law[8] and the failure to realize the full human potential of the injured.[9]

II. The Role of Compensation in Tort Law

A. Laurel and Hardy, Peanut Butter and Jelly, and Deterrence and Compensation?

Tort law's doctrinal linkage of compensation and deterrence makes no sense from the perspective of the plaintiff's need for compensation.[10] The need to restore the plaintiff bears no apparent relationship to the need to deter the defendant; rather, the restorative goal of compensation appears to be independent of the need for deterrence.[11] Furthermore, by awarding compensation to the plaintiff only when the defendant's conduct is in need of deterrence, the fault-based tort system creates a compensation gap that dramatically limits the use of tort law as a compensation system.[12] Why maintain a compensation system that is so poorly designed to fulfill its goal of compensation?

There are both historical and contemporary explanations for the linkage of compensation and deterrence in tort law. It is curious, however, that although the amount of compensation is based on the needs of the plaintiff, the justification for linking deterrence to compensation has nothing to do with the impact of the defendant's conduct on the plaintiff. Instead, it is based on the wrongfulness of the defendant's conduct. "[T]he fault principle...attempts to answer the question: 'When should we compensate a plaintiff?' by looking exclusively at the conduct of the defendant."[13] There is nothing in either the historical or contemporary theories that takes the restorative needs of plaintiffs

---

8. The notion that tort law, or any other body of law or legal decisionmaking, may have therapeutic or antitherapeutic affects is a question placed into focus by the lens of therapeutic jurisprudence. For a discussion of the various aspects of therapeutic jurisprudence, see generally David B. Wexler & Bruce J. Winick, Essays in Therapeutic Jurisprudence (1991) and David B. Wexler, Therapeutic Jurisprudence: The Law as a Therapeutic Agent (1990). Therapeutic jurisprudence seeks to examine the law's potential as a therapeutic agent; it posits that laws have both therapeutic and antitherapeutic consequences that should be empirically examined without subordinating other normative values. Daniel W. Shuman, Making The World A Better Place Through Tort Law?: Through The Therapeutic Looking Glass, X N.Y.L. Sch. J. Hum. Rts. 739, 739–40 (1993). Tort law is a particularly fertile field for the application of therapeutic jurisprudence because "[t]ort law's agenda for both deterrence and compensation are therapeutically driven—injury avoidance and restoration of the injured." Id. at 744.

9. See Albert W. Alschuler, Mediation With A Mugger: The Shortage of Adjudicative Services and the Need for A Two-Tier Trial System in Civil Cases, 99 Harv. L. Rev. 1808, 1809–10 (1986); Robert E. Keeton, Is There A Place for Negligence in Modern Tort Law?, 53 Va. L. Rev. 886, 888 (1967).

10. See David G. Owen, Deterrence and Desert in Tort: A Comment, 73 Cal. L. Rev. 665, 665–67 (1985).

11. See id. at 674–75.

12. Id.

13. P.S. Atiyah, Accidents, Compensation and the Law 471 (3d ed. 1980).

into account as a basis for awarding compensation rather than as an element of damages. To the contrary, consideration of the restorative impact of tort sanctions on the plaintiff as the basis for awarding compensation is atheoretical under all of these approaches.

Legal historians debate pre-nineteenth century common law tort liability's concern with fault and the exclusivity of strict liability.[14] Regardless of the outcome of this debate, negligence, with its fault-based premise, has come to dominate tort law in the twentieth century.[15] Accordingly, that fault-based premise has created an imposing hurdle for tort claims.

The view that fault is the only acceptable reason for loss shifting has been justified by some contemporary tort scholars on the basis of corrective justice considerations that link tort sanctions to the wrongfulness of the defendant's conduct.[16] Corrective justice theorists posit that people are morally responsible for the damage they have caused. Because corrective justice theorists regard tort sanctions as an appropriate response to a defendant's wrongful conduct, they argue that the defendant's wrongful conduct, rather than the plaintiff's restoration, should filter tort claims. What is troubling about this rationale is both that it assumes the plaintiff's injury is an appropriate measure of the wrongfulness of the defendant's conduct and that it ignores the plight of those injured in the absence of provable fault.

Distributive justice considerations offered by other contemporary tort scholars link compensation with proof of fault to achieve deterrence.[17] By awarding tort sanctions for faulty conduct, tort law is thought to send a message of general and specific deterrence to reduce the risk of harm in society. Whether the compensation gaps and externalities created by a fault-based tort system could be justified if they were shown to reduce the level of injury in society would present a difficult question. But, proof that the tort system deters with any degree of precision has not been made. The use of the tort system to deter unsafe behavior posits assumptions about how people behave and how tort sanctions

---

14. See Morton J. Horwitz, The Transformation of American Law, 1780–1860, at 85–99 (1977); Charles O. Gregory, Trespass to Negligence to Absolute Liability, 37 Va. L. Rev. 359 (1951); Gary T. Schwartz, Tort Law and the Economy in Nineteenth-Century America: A Reinterpretation, 90 Yale L.J. 1717 (1981); John H. Wigmore, Responsibility for Tortious Acts: Its History, 7 Harv. L. Rev. 315 (1894).

15. Fault is explicit in negligence and intentional torts. Although it does not purport to be a consideration in strict products liability, fault plays a major role in these determinations under the defectiveness label. Plaintiffs must prove that the product was defective; plaintiffs are not compensated merely because they show that they were injured by a product. The test for defective products now operates much like the test for negligence. James A. Henderson, Jr. & Theodore Eisenberg, The Quiet Revolution in Products Liability: An Empirical Study of Legal Change, 37 UCLA L. Rev. 479, 484–88 (1990). Even with the presence of strict liability, it is accurate to characterize tort law in the United States as a fault-based liability system.

16. Richard A. Epstein, Nuisance Law: Corrective Justice and Its Utilitarian Constraints, 8 J. Legal Stud. 49, 65–69 (1979); George P. Fletcher, Fairness and Utility in Tort Theory, 85 Harv. L. Rev. 537, 556–64 (1972).

17. Daniel W. Shuman, The Psychology of Deterrence in Tort Law, 42 Kan. L. Rev. 115, 118–19 (1993).

shape that behavior. There is nothing in any mainstream theory of human behavior, however, to suggest that tort law sanctions, as the tort system is presently structured, have the desired deterrent effect.[18] Thus, if there is anything to be said in favor of retaining the fault-based tort system in its present form, it must be found not in how it deters but how it compensates.

B. What's So Bad About A Little Revenge?

"Every kind of satisfaction, as it is a punishment to the offender, naturally produces a pleasure of vengeance to the injured party."[19] The yin and yang of tort law's beneficial restorative impact, if any, may be that the benefit derived by the plaintiff flows from the toll taken of the defendant. What is restoration for plaintiffs is revenge for defendants. Is there a difference between restoration (an attempt to return the victim to health) and revenge (an attempt to inflict harm on the injurer)?

Commentators have both touted and lambasted the revenge element of tort law. Is tort law a formalized system of revenge, and if so, is that all that bad? Is a discussion of the restorative effects of fault-based compensation simply an intellectualized veneer for revenge? If so, is revenge therapeutic; should it be a justification for the tort system?

One thoughtful critic, Albert Ehrenzweig, argued from a psychoanalytical perspective that tort law's goal of deterrence is a veneer and that negligence is a system of revenge.[20] Ehrenzweig maintained that a tort involves antisocial conduct.[21] The victim, who has abstained from some instinctual antisocial conduct, perceives an injustice that punishment has not occurred for another's failing to abstain from that same conduct.[22] The victim, now turned retributor, then has the opportunity to commit the same wrong under the guise of punishment.[23] Ehrenzweig therefore argued in favor of compensation without fault: "A maturing society will have to replace this fault formula by one less burdened with pseudo-moral considerations and more responsive to present needs, however devoid the new formula should prove of emotional satisfaction."[24]

For Ehrenzweig, the tort system is antitherapeutic and reinforces a psychopathology that psychotherapy should address. For other commentators, like David Owen, the tort system is itself therapeutic. Owen acknowledges that tort damages, particularly punitive damages, are a private revenge, but he

---

18. Id. at 165–66.

19. Jeremy Bentham, The Theory of Legislation 309 (1831).

20. Albert A. Ehrenzweig, A Psychoanalysis of Negligence, 47 NW. U. L. Rev. 855, 865–66 (1953).

21. See id. at 866.

22. Id.

23. Id.

24. Id. at 869; see also Erich Fromm, The Anatomy of Human Destructiveness (1973) (studying the nature and social conditions that foster human's obsession with death and dying, and concluding that radical changes are needed in our social and political structure).

argues that they restore the victim's "emotional equilibrium" and that they advance other important objectives including the reinforcement of social values.[25]

The differing views of Ehrenzweig and Owen prove once again that where you end up has a great deal to do with where you began. Unfortunately, there is little psychological research on revenge to assist in resolving these differing views.[26] Both Ehrenzweig and Owen agree that tort law may respond to significant emotional needs of victims. Where they differ is whether this is an appropriate function for tort law to serve. To make sense of their disagreement, it is helpful to examine what tort compensation hopes to achieve and how it does so.

C. Come Together, Right Now

The commonly understood goal of tort compensation is to restore the injured to their preaccident condition, to make them whole.[27] Jurors are instructed that "[t]he object of an award of damages is to place the plaintiff, as far as money can do it, in the situation he would have occupied if the wrong had not been committed."[28] Beyond that goal, about which little disagreement exists, it often appears that little agreement exists as to the goal's implementation, that is, the calculation of damage awards. Appellate opinions are criticized for providing infrequent and obscure guidance on the particulars of tort damage formulations, and trial judges are criticized for providing only vague guidance about tort damage calculations.[29] Yet, at bottom, there may be greater consensus than lawyers and judges often let on.

The consensus and its limits is perhaps best understood in the case of damages for medical services for nonpermanent personal injuries, such as a broken arm or leg. Tort damages are intended to compensate the plaintiff and advance the plaintiff's restoration by awarding a dollar amount sufficient to permit the plaintiff to purchase those health care services necessary for recovery. In the paradigm case, an injurer whose conduct breaks the plaintiff's leg is assessed damages, *inter alia*, in an amount that will permit the plaintiff to purchase hospital, physician, nursing, or rehabilitation services necessary to restore the leg to its former functioning.

But what of the pain and suffering or other intangible loss that the injury has caused the plaintiff? Damages for intangible injuries like pain and suffering or other psychological sequelae of wrongful conduct do not neatly fit this

---

25. David G. Owen, Punitive Damages in Product Liability Litigation, 74 Mich. L. Rev. 1257, 1279–81 (1976); see also Pietro Marongiu & Graeme Newman, Vengeance: The Fight Against Injustice (1987) (analyzing individual and collective forms of vengeance in western culture).

26. Noreen Stuckless & Richard Goranson, The Vengeance Scale: Development of a Measure of Attitudes Towards Revenge, 7 J. Soc. Behav. & Personality 25, 26 (1992).

27. Fowler V. Harper et al., The Law of Torts § 25.1, at 493 (2d ed. 1986); Allan C. Hutchinson, Beyond No-Fault, 73 Cal. L. Rev. 755, 761 (1985).

28. Graham Douthwaite, Jury Instructions on Damages in Tort Actions § 1-1, at 3 (2d ed. 1988).

29. Randall R. Bovbjerg et al., Valuing Life and Limb in Tort: Scheduling "Pain and Suffering", 83 NW. U. L. Rev. 908, 908–17 (1989).

paradigm. They present two sets of concerns, one pragmatic and the other theoretical. The pragmatic concern is that these intangible losses lack objective diagnostic criteria or a reliable method of valuation.[30] Therefore, they are thought to present special problems of assessment that frustrate accurate adjudication of these damage claims. Because these questions of diagnosis and valuation apply not only to the present system of tort law but also to insurance and no-fault compensation schemes,[31] the validity of these concerns is not critical to a comparison of the restorative impact of tort compensation with some other system of compensation and need not be addressed here. They must be addressed by any compensation scheme.

The theoretical concern about awarding damages for these intangible injuries reveals a significant gap in tort compensation theory. Unlike damages awarded to purchase medical services for nonpermanent physical injuries, the intangible losses represented by pain and suffering cannot be made whole by the purchase of tort-financed medical services in the same way that broken arms and legs can be mended. "It would hardly be possible ever to compensate a person fully for pain and suffering."[32] Tort law can award damages to pay for relaxation training, biofeedback, psychotherapy, cognitive-behavioral therapy, or hypnosis to help manage the pain,[33] for example, but tort damages cannot "buy out" the pain in the same way they can "buy out" the hospital bill. Because these losses do not fit neatly within the avowed goal of making people whole through tort compensation, tort law is faced with the decision whether to award damages for these injuries and, if so, how to justify them. After much resistance to awarding damages for psychological harm, tort law now uneasily

---

30. Calvert Magruder, Mental and Emotional Disturbance in the Law of Torts, 49 Harv. L. Rev. 1033, 1033 (1936). Magruder quotes from the oft-noted decision in Lynch v. Knight, 9 H.L. 577, 598 (1861) ("Mental pain or anxiety the law cannot value, and does not pretend to redress, when the unlawful act complained of causes that alone."). There is, however, extensive literature on the validation of claims for mental or emotional injury. See, e.g., Sanford L. Drob & Robert H. Berger, The Determination of Malingering: A Comprehensive Clinical-Forensic Approach, 15 J. Psychiatry & Law 519 (1987); Gary L. Hawk & Dewey G. Cornell, MMPI Profiles of Malingerers Diagnosed in Pretrial Forensic Evaluations, 45 J. Clinical Psychol. 673 (1989); Phillip J. Resnick, The Detection of Malingered Mental Illness, 2 Behav. Sci. & Law 21 (1984).

31. See Ellen S. Pryor, The Tort Law Debate, Efficiency, and the Kingdom of the Ill: A Critique of the Insurance Theory of Compensation, 79 Va. L. Rev. 91, 121–25 (1993). While many no-fault plans do away with compensation for intangible injuries, others include compensation for this loss. O'Connell & Simon, infra note 183, at 11. See generally Jean C. Love, Actions for Nonphysical Harm: The Relationship Between the Tort System and No-Fault Compensation (With an Emphasis on Workers' Compensation), 73 Cal. L. Rev. 857, 858–59 (1985) (discussing whether no-fault compensation plans cover claims for noneconomic losses).

32. Seffert v. Los Angeles Transit Lines, 364 P.2d 337, 345 (Cal. 1961) (Traynor, J., dissenting).

33. See, e.g., Francis J. Keefe et al., Behavioral and Cognitive-Behavioral Approaches to Chronic Pain: Recent Advances and Future Directions, 60 J. Consulting & Clinical Psychol. 528, 528 (1992); Robert J. Trifiletti, The Psychological Effectiveness of Pain Management Procedures in the Context of Behavioral Medicine and Medical Psychology, 109 Genetic Psychol. Monographs 251, 254 (1984).

awards damages for these injuries, albeit not in all cases, and often only when some special requirement not imposed for other types of loss is met.[34]

Tort law justifies an award of damages for intangible losses on the basis of two conceptually troubling premises that may yield divergent results.[35] One premise, a creative conceptualization of compensation, justifies an award of damages for intangible loss such as pain and suffering to permit the plaintiff to purchase an offsetting substitute pleasure.[36] That these damage awards offset or reduce the plaintiff's suffering lacks empirical validation.[37] Furthermore, this rationale justifies an award of damages for intangible loss only if the plaintiff survives and experiences the offsetting pleasures purchased with the damage award.[38]

Another premise, based upon deterrence, justifies an award of damages for intangible loss to avoid conferring on the defendant an entitlement to injure.[39] This justification is not based at all on compensation, but rather is simply an attempt to compute the full cost that the defendant should bear so that the damage award will have the appropriate deterrent effect. Because this rationale for awarding damages for intangible loss has nothing to do with its impact on the plaintiff, the plaintiff's survival or cognition is irrelevant.

Both the notion that we can offset intangible loss by awarding funds to purchase a substitute pleasure and the idea that we should value incalculable injuries to achieve deterrence are troubling explanations for damage awards for intangible loss. What is more troubling, however, is that absent from these justifications is some principled basis for tort compensation that distinguishes it from other models of compensation. If the only benefit plaintiffs can expect from tort compensation is the ability to purchase restorative goods or services or substitute pleasures, there is no particular reason, assuming that damages are calculated in an equivalent manner, that plaintiffs should care whether the payment is made by the defendant, an insurance company, or the government. Indeed, because the financial and emotional costs of obtaining tort compensation

34. Daniel W. Shuman, Psychiatric and Psychological Evidence 323–24, 326–27 (1986).

35. Stanley Ingber, Rethinking Intangible Injuries: A Focus on Remedy, 73 Cal. L. Rev. 772, 778–85 (1985).

36. Id. at 784.

37. The claim that although these losses are irreducible they are easier to bear on a tropical paradise vacation purchased with the tort award, Richard N. Pearson, Liability To Bystanders for Negligently Inflicted Emotional Harm—A Comment on the Nature of Arbitrary Rules, 34 U. Fla. L. Rev. 477, 502 (1982), is a simplistic construct of human nature that lacks support from any rigorous study of human behavior. The assumption that these substitute pleasures will be a distraction or that distractions are helpful in coming to terms with these losses is troubling. At best, money can only resolve monetary problems. In addition, the financial consequences of injury should already be addressed by damages for tangible loss. At worst, there is reason to be concerned that distractions may hurt the person who suffered the loss. Substitute pleasures may delay or thwart progression through the stages often assumed to describe the way in which people come to terms with loss—denial, anger, bargaining, depression, and acceptance. See, e.g., Elisabeth Kubler-Ross, On Death and Dying (1969).

38. McDougald v. Garber, 536 N.E.2d 372, 375 (N.Y. 1989).

39. Clarence Morris, Liability for Pain and Suffering, 59 Colum. L. Rev. 476, 478–79 (1959).

are higher than for other compensation systems, if money alone were the goal, and damages were calculated in equivalent ways, there is no reason for any plaintiff to choose tort compensation. If providing money to injured persons was the sole goal of tort compensation, it hardly seems likely that society could justify maintaining the present tort system with its costs and inefficiencies.

What should matter for both injured persons and a society concerned with compensation of the injured is whether the tort process has a differential restorative effect for both tangible and intangible loss. Does the receipt of compensation from the party who caused the harm, accompanied by a finding of responsibility, play a role in the restorative process that distinguishes tort compensation from first-party insurance or no-fault compensation schemes? To ask this question is to ask whether deterrence and compensation are not merely coincidental or even antagonistic goals of tort law, but integral components of the restorative process. The answer to this question holds the potential of a unifying theme for tort law's purportedly divergent goals.

III. The Psychology of Compensation

A. The Psychological Primacy of Compensation

Tort law looks to defendants in its attempt to deter injurious behavior and to plaintiffs in its attempt to compensate for the consequences of that behavior. This linkage posits a questionable synchronous relationship—the damage award necessary to compensate plaintiffs is the sanction necessary to deter defendants.[40] While critics categorize this linkage as "a clumsy and inefficient way...to achieve two distinct goals,"[41] the validity of the assumption that there is a linkage between deterring injurers and compensating the injured, let alone the validity of the assumption that tort law either deters or compensates, has been largely immune from scrutiny under the human behavior theories upon which tort law is implicitly constructed.

To explore these issues, I have begun an examination of the psychology of tort law. In the first part of this examination, *The Psychology of Deterrence in Tort Law*,[42] I examined the defendant-oriented deterrence function of tort sanctions from a psychiatric or psychological perspective of human behavior.

---

40. Because the two goals demand different results in some cases, jurors must decide whether to adjust the award based on the defendant's blameworthiness. A number of studies suggest that jury awards fuse liability and damages and that blameworthiness shapes the amount of the award. Edith Greene, On Juries and Damages Awards: The Process of Decisionmaking, Law & Contemp. Probs., Autumn 1989, at 225, 233; Dale W. Broeder, The University of Chicago Jury Project, 38 Neb. L. Rev. 744, 757–59 (1959). In one experiment, primary school aged children, when asked to determine the consequences of intentional and accidentally caused harm, awarded more compensation for victims of intentional harm, and overall evinced greater concern with punishing the wrongdoer than compensating the victim. Dale T. Miller & C. Douglas McCann, Children's Reactions to the Perpetrators and Victims of Injustices, 50 Child Dev. 861 (1979).

41. Marc A. Franklin, Replacing the Negligence Lottery: Compensation and Selective Reimbursement, 53 Va. L. Rev. 774, 790 (1967).

42. Shuman, supra note 17.

That examination concluded that no mainstream body of research on behavior supports the conclusion that tort law accurately or precisely deters injurious behavior, and that at best, it either over or under deters.[43] The organic and biological research, suggesting that behavior is internally cued by brain physiology, biochemistry, or molecular biology, reveals the limited capacity of tort law to shape behavior.[44] Psychodynamic psychological research, suggesting that behavior is the result of unconscious determinants, exposes the complex constellation of considerations that influence behavior and the limited capacity of tort law to shape that behavior.[45] Cognitive psychology research reveals that our decisionmaking is systematically flawed and that we are likely to overestimate tort risks and avoid desirable activity or underestimate tort risks and behave unsafely.[46] Behaviorist insights suggest that the tort system's use of delayed punishment rather than timely positive reinforcement is not an effective means of shaping desirable behavior.[47] Social learning theory, which suggests that punishment as well as positive reinforcement can change behavior, holds potential.[48] Because social learning theory posits that observing unpunished, inappropriate behavior reduces inhibitions to engage in that behavior, however, unless the percentage of meritorious tort cases brought is increased so that sanctions are observable with greater regularity, the tort system is likely to increase rather than decrease the frequency of undesirable behavior.[49] The collective wisdom from the mainstream body of research on human behavior is that tort law as presently structured is not likely to be successful in deterring unsafe behavior.[50]

That analysis of the deterrent effect of tort sanctions on defendants from the perspective of human behavior research did not evaluate the corresponding psychological impact of compensation on plaintiffs. Rather than join the ranks of those who have argued in favor of rejecting the tort system because it poorly serves deterrence, I suggested at the conclusion of that article that tort law's linkage of compensation with a determination of fault raised the need for an examination of how fault-based compensation affects plaintiffs.[51] I now take up that question. Just as tort scholarship has largely ignored the psychology of deterrence, what human behavior research has to say about how tort sanctions shape defendants' behavior, so it has also largely ignored the psychology of compensation, what human behavior research has to say about how tort sanctions shape plaintiffs' restoration.

Beyond reimbursing tangible loss or permitting the plaintiff to purchase therapeutic goods and services, how does tort compensation affect the process of healing? Does it transform injured persons from passive victims to proactive members of society? Does tort compensation permit injured persons to

---

43. Id. at 167.
44. Id. at 140–47.
45. Id. at 147–50.
46. Id. at 160–64.
47. Id. at 151–56.
48. Id. at 158.
49. Id. at 157–60.
50. Id. at 167.
51. Id. at 167–68.

tell their stories in a culturally meaningful setting that restores their role as valued members of society? Does tort compensation traumatize injured persons or encourage them to play the role of victims to maximize their compensation?

Surprisingly, the subject has not been addressed comprehensively. That is not to suggest that there is no visible evidence of tort law's impact on the process of healing. Apart from the historical evidence of tort law's roots, there is ample contemporary evidence to suggest that tort damages may play a powerful role in the restorative process.[52] Plaintiffs often report that they institute litigation because they expect it to be beneficial or therapeutic.[53] Students of human behavior note that punishment of wrongdoers "tends to relieve the outraged feelings of those who have been hurt; after its infliction their anger abates, and they tend to regard the incident as closed."[54] And, others speculate that even if fully compensated elsewhere, plaintiffs would nonetheless pursue tort litigation because of a "need for dignity, respect, empowerment, and an ideology of fairness that a system of justice provides."[55]

Fault, the defining element of tort law,

> may be attributed not to an eternal principle of justice but to a psychological reaction of a distinctly human kind. A person who has been wronged feels resentment, and society sympathetically identifies itself with the victim. The resentment of the victim and of society can be appeased by punishment (the criminal sanction) or satisfied by reparation (the civil sanction).[56]

The psychological primacy of compensation may not be adequately addressed by sterile payments to an injured person from a third party lacking responsibility for causing the harm to the plaintiff. The current tort system entails a determination of responsibility, albeit rife with loss-spreading principles. No-fault or first-party insurance systems, however, lack any mechanism for as-

---

52. Albert A. Ehrenzweig, Psychoanalytic Jurisprudence 243 (1971).

53. See, e.g., Gerald M. Stern, The Buffalo Creek Disaster 7 (1977) (discussing how the survivors of the disaster met to discuss suing the coal company); see also Neil Vidmar, Justice Motives and Other Psychological Factors in the Development and Resolution of Disputes, in The Justice Motive in Social Behavior 395 (Melvin J. Lerner & Sally C. Lerner eds., 1981). Whether plaintiffs ultimately find their experiences to be therapeutic is another matter. Robert Simon, a forensic psychiatrist at Georgetown Medical School, reports that the process often has the opposite effect for individuals who are not psychologically healthy and argues in favor of an obligation of lawyers to obtain informed consent from their clients about these consequences before proceeding with litigation. Letter from Robert Simon to Daniel Shuman (Jan. 31, 1994) (on file with author).

54. J.C. Flugel Man, Morals and Society: A Psycho-Analytical Study 145 (1945). Flugel explains that the infliction of punishment satisfies our superego, the source of our moral control. Id.

55. Leslie Bender Feminist (Re)Torts: Thoughts on the Liability Crisis, Mass Torts, Power, and Responsibilities. 990 Duke L.J. 848, 877; see also Jane B. Korn, The Fungible Woman and Other Myths of Sexual Harassment, 67 Tul. L. Rev. 1363, 1389–93 (1993) (arguing that sexual harassment and sexual assault claims in the work place should fall within the jurisdiction of the tort rather than the workers' compensation system because of the importance of adjudications of fault that occur in tort law).

56. Glanville Williams & B.A. Hepple, Foundations of the Law of Tort 116 (1976).

sessing responsibility. The abandonment of fault-based compensation further forsakes the psychological primacy of compensation.[57]

To understand the impact of this movement requires an examination of how tort compensation affects the restoration of the injured. Because the question of how tort compensation affects the behavior of tort plaintiffs is a question about the impact of law on human behavior, it is important to review the relevant research of those who study human behavior and how that behavior is shaped by the law. This body of research includes studies of how people respond to the judicial system more generally and social scientists' studies of human behavior without the context of the judicial system.

B. Secondary Gain Theory

One relevant body of empirical research consists of the studies that examine secondary gain theory by studying the impact of the termination of litigation on plaintiffs' psychological symptoms.[58] "A secondary gain is an advantage accruing subsequent to an illness or accident, which plays a part in creating and/or perpetuating" that illness or injury.[59] Central to secondary gain theory is that, unlike malingering, the injured plaintiff is not consciously aware of the role of the advantage in the perpetuation of the illness or injury.[60] Secondary gain theory posits that litigation is antitherapeutic because it reinforces psychopathology by holding out the possibility of a damage award.[61] Therefore, according to secondary gain theory, the receipt of a damage award and the termination of litigation should result in a decrease in psychopathology. The studies that address the impact of litigation on illness or injury reach divergent results. While some find a dramatic improvement in symptoms following the termination of litigation, others find that some plaintiffs improve before their claims are resolved and that some plaintiffs' significant symptoms persist long after termination of the litigation.[62]

Studies providing support for secondary gain theory find reduced reporting of psychopathology associated with the termination of litigation. In the most

---

57. In a related vein the abandonment of fault in divorce has been criticized as fostering the appearance of equality while in reality severely disadvantaging women. Martha A. Fineman, The Illusion of Equality: The Rhetoric and Reality of Divorce Reform 174 (1991).

58. See generally Renee L. Binder et al., Is Money A Cure? Follow-up of Litigants in England, 19 Bull. Am. Acad. Psychiatry & Law 151, 154–55 (1991). Although secondary gain research addresses physiological as well as psychological symptoms, psychological symptoms appear to be the most sensitive to this affect and have been the most controversial in tort law. "Most studies have found no differences in outcome measures between compensation and noncompensation patients with physical complaints." Zahava Solomon et al., Compensation and Psychic Trauma: A Study of Israeli Combat Veterans, 64 Am. J. Orthopsychiatry 91, 92 (1994). Thus, this examination is limited to psychological symptoms.

59. Lester Keiser, The Traumatic Neurosis 52 (1968).

60. Id. at 53. "The essential feature of malingering is the intentional production of false or grossly exaggerated physical or psychological symptoms, motivated by external incentives such as...obtaining financial compensation...." American Psychiatric Ass'n, Diagnostic & Statistical Manual of Mental Disorders, DSM-III-R 683 (4th ed. rev. 1994).

61. Keiser, supra note 59, at 56.

62. See id.

widely cited study supporting this conclusion, Henry Miller followed up on fifty persons who claimed psychiatric injuries in traffic and industrial accident cases in Britain after settlement of their compensation claims.[63] Within two years after settlement, Miller found disabling psychiatric symptoms present in only two of the fifty claimants.[64]

In a retrospective study in New Zealand, Roger Culpan and Christine Taylor followed up on seventy-one patients who had been referred by their attorneys to a private psychiatric clinic for evaluation following traffic or industrial accidents.[65] These authors' findings were not as dramatic as Miller's; they found that about half of the group either did not improve or deteriorated until their claims were settled.[66] In another study, Peter Denker used insurance company records to review disability insurance claims in New York.[67] Denker's findings also were not as dramatic as Miller's; he found evidence that in seven of fifteen cases involving lump sum payments, psychological symptoms were distinctly improved after the lump sum settlement.[68]

Studies not providing support for secondary gain theory find no consistent difference in reported psychopathology as associated with the termination of litigation. Reginald Kelly conducted two studies that found no association between termination of the litigation and improvement in psychological symptoms.[69] In 1972, Kelly conducted a prospective study in Britain of 170 patients in which he found that the vast majority of patients returned to work before their cases were resolved.[70] In a later study of fifty-one patients, Kelly found that approximately one-half of the patients returned to work before their cases were resolved, and of those who did not, only one out of twenty-six had returned to work eighteen months after their cases were resolved.[71]

In a follow-up study of 106 settled workers' compensation cases in Florida taken from a private psychiatric practice, Daniel Sprehe found no correlation between psychological improvement and settlement of the compensation claims.[72] The parties settled in seventy-nine cases; however, in seventy-eight percent of the cases, the plaintiffs reported no improvement in psychological symptoms.[73] In another study, George Thompson conducted a follow-up of 500 litigated cases involving claims for psychological injury.[74] He found that in

---

63. Henry Miller, Accident Neurosis, 1 Brit. Med. J. 919, 923 (1961).

64. Id. at 924–25.

65. Roger Culpan & Christine Taylor, Psychiatric Disorders Following Road Traffic and Industrial Injuries, 7 Australian & New Zealand J. Psychiatry 32 (1973).

66. Id. at 38.

67. Peter G. Denker, The Prognosis of Insured Neurotics: A Study of 1,000 Disability Insurance Claims, 39 N.Y. State J. Med. 238 (1939).

68. Id. at 246.

69. Reginald Kelly & B. Norman Smith, Post-Traumatic Syndrome: Another Myth Discredited, 74 J. Royal Soc. Med. 275, 275–76 (1981).

70. Id. at 275.

71. Id. at 275–76.

72. Daniel J. Sprehe, Workers' Compensation: A Psychiatric Follow-Up Study, 7 Int'l. J. L. & Psychiatry 165, 175 (1984).

73. Id. at 167.

74. George N. Thompson, Post-Traumatic Psychoneurosis—A Statistical Survey, 121 Am. J. Psychiatry 1043 (1965).

only fifteen percent of the thirty-eight percent of the cases followed to the conclusion of litigation was there a report of improvement in psychological symptoms.[75]

In a retrospective study in Britain, Michael Tarsh and Claire Royston followed up on thirty-five patients who had been referred by their attorneys to one of the authors for psychiatric evaluation.[76] The authors found no improvement in symptoms following compensation.[77] Even after financial recovery, most patients continued to suffer severe symptoms.[78]

One likely explanation for these widely differing results is that the relationship between psychopathology and litigation is more complex than secondary gain theory suggests and entails substantial individual variation in how plaintiffs experience litigation based on variables unrelated to the litigation. These variables include personality and familial support.[79] Another possible explanation for these widely differing results is sampling size and bias. It is difficult to obtain patient-litigants who will agree to be followed through the relevant time frames, and those who do may not be representative of the universe of plaintiffs. Thus, these studies generally have small sample sizes and use a retrospective study design. Those studies that use a longitudinal design often involve plaintiffs who were seen by the authors of the study in their capacity as expert witnesses on behalf of plaintiffs or insurance companies.

Apart from the failure to account for numerous individual variables and the methodological problems of sample size and researcher bias, another methodological problem limits the conclusions that may be drawn from these studies about the impact of tort compensation on restoration of the injured. None of these studies that address secondary gain includes a control group comprised of patients with comparable injuries who did not pursue litigation, thus interjecting the risk of a self-selection bias. Without the use of a control group, it is difficult to discern whether some other variable explains a correlation between the termination of litigation and the plaintiff's psychopathology.

In one of the few examinations of litigants and nonlitigants, Bonnie Green and her colleagues conducted a series of studies of the survivors of the Buffalo Creek, West Virginia dam collapse in 1972.[80] The researchers found no differ-

---

75. Id. at 1045.

76. Michael J. Tarsh & Claire Royston, A Follow-up Study of Accident Neurosis, 146 Brit. J. Psychiatry 18, 19–20 (1985).

77. Id. at 23–24.

78. Id. at 23; see also Thomas J. Reidy et al., Pesticide Exposure and Neuropsychological Impairment in Migrant Farm Workers, 7 Archives Clinical Neuropsychology 85, 93 (1992) (finding that migrant farmworkers who received workers' compensation for neurological impairment resulting from exposure to pesticides revealed significant impairment in neuropsychological test battery and no improvement in symptomology one year after resolution of their compensation claims).

79. Binder et al., supra note 58, at 158; see also Jack M. Fletcher et al., Behavioral Changes After Closed Head Injury in Children, 58 J. Consulting & Clinical Psychol. 93, 98 (1990) (finding that marriage, family, and sibling variables, rather than litigation, could explain differences in the behavioral adjustment of children with closed head injuries).

80. Bonnie L. Green et al., Buffalo Creek Survivors in the Second Decade: Stability of Stress Symptoms, 60 Am. J. Orthopsychiatry 43 (1990).

ence in the psychopathology of those who chose to litigate and those who did not, both before and after the termination of litigation.[81] In another study comparing litigants and nonlitigants, George Mendelson compared fifty-seven Australian patients seeking compensation for chronic low back pain with thirty-three patients complaining of low back pain who did not seek compensation.[82] He found no difference between these two groups in their reports of pain or psychopathology.[83] Most importantly, for the purpose of this inquiry, the only study comparing persons claiming similar injuries found no difference in the symptoms of those who pursued fault-based tort claims and those who pursued no-fault workers' compensation claims.[84] Of course, the failure to show convincingly that tort plaintiffs improve dramatically after compensation also casts doubt on the argument that tort litigation has a beneficial restorative effect.

The body of research addressing the effects of being a plaintiff does not show convincingly that, in general, claiming an injury plays a role in creating or perpetuating illness or injury. Even the worse case scenario of secondary gain theory, that plaintiffs improve dramatically after their claims are resolved and not a moment before, only describes what occurs but does not explain why it occurs. Improvement following tort compensation is consistent with both secondary gain theory and tort compensation having a beneficial restorative impact. If plaintiffs improve dramatically after they have received tort compensation, it may result from the removal of the negative effect of tort litigation or it may result from the receipt of its positive benefits.

C. Empowerment Theories

One group of social science theories posits that "one of the key factors in healing illness is mobilizing resources of power—typically by enhancing the individual's sense of personal empowerment (from external or internal sources)."[85] These theories are grounded in the "growing evidence in the medical and social psychological literature that illness and disease are closely

---

81. Id. at 51.

82. George Mendelson, Compensation, Pain Complaints, and Psychological Disturbance, 20 Pain 169 (1984); see also Frank Leavitt et al., Organic Status, Psychological Disturbance, and Pain Report Characteristics in Low-Back-Pain Patients on Compensation, 7 Spine 398 (1982). Leavitt and his colleagues studied 261 persons being treated for low-back pain. Id. at 399. Their study also showed little or no correlation between pain and psychopathology and whether the persons were or were not receiving compensation. Id. at 401.

83. Mendelson, supra note 82, at 176.

84. Cornelius J. Peck et al., The Effect of the Pendency of Claims for Compensation Upon Behavior Indicative of Pain, 53 Wash. L. Rev. 251, 266 (1978).

85. Meredith B. McGuire, Words of Power: Personal Empowerment and Healing, 7 Culture, Med. & Psychiatry 221, 222 (1983); see Peter L. Berger & Richard J. Neuhaus, To Empower People: The Role of Mediating Structures in Public Policy 7 (1977) (discussing the ways in which institutions controlled by faceless persons have resulted in a feeling of powerlessness in modern society); see also Anita Hodgkiss, Note, Petitioning and the Empowerment Theory of Practice, 96 Yale L.J. 569 (1987) (arguing that the radical lawyer's focus should be to encourage individual and collective empowerment).

linked with issues of power and domination."[86] The etiology of disempowerment differs depending upon the theory. What is common to these theories, however, is that healing entails empowerment. The method of achieving empowerment is linked to the etiology of the theory. These empowerment theories are of interest to a study of the psychology of tort compensation because tort litigants may enlist the coercive power of the judicial system to reshape the power imbalance in their relationships.[87]

1. Equity Theory

Equity theory in social psychology explains harm as the result of an inequity that occurs in a relationship.[88] "In general terms, an equitable relationship has been defined as one in which a person's ratio of outcomes to inputs is equal to the other person's outcome/input ratio."[89] Harm occurs when someone engages in an act that results in an inequitable relationship or distribution of harm.[90] When someone experiences a loss that is disproportionate to their perception of their responsibility for its causation, they experience an "aversive emotional state."[91] "One way a harm-doer can restore equity to his relationship with the victim is by making compensation to him."[92] Equity theory regards compensation by a harmdoer as a restorative act.[93]

Tortious injury results in an imbalance in the relationship between the injured and injurer. Viewed in this interdependent fashion suggested by equity theory, the payment of money to a plaintiff by some third person or entity contractually or statutorily obligated to make these payments is incomplete compensation. The harmful results of the inequity occasioned by the harmdoer's conduct endure unless addressed personally by the harmdoer. Indeed, equity theorists suggest that "society should be wary of introducing a compensation

---

86. McGuire, supra note 85, at 222; see Also Peter E.S. Freund, The Civilized Body: Social Domination, Control, and Health (1982).

87. This use of the judicial system to reshape personal relationships was observed by Laura Nader in her study of the Mexican Zapotec courts. Laura Nader, Styles of Court Procedure: To Make the Balance, in Law and Culture in Society 69 (Laura Nader ed., 1969). "The Zapotec ideal is not an 'eye for an eye,' but rather what restores personal relations to equilibrium." Id. at 73; see also Atiyah, supra note 13, at 553 ("When a person is involved in a dispute with another who he thinks has done wrong, and when that other refuses to admit that he has done wrong (and sometimes even when he does admit it), it may be a great satisfaction to the former to know that he has the right to summon the latter before one of Her Majesty's judges for a public confrontation in which the latter may be branded as in the wrong.").

88. Stewart Macauley & Elaine Walster, Legal Structures and Restoring Equity, in Considering the Victim: Readings in Restitution and Victim Compensation 291, 292 (Joe Hudson & Burt Galaway eds., 1975). For a cross-cultural perspective in restoring the balance in relationships, see Hiroshi Wagatsuma & Arthur Rosett, The Implications of Apology: Law and Culture in Japan and the United States, 20 Law & Soc'y Rev. 461 (1986).

89. Macauley & Walster, supra note 88, at 292.

90. Id.

91. Hensler et al., supra note 4, at 147.

92. Macauley & Walster, supra note 88, at 294.

93. See id.

procedure that erodes individuals' responsibility for restoring equity, thus weakening their adherence to equity norms."[94] Experiments by social psychologists reveal that victims feel most satisfied when compensated by the injurer rather than a third party.[95] Thus, the restorative act that is necessary to compensate the plaintiff is one that is performed personally by the harmdoer, or in the tort context, the defendant.

These insights from equity theory about the important role of injurers in restoring the injured suggest two lessons for tort law. First, society should be wary about the antitherapeutic consequences to the injured of replacing tort compensation with no-fault or first-party insurance programs. Second, society should rethink the operation of insurance and loss-spreading principles within tort law that minimize the individual responsibility of harmdoers and fail to address the imbalance resulting from injury.[96]

2. Feminist Theory

The defining tenet of feminist theory is that male-dominated institutions operate to disempower women. Feminist theorists view gender and power as inextricably linked in our society.[97] Proceeding from this premise, feminists view readjustment of this imbalance on a societal and individual level as the key to women's physical and emotional health and well-being. The process controls enjoyed by tort litigants[98] and the adjudication of liability (responsibility) that is a prerequisite to tort compensation suggest the responsiveness of tort law to injuries explained by feminist theory.

One example of this theory is the use of tort actions for victims of rape, which has been touted as empowering the victim.[99]

> [R]ape victims who disidentify themselves with stereotypical victim roles by taking their recovery into their own hands recover faster, more fully, and may protect themselves from future victimization by refusing to assume passive and dependent victim roles. In repudiating her assailant's power to silence her through shame, guilt and fear, the rape victim who launches a civil suit rejects her attacker's dominance and re-asserts her right to self-determination and sexual autonomy.[100]

---

94. Elaine Walster et al., New Directions in Equity Research, 25 J. Personality & Soc. Psychol. 151, 164 (1973).

95. Andre deCarufel, Victims' Satisfaction with Compensation: Effects of Initial Disadvantage and Third Party Intervention, 11 J. Applied Soc. Psychol. 445, 452 (1981).

96. See infra text accompanying notes 135–42.

97. Lynda M. Sagrestano, The Use of Power and Influence in a Gendered World, 16 Psychol. Women Q. 439, 439 (1992).

98. See discussion infra notes 121–28 and accompanying text.

99. See Holly J. Manley, Comment, Civil Compensation for the Victim of Rape, 7 Cooley L. Rev. 193, 202 (1990).

100. Nora West, Note, Rape in the Criminal Law and the Victim's Tort Alternative: A Feminist Analysis, 50 U. Toronto Fac. L. Rev. 96, 114 (1992); see also Bruce Feldthusen, The Civil Action for Sexual Battery: Therapeutic Jurisprudence, Ottawa L. Rev. (forthcoming). See generally Dale T. Miller & Carol A. Porter, Self-Blame in Victims of Violence, 39 J. Soc. Issues 139 (1983) (delineating types of victim self-blame and discussing their implication on the victimization process).

Rape victims who bring successful claims against their assailants may advance their restoration in ways that mental health care alone, paid by their health insurer, cannot.

Feminist theorists who address these issues, however, do not view the legal system as a wellspring of empowerment for all women. It would, therefore, be disingenuous to paint a picture of the legal system as a therapeutic agent receptive to the legitimate claims of victims. While the legal system offers an opportunity to correct imbalances of power, it nevertheless has often been accused of legitimizing these disparate social norms. For example, the legal system's reluctance to award damages for emotional harm has been attacked for failing to value injuries suffered by women, traditionally charged with the maintenance of relationships, while valuing property, traditionally a male charge.[101] Feminist theory highlights the potential of tort compensation either to restore by reshaping imbalanced relationships or to injure by reinforcing those imbalances.

The psychological problems reported by many victims of child sexual abuse is another illustration of the feminist approach to the use of the judicial system to reshape the power imbalance in relationships. Depression, anxiety, sexual dysfunction, self-destructive behavior and revictimization are symptoms frequently reported by victims of child sexual abuse.[102] These symptoms have been linked to "a profound sense of powerlessness engendered in victims of sexual abuse."[103] In addition to counseling, some therapists view the use of the judicial system by victims of child sexual abuse as an important tool in their healing because of its potential to empower them. "[W]hen children are able to bring the abuse to an end effectively, or at least exert some control over its occurrence, they may feel less disempowered."[104] Thus, those victims of child sexual abuse who are able to bring successful claims against their abuser also may advance their restoration in ways that payment for mental health care by their health insurers alone cannot.

D. Attribution Theory

Central to the concept of fault-based liability is that the plaintiff may recover only if the defendant, not the plaintiff, is primarily responsible for causing the injury. Thus, there is a financial incentive for plaintiffs to attribute re-

---

101. Martha Chamallas & Linda K. Kerber, Women, Mothers, and the Law of Fright: A History, 88 Mich. L. Rev. 814, 814 (1990); see also Robin L. West, The Difference in Women's Hedonic Lives: A Phenomenological Critique of Feminist Legal Theory, 3 Wis. Women's L.J. 81, 81–88 (1987).

102. Joan H. Liem et al., The Need for Power in Women Who Were Sexually Abused as Children, 16 Psychol. Women Q. 467, 468 (1992).

103. Id. Similarly, "[t]he rules that battered women try desperately to follow become established in a pattern of domination and control by the enforcement mechanism used by the batterer." Karla Fischer et al., The Culture of Battering and the Role of Mediation in Domestic Violence Cases, 46 SMU L. Rev. 2117, 2131 (1993).

104. David Finkelhor & Angela Browne, The Traumatic Impact of Child Sexual Abuse: A Conceptualization, 55 Am. J. Orthopsychiatry 530, 532 (1985).

sponsibility for their injury to defendants. In other words, it is necessary to blame to claim. Accordingly, it is not surprising to hear the assertion that "[w]here there is a prospect of compensation, the victim attributes fault in a way which justifies his claim."[105] When people attribute their injury to some external cause they are more likely to institute litigation. A Rand study of compensation for accidental injuries reveals that people "who mostly blame others for their injury are 12 times more likely to consider claiming than those who mostly blame themselves."[106] One potential antitherapeutic consequence of fault-based compensation is that it may encourage an attitude of helplessness, or blaming others for our misfortunes rather than taking personal responsibility for our lives.[107]

According to attribution theory research, learned helplessness occurs when people attribute success or failure to events outside themselves.[108] Viewed from the insights of attribution theory, fault-based compensation may encourage people to perceive others as at fault and themselves as victims of other's conduct, rather than encouraging them to perceive themselves as in control of their own lives. The consequences of making blaming a prerequisite to claiming[109] may extend beyond the triggering of those claims. The results of one study suggest that "[a]mong severe accident victims, blaming another and feeling that one could have avoided the accident were predictors of poor coping, whilst self-blame was a predictor of good coping."[110] Thus, a preliminary analysis of tort compensation viewed from the lens of attribution theory suggests antitherapeutic effects of tort recovery that may transfer to other segments of the plaintiff's life.

This generalization, however, is often misleading or inaccurate. External attribution of fault is not invariably antitherapeutic and internal attribution of fault is not invariably therapeutic. Victims of accidents and assault often blame themselves for their injuries because these internal attributions of events foster a sense of control over future events in their lives.[111] When the injured person

---

105. Lloyd-Bostock, supra note 6, at 101.

106. Hensler et al., supra note 4, at 144.

107. See generally Martha Minow, Surviving Victim Talk, 40 UCLA L. Rev. 1411, 1413–14 (1993) (discussing the "many attractions to victim status").

108. Harold H. Kelly & John L. Michela, Attribution Theory and Research, 31 Ann. Rev. Psychol. 457, 487–88 (1980).

109. The decision to institute personal injury litigation involves a process of "naming, the perception of an experience as an injury; blaming, the formation of views that some person or entity is responsible for the injury and obligated to remedy it; and claiming, or asserting a demand for redress." Dan Coates & Steven Penrod, Social Psychology and the Emergence of Disputes, 15 Law & Soc'y Rev. 655, 656 (1980–81).

110. V.E. Weighill, 'Compensation Neurosis': A Review of the Literature, 27 J. Psychosomatic Res. 97, 98 (1983). In another study of the relationship between childhood sexual abuse and adult functioning, those women abused as children who reported the most serious levels of psychological distress were those who perceived that they had little control over their environment. Erica R. Gold, Long Term Effects of Sexual Victimization in Childhood: An Attributional Approach, 5 J. Consulting & Clinical Psychol. 471 (1986).

111. Ronnie J. Bulman & Camille B. Wortman, Attributions of Blame and Coping in the "Real World": Severe Accident Victims React to Their Lot, 35 J. Personality & Soc. Psychol.

is not responsible for the injury or harm, however, internal causal attributions may be antitherapeutic. For example, in a study of how children and their parents attribute the cause of the child's cancer for which they have been told there is no known cause, both children and parents who attributed the cancer to external causes coped significantly better than those who made internal attributions of causation.[112] Self-blame without regard to an accurate appraisal of causal role in the event is "maladaptive, a correlate of depression, and a reflection of psychological problems."[113] Reinforcing inaccurate self-blame encourages low self-esteem and harsh self-criticism.[114] Thus, tort judgments may be an important attributional compass pointing the way for therapeutic assessments of blame.

Encouraging victim blaming in all cases has its own set of antitherapeutic risks.[115] In some instances, such as child sexual abuse, it is appropriate to acknowledge that the victim may lack the ability to control the event and to visit the entire responsibility on one party, the adult. We expect the adult to be responsible for avoiding these events and to suggest that the child should share responsibility is not likely to further any legitimate attributional goal—contributory negligence or assumption of the risk have no place here. Similarly, in the case of individuals who suffered injuries from in utero exposure to DES, there is no therapeutic benefit to the victim's internal attributions of fault. Other instances, such as misuse issues in product liability cases, are less subject to a bright-line test.[116] Accurate individualized judicial assessments of responsibility may lead to more therapeutic attributions.

E. Grief Work Theory

It is generally accepted by mental health professionals that to recover from the loss of a loved one, it is necessary to confront that loss, reflect on the events around the time of death and memories of the loved one, and work towards detaching from the deceased.[117] Another possible harmful effect of tort litigation in wrongful death actions is an interruption of the grief process, the

---

351, 360 (1977) (victims of spinal cord injury who felt that they could not have avoided the accident but nonetheless blamed themselves for their injury had less difficulty coping then those who blamed others).

112. David J. Bearison et al., Patients' and Parents' Causal Attributions for Childhood Cancer, 11 J. Psychosocial Oncology 47, 47–48 (1993); see also Ruth D. Abrams & Jacob E. Finesinger, Guilt Reactions in Patients With Cancer, 6 Cancer 474 (1953); Paul Chodoff et al., Stress, Defenses and Coping Behavior: Observations in Parents of Children With Malignant Disease, 120 Am. J. Psychiatry 743 (1964).

113. Ronnie Janoff-Bulman, Characterological Versus Behavioral Self-Blame: Inquiries into Depression and Rape, 37 J. Personality & Soc. Psychol. 1798, 1798 (1979).

114. Id. at 1799.

115. Miriam J. Stewart, Social Support: Diverse Theoretical Perspectives, 28 Soc. Sci. Med. 1275, 1275–76 (1989).

116. See Shuman, supra note 8, at 754.

117. Margaret Stroebe & Wolfgang Stroebe, Does "Grief Work" Work?, 59 J. Consulting & Clinical Psychol. 479, 479 (1991).

struggle to withdraw from investment in the deceased.[118] Involvement in wrongful death litigation may suspend the grief process if it results in limited processing of thoughts and feelings about the deceased or maintains a focus on the deceased that prevents withdrawal. Where genuine questions of responsibility for the death do not exist, litigation may interrupt the survivors' grief process by inappropriately focusing on the cause of the death rather than confronting its existence. Similarly, where litigation is not instituted in timely fashion or its resolution is prolonged, it may suspend or extend the grief process.

Conversely, involvement in wrongful death litigation may facilitate the grief process if it results in processing thoughts and feelings about the deceased shortly after the death.[119] When, for example, genuine questions of responsibility for the death do exist, litigation may facilitate the survivors' grief process by helping them sort through the events leading to the death or fulfill their sense of duty to the deceased. Particularly where the litigation is instituted shortly after the death and resolved expeditiously, it may accelerate the grief process.

Moreover, the assumption that everyone needs to engage in the same grief work is not supported by research.[120] Thus, it is difficult to generalize about the consequences of tort litigation on the grief process. Depending upon temporal and causal considerations and the individual circumstances of the plaintiff, tort litigation may facilitate or thwart the process of detachment from the deceased.

F. Procedural Justice Theory

The work of E. Allan Lind, Tom Tyler, and other procedural justice theorists examining psychological responses to the judicial process reveals that litigants are less concerned with outcome and more concerned with process considerations than is commonly assumed.[121] Without regard to outcomes, people are strongly affected by how decisions are made. The process concerns of litigants that arise from this body of research can be categorized as participation, dignity, and trust.[122] Litigants find procedures that allow them to participate, for

---

118. Paul C. Rosenblatt, Grief and Involvement in Wrongful Death Litigation, 7 Law & Hum. Behav. 351, 352 (1983).

119. Id. at 353.

120. Stroebe & Stroebe, supra note 117, at 481.

121. E. Allan Lind et al., In the Eye of the Beholder: Tort Litigants' Evaluations of Their Experiences in the Civil Justice System, 24 Law & Soc'y Rev. 953, 955 (1990). For an explanation of the basis and applications of procedural justice theory, see generally E. Allan Lind & Tom R. Tyler, The Social Psychology of Procedural Justice (1988); John Thibaut & Laurens Walker, Procedural Justice: A Psychological Analysis (1975); Tom R. Tyler, Why People Obey the Law (1990).

122. Tom R. Tyler, The Psychological Consequences of Judicial Procedures: Implications for Civil Commitment Hearings, 46 SMU L. Rev. 433, 439–40 (1992). This finding corresponds with James Pennebaker's research on expressed emotion, which found that discussing traumatic experiences is physically and psychologically beneficial. James W. Pennebaker & Joan R. Susman, Disclosure of Traumas and Psychosomatic Processes, 26 Soc. Sci. Med. 327, 330 (1988).

example by presenting evidence or telling their story, to be more fair, surprisingly even when they may have no opportunity to influence the outcome.[123] Litigants also want to be treated with dignity and do not regard procedures as fair that fail to recognize their importance as members of society.[124] Furthermore, litigants regard procedures as more fair, and believe they can trust the decisonmaker, when they think that the decisonmaker wants to treat them fairly.[125] While Lind and Tyler's work focuses on how people are affected by the judicial process and not on the restoration of injury, it provides important insights on why plaintiffs may experience a profoundly different effect from tort compensation than from first-party insurance or no-fault compensation.

A critical question for the psychology of tort compensation is how well the tort system responds to these concerns of participation, dignity, and trust as contrasted with no-fault compensation or first-party insurance. The adversary system used for tort litigation maximizes the plaintiff's opportunity to participate, both in the opportunity to state one's case and in the opportunity to influence the outcome. Tort litigation offers the plaintiff the opportunity to decide how to state one's case, what evidence to present, and whether to settle. Unlike no-fault or first-party insurance in which the claimant is unlikely to be given the opportunity to tell his or her story, tort litigation encourages this narrative. Thus, Lind found that tort litigants viewed trials as fairer than bilateral settlements, court annexed arbitration, or judicial settlement conferences because of the opportunity to participate in the process.[126]

The formality of the judicial system is intended to enhance its dignity. Formal notice, the right to be heard, and the right to confront adverse witnesses are institutionalized judicial rituals that strengthen its station. "[L]itigants feel that the court accords importance to the persons and subject matter involved in the dispute."[127] First-party insurance and no-fault systems do not prioritize the formalities that help dignify the judicial process; they regard those formalities as inefficient rituals antithetical to their goals.

Satisfaction is also tied to trust. People are more inclined to accept decisions from those whom they trust will be unbiased and will spend adequate time deciding their claims. The tort system's use of juries, beholden to no special interest, and their deliberative process advances that trust.[128] First-party insurance and no-fault systems typically use claims adjusters or governmental administrators who may be captives of the industry or some special interest and are not chosen by or directly answerable to the public. Consequently, these schemes lack those attributes of trust found in the judicial process.

---

123. Tyler, supra note 122, at 439–40.

124. Id. at 440–41.

125. Id. at 441–42.

126. Lind et al., supra note 121, at 980.

127. Id. at 981.

128. See Daniel W. Shuman et al., Jury Service—It May Change Your Mind: Perceptions of Fairness of Jurors and Nonjurors, 46 SMU L. Rev. 449, 470 (1992) (a study of jury service which revealed that for most people jury service enhances perceptions of the fairness of the criminal justice system).

If, as various empowerment theories suggest, people seek more from compensation decisions than money itself,[129] the work of the procedural justice theorists supports the restorative potential of tort compensation. The process control that allows an injured person to decide whether to institute a tort claim demands that the injurer answer questions about his or her conduct. Additionally, a person's sense of fairness and control over life may be enhanced by having a trusted decisionmaker determine the responsibility for the harm in a dignified proceeding. From a procedural justice perspective, tort litigation may be important to restore injured plaintiffs not only because the outcome vindicates the plaintiff, but also because the process itself may be therapeutic. Tort litigation provides the plaintiff an opportunity to tell an important story in a culturally meaningful context which manifests that society values the litigant. How well the process in fact fulfills that idealized goal in each case may be a matter of some dispute.

Not all victims leave the tort system feeling better. Cases are often dealt with by mass production techniques, litigants are often pressured to settle, and those who demand their day in court may be forced to wait years for trial. Tort litigants whose cases are resolved prior to trial may feel that their disputes were not important enough to warrant a trial and that they did not receive the court's full attention. Claimants excluded from any of this formality, however, may similarly feel that their disputes lacked importance or attention.

IV. Implications for Restoration of the Injured

A. Tinkering with the Tort System

Even if the tort system was remodeled to resolve cases quickly, inexpensively, and consistently, the requirement of a causal link between the plaintiff's injury and the defendant's blameworthiness would leave a gap resulting in serendipitous compensation. "Tort law thus has developed as a system of principles for redressing certain types of harm caused by certain types of behavior by certain types of injurers to certain types of victims—a 'system' incomplete at best."[130] Because a comprehensive system for redressing all harm, both that caused by culpable conduct and that not caused by culpable conduct, would require abandonment of fault-based liability,[131] a leap that may be viewed as an abandonment of personal responsibility,[132] some vestige of the tort system seems likely to remain if only as a moral signpost. Thus, although it is important to ask whether the restorative potential of tort law is worth the costs and inefficiencies of the fault-based system, it is also important to tinker with the existing tort system to enhance its restorative capacity.

---

129. See supra part III.C.
130. Owen, supra note 10, at 665–66 (footnotes omitted).
131. See id.
132. See J.M. Balkin, The Rhetoric of Responsibility, 76 Va. L. Rev. 197 (1990).

1. Less Than Complete Insurance

Although the tort system may play a marginal role in compensation for injury,[133] it occupies an important symbolic role that may best explain the energy and emotion it generates. Unfortunately, the pervasiveness of liability insurance may frustrate the use of tort sanctions to enforce personal responsibility. Liability insurance distributes the costs of tort liability throughout society rather than visiting those costs directly on the injurer.[134] There may be, however, some ways that the tort system might be accommodated to advance restoration beyond payment of compensation.

One way to enhance the restoration of plaintiffs, within the current structure of the tort system, is to require that defendants personally fund a portion of the plaintiffs' compensation. Liability insurance is pervasive and spreads the cost of compensation. It is not likely to disappear, and it serves many useful purposes, including the avoidance of uncompensated catastrophic loss.[135] By sheltering defendants completely from the direct financial impact of the judgment, however, liability insurance may frustrate any balance-reshaping effect of the judgment.[136] The transfer of funds from defendant to plaintiff is a restorative act that may help reshape the equitable balance in a relationship. The insights of empowerment theories suggest that the defendants' copayment of the cost of compensation may advance the plaintiffs' restoration.[137]

This suggestion is not simply a rehash of the argument about the impact of liability insurance on the deterrence goal of tort law.[138] That argument is concerned with how liability insurance may insulate defendants from the deterrent effect of the tort sanction. Although my argument suggests an interrelationship of deterrence and compensation, because of my doubts about the capacity of the current system to deter precisely,[139] it focuses not on how liability insurance shapes the behavior of injurers, but on how liability insurance shapes the restoration of the injured.

There is no research that supports a precise formula to calculate what amount the defendant should pay to restore the balance of power between the injured and the injurer. Furthermore, the absolute amount or percentage of the judgment or settlement paid by the defendant may not be as important to the plaintiff as the fact that the payment represents a change in that balance of power.[140] Indeed, as the amount of the judgment is based on compensable loss to the plaintiff rather than the power imbalance between the parties, the ab-

---

133. Hensler et al., supra note 4, at 175.

134. See Patricia M. Danzon, Medical Malpractice: Theory, Evidence, and Public Policy 118 (1985).

135. Gary T. Schwartz, The Ethics and the Economics of Tort Liability Insurance, 75 Cornell L. Rev. 313, 315 (1990).

136. Ingber, supra note 35, at 790.

137. See supra part III.C.1.

138. See, e.g., Louis L. Jaffe, Damages for Personal Injury: The Impact of Insurance, 18 Law & Contemp. Probs. 219 (1953); George L. Priest, Insurability and Punitive Damages, 40 Ala. L. Rev. 1009 (1989).

139. Shuman, supra note 17, at 165–66.

140. See Smith, supra note 1, at 794.

solute amount of the judgment may not be a reflection of the imbalance in the relationship or the symbolic amount that the defendant should pay personally to rectify it. The goal is to find an amount that is large enough to be meaningful, yet not so large as to encourage bankruptcy or risk leaving plaintiffs undercompensated.

One alternative for setting this amount in cases that proceed to trial with issues of comparative fault or causation is to use these assessments of fault or causation to set the amount that the defendant should pay personally. The amount might be computed by looking at the difference in the jury's assessment of the parties' relative fault or causation. If the defendant's fault or causation greatly exceeds the plaintiff's (by more than seventy-five percent, for example), the defendant might be required to pay a significant percent of the judgment personally (ten percent, for example). Correlatively, if the defendant's fault or causation exceeds the plaintiff's by only a small amount (less than twenty percent, for example), the defendant might be required to pay an insignificant percent of the judgment personally (one percent, for example). In cases that do not typically involve issues of comparative causation, these instructions might nonetheless be added to assist in assessing the defendant's personal responsibility for the judgment. Ultimately, a body of decisions might provide guidance for the settlement of other cases.

The decision whether to craft judicial or legislative rules that require defendants to pay a percentage or a minimum absolute amount to prevent defendants from insuring against one hundred percent of the risk should await the opportunity for private implementation of this approach. Given that many large businesses and governmental entities are now self-insured or purchase liability insurance with high deductibles or co-insurance,[141] market forces and education of counsel may encourage this result without the necessity of governmental coercion. Insurers may discover that plaintiffs are willing to accept lower dollar settlements when defendants agree to fund a symbolically significant portion of the settlement personally. Certainly, this is an issue that merits empirical research. Because most cases are resolved by settlement[142] and because there is an incentive for the insurer to encourage defendants to fund a portion of the plaintiffs' recovery, there may be no need for official coercion to encourage this arrangement. Insurers may incorporate this approach in their policies because it simultaneously reduces their exposure and mitigates the plaintiffs' injuries.

2. An Apology

An apology validates the victim's experience. Empowerment theories recognize that an apology is one way to acknowledge responsibility for harm and is

---

141. George Eads & Peter Reuter, Designing Safer Products: Corporate Responses to Product Liability Law and Regulation 110–11 (1983).

142. Over 90% of all cases filed in federal court are resolved without trial. See Report of the Proceedings of the Judicial Conference of the United States 4–5 (March 12, 1991); Report of the Proceedings of the Judicial Conference of the United States 40–41 (Sept. 23–24, 1991); Annual Report of the Director of the Administrative Office of the United States Courts 206–07 (1991); see also David M. Trubek et al., The Costs of Ordinary Litigation, 31 UCLA L. Rev. 72, 86 (1983).

an important component of the restorative process.[143] An apology simultaneously explicates the injurer's role in causing the harm and responds to the indignity of the harmful conduct by offering the injured an important showing of respect. There is good reason for tort law to encourage apology, or at least to avoid discouraging it.

The importance to injured persons that injurers acknowledge responsibility for harm also finds support in medical malpractice claims data. Studies of individuals who suffer harm in their medical care reveal that one significant variable explaining the likelihood of a tort claim is the perception that the physician has maintained good communication and has not attempted to deceive the patient.[144] When physicians are more forthright about what has occurred and assume responsibility for it, patients are less likely to sue. One plausible explanation for this phenomena is that the physician's acknowledgment of responsibility provides their patients with restorative benefits that others seek in tort litigation.

One way that tort law could encourage apology is to account for it in the computation of damages. This approach is not new and has a lengthy history in the law of defamation. A public apology is admissible in many jurisdictions to mitigate damages in defamation actions.[145] The research reported in this Article provides a good reason to expand this beyond defamation to other claims for intangible loss when the defendant makes a meaningful apology.[146]

Of what should a meaningful apology consist? Hiroshi Wagatsuma and Arthur Rosett suggest five conjunctive elements of a meaningful apology:

1. the hurtful act happened, caused injury, and was wrongful;
2. the apologizer was at fault and regrets participating in the act;
3. the apologizer will compensate the injured party;
4. the act will not happen again; and
5. the apologizer intends to work for good relations in the future.[147]

These requirements of an acknowledgment of responsibility and compensation for the injury occasioned are sensible but raise a number of questions when applied to tort law. How can the sincerity of the apology be judged? What

---

143. Wagatsuma & Rosett, supra note 88, at 487.

144. Gerald B. Hickson et al., Factors That Prompted Families to File Medical Malpractice Claims Following Perinatal Injuries, 267 JAMA 1359, 1362 (1992).

145. See, e.g., Fla. Stat. ch. 770.02 (1993) ("If...[an] apology...was...published...then the plaintiff in such case shall recover only actual damages."); Tex. Civ. Prac. & Rem. Code Ann. § 73.003(a)(3) (West 1986) ("To determine the extent and source of actual damages and to mitigate exemplary damages, the defendant in a libel action may give evidence of... any public apology...."); see also Townsley v. Yentsch, 135 S.W. 882, 885 (Ark. 1911); Linney v. Maton, 13 Tex. 449, 458 (1855).

146. The authority to impose this solution does not appear to pose serious constitutional problems. In addition to withstanding challenge in the defamation context, this approach has also been upheld in the criminal context under the federal sentencing guidelines which recognize acceptance of responsibility as a factor in sentence reduction. United States v. Saunders, 973 F.2d 1354, 1363–64 (7th Cir. 1992), cert. denied, 113 S. Ct. 1026 (1993); see David B. Wexler, Therapeutic Jurisprudence and The Criminal Courts, 35 Wm. & Mary L. Rev. 279, 287 (1993).

147. Wagatsuma & Rosett, supra note 88, at 469–70.

damages must the injurer compensate? Is the apology admissible against the defendant in a trial seeking other damages?

Because a defendant's apology is not regarded as hearsay under the admission exception to the hearsay rule and is not excludable as a compromise if made outside the context of settlement negotiations,[148] it is unlikely that a legally informed defendant would apologize unless the apology limited the defendant's liability. To provide an incentive for a defendant to apologize, the apology should limit liability for other intangible loss. Yet, if the apology commits the defendant to nothing more than penitent words, it would be difficult to gauge its sincerity. To provide some objective measure of sincerity, the apology should commit the defendant to pay actual compensation for tangible loss.

One alternative would be to preclude the recovery of punitive damages when a defendant makes a meaningful apology. As a consequence of the apology, which necessarily admits responsibility for the harm and thereby advances the restoration of the injured, the defendant would simultaneously limit his or her responsibility to pay punitive damages. Assessing defendants punitive damages may be sensible to enhance the deterrence of reprehensible conduct, but awarding punitive damages to a plaintiff is paradoxical because such damages are not intended to compensate for any loss the plaintiff has suffered.[149] An apology is responsive both to the extent of the plaintiff's loss and to the wrongfulness of the defendant's conduct. Particularly in cases where liability is clear and the real issue is the extent of punitive damages, this alternative may advance the resolution of the proceedings and the restoration of the plaintiff.

As punitive damages are relatively rare,[150] however, this proposal, while theoretically interesting, may affect few cases. A controversial proposal with more bite would link apology to a limitation of damages for all intangible losses. Because the decision to award damages for intangible losses makes sense, if at

---

148. A statement of a party sought to be introduced against that party falls within the admission exception/exclusion from the hearsay rule. Fed. R. Evid. 801(d)(2). If that statement is made within the context of settlement negotiations, it will be excluded to encourage civil compromises. Fed. R. Evid. 408.

149. Based, in part, upon the notion that punitive damages are not intended to compensate the plaintiff for any loss suffered, a number of states now provide for state allocation of a percent of private punitive damage awards. See, e.g., Colo. Rev. Stat. § 13-21-102(4) (West Supp. 1993) (33%); Fla. Stat. Ann. § 786.73(2)(b) (West Supp. 1994) (35%); Ga. Code Ann. § 51-12-5.1 (e)(2) (Supp. 1994) (75% in product liability cases only); Ill. Ann. Stat. ch. 735 para. 512-1207 (Smith-Hurd 1992) (discretion of the court); Iowa Code Ann. § 668A.1 (2)(b) (West 1987) (75% when defendant's conduct not directed specifically to plaintiff); Kan. Stat. Ann. § 60-3402(e) (Supp. 1993) (50% in medical malpractice); Mo. Rev. Stat. § 537.675(2) (Supp. 1992) (50%); N.Y. Civ. Prac. L. & R. § 8701(1) (McKinney Supp. 1994) (20%); Or. Rev. Stat. § 18.540(1)(c) (Supp. 1994) (50%); Utah Code Ann. § 78-18-1(3) (1992) (50%). For a discussion of the constitutionality of this approach, see Paul F. Kirgis, Note, The Constitutionality of State Allocation of Punitive Damage Awards, 50 Wash. & Lee L. Rev. 843 (1993).

150. Deborah Hensler, Summary of Research Results on the Tort Liability System 4 (1986); See Also Mark Peterson et al., Punitive Damages: Empirical Findings (1987); Michael Rustad, Demystifying Punitive Damages in Products Liability Cases: A Survey of a Quarter Century of Trial Verdicts (1991); Stephen Daniels & Joanne Martin, Myth and Reality in Punitive Damages, 75 Minn. L. Rev. 1 (1990).

all, as an aid in empowering plaintiffs by restoring imbalances in relationships, an apology may be an effective alternative to accomplish this goal. A defendant who makes a meaningful apology may advance the plaintiff's emotional healing more effectively than an award of damages for the intangible portion of the loss.

Another way in which the law could encourage apology is to consider it as an affirmative defense to certain torts whose principal concern is the protection of dignitary interests. Thus, in suits for injury to reputation or privacy, for example, a timely, sincere, and public apology may achieve all that tort sanctions can reasonably be expected to achieve both in terms of restoring the plaintiff and in deterring the defendant.[151] Indeed, at least in the Japanese culture, the "availability of social restorative mechanisms like apology obviates formal legal sanction in many cases."[152]

Some may respond to this proposal to use apology to limit damages for some or all intangible personal injury that plaintiffs may prefer money to an apology. This response assumes that plaintiffs enjoy an entitlement to damages for intangible personal injury that is immune from judicial or legislative action. Of course, plaintiffs do not. Judicial recognition of damage claims for intangible personal injury is relatively recent and far from firmly entrenched, and legislative limitation of these damage claims has become common. More importantly for the purpose of this Article, plaintiffs should be entitled to these damages only if they advance some goal of the tort system, that is, their restoration. Thus, those who maintain that they are entitled to these damage claims must explain how the claim advances their restoration more effectively than an apology.

B. Outside the Realm of the Tort System

While the tort system's symbolic role may remain an important part of our culture, its overall impact on compensating the injured is marginal. In the opinion of many observers, abolition of the tort system is imminent.[153] Even if its demise is not imminent, it may be possible to enhance the restorative capacity of other systems for injured persons who do not proceed through the tort system. Thus, a core issue to consider in the psychology of compensation is the implication of this research for systems in which compensation is not linked to fault.

1. The Criminal Justice System as an Alternative to Tort Findings of Fault

Proposals to remove fault from compensation encourage closer scrutiny of the criminal justice system. Not only is the deterrent capacity of the criminal justice system of increased importance without a fault-based tort system, but the criminal justice system also remains the primary source of formal judgments of responsibility for harmful conduct. Thus, it is appropriate to examine the restorative potential of the criminal justice system for victims as an alternative to tort law.

---

151. See Ingber, supra note 35, at 835–36.
152. Wagatsuma & Rosett, supra note 88, at 464.
153. Smith, supra note 1, at 765.

The focus of the criminal justice system is to bring the perpetrator to justice.[154] The constitutional parameters of the criminal justice system delineate the limits of governmental authority in its prosecution of the accused, but make no reference to the role or rights of the victim. In addition, a crucial assumption of American criminal law is that a criminal act is a wrong against society.[155] Thus, the interests of the victim have been considered relevant in the criminal justice system only to the extent that they coincide with the government's interest in bringing the perpetrator to justice.[156]

Therefore, it is appropriate to ask about the psychological impact of the criminal justice system on the recovery of victims. The restorative benefits of the American criminal justice system for crime victims appear to be the "vicarious thrill from seeing the criminal punished."[157] A violation of the criminal law, however, is an offense against the state, and prosecution normally lies within the sole discretion of the public prosecutor. Therefore, the receipt of these restorative benefits turns on choices made by the prosecutor of what evidence to present and in what form. The victim stands mute, except when instructed to speak, at the periphery of the criminal justice system. Beyond this doctrinal limitation on the ability of the victim of crime to participate in the prosecution of a defendant, the criminal justice system is regularly accused of being unresponsive and inhospitable to the needs of victims.[158]

Two movements in the criminal justice system, however, require additional evaluation. Increasingly, victim compensation statutes have authorized payments by the guilty party to the victim, and increasingly victims have been permitted to participate in the proceedings arising out of their injuries. Victim compensation within the criminal justice system is an old idea resuscitated by victims' rights advocates.[159] Statutory schemes in existence in many states authorize the victim to receive money from the state to compensate for certain losses sustained by criminal activity. Unlike the tort process, however, in victim compensation schemes there is no nexus between the victim and the criminal. Thus, the empowering potential of making the injurer pay after a determination of responsibility for harm does not exist in the victim compensation setting. While this observation is not a criticism of victim compensation schemes,

---

154. United States v. Leon, 468 U.S. 897, 953 n.12 (1984) (Brennan, J., dissenting) (citing Potter Stewart, The Road to Mapp v. Ohio and Beyond: The Origins, Development and Future of the Exclusionary Rule in Search-and-Seizure Cases, 83 Colum. L. Rev. 1365, 1400 (1983)).

155. United States v. Barnett, 330 F.2d 369, 415 (5th Cir. 1963), certified question answered by 376 U.S. 681 (1964).

156. Juan Cardenas, The Crime Victim in the Prosecutorial Process, 9 Harv. J.L. & Pub. Pol'y 357 (1986).

157. Richard E. Laster, Criminal Restitution: A Survey of its Past History and An Analysis of its Present Usefulness, 5 U. Rich. L. Rev. 71, 82 (1970).

158. See, e.g., Karen L. Kennard, Comment, The Victim's Veto: A Way to Increase Victim Impact in Criminal Case Dispositions, 77 Cal. L. Rev. 417, 417–18 (1989).

159. Roger E. Meiners, Victim Compensation: Economic, Legal, and Political Aspects 1–5 (1978). Prior to the end of the Anglo-Saxon period in England, no distinction existed between personal injury involving public and private wrongs, as we now recognize these separate notions of wrong. 2 W.S. Holdsworth, A History of English Law 33 (1909).

it shows a limitation of the ability of such schemes to aid in the restoration of the injured. Of course, a compelling reason for the enactment of these schemes is the inadequacies of the tort system—the necessity for proof of the defendant's fault and the ability of the defendant to satisfy a judgment.

Most reports of crime do not result in apprehension and prosecution of a suspect,[160] and most criminal defendants are assessed as indigents in need of appointed counsel.[161] Thus, victim compensation schemes operate more like no-fault schemes, in which payments are made without regard to the ability to identify the defendant or the financial ability of the defendant to satisfy a judgment. Only if a victim blames the state for a harm that resulted from the failure of the state to protect its citizens[162] does payment from the victim compensation fund purport to empower the victim.

Increasingly, as a matter of custom[163] and positive law,[164] victims are given the opportunity to be heard in bail, sentencing, and parole decisions, although their impact on these decisions is unclear. It is still the case, however, that the criminal justice system does not afford the victim substantial involvement in the charging or prosecution of a case.[165] One recent innovation is the Victim-Offender Reconciliation Program,[166] in which the victim and the offender negotiate directly with the assistance of a mediator. While increasing the opportunity for the victim to participate in some process with the injurer, victim-offender reconciliation programs address criminal wrongs as a matter appropriate for negotiation, rather than as a formal adjudication of responsibility. Instead of adjudications of fault, these programs offer victims the opportunity to live out "the Christian message of reconciliation and peace."[167] The victim is offered an opportunity to get answers about the circumstances of the offense and the offender or obtain an agreement for restitution, but not to obtain an adjudication of responsibility for it.[168] In effect, these programs say to victims, you can control the process as long as it does not involve punishment or a finding of wrongdoing. Yet, this is arguably exactly what victims need for their restoration.[169]

---

160. "Recent statistics show that for every one hundred violent crimes committed in the United States, fifty-five incidents are reported to the police; eighteen assailants are apprehended; eleven cases are filed for prosecution; nine defendants are convicted, six are incarcerated; four go to jail and two are sent to prison." Lois H. Herrington, Personal Responsibility in Criminal Law, 77 Cornell L. Rev. 1057, 1057 (1992).

161. See, e.g., Judith Resnik, Tiers, 57 S. Cal. L. Rev. 837, 1008 (1984).

162. Bruce R. Jacob, Reparation or Restitution by the Criminal Offender to His Victim, 61 J. Crim. L. & Criminology 152, 153 (1970).

163. Donald J. Hall, The Role of the Victim in the Prosecution and Disposition of a Criminal Case, 28 Vand. L. Rev. 931, 934–61 (1975).

164. See, e.g., Payne v. Tennessee, 501 U.S. 808, 824–27 (1991) (rejecting an attack on the constitutionality of permitting the use of a victim impact statement in a capital sentencing determination).

165. Hall, supra note 163, at 978–79.

166. Mark S. Umbreit, Mediation of Victim Offender Conflict, 1988 J. Disp. Resol. 85, 87.

167. Mark Umbreit, Crime and Reconciliation 99 (1985).

168. Id.

169. See infra note 177 and accompanying text.

2. Alternative Forums for Addressing the Psychology of Compensation

If there are restorative benefits to fault-based tort compensation, can these restorative benefits be enjoyed outside the tort system? Most injured persons do not pursue tort claims, and those who do are the targets of reformers who would abolish or severely limit those claims. What lessons can be learned about the restorative benefits of tort compensation to assist those for whom tort compensation is unavailable or undesirable?

At its restorative best, the tort system offers plaintiffs the opportunity to be heard in a dignified and culturally meaningful proceeding that conveys a message that society cares what happened and to have a judgment of responsibility made by a trusted decisonmaker who helps reshape the balance of power between the plaintiff and the defendant. There is no reason that injured parties must pursue these goals exclusively within the tort system or the criminal justice system. Although costly judicial apparatus may lend credence to the dignity and concern evinced by the proceedings, there are less costly and time consuming ways to achieve these same ends. Indeed, one factor that emerges from research on the effects of litigation is the correlation between improvement in psychological symptoms and "a longer time after resolution of the litigation and a shorter time between injury and litigation."[170]

It seems reasonable, having so framed the question, to ask whether the alternative dispute resolution movement, specifically mediation,[171] responds to these restorative concerns. There are numerous deontologically based objections to alternative dispute resolution—loss of the right to trial by jury, separation of powers, due process, and equal protection concerns—that focus on the consequential loss of rights as compared to a traditional trial by judge and jury.[172] Without passing judgment on these objections, the focus here is not on these legalistic claims, but on the impact of these differing procedures on the restorative process.

Mediation, though less formalistic than the traditional judicial system and offering less procedural control, may nonetheless offer plaintiffs an opportunity to be heard in a dignified proceeding that conveys a message that society cares and is presided over by a trusted individual.[173] What mediation lacks, like other forms of alternative dispute resolution, is the opportunity for a judgment of responsibility that may help reshape the balance of power between the injured and the injurer.[174]

---

170. Renee L. Binder et al., The Course of Psychological Symptoms After Resolution of Lawsuits, 148 Am. J. Psychiatry 1073, 1074 (1991).

171. I have chosen to include only mediation rather than arbitration not merely because arbitration is not an alternative system, but also because arbitration has developed into an institution beset with its own host of problems.

172. See G. Thomas Eisele, Differing Visions—Differing Values: A Comment on Judge Parker's Reformation Model for Federal District Courts, 46 SMU L. Rev. 1935 (1993).

173. Lind et al., supra note 121, at 980–83.

174. Even proponents of alternate dispute resolution note that even mandatory programs are "accorded too little binding authority." Robert M. Parker & Leslie J. Hagin, "ADR"

Mediation may help the parties find a dollar amount that fairly represents the risks of trial, but the mediator is only a neutral facilitator who assists the parties in resolving their dispute.[175] "The mediator...has no higher authority to invoke, and rebuffs requests to make findings of fact or decisions about blameworthiness."[176] When the parties, assisted by the mediator, cannot themselves agree about responsibility for harm, the mediator cannot make those judgments. Moreover, some disputes are not appropriate for compromise or negotiation. What a claim is worth is negotiable; whether or when it is acceptable to drive while intoxicated or abuse a child or a spouse is not negotiable, and the decision risks reinforcing the imbalance of power.[177] Therefore, while mediation may be the solution to many problems, it lacks a core component of the restorative benefits many plaintiffs seek in tort law— societal judgments of responsibility.[178]

People want to know that they are taken seriously by society and that moral relativity has its limits. Not all disputes are negotiable.[179] It is important for the restoration of victims that they be able to institute a process in which these societal judgments of fault and responsibility can be made.[180] Before people came to rely on courts, their neighborhood, religion, or profession served this function.[181] The conclusion that a person's neighborhood, religion, or profession no longer defines how that person finds his or her community does not

---

Techniques in the Reformation Model of Civil Dispute Resolution, 46 SMU L. Rev. 1905, 1910 (1993).

175. Leonard L. Riskin, The Special Place of Mediation in Alternative Dispute Processing, 37 U. Fla. L. Rev. 19, 24–27 (1985).

176. Charles A. Bethel & Linda R. Singer, Mediation: A New Remedy for Cases of Domestic Violence, 7 Vt. L. Rev. 15, 18 (1982).

177. Barbara Hart, Gentle Jeopardy: The Further Endangerment of Battered Women and Children in Custody Mediation, 7 Mediation Q. 317, 320–22 (1990).

178. See Fischer et al., supra note 103, at 2142 (arguing that mediation has serious problems when used for relationships that involve a culture of battering and may actually increase the risk of domestic violence). But see Kathleen O. Corocoran & James C. Melamed, From Coercion to Empowerment: Spousal Abuse and Mediation, 7 Mediation Q. 303 (1990).

179. See David M. Engel, The Oven Bird's Song: Insiders, Outsiders, and Personal Injuries in an American Community, 18 Law & Soc'y Rev. 550, 567–68 (1984).

180. See id.

181. Cf. id. (discussing the impact of social and economic changes on the role of formal law in mediation in a close-knit society). One provocative response that might be considered in light of this loss of a collective moral compass is revitalization of community to define these norms. See, e.g., Amital Etzioni, the Spirit of Community: Rights, Responsibilities, and the Communitarian Agenda (1993); Alasdair MacIntyre, after Virtue: A Study in Moral Theory (1981); Michael Sandel, Liberalism and the Limits of Justice (1982); Michael Taylor, Community, Anarchy and Liberty (1982). Of course, the communitarian concern with a shared common good as a response to individualism run amok risks that the restorative needs of the individual will not be given a high priority. See Derek L. Phillips, Looking Backward: A Critical Appraisal of Communitarian Thought 176 (1993) (noting that the societies identified by communitarians as ideological models were often based on the denial of basic human rights to women, minorities, and the poor).

compel a further conclusion that society's adjudicative function can only be performed by courts.[182]

V. Conclusion

It is appropriate to end with a caveat. None of the research examined in this Article proves that tort recovery has a therapeutic or antitherapeutic affect on plaintiffs. Hopefully, this examination will generate research directed towards this issue. The existing research does, however, strongly suggest that there are both potential restorative benefits and serious restorative disadvantages to fault-based compensation. These consequences should be explored more extensively before jettisoning fault-based tort compensation in favor of first-party insurance or no-fault compensation.

The lessons to be learned from this exploration point in the direction of enhancing the restorative potential of tort law and other systems that address injuries. These directions are neither inconsistent nor mutually exclusive. To discuss the therapeutic potential of tort law and other compensation systems recalls what therapists already know: No single therapy is right for everyone. Successful therapists, therefore, vary their techniques based upon what works with a patient. Some plaintiffs seek only money to compensate for their losses and may be equally satisfied with other systems of compensation that lack an adjudication of responsibility but are quicker and less costly.[183] Other plaintiffs seek only an adjudication of responsibility to assist in their restoration and turn to tort law because it is the only system for achieving this finding over which they can exercise process controls. Alternative forums for the adjudication of responsibility for harm may be equally psychologically satisfying for these persons and also may make these adjuducations more available to the majority of injured persons who do not pursue tort claims for their losses. For those plaintiffs who seek not only an adjudication of responsibility but also money damages for their losses, enhancing the restorative potential of tort law offers to fulfill the promise of tort law's goal of compensation.

---

182. For a discussion of a collection of nonjudicial and largely nonadjudicative alternative mechanisms for redress of grievances, see No Access to Law: Alternatives to the American Judicial System (Laura Nader ed., 1980).

183. O'Connell and Simon's study of automobile accident claimants compensated by the other driver's insurer revealed that claimants infrequently harbored anger or ill will toward the other driver and that payment for pain and suffering played no role in assuaging any anger that might exist. Jeffery O'Connell & Rita J. Simon, Payment for Pain & Suffering: Who Wants What, When & Why?, 1972 U. Ill. L.F. 1, 26. While individuals who sustain minor damage from minor automobile accidents might not be expected to harbor anger or ill will towards the other driver, individuals who suffer permanent disabling injuries resulting from grossly negligent conduct of other drivers might be expected to feel differently. O'Connell and Simon did not examine this issue.

Chapter 23

Limiting the Psychotherapist-Patient Privilege: The Therapeutic Potential

Jeffrey A. Klotz

The relationship between a psychotherapist[1] and patient is a special one. It has long been assumed that confidentiality and trust are the building blocks of an effective therapeutic alliance.[2] The security of the relationship between therapist and patient is expected to increase the patient's willingness to reveal all of his innermost feelings, desires, and emotions. It is this freedom of disclosure, thought to be essential to the nourishment of a healthy therapeutic relationship, that is itself thought to be essential to favorable treatment outcomes.[3]

The laws of evidence have recognized the importance of fostering the trust between psychotherapist and patient. The psychotherapist-patient privilege is the evidentiary device that recognizes the intimacy of this alliance. By preventing the mandatory disclosure of certain communications made to the therapist by the client, it is assumed that the privilege ensures the patient's full disclosure of personal details that aid in the treatment process.

The assumptions upon which the psychotherapist-patient privilege rests have been challenged in a series of empirical studies.[4] These "privilege studies"

---

1. As used in this essay, the term "psychotherapist" will refer to a broad group of individuals who provide psychological services to their clients. See Cal. Evid. Code § 1010 (West Supp. 1990).

2. The therapeutic alliance has been defined as "the interactive process between the patient and therapist that develops from the patient's need or desire to solve a health problem and the therapist's desire to assist the patient in this endeavor." Hipshman, "Defining a Clinically Useful Model for Assessing Competence to Consent to Treatment," 15 Bull. Am. Acad. Psychiatry L. 235 (1987).

3. Lambert, Shapiro & Bergin. "The Effectiveness of Psychotherapy," Handbook of Psychotherapy and Behavior Change 157–211 (S. Garfield & A Bergin eds. 3d ed. 1986), Buetler, Crago, & Arizmendi, "Therapist Variables in Psychotherapy Process and Outcome," Handbook of Psychotherapy and Behavior Change 280–281 (S. Garfield & A. Bergin eds. 3d ed. 1986). Orlinsky & Howard, "Process and Outcome in Psychotherapy," Handbook of Psychotherapy and Behavior Change 327–352 (S. Garfield & A. Bergin eds. 3d ed. 1986), Hymer, "The Therapeutic Nature of Confessions," 13 J. Contemp. Psychotherapy 129 (Fall & Winter 1982) (hereinafter Hymer).

4. Shuman & Weiner, "The Privilege Study: An Empirical Examination of the Psychotherapist-Patient Privilege," 60 N.C.L. Rev. 893–942) (1982) (hereinafter Shuman & Weiner); Weiner & Shuman, "Privilege—A Comparative Study," 12 J. Psychiatry & L. 373 (1984); Shuman, Weiner, & Pinard, "The Privilege Study (Part III): Psychotherapist-Patient Communications in Canada," 9 Int'l J. L. & Psychiatry 393 (1986) (hereinafter Shuman, Weiner & Pinard) (hereinafter, collectively, "the privilege studies").

suggest that the presence or absence of an absolute psychotherapist-patient privilege actually has little impact upon a patient's willingness to reveal personal thoughts to a psychotherapist. From these findings, one might understandably conclude, as do the authors of the privilege studies, that were the law purged of the psychotherapist-patient privilege, there would be little if any impact on treatment outcomes. However, the absence of an absolute psychotherapist-patient privilege *could* influence therapeutic results: The absence of the privilege could actually *prevent* harmful behavior. Were the absolute psychotherapist-patient privilege removed[5] from the typical therapeutic relationship, those patients who make potentially incriminating communications to their therapists (e.g., of the desire or intent to commit a crime) might be less likely to act on those urges. They might be deterred from engaging in behaviors that have foreseeable legal consequences in order to avoid disclosure of the communication in a future criminal proceeding. In short, the removal of the psychotherapist-patient privilege could be therapeutically beneficial.[6]

Psychotherapist-Patient Privilege

Background

A legal privilege, in general, is an evidentiary tool that, when invoked, allows the holder of the privilege to prevent the admission of relevant evidence into judicial proceedings. Privileges are the product of a balancing test. To qualify, the privileged relationship must be considered paramount to the fundamental principle that "the public...has a right to every man's evidence."[7] As Dean Wigmore has stated: "The injury to the relationship that would result from disclosure of the communication must outweigh the benefits of disclosure for purposes of the litigation."[8]

A privilege typically can be invoked by one who stands in special relationship to another to whom confidential information has been conveyed.[9] Typical

---

5. A suggestion of this essay is that short of eliminating the privilege entirely, the privilege should be unavailable in situations when the patient has acted on the harmful urges revealed to the therapist. Some jurisdictions already recognize a similar but broader exception to the privilege when the patient *threatens* future harm to identifiable victims. See note 23 infra. The proposed exception would rescind the privilege for any statements made by patients to therapists regarding intentions to commit future crimes, but only if the patient *acted* on those urges and was apprehended.

6. The proposal fits neatly within the framework of what Professor Wexler has called "therapeutic jurisprudence," the study of the role of the law as a therapeutic agent. D. Wexler, Therapeutic Jurisprudence: The Law as a Therapeutic Agent (Carolina Academic Press, 1990) (hereinafter D. Wexler).

7. United States v. Bryan, 339 U.S. 323, 331 (1950).

8. 8 J. Wigmore, Evidence § 2285 (McNaughton rev. ed. 1961).

9. Not all privileges are relational. Other privileges include the privilege to refuse to disclose one's vote at a political election (Proposed Fed. R. Evid. 507); the privilege to refuse to disclose one's trade secret (Proposed Fed. R. Evid. 508); the privilege to refuse to disclose secrets of state and other official information (Proposed Fed. R. Evid. 509) and the privilege of a government official to refuse to disclose the identity of an informer (Proposed Fed. R. Evid. 510).

privileged relationships include lawyer-client,[10] husband-wife,[11] clergyman-penitent,[12] physician-patient,[13] and psychotherapist-patient.[14] Proposed Federal Rule of Evidence 504(b), as originally submitted to Congress by the Supreme Court, reflects the prototypical statement of the general rule of the psychotherapist-patient privilege:

> A patient has a privilege to refuse to disclose and to prevent any other person from disclosing confidential communications, made for the purposes of diagnosis or treatment of his mental or emotional condition, including drug addiction, among himself, his psychotherapist, or persons who are participating in the diagnosis or treatment under the direction of the psychotherapist, including members of the patient's family.[15]

The psychotherapist-patient privilege is usually not absolute, as legislatures often carve out exceptions to it. Such exceptions, which vary considerably from state to state, include a patient-litigant exception,[16] a court-appointed therapist exception,[17] a crime or tort exception,[18] an exception for breach of duty arising out of the psychotherapist-patient relationship,[19] an exception in proceedings to determine the sanity of a criminal defendant,[20] an exception in proceedings to establish competency,[21] and an exception for children under sixteen years of age who are the victims of a crime.[22] There is also an exception that allows the therapist to protect against future crimes involving danger to the patient or others[23] and an exception in child

---

10. Proposed Fed. R. Evid. 503.

11. Proposed Fed. R. Evid. 505.

12. Proposed Fed. R. Evid. 506.

13. Uniform R. Evid 503.

14. Proposed Fed. R. Evid. 504.

15. Proposed Fed. R. Evid. 504, 56 F.R.D. 103, 240–241 (1973). Congress did not adopt this rule. Proposed Federal Rule 504 remains important, however, because it has been adopted in some states as the particular jurisdiction's version of the privilege. See generally J. Weinstein & M. Berger, Weinstein's Evidence. ¶¶ 504-1–504-72 (1989) (hereinafter J. Weinstein & M. Berger).

16. See, e.g., Cal. Evid. Code § 1016 (West 1966).

17. Id. § 1017 (West Supp. 1990).

18. Id. § 1018 (West 1966). Statutes differ from one jurisdiction to another as to the applicability of the psychotherapist-patient privilege in criminal proceedings. Some statutes make a blanket exception for all criminal proceedings; others provide that the privilege is removed when the defendant raises the issue of insanity. 47 Am. Jur. 2d Proof of Facts 721 (1987).

19. See, e.g., Cal. Evid. Code § 1020 (West 1966).

20. Id. § 1023.

21. Id. § 1025.

22. Id. § 1027 (West Supp. 1990).

23. Id. § 1024 (West 1966). These "dangerous patient" exceptions are closely related to, but distinct from, the duties imposed upon therapists by Tarasoff v. Board of Regents, 17 Cal. 3d 425, 551 P.2d 334, 131 Cal. Rptr. 14 (1976) (*Tarasoff II*), *vacating* 13 Cal. 3d 117, 529 P.2d 663, 118 Cal. Rptr. 129 (1974) (*Tarasoff I*), which confers upon a therapist the duty to use reasonable care to protect third persons threatened by their patients. See Howell & Ogles, "Psychologist-Client Privileged Communication Laws for the Fifty States: Duty to Report, Duty to Warn," 7 Am. J. Forensic Psychology 5 (1989) (hereinafter Howell &

abuse cases.[24]

A vast majority of states have enacted either a physician-patient, psychiatrist-patient, psychologist-patient, or psychotherapist-patient privilege.[25] Although these privilege statutes vary greatly, they tend to have certain features in common, such as the requirement that the person making or receiving the communication be a patient; that the communication be made to a psychotherapist in the course of a professional relationship; that the patient intend the communication to be and remain confidential; that the communica-

---

Ogles) (compares privileges with statutory and case law surrounding the duty to report and the duty to warn and protect); People v. Clark, 50 Cal. 3d 583, 789 P.2d 127, 268 Cal. Rptr 399 (1990), *reh'g denied and modified*; Shaw v. Glickman, 45 Md. App. 718, 415 A.2d 625 (1980); Mavroudis v. Superior Court for the County of Mateo, 102 Cal. App. 3d 594, 162 Cal. Rptr. 724 (1980)

> [T]he exception is applicable if the court finds that, prior to the time of the injury complained of, the therapist determined, or reasonably should have determined, that the therapist's patient presented a danger of violence to a readily identifiable victim and the disclosure of confidential communications was necessary to prevent the threatened danger.

Mavroudis, 162 Cal. Rptr. at 733. Duties to protect are much broader and a greater invasion on the privacy and autonomy of patients than are the related exceptions to privilege. The distinction is that *Tarasoff* imposes an affirmative duty upon a therapist to protect a specifically identifiable victim before harm occurs, whereas exceptions to the privilege allow the introduction into evidence of the statements themselves, assuming they become relevant in a subsequent proceeding. Typically, however, those states that abrogate the privilege for future crimes also impose adjoining duties on psychologists to protect third persons. Howell & Ogles, supra.

24. Some states have expressly exempted evidence of psychotherapists' child abuse reports from the application of the psychotherapist-patient privilege. See, e.g., Cal. Penal Code § 11171(b) (West 1982) (privilege is not applicable in any court proceeding to information reported pursuant to the Child Abuse Reporting Act). These exceptions are related to but distinct from child abuse reporting laws, enacted by legislatures in all fifty states, which often require specified individuals, including psychotherapists, to report suspected physical abuse to child welfare agencies. See, e.g., Cal. Penal Code §§ 11165–11174 (West 1982 & Supp. 1990) (child abuse reporting act); Note, "Vanishing Exception to the Psychotherapist-Patient Privilege: The Child Abuse Reporting Act," 16 Pac. L.J. 335 (1984); Howell & Ogles, note 23 supra. These duties to report, like the duties to protect or warn discussed in note 23 supra, are much broader and involve a greater intrusion into privacy and patient autonomy than do the exceptions to the psychotherapist-patient privilege. Statutes requiring reporting or warning call for intrusion into the privacy of the patient before the privilege issue ever matures. As a result, any harm as a result of the intrusion would already be felt by the patient prior to the introduction of therapeutic communications into a judicial proceeding. At least *Tarasoff*, the dangerous patient exception to the privilege, and child abuse reporting laws are premised on the same policies as proposed here: Prevention of harm in certain instances must supplant privacy interests of the patient. E.g., In re Kevin F., 261 Cal. Rptr. 413, 213 Cal. App. 3d 178 (App. 3 Dist. 1989).

25. Howell & Ogles, note 23 supra (as of 1989, forty-seven out of fifty states have the privilege. The article presents a tabular summary and review of the psychologist-client privilege statutory laws for the fifty states and the District of Columbia); see also J. Weinstein & M. Berger, note 15 supra, at ¶¶ 504-36–504-72, for a discussion of the varying states' adaptations of proposed Fed. R. Evid. 504.

tion not be made in the presence of a third person (unless the third person was present to further the patient's interest in the consultation or treatment), and so forth.[26]

Rationale

Effective psychotherapy often involves the sharing of intimate details of a most personal nature. The psychotherapist-patient privilege is premised primarily on Freudian psychoanalysis, which is based on the fundamental rule that the patient must fully disclose to the therapist his thoughts or feelings.[27] Any encumbrances on this disclosure apparently hinder effective therapy. It is assumed that patients are less likely to reveal this type of information if there is a chance that it will be made known to those outside the therapeutic relationship.[28] This notion is reflected in the Proposed Federal Rule of Evidence 504 advisory committee note:

> Among physicians, the psychiatrist has a special need to maintain confidentiality. His capacity to help his patients is completely dependent upon their willingness and ability to talk freely. This makes it difficult if not impossible for him to function without being able to assure his patients of confidentiality and, indeed, privileged communication...[T]here is wide agreement that confidentiality is the *sine qua non* for successful psychiatric treatment...Therapeutic effectiveness necessitates going beyond a patient's awareness and, in order to do this, it must be possible to communicate freely. A threat to secrecy blocks successful treatment.[29]

Five possible theoretical justifications for a psychotherapist-patient privilege have been articulated.[30]

> 1. **The absence of a privilege deters people from seeking needed therapy.** In the absence of a privilege, potential patients may refrain from seeking help for fear of being labeled mentally ill....The advantage of a privilege at this stage is the assurance of privacy, that the individual's status as the patient of a psychotherapist will not be revealed to others." [31]

---

26. 47 Am. Jur. 2d Proof of Facts 721, 743 (1987).

27. Shuman & Weiner, note 4 supra, at 897; 23 S. Freud, An Outline of Psychoanalysis, in Standard Edition of the Complete Psychological Works of Sigmund Freud 141 (1964).

28. Shuman & Weiner, note 4 supra, at 898.

29. Proposed Fed. R. Evid. 504 advisory committee note [quoting from the report of the Group for the Advancement of Psychiatry. Report No. 45, Confidentiality and Privileged Communication in the Practice of Psychiatry (Report No. 45, 1960)].

30. Shuman & Weiner, note 4 supra, at 898–899.

31. The authors of the first privilege study note that this premise is based upon an incorrect assumption regarding the operation of the law: The privilege does not generally prevent disclosure of an individual's status as a patient. *Id.* at 900–901. The majority of federal courts addressing the issue have failed to recognize the need for confidentiality as to the *fact* of treatment. Note, "The Case for a Federal Psychotherapist-Patient Privilege That Protects Patient Identity," 1985 Duke L. J. 1217 (1985); Alameda County v. Superior Court (Darlene W.), 239 Cal. Rptr. 400, 194 Cal. App. 3d 254 (1987) (identity of mental patient who allegedly raped another mental patient in county facility was not privileged against discovery

2. **The absence of a privilege delays people from seeking needed therapy.** Although the potential stigma that flows from the mental illness label may not result in a failure to seek therapy, it may result in delay in seeking therapy, thereby extending the duration of a patient's emotional problems. Thus, a privilege may result in more rapid consultation with a therapist.[32]

3. **The absence of a privilege impairs the quality of therapy.** Successful treatment requires frank disclosure that cannot occur without the assurance of confidentiality that aids in developing the trust necessary between therapist and patient.[33]

4. **The absence of a privilege causes premature termination of therapy.** The psychotherapist-patient relationship is based upon trust. If the therapist reveals a confidential patient communication under court order, that trust will be destroyed and the relationship will terminate prematurely. The privilege avoids the possibility of compelled judicial disclosure.[34]

5. **The absence of a privilege leads to compelled judicial disclosure of patient communications, which results in psychological harm to patients.** The absence of a privilege permits a court to order a therapist to disclose relevant patient communications. These communications, containing "the patient's inner most fears and fantasies," touch upon very sensitive components of the patient. Public revelation of this information will result in psychological harm to the patient.[35]

These questionable empirical assumptions[36] provided the basis for the privilege studies' scientific inquiry.

---

under psychotherapist-patient privilege by alleged victim in personal injury action against county); In re Zuniga, 714 F.2d 632 (6th Cir.), *cert. denied*, 464 U.S. 983 (1983). But see Scull v. Superior Court, 254 Cal. Rptr. 24, 206 Cal. App. 3d 784 (1988) (the mere disclosure of a patient's identity violates the psychotherapist-patient privilege because the harm to the patient's interest in privacy is exacerbated by the stigma that society often attaches to mental illness).

32. Again, the privilege does not generally prevent a person's status as a patient from being known. Note 31 supra.

33. Shuman & Weiner, note 4 supra, at 901, note that the effectiveness of psychotherapy in resolving mental or emotional problems is still in question. *See* Marshall, "Psychotherapy Works, but for Whom?" 207 Sci. 506 (1980); Durham & La Fond, "A Search for the Missing Premise of Involuntary Therapeutic Commitment: Effective Treatment of the Mentally Ill," 40 Rutgers L. Rev. 303–370. Also, as mentioned in note 27 supra, and accompanying text, this premise rests on the psychoanalytic philosophy of treatment, which is the only school of psychotherapy that requires full disclosure. Plaut, "A Perspective on Confidentiality," 131 Am. J. Psychiatry 1021 (1974). See discussion in Shuman & Weiner, note 4 supra, at 901–903.

34. Psychotherapists, however, have not generally advocated an absolute privilege, which implies that either therapists do not accept the validity of this premise, or, that they recognize that other societal concerns might be more important than those protected by the privilege. Shuman & Weiner, supra note 4, at 903. But see Freedman, Confidentiality, in Comprehensive Textbook of Psychiatry/III (H. Kaplan, A. Freedman, & B. Sadock eds. 1980).

35. This premise is weakened for the same reasons set forth in note 34 supra.

36. Shuman & Weiner, note 4 supra, note other arguments in favor of the psychotherapist-patient privilege that are not based upon any particular model of psychotherapy. The right to privacy argument asserts that the psychotherapist-patient relationship is an area of human relations into which the state should not intrude. Id. at 899; Shuman, Weiner, & Pinard, note 4 supra; Krattenmacker, "Testimonial Privileges in Federal Courts—Alterna-

The Privilege Studies

Prompted by the passage of a 1979 psychotherapist-patient privilege statute in Texas,[37] as well as the paucity of sound empirical research on the assumptions underlying the psychotherapist-patient privilege, the first of three studies was conducted[38] designed to test the empirical assumptions upon which the typical psychotherapist-patient privilege rests.[39]

Based upon the results of their empirical inquiries, the privilege researchers generally concluded that the presence of the absolute psychotherapist-patient privilege "is consequential in the inception and conduct of a therapeutic relationship for only a small percentage of individuals who might consider therapy for the treatment of an emotional problem."[40] More specifically, the authors concluded that:

1. Patients are probably not deterred from seeking psychiatric help to any significant degree by the absence of the privilege, partly because they are generally unaware of the privilege when deciding to seek therapy.[41]
2. The absence of privilege does not typically delay potential patients from seeking treatment.[42]

---

tives to the Proposed Rules of Federal Evidence," 62 Geo. L. J. 61, 85–86 (1973); Saltzburg, "Privileges and Professionals: Lawyers and Psychiatrists," 66 Va. L. Rev. 597, 622 (1980). Although the privilege is to be liberally construed in favor of the patient, and the court should heed the basic privacy interests involved in the privilege (Patterson v. Superior Court, San Mateo County, 193 Cal. Rptr. 99, 147 Cal. App. 3d 927 (1983)), this principle is limited when necessary to protect the safety of society. In re Kevin F., 261 Cal. Rptr. 413, 213 Cal. App. 3d 178 (App. 3 Dist. 1989). The present proposal is consistent with this policy that in certain instances in which harm is threatened by patients, the privacy interests of those patients must yield to the interests of public protection. See notes 8 and 24 supra. The limited exception that is suggested here attempts to protect the privacy interests of patients as much as possible by being narrow in scope, applying only after the patient has acted on his criminal impulses.

> Another justification offered for the privilege is that judicial determinations should not rely on inherently confusing psychiatric testimony. Shuman & Weiner, supra note 4, at 899–900; Slovenko, "Psychotherapist-Patient Testimonial Privilege: A Picture of Misguided Hope," 23 Cath. U.L. Rev. 649 (1974). A third position asserts that the privilege is necessary to protect psychotherapists from the "inconvenience and annoyance" frequently suffered by witnesses. Shuman & Weiner, note 4 supra, at 901; Katz, Privileged Communications: A Proposal for Reform, 1 Dalhousie L.J. 597 (1974).

37. Tex. Rev. Civ. Stat. Ann. art. 5561h (Vernon Supp. 1982).

38. Note 4 supra.

39. The authors attacked the empirical problem from several different angles. Shuman & Weiner, note 4 supra, at 917–924. The studies were basically divided into several questionnaire "sub-studies," including a "lay study," a "patient study," a "therapist study," and a "judge study." Although the generalizability and validity of the findings have been questioned (DeKraai & Sales, "Confidential Communications of Psychotherapists," 21 Psychotherapy 293 (1984) (hereinafter DeKraai & Sales) for the purposes of discussion, the validity of the privilege studies' findings will be assumed.

40. Shuman & Weiner, note 4 supra, at 927.

41. Id. at 924–925.

42. Id. at 925.

3. Patients often withhold information from their therapist, but this bears little relationship to fear of disclosure. The basic reason patients withhold information is because they fear the judgment of their therapists; the ethics of the therapist and confidentiality[43] are most important for therapeutic trust. Interestingly, psychologically sensitive information was withheld more often than legally sensitive information, and patients avoid withholding or discussing acts or thoughts of violence.[44] The presence of the privilege, then, does not greatly increase a patient's willingness to convey private thoughts.[45]

4. A threat to disclose or actual disclosure by a therapist causes a small number of premature terminations from therapy and probably deters a large percentage of these people from seeking further help. However, the incidence of actual disclosure may be minimal.[46]

5. Although actual disclosure can lead to premature termination in a few cases, there is no convincing evidence that psychological harm comes to those patients whose confidences have been revealed in judicial proceedings.[47]

6. The impact that the lack of privilege has on the accuracy of judicial proceedings is, at most, minimal.[48]

Proponents of an absolute psychotherapist-patient privilege argue that eliminating the privilege would be *antitherapeutic*, as it would reduce the likelihood of effective therapy. The privilege studies suggest that, at the least, this position is overstated, and that perhaps abolishing or limiting the application of the privilege would *not* have the devastating antitherapeutic effects that concern proponents of the privilege. Aside from a few isolated cases, eliminating the privilege would probably not be *antitherapeutic*; the therapeutic effects would, presumably, be *neutral*. The next logical step, then, would be to surmise how abrogating the absolute privilege might actually be *therapeutic*.[49] The possibility of taking that step is the thrust of this essay.

---

43. The concept of confidentiality must be distinguished from that of evidentiary privilege:

> An evidentiary privilege is a law that permits a person to prevent a court from requiring revelation of relational communications. Confidentiality refers to a duty, frequently an ethical limitation imposed by a profession, not to disclose relational communications. These ethical limitations prohibit gratuitous disclosure of patient communications—for example to one's spouse or friend. Thus, they provide substantial assurances that, in the ordinary course of events, nothing told to one's therapist will be disclosed to others. But they do not abrogate the duty to respond to compulsory judicial process.

Id. at 912 (footnotes omitted). Clearly, the concept of confidentiality is much broader than that of privilege. See generally DeKraai & Sales, note 39 supra.

44. Shuman, Weiner & Pinard, note 4 supra.

45. Shuman & Weiner, note 4 supra, at 925–926.

46. Shuman & Weiner, note 4 supra, at 926–927.

47. Id at 926, 927.

48. Id. at 927.

49. D. Wexler, note 6 supra, has suggested that under the rubric of "therapeutic jurisprudence," the law can be divided into three parts: substantive rules, legal procedures, and judicial and legal roles. Each of these, in turn, can have either therapeutic, neutral, or antitherapeutic effects.

Therapeutic Potential

Assuming that the findings of the privilege studies are valid, let us discuss how, in the absence of an absolute psychotherapist-patient privilege, the typical therapeutic relationship could be tailored to improve therapeutic results. Consider the following cases.

Case 1. Patient (*P*) consults Therapist (*T*) because *P* has recently been having the urge to shoplift every time *P* goes into a store, although *P* has never acted on those urges. *P* is concerned and hopes *T* can help him to curb these impulses.

Case 2. Because *P* has in the past had the urge to expose himself to strangers, he seeks the help of *T*, whom he believes will help him to overcome these desires and prevent future instances of indecent exposure.

Case 3. *P* seeks psychotherapy because *P* has been recently experiencing episodes during which thoughts of committing sexual violence almost overwhelm him. During the course of therapy, *P* reveals to *T* his strong desire to sexually assault an unspecified woman, although he has never done so.

Case 4. *T* is treating *P*, who initially came to *T* because *P* has a problem controlling his temper. During the course of therapy, *P* tells *T* of his problem and that sometimes he tries to pick fights or physically assault people. *P* expresses to *T* his urge to continue to do so.

In each of the preceding cases, the patient has expressed to the therapist the desire or intent to commit a future crime. When the patient comes to the therapist because of his or her criminal urges,[50] the therapist could, in the absence

---

50. Four therapeutic scenarios are possible. The following diagram may prove helpful:

Patient Acted on Criminal
Impulses in the Past?

		No	Yes
		A Case 1 Case 3	B Case 2 Case 4
Patient Seeking Treatment for Criminal Urges?	Yes		
	No	C X	D X

In the cases presented (Cells A and B), the patient probably had no pre-apprehension about *T*'s whistle-blowing since, after all, treatment was sought specifically for the criminal urges. Conceivably, patient candor in those instances will be less affected by the absence of a privilege. The destructive urges could also come to light, however, during treatment for another problem (Cells C and D). In those situations, the suggested therapeutic motivators might operate, but could conceivably be weaker. Since both *T* and *P* probably will not have foreseen these urges being communicated during therapy, patient candor regarding collateral criminal urges might be more inhibited than when treatment is sought specifically for those criminal urges, especially if *P* deems as unnecessary the revelation of criminal urges not specifically related to the problem that is the focus of treatment.

of a privilege, structure therapy in a way that could help deter these patients from committing the future criminal acts.

In the initial therapy session, it would be important for the therapist to tell the patient he or she would be *non-judgmentally* assessed by the therapist. It would be equally important for the therapist to inform the patient that subject to certain limitations,[51] *confidentiality* would be ensured, but that there is no absolute psychotherapist-patient privilege.[52] The therapist would need to, of

---

51. The therapist should, at this point, inform the patient of the other limits on confidentiality that may exist in the particular jurisdiction, such as duties to warn or report potential harm. See notes 23 and 24 *supra*.

52. Empirical research suggests that such "psychological Mirandizing" (i.e., informing patients as to the status of the law and the scope and limits of their rights) should not reduce the patients' willingness to disclose, and that in fact, omitting such a "warning" may be therapeutically damaging. In a survey of psychiatrists in clinical practice, Beck found that 40 percent had been involved in a case in which a *Tarasoff*-type warning was given to a potential victim. Warnings that were not initially discussed with the patient were found to have a harmful therapeutic effect. In other words, if the patient thinks all communications are absolutely confidential, yet later finds out that they are not, this might be what undermines trust and treatment outcomes, not the actual disclosure itself. Beck concluded that the important factor of these warnings is the integration into therapy, which can serve as a limit-setting function and decrease patient violence. Beck, "When the Patient Threatens Violence: An Empirical Study of Clinical Practice After *Tarasoff*," 10 Bull. Am. Acad. Psychiatry L. 189 (1982). Informing the patient of the status of privilege law might also serve such a "limit-setting" function. Apprising the patient of the limits of confidentiality has been viewed as:

> (1) an opportunity to discuss some of the difficulties and hazards along the therapeutic process, (2) an opportunity to collaborate with patients in the decision-making process about how the therapy should proceed, and (3) an aid in the establishment of the therapeutic alliance...and can provide patients a cognitive preparation for some of the struggles that lie ahead.

Jensen, Josephson, & Frey, "Informed Consent as a Framework for Treatment: Ethical and Therapeutic Considerations," 43 Am. J. Psychotherapy 378, 380–381 (1989).

Indeed, therapists might have an ethical obligation to inform patients of their limited rights. Failing to apprise patients of the limits on confidentiality, including exceptions to the absolute psychotherapist-patient privilege, might actually contravene the ethical requirement of informed consent. "The doctrine of informed consent imposes upon a therapist the duty to disclose to the patient all relevant information concerning the proposed treatment, including collateral hazards attendant thereto, so that the patient's consent to treatment will be an intelligent one." Comment, "Tarasoff v. Regents of the University of California," 22 N.Y.L. Sch. L. Rev. 1011, 1021, n. 49 (1977). Not surprisingly, therapists are often reluctant to discuss the limits of confidentiality with their patients. In fact, present practice seems to be based on deception: Therapists often get a patient to talk by allowing the patient to incorrectly believe that confidentiality is absolute. One study has suggested that even though therapists generally believe that most patients in fact incorrectly assume that information disclosed to their therapists is absolutely confidential, and 70 percent of the therapists surveyed reported their belief that confidentiality could properly be breached in some circumstances, only about 11 percent of therapists reported always discussing confidentiality; the majority did so only "sometimes." Note, "Where the Public Peril Begins: A Survey of Psychotherapists to Determine the Effects of *Tarasoff*." 31 Stan. L. Rev. 165 (1978). Most therapists discuss the limits of confidentiality only if the issue arises during the course of treatment, rather than raising the issue on their own initiative. Id.

course, make sure the patient was aware of the difference between confidentiality and privilege[53] so that the patient would not incorrectly believe that the absence of a legal privilege indicates the absence of an ethical duty to maintain confidentiality.[54] Such an introductory statement might take the following form:[55]

> Because you have voluntarily come to therapy, it is clear that you want to get better. I, too, share this objective. Throughout the course of treatment, it is very important that we build a trusting relationship. It is essential that you feel free to tell me anything and everything, and that you are not inhibited in any way in telling me your innermost thoughts and feelings. This will help me to help you get better. I will not judge you in any way by what you tell me. You must know then that everything you tell me during therapy is confidential. This means that, subject to certain limitations,[56] I must not tell others what you tell me. I cannot tell my friends, your friends, your family, anyone. I have an ethical duty in the ordinary course of events not to tell anyone what is said during our therapy sessions, and I promise you that what you tell me will be kept confidential.
>
> You must also be aware, however, that in this state, there is no absolute psychotherapist-patient privilege. What this means is that if, for some reason, what is said between us in therapy becomes relevant to a judicial proceeding, I could be compelled to tell the court the content of the communication. For example, if you are arrested for a crime, and go to trial, I can be compelled to disclose in the judicial proceeding what you have told me relating to the crime with which you have been charged, your intention to commit it, and so forth.

In short, the therapist would make it clear that the therapist could be required to testify as to the patient's confidential communications were legal proceedings instituted. In fact, this display of honesty and straightforwardness may actually bolster the patient's confidence in the therapist's integrity and truthfulness.[57] Be-

---

The suggested model (informing patients about the limits of confidentiality) would move us from the present deceptive model to a more realistic model based upon true informed consent. Saxton, "Confidentiality Dilemmas for Psychologists and Psychiatrists in the Criminal Justice System," 4 Am. J. Forensic Psychology 25 (1986) (suggesting that the limits of confidentiality should be expressed to inmate clients).

53. See note 43 supra.

54. Implicitly, however, if the therapist ever actually testifies, then confidentiality will have been broken. However, when required to do so by law, therapists are exempt from the duty to maintain confidentiality, so this does not really amount to a breach of confidentiality at all. Am. Psychological Ass'n, "Ethical Principles of Psychologists," 36 Am. Psychologist 633 (1981); Am. Psychological Ass'n. "General Guidelines for Providers of Psychological Services," 42 Am. Psychologist 712 (1987); DeKraai & Sales, note 39 supra.

55. This statement is suggestive only. Therapists should tailor it according to their specific therapeutic needs and according to the relevant laws in the particular controlling jurisdiction.

56. The therapist should insert here the applicable statutory or common law limits on confidentiality that apply in the particular jurisdiction.

57. The warning itself may seductively imply to the patient that the therapist is someone who can be trusted. Am. Psychiatric Ass'n, Psychiatry in the Sentencing Process: Report of the Task Force on the Role of Psychiatry in the Sentencing Process, in Issues in Forensic Psychiatry (1984).

cause the patient would know of the possibility[58] of judicial disclosure, yet would still reveal therapeutically significant yet potentially legally incriminating information (e.g., as in the previous cases, the desire to shoplift, indecently expose oneself, rape, or assault), the patient might actually seek to avoid the behavior that might in fact necessitate judicial intervention. In other words, before acting on his impulses, the patient might realize that were he arrested and charged with the offense he told his therapist he desired to commit, his statements might be used against him in a court of law, and might render certain "defenses" futile.[59] These realizations might dissuade the patient from acting on those criminal impulses discussed during therapy. In this way, the limited privilege would not only fail to impair the quality of treatment, but might also have the therapeutic "side-effects" of deterring future criminal behavior.

Applying this analysis to the case examples provided might prove helpful. In Case 1, *P* is seeking treatment for shoplifting, the very behavior hoped to be deterred. The criminal desires to shoplift did *not* surface as part of treatment for another disorder, nor has *P* acted on his impulses in the past. The only concern in this first case, then, is the deterrence of *P*'s *future* crime of shoplifting. At *P*'s initial consultation, *T* would deliver something similar to the suggested initial statement regarding confidentiality and privilege. Recall that, according to the privilege studies, *P* will still retain *T*'s services, and *P* will eventually talk about his desires to shoplift in the future; after all, this is why he came to *T* in the first place. Nor will *P* be dissuaded from divulging because of the lack of privilege, since confidentiality was guaranteed to the full extent that the law would allow. Then, if *P* were harboring the desire to steal while out shopping,

---

58. In making the initial statement to the patient, the therapist must at least tell the patient that given the limited applicability of a privilege, the *possibility* exists that legal procedure may require disclosure of the contents of the patient's therapy sessions, i.e., that *T* may be required to testify if *P* is apprehended for a future crime discussed during therapy. Indeed, if the issue of *T* testifying ever comes up, it is very likely that it will be *P* that calls *T* to testify on his behalf, such as in support of an insanity defense or in a plea for mitigation of punishment. In such instances, disclosure would be a virtual certainty, and there already typically exist exceptions to the psychotherapist-patient privilege. See, e.g., Hawaii Rev. Stat. § 626-1, Rule 504. 1(d)(3) (1985). Perhaps *T* could even tell *P* that it may be *P* that *wants T* to testify; *P* might therefore be even less likely to censure the revelation of criminal desires to *T* knowing it might be to his advantage in a future proceeding.

If, on the other hand, the *state* wanted to use the communications *against P*, several contingencies would have to occur before actual disclosure of the communications would be possible: (1) *P* must act on the impulse expressed to *T*, (2) *P* must be apprehended for that criminal act; (3) the state must learn that *P* was in treatment; (4) the state must learn the identity of *T*; (5) *T* must be located and subpoenaed; (6) *T*'s testimony must be deemed admissible. The probability of each contingency occurring will obviously vary from case to case and from jurisdiction to jurisdiction, depending on the facts of the case and the given jurisdiction's laws pertaining to the admission of such statements expressing the desire to commit crimes. Therefore, it is unlikely that any estimate of probability would be accurate for any particular patient.

59. Notice that in these examples, not only does the deterrent effect come from the fear of *T*'s testimony providing positive evidence against *P*, but it also comes from *P*'s realization that typical "defenses" might become unconvincing in light of the expressed intention to commit an act.

P might recall that he had expressed his desire to shoplift to *T*. *P* would know that if he acts on his impulses and is apprehended, *T* could be called by the state to testify against *P*. *T*'s statements could supply the element of intent to the prosecutor. Were *T* to tell the court of *P*'s intention to steal, the typical defense of "I didn't mean to steal; I simply forgot to pay for the item," would evaporate.[60] Realizing all of this, *P* might be deterred from stealing.

In Case 2, *P* would deliver his introductory statement, perhaps including a statement relating to disclosure of past completed crimes.[61] In the course of treatment for his urge to expose himself, *P* will obviously tell *T* about those intentions and desires. Then, if *P* later gets the urge to expose himself again, *P* would recall that *T* possesses critical evidence that could be used against him. *P* might also realize that a fabricated defense, such as "I was urinating," would also fail. As a result, *P* might be disinclined to act on his impulses.

In Case 3, the sexually violent tendencies harbored by *P* are discussed during treatment. *T* would tell *P* about the state of the law regarding the absence of the privilege, and of his potential obligation if subpoenaed to testify regarding the patient communications relevant to the pending proceeding. Presumably, *P* would still reveal to *T* his desires to rape. Then, when contemplating committing a rape, *P* might recognize that evidence of his intent could be presented by *T* if *P* were, in fact, caught. *P* might also realize that an attempt to fabricate a "consent defense" might be frustrated, given *T*'s testimony that *P*

---

60. See note 59 supra.

61. It is assumed that it would be therapeutically beneficial for *P* to reveal past instances of criminal conduct similar to those for which *P* is seeking treatment. Hymer, note 3 supra. Although therapists may have obligations to report or warn of intended dangerous conduct, "there is no similar general requirement as to *completed* criminal conduct, 'dangerous' or not, of which the psychotherapist becomes aware." Applebaum & Meisel, "Therapists' Obligation to Report Their Patients' Criminal Acts," 14 Bull. Am. Acad. Psychiatry L. 221, 221–222 (1986) [hereinafter Applebaum & Meisel]; Applebaum, "Confidentiality in the Forensic Evaluation," 7 Int'l. J.L. & Psychiatry 285 (1985). A separate question is whether a therapist *may* report the past crimes of a patient, wherein the therapist runs the risk of incurring liability for breach of confidentiality. Applebaum & Meisel, supra. Given the very unlikely risk of liability for failing to report patients' past completed crimes, fear of prosecution for failure to report a past crime should not be a factor in a therapist's decision to discuss a patient's past crimes, nor should a patient be concerned that a therapist might report the crime. Id.

Should *P* be concerned that *T* might testify if *P* were apprehended for those past crimes discussed during therapy? The answer to that question might depend on the status of privilege law in the given jurisdiction. Of course, if no privilege existed, the confession would not be privileged, and the therapist could be required to testify. Knowing this, *P* might be reluctant, therefore, to reveal instances of past crimes to *T*. In jurisdictions where such confessions are not privileged, *T* might suggest that *P* reveal instances of past crimes in a general manner only. Arguably, if *P*'s statements to *T* about past crimes were only that "I have exposed myself in the past," they might be more prejudicial than probative. Fed R. Evid. 403. A simpler solution might be to simply retain the privilege for confessions of past crimes, which are generally privileged (See Alvord v. Wainwright, 564 F. Supp. 459 (D.C. Fla. 1983), *aff'd in part, rev'd in part*, 725 F.2d 1282, *reh'g denied*, 731 F.2d 1486, *cert. denied*, 105 S. Ct. 355, 469 U.S. 956, 83 L. Ed. 2d 291), while abrogating the privilege for statements relating to future crimes.

expressed an intention to assault a woman sexually. Consequently, *P* might avoid engaging in the destructive behavior given the increased likelihood of conviction if apprehended.

A fourth scenario is presented by Case 4. *P* is seeking treatment for his temper, and during therapy expresses the likelihood or desire to assault in the future, noting that he has acted on these impulses in the past. In the introductory statement, *T* would mention the limits of confidentiality, including the caveat about revealing past crimes.[62] Again, according to the results of the privilege study, *P* would still not be deterred from revealing to *T* his assaultive urges despite the absence of the privilege. Then, when *P* felt assaultive, he might actually avoid the behavior that could lead to the disclosure of his proclivity to violence and intention to commit violent acts by either leaving the situation (e.g., leaving the bar) or choosing not to fight at all. He might also realize that a typical defense of "self-defense" would go by the wayside, given testimony of his expressed intention to assault. In this way, injury would be prevented both to an unsuspecting third party and to *P* who would avoid punishment.

Compare these four results to what would happen if the psychotherapist-patient privilege applied to expressed desires to commit future crimes. If the privilege were operative, in each of the case examples given, *P* would reveal to *T* his or her desire to commit crimes. This might improve treatment outcomes.[63] This benefit would also continue if the privilege were limited as suggested. However, without the exception to the privilege in place, if *P* felt the urge to act on his criminal or violent impulses, the only deterrent would be fear of criminal liability. Hopefully, this might itself be enough to prevent *P*'s harmful actions. This deterrent effect is operative regardless of the existence of the privilege. If, however, in situations where the privilege is unavailable for expressions of criminal urges, *T* were then to inform *P* about the possibility of compelled judicial disclosure of confidential communications, *P* might have an *additional* incentive not to act on the impulses. Despite the modest deterrent effect that might be realized, such additional motivation would be more than would be realized were the proposed exception not recognized.

The traditional benefits of the privilege appear to be present even in the absence of the privilege; the costs of limiting the privilege appear to be minimal. Given the additional deterrent effect that could be realized in the *absence* of the absolute privilege, perhaps under the traditional balancing test,[64] the benefits of eliminating the privilege should tip the scale toward a future crimes exception: If the benefits of a limited exception to the privilege now surpass the benefits of preserving the absolute privilege, and the costs of a limited eradication of the privilege are low, elimination of the psychotherapist-patient privilege for statements expressing intent to commit future crimes becomes a viable option.

---

62. See note 61 supra.
63. See note 3 supra and accompanying text.
64. See note 8 supra and accompanying text.

Conclusion

The therapeutic goal of disposing of the absolute psychotherapist-patient privilege is the prevention of harmful behavior before it occurs. Prevention is preferred to post-harm intervention, which is often costly and ineffective in the prevention of further harm to society.[65] Prevention not only safeguards against injury to people and society as a whole, but also benefits the person whose harmful behavior has been prevented. That patient avoids incarceration, commitment, fines, and other forms of legal liability. Moreover, the burden on the system is lessened because the patient has avoided contact with the legal system altogether. Even those few patients adversely affected by the absence of the privilege might later decide to seek treatment or reveal confidences to the therapist after learning of other patients who have overcome impulse disorders by doing so.

Implementation of this proposal might also contribute to the patient's longer term post-treatment success. Although the initial impetus for the patient's refraining from certain criminal acts might be the fear of the increased probability of incurring criminal liability due to the limited privilege, if the patient actually controls the problematic behavior, he or she might learn that it is possible to control those impulses, and that the control comes from within.[66] The target patients should learn to attribute the reasons for their newly found self-control to themselves rather than some external force, such as the fear of punishment or judgment of their therapist.[67] The therapist can be instrumental and should play a role in influencing the patient's reattributional processes.[68]

This does not suggest that crime will be eradicated or that patients with criminal propensities will be cured by this proposal. However, if therapists can use the status of the law (limited privilege) to benefit therapy, that potential therapeutic power should be harnessed. The law may play a minor role, but it will play *a* role, and we should let it play that role if therapeutic effects will be realized.

---

65. See generally Preventing Crime (J. Cramer ed. 1978).

66. This has been called "self-efficacy," where the patient comes to believe not only that the benefits of certain actions outweigh the costs, but that he or she is capable of learning and performing or avoiding those actions effectively. D. Meichenbaum & D. Turk, Facilitating Treatment Adherence (1987) (hereinafter D. Meichenbaum & D. Turk).

67. Fear- and guilt-arousing inducements, while they might be effective in some instances, can actually interfere with adherence to some treatment regimens by triggering defensive reactions. D. Meichenbaum & D. Turk, note 66 supra, at 204–208.

68. Id. at 201.

Chapter 24

The Psychotherapist-Patient Privilege: A Therapeutic Jurisprudence View

Bruce J. Winick

[This chapter analyzes an issue before the United States Supreme Court in its 1995 term. As this book was in press, the Court decided the case, affirming the lower court's recognition of a psychotherapist-patient privilege under the Federal Rules of Evidence. *Jaffee v. Redmond*, 116 S. Ct. 1923 (1996).]

Although all fifty states recognize some form of psychotherapist-patient privilege,[1] the issue remains unresolved for the federal courts under the Federal Rules of Evidence. In the revisions to the Federal Rules of Evidence drafted by the Judicial Conference and approved by the Supreme Court in 1972, proposed Rule 504 explicitly provided for a psychotherapist-patient privilege for confidential communications made in connection with treatment.[2] Congress, however, rejected this proposed rule.[3] Instead, Congress adopted Federal Rule of Evidence 501, a general rule of privilege granting the federal courts wide discretion to recognize evidentiary privileges "in the light of reason and experience."[4] The lower federal courts are split on whether this broad language should be construed to recognize a psychotherapist-patient privilege,[5] and now the Supreme Court has granted review of a case that recognized the privilege

---

1. Jaffee v. Redmond, 51 F.3d 1346, 1356 & n.17 (7th Cir. 1995), cert. granted, 116 S. Ct. 334 (1995); Anne D. Lamkin, Should Psychotherapist-Patient Privilege Be Recognized?, 18 Am. J. Trial Advoc. 721, 723–25 (1995) (all fifty states and the District of Columbia have recognized the psychotherapist-patient privilege in some form); e.g., Alaska R. Evid. 504 (1995); Cal. Evid. Code §§ 1010–26 (West 1994); Colo. Rev. Stat. § 12-43-214 (1995); Fla. Stat. § 90.503 (1994); Utah R. Evid. 506 (1994); Va. Code Ann. § 8.01-400.2. (1994).

2. Rules of Evidence for United States Courts and Magistrates, 56 F.R.D. 183, 240–41 (1972). The proposed Rule set forth ten specified privileges, including a psychotherapist-patient privilege. Id. at 230–58.

3. Cf. Act of Jan. 2, 1975, ch. 157, 88 Stat. 1926 (establishing rules of evidence, not including proposed Rule 504).

4. Fed. R. Evid. 501.77.

5. Compare In re Doe, 964 F.2d 1325 (2d Cir. 1992) and In re Zuniga, 714 F.2d 632 (6th Cir.), cert. denied, 464 U.S. 983 (1983) (both recognizing a psychotherapist-patient privilege) with United States v. Burtrum, 17 F.3d 1299 (10th Cir.) (holding that the privilege does not apply in the context of a child sex abuse case), cert. denied, 115 S. Ct. 176 (1994) and In re Grand Jury Proceedings, 867 F.2d 562 (9th Cir.) (no psychotherapist-patient privilege for target of grand jury), cert. denied, 493 U.S. 906 (1989) and United States v. Corona 849 F.2d 562 (11th Cir. 1988) (no physician-patient or psychotherapist privilege under the common law in federal criminal trials), cert. denied, 489 U.S. 1084 (1989) and United States v. Meagher, 531 F.2d 752 (5th Cir.) (no physician-therapist privilege under the common law in federal criminal trials), cert. denied, 429 U.S. 853 (1976).

and applied it to psychiatric social workers.[6] In that case, *Jaffee v. Redmond*, the Court will decide whether the psychotherapist-patient privilege should be recognized in federal cases that do not require application of state law on the issue.

The facts of the case are interesting and reveal the importance of the privilege question. Mary Lou Redmond, an Illinois police officer, responded to a call concerning a fight in progress at an apartment complex. Arriving at the scene alone, she was advised that there had been a stabbing in the building. In the events that followed, Officer Redmond fired her gun and killed Ricky Allen.

The facts were in dispute. According to Redmond's testimony, Allen was chasing another man in the building with a butcher knife and had failed to heed the officer's warnings.[7] In contrast, testimony by several of Allen's relatives who were witnesses to the shooting suggested that Allen was not armed and that Officer Redmond had emerged from her police car with her gun drawn and shot Allen without warning.[8] Allen's surviving family members brought an action against Redmond in federal district court in Illinois, alleging that the officer's unnecessary use of force had infringed Allen's constitutional rights in violation of the Federal Civil Rights Act and that she had caused his death in violation of the Illinois wrongful death statute.[9]

Several days after the shooting, Officer Redmond began to visit Karen Beyer, a clinical social worker licensed under the law of Illinois and employed by the village for which Redmond worked.[10] Redmond saw her several times a week for counseling over approximately a six-month period.[11] The plaintiffs in the civil court action thereafter sought discovery of statements Redmond had made to her therapist and copies of Beyer's therapy notes. The trial court denied Redmond's motion to quash these discovery orders on the basis of a psychotherapist-patient privilege, finding that the Federal Rules of Evidence did not recognize extending such a privilege to psychiatric social workers.[12] When Beyer refused to answer certain questions at the deposition and produce her notes, the plaintiffs moved to compel, and the trial court ordered further discovery on the issue. When Officer Redmond refused to answer questions concerning what she had said to the therapist about the shooting, and Beyer produced only redacted portions of her therapy notes, the trial court permitted a jury instruction allowing the jury to draw an adverse inference resulting from Redmond's refusal to comply with discovery.[13] The jury returned a verdict for

---

6. Jaffee v. Redmond, 51 F.3d 1346 (7th Cir. 1995).

7. Id. at 1349.

8. Id.

9. Id. at 1348.

10. Id. at 1350. Under Illinois law, a licensed clinical social worker must have a master's or doctoral degree in social work from an accredited graduate school of social work and at least three years of supervised clinical social work experience. Id. at 1350 n.3 (citing Ill. Rev. Stat. ch. 225, para. 20/9 (1994)).

11. Id. at 1350.

12. Id. In contrast, Illinois recognizes a privilege for psychiatric social worker-patient communications. See id. at 1351 (citing Ill. Rev. Stat. ch. 740, para. 110/2, 110/10 (1994)).

13. Id. at 1351.

the plaintiffs. On appeal, the United States Court of Appeals for the Seventh Circuit reversed, finding that the trial court had erred in refusing to recognize a therapist-patient privilege under the Federal Rules of Evidence.[14]

In refusing to adopt a psychotherapist-patient privilege legislatively, Congress expressed its intent "not to freeze the law of privilege."[15] Instead, Congress left the issue to the federal courts, inviting them to develop a federal common law of evidentiary privilege.[16] With the federal circuit courts of appeals divided, the Supreme Court now will decide the issue: Should a federal psychotherapist-patient privilege be recognized; and should it apply to psychiatric social workers?

The issue before the Supreme Court is not a constitutional question, although it arises in a context in which the relevant constitutional values push strongly in the direction of construing the Federal Rules to recognize the privilege. Among those areas of constitutional privacy that are a part of the liberty protected by the Due Process Clauses of the Fifth and Fourteenth Amendments is "the individual interest in avoiding disclosure of personal matters."[17] Another is the liberty interest in making personal health care decisions.[18] A refusal to recognize the therapist-patient privilege would frustrate both these interests. But the issue before the Court is not the constitutionality of a federal rule of evidence denying the privilege. The Federal Rules do no such thing. Indeed, they explicitly leave open issues of evidentiary privilege, allowing the federal courts the authority to develop a federal common law of privilege.[19]

---

14. Id. at 1358.

15. Trammel v. United States, 445 U.S. 40, 47 (1980). In rejecting the proposed codification contained in Rule 504, Congress did not intend to disapprove or foreclose any of the specified privileges contained therein. The legislative history reflects that Congress did not reject Proposed Rule 504 on the merits, but that the resolution of the controversy it created would unduly delay the adoption of the entire rules package that had been submitted. See S. Rep. No. 1277, 93d Cong., 2d Sess. 6 (1974); see also 120 Cong. Rec. 40,891 (1974) (statement of Rep. Hungate) ("[T]he privilege section of the rules of evidence generated more comment or controversy than any other section.").

16. See S. Rep. No. 1277, supra note 15, at 13:

It should be clearly understood that, in approving this general rule as to privileges, the action of Congress should not be understood as disapproving any recognition of a psychiatrist-patient, or husband-wife, or any other of the enumerated privileges contained in the Supreme Court rules. Rather, our action should be understood as reflecting the view that the recognition of a privilege based on a confidential relationship and other privileges should be determined on a case-by-case basis.

See also 120 Cong. Rec. 40,891, supra note 15 (statement of Rep. Hungate) ("Rule 501 is not intended to freeze the law of privilege as it now exists.").

17. Whalen v. Roe, 429 U.S. 589, 599 (1977).

18. See, e.g., Riggins v. Nevada, 504 U.S. 127, 137 (1992) (recognizing a constitutional liberty interest in avoiding unwanted antipsychotic medication); Washington v. Harper, 494 U.S. 210, 229 (1990) (same); Cruzan v. Director, Mo. Dep't of Health, 497 U.S. 261, 278 (1990) ("The principle that a competent person has a constitutionally protected liberty interest in refusing unwanted medical treatment may be inferred from our prior decisions."); Bruce J. Winick, On Autonomy: Legal and Psychological Perspectives, 37 Vill. L. Rev. 1705, 1732–35 (1992) (discussing liberty interest in making personal health care decisions).

19. Fed. R. Evid. 501.

However, because recognizing a therapist-patient privilege would further these constitutional values, and rejecting it would frustrate them, the task of rule construction inevitably will be affected by the constitutional questions lurking in the background. While they do not decide the issue, these constitutional values certainly point toward recognition of the privilege.

Apart from constitutional considerations, what factors should guide the Court in reaching its decision? The recognition of any privilege, by depriving the courts of probative evidence, will inevitably harm the truth-determination process. The question is whether the value of recognizing a specific privilege outweighs this harm.[20]

In addressing the question presented in *Jaffee v. Redmond*—whether the Federal Rules of Evidence should be construed to permit a psychotherapist-patient privilege, and if so, whether it should extend to psychiatric social workers—the Court is directed to construe the federal rules in a way that permits the development of a common law of federal evidence in accordance with "reason and experience."[21] These words suggest that the Court should be sensitive to the consequences of its action. "The life of the law," Holmes told us, "has not been logic: it has been experience."[22] Among the many public policy considerations that might enter into this determination, the Court should examine closely the therapeutic or antitherapeutic consequences of its decision.[23] A therapeutic jurisprudence analysis of the issues before the Court suggests that significant positive therapeutic consequences would follow if the psychotherapist-patient privilege were to be recognized, and corresponding negative therapeutic consequences would ensue if it is not.

In an increasingly complex and stressful society, characterized by erosion of family and community, it is not surprising that mental illness is so prevalent. A recent study estimated that more than fifty-two million Americans suffer from a specific diagnosable mental disorder each year.[24] This represents more than

---

20. In a classic formulation of the standard for recognition of an evidentiary privilege, Dean Wigmore stated:

   (1) The communications must originate in a confidence that they will not be disclosed.
   (2) This element of confidentiality must be essential to the full and satisfactory maintenance of the relation between the parties.
   (3) The relation must be one which in the opinion of the community ought to be sedulously fostered.
   (4) The injury that would inure to the relation by the disclosure of the communications must be greater than the benefit thereby gained for the correct disposal of litigation.

8 John H. Wigmore, Evidence § 2285, at 527 (John T. McNaughton ed., 1961).

21. Id.

22. Oliver W. Holmes, Jr., The Common Law 1 (Gryphon Editions 1982) (1881).

23. See, e.g., David B. Wexler & Bruce J. Winick, Essays in Therapeutic Jurisprudence (1992); Law in a Therapeutic Key: Developments in Therapeutic Jurisprudence (David B. Wexler & Bruce J. Winick eds., forthcoming 1996).

24. See Darrel A. Regier et al., The De Facto U.S. Mental and Addictive Disorders Service System, 50 Archives Gen. Psychiatry 85, 88 (1993); see also Daniel Goleman, Mental Disorders Common, but Few Get Treatment, Study Finds, N.Y. Times, March 17, 1993, at C13 (discussing study by Regier).

twenty-eight percent of the adult population, or more than one in four.[25] Moreover, the statistics present a conservative picture.[26] Close to nine million of those with mental disorder develop the problem for the first time each year.[27] Another eight million of these suffer from a relapse of a condition developed earlier.[28] This study also estimated that of the more than fifty-two million Americans who suffer from mental illness each year, only 28.5 percent get help.[29]

Were more to get help, the many individual and social problems engendered by this high prevalence rate of mental illness would be considerably reduced. Were mental health treatment and counseling to be sought by more Americans, many of the severe social problems that characterize modern life—including divorce, child abuse and neglect, alcoholism and drug abuse, homelessness, poverty, employee absenteeism, and even crime—would be diminished. Many mental health problems are preventable with only a minimal amount of counseling that can help the individual to solve a personal problem, reduce stress, or cope with difficulties. Many mental disorders respond effectively to the broad range of treatment modalities currently available.[30]

Why, then, don't more people with mental health problems seek treatment, and how can we encourage more of them to do so? While at one level, the problem may involve the supply of therapists and the expense of obtaining their services, at another it may involve concern, particularly in our increasingly litigious society, that the most intimate and personal details of human life, revealed within the therapeutic relationship, might be the subject of subpoena and court-ordered disclosure.

The existing empirical literature is inconclusive concerning whether legal recognition of a psychotherapist-patient privilege is an important factor in whether people seek mental health treatment. Some studies suggest that people generally are unaware of legal rules relating to evidentiary privileges for professional communications and that their behavior in regard to obtaining or avoiding treatment is little affected by such legal rules.[31] This is consistent with studies showing little impact on patients' behavior in seeking therapy resulting from the *Tarasoff* rule,[32] which imposes a duty on therapists to warn individu-

---

25. Regier et al., supra note 24, at 88, 90.

26. The researchers counted only people who met all the official psychiatric diagnostic criteria for a disorder. People with "problems in living," such as marital difficulties, were excluded. Goleman, supra note 24, at C13.

27. Regier et al., supra note 24, at 88.

28. Id.

29. Id. at 90.

30. See Allen E. Bergin & Michael J. Lambert, The Effectiveness of Psychotherapy, in Handbook of Psychotherapy and Behavior Change 3, 143 (Allen E. Bergin & Sol L. Garfield eds., 4th ed. 1994).

31. See Daniel W. Shuman et al., The Privilege Study (Part III): Psychotherapist-Patient Communications in Canada, 9 Int'l J.L. & Psychiatry 393 (1986); Daniel W. Shuman & Myron S. Weiner, The Privilege Study: An Empirical Examination of the Psychotherapist-Patient Privilege, 69 N.C. L. Rev. 893 (1982); Myron F. Weiner & Daniel W. Shuman, Privilege—A Comparative Study, 12 J. Psychiatry & L. 373 (1984).

32. See James C. Beck, When the Patient Threatens Violence: An Empirical Study of the Clinical Practice After *Tarasoff*, 10 Bull. Am. Acad. Psychiatry & L. 189 (1982); Shuman &

als who are at risk of harm at the hands of their patients when revelations in therapy suggest such a threat.[33] These findings, however, are far from conclusive.[34]

Professors Daniel Shuman and Myron Weiner have performed three separate studies of the consequences of the psychotherapist-patient privilege.[35] The first study sought to assess the impact of a Texas statute that, for the first time, had adopted a psychotherapist-patient privilege.[36] Shuman and Weiner administered questionnaires to groups of psychiatrists, patients, laypersons (a sample of evening adult education students), and judges. The authors found that, at the outset of therapy, confidentiality was articulated as a concern by only fifty-four percent of the patients, and that only twenty-seven percent of the patients were aware of the new psychotherapist-patient privilege.[37] In addition, fifty-five percent of the psychiatrists reported themselves as unaware of the existence of the new privilege,[38] while seventy-four percent of those in the layperson sample were unaware of the privilege.[39]

Laypersons not in therapy were used to assess the extent to which a privilege would be a significant factor in their hypothetical decision whether to enter therapy should they encounter problems.[40] The authors concluded that patients are probably not deterred from seeking therapy to any significant degree by the absence of a privilege.[41] Because ninety-three percent of the lay sample would have sought therapy for serious emotional problems, even though seventy-four percent of the group were unaware of the existence of the privilege, the authors concluded that "the existence of a privilege could not have provided an incentive or avoided a barrier to therapy for these persons."[42]

Even leaving aside a variety of methodological problems with this study—small sample sizes, large non-response rates, selection of the patient sample by the psychiatrists in a non-randomized fashion, and the assumption that lay adult education students without mental health problems behave in a way similar to individuals that have such problems—the data do not seem to support the conclusion that the privilege does not play an important role in patient decisionmaking about whether to seek therapy. Let us assume that patients generally are unaware of the existence of a psychotherapist-patient privilege, as this Texas study demonstrated soon after enactment of a statute adopting such

---

Weiner, supra note 31, at 914–15; Note, Where the Public Peril Begins: A Survey of Psychotherapists to Determine the Effects of *Tarasoff*, 31 Stan. L. Rev. 165 (1978).

33. Tarasoff v. Regents of Univ. of Cal., 551 P.2d. 334 (Cal. 1976) (en banc). The court vacated and modified its previous opinion, Tarasoff v. Regents of Univ. of Cal., 529 F.2d 553 (Cal. 1974) (en banc), after rehearing. *Tarasoff*, 551 P.2d at 334.

34. See Shuman & Weiner, supra note 31, at 927 (concluding that both sides of the debate "have overstated their cases").

35. See supra note 31.

36. Shuman & Weiner, supra note 31, at 896–97.

37. Id. at 920.

38. Id. at 938.

39. Id. at 930.

40. Id. at 919.

41. Id. at 924–25.

42. Id. at 925.

a privilege. If they are unaware of the privilege, then of course it would not affect their decisions whether to seek therapy. Can it be assumed, however, that patients will be unaware of the privilege question once the Supreme Court has decided the issue and it receives the usual extensive publicity that follows Supreme Court decisions on matters of public interest? The important question, left unanswered by this research, is whether a Supreme Court opinion on this question will significantly increase awareness of the privilege, and whether such awareness will affect patient decisionmaking concerning whether to seek therapy. A new state statutory enactment of a psychotherapist-patient privilege is unlikely to make the front pages or the evening news, while a Supreme Court decision *denying* such a privilege will.

In fact, the Shuman and Weiner research in Texas suggests that people's awareness of the absence of a psychotherapist-patient privilege will dramatically affect their behavior. Without mentioning the existence of a privilege, the lay group was asked whether they would reveal to a therapist information concerning a series of subjects that included speeding, cheating on income taxes, physical violence, sexual fantasies, and work failure. A high percentage responded that they would reveal information concerning all of these categories. The group was then asked whether they would discuss these issues with a therapist in the absence of a psychotherapist-patient privilege, and "the response rate declined markedly."[43] Thus, if patients become aware of the absence of a privilege, as it can be assumed they would were the Supreme Court to decide against the privilege, the Shuman and Weiner study suggests that patient behavior would very much be affected.

Shuman and Weiner conducted a second study relating to privilege in South Carolina and West Virginia, which at the time were the only two states that did not have a psychotherapist-patient privilege.[44] This study suffered from similar methodological problems as the Texas study, and had an even higher non-response rate.[45] Once again, patients were shown to be unaware of the status of the psychotherapist-patient privilege in their state. Forty-one percent of the South Carolina/West Virginia patients incorrectly assumed that they possessed a privilege.[46] The authors again concluded that the existence of the privilege has little effect on patient decisionmaking concerning whether to enter therapy, but their conclusion is subject to the same limitations as previously discussed with regard to the Texas study. One may question whether the widespread misunderstanding on the part of patients in South Carolina and West Virginia concerning the existence of the privilege would apply after a high visibility Supreme Court decision rejecting a privilege. This study, therefore, also provides little support for a conclusion that patient behavior concerning therapy would be unaffected by a Supreme Court decision rejecting the privilege.

---

43. Id. at 919–20. The items most affected by this change in response rate had legal consequences. Id.

44. Weiner & Shuman, supra note 31, at 374–78.

45. Id. at 377 (43% of patients in the South Carolina and West Virginia studies responded to questionnaires, compared to 51% in Texas; 45% of therapists in the Texas study responded, compared to only 19% in the South Carolina and West Virginia study).

46. Id. at 381.

In a third study, Shuman, Weiner, and a Canadian colleague, Professor Gilbert Pinard, compared responses by psychiatrists, patients, judges, and a lay group of university students in two Canadian provinces, Ontario, which had no privilege, and Quebec, which had a form of the psychotherapist-patient privilege.[47] Here, too, the study found widespread lack of awareness concerning the presence or absence of a privilege, leading the authors to conclude that privilege had little bearing on patient decisionmaking concerning therapy.[48] Once again, it is not surprising that a factor concerning which patients were unaware or confused had little bearing on their decisionmaking. Once again, it may be questioned whether a high visibility Supreme Court decision on the issue would give rise to an entirely different situation. In summary, these three studies shed little light on the question of whether a Supreme Court decision rejecting existence of a psychotherapist-patient privilege would affect patient decisionmaking concerning whether to enter therapy.

Even though the empirical evidence is inconclusive, an adverse impact on patients' willingness to enter therapy can be hypothesized should the Supreme Court reject the privilege. For most people, public revelation of private therapy disclosures would be extremely unpleasant and embarrassing. Moreover, it could produce significant negative consequences that might be harmful to them in such important areas of their lives as the family and the workplace. As a result, behavioral psychology would predict that people who are aware of this possibility may be seriously deterred from engaging in therapy.

It stands to reason that this consideration will affect human behavior in precisely this way. The case before the Court is illustrative. Would a member of a police force involved in a shooting that became the subject of a law suit for police misconduct seek out counseling concerning his or her job-related stress if intimate details revealed in therapy could be the subject of an evidentiary fishing expedition conducted by the civil plaintiff? Would the victim of a sexual assault seek counseling if she knew that the perpetrator's attorney could seek discovery of what she said in therapy in order to impeach her with it at trial? Would individuals undergoing the heartache and stress of divorce seek treatment knowing that their intimate disclosures could be used in divorce litigation or could be sought by the adverse spouse for use as a club in settlement negotiations?

The potential of future negative consequences will affect human behavior only if people can predict those consequences and are aware of the risk of their occurrence. Behavior is not reflexive or automatic; it is cognitively mediated.[49] Shuman and Weiner's research suggests that people are unaware of the existence or nonexistence of the psychotherapist-patient privilege,[50] but the previ-

---

47. Shuman et al., supra note 31, at 393.

48. Id. at 411–12.

49. Albert Bandura, Behavior Theory and the Models of Man, 29 Am. Psychologist 859, 860 (1974); Bruce J. Winick, Harnessing the Power of the Bet: Wagering with the Government as a Mechanism for Social and Individual Change, 45 U. Miami L. Rev. 737, 755 (1991).

50. See Shuman et al., supra note 31, at 411–12; Shuman & Weiner, supra note 31, at 930; Weiner & Shuman, supra note 31, at 381. Whether they understand the distinction between confidentiality and the existence of an evidentiary privilege, other empirical evidence strongly suggests that patients believe that what they tell their psychotherapists will be held

ous analysis questions this conclusion in the context of Supreme Court resolution of the privilege question.

While the issue of the psychotherapist-patient privilege may not occur to some people, it doubtless would be a concern to many deciding on whether to seek needed mental health treatment.[51] The publicity that surely would follow a Supreme Court decision on whether the privilege should be recognized will predictably bring the issue to heightened public awareness. Were the Court to reject the existence of the privilege, people considering whether to enter therapy would learn of it. Not only would they learn of it through the usual intense media coverage of Supreme Court decisions on issues of public interest, but clinicians would have an ethical duty to divulge to their patients that patient-therapist communications may not be totally confidential, and may be revealed in judicial proceedings.[52] This will have a predictable chilling effect on the willingness of individuals to enter or remain in therapy.

At precisely the time when more Americans need the services of mental health professionals, a total rejection by the Supreme Court of the psychotherapist-patient privilege will, therefore, have the predictable effect of discouraging those seeking such professional help. One reason that people with mental health problems do not seek treatment relates to the historic stigma associated with mental illness.[53] Although there have been many efforts to destigmatize

---

in strictest confidence. Paul S. Appelbaum et al., Confidentiality: An Empirical Test of the Utilitarian Perspective, 12 Bull. Am. Acad. Psychiatry & L. 109, 110 (1984) (reviewing studies).

51. See 2 Jack B. Weinstein & Margaret A. Berger, Weinstein's Evidence 504–18 (1995) ("Unlike the patient with physical ailments or complaints, who will likely consult a physician regardless of whether confidentiality is guaranteed, a neurotic or psychotic individual may seek help only if he is assured that his confidences will not be divulged, even in a courtroom."); Group for the Advancement of Psychiatry, Report No. 45, at 92 (1960) [hereinafter GAP Report], cited with approval in Revised Draft of Proposed Rules of Evidence for the United States Courts and Magistrates, 51 F.R.D. 315, 367 (1971) (Advisory Comm. Notes); Ralph Slovenko, Psychiatry and a Look at the Medical Privilege, 6 Wayne L. Rev. 175, 184 (1960).

52. The Ethical Principles of Psychologists and Code of Conduct, Standard 5.01, provides:

(a) Psychologists discuss with persons and organizations with whom they establish a scientific or professional relationship (including, to the extent feasible, minors and their legal representatives) (1) the relevant limitations on confidentiality, including limitations where applicable in group, marital, and family therapy or in organizational consulting, and (2) the foreseeable uses of the information generated through their services.

(b) Unless it is not feasible or is contraindicated, the discussion of confidentiality occurs at the outset of the relationship and thereafter as new circumstances may warrant.

Ethical Principles of Psychologists and Code of Conduct, Standard 5.01, in 47 Am. Psychologist 1597, 1606 (1992). Similarly, the Code of Ethics of the National Association of Social Workers provides that "[t]he social worker should inform clients fully about the limits of confidentiality in a given situation, the purposes for which information is obtained, and how it may be used." National Ass'n of Social Workers, NASW Code of Ethics § II.H.2 (1990).

53. See Report of the Task Panel on Public Attitudes and Use of Media for Promotion of Mental Health, in 4 Task Panel Reports Submitted to the President's Comm'n on Mental

mental illness, sadly such stigma continues. As a result, many people with mental health problems will enter therapy only if they can be assured that their doing so will not come to public attention. Should the Supreme Court reject the existence of a psychotherapist-patient privilege, people with mental health problems concerned about avoiding the embarrassment and social disadvantages of stigmatization will be discouraged from entering therapy.

Rejection by the Supreme Court of a psychotherapist-patient privilege can therefore have significant negative effects on the mental health of the nation. People with mental health problems will be discouraged from seeking therapy and their problems will only worsen, sometimes causing social catastrophe. This is a problem that affects more than just the one in four adult Americans suffering from a diagnosable mental disorder. Most of us will face one or more devastating experiences in our lives—death of a loved one, loss of a job, divorce, becoming the victim of a crime or a natural disaster, for example. Many are unable successfully to cope with these events, and could benefit from professional counseling. Research is increasingly showing that talking about these difficulties can improve mental health, while not talking about them may be unhealthy in a number of respects.[54] Psychologist James Pennebaker's research shows that the act of inhibition of thoughts and feelings imposes severe stress that, over time, gradually undermines the body's defenses, affecting immune function, the actions of the heart and vascular systems, and even the biochemical workings of the brain and nervous systems.[55] While inhibition is harmful, Professor Pennebaker has found that confiding our hidden thoughts and feelings can have profound health benefits.[56]

In general, it is best for the individual to disclose serious problems to a professional therapist, one licensed under state law who by reason of education and training has been certified as competent to perform this special function. Yet, the willingness of many people to seek out such professional therapists will be undermined to the extent they lack confidence in the therapist's ability to maintain confidentiality. Recognition of the psychotherapist-patient privilege will bolster this confidence. Refusing to do so may destroy it.

Moreover, a rejection of the privilege may seriously diminish the effectiveness of therapy for individuals who are in or decide to undertake therapy. It can be predicted that many patients, out of concern for potential disclosure,

---

Health 1864, 1870 (1978); Bruce J. Winick, The Side Effects of Incompetency Labeling and the Implications for Mental Health Law, 1 Psychol. Pub. Pol'y & L. 6, 11 n.40 (1995). Former patients have eloquently articulated the personal costs of the stigma of mental illness. See Judi Chamberlin, On Our Own 107–11 (1978); Betty Blaska, First Account: What It Is Like To Be Treated Like a CMI, 17 Schizophrenia Bull. 173 (1991); Judi Chamberlin, The Ex-Patients' Movement: Where We've Been and Where We're Going, 11 J. Mind & Behav. 323, 324–25 (1990). The National Alliance for the Mentally Ill (NAMI), the nation's largest support and advocacy organization for individuals with mental illness and their families, has recently launched a comprehensive, five-year education campaign, endorsed by the National Institute of Mental Health (NIMH), to fight stigma and discrimination. National Anti-Discrimination Campaign Announced at Convention, 17 NAMI Advocate 1, July–Aug. 1995, at 1, 4.

54. See generally James W. Pennebaker, Opening Up: The Healing Power of Confiding in Others (1990) (reporting extensive research).

55. Id. at 13.

56. Id. at 14, 21.

will inhibit their own disclosure to the therapist. Shuman and Weiner's research demonstrates this by showing a significant diminution in patients' willingness to disclose information to a therapist once they are told that such information will not be privileged.[57] The "fundamental rule" of psychotherapy, Freud wrote, is that the patient be totally forthcoming with the therapist, revealing everything no matter how insignificant it may seem.[58] Inhibition by the patient thus can doom the therapeutic enterprise.

To succeed, mental health treatment requires a high degree of trust and confidence by the patient in the therapist.[59] Establishing this trust and confidence at the outset of the therapeutic relationship may be essential for its ultimate success.[60] It is precisely at this point that a therapist will feel ethically obligated to reveal to the patient that the confidentiality of the patient's communications cannot be fully protected.[61] For at least some patients, the specter of their therapist as a weapon in the hands of an adversary in litigation will prevent formation of the therapeutic alliance.[62] Concern about disclosure of intimate and personal information confided in a therapist thus can have profoundly antitherapeutic effects for the individual, producing a distrust of the therapist that can make the therapeutic process impossible.

Would any positive therapeutic consequences result from a decision denying recognition of a psychotherapist-patient privilege? Jeffrey Klotz suggests that there may be potential therapeutic advantages in eliminating the privilege in certain circumstances.[63] He urges a future crimes exception, under which patient communications of a desire or intent to commit a crime would be exempt from the privilege. Klotz hypothesizes that patients, aware that their disclo-

---

57. See supra note 43 and accompanying text.

58. See 23 Sigmund Freud, An Outline of Psycho-Analysis, in Standard Edition of the Complete Psychological Works of Sigmund Freud 174 (James Strachey ed. & trans., 1964). See also GAP Report, supra note 51 (The psychiatrist's "capacity to help his patients is completely dependent upon their willingness and ability to talk freely. This makes it difficult if not impossible for him to function without being able to assure his patients of confidentiality and, indeed, privileged communication.").

59. See Mark B. DeKraai & Bruce D. Sales, Privileged Communications of Psychologists, 13 Prof. Psychologist 372, 372 (1982) (the establishment of a relationship of trust between client and therapist "has been deemed so essential by some that it has been argued that psychotherapy is rendered worthless in its absence"); Bruce J. Winick, The Right to Refuse Mental Health Treatment: A Therapeutic Jurisprudence Analysis, 18 Int'l. J. L. & Psychiatry 99, 111–12 (1994); see also Ryan D. Jagim et al., Mental Health Professionals' Attitudes Toward Confidentiality, Privilege, and Third Party Disclosure, 9 Prof. Psychologist 458, 458–59 (1978) ("The concept of confidentiality of client-therapist communications is at the core of the psychotherapeutic relationship.").

60. Winick, supra note 59, at 113–14.

61. "Mental health professionals must alert their patients at the outset of therapy about special conditions under which complete confidentiality cannot be maintained." Report of the Task Panel on Legal and Ethical Issues, in 4 Task Panel Reports Submitted to the President's Comm'n on Mental Health, supra note 53, at 1399; see also supra note 52 (quoting ethical guidelines of psychologists and social workers).

62. See Winick, supra note 59, at 113–14.

63. Jeffrey A. Klotz, Limiting the Psychotherapist-Patient Privilege: The Therapeutic Potential, 27 Crim. L. Bull. 416 (1991).

sures concerning a future crime could be used against them in court, may avoid behavior that might necessitate judicial intervention.[64] Fear of future disclosure, in Klotz's view, could have the therapeutic effect of deterring future criminal conduct. Klotz's proposal already is largely reflected in state law exceptions to the privilege.[65] Would such a future crimes exception to the privilege have this desired effect? Would it instead deter patients who intend to commit a crime from entering therapy, or from disclosing their intentions in therapy, in either case foreclosing the potential that a therapeutic intervention might prevent the crime? These are interesting and unresolved empirical questions that deserve investigation.

In any event, even if Klotz is correct and if more criminal behavior can be avoided by recognizing this exception than by refusing to do so, allowing a future crimes exception does not argue for rejecting the privilege altogether. The case before the Supreme Court does not require resolution of whether a future crimes exception should be recognized. It merely involves the question of whether the Federal Rules of Evidence should be read to permit a general privilege for psychotherapist-patient communications. Whether a future crimes exception or other exceptions should be recognized can await another day, perhaps when more information concerning the consequences of various exceptions will be available. The privilege recognized by the court of appeals in *Jaffee v. Redmond* is not an absolute one, but expressly contemplates possible exceptions.[66] The Supreme Court, therefore, can affirm *Jaffee's* general recognition of a psychotherapist-patient privilege and leave the details of when it should be overcome by countervailing needs to the lower federal courts to be developed in light of "reason and experience."[67]

That the psychotherapist-patient privilege recognized by *Jaffee* is less than absolute does not undermine its therapeutic potential. The court of appeals acknowledged that, in appropriate circumstances, the need for the information sought could outweigh the interest in preserving confidentiality.[68] Allowing the trial judge to engage in this weighing process strikes the balance appropriately between the interest in ascertaining truth and the privacy and therapeutic concerns involved. In this sense, the privilege functions as a cloak of confidential-

---

64. Id. at 429.

65. Id. at 429 n.58; see, e.g., Alaska R. Evid. 504(d)(2) (1995) ("crime or fraud"); Cal. Evid. Code § 1018 (West 1995); Conn. Gen. Stat. § 52-146c(b)(3) ("risk of imminent personal injury...or risk of imminent injury to...property"); Ill. Ann. Stat. ch. 740, para. 110/11(vi) (1993) (threats of violence); La. Code Evid. 510(B)(2)(e), (C)(2)(b) (1995); Mass. Gen. L. ch. 112, § 129A(2)-(3) (1991) (threat or clear and present danger that patient will kill or inflict serious injury); 1995 Nev. Stat. 640, § 19 ("immediate threat that the patient will harm himself or other persons"), R.I. Gen. Laws § 5-37.3-4(4) (Supp. 1994) (when third party "is in danger from a patient"); S.C. Code Ann. § 19-11-95(C)(3) (Supp. 1994) ("intention...to commit a crime or harm himself"); W. Va. Code § 27-3-1(b)(4) (1992) "[t]o protect against a clear and substantial danger of imminent injury"); Wyo. Stat. § 33-27-123(a)(iv) (Supp. 1995) (immediate threat of physical violence against a readily identifiable victim"); see also United States v. Snelenberger, 24 F.3d 799, 802 (6th Cir. 1994) (applying future crimes exception under Fed. R. Evid. 501), cert. denied, 115 S. Ct. 433 (1994).

66. See Jaffee v. Redmond, 51 F.3d 1346, 1357 (7th Cir. 1995).

67. Fed. R. Evid. 501.

68. See *Jaffee*, 51 F.3d at 1357.

ity, generally preserving the privacy of sensitive disclosures made in therapy, but a cloak that can be removed in appropriate circumstances when the demands of the justice system require it. The privilege makes such communications presumptively protected from disclosure and, in effect, places on the party seeking disclosure the burden of demonstrating the heightened relevance to the proceedings of obtaining the information in question. Only when such information is essential to the proof of crucial facts should the intimacy of the therapeutic relationship be invaded.

Even though the psychotherapist-patient privilege would not be absolute, recognition of its existence by the Supreme Court would provide an important signal to those considering whether to enter therapy that the confidentiality of their disclosures will generally be protected. The opposite signal would encourage litigants to seek confidential information from therapists even when such information is not crucial, as a means of harassment and in an effort to force a settlement that would avoid disclosure of embarrassing or personal information. The absence of a privilege would encourage significant abuse by unscrupulous lawyers that will be difficult and expensive for trial judges to control.

All fifty states recognize a psychotherapist-patient privilege.[69] Although state law recognizes the privilege, if the Supreme Court were to refuse to do so under the Federal Rules of Evidence, a therapist would feel obligated to reveal to a patient that the federal courts do not protect the privilege.[70] When a patient first seeks therapy and the therapist is faced with the ethical duty of discussing confidentiality and its possible exceptions, it will be difficult to predict, if a lawsuit involving the patient should occur, whether it will be in state court or federal court.[71] The uncertainty engendered by this disclosure alone could have a serious deterrent effect on a patient's willingness to enter therapy and could therefore frustrate state policy that recognizes the privilege in order to foster mental health and to protect personal privacy.

Refusing to recognize the privilege thus will impose a number of serious social costs. People in need of therapy will be deterred from seeking it, and those already in therapy may participate in it with less than the full candor needed for treatment success. Against these costs must be weighed the loss of probative evidence. But how much probative evidence will be lost by recognition of a psychotherapist patient privilege? Because rejection of the privilege would deter patients from entering therapy or from participating in it with full candor, the very evidence sought—the patient's confidential communications to the therapist—would never have come into existence in the first place. As a result, refusal to recognize the privilege will not materially assist the truth-determination process. Because little evidence will accordingly be lost, the therapeu-

---

69. See id. at 1356; see also sources cited supra note 1.

70. Given the unanimity in the states concerning recognizing the privilege under state law, rejection of the privilege for the federal courts can produce the additional undesirable effect of promoting forum shopping. Cf. Erie R.R. v. Tompkins, 304 U.S. 64 (1938).

71. In cases in which the parties to a lawsuit are citizens of different states or in which the claim arises under federal law (such as the Federal Civil Rights claim involved in *Jaffee*), a civil plaintiff may file suit in either state or federal court. See 28 U.S.C. § 1331 (1995) (federal question jurisdiction); id. § 1332 (diversity jurisdiction).

tic benefits of recognizing the privilege outweigh the social costs of non-recognition.

If the privilege is recognized, it should be extended to all mental health professionals licensed by the state, including psychiatric social workers. Given the largely unmet mental health needs of the nation, it is essential that psychiatric social workers play the significant therapeutic role that this expanding profession has served so well in recent years. There are approximately 30,642 psychiatrists, 56,000 psychologists and 81,000 psychiatric social workers practicing mental health counseling today.[72] In reality, an increasing amount of patient contact involves psychiatric social workers, rather than psychiatrists and psychologists. Recognizing a privilege that extends to psychiatrists alone, or to psychiatrists and psychologists, but not to psychiatric social workers, would in effect create a second-class professional relationship for people lacking the financial means to hire the more expensive psychiatrist or psychologist. The psychiatric social worker has become "the poor person's psychiatrist."[73] In addition to being unwise and antitherapeutic, construing the privilege not to extend to psychiatric social workers thus would raise grave equal protection problems. In fashioning a privilege, the Court should focus on the function of the counseling relationship rather than on the identity of the counselor. Focusing on the purpose of the communication rather than on the occupation of the counselor avoids the social inequality created by granting a privilege to one type of counselor, such as psychiatrists and psychologists whose clients tend to be more affluent, while denying the privilege to another type, such as social workers, whose clients tend to be poor.[74]

The Supreme Court will not decide *Jaffee v. Redmond* on the basis of equal protection. But the equal protection tensions that would be created by recognizing a psychotherapist-patient privilege that did not extend to licensed psychiatric social workers argue strongly for a more extensive privilege. There simply is no avoiding the reality that our nation's mental health needs have eclipsed the ability of psychiatrists and psychologists to meet them. More and more services will be delivered by psychiatric social workers. More and more people need and will accept their services. It is in the mental health interests of the nation to promote their role.

Viewed in this light, there simply is no basis for concluding that psychiatrists and psychologists require the cloak of confidentiality to play their role effectively but that psychiatric social workers do not. With the exception of the medication that physicians alone may prescribe, the treatment approaches utilized by psychiatrists, psychologists, and psychiatric social workers do not differ significantly. Apart from the organic interventions reserved for psychiatrists, the practice of verbal psychotherapy, although it may differ based upon

---

72. Thomas H. Dial et al., Human Resources in Mental Health, in Mental Health, United States 1990, at 196, 208 (Ronald W. Manderscheid & Mary A. Sonnenschein eds., 1990).

73. See *Jaffee*, 51 F.3d at 1358 n.19 (citing Developments in the Law—Privileged Communications, 98 Harv. L. Rev. 1530, 1550 (1985)); see also Comment, Underprivileged Communications: Extension of the Psychotherapist-Patient Privilege to Patients of Psychiatric Social Workers, 61 Cal. L. Rev. 1050, 1050 (1973).

74. See Kerry L. Morse, Note, A Uniform Testimonial Privilege for Mental Health Professionals, 51 Ohio St. L.J. 741, 745–47 (1990).

the therapist's particular clinical orientation, will not vary based on professional lines. All forms of psychotherapy require trust and confidence by the patient in the clinician. To the extent that the privilege is based upon a desire to foster the therapeutic relationship, there can be no principle basis for distinguishing psychotherapists based upon professional discipline. Given the largely unmet mental health needs of the nation, we should not undermine the ability of psychiatric social workers to help in the battle.

The Supreme Court, therefore, should read the Federal Rules of Evidence to recognize a psychotherapist-patient privilege that includes psychiatric social workers. Fine-tuning of the privilege, including the circumstances in which it should be outweighed in particular cases, may be left for future decision. Endorsement by the Court of a general privilege for therapist-patient communications would bring federal practice in line with the approach uniformly followed in the states and would best serve both constitutional and therapeutic values.

Chapter 25

Arbitral Therapy

Roger I. Abrams
Frances E. Abrams
Dennis R. Nolan

I. Introduction

Thirty-four years ago, the Supreme Court issued its famous *Steelworkers Trilogy* decisions that set the ground rules for the relationship between the courts and the labor arbitration process.[1] In *United Steelworkers v. American Manufacturing Co.*,[2] the first of the *Trilogy*, Justice William Douglas posited therapeutic effects for the labor arbitration process. The Court held that a trial court should order arbitration even of claims the trial judge believes meritless.[3] "The processing of even frivolous claims may have therapeutic values of which those who are not part of the plant environment may be quite unaware."[4]

In footnote 6, Justice Douglas quoted at length from an article by Professor Archibald Cox referring to the "cathartic value" of arbitration and explaining the value to the parties of arbitrating even frivolous claims:

---

1. United Steelworkers v. American Mfg. Co., 363 U.S. 564 (1960); United Steelworkers v. Warrior & Gulf Navigation Co., 363 U.S. 574 (1960); United Steelworkers v. Enterprise Wheel & Car Corp., 363 U.S. 593 (1960). Briefly, the Court ruled that a court is to enforce a contract promise to arbitrate, applying a presumption of arbitrability. See *American Mfg. Co.*, 363 U.S. at 568; *Warrior & Gulf* Navigation Co., 363 U.S. at 582–83. Courts should order arbitration without considering the merits of the grievances. See *American Mfg. Co.*, 363 U.S. at 568–69. After arbitration, the court should not substitute its views for that of the arbitrator and should enforce an arbitration award as long as it has 'drawn its essence' from the terms of the agreement. See *Enterprise Wheel & Car Corp.*, 363 U.S. at 597–99. Much has been written on the *Trilogy*'s meaning and its effect on labor-management relations. See, e.g., Benjamin Aaron, Judicial Intervention in Labor Arbitration, 20 Stan. L. Rev. 41 (1967); Bernard Dunau, Three Problems in Labor Arbitration, 55 Va. L. Rev. 427 (1969); Theodore J. St. Antoine, Judicial Review of Labor Arbitration Awards: A Second Look at Enterprise Wheel and its Progeny, 75 Mich. L. Rev. 1137, 1141 (1977).

2. *American Mfg. Co.*, 363 U.S. at 568.

3. Id. at 568–69.

4. Id.

"Frivolous cases are often taken, and are expected to be taken, to arbitration. What one man considers frivolous another may find meritorious, and it is common knowledge in industrial relations circles that grievance arbitration often serves as a safety valve for troublesome complaints. Under these circumstances it seems proper to read the typical arbitration clause as a promise to arbitrate every claim, meritorious or frivolous, which the complainant bases upon the contract. The objection that equity will not order a party to do a useless act is outweighed by the cathartic value of arbitrating even a frivolous grievance and by the dangers of excessive judicial intervention."[5]

Many participants in labor arbitration sense that the process may have therapeutic effects. The literature on labor arbitration[6] and later Supreme Court decisions[7] repeat Justice Douglas's dictum. There is a consensus that the therapeutic effect is a valuable,[8] although not primary, goal of the arbitration process.

It is thus surprising that no one has ever examined the bases of Justice Douglas's claim. Is labor arbitration really therapeutic? If so, for what types of problems? What elements of the arbitration process make it therapeutic? How does the therapy work?

Psychologists examine therapeutic relationships. The psychology literature discusses the elements of therapeutic relationships that foster positive benefits for clients. The legal literature, in contrast, pays little attention to the thera-

---

5. Id. at 568 n.6 (quoting Archibald Cox, Current Problems in the Law of Grievance Arbitration, 30 Rocky Mtn. L. Rev. 247, 261 (1958)).

6. See, e.g., Fairweather's Practice and Procedure in Labor Arbitration 231 (Ray J. Schoonhoven ed., 3d ed. 1991); William R. Casto, The Steelworkers Trilogy as Rules of Decision Applicable by Analogy to Public Sector Collective Bargaining Agreements: The Tennessee Valley Authority Paradigm, 26 B.C. L. Rev. 1, 8, 46 (1984); Lynette T. Oka, Disarray in the Circuits after Alexander v. Gardner-Denver Co., 9 U. Haw. L. Rev. 605, 608 (1987); Carlton J. Snow, The Steelworkers Trilogy in Oregon's Public Sector, 21 Willamette L. Rev. 445, 448, 527 (1985); Tara Selver, Note, Labor Law—The United States Supreme Court Alters National Labor Policy: Bowen v. United States Postal Service, 16 N.M. L. Rev. 153, 163 n.73 (1986).

7. See, e.g., Alexander v. Gardner-Denver Co., 415 U.S. 36, 55 (1974) (discussing the conciliatory and therapeutic processes of arbitration); Carey v. Westinghouse, 375 U.S. 261, 272 (1964) ("[T]he therapy of arbitration is brought to bear in a complicated and troubled area.").

8. There is one dissenter, however. In her article blasting modern labor-management relations law and processes, Professor Katherine Van Wezel Stone ridicules the therapeutic model, pejoratively terming the arbitrator the "plant psychiatrist." Katherine V. Stone, The Post-War Paradigm in American Labor Law, 90 Yale L.J. 1509, 1563 (1981); see also Stewart Macaulay, Private Government, in Law and the Social Sciences 445, 498–99 (Leon Lipson & Stanton Wheeler eds., 1986). According to Stone, the "goal of the psychiatric model of arbitration...is to break up the cohesiveness of the informal work group and to counteract its power over production." Stone, supra, at 1572. Under her analysis, arbitration serves as the opium of the workers. She rejects peaceful and positive labor relations in favor of workplace rebellion. For a powerful response, see Matthew W. Finkin, Revisionism in Labor Law, 43 Md. L. Rev. 23 (1984).

peutic aspects of the formal legal process. In one of the few explorations of the subject, David Wexler remarked that "the law's ignorance of the mental health disciplines should no longer be excused."[9] In this Article, we apply insights from psychology to understand better the possible therapeutic value of the labor arbitration process.

II. *The Arbitration Model*

Labor arbitration is an informal mechanism for resolving grievance disputes arising during the term of a collective bargaining agreement. Over the past century, both the parties to collective bargaining agreements and the labor arbitrators have shaped the arbitration process.[10] Without judicial or legislative prescriptions, labor and management have incrementally created a widely-accepted model of labor arbitration.[11]

Employers and unions initially try to resolve their differences through a contractual grievance procedure.[12] If they cannot resolve a dispute, the union may invoke arbitration. At the arbitration stage, a single neutral arbitrator, jointly selected by the parties, resolves the dispute.[13]

---

9. David B. Wexler, Therapeutic Jurisprudence: The Law as a Therapeutic Agent 3 (1990).

10. See Dennis R. Nolan & Roger I. Abrams, American Labor Arbitration: The Early Years, 35 U. Fla. L. Rev. 373 (1983); Dennis R. Nolan & Roger I. Abrams, American Labor Arbitration: The Maturing Years, 35 U. Fla. L. Rev. 557 (1983).

11. See generally Dennis R. Nolan, Labor Arbitration Law and Practice in a Nutshell (1979); R.W. Fleming, The Labor Arbitration Process (1965). Laypersons often confuse arbitration and mediation. They are very different problem-solving methods. Arbitration is a method of adjudication that leads to a decision by a neutral. Mediation is a process where a neutral attempts to assist the parties in reaching their own resolution of the dispute. Some work has been done to show that mediation does not exhibit the characteristics of psychotherapy. Joan B. Kelly, Mediation and Psychotherapy: Distinguishing the Differences, 1 Mediation Q. 33, 33–44 (1983) (recognizing that the mediation process is distinct from the counseling or psychotherapy process in terms of goals, techniques, diagnosis and placement of emotions). See generally Note, The Sultans of Swap: Defining the Duties and Liabilities of American Mediators, 99 Harv. L. Rev. 1876 (1986).

12. Grievance procedures typically contain a series of steps. Typically the aggrieved employee initiates the matter, bringing the problem directly to a supervisor, often with the assistance of a union steward. Almost all grievances are resolved at the first step of the process. The union processes unresolved matters through the grievance procedure to higher level management and union officials. At the final step, the union may bring the dispute to arbitration.

13. Arbitration systems vary widely. For example, many Teamsters Union trucking contracts provide for a bipartite panel with equal numbers of management and union representatives. See generally David E. Feller, Arbitration Without Neutrals: Joint Committees and Boards, 37 Proc. Nat'l Acad. Arb. 106 (1985) (presenting different views as to whether a joint board or committee decision is the equivalent of arbitration). Public-sector contracts often provide for a tri-partite panel. Each party selects its representative and the two panel members select the neutral arbitrator, who serves as the panel chair.

Arbitrators hear the case at a mutually convenient site. Lawyers often represent the parties, but more commonly non-lawyers represent one or both. The typical labor arbitrator is a white male in his sixties,[14] about half have law degrees, and most are educators who arbitrate part-time.[15]

The arbitrator holds an informal but orderly hearing, not bound by the rules of evidence, to gather evidence and hear arguments. Arbitrator (and former Secretary of Labor) W. Willard Wirtz stated that arbitrators

> have established the pattern of ordered informality; performing major surgery on the legal rules of evidence and procedure but retaining the good sense of those rules; greatly simplifying but not eliminating the hearsay and parole evidence rules; taking the rules for the admissibility of evidence and remolding them into rules for weighing it; striking the fat but saving the heart of the practices of cross-examination, presumptions, burden of proof, and the like.[16]

The arbitrator hears testimony from sworn witnesses on direct and cross-examination and receives pertinent documents. One or both parties may order a transcript. Most hearings last a single day, often only a few hours.

After the hearing, parties may submit written briefs. The arbitrator reviews the record in the case and within a month or two issues a written opinion containing reasons for the award. The collective bargaining agreement normally provides that the arbitrator's award is final and binding on the parties. Some public sector contracts still provide for advisory arbitration. As a labor-management relationship matures, parties usually develop confidence in the arbitration process and move toward a binding procedure.

All unionized sectors of the economy follow this arbitration model. Virtually all collective bargaining agreements contain arbitration provisions.[17] These provisions cover all types of workers-unskilled, skilled, and professional.

III. Is Arbitration Therapeutic?

Justice Douglas stated that "[t]he processing of even frivolous claims may have therapeutic values."[18] Before examining the possible bases for this claim, we must first identify what "therapeutic" means. Psychologists define the term in various ways. Therapy is a process "through which one person helps an-

---

14. Mario F. Bognanno & Clifford E. Smith, The Demographic and Professional Characteristics of Arbitrators in North America, 41 Proc. Nat'l Acad. Arb. 266, 273, 275 (1989). The profile of the typical arbitrator is changing, albeit slowly. Increasingly, women and minorities are entering the field. See Brian Bemmels, Arbitrator Characteristics and Arbitrator Decisions, 11 J. Lab. Res. 181, 184–85 (1990).

15. Bognanno & Smith, supra note 14, at 275, 277, 279.

16. W. Willard Wirtz, Due Process of Arbitration, 11 Proc. Nat'l Acad. Arb. 1, 13 (1958).

17. In its survey of major collective bargaining agreements, the Bureau of National Affairs reported in 1989 that 98% of its sample contained arbitration provisions. 2 Collective Bargaining Negot. & Cont. (BNA) 51:4 (1989).

18. United Steelworkers v. American Mfg. Co., 363 U.S. 564, 568 (1960).

other to find relief from emotional pain."[19] A therapeutic process is "cura-tive."[20] Individuals who believe a helper or counselor has "curative" powers often experience relief from their problems or emotional disorders.[21] Therapy is a verbal interaction that lessens anxiety, thereby leading to tension reduc-tion.[22] Simply telling one's story may prove helpful.[23]

The therapeutic experience requires the development of a relationship be-tween a client and therapist aimed toward ameliorating emotional symp-toms.[24] Although there are many therapeutic orientations, they share common characteristics, including "comfort, support, guidance, reassurance, guilt-re-duction through confession, and hope."[25] As the therapeutic relationship de-velops, a client experiences an atmosphere free of criticism and judgment.[26]

Different psychotherapies use specific techniques to relieve clients' prob-lems. Some focus solely on the relationship that develops between a client and therapist. An individual can change and experience relief by developing a sup-portive relationship with another person.[27] To understand the therapeutic as-pects of labor arbitration, we will use insights developed in group, family, couples, and brief psychotherapy, techniques most similar to arbitration. Al-though professionals who follow these models share similar techniques and a common conceptual framework, even they cannot agree why a therapeutic ef-fect occurs.[28]

The essence of the therapeutic experience in a group setting lies in "increas-ing people's knowledge of themselves and others, assisting people to clarify the changes they most want to make in their life, and giving people some of the tools necessary to make these desired changes."[29] Psychological studies suggest that the therapeutic process is useful to many professions and to all human re-lationships.[30]

---

19. Rosemary M. Balsam & Alan Balsam, Becoming a Psychotherapist 1 (1984).

20. Gerard Egan, The Skilled Helper 16 (1986); Webster's Ninth Collegiate Dictionary 1223 (1991).

21. Egan, supra note 20, at 16.

22. Balsam & Balsam, supra note 19, at 5.

23. Jeffrey M. Masson, Final Analysis 112 (1990); see also R. Slovenko, Psychiatry and Law 459 (1973) ("Psychotherapy is a planned technique of altering maladaptive behavior of an individual (or group) toward more effective adaptation. The essential ingredient of psy-chotherapy is the utilization of the therapist's personality interacting with the patient's per-sonality") (quoting Joel S. Handler, Psychotherapy and Medical Responsibility, Arch. Gen. Psychiatry 464 (1959)).

24. Dictionary of Behavioral Science 304 (Benjamin B. Wolman ed., 1973) (hereinafter Behavioral Science).

25. Id.; see also Longman Dictionary of Psychology and Psychiatry 605 (Robert M. Gold-enson ed., 1984).

26. Behavioral Science, supra note 24, at 305.

27. Id.

28. Irvin D. Yalom, The Theory and Practice of Group Psychotherapy 4 (3d ed. 1985).

29. Marianne S. Corey & Gerald Corey, Groups: Process and Practice 9 (1987).

30. See The Carl Rogers Reader 62 (Howard Kirschenbaum & Valerie L. Henderson eds., 1989) [hereinafter Rogers].

Justice Douglas cites Professor Cox's article referring to labor arbitration as "cathartic."[31] Catharsis is free expression,[32] a simple release of feelings, sometimes accompanied by an emotional expression such as tears, anger, or shouting.[33] Following catharsis, a person is calmer.[34] Labor relations professionals will easily recognize the accuracy of Professor Cox's description.

A. The Problems for Which Arbitration Might Be Therapeutic

Justice Douglas's brief reference to therapeutic and cathartic values does not explain how arbitration produces these results or even what problems the process might redress. Before we explore the possible therapeutic effects of arbitration, we must identify its possible beneficiaries and the possible problems it might solve. Arbitration might address both individual and organizational problems.

The individual grievant may have demonstrable economic and psychological problems as a result of the employer's alleged contract breach. Deprived of contract benefits or even of a job, the aggrieved individual feels constrained by an internal labor relations system. A purely internal dispute-resolution system may inhibit expression and may not afford a remedy. The lack of a satisfactory procedure may depress the grievant, leaving him or her suffering from low self-esteem, resentment toward his employer, and stress. Although management might admit its error within the grievance procedure, in some cases relief—both economic and psychological—requires invoking the arbitration process.

The union representing the grievant might have concerns of its own. These are most likely to be economic or political, but might also be psychological. The union as an institution may have no remedy other than to demand relief from management. During the term of the collective bargaining agreement, the union may not lawfully use its economic power.[35] Although a union may win some grievances through logical persuasion, at times management will not yield to the merits of the case. For example, the employer might deny a facially meritorious grievance to show support for its supervisors or for other "political" or tactical reasons. The union as an institution may as a result feel enervated and powerless. (Without an effective dispute-resolution mechanism, it may actually become so.)

Management officials also may experience psychological problems for which arbitration might be therapeutic. Although able to resist union claims through the grievance procedure, individual officials may feel that the employees do not respect them or their positions. Power does not necessarily mean comfort. In

---

31. United Steelworkers v. American Mfg. Co., 363 U.S. 564, 568 (1960) (citation omitted).

32. Rogers, supra note 30, at 69; Yalom, supra note 28, at 78.

33. Robert D. Nye, Three Psychologies 11 (1986); Thomas J. Scheff & Don D. Bushnell, A Theory of Catharsis, 18 J. Res. Personality 238, 238–46 (1984).

34. Scheff & Bushnell, supra note 33, at 239.

35. Most collective bargaining agreements contain no-strike provisions enforceable by injunction. If the parties include an arbitration clause but remain silent on a no-strike clause, the courts will imply a no-strike obligation during the term of the agreement. Gateway Coal Co. v. United Mine Workers, 414 U.S. 368, 380–84 (1974).

some cases, management officials might even experience guilt for their actions affecting the grievant.

B. How Arbitration Might Resolve These Problems

We might posit several ways in which arbitration might lessen or eliminate the psychological problems of the participants. For the individual grievant, arbitration provides the opportunity to explain to a neutral party the basis for the complaint. The arbitrator listens to the grievant and has the authority to grant relief. The arbitrator-grievant relationship may relieve the grievant's depression while enhancing self-esteem.

Arbitration might not relieve the grievant's resentment towards management. In an adversarial proceeding, both management and union may appeal less to reason than to partisanship. Similarly, arbitration is not a stress-free activity. Successful establishment of the arbitrator-grievant relationship may reduce the grievant's stress but may not eliminate it. Nevertheless, the employee may gain some comfort. Arbitrator and Professor Benjamin Aaron has suggested that the grievant's presence at the hearing watching management's witnesses subjected to "searching and often embarrassing cross-examination" may result in "a kind of catharsis that helps to make even eventual defeat acceptable" to the grievant.[36]

Arbitration can also reduce the union's psychological concerns. By participating in arbitration, the union shows its power and ability to represent its members' interests. It also proves its power to force management to justify its actions before a third party. The union may or may not win the particular grievance. Win or lose, however, the opportunity to challenge management's decision before an outside authority improves the union's image and self-image. Moreover, by depriving the employer of unilateral authority, the union strengthens its hand in future negotiations. Finally, arbitration serves as an acceptable source of difficult decisions the union may not be able, politically, to make on its own. An arbitrator can tell an influential grievant that he or she is wrong a lot easier than an elected union leader can.

Similarly, management officials have the opportunity to confirm their positions by explaining them to the neutral arbitrator. Like union officials, managers may value the outsider's ability to decide issues that are politically difficult. A labor relations manager may be in no position to tell the company's chief executive that a change in policy violates the contract; an arbitrator is.

C. Evidence of Arbitration's Therapeutic Effects

Unfortunately it is virtually impossible to design an empirical test of arbitration's vaunted therapeutic effects. The problems are practical, not theoretical. One could design a survey instrument to focus on the relationship between arbitration and therapy. It would ask employees who bring frivolous grievances whether they feel better after the arbitration proceeding. Practical details

---

36. Benjamin Aaron, The Role of the Arbitrator in Ensuring a Fair Hearing, 35 Proc. Nat'l Acad. Arb. 30, 32 (1983).

make this infeasible. For example, selecting a sample is a challenge. Which grievances are frivolous? (Not all losing grievances are frivolous.) Collecting data also would be difficult. Should the investigator administer the survey after the hearing, but before the losing award? Inevitably such a survey would produce unreliable conclusions and interpretations. Furthermore, the survey would produce only the most subjective impressions, and these are notoriously unreliable.[37]

Fortunately, though, ample anecdotal evidence supports Douglas's assertions. Union representatives tell arbitrators that they appreciate the opportunity to present a case in arbitration even when they lose. The cathartic effect is sometimes clear. Some grievants exhibit relief, a positive effect, and a calmed demeanor after a hearing. The grievant in a recent case heard by one of the authors, for example, became calmer as the hearing proceeded. He revealed his comfort by unfolding his arms and hands, sitting back in his chair in a relaxed manner and making eye contact with the arbitrator. Arbitration appears in some instances to soothe and relieve a grievant's pain.

The arbitration hearing may be, as Professor Cox said, a cathartic experience. It is a special time set aside for participants to tell their stories. Arbitrator William Simkin described the beneficial results:

> One of the fundamental purposes of an arbitration hearing is to let people get things off their chest, regardless of the decision. The arbitration proceeding is the opportunity for a third party, an outside party, to come in and act as a sort of father confessor to the parties, to let them get rid of their troubles, get them out in the open, and have a feeling of someone hearing their troubles. Because I believe so strongly that that is one of the fundamental purposes of arbitration, I don't think you ought to use any rules of evidence. You have to make up your own mind as to what is pertinent or not in the case. Lots of times I have let people talk for five minutes, when I know all the time that they were talking it had absolutely nothing to do with the case—just completely foreign to it. But there was a fellow testifying, either as a worker or a company representative, who had something that was important for him to get rid of. It was a good time for him to get rid of it.[38]

The hearing serves as a form of psychodrama.[39] Arbitration's ritualized ceremonies allow the actors to express important events from their work lives on a stage before an audience of their colleagues and an arbitrator.[40]

---

37. See generally Robert B. McCall, Fundamental Statistics for Psychology (2d ed. 1975) (providing examples of applied statistics in the field of the behavioral sciences).

38. Transcript of Proceedings, 3 Conference on Training of Law Students in Labor Relations 636–37 (1947), quoted in Frank Elkouri & Edna A. Elkouri, How Arbitration Works 298 (4th ed. 1985).

39. A psychodrama is "an extemporized dramatization designed to afford catharsis and social relearning for one or more of the participants from whose life history the plot is abstracted." Webster's Ninth New Collegiate Dictionary 689 (1991). Plato criticized the Greek theater for encouraging the expression of emotions, thereby jeopardizing civil stability. Michael P. Nichols & Jay S. Efran, Catharsis is Psychotherapy: A New Perspective, 22 Psychotherapy 46 (1985). Aristotle retorted that these plays were beneficial; they were "incidents arousing pity and fear in such a way as to accomplish a purgation (KATHARSIS) of such emotion." Id. at 47.

40. Professor Louis L. Jaffe described arbitration as "an arena, a theater," and referred to

D. The Limits of the Therapeutic Value of Arbitration

While a successful arbitration may be therapeutic and cathartic, that is not its primary goal. Labor and management agree to arbitration because it is a comparatively efficient and inexpensive method of resolving disputes with finality. An arbitration that does not resolve a dispute fails to achieve its primary goal, even if it helps the participants to feel better about themselves. The arbitrator is not a "labor relations physician."[41] Arbitrators rule on the merits based on the terms of the parties' collective bargaining agreement and the existing body of arbitral common law, not on how the losing party will feel about the outcome. Thus arbitration's therapeutic effects are collateral by-products of the decision-making process.

The therapeutic values of arbitration may be important nonetheless. They explain, at least in part, why parties might choose to arbitrate even frivolous matters. As political organizations, unions must sometimes arbitrate cases they know they will lose. Although they might welcome arbitration's therapeutic value to the grievants, they may really want to have a third party deny the grievance. By doing so, they may avoid potential liability for breach of their duty of fair representation and yet will bear no blame for the result.

Arbitration's therapeutic values may also explain, at least in part, why the Supreme Court would order a reluctant party to arbitrate even a frivolous grievance. The *Trilogy*'s principle of ordering the arbitration of even frivolous matters runs contrary to the traditional equity maxim that a court should not order parties to perform a futile act. If a grievance is frivolous, arbitrating the case would be a waste of time but for other benefits such as a therapeutic effect. The Court's decision might rest on any of several grounds. First, the Court might have believed that it was carrying out the intentions of the parties to the agreement, an appropriate goal in a contract case. The parties contracted for arbitration of *all* arbitrable matters, not merely the *meritorious* ones. Second, the Court might simply have decided as a matter of federal labor policy that arbitration is preferable to litigation or self-help measures, even if that policy obliges a court to order a futile act. Third, the Court might have recognized that courts are institutionally incapable of determining whether a grievance is frivolous. The risk of "false positives" is too high, especially when the parties have provided an alternative system for that decision. Finally, the Court might have favored arbitration because of judicial economy and institutional capabilities. When parties have their own system for resolving disputes, they should use it without unnecessary delay. This keeps the courts free for business only the courts can do.

---

the "scene, the dramatis personae" of the process. Louis L. Jaffe, Labor Arbitration and the Individual Worker, Annals Am. Acad. Pol. & Soc. Sci., May 1953, at 34, 40–41, quoted in Elkouri & Elkouri, supra note 38, at 12.

41. We have criticized this concept elsewhere. Dennis R. Nolan & Roger I. Abrams, The Labor Arbitrator's Several Roles, 44 Md. L. Rev. 873, 887–90 (1985). The term is from Lon L. Fuller's seminal article. Lon L. Fuller, Collective Bargaining and the Arbitrator, 1963 Wis. L. Rev. 3, 4.

IV. Arbitration's Therapeutic Elements

What aspects of arbitration might make it therapeutic? We can identify a series of the characteristics of the arbitration model that enhance its therapeutic value.

A. An Employee-Initiated Process

Even before the arbitration process begins, the parties' grievance procedure may offer therapeutic values. An aggrieved employee begins the grievance procedure by contacting a supervisor to complain about a contract violation. A union steward may or may not participate at this stage. This first step of the grievance procedure might be oral, although some collective bargaining agreements require a written grievance. By filing a grievance, the employee can command the attention of the supervisor. The employee exerts some control over his or her work life, even without getting immediate relief.

In the psychological counseling context, a client usually seeks help for a problem by contacting a therapist. Some therapists may require the client to write out the problem on a form, much like a grievance form. Admittedly, some therapy relationships are not consensual. A court, for example, may order an indicted person to seek counseling or else face trial. Even in that case, the client makes a 'choice,' although not a completely free one.[42]

By beginning the healing process, the client feels a sense of relief and hope even before meeting the counselor. It is helpful to know that something is happening. In both the counseling and the grievance situations, beginning the process is therapeutic in itself. That is so even if the party contacted cannot or will not solve the underlying problem. Of course, the grievant's supervisor does not act as a therapist. The therapeutic value of the grievance stage flows from the process of filing a grievance, not from the conduct of the supervisor.

Typically, the union, not the individual grievant, decides whether to arbitrate an unresolved dispute. The question whether to arbitrate arises, however, only because the aggrieved employee filed the grievance in the first instance. Using the grievance process, the employee moves from helplessness to seeking a remedy for an economic concern.

Clients seek therapy when faced with unresolved problems affecting their daily lives.[43] Unions seek arbitration for the same reason. A grievance festers in the workplace unless resolved in negotiation or arbitration. It may affect the morale of union members. The union must prove to its members that it will press their concerns even at the risk of losing.

The ability to file a grievance and to begin a counseling relationship gives the grievant and the client a sense of power and personal value. They can force others to pay attention to their problems. They learn how to call upon others

---

42. Cf. Rogers, supra note 30, at 64 (noting the importance of the initial decision to seek therapy, whether by one's own initiative or at the recommendation of a person charged with making the decision).

43. Leonard Small, The Briefer Psychotherapies 44 (1979).

for help. Thus, even if a grievance never goes to arbitration, the grievant gets attention. Even if therapy does not assuage all problems, the client learns how to seek help. Processing and arbitrating grievances also gives the union a chance to promote the best interests of the persons it represents.

B. Arbitrator Selection

Under the typical arbitration model, the union and the employer jointly select the arbitrator. Control over selection of the decision-maker may have a positive therapeutic influence. Although the grievant usually does not participate in the selection, his or her representative does. Even indirect participation will enhance the grievant's trust in the arbitrator.[44] For the union, of course, an equal say in selecting the adjudicator empowers the organization.

Participation in the selection of the arbitrator also promotes the grievant's anticipation of a favorable result. However, this may be deceptive. Only inexperienced participants think they can guarantee victory by selecting the right arbitrator. Acceptable labor arbitrators stay that way because they decide cases on the merits. In this way, arbitrators fulfill the parties' reasonable expectations.[45] This, however, may not be what the grievant foresees.

Parties select an arbitrator based on prior experiences, on recommendations, and on their review of published awards and other data. These are good sources upon which to base a choice. Both parties are likely to seek someone who understands the therapeutic potential of the arbitration process, although they might not use those terms.[46] For example, Arbitrator Richard Bloch recently noted the impact of the arbitrator's conduct of the hearing on the arbitrator's acceptability.[47] The same may be true for other aspects of an arbitrator's conduct affecting therapeutic values. References within the industrial relations community will report whether the arbitrator "runs a good hearing"

---

44. Under common arbitrator selection schemes, the arbitrator is not the first choice of either party. Upon request, appointing agencies, such as the American Arbitration Association or the Federal Mediation and Conciliation Service, supply a list of neutrals. Parties alternately strike from the list. The remaining person is appointed. Thus, in actuality the arbitrator may be the person least offensive to the two parties. Even so, each party (and the grievant, through the bargaining representative) will have some say in the chosen person.

45. See Roger I. Abrams, The Nature of the Arbitral Process: Substantive Decisionmaking in Labor Arbitration, 14 U.C. Davis L. Rev. 551 (1981). Compare the selection of the labor arbitrator with the court system for selecting a judge. The presiding judge is assigned at random without disputant control. Mere fortune—good or bad—determines who will sit as judge.

46. The Supreme Court stated in Alexander v. Gardner-Denver Co., 415 U.S. 36, 57 (1974), that "[p]arties usually choose an arbitrator because they trust his knowledge and judgment concerning the demands and norms of industrial relations." These "demands and norms" may well include an appreciation of the therapeutic values of arbitration.

47. Arbitrator Bloch suggests that the way the arbitrator conducts the hearing, in particular how he responds to evidentiary objections, is very important for the arbitrator's acceptability to the parties. Richard I. Bloch, Objections at the Hearing, 41 Proc. Nat'l Acad. Arb. 305 (1989).

by controlling the proceeding. For therapeutic reasons among others, parties want a fair, well-managed proceeding.[48]

Similarly, a client normally selects a therapist based on prior experience and on recommendations from doctors or friends. This client information may be incomplete or inaccurate, but even so the client believes the person selected will fulfill the therapeutic function. Choosing one's own therapist is an important step toward recovery.

The selection processes for therapists and arbitrators raise the positive expectations of clients and grievants and their unions. Someone the affected persons helped select—either directly or indirectly—will listen to the problem and work toward a resolution. That alone bodes well for the processes to come and their curative effects.

C. The Site of the Arbitration Hearing

Parties normally hold arbitration hearings in hotel meeting rooms or conference rooms at the workplace. A neutral, non-threatening location may enhance the therapeutic values of the process to the participants. Were the hearing held in a courtroom, for example, the formal surroundings might inhibit witnesses and thus dampen the potential therapeutic effect. A hearing held in the employer's office could be a chilling experience for employees. An unfriendly environment would likely inhibit the testimony of the grievant and co-workers, perhaps keeping them from frankly stating their recollections and expressing their views and emotions. Certain places promote candor; others do not.[49] The arbitrator is independent of the parties, although employed by both. A neutral site reflects this independence.

The setting for a client-therapist relationship is similarly important. The therapist must provide an environment suitable for exploring problems. The decor and arrangement of furniture in a therapist's office is an aspect of proxemics, the study of environmental or personal space.[50] The setting varies depending on the therapist's orientation. The therapist, however, will choose a setting to enhance the therapeutic effect. Most psychologists believe that an informal setting relaxes the client and encourages exchange of necessary information.[51] Others suggest that the setting should be nondescript, allowing the client to focus attention inward.[52]

---

48. This might paint too rosy a picture for some collective relationships. Adversaries in the workplace may use arbitration to score psychological points, gain advantages they could not get through negotiations, and recover damages for past injustices. They want a forum, whether fair or not. Therapy for such adversaries may be impossible.

49. Employees are trained from grade school to sit and be quiet in certain places. The boss's office and the courtroom are the functional equivalent of the principal's office and the classroom.

50. William H. Cormier & L. Sherilyn Cormier, Interviewing Strategies for Helpers 77 (1985).

51. See Augustus Y. Napier, The Family Crucible 2 (1978).

52. Masson, supra note 23, at 199.

In a counseling relationship, the distance a therapist sits from the client influences the therapeutic effect. A client will feel discomfort if the therapist sits too near or too far. A space of three to four feet best promotes communication. This distance diminishes anxiety and allows the client to focus on internal rather than external issues.[53]

Most psychologists try to design a therapeutic environment that is mildly stimulating. This allows the client to be alert but able to focus on issues without distraction. To benefit from counseling, the client must feel comfortable in the surroundings. Distracting furniture, colors and pictures might inhibit the interchange between therapist and client.[54]

Arbitration requires a greater degree of formality. Sitting around on soft chairs and couches discussing the workplace problem would not encourage the orderly collection of the data needed to adjudicate the dispute. A little formality silently conveys the importance of the proceeding. That, in turn, encourages truthfulness and mutual respect. The setting of the hearing also affects the legitimacy of the process. The arbitrator's decision will affect the employees' work lives. A completely informal environment might suggest that the arbitrator will not give the decision the proper attention.

The arrangement of tables in the arbitration hearing room may be important. The arbitrator sits on the same level as the parties, but at a separate table. This signifies a suitable detachment without the distancing effect of a judge's raised bench. Witnesses sit directly before or beside the arbitrator, allowing eye contact and an evaluation of demeanor. Some arbitrators insist on a U-shaped series of connected tables. Space between the arbitrator and the parties increases formality without helping fact-gathering.

The setting of arbitration and counseling is important to the therapeutic mix. Both are informal, although arrangement of the arbitration hearing room must emphasize efficient data collection over good feelings. Grievants and clients must feel comfortable in their respective settings. Neither procedure should tolerate artificial barriers to communication.

D. An Informal Hearing Not Bound by the Rules of Evidence

Arbitration hearings are orderly but informal. The atmosphere of informality at the hearing enhances the therapeutic value of the proceeding by encouraging those concerned to speak freely. The arbitrator wears business clothes, not a robe. Informal discussion may precede the hearing. The parties and the arbitrator relate to one another. The arbitrator normally introduces himself or herself to the parties and meets the grievant before the hearing.

On the other hand, the arbitration process demands some formality to demonstrate its importance, its seriousness, its distinctiveness, and its legitimacy. Thus the arbitrator does not wear casual clothes, follows a ritualized procedure,

---

53. These distances are appropriate for adult middle-class Americans. Other cultures might prefer a greater or lesser distance to achieve the same level of comfort. Cormier & Cormier, supra note 50, at 77.

54. Id. at 78.

sits apart, and addresses (and is addressed by) the advocates and witnesses by honorific titles ("Arbitrator Jones," "Ms. Smith").

A similar situation occurs in counseling, most particularly in family therapy which usually begins with a social stage of mutual introductions. The therapist tries to make the family feel comfortable in the office while maintaining a professional distance.[55]

During the arbitration hearing, the arbitrator gets the information needed to resolve the dispute. Through testimony and documents, the parties inform the arbitrator about their work relationship and the facts of the grievance. Parties can cross-examine witnesses to test their testimony and elicit additional information for the arbitrator. The arbitrator normally seeks to reduce conflict between the parties at the hearing because conflict may interfere with data collection.

A particularly important facet of arbitration is the opportunity for participants to explain events directly to an outside authority. The rules of the arbitration hearing foster the collection of this unfiltered data. Representatives of the parties may try to interfere with this process by lodging evidentiary objections. The experienced arbitrator will not permit objections to thwart introduction of this pertinent evidence.

Often one party uses a lawyer while the other does not. If evidentiary rules applied, the party lacking a lawyer would be at a great disadvantage in presenting its story to the arbitrator. Some traditional court rules of evidence designed to keep prejudicial information from the jury have no place in arbitration. An arbitrator is not an untutored juror. The skilled arbitrator, like a judge, can give evidence the weight it deserves.[56]

It may be therapeutic for the grievant to tell the story through his or her testimony. For best results, the grievant must perceive the hearing as more than a continuation of the employer-controlled grievance procedure. Evidentiary rules foreign to the participating workers should not inhibit the grievant's ability to tell the "truth" as he or she sees it.[57]

---

55. Jay Haley, Problem-Solving Therapy 16 (1976). At this stage in family therapy, the therapist attempts to involve all members of the family in defining the problem they seek to address. In arbitration, by comparison, management and the union each have a designated representative. See also Napier, supra note 51, at 2.

56. Arbitrators often accept evidence of questionable reliability, stating that they will give it "the weight it deserves." This often infuriates lawyer representatives who are accustomed to the rules of evidence. The greater risk, however, "is not that the arbitrator will hear too much irrelevancy, but rather that he will not hear enough of the relevant." Harry Shulman, Reason, Contract, and Law in Labor Relations, 68 Harv. L. Rev. 999, 1017 (1955).

57. Professor Reginald Alleyne argues that the "valuable therapeutic effect...is derived from the opportunity to present a case on matters relevant to the grievance." Reginald Alleyne, Delawyerizing Labor Arbitration, 50 Ohio St. L.J. 93, 100 (1989). To expedite proceedings, he would apply a simple test of relevancy. One problem with this approach is that an arbitrator rarely knows what is relevant until a substantial portion of the case is presented. Unlike court cases with formal documents framing the issues, arbitrators normally come to the hearing with little or no information about the dispute. Both for fact-finding and therapeutic reasons, therefore, the arbitrator should allow the parties to present their evidence and sort it out later for relevance.

Similarly, a therapist encourages the client to share information that will help the therapist better understand the client, from the client's frame of reference. No procedural "rules" inhibit this information transmittal, although some may help it. For example, therapy usually occurs at a set time and place. Moreover, confidentiality is an underlying principle of psychotherapy which encourages full and frank communication.[58]

One therapeutic advantage of an arbitration hearing is that the grievant expects a prompt resolution of the problem. The hearing itself normally lasts only a few hours. Either by contract or appointing agency rule, the arbitrator's award is normally due in 30 or 60 days. Arbitration is thus more like time-limited or brief psychotherapy than Freudian psychoanalysis, which often takes years.[59] A client facing a few therapeutic sessions will expect improvement.[60] Brief psychotherapy focuses on specific symptoms or identified issues,[61] much as arbitration focuses on particular alleged contract breaches rather than the whole bargaining relationship.[62]

One essential step in developing a brief psychotherapeutic relationship is fostering the client's emotional safety.[63] Clients need to know the therapist will respect rather than ridicule them. Similarly, in arbitration grievants must feel their concerns are important to the arbitrator. In contrast to their status at work, grievants in arbitration have special recognition. They deserve the attention of all the people gathered in the arbitration hearing room, especially that of the arbitrator. In brief therapy, the client often feels that the simple act of talking about the problem can be helpful, even if the discussion is only superficial.[64] Much the same occurs in arbitration.

Within the limits of an orderly proceeding, informality is an essential therapeutic aspect of labor arbitration. Beyond the necessary order, formality will likely decrease the proceeding's therapeutic value. This "ordered informality" also fosters the arbitrator's information-gathering because witnesses find it easy to convey their evidence and opinions. That in turn helps the arbitrator to complete the assigned task of resolving the dispute on the merits. Similarly, informality engenders trust and openness within the client-therapist relationship. It helps the client to speak freely and allows the therapist to understand the

---

58. Gerald Corey et al., Issues and Ethics in the Helping Professions 183 (1988). Although the arbitration process is normally private, it does not usually require the same degree of confidentiality.

59. Leonard Small reports that five or six sessions is adequate brief therapy in most instances. Small, supra note 43, at 122. The total time approximates the average arbitration hearing. See also Nye, supra note 33, at 38; Behavioral Science, supra note 24, at 304.

60. Small, supra note 43, at 44.

61. Simon H. Budman & Allan S. Gurman, Theory and Practice of Brief Therapy 27 (1988).

62. Arbitration also resembles crisis intervention, a form of brief therapy that addresses a critical period in a person's life. Small, supra note 43, at 27.

63. See Mary M. Goulding, Getting the Important Work Done Fast: Contract Plus Redecision, in Brief Therapy: Myths, Methods, and Metaphors 303 (Jeffrey K. Zeig & Stephen G. Gilligan eds., 1990).

64. Balsam & Balsam, supra note 19, at 165.

nature of the client's problem. Only then, with the therapist's help, can the client begin to resolve the problem.

E. The Grievant-Arbitrator Relationship

Of the many possible therapeutic aspects of arbitration, the most important to the individual grievant is the potential relationship with the arbitrator. The grievant's initial and final perceptions of the arbitrator will critically affect therapeutic values. The therapeutic key is the creation of a relationship between the grievant and the arbitrator within which the grievant trusts the arbitrator. The arbitrator's personal characteristics—expertise, openness, and the ability to control the proceeding, among others—foster this trust. The grievant-arbitrator relationship also resembles the relationships developed in group and family therapy.

During the grievance procedure, the grievant could not help but notice that management controlled the process. After all, management could, and did, deny the grievant's claim. At the arbitration hearing, in contrast, the grievant finds a new power, the arbitrator. The grievant sees how the arbitrator controls the proceeding. The arbitrator's control places the union and the employer on the same plane, thus raising the grievant's relative position. (For the same reason, arbitration enhances the union's position in the eyes of its members and in the eyes of the company.) Although the grievant has not seen the arbitrator before, he or she is likely to appreciate the neutral's ability to treat the grievant and union as management's equals.

Similar development occurs in therapy. Studies show that a therapeutic relationship between a client and a counselor evolves as the client comes to perceive the counselor as expert, attractive, and trustworthy.[65] When these three characteristics, known as "relationship enhancers," are present, counselors more readily influence clients.[66] A counselor's physical appearance, reputation, and professional status contribute to the client's perception and thus to the client's willingness to develop a productive relationship. Clients determine their counselor's competence by examining credentials and accomplishments. They consider such factors as specialized training, experience, status, attire, reputation, and physical attractiveness to determine their counselor's ability to help them.[67]

Arbitrators may exhibit these "relationship enhancers." Grievants perceive arbitrators as experts. The grievant expects to trust the arbitrator because the union, the grievant's representative, participated in the selection process. Appearance and demeanor can confirm (or defeat) that expectation. A self-assured arbitrator will impress a grievant. The arbitrator's role in the proceeding, directing both labor and management, supports the grievant's predisposition. The arbitrator's behavior should enhance the grievant's trust by showing sincerity, openness, and competence.

---

65. See Yalom, supra note 28, at 102–03.

66. Cormier & Cormier, supra note 50, at 44. Michael Kahn has written that "the relationship *is* the therapy." Michael Kahn, Between Therapist and Client 1 (1991).

67. Egan, supra note 20, at 19–21.

The grievant-arbitrator relationship parallels the client-therapist relationship. The client depends on visual cues, descriptive and behavioral, to form an opinion about the therapist. The client watches and listens, noting how the therapist makes eye contact, speaks, moves, and responds. These initial impressions strengthen the therapeutic relationship.[68] The client judges the counselor's openness, honesty, and candid description of the process. The relationship deepens when the client perceives the counselor as friendly and likeable. The therapist must maintain some distance, however. The client and therapist are not friends.[69] When the therapist projects professional characteristics, the client becomes trusting. Once secure, the client can reveal sensitive information.[70]

At its core, the therapist-client relationship depends upon trust.[71] Rogerian therapy, a humanistic, person-centered approach, focuses on factors that foster a trusting relationship. Thus, Carl Rogers explains that a therapist's personal characteristics and attitudes are essential to the development of the therapeutic relationship.[72] The therapist must show:

1. "*congruence*," Rogers's term for genuineness;[73]
2. "*unconditional positive regard*," which is "prizing," "acceptance," and "trust";[74] and
3. "*empathy*," an "understanding from the client's viewpoint."[75]

These aspects of a client-therapist relationship contribute to the therapeutic effect.[76]

A labor arbitrator who exhibits the same characteristics also will promote therapeutic values. This does not require partisanship favoring the grievant. A

---

68. See, e.g., Cormier & Cormier, supra note 50, at 37.

69. Kahn, supra note 66, at 2–3.

70. See, e.g., Cormier & Cormier, supra note 50, at 21.

71. Small, supra note 43, at 44 (1979); Behavioral Science, supra note 24, at 304.

72. Rogers, supra note 30, at 62, 135.

73. Id. (emphasis added). Congruence helps the counselor develop trust and rapport. Cormier & Cormier, supra note 50, at 22. The client perceives genuineness when the counselor behaves in a non-stylistic manner. Id. at 27. The counselor conveys genuineness with non-verbal behaviors, such as eye contact, smiling, and leaning forward towards the client. Id.

74. Rogers, supra note 30, at 136 (emphasis added). The therapist makes an effort to understand the client. By respecting the individual, the counselor demonstrates a commitment to the relationship, behaving in a non-judgmental manner with warmth. Cormier & Cormier, supra note 50, at 22. These behaviors show the client a commitment to work toward resolution by accepting the client as a person. Id. at 22, 31; see Rogers, supra note 30, at 136.

75. Rogers, supra note 30, at 62, 136 (emphasis added). A therapist demonstrates empathy by showing a desire to comprehend the client's feelings. See id. at 136. He or she does so by discussing what is important to the client and reflecting the client's feelings and statements. Using these skills, the counselor builds rapport and elicits information from the client, allowing the client to explore himself or herself. Cormier & Cormier, supra note 50, at 22. Empathy, like genuineness, is conveyed through non-verbal behaviors, such as direct eye contact, an open arm stance, and leaning forward. Id. at 23.

76. Yalom, supra note 28, at 48–49.

therapist's focus in individual therapy is the client's well-being, but the arbitrator's primary concern is the relationship between the employer and the union. At times the arbitrator must sacrifice a full therapeutic effect for the grievant to maintain the stability of the collective relationship. The arbitrator can listen and empathize without showing bias toward the grievant. Therapeutic effect does not depend upon partiality. It is enough for the arbitrator to treat the grievant with respect and listen to his or her story.[77]

We might compare arbitration to group therapy and the arbitrator to a group leader. Justice Douglas spoke particularly about the positive therapeutic effect on employees. Other members of the arbitration "group"—union grievance committee members and management representatives—also may benefit from participating in the process.

The goals in group therapy are "clear and specific," determined collectively by group members and the group leader.[78] Similarly, the goals in an arbitration hearing are clear and understood. The parties help the arbitrator collect enough information about a dispute to make an informed judgment based on the dispute. The members of the arbitration "group," union and management, have created the process. With the "group leader" arbitrator, they follow the rules of the proceeding.

Research by psychologists on group process suggests that the group leader's personal characteristics can determine the effectiveness of the process. A series of leadership elements are important to therapeutic effectiveness: "Courage, Willingness to Model, Presence, Goodwill and Caring, Belief in Group Process, Openness, Nondefensiveness in Coping with Attacks, Personal Power, Stamina, Willingness to Seek New Experiences, Self-Awareness, Sense of Humor, and Inventiveness."[79]

The best arbitrators exhibit the same characteristics. They face difficult cases courageously, without concern for personal self-interest.[80] They model appropriate behavior for the parties and their representatives. They involve themselves in the hearing and exhibit respect and caring for the parties. They believe in the process, approach the hearing without preconceptions, and remain open to new ideas and different lifestyles. Finally, they put aside personalities in dealing with the hearing's inevitable tensions.

Moreover, arbitrators are in control throughout the hearing, directing the proceeding in an efficient and productive manner. Arbitration can be exhausting, and arbitrators need stamina. Venturing to small towns and strange plants to hear disputes, arbitrators must be willing to experience the unknown. Throughout the proceeding, arbitrators must respect arbitration's goals while seeking the information necessary for a fair and informed decision. Arbitrators

---

77. Similarly, in group therapy, the therapist, although empathetic, must remain impartial. The therapist must treat both parties fairly and comprehend their differences. Rogers, supra note 30, at 347.

78. Corey & Corey, supra note 29, at 177.

79. Id. at 14–20 (using the listed characteristics as subheadings in the discussion of what makes an effective group leader).

80. See Rolf Valtin, A Word to the Arbitrator in Training, in A. Zack, Arbitration in Practice 1, 4 (Arnold M. Zack ed., 1984).

must maintain a sense of humor to keep the process in perspective.[81] Successful arbitrators must creatively respond to unforeseen events at the hearing.
They must also creatively draft an opinion that will meet the parties' needs
while staying true to the contract.

Yalom reports several therapeutic factors that occur in group therapy.[82] We
can identify their analogues in the arbitration hearing. First, group therapy results in the "instillation of hope" in the client. The therapist's effort to understand client disclosures is one of the most effective therapeutic behaviors.[83]
Similarly, the arbitration hearing fosters the grievant's hope for resolution of
the problem.[84] The hearing offers the grievant the opportunity to state the
problem and receive relief. Second, in group therapy one "imparts information," sharing personal pain or problems with other members of the group.
The arbitration hearing affords the grievant a similar opportunity to share
with others.

Yalom notes a third therapeutic factor: The group process shows the client
that his or her problem is not unique. At the arbitration hearing, the grievant
often learns that the arbitrator has heard similar disputes. This may give the
grievant a sense of relief at being normal.

Group therapy also fosters cohesiveness within the group, a bonding that
provides support and caring.[85] Similarly, the arbitration hearing allows the
grievant to bond with union representatives and fellow employees. During the
processing of the case, the grievant is the sole focus of the union's attention.
Cohesion is essential if the grievant is to feel that the "arbitration team" is
working on his or her behalf.

Finally, group therapy recreates the family setting. Arbitration, too, might
create a temporary family. The men and women in the hearing room usually
know each other well. They spend eight hours together every workday, more
waking time than they may spend with their real families. The members of the
"work family" in the arbitration hearing room may disagree, of course, but so
do real families.

The therapist/client and arbitrator/grievant relationships aid the processes'
curative effects. The therapist's and arbitrator's personal characteristics and

---

81. In his presidential address to the National Academy of Arbitrators, Arbitrator
William J. Fallon stated:

> The lighter touch . . . is an antidote to the tension, to the hostility, to the distrust that
> accompanies so much of what we do. What it can do is release that tension, per-
> haps draw people together, implant the idea that all problems are solvable among
> people of good will, and, not least, break up the sometime overwhelming monot-
> ony of each side relentlessly ignoring the other's point of view.

William J. Fallon, The Presidential Address: The Role of Humor in Arbitration, 39 Proc.
Nat'l Acad. Arb. 1, 5 (1987).

82. Yalom, supra note 28, at 3.

83. Rogers, supra note 30, at 346.

84. Hope has a positive effect on an individual's behavior. Small, supra note 43, at 43. It
should also improve an employee's ability to perform in a more adaptive manner. Under the
"expectation theory," an employee would modify current behavior in anticipation of resolution of the conflict. Id.

85. Corey & Corey, supra note 29, at 10, 176.

professional habits help develop these relationships. Over time, the client and grievant come to believe that the therapist and the arbitrator will help resolve their problems.

F. The Opportunity to Address the Arbitrator

At the close of the hearing, many arbitrators offer grievants a chance to speak freely on the record. This penultimate stage of the hearing fulfills the grievant's expectation about the relationship with the arbitrator. By offering the grievant a chance to speak, the arbitrator shows concern, empathy, and understanding of the grievant's turmoil and discomfort.[86]

This may be the most therapeutic moment of the arbitration hearing. Unencumbered by management or the union, the employee can speak freely. Sometimes the statements are very revealing. They may convince the arbitrator that a grievant cannot return to the workplace.[87] Other employees show contrition and rehabilitation.[88] Even if grievants say nothing, they are likely to appreciate the offer.

Carl Rogers stresses the importance of the client's expression of feelings. The therapist elicits these expressions by showing an understanding of the individual's problem and a willingness to listen.[89] Other therapeutic models insist that simply releasing unexpressed feelings is not enough to produce a therapeutic effect. There must be a cognitive element present, a knowing appreciation, and an understanding of the problem.[90]

A grievant who accepts the arbitrator's offer of a chance to speak freely may accomplish both exposition and understanding. On the other hand, the grievant may only feel a cathartic release.[91] In either case, the experience is psychologically helpful.

Psychologists have focused on the need to communicate feelings to others. Exposition in an empty room is neither cathartic nor therapeutic.[92] In the arbi-

---

86. Cf. Rogers, supra note 30, at 112, 136 (discussing the attitudes of an effective therapist); Cormier & Cormier, supra note 50, at 23 (discussing ways in which a counselor may both verbally and nonverbally convey understanding and empathy even where the client does not explicitly express underlying feelings).

87. National Academy of Arbitrators President William J. Fallon noted that Arbitrator Eva Robins once asked a grievant whether he wanted his job back. He replied: "Hell no, I don't want the job back or any back pay. I just want satisfaction." Fallon, supra note 81, at 5.

88. Professor A. Howard Myers explained that "[t]he arbitration hearing has been called the psychiatrist's couch of industrial relations," because the arbitrator can determine "motives" at the hearing. A. Howard Myers, Concepts of Industrial Democracy, 9 Proc. Nat'l Acad. Arb. 59, 74 (1956). For example, the grievant might reveal those motives when asked by the arbitrator to supplement the record.

89. Corey & Corey, supra note 29, at 5; see also Yalom, supra note 28, at 50.

90. Corey & Corey, supra note 29, at 5; see also Yalom, supra note 28, at 84, 226.

91. One could test this hypothesis by observing grievants' behavior on the work floor after the hearing. A positive behavioral change might indicate the employee both expressed feeling and understood the import of the proceeding.

92. Yalom, supra note 28, at 85.

tration hearing, the grievant has an audience consisting of coworkers, union leaders, managers, and—most importantly—the arbitrator.

The entire therapist-client session is a direct conversation between the two persons. In contrast, only a small part of the arbitration hearing involves a direct interchange between arbitrator and grievant. In this brief period, however, the arbitrator can learn a lot about the grievant. In addition, the interchange reinforces the grievant's perception of the process as fair, open, and curative.

G. The Opinion

The arbitration process is not over until the arbitrator issues an opinion explaining the basis of the award. The opinion explains a loss to the losing party.[93] Thus, the arbitrator should write the opinion in language the affected employees can understand. Employees may not agree with the outcome, but a well-written opinion can convince them that the arbitrator at least heard and understood their positions.[94]

According to the more directive theories of psychological treatment, the therapist gives feedback to the client. To communicate effectively with the client, the therapist must avoid jargon. Incomprehensible advice leaves the client without a way to solve the problem. Unlike an arbitrator, the therapist cannot order relief. The therapist can only make suggestions the client can follow to produce relief.

Arbitration is narrower in scope than therapy. It does not try to solve all the grievant's life problems. It focuses instead on resolving a single dispute. While therapy can also focus on a single problem, it often opens a broader range of issues for discussion and treatment. Arbitrators try to work as precisely as possible; therapists may have to address more general and unfocused concerns.

The arbitration opinion completes the therapeutic process. Even when the arbitrator denies the grievance, the grievant at least learns the reasons for the loss. The careful arbitration opinion therefore reinforces arbitration's therapeutic values. Justice Douglas did not promise victory, only process and therapy.

V. Therapeutic Values and Arbitral Legitimacy

With little explanation, Justice Douglas applauded arbitration's therapeutic values. We have tried to suggest how and when arbitration might be therapeutic. Therapy, however, is only one of several arbitral values, others of which deserve at least as much protection. The arbitrator should therefore try to accomplish the therapeutic goals of arbitration without losing sight of the other

---

93. See Roger I. Abrams & Dennis R. Nolan, Arbitral Craftsmanship and Opinion Writing, 5 Lab. Law. 195, 217 (1989).

94. See id. Professor Susan Fitzgibbon argues that "[t]he arbitral opinion contributes to the therapeutic effect [of] the process and the continuing relationship of the parties by explaining the reasoning behind the award, demonstrating that the arbitrator heard and considered the arguments of each side." Susan A. Fitzgibbon, The Judicial Itch, 34 St. Louis U. L.J. 485, 506 (1990).

goals. A purely therapeutic approach would not be desirable, nor would it fulfill the parties' needs and expectations. To the contrary, it could destroy the very legitimacy essential to arbitration's success.

The arbitration process must be legitimate, final, and binding. Some characteristics that enhance therapy, for example the joint selection of the arbitrator by the parties, also foster these other important values.[95] On the other hand, some characteristics could produce therapy at the expense of the other values. Here are a few examples.

A. Insufficient Formality

An unstructured, completely informal proceeding might be the best way to solve an individual's psychological problems. Nevertheless, it might destroy the parties' respect for arbitration as a quasi-judicial process.[96] Arbitration requires more than a helpful chat with a counselor about a workplace problem. Arbitrators who are too informal and too familiar with the parties may raise significant doubts about the legitimacy of their awards.

We conduct trials with substantial formality at least partly to enhance their legitimacy and power.[97] Arbitrators do not sentence people to death or even to jail, but they do address important employee job rights. Participants often refer (hyperbolically) to discharge as "industrial capital punishment." Because of the importance of the results to the participants, arbitration should have sufficient formality to provide the dignity and respect appropriate to the issue.

B. Insufficient Finality

The ultimate result of the arbitration process must be a binding resolution of the dispute. A purely therapeutic model might leave some substantive issues for the parties to resolve after the arbitrator's intervention is complete. A psychologist, for example, will try to encourage the client to develop remedial strategies to deal with difficult situations. Therapy teaches clients to exercise self-control. Although arbitrators commonly leave the back pay calculation to the parties for final resolution, they must address the merits with finality. Parties also may learn something about problem solving that would be useful in the future. This might be a collateral benefit of the process, but it is not its central focus. The most important task for the arbitrator is to resolve the dispute with finality.

C. Failure to Exercise Judgment

A therapist might avoid telling a client bluntly that he or she is wrong. An arbitrator may have to do so in an opinion. Failing to exercise judgment

---

95. Harry T. Edwards, Advantages of Arbitration over Litigation: Reflections of a Judge, 35 Proc. Nat'l Acad. Arb. 16, 25 (1983).

96. See generally Tom R. Tyler, Why People Obey the Law (1990) (discussing what the public expects of the legal system).

97. See generally Marc Galanter, Adjudication, Litigation, and Related Phenomena, in Law and the Social Sciences 151–229 (Leon Lipson & Stanton Wheeler eds., 1986) (discussing formal dispute resolution within a governmental framework).

would be neither honest nor "legitimate." Judgment is what the parties wanted when they agreed to arbitration and selected a neutral to judge the dispute.

D. Lack of Impartiality

A therapist might try to assure a client that he or she is on the client's side. The arbitrator, on the other hand, must maintain strict impartiality. The arbitrator's relationship with the grievant must not be misread as favoring the union's case. It is a difficult line for the arbitrator to walk between openness and taking sides.

E. Deciding the Particular Dispute

A therapist might decide to extend and expand treatment to help the client resolve many outstanding issues. By comparison, an arbitrator should seek a speedy resolution of the submitted dispute. A therapist offers advice; an arbitrator must *decide* the issue. A therapist often operates on subjective feelings; an arbitrator should strive to decide a case on the record. Thus, while there are parallels between arbitration and therapy, there are differences in purpose and process.

The key is balance. Informality in an arbitration proceeding may promote therapy without jeopardizing legitimacy if the arbitrator protects the basic integrity of the process.[98] The parties must see the arbitrator doing his or her primary job, collecting the information necessary to resolve the dispute. The arbitrator who allows employees to tell their story gains this information. With a balanced approach the arbitrator can relieve employee apprehension while maintaining the proper distance needed to protect arbitration's legitimacy. In the end, the correct balance allows arbitration to serve its essential goals.

VI. Threats to Therapeutic Values

Since the *Trilogy*, changes in the legal environment have tested arbitration's therapeutic values. Statutory changes have threatened to make labor arbitration more court-like.[99] Many parties now take statutory disputes to arbitration rather than to court because it is cheaper and more efficient.[100] The growth of public-sector arbitration has aggravated the problem because government employee cases normally involve laws and regulations. The infusion of legal terms and concepts into labor arbitration has made the process more like a court. These developments jeopardize arbitration's therapeutic values.

---

98. See Roger I. Abrams, The Integrity of the Arbitral Process, 76 Mich. L. Rev. 231, 252–54 (1977).

99. See St. Antoine, supra note 1, at 1144, 1161.

100. Alexander v. Gardner-Denver Co., 415 U.S. 36, 55 (1974) ("[T]he grievance-arbitration machinery of the collective-bargaining agreement remains a relatively inexpensive and expeditious means for resolving a wide range of disputes, including" Title VII claims); see Lea S. VanderVelde, Making Good on Vaca's Promise: Apportioning Back Pay to Achieve Remedial Goals, 32 UCLA L. Rev. 302, 385 (1984).

A dispute based on the reading of a statute is likely to be more formal than one that requires interpreting a privately-written contract. A swarm of lawyers descending on the local Holiday Inn conference room for an arbitration hearing brings with it legalisms and court-like trappings.[101] This is especially true if the attorneys are unschooled in the ways of alternative dispute resolution.[102] Federal sector arbitration, burdened by statutory review procedures, can be excessively formal.[103]

Fortunately, most arbitration cases remain unaffected by external law. There is no sign that arbitrators have changed the way they conduct hearings in a typical case. A just cause determination in a simple discharge case, a seniority case involving bumping rights in a layoff, a subcontracting case involving unit work—none of these requires much formality. The essential therapeutic nature can remain strong. Statutes need not require abandoning arbitration's therapeutic values.

VII. Conclusion

There is a solid basis for Justice Douglas's assumption that labor arbitration may be therapeutic. Many elements of the arbitration process resemble traditional psychotherapy. Of course, many aspects of psychotherapy have no role in arbitration. Parties apparently find arbitration valuable even when they lose. If they did not find it useful, labor and management would not include an arbitration clause in virtually every collective bargaining agreement.

Arbitrators may not see themselves as performing a therapeutic function. It is clearly not their primary duty. They are "creature[s] of the parties,"[104] appointed to interpret and apply the collective bargaining agreement, not labor relations physicians. The better arbitrators, however, do understand their role is multi-faceted. They must resolve particular disputes. They also have important obligations to the continuing relationship between labor and management. Finally, though, they also fulfill Justice Douglas's promise in the *Trilogy* by serving a therapeutic function.

---

101. See Alleyne, supra note 57, at 94–95 (noting that a "casual and short-term observer" may have difficulty distinguishing a trial from an arbitration proceeding).

The *Alexander* Court noted the importance of the arbitrator giving "full consideration to an employee's Title VII rights." See *Alexander*, 415 U.S. at 60 n.21 (concluding that in a Title VII case a judge might give greater deference to an arbitrator's prior ruling in the same matter if the arbitration met certain procedural requirements). Parties desiring to make the arbitration award final and binding will likely try to meet the required standards.

102. See generally Alleyne, supra note 57, at 93–106 (arguing for less formalism in arbitration proceedings).

103. See generally John Kagel, Grievance Arbitration in the Federal Service: Still Hardly Final and Binding?, 34 Proc. Nat'l Acad. Arb. 178, 178–79 (1982) (comparing statutory review of arbitration awards with the more limited use of review processes in traditional arbitration).

104. Labor Arbitrator Development: A Handbook 239 (Christopher A. Barrecca et al. eds., 1983) (using the term as a title of a section discussing the historical development of labor arbitration).

Labor and management should worry about the developments in labor arbitration that jeopardize its therapeutic values. Arbitration can accommodate a broad spectrum of issues, but it cannot maintain its therapeutic nature if court-like formality replaces ordered informality, if the rules of evidence strictly govern hearings, or if the employees cannot tell their stories to an informed neutral.

Labor arbitration differs from other alternatives to litigation because it is more than a mere substitute for court proceedings. As Justice Douglas said in the *Trilogy*, arbitration is a continuation of the collective bargaining process.[105] Excessive legalism endangers labor arbitration's procedural values. If we are to fulfill Justice Douglas's promise, we must preserve arbitration's therapeutic nature from these external threats. If we are to maintain arbitration's positive role in the workplace, we must protect those elements that help employees reach a better understanding of themselves and their behaviors.

---

105. United Steelworkers v. Warrior & Gulf Navigation Co., 363 U.S. 574, 581 (1960).

Chapter 26

Class, Personality, Contract, and Unconscionability

Jeffrey L. Harrison

> As soon as you're born they make you feel small
> By giving you no time instead of it all
> Till the pain is so big you feel nothing at all
> A working class hero is something to be.[1]

I. Introduction

My thesis begins with the idea of "entitlement"—not a legal entitlement, but a "sense of entitlement."[2] That is, a sense of deserving something. For most of us, it is important to feel that we have received that to which we are entitled. In the context of an exchange, it means that we want to feel we have been treated fairly or reached a state of "compensatory justice."[3] Part of my thesis is that this sense of entitlement is not evenly distributed among us. As an example, suppose that two individuals are hired as entry-level law professors. Before moving to their new locations, both inquire about their employer's will-

---

1. John Lennon, Working Class Hero, on Plastic Ono Band (Apple Records, Ltd. 1970)

2. I do not mean to imply that everyone will have difficulty understanding what I mean by a "sense of entitlement." But much of what I say in the following pages is devoted to the idea that not only do we each have a sense of entitlement, but that that sense is a function of factors that are unrelated to whether one really is "entitled" or "deserving." This broader statement may be difficult for some to comprehend. My sense is that the stronger one's sense of entitlement, the more they will have invested in believing that they are "truly" entitled. Thus, I suggest that the reader who finds what follows to be unacceptable, should ask him or herself whether they are motivated by something other than whatever errors or overstatements follow. See Reinhold Niebuhr, Moral Man and Immoral Society: A Study in Ethics and Politics 117 (1932) ("The most common form of hypocrisy among the privileged classes is to assume that their privileges are the just payments with which society rewards specially useful or meritorious functions."). I would like to thank Amy Mashburn for bringing Niebuhr's views on this matter to my attention.

3. By "compensatory justice" I am referring to the fairness of the exchange between individuals. See Michael Rosenfeld, Contract and Justice: The Relation Between Classical Contract Law and Social Contract Theory, 70 Iowa L. Rev. 769, 780 (1985) (defining "compensatory justice" as the reward of "just deserts" resulting from the conference of a benefit upon another).

ingness to pay moving expenses. The response to each is, "It is our policy to pay up to $3,000." One professor responds, "But that is not enough! I cannot possibly move my family for that amount." An argument ensues. The second professor simply processes this information and uses it in arranging her move.[4]

The difference in the responses reflects a difference in their expectations and their senses of entitlement. This difference may be explained by something quite concrete. For example, the first professor may have seen a memorandum indicating that the school traditionally had paid moving expenses for new members of the faculty. But one's sense of entitlement may also, and generally does, arise from less direct and more subtle influences. As a child the first professor may have heard repeatedly how smart, clever or attractive he was and, thus, began to feel as though he was somehow more worthy than others. Or, he may have attended a prestigious school where he was "taught" that graduates of that school are somehow special.[5] In contrast, the second faculty member may have been treated quite differently, that is, never taught that she is somehow special and more deserving.

This sense of entitlement is the cornerstone of this Article, but there are two more components. The first is that social class[6] is an important determinant of one's sense of entitlement. The second component is that individuals with a higher general sense of entitlement require more of whatever is at stake in an exchange, in order to achieve a state that they regard as compensatorily just, than those with a lower sense of entitlement. Together, these propositions produce the general thesis that social class and the resulting sense of entitlement have an impact on the terms of private orderings. Because individuals from higher social classes have a greater sense of entitlement, the terms of exchanges between different classes typically will favor those individuals. More generally, this means that the private orderings of people who belong to a class-oriented society will passively, though relentlessly, reinforce the existing class structure.[7]

---

4. In this example, gender specification is intentional.

5. Interestingly, sometimes a sense of entitlement can be purchased.

6. I make no attempt here to define social class in a precise way that will satisfy every critic of what is to follow. To me it involves weighing education, job status, income, and wealth. Harold Hodges suggests that classes are "the blended product of shared and analogous occupational orientations, educational backgrounds, economic wherewithal, and like experiences." Harold M. Hodges, Jr., Social Stratification: Class in America 13 (1984). I believe this is generally consistent with the measures used in Paul Fussell, Class: A Guide Through the American Class System (1983). In the first chapter of his book, Fussell offers interesting insights into how touchy discussions of class can be. I am indebted to my friend Walter Weyrauch for helping me understand the significance and signifiers of class.

7. Of course, for this to work smoothly, both classes must accept the legitimacy of their positions. See Peter M. Blau, Exchange and Power in Social Life 143–67 (1986) (distinguishing the various expectations of individuals and their relation to contemporary values and social standards); Jon Elster, Sour Grapes: Studies in the Subversion of Rationality 145 (1983) (explaining the necessity for oppressed and exploited classes to believe and accept the very social order that accepts them); L. Richard Della Fave, The Meek Shall Not Inherit the Earth: Self-Evaluation and the Legitimacy of Stratification, 45 Am. Soc. Rev. 955 (1980) (identifying the diverse collection of social mechanisms that generate, maintain and legitimize the notion of unequal distribution of resources); Robert Gordon, New Developments in Legal Theory, in the Politics of Law: A Progressive Critique 281, 286–87 (David Kairys

In essence, the source of the continual societal imbalances that flow from "freedom of contract" are largely the results of the damage that class stratification has already inflicted.[8]

I want to state this in terms that are slightly different but that may be more familiar. The idea that people act in accordance with their senses of compensatory justice means, in effect, that they have a generalized *preference* for sensing that they have received fair treatment.[9] When they find the terms of an exchange acceptable, this is an expression that this preference is satisfied. Much of my point is that this preference, or what it takes to satisfy it, is "taught" in large measure by one's social position and the laws that help preserve the social structure. In the terms economists use, this preference is determined endogenously—that is, it is not exogenous or simply a given.[10]

---

ed., 1982) (citing to Antonio Gramsci's theory of "hegemany" which suggests that class domination is most effective when both the dominant and dominated classes believe that there are no viable alternatives to the existing order).

An article that seems driven by the same concerns I have, but which takes a different perspective is Marc Galanter, Why the "Haves" Come Out Ahead: Speculations on the Limits of Legal Change, 9 Law & Soc. Rev. 95 (1974) (analyzing how the legal system operates by looking at the different kinds of parties involved and how their differences affect the rules and institutional facilities as opposed to looking at how the rules and facilities impact the parties).

8. A baseline source on this is Richard Sennett & Jonathan Cobb, The Hidden Injuries of Class (1973).

9. An obvious implication of equating this with a preference is to suggest that this sense of being treated fairly is just one of many sources of utility. I and many others do not believe, however, that all things that motivate us can be reduced to a single plane or class of utility. See, e.g., Amitai Etzioni, The Moral Dimension: Toward a New Economics 67–92 (1988) (suggesting that personal behavior is influenced by a vast array of pressures and obligations rather than the need to fulfill moral commitments instead of pleasure); Mark A. Lutz & Kenneth Lux, The Challenge of Humanistic Economics 9–22 (1979) (discussing the hierarchy of human needs, ranging from the basics, including food and shelter, to the less tangible, truth and justice); Nicholas Georgescu-Roegen, Choice, Expectations and Measurability, 68 Q. J. Econ. 503, 515 (1954) (summarizing the "Principle of the Irreducibility of Wants," which holds that the motives and feelings of individuals are so disproportionate in power and authority that human wants can not be reduced to a common basis); Jeffrey L. Harrison, Egoism, Altruism, and Market Illusions: The Limits of Law and Economics, 33 UCLA L. Rev. 1309, 1328–34 (1986) (explaining the idea of "lexical ordering," which states that those values that are afforded priority are not interchangeable with others); Amartya K. Sen, Rational Fools: A Critique of the Behavioral Foundations of Economics Theory, 6 Phil. & Pub. Aff. 317 (1977) (examining the problems that have arisen from the traditional economic assumption that individuals are motivated only by self-interest).

10. For a good discussion of the difficulties in dropping the assumption that tastes and preferences are a given and an example of the interesting work to which dropping that assumption can lead, see Kenneth G. Dau-Schmidt, An Economic Analysis of the Criminal Law as a Preference-Shaping Policy, 1990 Duke L. J. 1, 14–22. See also Mark Kelman, Consumption Theory, Production Theory and Ideology in the Coase Theorem, 52 S. Cal. L. Rev. 669, 677, 695 (1979) (comparing the Coase Theorem's desire to defend the concept of "state neutrality" against the specious claim of taste-neutrality which is inevitably undermined by existing liability rules); Robert A. Pollak, Endogenous Tastes in Demand and Welfare Analysis, 68 Am. Econ. Rev. Papers & Proc. 374 (May 1978) (applying welfare analysis and eco-

An important implication of this thesis is that Pareto superiority[11] may be an especially poor moral basis for enforcing interclass contracts. This follows from the likelihood that whether an exchange will leave both parties feeling better off is contingent on disparities in class, self-esteem, or personal sense of entitlement. If the disparities were less, the terms—distributive consequences—of some contracts would vary and other contracts may not exist at all. Just as contracts that are the result of coercion are not enforced because one's consent is induced artificially, contracts that come about because of our class-contingent notions of what we "deserve" seem equally artificial.[12]

The thrust of this argument is that "freedom" of contract is an illusion, in that we are taught from birth, by the fortuity of our class, that to which we should feel entitled. Furthermore, the conclusion that contract law principles are carefully designed to permit and facilitate inequality in exchanges seems accurate. For example, most questions in contract law are evaluated by objective standards, but the actual exchange itself, perhaps the only thing that really matters, is held to a subjective standard under the basic rule that the law will not address "adequacy of consideration."[13] Moreover, courts generally have avoided directly addressing questions of "substantive unconscionability," the one legal doctrine that would directly penetrate the fairness of the exchange.[14]

---

nomic analysis to the study of taste formation and change); Cass R. Sunstein, Legal Interference with Private Preferences, 53 U. Chi. L. Rev. 1129 (1986) (concluding that government action in the form of legal intervention is frequently justifiable regardless of the ancillary effects on private preferences).

For a typical example of the conventional approach in which law has no impact on preferences, see Alan Schwartz, A Reexamination of Nonsubstantive Unconscionability, 63 Va. L. Rev. 1053 (1977).

11. In this context Pareto superiority is achieved when two individuals can enter into an exchange that makes them both feel better off while no one is made worse off than they were prior to the exchange. See David W. Barnes & Lynn A. Stout, Cases and Materials on Law and Economics 11–12 (1992) (discussing the classification scheme devised by Vilfredo Pareto for making a neutral judgment as to wealth and utility maximization).

12. As the language in this sentence implies, there can be a number of ways in which an exchange can improve the position of the exchanging parties. Part of the argument to be developed later is that some exchanges that would tend to make both better off will not be acceptable because they offend the sense of compensatory justice of one of the parties.

Although he does not address this issue specifically, I think that the view of coercion in Mark Kelman, Choice and Utility, 1979 Wis. L. Rev. 769, 792–95, can be interpreted in such a way that the process of adaptation I am writing about ultimately can be seen as a response to coercion.

13. See Restatement (Second) of Contracts § 79 (1979) ("If the requirement of Consideration is met, there is no additional requirement of...equivalence in the values exchanged....").

14. A 1986 study reports that "since 1971, no court has declared a contract unconscionable solely on substantive unconscionability grounds." Craig Horowitz, Comment, Reviving the Law of Substantive Unconscionability: Applying the Implied Covenant of Good Faith and Fair Dealing to Excessively Priced Consumer Credit Contracts, 33 UCLA L.Rev. 940, 942 n. 14 (1986). On the other hand, in 1982 Melvin Eisenberg identified 10 cases in which a finding of unconscionability was based on price alone. Melvin A. Eisenberg, The Bargain Principle and Its Limits, 95 Harv. L. Rev. 741, 752 (1982); see also M.P. Ellinghaus, In Defense of Unconscionability, 78 Yale L. J. 757, 782–93 (1969) (discussing the case of in-

Yet, if subjective notions of fairness are class-contingent, it makes sense to employ an objective standard when examining the adequacy of consideration in contract cases, possibly through expanded reliance on substantive unconscionability.[15]

My argument is not that courts should apply the theory of unconscionability for the sole purpose of promoting equality. A more important point is that law can have an educative or "therapeutic"[16] function and that routine reliance on substantive unconscionability as a basis for not enforcing contracts can have the effect of elevating the sense of entitlement of the disadvantaged and decreasing the sense of entitlement of the privileged. Howard Lesnick captures the notion perfectly when he describes the possible liberation of the downtrodden so that they change from defendants to potential "counterclaimant[s]."[17]

In the pages that follow, I first explain in greater detail how one's sense of compensatory justice can affect his or her view of an exchange. Then, in Section III, I examine the two components of my thesis and indicate how they are supported by social science research in the areas of equity theory[18] and relative deprivation theory.[19] In Section IV, I illustrate more formally the way in which

---

voluntary bankruptcy); John A. Spanogle, Jr., Analyzing Unconscionability Problems, 117 U. Pa .L. Rev. 931, 952 (1969) (providing the example of price disparity and subsequent invocation of unconscionability theory).

Of course, courts respond to inequality in exchanges by using a variety of theories other than unconscionability. See E. Allan Farnsworth, Contracts 255–344 (2d ed. 1990).

15. By this I mean some version of the "reasonable person" standard. See James Gordley, Equality in Exchange, 69 Cal. L. Rev. 1587, 1637 n. 200 (1981).

16. The "therapeutic" effects of law in its various forms have been explored, primarily in the context of mental health law. See David B. Wexler & Bruce J. Winick, Essays in Therapeutic Jurisprudence (1991). It is from Wexler and Winick's work that I too became concerned with what might be termed "therapeutic effects," in the sense that I am interested in the healing potential of unconscionability. I am indebted to John Robertson who advised me of their work.

17. Howard Lesnick, The Wellsprings of Legal Responses to Inequality: A Perspective on Perspectives, 1991 Duke L.J. 413, 437. I am indebted to Jack Boger for telling me about this article.

18. See J. Stacy Adams, Inequity in Social Exchange, in 2 Advances in Experimental Social Psychology 267 (Leonard Berkowitz ed., 1965); Elaine Walster et al., New Directions in Equity Research, in 9 Advances in Experimental Social Psychology 1 (Leonard Berkowitz & Elaine Walster eds., 1972).

19. See W.G. Runciman, Relative Deprivation and Social Justice 9–35 (1966) (introducing notions of "relative deprivation" and "reference groups" and how both are derived from the truism that people's attitudes, aspirations and grievances largely depend on the frame of relevance within which they are conceived). For further discussion of the importance of relative deprivation theory, see Herbert Hovenkamp, Positivism in Law and Economics, 78 Cal. L. Rev. 815, 836–37 (1990) (distinguishing legal instruments employed for purposes of redistribution from the economist's perspective of maximizing efficiency); Kenneth Karst, Why Equality Matters, 17 Ga. L. Rev. 245, 261–62 (1983) (referring to culturally inbred understanding in America that winners and losers are natural consequences of a fair competition system); Richard H. McAdams, Relative Preferences, 102 Yale L. J. 1, 31–38 (1992) (examining the process of social comparison and its relation to the theory of relative deprivation); Deborah L. Rhode, The "No-Problem" Problem: Feminist Challenges and Cultural Changes,

equity theory and relative deprivation theory undermine Pareto superiority as a principled basis for the enforcement of contracts. In Section V, I address concerns that greater judicial intervention in private orderings would threaten personal autonomy, and review the suspicions and reservations that already have been voiced in the context of agreements resulting from efforts at informal dispute resolution. The questions raised in that much narrower context are based on concerns similar to those discussed in this Article. Finally, I defend a proposal to expand the concept and use of unconscionability. The critical question in this context is whether law as a preference-shaping variable can alter expectations and one's sense of entitlement in order to assist the disadvantaged to "prefer" better treatment.

Underlying my thesis are two, primarily implicit, subthemes. The first subtheme is the recognition of the false separation of microeconomic from macroeconomic issues. Concepts like social class and income distribution seem to fit into macroeconomic categories, but invariably they are the results of innumerable smaller transactions. Thus, income distribution cannot be divorced from basic wage determination. Accumulations of wealth or debt are simply the results of series of smaller individual transactions. Indeed, much of the overall thesis of this Article depends on the interdependence between individual transactions and broad-based measures of social class.

The second subtheme is the general notion that courts should be engaged more actively in the pursuit of compensatory justice. In this sense, what I present here is at odds with the view that distributive concerns are addressed best through a system of tax and transfer payments.[20] In fact, it seems likely that a system that renders disadvantaged people dependent on collective action, and allows individuals to rationalize their advantage-taking by reference to governmental efforts at redistribution, may actually undercut whatever potential exists for these problems to be addressed through private orderings.

I am not optimistic that my proposals will be adopted. After all, if it is true that "the ruling ideas of each age have ever been the ideas of the ruling class,"[21] there would appear to be little hope. On the other hand, instances in which people pass up free-riding opportunities,[22] and the capacity of individuals to empathize[23] and to conceive of justice as something other than what is

---

100 Yale L. J. 1731, 1773–76 (1991) (discussing the theory of relative deprivation in connection with legal norms and gender hierarchies); Judith Shklar, Giving Injustice Its Due, 98 Yale L. J. 1135, 1149–50 (1989) (looking at the societal tendency to blame the victims of injustice and how inherently unequal social circumstances contribute to such a practice).

20. On the distributive importance of contract law, see Duncan Kennedy, Distributive and Paternalistic Motives in Contract and Tort Law, with Special Reference to Compulsory Terms and Unequal Bargaining Power, 41 Md. L. Rev. 563 (1982); Anthony T. Kronman, Contract Law and Distributive Justice, 89 Yale L. J. 472 (1980); Frank I. Michelman, Norms and Normativity in the Economic Theory of Law, 62 Minn. L. Rev. 1015 (1978).

21. Karl Marx & Friedrich Engels, The Communist Manifesto 50 (D. Ryazanoff ed., 1930, reissued 1963).

22. "Free-riding" occurs when individuals attempt to enjoy the benefits resulting from the efforts of others without making their own contribution. See infra text accompanying notes 163–68.

23. See generally Lynn H. Henderson, Legality and Empathy, 85 Mich. L. Rev. 1574 (1987) (examining the stories of Supreme Court decisions from the perspective of empathy

always in their personal self-interest,[24] are all positive signs. Moreover, there will be no change unless we can continue to discuss the relationship between personality, economics, and justice.[25]

II. Value and Fairness in Exchange

When I say that the terms of the exchange generally will favor individuals from higher social classes,[26] I want my meaning to be clear. First, I am referring to an actual material concept of "terms of the exchange." In particular, I want to distinguish the subjective notion of sensing that one has been treated fairly and the actual material gain that one acquires from the exchange. Obviously, these two ideas are related in the sense that one's standard of "fair treatment" will affect the material outcome.

The difference between what a buyer might say an item is worth and what he or she is willing to pay another party for that item emphasizes the importance of this distinction. For example, suppose Tim shops for an automobile and, at one lot, spies a 1985 Ford. Tim decides the car is "worth" $5,200;[27] therefore, if he buys the car for anything less than $5,200, economists would say that he has received consumer surplus.[28] Furthermore, suppose the car salesperson is authorized to accept as little as $4,000 for the car. At this point, a possible exchange may leave both Tim and the car dealer feeling better off. In fact, so the economists' story goes, any price below $5,200 gives Tim con-

---

and its influence as the deliberation process); see also Toni M. Massaro, Empathy, Legal Storytelling, and the Rule of Law: New Words, Old Wounds?, 87 Mich. L. Rev. 2099 (1989) (advocating a more individualized approach to justice that departs from impersonal and uniform application of laws).

24. See generally Lawrence Kohlberg, The Psychology of Moral Development (1984) (collecting a series of essays discussing moral education and the development of morality); Lawrence Kohlberg, Moral Stages and Moralization, in Moral Development and Behavior 31 (Thomas Lickona ed., 1976) (outlining moral development of individuals and the theory of moralization that best explains such development).

25. See generally Kelman, supra note 12, at 778–95 (arguing that the assumption made by welfare economists that free choice maximizes welfare is flawed and ignores certain realities and constraints imposed by personality, background, and other factors).

26. Obviously, exchanges take place between people at all levels of social class. The idea here is that exchanges between individuals from similar classes cannot have any important distributive consequences. Thus, it is the ones between members of different classes that make the difference.

27. Typically, this is called the reservation price—the most Tim is willing to pay for the car. If Tim were the seller, this would be the least he would take for the car. The reservation price may change depending on whether one is the seller or buyer of a particular asset. This raises big problems in the field of law and economics. See Kelman, supra note 10; Duncan Kennedy, Cost-Benefit Analysis of Entitlement Problems: A Critique, 33 Stan. L. Rev. 387 (1981). See generally Harrison, supra note 9, at 1357–61 (discussing the effect of wealth on an individual's preferences). I want to steer clear (pun intended) of calling this the reservation price because I think the actual maximum he would pay will be influenced by the secondary decision discussed below.

28. This is a dollar measure of Tim's benefit from the bargain.

sumer surplus and any price in excess of $4,000 gives the car dealer producer surplus. The entire gain from the exchange is $1,200.[29]

But the story is far from over. As Paul Samuelson has written, "rational self-interest...does not necessitate that there will emerge...a Pareto-optimal solution that maximizes...profits, *in advance of and without regard to how that maximized profit is to be divided up....*"[30] What this suggests is that the formation of a contract consists of two steps. The first is the discovery of an exchange that potentially increases the profit or "surplus" of each party. From the buyer's standpoint, this means discovering an item that provides more utility than holding the money and spending it on a different item. The second step is a decision about how to divide that surplus.[31] In other words, having found an exchange that could make them both feel better off, the parties must agree on a fair division of the surplus created by the exchange. At this point, the decisionmaking has a more interpersonal focus. Instead of considering how his money might best be spent, each trader becomes concerned with how "good" the deal is relative to how good it is for the other party. At this microeconomic level, the parties "test" possible prices against their senses of compensatory justice.

If the desire to sense that they have been treated fairly has lexical priority or is sufficiently powerful,[32] the transaction will not be consummated when either party believes that the division of the surplus is compensatorily unjust. I do not address that possibility here, although it does have important implications.[33] Instead, my concern is with the actual division of the surplus and how it may vary from individual to individual in a systematic fashion.

For example, Tim and the salesperson must arrive at a price that both see as a fair division of the gain created by the exchange. For Tim, the price may not

---

29. See Richard A. Posner, Utilitarianism, Economics, and Legal Theory, 8 J. Legal Stud. 103, 120 (1979). Of course, whether this means that overall welfare is enhanced is a different matter. See Anthony T. Kronman, Wealth Maximization As a Normative Principle, 9 J. Legal Stud. 227 (1980) (attacking Judge Posner's theory of wealth maximization as "incoherent" and arguing that it produces morally objectionable results).

30. Paul A. Samuelson, The Monopolistic Competition Revolution, in 3 The Collected Scientific Papers of Paul A. Samuelson 18, 35 (Robert C. Merton ed., 1972). But see R.H. Coase, The Firm, the Market and the Law 159–63 (1988) (arguing that the number of cases in which the potential for Pareto optimality exists but in which no agreement is reached is necessarily so small as to be negligible).

31. Some interesting experimental results dealing with the division of the surplus created by an exchange are found in Elizabeth Hoffman & Matthew L. Spitzer, The Coase Theorem: Some Experimental Tests, 25 J. L. & Econ. 73 (1982) [hereinafter Hoffman & Spitzer, Experimental Tests]; Elizabeth Hoffman & Matthew L. Spitzer, Entitlements, Rights, and Fairness: An Experimental Examination of Subjects' Concepts of Distributive Justice, 14 J. Legal Stud. 259 (1985) [hereinafter Hoffman & Spitzer, Fairness].

32. I have shortened "lexicographical ordering" to "lexical." See John Rawls, A Theory of Justice 42–43 (1971). Here it simply means that there are certain principles that cannot be reduced to conventional notions of utility. See supra note 9.

33. One might regard this search for fairness as entailing transaction costs. If the transaction costs are too high, or there is no point that both parties regard as fair, the exchange will not occur.

be one that he would quote if asked what the car is "worth." The seemingly "objective" statement of the car's worth may be quite different than the most Tim would be willing to pay and still feel that he has been dealt with justly in the context of an interpersonal exchange. Suppose Tim asks the price of the car and is told it is $5,000. After a few minutes of bargaining, Tim and the salesperson agree on a price of $4,500. I think it is safe to assume that the price of $4,500 is one that is in some sense fair to him. Put differently, Tim does not feel strongly entitled to a lower price. We do not know that Tim would have agreed to a higher price. In fact, it may be that $4,500 was the highest price Tim actually was willing to pay because it was the highest price that would have left him with the feeling of having received the share of the division of the surplus to which he was "entitled."

Now suppose Thelma enters the picture and almost everything is the same. In response to a third party's inquiry as to the worth of the car she replies, "$5,200." This time the deal is struck at $4,900. At that price Thelma feels better off and as though she has received her fair share of the benefit created by the exchange.

Obviously Tim is better off than Thelma to the tune of $400. This is the case even though she may feel just as happy about the contract as Tim felt with his. The critical issue is what accounts for their ability to feel that they have both been treated justly even though the terms of the exchange are quite different. This can be traced to some personality difference that means Thelma's sense of compensatory justice either is satisfied more easily or is dependent on things other than the price of the automobile.

The temptation to suggest that the difference can be accounted for by differences in their negotiating skills or bargaining power is hard to avoid. Negotiating skills, however, are unlikely to determine one's feeling of entitlement. These skills are tools for achieving that to which one already feels entitled. Similarly, bargaining power suggests an imbalance in the market. If a good is scarce, sellers will have relatively greater bargaining power than buyers. But scarcity per se does not translate into the actual use of bargaining power.[34] Although scarcity may influence what one believes to be a fair price, the primary importance of bargaining power is to enable one to confidently "back up" the threats she makes in the negotiation process. The choice of whether to use that power again is largely a function of an independently determined sense of personal justice.[35]

---

34. The reader should not infer from my use of a two party bargaining example that I am suggesting that the issue discussed here arises only in the context of bilateral monopoly. Although very competitive markets may make advantage-taking by those with a strong sense of entitlement difficult, hardly any markets are so competitive that a sense of entitlement would be excluded as a variable in the determination of the terms of an exchange. Similarly, the fact that Thelma and Tim are buyers should not lead one to infer that my analysis is confined to decisions by buyers. Obviously, the disadvantaged are often sellers, probably most crucially in labor markets.

35. See Alvin E. Roth & J. Keith Murnighan, Information and Aspirations in Two-Person Bargaining, in Lecture Notes in Economic and Mathematical Systems: Aspiration Levels in Bargaining and Economic Decision Making 91, 102 (Reinhard Tietz ed., 1982) (proposing that higher aspirations lead to tougher bargaining).

The difference in the sense of entitlement or compensatory justice is far more pervasive than the bargains made in the preceding examples. Some students complain about low grades, others do not. Some people pay the auto repair bill without complaint, others are upset. Some people accept a wage without feeling resentment, others feel exploited.

Before attempting to pierce the matter of different expectations, two more points need to be made. The first is that the sense of what one is entitled to may be so ingrained that one can feel that she is entitled to less than someone else. For example, there is no guarantee that Thelma would become dissatisfied with her automobile deal if she heard about Tim's deal.[36] She might, but she also may reason that Tim "earned a better deal" by bargaining for a longer period of time.[37] Alternatively, she might believe that Tim, an important person in the community, was somehow simply more deserving.[38] Certainly, the news of Tim's more favorable deal may change Thelma's view of her own deal, but not if Thelma sees herself as less deserving than Tim.

The second point that must be addressed is that people can, and frequently do, make deals that leave them feeling that they have not been treated fairly.[39] Probably the best example of this kind of deal is an employment contract in which the employee feels underpaid but must take the job in order to make a living. Of course, as the next section explains, people in dissatisfying arrangements seem to have an infinite capacity to alter their perceptions of themselves or their expectations in order to preserve their dignity.

III. *Interpersonal Justice*

> Keep you doped with religion and sex and TV
> And you think you're so clever and classless and free
> But you're still fucking peasants as far as I can see
> A working class hero is something to be.[40]

Two leading theories that seek to explain why people react differently to different distributive outcomes are equity theory and relative deprivation theory. Although these areas of study have been considered together and efforts

---

36. See infra notes 64–84 and accompanying text.

37. This is different from feeling that Tim deserves a lower price because he is better at negotiating. Instead, this is accepting the legitimacy of a reward for the effort Tim has devoted to the negotiation.

38. "Status attribution" is one process through which Thelma may find the outcome just. See Della Fave, supra note 7, at 960–62 (discussing status attribution theory as the process by which an individual's overall class status is determined by examining that individual's known characteristics).

39. There are two explanations for this. First, at some price individuals are willing to be humiliated. Second, even though they may view the preservation of dignity through fairness in the exchange as lexically prior to most worldly sources of utility, they may, at the same time, regard survival and providing for their families as lexically prior to maintaining their own dignity.

40. Lennon, supra note 1.

made to integrate them,[41] they are sufficiently different to warrant separate consideration.

A. Equity Theory

Equity theory has its roots in social psychology.[42] Its fundamental proposition is that individuals tend to feel that outcomes are just when the following equation holds:

$$\frac{\text{outcomes of person A}}{\text{inputs of person A}} = \frac{\text{outcomes of person B}}{\text{inputs of person B}}[43]$$

In other words, a distribution is equitable when the ratios of outputs to inputs are perceived as being equal. Much of the work in equity theory is devoted to studying the responses of individuals when the ratios are not equal.[44] For example, workers who feel underpaid—the ratio of their "investments" to their income is lower than that of others—may not work as hard or may take longer breaks.[45] Conversely, someone who feels overpaid relative to another actually may increase productivity.[46]

The more important issue for the purpose of this Article is how individuals determine what factors they will count as relevant inputs and outputs. For example, if the disappointed new law professor in my initial example regards his inputs as higher because he attended an Ivy League school and his counterpart decides that her attendance at an Ivy League school is not an input of consequence, a disagreement will occur as to the equity of the employer's decision to give them equal moving allowances.

A good and especially accessible example of the implications of equity theory for the terms of contractual exchanges is found in the work of Elizabeth Hoffman and Matthew Spitzer in their experiments testing the Coase Theorem.[47] In a series of tests, Hoffman and Spitzer arranged for two individuals to divide the gains created by an exchange. In the experiments, each group of two

---

41. See Faye Crosby & A. Miren Gonzalez-Intal, Relative Deprivation and Equity Theories, in The Sense of Injustice: Social Psychological Perspectives 141 (Robert Folger ed., 1984); Joanne Martin & Alan Murray, Distributive Injustice and Unfair Exchange, in Equity Theory: Psychological and Sociological Perspectives 169 (David M. Messick & Karen S. Cook eds., 1983).

42. Crosby & Gonzalez-Intal, supra note 41, at 142.

43. Adams, supra note 18, at 276–88; Martin & Murray, supra note 41, at 171.

44. Reaction may be to increase or decrease inputs or to increase or decrease output. For an extensive bibliography, see J. Stacy Adams & Sara Freedman, Equity Theory Revisited: Comments and Annotated Bibliography, in 9 Advances in Experimental Social Psychology 43 (Leonard Berkowitz & Elaine Walster eds., 1976).

45. The response may be to alter inputs or to alter outputs. For an example of an input altering reaction, see research reported by Adams, supra note 18, at 286–87.

46. Id. at 284–88; J. Stacy Adams & William B. Rosenbaum, The Relationship of Worker Productivity to Cognitive Dissonance About Wage Inequities, 46 J. Applied Psychol. 161 (1962).

47. See Hoffman & Spitzer, Experimental Tests, supra note 31; Hoffman & Spitzer, Fairness, supra note 31.

was given a series of choices. Each choice resulted in a certain monetary pay-out to the participants. One of the players was designated the "controller" and was entitled to select any of the alternatives.[48] One of the alternatives maximized the payout to the controller and another maximized the total payout to both parties. The party who was not designated the controller could attempt to influence the choice of the controller by a side-payment. For purposes of testing the Coase Theorem, the issue was whether the two parties would bargain to reach the outcome that would result in the controller selecting the joint income-maximizing alternative.

Hoffman and Spitzer discovered that the parties nearly invariably did select the joint profit-maximizing outcome.[49] Perhaps more interesting was the manner in which the parties divided the profit. Initially one might hypothesize that the parties would settle on a split that would leave the controller no worse off than if he had selected his individual profit-maximizing outcome at the outset. As it turned out, the division of the payoffs differed dramatically depending upon the way in which the controller was selected. For example, in their initial experiments, Hoffman and Spitzer's experimental design called for the controller to be determined by the flip of a coin. In those cases, the predominant method of dividing the gain was in equal shares.[50]

In a second set of experiments, the controller was determined by playing a simple game. In these instances the researchers attempted to create in the winner a sense of moral authority suggesting that, by winning the game, the winner had "earned" the right to be controller.[51] In this set of experiments the controller was far less likely to receive less than the amount available from selecting his or her joint maximizing outcome.[52]

The Hoffman and Spitzer experiments suggest that both parties adopted the same view of the relevant inputs. Thus, in the first experiments, when the controller was selected by a random event, the inputs of the parties were the same. In order to keep the equity formula in balance, the payoff to the parties would also have to be the same. In the second set of tests, winning the game was regarded by both parties as a valid input and, therefore, a higher payoff was necessary to the controller in order to balance the equity formula.[53]

While the Hoffman and Spitzer experiments are marvelous illustrations of how the implications of equity theory can play out, they leave open the question of precisely how the parties avoid conflict about what inputs count. Studies in equity theory suggest two principal ways of avoiding the issue. First, in-

---

48. In the most basic of the "games" there were seven payoff choices with the total payoff ranging from $11.00 to $14.00. The $14.00 payoff possibility would result in a $10.00 to $4.00 split in the payoff. See Hoffman & Spitzer, Experimental Tests, supra note 31, at 86.

49. Id. at 92.

50. Id.

51. See Hoffman & Spitzer, Fairness, supra note 31, at 270–71.

52. Id. at 276.

53. Hoffman and Spitzer attribute a Lockean sense of distributive justice to the participants because they seemed to be guided by some notion of "desert" as opposed to strict self-interest in dividing the payoffs. See id. at 261.

dividuals tend to avoid making comparisons with cohorts who are dissimilar.[54] Second, when such comparisons are made, individuals tend to find justifications for what would appear to be unequal results by including as their counterpart's inputs such things as education or skill. In essence, they appear to "manufacture" equity.[55]

B. Relative Deprivation

Relative deprivation theory has its roots in sociology and political science.[56] It differs from equity theory in a number of respects, primarily its emphasis on social comparison. Rather than a tidy formula comparing ratios of inputs and outputs, this theory is characterized by a general process of comparing one's well-being with the position of others.[57]

As a general matter, one's view of her own situation is based on whether or not she feels deprived. Deprivation is more likely to occur when one lacks an outcome, compares herself to someone who has that outcome, feels entitled to that outcome, feels the outcome was feasible, and does not blame herself for not achieving the desired outcome.[58]

The critical feature of the theory is that it is capable of explaining why individuals or groups that are absolutely disadvantaged when compared with other groups actually may feel more content than members of those groups. The principal example offered to illustrate relative deprivation theory at work concerns studies of military personnel during the 1940s. The studies indicated that airmen were more dissatisfied than military police with the rate of promotion even though the airmen were promoted more rapidly. This phenomenon was explained by the fact that the airmen felt "relatively deprived."[59] In another study, company presidents expressed greater dissatisfaction than first-line supervisors earning only one-fourth as much as the presidents. In essence, based on comparisons with their "reference group," the company presidents felt deprived even though they were far better off in an absolute sense than the line supervisors.[60]

It is useful to note that relative deprivation can be seen as falling into one of two categories: egoistic deprivation and fraternal deprivation.[61] In the case of

---

54. See Martin & Murray, supra note 41, at 178, 181.

55. See Joanne Martin, Relative Deprivation: A Theory of Distributive Injustice for an Era of Shrinking Resources, in 3 Research in Organizational Behavior 53, 97 (L.L. Cummings & Barry M. Staw eds., 1981).

56. Crosby & Gonzalez-Intal, supra note 41, at 142.

57. See George C. Homans, Social Behavior: Its Elementary Forms 241–42 (rev. ed. 1974).

58. See Morty Bernstein & Faye Crosby, An Empirical Examination of Relative Deprivation Theory, 16 J. Experimental Soc.Psychol. 442 (1980); Faye Crosby, A Model of Egoistical Relative Deprivation, 83 Psychol.Rev. 85 (1976).

59. 1 Samuel A. Stouffer et al., The American Soldier: Adjustment During Army Life (1949). For a summary, see Adams, supra note 18, at 269.

60. Edward E. Lawler III & Lyman W. Porter, Perceptions Regarding Management Compensation, 3 Industrial Relations 41, 46–48 (1963).

61. See Runciman, supra note 19, at 96; Martin, supra note 55, at 60–67.

egoistic deprivation, the individual compares his plight with that of a similar referent, with the emphasis on the individual's own well-being. With fraternal deprivation, the scope of the comparison changes; the focus is on the plight of the group of which the individual is a member, as compared to a better situated group. The implications of this distinction are important because the type of discomfort associated with fraternal relative deprivation could result in the sort of action that changes the status of the entire group.[62] Individual transactions are more likely to raise issues of egoistic deprivation.[63]

Although relative deprivation provides a useful structure in which to analyze why the individual sense of distributive justice of some individuals is satisfied with so much less than it would take to satisfy another, it really only begins the analysis. Simply stated, if the theory is that we do not sense deprivation as long as we get that to which we think we are entitled and our entitlement is determined by some reference group, two critical questions emerge. First, how are reference groups selected? Second, if we do not feel deprived when we sense we could have controlled the outcome, what are the factors that determine when we assume responsibility for the outcomes we experience?

C. Thinking About Fairness

It is useful at this point to revisit the two law professors introduced at the outset and analyze their reactions from the perspectives of equity theory and relative deprivation theory. The first law professor experienced a sense of inequity or deprivation. In equity theory terms, he made a rough judgment that the reward to his inputs was disproportionately low when compared to that experienced by others with whom he chose to compare himself. Or, in relative deprivation terms, the moving allowance was inconsistent with his expectation based on how he believed similarly situated people, perhaps with comparable educations and work experience, were treated. Alternatively, the second professor, if one applies equity theory, felt that individuals with inputs similar to her own would receive roughly the same moving allowance as she did. Or, in terms of relative deprivation theory, she felt that her peers would receive a similar moving allowance. The key point is that, for purposes of equity theory analysis, the law professors applied different standards to identify and evaluate their "inputs" and, for purposes of relative deprivation analysis, they selected different reference groups.[64]

---

62. Martin, supra note 55, at 67–69, 99.

63. Martin & Murray, supra note 41, at 186.

64. This might be readily explained if it were discovered that the dissatisfied law professor was born into a well-to-do family, attended Ivy League schools, served in a prestigious judicial clerkship, and became friends with those possessing similar backgrounds. The second law professor might have come from a working class family, attended state schools, and worked in a small law firm. These different life experiences could account for their different reference points when applying their individual senses of justice to the $3,000 moving allowance. See generally Blau, supra note 7, at 143–67 (stating that past experience and reference standards influence expectations).

Equity theory and relative deprivation theory differ in a number of respects. While equity theory emphasizes inputs and outputs, relative deprivation theory provides a way of thinking about individual concerns and a broader sense of social deprivation. In addition, equity theory, with its possible tendency toward legitimizing the status quo, may contain a relatively conservative political bias.[65] Relative deprivation theory, with its emphasis on explaining why the disadvantaged do not experience a sense of injustice, can be seen as having a liberal bias in terms of its research agenda.[66]

For the purposes at hand, both equity theory and relative deprivation theory provide useful frameworks for explaining differences in the ways individuals respond to differences in the terms of exchanges. They do not, however, provide clear answers to the question of how uneven outcomes are ultimately accepted as legitimate. In other words, how is it determined "which inputs count" for purposes of equity theory and how does one learn to accept one reference group over another for purposes of relative deprivation theory?

Another question that appears in both theories but in different forms is that of individual responsibility. In relative deprivation theory, one of the elements necessary for a sense of deprivation to arise is that the deprived individual have no sense of self-blame for the outcome.[67] In other words, individuals do not feel deprived if they sense they could have controlled the outcome, even in a vague way, but did not. It is harder to find an analogous issue in equity theory because equity theory seems to focus on actual inputs and outputs.[68] Seemingly, by implication, the inputs are the responsibility of the individual. One would think, however, that there are instances in which an individual would feel that the inability to contribute more inputs is not in his or her power and, therefore, a difference in outputs is unjust.

Whatever potential there is for developing a sense of injustice in equity theory due to a "blameless" inability to contribute more inputs can be avoided by focusing on the selection of the individuals to whom comparisons are made. One of the clear conclusions of equity theory is that individuals prefer to make comparisons to those who are similar.[69] Thus, those who do experience a sense of personal responsibility and see themselves as controlling possible outcomes may tend to compare themselves with those who are also seen as similarly empowered. A second possibility lies in redefining what one believes to be just.[70] In other words, individuals, especially from lower socioeconomic levels, may gradually learn to accept that their inability to contribute more inputs is in reality their fault.[71]

---

65. Martin & Murray, supra note 41, at 173–77.

66. Id. at 185.

67. See Crosby, supra note 58, at 90.

68. Cf. Helmut Lamm et al., An Attributional Analysis of Interpersonal Justice: Ability and Effort As Inputs in the Allocation of Gain and Loss, 119 J. Soc. Psychol. 269 (1983) (comparing the effects on outcome when ability and effort are used as inputs).

69. See Martin & Murray, supra note 41, at 178.

70. See Joanne Martin, The Tolerance of Injustice, in Relative Deprivation and Social Comparison: 4 The Ontario Symposium 217 (James M. Olson et al. eds., 1986).

71. See Sennett & Cobb, supra note 8, at 20, 28, 249–50; Karen Cook, Expectations, Evaluations and Equity, 40 Am. Soc. Rev. 372 (1975) (discussing the impact of expectation

When attempting to address the questions of reference group selection, "which inputs count," and the role of self-blame, a pattern of answers emerges that suggests that disadvantaged people tend to adapt in order to accept "what is," as opposed to aspiring to some greater share of material allocations. In the context of equity theory, they gravitate toward choosing as their referents individuals who are similar and they are careful to define inputs in such a way that returns the equity equation to a position of equality. Similarly, those who otherwise might experience a sense of relative deprivation seem largely destined to compare themselves to those who are "equally deprived" and thus avoid the feeling of relative deprivation. In the words of G.C. Homans, "what people say ought to be is determined in the long run... by what they find in fact to be the case."[72] In effect, people tend to aspire to distributive goals that reflect existing allocations as opposed to utopian outcomes.[73]

Of course, much of this just begs the issue. What prevents the disadvantaged from redefining their inputs so that they experience a sense of inequity when they receive less than another? Why don't they choose to use as their point of comparison those who are better off? To rephrase the Homans' quotation: *Why* does "what is" turn into what is right?

Put differently, how does the process work through which social stratification is legitimized even in the eyes of those who are systematically disadvantaged? There are a number of factors that seem to interact. One is that we define ourselves as others define us and rely on their valuation to determine our own worth. Since the value of a person, by our cultural standards, is largely a function of his or her power, income, wealth, and education, individuals apply those standards in order to ascertain how deserving they are.[74]

As already noted, in order to feel deprived, one must escape a sense of personal responsibility for his or her position. It makes sense that a social structure that leaves us in relatively poor condition will still be regarded as just or at least as legitimate if we sense our relatively small allocation is traceable to our own shortcomings. As it turns out, the disadvantaged tend to assume responsibility for the inferior outcomes they experience.[75] And, interestingly, ex-

---

on the equity process); Morton Deutsch, Awakening the Sense of Injustice, in The Quest for Justice: Myth, Reality, Ideal 19, 24–27 (Melvin J. Lerner & Michael Ross eds., 1974) (arguing that the victim, in an effort to control feelings of injustice, identifies with the victimizer and internalizes the victimizer's derogatory attitudes); Janice Steil, The Response to Injustice: Effects of Varying Levels of Social Support and Position of Advantage or Disadvantage, 19 J. Experimental Soc. Psychol. 239 (1983) (finding that social support reduced the tendency of disadvantaged individuals to assume responsibility for their lower outcomes).

72. Homans, supra note 55, at 250.

73. See Joseph Berger et al., Structural Aspects of Distributive Justice: A Status Value Formulation, in 2 Sociological Theories in Progress 119 (Joseph Berger et al. eds., 1972) (detailing how normative expectations are violated when similar actors receive dissimilar rewards); Della Fave, supra note 7; Norma Sheplak & Duane Alwin, Beliefs About Inequality and Perceptions of Distributive Justice, 51 Am. Soc. Rev. 30 (1986).

74. See generally Della Fave, supra note 7 (arguing that social stratification is legitimized by social values).

75. See Sennett & Cobb, supra note 8, at 20, 28, 249–50; Della Fave, supra note 7, at 963; Steil, supra note 71, at 251. Ironically, they do not appear to take personal credit for good outcomes. See Lawrence Kutner, Parent and Child, N.Y. Times, Jan. 21, 1993, at C12.

periments suggest that even a supportive social structure cannot overcome this tendency.[76] The precise mechanism for this tendency toward self-blame among the disadvantaged is not clear, but certainly both the pervasiveness of the American Dream myth which drives home the notion that everything is available if one just tries hard enough,[77] and a desire to preserve one's psychological well-being by reducing the stress associated with perceiving injustice contribute to this tendency.[78]

A key element playing into the mix is self-esteem. As already suggested, our self-perceptions are influenced heavily by the views of others. Indeed, as a statistical matter, self-esteem among adults is correlated with social class.[79] The mechanism here is not hard to imagine. No one wants to live in a poor neighborhood; no one aspires to be poor. Being poor and relatively powerless contribute to feelings of shame. And being ashamed is synonymous with a lack of self-love or a sense of personal value.[80]

While the lack of self-esteem, without more, can help to explain the infrequency with which the absolutely deprived experience a sense of relative deprivation, an even more insidious element is at work in this process. One of the primary characteristics of those with low self-esteem is that they are easily influenced.[81] For example, in experiments involving rewards and in which subjects were paired with others, low self-esteem subjects were more likely to begin to imitate the reward allocation patterns of their partners than were high self-esteem subjects.[82] Similarly, subordinates with low self-esteem are more likely to adopt the values of their supervisors than those with high self-esteem.[83]

This influenceability or "plasticity" has clear implications for equity theory and relative deprivation theory, as well as for the cycle of social stratification

---

On the other hand, the privileged are likely to view those who are less well-off as responsible for their plight. See R.A. Steffenhagen & Jeff D. Burns, The Social Dynamics of Self-Esteem 135–36 (1987).

76. See Steil, supra note 71, at 239.

77. See Deutsch, supra note 71, at 29–30.

78. The effect is to reduce cognitive dissonance, see Leon Festinger, A Theory of Cognitive Dissonance 1–31 (1957), in order to avoid stress-related afflictions. See Martin, supra note 70, at 239–40.

79. See John P. Hewitt, Social Stratification and Deviant Behavior 47–49 (1970); Steffenhagen & Burns, supra note 75, at 134–41; Morris Rosenberg & Leonard I. Pearlin, Social Class and Self-Esteem Among Children and Adults, 84 Am. J. Soc. 53, 55–57 (1978).

80. See Gershen Kaufman & Lev Raphael, Dynamics of Power: Fighting Shame and Building Self-Esteem xiii, xvii, 35–36 (2d ed. rev. 1991).

81. See Joel Brockner, Low Self-Esteem and Behavioral Plasticity: Some Implications, in 4 Review of Personality and Social Psychology 237 (Ladd Wheeler & Philip R. Shaver eds., 1983); Arthur Cohen, Some Implications of Self-Esteem for Social Influence, in Personality and Persuasibility 102 (Carl I. Hovland & Irving L. Janis eds., 1959).

82. See Joel Brockner et al., Reward Allocation and Self-Esteem: The Roles of Modeling and Equity Restoration, 52 J. Personality & Soc. Psychol. 844, 847 (1987).

83. See Howard M. Weiss, Social Learning of Work Values in Organizations, 63 J. Applied Psychol. 711 (1978); Howard M. Weiss, Subordinate Imitation of Supervisor Behavior: The Role of Modeling in Organizational Socialization, 19 Organizational Behav. & Hum. Performance 89 (1977).

legitimization. Low self-esteem typically is associated with uncertainty and a lack of confidence in one's own attitudes.[84] Obviously, an important element in the perpetuation of a system of classes is the ability to convince those on the lowest rung that they are responsible for their position and that the values that those in power use to determine status are appropriate.

In summary, one's sense of whether she has been treated fairly is the product of comparisons to the input/output ratio of others or to the general welfare of some reference group. In equity theory, the central issue is which inputs are worthy of being counted. In terms of relative deprivation theory, the primary question is which group does the individual believe she has the "right" to be treated like. In equity theory, those in power determine which inputs count. In relative deprivation theory, those who are in worse positions than others accept comparisons with those who similarly are deprived because they believe that whatever position they hold in the social order is of their own making. Pervading, legitimizing, and sustaining both of these processes is the impact of social stratification on the sense that individuals have of their own worth or self-esteem. The unrelenting message is that those who receive less must have less to offer and are ultimately less worthy, and, having heard this message long enough, individuals become even more susceptible to it. Disadvantaged people tend not to question a world that tells them how little they have to offer, how little they are entitled to, and that they are ultimately to blame.

IV. Piercing Pareto Optimality

Equity theory and relative deprivation theory can be viewed as limiting the application of economics to law. Much of the contemporary criticism of law and economics asks whether private orderings ultimately result in efficient results. For example, both Pareto optimality and wealth maximization, the two leading measures of efficiency, depend on a variety of assumptions. The most important assumption is that the choices people make reveal their preferences.[85] More generally, Pareto optimality and wealth maximization require that we assume away the problems created by the possibilities of counter-preferential choice,[86] preference reversals,[87] dual preferences,[88] and the wealth ef-

---

84. See Hewitt, supra note 79, at 37–40; Brockner et al., supra note 82, at 846; Kutner, supra note 75; Weiss, supra note 83, at 712.

85. Compare Paul A. Samuelson, Consumption Theory in Terms of Revealed Preference, 15 Economica 243 (1948) (arguing that a consumer's behavior is based upon revealed preferences) with Amartya Sen, Behavior and the Concept of Preference, 40 Economica 241 (1973) (arguing that choices made do not always reveal a person's real preferences).

86. See Sen, supra note 9, at 328.

87. See generally Jon Elster, Ulysses and the Sirens 36–111 (1979) (discussing precommitment to a certain path as being imperfectly rational); Paul Slovic & Sarah Lichtenstein, Preference Reversals: A Broader Perspective, 73 Am. Econ. Rev. 596 (1983) (arguing that preference reversals fit in a larger picture posing a challenge to preference theories); Amos Tversky & Daniel Kahneman, The Framing of Decisions and the Psychology of Choice, 211 Science 453 (1981) (discussing reversals of preference obtained in choices regarding monetary outcomes and the loss of lives).

88. See Richard Thaler, Toward a Positive Theory of Consumer Choice, 1 J. Econ. Behav.

fect,[89] each of which suggests either that market choices may not reveal preferences or that the connection between preferences and utility maximization is not clear.[90]

What I am addressing here, however, involves an entirely different matter. I am assuming that choices *do* reveal preferences and that the preferences revealed *do* increase the utility of the choosers. If both of these conditions are met, then it seems hard to argue against the legitimacy of Pareto superiority as a principled basis for enforcing contracts, but the point of the foregoing discussion is that there are additional questions to be raised. These questions come from peeling back the skin of Pareto optimality in order to reveal the effect of class-based personality differences on preferences and the substance of exchanges that individuals regard as utility-maximizing.

Equity theory and relative deprivation theory suggest that both the Paretian standard and wealth maximization are extremely "thin" concepts. For instance, in the automobile example, if we stop our analysis at the level of efficiency, we would determine that both Tim and Thelma have experienced increases in their utility and the world is a generally happier place. But if we peel back even a single layer of this efficient outcome, we begin to ask why Thelma would believe she received fair treatment when she paid a much higher price than Tim. We may find that this efficient outcome in Thelma's case could only come about because Thelma had a low sense of entitlement. Moreover, if this lack of a sense of entitlement was determined by some combination of Thelma's social class and self-esteem, it is reasonable to ask whether we should feel morally comfortable with the different outcomes.

To expand on this, it is necessary to review the basic notions underlying the view that Pareto optimality supports the enforcement of contracts. First, this analysis requires a digression into the basic economic explanation for why exchanges take place.[91] One must start with what economists call *indifference curves*.[92] In Figure I, the X axis indicates the quantities of good X an individual might have and the Y axis indicates the amounts of good Y. Each curve plots the possible combinations of X and Y that give the individual the same amount of satisfaction. For example, X could be apples and Y bicycles. Each point along a specific curve represents a different combination of bicycles and apples, but each combination would leave this individual feeling equally well off. As the curve suggests, as the individual has fewer apples, she must have more bicycles to maintain the same level of satisfaction. On the graph, each curve represents a different level of satisfaction with the curves farther away

---

& Organization 39, 55–56 (1980) (discussing how individuals exercise self-control through precommitment to certain alternatives).

89. See supra note 27.

90. See generally Kelman, supra note 10 (remarking that legal rules may change consumer demand behavior); Kelman, supra note 12 (arguing that choices may be made because of duress).

91. I know this is going to be boring but please hang in there. It will be short and I think it helps illustrate my point. I would like to thank Jules Theeuwes for helping work through the indifference curve analysis.

92. Most basic economics texts have a good discussion of indifference curves. See, e.g., Jack Hirshleifer, Price Theory and Applications 62–122 (2d ed. 1980).

FIGURE I

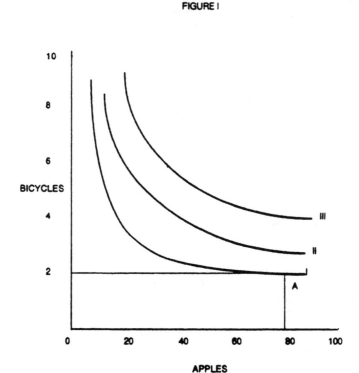

from the origin representing higher levels of utility.[93] The indifference map of Thelma might look like Figure I. If Thelma had eighty apples and two bicycles, she would be located at point A on curve I.

Of course, an exchange requires another participant. Thus, Figure II depicts the possible indifference curves for Tim. Again, each curve represents a separate level of satisfaction and shows the combinations of bicycles and apples that result in the same level of satisfaction. And, as in Figure I, as the curves move out from the origin, they represent different and higher levels of satisfaction. If we suppose Tim has twenty apples and eight bicycles, he will be located at point A on curve I.

This seemingly lopsided allocation of bicycles and apples obviously creates an opportunity for exchange. The two indifference maps can be combined into what is called an "Edgeworth Box."[94] In Figure III, the two sets of indifference curves are on the same graph with Thelma's origin located at the bottom left corner and Tim's origin at the upper right corner. Point A on the graph is on indifference curve I for both Thelma and Tim.

93. It is, perhaps, easier to understand what is happening as one moves to indifference curves that are farther from the origin if you realize that the graph actually has a third dimension coming off the page. On this third axis, one would be plotting utility. As the curves move out, one would be moving up the third axis. In a three dimensional depiction, the curves would gradually rise up off the page as they move farther from the origin.

94. See Hirshleifer, *supra* note 92, at 192–97 (discussing the "Edgeworth Box" as a tool to illustrate how exchange allows for mutually advantageous improvement in the allocation of consumption goods).

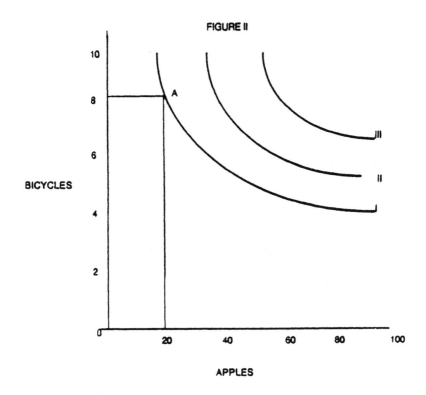

FIGURE II

BICYCLES

APPLES

The question for contract purposes and for purposes of Pareto superiority is whether the parties can exchange bicycles for apples in such a way that they are both better off. In other words, can they both move to higher indifference curves while being restricted by the fact that there are a total of one hundred apples and ten bicycles in the entire economy? There are, in fact, a number of possible points at which both parties would be better off.

To visualize this, consider point B where Thelma's indifference curve I is tangent to Tim's indifference curve III. The point represents thirty apples and three bicycles for Thelma and seventy apples and seven bicycles for Tim. At this point, Thelma is still on indifference curve I and is as happy as she was with eighty apples and two bicycles. Tim has moved up to indifference curve III and, therefore, is better off. In essence, Thelma has paid fifty apples for one bicycle. While this is actually an unlikely exchange because it leaves Thelma no better off, it forms the outside limit of a possible exchange. Similarly, point C, where Tim has five bicycles and fifty apples and Thelma has five bicycles and fifty apples, represents a point at which Thelma is better off and Tim stays on his original indifference curve. This point also represents a limit on their exchange because under no circumstances would Tim enter into an exchange that made him worse off.

Economists refer to the area between indifference curve I for Thelma and curve I for Tim as a lens.[95] All movements from the original allocation that

---

95. Id. at 195.

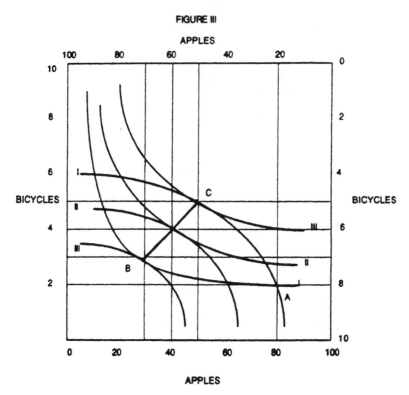

FIGURE III

will leave both parties better off are located within this lens. Only within this lens exist potential exchanges that move both parties to higher indifference curves.

Because both parties presumably desire to move to the highest possible indifference curve (i.e., that which is farthest from their respective origins), and because these moves must be consistent with moving to higher indifference curves of their partners, it is possible to narrow the focus even more. The critical points are those at which the indifference curves are tangent to each other. For each indifference curve of Thelma, there is an indifference curve for Tim that is tangent to Thelma's curve at some point. A line drawn through these points of tangency is called the *contract curve*.[96] The contract curve shows a series of possible exchanges or "prices" of apples in terms of bicycles, or vice versa, that will improve the positions of both parties. The actual price the parties will establish will be determined by their negotiations.

The full contract curve, as illustrated in Figure III, shows the points which are acceptable to both parties, assuming the parties are compensatorily insensitive.[97] Possibly, however, parties may view many of these points as involving

---

96. All of the points on the contract curve are Pareto superior to the original allocation. They are also Pareto optimal in that it is impossible to move from one point to another without leaving one of the parties worse off.

97. One might take the position that the sense of justice or injustice from an exchange of bicycles for apples is built into the curves. This would not be a correct interpretation of the curves. The curves do not "anticipate" exchange and the fairness of proposed exchanges. In-

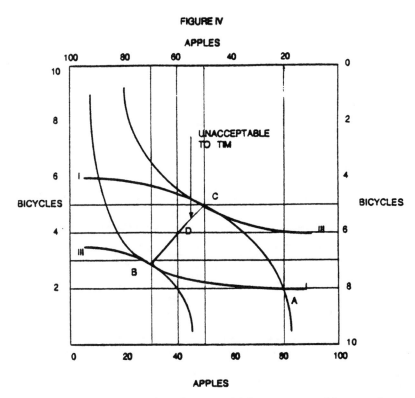

FIGURE IV

exchanges that are so uneven that they would be unacceptable to at least one of the parties on the grounds of being compensatorily unfair. In short, there are two curves: a contract curve, consisting of points that would involve Pareto superior exchanges and another curve that introduces and accounts for the interpersonal component of the exchange. The latter curve, as depicted by the bold portion of the full contract curve in Figure IV, is shorter than the original, "compensatorily insensitive" curve, and consists of the portions of the original curve that are acceptable to both parties. Equity and relative deprivation theory strongly suggest that, if a portion of the curve is not in play, that part will lie near the axis of the trading partner with the greater sense of entitlement. Thus, in Figure IV, the relevant portion of the curve excludes the segment closest to Tim's axis.[98]

---

stead, they represent different combinations of apples and bicycles that result in different levels of utility—a purely detached functional analysis. Certainly, when apples are reduced the person must receive bicycles in order to experience the same level of utility. The "fairness" of this substitution of apples for bicycles, or vice versa, is not a relevant factor as there is no interpersonal interaction.

98. I fully understand that some will reject the notion that a Pareto superior position would ultimately be unacceptable to a party. They might reason that an exchange that is not acceptable must not increase utility and, therefore, could not have been Pareto superior. As I have already noted, this does not worry me as I do not accept the view that all desired outcomes are reducible to a single "class" of utility. See supra note 9. For those wedded to the traditional notion of utility, however, I suggest adopting the view that the "cost" of an exchange is not just what one gives up in a material sense but any loss in status or pride that

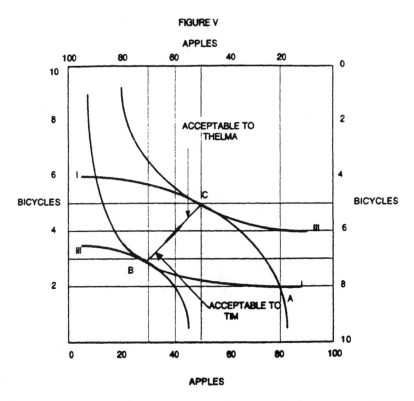

FIGURE V

At this point a variety of points remain that leave both parties feeling better off. Assume that Tim has the greater sense of entitlement and that the two parties agree on an exchange at point D which happens to require Thelma to give up forty apples for two bicycles. Both Tim and Thelma feel better off—i.e., are on higher indifference curves—and, assuming no ill effects on third parties, overall welfare is increased.

But now suppose everything stays the same except that Thelma's consciousness is raised and she reevaluates her personal sense of desert. As a consequence of this new higher self-esteem and sense of entitlement, the deal of two bicycles for forty apples just does not seem fair and is rejected by Thelma. Indeed, Thelma may now find that most of the terms of the exchange, as shown by the contract curve, no longer seem fair. Thus, as shown in Figure V, Thelma finds acceptable only those exchanges that are close to Tim's axis and Tim only finds acceptable those exchanges that are near the axis of Thelma. In effect, we

would go along with accepting the proposed terms. Under this interpretation, what I am saying here is that these psychic costs increase relatively rapidly for those with an elevated sense of entitlement as the material terms of the exchange become less favorable. By the same token, increasing the self-esteem and sense of entitlement of someone who was previously disadvantaged, also has the effect of making them require more of what is being traded for in order to give up what they have to trade. In short, the conclusions suggested here will not vary even if one feels compelled to go by the more conventional methodology.

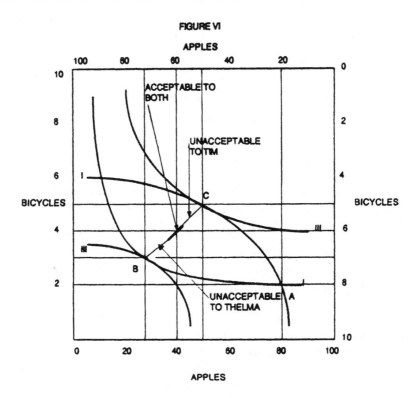

FIGURE VI

have a contract curve that includes no points upon which the parties can agree.

Another, and perhaps more likely, possibility is that the new-found sense of entitlement for Thelma does not eliminate all the possible exchange prices that could result in Pareto superior moves. Instead, as shown in Figure VI, the range of exchange possibilities has been substantially narrowed, thereby decreasing the likelihood of finding a mutually agreeable exchange term. After all, even along the full contract curve in Figure III, the parties may negotiate long and hard and still walk away without an agreement. In Figure VI, however, the opportunities are few, increasing the likelihood that no mutually agreeable point will be found. This may be tantamount to raising transaction costs and higher transaction costs decrease the likelihood of striking a bargain.

In general terms, the curves illustrate that by changing the personality of one of the participants so that that person has a higher sense of entitlement, we may decrease the likelihood that a once mutually beneficial exchange will take place. Increasing a person's sense of self-worth may decrease his opportunities for arriving at Pareto superior positions. Conversely, by depriving him of self-esteem we can create an interpersonal environment consisting of many more opportunities for increases in efficiency through Pareto superior moves. In its barest form, this means that the more demeaning an environment, the more likely it is that "efficient" exchanges will take place. But "efficient" exchanges that are only possible because of the deprivations that exist in society should make us think twice about whether they have the moral legitimacy necessary to be enforced by contract law.

More importantly, from the standpoint of this Article, a change in the parties' relative senses of compensatory justice affects the division of the surplus created by the exchange. When the division consistently is lopsided in favor of the more privileged party, questions of moral legitimacy also arise.

Let me put this latter point in more vivid terms. Suppose a black child grows up in a racist community and knows nothing other than being treated with suspicion and disdain. When he grows up, he is perfectly happy with a job similar to that occupied by whites but for which he is paid a salary equal to only two-thirds that paid to whites. Moreover, the employer would not pay a salary as high as that paid to a white person. Presumably, we have increased efficiency due to the fact that the employer and employee have moved to higher indifference curves. But the division of the surplus from the trade, and perhaps the existence of the contract itself, can be explained by the fact that the black employee has been taught to be satisfied with less than his white counterpart. In terms of *equity theory*, he has been taught that his inputs are, in a literal sense, less worthy. In terms of *relative deprivation theory*, he does not feel as though the wage is unfair because it is equal to that received by those to whom he compares himself.

We are faced, however, with the possibility that through years of consciousness-raising the black person is able to overcome his sense of inferiority.[99] By viewing his inputs as being as valuable as those contributed by whites or by broadening the range of those included in his social comparison process and thus experiencing a sense of relative deprivation, he now finds the lower salary unacceptable. The loss of dignity would be too great to offset the financial gain. One possibility is that a higher wage will be received. On the other hand, if the employer sticks to his race-based wage structure, the employment contract will not be made, and arguably, a possible Pareto superior exchange will be foregone because of the employee's new self-valuation.

The same sort of analysis can be applied to the situation found in *Williams v. Walker-Thomas Furniture Co.*[100] Suppose that the exchange in that case,

---

99. This consciousness-raising has the effect of "delegitimizing the stratification." See Della Fave, supra note 7, at 966–68 (arguing that delegitimization comes when incongruence develops between distribution of primary resources and self-evaluations); Deutsch, supra note 71, at 33–34 (arguing that raising a sense of injustice to people's consciousness creates a source of social organization and cohesion); Martin, supra note 55, at 66–67 (noting studies that demonstrate that Northern blacks had a greater sense of entitlement than Southern blacks because Northern blacks compared their economic status with that of whites while Southern blacks restricted such comparison to other blacks).

100. 350 F.2d 445 (D.C.Cir.1965). Mrs. Williams made a series of credit purchases from the Walker-Thomas store totalling over $1800. Id. at 447 n. 1. The collateral for each purchase was not just the item purchased but all items on which she had an outstanding balance. Id. at 447. Each payment was credited to each item on a proportionate basis. Id. Thus, under the terms of the agreement, "'the amount of each periodical installment payment... shall be inclusive of and not in addition to the amount of each installment payment...under prior...accounts; and all payments made...shall be credited pro rata on all outstanding... accounts....'" Id. (quoting the contract) (alterations in original). In effect, Williams could not pay off any one item until all the items were paid off. Id. At a point when her balance was $164, Williams purchased another item. Id. at 447 n. 1. Upon her default, the Walker-Thomas store attempted to repossess all of the items she had purchased under the "add-on"

even if Williams fully understood the add-on clause in her contract with Walker-Thomas, fell squarely on the contract curve. In that instance, both parties would have experienced increases in utility. Again, the possibility looms that the bargain was only possible because of Williams' low self-image—"it's not a great deal," she realizes, "but that's what those of us in the inner city must be happy with and it is what we deserve."

Suppose Williams begins to spend time around people who help her to develop a greater sense of personal dignity or that because the terms offered to her have been labelled "unconscionable" by a court, exchanges that once seemed fair to her no longer seem fair.[101] The terms offered by Walker-Thomas seem unacceptable because she now feels relatively deprived. It is important to note that she rejects the Walker-Thomas offer not simply because she thinks there are better deals elsewhere, but because she now feels deserving of those exchanges.

In both the employment example and the *Walker-Thomas* possibility, the question is whether the terms of the exchange or the exchange itself are possible only because of the respective classes, and resultant self-images, of the parties. Whatever the philosophical basis, I think that at some level, exchanges and terms that exist as consequences of the difference in senses of entitlement make us uncomfortable. Indeed, it is a very shallow notion of fairness that is based on a concept of efficiency that is, at least in some part, dependent on the deprivation and devaluation of individuals.

V. Preferences, Personal Autonomy, and Distributive Outcomes

A. Adaptations to Class

The preceding section spells out in technical economic terms why relative deprivation theory and equity theory provide strong foundations for excusing individuals from their contracts. A line of reasoning opposing such action could be based on the view that people, in terms of preference, are as we find them[102] and interference with their private orderings impinges on their liberty by substituting their preferences and personalities with those we wish they had. In addition, any response that excuses them from their choices might be regarded as unduly paternalistic. More specifically, one might argue that I sim-

---

terms. Id. at 447.

For defense of this type of contract provision, see Richard A. Epstein, Unconscionability: A Critical Reappraisal, 18 J. L. & Econ. 293, 306–07 (1975). See also Schwartz, supra note 10 (arguing that inadequate information should be the only factor of nonsubstantive unconscionability to invalidate an agreement). For a different view, see Robert Braucher, The Unconscionable Contract or Term, 31 U. Pitt. L. Rev. 337, 343–44 (1970).

101. See infra notes 170–82 and accompanying text.

102. See George J. Stigler & Gary S. Becker, De Gustibus non Est Disputandum, 67 Am. Econ. Rev. 76 (1977) (asserting that tastes are stable over time and do not vary widely between different people).

ply am saying that *my* preference is that disadvantaged people act more as-sertively in bargaining contexts.[103] At a different and more troublesome level, though, the intervention may reflect a desire that individuals have a sense of compensatory justice that mirrors our own.[104]

An easy response to these objections may be that we really are not interfer-ing with preferences at all. Arguably, every self-interested and rational person wants as much of the surplus created by the exchange as possible. In addition, it is hardly paternalistic to help someone achieve a goal—greater wealth—which we know they desire but which they do not believe they deserve. Indeed, as a general rule, it does not seem to be paternalistic to intervene if the subject of our intervention would immediately defend our actions, as seems likely in this context.[105] Even if they do not want more, it seems safe to predict that they would prefer to have a greater sense of desert. That is, they might say, "Yes, I would like to feel more deserving."

But all of this makes it too easy to avoid the issues of autonomy when in-terfering with the joint decisions individuals have made about distributive out-comes. First of all, we may be dealing with a preference that transcends day-to-day preferences, such as wine rather than soft drinks or Mozart rather than the Rolling Stones. Arguably, people accept less because they honestly have their own standards for distributive outcomes and strive to achieve "fairness" as they see it. In other words, they may adhere to their own belief as to what constitutes compensatory justice as a matter of principle or lexical ordering. If this is the case, intervening on the basis of what we would like them to prefer as a matter of compensatory justice is not much different than attempting a re-ligious conversion.

Another possibility is that individuals are comfortable with less because they desire to avoid the risk of humiliation if they ask for more and are re-fused. Indeed, embedded in the analysis of equity theory and relative depriva-tion theory is a preference-like notion that has to do with how much of the surplus from the exchange is enough to make these individuals feel they have been treated fairly. In essence, some individuals "prefer," or are comfortable with, less of the surplus. In utilitarian terms, one might argue that there is safety in asking for less and in "staying in one's place." A related but slightly different possibility is that one may derive some perverse pleasure from being what outsiders may regard as deprived. This would also have a utilitarian basis with the individual preferring to think of herself or to have others think of her as a "victim." In all of these cases, interfering with the compensatory preference is far more fundamental than helping someone to overcome her preference for smoking or television or even for contracts with disclaimers.

---

103. See Harrison, supra note 9, at 1361–62 (questioning how much weight one's own preferences should be given when making policy decisions regarding the preferences of oth-ers). See generally C. Dyke, The Vices of Altruism, 81 Ethics 241 (1971) (positing that when one has fewer alternatives, self-interest is more motivating than the common good).

104. In a sense, we want them to feel they deserve a greater share of the gains from the exchange.

105. See Kennedy, supra note 20, at 572.

A 1986 article by Cass Sunstein is helpful in questioning the legitimacy of interfering with preferences.[106] Sunstein meticulously lays out the reasons we are sometimes able to overcome our hesitancy to interfere with expressed preferences. His "catalogue," includes four categories. First is the possibility that a majority will choose to "bind itself against the satisfaction of its own misguided choices."[107] In effect, the majority may choose to eliminate some choices in order to channel behavior toward choices that they would prefer to have. The second category involves preferences that are themselves the product of legal rules.[108] The third category concerns efforts to curb choices that depend on "addictions, habits, or myopic behavior."[109] Finally, preferences that stem from "cognitive distortions"[110] may also be fair game for interference. The simplest example of a cognitive distortion is a choice that results from a lack of information.

I am tempted to say that interfering with contracts purely on the basis of the questionable legitimacy of the compensatory outcomes can be justified entirely by reference to Sunstein's fourth category. In effect, the personal sense of compensatory justice that drives one to reveal a preference for a lopsided distribution is a function of the lack of accurate information the individual has about his own moral worth or the value of his own inputs as compared to the value of the inputs of others. For example, a belief that individuals are of equal moral worth may lead one to believe that he need not take a smaller share of the surplus created by exchanges.[111] Similarly, knowledge that the definition of "valued inputs" is a function of inequities in class and power may reduce the tendency to accept subordinate status. In effect, preferences based on inadequate or inaccurate information are fair game for judicial interference.[112] Although this argument is appealing in some sense, it does not really seem to match the sorts of cognitive errors that Sunstein sees as fitting into category four.[113] This lack of information is not of the same ilk as smoking when one has not heard of the health risks associated with smoking.

This category, however, can blend with category two, which deals with the adaptations that individuals make to existing laws or power imbalances that

106. Cass A. Sunstein, Legal Interference with Private Preferences, 53 U.Chi. L. Rev. 1129 (1986).

107. Id. at 1138.

108. Id. at 1138–39; see also Elster, supra note 7, at 141–48.

109. Sunstein, supra note 106, at 1139.

110. Id.

111. In essence, the "choice" to take less may be a result of class-driven feelings of self-esteem. Low self-esteem is then the result of a faulty self-valuation process. In other words, the choice to take less may be the result of inaccurate information about one's value vis-a-vis that of others.

112. They are fair game in the sense that the "preference" revealed is based on inaccurate information. They are also fair game due to the possible therapeutic value of having courts routinely vindicate those who have undervalued themselves. See infra notes 175–82 and accompanying text.

113. See Sunstein, supra note 106, at 1166–69 (stating that intervention in decisionmaking is less objectionable when one does not know all the relevant information).

themselves result from the legal system. Before addressing this blending possibility, I will focus on the two types of adaptations that could account for the tendency of disadvantaged individuals to prefer to accept without protest the preferences others have for what the disadvantaged person should feel about compensatory fairness.

Adaptation in this context means that the preferences expressed by individuals are not their own, in a true sense, but are dependent on law.[114] The first type of adaptation is fairly straightforward. Despite what most contract law professors teach their students, the common person generally believes that a "contract is a contract." In fact, the doctrine that the law will not refuse to enforce a contract simply because of the lack of adequate consideration seems well known, at least at an intuitive level, to virtually everyone. For example, if contract law fails to directly address issues of adequacy of consideration, and bargains like those in *Williams v. Walker-Thomas Furniture Co.*[115] are enforced routinely, one begins to accept those bargains as "just." After all, laws are designed to promote justice, aren't they? Furthermore, the inequality of the division of the surplus also will be viewed as having the moral authority of the law.[116] In short, people's views of what is "just" are to some extent dependent on what the law implicitly labels as "just." Moreover, if they have been on the short end of a deal, are from a low social class and, consequently, have low self-esteem, they will be quick to accept the views of others that they have only themselves to blame.[117]

This general response to an intuitive sense of the law is probably not enough to explain why some individuals seem to prefer, or feel comfortable with, consistently being on the short end of bargains, whether in employment contracts, housing contracts, automobile sales contracts, or insurance contracts. A broader adaptation that accounts for this "willingness" routinely to be the contract victim can be explained by reference to "ideology." Sunstein describes these preferences as "desires and beliefs that derive from relations of power."[118] In this context, the "preference" is really a psychological adjustment or resignation to power imbalances that cannot be overcome.[119] It is, in fact, a way of avoiding the dissonance and stress that would occur if one began to question the legitimacy of his status.

The manifestation of this adaptation can be found in the responses individuals express when asked about apparent inequities. For example, Professor

---

114. One might view the distinction as being between "pure preferences" and "dependent preferences" with the latter reflecting adaptations to law and ideology.

115. 350 F.2d 445 (D.C.Cir.1965).

116. Cf. Hoffman & Spitzer, Fairness, supra note 31 (using a laboratory test to ascertain the source of generally held notions of fairness or morality and discussing the implications of the test results for the legal system).

117. See supra notes 75–84 and accompanying text.

118. Sunstein, supra note 106, at 1152; see also Elster, supra note 7, at 145 (positing that the oppressed have a tendency to regard their oppressive social order as being just, and that this tendency may be due to an illusion among the oppressed that they owe their livelihood to their oppressors).

119. Cf. Kelman, supra note 12 (arguing that consumers will attempt to evade the duress of market powers when possible).

Joanne Martin offers a variety of ways in which individuals learn to adapt to injustice.[120] Two of the more powerful descriptions are as follows:

> (He), youngest of three children, lived with his mother in an 8-story apartment in the South Bronx, a mostly black and Puerto Rican neighborhood. "I didn't know any different. I didn't have anything to compare it to....I didn't see it as tough. It was my home."
>
> ....
>
> An Appalachian woman was hired by the Office of Economic Opportunity to work as a community organizer in her own impoverished black neighborhood. She spent her time making fruit pies for her poorer neighbors. When asked by a friend how she felt about the amount of money she was earning in this job (her income was slightly above the poverty line), she replied, "I am very content; I have more than my neighbors." Her friend continued, "What about the people on 'the hill'?" (This was a wealthy residential area, clearly visible from the organizer's front yard.) She answered, "My life is here. I don't think about them."[121]

At this point, the matter of preference determination merges with relative deprivation theory and equity theory. The valuations either of the relative inputs and outputs in the context of equity theory or of the lack of a sense of deprivation among those who objectively are deprived in the case of relative deprivation theory are hard to equate with the true or "pure" preferences of the individuals. They are preferences influenced by, perhaps even created by, outside factors.

As I mentioned, the adaptation rationale for not taking observed indications of preferences at face value blends with Sunstein's category four which deals with problems stemming from inadequate information.[122] This blending is important because the problem of adaptive preferences would be far less troublesome if individuals had the information to assess their own preferences, to evaluate how they are formed, and to at least consider the possibility of having preferences other than the ones they have. Not only are the preferences not independent of law, but, as a cognitive matter, individuals are without the type of information or introspection that would permit them to alter their expectations for themselves.[123]

Seen in this light, there is no powerful autonomy-based moral objection to intruding on individuals' choices to consistently undervalue themselves and their contributions as compared to the contributions of others. To view the process as one of interfering with liberty is simply to legitimize the system that has distorted the self-valuations and senses of entitlement that individuals have.

B. A Comparison to Informal Dispute Resolution

An analogy can be drawn here to the arguments that have been made in the context of informal dispute resolution. Informal dispute resolution can injure

---

120. See Martin, supra note 70.

121. Id. at 217.

122. See supra note 110 and accompanying text.

123. For one description of the difficulties involved in overcoming one's adaptive preferences, see Kaufman & Raphael, supra note 80, at 30–52 (discussing the development of inner security and self-esteem).

the powerless at both a macro level and a micro level. At the macro level, it may siphon off disputes that, if resolved in a formal setting, could begin a general movement toward reform.[124] It also can dampen the festering social discontent that otherwise might lead to collective action for change.[125]

The micro level dangers are more interesting for the purpose of this discussion because informal dispute resolution typically involves the negotiation of a contract. Although the contracts entered into as a means of settling disputes, where the pressures to contract are great, may be seen as different from those made in a more voluntary context, the concerns raised carry over to day-to-day private orderings. Indeed, contracts about the necessities of life and employment are even less voluntary than those designed to settle disputes.

Increasingly, legal scholars have expressed concerns that informal dispute resolution is dangerous to those groups who, in terms of this Article, have a relatively low sense of entitlement.[126] These scholars claim that weaker parties are actually better off when disputes are resolved in a formal, as opposed to an informal, setting.[127] To be specific, the case has been made that the formal setting encourages the parties, including the stronger parties, to aspire to higher values.[128] In addition, the formal setting insulates the parties and avoids the intimate contact that allows the stronger party to dominate.[129]

---

124. See Owen Fiss, Against Settlement, 93 Yale L. J. 1073, 1086 (1984) (arguing that settlement masks society's "basic contradictions"); Richard Hofrichter, Neighborhood Justice and the Social Control Problems of American Capitalism: A Perspective, in 1 The Politics of Informal Justice 207, 223–24 (Richard L. Abel ed., 1982).

125. See Richard Hofrichter, Neighborhood Justice in Capitalist Society: The Expansion of the Informal State 82 (1987) (discussing how informality facilitates early intervention which helps to prevent social disruption); Richard L. Abel, The Contradictions of Informal Justice, in 1 The Politics of Informal Justice 267, 280–95 (Richard L. Abel ed., 1982) (describing how informal legal institutions neutralize conflict by responding to grievances before they ripen into serious challenges to the State).

126. See Richard L. Abel, Conservative Conflict and the Reproduction of Capitalism: The Role of Informal Justice, 9 Int'l J. Soc. L. 245, 257 (1981) (noting how in a class society informalism benefits those with greater power); Trina Grillo, The Mediation Alternative: Process Dangers for Women, 100 Yale L. J. 1545, 1564–67 (1991) (discussing how certain groups tolerate injustice because they do not feel entitled to assert their rights); Frances Olsen, The Family and the Market: A Study of Ideology and Legal Reform, 96 Harv. L. Rev. 1497, 1541–42 (1983) (asserting that "deformalized" procedure, e.g., family court, may have adverse effects on women in that attempts at conciliation often subject women to more injury and welfare of the weaker parties often depends on "the uncontrolled discretion of state agencies").

127. See Abel, supra note 126, at 295–301; Richard Delgado et al., Fairness and Formality: Minimizing the Risk of Prejudice in Alternative Dispute Resolution, 1985 Wis. L. Rev. 1359, 1387–88.

128. See Delgado et al., supra note 127, at 1387–88; John Thibaut et al., Procedural Justice as Fairness, 26 Stan. L. Rev. 1271, 1288–89 (1974) (suggesting that the adversary system is perceived as more just and encourages more diligent representation of parties by their attorneys).

129. See Abel, supra note 127, at 257; Delgado et al., supra note 127, at 1388; Grillo, supra note 126, at 1550, 1597–600; Olsen, supra note 126, at 1542.

Mediation is a good example of a method of informal dispute resolution that gives rise to these concerns.[130] Ideally, mediation allows the parties to define what they consider to be a "just" outcome. In effect, the parties come together with the goal of achieving an outcome that is consistent with each party's sense of justice as influenced by ideology.[131] Their sense of justice in this context, however, is largely a function of their personal sense of entitlement. The "preferences" and, therefore, the outcome, of the informal process can be less equal than that resulting from a more formal setting in which the ritual may elevate the integrity of the weaker party. As Richard Abel, the leading critic of informal dispute resolution, posits: "compromise produces unbiased results only when opponents are equal; compromise between unequals inevitably reproduces inequality."[132] Moreover, the outcome is more dangerous in that the sense of being treated in an arbitrary fashion, which might provide the basis for reform, is lost.[133]

Writers have noted especially the dangers of informal dispute resolution for women.[134] For example, if in fact women are more altruistic than men, in that they are more nurturing and interested in preserving relationships, the informal setting in which they negotiate with men who do not share the same values can result in material disadvantages for women. In essence, if the cost of individual material gain is the destruction of the relational interest, some women do not feel entitled to pay the price.[135] This sense of the proper role, "place," or even behavior of women in informal dispute resolution can be generalized to the sense of "place" or entitlement of any person engaged in a negotiation.[136]

The day-to-day private orderings of individuals embody all of the dangers of informal dispute resolution and then some. The absence of formality liber-

---

130. See, e.g., Hofrichter, supra note 125, at 82; Grillo, supra note 126 (challenging the notion that mediation is fairer or more humane); Lisa G. Lerman, Mediation of Wife Abuse Cases: The Adverse Impact of Informal Dispute Resolution on Women, 7 Harv. Women's L. J. 57, 71–97 (1984) (discussing the various criticisms of mediation in the wife-abuse context, and arguing that prosecution is the only appropriate remedy); Laurie Woods, Mediation: A Backlash to Women's Progress on Family Law Issues, 19 Clearinghouse Rev. 431 (1985) (arguing that mediation in family law disputes denies women the opportunity to develop and enforce new rights).

131. See generally Leonard Riskin, Mediation and Lawyers, 43 Ohio St. L. J. 29, 34–35 (1982) (stating that certain assumptions of the parties to a "mediation affect the procedures and results achieved in [the] mediation[ ]").

132. Abel, supra note 126, at 257.

133. Id. at 259.

134. Sources discussing the problems resulting from mediation or general lack of formality in the context of family and gender-related disputes include: Grillo, supra note 126; Lerman, supra note 130; Olsen, supra note 126; Janet Rifkin, Mediation from a Feminist Perspective: Promise and Problems, 2 Law & Ineq. J. 21 (1984) (examining mediation in the separation and divorce context and the sexual harassment context and discussing a variety of criticisms of mediation); and Woods, supra note 130.

135. See, e.g., Grillo, supra note 126, at 1601–05 (arguing that women have a relational sense of self, focusing on connections with others rather than on individualism).

136. See Hofrichter, supra note 125, at 73; Abel, supra note 126, at 257; Delgado et al., supra note 127, at 1360.

ates the parties to respond to their baser motivations. The close interpersonal contact forces the weaker party, typically the party with greater plasticity,[137] to listen to the stronger party's view on what is fair. An important distinction exists between day-to-day private orderings and informal dispute resolution that means the former is even more likely to be damaging to weaker parties. In informal dispute resolution there is at least a quasi-formality in the sense that even the weaker party recognizes the existence of a dispute and the need to defend her own interests, however those interests might be defined. In the day-to-day context, though, even those guards are down.

VI. Unconscionability and Entitlement

Although courts can adopt a variety of contract doctrines in order to respond indirectly to advantage-taking,[138] the most direct response to contracts resulting in uneven exchanges would be an expanded notion of unconscionability. I do not intend here to go into great detail about how this might be done.[139] In the first section below, I sketch how my version of unconscionability would differ from the way in which it currently is applied. In the second section, I will discuss in more general terms the potential of an expansion of substantive unconscionability as a means of educating individuals and shaping their senses of entitlement. I respond to the typical "law and economics" concerns about expanding unconscionability by illustrating how the perspective changes when unconscionability is used as a preference-shaping tool.

A. Revising Unconscionability

As every first year law student knows, a consideration of unconscionability begins with Arthur Leff's analysis.[140] Professor Leff divides the topic into two categories: problems in the bargaining process, *procedural* unconscionability, and pure unfairness in the exchange, *substantive* unconscionability.[141] Al-

---

137. See supra notes 78–79 and accompanying text.

138. See, e.g., Farnsworth, supra note 14, §4 (discussing the doctrines of mental infirmity, incompetency, misrepresentation, and fraud); Ellinghaus, supra note 14, at 788 (citing Lon L. Fuller & Robert Braucher, Basic Contract Law 180–81 (1964), for the proposition that there are at least nine established contract doctrines in response to advantage-taking); Gordley, supra note 15, at 1649–55 (suggesting that many cases decided under common contract doctrines were actually decided under unconscionability standards); Horowitz, supra note 14, at 941 (noting the theories of duress, fraud, and lack of capacity).

139. I do not mean to suggest that there are not details to work out. I have a sense, however, that anyone agreeing with the propositions set forth will agree that an express expansion of unconscionability is quite practical. On the other hand, readers who reject most of what has been said and what is to come will be more likely to think of such a change as impractical.

140. Arthur A. Leff, Unconscionability and the Code—The Emperor's New Clause, 115 U. Pa. L. Rev. 485 (1967).

141. Id. at 486–87, 489–501, 509–16.

though his two-pronged analysis is an interesting way to approach the issue, it is not terribly useful.[142] If there is procedural unfairness, but not unfairness in the exchange, there is no issue to address. In all likelihood, however, when there is substantive unfairness, procedural unfairness of some form is also nearby.[143] If so, there seems to be little need to fit it into an appropriate procedural pigeonhole.

To a great extent, Melvin Eisenberg takes this view in his important and thorough article, *The Bargain Principle and Its Limits*.[144] Professor Eisenberg identifies a trend toward reacting to unfairness without regard to some sign of a procedural defect, but there remains a great deal of ambivalence toward responding solely to unfairness in the bargain.[145] Thus, although the *Restatement (Second) of Contracts* discusses the "theoretical" possibility of such a response, it notes that "[o]rdinarily,... an unconscionable contract involves other factors as well as overall imbalance."[146] The Restatement suggests that unequal bargaining power accompanied by terms that are favorable to the stronger party may mean that "the weaker party had no meaningful choice, no real alternative, or did not in fact assent or appear to assent to the unfair terms."[147]

This discomfort with responding directly to simple unfairness in the exchange ironically is exhibited in Professor Eisenberg's article itself. Although his thesis seems to state that courts are more ready than ever to dispense with the need for a procedural element of unconscionability, much of the article is devoted to the discussion of unconscionability categories that look remarkably like different versions of procedural unfairness.[148] In this context he discusses four categories of cases in which the enforcement of bargains might be limited on the basis of unconscionability. The first category involves bargains made when one of the parties was in distress and had little choice but to accept the offer made by the other party.[149] Professor Eisenberg's second category involves "transactional incapacity" which seems to include those instances in which even people of average intelligence may not be capable of understanding the implications of complex bargains.[150] The third category, "unfair persuasion," involves the "use of bargaining methods that seriously impair the free and competent exercise of judgment."[151] The final category envisions "price ig-

---

142. See Eisenberg, supra note 14, at 754 (stating that "[t]he distinction between procedural and substantive unconscionability is too rigid to provide significant help").

143. See Richard J. Hunter, Jr., Unconscionability Revisited: A Comparative Approach, 68 N. D. L. Rev. 145, 169 (1992) ("[T]here will be few instances where a contract is so one-sided as to [be substantively unconscionable] absent some strong evidence of [procedural unconscionability].").

144. Eisenberg, supra note 14.

145. Id. at 752–54.

146. Restatement (Second) of Contracts § 208 cmt. c (1979).

147. Id. § 208 cmt. d.

148. See Eisenberg, supra note 14, at 754–85.

149. Id. at 754–63.

150. Id. at 763–73.

151. Id. at 773–74.

norance" in which the price offered is taken as a kind of warranty that it is representative of the "prevailing price."[152]

While I probably could squeeze any exchange that I would regard as unconscionable into one of Professor Eisenberg's categories,[153] that exercise would be unnecessary, because even Professor Eisenberg does not view his list of categories as being all-inclusive. Instead, he states that "unconscionability is a paradigmatic concept that can never be exhaustively described."[154] In addition, the critical element of Professor Eisenberg's methodology was to identify cases in which neither "fairness nor efficiency support the bargain principle's application."[155] This, in large measure, is consistent with the analysis in the preceding two sections. If one's consent to the terms of a contract is the function of class-based injuries, it is hard to defend the bargain on either fairness or efficiency grounds.[156]

I would deviate from the Eisenberg model in one important way—the classification of unconscionability cases is not only unnecessary but counterproductive. I am concerned about an approach in which the disadvantaged party is seen as a victim that the law has more or less rescued.[157] This suggests some element of subordination which, in a subtle way, cuts against the elevating and vindicating effects that are more productive. In order for routine use of unconscionability to have the effect I am suggesting, it is important to avoid the taxonomy of victims.[158] More specifically, I think the therapeutic effects of more

---

152. Id. at 778–85.

153. For example, although Professor Eisenberg's "unfair persuasion" category seems to involve methods used by advantage-taking parties, much of the problem discussed in this paper has to do with the possibility that some classes of people are more easily persuaded than others. This could be regarded as "unfair persuasion."

154. Eisenberg, supra note 14, at 754.

155. Id.

156. Both the fairness and efficiency elements of Pareto superiority are grounded in the idea that the parties have consented. When that consent is contingent on class-based injuries it is hard to defend the exchange from the standpoint of fairness or efficiency.

157. Professor Lesnick states that the "radical" approach to greater use of unconscionability would involve recognition that the party "see himself as a victim of abuse, rather than as someone who...has made a mess of things." Lesnick, supra note 17, at 437. Certainly this is consistent with the view here that class stratification is maintained in part because those who are worse off believe they are responsible for their position. While I agree with Professor Lesnick, my point here is that an affirmative showing of one's weakness in a judicial setting seems inconsistent with the proper type of consciousness-raising.

I realize that not requiring a party to prove his or her weakness would mean that the proposal would not limit the use of unconscionability to those who are from lower classes who have dealt with higher class advantage-takers. The fact that bargains between disadvantaged parties, between advantaged parties, and between parties from different classes in which the party from the lower class has somehow received the larger share of the gain from the exchange may be affected, does not seem to me to be very important. The bargains between individuals from the same class will have no distributive impact. Thus, it becomes an empirical question of whether the advantaged or disadvantaged segments of society will benefit more from an expanded application of unconscionability. My sense is that members of the class that is more often on the short end of the bargain will more often wish to avoid the contract.

158. I am sure the comparison is not entirely accurate and I have been unable to track down its origins, but I am reminded by Toni Massaro of the shift from the phrase "rape vic-

routine use of unconscionability would be undercut terribly if the party wishing to avoid the contract were required to prove that he truly was poor, passive, helpless, or lacked self-esteem.

I envision three basic distinctions between the use that I see for unconscionability and the way it is currently applied. First, the focus would be strictly on substantive fairness without any requirement that unconscionability have a procedural element. Thus, the sole question would be whether the exchange was fair.[159] In the terms of Professor Gordley's article, *Equality in Exchange*,[160] I would look to whether one party has been "enriched at the other's expense."[161] No real investigation into procedural niceties is required here. The second variation would be that the "fairness of the exchange" be a question of fact.[162] This cuts against the origins of unconscionability as an equitable doctrine, but should not prevent the adoption of a jury question approach. The objective is to evaluate the issue of fairness from a more general social norm, rather than from a judge's possibly privileged perspective. Finally, any finding of substantive unconscionability should be accompanied by a form of public notice. In essence, the community should be notified of those individuals or firms that have been found to have acted "unconscionably." I will discuss the importance of this latter element when I return to the educative value of unconscionability in the following section.

B. The Educative Effect of Unconscionability

As I noted in the Introduction, my principal point is to suggest that the routine use of unconscionability may have the effect of altering the expectations that individuals have about the bargains they make and what they deserve in those bargains. This is not meant to imply that I personally do not favor the use of unconscionability strictly as a means of achieving equality. My point is that if routine use of unconscionability had the desired effect of teaching the traditionally disadvantaged that they are as deserving as the relatively privileged, then the need for judicial intervention at all levels, which has as its goal the equalization of individuals in a material sense, could be greatly lessened. In

---

tim" to "rape survivor." See Massaro, supra note 23, at 2112.

159. This view is hardly unprecedented even in the United States. See Eisenberg, supra note 14, at 752–53; Gordley, supra note 15, at 1645–55; see also A.H. Angelo & E.P. Ellinger, Unconscionable Contracts: A Comparative Study of the Approaches in England, France, Germany, and the United States, 14 Loy. L. A. Int'l & Comp. L. J. 455 (1992) (comparing common law and civil law jurisdictions and finding a focus on "usurious price" only in some jurisdictions); Franco Taisch, Unconscionability in a Civil Law System: An Overview of Swiss Law, 14 Loy. L. A. Int'l & Comp. L. J. 529 (1992) (finding that the Swiss law dealing with unconscionability focuses on disparity of consideration and weakness of one party).

160. Gordley, supra note 15.

161. Id. at 1637.

162. Competitive market price and the seller's cost would be evidence of the fairness of the exchange. See Eisenberg, supra note 14, at 749–50 (arguing that "[i]f the price was not set by a mechanism that is regarded as fair, such as a competitive market, it may not be unfair to revise it judicially"); Gordley, supra note 15, at 1613–14 (arguing that "a price that covers costs is both an ideal minimum and an ideal maximum because at that price the wealth of the parties remains constant").

effect, there is an immediate and short-run equalizing effect and, perhaps more important, a longer run "therapeutic" effect.

To some extent—and I cannot say exactly to what extent—my admittedly slight optimism that a generalized sense of equal self-esteem and entitlement could be achieved is fueled by the numerous examples of behavior indicating that individuals have, at some level, a consciousness about standards of fairness that exists apart from narrowly defined notions of self-interest. Whether leaving a tip at a restaurant on an interstate highway,[163] donating to public television[164] or a blood bank,[165] voting,[166] or increasing one's efforts to adjust for what would otherwise be excessive payment,[167] the strong implication is that individuals, for whatever reason, seem to free-ride in far fewer instances than there are opportunities available. The implication is that even members of advantage-taking classes have the capacity to act altruistically and define their interests more broadly than those that are narrowly self-serving.[168] It is even possible that this willingness not to always take advantage of the weakness of others is a trait that can be reinforced.

In its full-blown version, the possibility exists that individuals take advantage of their power vis-a-vis others as a defensive strategy because the assumption is that others are likely to be acting with the same selfish motives. If so, one could view a sense of compensatory justice requiring roughly equal exchanges as a type of public good—something that individuals desire but that few will act on, because unless everyone acts similarly, the objective cannot be met.[169]

Aside from these possibly fanciful hopes about human nature, there is substantial support for the belief that law can have the sort of preference-shaping effect that I am discussing. For example, in a recent article, Professor Kenneth

---

163. See Robert H. Frank, If Homo Economicus Could Choose His Own Utility Function, Would He Want One with a Conscience?, 77 Am. Econ. Rev. 593, 593 (1987).

164. See Howard Margolis, Selfishness, Altruism, and Morality 12 (1982).

165. See Richard M. Titmuss, The Gift Relationship (1971) (studying the scientific, social, economic, and ethical implications of the procurement, processing, and distribution of human blood).

166. On the rationality of voting from the standpoint of individual self-interest, see Anthony Downs, An Economics Theory of Democracy (1957) (approaching the problem of democratic government from an economic standpoint); Margolis, supra note 164, at 92–95; Stephen G. Salkever, Who Knows Whether It's Rational to Vote?, 90 Ethics 203 (1980) (arguing that voting cannot be explained by either an economic (cost-benefit) analysis or a political (duty-bound) analysis, but can only be explained on a situational, case-by-case basis).

167. See Adams, supra note 18, at 284–85.

168. See Harrison, supra note 9, at 1338–51 (arguing that a person who makes a donation with the hope of receiving something has not performed an altruistic act).

169. This, of course, raises the familiar problem of the "prisoner's dilemma." See Generally Robert Axelrod, The Evolution of Cooperation (1984) (utilizing a computer study of the prisoner's dilemma as the point of departure for a discussion of the problem of cooperation given an underlying pursuit of self-interest); R. Duncan Luce & Howard Raiffa, Games and Decisions 88–113 (1957) (providing a discussion of two-person, non-zero-sum, non-cooperative games such as the prisoner's dilemma).

Dau-Schmidt[170] makes the crucial distinction, primarily in the context of criminal law, between "(1) shaping the individual's opportunities to give incentive for desired behavior, or (2) shaping the individual's preferences by increasing her taste for desired behavior."[171] From the perspective of mental health law, Professors David Wexler and Bruce Winick have done path-breaking work dealing with "therapeutic jurisprudence."[172] By therapeutic jurisprudence, they mean "the extent to which substantive rules, legal procedures, and the roles of lawyers and judges produce therapeutic or antitherapeutic consequences."[173] More directly, to what extent can law have a healing effect?[174]

It may seem odd to draw on scholarship from criminal law and mental health law in an argument for expanded use of unconscionability, but the matters discussed in this Article skirt the edges of both these fields. "Unconscionability" has a distinctly moral connotation.[175] Furthermore, by suggesting that routine reliance on unconscionability may reshape the preferences of both the advantaged and disadvantaged, I am arguing that law can be used to repair some of the psychic harm caused by rigid class stratification.

In a transaction that a court determines to be unconscionable, especially if the identity of the unconscionable party is publicized, the unconscionable party is likely to feel shame and "a negative, downward change in...self-concept"[176] is likely to be triggered. Perhaps more important are the affirming and educative effects on the person who has not acted unconscionably.[177] According to Professors Wexler and Winick, "the intensity and durability of a stigmatizing label can have major consequences for the labeled person."[178] But they

---

170. Dau-Schmidt, supra note 10.

171. Id. at 1. See generally John R. McKean & Robert R. Keller, The Shaping of Tastes, Pareto Efficiency and Economic Policy, 12 J. Behav. Econ. 23 (1983) (analyzing the treatment of tastes and attempts to incorporate tastes and preferences into welfare theory); Carl C. von Weizsacker, Notes on Endogenous Change of Tastes, 3 J. Econ. Theory 345 (1971) (arguing that the variables about which economists are usually concerned are not flexible enough to cope with endogenously changing tastes).

172. Wexler & Winick, supra note 16.

173. Id. at ix.

174. See id. at 8 (citing Parham v. J.R., 442 U.S. 584 (1979), to illustrate implicit Supreme Court recognition of "therapeutic jurisprudence").

175. Even Professor Leff, who found little clarity in § 2-302 of the Uniform Commercial Code, which addresses unconscionability, noted that, "[i]f reading...[§ 2-302] makes anything clear it is that reading...[the] section alone makes nothing clear about 'unconscionability' except perhaps that it is pejorative." Leff, supra note 140, at 487 (citation omitted).

176. Toni M. Massaro, Shame, Culture, and American Criminal Law, 89 Mich. L. Rev. 1880, 1886 (1991).

177. See Joshua Dressler, Understanding Criminal Law 8 (1987) (stating that the act of denouncing crime serves several important societal functions, including expression of anger and stigmatization of the offender); see also Johs Andenaes, General Prevention—Illusion or Reality?, 43 J. Crim. L. Criminology & Police Sci. 176, 179–80 (1952) (suggesting that a concrete expression of society's disapproval of an act creates conscious and unconscious inhibitions within the public against committing the act).

178. Wexler & Winick, supra note 16, at 306.

also note the importance of studying the reaction of "others" to the label-ing.[179] It is important to note that the affirming effects on individuals are quite different from finding that they were indeed victimized by the advantage-taker. The sense, especially in a transactional setting, is that one party "played by the rules," while the other party did not. This affirmation can have the generalized impact of affirming the total person and his personal sense of self-worth. Moreover, as far as the disadvantaged are concerned, to the extent that their diminished sense of entitlement is a function of low self-esteem[180] and person-ality plasticity,[181] the effect is in a very real sense a therapeutic or healing one. Here the wounds are what Sennett and Cobb, in their seminal work, call the "hidden injuries of class."[182]

My proposals, especially for those who think in traditional economic ways, are not without some risk. There are two risks to consider. First, broader ap-plication of substantive unconscionability may dampen the incentives to im-prove for those who have made what turn out to be unfavorable exchanges. Second, the routine use of unconscionability is comparable to the use of price ceilings and may affect the poor disproportionately.[183] In both cases, allowing individuals to escape lopsided bargains ultimately can make them worse off. To some extent, my points about the use of unconscionability as a preference-shaping tool can be illustrated by contrasting that view with the conventional economic objections to the use of unconscionability.

The first argument is that only by forcing those who are disadvantaged to live with their bargains can we provide them with the motivation to read the small print, to become better educated, and to assert themselves.[184] If one sub-

---

179. Id.; cf. Laurence R. Iannaccone, Sacrifice and Stigma: Reducing Free-Riding in Cults, of Communes, and Other Collectives, 100 J. Pol. Econ. 271, 289–90 (1992) (discussing the use of nonproductive costs, such as painful initiation rites, to weed out potential free-riders in collective communities).

180. See supra notes 79–80 and accompanying text.

181. See supra notes 81–84 and accompanying text.

182. Sennett & Cobb, supra note 8.

183. See Epstein, supra note 100, at 305–15 (arguing that when substantive uncon-scionability is used it has the effect of undercutting the private contract which ends up caus-ing more social harm than good); Schwartz, supra note 10, at 1057–63 (stating the proposi-tion that when a contract provision that might be considered oppressive, such as a warranty disclaimer, is invalidated by the court, this produces an undesirable result because the poor may not be able to afford the required warranty).

184. One could view the matter as a unilateral mistake. In these instances, the general rule is that one is not excused from the contract unless enforcement would be uncon-scionable or the other party had reason to know of the mistake. Restatement (Second) of Contracts § 153 (1979). The basic law and economics view on unilateral mistake, as I un-derstand it, is that excusing parties too frequently when they have made a "mistake" may re-duce incentives to produce or acquire information. See Richard A. Posner, Economic Analy-sis of Law § 4.6 (4th ed. 1992) (arguing that rules requiring disclosure of information are inefficient and result in lessened incentives to acquire and use information). In the context of this Article, the argument would be that routine application of unconscionability would re-duce the incentive to read small print and search for better terms. I am indebted to Dan Yea-ger for making the suggestion that this is an argument against the position I have taken in this Article.

scribes to this argument, then he or she disagrees with the core elements of this Article. A person taking this view would have to believe that finding against those who have been disadvantaged actually has a motivating and uplifting effect. The counterargument, as suggested in the previous section, is that law teaches people about their value and what is regarded by society as just, and that people adapt their own beliefs to these teachings.[185] Thus, the real impact of decisions that refuse to respond to advantage-taking is to make advantage-taking seem more legitimate to all affected. Empirical evidence strongly suggests that this would be especially true of the lower class and higher plasticity individuals.[186]

For example, contrast a very narrow standard under which all bargains are enforced, no matter how uneven the division of the surplus, with a policy that routinely refuses to enforce bargains involving undue advantage-taking. Certainly the second policy would be more likely to teach both parties that they are of equal moral worth and that the law does not countenance advantage-taking. As the advantage-takers are delegitimized, the self-esteem and assertiveness of the less advantaged seems likely to grow. As it grows, they are less in need of judicial intervention.

The second line of argument, based on unconscionability as the imposition of price ceilings, fits nicely into the *Williams v. Walker-Thomas Furniture Co.*[187] fact pattern, but can be applied more generally. Those making the price ceiling argument foresee alternate scenarios. The first scenario is that the merchants are making money hand-over-fist and that this is good, because competing merchants will soon see the opportunities for profits by operating in that market and will enter the market, thereby forcing prices down.

The price ceiling will retard this entry. This scenario has a number of responses. First, it requires one to have tremendous faith in the market and believe that the firm will not engage in conduct that would delay or prevent entry of competitors.[188] In addition, one has to ignore the fact that monopolies, when faced with price ceilings, may find it profitable to increase output. Putting this possibility aside, is it necessary for some buyers to pay supracompetitive prices in order that others will have lower prices in the future? If an expansive definition of unconscionability is a form of price regulation and constitutes the setting of a price ceiling, then shortages will result, translating into long lines of consumers at the stores forced to charge prices that permit only a normal profit. According to economic theory, as long as new entrants can be assured of at least earning a normal profit, they will enter the market. In essence, waiting in line would provide the rationing that higher prices would provide under the typical regime. The point is that limiting the prices will not mean that there will not be new entrants *and* increases in sales.

In the second scenario the merchants in the high crime, high insurance rate, high credit risk neighborhoods are barely making a profit. If they are not per-

---

185. See supra notes 118–25 and accompanying text.

186. See supra notes 81–84 and accompanying text.

187. 350 F.2d 445 (D.C.Cir.1965). See supra note 100 (providing a description of this case).

188. Efforts to preserve monopoly power have been identified as one of the social costs of monopoly. Posner, supra note 184, at 279–80.

mitted to charge prices for appliances that are greatly in excess of those charged at suburban discount stores or cannot routinely use add-on clauses on credit sales, they will be unable to operate and earn a normal profit.[189] Eventually, they will leave the neighborhood and reduce the choices available to the consumers in the area. There are two responses to this scenario. The first is to ask whether the risks of default and even the risks of crime in the neighborhood are not themselves responses to the high prices and onerous credit terms of the sellers. Certainly, the lower one's payments the more likely he or she is to make them. And the type of resentment that can build when prices are high and the buyers have no choice can lead to frustration that results in a violent reaction. The point is that the impact of "price ceilings" on the risks faced by merchants is at least an empirical question.

The second, and more important, response requires one to recall that the willingness to pay the prices offered or accept certain credit terms can be a function of the buyers' sense of entitlement. If this is true, and it is true that that sense of entitlement is shaped by the law's persistence in enforcing these exchanges and its general tendency to reinforce class distinctions, is there really any harm if the law shifts and the store does leave the neighborhood?[190]

To see this in a different light, suppose a series of judicial opinions finding several bargains unconscionable forced merchants to adopt new policies that meant that they could not operate profitably in the neighborhood. Suppose further that the people who shopped at the stores understood that the prices and credit terms were regarded as exploitative and unenforceable. Critics of the expansion of unconscionability would suggest, because the customers are now denied a choice that once existed, that the stores' customers would be up in arms.[191] The reasoning, in economic terms, would be that there were Pareto superior moves available to both buyers and sellers and the unconscionability rulings have now removed those opportunities. The problem with this argument is that it assumes that the preferences of the buyers with respect to their sense of compensatory justice is independent of the repeated findings that the prior exchanges were unconscionable.

Once the information is available that the merchants' departure was a result of what the public generally regarded as unfair dealings, it seems quite unlikely that the former customers would experience a sense of loss. In effect, the law would inform them that they deserved better and that their preferences with respect to the terms of exchanges would reflect that knowledge. Please note that the argument is not that the broader use of unconscionability has made people better off,[192] but rather that whether they would feel worse off when

---

189. A "normal" profit would be a return to investors sufficient to justify continued investment in the enterprise.

190. Admittedly, there will be short-run harm if consumers are denied access to necessities that are unavailable elsewhere. Presumably, prices that reflect the costs of supplying necessities would not be routinely regarded as unconscionable.

191. See Schwartz, supra note 10, at 1057–63 (providing an example of this type of thinking).

192. I do believe, however, that the long-term effects will be to improve the position of those who are worse off because they will value themselves more and will bring this valuation to their private orderings.

these opportunities are eliminated is, at least, an empirical question. If they do not, it is foolish to say the use of unconscionability has actually made them worse off.

One final note may be in order on this last point. Some may say that the sort of "engineering" that I am proposing in order to convince the buyers that they really did not want those lopsided bargains in the first place, is unacceptable interference with their autonomy. This may be true. On the other hand, it is important to recall that their initial acceptance of bargains that would violate the sense of compensatory justice of those from higher classes is no less a product of "engineering." Consequently, the autonomy exercised in accepting those bargains cannot be defended as more legitimate or as a more accurate indicator of their true preferences.

VII. Conclusion

In this Article, I have attempted to explore the mechanism through which inequality and class stratification are perpetuated. At one level, the stratification continues because individuals in their private orderings permit it to continue. Those who have less tend to agree to continue to take less. At this simplistic level, however, terms like "agree" and "consent" have only the thinnest of meanings.

Individuals who "consent" to uneven bargains are responding to a system in which they have been taught that they deserve less than others. Whether it is in the way the privileged have defined which inputs count in determining the rewards to which individuals are entitled or the tendency for individuals to assess their well-being by comparing themselves to those who are similarly deprived, those from the lower class sense that they have been treated justly even when they receive unequal treatment. They tend to blame themselves for their plight and they are easily convinced that it is a consequence of personal shortcomings instead of systemic bias.

The fact that individuals have adjusted their sense of compensatory justice so that it reflects the needs of class preservation raises two issues. First, if the terms, and to some extent the existence, of interclass contracts are contingent on class-based differences, is Pareto superiority a morally sound basis for enforcing contracts? Here the argument is made that, if lopsided exchanges only seem acceptable because individuals are accustomed to being deprived, there seems little moral basis for holding them to their contracts.

The second issue is whether contract law can be adapted as a preference-shaping and therapeutic tool in order to heal the "hidden injuries of class" that account for the apparent willingness of the disadvantaged to play their role in the cycle of exploitation. I have suggested that fuller development of substantive unconscionability with public notice of when parties have acted unconscionably may serve this end. The goal would be to educate and vindicate those who are traditionally disadvantaged so that they may adjust their sense of entitlement. Such an approach seems preferable to efforts to help those who are deprived in ways that only make them more dependent.

Chapter 27

Lawyers in Distress

Amiram Elwork
G. Andrew H. Benjamin

Until recently very little was known about the mental and emotional functioning of attorneys.[1] It now appears that a large proportion of them are either very dissatisfied with their careers or suffer from some form of mental illness or substance abuse.[2] Although this problem has been receiving increased attention in legal magazines[3] and in the popular media,[4] so far it has got scant attention from scholars in either the legal or the mental health communities. The purpose of this article is to help justify and stimulate such attention.

As we detail below, several studies have shown that lawyers experience more mental health problems than the population at large.[5] These data suggest the possibility that at least some of the stressors they experience are related to the specific characteristics of the legal system and legal process. In addition, other studies suggest that stress among lawyers is not simply a private matter; the adequacy with which the rights of litigants are represented and the integrity of the legal process itself are also negatively affected.[6]

---

1. O. Maru, Research on the Legal Profession (2nd ed., 1986).

2. American Bar Association, "At the Breaking Point: The Report of a National Conference on the Emerging Crisis in the Quality of Lawyers' Health and Lives, and Its Impact on Law Firms and Client Services" (1991) [hereinafter cited as ABA, "At the Breaking Point"]; American Bar Association, "The State of the Legal Profession—1990: Report of the Young Lawyers Division" (1991) [hereinafter cited as ABA, "The State of the Legal Profession"]; G.A.H. Benjamin, E.J. Darling & B.D. Sales, The Prevalence of Depression, Alcohol Abuse, and Cocaine Abuse Among United States Lawyers, 13 International Journal of Law and Psychiatry 233 (1990).

3. See, e.g., A. Elwork, The Workaholic Lawyer, 15(2) The Pennsylvania Lawyer 6 (1993); S. Goldberg, One in Five Lawyers Dissatisfied, 76(10) ABA Journal 36 (1990); M.M. Shultz, Study Sends Message to Law Firms, The National Law Journal, Nov. 26, 1990, at 22, col. 1.

4. See, e.g., M. Jordan, More Attorneys Making a Motion for the Pursuit of Happiness, The Washington Post, September 4, 1993, at 3A; J. Schroer, Discontented Lawyers Flee Profession, USA Today, Oct. 7, 1993, at 1B.

5. Benjamin, Darling & Sales, supra note 2; W.W. Eaton, J.C. Anthony, W. Mandel & R. Garrison, Occupations and the Prevalence of Major Depressive Disorder, 32 Journal of Occupational Medicine, 1079 (1990).

6. R.E. Mallen & J.M. Smith, Legal Malpractice, at 166–168 (3rd ed., 1989); V. Slind-Flor, Lawyer Depression Often Behind Malpractice, The Los Angeles Daily Journal, March 26, 1989, at 5; D.L. Spillis, An Overview of Lawyer Assistance Programs in the United States: Report of the ABA Commission on Impaired Attorneys (February 1991); Standing

Clearly these profession-specific aspects of the problem could benefit from an analysis by interested legal and mental health professionals. In applying their special expertise to "lawyers in distress," they can help answer such questions as: What variables within the legal environment in particular cause or contribute to lawyers' distress? To what extent does the level of stress experienced by lawyers hurt their representation of litigants and the integrity of the legal process? How can the legal system be reformed to help reduce stress among lawyers?

A Framework for the Study of Stress among Lawyers

To develop an even more concrete description of the ways in which legal and mental health researchers can contribute to this area, we thought it would be useful to conceptualize them within the context of a meta-theoretical framework. Indeed, this made it easier to recognize the full significance of the current "hodgepodge" of research findings on lawyers and to present them in an integrated fashion. In addition, it helped reveal the many issues that have yet to be studied.

In conceiving our framework, we first reviewed the growing number of occupational stress models,[7] which are themselves based on a number of well-known general stress models.[8] Although occupational stress experts often disagree about terminology and the relative importance of different factors, they do tend to agree on the major categories of variables that are relevant to this topic. We applied these categories to the specific characteristics of law practice and created the conceptual model represented in the figure on page 579.

We then used this framework to structure a review of what is currently known and what has yet to be learned about lawyers. The next section presents a review of what is known about the environmental and personality-related stressors that affect the typical lawyer. This is followed by an examination of the consequences of such stressors on lawyers, litigants and the legal system. Finally, a number of individual interventions and systemic reforms are recommended and discussed.

Two general comments should be made about the current research literature on lawyers. First, many of the studies done to date in this area can be criticized for various methodological deficiencies (e.g., excessive reliance on subjective self-reports, small samples). Although it is beyond our scope to critique each study in detail, the reader should be cautioned that many of the findings we re-

---

Committee on Lawyers' Professional Liability, The Lawyer's Desk Guide to Legal Malpractice, at 105 (1992).

7. See, e.g., J.J. Hurrell, L.R. Murphy, S.L. Sauter & C.L. Cooper, Occupational Stress: Issues and Developments in Research (1988); R.L. Kahn & P. Byosiere, Stress in Organizations, in Handbook of Industrial and Organizational Psychology 571 (Vol. 3, 2nd ed., 1992).

8. See, e.g., R.S. Lazarus & S. Folkman, Stress, Appraisal and Coping (1984); H. Selye, History and Present Status of the Stress Concept, in Handbook of Stress 7 (1982).

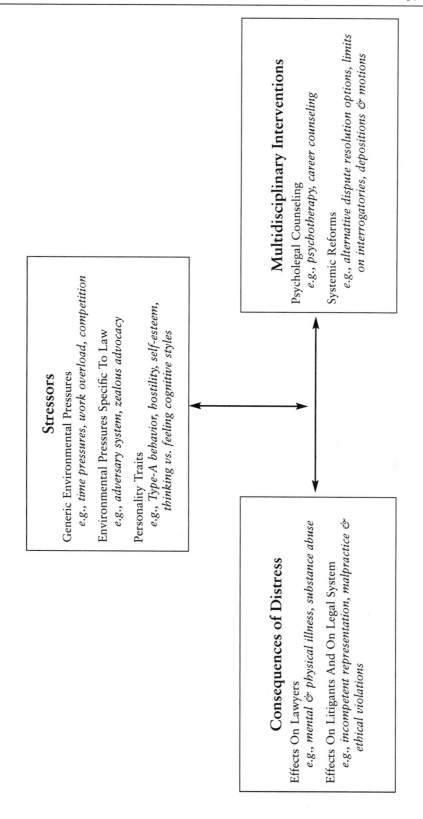

Framework for the study of stress among lawyers

Stressors

Generic Environmental Pressures
e.g., time pressures, work overload, competition

Environmental Pressures Specific To Law
e.g., adversary system, zealous advocacy

Personality Traits
*e.g., Type-A behavior, hostility, self-esteem,
thinking vs. feeling cognitive styles*

Multidisciplinary Interventions

Psycholegal Counseling
e.g., psychotherapy, career counseling

Systemic Reforms
*e.g., alternative dispute resolution options, limits
on interrogatories, depositions & motions*

Consequences of Distress

Effects On Lawyers
e.g., mental & physical illness, substance abuse

Effects On Litigants And On Legal System
*e.g., incompetent representation, malpractice &
ethical violations*

port are suggestive rather than definitive and need replication. Instead of repeating this point a number of times, we have chosen to state it just once, here.

In addition, it is important to note that some of the researchers who have
studied lawyers hitherto were primarily interested in demonstrating a psychological hypothesis rather than gaining insight into lawyers per se. That is, they
chose to study lawyers only as a way of extending the applicability of their
theories to yet another subject pool, or because it was convenient to do so. Although many of their findings were instructive to our discussion and worthy of
inclusion, we hope this article will stimulate a different sort of research program, one that focuses on lawyers and the legal system for their own sake.

Stressors

In 1990 the ABA Young Lawyers Section conducted the second wave of a
national longitudinal study about the legal profession.[9] Over 3,000 attorneys
completed a lengthy and detailed questionnaire, partly for the purpose of determining whether the disturbing results of earlier studies were reliable.[10] The
data confirmed what many lawyers had complained about for years: a significant number of them were increasingly dissatisfied with their careers. To a
great extent, lawyers linked their career dissatisfaction to increased levels of
mental and physical stress. More than 70% complained that they were required to endure intolerable daily pressures and tensions.

Generic environmental pressures

Predictably, lawyers attribute their stress to variables that are generally cited
by occupational experts as being operative in a number of professions: work
overload, time pressures, poor relationships at work, inadequate support,
competition, etc.[11]

In 1990, for example, close to 50% of the lawyers surveyed claimed that
time famine due to their workaholic schedules allowed too little time for themselves or for their families.[12] Many lawyers also attributed their increased levels of dissatisfaction to negative environmental working conditions such as interpersonal coldness, lack of respect from superiors, political intrigue and
backbiting, promotion based on subjective factors rather than competence,

---

9. ABA, "The State of the Legal Profession," supra note 2; S. Goldberg, Satisfaction,
75(4) ABA Journal 40 (1989); Shultz, supra note 3.

10. M.C. Fisk, A Measure of Satisfaction, 12(38) The National Law Journal, S2–S12
(1990); Goldberg, supra note 3; R.L. Hirsch, Are You on Target? 12(1) Barrister 17 (1985);
S.E. Jackson, J.A. Turner & A.P. Brief, Correlates of Burnout Among Public Service Lawyers,
8(4) Journal of Occupational Behavior 339 (1987); P. Reidinger, It's 46.5 Hours a Week in
Law, 72(9) ABA Journal 44 (1986); R.S. Smith, A Profile of Lawyer Lifestyles, 70(2) ABA
Journal 50 (1984).

11. See, e.g., C.L. Cooper, Job Distress: Recent Research and the Emerging Role of the
Clinical Occupational Psychologist, 39 Bulletin of the British Psychological Society 325
(1986).

12. ABA, "The State of the Legal Profession," supra note 2.

poor clerical and paralegal assistance, and inadequate opportunity for advancement. With another 200,000 lawyers joining the ranks by the end of the decade, thereby swelling the profession to 1,000,000 members by the year 2000, many lawyers also blamed part of their stress on increasing competition.

Other descriptive accounts of what it is like to be a lawyer today often paint a picture of working conditions remarkably similar to those of the "sweat shops" blue-collar workers endured several generations ago.[13] Many law firms have one central motivation that overshadows all others: profit. Such law firms push productivity to the limits of human capacity and constantly function in a crisis mode. "Workaholism" is a requirement, whereas personal fulfillment is considered a luxury. Indeed, billable-hour expectations have nearly doubled in the last 15 years, and are now commonly 2,000–2,500 hours per year.[14] Often staff feel as though they are commodities that can be used, discarded, and replaced with little difficulty.

It should be noted that a greater number of female attorneys express job dissatisfaction and an even more negative work environment than their male cohorts.[15] In addition to reporting the same negative working conditions that men do, they also report experiencing sexual harassment and job discrimination, which in turn makes it more difficult for them to get promotions and pay raises. Female lawyers also may experience greater role conflicts; they, more than men, are pressured to delay or forgo childbearing, to assume unequal family responsibilities for child and elder care, or to parent children alone.[16]

Environmental pressures specific to law

It is our contention that the generic variables listed above are only part of the causal chain that leads to stress among lawyers. We propose that factors such as time pressure, work overload, and interpersonal problems interact with other underlying causes of stress, some of which are indigenous to the practice of law.

For example, it is not enough to know that many lawyers are workaholics and to assume that this is directly responsible for their stress. As has been re-

---

13. E.A. Adams, Legal Career Exacts Steep Personal Price, New York Law Journal, Feb. 7, 1994, at 1; M.A. Altman, Life After Law (1991); D.L. Arron, Running From the Law: Why Good Lawyers Are Getting Out of the Legal Profession (1991); W. Bachman, Law v. Life (1995); B. Sells, The Soul of the Law (1994).

14. Commission on Women in the Profession (ABA), "Lawyers and Balanced Lives: A Guide to Drafting and Implementing Workplace Policies for Lawyers" (1990).

15. Adams, supra note 13; ABA, "The State of the Legal Profession," supra note 2; S.R. Anleu, Women in Law: Theory, Research and Practice, 28 Australian and New Zealand Journal of Sociology 391 (1992); R.L. Hirsch, Will Women Leave The Law? 16(1) Barrister 22 (1989); P. MacCorquodale & G. Jensen, Women in the Law: Partners or Tokens? 7 Gender and Society 582 (1993); J. Rosenberg, H. Perlstadt & W.R. Phillips, Now That We Are Here: Discrimination, Disparagement and Harassment at Work and the Experiences of Women Lawyers, 7 Gender and Society 415 (1993); A.L. Weinberg & C.K. Tittle, Congruence of Ideal and Real Job Characteristics: A Focus on Sex, Parenthood Status, and Extrinsic Characteristics, 30 Journal of Vocational Behavior 227 (1987).

16. Commission on Women in the Profession, supra note 14.

ported by one researcher, law professors work as many hours as practicing attorneys, but they do not seem to exhibit the same symptoms of burnout.[17] To fully understand the problem, we need to know what it is about the practice of law that either leads to workaholism or when combined with it becomes harmful. At this deeper level of analysis, our empirical knowledge about the stressors endemic to the legal environment is limited.

Nevertheless, we know enough to suggest several obvious hypotheses that need further exploration. For example, it is generally known that our adversarial legal system encourages suspiciousness, hostility and aggression. These may be among the underlying variables that raise performance anxiety, encourage workaholism, and damage relationships. Indeed, preliminary empirical findings confirm that lawyers tend to be more suspicious and cynical than the general population.[18] In addition, they are more authoritarian, dogmatic, and aggressive.[19] Lawyers don't see the adoption of a dog-eat-dog Machiavellian world view as cynical—just as realistic.[20]

The relative extent to which the practice of law attracts persons with such traits or encourages their expression is not clear and needs to be researched. Undoubtedly, however, the adversarial nature of our legal system is at least a contributing factor in encouraging paranoia and aggressive feelings and behaviors among all lawyers. In this way, our adversarial system is likely to have an effect on their mental health.

Another aspect of the legal environment that may distress some lawyers is the weight placed on detail-oriented rational analysis within a context where mistakes can be very costly. Even though this hypothesis has yet to be tested, we do know that lawyers have an extremely strong preference for logical "thinking" over value-laden "feeling" in making their decisions.[21]

---

17. B.S. Gould, Beyond Burnout, 10(3) Barrister 4 (1983).

18. G.A.H. Benjamin, A. Kaszniak, B.D. Sales & S.B. Shanfield, The Role of Legal Education in Producing Psychological Distress Among Law Students and Lawyers, American Bar Foundation Research Journal 225 (1986); L.D. Eron & R.S. Redmount, The Effect of Legal Education on Attitudes, 9 Journal of Legal Education 431 (1957); R. Frances, G. Alexopoulos & V. Yandow, Lawyers' Alcoholism, 4(2) Advances in Alcohol and Substance Abuse 59 (1984); M.D. Gupta, Machiavellianism of Different Occupational Groups, 18(2) Indian Journal of Psychometry and Education 61 (1987); R. Tomasic, Social Organization Amongst Australian Lawyers, 19(3) Australian and New Zealand Journal of Sociology 447 (1983).

19. P.B. Forsyth & T.J. Danisiewicz, Toward a Theory of Professionalization, 12(1) Work and Occupations 59 (1985); J.P. Heinz & E.O. Laumann, Chicago Lawyers: The Social Structure of the Bar (1984); C.J. Hosticka, We Don't Care About What Happened, We Only Care About What Is Going to Happen: Lawyer-Client Negotiations of Reality, 26(5) Social Problems 599 (1979); S. Reich, California Psychological Inventory: Profile of a Sample of First-Year Law Students, 38 Psychological Reports 871 (1976); N. Solkoff & J. Markowitz, Personality Characteristics of First-Year Medical and Law Students, 42 Journal of Medical Education 195 (1967).

20. Tomasic, supra note 18.

21. L.J. Landwehr, Lawyers as Social Progressives or Reactionaries: The Law and Order Cognitive Orientation of Lawyers, 7 Law and Psychology Review 39 (1982); P. Miller, Personality Differences and Student Survival in Law School, 19 Journal of Legal Education 460 (1967); D.C. Moss, Lawyer Personality, 77(2) ABA Journal 34 (1991); I.B. Myers & M.H. McCaulley, A Guide to the Development and Use of the Myers-Briggs Type Indicator 249

Finally, another set of variables that needs to be considered involves "role conflict and ambiguity." These variables are frequently cited as important in the general occupational stress literature,[22] and it appears that they are operative in the legal environment as well, but in unique ways.[23] For example, lawyers report feeling conflicted between their roles as officers of the court and as advocates for their clients; they find that their duty to uphold justice or do what is right in a universal sense often conflicts with their duty to zealously promote their clients' special interests. Even though a failure to fulfill the latter role is cause for malpractice, it also is the reason that the legal profession is viewed with such antipathy by our society, which itself causes stress.

Role conflicts for lawyers also arise from the fact that they often are forced to hurt people, and to do so in the context of already tragic circumstances. For example, lawyers who practice criminal law come in contact with victims of terrible violence; those in family law have to deal with adults and children whose lives are shattered by bitter divorces. In addition to the stress that frequent contact with human tragedies brings, lawyers frequently must force such persons through a process that can itself be very damaging to all concerned.

Personality traits

Career counselors[24] as well as occupational stress researchers [25] have recognized the importance of considering how individual differences interact with environmental factors. It is widely assumed that certain personal traits tend to ameliorate the negative effects of stressful work. The research literature has focused on traits such as Type A behavior, hostility, self-esteem, locus of control, optimism, and psychological hardiness.[26] Coincidentally, several researchers have used lawyers as their primary subjects. The data tend to suggest only that

(1985). See also J.A. Lau, Lawyers vs. Social Workers: Is Cerebral Hemisphericity the Culprit? 62(1) Child Welfare 21 (1983).

22. Kahn & Byosiere, supra note 7; V.J. Sutherland & C.L. Cooper, Sources of Work Stress, in Occupational Stress: Issues and Developments in Research 3 (1988).

23. ABA, "The State of the Legal Profession" supra note 2; Benjamin, Darling & Sales, supra note 2; S. Benson, Why I Quit Practicing Law, Newsweek, Nov. 4, 1991, at 10; E.H. Greenbaum, Lawyers' Relationship to Their Work: The Importance of Understanding Attorneys' Behavior, 53 Legal Education 651 (1978); D.L. Sassower, Marriages in Turmoil: The Lawyer as Doctor, 7 Journal of Psychiatry and Law 333 (1979); J.S. St. Lawrence, M.L. McGrath, M.E. Oakley & S.C. Sult, Stress Management Training for Law Students: Cognitive-Behavioral Intervention, 1(4) Behavioral Sciences and the Law 101 (1983).

24. J.L. Holland, Making Vocational Choices: A Theory of Vocational Personalities and Work Environments (2nd ed., 1983); R.L. Lowman, The Clinical Practice of Career Assessment: Interests, Abilities, and Personality (1991).

25. C.L. Cooper & R. Payne, Personality and Stress: Individual Differences in the Stress Process (1991); Kahn & Byosiere, supra note 7; S.C. Kobasa, Conceptualization and Measurement of Personality in Job Stress Research, in Occupational Stress: Issues and Developments in Research 100 (1988).

26. Kahn & Byosiere, supra note 7; Kobasa, supra note 25; J. Schaubroeck & D.C. Ganster, Associations Among Stress-Related Individual Differences, in Personality and Stress: Individual Differences in the Stress Process 34 (1991).

what is true for other professions is true for lawyers as well. Nevertheless, these findings are instructive to our discussion.

For example, Kobasa[27] found that symptoms of anxiety and stress in lawyers are inversely related to the "hardiness" of their personalities. Hardy personalities are characterized by traits such as flexibility and tolerance of change, a balanced commitment to work and to personal life, and a belief that one can control one's destiny.[28] In another study, researchers found that the level of hostility, cynicism and aggression felt by lawyers during law school was highly correlated with their mortality rate some 30 years later.[29] For a lawyer who had scored in the high range (upper 16%) on a hostility scale derived from the Minnesota Multiphasic Personality Inventory, the risk of dying was 5.5 times higher than for a lawyer who had scored in the low range (lower 16%).

Gender-related personality differences also have been found to correlate with stress. For the population at large at least, it has been shown that women tend to get emotionally sensitized by stress, whereas men tend to repress their emotions but express stress behaviorally.[30] Thus in addition to the environmentally related factors discussed previously, such gender differences may partly explain why female lawyers express more discontent than male lawyers with their careers.[31]

Are there specific personality traits, aptitudes, interests and values that are best suited for resisting the stressors of a law practice? Presently not enough is known to reliably answer this question. However, what little has been written about lawyers in this regard has focused on their decision-making styles.

For example, it is a well accepted perception that lawyers tend to make decisions by using detailed logical analysis rather than values and feelings.[32] Indeed, one researcher found that instead of using their conscience, lawyers prefer to solve ethical dilemmas by relying on authoritatively fixed rules that protect the social order.[33] Another researcher reported that attorneys who are

---

27. S.C. Kobasa, Commitment and Coping in Stress Resistance Among Lawyers, 42(4) Journal of Personality and Social Psychology 707 (1982); S.C. Kobasa, The Hardy Personality: Toward a Social Psychology of Stress and Health, in The Social Psychology of Health and Illness (1982). Also see M. Sweetman, D.C. Munz & R.J. Wheeler, Optimism, Hardiness, and an Explanatory Style as Predictors of General Well-Being Among Attorneys, 29 Social Indicators Research 153 (1993).

28. J.C. Quick, D.L. Nelson & J.D. Quick, Stress and Challenge at the Top (1990).

29. J.C. Barefoot, K.A. Dodge, B.L. Peterson, W.G. Dahlstrom & R.B. Williams, The Cook-Medley Hostility Scale: Item Content and Ability to Predict Survival, 51 Psychosomatic Medicine 46 (1989).

30. R. Jenkins, Demographic Aspects of Stress, in Personality and Stress: Individual Differences in the Stress Process, 107 (1991); R.J. Lueger & R.G. Evans, Emotional Expressivity and Sex-Role Perceptions of Repressors and Sensitizers, 45(3) Journal of Personality Assessment 288 (1981); Y. Rofe & I. Lewin, Daydreaming in a War Environment, 4(1) Journal of Mental Imagery 59 (1980); A.K. Sahar & A. Kureshi, A Study of Peptic Ulcer in Relation to Repression-Sensitization, 6(1) Journal of Personality and Clinical Studies 47 (1990).

31. ABA, "The State of the Legal Profession," supra note 2.

32. Lau, supra note 21.

33. Landwehr, supra note 21.

most likely to be satisfied with their careers tend to be practical and logical rather than altruistic and socially oriented.[34]

These data are in general concordance with the findings of several other researchers who have used the Myers-Briggs Type Indicator to classify lawyers. (The MBTI is a psychological instrument based on Carl Jung's personality theory.) A consistent finding has been that the majority of lawyers prefer to make judgments on the basis of "thinking" or impersonal logical analysis rather than of "feeling" or person-centered values.[35] A recent study done with a large national sample of lawyers showed that more than 75% of them are "thinkers."[36] One researcher found that law students who are "feelers" have a dropout rate that is four times higher than that of "thinkers."[37]

These studies suggest that "thinkers" may be better suited for the ways in which law is currently practiced. Much of law involves the processing of formalized rules, so it makes sense that those with a preference for objective logical analysis would be attracted to it. In addition, however, it may be that the "thinking" style is less sensitive to the emotional conflicts that the practice of law may evoke. "Feelers" care more about the human element and experience more empathy for others. In an adversarial context where suffering and hostility are common, "feelers" may experience more distress than "thinkers." Similarly, "feelers" may experience more emotional conflict over their duty to zealously represent their clients' interests without regard to their own set of values.

Of course, it is possible that "thinkers" simply repress their emotions and after a time may experience the negative mental health consequences of doing that. In addition, it may be that "thinkers" are less sensitive to interpersonal matters and are not as effective as "feelers" at resolving conflicts through the use of alternative methods such as mediation. That is, one of the factors that may contribute to the general adversarial nature of law is that the majority of lawyers are "thinkers" and as such are generally less sensitive to interpersonal matters.

Obviously much more research needs to be done to find a fuller answer to the question we posed earlier. In addition to searching for individual traits that are well suited for the general practice of law, it may be fruitful also to take into account the various specialties within law. For example, environmental law may require different traits than family law.

Consequences of Distress

The possible ramifications of high stress among lawyers are very predictable. The available data suggest that it places lawyers at high risk for men-

---

34. G.W. LaRussa, Portia's Decision: Women's Motives for Studying Law and Their Later Career Satisfaction as Attorneys, 1 Psychology of Women Quarterly 350 (1977). Also see R. Granfield & T. Koenig, The Fate of Elite Idealism: Accommodation and Ideological Work at Harvard Law School, 39 Social Problems 315 (1992).

35. Myers & McCaulley, supra note 21, at 248–249.

36. L. Richard, The Lawyer Types, 79(7) ABA Journal 74 (1993).

37. Miller, supra note 21.

tal and physical illness and that it results in a higher than expected rate of professional incompetence. The latter outcome damages the rights of litigants and the integrity of the legal system.

Effects on lawyers

Recent surveys in the states of Washington and Arizona have demonstrated that one-third of all lawyers appear to be suffering from either depression or substance abuse.[38] In the Washington sample, for example, it was found that 14% reported symptoms of clinical depression, 13% reported symptoms of problem drinking, and 5% suffered from both disorders. These statistics were twice the national prevalence rates for these two disorders.[39] Another study confirmed that compared with 104 other occupational groups in the United States, lawyers were the most likely to suffer from depression and 3.6 times more likely than average.[40]

The magnitude of their results compelled these researchers to conclude that lawyers' profession-specific occupational stresses are what causes such high levels of mental illness and substance abuse. Occupational stress among lawyers also has been proposed as a major contributing factor to physical illnesses such as coronary heart disease.[41]

It should be noted that law students report negative experiences similar to those of practicing attorneys. Even though people who select the law as a profession are as healthy as the general population, it has been found that they become comparatively less healthy soon after entering law school.[42] This suggests that the acculturation process to which nascent lawyers are exposed helps establish dysfunctional patterns of behavior that eventually lead to greater career dissatisfaction and negative health consequences.[43]

---

38. Benjamin, Darling & Sales, supra note 2; Benjamin, Kaszniak, Sales & Shanfield, supra note 18.

39. Benjamin, Darling & Sales, supra note 2.

40. Eaton, Anthony, Mandel & Garrison, supra note 5.

41. Barefoot, Dodge, Peterson, Dahlstrom & Williams, supra note 29; E.H. Friedman & H.K. Hellerstein, Occupational Stress, Law School Hierarchy and Coronary Artery Disease in Cleveland Attorneys, 36 Psychosomatic Medicine 72 (1968); J.M. Rhoads, Overwork, 24 Journal of the American Medical Association 2615 (1977); H.I. Russek & L. Russek, Is Emotional Stress an Etiological Factor in Coronary Heart Disease? 17 Psychosomatics 63 (1976).

42. Benjamin, Kaszniak, Sales & Shanfield, supra note 18; M. Hedegard, The Impact of Legal Education: An In-Depth Examination of Career-Relevant Interests, Attitudes, and Personality Traits Among First-Year Law Students, 1979 American Bar Foundation Research Journal 791 (1979).

43. See, e.g., P. Beck & D. Burns, Anxiety and Depression in Law Students: Cognitive Intervention, 30 Journal of Legal Education 270 (1979); Benjamin, Kaszniak, Sales & Shanfield, supra note 18; B. Diamond, Psychological Problems of Law Students, in Looking at Law School (1977); L. Dubin, The Role of Law School in Balancing a Lawyer's Personal and Professional Life, 10(1) The Journal of Psychiatry & Law 57 (1982); F.J. Gutierrez, Counseling Law Students, 64(2) Journal of Counseling and Development 130 (1985); M. Heins, S.N. Fahey & R. Henderson, Law Students and Medical Students: A Comparison of Perceived Stress, 33 Journal of Legal Education 511 (1983); M. Heins, S.N. Fahey & L.I. Lei-

Effects on litigants and on legal system

Logic suggests that occupational distress among lawyers has a deleterious effect on their ability to function effectively (e.g., meet deadlines, detect conflict). Although such a causal link needs much more comprehensive empirical verification than it has received so far, what we do know to date strongly confirms this hypothesis. The implications for clients of distressed lawyers and for the entire legal process are alarming.

Preliminary evidence within several jurisdictions suggests that mental illness and substance abuse are leading causes of malpractice suits and ethical disciplinary actions against attorneys. For example, it has been estimated that 60% of the recently taken disciplinary actions against lawyers in California and in Oregon involved chemical dependency or stress-related mental illness.[44] Since many impaired attorneys are either not identified by their clients or colleagues or formally charged with any infractions, we can assume that the actual magnitude of the problem is larger than measured, and that the majority of inadequately represented clients never have their grievances acknowledged or redressed.

The client group that is most likely to be negatively affected by distressed lawyers is the poor. For example, it has been estimated that public defenders represent 65% of all criminal defendants in this country;[45] unfortunately, public defenders are also among the most overworked and "burned out" groups of lawyers.[46] One legal scholar documented the problem with the illustration of a case called Cooper v. Fitzharris:[47]

> The district court found, after an evidentiary hearing, that counsel's failures were the "product of an overwhelmingly heavy caseload...." Counsel testified that she had conducted no legal research, and that she collapsed in court a few months after the defendant's conviction, her health seriously threatened by carrying a caseload of approximately 2,000 different cases per year. She resigned from the Public Defender Office after concluding that she was "actually doing the defendants more harm by just presenting a live body than if they had no representation at all."[48]

---

den, Perceived Stress in Medical, Law, and Graduate Students, 59(3) Journal of Medical Education 169 (1984); R. Kellner, R.J. Wiggins & D. Pathak, Distress in Medical and Law Students, 27(3) Comprehensive Psychiatry 220 (1986); Report of the AALS Special Committee on Problems of Substance Abuse in the Law Schools, 44 Journal of Legal Education 35 (1994); L. Silver, Anxiety and the First Semester of Law School, 4 Wisconsin Law Review 1201 (1968); St. Lawrence, McGrath, Oakley & Sult, supra note 23.

44. Spillis, supra note 6, at 1–2.

45. R. Klein, The Relationship of the Court and Defense Counsel: The Impact on Competent Representation and Proposals for Reform, 29(3) Boston College Law Review 531 (1988).

46. Jackson, Turner & Brief, supra note 10.

47. Cooper v. Fitzharris, 551 F.2d 1162 (9th Cir. 1977), aff'd on reh'g, 586 F.2d 1325 (9th Cir. 1978) (en banc), cert. denied, 440 U.S. 974 (1979).

48. Klein, supra note 45, at 534.

Multidisciplinary Interventions

There is a variety of possible solutions to the problems we have discussed. One approach is to develop "psycholegal" counseling methods specifically designed to treat and prevent mental illness in individual lawyers. Another approach is to intervene at the systemic-organizational level and reduce the environmental factors that cause distress. Both types of interventions can be developed and implemented most effectively through multidisciplinary efforts that involve legal and mental health professionals.

Psycholegal counseling

The idea that lawyers in distress could benefit from psychological interventions designed specifically for them is not new. Several models for the implementation of this idea already exist. Although the efficacy of such models has not been assessed, they do provide the groundwork for an excellent beginning.

For example, several mental health professionals have reported on their efforts to design counseling programs for law students.[49] In addition, a number of jurisdictions have established lawyers' assistance programs (LAPs). Although most LAPs rely solely on peer counselors and offer limited psychological services, some jurisdictions provide comprehensive services that combine the efforts of professional mental health staff with those of trained peer counselors.[50]

Comprehensive LAPs deliver educational and prevention programs, formalized procedures for identifying distressed lawyers, evaluations with measures that depend on lawyer norms, and various types of therapeutic interventions such as peer counseling and individual and group psychotherapy.[51] Services are provided in the context of confidentiality rules that encourage attorneys to seek help. One jurisdiction has reported that in just four years its LAP has caused malpractice claims against lawyers to drop from 10% to 7% and malpractice premiums to decrease by 28%.[52]

Most therapeutic programs serving law students or lawyers focus on general stress- and time-management techniques or on cognitive-behavioral interventions designed to improve problem-solving competencies. Primarily these programs tackle the "generic" stressors (e.g., work overload) discussed earlier, which impinge on lawyers as well as on many other professionals.

To fully realize the potential of what Elwork[53] has called "psycholegal treatment," however, these services also need to deal with the "nongeneric" stress factors we discussed in a preceding section: the specific environmental stressors

---

49. Beck & Burns, supra note 43; Gutierrez, supra note 43; St. Lawrence, McGrath, Oakley & Sult, supra note 23.

50. G.A.H. Benjamin, B.D. Sales & E. Darling, Comprehensive Lawyer Assistance Programs: Justification and Model, 16 Law and Psychology Review 113 (1992).

51. Benjamin, Sales & Darling, supra note 50.

52. Oregon State Bar Professional Liability Fund, Annual Report (Unpublished report, Oregon Bar Assoc., 1990).

53. A. Elwork, Psycholegal Treatment and Intervention: The Next Challenge, 16(2) Law and Human Behavior 175 (1992); A. Elwork, Stress Management for Lawyers (1995).

that are indigenous to the practice of law, and the personal traits commonly found in lawyers that heighten the effects of environmental stressors. For example, techniques can be developed to help lawyers learn effective ways of resisting the stressors generated by the adversarial nature of the legal system and the uniquely conflicting roles lawyers are expected to play in court.

A fully developed psycholegal treatment model could also focus on teaching mental health professionals how to deal with the typical problems encountered in treating lawyers.[54] For example, it has been observed that lawyers are experts at defending themselves through the use of denial and rationalization, that they are not accustomed to dependency roles, and that they sometimes intimidate their therapists by their "cross-examining" methods.[55] In addition, it appears that the strong cognitive abilities of lawyers combined with the weak development of their affective abilities may interfere with creating strong therapeutic alliances with counselors. Lawyers may lend greater credibility to and relate better with therapists who are especially knowledgeable about the practice of law.

Career assessment and counseling for lawyers is another area of intervention that holds much promise.[56] Already a small number of practitioners have used psychological methods and tests to help distressed law students and attorneys consider alternative specialties within law as well as career paths outside of law.[57] In addition, psychological methods have been used to develop ways of evaluating lawyers' job satisfaction and performance.[58] To date, however, these efforts have been very elementary. Given lawyers' great need for career-related guidance, much more work needs to be done in this area. Again, a psycholegal perspective would be more likely to result in career assessment techniques that meet the unique as well as the generic needs of lawyers.

Systemic reforms

Up to now, efforts to reduce stress among lawyers have focused on what individuals can do. They have emphasized helping lawyers increase their resistance to the environmental stressors that exist, rather than reducing the presence of the stressors themselves. To the extent that these stressors are caused

54. Benjamin, Sales & Darling, supra note 50; Frances, Alexopoulos & Yandow, supra note 18.

55. Frances, Alexopoulos & Yandow, supra note 18.

56. P.F. Buller & C.L. Beck-Dudley, Performance, Policies and Personnel, ABA Journal 94 (1990); T.F. Gibbons, Law Practice in 2001, 76(1) ABA Journal 69 (1990).

57. A. Abbey, C. Dunkel-Schetter & P. Brickman, Handling the Stress of Looking for a Job in Law School: The Relationship Between Intrinsic Motivation, Internal Attributions, Relations with Others, and Happiness, 4(3) Basic and Applied Social Psychology 263 (1983); S.J. Bell & L.R. Richard, Anatomy of a Lawyer: Personality and Long-Term Career Satisfaction, in Full Disclosure: Do You Really Want to Be a Lawyer? 139 (1989); M. Byers, D. Samuelson & G. Williamson, Lawyers in Transition: Planning a Life in the Law (1988); Gutierrez, supra note 43.

58. L.M. Hough, Development and Evaluation of the "Accomplishment Record" Method of Selecting and Promoting Professionals, 69(1) Journal of Applied Psychology 135 (1984); E. Malinowska-Tabaka, Complex Measures of Job Satisfaction/Dissatisfaction Among Professionals, 19(4) Social Indicators Research 451 (1987).

by laws, legal processes and legal institutions, another viable way of reducing stress among lawyers is to reform the system.

One way to approach this task is to adopt a concept recently introduced by Wexler[59] called "therapeutic jurisprudence." The idea is that more multidisciplinary attention needs to be focused on how laws themselves cause psychological dysfunction and on how they can be improved. A similar tactic can be applied to evaluate and reform laws and policies that affect the behaviors of attorneys in ways that are detrimental to their health.

For example, a number of jurisdictions are experimenting with what have been called "alternative dispute resolution" methods, such as divorce mediation. Although these programs were not conceived with this end in mind, their existence offers researchers an opportunity to ascertain their effect on lawyers' health. If, as discussed earlier, much of the stress lawyers experience is caused by the adversarial nature of litigation, then alternative dispute resolution options should have a positive benefit in this regard.

As another example, jurisdictions vary in the limits their rules place on the number of interrogatories, scope of depositions, and number of motions and pleadings they allow in a single case. Again, this offers researchers the opportunity to explore whether variations in rules of procedure have an effect on the level of combativeness that exists among attorneys. If our previous hypotheses are correct, streamlined procedures should curtail the worst type of aggression that the adversary system tends to encourage, thereby decreasing the stress that many lawyers experience.

The various ways in which courts schedule their cases also need to be empirically explored. A common complaint among lawyers is that certain current scheduling policies do not allow for enough predictability or advance notice, thus placing attorneys under much time pressure and psychological distress. In some courts lawyers actually find themselves trying multiple cases at the same time.[60]

Ethical guidelines regulating the practice of law also may need to be examined for their potential effects on the health and welfare of attorneys. For example, as was discussed earlier, a lawyer's multiple duties to represent clients, to act with professionalism and to serve as an officer of the court often result in difficult conflicts that lead to distress. Programs such as the American Inns of Court have provided a social forum in which lawyers can experiment with difficult ethical dilemmas while feeling supported by colleagues from the bench and practice.[61] Researchers could add an empirical dimension to this experimentation by actually measuring the effects of alternative ethical guidelines on lawyers' behaviors.

---

59. D.B. Wexler, Therapeutic Jurisprudence: The Law as a Therapeutic Agent (1990); Wexler, Therapeutic Jurisprudence and Changing Conceptions of Legal Scholarship, 11 Behavioral Sciences and the Law 17 (1993).

60. J. Capeci, Double Trials Tax Lawyers' Schedules: Precedent in Brooklyn? The National Law Journal, Oct. 7, 1985, at 3.

61. S. Christensen, The Concept and Organization of an American Inn of Court: Putting a Little More English on American Legal Education, Federal Rules Decisions, June 1982, at 807; J. Jenkins, The Quiet Crusade, Federal Bar News & Journal, June 1992, at 318.

Another set of policies in need of examination is those that tend to discourage lawyers from seeking psychological treatment. For example, some of the Lawyers' Assistance Programs around the country have failed to establish confidentiality protections for participants. Absent such protection, few lawyers seek services from these programs, chilled by the concern that their problems may be disclosed to disciplinary authorities. Similarly, many law students are reluctant to seek psychological treatment for fear that they will have to reveal such information upon applying for admission to their bar (e.g., Florida).

Another set of policies that needs to be examined is those that regulate the education of lawyers. A number of authors have concluded that the high levels of stress attorneys experience begin in law school.[62] In teaching students to "think like a lawyer," law schools often also teach them how to be impersonal in their professional dealings. This has its advantages, but it can have long-term negative mental health consequences as well. Similarly, too much of the "Socratic method" may increase hostility and damage students' personal development.

Reformers recommend that law school curricula and policies place greater importance on the human aspects of practicing law.[63] This could include course offerings that help law students develop better human relations and counseling skills, as well as negotiation and mediation capabilities. In addition, it has been suggested that law schools encourage more student-faculty interactions and teach law students how to develop greater balance between their professional and personal lives. For similar reasons, bar associations should consider approving continuing legal education credits for courses that focus on increasing interpersonal and psychological skills; current policies restrict CE courses to very traditional legal topics.

Finally, employment policies within law firms also have been criticized in the last few years and are thought to contribute to lawyers' distress. A number of national as well as local bar organizations have held conferences and issued reports recommending a variety of modifications.[64] These have included the endorsement of alternative work schedules, a reduction in the billable-hours requirements, improved communications with associates and clients, greater training opportunities, and more mentoring experiences.

---

62. See, e.g., Dubin, supra note 43; Gutierrez, supra note 43; Lawrence, McGrath, Oakley & Sult, supra note 23; A.S. Watson, Lawyers and Professionalism: A Further Psychiatric Perspective on Legal Education, 8 Journal of Law Reform 248 (1975).

63. Benjamin, Kaszniak, Sales & Shanfield, supra note 18; Dubin, supra note 43; Gutierrez, supra note 43; F.K. Zemans & V.G. Rosenblum, The Making of a Public Profession (1981).

64. ABA, "At the Breaking Point," supra note 2; Commission on Women in the Profession, supra note 14; P.C. Heintz & C.A. Ingram, Slaying the Dragon: A Plan to Combat Lawyer Dissatisfaction, 54(2) The Shingle: Philadelphia Bar Association Quarterly Magazine 20 (1991).

Conclusion

A systematic effort by the law-mental health community to understand, evaluate and improve the welfare of attorneys can have a significant influence on their lives as well as on the lives of those who will receive more effective legal representation. The model introduced in this article can be applied to all the other professionals who play a role in our legal system, including judges, legislators, regulators, and police officers. It emphasizes the usefulness of reversing the usual direction through which we analyze cause-and-effect relationships within our legal system. That is, the norm is to examine how various actors affect the legal system. Perhaps it is time we began to explore how the legal system affects its various actors, and how that reflexively influences the legal process.

II.
Commentary
about
Therapeutic
Jurisprudence

Chapter 28

Therapeutic Jurisprudence: From Idea to Application

David Finkelman
Thomas Grisso

[This selection is the introduction to a Symposium issue of the New England Journal on Criminal and Civil Commitment, volume 20, #2, 1994, entitled "Therapeutic Jurisprudence: Bridging the Gap from Theory to Practice."]

I. Introduction

Our purpose in this Article is to provide a foundation and context for the articles that follow in this special collection of works on therapeutic jurisprudence. The motivation for producing these articles arose from a professional conference in June, 1992, organized by the Law and Psychiatry Program at the University of Massachusetts Medical Center, and sponsored by the Division of Forensic Mental Health of the Massachusetts Department of Mental Health in conjunction with Bridgewater State Hospital.

At that conference, several forensic mental health professionals[1] presented their reflections on the value of the concept of therapeutic jurisprudence in understanding the therapeutic and anti-therapeutic consequences of laws and legal procedures. Their focus was on the consequences that they witnessed in their day-to-day work with mentally ill persons in the civil, criminal, and juvenile sectors of Massachusetts' mental health and court systems.

Our Article focuses on two contexts within which to consider the articles appearing in this Symposium. First, we reflect on the role of therapeutic jurisprudence as a concept in the historical context of other movements in the study of jurisprudence, especially as a derivative of the legal realism movement. Second, we explain the potential value of including "front-line" forensic mental health professionals in the discourse about therapeutic jurisprudence during these formative years of the concept.

* * *

---

1. A forensic mental health professional is a psychologist, psychiatrist, or social worker who provides specialized mental health services in legal settings (e.g., courts or correctional institutions).

II. Some Historical Background Regarding Therapeutic Jurisprudence

Therapeutic jurisprudence studies "the extent to which substantive rules, legal procedures, and the roles of lawyers and judges produce therapeutic or antitherapeutic consequences."[2] In so doing, it draws on relevant psychological and psychiatric research and theory. David Wexler and Bruce Winick argue that therapeutic or antitherapeutic consequences are only one factor that should be taken into account in evaluating legal rules and procedures, and in deciding whether and how a rule or procedure should be changed.[3]

Therapeutic jurisprudence has been remarkably influential in its short history. It was first introduced by Wexler in a paper written in the summer of 1987 for a workshop sponsored by the National Institute of Mental Health.[4] By 1991, two edited volumes on the topic had appeared.[5] Since then, it has influenced the thinking of an increasing number of scholars in both the legal and mental health fields.[6]

A. Comparison to Other Movements

Therapeutic jurisprudence can be seen as one of a number of heirs to the legal realism movement that flourished earlier in this century. The legal realist view can be contrasted with the concept of law, dominant throughout much of the 19th century, that has variously been termed "formalistic," "logical," "conceptual," and, perhaps most descriptively, "mechanical," as in Pound's[7] famous phrase, "mechanical jurisprudence."[8] From this latter point of view, the judicial task was simply to locate the pertinent law (in the Constitution, statutes, or common law) and apply it in a straightforward way to the task at hand. This meant that the *consequences* of a legal decision were irrelevant; all that was important was that the law was being applied correctly. Also central to this conception of legal activity was the view of law as an *autonomous* dis-

---

2. David B. Wexler & Bruce J. Winick, Therapeutic Jurisprudence as a New Approach to Mental Health Law Policy Analysis and Research, 45 U. Miami L. Rev. 979, 981 (1991).

3. Id.

4. David B. Wexler, Putting Mental Health Into Mental Health Law: Therapeutic Jurisprudence, 16 Law & Hum. Behav. 27, 27–28 (1992).

5. See generally Therapeutic Jurisprudence: The Law as a Therapeutic Agent (David B. Wexler ed., 1990); Essays in Therapeutic Jurisprudence 9 (David B. Wexler & Bruce J. Winick eds., 1991).

6. See, e.g., Michael L. Perlin, Tarasoff and the Dilemma of the Dangerous Patient: New Directions for the 1990's, 16 Law & Psychol. Rev. 29, 29–63 (1992); Norman G. Poythress & Stanley L. Brodsky, In the Wake of a Negligent Release Lawsuit: An Investigation of Professional Consequences and Institutional Impact on a State Psychiatric Hospital, 16 Law & Hum. Behav. 155 (1992); Robert F. Schopp, Therapeutic Jurisprudence and Conflicts Among Values in Mental Health Law Scholarship, 11 Behavioral Sci. & L. 31 (1993).

7. Roscoe Pound, Mechanical Jurisprudence, 8 Colum. L. Rev. 605 (1908).

8. See Laura Kalman, Legal Realism at Yale: 1927–1960 (1986); John Monahan & Laurens Walker, Empirical Questions Without Empirical Answers, 1991 Wis. L. Rev. 569; Joseph. W. Singer, Legal Realism Now, 76 Cal. L. Rev. 9 (1988).

cipline; the law was seen as self-contained, relying on no external sources to guide it. Concretely, this meant that decisions should be based on what Thomas Hafemeister and Gary Melton termed "primary sources," that is, prior cases, statutes, and regulations.[9]

One of the best-known early critics of this view was Oliver Wendell Holmes. In one of his most frequently-cited passages, from the opening of *The Common Law*, Holmes challenged the "mechanical" view:

> The life of the law has not been logic: it has been experience. The felt necessities of the time, the prevalent moral and political theories, intuitions of public policy, avowed or unconscious, even the prejudices which judges share with their fellow-men, have had a good deal more to do than the syllogism in determining the rules by which men should be governed.[10]

Holmes' criticisms were amplified and extended by Roscoe Pound, who developed a point of view called "sociological jurisprudence."[11] Some of the themes of therapeutic jurisprudence are clearly foreshadowed in Pound's writings. Pound wanted the law "to take more account, and more intelligent account, of the social facts upon which law must proceed and to which it is to be applied."[12] More specifically, he called for "study of the actual social effects of legal institutions and legal doctrines."[13] If we think of "therapeutic effects" as one form of "social effects," the relevance of Pound's views for therapeutic jurisprudence becomes clear.

Pound's views were in turn extended by the legal realists. This label was applied to a large and diverse group of people, but White suggests that Karl Llewellyn and Jerome Frank were the primary exponents of realism.[14] Frank's approach might seem at first glance to bear a close relation to therapeutic jurisprudence because of the psychological bent of his writings. After his own psychoanalysis in 1927, Frank viewed the legal profession from a distinctly psychoanalytic orientation. He called for "training in the best available methods of psychology,"[15] but by this he seems to have meant simply that judges should be psychoanalyzed. This is far removed from the main concerns of therapeutic jurisprudence.

A closer relationship between legal realism and therapeutic jurisprudence can be seen in the empirical orientation of some of the realists. Although most of their empirical investigations did not involve psychology directly, focusing instead on such matters as court administration, bankruptcy, the banking sys-

---

9. Thomas L. Hafemeister & Gary B. Melton, The Impact of Social Science Research on the Judiciary, in Reforming the Law: Impact of Child Development Research 27 (Gary B. Melton ed., 1987).

10. Oliver W. Holmes, The Common Law 5 (Harvard University Press 1963) (1881).

11. See Roscoe Pound, The Scope and Purpose of Sociological Jurisprudence, 25 Harv. L. Rev. 489 (1912).

12. Id. at 512–13.

13. Id. at 513.

14. G. Edward White, From Sociological Jurisprudence to Realism: Jurisprudence and Social Change in Early Twentieth Century America, 58 Va. L. Rev. 999, 1017 (1972).

15. Jerome Frank, Courts on Trial 247 (1949).

tem, and compliance with traffic rules,[16] some of them did involve psychology; Robert Hutchins and Donald Slesinger,[17] for example, attempted to apply research in the psychology of memory to evidence law.

The realists also grappled, as do the advocates of therapeutic jurisprudence, with the relationship of the descriptive and the normative in their work, and came to similar conclusions. According to Karl Llewellyn, the realists advocated

> the *temporary* divorce of Is and Ought for purposes of study.... The argument is simply that no judgment of what Ought to be done in the future with respect to any part of law can be intelligently made without knowing objectively, as far as possible, what that part of law is now doing.[18]

David Wexler and Robert Schopp make a similar point: "As a research program, therapeutic jurisprudence does not resolve conflicts among competing values. Rather, it seeks information needed to promote certain goals and to inform the normative dispute regarding the legitimacy or priority of competing values."[19]

Legal realism as an identifiable movement had lost its force and vitality by the 1950s,[20] but many of its ideas have been incorporated into the fabric of contemporary legal thinking. It has become a cliche to say, "we are all realists now."[21] Most contemporary schools of legal thought have appropriated realist insights; these include the law and society movement,[22] law and economics,[23] critical legal studies,[24] feminist legal theory[25] and social science in law.[26] Of these, it is clearly the latter of the five that is closest in spirit to therapeutic jurisprudence. Indeed, as Wexler and Schopp point out, "therapeutic jurisprudence can be understood as a special application of the more general field of 'social science in law.'"[27] But there are ties to other movements as well; a par-

---

16. John Monahan & Laurens Walker, Social Science in Law: Cases and Materials 21 (2d ed. 1990).

17. Robert M. Hutchins & Donald Slesinger, Some Observations on the Law of Evidence—Memory, 41 Harv. L. Rev. 860 (1928).

18. Karl N. Llewellyn, Some Realism About Realism—Responding to Dean Pound, 44 Harv. L. Rev. 1222, 1236–37 (1931).

19. David B. Wexler & Robert F. Schopp, Therapeutic Jurisprudence: A New Approach to Mental Health Law, in Handbook Psychol. & L. 361, 373 (Dorothy S. Kagehiro & William S. Laufer eds., 1992).

20. Monahan & Walker, supra note 16, at 27.

21. Id.

22. Laurence M. Friedman, The Law and Society Movement, 38 Stan. L. Rev. 763 (1986).

23. Richard A. Posner, Economic Analysis of Law 16 (3d ed. 1986).

24. Roberto M. Unger, The Critical Legal Studies Movement 1 (1986).

25. Catherine A. McKinnon, Feminism Unmodified: Discourse on Life and Law 26–27 (1987).

26. Monahan & Walker, supra note 16, at 29.

27. Wexler & Schopp, supra note 19, at 373.

allel can be drawn between the therapeutic jurisprudence focus on therapeutic impact, and the law and economics advocates' emphasis on efficiency.

Although there are similarities between therapeutic jurisprudence and other movements in legal scholarship, both past and present, therapeutic jurisprudence makes a unique contribution. It has focused primarily on mental health law and, although this area certainly has received a great deal of scholarly attention, little of it is of the sort suggested by therapeutic jurisprudence advocates. Indeed, the use of empirical evidence and psychological theory in the manner suggested by therapeutic jurisprudence supporters has been evident to a much greater extent in other areas in which psychology and the law interact, including child development research,[28] eyewitness testimony,[29] and the psychology of the jury.[30] By applying psychological research and theory to mental health law in particular, therapeutic jurisprudence promises to reinvigorate the area and, if successful, to produce better mental health law, and better treatment for those who find themselves involved in the mental health law system.[31]

B. Some Difficulties with the Therapeutic Jurisprudence Approach

Therapeutic jurisprudence is sometimes criticized for being but a short step (both lexically and conceptually) from the "therapeutic state."[32] It is argued that application of the concept could easily lead us back to the days in which the power of mental health professionals often went largely unchecked. This is a danger of which Wexler and Winick are well aware, and they have taken pains to emphasize that therapeutic considerations are not the only ones that must be taken into account; indeed, in many circumstances, other considerations should override therapeutic ones.[33] It would indeed be ironic if therapeutic jurisprudence were used to defend the concept of the therapeutic state, because some of Wexler's best known early works were highly critical of the substantial legal power wielded by mental health professionals.[34]

Another difficulty concerns the role of empirical investigation. Therapeutic jurisprudence has both an empirical and nonempirical dimension,[35] but the

---

28. Gerald Koocher, Children Under Law: The Paradigm of Informed Consent, in Reforming the Law: Impact of Child Development Research 3 (Gary B. Melton ed., 1987).

29. Gary L. Wells & Elizabeth F. Loftus, Eyewitness Research: Then and Now, in Eyewitness Testimony: Psychological Perspectives 1 (Gary Wells & Elizabeth Loftus eds., 1984).

30. Valerie P. Hans & Neil Vidmar, Judging the Jury 79 (1986); Reid Hastie et al., Inside the Jury 15 (1983).

31. More recently, therapeutic jurisprudence has expanded its purview. As Wexler points out in his contribution to this series, the therapeutic jurisprudence approach has been applied to topics as diverse as tort law, criminal law and procedure, and family law. David B. Wexler, An Orientation to Therapeutic Jurisprudence, 20 New Eng. J. on Crim. & Civ. Confinement 17 (1994).

32. Nicholas N. Kittrie, The Right to Be Different: Deviance and Enforced Therapy 11 (1971).

33. Wexler & Winick, supra note 2, at 982.

34. See, e.g., David B. Wexler, Therapeutic Justice, 57 Minn. L. Rev. 289, 291 (1972).

35. Wexler & Winick, supra note 2, at 984.

empirical dimension is critical: determining whether a legal rule or procedure is therapeutic requires some degree of empirical investigation.[36]

The fate of empirical research among the legal realists has been that many of those who were initially enthusiastic about the promise and potential of such research (including, for example, Thurman Arnold and Robert Hutchins) later became skeptical of the enterprise.[37] Although some of the reasons for the decline in their enthusiasm may be less relevant now (for example, many of the methodological and statistical techniques in use at the time appear unsophisticated by contemporary standards), many of the fundamental problems remain. It is often extremely difficult to design research that represents testable questions and provides meaningful answers, especially with the additional constraint of ethical considerations that must be addressed in any study involving human beings. In short, there can be empirical questions without empirical answers,[38] as Wexler himself recognizes.[39]

Furthermore, ambiguity resides in the word "therapeutic." It may not be easy to determine whether changing a legal rule or procedure had a therapeutic effect. Consider some of the difficulties in conducting psychotherapy outcome research. In attempting to assess the efficacy of psychotherapy, one might query the client, the therapist, or the client's family or friends; employ one or more psychological tests; or observe some aspect of the client's behavior, among other possibilities.[40] The difficulty is that the information garnered from these different sources may be discrepant. Consider a related problem in family therapy: it is well-known that an improvement in one family member may be accompanied by deterioration in one or more family members.[41] Research in therapeutic jurisprudence then may face some of the same difficulties.

A final problem is one that this special section hopes to alleviate. It is that therapeutic jurisprudence has, to this point, been primarily the province of academic scholars. We believe that if therapeutic jurisprudence is to prove beneficial to mental health law, it will have to be heuristically and practically useful to professionals in mental health and forensic mental health systems—professionals who, by training, are likely to be most concerned with the therapeutic consequences of law. In the next section, we discuss why we believe that psychiatrists, psychologists, and other mental health professionals in these systems are in a unique position to use the therapeutic jurisprudence perspective in their work to further the objectives of that perspective. In addition,

---

36. Most of the work that has been conducted under the therapeutic jurisprudence rubric thus far has not been empirical. It could rather be characterized as informed speculation based on psychological theory or clinical experience as to whether some aspect of the legal system is therapeutic and how changing the law might shift the system in a more therapeutic direction. But our main point is simply a reminder of the difficulties that attend empirical research on complex legal and social issues.

37. Kalman, supra note 8, at 34–35.

38. Monahan & Walker, supra note 18, at 16.

39. David B. Wexler, Therapeutic Jurisprudence and Changing Conceptions of Legal Scholarship, 11 Behavioral Sci. & L. 17, 29 (1993).

40. Robert C. Carson & James N. Butcher, Abnormal Psychology and Modern Life 662 (9th ed. 1992).

41. Jay Haley, Leaving Home: The Therapy of Disturbed Young People 7 (1980).

we believe that they have a special role to play in contributing to the maturation of the concept itself. The next section explains our reasoning, as well as the process by which the present collection of articles arose.

III. Viewing Massachusetts through the Therapeutic Jurisprudence Lens

A. Therapeutic Jurisprudence from the Bottom Up

The concept called therapeutic jurisprudence arose in the rarefied atmosphere of legal scholarship and theory. It appears to have originated as an idea: What would mental health law be like if it shifted gears from the recent historical emphasis on rights and legal due process for mentally ill persons? What if one put "mental health" back into "mental health law?" If theoretical discourse about therapeutic jurisprudence eventually has an impact on the welfare of mentally ill persons, this benefit will have largely developed "from the top down": from theory to practice and procedure.

There are certain advantages of a "top-down" approach to developing a new perspective. Not the least of these is that the scholars who introduce the perspective are sufficiently articulate to focus attention on it and to frame it in such a way that it can become the subject of debate and refinement.

Yet there can be disadvantages to the top-down development of an idea when it remains exclusively or too long in the hands of scholars and theorists. Most of these disadvantages are related to the dangers of isolation of scholarly discourse from the "real world," from everyday events of the admitting room in the forensic hospital, of the examination room in the court clinic, of the suicide-proof holding cell, and of the life-in-limbo of the patient who is hospitalized after a finding of not guilty by reason of insanity.

First, theoretical discourse needs information from the real world of forensic mental health in order to fuel its debate. No idea can live forever on abstractions. It must have real-world observations that will assist in generating and expanding the original idea. Direct observation can provide concrete examples that improve one's communication of the abstract principle or the theoretical notion.

Second, therapeutic jurisprudence discourse needs to be challenged by observations that come from sources other than the scholars who generated the idea. Theoretical arguments are hard to test when the arguments use practical examples that are drawn only from the minds of the debaters. It is too easy to manufacture situations that fit one's purpose. Moreover, scholars who generate theory may do so from an academic base that does not always reflect reality. Theoretical arguments eventually should have to face real-world events, in all of their unruliness and unpredictability. Thus, observations in forensic and mental health practice can challenge ideas that otherwise might enjoy academic immunity at the expense of our enlightenment.

Third, a theory or scholarly paradigm increases in importance if it is found that it has heuristic value in the hands of those whose needs are different from those who originated the idea. When given to forensic mental health professionals in the trenches, can the therapeutic jurisprudence perspective help them to understand their work or phenomena that surround them every day? Do things become clearer for them when they view their world through a "therapeutic jurisprudence lens?" Does the therapeutic jurisprudence paradigm help them to imagine different ways in which their objectives could be achieved?

Therapeutic jurisprudence discourse is in need of observations and ideas that can fuel and challenge it "from the bottom up." This requires the involvement of thoughtful individuals who occupy the front line of forensic mental health services, where the appropriate real-world observations may be made. If informed of the therapeutic jurisprudence paradigm, they could use it to gather observations to feed the debate, to challenge it, and to test its heuristic value in a world dominated by complex political and practical demands.

There is every reason to believe that the thoughtful forensic psychiatrist or forensic psychologist in the public sector forensic mental health system would grasp quickly the basic notion of therapeutic jurisprudence and the issues that it attempts to address. This is because they can find in the concept a crystallization of conflicts that forensic mental health professionals long have felt in their everyday work. Their professional training has taught them to be clinicians who recognize a duty to diagnose and relieve human suffering, but they have chosen to work in clinical settings that are quite unlike the clinics in which they originally trained. The prison hospital, the court clinic, and the pretrial detention center have several objectives, only one of which is the diagnosis and treatment of mental disorder. Other objectives include the protection of defendants' rights, protection of the interests of society (including its interests in both safety and retribution), and enhancement of the daily procedural interests of the legal system.

Every forensic mental health professional, therefore, is aware, acutely or vaguely, of tensions between these legal objectives and the purely clinical objectives that are central to the traditions of psychiatry and clinical psychology. Inherent in the life of these clinicians—if they do not become inured to their circumstances—is a struggle to define their identity, such that the traditional therapeutic purposes of their professions can be accomplished in the context of a health system that demands the fulfillment of sometimes conflicting legal purposes. These are the same tensions that are highlighted in the notion of therapeutic jurisprudence: the potentially antitherapeutic consequences of legal protections for defendants, and the search for ways to satisfy therapeutic objectives without compromising the ultimate objectives of the legal system.

Front-line forensic mental health professionals, therefore, have the potential to be important "bottom-up" contributors to therapeutic jurisprudence discourse. They are not strangers to the concept, for it has been part of their lives for some time in a less systematic guise. Moreover, they are in a unique position to observe and describe real phenomena, in all their complexity, about which the therapeutic jurisprudence discourse is ultimately concerned.

* * *

C. Therapeutic Jurisprudence in Massachusetts

We felt that the diversity and integration of the Massachusetts forensic mental health system made it an ideal context within which to generate real-world observations that might stimulate and challenge the growing discourse about therapeutic jurisprudence. Moreover, the quality of the system's forensic mental health professionals suggested that they were capable of generating relevant insights into the functions of the mental health and legal systems in which they work.

Toward this end, in 1992 the Law-Psychiatry Program of UMMS developed a special conference for the Massachusetts forensic mental health system, focusing on the application of the therapeutic jurisprudence paradigm to enhance our understanding of the system. Prior to the conference, pairs of senior forensic professionals had been assigned the task of learning the therapeutic jurisprudence concept, then observing through the therapeutic jurisprudence "lens" the legal and forensic procedures in which they functioned daily. They were asked to select some aspect of the forensic mental health process with which they were already thoroughly familiar, and to (a) describe it from a therapeutic jurisprudence perspective, (b) identify issues and conflicts raised by that application (e.g., antitherapeutic aspects of current legal and mental health procedures), and (c) if possible, use the therapeutic jurisprudence concept to generate alternative mechanisms for satisfying both legal and mental health objectives in the procedural area that they had chosen to discuss.

The results of this project were the papers that appear in this series. They deal with issues in civil commitment, criminal evaluations and treatment, and juvenile court procedures, as seen through the eyes of professionals on the front line of forensic mental health services in Massachusetts. The papers are preceded by a brief introduction to the therapeutic jurisprudence concept that they were asked to use, as described by * * * Professor David Wexler. Their observations and ideas then are discussed by Professor Michael Perlin, a leading scholar in mental health law and contributor to the therapeutic jurisprudence literature.

The sequence of these papers, therefore, takes the concept from its academic and theoretical origins, putting it (top down) into the hands of professionals in the real world of forensic mental health, who then give their observations (bottom up) back to the scholars for their reflection on the value of the exercise. We believe the result is enlightening not only for its substance, but also as a model for driving the development of other ideas in mental health law that are intended to have both theoretical and practical significance.

Therapeutic Jurisprudence and Changing Conceptions of Legal Scholarship

David B. Wexler

Mental health law scholarship is in a state of flux. The doctrinal, constitutionally-oriented scholarship that has characterized the field over the last two decades is losing its driving force. There is, however, an emerging interest in new, interdisciplinary approaches to the field. One such approach is therapeutic jurisprudence—the study of the role of the law as a therapeutic agent.[1]

In many ways, the change in mental health law scholarship is symptomatic of a change in legal scholarship generally. And the change in legal scholarship is in turn related to changing conceptions of the law. This article examines those changing conceptions of law and legal scholarship and relates them to developments in therapeutic jurisprudence.

Legal Scholarship

In a recent article in the *Michigan Law Review* entitled "The Concept of Law and the New Public Law Scholarship,"[2] Professor Edward Rubin traces the recent change in legal scholarship, with particular reference to public law and administrative law scholarship. This section of the essay will summarize Rubin's essential conclusions regarding public law scholarship. The next section will look at changing mental health law scholarship and at therapeutic jurisprudence. The purpose of this article is to show how therapeutic jurisprudence may be regarded as a mental health law counterpart of the "New Public Law" scholarship.

Rubin begins by noting that most legal scholarship, whether of the older or newer variety, is distinguishable from the scholarship of most other academic disciplines by its prescriptive nature. Its purpose, in other words, is "to frame recommendations to responsible decisionmakers."[3]

---

1. David B. Wexler, Therapeutic Jurisprudence: The Law as a Therapeutic Agent (1990); David B. Wexler & Bruce J. Winick, Essays in Therapeutic Jurisprudence (1991).

2. Edward L. Rubin, The Concept of Law and the New Public Law Scholarship, 89 Mich. L. Rev. 792 (1991).

3. Id. at 796. Of course, some legal scholarship—such as legal history and sociology of law—is not prescriptive. The great bulk of legal scholarship—that performed by academic lawyers on law school faculties—is, however, prescriptive in nature. Rubin notes that the quality of a legal scholar's prescriptive work ought not to be judged by whether it is adopted, but by whether other scholars accept its "logic, creativity, and judgment." Id. at 796. Hence, the work is addressed in a technical sense to law and policymaking bodies, but is in reality

Under the "old" concept of law, the "law" was thought of as judge-made and, before legal realism, as judge "discovered." Such judge-made law developed incrementally, on a case-by-case basis. Courts would carefully examine prior precedent, reason by analogy, and try to extract overarching principles from previously decided cases. More recently, judges have been explicitly willing to consider policy arguments in developing doctrine.[4] With or without policy arguments, the overall goal of the common law is to achieve an intellectual coherence.[5] Indeed, even other areas, including the Supreme Court's meticulously developed body of constitutional law, "aspire to this same coherence and thus encourage and respond to similarly theoretical arguments."[6]

Traditional legal scholarship comported well with the "old" concept of law. Originally, legal scholars helped courts and practitioners extract the principles embedded in the case law and communicated those principles in treatises. Later, law reviews became the principal scholarly forum. Law review articles served the same extracting, synthesizing, and disseminating function as the treatises. Even more, however, law reviews served to critique the intellectual coherence of given bodies of judge-made law, and presented well-reasoned proposals, based on precedent and policy, for particular doctrinal developments. Tied closely to the common law feature of incrementalism, law review articles most typically recommended to courts how best to grapple with pending or "next generation" legal issues.

Of course, this description of law review writing applies even now to many of the law review articles being written (although the highest prestige law reviews rarely print "straight" doctrinal pieces). But there is also a discernable "new" legal scholarship that derives largely from a "new" concept of law.[7]

The "new" concept of law flows from the reality of the modern administrative state and from the recognition that legislatures and administrators, rather than judges, are today the primary lawmakers. Today's primary (non-judicial) lawmakers are not particularly interested in legal principles and meticulous reasoning processes. To them, the law is an instrumentality designed to deal with a particular problem; law is successful if its results satisfactorily tackle the problem. Incrementalism is not a necessary part of this lawmaking process. Reasoning by analogy is inappropriate. Prior legislation is looked to as "data"[8]—it is looked to for its efficacy rather than for its precedential value.

---

largely read and evaluated by scholars. Nonetheless, although, in light of political realities, scholars cannot except their recommendations to be accepted as a whole, some portion of some recommendations are likely to be accepted on an occasional if not a regular basis. Id. at 830. Moreover, the recommendations may create general moods or catalysts for action. Id. Indeed, "once a body of prescriptive scholarship exists, it may influence the legislators' estimation of political advantage." Id. at 831.

4. Id. at 802, 809.

5. Id. at 833.

6. Id. at 833.

7. Rubin notes that two distinctly new trends in legal scholarship—critical legal studies and law and economics—have shockingly "remained bound to the judicial orientation of standard scholarship." Id. at 810.

8. Id. at 823.

Increasingly, in other words, the referent of legal analysis is social problems, not the body of law itself.

The "new" legal scholarship addresses recommendations to legislatures and administrators rather than to the judiciary. According to Rubin, the reasoning represents a "shift from process justification to cause-and-result justification."[9] When shifting "from analogical to instrumental thinking,"[10] scholars are "not searching for solutions which are intellectually coherent with a pattern of previous decisions, but for solutions that effectively [achieve] specific goals."[11] A new series of questions are posed by the new brand of scholarship:

> Which rules work best in general? Which work best for particular purposes? Under what circumstances is specificity desirable, and under what circumstances is it counterproductive? What is the best mechanism for enforcing various provisions? How important is public participation for achieving the purpose and how can such participation be secured?[12]

The "New Public Law" scholarship asks legal scholars to be sensitive to "insights and techniques from social science disciplines."[13] They should use studies of the law's effects[14] and, in collaboration with social scientists, might participate in the development of such studies. The crucial task of the legal scholar, however, is not so much to generate data but rather to use data in framing recommendations[15] and to suggest important and relevant lines of inquiry to social scientists.

Ultimately, general theories may emerge regarding such matters as "when private causes of action are effective, what kind of agencies can implement specific programs, how statutory language can be used to control adjudicatory behavior, or which enforcement strategies an agency should use in particular circumstances."[16] Perhaps such scholarship will eventually be marshalled in a new breed of treatise.[17]

Normatively, the "New Public Law" scholarship is based on the assumption that the enhancement of "the welfare of our society", and the promotion of compliance with "the essential, deontological norms in which we believe," are "achievable by governmental action," and that "the performance of our government can be improved, that there are techniques of governance that can be discovered, adopted, and applied."[18]

---

9. Id. at 820.

10. Id. at 812.

11. Id. at 819.

12. Id. at 815.

13. Id. at 827.

14. Id.

15. Id. at 828.

16. Id. at 827.

17. Id. See Ted Schneyer, Uniting the Balkans: Wolfram on Legal Ethics, 37 J. Legal Ed. 434, 438 (1987) (book review) (treatise writing as scholarship).

18. Rubin, supra note 2, at 836.

Therapeutic Jurisprudence and the New Legal Scholarship

Without question, "traditional" mental health law scholarship was grounded in the "old" concept of law, albeit with a strong constitutional component. The core of traditional mental health law is probably the civil commitment system. Civil commitment is, of course, governed by codes, but scholarly attention was attracted almost exclusively to constitutional controversies, largely of the procedural due process variety. The body of mental health law of interest to legal scholars was basically judge-made doctrine, developed incrementally and through a process of analogical reasoning. In the area of civil commitment of the mentally ill, the analogy was almost always to the area of constitutional criminal procedure:

> The Supreme Court has said indigent criminal defendants and juveniles alleged to be delinquent have a right to appointed counsel. Since civil commitment can also lead to a deprivation of liberty, shouldn't proposed patients have a similar right to counsel?
>
> What about the right to jury trial? Criminal defendants have a right to jury trial. But the Supreme Court has held that the right to jury trial does not extend to juvenile delinquency proceedings. Since civil commitment is closer to juvenile delinquency proceedings than to criminal proceedings, perhaps no right to jury trial should attach in commitment proceedings.
>
> What standard of proof is appropriate in civil commitment cases? Criminal cases of course require proof beyond a reasonable doubt. Traditional civil cases, on the other hand, require only a mere preponderance of the evidence. Is civil commitment "truly" criminal or is it civil? Or is it perhaps a hybrid? And if it is a hybrid, should a compromise standard of "clear and convincing" evidence suffice?[19]

As noted elsewhere,[20] that sort of mental health law and its accompanying scholarship is losing its lustre. To a considerable extent, traditional mental health law scholarship was successful in incorporating basic procedural safeguards into the mental health system, and many mental health law scholars believe it is now time to move on to other matters. In any event, recent developments make it clear that the constitutional rights revolution is, at least for the time being, over. Indeed, the current decline of traditional mental health law scholarship seems largely attributable to the fact that the scholarship was built

---

19. David B. Wexler, Putting Mental Health into Mental Health Law: Therapeutic Jurisprudence, 16 Law & Hum. Behav. 27, 28–29 (1992). See also Tom R. Tyler, The Psychological Consequences of Judicial Procedures: Implications for Civil Commitment Hearings, 46 SMU L. Rev. 433 (1992) (blending procedural justice and therapeutic jurisprudence perspectives); Michael L. Perlin, Pretexts and Mental Disability Law: The Case of Competency, 46 U. Miami L. Rev. (1992) (pondering the therapeutic or antitherapeutic impact of courts condoning "pretextuality" at involuntary civil commitment and incompetency to stand trial hearings).

20. David B. Wexler & Bruce J. Winick, Therapeutic Jurisprudence as a New Approach to Mental Health Law Policy Analysis and Research, 45 U. Miami L. Rev. 979 (1991).

on a constitutional criminal procedure foundation that is itself now crumbling.[21] But independent of the Supreme Court's lack of interest in forging on to new constitutional frontiers, the doctrinal approach to mental health law scholarship is, at least after 20 years, simply sterile.[22] The scholarly malaise regarding the manipulation of mental health law doctrine signals the need for new approaches and may be evidence of a changing conception of law and legal scholarship.

Some legal scholars are now striking out in a new, highly interdisciplinary direction, and are developing an approach known as therapeutic jurisprudence. Therapeutic jurisprudence suggests that the law itself can be seen to function as a therapist or therapeutic agent. Legal rules, legal procedures, and the roles of legal actors (principally lawyers and judges) may be viewed as social forces that sometimes produce therapeutic or antitherapeutic consequences. The prescriptive focus of therapeutic jurisprudence is that, within important limits set by principles of justice, the law ought to be designed to serve more effectively as a therapeutic agent.[23] Therapeutic jurisprudence in no way suggests that therapeutic considerations should trump other considerations. It suggests that, other things being equal, mental health law should be restructured to better accomplish therapeutic goals. But whether other things are equal is often debatable, and therapeutic jurisprudence does not resolve that debate.

The therapeutic jurisprudence "lens" enables us to ask a series of questions regarding legal arrangements and therapeutic outcomes that likely would have gone unaddressed under the traditional doctrinal approach to mental health law and scholarship. Therapeutic jurisprudence will lead us to raise questions, the answers to which are empirical[24] and normative. The key task is, of course, to determine how the law can use mental health information to improve therapeutic functioning without impinging upon justice concerns.

In digesting the therapeutic jurisprudence literature presented below, the reader should keep in mind the hypothesis-generating role of therapeutic jurisprudence. That is, the overall project of therapeutic jurisprudence should not stand or fall on the reader's assessment of the empirical accuracy of particular illustrations. Indeed, the illustrations themselves typically call for further empirical research.

---

21. Id.

22. Daniel W. Shuman, Overview, 46 SMU L. Rev. 323 (1992) (introduction to mental disability law symposium); Wexler, supra note 19, at 29.

23. D. Wexler, supra note 1; D. Wexler & B. Winick, supra note 1. The normative question is extensively explored in Robert F. Schopp, Therapeutic Jurisprudence and Conflicts Among Values in Mental Health Law (this issue).

24. Because of methodological considerations, the empirical questions will in practice vary markedly in their receptivity to actual empirical analysis. Legal scholars should not "censor" these questions under some prior restraint notion of methodological difficulty. Instead, the questions should be asked, and social scientists and ethicists should be given the opportunity of thinking through the propriety of conducting the research. Indeed, policy recommendations may often be permissibly made on the basis of empirical questions that yield suggestions but that lack definitive empirical answers. See John Monahan & Laurens Walker, Empirical Questions Without Empirical Answers, 1991 Wis. L. Rev. 569 (1991).

An examination of the emerging therapeutic jurisprudence scholarship reveals patterns that track quite closely the new directions in legal scholarship described by Rubin. Much of the scholarship in therapeutic jurisprudence continues to be technically directed to the appellate arena of lawmaking. The unique contribution of therapeutic jurisprudence in that arena, however, is to argue for the acceptance or rejection of a legal doctrine on the basis of policy arguments grounded in mental health information or psychological theory. A conceptual analysis may be undertaken simply to show how the policy-driven proposed doctrine is consistent with an intellectually coherent body of law.

A case in point of appellate-oriented therapeutic jurisprudence scholarship is Winick's article on the *Zinermon*[25] case. In *Zinermon*, the Supreme Court called into question the competence of patients to consent to voluntary hospitalization. Zinermon was himself so delusional that he was unaware he was entering a mental hospital. In its *Zinermon* opinion, however, the Supreme Court used unnecessarily broad language in its constitutional condemnation of Zinermon's "voluntary" admission. Some *dicta* in the opinion can, therefore, be read as seriously limiting the voluntary admission process.

Relying on the vast literature relating to the psychological value of choice, Winick has urged appellate courts to construe the *Zinermon* rule narrowly.[26] Looking to principles of cognitive and social psychology to support the presumed therapeutic advantages of voluntary hospitalization over involuntary commitment, Winick suggests *Zinermon*, if taken literally, could undermine much of the therapeutic value of the voluntary hospitalization process. His thesis is that voluntary hospitalization is more likely than involuntary hospitalization to be efficacious, and that the potential for success is enhanced when the patient is treated as competent and when his or her choices are honored. Winick, therefore, engages in a careful doctrinal analysis—such as separating the Court's "holding" from its "*dictum*"—in order to convince appellate courts that they *need* not read *Zinermon* literally and broadly. It is, however, his psychologically-driven, therapeutically-oriented policy argument that is offered to persuade the courts that they *should* read *Zinermon* narrowly.[27]

---

25. Zinermon v. Burch, 110 S. Ct. 975 (1990).

26. Bruce J. Winick, Competency to Consent to Voluntary Hospitalization: A Therapeutic Jurisprudence Analysis of Zinermon v. Burch, 14 Int'l J. L. & Psychiatry 169 (1991). Of course, to the extent that coercive influences drive patient decisionmaking, Winick recognizes that the value of "choice" may evaporate. Id. at 193. For a recent empirical study of coercive influences in voluntary hospital admission, see Susan C. Reed & Dan A. Lewis, The Negotiation of Voluntary Admission in Chicago's State Mental Hospitals, 18 J. Psychiatry & L. 137 (1990).

27. In a separate piece based on the importance of choice, Winick suggests that therapeutic value may well flow from the judicial recognition of a right to refuse treatment. Bruce J. Winick, The Right to Refuse Treatment: A Therapeutic Jurisprudence Analysis, 15 Int'l J.L. & Psychiatry (1992). For additional therapeutic jurisprudence questions regarding the right to refuse treatment, see Michael L. Perlin, Reading the Supreme Court's Tea Leaves: Predicting Judicial Behavior in Civil and Criminal Right to Refuse Treatment Cases, 12 Am. J. Forensic Psychiatry 37, 54 (1991). See also Bruce J. Winick, Competency to be Executed: A Therapeutic Jurisprudence Perspective, 10 Behav. Sci. & L. 317 (1992) (constitutional question in capital context). For other constitutional questions viewed through a therapeutic jurisprudence lens, see Fred Cohen, Liability for Custodial Suicide: The Information Base Re-

Therapeutic jurisprudence scholars have also addressed appellate courts in areas not involving constitutional concerns. Both Schopp and Shuman, for example, have examined particular aspects of tort doctrine through a therapeutic jurisprudence lens.

Schopp has looked at certain aspects of a psychotherapist's *Tarasoff*[28] duty to protect third persons from dangers posed by the therapist's patient.[29] Schopp does not enter the debate over whether the *Tarasoff* obligation is itself therapeutically detrimental (by pitting the therapist against the patient),[30] or whether the obligation might in the aggregate prove to be therapeutic.[31] The "therapeutic" thesis is that since homicidal threats are overwhelmingly made against family members and intimates who themselves play a substantial role in contributing to the violence, *Tarasoff* may prompt therapists to make contact with potential victims—persons who might profitably be brought into some sort of "couple" or "conjoint" therapy.

Assuming the existence of a *Tarasoff* rule, Schopp shows how therapeutic jurisprudence considerations might inform the debate over whether the obligation should constitute only a duty to warn or a more general duty to protect. Moreover, he discusses whether a therapist's obligation should be limited to situations involving "specific threats against identifiable victims" (STIV), or whether, under the "zone of danger" (ZOD) test, it should apply *whenever* the patient poses a foreseeable danger—and extend to *all* victims within the zone of danger.

Basing his therapeutic jurisprudence analysis on a "consistent body of research [indicating] that successful therapy depends heavily on a therapeutic relationship in which the patient perceives the therapist as concerned about and dedicated to the patient's well-being,"[32] Schopp worries that the tort regulation of psychotherapy might sometimes be self-defeating. Tort law tries to influence a therapist's fiduciary obligations—to put the *patient's* interests first—by appealing to the *self*-interest of the therapist in avoiding liability. A tort rule governing psychotherapists would be particularly self-defeating if it "encourages prudent therapists to practice their professions with a wary eye toward potential liability rather than with full attention on their patients' interests."[33]

---

quirements, Jail Suicide Update, summer 1992, at 1 (constitutional suicide prevention duty); Daniel W. Shuman, Calling in the Cavalry: The Duty of the State to Rescue the Vulnerable in the United States (unpublished manuscript 1992) (discussing advisability of a constitutional duty to rescue victims of child abuse).

28. Tarasoff v. Regents of the Univ. of Calif. 131 Cal. Rptr. 14 (1976).

29. Robert F. Schopp, The Psychotherapist's Duty to Protect the Public: The Appropriate Standard and the Foundation in Legal Theory and Empirical Premises, 70 Neb. L. Rev. 327 (1991).

30. Alan A. Stone, The *Tarasoff* Decisions: Suing Psychotherapists to Safeguard Society, 90 Harv. L. Rev. 358 (1976).

31. David B. Wexler, Patients, Therapists, and Third Parties: The Victimlogical Virtues of *Tarasoff*, 2 Int'l J.L. & Psychiatry 1 (1979). See also Michael L. Perlin, *Tarasoff* and the Dilemma of the Dangerous Patient: New Directions for the 1990's, 16 Law & Psychol. Rev. 29 (1992) (therapeutic jurisprudence questions posed by *Tarasoff*).

32. Schopp, supra note 29, at 354.

33. Id. at 354. See also Stanley L. Brodsky, Fear of Litigation in Mental Health Professionals, 15 Crim. Just. & Behav. 492 (1988).

Schopp suggests that the self-defeating feature of a therapist's duty to warn or protect potential victims can be greatly reduced by the law "providing a crystallized trigger that clearly identifies cases in which the...duty to warn applies."[34] That way, "therapists could then put this concern [of potential patient dangerousness] aside until the triggering conditions occurred."[35] They "could attend to their fiduciary responsibilities most of the time, but sacrifice these concerns when the duty to warn demanded it."[36]

Schopp regards the STIV standard as just such a crystallized trigger. A therapist could go about his or her duty, putting the patient's interests first and not thinking at all in self-interested legal liability terms, unless and until the patient makes a specific threat against an identifiable victim. If and when such a threat occurs, the balance would, for public policy purposes, shift.[37]

Schopp proposes to enhance therapeutic outcome through tort rules directed at psychotherapists. Shuman, on the other hand, hopes to improve therapeutic outcome through a proposed rule directed at emotionally stressed accident-prone persons.[38] Drawing on the literature linking stressful life events to high accident rates, Shuman postulates that accident proneness would decrease if non-mentally ill but emotionally stressed individuals were encouraged to seek effective treatment.

Shuman believes that traditional tort law, with its "objective" standard of care, does not play a role in encouraging such treatment-seeking behavior. The objective standard assesses negligence according to an abstract, idealized notion of the "reasonable" person. Accordingly, the objective standard would not have the jury take into account the defendant's *special* stressful situation

---

34. Schopp, supra note 29, at 355.

35. Id.

36. Id.

37. In contrast to the STIV, the ZOD (zone of danger) standard is a vague, non-crystallized "trigger" that leaves a therapist at sea with regard to when a protective duty arises. Just as triggers may be crystallized or non-crystallized, so too may be the underlying duty. A duty to warn is crystallized insofar as it requires specific action; a duty to protect, on the other hand, is general and might be discharged in various ways. Schopp has noted the various potential combinations:

> When courts adopt the STIV standard for the duty to warn, they establish a fully crystallized standard of care, and when they adopt the STIV for the general duty to protect, they establish a crystallized trigger for a broad general duty. Analogously, when courts adopt the ZOD standard for the duty to protect, they crystallize neither the duty nor the trigger, and when they apply the ZOD standard to the duty to warn, they establish a crystallized duty without a crystallized trigger.

Id. at 353. Schopp notes that the therapeutic or antitherapeutic consequences of the various combinations are of course empirical matters. Nonetheless, given his assumption that therapy works best when a therapist can think in undiluted terms about the patient's interest only, Schopp hypothesizes that a ZOD trigger combined with a crystallized duty to warn "draws the worst from both worlds." Id. The ZOD "trigger" will lead the therapist constantly to practice with "a wary eye toward potential liability," id. at 354, and the crystallized duty to warn will require a warning even in circumstances where the therapist has "good reason to believe that warnings will exacerbate the danger of harm." Id. at 353.

38. Daniel W. Shuman, Therapeutic Jurisprudence and Tort Law: A Limited Subjective Standard of Care, 46 SMU L. Rev. 409 (1992).

and the measures the defendant has taken to relieve the stress—and to relieve the concomitant accident proneness. Shuman urges appellate courts to depart from the objective standard and to adopt a limited "subjective" standard of care in certain situations. Under a limited subjective standard, the jury would learn of the defendant's stress and of therapeutic measures undertaken to relieve it. Given the defendant's situation and therapeutic efforts, a jury would presumably be less inclined to find negligence than it would be if it knew nothing of the defendant's stress and judged the defendant's behavior under an objective reasonable person standard. Indeed, the jury would be specifically instructed to evaluate the defendant's conduct under a subjective standard. Shuman hopes that the use of a limited subjective standard might actually prompt persons suffering considerable stress to seek professional assistance.[39]

The constitutional and tort law proposals described above are obviously aimed primarily at appellate court lawmakers, although many of the proposed policies could, of course, also be achieved through legislative efforts.[40] Other recent therapeutic jurisprudence writings, however, are clearly addressed to audiences other than appellate judges.

In a recent piece by Wexler and Winick[41] and in another by Klotz, Wexler, Sales, and Becker,[42] commentators have applied a therapeutic jurisprudence approach to generate questions and suggestions about sex offenders and the plea process. These pieces draw upon the literature suggesting sex offenders are notorious in their harboring of "cognitive distortions" denying or minimizing their culpability. Therapists, therefore, often begin therapeutic efforts with a process of "cognitive restructuring," an endeavor that seeks to induce offenders to confront their distortions and admit their criminal behavior.

A therapeutic jurisprudence approach to the sex offense area might lead us to ask whether the law (rules, procedures, or roles of lawyers and judges) in the context of sex offenders operates therapeutically or antitherapeutically. For

---

39. If an individual suffering considerable emotional stress goes to a physician, counselor, or walk-in clinic, the appropriate professional could advise the individual to accept—or continue with—psychotherapy. In encouraging the individual to receive treatment, the professional could emphasize that attending therapy sessions might reduce the risk of an accident and, if an accident should nonetheless occur, should reduce the risk of legal liability. In that way, tort law might serve a deterrent—and therapeutic—function. Perhaps the therapeutic impact will be strongest among "law-regarding" potential defendants, such as professionals worried about malpractice liability, and weakest among the ordinary automobile driver.

40. An interesting application of therapeutic jurisprudence in the tort context also appears in Norman G. Poythress & Stanley L. Brodsky, In the Wake of a Negligent Release Law Suit: An Investigation of Professional Consequences and Institutional Impact on a State Psychiatric Hospital, 16 Law & Hum. Behav. 155 (1992). That inquiry is more descriptive than prescriptive, however, and thus is not addressed to the appellate judiciary. See also James L. Stirling, Jr., "Litigaphobia" in Alabama's State Mental Hospitals: Can Qualified Immunity Put the King's Men Back Together Again?, 15 Law & Psychol. Rev. 185 (1991) (recommending legislative solutions).

41. David B. Wexler & Bruce J. Winick, Therapeutic Jurisprudence and Criminal Justice Mental Health Issues, 16 Mental & Physical Disability L. Rep. 225 (1992).

42. Jeffrey A. Klotz, David B. Wexler, Bruce D. Scales & Judith V. Becker, Cognitive Restructuring through Law: A Therapeutic Jurisprudence Approach to Sex Offenders and the Plea Process, 15 U. Puget Sound L. Rev. 579 (1992).

example, does the law in this area promote cognitive restructuring? Or does it instead promote cognitive distortion (and thus perhaps contribute to psychological dysfunction and criminality)?

In that connection, consider the following: in terms of plea bargaining, in jurisdictions where judges have considerable discretion in imposing sentence, offenders will often engage in "sentence" bargaining, where they will plead guilty to the charged offense in exchange for leniency in the sentence imposed. In jurisdictions with heavy mandatory sentencing provisions for certain offenses (such as sex offenders), however, judicial discretion is lacking; discretion in such jurisdictions is in essence transferred to prosecutors in their charging decisions. In those jurisdictions, offenders will often engage in "charge" bargaining, where they are charged with crime X, but acquire sentence leniency by pleading to lesser offense Y. Therapeutic jurisprudence would lead us to ask whether, by encouraging defendants to plead to conduct different from—and less serious than—the conduct they actually engaged in, charge bargaining contributes to cognitive distortion more so than does sentence bargaining.

Similarly, do sex offenders disproportionately seek to plead "no contest," where they take the consequences of a guilty plea without admitting guilt? Do no contest pleas lead to a missed opportunity for the law to engage the defendant in cognitive restructuring? If no contest pleas were unavailable, would defence lawyers seeking to arrange plea bargains for their clients be more inclined to encourage their clients to face the facts, thereby in essence performing a cognitive restructuring function?

Finally, when a judge accepts a guilty plea, the court possesses considerable discretion in how to establish the required "factual basis" for the plea. The nature and detail of the court's questioning of the defendant might bear heavily on whether cognitive distortion or cognitive restructuring results.

Once the empirical evidence is in, to whom will the policy recommendations regarding sex offenders be made? If charge bargaining is antitherapeutic, at least in sex offense cases, that is a matter that presumably ought to be factored into the question whether mandatory sentencing for such offenses ought to continue. The primary message is indeed to the *legislature*. Secondarily, however, *prosecutors* might think twice about engaging in charge bargaining in certain contexts. If no contest pleas are antitherapeutic in the sex offender context, again legislators might wish to take action to make such pleas unavailable (generally or in specific sorts of cases). Regardless of what the legislature does, however, *trial judges* might decide to accept no contest pleas in sex cases reluctantly if at all. Finally, if detailed questioning of the offender on the record yields greater cognitive restructuring than does cursory questioning, trial courts might begin to take quite seriously their role in establishing a factual basis for sex offense pleas.

Note that the concept of "law" for this therapeutic jurisprudence exercise consists of (1) legislation, (2) administration and enforcement of the law (by the public prosecutor), and (3) judicial behavior unrelated to the creation of legal doctrine. Prescriptive scholarship and "law reform" might, therefore, often be addressed to functionaries in the system, urging them, for therapeutic reasons consistent with principles of justice, to change their behavior or their ordinary course of doing business.

When the functionaries in the legal system operate with wide discretion—when they exist in an unconstrained (or "unimpacted")[43] legal field—we must face Appelbaum's concern, expressed in the somewhat different context of civil commitment, that "to the extent that judges, attorneys, or mental health professionals must alter their behavior to effect the aims of therapeutic jurisprudence, the call for them to do so presumes a preexistent willingness."[44] If those actors lack a pre-existing willingness to engage in the suggested behavior, the message, theory, empirical support, and practicability of the suggested behavior must be convincingly provided in the scholar's prescription.[45] Of course, certain actors—perhaps especially judges—may be hesitant to perform a supposedly therapeutic role, as opposed to a strictly legal or judicial one. Like it or not, however, judicial behavior may produce therapeutic or antitherapeutic consequences, and judges may therefore ultimately decide (or be persuaded) to behave in a manner most beneficial to society. Today's law students, more accustomed than their predecessors to thinking about the law in interdisciplinary terms, may, when they ascend to the bench, be reasonably comfortable with such an expanded role.

Another example of therapeutic jurisprudence scholarship aimed at the behavior of trial judges is my proposed incorporation of psychological health care compliance principles in the insanity acquittee conditional release process.[46] Psychologists have discerned certain principles that health care professionals might employ in order to increase patients' medication and treatment adherence. One such principle is that those who enter into behavioral contracts to comply are likely to have greater compliance than those who do not; another is that compliance is enhanced by making a "public commitment" to comply; relatedly, if family members are aware of a patient's agreement to comply, the rate of patient compliance is likely to be higher.

By using these principles, courts might be able to structure conditional release proceedings to better serve a risk management function. Those hearings might then be used not simply to *predict* whether a patient will continue to take medication if released, but to actually *influence* and *facilitate* that compliance. A judge familiar with the principles and willing to use them might ask

---

43. See Duncan Kennedy, Freedom and Constraint in Adjudication: A Critical Phenomenology, 36 J. Legal Educ. 518 (1986).

44. Paul S. Appelbaum, Civil Commitment from a System Perspective, 16 Law & Hum. Behav. 61, 69 (1992).

45. And, of course, remember Rubin's consolation that the scholarship need not be evaluated by whether it is immediately accepted in practice. See *supra* note 3.

An actor who possesses considerable discretion—who is legally unconstrained—may decide to exercise his or her discretion in a particular way in order to constrain the behavior of another actor. And the first actor might act to constrain the second actor so as to help achieve a possibly therapeutic effect. For example, if a judge decides not to accept a no contest plea in a sex offender case, the defense counsel's role in achieving a satisfactory plea bargain for his or her client might now be more constrained and more difficult; the defense counsel, in turn, might exert more pressure on the client. That pressure, however, might serve a cognitive restructuring function.

46. David B. Wexler, Health Care Compliance Principles and the Insanity Acquittee Conditional Release Process, 27 Crim. L. Bull. 18 (1991).

whether the patient, hospital, and community facility have signed a behavioral contract; the hearing might be deferred in the event such a contact had not yet been negotiated and signed. The judge might use the hearing as a forum in which a patient might make a public commitment to comply with certain release conditions, and the judge might arrange for certain agreed-upon family members to be present at the hearing. By following these principles, therapeutic compliance and public safety may presumably be enhanced without any sacrifice to liberty/justice principles.

In the proposed health care compliance scheme, *judges* are encouraged to use *psychological* principles to promote compliance with court orders. By contrast, in his look at the psychotherapist-patient privilege, Klotz[47] uses a therapeutic jurisprudence perspective to argue that *psychotherapists* ought to use *legal principles* to enhance treatment goals.

Klotz builds upon the empirical "privilege study" conducted by Shuman and Weiner.[48] Shuman and Weiner concluded that, contrary to the conventional wisdom, the presence or absence of a psychotherapist-patient privilege actually has very little therapeutic impact. Relying on deterrence theory in conjunction with the Shuman and Weiner findings, Klotz suggests that the *absence* of an absolute psychotherapist-patient privilege could actually be *therapeutically beneficial.* Klotz reasons that those patients who come to therapy in order to receive treatment for behaviors that may result in criminal conduct are likely to speak with their therapists about their criminal desires. But:

> were the absolute psychotherapist-patient privilege removed from the typical therapeutic relationship, those patients who make potentially incriminating communications to their therapist (e.g., of the desire or intent to commit a crime) might be less likely to act on those urges. They might be deterred from engaging in behaviors that have foreseeable legal consequences in order to avoid disclosure of the communication in a future criminal proceeding. In short, the removal of the psychotherapist-patient privilege could be therapeutically beneficial.[49]

The Klotz suggestion is really addressed to two audiences: (a) the legislature, which, if Klotz is right, ought to eliminate or limit the psychotherapist-patient privilege, and (b) psychotherapists, who would presumably need to know about the content of the privilege law and about the postulated therapeutic and deterrent benefit that ought to flow from communicating the status of the law to their patients.[50]

---

47. Jeffrey A. Klotz, Limiting the Psychotherapist-Patient Privilege: The Therapeutic Potential, 27 Crim. L. Bull. 416 (1991).

48. Daniel W. Shuman & Myron S. Weiner, The Privilege Study: An Empirical Examination of the Psychotherapist-Patient Privilege, 60 N.C. L. Rev. 893 (1982).

49. Klotz, supra note 47, at 417.

50. Klotz suggests, id. at 428, that a psychotherapist might make an introductory statement explaining to the patient the concept of confidentiality and assuring the patient that confidentiality will be respected unless it is legally or ethically necessary for the therapist to make a disclosure. As an example of a legal restriction on confidentiality, the therapist might then state:

> [For example,] in this state, there is no absolute psychotherapist-patient privilege. What this means is that if, for some reason, what is said between us in therapy becomes relevant to a judicial proceeding, I could be compelled to tell the court the

The Klotz example shows us how, in therapeutic jurisprudence terms, even private therapists might be regarded as "administrators" or "enforcers" of the pertinent law. One way for the law to reach and influence the behavior of this type of functionary is by rules such as *Tarasoff* that serve to guide and constrain the behavior of mental health professionals. The Klotz example is, however, quite different: If mental health professionals are, as a matter of law, relatively or wholly unconstrained in their discretion whether or not to notify patients of limitations in the privilege law,[51] the suggestions of scholars will need to convince the professionals that it is indeed in their professional interest to use or "administer" the law in the recommended manner.

Conclusion

What might we conclude from our examination of the emerging therapeutic jurisprudence literature? Changes in our conception of the law and in our mode of conducting legal scholarship is occurring in many areas, and mental health law is no exception. In some ways, therapeutic jurisprudence seems to be mental health law's counterpart to what Rubin describes as the "New Public Law" scholarship. Therapeutic jurisprudence has important constitutional law and common law components, and it has clearly not abandoned the appellate arena. In that arena, however, it sees its role as providing empirically- or theoretically-derived, therapeutically-oriented, justice-compatible policy arguments as the basis for urging new legal and constitutional doctrine. Therapeutic jurisprudence has begun its foray into the legislative arena, but obviously has only begun to scratch the surface of that promising scholarly enterprise. In some ways, the conception of law harbored by therapeutic jurisprudence scholars is remarkably broad, and includes the behavior of trial judges, the exercise of prosecutorial discretion,[52] the performance of trial lawyers,[53] and the behavior of mental health professionals and others.

---

content of the communication. For example, if you are arrested for a crime, and go to trial, I can be compelled to disclose in the judicial proceeding what you have told me relating to the crime with which you have been charged, your intention to commit it, and so forth.

51. Depending upon the jurisdiction, and upon professional ethics requirements, a psychotherapist may be either entirely unconstrained about whether to tell the patient anything about the limitation of the privilege (and related matters), or the therapist might be under some obligation to disclose the limits of the privilege (and other limits). The law and practice is at present quite unsettled. Id. at 427 n. 52. Psychotherapists may be as reluctant to use the law in their work as members of the bench and bar may be about using therapeutic concepts. Increased interdisciplinary education will, however, expectedly reduce that reluctance. Psychotherapists sensitive to the law and to legal context may be able to devise effective "psycholegal" treatments. See Amiram Elwork, Psycholegal Treatment and Intervention: The Next Challenge, 16 Law & Hum. Behav. 175 (1992).

52. For a therapeutic jurisprudence example of the suggested exercise of prosecutorial discretion, see David B. Wexler, Inducing Therapeutic Compliance through the Criminal Law, 14 Law & Psychol. Rev. 43 (1990) (discussing possible reckless endangerment prosecutions against those who refuse to take reasonable steps to reduce their dangerous propensities).

53. Michael L. Perlin, Fatal Assumption: A Critical Evaluation of the Role of Counsel in

The questions asked by therapeutic jurisprudence scholars parallel closely the ones asked by the new brand of public law scholars. In light of what we have seen regarding *Tarasoff* and "crystallized triggers," and in light of what we have seen regarding the possible judicial use of health care compliance principles such as public commitment and the involvement of family members, consider, in a therapeutic jurisprudence context, the relevance of the questions posed earlier by Rubin:

> Which rules work best in general? Which work best for particular purposes? Under what circumstances is specificity desirable, and under what circumstances is it counterproductive? What is the best mechanism for enforcing the various provisions? How important is public participation for achieving the purpose and how can such participation be secured?[54]

Not surprisingly, given the similarities we have seen between the two, therapeutic jurisprudence and the "New Public Law" scholarship share basic normative assumptions. Recall that, according to Rubin, the latter body of scholarship works from the assumption that the enhancement of "the welfare of our society," and the promotion of compliance with "the essential, deontological norms in which we believe," are "achievable by governmental action," and that "the performance of our government can be improved, that there are techniques of governance that can be discovered, adopted, and applied,"[55] Therapeutic jurisprudence, as an application of the social science in law (SSL) enterprise, is in accord. Consider, in closing, the striking similarity between Rubin's remarks and those of Melton, who notes that SSL scholars share a "commitment to the question of social welfare" and also share "beliefs that the law is a useful means to that goal, that the law is reformable, and that social science can assist the law in its mission."[56] Therapeutic jurisprudence scholarship can assist in the "law and mental health" aspect of the law's mission.

Mental Disability Cases, 16 Law & Hum. Behav. 39, 57–58 (1992). See also note 45 supra (role of defense counsel).

54. Rubin, supra note 2, at 815. Therapeutic jurisprudence represents a new brand of scholarship designed to address those sorts of questions in a particular context. Ultimately, with cooperation between legal scholars and social scientists, we may end up with a body of material answering these questions and illuminating the relationship between "legal arrangements and therapeutic outcomes." Some day, such materials may even be synthesized and categorized in a new brand of treatise, as Rubin speculates may eventually occur with the "New Public Law" scholarship. Id. at 827.

55. Rubin, supra note 2, at 836.

56. Gary B. Melton, Law, Science and Humanity: The Normative Foundation of Social Science in Law, 14 Law & Hum. Behav. 315, 321 (1990).

Chapter 30

Legal Psychology and Therapeutic Jurisprudence

Mark A. Small

Two academic fields represent the bulk of scholarly work done at the crossroads of psychology and law—legal psychology and psychological jurisprudence. Legal psychology is the scientific study of human behavior relevant to law, and consists of those theories that describe, explain, and predict human behavior by reference to law.[1] In contrast, psychological jurisprudence consists of those theories that describe, explain, predict and proscribe law by reference to human behavior.[2] This Article explores the relationship between legal psychology and a particular version of psychological jurisprudence called therapeutic jurisprudence. The Article concludes that therapeutic jurisprudence provides a framework that only partly captures the field of legal psychology, and argues for construction of a psychological jurisprudence with a broader scope.

Part I discusses three primary ways in which law and psychology relate. These relationships include: a) how law regulates the practice of psychology; b) how law uses psychology, and c) how psychology uses the law. Part II of this Article proposes a definition and description of the content of legal psychology. Part III reviews therapeutic jurisprudence; a particular version of psychological jurisprudence increasingly appearing in the legal literature.[3] Part IV describes the current relationship between legal psychology and therapeutic jurisprudence. Part IV also argues that the relationship between law and psychology would be enhanced by developing a psychological jurisprudence that is more inclusive of legal psychology.

---

1. Despite a few books with the title "legal psychology," there is no common definition of legal psychology in the literature. The broad working definition offered here and explained infra at section II.A., would probably be agreed upon by most working in the field. The earliest book with such a title was Harold E. Burtt, Legal Psychology (1940).

2. For a general description of current approaches to psychological jurisprudence, see Mark A. Small, Advancing Psychological Jurisprudence, 11 Behav. Sci. & L. 3 (1993).

3. See, e.g., David B. Wexler, Therapeutic Jurisprudence: The Law as a Therapeutic Agent (1990); David B. Wexler & Bruce J. Winick, Essays in Therapeutic Jurisprudence (1991); David B. Wexler, Putting Mental Health into Mental Health Law: Therapeutic Jurisprudence, 16 L. & Hum. Behav. 27 (1991); David B. Wexler & Bruce Winick, Therapeutic Jurisprudence as a New Approach to Mental Health Law Policy Analysis and Research, 45 U. Miami L. Rev. 979 (1991); Robert F. Schopp, Therapeutic Jurisprudence and Conflicts Among Values in Mental Health Law, 11 Behav. Sci. & the L. 17 (1993); Daniel W. Shuman, Therapeutic Jurisprudence and Tort Law: A Limited Subjective Standard of Care, 46 SMU L. Rev. (1992); Jeffrey A. Klotz, et al., Cognitive Restructuring Through Law: A Therapeutic Jurisprudence Approach to Sex Offenders and the Plea Process, 15 U. Puget Sound L. Rev. 579 (1992).

I. Law and Psychology

To understand the field of legal psychology, it is helpful to understand the context of law/psychology relationships. Allowing for some overlap, law and psychology relate to one another in three basic ways. First, law regulates the practice of psychology. This relationship is predicated upon the fact that psychology is, in part, a profession that provides services which affect citizens.[4] Second, the law requests and demands the field of psychology to provide information that is useful to the courts. These requests and demands generally take the form of court ordered psychological evaluations and/or testimony regarding clinical and empirical information that is useful for resolving legal issues.[5] Although the law's use of psychology could be included within the broader field of social science in law,[6] there are applications that are uniquely psychological. The final manner in which law and psychology relate concerns how psychology uses law in attempting to influence law and policy.

There are corresponding, yet distinct, academic role models associated with each of these three relationships between law and psychology. A portrayal of each academic role model provides one with an understanding of the cast of characters who comprise the academic discipline of law and psychology. The dominant role model associated with each relationship of law and psychology is described. There is a notably "applied" character to this cast, which is discussed in later sections.[7]

A. Law's Regulation of Psychology

The legal regulation of psychology essentially takes three forms. The first identifies the circumstances in which one may be called a "psychologist" and thus hold out a shingle for the provision of psychological services. The second regulates what can actually take place during the provision of psychological services. A third deals with legal regulation within state mental health systems.

The authority to enact and enforce licensing laws derives from state police powers which authorize states to protect the health, welfare, and safety of their citizens. States have long regulated various professions,[8] and all states have some requirements that must be met to be a "psychologist." For example, Illinois law states that "No individual, partnership association or corporation shall, without a valid license as a clinical psychologist issued by the De-

---

4. See American Psychological Association, Ethical Principles of Psychologists and Code of Conduct, 47 Am. Psychol. 1597 (1993).

5. See Gary B. Melton, et al., Psychological Evaluations for the Courts: A Handbook for Mental Health Professionals and Lawyers (1987).

6. For an overview, see David L. Faigman, To Have and Have Not: Assessing the Value of Social Science to the Law as Science and Policy, 38 Emory L.J. 1005 (1989).

7. See infra notes 16–18 and accompanying text.

8. For example, the earliest laws to directly regulate the medical profession were enacted in Virginia in 1639. R.C. Derbyshire, Medical Licensure and Discipline in the United States 2 (1969).

partment, in any manner hold himself out to the public as a psychologist or clinical psychologist...."[9]

Laws not only regulate who may call themselves a psychologist, but also place limitations on confidentiality between the psychologist and client, thus regulating what occurs within the psychologist/client relationship. An early limitation was imposed by a California court in *Tarasoff v. Regents of Univ. of Calif.*[10] In *Tarasoff*, the Court held that a "therapist owes a legal duty not only to his patient, but also to his patient's would be victim and is subject in both respects to scrutiny by judge and jury."[11] More recent limits on the therapeutic relationship have to do with statutorily imposed duties to report suspected child abuse and neglect. Between 1963 and 1966, all fifty states and the District of Columbia passed some type of statute requiring health care professionals to report suspected abuse and neglect.[12] Accordingly, states mandate that psychologists report any patient who is suspected of child abuse and neglect, regardless of the effect on the therapeutic relationship.

Along with the legal regulation of clinical psychologists who provide assessment and therapeutic services, the law also regulates the conduct of research psychologists who use humans as subjects for various studies. The doctrine of informed consent requires all subjects, whether the recipients of services or the subjects of studies, to knowingly, intelligently, and voluntarily consent to psychological procedures. Because of early abuse in the use of deception in research[13] and the recognition of possible harms to the subject, society, and profession,[14] federal laws now require informed consent of all participants, and all universities have instituted internal review boards to approve research using human subjects.

The field of mental health law comprises the final manner in which the law regulates psychology. While certain laws govern the private practice of clinical and research psychologists, a substantial body of law governs the provision of psychological services by the state.[15] When the state rather than the private sector provides mental health services, a host of separate and distinct laws apply, not the least of which define the criteria and procedures for involuntary civil commitment. The field of mental health law arguably dominates this subdomain of legal regulation of psychology, partly as a result of the numerous laws and cases written to articulate the permissible parameters of providing psychological services to those involuntarily deprived of their liberty.

---

9. Ill. Rev. Stat. ch. 111, para. 5353(3)(a) (1991).

10. 17 Cal. 3d 425, 442, 551 P.2d 334, 347, 131 Cal. Rptr. 14, 27 (1976).

11. Id. at 439.

12. Mark A. Small, Policy Review of Child Abuse and Neglect Reporting Statutes, L. & Pol'y (forthcoming 1993).

13. Diana Baumrind, Some Thoughts on Ethics of Research: After Reading Milgram's "Behavioral Study of Obedience," 19 Am. Psychol. 421, 422 (1964).

14. Diana Baumrind, Research Using Intentional Deception: Ethical Issues Revisited, 40 Am. Psychol. 165, 168–70 (1985).

15. For an overview of mental health law, see Ralph Reisner & Christopher Slobogin, Law and the Mental Health System (1990).

The academic role model associated with this area of psychology and law, will be referred to as the Practitioner/scientist. The Practitioner/scientist is primarily interested in how the law affects the practice of psychology, both as a private and public enterprise. Thus, a typical research study by a Practitioner/scientist would examine the effect mandatory child abuse and neglect reporting statutes might have on the therapeutic relationship[16] or the effect the duty to protect third parties might have on the therapeutic relationship.[17] A Practitioner/scientist might also research how changes in the statutory criteria of civil commitment affect the number of those committed to institutions,[18] or how informed consent procedures might affect participation in research.

B. The Law's Use of Psychology

Although there are several potential uses for social science in law,[19] the contributions from psychology have primarily emerged from two sources—forensic clinical psychology and forensic experimental psychology.

1. Forensic Clinical Psychology

Law's use of psychology, especially clinical assessment, has been around for some time.[20] The field is now moving beyond what could be called a cottage industry.[21] Psychologists requested to perform clinical evaluations for the courts are referred to as forensic clinical psychologists. In civil law, forensic clinical psychologists are now routinely called upon to testify in cases of child custody, workmen's compensation, and negligence suits alleging psychological trauma and pain.[22] In criminal law, forensic clinical psychologists are called upon to testify about a variety of issues including defendants' competency to stand trial, defendants' mental status at the time of the offense, as well as providing recommendations for sentencing.[23]

Forensic clinical psychology has met with criticisms from experts both outside and from within the field. Initially, forensic psychologists were embraced by those outside the field as an important ally to legal decision makers. However, legal scholars have since criticized psychologists for delivering little of

---

16. See Holly Watson & Murray Levine, Psychotherapy and Mandated Reporting of Child Abuse, 59 Am. J. Orthopsychiatry 246 (1989).

17. See Givelber, et al., Myth and Reality: An Empirical Study of Private Law in Action, 1984 Wis. L. Rev. 443.

18. Roger Peters, et al., The Effects of Statutory Change on the Civil Commitment of the Mentally Ill, 11 L. & Hum. Behav. 73 (1987).

19. John Monahan & Laurens Walker, Social Science in Law: Cases and Materials 33 (1989).

20. See, e.g., Stanley Brodsky, Psychologists in the Criminal Justice System (1973).

21. Thomas Grisso, The Economic and Scientific Future of Forensic Psychological Assessment, 42 Am. Psychol. 831 (1987).

22. See Gary B. Melton, et al., Psychological Evaluations for the Courts: A Handbook for Mental Health Professionals and Lawyers 272, 329 (1987).

23. Id. at 93, 111, 166.

what was initially promised.[24] Additionally, legal scholars have criticized forensic clinical psychologists for usurping the role of the legal decision maker.[25] The contributions of forensic clinical psychologists have also been criticized by experts within the field.[26] Identifying two major flaws, Professor Grisso described the product offered by forensic psychologists as being neither "forensic"[27] nor particularly "psychological."[28]

2. Forensic Experimental Psychology

Experimental forensic psychology generally refers to non-clinical psychologists who research and testify about a broad array of topics ranging from jury behavior to the accuracy of eyewitness identification. While use of forensic experimental psychologists is increasing,[29] they are outnumbered by their forensic clinical counterparts,[30] who appear more frequently in courts because of the relevance of their expertise to a broader range of legal questions.

To illustrate the work characteristics of forensic experimental psychologists, it is helpful to look at a survey conducted in 1989 in which sixty-three experts were asked to rate the reliability of twenty-one eyewitness phenomena that have been under empirical investigation.[31] The following examples are taken

---

24. David Bazelon, Psychiatrists and the Adversary Process, 230 Sci. Am. 18 (1974).

25. Stephen J. Morse, Law and Mental Health Professionals: The Limits of Expertise, 9 Prof. Psych. Res. & Prac. 389, 391 (1978); Gary Melton & Susan Limber, Psychologists' Involvement in Cases of Child Maltreatment: Limits of Role and Expertise, 44 Am. Psychol. 1225, 1230 (1989).

26. See generally, Thomas Grisso, Evaluating Competencies: Forensic Assessments and Instruments (1986); Thomas Grisso, The Economic and Scientific Future of Forensic Psychological Assessment, 42 Am. Psychol. 831, 834 (1987); Gary B. Melton et al., Psychological Evaluations for the Courts: A Handbook for Mental Health Professionals and Attorneys 3 (1987); Norman G. Poythress, Concerning Reform in Expert Testimony: An Open Letter from a Practicing Psychologist, 6 L. & Hum. Behav. 39, 40 (1982).

27. Because too many psychologists assume that they can follow templates used in regular clinical practice, many so called "forensic" evaluations are simply "clinical" evaluations dressed up in legal jargon and provided to legal decision-makers. Thus, these evaluations prove to be of limited utility to legal decision-makers because they do not address the specific legal questions at issue. "Often such assessments are doomed from the start, because the special legal constructs that the court must address—ranging from the various legal competencies to dangerousness—are quite different from general clinical constructs of personality and psychopathology." Grisso, supra note 26, at 834.

28. Grisso's second criticism is that it is often hard to distinguish the work of forensic psychologists from that of other mental health professionals. Moreover, the theoretical and empirical approaches that make psychology unique as a discipline have largely gone untapped. Assessment theory and measurement, cognitive, developmental and social psychology have, thus far, had little impact on the development of the discipline of forensic psychology. Id.

29. Michael McCloskey, et al., The Experimental Psychologist in Court: The Ethics of Expert Testimony, 10 L. & Hum. Behav. 3 (1986).

30. Grisso, supra note 26.

31. See Saul M. Kassin, et al., The "General Acceptance" of Psychological Research on Eyewitness Testimony, 44 Am. Psychol. 1090–99 (1989).

from the twenty-one phenomena used in that study and are listed to present a flavor of the work of forensic experimental psychologists:

> The presence of a weapon impairs an eyewitness' ability to accurately identify the perpetrator's face....Police instruction can affect an eyewitness's willingness to make an identification and/or the likelihood that he or she will identify a particular person....The rate of memory loss for an event is greatest right after the event, and then levels off over time....White eyewitnesses are better at identifying other White people than they are at identifying Black people....Eyewitnesses testimony about an event can be affected by how the questions put to that witness are worded....Hypnosis increases suggestibility to leading and misleading questions....Women are better than men at recognizing faces.[32]

Although the accuracy of eyewitness identification and jury behavior have occupied the bulk of research by forensic experimental psychologists,[33] there are other promising areas currently under investigation.[34]

3. A Paradigm for the Use of Social Science in Law

The use of forensic clinical and experimental psychology by law is part of a broader movement by the courts to utilize social science information. In a series of articles, Professors Monahan and Walker have produced a conceptual bridge that is useful for understanding how social science can be used by legislatures and courts.[35] Professors Monahan and Walker "suggest a paradigm in which law-changing research is 'social authority,' case-specific research is 'social fact,' and a newer hybrid combination of these two is 'social framework.'"[36] In this paradigm, the central concept is social authority, where courts would "treat social science research much as they would legal precedent under the common law."[37] Professors Monahan and Walker recently summarized their perspective in outline form to provide courts with a step-by-step procedure to utilize when faced with an empirical question concerning human behavior.[38] Monahan and Walker have provided a great service in providing a

---

32. Id. at 1091.

33. See infra notes 77–78 and accompanying text.

34. See Dorothy Kagehiro & William Laufer, Handbook of Psychology and Law 487–555 (1992).

35. See Laurens Walker & John Monahan, Social Authority: Obtaining, Evaluating, and Establishing Social Science in Law, 134 U. Pa. L. Rev. 477 (1986); Laurens Walker & John Monahan, Social Frameworks: A New Use of Social Science in Law, 73 Va. L. Rev. 559 (1987); Laurens Walker & John Monahan, Social Facts: Scientific Methodology as Legal Precedent, 76 Cal. L. Rev. 877 (1988); John Monahan & Laurens Walker, Social Science Research in Law: A New Paradigm, 43 Am. Psychol. 465 (1988).

36. John Monahan & Laurens Walker, Social Science Research in Law: A New Paradigm, 43 Am. Psychol. 465 (1988).

37. Id. at 466.

38. According to this approach, courts should adhere to the following steps:

1. Determine whether the substantive law governing the case raises an empirical issue to which social science research may be pertinent.

2. If so, determine whether the empirical issue bears on an assumption underlying the choice of a legal rule that has general applicability, a factual dispute pertaining only to the parties before the court, or a mixture of the two in which general empirical information provides a context for determining a specific fact.

context in which the courts may use social science information (including psychology), though there is still some confusion among legal scholars regarding social science in law paradigms.[39]

The academic role model associated with providing information that is useful to the courts could be called the "Technician."[40] Technicians have a set of technical social science skills needed to generate knowledge that is relevant to legal decision makers. Technicians might also be called handmaidens; essentially doing the law's bidding by providing facts and figures upon request. As an indication of the growing popularity of the use of social science, a number of books are now available to assist lawyers in understanding the services offered by technicians.[41]

---

3. If the empirical issue concerns an assumption underlying the choice of a legal rule of general applicability:

    a. receive social science studies in briefs submitted by the parties or amici.

    b. if the parties or amici do not submit social science studies, request such studies from the parties or amici, or obtain them from the court's own sua sponte investigation of published sources.

    c. evaluate any available research by determining whether the research has survived the critical review of the scientific community, has used valid research methods, is generalizable to the legal issue in question, and is supported by a body of related research.

    d. if no acceptable research is available, candidly state this conclusion in the opinion. In common law cases, rely upon the empirical assumption that appears to the most plausible. In reviewing state action, rely upon the legally appropriate standard of review in determining where to place responsibility for resolving the empirical issue.

4. If the empirical issue concerns a factual dispute bearing on only the parties before the court:

    a. determine the party with the burden of proving the contested fact.

    b. determine whether the law governing the case makes empirical research an appropriate form of evidence for meeting this burden.

    c. if empirical research does constitute an appropriate form of evidence, allow the admission of direct and rebuttal expert testimony subject to the applicable federal or state rules of evidence.

    d. if the party with the burden of proof does not produce relevant expert testimony, weigh this omission in determining whether the burden has been met.

5. If the empirical issue concerns the provision of a general context within which to determine a fact pertaining only to the parties:

    a. obtain and evaluate social science research as specified in 3a–3c, above.

    b. in cases tried before a jury, communicate the conclusions by means of jury instructions.

John Monahan & Laurens Walker, Judicial Use of Social Science Research, 15 L. & Hum. Beh. 571 (1991).

39. Compare Peggy C. Davis, "There is a Book Out...": An Analysis of Judicial Absorption of Legislative Facts, 100 Harv. L. Rev. 1539 (1987), with Michael J. Saks, Judicial Attention to the Way the World Works, 75 Iowa L. Rev. 1011 (1990).

40. The term is borrowed from David M. Trubek, Back to the Future: The Short Happy Life of the Law and Society Movement, 18 Fla. St. U. L. Rev. 1, 26 (1990).

41. See David W. Barnes, Statistics as Proof: Fundamentals of Quantitative Evidence (1983); David W. Barnes & John M. Conley, Statistical Evidence in Litigation (1986);

C. Psychology's Use of the Law

Psychology's efforts to influence the law can be described at both the individual and organizational level. The majority of effort is probably concentrated at the individual level where psychologists employed in various agencies and bureaucracies attempt to change law and policies from within institutions. Relying on training in the social science of psychology, individual efforts attempt to insure that laws and policies are supported, when possible, by the empirical literature. Efforts are also made at the organizational level to influence law and policy, the most notorious examples being those when the American Psychological Association (APA) submits *amicus curiae* briefs.

In recent years, the APA has formally submitted *amicus curiae* briefs in several cases.[42] A professional organization that asks (or is asked) to serve as a "friend of the court" faces several difficult ethical questions. First is the question of whether to submit a brief, and if this decision is in the affirmative, then in considering what duties and responsibilities inhere in the *amicus curiae* role. Although a number of psychologists have participated in a variety of cases to make apparent the ethical issues and problems that arise in regard to this type of advocacy, the process of brief writing is still a relatively new phenomenon to most psychologists. Accordingly, many psychologists are still in the process of defining what they consider the proper nature and extent of psychological advocacy at the appellate level.[43] The APA has been active at both the federal and state levels in submitting amicus curie briefs. The two cases that follow arguably illustrate examples of APA brief writing success, defined here as having an influence on the court's reasoning.

At the federal level, in April of 1987, the APA filed an *amicus curiae* brief in the case of *Kentucky v. Stincer*.[44] The issue before the Court in *Stincer* was whether exclusion of a defendant from a pretrial hearing, convened to determine the competency of child witnesses, violated the defendant's Sixth Amendment right to confront the witness.[45] The purpose in filing the brief was to "inform the Court...of the extent to which current empirical and clinical mental health data support assumptions regarding the traumatic effects of such confrontation on child witnesses as a basis for dispensing with defendant's rights...."[46] The APA argued that the current state of empirical and clinical

---

Noreen L. Channels, Social Science Methods in the Legal Process (1984); Wayne C. Curtis, Statistical Concepts for Attorneys: A Reference Guide (1984); David Vinseon & P. Anthony, Social Science Research Methods for Litigation (1985).

42. Charles R. Tremper, Organized Psychology's Efforts to Influence Judicial Policy-Making, 42 Am. Psychol. 496, 499 (1987).

43. Compare Rogers Elliot, Social Science Data and the APA: The "Lockhart" Brief as a Case in Point, 15 L. & Hum. Behav. 59 (1991), with Phoebe C. Ellsworth, To Tell What We Know or Wait of Godot?, 15 L & Hum. Behav. 77; or compare Ralph Underwager and Hollida Wakefield, Poor Psychology Produces Poor Law, 16 L. & Hum. Behav. 233 (1992), with Gail S. Goodman, et al., The Best Evidence Produces the Best Law, 16 L. & Hum. Behav. 244 (1992).

44. 482 U.S. 730 (1986).

45. Id. at 732.

46. Amicus Curiae Brief of American Psychological Association, at 3, Kentucky v. Stincer, 482 U.S. 730 (1986) (No. 86-572).

findings regarding the effects on child sexual assault victims was "tentative."[47] Therefore, a defendant's confrontation right should only be abrogated in cases where the risk of trauma is documented, and its nature and potential duration are believed to be substantial.[48]

The APA's brief went on to say that "not only is there very little evidence to support the general proposition that face-to-face confrontation by child victims of sexual abuse with their alleged abusers has any more negative psychological effects than such confrontation has for adults,"[49] but there is some evidence to indicate that children actually benefit from the experience.[50] The Supreme Court never reached the issues raised by the APA, deciding that the defendant's confrontation right was not violated by exclusion from the competency hearing.

In March, 1990, the APA filed an amicus curiae brief in Maryland v. Craig.[51] Noting that the empirical evidence was much stronger than that presented in Stincer, the brief stated, "The resulting body of research supports the proposition that children as a class may be especially likely to be emotionally distressed by courtroom confrontation with their alleged abusers."[52] However, a "substantial number of children are capable of testifying fully and accurately under conventional criminal procedures without serious and lasting harm."[53] Unfortunately, the basis for determining which children require protection is not yet well developed,[54] and there is no evidence to suggest which procedures may ameliorate harm most effectively.[55] The brief advocated the position eventually adopted by the Court—a case-by-case determination of whether the risk of trauma outweighs a defendant's confrontation right.[56]

An example of the APA's brief writing at the state appellate level involved a challenge to Kentucky's sodomy law, which banned oral and anal sex between homosexuals but not heterosexuals. "Citing an American Psychological Association brief on gay and lesbian sexuality and the effects of discrimination on homosexuals, the Supreme Court of Kentucky voted 5–4 September 24, 1992, to strike down Kentucky's 17-year-old sodomy law."[57] The APA brief made three points:

> One elaborates on the right-to-privacy issue from a psychological standpoint, stating that homosexual intimacy doesn't hurt others and is necessary for gays' psychological health. . . . In its second point, the brief states that both social-sci-

---

47. Id. at 5.

48. Id.

49. Id.

50. Id.

51. Amicus Curiae Brief for the American Psychological Association, at 5, Maryland v. Craig, 110 S. Ct. 3157 (1990) (No. 89-478).

52. Id. at 3.

53. Id.

54. As noted in the brief, "Given ethical and practical constraints, systematic field research is extremely difficult to conduct in this area." Id. at 14 n28.

55. Amicus Curiae Brief for the American Psychological Association, supra note 46, at 4.

56. Id. at 4.

57. Tori de Angelis, Kentucky High Court Repeals Sodomy Law, Am. Psychol. Assoc. Monitor, December 1992, at 1.

ence research and opinion support the courts' contention that the Kentucky statute violates Mr. Wasson's right to equal protection. In its third point, the brief points out that the Kentucky law banning sodomy stymies public-health efforts to combat AIDS, and harms gay mental health.[58]

The academic role model associated with the study of conducting research for the express purpose of influencing law and policy could be titled "Social Problem Solver."[59] Social Problem Solvers are scientists with a social mission, "attracted to the law because an alliance with it would give them access to centers of power and opportunities to participate in social reform programs."[60] The Social Problem Solvers in law and psychology direct efforts at both the individual and organizational level to influence law and policy.

II. *Legal Psychology*

A. The Definition of Legal Psychology

Most scholars working within the field of psychology and law generally work within one or more of the above described domains as Practitioner/scientists, Technicians, or Social Problem Solvers. One of the academic fields responsible for providing a home for the work of psycholegal studies is legal psychology. Legal psychology is a field of inquiry that focuses on applying the science of psychology to law. Accordingly, legal psychology would be defined as "the scientific study of human behavior relevant to laws and legal systems." It is important to note that legal psychology is a science; it applies the scientific method of systematic observation, description, and measurement to the study of behavior that is legally relevant. As a science, legal psychology contrasts with law which relies primarily on logic as a foundation of knowledge.

The "psychology" in legal psychology comes from the focus on behavior, predominantly that of individuals. In legal psychology the unit of analysis can be defined either at the individual or group level. At the individual level, judges, witnesses, citizens, children, and criminals are all studied. Individuals within groups (e.g., jurors, legislators) and even groups themselves (e.g. juries, legislatures, supreme courts) are also studied. Moreover, the particular phenomenon (unit of analysis) to be studied can be either behavior or mental processes.

What makes legal psychology "legal" is the application of the study of behavior and mental processes to laws and legal systems. Whereas other sub-disciplines of psychology may study behavior either in relative isolation (e.g., biological psychology) or a particular context (social psychology), legal psychology works within the legal context of substantive or procedural law. Thus far, the substantive and procedural fields that have dominated legal psychology are criminal law and mental health law.[61]

---

58. Id. at 30.

59. Again, the term is borrowed from Trubek, supra note 40, at 26.

60. Id.

61. See, e.g. Dorothy K. Kagehiro & William S. Laufer, Handbook of Psychology and Law (1992).

B. Goals of Legal Psychology

The primary purpose of psycholegal research is to challenge specific behavioral assumptions.[62] Typical examples of research empirically testing behavioral assumptions include looking at children's competence to consent,[63] juveniles' understanding of Miranda warnings,[64] and jurors' understanding of instructions.[65] While testing assumptions implicitly or explicitly runs through much of the psycholegal literature, three other purposes are frequently found—measuring the effects of a law against stated goals, contributing to subsequent decision making, and testing theory in real world settings.

1. Measuring the Effects of a Law Against Stated Goals

In conducting research for this purpose, the academic can examine both direct and indirect effects, anticipated as well as unanticipated consequences of laws. The most common type of study examines direct effects. Examples include analyzing the effects of changing civil commitment procedures on the civil commitment of the mentally ill,[66] and analyzing the effects of lowering or raising the minimum drinking age on injuries and deaths of different age groups.[67]

Studies focusing on indirect effects are less common. One study examined a Massachusetts law requiring mandatory monetary deposits on glass beverage containers.[68] The intent of the "bottle bill" was to provide an incentive to recycle. However, the study examined the effect of the bill on the incidence of lacerations in childhood. The bill, essentially passed to encourage recycling, was found to have the additional benefit of reducing the number of children who injured themselves on broken glass.[69]

2. Contributing to Subsequent Decision Making

Research conducted for the purpose of contributing to subsequent decision making can be divided into two types, formative and summative.[70] Formative research produces information that can be fed back to law makers for adjust-

---

62. See, e.g., Michael J. Saks, The Law Does Not Live by Eyewitness Testimony Alone, 10 L. & Hum. Behav. 279 (1986).

63. See, e.g., Gary B. Melton, et al., Children's Competence to Consent (1983).

64. See, e.g., Thomas Grisso, Juveniles' Capacity to Waive Miranda Rights: An Empirical Analysis, 68 Cal. L. Rev. 1134 (1980).

65. See, e.g., Harvey S. Perlman, Pattern Jury Instructions: The Application of Social Science Research, 65 Neb. L. Rev. 520 (1986).

66. See, e.g., Roger Peters, et al., The Effects of Statutory Change on the Civil Commitment of the Mentally Ill, 11 L. & Hum. Behav. 73 (1987).

67. For a review, see Richard Bonnie, The Efficacy of Law as a Paternalistic Instrument in Nebraska Symposium on Motivation: The Law as a Behavioral Instrument 131, 150 (Gary B. Melton ed. 1987).

68. See M.D. Baker et al., The Impact of Bottle Bill Legislation on the Incidence of Lacerations in Childhood, 76 Am. J. of Pub. Health 1243 (1986).

69. Id.

70. Carol H. Weis, Evaluation Research: Methods of Assessing Program Effectiveness (1972).

ing and fine tuning laws. An example of formative research is to look at the effectiveness of various rules of civil procedure, which are the rules governing attorney conduct in civil trial cases. Under these rules, sanctions are available against attorneys who abuse the legal process. An academic could study the effectiveness of sanctions in deterring abusive practices and relaying that information to law makers to make appropriate adjustments.

Summative research refers to information about whether or not decision makers should adopt or drop particular laws or policies. For example, a recent study examined the role of bias in death sentences in Georgia.[71] The study found that a Black defendant who kills a white victim is significantly more likely to be sentenced to death than a white defendant who kills a black victim.[72] This, along with other evidence, failed to convince the United States Supreme Court that Georgia's system for administering the death penalty was unconstitutional.[73] However, other state courts whose death penalty processes are similar, are free to consider such empirical evidence.[74]

3. Testing Theory in "Real" World Settings

A third purpose is to test out psychological theories in an environmentally valid setting. The legal system provides an ideal backdrop for testing out various theories. Trial procedures offer settings for testing hypotheses about the accuracy of eyewitness' recall and the influence of variables on group decision making. Unfortunately, many studies have simply simulated the legal process, using vignettes and mock jurors. Although more recent research focuses on field methods,[75] many earlier studies raise questions of external validity.

Generally, researchers interested in empirically testing behavioral assumptions in the law follow a simple strategy.[76] First, some behavioral assumption in the law is discovered. Then the researcher determines how the assumption relates to a body of law. Psychologists next determine the applicability of any relevant psychological theory, and assess the merits for testing the assumption. An appropriate methodology is chosen for testing the assumption. Finally, the information is disseminated to appropriate lawmakers.

---

71. See David C. Baldus, et al., Law and Statistics in Conflict: Reflections on McCleskey v. Kemp in Handbook of Psychology and Law 251, 255 (Dorothy K. Kagehiro & William S. Laufer eds. 1992).

72. Id. at 259.

73. McCleskey v. Kemp, 481 U.S. 279 (1987).

74. Indeed, a reading of Supreme Court death penalty cases would lead one to the conclusion that marshalling empirical evidence to persuade the Supreme Court that a state's program for administering the death penalty is unconstitutional is no longer viable. See Mark A. Small, A Review of Death Penalty Caselaw: Future Directions for Program Evaluation, 5 Crim. Just. Pol'y Rev. 114 (1991).

75. See Peter D. Blanck, The "Process" of Field Research in the Courtroom: A Descriptive Analysis, 11 L. & Hum. Behav. 337 (1987).

76. The following strategy is given in more detail and applied to privacy torts in Mark A. Small & Richard L. Wiener, Rethinking Privacy Torts: A View toward a Psycholegal Perspective in Handbook of Psychology and Law 455, 467 (1992).

C. Theory in Legal Psychology

Given this definition and these goals of legal psychology, what is the work product of psycholegal studies? The following informal analysis was undertaken to specifically examine the content of psycholegal studies. A useful tool to measure the character and maturity of a discipline is to examine how the field has developed theory. Progress in psychological theorizing can be described as a three stage model. In Stage I, researchers simply attempt to define or describe a particular phenomenon. As noted, in psycholegal studies, the phenomenon or stimulus that gives rise to work in this stage of psychological theorizing is usually some assumption that the law makes about human behavior; an assumption that can be tested using empirical analysis. In Stage II, investigators construct descriptive theories that account for observed behaviors. Finally, in Stage III, explanatory accounts are presented to specify universal theory, independent of domain specific mechanisms.

1. Analysis of Law and Human Behavior Articles

Articles appearing in *Law and Human Behavior* for the last five years were analyzed by way of a three stage model of psychological theorizing.[77] A total of 28 issues, appearing from June 1986 to December 1991, were reviewed. Within these issues, a total of 150 articles were selected. Only those manuscripts designated as "Articles" in *Law and Human Behavior* were reviewed. Other manuscripts, which appeared under a section of the journal entitled "Comments," "Adversary Forum," "Book Review," or some other designation were excluded. Of the 150 articles, 49 were single-authored, 54 were co-authored, and 47 had three or more authors (26 had 3 authors, 12 had 4 authors, 5 had 5 authors, 4 had 6 or more authors). For those who keep track of such things, exactly half of the titles contained colons.

The 150 articles comprised the work of 327 authors, of whom approximately 104 were women. The breakdown for primary institutional affiliation for authors was as follows: Psychology Department (226), Treatment Facility (26), Criminal Justice or Justice Studies (16), Public or Private Research Facility (e.g., ABA, RAND) (14), Psychiatry or Medicine Dept. (12), Law School (12), Sociology/Social Ecology (7) and Others (14).

The articles were divided into two categories, experimental and non-experimental. Of the 150 articles, 105 were experimental, 45, non-experimental. While the non-experimental papers were too diverse to properly classify, the experimental articles fell into the following categories. Jury decision making was the largest category with 44 entries. A second category entitled "Other Decision Making" had 14 entries, broken down as follows; Parole (1), Children (5), Judicial (3), Couples (1), MI Patients (2), Forensic Clinician (1), and Individual (1). Eyewitness was the next largest category with 13 entries, then

---

77. Law and Human Behavior was chosen because it is the flagship journal of the American Psychology-Law Society and arguably prints works that are representative of the field of legal psychology.

Forensic Assessment & Treatment (10), Test Changes in Law (5), Relationship of MI to Violence (5), and Others (13).

Of the 105 experimental articles, the vast majority (96) fell within Stage I of psychological theorizing. Most of the articles' topics were driven by the law. Somewhere within the law or legal process, an assumption was made about human behavior (usually the ability to decide) and researchers went about testing the validity of the assumption. Rather than testing a psychological theory by using the law and or legal process as a natural world laboratory, the research focused on validating behavioral assumptions contained within the law.

Some articles (9) did attempt to pose descriptive theories to account for observed behaviors (Stage II). Examples include a three step model constructed to explain custody decisions,[78] a model for capital penalty decision making,[79] a brief description of a "common law" of responsibility attributions,[80] a path model for understanding the factors that mediate the effects of jury nullification information and challenges to such information on the outcome of criminal trials,[81] and, finally, a path analysis of juror judgment process for impeachment evidence.[82] No articles fell into Stage III, where explanatory accounts are presented.

A greater percentage (7/45) of the non-experimental papers fell within Stage II of the psychological theory model. Examples include a discussion of the use of decision theory in the analysis of legal procedure,[83] a model asserting the conditional probabilities leading to the likelihood that an individual accused of spousal abuse will be punished by the courts,[84] a decision making approach to tax paying,[85] an explanatory account of how jurors construe insanity independent of specific insanity tests,[86] an argument that the process for line-up identification procedures should be consistent with memory research,[87] and the use

---

78. See, e.g., Carol R. Lowery, Maternal and Joint Custody: Differences in the Decision Process, 10 L. & Hum. Behav. 303 (1986).

79. See, e.g., Lawrence T. White, Juror Decision Making in the Capital Penalty Trial: An Analysis of Crimes and Defense Strategies, 11 L. & Hum. Behav. 113 (1987).

80. See, e.g., Joseph J. Sanders & V. Lee Hamilton, Is There a "Common Law" of Responsibility?: The Effect of Demographic Variables on Judgments of Wrongdoing, 11 L. & Hum. Behav. 277 (1987).

81. See, e.g., Irwin A. Horowitz, Jury Nullification: The Impact of Judicial Instructions, Arguments, and Challenges on Jury Decision Making, 12 L. & Hum. Behav. 439 (1988).

82. See, e.g., Sarah Tanford & Michele Cox, The Effects of Impeachment Evidence and Limiting Instructions on Individual and Group Decision Making, 12 L. & Hum. Behav. 477 (1988).

83. See, e.g., Terry Connolly, Decision Theory, Reasonable Doubt, and the Utility of Erroneous Acquittals, 11 L. & Hum. Behav. 101 (1987).

84. See, e.g., Donald G. Dutton, The Criminal Justice Response to Wife Assault, 11 L. & Hum. Behav. 189 (1987).

85. See, e.g., John S. Carrol, Compliance with the Law: A Decision-Making Approach to Taxpaying, 11 L. & Hum. Behav. 319 (1987).

86. See, e.g., Norman J. Finkel & Sharon F. Handle, How Jurors' Construe Insanity, 13 L. & Hum. Behav. 41 (1989).

87. See, e.g., C. A. Elizabeth Luus, & Gary Wells, Eyewitness Identification and the Selection of Distractors for Lineups, 15 L. & Hum. Behav. 43 (1991).

of psychological theories to account for third party consent in search and seizure cases.[88]

2. Discussion and Conclusions

In summary, researchers in legal psychology typically sought to test assumptions made about human behavior, but only occasionally used psychological theories to do so. The task of creating and applying theory in legal psychology belongs to the "True Scientist." Professor Trubek describes the True Scientist as follows:

> The true scientist believes that society obeys natural laws. He searches for the underlying forces that govern the behavior of groups and individuals. He sees the natural sciences as the model for social science. He believes that "theory" is a statement of empirically observed regularities. Whether he favors grand or middle range theory, the true scientist aspires to produce a body of certifiable knowledge which will hold true for all time and all places. To be certifiable as scientific, this knowledge must be supported by empirical evidence which meets the evidentiary standards of the social science community.[89]

The minimal role of psychological theorizing could be explained if a number of studies made use of legal theory, generally referred to as jurisprudence. However, in no case was the empirical research driven by legal theory. Only two of the 150 articles, both non-empirical, could be said to relate to legal theory. Haney detailed a jurisprudential analysis to account for the observed discrepancy between values and protections for values.[90] Melton discussed the normative foundation for psycholegal studies based on a psychological jurisprudence.[91]

In summary, the role of theory (either legal or psychological) in psycholegal studies is minimal. Several possible factors may account for the minor role theory plays in psycholegal studies. One obvious factor, and limitation of this study, is that more theoretical psycholegal work may be reported in journals not included in the present survey. Another factor may be the youth of the field. Another explanation may be that, by its nature, psycholegal study is primarily an applied discipline, not inclined to attract much theoretical interest. Finally, it may be that the primary theory to be logically used is legal theory, and many researchers lack an understanding of jurisprudence. To provide such an understanding, proponents of psychological jurisprudence have attempted to provide a legal context for empirical research. As one particular brand of psychological jurisprudence, therapeutic jurisprudence has been offered as a framework to guide the future work of legal psychologists.

---

88. See, e.g., Dorothy K. Kagehiro, et al., Reasonable Expectations and Thirdparty Consent Searches, 15 L. & Hum. Behav. 121 (1991).

89. The term is borrowed from David M. Trubek, Back to the Future: The Short Happy Life of the Law and Society Movement, 18 Fla. St. U. L. Rev. 1, 26 (1990).

90. Craig Haney, The Fourteenth Amendment and Symbolic Legality: Let Them Eat Due Process, 15 L. & Hum. Behav. 183 (1991).

91. Gary B. Melton, Law, Science, and Humanity: The Normative Foundation of Social Science in Law, 14 L. & Hum. Behav. 315 (1990); but see Mark A. Small, The Normative Foundation of Social Science in Law Revisited, 15 L. & Hum. Behav. 325 (1991).

III. *Therapeutic Jurisprudence*

In two books,[92] Professors Wexler and Winick lay the foundation for therapeutic jurisprudence, defined as "the study of the use of the law to achieve therapeutic objectives,"[93] or more elaborately, "the extent to which substantive rules, legal procedures, and the roles of lawyers and judges produce therapeutic or anti-therapeutic consequences."[94] Mental health law would better serve society if major efforts were undertaken to study, and improve, the role of the law as a therapeutic agent.[95] Modestly, "therapeutic jurisprudence simply seeks to focus attention on an often neglected ingredient in the calculus necessary for performing a sensible policy analysis of mental health law and practice—the therapeutic dimension—and to call for a systematic empirical examination of this dimension."[96]

The approach outlined by Wexler and Winick involves empirically examining how substantive mental health law and legal actors produce effects that are therapeutic, anti-therapeutic, both or neither. Both books adopt a similar format—an introduction to the field followed by examples of scholarship of therapeutic jurisprudence. After the introduction, *Therapeutic Jurisprudence* is divided into four parts: a) law-related psychological dysfunction; b) therapeutic aspects of the law; c) therapeutic aspects of the legal process, and d) therapeutic aspects of lawyer roles. Within each division are previously published articles that illustrate work on therapeutic jurisprudence.[97]

In contrast, *Essays in Therapeutic Jurisprudence* is divided into five parts: a) therapeutic jurisprudence; b) consent to treatment and hospitalization; c) tort regulation and the therapeutic enterprise; d) marshalling evidence—threats, contracts, and wagers, and e) teaching and research.[98] All the chapters within these divisions are articles of recent vintage (post-1989).[99] With the exception of two chapters co-authored by Robert Schopp, all are authored by Wexler, Winick or both. The two books are meant to be companion pieces.

Therapeutic jurisprudence has attracted a good deal of attention recently and necessarily invites reflection and review by those interested in the field of mental health law and jurisprudence. This short review, highlights the promise and peril of therapeutic jurisprudence. A primary concern is that therapeutic jurisprudence might dislodge mental health law from its traditional focus on the rights of citizens who voluntarily or involuntarily become involved with the mental health system. After this review, the following section relates therapeutic jurisprudence to legal psychology.

---

92. David B. Wexler, Therapeutic Jurisprudence: The Law as a Therapeutic Agent (1990) [hereinafter Wexler]. David B Wexler & Bruce J. Winick, Essays in Therapeutic Jurisprudence (1991) [hereinafter Wexler & Winick].

93. Wexler, supra note 92, at 4.

94. Wexler & Winick, supra note 92, at ix.

95. Wexler, supra note 92, at vii.

96. Wexler & Winick, supra note 92, at xi.

97. For further description, see the review by Murray Levine, Law and Psychiatry or Law Versus Psychiatry?, 36 Contemporary Psych. 931 (1991).

98. See Wexler, supra note 92.

99. Id.

A. The Promise: Therapeutic Jurisprudence as Social Science

The most striking aspect of therapeutic jurisprudence is its unabashed declaration of the value of studying the therapeutic effects of laws; particularly mental health laws. Wexler and Winick are careful to assure us that understanding the therapeutic effects of law is just one factor to be considered in deciding mental health policy issues,

> By suggesting the need to identify the therapeutic and anti-therapeutic consequences of legal rules and practices, we do not necessarily suggest that such rules and practices be recast to accomplish therapeutic ends or avoid anti-therapeutic results. Whether they should is, of course, a normative question that calls for a weighing of other potentially relevant normative values as well, such as consideration of patient autonomy, constitutional rights, community safety, etc.[100]

Thus, the discovery that a particular law "is" therapeutic does not necessarily lead to the conclusion that the law "ought" to be reformed to reflect therapeutic values. However, the distinction between "is" and "ought" is a slippery one at best. By re-orienting the field to systematically studying therapeutic effects, this value could gain considerable importance in future mental health policy calculations.

Assuming for a moment that the field of mental health law will be reoriented, why are the therapeutic effects of laws so important? It would have been just as easy to proclaim equality as a paramount value in mental health law and systematically study the discriminatory effects of laws and legal actors on minority members in the mental health system. Similarly, dignity has been proposed as an overriding construct for a psychological jurisprudence, and systematic study could have been given to the effect of mental health laws on human dignity.[101] An advantage of these latter values is their recognition as longstanding democratic values with constitutionally historic roots.

Therapeutic jurisprudence acknowledges the role of other values in mental health policy:

> We assume general agreement that, *other things being equal*, mental health law should be restructured to better accomplish therapeutic values. But whether other things are equal in a given context is often a matter of dispute. Therapeutic jurisprudence, although it seeks to illuminate the therapeutic implications of legal practice, does not resolve *this dispute*, which requires analysis of the impact of alternative practices on other relevant values.[102]

Yet, it seems natural that social science should organize (or at least intentionally disorganize) mental health law around therapeutic consequences, particularly when laws rest on therapeutic assumptions. For example, the Supreme Court's decision in *Parham v. J.R.*,[103] rested partly on assumptions that a hearing for the civil commitment of adolescents: a) "would exacerbate whatever

---

100. Wexler & Winick, supra note 92, at vii.
101. For a discussion of the role of values in psychological jurisprudence see Small, supra note 2.
102. Wexler & Winick, supra note 92, at xii (emphasis in original).
103. 442 U.S. 584 (1979).

tensions already existed between the child and the parent;" b) "will adversely affect the ability of the parents to assist the child while in the hospital," and c) "make his subsequent return home more difficult."[104] Wexler aptly points out that such assumptions are ripe for study; "the federal system has provided us with a natural laboratory: some states have followed *Parham*'s cue and have dispensed with juvenile commitment hearings, while others have decided to exceed the constitutional minima of *Parham* and have provided for hearings in juvenile commitment cases."[105] The promise of therapeutic jurisprudence is that it offers a coherent framework for empirically testing therapeutic assumptions in laws.

B. The Peril: Therapeutic Jurisprudence as Law

The leap to therapeutic jurisprudence comes in part from a dissatisfaction with the current state and direction of mental health law scholarship. Therapeutic jurisprudence, its authors boldly believe, "can breathe new life into the area of mental health law—an area that, as traditionally approached, has largely lost its academic appeal."[106] Wexler argues that the field of mental health law has declined in large part due to its dependence on a "rights analysis." Mental health law was largely created by granting mental patients the same rights given other institutionalized populations (notably, criminals). As the importance of rights in other areas of law has descended, so has the field of mental health law. Therapeutic jurisprudence is offered to both fill the vacuum and reorient the field.

While the field of mental health law may have grown sterile (as Wexler maintains), there is support for the argument that it was never overly fertile. Mental health law was created in large part by those advocating reform of the atrocious conditions in mental institutions and sloppy institutionalization practices. Many of the reforms brought about by mental health litigation (primarily the improvement of standards and services in institutions and the alteration of procedures by which persons could be institutionalized) were the result of specifically targeted concerns. The reforms successfully accomplished a move away from a medical model of mental health policy toward a libertarian model that afforded rights and protections to a vulnerable population.

The most recent trend in mental health law returns power to mental health professionals in charge of making decisions about the practices of mental health policy. Leading the charge, the Supreme Court in *Youngberg v. Romeo*,[107] held that courts must defer to the judgment of mental health professionals in determining what treatment services are constitutionally guaranteed to institutionalized persons. As *Youngberg*'s progeny of cases attest, courts' deference to mental health professionals' opinions concerning mental health policy administration shows no signs of abating.[108] A similar, if not

---

104. Id. at 591.

105. Wexler, supra note 92, at 15.

106. Wexler & Winick, supra note 92, at xiv.

107. 457 U.S. 357 (1982).

108. See Washington v. Harper, 110 S. Ct. 128 (1990). For a discussion of how mental health professionals might use such decisions to provide services that might not otherwise be

more pronounced, deference exists in cases involving adolescents in which the Supreme Court held that a full hearing is not necessary; the commitment decision could be made by a neutral administrator.[109]

The effect of this judicial trend of deference to professional judgment is to place the responsibility for mental health policy more firmly in the hands of mental health professionals. For therapeutic jurisprudence, this trend has mixed implications. On the one hand, if mental health professionals are to be the primary decision makers in matters of mental health policy, it is wise that they obtain information about the therapeutic effects of the legal context in which they work. Ostensibly, they are well positioned to both understand obstacles to therapeutic objectives as well as implement necessary changes.

On the other hand, it was because of abuse and neglect of the "therapeutic" goals of laws that the field of mental health law was originally created. Although mental health law may better serve society if it is founded upon accurate therapeutic assumptions, it does not necessarily follow that mental health law will better serve society if it is removed from focusing on the rights of citizens and patients. Law is the last, and frequently only, refuge for the oppressed mentally ill. A continued focus on the rights of the mentally ill is necessary to insure that there is no return to the "old" days. Moreover, much empirical work remains to be done on how and whether basic rights are still being violated. Thus, it is premature to abandon the traditional field of inquiry. A potential peril lies in removing mental health law from its freshly liberating position and returning it to its dark, paternalistic past.

IV. Legal Psychology and Therapeutic Jurisprudence

In a detailed analysis of the Supreme Court's apparent deliberate disregard for psychological research in deciding trial procedure cases, Professor Tanford makes the argument that "for a body of empirical research to command a place in jurisprudence, the science must reflect some of the same values as a particular body of law. The more the two value systems converge, the more completely will law accept the science."[110] If this is true, then therapeutic jurisprudence is well suited to provide empirical results for mental health law. Empirically documenting the nature and extent of therapeutic effects of laws and procedures is consistent with the therapeutic value implicit in most mental health laws. Social science could advance mental health law by insuring that laws based on therapeutic assumptions are accurately founded, and for laws not founded upon therapeutic assumptions, then at least the therapeutic effects are known.

The broader question asks whether therapeutic jurisprudence offers a theoretical framework that can be utilized within the field of legal psychology. Professors Wexler and Winick claim that therapeutic jurisprudence has the poten-

---

available see Mark A. Small & Randy K. Otto, Utilizing the "Professional Judgment Standard" in Child Advocacy, 20 J. Clinical Child Psych. 71 (1991).

109. See, e.g., *Parham*, 442 U.S. 584 (1979).

110. J. Alexander Tanford, The Limits of a Scientific Jurisprudence: The Supreme Court and Psychology, 66 Ind. L. Rev. 137, 167 (1989).

tial of transcending the narrow confines of mental health law; "Although therapeutic jurisprudence probably ought to begin by focusing on mental health law, it can obviously have implications and applications far beyond the mental health law area."[111] When compared with the academic fields of law and legal psychology, this claim becomes problematic.

The strength of therapeutic jurisprudence is that the promoted value of "therapy" is consistent with the therapeutic value long prized and implicit in mental health law. When one moves to other areas of law, the value of therapy takes on considerably less significance, and at times becomes irrelevant. For example, there seems little benefit in empirically analyzing issues in antitrust law, secure transactions, or water law according to therapeutic outcomes. These and other areas of law were created to serve a variety of purposes, perhaps least (if at all) among them is that there is or should be a therapeutic outcome that is of consequence.

When compared with the field of legal psychology, the ability of therapeutic jurisprudence to expand beyond the realm of mental health law depends in part on its ability to attract those who work within the field of legal psychology. While there is currently some overlap between the goals of legal psychologists and those advocated by therapeutic jurisprudence, at this time therapeutic jurisprudence as a template fails to cover the diversity of work being done within the field of legal psychology. An additional issue for consideration is the composition of those who will produce therapeutic jurisprudence scholarship.

As noted, the cast of psycholegal scholars at different times play the roles of Practitioner/scientist, Technician, Social Problem Solver, and occasionally, True Scientist. These roles were created largely in response to scripts written by the law (broadly defined). Practitioner/scientists emerged when citizens needed protection from the state (and psychologists). Technicians emerged when the legal enterprise needed quantitative information. Social Problem Solvers emerged when the law required evaluation of whether socially desirable goals were being met. The law has yet to write a script for therapeutic jurisprudence. Therapeutic jurisprudence may be important, but the case has yet to be made that it is imperative.

V. Conclusion

The primary advantage of therapeutic jurisprudence is that it advances mental health law by insuring that laws based on therapeutic assumptions are accurately founded, and for laws not founded upon therapeutic assumptions, then at least the therapeutic effects are known. The research agenda outlined for mental health law by therapeutic jurisprudence is both ambitious and daunting, and could be considered a success if it results in nothing more than empirical attention to the mental health law field.

A disadvantage of therapeutic jurisprudence is the danger that lies in mental health professionals who are granted more power by the courts in determining

---

111. David B. Wexler & Bruce J. Winick, Therapeutic Jurisprudence as a New Approach to Mental Health Law Policy Analysis and Research, 45 U. Miami L. Rev. 979, 982 n.10 (1992).

rights, and those interested in mental health law (traditionally advocates for patient rights) responding with a reorientation toward examining therapeutic effects of mental health laws. While therapeutic jurisprudence holds the promise of bringing social science to bear on examining therapeutic effects, there is the potentially perilous possibility that mental health law will discourage research on protecting rights; an historically valuable direction where arguably much empirical work remains to be done. Finally, there may be limits to the ability of therapeutic jurisprudence to expand beyond the field of mental health law or to capture the diversity of the field of legal psychology, both of which are necessary for a comprehensive psychological view of the law.

Chapter 31

New Approaches to Mental Health Law: Will the UK Follow the US Lead, Again?

David Carson
David B. Wexler

The 1960s and 1970s witnessed a growing concern in the United States (USA) about the position of mentally disordered people. Lawyers sought to establish rights and protections for mentally disordered patients, often calling in aid the authority of the US Constitution. This "legal-rights movement," along with contemporaneous anti-psychiatry and deinstitutionalisation movements, was regularly perceived as setting lawyers and individual rights in opposition to clinicians and medical paternalism. It had important successes (Herr *et al.*, 1983). Similar concerns were expressed in the United Kingdom (UK), but less powerfully and usually some years after their articulation in the USA. "Despite the much-vaunted concern of the common lawyer for individual freedom, lawyers in this country played little part in all this ferment" (Hoggett, 1990, p. 3). Nevertheless the legal rights movement was exported from the USA to Canada and the UK (Rappeport, 1987). In the UK it led to the Mental Health Act 1983.

Ten years on, organisations such as the Mental Health Act Commission, established by the Act of 1983, are calling for a comprehensive review of the Act (Mental Health Act Commission, 1993) and the House of Commons Select Committee on Health is describing the Act as "obsolescent though far from obsolete" (Health Committee, 1993, para. 87). Will any new legislation continue this "legal rights" perspective or will it simply involve a swing of the pendulum back towards giving clinicians greater discretion? Will it take account of the new, radically different approaches to mental health law that have developed in the USA in recent years? This approach, essentially interdisciplinary and co-operative (Keilitz and Roesch, 1992), contrasts markedly with the antagonistic and adversarial model of mental health law; law versus psychiatry, rights or treatment. It is concerned to see that services in the community, as well as in institutions, are effective (Petrila, 1992).

This article aims to highlight (not to review) recent developments in the USA, particularly those associated with therapeutic jurisprudence. It then adopts a broad conception of "mental health law" and a deliberately diverse range of topics to consider a number of examples, indicating how a more interdisciplinary and co-operative approach might advantage patients and clients without compromising basic legal rights. Whilst noting certain advantages that the UK has over the USA, the paper concludes that much depends upon a willingness to find new ways of interdisciplinary and interprofessional working.

* * *

Pendulum Laws

Reform of mental health laws in the UK has been likened to the swings of a pendulum (Jones, 1972), between providing clinicians with broad discretion or prescribing detailed regulation. The Lunacy Act 1890, "a 'close-textured' statute, in which everything is prescribed in great detail, and nothing is left to chance or professional discretion" (Jones, 1991, p. 95) was superseded by the Mental Health Act 1959, "a normative Act—relatively brief, non-prescriptive, and concentrating upon the principles of good service rather than on offences and penalties" (Jones, 1991, pp. 99–100). Viewed from an historical perspective the 1983 Act was another swing of the pendulum between regulation and legal perspectives. However, concern, particularly about the degree of power which the 1959 Act gave to clinicians, was articulated to great effect by Larry Gostin, a US trained lawyer who was legal officer of MIND, the leading mental health pressure group in the UK. His work had a powerful influence leading to the Mental Health Act 1983 (Gostin, 1975, 1977, 1983).

With that Act the pendulum once again swung from reliance upon clinicians' discretion and good faith, towards providing clinicians with more explicit tests and procedures, providing more occasions when clinicians must justify their actions, providing more Mental Health Review Tribunal hearings. "Once again we have 'close-textured' prescriptive law, characterised by prohibitions and penalties" (Jones, 1991, pp. 99–100). The 1983 Act has led to more litigation; in a few years a much more extensive body of case-law has developed than existed under the 1959 Act (Hoggett, 1990). The rights approach has led to some important changes; although some doubt whether the legal rights approach made any real gains in the USA (Rappeport, 1987; Stone, 1982). The gains, at least in the UK, have tended to be procedural; have regulated rather than ensured treatment. For example, in *R. v. Hallstrom, ex parte* W ([1986] Q.B. 1090) the courts declared unlawful the "compulsory supervision" of patients in the community by keeping them technically detained in hospital but allowing them long leave at home.

In both the USA and the UK lawyers' attention has been on rights in institutions rather than rights in the community, even though that is where the focus for providing care has moved, encouraged by the deinstitutionalisation and legal rights movements (Brown, 1985; Griffiths, 1988, 1989). "Clinical experience in New South Wales, Victoria, New Zealand and some states of the USA shows that hospital oriented statutes imperfectly apply to community oriented services" (Health Committee, 1993, para. 6). Indeed, because of the 1983 Act's failure to make adequate provision for patients in the community as well as in hospitals, the UK Government proposes introducing a new statutory procedure for "supervised discharge," whilst stressing that greater use could be made of existing legal powers (Department of Health, 1993; see also Fennell, 1993; Gunn, 1986).

* * *

TJ in the UK: Disincentives to Treatment

Whilst US and UK laws are often significantly different there are a number of parallels. Although in both countries there would appear to be a concern to ensure that those who have need for treatment or other forms of help can obtain it, the law may provide a disincentive. For example, in the USA, in certain circumstances, it is against the legal interests of a defendant with a learning disability to acknowledge that disability. His or her learning disability is noted by clinicians and others but, sometimes, it is then "unidentified" in order to take advantage of the wider range of "disposal" opportunities open to people without such disabilities (Petrella, 1992). Recognising the disability formally would limit the disposal options. In the UK it is unwise for someone who has committed a crime whilst in a diabetic coma (*Hennessy* [1989] 2 All E.R. 9), whilst sleep-walking (*Burgess* [1991] 2 W.L.R. 120; but note that the Canadian Supreme Court took a different approach in *Parks* (1993) 95 D.L.R. 27), or whilst having an epileptic seizure (*Sullivan* [1984] A.C. 156) to identify the cause as such, unless he or she is prepared to accept the consequence of a not guilty but insane verdict.

This tendency, to provide disincentives to seeking treatment, is not limited to the criminal law. In order to reduce the number of car accidents Shuman (1992b) proposes that the standard of care, in the law of negligence, should take account of whether defendants, including those experiencing stress, have sought appropriate medical care. Tort law provides a disincentive.

> "Those who respond to the objective standard's therapeutic incentive and receive a thorough psychiatric or psychological diagnosis fare even worse under tort law than those who ignore the symptoms of their illness. Tort law imposes a greater burden on those who discover specific knowledge of risk." (Shuman, 1992b)

Those who sought and followed appropriate treatment before the accident occurred, Shuman and many others argue, should be less liable, should be judged by a lower standard of care than those who knew of an illness, or the desirability of seeking attention, but did not act. The effect of any such practice in the UK would be mediated by insurance policies. However, those insurance policies could provide special rates, perhaps required or encouraged by the law, for those who sought medical attention rather than avoided it.

Disincentives to seeking appropriate treatment may be traced to the law's predeliction for the use of dichotomous categories. These encourage erroneous stereotypes of mentally disordered people as being either/or; for example, either capable or incapable of understanding the consequences of their actions or intending them. People, including those with mental disorders, often know when they have problems, know when they have difficulties controlling their behaviour. They also have insight, to different degrees, into the nature and extent of their problems, just like those who have problems with their use of alcohol or nicotine.

Was the father who sexually abused his child, suddenly, unexpectedly and overwhelmingly, overcome by some form of irresistible impulse at a particular defining moment in time? Or did he realise that he was "attracted" to his child for sexual or other inappropriate reasons, to which he eventually gave way? In practice, individuals, such as child sex abusers, are more or less likely to appreciate that they have problems and more or less likely to realise that they might be able to do something, and ought to do something, about them. Their knowledge of what options are open to them, how practical action on those options is, and what the balances in favour of action or inaction are, depends crucially upon the law and the publicity and education provided about it. However, our law, both in its black letter form and in practice, provides disincentives to people who need help in order to avoid or to reduce the likelihood of committing crimes. Our legal industry, like medicine, is preoccupied with responding to pathologies rather than establishing preventative systems.

Consider the father who feels "attracted" towards his child. Should he tell anyone? If he did tell someone, say a doctor, would it be kept confidential, at least so long as he actively engaged in therapy? If he told his wife or an adviser during conciliation proceedings, the Court of Appeal has decided that the information could be divulged in proceedings under the Children Act 1989, at least (*Re D (minors)* [1993] 2 W.L.R. 721). That decision was based on *W. v. Egdell* ([1990] 1 All E.R. 835) where a psychiatrist, who had been asked to prepare a report to assist a patient's case for discharge by a Mental Health Review Tribunal, was found not to have been in breach of confidence when, concluding that the patient still posed danger to the public and finding that his report was not going to be made available to the Tribunal, he sent copies of it to the Tribunal and other relevant organisations.

Analysis of legal doctrine will reveal that prior social duty would justify breach of such a confidence, certainly where one assault had already taken place but therapy was sought before it was repeated (Brazier, 1992). But is that useful? Surely the first objective should be prevention, not punishment after the event. If people are less likely to commit offences when provided with therapy or other forms of intervention which they are prepared to accept, then there ought to be positive or negative, direct or indirect, incentives. Doctors and others might be authorised, with the authority being translated into positive procedure guides as well as being a bald statement of law, to maintain confidentiality in such circumstances. Prosecutions could be held in abeyance for so long as treatment is actively pursued and further offences are not committed. Those whom it can be shown had insight into their problems, who knew that confidential services were available to assist them or could have known this with reasonable diligence, but who failed to seek such services, could be punished more severely.

Of course such proposals will offend those who see the criminal justice system's primary goals in terms of punishing, but protecting the rights of, offenders. The argument is that we should consider whether other valuable goals, including primary and secondary prevention and the interests of victims, can be achieved by other means. It need not be perceived as a clash of systems, child protection or criminal justice, but an attempt to marry objectives. The child victim of an incestuous sexual assault may not actually want her father prosecuted and imprisoned, with all the practical consequences that that is likely to have for her and her family. She may be satisfied with being believed and being assured that it will not occur again. Involving victims, such as by encouraging civil actions for assault, will improve their sense that justice has been done (Tyler, 1992), will be important for their therapy, and will empower them in a way which may help prevent repetition (Carson, 1994a). The primary, although implicit, message of our law, to perpetrators of such crimes, ought not to be: "If you are going to assault a child then make sure you threaten her or him so much, such as by regular repetition, that he or she will be too frightened to tell, and will be liable to be disbelieved for not having told earlier."

It might be argued that, by providing disincentives to treatment, the law is serving an important function of discouraging the medicalisation of moral or legal issues. That someone feels disposed to commit a crime even if, like child sexual abuse, that crime is replete with stereotypes and assumptions, does not, by itself, justify any assumption that that person is mentally disordered or otherwise "ill" or "sick." "Treatment" and "therapy," with all their assumptions of medical benevolence, may be inappropriate; the individual requires punishment or, at least, deterrence. First, there is no assumption that the "treatment" must be of a medical form or only provided by medically qualified people. Second, punishment is inappropriate where no crime has yet been committed and relying upon deterrence is risky. Third, the critical role of consent has not been questioned. The values implicit in a therapeutic jurisprudence approach do not "trump" (Wexler, 1993c) other values, particularly core civil liberty considerations. Indeed a therapeutic jurisprudence approach is liable to put greater emphasis upon the importance of consent given its empirically demonstrated role in aiding the attainment of therapeutic goals (Winick, 1991a). Traditional approaches to mental health law, which emphasise the role of legal doctrine, have produced in the UK the dichotomous categories of detained or "voluntary" patient. However, the genuineness of the "voluntary" category is regularly doubted because the patient might be "threatened" with detention if he or she did not agree to be a voluntary patient. A willingness to consider different approaches will be necessary if such conundrums are to be tackled. Treatment is more likely to be effective if it is consensual, if the patient is motivated. A therapeutic jurisprudence approach would encourage everyone, clinicians and lawyers, to find ways of gaining the patient's full-hearted consent because of its treatment efficacy and because of the legitimacy it provides for the treatment. The potential of the law of contracts, which *inter alia* has the advantages of encouraging patient motivation and explicit input and outcome measures, should be considered. Winick (1991b) has proposed an analogous system based upon patients "wagering" with the government. A therapeutic jurisprudence should lead to many fewer, not more, patients being compulsorily treated. To promote it is not to say that certain people need treatment, in their objective best interests, therefore let us devise ways of authorising this in law. Rather it is to recognise that many people need and will benefit from treatment and, provided that their rights are respected, indeed that their autonomy will be enhanced, it encourages lawyers to ensure that the law does not frustrate them in their wish to be treated. The law should not be preoccupied with issues of compulsory treatment to the exclusion of the problems surrounding the consequences of people not obtaining treatment and other services.

TJ in the UK: Procedural Considerations

A therapeutic jurisprudence approach can inform procedures as well as substantive laws. For example, there is continuing concern about abuses occurring in some of our hospitals for people with mental disorders. This has led to new and improved complaints procedures, sometimes providing for legal representation of the parties. What are the principal objects of such schemes? A fair hearing and a correct interpretation of the dispute? That might just be achieved. Or should the principal objects include the prevention of abuses in the first place? Given the reality of hospitals, particularly secure hospitals where the most difficult-to-manage patients are placed (and the greatest opportunities for misunderstandings and disputes about facts are likely to arise), patients must be expected to be reluctant to complain. They are relatively powerless. Their complaints naturally appear as criticisms and as challenges to staff. A patient who is prepared to complain is isolating himself or herself, is inviting problems including having the incident recorded as symptomatic of his or her disorder.

Managers need a regular flow of information in order to know what is happening in their service. Why not put the emphasis on comments rather than on criticisms? It is much easier to ask for information and to style it in a non-threatening and non-confrontational manner: "Should I have been refused that opportunity?" rather than "You are biased against me and refused me that opportunity." With a complaint the initiative is placed upon the complainant to develop a theory about why something happened. With a comment the initiative is on the authorities to explain. The objectives of a complaints scheme need not be compromised just by broadening the analysis of the problem and considering non-traditional legal responses. Of course brutality and other abuses in closed institutions such as hospitals will not be prevented by simply changing complaints systems into comments schemes. Nobody would seriously suggest that! This is just one idea, one contribution that might be developed if a less traditional approach was taken seeking the maximisation of a wider range of goals.

In this example the needs of managers for information and the organisation for dialogue were added to the traditional dispute resolution model which awaits a query being concretised into an issue and then a problem. More people are likely to seek explanations, or to make comments, than to criticise. It will be easier to transform the making of comments into a valued, regular and recognised activity than to transform the making of complaints. Managers ought to be able to recognise, and be able to explain to other people, that a unit which receives many more comments (or criticisms) than another may be a much better unit than one with fewer comments or criticisms. It could be that the regime in the first unit respects its clients, that it encourages and welcomes the expression of views, whilst the second unit is repressive. It would be easier for managers to get this philosophy adopted if they concentrated upon schemes seeking comments rather than complaints.

Therapeutic jurisprudence could also inform and improve decisionmaking. Mental Health Review Tribunals have to decide whether detained patients should be discharged from hospital or not (Mental Health Act 1983, Part V). They have a power to make recommendations. Based upon this organisational scheme and tribunal model, the Parole Board can now order the release of discretionary life sentence prisoners, or make recommendations (Criminal Justice Act 1991, s. 34). From detention in hospital or prison, to discharge or release into the community, is a remarkably large step to take, which makes the decision more difficult to manage and therefore dangerous. Although such action may satisfy our craving for dramatic decisions, would not smaller steps, which the professionals involved are more used to planning and taking, be wiser and more open to control? The

Court of Appeal, in *R.* v. *Parole Board, ex parte Telling* (unreported, 1993, *Lexis*, 6 May), rejected criticism of a discretionary lifers panel decision for not taking a big enough step. But it did so by undertaking a traditional doctrinal analysis, of such concepts as dangerousness and reasonableness, rather than by adopting an analysis of the quality of the decision-making systems adopted (Carson, 1993b).

Adopting a variety of expressions, both the mental health and the criminal justice systems focus on the "dangerousness" of the patient or prisoner (for example, see Floud and Young, 1981). That is an exceptionally difficult, if not impossible, criterion to assess. It has led to extensive debates, including whether there is a sufficient body of knowledge to justify expert witnesses giving evidence on the topic (Faust and Ziskin, 1988; Hoge and Grisso, 1992). But the debate has moved on—it may perhaps have done so in the UK (Carson, 1990) earlier than in the USA (Steadman *et al.*, 1993)—and away from dichotomous legal concepts, artifically and dangerously taken on, and concentrating upon, one particular day, to a focus upon the quality of the decision-making and a wider, more relevant range of variables (Carson, 1994b).

A focus upon the quality of decision-making, such as by the development and positive monitoring of risk-taking policies (Carson, 1990), provides valuable opportunities. For clinicians there is the opportunity for endorsement of their small-step controlled approach, allowing progressively more freedom and responsibility to patients. For lawyers there is the opportunity to scrutinise whether an appropriate programme of risk-taking, oriented towards their clients' growing competence and discharge, is being *actively* pursued. For patients there is the reassurance that the consequence of inappropriately *not* taking risks is available for scrutiny. For the public there is the reassurance that the critical situational and management factors of risk-taking are being taken into account.

Therapeutic jurisprudence also suggests that psychological principles can be brought into conditional release determination in order to increase a patient's compliance with orders to take medication and the like. For instance, health care psychology suggests that compliance with medical advice will be greater if a behavioural contract is signed by the patient and the provider, if family members are made aware of the terms of the agreement, and the patient makes a public commitment to comply. If these principles were incorporated into the legal release decision-making procedure then patient compliance with treatment orders would be expected to increase, although that is of course an empirical question which therapeutic jurisprudence encourages. (Wexler and Winick, 1991)

Another example, in the UK, is the law concerning decision-making by mentally incapable adults. When do they have capacity to make which decisions about financial, medical, sexual, personal, or any other issue of direct or indirect legal significance to them and others and, if they lack capacity, who should make which decisions for them, when and how? The Law Commission, which is considering new legislation on these issues, is, in essence, treating it as a technical legal problem, where the mentally incapacitated adult constitutes the problem, which simply requires the development of a legal framework attracting as much consensus as is possible (Law Commission, 1993a, 1993b, 1993c). It could, instead, focus upon the potential for people who are not incapacitated to structure and simplify the decisions that need to be taken by people who may, otherwise, be incapable. It could focus on the potential for dis-disabling people by providing them with skills. The law could also encourage people to deal fairly with each other; for instance, by further developments in the law of undue influence. It could take a realist approach focusing upon the substantive, not just the formal, quality of the interactions between people who may be incapable and others who are not incapable on that particular issue (Carson, 1993a).

Potential for TJ in the UK

Whilst therapeutic jurisprudence was developed in the USA, which is much further ahead in the statement of the empirical issues that need investigation, there are a number of reasons why therapeutic jurisprudence should have a particularly fecund future in the UK. First, the UK does not have a written constitution with the same prominence in legal theory as does the USA. That should make us less preoccupied with doctrinal analysis, although the European Convention on Human Rights still attracts such attention. Law reform proposals are being developed with an eye to whether the letter of the Convention, and interpretations of it, might be breached (Law Commission, 1993a, 1993b, 1993c; Department of Health, 1993). That would be unexceptional if those discussions also considered the spirit and principles behind the Convention and, perhaps, wondered aloud whether some of the Convention's requirements have grown dated.

Second, we are more accustomed to the use of codes as a legislative tool. Particularly if they are given some legal muscle, such as a requirement that they be taken into account should a dispute ever get so far as a court, codes are peculiarly adaptable to a range of different circumstances. They are also relatively inexpensive to draft and redraft as circumstances change and standards improve, and they permit individualisation in a way that formal legislation cannot achieve.

Third, we have a more unified system for the organisation, financing and delivery of services to people with mental disorders, at least in comparison with the USA with its range of public and private, federal and state provision. One critical failure of the "legal rights" approach has been its inability to ensure that services are actually provided. In the UK hopes have been pinned on public law remedies and judicial review of the implementation of statutory duties to provide services. If private law remedies, such as for managerial negligence (leading to the inefficient design and delivery of services) or for breach of contract, were emphasised then more progress might be made.

Whilst the present UK Government emphasises the ideology of contracts—for example, turning health authorities into purchasers of health care and hospitals into providers—it has not put contractual muscle behind it. "Contractual" disputes, between purchasers and providers, cannot be referred to the courts for resolution (National Health Service and Community Care Act 1990, section 4(3)). Customers of public health and social services do not, currently, have a contractual basis upon which to sue. Particularly with the growing recognition that traditional statutes such as the Mental Health Act 1983 may be appropriate for regulating institutional care but are not appropriate for supporting the development of community care, we should consider the potential of contract law.

First, clients could be provided with vouchers with which to make a direct choice of preferred service (Winick, 1993), from a range of services acceptable to and notified by the agency that will redeem the voucher. In that way the client would be providing consideration for the services received and the agency could be relieved of the potential embarrassment of having to sue for breach of contract. A social services department, for example, may be inhibited about removing a contract from an agency through concern about how else it is going to ensure that services are provided, particularly at that price. It may also feel that the breached term of the contract is insufficiently serious to damage relations between it and the agency, a major consideration in practice (Cotterrell, 1984).

Second, the contributions that clients often have to make towards the costs of certain services might be organised into a form of consideration, instead of just being part of a means test applied to aid the funding of the service. Third, those who are responsible for ensuring that care is provided to the clients, such as case managers and their statutory authority employers, could be encouraged to make it a registration requirement that service providers offer their clients a contract which covers certain minimal conditions, when providing services under such as the registered homes legislation (Registered Homes Act 1984, as amended by the Registered Homes (Amendment) Act 1991). Since original submission the Divisional Court, in R. v. *Newcastle upon Tyne City Council, ex parte Dixon* (*The Times* 26 October 1993), decided that it was lawful for registration authorities to impose additional contractual obligations upon private and voluntary sector service providers.

* * *

Is "therapeutic jurisprudence" distinctive? Yes. Does it involve anything more than investigating whether the law is effective and, if not, why not? Yes. As indicated at the start of this paper the history of mental health law has been characterised by broad swings between detailed legal regulation and relative clinical autonomy. The relationship between lawyers and psychiatrists (and other service providers) has basically been antagonistic rather than co-operative. Therapeutic jurisprudence is distinctive because it advocates interdisciplinary co-operation without requiring anyone to give up their core concerns, be that for seeing patients treated or seeing patients' legal rights are protected. It provides lawyers with a means (or lens) with which they can look to their clients' broader interests. It does not involve placing a misplaced faith in or having a reified image of therapy and paternalistic medical goals. By questioning what the therapeutic goals are, and by empirically testing whether they are actually achieved, it actually involves testing those goals in a more effective manner than can generalised scepticism. It is crucial to emphasise the fact that therapeutic jurisprudence carefully acknowledges the value debates in which it participates and that it does *not* seek to "trump" (Schopp, 1993; Wexler, 1993c) other values, such as legal interests, but rather to suggest that, wherever other things are at least equal, law ought to aid, rather than harm or hinder, therapeutic outcomes.

Therapeutic jurisprudence involves opening up more choices for more people to take; it need not be a case of law *or* psychiatry, but rather one of law *and* psychiatry. But it requires a willingness to consider different ways of working. That may prove to be its greatest challenge in the UK. The momentum of the pendulum may yet prove too powerful so that we continue with our relatively unproductive adversarial approach to mental health law.

References

M. Brazier, Medicine. Patients and the Law (1992) (2nd edn.) Harmondsworth. Mx: Penguin.

P. Brown (ed.), Mental Health Care and Social Policy (1985) Boston, MA: Routledge & Kegan Paul.

D. Carson (ed.), Risk-taking in Mental Disorder; Analyses, Policies and Practical Strategies (1990) Chichester: S.L.E. Publications.

D. Carson, "Disabling progress; the Law Commission's proposals on mentally incapacitated adults' decision-making" (1993a) Journal of Social Welfare and Family Law: 304–320.

D. Carson, note and commentary on R. v. Parole Board, *ex parte* Telling (1993b) Expert Evidence 2, 2: 82–84.

D. Carson, "The law's contribution to protecting adults with learning disabilities from sexual abuse" (in press) in J. Harris and A. Croft (eds.) People with Learning Difficulties at Risk of Physical or Sexual Abuse (1994a) Kidderminster: British Institute of Learning Disabilities.

D. Carson, "Dangerousness decisions: the case of discretionary life sentence prisoners" (1994b) (under review).

R. Cotterrell, The Sociology of Law: An Introduction (1984) London: Butterworth.

Department of Health, Legal Powers on the Care of Mentally Ill People in the Community; Report of the Internal Review (1993) London: Department of Health.

D. Faust and J. Ziskin, "The expert witness in psychology and psychiatry" (1988) Science 241: 31–35.

P. Fennell, "Arrest or injection?" (19 March 1993) New Law Journal 143: 395–396, 398.

J. Floud and W. Young, Dangerousness and Criminal Justice (1981) London: Heinemann.

L. Gostin, A Human Condition: The Mental Health Act from 1959 to 1975: Observations, Analysis and Proposals for Reform, Vol. 1 (1975) London: MIND.

L. Gostin, A Human Condition: The Law Relating to Mentally Abnormal Offenders: Observations, Analysis and Proposals for Reform, Vol. 2 (1977) London: MIND.

L. Gostin, "The ideology of entitlement: the application of contemporary legal approaches to psychiatry" in P. Bean (ed.) Mental Illness: Changes and Trends (1983) Chichester, Sx: Wiley.

R. Griffiths, Community Care: Agenda for Action, a Report to the Secretary of State for Social Services (1988) London: HMSO.

R. Griffiths, Caring for People: Community Care in the Next Decade and Beyond (1989) London: HMSO.

M. J. Gunn, "Mental Health Act guardianship: where now?" (1986) Journal of Social Welfare Law 290: 144–152.

Health Committee, Community Supervision Orders, House of Commons paper, 667-1, 1992–93 session (1993) London: HMSO.

S.S. Herr, S. Arons and R.E. Wallace, Legal Rights and Mental Health Care (1983) Lexington, MA: Lexington Books.

S.K. Hoge and T. Grisso, "Accuracy and expert testimony" (1992) Bulletin of the American Academy of Psychiatry and Law 20: 67–76.

B.M. Hoggett, Mental Health Law (1990) (3rd edn.), London: Sweet & Maxwell.

K. Jones, A History of the Mental Health Services (1972) London: Routledge & Kegan Paul.

K. Jones, "Law and mental health: sticks or carrots?" in G.E. Berrios and H. Freeman (eds.) 150 Years of British Psychiatry, 1841–1991 (1991) London: Gaskell.

I. Keilitz and R. Roesch, "Improving justice and mental health systems interactions: in search of a new paradigm" (1992) Law and Human Behavior 16, 1: 5–26.

Law Commission, Mentally Incapacitated Adults and Decision-Making: A New Jurisdiction, Consultation Paper No. 128 (1993a) London: HMSO.

Law Commission, Mentally Incapacitated Adults and Decision-Making: Medical Treatment and Research, Consultation Paper No. 129 (1993b) London: HMSO.

Law Commission, Mentally Incapacitated Adults and Decision-Making: Public Law Protection, Consultation Paper No. 130 (1993c) London: HMSO.

Mental Health Act Commission, Evidence to the Department of Health (1993) Nottingham: Mental Health Act Commission.

R.C. Petrella, "Defendants with mental retardation in the forensic services system" in R.W. Conley, R. Luckasson and G.N. Bouthilet (eds.) The Criminal Justice System and Mental Retardation (1992) Baltimore, MD: Paul H. Brookes.

J. Petrila, "Redefining mental health law: thoughts on a new agenda" (1992) Law and Human Behavior 16, 1: 89–106.

J.R. Rappeport, "Belegaled: Mental Health Law in the United States, 1986" (1987) Canadian Journal of Psychiatry 32: 719–727.

R.F. Schopp, "Therapeutic jurisprudence and conflicts among values in mental health law" (1993) Behavioural Sciences and the Law 11, 1: 34–45.

D.W. Shuman, "Therapeutic jurisprudence and tort law: a limited subjective standard of care" (1992b) SMU Law Review 46, 2: 409–432.

J. Steadman, J. Monahan, P.C. Robbins, T. Grisso, D. Klassen, E.P. Mulvey and L. Roth, "From dangerousness to risk assessment: implications for appropriate research strategies" in S. Hodgins (ed.), Mental Disorder and Crime (1993) Newbury Park, CA: Sage, pp. 39–62.

A.A. Stone, "Psychiatric abuse and legal reform: two ways to make a bad situation worse" (1982) International Journal of Law and Psychiatry 5: 9–28.

T.R. Tyler, "The psychological consequences of judicial procedures: implications for civil commitment hearings; (1992) SMU Law Review 46, 2: 433–445.

D.B. Wexler, "Justice, mental health, and therapeutic jurisprudence" (1993c) (in press) Cleveland State Law Review.

D.B. Wexler and B.J. Winick, Essays in Therapeutic Jurisprudence (1991) Durham, NC: Carolina Academic Press.

B.J. Winick, "Competency to consent to treatment: the distinction between assent and objection" in D.B. Wexler and B.J. Winick (eds.), Essays in Therapeutic Jurisprudence (1991a) Durham, NC: Carolina Academic Press.

B.J. Winick, "Harnessing the power of the bet: wagering with the government as a mechanism for social and individual change" in D.B. Wexler and B.J. Winick (eds.), Essays in Therapeutic Jurisprudence (1991b) Durham, NC: Carolina Academic Press.

B.J. Winick, "Rethinking the health care delivery crisis: the need for a therapeutic jurisprudence" (1993) Journal of Law and Health 7, 1: 49–54.

Chapter 32

The Jurisprudence of Therapeutic Jurisprudence

Bruce J. Winick

I. Introduction

Therapeutic jurisprudence has grown considerably since its inception in the early 1990s. It has generated interest among scholars from law and the social sciences, and an already large body of work applying its approach to a wide range of legal issues.[1] It has also produced a body of commentary raising dilemmas and questions about its definition and approach, and discussing the limits and potential dangers of the enterprise.[2] This essay offers a further elaboration of the theory of therapeutic jurisprudence, and a response to the major issues raised by its critics.

Commentators have raised a number of questions concerning therapeutic jurisprudence: What is therapeutic jurisprudence, and how should it be defined? In what sense is it a school of jurisprudence, and how does it differ from other schools of jurisprudence? Is it merely "old wine in new bottles?"[3] Is therapeutic jurisprudence a conservative, paternalistic approach to the law that serves to reinforce the existing distrubution of power between mental health

---

1. See Law in a Therapeutic Key: Developments in Therapeutic Jurispurdence, Part II (David B. Wexler & Bruce J. Winick eds., forthcoming 1996) [hereinafter Law in a Therapeutic Key] (collecting examples).

2. For examples of therapeutic jurisprudence scholarship, see Michael L. Perlin, The Jurisprudence of the Insanity Defense (1994); David B. Wexler & Bruce J. Winick, Essays in Therapeutic Jurisprudence (1991) [hereinafter Essays in Therapeutic Jurisprudence]; Bruce J. Winick, Therapeutic Jurisprudence Applied: Essays on Mental Health Law (forthcoming 1996) [hereinafter Therapeutic Jurisprudence Applied]; Bruce J. Winick, The Right to Refuse Mental Health Treatment (forthcoming 1997) [hereinafter Right to Refuse]; Law in a Therapeutic Key, supra note 1; Law, Mental Health, and Mental Disorder (Bruce D. Sales & Daniel W. Shuman eds., 1996) [hereinafter Law, Mental Health, and Mental Disorder]; Therapeutic Jurisprudence: The Law as a Therapeutic Agent (David B. Wexler ed. 1990); Bibliography, in Law in a Therapeutic Key, supra note 1 (listing approximately 145 articles in therapeutic jurisprudence).

3. See Bruce D. Sales & Daniel W. Shuman, The Newly Emerging Mental Health Law, in Law, Mental Health, and Mental Disorder, supra note 2, at 2, 6; Daniel W. Shuman, Making the World a Better Place Through Tort Law? Through the Therapeutic Looking Glass, 10 N.Y.L. Sch. J. Hum. Rts. 739, 743 (1994).

professionals and people with disability?[4] Does therapeutic jurisprudence have a normative agenda? Should the value of promoting psychological and physical health outweigh other public policy concerns or constitutional principles? Is therapeutic jurisprudence built upon a weak foundation because it is based on social science, which has inherent limitations, particularly when applied to study the legal system?[5] How should the law regard legal issues when their therapeutic implications are indeterminate? What is the future direction of therapeutic jurisprudence? This essay analyzes these questions about the jurisprudence of therapeutic jurisprudence.

Let us begin with a brief definition of therapeutic jurisprudence. Therapeutic jurisprudence is the study of the role of the law as a therapeutic agent. It is an interdisciplinary enterprise designed to produce scholarship that is particularly useful for law reform. Therapeutic jurisprudence proposes the exploration of ways in which, consistent with principles of justice and other constitutional values, the knowledge, theories, and insights of the mental health and related disciplines can help shape the development of the law. Therapeutic jurisprudence builds on the insight that the law itself can be seen to function as a kind of therapist or therapeutic agent. Legal rules, legal procedures, and the roles of legal actors (such as lawyers and judges) constitute social forces that, whether intended or not, often produce therapeutic or antitherapeutic consequences. Therapeutic jurisprudence calls for the study of these consequences with the tools of the social sciences in order to identify them and to ascertain whether the law's antitherapeutic effects can be reduced, and its therapeutic effects enhanced, without subordinating due process and other justice values.

Part II of this essay examines the relationship between therapeutic jurisprudence and other schools of jurisprudence, addressing the question whether therapeutic jurisprudence is merely "old wine in new bottles?" This Part also analyzes therapeutic jurisprudence's normative focus and its limits. Part III analyzes how "therapeutic" should be defined, and addresses the question of whether therapeutic jurisprudence is paternalistic in orientation or is committed to a conception of therapeutic or of the therapeutic process associated with the mental health professions of psychiatry and psychology.

Part IV analyzes the empirical indeterminacy dilemma—the question of whether the inherent limitations of social science research doom the therapeutic jurisprudence enterprise on which it is based. Part V analyzes how therapeutic and other sometimes conflicting values can be reconciled and discusses the problem of how the law should respond when they cannot be. Part VI describes the path of therapeutic jurisprudence, showing how the approach has developed from a lens for examining mental health law to a therapeutic approach to the law as a whole, and how scholarly attention has moved from an analysis of the therapeutic consequences of legal rules and procedures to consider as well

---

4. John Petrila, Paternalism and the Unrealized Promise of Essays in Therapeutic Jurisprudence, 10 N.Y.L. Schl. J. Hum. Rts. 877 (1993) (book review).

5. See Christopher Slobogin, Therapeutic Jurisprudence: Five Dilemmas to Ponder, 1 Psychol. Pub. Pol'y & L. 193, 204–08 (1995) (discussing the "dilemma of empirical indeterminacy").

how legal actors can apply existing law more therapeutically. This part also discusses the emerging comparative law direction in therapeutic jurisprudence, and points out several ways in which a comparative law approach presents new research opportunities.

II. Therapeutic Jurisprudence and Other Schools of Jurisprudence: Old Wine in New Bottles?

Law once was regarded as a set of formal principles that ordered human behavior, the structural pillars of our political reality. Under the Nineteenth Century conception, judges were understood as finding and applying the law in a mechanical way, as though operating within a system of deductive logic.[6] Judges did not "make" the law; they simply located it in the common law or in legislation, and applied it. The judicial process was thought of more as a science than as politics, and the consequences of a legal decision were treated as largely irrelevant.

We have come to understand this as a naive and artificial conception. "The life of the law," Holmes taught us, "has not been logic: it has been experience."[7] The insights of such movements as the sociological jurisprudence of Roscoe Pound[8] and the legal realism of Karl Llewellyn and others[9] have led us to see law as part of a rich tapestry of human interactions. We have learned to look beyond law's formalisms to see the deeper structures lying within. In some ways, law is but a casement that masks the all-important play of political, economic, and social forces. As post-realists, we understand that there is a wide gulf between law on the books and law in action. Law is not an artifact on display in the museum: it is a living, breathing organism. Law functions within a particular society, absorbing and reflecting the culture in which it exists. Judges, although acting within a framework of precedent, are political actors who make law in the process of applying it.

To understand how law functions we must understand political science, economics, anthropology, sociology, and psychology, and we must examine law with the tools of these disciplines. Modern approaches to law have been interdisciplinary and empirical in character. We have seen the rise of law and eco-

---

6. See Roscoe Pound, Mechanical Jurisprudence, 8 Colum. L. Rev. 605 (1908).

7. Oliver W. Holmes, Jr., The Common Law 1 (Gryphon Editions) (1982) (1881). According to Holmes, the notion of law as a form of syllogistic reasoning was artificial, and failed to take account of such significant determinants of legal decisionmaking as the "felt necessities of the time, the prevalent moral and political theories, intuitions of public policy, avowed or unconscious, even the prejudices which judges share with their fellow-men...." Id.

8. Roscoe Pound, Outline of Lectures on Jurisprudence (5th ed. 1943); Roscoe Pound, The Scope and Purpose of Sociological Jurisprudence, 25 Harv. L. Rev. 489, 512–13 (1912) (calling for "study of actual social effects of legal institutions and legal doctrines").

9. See, e.g., William Twining, Karl Llewellyn and the Realist Movement (1973); Karl N. Llewellyn, Some Realism About Realism—Responding to Dean Pound, 44 Harv. L. Rev. 1222 (1931); G. Edward White, From Sociological Jurisprudence to Realism: Jurisprudence and Social Change in Early Twentieth Century America, 58 Va. L. Rev. 999 (1972).

nomics,[10] law and society,[11] law and psychology,[12] and social science in law.[13] With these varying interdisciplinary approaches we look beyond the facade of the law to penetrate its inner workings.

It is precisely within these interdisciplinary traditions that therapeutic jurisprudence is situated. Much like law and psychology and social science in law, therapeutic jurisprudence looks at law with the tools of the behavioral sciences. But therapeutic jurisprudence has a more narrow focus. Unlike these other interdisciplinary approaches, it does not seek *generally* to examine law in order to test its assumptions or measure its effectiveness or impact.[14] It is concerned with a more narrow set of consequences. Therapeutic jurisprudence seeks to apply social science to examine law's impact on the mental and physical health of the people it affects.[15] It recognizes that, whether we realize it or not, law functions as a therapeutic agent, bringing about therapeutic or antitherapeutic consequences.

These are not law's only consequences, of course, or the only ones worth noting. Law may produce economic effects, sometimes redistributing wealth and sometimes imposing transaction costs that retard economic productivity. Law may produce environmental consequences, sometimes setting up disincentives to the maintenance of environmental quality and sometimes producing incentives to minimize pollution. Sometimes the law promotes caution, and sometimes heedlessness.

A sensitive policy analysis of law should seek to measure and weigh all of the various costs and benefits of legal rules. One important but previously neglected aspect of this policy calculus is the therapeutic impact of law. Therapeutic jurisprudence accordingly calls for a systematic study of law's therapeu-

---

10. See, e.g., A. Michael Polinsky, An Introduction to Law and Economics (2d ed . 1989); Richard A. Posner, Economic Analysis of Law (3d ed. 1986); Law and Economics (Jules Coleman & Jeffrey Lange eds., 1992).

11. See, e.g., Law and Society (Roger Cotterrell ed., 1994); Laurence M. Friedman, The Law and Society Movement, 38 Stan. L. Rev. 763 (1986); David M. Trubek & John Esser, Critical Empiricism in American Legal Studies: Paradox, Problem, or Pandora's Box, 14 Law & Soc. Inquiry 3 (1989).

12. See, e.g., Law and Psychology (Martin Levine ed., 1995); Law and Psychology: The Broadening of the Discipline (James R.P. Ogloff ed., 1992); Craig Haney, Psychology and Legal Change: The Impact of a Decade, 17 Law & Hum. Behav. 371 (1993); Gary B. Melton, Law, Science and Humanity: The Normative Foundation of Social Science in Law, 14 Law & Hum. Behav. 315 (1990); Gary B. Melton, The Law is a Good Thing (Psychology is Too): Human Rights in Psychological Jurisprudence, 16 Law & Hum. Behav. 381 (1992); Mark A. Small, Advancing Psychological Jurisprudence, 11 Behav. Sci. & L. 3 (1993); Mark A. Small, Legal Psychology and Therapeutic Jurisprudence, 37 St. Louis U. L.J. 675 (1993).

13. See, e.g., John Monahan & Laurens Walker, Social Science in Law (3d ed. 1994); David L. Faigman, To Have and Have Not: Assessing the Use of Social Science to the Law as Science and Policy, 38 Emory L.J. 1005 (1989).

14. See Austin Sarat, Legal Effectiveness and Social Studies of Law: On the Unfortunate Persistence of Research Tradition, 9 Legal Stud. F. 23 (1985) (discussing the legal effectiveness tradition in social research on law).

15. See Slobogin, supra note 5, at 196.

tic or antitherapeutic effects. These are not the only effects worth studying, but they should not be ignored.

Therapeutic jurisprudence thus is largely a form of consequentialism.[16] Although law is designed to serve various normative ends, scholars should study the extent to which these ends actually are furthered in practice. Once it is understood that rules of substantive law, legal procedures, and the roles of various actors in the legal system such as judges and lawyers have either positive or negative effects on the health and mental health of the people they affect, the need to assess these therapeutic consequences should not be neglected. Accomplishing positive therapeutic consequences or eliminating or minimizing antitherapeutic consequences thus emerges as an important objective in any sensible law reform effort.

Unlike law and psychology and social science in law, which are empirically-based ways of looking at law that often purport to have no normative agenda, therapeutic jurisprudence is normative in its orientation. It posits that the therapeutic domain is important and ought to be understood and somehow factored into legal decisionmaking. Therapeutic jurisprudence suggests that, *other things being equal*,[17] positive therapeutic effects are desirable and should generally be a proper aim of law, and that antitherapeutic effects are undesirable and should be avoided or minimized. Because this normative agenda drives therapeutic jurisprudence research, it is not the neutral, value-free mode of scholarly inquiry that law and psychology and social science in law often try to be. In this respect, therapeutic jurisprudence is more like law and economics,[18] critical legal studies,[19] feminist jurisprudence[20] and critical race theory[21]—all of which are schools of jurisprudence that examine law with a

---

16. See, e.g., Consequentialism (Philip Pettit ed., 1993); Consequentialism and Its Critics (Samuel Scheffler ed., 1988). Consequentialism can be traced to the utilitarianism of Jeremy Bentham. See Jeremy Bentham, Fragments on Government and Introduction to the Principles of Morals and Legislation (W. Harrison ed., 1948)

17. Of course, other things may rarely be equal. Thus, although therapeutic jurisprudence is normative in orientation in that it suggests that law in general should seek to further therapeutic ends, it does not suggest that therapeutic ends are the only ones that law should seek to accomplish, or the most important ends. Law properly attempts to further many ends, and therapeutic jurisprudence does not seek to subordinate these other ends to therapeutic ones. Countervailing normative considerations may often justify a legal rule or practice found to produce antitherapeutic consequences, and therapeutic jurisprudence does not purport to be a method of determining which factor should predominate in legal decisionmaking. Wexler & Winick, supra note 1, at xi–xii; David B. Wexler, Justice, Mental Health and Therapeutic Jurisprudence, 40 Clev. St. L. Rev. 27 (1992); see infra Part V.

18. See supra note 10.

19. See, e.g., Roberto M. Unger, The Critical Legal Studies Movement (1986); Critical Legal Studies (James Boyle ed., 1993); Richard Michael Fischl, Some Realism About Critical Legal Studies, 41 U. Miami L. Rev. 505 (1987).

20. See, e.g., Catherine A. McKinnon, Feminism Unbounded: Discourse on Life and Law (1987); 1 & 2 Feminist Legal Theory (Frances Olsen ed., 1995); Cass Sunstein, Feminism and Legal Theory, 101 Harv. L. Rev. 826 (1988) (book review).

21. See, e.g., Derrick Bell, And We are not Saved: The Elusive Quest for Racial Justice (1987); Patricia J. Williams, The Alchemy of Race and Rights (1991); Critical Race Theory (Kimberly Crenshaw et al. eds., 1996).

particular normative orientation.[22] One need not reject the normative goals of any of these other schools in order to accept therapeutic jurisprudence. Indeed, sometimes they overlap. Treating women with equality in the workplace, for example, might be defended not only on feminist grounds, but also as serving efficiency and therapeutic values. In any case, all of these consequences are relevant to a comprehensive assessment of law.

All of these schools of jurisprudence seek to advance the well-being of people whose welfare is affected by the law. Critical legal studies, feminist jurisprudence, and critical race theory seek to advance the well-being of particular groups—the politically oppressed, women, and racial minorities. Therapeutic jurisprudence, although it focuses on a more narrow aspect of well-being (the therapeutic), is not limited in its concern to particular groups. It seeks to promote the psychological and physical well-being of people generally.

How significant are these differences between therapeutic jurisprudence and other schools of jurisprudence? Is therapeutic jurisprudence merely "old wine in new bottles"?[23] It may be, as Slobogin notes, that the distinctiveness of therapeutic jurisprudence is more a matter of emphasis than of kind.[24] Nonetheless, therapeutic jurisprudence contributes by bringing under one conceptual umbrella many legal areas that previously had not been thought to be related.[25] Moreover, its principal power is to generate questions that otherwise might well go unasked. Perhaps the best way to approach the question of the distinctiveness of therapeutic jurisprudence[26] is to ask how likely, *without* a therapeutic jurisprudence perspective, would it have been that we would ask the following questions (representative of therapeutic jurisprudence): Can a judge's colloquy with a criminal defendant at a plea hearing influence the defendant's acceptance of responsibility?[27] Can a judge conduct a sentencing hearing in a manner likely to increase a criminal defendant's compliance with conditions of probation?[28] Is "sentence bargaining" less likely to interfere with later efforts at offender rehabilitation than "charge bargaining"?[29] Can "teen courts" increase empathy in delinquent youths by having those youths serve as attorneys for victims in teen court proceedings?[30] Might a fault-based tort system promote recovery better than a no-fault system?[31] Would expansion of the unconscionability doctrine under the Uniform Commercial Code increase the

---

22. See Slobogin, supra note 5, at 199–200.

23. See supra note 3 and accompanying text.

24. Slobogin, supra note 5, at 200.

25. Wexler & Winick, supra note 1, at x; David B. Wexler, Reflections on the Scope of Therapeutic Jurisprudence, 1 Psychol. Pub. Pol'y & L. 220, 228 (1995).

26. See supra note 3.

27. See David B. Wexler & Bruce J. Winick, Therapeutic Jurisprudence and Criminal Justice Mental Health Issues, 16 Mental & Physical Disability L. Rep. 225, 229–30 (1992).

28. See David B. Wexler, Therapeutic Jurisprudence and the Criminal Courts, 35 Wm. & Mary L. Rev. 279 (1993).

29. See Wexler, supra note 28; Wexler & Winick, supra note 27, at 229–30.

30. See Allison R. Shiff & David Wexler, Teen Court: A Therapeutic Jurisprudence Perspective, 32 Crim. L. Bull. (forthcoming 1996).

31. See Daniel W. Shuman, The Psychology of Compensation in Tort Law, 43 U. Kan. L. Rev. 39 (1994).

self-esteem of economically disadvantaged consumers by empowering them to fight back against merchants with greater economic power?[32]

Like law and economics, therapeutic jurisprudence is essentially a consequentialist approach to law. Both evaluate law based on its consequences. Therapeutic jurisprudence focuses on a particular kind of consequence—the therapeutic—and calls for study of law's impact on health and mental health. This assessment should be scientific, but once the assessment is performed, the use to which it should be put raises questions of value that science cannot answer.[33]

Even though there may be societal consensus that positive therapeutic consequences are to be valued, identifying law's therapeutic or antitherapeutic effects—the research agenda of therapeutic jurisprudence—does not necessarily argue for legal change. Therapeutic jurisprudence seeks to avoid the difficulties that sometimes were encountered by another branch of interdisciplinary legal scholarship—the law and economics movement. In its criticism of certain legal rules as inefficient, law and economics scholarship sometimes treated efficiency and wealth maximization as a transcending norm. Any form of consequentialism must be careful to avoid equating a description of a rule's consequences with a normative conclusion about the rule's value. There is an essential difference between descriptive and normative propositions.[34] While descriptive statements can be verified empirically, normative statements cannot be. Normative statements are not true or false. We either agree or disagree with them depending upon our value preferences. Within any particular society there may, of course, be consensus concerning certain values. Although there may be generally accepted conventions that allow us to argue about conflicts concerning normative matters, unless there is agreement about norms or about principles identifying a hierarchy of values, such disputes cannot be resolved by argument alone or by empirical research.

Once we understand this essential difference between descriptive and normative propositions, we must recognize that empirical verification of the truth concerning a particular set of facts cannot justify a normative conclusion concerning, for example, how a rule of law should be changed. One cannot reason from the "is" to the "ought" without explicitly or implicitly adopting a particular normative viewpoint, at least not without violating what G. E. Moore called the "naturalistic fallacy."[35] While efficiency is an important value, it is

---

32. See Jeffrey L. Harrison, Class, Personality, Contract and Unconscionability, 33 Wm. & Mary L. Rev. 445, 445–51, 493–500 (1994).

33. See Wexler & Winick , supra note 2, at xi–xii; David Finkelman & Thomas Grisso, Therapeutic Jurisprudence: From Idea to Application, 20 N. Engl. J. Crim. & Civ. Confinement 243, 247 (1994); Robert F. Schopp, Therapeutic Jurisprudence and Conflicts Among Values in Mental Health Law, 11 Behav. Sci. & L. 31 (1993); David B. Wexler & Robert F. Schopp, Therapeutic Jurisprudence: A New Approach to Mental Health Law, in Handbook of Psychology and Law 361, 373 (Dorothy S. Kagehiro & William S. Laufer eds., 1992).

34. See, e.g., Richard B. Brandt, Ethical Theory: The Problems of Normative Ethics 163 (1959); Paul Edwards, The Logic of Moral Discourse 209 (1955); Alan Montefiore, A Modern Introduction to Moral Philosophy 120–32 (1958); George E. Moore, Principia Ethica 66 (1903); Paul W. Taylor, Normative Discourse 240–51 (1961).

35. Moore, supra note 34, at 66.

not the only value. Thus, one may criticize a legal rule's impact on efficiency—showing, for example, that the requirement that welfare recipients receive an adversarial hearing before their benefits may be terminated imposes high fiscal and administrative costs. Such criticism, however, should not ignore the values apart from efficiency—accuracy, litigant satisfaction, and participatory or dignitary values—that such hearings serve. Some legal rules are defensible even if they are shown to impose costs and inefficiencies.

Similarly, although in general positive therapeutic consequences should be valued and antitherapeutic consequences should be avoided, there are other consequences that should count, and sometimes count more. There are many instances in which a particular law or legal practice may produce antitherapeutic effects, but nonetheless may be justified by considerations of justice or by the desire to achieve various constitutional, economic, environmental, or other normative goals. An example is provided by the Supreme Court's decision in *Ford v. Wainwright*,[36] barring execution of death row prisoners who become legally incompetent. This legal rule is justified on moral and constitutional grounds even though it may produce mental illness or malingering. Therapeutic jurisprudence therefore does not suggest that therapeutic considerations should outweigh other normative values that law may properly seek to further. Rather, it calls for an awareness of these consequences and enables a more precise weighing of sometimes competing values.

III. The "Therapeutic" in Therapeutic Jurisprudence

Therapeutic jurisprudence thus is an interdisciplinary approach to law. It is empirically based but also normative in its orientation. It takes as its particular focus the effect of law on the health and mental health of the individual. But how is "health" or "therapeutic" to be defined? Is therapeutic jurisprudence an attempt to justify government paternalism? Does it envision a therapeutic state, some brave new world in which Platonic guardians use law to achieve their conceptions of good health and social adjustment? Are the conceptions of "therapeutic" embraced by mental health professionals to be favored, or those of patients.

Although therapeutic jurisprudence suggests that law should be used to promote mental health and psychological functioning, it does not suggest that psychological and physical health is a transcending norm. Nor does it endorse the paternalistic concept of the "therapeutic state"[37] or what Wexler has criticized as "therapeutic justice."[38] Indeed, the existing body of therapeutic jurisprudence work is anything but paternalistic. My work, for example, has praised the law's commitment to the principle of individual autonomy on the basis that self-determination is therapeutically advantageous.[39] It has criticized

---

36. 477 U.S. 399 (1986); see Bruce J. Winick, Competency to be Executed: A Therapeutic Jurisprudence Perspective, 10 Behav. Sci. & L. 317 (1992).

37. Wexler & Winick, supra note 2, at xi.

38. David B. Wexler, Therapeutic Justice, 57 Minn. L. Rev. 289 (1972).

39. Bruce J. Winick, On Autonomy: Legal and Psychological Perspectives, 37 Vill. L. Rev. 1705 (1994).

the labeling of people with mental illness as incompetent (a prerequisite for the exercise of governmental paternalism) on the ground that such labeling produces serious adverse social and psychological consequences.[40] It has endorsed the right to refuse treatment on the basis that recognition of such a right would be therapeutically beneficial.[41] It has proposed that mental illness be defined narrowly for purposes of civil commitment and involuntary treatment, thereby limiting the range of paternalistic governmental interventions imposed upon those with mental illness.[42] In addition, it has criticized the incompetency-to-stand-trial doctrine on the basis that it imposes severe burdens on criminal defendants and in practice is often a misguided paternalistic intervention.[43] Much of this work, rather than defending government paternalism, is animated by the insight that such paternalism is often antitherapeutic, and that legal protection for individual autonomy can have positive therapeutic value.

Therapeutic jurisprudence therefore does not embrace a conception of "therapeutic" that is tied to notions of paternalism. To the contrary, the thrust of much of the existing therapeutic jurisprudence work is that the individual's own views concerning his or her health and how best to achieve it should generally be honored. Beyond this, therapeutic jurisprudence has left the concept of "therapeutic" intentionally vague.

In defining "therapeutic" broadly to include anything that enhances the psychological or physical well-being of the individual, therapeutic jurisprudence has left the concept of "therapeutic" ambiguous and open to argument about what should count as therapeutic. As Wexler has put it, "as a mere heuristic, therapeutic jurisprudence has eschewed a tight definition of 'therapeutic,' and has similarly left open the nature of the party or person upon whom the therapeutic or anti-therapeutic consequences might be visited.[44] Opting not to adopt a tight definition of "therapeutic" allows scholars to "roam within the intuitive and common sense contours of the concept."[45] The focus is on mental health and psychological aspects of health viewed broadly.

In order to explore the broad contours of the concept of "therapeutic," let us consider several examples. At the core of the concept is the concern for avoiding or ameliorating psychopathology in a traditional sense, and this has

---

40. Bruce J. Winick, The Side Effects of Incompetency Labeling and the Implications for Mental Health Law, 1 Psychol. Pub. Pol'y & L. 6 (1995).

41. Bruce J. Winick, The Right to Refuse Mental Health Treatment: A Therapeutic Jurisprudence Analysis, 17 Int'l J. L. & Psychiatry 99 (1994).

42. Bruce J. Winick, Ambiguities In The Legal Meaning and Significance of Mental Illness, 1 Psychol. Pub. Pol'y & L. 534 (1995).

43. Bruce J. Winick, Presumptions and Burdens of Proof in Determining Competency to Stand Trial: An Analysis of Medina v. California and the Supreme Court's New Due Process Methodology in Criminal Cases, 47 U. Miami L. Rev. 817 (1993); Bruce J. Winick, Reforming Incompetency to Stand Trial and Plead Guilty: A Restated Proposal and a Response to Professor Bonnie, 85 J. Crim. L. & Criminology 571 (1995) [hereinafter Reforming Incompetency]; Bruce J. Winick, Restructuring Competency to Stand Trial, 32 UCLA L. Rev. 921 (1985) [hereinafter Restructuring Competency].

44. David B. Wexler, New Directions in Therapeutic Jurisprudence: Breaking the Bounds of Conventional Mental Health Law Scholarship, 10 N.Y.L. Sch. J. Hum. Rts. 759, 765 (1993).

45. Wexler, supra note 25, at 221.

been the subject of much of the therapeutic jurisprudence literature dealing with mental health law.[46] But "therapeutic" extends beyond this to encompass various health and social problems that seem to have a psychological component, such as drug abuse,[47] sex offenses,[48] juvenile delinquency,[49] domestic violence,[50] and child abuse.[51] Moving further away from the core, it may include the problems of those suffering tort injury,[52] victims of crime,[53] employees suffering job-related injuries,[54] lawyers suffering from occupational stress,[55] and people suffering from disabilities[56] and medical problems generally.[57] Even

---

46. E.g., Winick, Therapeutic Jurisprudence Applied, supra note 2 (analyzing the impact of legal rules governing civil commitment, involuntary treatment, competency to stand trial, treatment decisionmaking, and the psychotherapist-patient privilege on the mental health of patients subjected to them); Symposium, Therapeutic Jurisprudence: Restructuring Mental Health Law, 10 N.Y.L. Sch. J. Hum. Rts. 623–926 (1993); Tom R. Tyler, The Psychological Consequences of Judicial Procedures: Implications for Civil Commitment Hearings, 46 SMU L. Rev. 433 (1992).

47. E.g., Jack Lehman, The Movement Toward Therapeutic Jurisprudence: An Inside Look at the Origin and Operation of America's First Drug Court, 10 NJC Alumni 13 (Spring 1995); David B. Wexler, Some Therapeutic Jurisprudence Implications of the Outpatient Civil Commitment of Pregnant Substance Abusers, 15 Politics & Life Sci. 73 (1996); Bruce J. Winick, Harnessing the Power of the Bet: Wagering With the Government as a Mechanism for Social and Individual Change, 45 U. Miami L. Rev. 737, 772–88 (1991).

48. E.g., Bruce Feldthusen, The Civil Action for Sexual Battery: Therapeutic Jurisprudence?, 25 Ottawa L. Rev. 205 (1993); Jeffrey A. Klotz, Sex Offenders and the Law: New Directions, in Mental Health and Law: Research, Policy, and Services 257 (Bruce D. Sales & Saleem A. Shah eds., 1996); Jeffrey A. Klotz et al., Cognitive Restructuring Through Law: A Therapeutic Jurisprudence Approach for Sex Offenders and the Plea Process, 15 U. Puget Sound L. Rev. 579 (1992).

49. Shiff & Wexler, supra note 30.

50. Leonore M. Simon, A Therapeutic Jurisprudence Approach to the Legal Processing of Domestic Violence Cases, 1 Psychol. Pub. Pol'y & L. 43 (1995); see also Liz Balmaseda, Two Judges Use Therapy to Curb Home Violence, Miami Herald, Apr. 7, 1993, at 1B (reporting judicial use of therapeutic jurisprudence to fashion innovative remedies in domestic violence court).

51. Murray Levine, A Therapeutic Jurisprudence Analysis of Mandated Reporting of Child Maltreatment by Psychotherapists, 10 N.Y. L. Sch. J. Hum. Rts. 711 (1993).

52. Daniel W. Shuman, The Psychology of Compensation in Tort Law, 43 U. Kan. L. Rev. 39 (1994); Daniel W. Shuman, Therapeutic Jurisprudence and Tort Law: A Limited Subjective Standard of Care, 46 SMU L.Rev. 409 (1992).

53. Richard P. Wiebe, The Mental Health Implications of Crime Victims' Rights, in Law, Mental Health, and Mental Disorder, supra note 1, at 414.

54. William E. Wilkinson, Therapeutic Jurisprudence and Workers' Compensation, 30 Ariz. Att'y 28 (April 1994).

55. Amiram Elwork & G. Andrew H. Benjamin, Lawyers in Distress, 23 J. Psychiatry & L. 205 (1995).

56. Rose A. Daly-Rooney, Designing Reasonable Accommodations Through Co-Worker Participation, Therapeutic Jurisprudence, and the Confidentiality provision of the Americans with Disabilities Act, 8 J.L. & Health 89 (1994).

57. Bruce J. Winick, Rethinking the Health Care Delivery Crisis: The Need for a Therapeutic Jurisprudence, 7 J. L. & Health 49 (1993).

people in the criminal justice system who may not have mental health problems *per se* may be thought of as having problems within the purview of therapeutic jurisprudence. Dealing with problems of sentencing, offender rehabilitation, and deterrence involve aspects of psychological functioning and social adjustment that make them an appropriate concern of therapeutic jurisprudence scholars.[58]

But even these may not mark the outer contours of the province of therapeutic jurisprudence. Inducing individual and social change through legal approaches that employ such techniques as "wagering" or behavioral contracting, which harness a variety of psychological mechanisms to increase motivation and psychological functioning, has also been the subject of therapeutic jurisprudence speculation.[59] Using psychological approaches to increase worker productivity alone might not seem to qualify. But when legal rules themselves produce psychologically dysfunctional behavior and dampen motivation to succeed—such as several aspects of our existing welfare program[60] and civil service system,[61] and the Armed Services' "Don't-Ask, Don't-Tell" policy[62]—consideration of legal change to eliminate or minimize such dysfuntional effects would seem a proper subject for therapeutic jurisprudence work. Moreover, even when legal rules have not themselves induced psychologically dysfunctional behavior, a proper concern of therapeutic jurisprudence is consideration of alternative legal arrangements that might produce more functional behavior, such as the contention that the expansion of the unconsciounabilty doctrine under the Uniform Commercial Code would increase the self-esteem of economically disadvantaged consumers by providing them with a mode of empowerment—a legal tool to fight back against those who might exploit them economically.[63] Is increasing self-esteem, with a resulting increase in psychological functioning, a "therapeutic" consequence of such a change in law? I argue that it is in the sense that such a goal might be an appropriate one for psychological counseling. If a problem or goal is one for which an individual might consult a mental health therapist or counselor, it would qualify as a proper subject of therapeutic jurisprudence work. Any consequence that is arguably therapeutic and in at least some sense related to psychological functioning would seem to be within the broad contours of therapeutic jurisprudence.

Sometimes, of course, therapeutic considerations arguably will conflict. Legal rules may affect an individual both positively and negatively. Let us consider, for example, the case of physician-assisted suicide. In a jurisdiction

---

58. Robert J. Kane, A Sentencing Model for the 21st Century, Fed Probation 10 (Sept. 1995); Keri A. Gould, Turning Rat and Doing Time for Uncharged, Dismissed, or Acquitted Crimes: Do The Federal Sentencing Guidelines Promote Respect for the Law?, 10 N.Y.L. Sch. J. Hum. Rts. 835 (1993); Wexler, supra note 28; Wexler & Winick, supra note 27.

59. David B. Wexler, Health Care Compliance Principles and the Insanity Aquittee Conditional Release Process, 27 Crim. L. Bull. 18 (1991); Winick, supra note 47.

60. Id. at 793–97.

61. Id. at 788–93.

62. Kay Kavanagh, Don't Ask, Don't Tell: Deception Required, Disclosure Denied, 1 Psychol. Pub. Pol'y & L. 142 (1995).

63. Harrison, supra note 32.

which allows this form of euthanasia, either statutorily as in Oregon[64] or judicially,[65] individuals aware that they may control their death may feel a measure of psychological ease and empowerment that would count as a positive therapeutic consequence. On the other hand, some may acquire a fear and distrust of physicians generally, based on a misconception that visiting a physician when old and infirm may produce an unwanted physician-assisted death, perhaps abetted by relatives wishing to conserve the assets of their future testator. This fear, accompanied by the anxiety and potential psychologically dysfunctional response of ignoring a legitimate need for medical assistance, could arguably count as a negative therapeutic consequence of such laws. Which consequence is more or less therapeutic, of course, is a normative question, not a clinical one. Identifying these therapeutic consequences, even if not resolving the conflict they might present, is certainly an appropriate task of therapeutic jurisprudence scholarship. How such a conflict should be resolved goes beyond the capabilities of therapeutic jurisprudence, except, perhaps, when the balance tips decidedly in one direction or another. In most cases, however, the conflicting therapeutic consequences of a particular legal rule or proposal for change are weights on the scale to be considered along with other relevant values in the balancing that is inherent to legal decisionmaking. Therapeutic jurisprudence cannot resolve this debate, but can enrich the decisionmaking process.

Defining therapeutic jurisprudence broadly thus cedes to therapeutic jurisprudence scholars wide latitude in selecting their scholarly agendas. Working within these broad contours, of course, researchers must settle on the definition of "therapeutic" that they will apply in their work, and should be explicit about this.[66] There may, of course, be different perspectives on what should count as therapeutic. In cases in which a rule of law may impose conflicting therapeutic effects on different groups, there also may be disagreement about which group's interests should be considered more important. Therapeutic jurisprudence prefers to leave these matters open for analysis and scholarly debate. In that debate, however, special efforts should be made to take account of the patient (or consumer) viewpoint concerning what is therapeutic.[67] As a result, therapeutic jurisprudence is not committed to professional notions of what is therapeutic, is not a servant of the professions of psychiatry and

---

64. Or. Ballot Measure No. 16, reprinted in Kane v. Kulonguski, 871 P.2d 993, 1001–06 (Or. 1994).

65. Compassion in Dying v. Washington, 79 F.3d 790 (9th Cir. 1996); Quill v. Vasco, 80 F.3d 716 (2d Cir. 1996); see Sylvia A. Law, Physician-Assisted Death: An Essay on Constitutional Rights and Remedies, 55 Md. L. Rev. 292 (1996).

66. Wexler, supra note 25, at 222. "Making the definition reasonably explicit will ease the empirical measurement of dependent variables or outcome measures and will also raise the issue for normative debate in the political arena." Id. See also Slobogin, supra note 5, at 28.

67. David B. Wexler & Bruce J. Winick, Patients, Professionals, and the Path of Therapeutic Jurisprudence: A Response to Petrila, 10 N.Y.L. Sch. J. Hum. Rts. 907 (1993); Wexler, supra note 25, at 221; see, e.g., Julie M. Zito et al., Toward a Therapeutic Jurisprudence Analysis of Medication Refusal in the Court Review Model, 11 Behav. Sci. & L. 151 (1993).

psychology, and is by no means a device to reinforce or rationalize existing power imbalances between clinicians and their patients.

IV. The Dilemma of Empirical Indeterminacy

Therapeutic jurisprudence suggests that behavioral science research and theory be used to enhance the therapeutic impact of legal rules and practices. Some therapeutic jurisprudence work seeks to apply psychological and social science theory to speculate about the therapeutic consequences of a particular legal rule.[68] Several scholars have themselves conducted empirical research seeking to measure such therapeutic consequences.[69] Therapeutic jurisprudence's reliance on social science research, however, creates what Slobogin has referred to as "the dilemma of empirical indeterminacy."[70] Therapeutic jurisprudence depends upon an ability to measure the therapeutic effect of a legal rule or practice. Are the tools of social science adequate for the task? Slobogin discusses the lack of "science" in social science, and the special difficulties of applying social science methods in the legal context.[71] The best type of research is the "true experiment," with random assignment of identical populations to an experimental and a control group in order to isolate the variable under investigation.[72] Experimentation in the legal system, however, can only rarely employ true randomization.[73] Constitutional and ethical restrictions in performing experimentation with human subjects render social science research of this kind less than perfect science. An inherent problem with therapeutic jurisprudence's reliance on social science data, therefore, will mean that the conclusions of therapeutic jurisprudence work will be "subject to all of the vagaries that afflict social science itself."[74]

Does this mean, however, that therapeutic jurisprudence rests upon a "shaky foundation?"[75] I think not. To identify the uncertainties and imperfections of social science research is not to negate its usefulness to the law.[76] Although imperfect, particularly when compared to at least some research in the physical sciences, social science research can be of enormous help in the resolution of legal problems. Courts, legislatures, and administrative agencies in-

---

68. See Law in a Therapeutic Key, supra note 1, Part I (collecting examples).

69. See id., Part III (collecting examples).

70. Slobogin, supra note 5, at 204.

71. Id.

72. Id.

73. For an analysis of constitutional and other legal limits on research with human subjects, see Bruce J. Winick, Legal Limitations on Correctional Therapy and Research, 65 Minn. L. Rev. 331, 403–20 (1981).

74. Slobogin, supra note 5, at 207.

75. Id. at 204.

76. See Faigman, supra note 13, at 1051 ("The uncertainties that will continue to attach to even the best social research should only qualify its value.... An inability to explain completely human behavior hardly undermines the value of social science to the legal process."); Slobogin, supra note 5, at 208.

volved in the fashioning of legal rules frequently rely on the fruits of social science research. The perhaps inevitable indeterminacy of such research does not vitiate its usefulness; it merely requires caution in its use. Courts and other legal bodies will sometimes use such research in their decisionmaking,[77] and sometimes will reject it.[78] There rarely can be certainty in the legal system. Decisions—judicial, legislative, and administrative—often need to be made in the face of uncertainty, and frequently are made based on available knowledge, however imperfect. Therapeutic jurisprudence work will increase the knowledge base and thus enhance the quality of legal decisionmaking even though its conclusions may lack certainty.

How should the law deal with such empirical uncertainty? There are, as John Monahan and Laurens Walker have suggested, empirical questions without empirical answers.[79] Monahan and Walker discuss the way courts should respond when deciding legal issues in areas involving empirical uncertainty. They suggest that if empirical uncertainty exists as to propositions underlying general rules of law (the kind involved in what is sometimes referred to as rulemaking), rather than those relating merely to the resolution of a particular case (the kind involved in what is sometimes referred to as adjudication), then courts may treat theoretical speculation, even if untested, as the equivalent of precedential authority, which can form the basis for the legal rule.[80] Under this view, courts involved in resolving open legal questions may base their decisions on therapeutic jurisprudence speculation about what results of empirical research might demonstrate. This approach has the virtue of leaving such questions open for possible revision in light of future empirical research, and of encouraging such research to be performed.[81] If, as Monahan and Walker suggest, it is legitimate for courts to rely upon untested or inconclusively tested social science theory in reaching decisions, then surely it is legitimate for them to rely upon social science empirical evidence, even if indeterminate. Therapeutic jurisprudence work thus can become the grist for legal advocacy in the judicial, legislative, and administrative arenas, and ultimately can provide valuable material from which legal decisionmakers can craft legal rules.

V. Balancing Therapeutic and Other Values: Convergence and Conflict

How should legal decisionmakers use therapeutic jurisprudence material, and how can the potential be avoided that they will abuse it? How should conflicts between therapeutic and other values be resolved? Since therapeutic ju-

---

77. See, e.g., Ballew v. Georgia, 435 U.S. 223 (1978) (social science research relied upon to hold unconstitutional reduction in jury size below six).

78. See, e.g., McCleskey v. Kemp, 481 U.S. 279 (1987) (rejecting challenge based on social science research to administration of death penalty as discriminatory based on the race of the victim).

79. John Monahan & Laurens Walker, Empirical Questions Without Empirical Answers, 1991 Wis. L. Rev. 569.

80. Id. at 570–71, 593.

81. Id. at 593.

risprudence endorses health as a good, but does not consider other goods irrelevant or unimportant, in cases in which these other values converge with positive therapeutic effects, the direction of law reform will be clear. When there is conflict among them, however, therapeutic jurisprudence is not a method of resolving the conflict.

These points can be illustrated by my research on the right to refuse mental health treatment.[82] The right to refuse treatment can be justified on constitutional grounds and the respect for individual autonomy that is central to much of the ethical and political theory that our legal and political system is based on.[83] If recognition of the right, however, could be shown to cause serious harm to those with mental illness who might assert it, then concerns for beneficence might lead courts and legislatures to deny the right in certain circumstances or to construe it narrowly. However, my therapeutic jurisprudence analysis of the right suggests, based on psychological and psychodynamic theory, that recognition of the right can have positive therapeutic value and can actually increase the therapeutic efficacy of treatment that patients, given a choice to participate in or to refuse treatment, choose to accept.[84]

This conclusion, of course, is the product of a theoretical therapeutic jurisprudence analysis, one that applies social science theory, often drawn from research in other contexts, to speculate about the consequences of legal practices. Although this conclusion is consistent with informed clinical experience, it merits empirical investigation. Should my theoretical analysis of the therapeutic values of a right to refuse treatment be confirmed by empirical research, it would suggest a convergence between therapeutic values and the constitutional and political values often invoked in support of the right. This convergence of relevant values would argue for a broad and generous recognition of the right to refuse. Let us assume, on the other hand, that a therapeutic jurisprudence analysis of the right to refuse treatment reaches the opposite conclusion. If recognition of the right were shown to be injurious to the mental health of those with mental illness, there could be a conflict between therapeutic values and the constitutional and political values that support the right. Resolution of this conflict would require use of an overarching theory of value that would assign weights to the various values in question.

While therapeutic jurisprudence is premised on the notion that, other things being equal, health is a value that law should seek to foster, it makes no attempt to assign relative values to the various other goals of law. To resolve such conflicts of value, one must go outside therapeutic jurisprudence to some ethical or political theory that establishes a hierarchy of values. In our political system this balancing is often performed by the legislature, which, within our democratic traditions, attempts to reflect the will of the citizenry. When fundamental constitutional rights are involved, the task is often performed by the courts, and ultimately by the Supreme Court, the institution in our governmental structure that is assigned the role of safeguarding constitutional values and protecting them from erosion by majoritarian pressures.

---

82. Winick, Right to Refuse, supra note 2.
83. Id. chs. 10–14.
84. Id. ch. 17; see also Winick, supra note 41.

Therapeutic jurisprudence's contribution to this balancing process is its identification of a previously neglected ingredient in the policy analysis of law—the therapeutic dimension. Those with strongly held deontological views about the aims of law might be concerned that therapeutic jurisprudence will endanger acceptance of their normative vision of law. If one's view is that law, above all, should increase productivity in society, or promote equality, or foster self-actualization, or further the interests of a particular social class, for example, then therapeutic jurisprudence might appear threatening. Legal rules thought to be embedded might instead become contingent upon the results of empirical research. If a therapeutic jurisprudence analysis of a particular legal rule or practice might challenge its continued wisdom, then a proponent of that rule or practice might prefer that such therapeutic jurisprudence analysis never occur.

At bottom, however, this concern about the potential of therapeutic jurisprudence to challenge a particular normative vision of law is anti-intellectual and should be dismissed. It is the task of scholarship to advance knowledge even if it might challenge deeply held values. If the assumptions upon which a society's values are based are erroneous in some way that scholarship can demonstrate, then those values are in need of reexamination. Such reexamination does not mean that a society will discard its basic values, but the scholarly and public debate about them will inevitably be healthy,[85] and often will result in legal change that better effectuates the society's values. All scholarship must be welcome in the marketplace of ideas, and all of our beliefs must perpetually be tested in the competition of that marketplace.[86] The quest for truth sometimes can make us question basic assumptions. While it may be uncomfortable and sometimes even painful to do this, we must be brave enough to open our eyes to knowledge and to dare to see the world clearly, as it is, rather than as we might wish it to be.

Let us return to the example of the right to refuse treatment. My work on the right to refuse treatment endorses the normative constitutional and political values typically evoked to support recognition of the right. So important are the First Amendment freedom from governmental intrusion into mental processes and the due process protections for individual autonomy and bodily privacy that recognition of a right to refuse intrusive treatments that impinge on these values can be defended even if the results of doing so were antitherapeutic. But the dimensions of the right might differ depending on whether the consequences of its recognition were in fact antitherapeutic. Were it to be demonstrated that recognition of the right produced antitherapeutic consequences, the question would be how to strike an appropriate balance between the constitutional values at stake and the value of beneficence in a way that would best accommodate these sometimes conflicting values. Demonstration

---

85. To the extent that therapeutic jurisprudence research highlights conflicts between countervailing values, it will force a confrontation of those competing values that can lead to needed legal change. Moreover, public discourse and debate about such conflicting values can be healthy for the society and for the participants in the debate. See Sales & Shuman, supra note 3, at 12 ("talking openly about conflict has therapeutic value").

86. See Abrams v. United States, 250 U.S. 616, 630 (1919) (Holmes, J., dissenting, joined by Brandeis, J.).

of such a conflict between values will cause us to reexamine the purposes that the constitutional right seeks to accomplish and whether these objectives can be accomplished in other ways. It will increase our understanding about how rights actually operate, and will enrich the ensuing debate about how they should be applied. When the relevant constitutional and therapeutic values converge, on the other hand, recognition of a broader right to refuse will be appropriate. Therapeutic considerations, quite simply, cannot be ignored in the decisionmaking process any more than we can ignore other considerations, such as cost, for example. How these considerations should be weighed in the inevitable balancing process that law-making at both the legislative and judicial levels entails is itself a normative question to be resolved by our political institutions within the framework of the democratic process.

Another example of the balancing of sometimes competing values in resolving legal issues arises in the context of the psychotherapist-patient privilege. Recognition of such an evidentiary privilege can be justified on deontological grounds—protection of the privacy of intimate disclosures made in a therapeutic relationship. In addition, it may be justified on consequentialist grounds— that refusal to recognize the privilege will deter many who need mental health services from obtaining them, and will discourage the full and candid disclosure of information in the therapeutic relationship that may be essential for its success.[87] Professor Daniel Shuman's empirical work on the privilege has questioned the extent to which the consequentialist defense of the privilege is valid.[88] My therapeutic jurisprudence analysis of the privilege, however, comes to the opposite conclusion, at least in the context presented to the Supreme Court in *Jaffee v. Redmond*,[89] raising the question of whether the Federal Rules of Evidence should be construed by the Court to recognize a psychotherapist-patient privilege. Perhaps, as Shuman suggests, the privilege should be recognized on deontological grounds even if there is no therapeutic value in doing so.[90] A proponent of the privilege might worry about the performance of empirical work of the kind Shuman has done (testing the consequentialist rationale for the privilege) on the ground that the results of such research might weaken the argument for the privilege's recognition. In my view, however, there is intrinsic value in performing the kind of research that Shuman has done. Such research might produce results that validate the consequentialist argument (as my theoretical speculation suggests it would[91]), thereby strengthening the case for recognition of the privilege. But even if it does not (as Shuman's work sug-

---

87. Bruce J. Winick, The Psychotherapist-Patient Privilege: A Therapeutic Jurisprudence View, 50 U. Miami L. Rev. 249 (1996).

88. See generally Daniel W. Shuman et al., The Privilege Study (Part III): Psychotherapist-Patient Communications in Canada, 9 Int'l J.L. & Psychiatry 393 (1986); Daniel W. Shuman & Myron S. Weiner, The Privilege Study: An Empirical Examination of the Psychotherapist-Patient Privilege, 60 N.C.L. Rev. 893 (1982); Myron S. Wiener & Daniel W. Shuman, Privilege—A Comparative Study, 12 J. Psychiatry & L. 373 (1984).

89. 51 F. 3d 1346 (7th Cir.), cert. granted, 116 S. Ct. 334 (1995). The Court recently affirmed recognition of the privilege based in part on the consequentialist arguments. Jaffee v. Redmond, 116 S. Ct. 1923 (1996).

90. Shuman et al., supra note 88, at 417.

91. Winick, supra note 87.

gests[92]), such research will facilitate our full understanding of the issues and improve the quality of their resolution.

Scholars, of course, engage in an act of judgment when they select particular issues for examination with the lens of therapeutic jurisprudence. When constitutional or other strongly held normative values support a rule in a way that is morally or politically unchangeable, the value of conducting a therapeutic jurisprudence analysis of the consequences of the rule will be considerably reduced. Because therapeutic jurisprudence has a law reform as well as scholarly agenda, its practitioners presumably will wish to select issues for examination that can at least potentially lead to legal change in line with their own and the society's strongly held normative values. In this sense, a particularly appropriate focus for therapeutic jurisprudence scholarship would seem to be a seeking for convergence between therapeutic values and cherished constitutional, moral, or other normative values. Rather than choosing areas for therapeutic jurisprudence work in which there is likely to be conflict between therapeutic consequences and important normative values, the therapeutic jurisprudence scholar would be better off exploring areas in which such values appear likely to converge. Seeking such convergence, as I have found in my own work in the area of mental health law, can be quite rewarding and can produce significant original proposals for law reform that are not politically implausible.[93]

VI. *The Path of Therapeutic Jurisprudence*

A. From Mental Health Law to a Mental Health Approach to Law Generally

Therapeutic jurisprudence started, predictably, with the area of mental health law.[94] The field has since grown considerably beyond mental health law. A soon-to-be published anthology of essays that explicitly apply a therapeutic jurisprudence approach illustrates this development.[95] It contains work by the growing number of law professors, judges, and scholars in psychology, criminology, philosophy, and psychiatry who now use therapeutic jurisprudence in their work. These essays apply the therapeutic jurisprudence approach to legal issues across a wide variety of legal subjects. The field thus has transcended mental health law, and therapeutic jurisprudence has now been applied to ana-

---

92. See sources cited in supra note 88.

93. See Winick, Therapeutic Jurisprudence Applied, supra note 2 (seeking and finding convergence between constitutional and therapeutic values in such areas as the use of incompetency labeling, the right to refuse treatment, the definition of mental illness for various legal purposes, voluntary hospitalization, the psychotherapist-patient privilege, incompetence in the criminal process, and the use of advance directive instruments); Winick, Right to Refuse, supra note 2 (seeking and finding convergence between constitutional and therapeutic values in defining and implementing the right to refuse mental health treatment).

94. See, e.g., Wexler & Winick, supra note 1. For a comprehensive therapeutic jurisprudence analysis of mental health law, see Winick, Therapeutic Jurisprudence Applied, supra note 2.

95. Law in a Therapeutic Key, supra note 1, Part I (collecting examples of therapeutic jurisprudence work across a wide spectrum of legal areas).

lyze issues in correctional law, criminal law, family law and juvenile law, sexual orientation law, disability law, health law, evidence law, personal injury law, labor arbitration law, contract and commercial law, workers' compensation law, probate law, and the legal profession.

Therapeutic Jurisprudence thus has emerged as an interdisciplinary scholarly approach for examining legal issues that cut across a wide spectrum of legal subjects. The original work has also now provoked a second generation of therapeutic jurisprudence scholarship—commentary about therapeutic jurisprudence itself, consisting of further elaborations of the theory, assessments, proposals for development, and critiques.[96] In addition, although therapeutic jurisprudence started with theoretical work applying social science principles to law, social scientists themselves now have begun the difficult empirical work of testing therapeutic jurisprudence hypotheses.[97]

B. Applying the Law Therapeutically

Therapeutic jurisprudence scholars initially were interested in examining substantive legal rules and legal procedures for their therapeutic and antitherapeutic effects. They examined legal statutes, common law doctrines, and recent cases with the therapeutic jurisprudence lens. More recently, scholars have begun to use the therapeutic jurisprudence lens to examine how the law is applied by various actors in the legal system. Even when a particular rule or practice is required to accomplish other goals, there may remain considerable room for applying law more therapeutically and less antitherapeutically.[98] Judges and attorneys play an important role in facilitating people's understanding of the law's requirements. What judges and lawyers say to the consumers of law may have a significant impact on their appreciation of those requirements and may help people to adapt to them in ways that have positive effects on their health and mental health. My study of the problems of incompetency labeling provides an illustration.[99] The negative social and psychological effects of such labeling are considerable, calling for a number of legal changes that can avoid or minimize these serious antitherapeutic consequences. Among them are suggested ways in which judges and attorneys, in cases in which the law finds it necessary to label a mentally ill individual as incompetent, can attempt to reframe the labeling experience for the individual in order to decrease at least some of the negative self-attributional effects that such labeling can produce.[100] Judges and lawyers accordingly need to have a special appreciation of their roles in this regard and of the potential for promoting well-being and minimizing harm. If those involved in law-making, in law-applying, and in law-related counseling begin to see themselves as therapeutic agents, they can enhance considerably the potential of law as a helping profession.

---

96. See Law in a Therapeutic Key, *supra* note 1, Part II (collecting examples).

97. See *id.*, Part III (collecting examples).

98. See David B. Wexler, *Applying the Law Therapeutically*, 5 Applied & Preventive Psychol. (forthcoming 1996).

99. Winick, *supra* note 40.

100. *Id.* at 40–41.

Existing law can be applied therapeutically not only by judges and lawyers. The actions of other actors in the legal process also may produce therapeutic or antitherapeutic effects. An example involves police officers assigned the task of transporting to the hospital individuals for whom an emergency commitment order has been issued. At the 1996 meeting of The American Psychology-Law Society, preliminary data was presented concerning research conducted under the auspices of the MacArthur Network on Mental Health and the Law relating to coercion in the mental health system. The researchers had studied perceptions of coercion, examining factors that led patients to feel coerced. Patients transported to the hospital by police officers who took them into custody without more than a rudimentary explanation felt coerced. On the other hand, when police officers acted more humanely toward patients, explaining that they were merely acting in accordance with a court order and that the patient would have an opportunity to talk with hospital doctors concerning their need for hospitalization and to have a subsequent hearing on the issue, patients felt less coerced. Although not discussed at the conference, these findings may have therapeutic implications for the patients involved. Psychological theory would suggest that people who feel themselves to have been coerced may respond adversely, exhibiting a form of psychological reactance that might frustrate achievement of the treatment or other goal.[101] As a result, patients transported to the hospital for emergency commitment by police officers who were more communicative and treated them in ways that they perceived as more fair and humane predictably would have a better therapeutic response to hospitalization than those involved with police officers who treated them more like criminals. If this is so, it would suggest that different styles of handling emergency patients by police officers assigned the task of transporting them to the hospital could have an important impact on the patient's response to hospitalization and treatment, and would suggest the value of training programs designed to educate such police officers concerning how they might apply the law more therapeutically.

The concept that legal actors should seek to apply the law therapeutically raises what Slobogin has called the "rule of law dilemma."[102] Slobogin warns that "any attempt to individualize the law may undermine it."[103] Slobogin's concern is that placing a high degree of authority in clinicians and others delegated the power to apply the law may produce abuse. This concern is a traditional dilemma of administrative law. When low level and low visibility administrative officials are vested with discretion, the potential for arbitrary and discriminatory application of law is always present.

How can the potential for abuse be minimized? Administrative law has devised a number of approaches.[104] Legislatures should set forth statutory standards to channel and limit administrative discretion. Even within the interstices of such statutory standards, when administrative practices have

---

101. See Sharon S. Brehm & Jack W. Brehm, Psychological Reactance: A Theory of Freedom and Control (1981).

102. Slobogin, supra note 5, at 208–10.

103. Id. at 210.

104. See, e.g., Kenneth C. Davis, Police Discretion (1975) (applying administrative law models to deal with problems of police abuse).

developed to the point that administrative standards of practice have emerged, these standards should be codified through administrative rulemaking.[105] When administrative action affects an individual's liberty or property, some kind of administrative hearing should be provided at which the individual is afforded the opportunity to present arguments and evidence. Finally, judicial review of administrative action always is possible, allowing courts to scrutinize administrative behavior to prevent unauthorized administrative action, action inconsistent with the Constitution or relevant statutes, and action that is arbitrary, discriminatory, or that constitutes an abuse of discretion.[106]

These and other measures can be adapted to limit the potential that clinicians, police officers, schools, welfare agencies, and others given discretion to apply the law therapeutically will abuse their authority. Therapeutic jurisprudence has always suggested that therapeutic goals should be achieved only within the limits of considerations of justice. These include our basic notions of the "rule of law"—that the law should be applied fairly, evenhandedly, and non-discriminatorily. Legal actors should seek to apply the law therapeutically, but only when consistent with these values.

C. The Comparative Law Perspective of Therapeutic Jurisprudence

In another recent development, therapeutic jurisprudence has begun to attract attention by scholars and professionals in other countries.[107] This emerging comparative law approach holds great promise for enriching the field of therapeutic jurisprudence. Therapeutic jurisprudence presents a new set of opportunities for those interested in comparative law research. Unlike traditional approaches to mental health law, therapeutic jurisprudence is not constitutionally driven. It does not depend upon a Supreme Court aggressively applying the Constitution to expand the rights of those with mental illness. As a result, therapeutic jurisprudence can be more international and comparative in scope, allowing for greater opportunities for interchange between scholars of different nations. A comparative perspective can provide an international laboratory for therapeutic jurisprudence research in a number of ways. It may be that legal rules or approaches in other countries are more (or less) antitherapeutic than our own. An understanding of the laws of other countries and of their therapeutic consequences might therefore be quite illuminating concerning how our own law functions. In addition, therapeutic jurisprudence analyses of American law may provide insights for other countries engaged in a process of examining their own laws. A comparative perspective can also make available international laboratories for therapeutic jurisprudence research that might be

---

105. Such rulemaking should involve prepublication of a proposed administrative rule and an opportunity for public comment. See Administrative Procedure Act, 5 U.S.C. § 553(c) (1994) (notice and comment rulemaking).

106. See id. at § 706.

107. See David Carson, Therapeutic Jurisprudence for the United Kingdom?, 6 J. Forensic Psychiatry 433 (1995); David Carson & David B. Wexler, New Approaches to Mental Health Law: Will the UK Follow the US Lead, Again?, 1 J. Soc. Welf. & Family L. 79 (1994); Feldthusen, supra note 48.

difficult to perform or even to envision domestically. By this, I do not mean to suggest the use of unethical laboratories, *i.e.*, those displaying less concern for the protection of the rights of human subjects. Instead, I refer to the consequences of the fact that law in America functions within a constitutional framework that often limits the potential for legal change. This is not always true in other countries, with the result that legal practices in other countries may shed considerable light on our understanding of law's impact on therapeutic values. Moreover, in other respects, the potential of legal change to accomplish therapeutic objectives may exist in other legal regimes that are not possible or are not thought to be possible under American law. Actual or assumed domestic legal restrictions thus might make a change in legal arrangements appear impossible. This appearance alone will make it unlikely that research will be conducted concerning the impact of those legal rules that are thought of as unchangeable.

Research in other nations that do not have such restrictions may cause us to question the continued wisdom of a domestic legal rule thought to be unchangeable. I do not suggest that we use such research to question domestic rules that are constitutionally required. For example, research in another country showing that a high degree of communal involvement in the raising of children increases the mental health of children and their families[108] would not cause us to reexamine due process protection for a sphere of family privacy that allows a significant degree of parental autonomy, free of government control, over the rearing and education of children.[109] It might, however, make us think about ways, consistent with parental autonomy, of providing services and opportunities to parents (that they could be free to accept or reject) that might increase the degree of participation by grandparents, foster grandparents, neighbors, and teachers in the child-rearing process.

The United States Constitution itself may prevent abandonment of a legal rule that research in foreign laboratories suggests may be antitherapeutic. While abandonment of the rule may be impossible, changes in the way it is applied designed to minimize antitherapeutic effects in some instances may be considered. When the Constitution does not require a particular rule, on the other hand, comparative law research may be especially useful in the law reform effort.

There also may be occasions in which constitutional doctrine is mistakenly regarded as preventing legal change, and in which comparative therapeutic jurisprudence work may prompt us to question our mistaken assumptions. An example is gun control. A substantial segment of the population may mistakenly regard the Second Amendment to the Constitution as precluding government efforts to prohibit or curtail the private possession of handguns. This mistaken view may seriously diminish the pressure for legislative response. Were comparative therapeutic jurisprudence research in a society that bans handguns to demonstrate significant positive consequences to mental and physical health, this research might prompt clarification of the Second Amendment's reach and pave the way for legislative action.

---

108. See Hillary Rodham Clinton, It Takes a Village and Other Lessons Children Teach Us (1996).

109. E.g., Pierce v. Society of Sisters, 268 U.S. 510 (1925); Meyer v. Nebraska, 262 U.S. 590 (1923).

Sometimes what is thought to be a constitutionally required rule may instead be dicta, a judicial statement not having the force of precedent. In such cases, comparative therapeutic jurisprudence work can prompt reexamination of such dicta. My prior work on incompetency in the criminal process[110] illustrates this potential. In a series of articles, I proposed that the American competency-to-stand-trial process be restructured to differentiate between two categories of cases. One category involves defendants who seek to obtain an incompetency adjudication based upon their mental illness in order to permit a delay in the proceedings so that they may obtain needed treatment. The other involves defendants who wish to stand trial or plead guilty notwithstanding their mental illness and therefore seek to resist an adjudication of incompetence. I proposed that these two types of cases be treated differently. As long as counsel concurs in the defendant's judgment, the proposal, with several exceptions, would allow defendants able to articulate a preference for trial or guilty plea to avoid an incompetency adjudication, even though their competency is diminished by mental illness. For defendants who do not have such a preference, however, but wish to assert their mental illness as a basis for postponing their trial, I proposed substituting a system of trial continuances for the formal competency evaluation process.

This latter suggestion could be the subject of empirical investigation in a domestic laboratory if a jurisdiction were willing to experiment with this proposal. However, the proposal that defendants of marginal competence be permitted to stand trial or plead guilty may appear impossible to implement without violating constitutional doctrine. The Supreme Court's dicta in its 1966 opinion in *Pate v. Robinson*,[111] often repeated in recent decisions,[112] has been read to stand for the broad proposition that the Constitution places an absolute prohibition on the trial of an incompetent defendant. This assumption has hampered empirical research in this area and has made the radical restructuring of incompetency doctrine proposed in my prior work seem legally impossible. My prior articles argue that the language in *Pate* is dicta and need not be read as barring the proposal made.[113] However, even if dicta, it is unlikely that states would be willing to experiment with the proposal because of the risk that ensuing convictions might be overturned. Although my prior work suggests that there would be therapeutic as well as other advantages in permitting the trial or guilty plea of defendants in this category, the constitutional concerns would make it unlikely that this aspect of the proposal would be tested in a domestic laboratory.

Other countries, however, are free of the restrictions of the *Pate v. Robinson* gloss on due process, and therefore may be more willing to experiment with this proposal. The experience in these jurisdictions could be used to probe the wisdom of the proposals made in my articles, and these countries could become laboratories for empirical research on the question. Should research in

110. Reforming Incompetency, supra note 43; Restructuring Competency, supra note 43.

111. 383 U.S. 375, 378, 384–86 (1966).

112. E.g., Cooper v. Oklahoma, 116 S. Ct. 1373, 1376 (1996); Godinez v. Moran, 113 S. Ct. 2680, 2685, 2688 (1993); Medina v. California, 505 U.S. 437, 438, 448–49, 453 (1992).

113. Reforming Incompetency, supra note 43, at 584; Restructuring Competency, supra note 43, at 968–69.

these jurisdictions document the asserted values of the proposed restructuring of incompetency doctrine, then it would be open for American courts to discard the *Pate v. Robinson* dicta and implement legal change. As these examples illustrate, the opportunities for interesting comparative work in the area of therapeutic jurisprudence abound.

VII. Conclusion

Therapeutic jurisprudence is a school of jurisprudence within the tradition of sociological jurisprudence and legal realism. Like psychology and law and social science in law, it is an interdisciplinary and empirical approach to the study of law. Unlike these schools, but like law and economics, critical legal studies, feminist jurisprudence, and critical race theory, it is normative in orientation. It calls for the application of social science theory and research to enhance law's therapeutic impact. But it recognizes that, although psychological and physical health is a desirable aim of law, it is not the only aim. When therapeutic and other normative values conflict, its contribution is to sharpen the debate, but it cannot resolve it. On the other hand, when therapeutic and other normative values converge, therapeutic jurisprudence helps to identify the path of true law reform. By providing a new lens through which to examine law, it promises to produce new insights and a newly invigorated interdisciplinary approach to law that will enrich legal policy analysis and improve law's functioning and its ability to increase the well-being of our society.

Chapter 33

Speaking Truth to Power: Rights, Therapeutic Jurisprudence, and Massachusetts Mental Health Law

Joel Haycock

I. Introduction

In 1866, the famous New Hampshire Supreme Court Justice Charles Doe argued that nothing could be a fact in law if it were not a fact in science, and nothing would be health in law which was disease in fact.[1] Through the perspective of therapeutic jurisprudence, David Wexler and colleagues propose to gently extend Judge Doe's axiom: that cannot be true, or good in mental health law if not true in mental health practice; that cannot be healthy in mental health law which is antitherapeutic in its effects.

In an important statement of the case for this gentle extension, David Wexler offers three reasons for a new approach to mental health legal scholarship. First, Wexler warns that the emphasis on rights in traditional mental health legal scholarship has become both sterile and risky. It has become risky

> because if scholarship is exclusively dependent upon the recognition or the pursuit of certain rights, then as society and the composition of the Supreme Court change, making the viability or the attainment of those rights less likely, the entire branch of scholarship is likely to die on the vine.[2]

Note that this is a conjunctural, almost tactical point, rather than a theoretical one.

Second, Wexler argues that mental health law has been impoverished by its association with the civil libertarian attack on psychiatry and related disciplines.

> Because of its recent history and its antagonism toward psychiatry and related disciplines...modern mental health law has not profited from truly interdisciplinary cooperation and interchange—from having the knowledge, theories, and insights of the mental health disciplines help *shape* the law, the legal system, and the behavior of legal actors, just as economic principles have been

---

1. See generally State v. Pike, 49 NH 399, 408–44 (1869) (Doe, J., dissenting).

2. David B. Wexler, Putting Mental Health Into Mental Health Law: Therapeutic Jurisprudence, in Essays in Therapeutic Jurisprudence 5 (David B. Wexler & Bruce J. Winick eds., 1991) [hereinafter Wexler 1991b].

used to inform legal development in certain other areas of the law, such as antitrust.[3]

The third point reflects a theoretical position on the nature of law and consequently the nature of mental health law. In this view, legal questions inevitably involve issues of social policy. Thus, legal questions in the mental health area concern mental health social policy issues. "Therapeutic jurisprudence is the study of the role of the law as a therapeutic agent. It looks at the law as a social force that, like it or not, may produce therapeutic or antitherapeutic consequences."[4] Furthermore, "[t]he task of therapeutic jurisprudence is to identify—and ultimately to examine empirically—relationships between legal arrangements and therapeutic outcomes."[5] In Wexler's view, mental health legal scholarship has tended to ignore therapeutic outcomes, failing to benefit from research advances in the mental health disciplines.

> The law's ignorance of the mental health disciplines should no longer be excused. First of all, courts already *do* occasionally consider (or purport to consider) the anticipated therapeutic outcomes of their rulings, so it is best to focus scholarly attention on such matters to assist courts in reaching correct results.[6]

Therapeutic jurisprudence would then synthesize principles of justice with the contributions of mental health research. Having weathered the "rights" revolution of the 1970s and survived its association with radical critiques of psychiatry,

> mental health law is now in a reasonably good position both to evaluate mental health information and, because of the law's historical origin and consequent 'rights' orientation, to appreciate the crucial importance of certain principles of justice (e.g., the need for counsel; the need for a fair fact-finding mechanism).[7]

Wexler's call for a shift to a therapeutic jurisprudence perspective, therefore, rests on two different and logically separable points. The first asks that we evaluate "the extent to which the law itself causes or contributes to psychological dysfunction."[8] This seems like a robust and illuminating enterprise. The other and more controversial point is a call for shifting, rather than simply complementing, the focus of mental health law away from its traditional concern with "rights" to an "alternative route," one "that exploits meaningful insights from the mental health disciplines and allows the law to better serve as a therapeutic agent."[9]

The theoretical position arguably bears the influence of several productive, even sometimes opposing traditions of legal scholarship, with roots both in Roscoe Pound's sociological jurisprudence[10] and especially in the later move-

---

3. David B. Wexler, An Introduction to Therapeutic Jurisprudence, in Essays in Therapeutic Jurisprudence 17 (David B. Wexler & Bruce J. Winick eds., 1991) [hereinafter Wexler 1991a].

4. Wexler 1991b, supra note 2, at 8.

5. Id.

6. Wexler 1991a, supra note 3, at 17.

7. Id. at 18.

8. Id. at 19.

9. Id. at 18.

10. Roscoe Pound, Outline of Lectures on Jurisprudence (5th ed. 1943).

ment of legal realism.[11] From the perspective of legal realism, legislators, judges, legal scholars and others argue or decide social policy questions based on their psychological and sociological assumptions as well as their political values. They "then rationalize their decisions by invoking legal rules and principles."[12] They should "consciously and frankly engage in sophisticated and fact-sensitive social science analysis"[13] so that they can make better policy.

Mental health law and legal procedure are replete with assumptions about human psychology and mental health treatment. Those assumptions should be dragged into view and examined. Wexler is right to stress that current mental health law and legal procedures are insufficiently empirically-referenced. Law and procedure should be evaluated in light of research advances in these areas. Wexler's argument seems more contestable when he advocates a shift in mental health legal scholarship away from rights, however, perhaps especially as it concerns the criminal justice area.

The scope of the therapeutic jurisprudence perspective in the criminal justice system differs substantially from its potential scope in civil commitment or juvenile justice. The jurisprudence of involuntary civil commitment and juvenile justice is based on the state's *parens patriae* authority. The principle of *parens patriae* empowers the state to act in the "best interests" and on behalf of those individuals who cannot care adequately for themselves.

The jurisprudence of criminal law is based upon the state's "police power." The state is authorized to use police power to protect the public safety against individuals who might threaten the general welfare of society.[14] The criminal justice system does not function on behalf of individuals, but rather on behalf of the social order. "While the criminal justice system may seek to rehabilitate offenders, it serves other purposes that are at least as important, such as retribution and deterrence."[15]

It is not hard to see why the concept of therapeutic jurisprudence has gripped the imagination of so many people in the mental health field over the last several years. Therapeutic jurisprudence offers the hope to mental health professionals that the law will finally go to school, this time not law school, but rather their school. Through therapeutic jurisprudence, the mental health professional's "knowledge, theories, and insights" will "shape the law, the legal system, and the behavior of legal actors."[16] Therapeutic jurisprudence appears to give voice to the frustration or sense of grievance occasionally experienced by mental health professionals preparing evaluations for the courts, namely that the law lacks respect for their expertise. How welcome then to hear legal scholars declare that "the law's ignorance of the mental health disciplines should no longer be excused."[17]

---

11. See Karl Llewellyn, The Common Law Tradition: Deciding Appeals (1960); William Twining, Karl Llewellyn and the Realist Movement (1973).

12. Richard Michael Fischl, Some Realism About Critical Legal Studies, 41 U. Miami L. Rev. 505, 520 (1987).

13. Id.

14. Samuel J. Brakel et al., The Mentally Disabled and the Law 24–26 (3d ed. 1985).

15. Gary B. Melton et al., Psychological Evaluations for the Courts 211 (1987).

16. Wexler 1991a, supra note 3, at 17.

17. Id.

That mental health law or procedure in the criminal justice system "causes or contributes to psychological dysfunction,"[18] therefore may have less relevance to, and less weight on, legal outcomes than mental health professionals might hope. Mental health law in the criminal justice system is not formed with a view to the best interests of the patient, detainee, prison inmate or defendant. Rather, it is formed through a combination of interests in which the defense of social order, liberty interests, constitutional rights,[19] and occasionally therapeutic outcomes, compete for attention.

Especially in the criminal justice system, the interplay of these other interests ensures that the interpretation and ultimate social value of therapeutic consequences will be sharply contested. Like Wexler, we want the courts to reach "correct results."[20] Nonetheless, in a society composed of competing social actors, moral values, and political ideologies, there are no indisputably "correct results" to which science (such as can be found in the mental health field) can now lead the law.

Just as assumptions about therapeutic consequences may influence judicial reasoning about mental health law, so political and social values will influence the reading of mental health "knowledge, theories and insights" by courts, legislators, and also by mental health researchers. For more than a hundred years, psychiatrists have complained about the demoralizing spectacle of having mutually exclusive expert psychiatric opinions rendered in criminal trials, complained not least because it has continually undermined the scientific authority of the mental health disciplines in the public and judicial minds. No less than society, the mental health field is composed of competing social actors (sometimes just actors), moral values, and political ideologies. There is no reason to suppose that when modern mental health law finally attends psychology graduate school, the instructors it encounters will speak with one voice on therapeutic or antitherapeutic consequences.

The jurisprudential authority for law in the areas of civil commitment and juvenile justice is derived from the state's *parens patriae* powers. For this reason, therapeutic jurisprudence may there represent a reasonable refocusing of energies away from a repetitive insistence on rights. If the appeal is (at least putatively) to the individual's best interests in the first place, then the introduction of new mental health research regarding what constitutes the individual's psychological best interest, or what procedures are not in the individual's therapeutic interests, or how he or she might make the greatest or most durable therapeutic gains, form a logical part of a coherent discourse. This may also apply to certain rights-driven changes in mental health law in the criminal justice area. Yet given that the purposes of the criminal justice system are chiefly concerned with protection of the social order and may only incidentally bear

---

18. Id. at 19.

19. See generally Estelle v. Gamble, 429 U.S. 97 (5th Cir. 1974); Ramos v. Lamm, 639 F.2d 559 (10th Cir. 1980); Bowring v. Godwin, 551 F.2d 44 (4th Cir. 1977); Fred Cohen, U.S. Dep't of Justice, Legal Issues and the Mentally Disordered Prisoner (1988) (discussing treatment only for "serious" medical or psychological needs).

20. Wexler 1991a, supra note 3, at 17.

on therapeutic goals, the question becomes whether therapeutic jurisprudence represents an effective or prudent *redirection* for mental health law in this area. Where the jurisprudential authority derives from the state's police power, pointing out that a particular law may aggravate psychological dysfunction seems considerably less compelling.

II. Massachusetts General Laws, Chapter 123, Section 18A

To illustrate these problems, let us consider a law that affected all involuntarily committed patients in the civil and criminal systems. Section 18A of chapter 123 of the Massachusetts General Laws was an amendment quietly passed into law during the summer of 1991, and innocuously entitled, *Contributions Towards Cost of Appointed Counsel*. The new law became effective on July 1, 1991 and remained in effect until Judge Rya Zobel issued a preliminary injunction on April 22, 1992. Through the winter of 1991–1992 the law was reluctantly enforced in state institutions.[21]

This new law stipulated that a psychiatric patient in a Department of Mental Health facility or in Bridgewater State Hospital who had funds held in trust "shall contribute toward the cost of any counsel appointed" for that patient in involuntary commitment proceedings to a psychiatric hospital or regarding the involuntary administration of psychotropic medication.[22] The law required the Department of Mental Health or the Department of Correction to turn over such funds, not exceeding five hundred dollars per instance, to the state treasurer.[23] No economic means test accompanied the legislation. Regardless of how little money the patients had, the law required the affected Departments to take it.

This legislation was doubtless passed with the help of stories about the occasional psychiatric patient receiving large monthly checks from the Veteran's Administration. Such tales are the mental health equivalent of those hoary anecdotes, beloved by politicians, about the welfare mother picking up her check in a Cadillac. The reality is quite different.

Take the situation of an average involuntarily committed psychiatric patient. Whether or not the patient originally came from straitened circumstances, the burden of his mental disorder is extreme.[24] He has almost no money. Anecdotes about VA checks notwithstanding, ninety-four percent of Bridgewater State Hospital patients have less than two hundred dollars, and eighty-nine percent have less than one hundred dollars in their accounts. What a patient has is "held in trust" since he is not allowed to have money on his person.

---

21. Mass. Gen. L. ch. 123, § 18A (1992) (originally enacted as of July 1, 1991, 1991 Mass. Acts 138, §§ 275, 393 (1991)).

22. Id.

23. Id.

24. These examples come from Bridgewater State Hospital, and therefore involve only male patients.

There is very little paid work available in most state psychiatric institutions. At Bridgewater State Hospital, the maximum that a patient can earn is two dollars a day, but only a small fraction of the patients have paid work. With these few dollars, a patient can purchase deodorant, cigarettes, stamps, a piece of fruit, or a cold soda or an ice cream in the summer. Until recently, indigent patients at all state hospitals were allowed to send four free letters per week, but a strict means test has now limited free mail. Some who do receive social security checks send a portion to their families as reimbursement for collect telephone calls. Patients are only allowed to call collect.

The state legislature decided to sanction the seizure of funds under the statute, "whenever" the hospital holds *any* funds for such a man. In the first week of March, 1992, patients with fifty dollars in their accounts had over one hundred dollars deducted, and were left not only penniless, but with a debt. Other patients at Bridgewater State Hospital with eighty dollars in their accounts had forty dollars taken from them to cover the cost of hearings which had occurred the previous summer. Given time-limited commitments and time-limited substituted judgments, new hearings were already scheduled for some of those same patients. These patients therefore, could expect the remaining forty dollars to be seized in short order.

The patient has two choices. He can decide to waive legal representation when the hospital attempts to commit or involuntarily treat him, thereby saving his forty dollars. This allows him to retain the ability to purchase cigarettes, sodas, or stamps. Or, he can contest his hearings. Should the patient lose the hearing, he will find himself without any money at all, or perhaps with a debt that he will in effect gradually work off until the end of the current commitment. At the end of the current commitment a new hearing will take place, followed by a fresh seizure of funds. This assumes that the patient does not avail himself of his right to appeal his commitment to the Superior Court, the cost of which would require another "contribution."

The law thus penalizes those psychiatric patients who exercise their constitutional rights, while rewarding those compliant or simply needy individuals who decide to forgo legal representation. The Commonwealth implicitly tries to buy the rights of involuntarily committed, indigent mental patients with cigarettes, soda, and fruit, commodities many of them will lose if they choose to challenge the wisdom of their doctors.

A seriously mentally ill patient, with eighty dollars in his account is by any definition indigent. While seizing those few dollars under any circumstances is cruel, penalizing that man for asserting his rights against the police power of the Commonwealth is vindictive.

There are further dizzying complications, as there frequently are in the Kafka-esque world that still often surrounds the mentally ill. Who would be competent to waive their right to counsel? A number of psychiatric patients are involuntarily hospitalized, at Bridgewater and elsewhere, as legally incompetent to stand trial. Many more, pursuant to the *Rogers*[25] decision, have been declared by Commonwealth courts incompetent to make treatment decisions

---

25. Rogers v. Comm'r of Dep't of Mental Health, 458 N.E.2d 308 (Mass. 1983).

for themselves.[26] It is safe to say that a number of those patients who would be tempted to forgo legal representation in order to conserve their eighty dollar accounts might not be considered by their mental health professionals competent to make that judgment. They would be *forced* to have legal representation, then forced to pay for it, and if they lost the case, forced to go through the process again.

The ultimate decision concerning involuntary commitment or forcible medication cases is one of social policy, where liberty interests, constitutional rights, humane considerations and public safety questions are all at issue. To balance these conflicting concerns we usually require an adversarial process.

But perhaps adversarial processes are no longer for the indigent. When the indigent mentally ill assert their claims regardless, we will taunt them by denying them the ability to purchase cigarettes, soda or stamps. In this way we will teach them a lesson about the world in which they are to reintegrate themselves, about the responsible citizenship they will exercise once outside.

Let those who are going to contest doctors' professional judgment have their funds seized, so that they may beg a soda from their fellow patients, pick up butts from the hospital ashtrays, or perhaps threaten others for pretzels. In this way they will better prepare themselves for life in our communities, where they must beg for spare change, collect empties from dumpsters, and search the sidewalks for pieces of cigarettes.

There are several ways of evaluating this Massachusetts law.[27] One method is derived from the concept of therapeutic jurisprudence. This approach would point out the multiple and flagrant antitherapeutic effects of the statute. But section 18A was not written with therapeutic effects in mind, and the recitation of its antitherapeutic consequences did not carry much weight with those who passed it. The law was enacted as part of a general policy aimed at finding revenue streams, even trifling ones, and at dismantling what have come to be derisively labelled "entitlement programs," policies from which the poor benefit (as opposed to tax deductions for mortgage interest, which, since they benefit other classes, are obviously not "entitlement programs").

Whatever the legislative intent of section 18A, the law was also enacted as part of a general trend towards punishing public charges, and limiting their access to the courts. There is a point where regressive taxation policy and the punitive Zeitgeist meet, and that point is embodied in *Contributions Toward Costs of Appointed Counsel*.

Not surprisingly, the criticism of the law was a "rights-led" attack, and not an appeal to its antitherapeutic outcomes. The law was challenged for violating the constitutional rights to due process, to counsel, to equal protection under the law and to access to the courts. These challenges have temporarily succeeded. Against the police power of the state, the "traditional" concern with individual rights continues to have a force that eludes other types of appeal, such as antitherapeutic effects.

---

26. Indeed, presumably if more patients waived their right to counsel in hearings regarding their competence to make treatment decisions, even greater numbers of them would be found incompetent to make those decisions.

27. Mass. Gen. L. ch. 123, § 18A (1992); see supra note 21.

III. Three Issues Bearing on the Mental Health Treatment of Prisoners

Convicted prisoners represent the bulk of forensic psychiatric inpatients. For at least fifteen years, prisoners have accounted for more admissions to mental hospitals and represent, on any given day, a higher percentage of total forensic inpatients, than the combined total of those hospitalized after having been adjudicated incompetent to stand trial, found not guilty by reason of insanity or adjudged mentally disordered sex offenders.[28] How the law, its accompanying legal procedures, and legal actors impede or facilitate the mental health assessment and treatment of detainees and prisoners arguably represents the core of forensic mental health in and out of hospital contexts.

The first issue concerns the forcible administration of psychotropic medication to convicted prisoners. In *Washington v. Harper*,[29] the United States Supreme Court made three findings. First, the Court held that the state had a "legitimate interest in combating the danger posed by a violent, mentally ill inmate."[30] The Court held that any constitutional claim that prisoners might raise against the state should be evaluated according to the so-called "reasonableness" test. In *Turner v. Safley*,[31] and *O'Lone v. Estate of Shabazz*,[32] the Court held that the proper standard for determining the validity of a prison regulation was to ask whether the regulation is "reasonably related to legitimate penological interests."[33]

Although "inmates retain at least some constitutional rights despite incarceration…prison authorities are best equipped to make difficult decisions regarding prison administration."[34] This application of review, the "reasonableness" standard, "applies to all circumstances in which the needs of prison administration implicate constitutional rights."[35] Second, given the state's compelling interest in social order within its prisons, the state need not find a prisoner incompetent to make treatment decisions, and need not then "obtain court approval of the treatment using a 'substituted judgment' standard."[36]

Third, the Due Process Clause does not require a judicial hearing prior to involuntarily treating a mentally ill prisoner with antipsychotic medication.

---

28. Cohen, supra note 19, at 4; Eliot Hartstone et al., Vitek and Beyond: The Empirical Context of Prison-to-Hospital Transfers, 45 Law & Contemp. Probs. 125, 135 (1982).

29. 494 U.S. 210 (1990).

30. Id.

31. 482 U.S. 78 (1987).

32. 482 U.S. 342 (1987).

33. Harper, 494 U.S. at 223.

34. Id.

35. Id. at 223–24. The reasonableness standard in judging prison regulations contrasts with the strict scrutiny/least intrusive standard, which holds that a restriction on inmates' constitutional rights can be justified "only if it further[s] an important or substantial governmental interest unrelated to the suppression" of that right (suppression of expression, for example) and the restriction extends no further than necessary to protect the interest. Cohen, supra note 19, at 28. See also Procunier v. Martinez, 416 U.S. 396 (1974) (discussing strict scrutiny).

36. Harper, 494 U.S. at 226.

Harper's substantial liberty interest, when considered with the government interests involved and the efficacy of the particular procedural requirements, is "adequately protected, and perhaps better served, by allowing the decision to medicate to be made by medical professionals rather than a judge."[37] The Court rejected the respondent's argument that the institutional hearing provided by the State of Washington at its Special Offender Center must "be conducted in accordance with the rules of evidence" and the state court's "clear, cogent, and convincing standard of proof."[38] "This standard is neither required nor helpful when medical personnel are making the judgment required by the regulations here."[39]

The Supreme Court believes prison authorities are sufficiently equipped to decide what is "'reasonably related to legitimate penological interests'"[40] and medical professionals are best equipped to decide on involuntary medication.[41] Yet, the forcible administration of medication in prison settings is a daunting spectacle and should give pause to anyone concerned with the mental health of prisoners, not to mention their constitutional rights. Once the inmate fails to arrive at the medication line, the nurse or doctor proceeds to his or her cell, accompanied by correction officers. An exchange usually ensues, in which the inmate refuses to come out of the cell to receive the medication. At this point, a special tactical operations unit is usually notified, the tier or unit is typically locked down, and a specially equipped extraction team, replete with shields, visors, special uniforms, and command codes, arrives to "extract" the prisoner from the cell. The extraction team forcibly places the prisoner against a wall, where the medication is administered by injection. Amid the shouting from other prisoners down the tier, from the extraction team, and from the furious, resistant, and ultimately helpless inmate, some staff member invariably tells him, not that the court has ordered this medication, but rather that "the doctor says you need your medication."[42]

---

37. Id. at 229–31.

38. Id. at 235.

39. Id.

40. Id. at 223 (quoting Turner v. Safley, 482 U.S. 78, 89 (1987)).

41. Id. at 235.

42. To its great credit, the Massachusetts Department of Correction has long agreed as a matter of informal practice (though not formal procedure) not to pressure for the forcible medication of any of its prisoners. In Massachusetts, there are stringent due process requirements for the involuntary administration of antipsychotic medications to any hospitalized patient, including prisoners. Rogers v. Comm'r of Dep't of Mental Health, 458 N.E.2d 308 (Mass. 1983). In Rogers, the court held a patient's liberty interests required court approval of the forcible administration of psychotropic medication. Id. at 310–11. Before judicial authorization for such treatment can be given, the Commonwealth must prove both that the individual is incompetent to make treatment decisions and that were the patient competent, he or she would agree to the treatment advocated by the hospital. Id. at 313–14. These are civil proceedings, and in Massachusetts the judicial hearing may take place in either the district court having jurisdiction over the hospital confining the patient or in probate court. Id. at 314–15. District and probate substituted judgments have different spheres of application: A district court judgment is bounded by the patient's hospital commitment, and so does not follow him or her out of the hospital, whereas a probate court decision follows the patient throughout the state, including hospital, prison or jail. Probate orders, therefore, bring with

Two other procedures bearing on the treatment of prisoners' mental health needs concern the management of suicidal patients and parole decisions. These procedures or practices were not explicitly fashioned with an eye to the Supreme Court's reasonableness standard, but rather from the traditional penological concern for order and stability which the Supreme Court's current standard rationalizes.

In many prison systems, including Massachusetts, New York, and the federal system, acts of self-injury such as non-fatal cutting result in disciplinary reports and sometimes in disciplinary sanctions. Further, being placed on an at-risk status, mental health observation, or psychotropic medication sometimes can formally or informally result in a prisoner's retention in higher security, a denial of transfer to lower security such as pre-release status, or following a transfer to lower security, a transfer back to a high security unit. This occurs because placement on at-risk status or admitting to feelings of depression or suicidal despair are frequently considered signs of poor adjustment. The following is an example from the initial classification report on a prisoner plagued by suicidal thoughts. "Inmate Donald X has made a poor adjustment to his first incarceration. He was moved from [the unit for new inmates] to the Health Service Unit (HSU) as he stated that he felt like committing suicide. In HSU he was on ten minute observation and has now returned to [the unit for new inmates]. He has not received any [discipline] reports or work details. He takes [an antipsychotic agent] for manic depression and is monitored by Health Service Unit staff."[43] Consider also the case of Mr. Jones, denied transfer to the minimal security of a pre-release center because of adjustment difficulties, as evidenced by being placed on at-risk status.[44]

While inmates cannot be denied parole because of a mental disorder, over the years the Massachusetts parole board has sought reassurance that an established mental disorder or a history of psychiatric hospitalization does not complicate parole prospects, and that the inmate has adequate arrangements for aftercare. Until recently the parole board did not consider anyone for parole who was currently an inpatient at Bridgewater State Hospital. The Massachusetts Parole Board has, to date, not seen patients with certain kinds of charges. A study several years ago found that inmates with ongoing relationships with the prison mental health service were significantly more likely to be turned down by the parole board.[45] Prisoners continue to believe that being on psychotropic medication, or being an inpatient at Bridgewater State Hospital, will at best complicate or prejudice their chances of receiving parole, and at worst result in the denial of parole.

---

them a potential dispositional and management flexibility that the district court orders do not. At Bridgewater State Hospital, which operates under the agency authority of the Department of Correction, the clinical staff will not seek, and indeed has occasionally actively opposed, probate court Rogers orders for prisoners who might then be returned to correctional settings.

43. This is not a published legal case, but rather a clinical vignette. It is not a hypothetical case; thus, confidentiality precludes any further identification.

44. See supra note 43.

45. Susan Lantagne & Cynthia Jeffers (1988) (unpublished manuscript, on file with author).

These procedures, like those allowed in *Harper*,[46] threaten irreparable disruption in treatment relationships with prisoners. Some prisoners flee their entanglements with mental health providers, in the hope of bolstering their chances of getting classified to lower security or making parole, or in the worst cases, simply avoiding the extraction team and the accompanying needle. Prisoners may also refuse contacts or communications which might lead to a further involvement with mental health professionals, such as placement on at-risk status, placement on medication, transfer to a psychiatric facility or simply identification as a mental health patient. Prisoners may withhold information that would lead to greater mental health involvement. They may break off or choose not to initiate working alliances with mental health staff. They may even terminate therapy or medication at ill-advised times, or struggle destructively to get discharged from a psychiatric hospital.

Case law and procedures like these entail stark antitherapeutic effects, and a jurisprudence rooted in the recognition of those effects is urgently needed. One may have to resort increasingly to such a jurisprudence if, as Wexler predicts, avenues for rights-based redress are closed.[47] But the most powerful way of stating the effects of such procedures might be that these prisoners suffer discrimination as psychiatric patients. As such, the most powerful means of redress may still lie within a rights-based appeal.

IV. Conclusion

Particularly in light of Professor Wexler's own distinguished record[48] and Professor Winick's careful insistence that "therapeutic values...may not be dispositive of the legal issue,"[49] the above discussion may seem needlessly cautious. As a research agenda, therapeutic jurisprudence holds out enormous promise—a promise abundantly evident in the stream of provocative legal scholarship it has engendered. A given research agenda is always judged by its productivity: the importance of therapeutic jurisprudence therefore depends partly on the fruitful lines of research it opens.

In directing us to explore the therapeutic outcomes associated with particular legal arrangements, therapeutic jurisprudence expands the scope and power of mental health legal scholarship. It has other equally important implications: it can energize and widen the work of patient advocacy, legal representation, and forensic mental health clinical practice. It would seem that any practicing clinician could only cheer such a development, and cheers in considerable measure are more than warranted.

---

46. 494 U.S. 210 (1990).

47. One may also need to couch the argument in a social control mode (treatment will bring a safer, more secure facility or enhance public safety in the long run) if no other hearing can be obtained. But of course social control arguments for treatment are not necessarily true. Draconian security works, more often than not, for longer rather than shorter periods.

48. See, e.g., David B. Wexler & Samuel E. Scoville, The Administration of Psychiatric Justice: Theory and Practice in Arizona, 13 Ariz. L. Rev. 1 (1971).

49. David B. Wexler & Bruce J. Winick, Therapeutic Jurisprudence as a New Approach to Mental Health Law Policy Analysis and Research, 45 U. Miami L. Rev. 979, 996 (1991).

But the project of therapeutic jurisprudence also carries risks. One stated goal of that project is to loosen the close dependence of mental health legal scholarship on doctrinal and constitutional approaches.[50] In the criminal justice system, to stray from rights-based perspectives always entails grave risks. If therapeutic jurisprudence is understood as a complement to and deepening of such rights-based perspectives, a complement in which mental health insights inform doctrinal and constitutional approaches, then the risks will be minimized. But if therapeutic jurisprudence is construed as a shift from, or an alternative to, rights-based perspectives, then real risks exist.

The doctrinal authority for criminal justice does not begin with the therapeutic interests of the individual, and mental health in the criminal justice arena does not generally operate under a *parens patriae* umbrella. Regardless of the intentions or effects of mental health practitioners, mental health clients or patients in the criminal justice system are treated not so much for their own sake, but often for our collective sake, because they frighten us as a society, or because their psychological difficulties disrupt the orderly workings of our current criminal justice institutions. Mental health care within those institutions is forced to respond to systemic interests rather than individual ones. It is those systemic interests that are by necessity in some contradiction with, and sometimes flatly inimical to, the needs of mental health patients.

In evaluating the effectiveness of new directions in mental health law, we need to listen for the vulnerabilities created for the objects of that law within systems not designed for their care. Working from the perspective of therapeutic jurisprudence, or of any other new direction in mental health law, we need to bear three considerations in mind; considerations of power, the need for protection *from* mental health, and considerations of empowerment.

Regardless of other weaknesses, doctrinal and constitutional approaches to mental health law have served as an effective counter-weight to the police power of the state. The first question before therapeutic jurisprudence—and perhaps the one most easily answered—is whether therapeutic jurisprudence is construed as reinforcing or weakening that counterweight. From their writings, there is no question that Wexler and Winick have no intention of, and have explicitly warned against, retreating from the protections embodied in traditional mental health law.[51]

The potential risks associated with a new direction in mental health law do not lie simply in the formal scholarship. They also inhere in how that perspective is understood by clinicians on the front lines or in the trenches (military metaphors that implicitly raise complicated questions of whom we are fighting for, against, and with), by attorneys and by patients. Regardless of research advances, the goals and values of mental health face enormous pressures within the criminal justice system. Historically, mental health has not been able to withstand these pressures without the protection of doctrinal and constitutional law.

There is always a risk that one day we will assume that mental health has once more become purely and securely benevolent. This presents the second

---

50. Wexler 1991b, supra note 2.

51. See generally David B. Wexler, An Orientation to Therapeutic Jurisprudence, 20 New Eng. J. on Crim. & Civ. Confinement 259 (1994).

question confronting therapeutic jurisprudence: Does therapeutic jurisprudence educate us to that danger, or conversely, fail to challenge that assumption? Failing that education, will practitioners construe the theory as therapeutic paternalism, a new version of doctor knows best? Within the criminal justice system, a new direction in mental health law must also help protect the objects of that law and of our care from mental health itself. Within that system, therapeutic jurisprudence risks being construed unilaterally from the perspective of the producers of mental health, the clinicians, and the consumers of their services, the courts and other criminal justice agencies, rather than from the perspective of the objects of mental health law.

What Wexler calls the "civil liberties revolution"[52] did not take place because one day a conference of lawyers and legal scholars decided this was an interesting direction to take the law. As Wexler knows intimately, it was not simply "litigation and scholarship" that "served to expand the rights of criminal suspects, defendants, prisoners, and ultimately mental patients and respondents in civil commitment hearings."[53] The civil liberties revolution came about in large part because of the existence of social movements, of movements for redress, in which the central actor was the civil rights movement. The civil rights movement had a natural effect on law in criminal justice and mental health. This was not a world the lawyers made. While lawyers and legal scholars helped shape it, they also trailed behind it, sometimes at a great distance.

Besides the cogent argument offered by Wexler, another reason for the sterility and riskiness of rights-driven mental health law stems from the current absence of any social echo in the objects of that law. The richness and productivity of rights-driven law had to do with the way it reflected the practical exercise of rights, even where the law did not yet recognize them; and in turn with the way rights-driven legal scholarship empowered people to assert their rights.

This is the third standard against which to judge the research agenda of therapeutic jurisprudence: the success of therapeutic jurisprudence will depend in part on the degree to which it empowers the objects of therapeutic and judicial attention. We know that therapy is neither something that one person does to another, nor something that one person says to another, but rather joint work, joint dialogue, joint discourse. If we are going to use the law to advance therapeutic or treatment ends, patients cannot simply be the objects of law-driven treatment. They also have to be allies in it, joint discussants.

The relationship here, particularly in the criminal justice area, needs to be clear. They, forensic mental health patients or clients, do not mainly owe their care to us; we mainly owe our jobs to them. But for their movements, their court suits, even sometimes their work stoppages and riots, most of us would not be here. Would not be here because their rights to our care would not be established, and would not be here because the potential dangerousness of the court-involved mentally-ill, and the potential dangers of ignoring the mental health needs of people involved in the criminal justice system, would not be es-

---

52. Wexler 1991b, supra note 2, at 3.
53. Id. at 3–4.

tablished. And but for concern about dangerousness, the need for experts about the care of those people would not exist, and courts would not mandate, and legislatures not fund, some of our services.

The question before therapeutic jurisprudence is to what extent do its analyses and criticisms of law, its suggestions regarding reform, and its very language, enable those persons to act on their own behalf and to engage in treatment. To what extent does its language become part of their language. There are many ways in which the law and legal procedures discourage treatment. Therapeutic jurisprudence represents a means for redress, and for reform, and to that extent, it is salutary and illuminating.

In that way, therapeutic jurisprudence can complement rights-driven mental health law. But before we shift away from rights-driven mental health law, before we shelve it as "traditional," before we decide that a continued concern with rights in the face of what Wexler calls "changes" in society and the composition of the Supreme Court will lead to an entire branch of scholarship "d[ying] on the vine,"[54] we need to remember where the power of the "civil liberties revolution" rested.

The power of the rights revolution in all areas of law stemmed from its ability to inspire people. Since the Enlightenment, or at least the Declaration of the Rights of Man, men and women, particularly the dispossessed and marginal, have reached for the language of rights whenever they had to speak truth to power. On every ward in every psychiatric hospital, when faced with medical, judicial, or even budgetary authority, patients talk about their rights.

Part of Wexler's argument for a shift from traditional rights-based perspectives rests on a conjunctural analysis. In the face of the changing composition of the Supreme Court and corresponding ideological trends in the country at large, Wexler warns that a continued focus on rights-based appeals has led to an attrition in mental health legal scholarship. But social, political, and legal conjunctures change. We live in a difficult time for law and society. At the time of the conference, I was reminded of this watching the television and listening to the radio, and hearing Henry Hyde and Arlen Specter expatiate about the need for federal action to examine whether civil rights violations occurred in the Rodney King case. These particular individuals are not strong constitutional scholars. If they momentarily rallied to this particular viewpoint, it was not simply because their close readings of the Fourteenth Amendment had convinced them that important constitutional issues are at play.

Similarly, we should not view the changes in the Supreme Court or federal appeals courts as facts of nature. Among its other merits, therapeutic jurisprudence may well help shelter mental health legal scholarship—and more importantly, mental health patients' rights—from "the precise composition of the U.S. Supreme Court."[55] But courts now deaf to rights-based appeals may suddenly discover overriding constitutional interests when the social costs of ignoring those interests become sufficiently high. This is another way of stating that even a bad court will do some of the right things if the social costs of not doing them are made great enough. Perhaps even a very good court will fail the rights of some people if the social penalties of failing them appear trifling.

---

54. Wexler 1991b, supra note 2, at 5.
55. Wexler 1991b, supra note 2, at 15.

To take an example from the prisons: as long as prison authorities can reasonably argue that they are uniquely situated to ensure, and indeed, can ensure the security of correctional institutions with draconian policies, the current judicial deference to prison administrators will likely continue. We should remember, however, that prison administrators were equally uniquely situated long before the civil rights revolution, and that did not make for uniformly safe, humane, or secure prisons. If the utopian dream of the technologically secured prison one day brings massive unrest, the claims to maintenance-of-order expertise will once again ring hollow, and courts may conclude that constitutional rights override after all, and the "reasonableness" standard currently in vogue may no longer be so persuasive.

In the nineteenth century, in France, England, and the United States, established opinion often made reference to the dangerous classes.[56] The dangerous classes included "pauper lunatics," among whom were found the forebears of today's forensic patients, the unemployed, persons labelled as vagrants, persons involved in crime or who simply fell afoul of the law, almshouse or workhouse inmates, debtors, women who gave birth out of wedlock, etc. But in sum, the dangerous classes meant the lower classes.

Wexler calls for putting mental health back into mental health law. To have rights that the established order is "bound to respect," rights that remain in Wexler's phraseology "viable," the lower classes have to retain some measure of that perceived dangerousness. If one can act with impunity towards them, then in the name of fiscal restraint and a "fresh approach to government," some social policy makers will attempt to act with impunity towards them. This is what we might call the "schizophrenics with guns" qualifier that many social policy makers carry around in their heads as they try to determine how far they can go in abandoning all public care for the mentally ill. So as we put mental health back into mental health law, let us also smell the smoke that still lingers from the Los Angeles riots, smoke that has suddenly put a little danger back into the lower classes. For when the danger entirely leaves the dangerous classes, the rights of these people recede. When the danger comes back, their rights will again be respected, and rights-based mental health law will again blossom on the vine.

---

56. See Charles L. Brace, The Dangerous Classes of New York and Twenty Years' Work among Them (1872).

Chapter 34

Paternalism and the Unrealized Promise of *Essays in Therapeutic Jurisprudence*

John Petrila

In *Essays in Therapeutic Jurisprudence*,[1] David Wexler and Bruce Winick argue that mental disability law has too long ignored the consequences of the rules it establishes. In their view, academicians and practitioners interested in mental disability law have focused almost exclusively on questions of ideology and rights, forfeiting valuable examination of the outcomes caused by judicial and legislative decisions. In attempting to eliminate the intellectual "sterility" which they believe characterizes mental disability law, they propose therapeutic jurisprudence as a way to examine "the extent to which substantive rules, legal procedures, and the roles of lawyers and judges produce therapeutic or antitherapeutic consequences."[2]

In practice, this would result in a much greater reliance by legal decision makers on empirical data produced by social scientists:

> "Legal judgments...are often based on factual predicates that remain unexamined empirically and that might turn out not to be true...Our aim is to suggest that legal decision makers explicitly take account of this impact, that they become more sophisticated about and make better use of the insights and methods of the behavioral sciences, and that social scientists audit law's success or failure in this regard."[3]

Wexler and Winick describe their mission in rather modest terms: therapeutic jurisprudence "simply seeks to focus attention on an often neglected ingredient in the calculus necessary for performing a sensible policy analysis of mental health law and practice—the therapeutic dimension—and to call for a systematic empirical examination of this dimension."[4] Despite this modest claim, they believe that therapeutic jurisprudence principles have general applicability far beyond mental disability law and "will also have applications in forensic psychiatry generally, in health law, in a variety of allied legal fields (criminal law, juvenile law, family law) and probably across the entire legal spectrum."[5]

---

1. Essays in Therapeutic Jurisprudence (David B. Wexler & Bruce J. Winick, eds., 1992).
2. David B. Wexler & Bruce J. Winick, Introduction to Essays, supra note 1, at ix.
3. Id. at xi.
4. Id.
5. Id. at x.

While there is no evidence that courts have as yet been responsive to therapeutic jurisprudence,[6] it has struck a responsive chord among academicians. *Essays* has garnered high praise from some of the leading figures in the mental disability law field,[7] and a literature devoted to the subject of therapeutic jurisprudence is emerging.[8]

The popularity of therapeutic jurisprudence among academicians may be attributable in part to its seemingly undeniable logic. The argument that people involved in the development of mental disability law (or for that matter any area of law) should examine the consequences of legal rules, principles, and procedures, is difficult to dispute.

At the same time, therapeutic jurisprudence may be criticized on a number of grounds. First, academicians and others (including people who have received treatment in the mental health system) may dispute the assumption that an attempt to obtain therapeutic outcomes should play a dominant (or for that matter any) role in judicial decision making.[9] Second, the claim that therapeutic jurisprudence represents a new way of thinking about disability issues seems overstated; as the authors acknowledge, the United States Supreme Court has given at least lip service to the idea that legal principles established

---

6. A Lexis search performed on Oct. 25, 1993, searching all federal and state court cases for the term "therapeutic jurisprudence" found no cases. At the same time, it is evident that courts attempt to examine the impact of their decisions on individuals without using the label created by Wexler and Winick. See infra note 10 and accompanying text. But see Liz Balmaseda, Two Judges Use Therapy to Curb Home Violence, Miami Herald, Apr. 7, 1993, at 1B (reporting that Judges Cindy Lederman and Linda Dakis use "therapeutic jurisprudence" in applying innovative remedies from the bench to break the cycle of domestic violence).

7. Essays, supra note 1, at jacket (containing praise from a number of leading academicians in the mental disability law field). John Monahan writes that "what mental health law craves are new ideas, and Essays in Therapeutic Jurisprudence is brimming with them...two of the most creative scholars in the field have produced a work that can genuinely be called exciting." Id. Paul Appelbaum claims that "therapeutic jurisprudence is a tonic for what ails mental health law...[it] will set the agenda for the next generation of reform in the civil and criminal systems that deal with the mentally ill." Id. Richard Bonnie writes that "these essays will leave an enduring mark on the field." Id. Wexler describes therapeutic jurisprudence as a "fresh approach to mental health law." Id. See Jeffrey A. Klotz et al., Cognitive Restructuring Through Law: A Therapeutic Jurisprudence Approach to Sex Offenders and the Plea Process, 15 U. Puget Sound L. Rev. 579, 579 n.1 (1992) (citing Essays as providing "concrete illustrations and applications of the approach.").

8. See Robert F. Schopp, Therapeutic Jurisprudence and Conflicts Among Values in Mental Health Law, 11 Behavioral Sci. & L. 31, 32 (1993) (supporting the use of empirical data in legal decision making, but acknowledging the fact that "empirical premises alone cannot determine the correct choice."); David B. Wexler, Therapeutic Jurisprudence and Changing Conceptions of Legal Scholarship, 11 Behavioral Sci. & L. 17, 29 (1993) (tracing the parallel between questions asked by therapeutic jurisprudence scholars and those asked by public law scholars); David B. Wexler & Bruce J. Winick, Therapeutic Jurisprudence and Criminal Justice Mental Health Issues, 16 Mental & Physical Disability L. Rep. 225, 225 (1992) (illustrating the application of therapeutic jurisprudence to criminal justice/mental health issues); see also Mark A. Small, Legal Psychology and Therapeutic Jurisprudence, 37 St. Louis U. L.J. 675 (1993).

9. See infra note 38 and accompanying text.

in mental disability litigation should consider whether those principles will have a therapeutic impact.[10] In addition, other academicians have expressed similar views under different labels.[11]

Third, a close reading of therapeutic jurisprudence, particularly as it is presented in *Essays*, suggests that the uncritical enthusiasm with which therapeutic jurisprudence has been embraced should be tempered by more critical analysis of the key assumptions made by Wexler and Winick. The core premise

---

10. Parham v. J.R., 442 U.S. 584 (1979) (upholding the constitutionality of a Georgia law, in considering voluntary admission of a ward of the state by the Department of Family and Children Services to Central State Regional Hospital (a mental health institution), which provided at that time:

> The superintendent of any facility may receive for observation and diagnosis...any individual under 18 years of age for whom such application is made by his parent or guardian...If found to show evidence of mental illness and to be suitable for treatment, such person may be given care and treatment at such facility and such person may be detained by such facility for such period and under such conditions as may be authorized by law.

Ga. Code Ann. § 88-503.1 (1975)). The decision permitted civil commitment of children without judicial hearing in part because of the concern of the majority that the imposition of judicial process might impede the treatment of children. *Parham*, 442 U.S. at 610. Writing for the majority, Chief Justice Burger noted that:

> Moreover it is appropriate to inquire into how such a hearing would contribute to the successful long-range treatment of the patient. Surely, there is a risk that it would exacerbate whatever tensions already exist between the child and the parents. Since the parents can and usually do play a significant role in the treatment while the child is hospitalized and even more so after release, there is a serious risk that an adversary confrontation will adversely affect the ability of the parents to assist the child while in the hospital.

Id. at 610. But see Michael L. Perlin, An Invitation to the Dance: An Empirical Response to Chief Justice Warren Burger's 'Time-Consuming Procedural Minuets' Theory in Parham v. J.R., 9 Bull. Am. Acad. Psychiatry & L. 149 (1981) (disagreeing with the Court's logic). Perlin criticizes the Supreme Court's omission of "supporting citation, reference to the court record or analysis of behavioral research" in light of the fact that it "embraced the basic propositions proffered by amicus American Psychiatric Association (APA) without much consideration of its supporting data. On the other hand, it totally failed to acknowledge, consider, deal with or rebut the data presented by another amicus, the Division of Mental Health Advocacy of the New Jersey Department of the Public Advocate." Id. at 152–53 (footnotes omitted). The amicus curiae brief submitted by the APA concluded that psychological harm would be inflicted upon the child during due process hearings because of "the unique emotion-laden nature of the parent-child conflicts" that would be aired, basing its conclusions on several cited articles considering the traumatic effect of hospitalization on parents; in contrast the amicus curiae brief submitted by the Division of Mental Health Advocacy of the New Jersey Department of Public Advocacy highly recommended due process hearings based upon experience in providing legal representation of juveniles facing involuntary civil commitment proceedings, accumulated statistics, and records of dispositions acquired since 1975. Id. at 154–56 (footnotes omitted).

11. See Craig Haney, Psychology and Legal Change: The Impact of A Decade, 17 Law & Hum. Behav. 371 (1993) (reviewing the literature on psychology and its potential contribution to law and discussing the need for the law and psychology field to become more inclusive in its perspective). Haney welcomes other points of view, particularly from feminists and racial minorities. Id. at 387–92.

of *Essays* is an assumption of "general agreement that, *other things being equal,* mental health law should be restructured to better accomplish therapeutic values."[12] As will be discussed in more detail below, this assumption is questionable. In addition, in making this assumption, the authors ignore the emerging consumer/survivor movement in mental health, which challenges the basic premises upon which mental health policy, practice, and law rest. Academicians, researchers, lawyers, and mental health professionals may agree that the premise that the law should seek therapeutic outcomes is an article of faith while those most affected by the law and mental health practice may strongly disagree.

Significantly, *Essays* fails to question *who decides* what represents a therapeutic outcome. Instead, *Essays* simply assumes that research scientists and lawyers will decide whether a particular legal rule or intervention has therapeutic value. People treated voluntarily or coercively by mental health professionals and subject to legal rules governing the conditions and terms of that treatment are largely ignored. As a result, people who can provide the best information about the therapeutic or antitherapeutic consequences of legal/therapeutic interventions are excluded from participating in the analysis of what is or is not in their interest. Therapeutic jurisprudence as it has been conceptualized to date is a conservative, arguably paternalistic, approach to mental disability law. It relegates to research psychologists and lawyers decision making authority over issues of critical importance to individuals who find themselves the subject of mental health treatment and legally sanctioned coercion. In its current state therapeutic jurisprudence, while often cloaked in the language of autonomy and choice, simply reinforces the existing distribution of power in the relationship between treater and treated. In some critical areas it would result in even more power accruing to professional interests. Until this core problem is addressed, therapeutic jurisprudence will have little if any practical impact on many of the questions its authors would like to address and as a concept one may reasonably predict that it will be actively resisted by many in the consumer/survivor movement as simply another in a long series of efforts to assure continued professional dominance over mental health services and disability law.

Book Contents

Essays in Therapeutic Jurisprudence is a collection of essays authored by Wexler, Winick, and Robert F. Schopp, either together or individually, which explore applications of the principles of therapeutic jurisprudence to a variety of legal topics. Like an earlier work by Wexler on the same topic,[13] most of the material has been published elsewhere.

The book is divided into five parts. Part I, entitled *Toward a Therapeutic Jurisprudence,* consists of two chapters in which Wexler establishes the rationale and conceptual framework for therapeutic jurisprudence. In Chapter 1, Wexler argues that mental health law has been largely "doctrinal, constitutional, and

---

12. Introduction, supra note 2 at xii.

13. Therapeutic Jurisprudence: The Law as a Therapeutic Agent (David B. Wexler, ed., 1990).

rights-oriented," an approach which is heavily dependent on judicial decisions setting forth constitutional principles.[14] In Wexler's view this approach is "both risky and, after twenty years, sterile."[15] Wexler believes that as a result of the ideological conflicts which governed mental disability law in its early phases, lawyers and judges lack trust in mental health professionals, which in turn has led to a reluctance to consider behavioral science contributions in articulating and evaluating the consequences of legal principles.[16] Therapeutic jurisprudence, "the study of the role of the law as a therapeutic agent," is his antidote.[17] This chapter concludes with a description of the format of a "paradigmatic therapeutic jurisprudence piece written by an academic lawyer."[18]

In Chapter 2 Wexler describes four overlapping areas of inquiry for therapeutic jurisprudence.[19] These include the role of the law in producing psychological dysfunction; therapeutic aspects of legal rules; therapeutic aspects of legal procedures; and therapeutic aspects of judicial and legal roles. He uses a variety of examples, including civil commitment and treatment of people found incompetent to stand trial, to suggest ways in which inquiry by behavioral scientists may lead to more informed judgments regarding the therapeutic consequences of legal rules and processes.

Part II of the book includes two chapters written by Bruce Winick.[20] In these chapters Winick develops an argument for utilizing a model of compe-

---

14. David B. Wexler, Putting Mental Health into Mental Health Law: Therapeutic Jurisprudence, in Essays, supra note 1, at 3.

15. Id. at 5.

16. "The lesson—learning to be skeptical of supposed scientific expertise—is an important one, and I doubt the law will ever again simply defer to psychiatry and the related disciplines." Id. at 7. But see Youngberg v. Romeo, 457 U.S. 307, 322–24 (1982) (announcing that courts were to defer to professional judgment in litigation involving the rights of people who were institutionalized in state mental disability facilities). Cf. Susan Stefan, Leaving Civil Rights to the "Experts": From Deference to Abdication Under the Professional Judgment Standard, 102 Yale L.J. 639 (1992) (describing professional judgment as a standard that the Court does not truly understand).

> Courts...bas[e] the professional judgment standard on a powerful mythology about professionals in the private sphere, but almost always apply it in a public sector context. The Court's image of freely chosen professional-client interaction is thus transplanted to institutional settings where the professionals are state actors, the professional-client relationship is permeated with state concerns and conflicts of interest, and the clients are an indigent and captive population.

Id. at 644.

17. David B. Wexler, Putting Mental Health into Mental Health Law: Therapeutic Jurisprudence, in Essays, supra note 1, at 8.

18. A typical article written in a therapeutic jurisprudence framework will include an introduction, a description of applicable law, a discussion of relevant psychological principles and findings, application of psychological principles and findings to the legal matter at issue, and a conclusion. Wexler, supra note 14, at 13–14.

19. David B. Wexler, An Introduction to Therapeutic Jurisprudence, in Essays, supra note 1, at 17.

20. Bruce J. Winick, Competency to Consent to Treatment: The Distinction between Assent and Objection, in Essays, supra note 1, at 41 [hereinafter Competency to Consent to Treatment]; Bruce J. Winick, Competency to Consent to Voluntary Hospitalization: A Ther-

tency which in most situations would presume that a person being treated or seeking treatment for mental illness is competent to make such a decision. A formal adjudication of competency would occur only if the person objected to treatment, or if it was decided (by whom is not clear) that the proposed treatment or intervention may be sufficiently risky and the person's competency sufficiently marginal that an inquiry into competency would be conducted.[21] As the discussion below suggests, these chapters rest on assumptions about the operation of the mental health system and the relationship between treater and treated that are suspect at best.

In Part III, David Wexler, collaborating with Robert Schopp, examines the problem of hindsight bias in the tort system. In Chapter 5 they discuss two proposals for ameliorating the problem of hindsight bias by fact finders in malpractice litigation.[22] They suggest that the elimination of hindsight bias may be more important in some types of cases than in others, contrasting malpractice cases where suicide by prescribed medication has occurred with negligent release cases in which violence toward another has resulted. Chapter 6 continues the discussion of malpractice litigation and the tort system.[23] Wexler and Schopp argue that efforts by mental health professionals to establish clear standards of care in areas susceptible to malpractice litigation may subvert both the therapeutic outcomes sought by the mental health system and the goals of the legal system.[24] Briefly, Schopp and Wexler argue that if fixed stan-

apeutic Jurisprudence Analysis of Zinermon v. Burch, in Essays, supra note 1, at 83 [hereinafter Winick, Competency to Consent to Hospitalization].

21. Winick, Competency to Consent to Treatment, supra note 20, at 51–67.

22. David B. Wexler & Robert F. Schopp, How and When to Correct for Juror Hindsight Bias in Mental Health Malpractice Litigation: Some Preliminary Observations, in Essays, supra note 1, at 135. See Harold Bursztajin et al., "Magical Thinking," Suicide, and Malpractice Litigation, 16 Bull. Am. Acad. Psychiatry & L. 369 (1988). One solution to the disadvantage of "determination [s] made in retrospect" in negligence litigation cases is "a carefully documented risk-benefit analysis shared with the patient through the informed consent procedure." Id. at 369, 375 (footnote omitted). See also Norman G. Poythress Jr., Negligent Release Litigation: A Proposal for Procedural Reform, 17 J. Psychiatry & L. 595, 600–03 (1989) (suggesting bifurcated proceedings to allow juries to rule separately on negligence and harm inquiries).

23. Robert F. Schopp & David B. Wexler, Shooting Yourself in the Foot with Due Care: Psychotherapists and Crystallized Standards of Tort Liability, in Essays, supra note 1, at 157.

24. In recent years, efforts by psychiatry and other branches of medicine to create "practice standards" or "practice guidelines" have increased, both in response to malpractice litigation and to cost-containment efforts by insurers. See, e.g., American Psychiatric Association, Practice Guidelines for Eating Disorders, 150 Am. J. Psychiatry 207 (1993); American Psychiatric Association, Practice Guidelines for Major Depressive Disorder in Adults, 150 Am. J. Psychiatry (Supp. 1993); Consensus Development Conference Panel, Diagnosis and Management of Asymptomatic Primary Hyperparathyroidism: Consensus Development Conference Statement, 114 Annals of Internal Med. 593 (1991); Seymour Perry, The NIH Consensus Development Program: A Decade Later, 317 New Eng. J. Med. 485, 485 (1987) (discussing the effects of the 1977 National Institute of Health (NIH) program report calling for technology assessment to reduce health care costs and improve health care quality). Some states have mandated the creation of practice standards as part of legislative efforts to regularize practice. E.g., Fla. Stat. Ann. § 408.02 (West 1992) (directing state government, working with the state medical associations, to adopt and implement "scientifically sound medical

dards of care are established, mental health professionals in their desire to adhere to such standards (thereby enjoying some presumed insulation from malpractice judgments) may act according to their own, rather than their patients', interest in making certain judgments. This in turn would undermine
their view of the law's goal in applying tort principles as the reinforcement of
the fiduciary relationship between treater and treated.[25]

---

practice parameters for their respective practices in the state to eliminate unwarranted variations in the delivery of health care." In developing these parameters, the state was to use "reliable methodologies that integrate relevant research findings" and utilize "appropriate clinical expertise" as well. The parameters, once developed, are to be distributed to physicians
and other providers across the state, and are to be used as well in conducting utilization review in the Medicaid program. Fla. Stat. Ann. § 408.02(1) (West 1992)).

25. Schopp and Wexler argue that in cases other than assault on a patient and other egregious conduct "both professional organizations and courts should refrain from establishing...concrete professional rules or crystallized legal duties" because therapists will then attempt to conform their conduct to those rules and risk acting in their own rather than their
client's interests. Schopp & Wexler, supra note 23, at 182–83. The authors also argue that as
a general rule, courts should adopt as the relevant standard in tort litigation the standard of
"ordinary care and competence" provided by a member in good standing within the profession. Id. at 161. The authors come close to an argument that mental health professionals
should be exempt from ordinary tort principles suggesting that "[a]t first glance, these arguments may seem to generate the intuitively implausible claim that no one should ever be held
liable in tort for violating a fiduciary duty." Id. at 174. While not arguing for an exemption,
Schopp and Wexler do counsel almost complete deference to professional views as to what
constitutes acceptable treatment, based on the assumption that the tort system should operate to reinforce the fiduciary responsibilities of treater to the person in treatment. Id. While
this may be one goal of the tort system, it is certainly not the only one nor is it even the primary one. See W. Page Keeton et al., Prosser and Keeton on the Law of Torts § 1, at 6 (5th
ed. 1984) ("The law of torts, then, is concerned with the allocation of losses arising out of
human activities...'The purpose of the law of torts is to adjust [these] losses, and to afford
compensation for injuries sustained by one person as the result of the conduct of another.'").

Some readers may find this chapter problematic in other ways. For example, Schopp and
Wexler use the term "psychotherapy" as roughly synonymous with "mental health care." Id.
at 160 n.8. This is an uncommonly broad use of that term. The authors rest their argument
for deference in part on the statement that "outcome research increasingly supports the contention that psychotherapy produces statistically significant and clinically meaningful improvements for patients. These positive results tend to last and to exceed the effects of
placebo or pseudo-therapy control groups." Id. at 173. Contra Martin L. Gross, The Psychological Society: The Impact—and the Failure—of Psychotherapy, Psychoanalysis and the
Psychological Revolution (1978). Gross discusses research studies that conclude that psychotherapy "has only little, or modest healing powers." Id. at 24–31. He quotes Dr. Lester
Luborsky of the University of Pennsylvania in his opinion that "[i]t cannot be determined
whether the type of individual who profits most would also have profited from another form
of treatment or from change-inducing experiences which usually are not designated as psychotherapy—or indeed from nothing more than the mysterious change attributed to the passage of time." Id. at 54. See, e.g., Janice L. Krupnick & Harold A. Pincus, The Cost-Effectiveness of Psychotherapy: A Plan for Research, 149 Am. J. Psychiatry 1295 (1992). Mental
health professionals have experienced increased difficulty in obtaining reimbursement for
their services because of a paucity of data which could convince payers of care that the cost
effectiveness of those services has been demonstrated. Id. Krupnick and Pincus recognize the
need for research in the area of cost-effectiveness in the area of psychotherapy to meet an in-

Part IV, called *Marshalling Motivation: Threats, Contracts, and Wagers*, consists of three chapters devoted to applying various behaviorist theories to assure better compliance with treatment regimens. In Chapter 7 Wexler suggests using a criminal charge of reckless endangerment against people on conditional release or outpatient status who decline to take their medication.[26] He argues that negative consequences may occur if a person does not take medication that has been prescribed, urging that criminal law reckless endangerment statutes be applied to such situations as they are in other cases, for example, when people diagnosed as alcoholics do not follow treatment regimens designed to prevent harm. Wexler focuses on those "who have a history of violent behavior when they fail to take antipsychotic medication."[27] While some people who have been diagnosed as schizophrenic may present a danger to others in some circumstances (as do other people with other characteristics) his arguments ignore reports from psychiatrists that people decline to take prescribed medication for a variety of reasons.[28] In Chapter 8 Wexler describes a series of principles developed in the general health system designed to increase adherence to prescribed treatment.[29] He then applies the principles to two alternative forms of monitoring the status and treatment adherence of individuals conditionally released after acquittal by reason of the insanity defense. In some jurisdictions judges oversee the release process, while in others that function is performed by an administrative board. Wexler speculates that the judicial model may be superior to the administrative model because it permits the judge to reinforce for the individual the importance of following the prescribed treatment regimen.[30]

Part IV concludes with Chapter 9, the longest chapter in the book.[31] In this chapter, Winick argues that government should use the "psychological power of the bet" to accomplish a variety of social goals. In his scheme, government would "wager" with citizens in an effort to achieve particular outcomes. For example, individuals could choose to "bet" the government regarding their eventual completion of a program designed to address drug addiction. If a citizen chose voluntarily to enter this arrangement, he or she could "win" money or other rewards established by government by reaching the goal agreed upon at the start. Conversely, if the person failed ("lost the bet") he or she would suffer an agreed upon consequence.[32]

---

creasing demand for accountability by governmental bodies, to serve as a guide to clinical practice, and to provide a basis for informed policy and reimbursement decisions, for example, in speeding recovery and shortening hospital stays for cardiac patients. Id. at 1302.

26. David B. Wexler, Inducing Therapeutic Compliance Through the Criminal Law, in Essays, supra note 1, at 187.

27. Wexler, supra note 26, at 193.

28. Paul S. Appelbaum & Thomas Gutheil, Clinical Handbook of Psychiatry and the Law 114–19 (2d ed. 1991) (noting that "origins of treatment refusal are manifold").

29. David B. Wexler, Health Care Compliance Principles and the Insanity Acquittee Conditional Release Process, in Essays, supra note 1, at 199.

30. Id. at 217–18.

31. Bruce J. Winick, Harnessing the Power of the Bet: Wagering with the Government as a Mechanism for Social and Individual Change, in Essays, supra note 1, at 219.

32. This chapter does not define what the person would lose or by what process, nor does it discuss the unequal bargaining power that government would have relative to an individ-

In Part V, *Teaching and Research*, Wexler makes a series of interesting observations about revitalizing the teaching of mental disability law through use of therapeutic jurisprudence principles.[33] He describes a number of traditional law/mental health issues that might be re-examined "using the therapeutic jurisprudence lens."[34] These include the right to refuse treatment, treatment for incompetent death row inmates, and treatment for incompetency to stand trial. Wexler ends this chapter, and the book, by arguing that the use of therapeutic jurisprudence will result in an international research agenda in mental disability law by creating a framework for the pursuit of multi-national research.

Comments

The authors apply therapeutic jurisprudence principles to a broad range of legal issues. In many cases an analysis using therapeutic jurisprudence principles may yield more informed outcomes than might otherwise occur when legal principles are based wholly on anecdotal or case-specific information. The authors also make clear that they do not intend that the law be given over wholly to research scientists; they acknowledge that in certain circumstances normative constitutional principles should prevail regardless of what social science research suggests about the therapeutic or antitherapeutic consequences of those principles.[35] The chapters written by Winick stress the legal and clinical importance of the values of autonomy and voluntariness as principles that should govern decision making by individuals with mental disability.

However, *Essays* falls short when it suggests therapeutic jurisprudence can reinvigorate mental disability law, because it does nothing to challenge professional domination of mental disability law and treatment. It fails to take account of the growing challenge to professional hegemony represented by the

---

ual who in many of the examples Winick uses would lack economic or other resources that would make "entering the wager" truly voluntary.

33. David B. Wexler, Training in Law and Behavioral Sciences: Issues from a Legal Educator's Perspective, in Essays, supra note 1, at 293.

34. Id.

35. Wexler explains "[w]e do not suggest that all constitutional restrictions be open to reconsideration in light of the results of a therapeutic jurisprudence assessment. Many constitutional rules—Ford v. Wainwright's ban of execution of a person found to be incompetent, for example—will be fully justified on normative grounds even if they produce negative therapeutic consequences." David B. Wexler & Bruce J. Winick, Therapeutic Jurisprudence as a New Research Tool, in Essays, supra note 1, at 320 (footnote omitted); Ford v. Wainwright, 477 U.S. 399 (1986) (reversing State decision inflicting the death penalty upon an insane prisoner as a violation of the Due Process Clause and the Eighth Amendment). Discussing the *Wainwright* holding, Wexler defines the operative normative principle as "the notion that it does not comport with human dignity to execute a defendant who is so mentally ill that he is unable to understand and appreciate why he is being put to death." Wexler & Winick, supra, at 313. One of the difficulties with the approach to therapeutic jurisprudence outlined in Essays is that the authors provide few criteria other than vaguely defined "normative principles" like that noted as the justification for the Court's ruling in *Wainwright*. As a result, the application of therapeutic jurisprudence principles appears somewhat arbitrary and dependent on the subjective preferences of people writing about it.

consumer/survivor movement in mental health[36] and relies upon a set of assumptions which warrant close examination. These assumptions may be characterized as described below.

First, as noted earlier, the authors assume "general agreement that, *other things being equal*, mental health law should be restructured to better accomplish therapeutic values."[37] This assumption on its face is highly questionable. Criticisms of the "therapeutic state" are common in both popular and professional literature;[38] the views of people who do not share the belief that law should be devoted to accomplishing therapeutic values should not simply be discounted. *Essays* also fails to articulate clear decision rules for determining when "other things are equal" and whether and under what circumstances therapeutic values must yield to other values.[39] As a result *Essays* assumes the triumph of therapeutic values in ways that appear to be arbitrary. For exam-

---

36. The nomenclature used to describe people who have been treated in or confined by the mental health system has become an issue. Some publications use terms like "survivor," "consumer," "user," and "client" interchangeably. See Mary O'Hagan, Stopovers on My Way Home from Mars: A Winston Churchill Fellowship Report on the Psychiatric Survivor Movement in the USA, Britain and the Netherlands (1991). Mental patients' liberation groups "develop[ed] different terminologies to describe themselves and their work" including but not limited to "ex-patient," "ex-psychiatric inmate," "client," "consumer," or "psychiatric survivor." Judi Chamberlin, The Ex-Patients' Movement: Where We've Been and Where We're Going, 11 J. Mind & Behav. 323, 326–28 (1990). The differences in terminology reflect the differing priorities and emphases of the users: those calling themselves "inmates" or "survivors" generally adopt a more militant stance toward the mental health system. Id. The phrase used most frequently in Essays to describe people who have been diagnosed as mentally ill is the phrase "mental patient," a phrase exclusively used by professionals.

37. Wexler & Winick, supra note 2, at xii.

38. Louise Armstrong, And They Call it Help (1993) (describing in highly critical terms the explosion of psychiatric hospitalization of children that occurred in the 1980's, principally in private, for profit, psychiatric hospitals). Armstrong reveals the trials and tribulations of those who have been abused in the psychiatric system (whom she labels psychiatric survivors). Id. at 3–4. The book relies heavily on accounts gathered from children who had been hospitalized, recounts the concerted efforts of hospitals and other providers to gain patients, and expounds the U.S. House of Representatives Select Committee on Children, Youth, and Families hearing entitled The Profits of Misery: How Inpatient Psychiatric Treatment Bilks the System and Betrays Our Trust, chaired by Representative Pat Schroeder. Id. at 265–71. See also Cry of the Invisible (Michael Susko ed. 1991) (detailing encounters by homeless persons who have been diagnosed as mentally ill); Thomas S. Szasz, Law, Liberty and Psychiatry: An Inquiry into the Social Uses of Mental Health Practices 39 (1968) (characterizing commitment proceedings as an example of how "commitment serves the institutional values of psychiatry as a system of social control...Its controlling function is hidden under a facade of medical and psychiatric jargon, and is buttressed by a self-proclaimed desire to help or treat so-called mentally ill persons." Id.). Thomas S. Szasz, The Myth of Mental Illness: Foundations of a Theory of Personal Conduct 296 (1961) [hereinafter The Myth of Mental Illness] (denying the existence of mental illness and defining psychiatrists' concerns as "deal[ing] with personal, social and ethical problems in living."). See generally Symposium, Challenging the Therapeutic State: Critical Perspectives on Psychiatry and the Mental Health System, 11 J. Mind & Behav. 247 (1990) (challenging a variety of mental health practices in a diverse collection of articles).

39. See supra note 35.

ple, in arguing for a model of decisionmaking that would presume the competency of the individual, Winick writes:

> The presumption of competency attaching to the expression of choice would be rebuttable and vary with the degree of autonomy present and the risk/benefit ratio of the intervention the individual seeks to elect. When, for example, the risk/benefit ratio is highly questionable, it may be appropriate to find a marginally competent individual incompetent and prevent him from acting in accordance with his expressed preference.[40]

This is an argument that autonomy will be honored as a core value and the individual will be permitted to exercise choice only until others decide that even a "marginally competent" individual has chosen badly. Such a result is arbitrary (there are no stated, objective rules for determining when the "marginally competent" person will lose the power to decide) and paternalistic (the person loses the power to decide when someone else will decide that it is appropriate for her to lose it). While this may be well-intended paternalism it is paternalism nonetheless. It suggests that *Essays* does not articulate the discernible limits on the exercise of therapeutic values that it endorses.

Second, *Essays* fails to answer the more important question of *who decides* what constitutes a therapeutic outcome. While Wexler and Winick do not address this point directly, they suggest at least implicitly that research scientists and lawyers sensitive to research data will make such decisions. In concluding Part I, which establishes the rationale for pursuing a therapeutic jurisprudence agenda, Wexler writes:

> [I]n the aftermath of [therapeutic jurisprudence] research and thinking, the accumulated body of knowledge may be useful to practicing legal and mental health professionals. Indeed, with such knowledge, the professionals might strive together to reform the law and the legal system to help counteract mental illness and to help promote mental health.[41]

While the authors suggest several times that the legal system should consider but not simply defer to research conclusions regarding the therapeutic value of certain legal principles or processes some of their other suggestions are contradicting. While arguing for a departure by lawyers from an adversarial role in some circumstances, Wexler writes:

> [L]awyers may, for example, ask a client to consider whether the pursuit of a certain grievance is in actuality an attempt to resist therapy.
>
> For lawyers properly to play such a role, however, further work needs to be performed in marshalling mental health insights, in documenting the extent to which lawyers can be trained to function as therapeutic agents, and in examining the ethical implications of that revised role.[42]

---

40. Winick, Competency to Consent to Treatment, supra note 20, at 66.

41. David B. Wexler, An Introduction to Therapeutic Jurisprudence, in Essays, supra note 1, at 38.

42. Id. at 36–37.

While the suggestion that lawyers on occasion may and should abandon a re-flexively adversarial role may have merit,[43] the more important point that needs critical examination is the assumption that lawyers and mental health professionals should act in concert to identify and promote therapeutic values as one of the core functions of the legal system.

These two assumptions rest in turn on a third assumption, which informs many of the major conclusions of *Essays*. This is the assumption that in virtually all circumstances the legal system should defer to the prescriptions of treaters. The rationale for this conclusion, discussed most comprehensively in the chapters on assent and voluntary admissions, is that physicians have a fiduciary duty to their patients and therefore it generally may be assumed absent an objection by the patient that the proposed treatment is in the person's best interest.[44] In the model of consent and competency proposed by Winick, individuals generally would be considered competent unless objecting to a decision by a mental health professional. He argues:

> Other than in contexts in which a high possibility of conflict of interest between physician and patient exists, the physician's recommendation provides strong evidence that the risk/benefit ratio of the patient's choice is an acceptable one and that the patient's decision is thus not unreasonable...We should hesitate to interfere with a patient's assent to a treatment recommended by his physician since the physician's recommendation ordinarily provides rather strong evidence that the patient's choice, rather than being injurious to his welfare, will further it.[45]

This characterization of the physician-patient relationship underlies his arguments in the chapter on voluntary hospitalization as well.[46] This chapter is a

---

43. See David B. Wexler, Mental Health Law: Major Issues 99 (1981) (suggesting that counsel thoroughly study the facts of the case; communicate with the patient, family, and friends; fully understand the events preceding the filing of the petition; investigate the patient's and family's financial conditions; and explore the treatment and custodial resources of the community, ensuring application of resources to "meet the needs of the client as alternatives to involuntary commitment."); Samuel J. Brakel, Legal Aid in Mental Hospitals, 1981 Am. B. Found. Res. J. 23, 93 (1981) (illuminating the role of law and lawyers "in improving the treatment of the mentally ill" or "of doing considerable damage" through a comparison of studies from several states); Robert D. Miller et al., Litigiousness as a Resistance to Therapy, 14 J. Psychiatry & L. 109, 119 (1986) (footnote omitted) (describing "how adversarial legal proceedings can reinforce adolescents' resistance to therapy by supporting their challenges to authority as represented by their therapists. On the other hand, when advocates recognize the resistance involved in some grievances, they can provide significant assistance...Patients will often accept interpretations from attorneys or advocates when they won't listen to clinical staff.").

44. Winick's chapters are discussed in detail because they rely explicitly on an idealized model of the mental health system and treatment relationship permitting a conclusion that prescriptions of treaters should generally receive deference from the legal system. Wexler's chapters support the same conclusion.

45. Winick, Competency to Consent to Treatment, supra note 20, at 66–67 (footnotes omitted).

46. See id. at 83–134.

critique of the decision by the United States Supreme Court in *Zinermon v. Burch*.[47] In *Zinermon*, the Supreme Court held that an individual who had admitted himself voluntarily to a Florida state psychiatric hospital could bring a federal civil rights action alleging that his rights had been violated when the hospital did not inquire into his competency to admit himself voluntarily to the hospital.[48] Winick focuses on dicta in the Court's decision which appears to impose an obligation upon states to inquire into a person's competency as a condition of voluntary admission.[49] Concerned that this will impose an unduly high standard of competency thereby discouraging voluntary admissions, he proposes instead a model which he believes would encourage voluntary admissions, noting that "[t]here is considerable value in allowing patients to choose hospitalization voluntarily, rather than imposing it upon them. Indeed, making patients feel that the decision has been made for them could undermine the therapeutic value of choice."[50] Winick concludes that an informal review of the competency of the person seeking admission will suffice to protect people against unwarranted admissions, and argues that the cost of an erroneous admission is not high. After reviewing the risks of error to the individual in other contexts (for example, the erroneous admission of a child to a psychiatric hospital or an erroneous injection of medication) he concludes:

> These potential social and individual costs of error do not seem present to the same extent in the voluntary hospitalization context. Nor does it present a similar potential for conflict of interest which could increase the risk of error. The costs to the individual of an erroneous hospital admission are mitigated by the fact that a voluntary patient may always elect to revoke his consent to admission at any time, thereby triggering either discharge or a formal involuntary commitment hearing within a several day period to determine the need for continued hospitalization.[51]

In both the treatment and voluntary admission contexts Winick assumes that the physician's fiduciary responsibilities will ameliorate the risk of error. He writes:

---

47. 494 U.S. 113 (1990) (deciding whether or not an individual's rights were violated when he voluntarily admitted himself to a mental health facility while in a confused state during which he was largely unaware of his surroundings).

48. Id. at 980–982 (quoting Fla. Stat. Ann § 394.465(1)(a) (West 1992) (authorizing admittance for treatment to any adult "'making application by express and informed consent'" if he is "'found to show evidence of mental illness and to be suitable for treatment'", and quoting Fla. Stat. Ann. § 394.455(22) (West 1992) ("'[e]xpress and informed consent' is defined as 'consent voluntarily given in writing after sufficient explanation and disclosure...to enable the person...to make a knowing and willful decision without any element of force, fraud, deceit, duress, or other form of constraint or coercion.'")).

49. Id. at 987 (footnote omitted) ("[T]he very nature of mental illness makes it foreseeable that a person needing mental health care will be unable to understand any proffered 'explanation and disclosure' of the subject matter of the forms that person is asked to sign, and will be unable 'to make a knowing and willful decision' whether to consent to admission.").

50. Winick, Competency to Consent to Hospitalization, supra note 20, at 109.

51. Id. at 119.

> The fact that the physician is an employee of the treating institution does not alone create a conflict of interest in violation of due process, at least where he is independent and has a professional duty to act in the best interests of the patient, and can place his fiduciary duty to the patient over any interests of his institutional employer.[52]

This statement is striking because the only evidence provided for the conclusion that physicians do not experience conflicts between their patients and their employers are two opinions of the United States Supreme Court noteworthy primarily for their willingness to defer to the judgment of professionals.[53]

---

52. Winick, Competency to Consent to Treatment, supra note 20, at 66 n.93.

53. The two decisions cited by Winick are Washington v. Harper, 494 U.S. 210 (1990) and Parham v. J.R., 442 U.S. 584 (1979). Parham is discussed supra note 10. In Washington, a majority of the Court ruled that administrative processes were sufficient to address objections by prisoners to taking anti-psychotic medication. The Court wrote that "[i]t is only by permitting persons connected with the institution to make these decisions that courts are able to avoid 'unnecessary intrusion into either medical or correctional judgments.'" 494 U.S. at 235 (citing Vitek v. Jones, 445 U.S. 480, 496 (1980).

This is not the only place in Essays in which the authors do not support their conclusions with empirical evidence. This lack of citation to empirical evidence is noted here principally because this is a book devoted to bringing empiricism to bear on the law. The most obvious examples occur in Harnessing the Power of the Bet, in which Winick argues for government sponsored wagers with citizens to achieve social policy ends. At one point, in asserting that government would have to construct different wagers for different groups of people, he draws a sweeping class-based distinction without any citation to empirical evidence. He writes:

> For people with middle-class values or backgrounds, who may have a strong ability to delay gratification, the promise of a reward in the future may be sufficient to motivate present behavior. Thus, middle-class students will work hard to achieve future reinforcement in the form of good grades provided at the end of a semester and increased educational and occupational opportunities that may come many years later. Others, however, including many of the disadvantaged whose social or health problems government is most interested in solving, *often are more present-oriented, valuing present utility and heavily discounting the future. For them, the concept of future benefits may have little meaning and may not effectively influence behavior.*

Winick, supra note 31, at 237 (emphasis added) (footnote omitted). This statement is not only unsupported by even a single footnote, but in context gives the chapter a comparatively elitist tone, reinforced a few pages later in discussing the applicability of wager theory to drug addiction. After first reviewing a number of theories about drug addiction, Winick writes:

> I can confirm much of the validity of the behavioral model of addiction out of a personal experience with drug addiction. The substance I became hooked on was cappuccino...I do not suggest that all drugs function the same, of course; some—cocaine, for example—are undeniably more powerful as reinforcers than others, and significantly more addicting than caffeine...Nevertheless, despite these differences and many others, the experience of becoming addicted to caffeine and that of becoming addicted to these other substances bear important similarities. Indeed, I believe that my experience with caffeine is not unrepresentative of the basic experience of becoming addicted to other drugs.

Id. at 253. Even assuming with the author that all addiction has something in common, com-

This is not to suggest that the authors are blind to the importance of individual choice in therapeutic relationships. Winick, in particular, notes that therapeutic relationships based on the participation of the person subject to treatment are more likely to yield good outcomes.[54] His argument that competency generally should be presumed and deference given to the judgments of treaters is based in part on an assumption that doing so will give individuals more choice. However, the conclusion that the proposed model will expand choice rests on an idealized world where those providing treatment and those subject to it almost always reach the same conclusion, and where the clinical relationship exists devoid of economic and institutional pressures. This is not the world described by individuals who have written about their experiences with the mental health system.

Research has exposed the lack of voluntariness of many of the "voluntary" decisions made by people entering the mental health system and the degree to which institutional pressures distort the relationship between treater and treated.[55] It is even more interesting to observe how starkly different the world

---

paring an addiction to cappuccino with an addiction to crack cocaine is a completely academic exercise. In addition, drawing a conclusion about the correctness of a particular theory of drug addiction based solely on a personal experience with caffeine in a book devoted to empiricism is an invitation to the reader to dismiss the serious points the authors are trying to make.

54. Winick observes that "an important rationale underlying the informed consent doctrine is that giving the patient choice in medical decision making enriches and improves the decision making process." Winick, Competency to Consent to Treatment, supra note 20, at 79–80 n.152. However, he fails to note problems that may arise in implementing informed consent principles in the context of a psychiatric-patient relationship.

55. But see Susan C. Reed & Dan A. Lewis, The Negotiation of Voluntary Admissions in Chicago's State Mental Hospitals, 18 J. Psychiatry & L. 137 (1990) (exploring the process by which a high rate of voluntary admissions is achieved). In a study of admissions to four state mental health centers, Reed and Lewis found that employees of those centers were under enormous pressure to avoid judicial hearings on people entering the centers and as a result sought to make virtually every admission a "voluntary" one. The primary pressure on employees was to continue to have beds available for new admissions—court hearings also meant time away from treatment. Reed and Lewis found that staff employed three discrete strategies to obtain a "voluntary" admission. The first was labeled "persuasion/coercion" where people were told (though it was untrue) that they would be held longer if they did not sign voluntary papers. Id. at 148–49. The second strategy was "barter" in which people were told that they would not have the privileges of other patients if they forced a court hearing. The third strategy was simply to stall if the person insisted on a hearing by asking the court for adjournments until the person was ready for discharge. Id. at 152. Reed and Lewis, who drew many of their observations by speaking with people who had been hospitalized, concluded that "..laws that have attempted to prevent the threatening of patients with commitment appear to have been ineffective." Id. at 158. Some clinicians have also recognized that informed consent is not always taken seriously by mental health professionals.

> The legal requirements (for informed consent) have gone as far as they can. The framework for respect has been created and codes of behavior have been prescribed. And that has not been enough...Even granting the unlikely assumption that elements of physicians' overt behavior could be controlled by law, it is clear that attitudinal change must be accomplished by different means. Physicians must come to accept the values underlying informed consent before they will behave ac-

portrayed in *Essays* is from the world portrayed in the growing literature that is emerging written by individuals who have been treated in the mental health system. This literature provides a useful counterpoint for examining some of the core assumption of *Essays*.

Judi Chamberlin traces the roots of the consumer/survivor movement in mental health to approximately 1970.[56] Writings by people who have been pa-

---

cordingly.

. . . .

Currently, physicians in residency training learn from what they see around them that informed consent is a nuisance, an alien imposition of the legal system that must be tolerated . . .

Paul S. Appelbaum et al., Informed Consent: Legal Theory and Clinical Practice 264–266 (1987).

Other factors, such as poverty and race also affect the amount of information physicians give to patients about treatment. See 2 President's Commission for the Study of Ethical Problems in Medicine and Biomedical and Behavioral Research, Making Health Care Decisions: A Report on the Ethical and Legal Implications of Informed Consent in the Patient-Practitioner Relationship 62, 97–98, 121, 124 (1982). There are also gender biases that influence the delivery of health care. Even though "women use more physician services than men, . . . physicians appear to be more likely to prescribe drugs of all types for women than for men." Ann A. Hohmann, Gender Bias in Psychotropic Drug Prescribing in Primary Care, 27 Medical Care 478 (1989) (footnotes omitted). See also Rachel E. Perkins & Len A. Rowland, Sex Differences in Service Usage in Long-Term Psychiatric Care: Are Women Adequately Served? 158 Brit. J. Psychiatry 75, 78 (1991) (discovering that a lack of "consideration of the gender-specific needs of female patients in either the planning of services or their delivery" resulted in an inadequate level of rehabilitation); Nancy G. Kutner & Donna Brogan, Sex Stereotypes and Health Care: The Case of Treatment for Kidney Failure, 24 Sex Roles 279, 288 (1990) (concluding that "stereotypic views of women's and men's social needs should be considered as one of the factors, [other than "legitimate medical" factors] potentially contributing to differential kidney transplant rates for women and men."); Jane Levitt, Men and Women As Providers Of Health Care, 11 Soc. Sci. & Med. 395 (1977) (encouraging "change to both the sex differential in the provision of health care and the mode of practice of medicine to which it is tied" (referring to the current mode of medicine "oriented toward specialized acute care inpatient hospital treatment with priority given to high-level technology, surgery, and drug therapy." Id. at 397.). It is also clear that changes in reimbursement systems are exerting enormous pressure on the relationship between physician and patient, as the cost of services must be considered more explicitly in individual clinical relationships. E. Haavi Morreim, Cost Containment: Challenging Fidelity and Justice, 18 Hastings Center Rep. 20, 20 (1988). "Because physicians largely control healthcare resources, they are caught in a bind. Somehow they must both loyally favor their own patients, yet justly show them no favoritism as they help to distribute resources impartially." Id. at 22.

56. Judi Chamberlin, The Ex-Patients Movement: Where We've Been and Where We're Going, 11 J. Mind & Behav. 323 (1990). Chamberlin describes the establishing principles of the ex-patients' movement which include the exclusion of non patients, consciousness raising, and self help and empowerment. Id. at 327. In recounting the history of people formerly treated by the mental health system establishing a movement of their own, Chamberlin distinguishes between "mental patients' liberation" and "anti-psychiatry." Chamberlin describes the latter as "largely an intellectual exercise of academics and dissident mental health professionals . . . [who have made] little attempt . . . to reach out to struggling ex-patients or to include their perspective." Id. at 324. Chamberlin provides valuable insights into the history of the "ex-patients" movement, and notes the differences of view among those in that move-

tients within the mental health system suggest fundamental differences with the mental health establishment regarding priorities of need, the amount of true choice presented to people seeking or being subjected to treatment, and the amount of "helping" that occurs within the mental health system. These differences are significant and need to be examined by academicians and practitioners in the disability law field because they go to the heart of Wexler's and Winick's arguments that law should attempt to create therapeutic outcomes as defined by professionals.

Studies conducted to date show little correlation between professional identification of what people in treatment need and self-identified need. For example, in an early study, staff on a psychiatric unit viewed the gaining of "insight" on the part of people in the role of patient as the primary goal of treatment, while those who were hospitalized ranked this last in importance.[57] In other studies, professionals reported that "client resistance" was the biggest barrier to service utilization by a group of 286 people in community treatment, with financial issues and transportation being ranked much lower. In contrast, 100% of the people in treatment reported that financial problems were the biggest barrier to utilizing service and obtaining necessary supports, with transportation and the lack of availability of services also noted as major problems.[58] Similar findings have been reported comparing consumer and professional opinions regarding housing.[59]

These studies are important because they suggest that mental health professionals and people treated by them view need in fundamentally different ways.

---

ment devoted to "a basic liberation principle [is] that people must speak for themselves" and a reformist "consumerism which developed as the psychiatric establishment began to fund ex-patient self-help." Id. at 333–34. See generally Judi Chamberlin, On Our Own (1978).

57. Joel E. Dimsdale et al., Conflict in Treatment Goals Between Patients and Staff, 14 Social Psychiatry 1, 3 (1979) (confirming that "patients and staff operate on very different wavelengths as far as their ideology about goals for therapy..." especially concerning insight); see Priscilla Ridgway, The Voice of Consumers in Mental Health Systems: A Call for Change, A Project of the Center for Community Change Through Housing and Support, University of Vermont, Dec. 1988.

58. See Mary M. Lynch & Jean M. Kruzich, Needs Assessment of the Chronically Mentally Ill: Practitioner and Client Perspectives, 13 Administration Mental Health 237 (1985) (discussing the confusion regarding the types of services required to enable the chronically mentally ill (CMI) to function independently in the community).

59. A study of client housing preferences revealed that three-quarters of a hospital staff believed that individuals in their care required highly structured housing while only one-quarter of those hospitalized wanted such housing. Phyllis Solomon et al., A Comparison of Perspectives on Discharges of Extended Care Facility Clients: Views of Families, Hospital Staff, Community Mental Health Workers, and Clients, 15 Admin. Mental Health 166 (1988) (reporting study results that a majority of mentally disabled persons confined to institutions prefer solitary and independent living conditions upon discharge, in contrast to family and staff concerns that released clients would not be able to control their own behavior in that type of setting). See also Howie T. Harp, Taking Issue: Taking a New Approach to Independent Living, 44 Hosp. & Community Psychiatry 413 (1993) (describing the desire of "most consumers of mental health services" to live independently); Priscilla Ridgway & Anthony Zipple, The Paradigm Shift in Residential Services: From the Linear Continuum to Supported Housing Approaches, 13 Psychosocial Rehabilitation J. 11 (1990).

This suggests in turn that the idea of choice presented in *Essays* is for many people a false one: even where autonomy is preserved in an individual therapeutic relationship, the universe of choices available to a person often does not include the very things identified as most pressing.

People who have undergone treatment in the mental health system also report a much less idealized experience than that imagined in *Essays*. One unpublished report, summarizing interviews with forty-six people (including thirty-four who were former or present consumers) notes that "while respondents cited a variety of sources of stigma, *most frequently mentioned were the attitudes and practices of the mental health system and its workforce.*"[60] Interviewees characterized a number of specific practices as stigmatizing, including issues of power and control particularly: forced treatment and its threat, reinforcement of the point of view that people in the role of patient had lower status than professional staff, forced separation in many mental health programs of people with psychiatric disabilities from ordinary community life, the absence of challenge or an orientation to personal growth in the mental health system, and a pervasive lack of privacy.

Some former patients have recounted in personal terms the sense of powerlessness which accompanies the onset of serious psychiatric illness. This powerlessness is often reinforced by the mental health system. Two of these accounts are quoted at some length, because they challenge the core premise of *Essays* that researchers, practitioners, and lawyers, working in concert, are capable of defining and implementing therapeutic values.

Patricia Deegan, a nurse, recently described her reactions as she was being told by her doctor that she had been diagnosed as a chronic schizophrenic.[61]

> I remember that as these words were spoken to me by my psychiatrist it felt as if my whole teenage world—in which I aspired to dreams of being a valued person in valued roles, of playing lacrosse for the US Women's Team or maybe joining the Peace Corp—began to crumble and shatter. It felt as if these parts of my identity were being stripped from me. I was beginning to undergo that radically dehumanizing and devaluing transformation from being a person to being an illness; from being Pat Deegan to being 'a schizophrenic.' As I look back on those days I am struck by how all alone I was. This profound sense of being all alone only served to compound my sense of feeling worthless and of having no value...in a very fundamental way I experienced myself as being all alone, adrift on a nameless sea without compass or bearing. And that deep sense of loneliness came from the fact that although many people were talking to me about my symptoms, no one was talking to me about how I was doing.[62]

Betty Blaska describes in *her* account the lack of power and autonomy that characterizes the daily lives of many people treated for mental illness.[63]

---

60. Deborah E. Reidy, "Stigma is Social Death": Mental Health Consumers/Survivors Talk About Stigma in Their Lives. Education for Community Initiative (Feb. 1993) (unpublished manuscript on file with author).

61. Patricia Deegan, Recovering Our Sense of Value After Being Labeled Mentally Ill, Psychosocial Nursing, Apr. 1993, at 7.

62. Id.

63. Betty Blaska, First Person Account: What It Is Like to Be Treated Like A CMI, 17

The first time you experience dystonia from the neuroleptics they've given you, you're extremely frightened. Your tongue is rigid and you're unable to control its movements. You rush to the nurse's station and they're all huddled inside the little cage's protective walls. They won't leave it for fear of contamination. They are puzzled by your presence and seem greatly inconvenienced by it. You can't speak because of your tongue's movements. Yet they wait impatiently for you to tell them what's wrong. And you wonder what's wrong with them. Can't they see your predicament? But, no. It's not that they don't see. They don't feel. Because you don't count. You're on your way to becoming a CMI.[64]

Blaska continues a description of her experiences:

As an inpatient in what's called a 'mental institution' you go to something they call OT—occupational therapy. Everything here is called therapy—even when it isn't. And today it's 'assertiveness' class! Whoopie! Someone back in the 1960s decided that the hallmark of a mentally healthy person was being assertively able to choose and refuse, speak, act, and listen. This is a mockery inside a place called a "mental institution" because here no mental patient is free to choose, refuse, speak, or act. You can't even listen to each other without someone spying, reporting, recording, and charting. And then calling you paranoid if you notice. Or object.

And when you refuse an activity or "therapy"—which they tell you is your right—and which they've taught you to do in their 'assertiveness' class, then they badger you by sending nurse after nurse, attendant after attendant, into your room to remind you that "It's 1:00. Time for OT!" Your refusals mean nothing. They badger you until you either give in and go, or they've frustrated you to tears. Or enraged you to anger. And then they can justify calling you by the malignant label they've designated you by—resisting treatment or "noncompliant," passive dependent, passive aggressive, paranoid, or borderline personality disorder. They're all different labels. But they all mean the same thing: you're not really you. You're just a CMI. And that justifies their dehumanization of you.

. . . .

And of course you've lost your job. Who could work amid all this drug experimentation? And the myriad of drug side effects—nausea, diarrhea, dizziness. Vision so bad you can't cross the street because you can't judge the cars' distance from you. Drug-induced psychosis so bad you can't leave your bed or look out the window for the terror you feel. Blood pressure so low you can't stand for very long, and your voice so weak you can't be heard across a telephone wire.[65]

In recent years, some professional attitudes have begun to change—in the last few years, particularly with the growth of the psychosocial rehabilitation

---

Schizophrenia Bull. 173 (1991).

64. Id. Blaska uses "CMI" as shorthand for "chronically mentally ill," the label often applied to people who have been treated more than once or for more than a brief period of time for mental illness. Blaska uses the acronym to reinforce the depersonalization experienced by many people treated for mental illness, who often become known more frequently by a label attached by others than by their name.

65. Id. at 174–175.

movement[66] and services designed by consumers,[67] some mental health services informed by true respect for individual autonomy and choice have emerged. However, we professionals who make our livelihoods and careers in mental disability law often fail to seek the opinions of those most affected by the work we do. Legal decisions often devalue individuals who have been labeled mentally disabled, and often mask stereotypical views of those who are disabled.[68] Yet even public mental health systems have created formal roles for consumers,[69] and, in general medicine an influential body of work is emerging which relies principally on the reports of patients in assessing the quality and effect of medical interventions.[70]

Essays, however, like most of the mental disability law literature, is virtually devoid of any reference to experiences like those recounted above, or to the literature that suggests that the people providing treatment and the people receiving it may have fundamentally different views on questions of need and

---

66. The psychiatric rehabilitation movement is a philosophy of treatment which explicitly seeks not only the participation of the person diagnosed as mentally ill in treatment but looks to the person to be primarily responsible for designing the goals and substance of the treatment process. It also seeks to combine social supports like case management and housing with more traditional medical treatment. William Anthony et al., Psychiatric Rehabilitation (1990); William Anthony, Principles of Psychiatric Rehabilitation (1979).

67. See, e.g., Judi Chamberlin & Joseph A. Rogers, Planning a Community-Based Mental Health System: Perspective of Service Recipients, 45 Am. Psychologist 1241 (1990); Judi Chamberlin et al., Consumers, Families, and Community Support Systems, 12 Psychosocial Rehabilitation J. 93 (1989); Esso Leete, A Consumer Perspective On Psychosocial Treatment, 12 Psychosocial Rehabilitation J. 45 (1988); Howie T. Harp, National Institute on Disability and Rehabilitation Research Consensus Validation Conference on Strategies to Secure and Maintain Employment for People with Long Term Mental Illness, Empowerment of Mental Health Consumers in Vocational Rehabilitation (1992).

68. See Michael L. Perlin, On "Sanism", 46 SMU L. Rev. 373, 376–77 (1992) (urging a total restructuring and re-education of counsel, judges and legislators, "both substantively and attitudinally" to eliminate bias against mentally disabled persons especially in the drafting of statutes or writing of opinions). Cf. Michael L. Perlin, Morality and Pretextuality, Psychiatry and Law: Of 'Ordinary Common Sense,' Heuristic Reasoning, and Cognitive Dissonance, 19 Bull. Acad. Of Psychiatry & L. 131 (1991).

69. A report by the National Association of State Mental Health Program Directors (the association of state commissioners of mental health) reported that 65% of state mental health agencies provided at least some financial support for consumer-run and family-run programs (the family and consumer/survivor movements are separate movements in most respects), and that 19 states had established consumer offices or had definite plans to start such an office. National Association of State Mental Health Program Directors Studies, Survey #92-720, (Mar. 22, 1993).

70. E.g., New Patient Preference Tools Force Tough Choices, 4 Rep. Med. Guidelines & Outcome Res. 1,2 (1993). Dr. Robert Nease has developed a computer program to assess the tradeoffs people with angina are willing to make when presented with competing treatment choices. Such information will be used in the development of practice guidelines, which to date have been developed with little information about patient choices. See, e.g., Bob Curley, Managed Care Study to Examine Outcomes and Satisfaction, Mental Health Weekly, Aug. 24, 1992, at 4 (announcing the use of "the Health Status Questionnaire (SF-36) and a self-evaluation instrument to measure quality of life and improvement in symptoms" by a managed care company to measure satisfaction (by clients) with its services).

whether the mental health system is in fact infused with therapeutic values. This is not a minor point, because *Essays* depends on a particular point of view about the way in which the mental health system works. That point of view is in many ways highly idealized, and assumes the existence of choices that often simply do not exist. It is ultimately paternalistic, because it honors autonomy as a value only until professionals decide that other values should triumph. It holds therapeutic jurisprudence subordinate to constitutional values but reinforces the existing distribution of power between professionals and people with disability. Until these issues are confronted directly, in therapeutic jurisprudence specifically and in mental disability law generally, the promise that the theory of therapeutic jurisprudence has for reinvigorating mental disability law will go unrealized.

Chapter 35

Patients, Professionals, and the Path of Therapeutic Jurisprudence: A Response to Petrila

David B. Wexler
Bruce J. Winick

In his book review *Paternalism and the Unrealized Promise of Essays in Therapeutic Jurisprudence*,[1] Professor John Petrila indicts our compilation, *Essays in Therapeutic Jurisprudence*,[2] and therapeutic jurisprudence generally, for subordinating patient/consumer interests and endorsing professional dominance. The indictment lacks probable cause. It evidences a lack of familiarity with (or a disregard of) much of the therapeutic jurisprudence literature[3] * * * and seriously misreads *Essays*. Indeed, Petrila puts words in our mouths and then critiques us for writing a book we did not (and would not) write.[4]

Despite an introduction to *Essays* that carefully highlights the importance of values such as autonomy and the integrity of the fact-finding process, and that repeatedly warns that we are *not* suggesting that therapeutic interests "trump" other values, Petrila says we are saying otherwise. And as to *who* decides what is therapeutic (or, presumably,[5] when therapeutic interests should trump other interests), Petrila says:

> *Essays* fails to answer the more important question of *who decides* what constitutes a therapeutic outcome. While Wexler and Winick do not address this point directly, they suggest at least implicitly that research scientists and lawyers sensitive to research data will make such decisions. In concluding Part

---

1. 10 N.Y.L. Sch. J. Hum. Rts. 877 (1993) (this issue).

2. Essays in Therapeutic Jurisprudence (David B. Wexler & Bruce J. Winick eds., 1993).

3. See generally Bibliography of Therapeutic Jurisprudence, 10 N.Y.L. Sch. J. Hum. Rts. 915 (1993).

4. Petrila challenges our notion that we *should* be concerned with the therapeutic implications of the law. The therapeutic jurisprudence approach, however, sheds light on the fact that the law (rules, procedures, and legal rules) often produces therapeutic or antitherapeutic consequences, and it does so whether we want it to or not. Would Petrila really have us *ignore* these matters, rather than study them and grapple with them in an effort to improve the situation? Would ignoring these consequences be in the interests of patients and consumers? Would he be unconcerned that the current criminal justice system might itself traumatize sexual battery victims or child victim/witnesses? Would he suggest a judge imposing probation conditions not be concerned with the type of judicial behaviors (e.g., speaking clearly and simply, asking defendant to express his or her understanding) that might lead a defendant to follow—rather than to disregard—the imposed conditions?

5. See David B. Wexler, Justice, Mental Health, and Therapeutic Jurisprudence, 40 Clev. St. L. Rev. 517, 518.

I, which establishes the rationale for pursuing a therapeutic jurisprudence agenda, Wexler writes: "[in] the aftermath of [therapeutic jurisprudence] research and thinking, the accumulated body of knowledge may be useful to practicing legal and mental health professionals. Indeed, with such knowledge, the professionals might strive together to reform the law and the legal system to help counteract mental illness and to help promote mental health."[6]

Absolutely nothing in the above quotation suggests that lawyers, researchers, or mental health professionals should formulate law reform proposals without regard to the patient/ consumer perspective. Further, there is an obvious and crucial difference between "striving" to change the law and having the actual power to change it. Ultimately, it is lawmakers, not researchers, who must be convinced of the merits of a proposal. In fact, in a recent piece by Wexler, cited by Petrila in his review, Wexler notes the importance of therapeutic jurisprudence scholars addressing their policy recommendations in a convincing manner to legislators, trial and appellate judges, administrators, and other *true* decisionmakers.[7]

We have repeatedly emphasized the fact that therapeutic jurisprudence is merely a "lens" designed to shed light on interesting and important empirical and normative issues relating to the therapeutic impact of the law. The therapeutic jurisprudence perspective sets the stage for the articulation and debate of those questions,[8] and hence has the potential of reinvigorating the field,[9] but it does not itself provide any of the answers. As noted in the introduction,

---

6. Petrila, supra note 1, at 891–92 (quoting David B. Wexler, An Introduction to Therapeutic Jurisprudence, in Essays, supra note 2 at 38).

7. David B. Wexler, Therapeutic Jurisprudence and Changing Conceptions of Legal Scholarship, 11 Behavioral Sci. & L. 17 (1993). See also Harry T. Edwards, The Growing Disjunction Between Legal Education and the Legal Profession: A Postscript, 91 Mich. L. Rev. 2191, 2196, n.20 (1993), where Judge Edwards, speaking of "practical interdisciplinary scholarship," notes that "Professor Wexler analyzes a number of articles—directed to judges, legislators, and other public decisionmakers—that address concrete problems in mental health law."

8. David B. Wexler, Justice, Mental Health, and Therapeutic Jurisprudence, 40 Clev. St. L. Rev. 517 (1992); Robert F. Schopp, Therapeutic Jurisprudence and Conflicts Among Values in Mental Health Law, 11 Behavioral Sci. & L. 31 (1993) (stressing importance of autonomy values).

9. Petrila questions the "newness" of therapeutic jurisprudence. So do we. Therapeutic jurisprudence is merely a sharper conceptualization of and focus on work that a number of us—including many Symposium participants—had been engaging in earlier. In fact, David B. Wexler's first book, Therapeutic Jurisprudence: The Law as a Therapeutic Agent (David B. Wexler ed., 1990) [hereinafter Law as Agent], was composed of an introductory chapter explaining therapeutic jurisprudence, followed by selections from pre-existing works by a number of writers that fell "implicitly" in the therapeutic jurisprudence framework. Essays, in contrast, consists of articles written explicitly from a therapeutic jurisprudence perspective. This sharpened focus has, we believe, helped generate much scholarship that otherwise likely would have gone unwritten, and, as David B. Wexler, New Directions In Therapeutic Jurisprudence: Breaking the Bounds of Conventional Mental Health Law Scholarship, 10 N.Y.L. Sch. J. Hum. Rts. 759, 765 (1993) (this issue) [hereinafter New Directions] and Bibliography, supra note 3, indicate, has created a community of therapeutic jurisprudence scholars interested in law/mental health issues in *many* fields of law, not simply in conventional mental health law. In that sense, we hope therapeutic jurisprudence has helped reinvigorate and restructure the law/mental health field.

"[t]herapeutic jurisprudence, although it seeks to illuminate the therapeutic implications of legal practices, does not resolve *this* dispute, which requires analysis of the impact of alternative practices on other relevant values."[10] Petrila faults us at once for *not* providing the answers and (incorrectly) for *providing* the answer that professionals decide what is meant by therapeutic and when therapeutic interests should prevail.

As Wexler points out, therapeutic jurisprudence, as a mere lens for better seeing the (legal) world, does not (and ought not) provide a tight definition of "therapeutic."[11] This flexibility has left scholars free to examine the issue in a number of important and interesting contexts. Significantly, the patient/consumer perspective has weighed heavily in those efforts.

For example, Tom Tyler has indicated how the importance of giving patient/respondents "voice" in commitment proceedings is of likely therapeutic significance.[12] In a recent piece looking at alternative commitment hearing structures, Wexler asks which procedure *respondents* would find fairer.[13] In *Law as Agent*, Wexler addressed right-to-refuse treatment questions by including an essay by psychiatric researchers who approached the matter by interviewing about-to-be released patients.[14] And psychologist Julie Zito and associates, in a recent therapeutic jurisprudence right-to-refuse inquiry, interviewed patients as well as doctors.[15]

In addition, as therapeutic jurisprudence takes us beyond the subject matter of traditional mental health law, commentators and investigators are asking how the law impacts therapeutically or antitherapeutically on persons other than traditional patients. For example, Gould proposes research to ascertain whether criminal defendants will find the U.S. Sentencing Guidelines fair— and, if not, how that will impact on their respect for the law, institutional behavior, and recidivism.[16] Feldthusen examines how sexual battery victims are treated in the criminal justice system and listens to what those victims have to say in analyzing whether there is therapeutic value in bringing tort actions against perpetrators.[17] Shuman begins the inquiry into whether accident victims will respond better to a fault-based, as opposed to a no-fault, compensa-

---

10. David B. Wexler & Bruce J. Winick, Introduction to Essays, supra note 2, at xii.

11. Wexler, New Directions, supra note 9.

12. Tom R. Tyler, The Psychological Consequences of Judicial Procedures: Implications for Civil Commitment Hearings, 46 SMU L. Rev. 433 (1992).

13. Wexler, supra note 8, at 524 ("[W]hich proceeding would the typical respondent find fairer?").

14. Harold I. Schwartz et al., Autonomy and the Right to Refuse Treatment: Patients' Attitudes After Involuntary Medication, in Law as Agent, supra note 9, at 189. See also Daniel W. Shuman & Myron S. Weiner, The Privilege Study: An Empirical Examination of the Psychotherapist-Patient Privilege, in Law as Agent, supra note 9, at 75 (discussing "privilege study" by authors conducted through questionnaires to patients as will therapists).

15. Julie Magno Zito et al., Toward a Therapeutic Jurisprudence Analysis of Medication Refusal in the Court Review Model, 11 Behavioral Sci. & L. 151 (1993)

16. Keri A. Gould, Turning Rat and Doing Time for Uncharged, Dismissed, or Acquitted Crimes: Do the Federal Sentencing Guidelines Promote Respect for the Law?, 10 N.Y.L. Sch. J. Hum. Rts. 835, 870 (1993) (this issue).

17. Bruce Feldthusen, The Civil Action for Sexual Battery: Therapeutic Jurisprudence?, 25 Ottawa L. Rev. (forthcoming 1994).

tion scheme.[18] And, as noted in Wexler's *New Directions* article, Shuman and associates have taken the trouble to ask persons who have served as jurors in traumatic criminal cases how that experience has affected them emotionally.[19] All of these inquiries, and more, have been made in the name of therapeutic jurisprudence research.

Thus, Petrila's claim that *Essays* takes us down the wrong path seems incorrect. Properly understood, therapeutic jurisprudence simply is a path to greater enlightenment about the law. Petrila also misinterprets us in his examination of some of the specific chapters in Essays. Let us look at some of those examinations.

Petrila discusses Wexler's essay regarding possible reckless endangerment prosecutions against persons who are dangerous without medication and who culpably fail to take the medication.[20] Petrila says Wexler's "focus" is on persons with schizophrenia, and chastises Wexler because (a) most persons with schizophrenia are not dangerous, and (b) persons with schizophrenia stop taking medication for a number of understandable reasons.[21] It is surprising that Petrila does not mention serotonin-deficient persons, for the springboard and the clear focus of Wexler's essay was not persons with schizophrenia, but violent offenders with a low serotonin function. When schizophrenia was mentioned, it was mentioned only (a) in the context of that subset of patients "who have a history of violent behavior when they fail to take antipsychotic medication,"[22] and (b) with the recognition of the complication, not as likely to be present in the serotonin example, that the failure to take antipsychotic medicine "may not be *culpable* with regard to the treatment refusal."[23]

Petrila particularly misconstrues Winick's chapters regarding patient "assent" to hospitalization and treatment.[24] Winick analyzes the difficult area of competence to consent to hospitalization and treatment, and concludes that, in part to maximize and to capitalize therapeutically on the patient's choice, the law ought to be fairly flexible in finding a patient competent when the patient and doctor agree, though not in situations where the patient's objection to recommended treatment is sought to be overridden on the ground that the patient is incompetent.[25]

By minimizing Winick's discussion of the legal treatment of patient/physician disagreement, Petrila makes it appear that Winick argues for an expansive

---

18. Daniel W. Shuman, Making the World a Better Place Through Tort Law: Through the Therapeutic Looking Glass, 10 N.Y.L. Sch. J. Hum. Rts. 739) (1993) (this issue).

19. Wexler, New Directions, supra note 9, at 769–70 (Para. beginning "While Feldthusen...").

20. Petrila, supra note 1, at 886–87.

21. Id.

22. David B. Wexler, Inducing Therapeutic Compliance Through the Criminal Law, in Essays, supra note 2, at 193.

23. Id. at 195 (emphasis in original).

24. Petrila, supra note 1, at 893–99.

25. See Bruce J. Winick, Competency to Consent to Treatment: The Distinction Between Assent and Objection, in Essays, supra note 2, at 41 [hereinafter Winick, Competency to Consent to Treatment]; Bruce J. Winick, Competency to Consent to Voluntary Hospitalization: A Therapeutic Jurisprudence Analysis of Zinermon v. Burch, in Essays, supra note 2, at 83 [hereinafter Competency to Consent to Hospitalization].

view of patient competence in order to further the interests of the *doctor*.[26] In fact, under Winick's proposal, flexibility in finding competence follows entirely from the *patient's* expressed interest.

Petrila accuses Winick of having an "idealized" view of doctor/patient relations, and of downplaying the reality of hospital life and its coercive pressures.[27] But Winick expressly *acknowledges* that in "some (perhaps many) understaffed civil mental hospitals...practices have sadly evidenced a conflict of interest on the part of staff physicians..." that should render inapplicable the presumption of competency that he argues is otherwise appropriate in the patient assent context.[28]

Ironically, it is Petrila's artificial and idealized view of the *legal* system that makes *his* supposed "real world" analysis falter: Petrila critiques Winick's supposed naivete, but does not consider the real world likely implications of *rejecting* Winick's view. If one rejects Winick's view of respecting the treatment assent of a patient of somewhat questionable competency, then a competency inquiry will be triggered. That inquiry, according to the non-idealized and non-artificial view confirmed by empirical studies that Winick cites,[29] will almost invariably lead to a decision to *treat* the patient according to the plan proposed by the *doctor*. And the patient will probably be given the message that, because of seeming mental incompetence, his or her input or "voice" is of no great concern to the decisionmakers.

However a reader or policymaker may ultimately come out with regard to the difficult question of patient "assent," it is clear that Winick's proposal attempts to give meaning to a *patient's* expressed desire and is emphatically *not* designed further to empower physicians. Winick's recent law review article on autonomy, and his defense in this Symposium of a broadened right to refuse treatment, underscore the importance he gives to patient decisionmaking and choice.[30]

For Petrila to derive from Winick's analysis of the difficult problem of patient assent, or from a reading of *Essays* generally, a view of therapeutic jurisprudence as uninterested in a patient/consumer perspective is a serious flaw and a total misunderstanding of our intentions and aspirations. On the other hand, that a person of Petrila's knowledge, intellect, and accomplishment should so badly misread us will surely lead us, and undoubtedly others working in therapeutic jurisprudence, to be constantly vigilant in seeking out a patient/consumer perspective,[31] as Perlin emphasizes in his introduction to this

---

26. Petrila, supra note 1, at 890–91.

27. Petrila, supra note 1, at 897.

28. Winick, Competency to Consent to Treatment, supra note 25, at 66 n.93.

29. Id. at 79 nn.148–49; Winick, Competency to Consent to Voluntary Hospitalization, supra note 25, at 120 nn.165–66.

30. Bruce J. Winick, On Autonomy: Legal and Psychological Perspectives, 37 Vill. L. Rev. 1705 (1992); Bruce J. Winick, Psychotropic Medication in the Criminal Trial Process: The Constitutional and Therapeutic Implications of Riggins v. Nevada, 10 N.Y.L. Sch. J. Hum. Rts. 637 (1993) (this issue).

31. Sometimes, studies of that perspective may yield results that differ from the experiences of those ex-patients who regard themselves as victims or survivors. For instance, a recent analysis of transcripts of interviews with recently admitted patients revealed that:

symposium,[32] and in using empirical work very carefully (another critique offered by Petrila)[33]—themes that ran through the papers, audience discussion, and "corridor talk" at the New York Law School Symposium on Therapeutic Jurisprudence.

Rather than being unduly deferential to professional discretion, as Petrila suggests, therapeutic jurisprudence calls for a "healthy skepticism toward claims of clinical expertise."[34] Rather than ignoring the patient/consumer perspective, therapeutic jurisprudence seeks to focus attention on the extent to which legal practices have actually served their therapeutic interests (and on the extent to which they may unintentionally yield antitherapeutic results). By asking hard questions about the impact of law on the people it is designed to affect, therapeutic jurisprudence seeks to bring about a restructuring of mental health law more responsive to the interests, and desires, of its consumers.

When the admission process violates [relevant] moral norms—when the patient is excluded from participation in the decision about whether he or she should be hospitalized, when the actions of others appear to be selfishly motivated, or when others lack the personal or professional qualifications to intervene, or lie to or disrespect the patient—coercion may be more likely to be perceived, and resented. *When these moral norms are adhered to, many apparently coercive acts seem to be accepted by the patient as morally legitimate.*

Nancy S. Bennett et al., Inclusion, Motivation, and Good Faith: The Morality of Coercion in Mental Hospital Admission, 11 Behavioral Sci. & L. 295, 305 (1993) (emphasis added).

32. Michael J. Perlin, What Is Therapeutic Jurisprudence?, 10 N.Y.L. Sch. J. Hum. Rts. 623 (1993) (this issue).

33. It is puzzling, however, that Petrila criticizes Winick's discussion of deferred gratification (and its absence) for failure to cite authority, when Winick *cites* some authority and specifically calls for additional empirical work to examine the assumption made. Bruce J. Winick, Harnessing the Power of the Bet: Wagering with the Government as a Mechanism for Social and Individual Change, in Essays, supra note 2, at 237 nn.68 & 69.

34. Wexler & Winick, supra note 10, at xi.

Chapter 36

Justice, Mental Health, and Therapeutic Jurisprudence

David B. Wexler

Mental health law advocates and even scholars have typically been hostile toward, afraid of, or at best indifferent to, the mental health disciplines (mainly psychiatry and psychology) and their practitioners. The reason for this is that modern mental health law, as part of the civil liberties revolution, was conceived to correct the abusive exercise of state psychiatric power.[2] As such, it took its place as part of the anti-psychiatry movement.

Learning to be skeptical of supposed scientific expertise is an important lesson, and the law should never simply defer to psychiatry and the related disciplines.[3] But to the extent that the legal system (and even legal academics) now *ignore* developments in the mental health disciplines, the lesson of healthy skepticism has been overlearned. It is my thesis, then, that those of us interested in "justice" in mental health law ought not to adopt the shortsighted and anti-intellectual stance of ignoring or shunning the mental health disciplines. Indeed, as I hope to show in this essay, an appreciation of the mental health disciplines can in many instances help to create a more just legal system and should surely contribute meaningfully and refreshingly to the dialogue on rights and justice.

The vehicle for bringing mental health insights into the study of law is therapeutic jurisprudence—the study of the role of the law as a therapeutic agent.[4] Therapeutic jurisprudence is a truly interdisciplinary enterprise that proposes that we explore ways in which, consistent with principles of justice, the knowledge, theories, and insights of the mental health and related disciplines can help *shape* the development of the law.

---

2. See Bruce J. Ennis, Prisoners of Psychiatry (1972). Often, however, the judiciary encouraged the exercise—and misuse—of psychiatric power, sometimes through discouraging effective advocacy by attorneys. Norman G. Poythress Jr., Psychiatric Expertise in Civil Commitment: Training Attorneys to Cope with Expert Testimony, 2 Law & Hum. Behav. 1, 16 (1978); Michael L. Perlin, Fatal Assumption: A Critical Evaluation of the Role of Counsel in Mental Disability Cases, 16 Law & Hum. Behav. 39, 44–45 n.33 (1992) [hereinafter Fatal Assumption] (referring to personal advocacy experience and the advocacy experience of colleague, Professor Keri Gould).

3. For current examples of inappropriate deference—even abdication—by the appellate judiciary, see Susan Stefan, Leaving Civil Rights to the "Experts": From Deference to Abdication Under the Professional Judgment Standard, 102 Yale L.J. 639 (1992).

4. See generally David B. Wexler & Bruce J. Winick, Essays in Therapeutic Jurisprudence (1991) [hereinafter Essays]; David B. Wexler, Therapeutic Jurisprudence: The Law as a Therapeutic Agent (1990) [hereinafter Therapeutic Jurisprudence]; David B. Wexler, Therapeutic Jurisprudence and Changing Conceptions of Legal Scholarship, 11 Beh. Sci. & L. 17 (1993) (discussing recent therapeutic jurisprudence scholarship).

Therapeutic jurisprudence suggests that the law itself can be seen to function as a kind of therapist or therapeutic agent. Legal rules, legal procedures, and the roles of legal actors (such as lawyers and judges) constitute social forces that, like it or not, often produce therapeutic or antitherapeutic consequences. Therapeutic jurisprudence proposes that we be sensitive to those consequences, rather than ignore them, and that we ask the question whether the law's anthitherapeutic consequences can be reduced, and its therapeutic consequences enhanced, without subordinating due process and justice values.[5] Therapeutic jurisprudence in no way suggests that therapeutic considerations should trump other considerations. Therapeutic considerations are but one category of important considerations, as are autonomy, integrity of the fact-finding process, community safety, and many more. Therapeutic jurisprudence does not itself purport to resolve the value questions: instead, it sets the stage for their sharp articulation.[6]

Often, legal arrangements or legal doctrines can be established that promote therapeutic outcomes while, at the same time, advancing (or leaving unaffected) liberty or justice interests. As Professor Schopp has noted, "early work in the agenda of therapeutic jurisprudence has tended to seek this convergence...."[7]

Some of my own writings seem illustrative of the desire to seek convergence between therapeutic and justice interests. One piece, for example, shows how psychological principles for increasing patient compliance with medical advice can be imported into the legal system and used by judges to increase an insanity acquittee's (or a probationer's) compliance with conditions of release (e.g., taking medication, keeping appointments, etc.).[8]

The psychological principles suggest that when one signs a behavioral contract, one is more likely to comply than if one does not embody the agreement in a behavioral contract. Also, one who makes a "public" commitment to comply—a commitment to persons above and beyond the medical provider—is more likely to comply than is one who makes no such public commitment. Relatedly, if family members are involved and aware of a patient's agreement, the patient is more likely to comply with the conditions than if family members are uninvolved in the process.

Therapeutic jurisprudence would suggest that trial judges shaping conditional release orders might increase compliance with such orders if a patient/defendant were asked to embody the conditional release plan in a behavioral contract, and if the hearing were used as a forum for the patient/defendant to make a "public" commitment to comply—a commitment made in the presence of the judge and agreed-upon family members. Such a procedure would tap therapeutic potential without offending our notions of justice.

---

5. Michael L. Perlin, 1 Mental Disability Law: Civil & Criminal § 1.05a (Supp. 1992).

6. Therapeutic jurisprudence will also often force the mental health disciplines to demonstrate the efficacy of their procedures. John W. Parry, Psychiatric Treatment and Justice at Odds, 15 Ment. & Phys. Disab. L. Rep. 119, 120 (1991) (book reviews).

7. Robert F. Schopp, Therapeutic Jurisprudence and Conflicts Among Values in Mental Health Law, 11 Beh. Sci. & L. 31 (1993).

8. David B. Wexler, Health Care Compliance Principles and the Insanity Acquittee Conditional Release Process, in Essays, supra note 4, at 199.

Another "convergence" piece draws on the clinical insight that offenders—and particularly sex offenders—harbor "cognitive distortions" about their offending behavior and therefore tend to deny or minimize their involvement in criminal activity.[9] As a first step in therapy, mental health practitioners seek to perform a task of "cognitive restructuring"—an attempt to break through offender denial by having the offender admit to the underlying conduct and its details.

Therapeutic jurisprudence might ask whether the law operates antitherapeutically, by promoting cognitive distortion, or whether it operates therapeutically, by setting the stage for cognitive restructuring. Since most offenders plead guilty, the plea process might be a profitable stage to examine for therapeutic jurisprudence implications. For example, when a trial judge accepts a guilty plea and goes through the process of establishing a factual basis for that plea, the behavior of the judge may be looked at in therapeutic jurisprudence terms. If the judge involves the defendant only minimally, and looks to the record and to statements by the prosecutor and defense counsel to establish the factual basis of the plea, a defendant harboring cognitive distortions might not have those distortions confronted head-on by the plea process and the colloquy with the judge. On the other hand, if the judge conducts a change of plea hearing so as to involve the defendant personally and heavily in the process of ascertaining a factual basis for the plea, the court may actually be performing a therapeutically valuable cognitive restructuring function.

In terms of our search for convergence of therapeutic and justice goals, it is interesting to note the research of legal anthropologist Susan Philips, who observed and analyzed a number of plea hearings.[10] Philips concluded that civil libertarian judges were "procedure oriented" and involved the defendant heavily in the process of establishing a factual basis for the plea. It was the politically conservative judges who were "record oriented" and who tended to establish the factual basis with minimal involvement of the defendant. Those judges regarded the defendant as someone who might mess up and muddy an otherwise clean change of plea record, perhaps rendering the plea more vulnerable to collateral or appellate attack.

Although the early work in therapeutic jurisprudence has indeed tended to seek out areas where there is a convergence between therapeutic and justice interests, such convergence is by no means inevitable. When there is a potential conflict, therapeutic jurisprudence does not itself attempt to resolve the debate. Therapeutic jurisprudence performs a service, however, by bringing the debate to the fore.

Professor Schopp, for example, has advanced the discussion of rights and justice by noting that a conflict between therapeutic interests and individual

---

9. David B. Wexler and Bruce J. Winick, Therapeutic Jurisprudence and Criminal Justice Mental Health Issues, 16 Mental & Phys. Disab. L. Rep. 225, 229–30 (1992). See also Jeffrey A. Klotz et al., Cognitive Restructuring Through Law: A Therapeutic Jurisprudence Approach to Sex Offenders and the Plea Process, 15 U. Puget Sound L. Rev. 579, 581–82 (1992).

10. Susan U. Philips, Ideological Diversity in Courtroom Discourse: Due Process Judicial Discretion and the Guilty Plea (tentative title of book manuscript in preparation) (on file with author).

liberty might be resolved through a "constraint" approach or through a "balancing" approach:

> When therapeutic interests conflict with individual liberty, one can advocate either of two plausible relationships between the competing values. First, one can grant a priority to one value over the other such that the first serves as a constraint on the second. According to this approach, for example, liberty might constrain therapeutic efforts such that any therapeutic program must give way when it conflicts with protective liberty, regardless of the magnitude of the potential gains or losses to each value. Alternately, one can balance the two competing values, selecting a rule or deciding a case by weighing the relative gains and losses to each value in the circumstances.[11]

Apart from the "constraint" and "balancing" inquiry, any potential conflict is likely to require us to think more clearly than we currently do about exactly what we mean by particular rights. A potential conflict will force us to focus on what the right entails, what its purpose is, and how it is likely to work in the real world.

Let me provide a concrete example that arose in my teaching. In my Therapeutic Jurisprudence Seminar, students are required to submit a short (e.g., 2–3 page) weekly reaction paper on the assigned readings. The reaction papers typically form the basis of classroom discussion.[12] One week, the topic for discussion was the therapeutic or antitherapeutic aspects of the legal process, with particular attention paid to the civil commitment hearing. The reading assignment included four chapters from one of the assigned texts,[13] as well as a recent law review article.[14] Some of the pieces emphasize the potential harm that could occur by having an emotionally troubled person (particularly an adolescent) listen to adverse testimony at a civil commitment hearing. Other readings addressed the importance of such hearings for communicating to the person exactly what it is about his or her behavior that society finds troubling and unacceptable. An assigned article by Tom Tyler suggested that according a patient respect and giving him or her "voice" in the proceeding would likely lead to greater acceptability of even an adverse judgment and would lead to greater therapeutic efficacy.[15]

Against the background of those readings, Marc Natelsky, one of the seminar students, proposed a "model" that he thought would increase the factual

---

11. Schopp, supra note 7, at 32.

12. For more on the teaching of therapeutic jurisprudence, see Essays, *supra* note 4, 292–301.

13. The assignment included one case, Parham v. J.R., 442 U.S. 584 (1979), as well as John J. Ensminger & Thomas D. Liguori, The Therapeutic Significance of the Civil Commitment Hearing: An Unexplored Potential, in Therapeutic Jurisprudence, supra note 4, at 245; Marc Amaya & W.V. Burlingame, Judicial Review of Psychiatric Admissions: The Clinical Impact on Child and Adolescent Inpatients, in Therapeutic Jurisprudence, supra note 4, at 281; Michael L. Perlin, An Invitation to the Dance: An Empirical Response to Chief Justice Warren Burger's "Time-Consuming Procedural Minuets" Theory in Parham v. J.R., in Therapeutic Jurisprudence, supra note 4, at 293.

14. Tom R. Tyler, The Psychological Consequences of Judicial Procedures: Implications for Civil Commitment Hearings, 46 SMU L. Rev. 433 (1992).

15. *Id.* at 439–40.

integrity of the process, clarify the roles of the participants, give the respondent "voice", and, at the same time, operate without some of the antitherapeutic aspects of the hearing that are worrisome to some commentators. Here is a somewhat abbreviated version of his reaction paper, which seems to propose a model that bears some similarity to the Continental system of criminal adjudication:

> This week's assignments in TJ discuss at length the possible therapeutic benefits that may be realized through a retooling of the civil commitment hearing. The greatest difficulty...appears to be that of assigning proper...roles for the judge and attorneys.
>
> The traditional respective roles of judge as impartial arbiter and of defense attorney as dogged advocate are problematic, because both roles must be essentially compromised in order for the patient to secure the care he may need. The judge must interact closely with professionals, to whom he often defers...due to a lack of knowledge of the field. The defense attorney is often placed in the uncomfortable position of denying hospitalization to someone who truly needs inpatient care, and might harm self or others if released, due to the attorney's efforts....The defense attorney might be violating the duty of loyalty in a majority of cases, as he is no longer playing the traditional role of ardent defender.
>
> Because the role of judge and defense counsel have become so compromised in civil commitment hearings, I propose an alternative that might replace both traditional roles, while still meeting constitutional due process mandates. Because the judge and defense attorney are no longer, respectively, impartial and zealous, I believe that the roles of judge and defense attorney can be combined into a fact-finder...role;...the fact-finder represents the interests of no party, responsible only for deciding whether a given hospitalization is necessary based on open testimony and records. The fact-finder must hear all witnesses, gather all pertinent evidence, and interview the family, if necessary. The patient... must be given a forum to present his views...This [procedure] would be available to minors and adults.
>
> Precisely because due process is so vital, I believe that this type of [procedure] is necessary. Under the current system, prosecutors are often ignorant of the nature of their cases until the morning of the trial. Judges are easily swayed by professionals, and patients are rarely given a forum. Defense attorneys are necessarily compromised by the gravity of the situation, and the incongruity of a "vigorous defense" when release may, in a given case, be the very worst thing for the patient. Under a fact-finder system, the judge would assume a role...responsible for gathering the facts of the case. The "civil commitment arbitrator" would be much more effective than players in the current system, in that he would be held to a high standard of having extensive knowledge in the field...and would be responsible for maintaining a reasonable knowledge of mental health law and issues. This knowledge is sorely lacking presently, with neither judge, defender, nor prosecutor possessing enough knowledge to really be effective....

Natelsky's "model"—which should obviously be regarded as food for thought rather than as a fully developed proposal—raises some very interesting questions, as indeed it did in the seminar session in which it was discussed. First of all, the proposed procedure is recommended both for the commitment of minors and for the commitment of adults. In the context of minors, if the procedure is invoked in situations where the parents are seeking commitment and where the hospital is willing to accept the juvenile, the proposal seems plainly constitutional. After all, in that setting, the suggested safeguards far exceed the minimal due process protections accorded juveniles by the Supreme Court decision in *Parham v. J.R.*[16]

Indeed, since the proposal clearly exceeds constitutional requirements, a state would be free to institute these procedures, and researchers and policy-makers might then be able to assess the relative therapeutic and other merits of the proposal in comparison with the "ordinary" *Parham* protections generally in operation. For example, will juveniles given "voice" under the proposal more readily accept an order of commitment, cooperate more fully with treatment teams, and have a more favorable therapeutic outcome than those accorded the barebones *Parham* protections?

In the adult commitment context, the proposal clearly conflicts with our traditional notions of the right to an adversary hearing and the right to counsel. But the proposal forces us to think through the ways in which the proposal differs from our traditional rights and what it is about those rights that we hold dear.

Under Natelsky's scheme, some important fact-gathering by the investigative/judicial official will apparently take place outside the presence of respondent. Such a proposal therefore raises questions about a cluster of rights,[17] including the right, in theory and practice, to face-to-face confrontation.

Does or should the right to face-to-face confrontation apply to a civil commitment hearing as well as to a criminal hearing? How important is face-to-face confrontation in a jurisdiction where respondent's presence at the hearing can be waived "by such person or by adversary counsel acting in her behalf and for good cause shown?"[18] How important is the right in jurisdictions where counsel routinely waives respondent's presence or where patients overwhelmingly choose not to attend?[19] How important is the right in jurisdictions where the respondent is required to appear at the hearing but where live medical testimony will not be offered unless the respondent, before the hearing, notifies the court that he or she wishes to cross-examine the examining physician?[20] Is the purpose of face-to-face confrontation tied exclusively to promoting the integrity of the fact-finding process? If so, is the Natelsky proposal likely to yield at least as accurate a factual picture as would a traditional civil commitment hearing? Are there some other values protected by face-to-face confrontation? Are there ways of modifying the proposal to accommodate those values?

---

16. 442 U.S. 584 (1979).

17. If civil commitment is analogized to a criminal proceeding, these rights would include the right to notice, to a public trial, to the presence of respondent, to cross-examination and the exclusion of hearsay, to compulsory process, and to effective counsel. Ralph Reisner & Christopher Slobogin, Law and the Mental Health System: Civil and Criminal Aspects 716–23 (2d ed. 1990).

18. Greene v. State, 537 S.W.2d 100, 102 (Tex. Ct. App. 1976).

19. See Fred Cohen, The Function of the Attorney and the Commitment of the Mentally Ill, 44 Tex. L. Rev. 424, 428–29 (1966). The author visited the Austin State Hospital, Austin, Texas, to observe commitment hearings. Of forty hearings observed in one day, only 2 were attended by the patient/respondent.

20. See David B. Wexler, The Waivability of Recommitment Hearings, 20 Ariz. L. Rev. 175, 181 n.31 (1978) (citing Conn. Gen. Stat. Ann. § 17-178(c) (West Supp. 1978).

How should procedural law reform proposals be constitutionally assessed, given the massive difference between the theory and reality of adversary commitment hearings? Those familiar with hearings[21] know that the Supreme Court unfortunately understated the situation when it noted that "the supposed protections of an adversary proceeding to determine the appropriateness of medical decisions for the commitment and treatment of mental and emotional illness may well be more illusory than real."[22] When traditional "adversary" hearings typically take only a matter of minutes,[23] can we really say the traditional due process right is meaningful? Which proceeding would the typical respondent find fairer? A currently conducted hearing or the procedure proposed by Natelsky? Putting aside for the moment the question of counsel, if a state were genuinely interested in implementing the Natelsky adjudicative model, should we mechanically condemn the procedure as unconstitutional and insist upon continuing the sham that may well now exist in that state?

And with respect to counsel, is the absence of counsel really worse than counsel who performs in a wholly perfunctory—or even compromised—fashion?[24] Again, which system would a respondent find fairer? If some sort of ally/mouthpiece is necessary, must it take the form of counsel? Why not a lay advocate from a Protection and Advocacy agency? Which of the two (agency lay advocate or appointed attorney) would likely know more? Be better motivated to help the client? Be more willing to act as a true advocate? Perform better?

My overall point, then, is that by attending carefully to the therapeutic or antitherapeutic implications that often inescapably flow from various rules of law, legal procedures, and the roles of legal actors, we will in no way disserve justice. Instead, we may find creative ways of crafting legal arrangements whereby we can preserve justice and increase therapeutic benefit. In cases where convergence is not possible, therapeutic jurisprudence does not call for elevating therapeutic values. Sometimes, other values will surely prevail even if the results are antitherapeutic. The constitutional rule prohibiting the execution of the mentally incompetent is a clear example.[25] In many instances, we

---

21. See, e.g., Fatal Assumption, supra note 2; David B. Wexler & Stanley E. Scoville, The Administration of Psychiatric Justice: Theory and Practice in Arizona, 13 Ariz. L. Rev. 1 (1971); Cohen, supra note 19.

22. Parham v. J.R., 442 U.S. 584, 609 (1979). For a recent study indicating that the supposed protections for an adversary proceeding remain more illusory than real, see Jane Hudson, Progress Made in Representation in Civil Commitment Hearings, 19 Centerline 2 (Winter 1993) (reporting on a recent study by the Arizona Center for Law in the Public Interest that focuses on representation in Maricopa County, Arizona).

23. *Parham*, 442 U.S. at 609 n.17.

24. See generally Fatal Assumption, supra note 2. See also Michael L. Perlin, Pretexts and Mental Disability Law: The Case of Competency, 47 U. Miami L. Rev. (forthcoming 1993) (antitherapeutic aspects flowing from the pretext of a system claiming to provide vigorous counsel).

25. Ford v. Wainwright, 477 U.S. 399 (1986).

A normative principle—the notion that it does not comport with human dignity to execute a defendant who is so mentally ill that he is unable to understand and appreciate why he is being put to death—drives the Ford analysis, and in our view this normative principle justifies the Court's decision in Ford even if it is shown to

may conclude that therapeutic concerns should be operative only within certain limits which are themselves fixed by concepts of justice. A criminal law analogy would be sentencing schemes that allow sentencing for utilitarian purposes, but only within a time frame fixed by notions of just deserts.[26] In still other cases of potential conflict, we will need to precisely define the conflict, and that ought to shed new light on the rights and justice concerns at issue.

In terms of rethinking the purpose and application of constitutional rights, Professor Slobogin's recent exercise of casting aside the shackles of caselaw and probing more deeply the fundamental values served by the Fourth Amendment[27] can serve as a model for more meaningful justice discussions in the law and mental health field. Instead of being prompted to think about rights because of the influence of another discipline (e.g., psychology or psychiatry), Slobogin's contribution was apparently aided by a comparative law perspective (faculty workshops on search and seizure that Slobogin conducted in Australia). Here is how Slobogin viewed his task:

> How would we regulate searches and seizures if the Fourth Amendment did not exist?...Starting on a blank slate, as it were, should free us from current preconceptions about the law of search and seizure, ingrained after years of analyzing current dogma. Viewed from this fresh perspective we might gain a better understanding of the values at stake when the state seeks to obtain evidence or detain suspects. This new understanding in turn should invigorate criticism of current law, and might even lead to fundamental reinterpretations of the Fourth Amendment's language.[28]

Slobogin's refreshing approach is reminiscent of the Warren Court's invitation, apparently never accepted by policymakers or scholars, to think through the true bases of *Miranda*[29] and the line-up cases.[30] Recall that the *Miranda* Court required specific warnings and waivers, including advice regarding appointed counsel during interrogation, "unless other fully effective means are devised to inform accused persons of their right of silence and to assure a continuous opportunity to exercise it...."[31] With lineups, the Court's right to counsel was not intended as a "constitutional straightjacket".[32] "Legislative or other regulations...which eliminate the risks of abuse and unintentional suggestion at lineup proceedings and the impediments to meaningful confrontation at trial may...remove the basis for regarding the stage as 'critical'".[33]

In my experience, this sort of analysis in the mental health law context is often sparked by attempts, such as the above-noted seminar paper, seeking simultaneously to explore justice and therapeutic concerns. In many contexts,

---

be antitherapeutic in effect [by encouraging and rewarding incompetence].
Essays, supra note 4, at 313 n.23.

26. Norval Morris, The Future of Imprisonment (1974).

27. Christopher Slobogin, The World Without a Fourth Amendment, 39 UCLA L. Rev. 1 (1991).

28. Id. at 3–4.

29. Miranda v. Arizona, 384 U.S. 436 (1966).

30. See, e.g., United States v. Wade, 388 U.S. 218 (1967).

31. 384 U.S. at 444. See also id. at 467.

32. 388 U.S. at 239.

33. Id.

surely including traditional mental health law, "rights" talk has become stale.[34] Just as a comparative law perspective may rejuvenate the study of rights in constitutional criminal procedure, perhaps the therapeutic jurisprudence perspective will revivify rights talk in mental health law—and in our teaching and scholarship.

34. Ingo Keilitz, Justice and Mental Health Systems Interactions, 16 Law & Hum. Behav. 1, 2 (1992); Daniel W. Shuman, Overview, 46 SMU L. Rev. 323, 324 (1992) (introduction to mental disability law symposium).

Therapeutic Jurisprudence and Conflicts among Values in Mental Health Law

Robert F. Schopp

I. Introduction

Therapeutic Jurisprudence provides a conceptual structure for a specific type of research agenda in mental health law. It emphasizes the inherently interdisciplinary nature of mental health law, promoting research designed to inform the development of legal rules, procedures, and roles in a manner that promotes the therapeutic mission of the mental health system.[1]

Many of the important developments in legal doctrine and scholarship in mental health law during the past quarter century have been directed toward establishing a body of legal rules and procedures designed to protect individual liberty. Legal doctrine established from this perspective sometimes constrains the manner in which the mental health system can pursue its therapeutic mission, but in other circumstances legal protection of liberty and the therapeutic mission of the mental health system converge. Early work in Therapeutic Jurisprudence seeks this convergence, exploring potential developments in mental health law intended to promote both liberty and therapeutic effectiveness.[2] In some circumstances, however, legal doctrine designed to maximize therapeutic effectiveness will do so at the expense of individual liberty, while uncompromising protection of liberty will impede effective treatment.

When therapeutic interests conflict with individual liberty, one can advocate either of two plausible relationships between the competing values. First, one can grant a priority to one value over the other such that the first serves as a constraint on the second. According to this approach, for example, liberty might constrain therapeutic effort such that any therapeutic program must give way when it conflicts with protected liberty, regardless of the magnitude of the potential gains or losses to each value. Alternatively, one can balance the two competing values, selecting a rule or deciding a case by weighing the relative gains and losses to each value in the circumstances. Some passages in Thera-

---

1. David B. Wexler & Bruce Winick, Essays in Therapeutic Jurisprudence 3–38 (1991); David B. Wexler & Robert F. Schopp, Therapeutic Jurisprudence: A New Approach to Mental Health Law, in Handbook of Psychology & Law 361 (Dorothy K. Kagehiro & William S. Laufer eds. 1992). For a more detailed discussion of Therapeutic Jurisprudence, see the article by David Wexler in this volume.

2. Wexler & Winick, id at 199–290; David B. Wexler, Therapeutic Jurisprudence 165–87 (1990).

peutic Jurisprudence scholarship apparently treat liberty as a constraint on therapeutic programs, while others seem to endorse the balancing approach.[3]

Empirical data can inform the decision to endorse one of these approaches by providing a reasonable estimate of the likely results of each, but empirical premises alone cannot determine the correct choice. The justification for endorsing a particular relationship between these two values must take the form of normative argument, appealing to broader moral principles underlying the legal and ethical systems in which mental health law and treatment are embedded.[4] This paper examines this normative issue, advancing a theoretical framework for addressing the tension between liberty and therapeutic effectiveness that permeates mental health law. Therapeutic Jurisprudence neither fosters nor encounters any unique difficulty of this type. By pursuing legal developments likely to promote therapeutic effectiveness, however, it draws attention to the previously exiting tension between these values in mental health law.

The argument proceeds in the following manner. Part II explicates the conflict, interpreting it as a special case of a more general problem in the law and ethics of health care. Part III examines several theoretical issues involving the parameters of the more abstract values underlying mental health law specifically and health care generally. Part IV develops the framework as applied to several types of difficult cases. This section does not purport to provide a mechanical procedure or easy answers for these cases. Rather, it advances a framework intended to inform the inquiry through the application of the more abstract underlying values. Part V concludes the argument.

II. Mental Health Law and Patient-Centered Health Care

A. Conflicting Values in Mental Health Law

Controversial developments in contemporary case law, statutory law, and the associated commentary involve apparent conflicts between therapeutic goals and the need to protect liberty. Although the participants in these debates sometimes differ regarding the therapeutic efficacy of specific forms of treatment or of involuntarily administered treatment generally, they also dispute the relative importance of effective treatment as compared to the right to accept or reject such care for oneself. Recent disputes regarding the appropriate statutory criteria for involuntary civil commitment involve both levels of dispute.[5] Empirical evidence supporting the therapeutic effectiveness of invol-

---

3. Wexler & Winick, supra note 1, compare 18 with 29–30.

4. When David Wexler initially advanced the Therapeutic Jurisprudence framework, some colleagues interpreted it as undermining individual liberty and advocating a return to the "psychiatrization" of mental health law. Wexler and I provided a preliminary response to this concern in an earlier work. Wexler & Schopp, supra note 1, at 373–78.

5. See generally Mary Durham & John Q. LaFond, A Search for the Missing Premise of Involuntary Therapeutic Commitment: Effective Treatment of the Mentally Ill, 40 Rutgers L. Rev. 303 (1988) (contending that no evidence demonstrates the clinical effectiveness of treatment administered to involuntarily confined patients) [hereinafter Durham & LaFond, The

untary treatment would supply a premise that is necessary but not sufficient for the justification of involuntary commitment solely for the purpose of providing treatment. A complete justification must also provide normative argument establishing the relative importance of liberty and effective therapy.

One who interpreted mental health law as an enterprise designed entirely to protect the liberty of citizens who encounter the mental health system would treat rights as a constraint on the pursuit of therapy. Treatment would be properly pursued only insofar as it did not infringe on individual liberty. As manifested in statutes and judicial opinions, however, mental health law is intended both to protect liberty and to promote well-being by providing for the care and treatment of those in need.[6]

A series of cases addressing the right of involuntarily confined patients to refuse psychotropic medication directly raises the conflict between the therapeutic mission of the mental health system and the individual's right to accept or reject potentially beneficial treatment. In *Washington v. Harper*, for example, a prisoner asserted a right to refuse antipsychotic medication, absent a judicial determination of incompetence. This prisoner did not contest the state's claim that he had been psychotic and assaultive and that the medication had previously improved his condition. Rather, he claimed the liberty to refuse admittedly beneficial treatment absent a judicial determination.[7]

Understood merely as an empirical research agenda, Therapeutic Jurisprudence does not address these normative concerns regarding the priority of liberty and therapeutic effectiveness. This research agenda is motivated by more than idle curiosity, however, in that it is designed to promote the design, interpretation, and application of mental health law in a manner that supports the therapeutic mission of the mental health system. As an agenda based on the premise that the law ought to promote therapeutic effectiveness, Therapeutic Jurisprudence calls our attention to the ongoing tension among the values underlying mental health law. In addition to seeking circumstances in which the interests in protecting liberty and in promoting therapeutic results converge, any realistic approach to mental health law must address those cases in which these values diverge.[8]

Missing Premise]; Mary Durham & John Q. LaFond, The Empirical Consequences and Policy Implications of Broadening the Statutory Criteria for Civil Commitment, 3 Yale L. & Pol'y Rev. 395 (1985) (arguing that more inclusive commitment criteria create a new class of chronically mentally ill patients and deprive voluntary patients of access to treatment); Stephen J. Morse, A Preference for Liberty: The Case Against Involuntary Commitment of the Mentally Disordered, 70 Calif. L. Rev. 54 (1982) (arguing that a normative priority for liberty should preclude involuntary civil commitment, regardless of treatment effectiveness); Alan Stone, Broadening the Statutory Criteria for Civil Commitment: A Reply to Durham and LaFond, 5 Yale L. & Pol'y Rev. 412 (1987) (rejecting the arguments of Durham and La-Fond, 1985).

6. Wexler & Schopp, supra note 1, at 361–62.

7. Washington v. Harper, 494 U.S. 210, 213–18 (1990); see also, Rennie v. Klein, 653 F.2d 836 (3rd Cir. 1981), *vacated and remanded* 102 S. Ct. 3506 (1982); Rogers v. Okin, 643 F.2d 650 (1st Cir. 1980), *vacated and remanded sub norm.* Mills v. Rogers, 457 U.S. 291 (1982); Alexander D. Brooks, Law and Antipsychotic Medication, 4 Behav. Sci. & L. 247, 253–54 (1986). For further discussion of Harper, see infra note 30 and accompanying text.

8. Wexler & Schopp, supra note 1, at 373–78.

In order to provide a more satisfactory approach to mental health law, scholars must pursue the empirical agenda of Therapeutic Jurisprudence in the context of a normative framework addressing the values that underlie the law and ethics of health care generally and of mental health care specifically. A comprehensive approach to these issues must address both the empirical questions regarding the manner in which mental health law can promote therapeutic effectiveness and the normative questions regarding the parameters within which it should do so, particularly when the project conflicts with liberty.

B. Patient-Centered Health Care, Autonomy, and Well-Being

The widely endorsed patient-centered approach to health care contemplates a process of shared decision-making in which competent patients retain final authority over their own treatment. Providers diagnose their patients and recommend treatment, explaining the advantages and disadvantages of the available alternatives. Patients exercise the right to informed consent and the concomitant right to refuse treatment by selecting from among the options.[9]

The moral principle of autonomy as a right to self-determination within a sphere of personal sovereignty supports the right to informed consent.[10] Health care delivery traditionally emphasizes the principle of beneficence, requiring that the provider actively promote the well-being of the patient.[11] The doctrine of informed consent promotes both values in most circumstances. It supports autonomy because under the appropriate conditions, either informed consent or treatment refusal constitutes exercise of self-determination. It promotes well-being according to any of the widely endorsed conceptions of well-being because in ordinary circumstances, fully informed patients are in the best position to make treatment decisions likely to promote their interests.[12]

When competent patients refuse treatment reasonably expected to produce a clear balance of benefits over costs, however, institutional decision makers confront a direct conflict between autonomy and well-being because they must either respect the patient's choice at the expense of well-being or override that

---

9. Cruzan v. Director, Missouri Dept. of Health, 110, S. Ct. 2841, 2846–52 (1990); Tom L. Beauchamp & James F. Childress, Principles of Biomedical Ethics 74–79 (3d ed. 1989); Allen Buchanan & Dan Brock, Deciding for Others 26–29, 90–93 (1989); Ruth R. Faden & Tom L. Beauchamp, A History and Theory of Informed Consent 274–97 (1986); W. Page Keeton et al., Prosser and Keeton on the Law of Torts 189–93 (5th ed. 1984). Although the patient-centered model is well established in law and commentary, some writers contend that the traditional paternalistic approach still dominates in clinical practice. This model emphasizes the principle of beneficence, authorizing the physician to treat the patient in the manner the physician considers most likely to promote the patient's best interests. Both the paternalistic and the patient-centered approaches pursue the patient's interests, but the latter attributes authority and responsibility for treatment decisions to the patient while the former allocates this authority and responsibility to the physician. Faden & Beauchamp, supra note 9, at 53–101.

10. Beauchamp & Childress, supra note 9, at 67–74; Buchanan & Brock, supra note 9, at 36–40; Joel Feinberg, Harm to Self 27–97 (1986).

11. Beauchamp & Childress, supra note 9, at 194–97.

12. Buchanan & Brock, supra note 9, at 29–30, 36–40.

choice in order to promote well-being. The perennial debate in mental health law regarding such issues as the appropriate standard for involuntary civil commitment and the committed patient's right to refuse treatment instantiate this potential tension between the more abstract values underlying the law and ethics of health care.

III. Autonomy, Well-Being, and Health Care

A. Autonomy

Although autonomy is widely accepted as a core value in contemporary health care ethics, the precise conception of autonomy at issue often remains vague. When used to identify a right, "autonomy" refers to a right to self-determination within a sphere of personal sovereignty. The individual who holds this right enjoys discretionary authority within this sphere in that the individual's competent, voluntary decision is necessary and sufficient to settle matters falling within the scope of the right. Theorists differ as to the proper boundaries of this sphere, but it generally encompasses central self-regarding life decisions regarding one's body, work, family, privacy, and property.[13]

Autonomy-as-a-condition is a set of virtues derived from the conception of a person as a self-governing being. These include self-reflection, direction, reliance, and control; moral authenticity and independence; and responsibility for self.[14] Those who have attained a relatively advanced development of these virtues critically reflect upon and endorse or alter their own motives and values. Autonomous persons develop integrated lives by reviewing and shaping their projects, motives, and conduct according to their higher order values. They are self-governing in that they define their lives and the principles they live by through this process of self-evaluation and development. By doing so, they reaffirm their lives as their own.[15]

In order to exercise sovereign self-determination and develop the virtues of autonomy as a condition, individuals need autonomous capacities. These are the psychological capacities such as consciousness, understanding, and reasoning used in critical self-reflection, deliberation, and decision-making.[16] For the sake of clarity, I reserve "autonomy" for the comprehensive value embracing all senses in which the term is used. I use "autonomous virtues" for autonomy-as-a-condition, referring to autonomy-as-a-right as "sovereignty" and to autonomy-as-capacity as "autonomous capacities."

Autonomous capacities serve as a necessary condition for sovereignty and autonomous virtues in that one who lacks sufficient autonomous capacities

---

13. Feinberg, supra note 10, at 52–56.

14. Id. at 31–44.

15. Gerald Dworkin, The Theory and Practice of Autonomy 24–33, 110–11 (1988) [hereinafter Dworkin, Theory and Practice]; Gerald Dworkin, The Concept of Autonomy, in The Inner Citadel 54 (John Christman ed. 1988) [hereinafter Dworkin, The Concept of Autonomy].

16. Feinberg, supra note 10, at 28–31; Dworkin, Theory and Practice, supra note 15 at 13–20; Dworkin, The Concept of Autonomy, supra note 15 at 54.

cannot develop the corresponding autonomous virtues and does not qualify for sovereignty. Increased capacities beyond the threshold required to qualify for sovereignty can improve one's ability to exercise this right, but they cannot increase the degree to which one is sovereign because sovereignty as discretionary control does not admit of degrees. Either the individual possesses complete authority within the identified domain of self-regarding decisions, or others retain some authority to intervene. If others retain such authority, the individual lacks discretionary control and thus, does not enjoy sovereignty. Individuals manifest autonomous virtues in various degrees, however, and the extent to which they develop these virtues depends in part on the degree of autonomous capacities they possess.[17]

B. Informed Consent, Autonomy, and Well-Being

The patient-centered model of health care protects individual sovereignty by requiring informed consent. Autonomous acts must involve the exercise of autonomous capacities; that is, the actor must act intentionally, voluntarily, and with understanding of important relevant information. By granting informed consent for health care, patients exercise this sovereignty through an autonomous act, authorizing the treatment and accepting responsibility for the decision.[18]

In ordinary circumstances, the requirement of informed consent promotes well-being as well as sovereignty. Some theorists identify individual well-being with some form of preference satisfaction, while others endorse an objective criterion of well-being such as happiness or self-fulfillment. According to either type of theory, people have welfare interests in certain states of affairs which allow them to pursue their ultimate good. An interest qualifies as a welfare interest to the extent that it is one which virtually all persons must attain to some minimal degree in order to be able to effectively pursue the other aspects of their well-being. These welfare interests include some minimal level of tangible goods, health, psychological functioning, and freedom to act as they see fit. Attainment of most plausible conceptions of individual well-being will be very difficult or impossible unless these welfare interests are met.[19] The right to informed consent ordinarily allows patients the opportunity to select health care in light of the likely effects of that care on their welfare interests and their ultimate good.

Certain patients, however, do not select health care likely to maximize their well-being. Some of these patients fail to make decisions in their own best interest because they lack the minimal capacities required to render them competent to manage their own health care. Others possess ordinary psychological

---

17. Feinberg, supra note 10, at 28–31.

18. Beauchamp & Childress, supra note 9, at 74–79; Buchanan & Brock, supra note 9, at 36–40; Faden & Beauchamp, supra note 9, at 235–87; Dworkin, Theory and Practice, supra note 15, at 101–20.

19. Buchanan & Brock, supra note 9, at 29–36; Joel Feinberg, Harm to Others 31–64 (1984).

capacities but decide in a manner inconsistent with their own long term interests due to fear, anger, stubbornness, miscalculation, or failure to consider some of the interests involved.

Incompetent patients suffer impairment of the autonomous capacities which serve as a necessary condition for sovereignty and autonomous virtues. A thorough discussion of incompetence would require careful examination of traditional difficult legal, psychological, and philosophic issues including competing theories of cognition, decision-making, responsibility, moral agency, and free will among others.[20] Such an inquiry would extend well beyond the scope of this article. It is sufficient here to say that certain types of psychological dysfunction undermine the autonomous capacities required to meet the threshold for sovereignty. A legal standard of competence that deprives these individuals of the right to informed consent and the concomitant right to refuse treatment does not violate the principle of autonomy. Throughout this paper, I will use "incompetent" to refer to those who suffer psychological dysfunction sufficient to prevent them from qualifying for sovereignty.[21]

Well-being assumes additional importance for these incompetent individuals. Most of them possess autonomous capacities and autonomous virtues to some degree, and most have the potential to further develop these traits. Some severely impaired patients, however, lack both the capacities required to qualify for sovereignty and the potential to develop further their autonomous capacities and virtues. In such cases, providers adhering to the patient-centered approach can only maximize other aspects of well-being.

Romeo, the severely retarded resident of a state institution in *Youngberg v. Romeo*, for example, lacked the capacity to significantly improve his cognitive functions. He sustained many injuries as a result of his aggressive conduct in the institution. The staff frequently placed him in physical restraints in order to prevent him from further injuring himself or others. The Supreme Court found a state obligation to provide minimally adequate training to promote safety and freedom from undue restraint. Romeo's lack of potential to significantly improve his autonomous capacities limited providers to promoting other aspects of his well-being by training him in a manner intended to reduce his violent behavior, decreasing the probability of injury and increasing freedom from restraint.[22]

---

20. See e.g., Buchanan & Brock, supra note 9, at 1–86; Faden & Beauchamp, supra note 9, at 274–97; Harry G. Frankfurt, The Importance of What We Care About 11–25 (1988); Robert F. Schopp, Automatism, Insanity, and the Psychology of Criminal Responsibility 219–51 (1991).

21. Due to lack of space I set aside two related issues. First, I do not attempt to give an account of the types and degrees of psychological impairment that should render one incompetent and ineligible for sovereignty. Second, I do not address the evidentiary issue regarding the type of evidence that would be sufficient to show that an individual suffered such impairment. As with other legal determinations that require evaluation of a person's psychological capacities and impairments, experts could provide descriptions of the individual's level of functioning, but the decision regarding the type and degree of capacities required for sovereignty remains an issue of political morality beyond the competence of experts.

22. Youngberg v. Romeo, 457 U.S. 307, 309–11, 319 (1982).

C. Autonomy, Liberty, and Freedom

By reducing Romeo's injurious behavior and the concomitant need for physical restraint, appropriate treatment might have increased his freedom of action without affecting his lack of sovereignty. Courts and commentators ordinarily address civil commitment, the right to refuse treatment, and other intransigent issues in mental health law as difficult cases involving conflicts between individual liberty and the need for effective treatment.[23] It may be helpful to consider these issues as specific instances of the more general concern regarding the relationship between the principles of autonomy and well-being underlying the broader field of health care delivery.

Freedom, liberty, and sovereignty are closely related but not identical. Freedom is the presence of open options. People have open options when they lack external personal constraints such that they can either perform an action or refrain from performing it as they choose. The more options people have open, the more freedom they have. Liberty is the absence of rule-imposed limits on freedom of action within a political system.[24] Thus, liberty is a narrower concept than freedom in that liberty involves only a lack of legal constraints, but freedom requires the absence of any constraints from personal sources.

In certain circumstances, people might be at liberty to perform certain acts but not free to do so, or they might be free to engage in conduct they are not at liberty to perform. People are at liberty to engage in activity but not free to do so when some personal source of constraint other than a political rule prevents them from performing the activity. People can be free to engage in activity they are not at liberty to pursue when the political rules forbidding such conduct are not enforced.[25] Suppose, for example, the law in a particular jurisdiction grants civilly committed patients a right to refuse medication absent an emergency or a judicial determination of incompetence.[26] Suppose also, however, that the legal system fails to enforce this law despite routine violations in the public institutions. Committed patients in this jurisdiction would be at liberty to refuse treatment, but they would not be free to do so effectively. The staff of the public institution would be free to administer treatment without consent, although they would not be at liberty to do so.

Sovereignty is a moral right that constitutes part of the moral value of autonomy. A legal system representing an underlying political philosophy vesting primary significance in this value must protect liberty regarding actions falling within the sphere of sovereignty because legal rules restricting liberty within this domain would violate the individual's standing as sovereign. A corresponding degree of freedom is necessary to give this sphere of sovereignty and liberty practical effect. One could endorse various liberties for reasons other than respect for autonomy. Those who vest value in efficiency or productivity,

---

23. See, e.g., sources cited supra notes 5,7.

24. Feinberg, supra note 10, at 62–68.

25. Id. at 63. Those who are at liberty to perform certain acts but not free to do so because the law protecting such liberty is not enforced enjoy *de jure* but not *de facto* liberty. This paper does not require explication of this distinction.

26. E.g., Rogers v. Com'r of Dept. of Mental Health, 458 N.E.2d 308, 314–15, 321–23 (1983).

for example, might support liberty to contract for one's labor or to participate in the marketplace as likely to maximize these values. Individual autonomy is widely recognized, however, as the primary value underlying the right to informed consent regarding health care.[27]

Some patients lack the capacities that would enable them to competently exercise the right to informed consent and qualify for sovereignty. Most of these people possess some degree of autonomous capacities or virtues or the potential to develop these traits. Autonomy retains normative force as a fundamental value for those patients. A comprehensive respect for the value of autonomy demands both deontic and consequentialist components.[28] The deontic value of autonomy requires respect for competent self-regarding choice as an exercise of sovereignty, although it allows temporary intervention to ascertain the competent, informed, and voluntary status of the choice.[29] This aspect of the value is deontic in that it vests significance in the intrinsic nature of the choice as an exercise of sovereignty by a competent moral agent, rather than in any expectations regarding its consequences.

The consequentialist aspect of the value, in contrast, emphasizes the expected consequences of any decision or action on the development of autonomous capacities and virtues. Those who recognize the consequentialist value of autonomy attribute positive normative force to an act insofar as it promotes development of these traits and negative normative force insofar as it undermines them. Acts which encourage development of autonomous capacities and virtues also increase the probability that certain individuals will qualify for sovereignty.

The consequentialist aspect of the value for autonomy commands weight both in itself and as an aspect of the patient's well-being. It commands independent weight because autonomous capacities and virtues constitute part of the comprehensive value for autonomy. Thus, recognizing the principle of autonomy commits one to promoting development of autonomous capacities and virtues. Concern for patients' well-being demands concern for development of their autonomous capacities because patients retain welfare interests in maintaining these psychological capacities that enable them to effectively pursue their ultimate interests. Finally, self-fulfillment in the form of development of the autonomous virtues constitutes at least part of a person's well-being in a political system vesting fundamental value in autonomy.

IV. Difficult Cases for Mental Health Law

A. Priorities Between Autonomy and Well-Being

Autonomy and well-being converge in ordinary circumstances when competent patients exercise the right to informed consent in a manner calculated to promote their most important interests. In some cases involving incompetent

---

27. Beauchamp & Childress, supra note 9, at 67–74; Buchanan & Brock, supra note 9, at 36–40.

28. Beauchamp & Childress, supra note 9, at 25–26.

29. Feinberg, supra note 10, at 12–14.

patients, autonomy and well-being converge in that others who treat patients in order to promote well-being also promote the consequentialist aspect of autonomy without violating sovereignty because the patient in question lacks the capacities necessary to qualify for sovereignty. Treating grossly impaired and assaultive patients without their consent, for example, may improve their cognitive functioning and reduce assaultive behavior, allowing more freedom from restraint, decreasing risk of injury, and improving autonomous capacities.

In *Washington v. Harper*, the Court allowed involuntary treatment with antipsychotic drugs of seriously mentally ill prisoners who are dangerous to themselves or others when the treatment is in their medical interests.[30] If the criterion of "serious mental illness" is interpreted as limited to psychological impairment sufficient to undermine the capacities necessary to qualify for sovereignty, then the *Harper* rule allows treatment to enhance well-being and the consequentialist aspects of autonomy without violating the deontic component of that value. Such treatment would be expected to improve well-being by increasing safety from injury, freedom of motion, and autonomous capacities. If the treatment improved these capacities sufficiently to restore these patients to competence, it would enable them to qualify for sovereignty.

Although this treatment would advance well-being at the expense of the patient's freedom to choose, it would not violate the principle of autonomy. Rather, it would enhance the consequentialist aspect of autonomy in circumstances in which the deontic aspect did not apply due to the patient's failure to qualify for sovereignty. Thus, liberty would not converge with effective treatment in these circumstances, but the underlying values of autonomy and well-being would converge. Any plausible legal system must allow constraints on individual liberty in order to prevent harm to others or harm to self by clearly incompetent individuals such as infants. Many provisions of the criminal law and mental health law, for example, define limits on individual liberty. In order to determine the appropriate scope and justified constraints on liberty, one must appeal to the broader political morality underlying the legal system. To the extent that specific liberties rest on the more abstract moral principle of autonomy, limitations on liberty that do not violate autonomy do not violate the principles of political morality underlying mental health law.

In some cases, however, it may be possible to influence an incompetent patient's behavior through several methods, each of which will improve different aspects of her well-being, requiring a choice regarding the most important components of well-being to pursue. For example, medication might reduce a severely disturbed patient's injurious behavior by sedating her in a manner that reduces even further her already impaired alertness and capacity to comprehend and make conscious choices, thus undermining her already impoverished autonomous capacities. A strictly applied behavioral program involving both positive and aversive consequences for her behavior, in contrast, might spare her the reduced autonomous capacities at the cost of inflicting the aversive consequences.

---

30. Washington v. Harper, 494 U.S. 210, 227 (1990). Although the Court's opinion focused heavily on procedural issues, I am only concerned here with the substantive standard. The Court did not explicate "serious mental illness." I discuss it here as an hypothetical example of a case in which autonomy and well-being would converge if the Court limited "serious mental illness" to impairment sufficient to undermine sovereignty.

Decision makers who encounter difficult cases must establish priorities between autonomy and well-being as well as among various components of these basic values. Some writers advocate a categorical priority for sovereignty over well-being, rejecting any paternalistic intervention in competent self-regarding decisions. Others balance sovereignty against well-being in each case.[31]

Theorists from both schools can accept intervention contrary to incompetent choices when doing so is necessary to promote well-being, but they may differ regarding which aspect of well-being to emphasize. Those who endorse a comprehensive priority for all aspects of autonomy refuse to sacrifice either the deontic or consequentialist components of this value in order to promote well-being. These theorists opt to maximize autonomous virtues and capacities at the expense of other components of well-being. In contrast, those who balance autonomy and well-being as well as some who advocate a priority for sovereignty balance the consequentialist values for autonomous virtues and capacities against other aspects of well-being. That is, some theorists might consistently endorse the priority of sovereignty over well-being but balance the consequentialist aspects of autonomy against other components of well-being.

Consider, for example, the following cases. John is an elderly widower with serious, chronic coronary disease. He knows that smoking and drinking markedly increase the danger of a fatal heart attack. John continues to smoke regularly and meets with three old friends to share a bottle of bourbon twice a week, explaining that he continues to smoke and drink despite the immediate danger of fatal consequences because these activities provide the greatest enjoyment in his life.

Jane is a moderately retarded adult who suffers a painful form of cancer. The only effective treatment for the pain is medication that significantly sedates Jane, decreasing her alertness and mental acuity, reducing her already impaired autonomous capacities and virtues. Due to Jane's incompetence, a surrogate must decide either to administer the medication, reducing the pain and her already impoverished autonomous capacities and virtues, or to withhold the treatment, maximizing her autonomous capacities and virtues but leaving the pain unabated. In short, the surrogate must grant priority either to the physical comfort that constitutes one aspect of Jane's well-being or to the autonomous capacities and virtues that constitute the consequentialist aspect of autonomy and another component of her well-being.

Ordinary practice and contemporary law would respect John's sovereign choice but call upon a surrogate to decide for Jane. Some readers would probably share the intuitive judgments that John's sovereignty ought to prevail over his well-being as evaluated from an external perspective and that the surrogate ought to opt for the medication, weighing Jane's physical comfort more heavily than the resulting cost to her autonomous capacities and virtues. Can one consistently advocate a priority for the deontic aspect of the value of autonomy over well-being by endorsing respect for John's sovereignty, yet sacrifice the consequentialist aspect of the value for autonomy to other aspects of Jane's well-being? What justifies a priority for the deontic aspect of the value for autonomy but allows balancing of the consequentialist aspect?

---

31. Compare Feinberg, supra note 10, at 57–62 (endorsing priority) with Buchanan & Brock, supra note 9, at 40–47 (balancing values).

Those who vest nonderivative value in autonomy can recognize human well-being as an additional important value, but they cannot balance well-being against the deontic aspect of autonomy when the two conflict. Those who accept a conception of autonomy including individual sovereignty must grant priority to that right over well-being for two reasons. The first is conceptual. When sovereignty is understood as discretionary control within a domain of essentially self-regarding issues, an institutional authority to paternalistically intervene in decisions within that domain violates sovereignty.

A legal institution claiming authority to prevent John from acting on unreasonable or self-defeating decisions, for example, would undermine an attribution of sovereignty to him. A social structure that grants such authority to override John's competent choice within his domain of "sovereignty" undermines his status as sovereign. John cannot enjoy discretionary control over any decision regarding which any other person or institution holds the authority to intervene because this external authority renders incoherent the claim of discretionary control. The other party's authority recasts his putative right to self-determination as a privilege, revocable at the judgment of those wielding that authority. Thus, the mere fact that others hold this authority undermines his claim to sovereignty, regardless of whether they choose to exercise it.[32]

The second argument for the priority of sovereignty involves the relationship between that right and the well-being of a competent adult. By exercising sovereignty, each competent person defines and pursues those aspects of well-being that are central to the life he or she has chosen. If the state claimed the authority to monitor and supervise all aspects of each person's life, leaving no domain of individual discretion within which that person independently defined his or her own projects and made his or her own decisions, it would dilute the credit and responsibility individuals could claim for their own lives. Individuals merit praise or blame and define their lives and the principles by which they live through the exercise of sovereign discretion. They create their own lives as extended projects which are uniquely their own by exercising sovereign discretion regarding the central self-defining choices.

Certain interests, including food, shelter, and safety among others, form part of virtually everyone's well-being. These interests, however, are common to all people and, indeed, to non-human animals. They do not address those aspects of each person's life that define that person as a unique individual. These interests contribute to one's good as a sentient being, but they do not in themselves constitute well-being unique to humans generally or to this person specifically. Neither do they reflect the defining characteristics of moral agency or of this particular person. Only by exercising sovereignty can one define one's life and embrace certain interests as one's own well-being.[33] Thus, others

---

32. It does not follow from this that legal institutions cannot monitor and intervene in conduct that threatens harm to others. Such behavior does not constitute the exercise of sovereignty because it extends beyond the essentially self-regarding domain. The state can respect individual sovereignty, yet retain legitimate authority to prevent acts which extend beyond the sphere of sovereignty to harm others.

33. Dworkin, Theory and Practice, supra note 15, at 13–33, 110–14; Feinberg, supra note 10, at 57–61; James Rachels & William Ruddick, Lives and Liberty, in The Inner Citadel 221 (John Christman ed. 1988).

can act to promote various states of affairs that would be good for John, but only by exercising sovereignty can John render them part of his unique personal good. Sovereignty takes priority because it enables John to define his own life and embrace various aspects of well-being as his well-being.

The priority for sovereignty supports both the principle of autonomy and the principle of beneficence insofar as the latter principle addresses the uniquely human well-being this person has adopted as his or her own. Absent the individual exercise of and social respect for sovereignty, those who act on the principle of beneficence can promote only the relatively impoverished notion of well-being common to all people and perhaps to other sentient beings.

These arguments for the priority of sovereignty extend to improvements in autonomous capacities sufficient to qualify an individual for sovereignty. Such increases take priority over other aspects of well-being because they provide persons with the opportunity to exercise sovereignty, defining their lives and their well-being. Merely incremental increases in autonomous capacities below the threshold that qualifies one for sovereignty lack this effect. Thus, one can advocate a priority for sovereignty but balance these consequentialist aspects of the value for autonomy against other components of the individual's well-being because the latter lack the special significance of the former in enabling the individual to define his or her life. For these reasons, one can coherently embrace the intuitive judgment that we ought to respect John's sovereign choice while concluding that reducing Jane's pain makes a contribution to her well-being sufficient to compensate for the marginal loss in her autonomous capacities.

B. Priorities Within Autonomy

Other cases require choices between the deontic and consequentialist aspects of autonomy. Mary is chronically moderately depressed, but she suffers no major cognitive dysfunction. She remains civilly competent and she understands her condition, its pattern of periodic exacerbation and partial remission, and the proposed treatments.[34] Mary endangers neither her own life nor others' well-being, but she fails to develop her talents, pursue any interests or projects, enrich her life, or voluntarily accept treatment. Her history of responsiveness to structured treatment and her fear of civil commitment suggest that threats to initiate commitment proceedings would probably motivate her participation in an outpatient program which would likely improve her well-being, including her autonomous capacities and virtues. When a competent patient refuses treatment likely to improve well-being in a manner that promotes autonomous capacities or virtues, the deontic value for autonomy conflicts with the consequentialist aspect of the same value.

The reasoning that supports the priority for sovereignty over well-being but allows balancing of the consequentialist aspect of autonomy against other components of well-being also supports the priority for the deontic value of

---

34. The appropriate criteria of competence for such decisions remains controversial. For the purpose of this paper, I will simply stipulate that Mary is significantly depressed yet competent. For discussion of appropriate standards of competence, see Buchanan & Brock, supra note 9, at 17–86; Faden & Beauchamp, supra note 9, at 274–336.

autonomy over the consequentialist aspect. The conceptual argument that precludes balancing sovereignty against well-being also precludes balancing sovereignty against the consequentialist aspects of autonomy that constitute components of well-being. Recognizing the state's authority to intervene in sovereign choice in order to promote autonomous capacities or virtues would undermine the individual's sovereignty, even if the state never exercised this authority. Thus, one cannot consistently vest nonderivative value in a conception of autonomy that includes sovereignty yet recognize the state's authority to balance sovereignty against well-being, including those components of well-being that also constitute the consequentialist aspect of autonomy.

The second argument addressing the relationship between autonomy and a person's well-being also applies. To promote this person's good is to promote the human good that she chooses, pursues, and endorses as her own.[35] Violating her sovereignty, and thus the deontic value of autonomy, in favor of any aspect of her well-being alienates that good from this person, undermining both the values for autonomy and for well-being. Such interventions sever this component of well-being from the person, rendering it no longer fully hers. Paternalistic interventions, such as initiating commitment proceedings or threatening to do so, may improve her well-being, including her autonomous capacities and virtues, but they do so at the expense of rendering that well-being less uniquely and personally Mary's. This component of Mary's well-being becomes alienated from her because its attainment can no longer be attributed to her.[36]

Some theorists might deny any nonderivative value for sovereignty. Some utilitarians, for example, might reject the patient-centered approach to health care in favor of the paternalistic model, or they might support the patient's right to informed consent as a general rule subject to being overridden when paternalistic intervention would maximize happiness.[37] This paper cannot resolve fundamental questions of moral philosophy such as the relative merit of utilitarian and autonomy based theories. The arguments presented above suggest, however, that those who vest nonderivative value in autonomy cannot endorse a balancing approach to cases in which sovereignty conflicts with well-being, including those components of well-being that also constitute the consequentialist aspect of autonomy.

Legal institutions, including those representing a political morality vesting nonderivative value in autonomy, must address circumstances of uncertainty through the efforts of fallible agents. For this reason they must be designed with an eye toward error preference as well as moral principle. Any legal institution that allows intervention into incompetent choices or temporary intervention into questionable choices in order to evaluate decisions for competence risks inaccurate evaluation, resulting in unjustified interference with

---

35. Frankfurt, supra note 20, at 88–94.

36. This discussion addresses only hard paternalism. For a discussion of the distinction between hard and soft paternalism, see Feinberg, supra note 10, at 12–16.

37. For the purpose of this paper, we can describe Utilitarianism roughly as the moral theory that identifies happiness as the good and considers right the conduct that maximizes the good. For a discussion of this theory, see, e.g., J.J.C. Smart & Bernard Williams, Utilitarianism (1973).

sovereignty.[38] Yet, institutions that did not allow such intervention would allow unjustifiable harm to well-being due to incompetent decisions.

Although those who endorse a nonderivative value for autonomy as a fundamental value must reject balancing of sovereignty and well-being in principle, they can accept legal institutions that risk occasional infringements of sovereignty to protect well-being in practice. Legal institutions address practical problems and they express societal value structures. Although institutions that allow intervention in incompetent choices risk occasional violation of sovereignty for well-being in practice, they do not accept balancing in principle because they explicitly repudiate any such infringement as an error, recognizing the aggrieved party's claim to legal remedy. By doing so, these institutions retain the principled priority of sovereignty as a right to self-determination within the identified domain. Thus, they express a value structure rejecting interference with individual sovereignty.

V. Conclusion

By advocating a research agenda intended to promote the design, interpretation, and implementation of mental health law in a manner that promotes therapeutic effects, Therapeutic Jurisprudence draws attention to a normative concern that permeates mental health law. Courts, legislatures, and commentators have traditionally framed perennially troubling issues such as the appropriate criteria for involuntary civil commitment and the right to refuse treatment as conflicts between individual liberty and effective treatment. To the extent that a research program such as Therapeutic Jurisprudence can recommend legal rules or procedures expected to promote therapeutic effects without violating liberty, it can ameliorate this tension. In contrast, empirical evidence suggesting that infringements on liberty would promote therapeutic results would accentuate the importance of establishing the appropriate relationship between these values.

These issues reflect the broader tension between the more abstract values of autonomy and well-being that underlie the law and ethics of health care. This paper suggests that a satisfactory approach to these problems may require examination of these more abstract values as applied to these troubling cases.

Mary Durham and John LaFond contend that available evidence fails to support the effectiveness of treatment of involuntarily committed patients, and Wexler argues that libertarian civil commitment criteria may be therapeutic for some patients.[39] Empirical research confirming these claims would suggest that stringent civil libertarian commitment criteria protect liberty and therapeutic effectiveness in these cases. Should empirical evidence demonstrate that more inclusive commitment criteria would promote effective treatment for these patients, however, mental health law must directly address the normative priorities. The argument regarding Mary presented previously contends that liberty

---

38. Buchanan & Brock, supra note 9, at 40–47.

39. See respectively, Durham & LaFond, The Missing Premise, supra note 5; Wexler, supra note 2, at 165–87.

must prevail because the deontic value for autonomy takes priority over well-being and the consequentialist aspect of autonomy in these circumstances.[40]

One can coherently deny any nonderivative value for autonomy, but one who recognizes autonomy as a fundamental value cannot consistently advocate balancing the deontic value for sovereignty against the patient's well-being. The patient-centered approach to health care and the legal right to informed consent suggest that some legal and ethical institutions endorse the priority for sovereignty as a fundamental value underlying the law and ethics of health care. This priority for sovereignty rejects paternalistic intervention intended to promote the competent patient's well-being, including those components of well-being that also constitute the consequentialist aspects of autonomy. When incompetence justifies paternalistic intervention to protect the incompetent patient's well-being, however, this reasoning does not demand a priority for promoting autonomous capacities and virtues over other components of well-being. Recognition of the fundamental value for autonomy entails a priority for the deontic aspect of sovereignty but not for the consequentialist components of autonomous virtues and capacities.

---

40. See supra note 34–36 and accompanying text.

Chapter 38

Therapeutic Jurisprudence and the Civil Rights of Institutionalized Mentally Disabled Persons: Hopeless Oxymoron or Path to Redemption?

Michael L. Perlin
Keri K. Gould
Deborah A. Dorfman

* * *

[T]o the best of our knowledge, there have been no systemic investigations of these case law developments from a therapeutic jurisprudence perspective. If therapeutic jurisprudence is truly to "inform doctrinal and constitutional approaches," will it do so in a way that "deepen[s] rights-based perspectives" or will it augur "a shift from...rights-based perspectives"?[28] This article is part of a preliminary inquiry into this issue.

Indeed, one of the most important controversies that has emerged from the first generation of therapeutic jurisprudence scholarship[29] is the question of whether, as a result of therapeutic jurisprudence, mental disability law will be more "therapeutic" or more "jurisprudential."[30] Some of the most important criticism of therapeutic jurisprudence flows from what is perceived as its willingness to subordinate civil libertarian concerns to therapeutic interests;[31] at

---

28. Joel Haycock, Speaking Truth to Power: Rights, Therapeutic Jurisprudence, and Massachusetts Mental Health Law, 20 New Eng. J. Crim. & Civ. Confinement 301, 315 (1994) ("if therapeutic jurisprudence is construed as a shift from, or an alternative to, rights-based perspectives, then real risks exist").

29. See, e.g., TJ, supra note 2; Essays, supra note 2; Wexler, supra note 1; David Wexler, Justice, Mental Health, and Therapeutic Jurisprudence, 40 Clev. St. L. Rev. 517 (1992); Wexler, supra note 3; Michael L. Perlin, What Is Therapeutic Jurisprudence? 10 N.Y.L. Sch. J. Hum. Rts. 623 (1993); see generally Bibliography of Therapeutic Jurisprudence, supra note 5; 1 Perlin, supra note 5, § 1.05A (1994 Supp.).

30. For the sharpest criticism of therapeutic jurisprudence, see John Petrila, Paternalism and the Unfulfilled Promise of Essays in Therapeutic Jurisprudence, 10 N.Y.L. Sch. J. Hum. Rts. 897 (1993).

31. See Petrila, supra note 30, at 893 (Essays, supra note 2, is premised on "the assumption that in virtually all circumstances the legal system should defer to the prescriptions of treaters"). But compare David Wexler & Bruce Winick, Patients, Professionals, and the Path of Therapeutic Jurisprudence: A Response to Petrila, 10 N.Y.L. Sch. J. Hum. Rts. 907, 914

the same time, some of the enthusiasm that therapeutic jurisprudence has engendered may flow implicitly from the same assumption.[32] On the other hand, Wexler and Winick recognize explicitly that therapeutic jurisprudence cannot and must not trump civil libertarian interests.[33] Other therapeutic jurisprudence "fellow travelers" (including the authors of this article) write from what is clearly a civil rights-expanding perspective.[34]

We reconsider from a therapeutic jurisprudence perspective the rights of institutionalized mentally disabled persons (and persons subject to the civil commitment process) in an effort to determine both whether therapeutic jurisprudence truly is compatible with a civil rights perspective, and if it is, whether litigants representing mentally disabled individuals should look more closely to therapeutic jurisprudence as a source for their clients' legal rights.[35]

Our tentative thesis is that both these propositions are true. In other words, all of the important mental disability law civil rights decisions (especially some of those that prominent critics of mental disability law reform, e.g., E. Fuller Torrey, H. Richard Lamb, and Samuel Jan Brakel, criticize most severely)[36] have a strong therapeutic jurisprudence component. Furthermore, as judges become (generally) more disinterested in and/or hostile toward Fourteenth

---

(1993) (therapeutic jurisprudence calls for a "healthy skepticism toward claims of clinical expertise"), quoting David Wexler & Bruce Winick, Introduction, in Essays, supra note 2, at xi.

32. See, e.g., Petrila, supra note 30, at 878–89 n. 7 (quoting Paul Appelbaum's claim that "therapeutic jurisprudence is a tonic for what ails mental health law").

33. Wexler, supra note 3, at 762:

> Therapeutic jurisprudence in no way supports paternalism, coercion, or a therapeutic state. It in no way suggests that therapeutic considerations should trump other considerations...

34. The authors locate themselves in that mode. See, e.g., Michael L. Perlin, Hospitalized Patients and the Right to Sexual Interaction: Beyond the Last Frontier? 20 N.Y.U. Rev. L. & Soc. Change 517 (1993–94); Michael L. Perlin, Fatal Assumption: A Critical Evaluation of the Role of Counsel in Mental Disability Cases, 16 Law & Hum. Behav. 39 (1992) [hereinafter Perlin, Fatal Assumption]; Perlin & Dorfman, Sanism, supra note 12; Perlin & Dorfman, supra note 11; Perlin & Gould, supra note 3; Gould, supra note 3; Deborah A. Dorfman, Through a Therapeutic Jurisprudence Filter: Fear and Pretextuality in Mental Disability Law, 10 N.Y.L. Sch. J. Hum. Rts. 805 (1993) [hereinafter Dorfman, Fear and Pretextuality]; Deborah A. Dorfman, Effectively Implementing Title I of the Americans With Disabilities Act: A Therapeutic Jurisprudence Analysis, 8 J.L. & Health (1994) (in press).

35. Many years before therapeutic jurisprudence was conceived of, one of us (then a litigator) did exactly this in arguing that one aspect of a constitutional right to treatment was a right to participate in voluntary, therapeutic compensated work programs. See Michael L. Perlin, The Right to Voluntary, Compensated, Therapeutic Work as Part of the Right to Treatment: A New Theory in the Aftermath of *Souder*, 7 Seton Hall L. Rev. 298 (1976). This effort was at least partially successful. Compare Davis v. Balson, 461 F. Supp. 842, 853 (N.D. Ohio 1978) (citing Perlin, supra, but rejecting plaintiffs' constitutional argument based on that theory), with Schindenwolf v. Klein, No. L41293-75 P.W. (N.J. Super. Ct., Law Div. 1979), reprinted in 2 Perlin, supra note 5, §6.23 (mandating that 25% of all New Jersey patients participate in such programs) (consent order).

36. See, e.g., Perlin, supra note 10; Michael L. Perlin, Book Review, 8 N.Y.L. Sch. J. Hum. Rts. 557, 558–61 (1991) (reviewing Ann Braden Johnson, Out of Bedlam: The Truth about Deinstitutionalization (1990)).

Amendment arguments,[37] it is essential that litigators representing mentally disabled litigants familiarize themselves with therapeutic jurisprudence and couch their arguments in therapeutic jurisprudence perspectives. The track record here has been mixed,[38] but we believe that this strategy promises more than any other alternative that has been offered. In summary, we believe that a "therapeutic" civil rights jurisprudence is not an oxymoron; rather, we believe that therapeutic jurisprudence analyses may be a strategy to redeem civil rights litigation in this area and to reinvigorate this body of mental disability law.

The article proceeds as follows. First, we present a brief explanation of the development of therapeutic jurisprudence as an interpretive tool in mental disability law and examine the questions that therapeutic jurisprudence seeks to ask about mental disability law matters. Next, we consider three discrete areas of mental disability law from three differing therapeutic jurisprudence perspectives[39]: the involuntary civil commitment process (where we look most closely at the text of the case law), the right to treatment (where we look most closely at the filings and pleadings of plaintiff's counsel), and the right to refuse treatment (where we look more at the subsequent empirical research). We then offer some modest conclusions.

II. Involuntary Civil Commitment

A. Introduction

We contend that therapeutic jurisprudence encourages mental health lawyers to engage in appropriate civil rights lawyering.[40] A practice that is

---

37. See Perlin, Pretextual Bases, supra note 12. "Pretextuality" refers to courts' acceptance (either implicit or explicit) of testimonial dishonesty and their decisions to engage in dishonest (frequently meretricious) decisionmaking in mental disability law cases. This pretextuality infects all participants in the system, breeds cynicism and disrespect for the law, demeans participants and reinforces shoddy lawyering, blase judging and, at times, perjurious testimony. See generally Michael L. Perlin, Morality and Pretextuality, Psychiatry and Law: Of "Ordinary Common Sense," Heuristic Reasoning, and Cognitive Dissonance, 19 Bull. Am. Acad. Psychiatry & L. 131 (1991) [hereinafter Perlin, Morality]; Michael L. Perlin, Pretexts and Mental Disability Law: The Case of Competency, 47 U. Miami L. Rev. 625 (1993) [hereinafter Perlin, Pretexts].

38. See, e.g., Michael L. Perlin, Invitation to the Dance: An Empirical Response to Chief Justice Warren Burger's "Time-Consuming Procedural Minuets" Theory in Parham v. J. R., 9 Bull. Am. Acad. Psychiatry & L. 149 (1981) (discussing Supreme Court's failure to acknowledge amicus brief of NJ Division of Mental Health Advocacy offering an empirical perspective in Parham v. J.R., 442 U.S. 584 (1979) (allowing for looser involuntary civil commitment criteria in juvenile commitment cases)).

39. We have not undertaken a therapeutic jurisprudence analysis of all of the case law in this area. Rather, we have chosen to look at these three areas of mental disability/civil rights law from three alternative therapeutic jurisprudence perspectives to see how these differing perspectives illuminate the questions we are addressing.

40. In this context, civil rights lawyering refers to the work done by public interest lawyers—a group that includes attorneys representing people institutionalized in psychiatric facilities—in their efforts to secure civil rights for members of groups that fall into the category generally defined in United States v. Carolene Products Co., 304 U.S. 144, 152 n.4

based on the tenets of therapeutic jurisprudence forces such lawyers to adopt a multidisciplinary investigation and evaluation of the therapeutic effects of the lawyering process and the case's ultimate disposition. In therapeutic jurisprudence, the client's perspective should determine the therapeutic worth or impact of a particular course of events. As a scholarly matter, we find it useful to use therapeutic jurisprudence as a framework within which to investigate and reformulate areas of law reform aimed at resolving difficult societal dilemmas.[41] As a practical legal tool, we believe that therapeutic jurisprudence has far-reaching potential.[42]

B. Before the Civil Rights Revolution

Since the mid-1960s, civil commitment—the power of the state to involuntarily confine someone on the basis of a finding of mental illness and related factors—has remained at the center of mental disability litigation.[43] Prior to that time, civilly committed persons generally found themselves involuntarily detained in locked mental institutions for indefinite periods of time with little or no recourse to legal process.[44] The lengthy period of commitment often effectively translated into the equivalent of a "life sentence."[45] Civil commitment procedures had not been closely scrutinized by courts,[46] and the Supreme Court of at least one state simply found that involuntary civil commitment was not the sort of liberty loss protected by the Due Process Clause of the Fourteenth Amendment.[47]

Lawyers or advocates of any sort were rarely involved in release or retention decisions.[48] Hospital personnel generally had exclusive control over all ad-

---

(1938); see generally 1 Perlin, supra note 5, § 1.03 at 5–7. On the role of lawyers representing public agencies in this context, see David Wexler, Inappropriate Patient Confinement and Appropriate State Advocacy, in TJ, supra note 2, at 347.

41. Gould, supra note 3; Keri A. Gould, Therapeutic Jurisprudence and the Arraignment Process; The Defense Attorney's Dilemma: Whether to Request a Competency Evaluation? in Mental Health Law and Practice Through the Life Cycle 67 (S. Verdun-Jones & M. Layton eds., 1994); John Ensminger & Thomas Liguori, The Therapeutic Significance of the Civil Commitment Hearing: An Unexplored Potential, in TJ, supra note 2, at 245.

42. Deborah A. Dorfman is currently representing mentally disabled persons through her work with the Legal Center for People With Disabilities in Salt Lake City, Utah. Keri K. Gould was formerly a senior attorney for New York's Mental Hygiene Legal Service. Michael L. Perlin was director of the Division of Mental Health Advocacy in the NJ Department of the Public Advocate.

43. See, e.g., 1 Perlin, supra note 5, §§ 2.06–2.08, 2.14–2.15; Perlin, Law and Disability, supra note 5, § 1.03. For recent cases, see e.g., 1 Perlin, supra note 5, § 3.45 at 95–100 (1994 Supp.).

44. See Perlin, Law and Disability, supra note 5, § 1.01. For a recent comprehensive overview, see Thomas Hafemeister & John Petrila, Treating the Mentally Disordered Offender: Society's Uncertain, Conflicted, and Changing Views, 21 Fla. St. U. L. Rev. 729 (1994).

45. See Jackson v. Indiana, 406 U.S. 715, 719 (1972).

46. See Hafemeister & Petrila, supra note 44, at 733; see generally 1 Perlin, supra note 5, §§ 2.03–2.04.

47. Prochaska v. Brinegar, 102 N.W. 2d 870, 872 (Iowa 1960).

48. Perlin, Fatal Assumption, supra note 34.

ministrative decisions, with few incentives to terminate custody.[49] Hospitals were traditionally "closed" institutions, and courts abided by the hands-off policy in rejecting requests for judicial oversight.[50]

New treatment modalities developed in the 1950s—specifically, the creation of antipsychotic drugs such as Thorazine[51]—combined with the changing political climate of the 1960s to bring dramatic changes to the way psychiatric facilities were run. Perhaps even more important, press exposes led to public perceptions that psychiatric facilities were often exploitative "snake pits."[52] In addition, funding became available on a larger scale for the first time through the passage of the Community Mental Health Centers Act of 1963.[53] As a result of these factors, psychiatric facility censuses were dramatically decreased.[54]

C. The Civil Rights Revolution

David Wexler has clearly and concisely set out the impact of the civil rights revolution on involuntary civil commitment law:

> In the very late 1960s, a revolution began in civil commitment legislation. From then until the mid or late 1970s, nearly every state revised its mental health code.... The revolution, motivated by civil libertarian concerns, prompted a re-thinking of such questions as who should be forcibly committed, on what grounds, for how long, and with what sort of procedural safeguards. The result was a setting of durational limits on the length of commitment, a massive increase in procedural protections and, substantively, stricter and more explicit commitment criteria.[55]

Not incidentally, the initiation of more formal hearings forced medical personnel to alter the manner in which they testified.[56] For the first time, psychia-

---

49. Hafemeister & Petrila, supra note 44, at 733.

50. Perlin, Law and Disability, supra note 5, § 2.08 at 218 n.32 (discussing Banning v. Looney, 213 F.2d 771 (10th Cir. 1954), cert. denied, 348 U.S. 859 (1954)).

51. Perlin, Law and Disability, supra note 5, § 2.08 at 214; see generally Sheldon Gelman, Mental Hospital Drugs: Professionalism and the Constitution, 72 Geo. L. J. 1725 (1984); Bruce Winick, The Right to Refuse Mental Health Treatment: A First Amendment Perspective, 44 U. Miami L. Rev. 1 (1989).

52. Geraldo Rivera's stark videotape depiction of the Willowbrook facility was the most influential of these. See David Rothman & Sheila Rothman, the Willowbrook Wars (1984): see generally Teresa Harvey Paredes, The Killing Words? How the Quality-of-Life Ethic Affects Persons With Severe Disabilities. SMU L. Rev. 805, 808 n.28 (1992).

53. Michael L. Perlin, Competency, Deinstitutionalization, and Homelessness: A Story of Marginalization 28 Hous. L. Rev. 63 (1991).

54. Perlin, Law and Disability, supra note 5, § 2.52, at 379–81, and sources cited supra notes 2–13.

55. David Wexler, Grave Disability and Family Therapy: The Therapeutic Potential of Civil Libertarian Commitment Codes, in TJ, supra note 2, at 165.

56. However, there may be hidden effects as well. A study comparing prereform and postreform commitment decision making in Dane County, Wisconsin (the county of origin for the case of Lessard v. Schmidt discussed extensively infra part I.D.1), found that there were fewer final hearings postreform and that a significant proportion of detainees still evidenced behavior leading to emergency detention that involved no actual harm. Michael Leiber & Sean Anderson, A Comparison of Pre-Reform and Post-Reform Civil Commitment

trists were subjected to rigorous cross-examination[57] and were required to substantiate their medical opinions rather than merely make medical conclusions. At the same time, psychiatric diagnostic and predictive skills were more closely scrutinized.[58] Lawyers were often successful in convincing courts that psychiatric diagnoses and predictions of dangerousness were inaccurate.[59] The meaning of *dangerousness* also became an important area of litigation.[60] Critics charged that the concept was "vague" and "amorphous," and its "elasticity" has made it "one of the most problematic and elusive concepts in mental health law."[61]

It was against this backdrop that many of the seminal cases litigating the boundaries of involuntary commitment of persons considered to be mentally ill were decided. We contend that the formalization of mental health law advocacy was patient centered, rights driven, and therapeutic in outcome.[62] These early cases were calculated to restore a modicum of dignity to those institutionalized pursuant to what were (almost without exception) archaic, paternalistic, and ultimately antitherapeutic laws. It is also not coincidental that the majority of those subjected to involuntary civil commitment are poor, elderly, uneducated, or female.[63] They are the people society renders the most

---

Decisionmaking in Dane County, Wisconsin, 20 N. Eng. J. Crim. & Civ. Confinement 1 (1993).

57. This of course assumes a fact never in evidence: that the lawyers assigned to represent mentally disabled individuals were able (or cared) to do a competent job of such cross-examination. See generally Perlin, Fatal Assumption, supra note 34.

58. Joseph Cocozza & Henry Steadman, The Failure of Psychiatric Predications of Dangerousness: Clear and Convincing Evidence, 29 Rutgers L. Rev. 1084 (1976); Alan Dershowitz, The Law of Dangerousness: Some Fiction About Predictions, 23 J. Legal Educ. 24 (1970); Bruce Ennis & Thomas Litwack, Psychiatry and the Presumption of Expertise: Flipping Coins in the Courtroom, 62 Cal. L. Rev. 693 (1974). This battle still rages. Compare Richard Rogers et al., Can Ziskin Withstand His Own Criticisms? Problems With His Model of Cross-Examination, 11 Behav. Sci. & L. 223 (1993), to Jay Ziskin, Ziskin Can Withstand His Own Criticisms: A Response to Rogers, Bagby and Perera, 15 Am. J. Forensic Psychiatry 41 (1994).

59. E.g., People v. Murtishaw, 631 P.2d 446 (Cal. 1981), cert. denied, 455 U.S. 922 (1982).

60. 1 Perlin, supra note 5, § 2.07.

61. Id. at 71 (citing sources), and at 73 (Comment to section).

62. See generally Lafond & Durham, supra note 26, at 82–99 (setting out historical and political perspective).

63. See, e.g., Leiber & Anderson, supra note 56, at 20 (females and those who lack support in the community remained committed for longer terms than younger individuals, males, and those who had an external support network). See generally Susan Stefan, The Protection Racket: Rape Trauma Syndrome, Psychiatric Labeling, and Law; 88 NW. U. L. Rev. 1271 (1994) (discussing statistically significant number of institutionalized women who have suffered from sexual abuse and violence, and discussing ways in which involuntary commitment leads to treatment that often exacerbates conditions that caused their suffering in the first place—silencing, infantilization, lack of control, forcible physical intrusion and restraint against their will, and an inability to escape. Id. at 1312–19). See also Susan Stefan, Silencing the Different Voice: Competence, Feminist Theory and Law, 47 U. Miami L. Rev. 763, 764 (1993).

visible within the community, and they are virtually invisible when expelled from the community.

Therapeutic jurisprudence proposes that we be sensitive to the consequences of governmental action and it asks whether the law's antitherapeutic consequences can be reduced and its therapeutic consequences enhanced without subordinating due process and justice values.[64] In civil commitment case law, rarely is any reference made to the patient's perceived therapeutic response to the legal procedures or terms and conditions of the commitment.[65]

D. The Case Law

By the mid-1970s, it was universally accepted that some finding of mental illness was a prerequisite to involuntary commitment, following the U.S. Supreme Court's decision in *Jackson v. Indiana*[66] that "at the least, due process requires that the nature and duration of commitment must bear some reasonable relationship to the purpose for which the individual is committed."[67] *Jackson's* principles were first given importance in an involuntary civil commitment context in *Lessard v. Schmidt*.[68] *Lessard* struck down Wisconsin's involuntary civil commitment scheme and established guidelines as to the meaning of *dangerousness* that served as the model for the first generation of such challenges.[69]

1. Lessard v. Schmidt. *Lessard* was a class action brought on behalf of all adults then being held involuntarily pursuant to any emergency, temporary, or permanent provision of Wisconsin's involuntary civil commitment statutes.[70] It challenged a state statute that allowed for commitment of an individual if the hearing court was "satisfied that he is mentally ill or infirm or deficient and that he is a proper subject for custody and treatment."[71] According to plaintiffs, the law failed to "describe the standard for commitment so that persons may be able to ascertain the standard of conduct under which they may be detained with reasonable certainty."[72]

---

64. Wexler, supra note 3, at 762.

65. See generally, e.g., cases discussed in 1 Perlin, supra note 5, chapters 2, 3; and in Perlin, Law and Disability, supra note 5, chapter 1.

66. 406 U.S. 715 (1972).

67. Id. at 738. See generally Perlin, Law and Disability, supra note 5, § 1.03; 3 Perlin, supra note 5, § 2.08.

68. 349 F. Supp. 1078 (E.D. Wis. 1972), vacated and remanded, 414 U.S. 473, on remand, 379 F. Supp. 1376 (E.D. Wis. 1974), vacated and remanded, 421 U.S. 957 (1975), reinstated, 413 F. Supp. 1318 (E.D. Wis. 1976).

Text accompanying footnotes 69–88 is generally adapted from Perlin, Law and Disability, supra note 5, § 1.04 at 25–28.

69. Professor Dix is clear: "Judicial activism began in 1972...in *Lessard* v. Schmidt." George Dix, Major Current Issues Concerning Civil Commitment Criteria, 45 Law & Contemp. Probs. 137 (Summer 1982). Compare Fhagen v. Miller, 278 N.E. 2d 615, 617–18 (N.Y. 1972), cert. denied, 409 U.S. 845 (1972) (rejecting similar challenge to New York state law) (decided nine months before *Lessard*).

70. *Lessard,* 349 F. Supp. at 1082.

71. Wis. Stat. Ann. § 51.02(5)(c) (West 1957).

72. *Lessard,* 349 F. Supp. at 1082.

In approaching the case, the court looked carefully at the common-law and historical roots of the state involuntary civil commitment power.[73] In involuntary civil commitment proceedings, it found that the same "fundamental liberties" as are in criminal cases are at stake[74]; the police power must thus similarly be "tempered with stringent procedural safeguards designed to protect the rights of one" subject to such power.[75] However, its review of the pertinent history suggested that, traditionally, involuntary civil commitment procedures have not "assured the due process safeguards against unjustified deprivation of liberty that are accorded those accused of crime."[76]

The court then examined the state's statutory definition of "mental illness"[77] in light of the U.S. Supreme Court's decision in *Humphrey v. Cady*,[78] which, in *dicta*, had interpreted the section in question to require that a person's "potential for doing harm, to himself or to others, is great enough to justify such a massive curtailment of liberty."[79] The *Lessard* court construed this statement to mean that "the statute itself requires a finding of 'dangerousness' to self or others in order to deprive an individual of his or her freedom."[80]

The use by the *Humphrey* court of the phrase "great enough" and its description of commitment as such a "massive curtailment" of liberty implied "a balancing test in which the state must bear the burden of proving that there is an extreme likelihood that if the person is not confined he will do immediate harm to himself or others."[81] Although predictions of future conduct are "always difficult" and confinement based on such predictions "must always be viewed with suspicion,"[82] civil confinement could be justified if the "proper" burden of proof were to be satisfied, and "dangerousness [were to be] based upon a finding of a recent overt act, attempt or threat to do substantial harm to oneself or another."[83]

---

73. The court began with the principle that the state's power to deprive a person of "the fundamental liberty to go unimpeded about his or her affairs" must be based on a "compelling" state interest in such a deprivation, Id. at 1084 (citing J. S. Mill, On Liberty 18 (Gateway, Inc. ed., 1962)); compare Jonas Robitscher, Legal Standards and Their Implications Regarding Civil Commitment Procedures, in Dangerous Behavior: A Problem in Law and Mental Health 61, 69–70 (C. J. Frederick ed., 1974) (criticizing this citation to Mill as a "bludgeon of reason" and an incomplete statement of Mill's philosophy).

74. *Lessard*, 349 F. Supp. at 1084.

75. Id.

76. Id.

77. Mental illness was defined as "mental disease to such extent that a person so afflicted requires care and treatment for his own welfare, or the welfare of others, or of the community." Wis. Stat. Ann. § 51.75, art. II(f) (West 1971).

78. 405 U.S. 504 (1972).

79. *Lessard*, 349 F. Supp. at 1093 (quoting *Humphrey*, 405 U.S. at 509).

80. *Lessard,* 349 F. Supp. at 1093.

81. Id.

82. Id.

83. *Lessard,* 349 F. Supp. at 1093. The court added that even an overt attempt to harm oneself substantially cannot be the proper foundation for a commitment unless the person in question is found to be mentally ill and an immediate danger at the time of the hearing of doing further harm to his or herself, id. at 1093 n.24, noting that the considerations that permit society to detain those likely to harm others because of mental illness "do not necessar-

Lessard was the forerunner of a generation of involuntary civil commitment cases,[84] all making some sort of finding that there must be a "real and present danger of doing significant harm" to show dangerousness sufficient to support such a commitment.[85] The cases were not unanimous (e.g., as to the need for an actual overt act).[86] Nevertheless, they reflected a clear "[break] with a century-old tradition that 'civil' commitment of the mentally ill, whether for their own good or that of society, demands fewer procedural protections than does incarceration for punishment."[87] More than 20 years after the case was decided, *Lessard* remains the "high-water mark in 'dangerousness' law."[88]

We contend that much of the *Lessard* court's opinion was based on a therapeutic jurisprudence perspective. In evaluating Wisconsin's commitment statutes, the court chose to look at the effects of civil commitment on those committed.[89] The court considered evidence that lengthy hospitalization, particularly involuntary hospitalization, may greatly increase the symptoms of mental illness and make adjustment to society more difficult.[90]

In addition, the court considered the substantial loss of substantive civil rights suffered by persons adjudicated mentally ill and unable to care for themselves or in need of hospitalization.[91] On the other hand, the court gave little credence to the state's contention that notice and an evidentiary hearing within the first few days of confinement may be psychologically harmful to the patient.[92] In fact, the

---

ily apply to potential harm to oneself." Id.

84. See Comment, Progress in Involuntary Commitment, 49 Wash. L. Rev. 617, 618 (1974) (*Lessard* was "the most sweeping judicial change to date"), and id. at n.4 ("*Lessard* opinion seems destined to be a classic"); John Myers, Involuntary Civil Commitment of the Mentally Ill: A System in Need of a Change, 29 Vill. L. Rev. 367, 378–79 (1983–84) (*Lessard* was a "landmark case" that articulated standards that have been "widely followed by courts and legislatures throughout the country"); Thomas Zander, Civil Commitment in Wisconsin: The Impact of Lessard v. Schmidt, 1976 Wis. L. Rev. 503, 559 ("The *Lessard* decision will find its place in history not merely as the first comprehensive federal court decision on the constitutionality of civil commitment, but also as one of the first major judicial recognitions of civil commitment as more than a court authorized medical decision").

85. See, e.g., Doremus v. Farrell, 407 F. Supp. 509, 514–15 (D. Neb. 1975) (commitment standards must be "(a) that the person is mentally ill and poses a serious threat of substantial harm to himself or to others; and (b) that this threat of harm has been evidenced by a recent overt act or threat").

86. See generally Perlin, Law and Disability, supra note 5, § 1.05 (citing cases).

87. Robitscher, supra note 73, at 69.

88. Alexander Brooks, Notes on Defining the "Dangerousness" of the Mentally Ill, in Frederick, supra note 73, at 49.

For an analysis of case law rejecting *Lessard*'s expansive construction of both substantive and procedural due process protections in the involuntary civil commitment context, see e.g., 1 Perlin, supra note 5, § 2.13 (discussing cases rejecting "overt act" requirement), §§ 3.09, 3.13 (discussing cases rejecting *Lessard*'s mandate of an immediate preliminary hearing, and its strict reading of time limitations between hospitalization and final commitment hearings).

89. *Lessard*, 349 F. Supp. at 1084.

90. Id. at 1087.

91. Id. at 1090–91.

92. Id. at 1091 ("Those who argue that notice and a hearing at this time may be harmful to the patient ignore the fact that there has been no finding that the person is in need of hospitalization").

Lessard opinion contains at least one explanatory passage that seems to qualify as one of the true judicial forerunners of therapeutic jurisprudence:

> [The] conclusion [that due process is mandated at involuntary civil commit-ment hearings] is fortified by medical evidence that indicates that patients re-spond more favorably to treatment when they feel they are being treated fairly and are treated as intelligent, aware, human beings. In [the named plaintiff's] case, for example, Dr. Kennedy testified that her improvement had occurred "following a period of involvement with not only hospital individuals and hos-pital staff influence, but an involvement with other environmental influences that have included a number of judicial involvements, legal involvements."[93]

In using a therapeutic jurisprudence perspective, the court was able to fash-ion a workable standard that took into account the concerns of the state to protect society,[94] provide appropriate care and treatment to its mentally ill cit-izens,[95] and protect the dignity and civil rights of persons thought to be in need of involuntary civil commitment.

*   *   *

III. *The Right to Treatment*

A. Introduction

The area of right-to-treatment law is perhaps the best fit between therapeu-tic jurisprudence and patients' civil rights. The right-to-treatment movement grew consciously out of dissatisfaction in the 1950s and 1960s with the non-therapeutic and antitherapeutic condition of large public state institutions for mentally disabled persons.[146] The earliest cases—especially *Wyatt v. Stickney*—made the overt link between therapeutic rights and constitutional rights.[147] Early cases that flowed from *Wyatt*—both right-to-treatment cases and "other institutional rights" cases—often relied specifically on therapeutic justifications for constitutional holdings.[148]

*   *   *

B. *Wyatt* and Its Progeny

By 1960, social reformers had become a major voice in the call to restruc-ture state public mental hospitals. The president of the American Psychiatric

---

93. Id. at 1101–1102.

94. Through its acknowledgement of the state's police powers. Id. at 1084–85.

95. Through its acknowledgement of the state's *parens patriae* powers. Id.

146. See 2 Perlin, supra note 5, § 4.04.

147. 325 F. Supp. 781 (M.D. Ala. 1971), suppl., 334 F. Supp. 1341 (M.D. Ala. 1972), 344 F. Supp. 373 (M.D. Ala. 1972), 344 F. Supp. 387 (M.D. Ala. 1972), aff'd sub. nom. Wyatt v. Aderholt, 503 F. 2d 1305 (5th Cir. 1974).

148. See generally infra Part II. C.

Association called the facilities "bankrupt beyond remedy"[154]; the social critic Albert Deutsch testified before Congress regarding his earlier investigations of state hospitals with these chilling words:

> Some physicians I interviewed frankly admitted that the animals of nearby piggeries were better housed, fed and treated than many of the patients on their wards. I saw hundreds of sick people shackled, strapped, straitjacketed, and bound to their beds. I saw mental patients forced to eat meals with their hands because there were not enough spoons and other tableware to go around—not because they couldn't be trusted to eat like humans.... I found evidence of physical brutality, but that paled into insignificance when compared with the excruciating suffering stemming from prolonged, enforced idleness, herdlike crowding, lack of privacy, depersonalization, and the overall atmosphere of neglect. The fault lay...with the general community that not only tolerated but enforced these subhuman conditions through financial penury, ignorance, fear and indifference.[155]

At about the same time, Morton Birnbaum (a physician and attorney) published his seminal article in the *American Bar Association Journal* calling for a declaration of "the recognition and enforcement of the legal right of a mentally ill inmate of a public mental institution to adequate medical treatment for his mental illness"[156] and for courts to openly consider the question of whether "the institutionalized mentally ill person receives adequate medical treatment so that he may regain his health, and therefore his liberty, as soon as possible."[157] Birnbaum located the constitutional basis of this right to treatment in the Due Process Clause: "Substantive due process of law does not allow a mentally ill person who has committed no crime to be deprived of his liberty by indefinitely institutionalizing him in a mental prison."[158] This article was widely acknowledged as "supplying much of the theoretical support for the subsequent development of the right-to-treatment litigation."[159]

The existence of a *statutory*[160] right to treatment was first judicially recognized by the District of Columbia Circuit Court of Appeals in the unlikely setting of a habeas corpus case brought by an insanity acquittee. There, in *Rouse v. Cameron*,[161] the court found that a District of Columbia hospitalization law established such a statutory right, reasoning that "the purpose of involuntary hospitalization is treatment, not punishment," quoting a statement by the act's

154. Harry Solomon, Presidential Address: The American Psychiatric Association in Relation to American Psychiatry, 115 Am. J. Psychiatry 1, 7 (1958).

155. Constitutional Rights of the Mentally Ill, Hearing Before the Senate Subcomm. on Constitutional Rights of the Judiciary, 87th Cong., 2d Sess. 40–42 (1961) (statement of Albert Deutsch), quoted in 2 Perlin, supra note 5, § 4.04 at 14–15.

156. Birnbaum, supra note 21.

157. Id. at 502.

158. Id. at 502–503.

159. 2 Perlin, supra note 5, § 4.03 at 12–13.

160. D. C. Code § 21-562 (1966); see generally 2 Perlin, supra note 5, § 4.04 at 15–19.

161. 373 F. 2d 451 (D.C. Cir. 1966).

sponsor that when a person is deprived of liberty because of need of treatment, and that treatment is not supplied, such deprivation is "tantamount to a denial of due process."[162] The hospital thus needed to demonstrate that it had made a "bona fide effort" to "cure or improve" the patient, that inquiries into the patient's needs and conditions be renewed periodically, and that the program provided be suited to the patient's "particular needs."[163]

Rouse was the subject of considerable academic and scholarly commentary—most of which was favorable[164]—but was nonetheless criticized sharply by the American Psychiatric Association for interfering with medical practice: "The definition of treatment and the appraisal of its adequacy are matters for medical determination."[165] This position, to be sure, was not unanimously held by the psychiatric establishment—Alan Stone, for instance, referred to it as a "monument to bureaucratic myopia"[166]—but it provides a context through which some of the incessant criticisms of the mental health advocacy movement can be reexamined: that the trade association for the service providers most closely linked with inpatient mental health care took the position that the hands-off doctrine[167] required a policy of judicial nonintervention in the relationship between institutionalization and constitutional rights.

The most important case finding a *constitutional* right to treatment was, without doubt, *Wyatt v. Stickney. Wyatt* was clear:

> The purposes of involuntary hospitalization for treatment purposes is *treatment* and not mere custodial care or punishment. This is the only justification from a constitutional standpoint, that allows civil commitment to [a state hospital]....
> To deprive any citizen of his or her liberty upon the altruistic theory that the confinement is for humane therapeutic reasons and then fail to provide adequate treatment violates the very fundamentals of due process.[168]

It subsequently found three "fundamental conditions for adequate and effective treatment": (a) a humane psychological and physical environment, (b) qualified staff in numbers sufficient to administer adequate treatment, and (c) individualized treatment plans.[169] Following a hearing (to which the court had invited a broad cross-section of interested professional associations to participate), the court issued supplemental orders detailing the "medical and consti-

---

162. Id. at 455.

163. Id.

164. See generally 2 Perlin, supra note 5, § 4.05 at 19–24.

165. Council of the American Psychiatric Association. Position Statement on the Question of the Adequacy of Treatment, 123 Am. J. Psychiatry 1458 (1967).

166. Alan Stone, The Right to Treatment and the Medical Establishment, 2 Bull. Am. Acad. Psychiatry & L. 159, 161 (1974).

167. See, e.g., Banning v. Looney, 213 F. 2d 771 (10th Cir. 1954), cert. denied, 348 U.S. 859 (1954).

168. 325 F. Supp. 781, 784–85 (M.D. Ala. 1971), suppl., 334 F. Supp. 1341 (M.D. Ala. 1972), 344 F. Supp. 373 (M.D. Ala. 1972), 344 F. Supp. 387 (M.D. Ala. 1972), aff'd sub. nom. Wyatt v. Aderholt, 503 F. 2d 1305 (5th Cir. 1974).

169. 334 F. Supp. at 1343.

tutional minimums...mandatory for a constitutionally acceptable minimum treatment program."[170] These standards covered the full range of hospital conditions, including environmental standards, civil rights, medical treatment criteria, staff qualifications, nutritional requirements, and need for compliance with Life Safety Code provisions.[171]

On what sources did *Wyatt* draw? An examination of the transcript, briefs, and court documents in *Wyatt* (and in *NYSARC v. Rockefeller*, a parallel suit brought in federal court in New York on behalf of residents of the Willowbrook facility for mentally retarded individuals [the *Willowbrook* case])[172] reveals that therapeutic motivations drove each and every important aspect of the litigation in question.

The complaint in *Willowbrook*, for instance, specifically articulated therapeutic ends:

> 32. Care, treatment, education and training are all included within a broader concept referred to by mental retardation professionals as "habilitation." The goal of habilitation is to assist each mentally retarded person to lead a life as close to normal as is possible.
>
> ...
>
> 35. Defendants, however, have created, fostered, and condoned conditions, policies and practices at Willowbrook that are directly contrary to professionally accepted concepts of habilitation. As a consequence, Willowbrook is not a therapeutic institution. It more closely resembles a prison, and the residents confined therein have therefore been denied due process of law.
>
> ...
>
> 37. A...prerequisite to an adequate habilitation program is a humane physical and psychological environment. The environment at Willowbrook is inhumane and psychologically destructive. Examples of the anti-therapeutic environment include...
> [listing examples].
>
> ...
>
> 54. Because of the foregoing, the vast majority of residents at Willowbrook have actually regressed and deteriorated since their admission...
>
> 55. Because of the foregoing, residents have been deprived of the habilitation necessary to enable them to speak, read, communicate, mix and assemble with others...
>
> 56. Because of the foregoing, residents have been deprived of their rights to privacy and dignity protected by the Fourteenth Amendment.
>
> ...
>
> 59. Because of the foregoing, residents have been denied due process and equal protection of the law, in violation of the Fourteenth Amendment.[173]

---

170. Id., 344 F. Supp. at 376.

171. Id. at 379–86; see generally 2 Perlin, supra note 5, § 4.07, at 34–35.

172. New York State Ass'n for Retarded Children, Inc. v. Rockefeller, 357 F. Supp. 752 (E.D.N.Y. 1973) [hereinafter *Willowbrook*].

173. Excerpts from Complaint in New York State Association for Retarded Children v. Rockefeller, 1 Legal Rights of the Mentally Handicapped 591 (B. Ennis & P. Friedman eds. 1973) [hereinafter *Legal Rights*].

At trial, experts and even defendants' witnesses testified as to the regression suffered by Willowbrook residents.[174] The consent order eventually entered in this case[175] was overtly premised on therapeutic ends:

> [The] conditions [at Willowbrook] are hazardous to the health, safety, and sanity of the residents. They do not conform with the standards published by the American Association of Mental Health Deficiency in 1964, or with the proposed standards published on May 5, 1973 by the United States Department of Health, Education and Welfare.[176]

Under the court's analysis, residents were entitled to, *inter alia*, "protection from assaults by fellow inmates or by staff," to "correction of conditions which violate 'basic standards of human decency'," to medical care, to exercise and outdoor recreation, to adequate heat during cold weather, and to the "necessary elements of basic hygiene."[177]

The conditions that faced the court in *Wyatt* were, to be charitable, abysmal. During the course of trial, the following uncontradicted facts were found:

> A resident was scalded to death by hydrant water, . . . a resident was restrained in a strait jacket for nine years in order to prevent hand and finger sucking, . . . and a resident died from the insertion by another resident of a running water hose into his rectum.[178]

In each instance, the court noted that the incidents could have been avoided "had adequate staff and facilities been available."[179]

In the pretrial aspects of *Wyatt,* an expert testified as to the way that the operation of the Partlow facility "foster[ed] dehumanization" and reflected a "long-

---

174. See, e.g., Excerpt from Plaintiffs' Post-Trial Memorandum in New York State Association for Retarded Children v. Rockefeller, in 2 Legal Rights, supra note 173, at 747 (1973) (defendant Grunberg testified that patient records revealed "regression after institutionalization at Willowbrook"; expert witness Clements testified Willowbrook failed to provide even a "minimal level of custodial care"; expert witness Roos testified that condition of Willowbrook residents was largely function of "long exposure to noxious debilitating environmental conditions"); see also id. at 770 ("It is obvious that there were many children who could possibly have walked if they had proper [physical] therapy from the beginning. It is questionable whether they could ever walk now. Their chances will definitely decrease as the time passes without proper developmental therapy") (emphasis in original) (quoting from posttrial memorandum, relying on case record).

175. 2 Perlin, supra note 5, § 4.28, at 136 (reprinting New York State Association for Retarded Citizens v. Carey, No. 72-C-356/357 (E.D.N.Y. 1975), approved, 393 F. Supp. 715 (E.D.N.Y. 1975).

176. *Willowbrook,* 393 F. Supp. at 755–56.

177. Id. at 764–65.

178. Wyatt, 344 F. Supp. at 394 n.13.

179. Id. For an even more graphic description of the way that Alabama state residents were fed in the facilities that were the subject of the *Wyatt* suit, see James Folsom, The Early Constructive Approach to *Wyatt* by the Department of Mental Health, in Wyatt V. Stickney: Retrospect and Prospect 41 (L. R. Jones & R. Parlour eds., 1981) [hereinafter Retrospect and Prospect] (describing process as "patients being slopped like hogs").

term warehousing operation"[180] and a "deprived environment"[181] in which staff had "little understanding as to the nature of the residents' disabilities"[182] and exhibited a "self-defeatist attitude" that "generates deterioration in the residents,"[183] and conditions on wards reflected "massive evidence of deprivation—emotional, social,... physical."[184] Briefs filed with the court relied on behavioral and medical experts to support arguments that institutional settings such as were present in Alabama "encourage disability rather than overcom[e] it," that such hospitalization is inevitably a "regressive experience with far reaching destructive repercussions," that such hospitalization is "anti-therapeutic" and "negative," and that continued exposure to such conditions "has severely debilitating effects on the social and psychological condition of patients."[185]

The court's original orders in *Wyatt*[186] drew specifically on many of the sources in coming to the conclusion that conditions at Alabama facilities violated the Due Process Clause.[187] Even that aspect of *Wyatt* that appears to be the most purely legal—its invocation of the least restrictive analysis doctrine for institutional decision making[188]—is premised on therapeutic ends.[189]

---

180. See 2 Perlin, supra note 5, § 4.18, at 75, 80–81 (reprinting deposition testimony of Philip Roos).

181. Id. at 87.

182. Id. at 89.

183. Id. at 94.

184. Id. at 95. Compare Philip Roos, Basic Facts About Mental Retardation, in 1 Legal Rights, supra note 173, at 17, 23 ("Retarded persons should be viewed developmentally, capable of growth or learning, regardless of level of retardation or age").

185. The Right to a Durational Limitation on Involuntary Commitment, in 1 Legal Rights, supra note 173, at 437, 442–43 (excerpt from posttrial memorandum in *Wyatt*).

186. For an analysis of subsequent litigation, see 2 Perlin, supra note 5, § 4.17 at 5–6 n.317.1 (1994 Supp.).

187. See, e.g., *Wyatt*, 344 F. Supp. at 376–86; see also 2 Perlin, supra note 5, § 4.07 at 34–35:

> The standards ranged in subject matter from the global (e.g., "Patients have a right to privacy and dignity") to the specific (e.g., "Thermostatically controlled hot water shall be maintained [at 180 degrees] for mechanical dishwashing")....
> They covered the full range of hospital conditions, including environmental standards, civil rights, medical treatment criteria, staff qualifications, nutritional requirements, and need for compliance with Life Safety Code provisions.

On the question of the therapeutic jurisprudence aspects of the privacy standards, see Joseph O'Reilly & Bruce Sales, Setting Physical Standards for Mental Hospitals: To Whom Should the Courts Listen, 8 Int'l J. L. & Psychiatry 301 (1986), and Joseph O'Reilly & Bruce Sales, Privacy for the Institutionalized Mentally Ill: Are Court-Ordered Standards Effective? 11 Law & Hum. Behav. 41 (1987).

188. Id.

189. See, e.g., David Chambers, Right to the Least Restrictive Alternative Setting for Treatment, in 2 Legal Rights, supra note 173, at 991, 1011 (theoretical support for application of least restrictive alternative principle to mental disability litigation, focusing on harms that often befall patients in large mental institutions, including "physical deterioration (loss of speech, inertia, passivity, etc.),... psychological deterioration (loss of social skills, loss of self-esteem, loss of identity, withdrawal, extreme dependency),... loss of liberty and dignity

On appeal, *amici* supporting *Wyatt* plaintiffs stressed the precise link between therapeutic outcome and constitutional rights, calling the court's attention to the fact-finding made below:

> [T]he dormitories are barn-like structures with no privacy for the patients. For most patients there is not even a space provided which he can think of as his own. The toilets in the restrooms seldom have partitions between them. There are dehumanizing factors which degenerate the patients' self-esteem. Also contributing to the poor psychological environment are the shoddy wearing apparel furnished the patients, the non-therapeutic work assigned to patients, and the degrading and humiliating admissions procedures which creates in the patient an impression of the hospital as a prison or as a crazy house.[190]

In the same brief, *amici* stressed findings made by defendants' experts:

> [The hospital] impressed me as a depressing and dehumanizing environment, reminding me of graveyard lots where the patients are essentially living out their lives without the rights of privacy (or ownership).[191]

Quoting further testimony:

> Residents with open wounds and inadequately treated skin diseases were in immediate danger of infection because of the unsanitary conditions existing in the wards, including urine and feces on the floor....There was evidence of insect infestation, including cockroaches in the kitchens and dining rooms.[192]
>
> Not only are inmates of Alabama's mental institutions deprived of treatment, they are deprived of even the most minimal stimulation and activity, with the result that their condition seriously deteriorates.[193]

On appeal, the Fifth Circuit substantially affirmed. It noted that there was "no significant dispute" about the level of conditions in the Alabama facilities in question,[194] relying on its recent decision in *Donaldson v. O'Connor*[195]:

> In *Donaldson,* we held that civilly committed mental patients have a constitutional right to such individual treatment as will help each of them to be cured or to improve his or her mental condition. We reasoned that the only permissible justifications for civil commitment, and for the massive abridgments of constitutionally protected liberties it entails, were the danger posed by the individ-

---

(lack of privacy, lack of movement, exposure to violence, extreme regimentation). Professor Chambers's work has been influential in the development of the least restrictive alternative doctrine.) See David Chambers, Alternatives to Civil Commitment of the Mentally Ill: Practical Guides and Constitutional Imperatives, 70 Mich. L. Rev. 1107 (1972). See e.g., Morales v. Turman, 383 F. Supp. 53, 125 (E.D. Tex. 1974), rev'd, 535 F. 2d 864 (5th Cir. 1976), rev'd 430 U.S. 322 (1977); Scott v. Plante, 641 F. 2d 117, 131 (3d Cir. 1981), vacated, 458 U.S. 1101 (1982); In re W. H. 481 A. 2d 22, 25 (Vt. 1984); Matter of Stokes, 546 A. 2d. 356, 360 (D.C. 1988) (all citing Chambers, supra).

190. Brief of Amicus Curiae on Appeal to the Fifth Circuit in Wyatt v. Stickney, in 1 Legal Rights, supra note 173, at 333, 354.

191. Id. at 367.

192. Id. at 367–68.

193. Id. at 377.

194. *Wyatt,* 503 F. 2d at 1310.

195. 493 F.2d 507 (5th Cir. 1974), vacated, 422 U.S. 563 (1975). See generally infra Part I.

ual committed to himself or others, or the individual's need for treatment and care. We held that where the justification for commitment was treatment, it offended the fundamentals of due process if treatment were not in fact provided; and we held that where the justification was the danger to self or to others, then treatment had to be provided as the *quid pro quo* society had to pay as the price of the extra safety it derived from the denial of individuals' liberty.[196]

Wyatt was characterized as "the most significant case in the history of forensic psychiatry" and "the foundation of modern psychiatric jurisprudence."[197] Furthermore, it crystallized the issue: The right to treatment was consciously intended to achieve therapeutic gains.[198] Post-*Wyatt* cases endorsed the link, both in "pure" right-to-treatment cases,[199] in institutional rights cases that focused on one or more aspect of *Wyatt*—for example, the right to be paid for institutional labor[200] or the right to freedom in religious practice,[201] and in early deinstitutionalization cases.[202]

*   *   *

IV. The Right to Refuse Treatment

A. Introduction

The right to refuse treatment has a strong therapeutic jurisprudence component. Although public attention has been focused primarily on what is often seen as the antitherapeutic aspect of this right,[280] we believe that there are significant benefits here as well: due process rights for the mentally disabled, better checks on doctors and clinical staff to ensure that medication and other

---

196. *Wyatt*, 503 F.2d at 1312.

197. Milton Greenblatt, Foreword, in Retrospect and Prospect, supra note 179, at ix, x.

198. See David Wexler, An Introduction to Therapeutic Jurisprudence, in TJ, supra note 2, at 3, 9 (citing Perlin, supra note 35).

199. E.g., Davis v. Watkins, 384 F. Supp. 1196 (N.D. Ohio 1974); Rone v. Fireman, 473 F. Supp. 92 (N.D. Ohio 1979).

200. Schindenwolf v. Klein, No. L41293-75P.W. (N.J. Super Ct., Law Div. 1979), order reprinted in 2 Perlin, supra note 5, § 6.23 at 509–19. For the complaint in Schindenwolf (setting out this link), see id., § 6.22, at 495–509.

201. Falter v. Veteran's Administration, No. 79-2284 (D.N.J. 1979) (complaint), reprinted in id., § 6.05, at 446–66.

202. Halderman v. Pennhurst State School & Hospital, 446 F. Supp. 1295 (E.D. Pa. 1978), modified, 612 F.2d 84 (3d Cir. 1979), rev'd, 451 U.S. 1 (1981), reinstated, 673 F.2d 647 (3d Cir. 1982), rev'd, 465 U.S. 89 (1984) (Pennhurst), discussed extensively in Perlin, Law and Disability, supra note 5, § 2.48. See e.g., Excerpt from Original Plaintiff's Brief in Halderman, reprinted in 2 Legal Rights of Mentally Disabled Persons 715, 725 (P. Friedman ed., 1979) (arguing that isolation and confinement "are counterproductive in the habilitation of the retarded").

280. See, e.g., Stephen Rachlin, One Right Too Many, 3 Bull. Am. Acad. Psychiatry & L. 99 (1975); Darryl Treffert, Dying With Their Rights On, 130 Am. J. Psychiatry 1041 (1973); Thomas Gutheil, The Boston State Hospital Case: "Involuntary Mind Control," the Constitution, and the "Right to Rot," 137 Am. J. Psychiatry 720 (1980).

treatment are not being administered as a means of punishment or convenience, and improved protection from administration of inappropriate medications or medications causing severe side effects, among others.

* * *

C. Empirical Research

1. *Introduction.* Much of the empirical research in the area of the right to refuse treatment for mentally disabled persons has focused on such areas as numbers, characteristics and treatment outcomes of medication refusers, and comparisons of clinical and judicial review regarding petitions for involuntary medication.[298] The results of these studies shed a great deal of light on the therapeutic jurisprudence value of the right to refuse mental health treatment and the current implementation of this law. In this section, we examine the empirical research on the right to refuse treatment and how well this right is being enforced.

2. *The therapeutic jurisprudence effect of the right to refuse treatment.*[299] Empirical research shows that the right to refuse medication often has therapeutic value.[300] One therapeutic benefit is that it expands the due process rights of mentally disabled individuals by providing them a judicial or administrative hearing on the issue of their capacity to refuse treatment.

This expansion of rights is therapeutic on several levels. First, studies comparing clinical and judicial review of involuntary mental health treatment show that there are therapeutic jurisprudence benefits of judicial review in that it affords mentally disabled persons the opportunity to present their case in a more formal legal setting.[301] A study by John Ensminger and Thomas Liguori, for example, found that more formal court proceedings may have therapeutic value. Ensminger and Liguori explain the therapeutic value of formal hearings in the civil commitment process, arguing that such hearings are therapeutic be-

---

298. A seriously underdiscussed issue is that of the economic status of state hospital patients, especially chronic patients. On the impoverished economic status of such persons in general, see Hendrik Wagenaar & Dan Lewis, Ironies of Inclusion: Social Class and Deinstitutionalization, 14 J. Health Pol. Pol'y & L. 503 (1989).

299. For an excellent and comprehensive overview of these issues, see Bruce Winick, The Right to Refuse Treatment: A Therapeutic Jurisprudence Analysis, 17 Int'l J. L. & Psychiatry 99 (1994).

300. See generally id. at 100–111 (on the relationship between therapeutic jurisprudence and the psychology of choice in the right to refuse treatment context); id. at 111–16 (effective implementation of the right to refuse treatment enhances the therapeutic relationship, making it into "a tool that is both more humane and more effective"; implementation of the right to refuse treatment best insures that therapeutic relationship will be "characterized by voluntariness rather than coercion").

301. See Cournos et al., supra note 6, at 854; see also Paul Sauvayre. The Relationship Between the Court and the Doctor on the Issue of an Inpatient's Refusal of Psychotropic Medication, 36 J. Forensic Sci. 219, 221 (1991) (citing Irwin Hasenfeld and Barbara Grumet, A Study of the Right to Refuse Treatment, 12 Bull. Am. Acad. Psychiatry & L. 65 (1984) (patients who initially refuse treatment and complete a judicial hearing as to their capacity to refuse treatment did better after discharge than those who complied with treatment)).

cause they force the individual to face reality and also give them an opportunity to present and hear evidence in a meaningful court procedure.[302] These same benefits can be attributed to medication hearings, particularly as these hearings are, in some jurisdictions, more formal than commitment hearings.[303]

Another benefit of due process is that it provides the appearance of fairness. The perception of receiving a fair hearing is therapeutic because it contributes to the individual's sense of dignity and conveys that he or she is being taken seriously.[304] Other studies show that medication judicial-administrative proceedings can be therapeutic because they allow patients the opportunity to discuss thoroughly the medications and their benefits and risks with their doctors.[305] By holding medication hearings, doctors must again discuss the medications, their purpose, and potential side effects.[306] At the same time, patients have the opportunity to explain the reasons they do not want the medication and ask questions about the drugs.[307] This may be therapeutic because the patients' medication concerns can be better considered in making medication determinations, thus enhancing the efficacy of medication decisions.[308] This benefit is particularly important at large public hospitals where doctors, because of large caseloads, often have less time to spend with their patients on a day-to-day basis. Furthermore, when doctors know that patients do not have to agree with their prescribed regimen, one can expect that doctors will better explain to patients why they believe a certain medication is appropriate, thus further enhancing the therapeutic relationship.[309]

The research also shows that the right to refuse treatment and the legal procedures surrounding these rights also help to prevent the inappropriate use of psychiatric medication, such as using it as a means of punishment or convenience.[310] Misuse of psychotropic medication has been recognized as a signifi-

---

302. Ensminger & Liguori, supra note 41 at 243, 245.

303. In California, for example, the burden of proof to show that a mental health patient lacks capacity to refuse medication is higher than to civilly commit that same patient. In an administrative capacity hearing, the burden of proof is clear and convincing evidence; in an administrative civil commitment hearing for a "14-day hold," the burden of proof is only probable cause. Cal. Welfare & Institutions Code § 5256.6. Compare Heller v. Doe, 113 S. Ct. 2637 (1993) (two-tier commitment system allowing for commitment of mentally retarded persons on a lesser standard of proof (clear and convincing evidence) that for mentally ill persons (beyond a reasonable doubt) is not violative of the equal protection clause).

304. See Note, The Role of Counsel in the Civil Commitment Process: A Theoretical Framework, in TJ, supra note 2, at 309, 323 n.83; see also Tom R. Tyler, The Psychological Consequences of Judicial Procedures: Implications For Civil Commitment Hearings, 46 SMU L. Rev. 433, 444 (1992) (discussing therapeutic value of judicial civil commitment hearings, and stressing that individuals benefit from hearings in which they can take part, are treated with dignity, and which are "fair").

305. Cournos et al., supra note 6, at 854; see also Zito et al., supra note 6, at 336.

306. Cournos et al., supra note 6, at 854.

307. Id.

308. Zito et al., supra note 6, at 336.

309. See Winick, supra note 299.

310. Davis v. Hubbard, 506 F. Supp. 915, 926–27 (N.D. Ohio 1980); see also Mary C. McCarron, The Right to Refuse Antipsychotic Drugs: Safeguarding the Mentally Incompetent Patient's Right to Procedural Due Process, 73 Maro. L. Rev. 477, 484 (1990).

cant concern justifying the need for checks on doctors and staff by courts as well as social scientists.[311]

Similarly, medication hearings serve as a check to ensure that doctors are not prescribing the wrong medications or the wrong dosages or ignoring patients' concerns regarding side effects.[312] A 1986 study, for example, comparing medical and judicial perceptions of the problem of side effects of psychiatric medication indicated that, whereas both groups valued such treatment, judges were concerned more about the risk of side effects than were the doctors.[313] This check is important as psychiatric medication can be antitherapeutic—even where administered in good faith—if there is a misdiagnosis, a failure to monitor the patient after the drugs are given, or if the beneficial effects of the medications are outweighed by the side effects.[314]

Despite the therapeutic components of the right to refuse treatment, there are arguments that this right has antitherapeutic aspects. For example, some argue that allowing mental health patients the right to refuse treatment will cause them to remain involuntarily committed for a longer period of time. Some researchers argue that treatment refusers stay hospitalized up to twice as long as those who consent to treatment.[315] However, other studies have shown that it is not necessarily the case that refusers are hospitalized longer than those who consent.[316]

A 1986 study by Julie Zito and her colleagues, for example, found that in fact there was no significant difference between refusers and consenters in

---

311. See, e.g., Washington v. Harper, 494 U.S. 210, 242–43 (1990) (Stevens, J., dissenting); Riggins v. Nevada, 112 S. Ct. 1810, 1817 (1992) (Kennedy, J., concurring); Heller v. Doe, 113 S. Ct. 2637, 2650 (1993) (Souter, J., dissenting). In *Harper*, Justice Stevens expressed his concerns that the failure to require that medication decisions be made by an independent party could lead to the improper use of medication for control purposes rather than for treatment. Id. at 245–46; see also, e.g., Rennie v. Klein, 476 F. Supp. 1294, 1299 (D.N.J. 1979) (evidence at trial indicated that psychiatric medications were being used routinely as a means of patient control and as a substitute for treatment); modified and remanded, 653 F.2d 836 (3rd Cir. 1981), vacated and remanded, 458 U.S. 1119 (1982).

312. *Rennie*, 476 F. Supp. at 1305–1306.

313. Harold Bursztajn et al., Medical and Judicial Perceptions of the Risks Associated With the Use of Antipsychotic Medication, 19 Bull. Am. Acad. Psychiatry & L. 271, 273–74 (1991).

314. Dorfman, Fear and Pretextuality, supra note 34, at 816–19 (citing McCarron, supra note 307, at 481–82); Delila M. J. Ledwith, Jones v. Gerhardstein: The Involuntarily Committed Mental Patient's Right to Refuse Treatment With Antipsychotic Drugs, 1990 Wis. L. Rev. 1367, 1373 (1990).

315. See Steven K. Hoge et al., A Prospective, Multicenter Study of Patient's Refusal of Antipsychotic Medication, 47 Arch. Gen. Psychiatry 949 (1990); Shelly Levin et al., A Controlled Comparison of Involuntarily Hospitalized Medication Refusers and Acceptors, 19 Bull. Am. Acad. Psychiatry & L. 161, 169 (1991).

316. On the competency of patients with schizophrenia to engage in such decisionmaking, see e.g., Barry Rosenfeld et al., Decision Making in a Schizophrenic Population, 16 Law & Hum. Behav. 651, 660 (1992) (after differences in verbal functioning controlled for, no differences remained between abilities of schizophrenic patients and nonpatients to consistently weigh risks, benefits and probabilities).

length of hospital stay.[317] Rather, the study found that the difference in length of stay related to the diagnosis of the patient. Specifically, they found that schizophrenic patients tended to consent more often than those with bipolar and schizoaffective disorder. Because of their diagnosis, however, schizophrenic patients were hospitalized for longer periods of time, although they tended to consent to medications.[318]

Another concern regarding the therapeutic value of the right to refuse treatment for mental health patients is that patients will become less compliant with medications overall.[319] However, in a study comparing patients refusing drugs, mental health diagnosis, and length of hospital stay, Zito and her colleagues found that the rate of medication noncompliance was no different before due process requirements were established than afterward.[320]

Although some argue that the right to refuse treatment has a number of disadvantages, the empirical research on this issue demonstrates that there is a significant therapeutic value in affording mental health patients the right to refuse treatment.

3. Antitherapeutic results of the current means of implementing the right to refuse treatment. Although empirical evidence indicates that the right to refuse treatment does have therapeutic jurisprudence value, research shows that the manner in which this right is enforced is not always as therapeutic. For example, research indicates that whereas the purpose of judicial review for patients wishing to refuse psychiatric treatment is meant to ensure that mental health patients are afforded due process protections, this is not always the case. Judges regularly defer to experts,[321] almost always approving involuntary medication applications.[322] Whereas such deference may be appropriate in instances where the physician has met the burden of proving that the patient lacks the capacity to refuse antipsychotic medication, automatic deference without a careful assessment of the evidence presented can render the right to refuse treatment meaningless and antitherapeutic.

Another problem is the general lack of interest of judges, lawyers, and society in mental disability law, a lack of interest often exacerbated in cases seeking to vindicate the civil rights of institutionalized mentally disabled per-

---

317. Zito et al., supra note 6, at 328.

318. Id.

319. Id. at 334.

320. Id.

321. Cournos et al., supra note 12; see also Michael G. Farnsworth, The Impact of Judicial Review of Patients' Refusal to Accept Antipsychotic Medications at the Minnesota Security Hospital, 19 Bull. Am. Acad. Psychiatry & L. 33, 40 (1991); Perlin, Morality, supra note 18; see also Stefan, supra note 218 (discussing the inappropriate reliance on the professional judgment standard by courts in "negative rights" claims such as the right to refuse treatment, and the problems of excessive expert deference).

322. Sauvayre, supra note 301, at 221 (citing studies indicating that most medication hearings are decided in favor of the physician). These studies include one by Cournos et al., supra note 6 (petition for involuntary medication granted in 95% contested cases), and by Jorge Veliz and William James, Medicine Court: *Rogers* In Practice, 14 Am. J. Psychiatry 62 (1987) (in 100% of the cases of involuntary medication studied, the court ruled in favor of medicating the patient).

sons.[323] Such disinterest conveys the message that patients' rights, including the right to refuse treatment, are not important.

The prevalence of ineffective assistance of counsel in mental disability cases, including medication hearings, further hampers the adequate implementation of the right to refuse treatment.[324] For those with mental disabilities, there is a dearth of competent counsel.[325] This problem results from a variety of factors, including mere ignorance of the law,[326] attorneys' fear of their own clients,[327] and a feeling of responsibility or blameworthiness for the acts of their clients.[328] As a result, advocates and attorneys run the risk of compromising their client's civil rights by either not zealously representing their client or not choosing to represent their client's expressed interest and instead representing what they—the attorneys and the advocates—feel is the client's best interest or in society's best interest. In the context of the right to refuse treatment, this lack of zealous advocacy can lead to unnecessary forced medication as well as an increased perception (and potential reality) by doctors, courts, and patients that the right to refuse treatment is illusory.

With the many difficulties in implementing the right to refuse treatment, many patients have grown to doubt the value of their own civil rights. Many patients view the right to refuse and the hearings as a sham.[329] They are leery of the entire process and thus are often deterred from exercising their rights. When patients feel that it is useless or meaningless to exercise their right to refuse treatment, not only may they get unwanted treatment, but they also cannot get the therapeutic benefits of having the right to refuse treatment, as discussed above.

Finally, a significant problem with the implementation of judicial review is

---

323. Perlin & Dorfman, Renaissance, supra note 11; see generally Joel Haycock et al., Mediating the Gap: Thinking About Alternatives to the Current Practice of Civil Commitment, 20 N. Eng. J. Crim. & Civ. Confinement 265, 272 (1994), quoting Perlin & Dorfman, Sanism, supra note 12 ("Mental disability law generally regulates powerless individuals represented by passive counsel in invisible court proceedings conducted by bored or irritated judges").

324. See Perlin, Fatal Assumption, supra note 34 (on inadequate role of counsel in involuntary civil commitment cases).

325. Id. at 42.

326. Dorfman, Fear and Pretextuality, supra note 34, at 815 (citing Matter of Brazleton, 604 N.E. 2d 376, 376–377 (Ill. App. 1992)). In Brazleton, counsel, who had been appointed to appeal an involuntary commitment order sought leave to withdraw, on the basis of the conclusion that counsel made that the appeal lacked merit and would be frivolous. The appellate court denied the motion as the attorney failed to present any issues which could be raised to support his client or any potential arguments that could be made. Furthermore, the appointed counsel incorrectly believed that the burden on the state was preponderance of the evidence; in 1979, some thirteen years before, the United States Supreme Court had ruled in Addington v. Texas, 441 U.S. 418 (1979), that the burden was at least clear and convincing evidence.

327. Perlin, Fatal Assumption, supra note 34, at 42.

328. Eric Turkheimer & Charles D. H. Parry, Why the Gap? Practice and Policy in Civil Commitment Hearings, 47 Am. Psychologist 646, 650 (1992).

329. Lisa A. Callahan, Challenging Mental Health Law: Butting Heads With a Billygoat, 4 Behav. Sci. & L. 305, 313 (1986) (patient interviews regarding the value of due process procedures used to determine whether a patient could be involuntarily medicated indicated that many were dissatisfied with the process and found it to be a sham).

that of frequent delays.[330] Such delay causes unnecessarily long involuntary commitment that compromises the liberty interests of patients to be free from involuntary confinement.

Much of the research done on the implementation of due process procedures for mental health patients wishing to refuse medications indicates that there is no significant difference in results obtained before and after right to refuse laws were enacted.[331] This evidence and the other implementation problems suggested by research results indicates a need to review the means of enforcing the right to refuse treatment.

D. Conclusion

The empirical research done regarding the right to refuse treatment for mental health patients coupled with a survey of the practical implementation of this right indicates that patients' rights advocates and attorneys, in enforcing the right to refuse treatment, could benefit from using therapeutic jurisprudence. Therapeutic jurisprudence provides a tool to allow counsel representing persons with mental disabilities to identify antitherapeutic problems and to attempt to resolve these issues so as to enhance patients' civil rights in a therapeutic manner. Finally, therapeutic jurisprudence is a potential means for attorneys and advocates representing medication refusers to see how they can improve the quality of their advocacy to ensure that the expressed interest of their clients is represented.

V. Conclusion

Three years ago, one of us reviewed Ann Braden Johnson's masterful (yet largely unsung) book, *Out of Bedlam: The Truth About Deinstitutionalization*, and discussed what the public saw as the causal link between constitutionally based mental disability law decision making and homelessness:

> Nurtured by radical psychiatrists (such as Thomas Szasz and R. D. Laing), spurred on by politically-activist organizations pushing egalitarian social agendas (such as the ACLU), a cadre of brilliant but diabolical patients' rights lawyers dazzled sympathetic and out-of-touch judges with their legal *legerdemain*—abetted by wooly-headed social theories, inapposite constitutional arguments, some oh-my-god worst-case anecdotes about institutional conditions, and a smattering of "heartwarming, successful [deinstitutionalization] case [studies]"—as a result of which courts entered orders "emptying out the mental institutions" so that patients could "die with their rights on." When cynical bureaucrats read the judicial handwriting on the hospital walls, they then joined the stampede, and the hospitals were thus emptied. Ergo deinstitutionalization. Ergo homelessness. Endgame.[332]

For years, social critics—H. Richard Lamb, E. Fuller Torrey, Rael Isaac, and

---

330. Farnsworth, supra note 318, at 40.

331. See Paul S. Appelbaum and Steven K. Hoge, The Right to Refuse Treatment: What the Research Reveals, 4 Behav. Sci. & L. 279 (1986).

332. Perlin, supra note 36, at 559–60 (footnotes omitted).

Virginia Armat—have scapegoated patients' rights lawyers as the true villains in the development of mental disability law.[333] A reexamination of the key cases in question—including *specifically* ones that these critics list as the true *bete noires*[334]—suggests that this analysis is simply "dead wrong."[335] Therapeutic jurisprudence helps illuminate why and how the analysis is wrong.

A reexamination of involuntary civil commitment, right to treatment, and right-to-refuse-treatment law from a therapeutic jurisprudence perspective provides some important insights. First, it is clear that therapeutic jurisprudence is compatible with an expanded rights-based perspective in all three areas. This is clearest in the right-to-treatment area but is also substantially present in the others as well. Second, it is clear that the antitherapeutic effects often associated with these areas of civil rights law (especially with the right to refuse treatment) are often attributable to antitherapeutic aspects of the judicial process (e.g., unnecessarily delayed hearings)[336] and to economic externalities (e.g., the lack of treatment alternatives that confront indigent persons).[337]

* * *

Joel Haycock and John Petrila have recently expressed concern that therapeutic jurisprudence may lead to a diminution of rights-based interests in mental disability law.[344] Elsewhere, we have articulated our visions of a sanist-based and pretexts-ridden mental disability law system.[345] We have previously attempted to combine these concerns by looking to therapeutic jurisprudence as a means of exposing the sanist and pretextual bases of that system.[346] The legal research that we have conducted for this article has confirmed our intuitive feelings: that therapeutic jurisprudence analyses largely support a rights-based perspective in mental disability law; that therapeutic jurisprudence can be an effective tool for ferreting out the law's sanist and pretextual bases; that it is *not* oxymoronic to characterize a constitutionally grounded jurisprudence as "therapeutic"; and that, finally, as the pendulum continues to swing (and as public ire grows over the perceived rights-based excesses of mental disability law),[347] therapeutic jurisprudence may indeed offer a path to redemption for a constitutionally based mental disability law jurisprudence.

---

333. See, e.g., Torrey, supra note 135, at 156–59; H. Richard Lamb, Deinstitutionalization and the Homeless Mentally Ill, 35 Hosp. & Community Psychiatry 899, 902 (1984); Rael Isaac & Virginia Armat, Madness in the Streets: How Psychiatry and the Law Abandoned the Mentally Ill 107–60 (1990).

334. See Perlin, supra note 53, at 87–88 (discussing Torrey's criticisms of Lessard v. Schmidt, O'Connor v. Donaldson, and Wyatt v. Stickney).

335. Perlin, supra note 36, at 560.

336. See supra Part III.

337. See Wagenaar & Lewis, supra note 298.

344. See Petrila, supra note 30; Haycock, supra note 28.

345. See supra note 34, citing sources.

346. See especially Perlin, Law and Disability, supra note 5; Perlin, Pretextual Bases, supra note 12; Dorfman, Fear and Pretextuality, supra note 34.

347. See Michael L. Perlin, "Tea Leaves Here, Tea Leaves There: The Supreme Court's Mental Disability Law Docket, the Legislatures, the Public, and You" (paper presented to National State Mental Health Program Directors' annual Forensic Directors conference, Sept. 1994, Tampa, FL); on the pendulum metaphor, see e.g., 1 Perlin, supra note 5, § 1.04 at 24 n.134 (citing sources).

Chapter 39

Therapeutic Jurisprudence: Five Dilemmas to Ponder

Christopher Slobogin

Therapeutic jurisprudence is no longer a fledgling movement. The number of scholars who purport to be viewing law through the therapeutic jurisprudence "lens" has grown appreciably in the short time since David Wexler and Bruce Winick introduced the idea in the early 1990s.[1] A perspective that originated within a small circle of academicians best known for their involvement in the mental health law field has since made itself felt in areas as disparate as tort,[2] contract,[3] and criminal law,[4] in articles written by practitioners as well as law professors.[5] With its growth from infancy into young maturity, the time has come for an assessment of its likely impact and its potential pitfalls. This article is among the preliminary efforts in that vein.[6]

Therapeutic jurisprudence, as described by its progenitors, is "the study of the role of the law as a therapeutic agent."[7] It is meant to encourage explo-

---

1. Essays in Therapeutic Jurisprudence (David B. Wexler & Bruce J. Winick eds., 1991). See also, Therapeutic Jurisprudence: The Law as Therapeutic Agent (David B. Wexler ed., 1990).

2. See e.g., Daniel W. Shuman, Therapeutic Jurisprudence and Tort Law: A Limited Subjective Standard of Care, 46 S.M.U.L. Rev. 409 (1992).

3. Jeffrey L. Harrison, Class, Personality, Contract, and Unconscionability, 35 Wm. & Mary L. Rev. 445 (1994).

4. See, e.g., David B. Wexler, Inducing Therapeutic Compliance Through the Criminal Law, 14 Law & Psychol. Rev. 43 (1990).

5. Robert L. Sadoff, Therapeutic Jurisprudence: A View from a Forensic Psychiatrist, 10 N.Y.L.S. J. Hum. Rts. 825 (1993); Deborah A. Dorfman, Through a Therapeutic Jurisprudence Filter: Fear and Pretextuality in Mental Disability Law, 10 N.Y.L. Sch. J. Hum. Rts. 805 (1993).

There are several compendiums of articles explicitly or implicitly adopting the therapeutic jurisprudence approach. In addition to the two books mentioned in note 1, supra, and this inaugural issue of Psychology, Public Policy, and Law, see 64, 2 Am. J. Orthopsychiatry; 20 New Engl. J. on Crim. & Civ. Confinement, Summer 1994; S.M.U.L.J. Part 2; N.Y.L. Sch. J. Hum. Rts. (Part 3). See also Bibliography of Therapeutic Jurisprudence Literature, 10 N.Y.L. Sch. J. Hum. Rts. 915 (1993).

6. See also John Petrila, Paternalism and the Unrealized Promise of Essays in Therapeutic Jurisprudence, 10 N.Y.L. Sch. J. Hum. Rts. 877 (1994) (book review); James D. Acker, Book Review, 20 J. Psychiatry & L. 273 (1992); Gary Melton, Book Review, 39 Contemp. Psychol. 215 (1994).

7. Wexler & Winick, supra note 1, at 8.

ration of substantive and procedural law to determine its therapeutic and countertherapeutic effects. Although, as with most disciplines, rational speculation is permitted, those applying this perspective usually attempt to determine the effect of a rule or practice through resort to empirical research carried out by behavioral scientists; thus, therapeutic jurisprudence, Wexler says, is "truly interdisciplinary."[8] As such, he hopes it will avoid a narrow doctrinal focus (which he claims is characteristic of "traditional" mental health law[9]) and influence legislators and administrators as well as the courts.[10]

As an illustration of therapeutic jurisprudence, consider one of Wexler's favorite examples.[11] Building on health care compliance principles summarized by two psychologists (Meichenbaum and Turk), Wexler has proposed several changes in the typical procedure used for conditionally releasing insanity acquittees. Instead of the nonexistent or perfunctory hearing now held, Wexler suggests that the acquittee eligible for release be required to agree to the release conditions in open court and in front of significant others and that the judge (or prosecutor, if there is one) engage the acquittee in "mild counterarguments" suggesting the conditions will be breached. These proposals are designed to encourage the acquittee to endorse rather than merely assent to the conditions and thus increase the chance the acquittee will abide by and benefit from them. Wexler urges that they be tested empirically to see if they do in fact encourage compliance.

Other examples of therapeutic jurisprudence come from the "co-founder" of the movement, Bruce Winick. Winick has plumbed psychological theory and research in an effort to show the "therapeutic value of choice." He contends that people who are involved in choosing a given goal feel more committed to the goal, are more likely to accomplish it, and improve in self-esteem. Building on this premise, he has written a number of articles arguing that a mentally ill person's choice should be honored whenever possible, including when a person of limited competency assents to recommended treat-

---

8. David B. Wexler, New Directions in Therapeutic Jurisprudence: Breaking the Bounds of Conventional Mental Health Law Scholarship, 10 N.Y.L. Sch. J. Hum. Rts. 759, 761 (1993).

9. See, e.g., Wexler & Winick, supra note 1, at 3 ("mental health law has been doctrinal, constitutional and rights-oriented," and the typical mental health law course has relied "heavily, if not exclusively, on judicial opinions in an effort to extract and critique doctrinal development").

10. See generally David B. Wexler, Therapeutic Jurisprudence and Changing Conceptions of Legal Scholarship, 11 Behav. Sci. & L. 17 (1993).

11. Wexler originally published the article described below in 27 Crim. L. Bull. 18 (1991), under the title Health Care Compliance Principles and the Insanity Acquittee Conditional Release Process. It was reprinted in Wexler & Winick, supra note 1, at 199, and further references to it in this article will be from this source. Wexler has used the gist of the article as an example of therapeutic jurisprudence in a number of other pieces. See, e.g., the introduction to Wexler & Winick, supra note 1, at 13–14; Putting Mental Health into Mental Health Law, 16 L. & Hum. Behav. 27, 36–37 (1992); Therapeutic Jurisprudence and the Criminal Courts, 35 Wm. & Mary L. Rev. 279, 291–98 (1993); Wexler, supra note 10, at 27 (1993); and most recently, Wexler, supra note 8, at 762–63.

ment[12] or hospitalization,[13] in the context of making "bets" with the government as to the outcome of a treatment program,[14] and when a person refuses mental health treatment.[15]

Wexler's and Winick's articles are paradigmatic of therapeutic jurisprudence. They rely on behavioral science research and theory in making suggestions designed to enhance the therapeutic impact of substantive and procedural law and of the judge's, lawyer's, and clinician's roles in applying it. When relevant behavioral science data do not exist, they construct testable hypotheses that they hope will inspire empirical work.[16]

Whereas these examples are limited in scope and involve the relative backwater of mental health law, others have made use of therapeutic jurisprudence in more ambitious undertakings outside of that substantive area. For instance, Daniel Shuman has argued that therapeutic jurisprudence may be useful in evaluating the worth of a fault-based tort system: It is possible, he suggests, that such a system has more of a "restorative effect" on claimants than a system based on insurance or no-fault approaches to compensation.[17] Similarly, Jeffrey Harrison has referred to the concept in arguing for a broadening of the unconscionability rubric in contract law; he contends that easing the limitations on claims of unconscionability is a good idea in part because it will increase the self-esteem of those victimized by unfair contracts.[18]

---

12. Bruce J. Winick, Competency to Consent to Treatment: The Distinction Between Assent and Objection, 28 Hous. L. Rev. 15 (1991), reprinted in Wexler & Winick, supra note 1, at 41.

13. Bruce J. Winick, Competency to Consent to Voluntary Hospitalization: A Therapeutic Jurisprudence Analysis of Zinermon v. Burch, 14 Int'l J. L & Psychiatry 169 (1991), reprinted in Wexler & Winick, supra note 1, at 83.

14. Bruce J. Winick, Harnessing the Power of the Bet: Wagering with the Government as a Mechanism for Social and Individual Change, 45 U. Miami L. Rev. 737, 752–72 (1991), reprinted in Wexler & Winick, supra note 1, at 219.

15. Bruce J. Winick, New Directions in the Right to Refuse Mental Health Treatment: The Implications of Riggins v. Nevada, 2 Wm. & Mary Bill of Rts. J. 205 (1993); Bruce J. Winick, The Right to Refuse Mental Health Treatment: A Therapeutic Jurisprudence Analysis, 17 Int'l J. L. & Psychiatry 99 (1994) (hereinafter Right to Refuse). Winick has also used the therapeutic value of choice idea in articles arguing for reform of the criminal system, particularly in connection with procedures for evaluating and adjudicating competency to stand trial. Bruce J. Winick, Presumptions and Burdens of Proof in Determining Competency to Stand Trial: An Analysis of Medina v. California and the Supreme Court's New Due Process Methodology in Criminal Cases, 47 U. Miami L. Rev. 817, 855–57 (1993); cf. Bruce Winick, Incompetency to Stand Trial: An Assessment of Costs and Benefits, and a Proposal for Reform, 39 Rutgers L. Rev. 243, 271–72 (1987).

16. See the chapter titled Therapeutic Jurisprudence as a Research Tool, in Wexler & Winick, supra note 1, at 303–320. This chapter also looks at the possibility of "comparative" research, aimed at learning how other countries handle similar problems.

17. Daniel W. Shuman, Making the World a Better Place Through Tort Law?: Through the Therapeutic Looking Glass, 10 N.Y.L. Sch. J. Hum. Rts. 739, 755–56 (1994) [hereinafter Shuman]. See also Daniel W. Shuman, The Psychology of Compensation in Tort, 43 Kan. L. Rev. 39 (1994).

18. Harrison, supra note 3, at 493–500.

The types of proposals generated by those who claim to be applying a therapeutic jurisprudence perspective are innovative and worthwhile (a point reiterated throughout this article, particularly in the conclusion). Like any jurisprudence, however, therapeutic jurisprudence faces several conceptual and practical dilemmas, and unless these dilemmas are recognized, it cannot be evaluated fully and may fall short of its significant promise. In this article, five such dilemmas are described: (a) the *identity* dilemma, (b) the *definitional* dilemma, (c) the dilemma of *empirical indeterminism*, (d) the *rule of law* dilemma, and (e) the *balancing* dilemma. Analysis of these dilemmas raises substantial questions about the viability of therapeutic jurisprudence (which, for convenience, will often be abbreviated to "TJ" in the remainder of this article). The intent, however, is not to "trash" this new movement but to anticipate the problems it may face, and perhaps help avoid them.

I. *The Identity Dilemma*

The first question one might ask about therapeutic jurisprudence is what is meant by the term *therapeutic*. Wexler, for one, would prefer to keep the concept vague. As he states, "as a mere heuristic, therapeutic jurisprudence has eschewed a tight definition of 'therapeutic,' and has similarly left open the nature of the party or person upon whom therapeutic or antitherapeutic consequences might be visited."[19] Nonetheless, exploring what the concept *might* mean is useful as a way of considering whether TJ offers anything unique to legal discourse. Perhaps it is nothing more than routine legal analysis dressed up with a fancy name. Or perhaps it is so similar to one or more other jurisprudences (e.g., legal realism, law and economics, or feminist theory) that it is merely redundant.

At its broadest, *therapeutic* could simply mean beneficial, whereas *counter-* or *anti-therapeutic* could mean harmful. Defined in this way, however, the concept is indistinguishable from any other analytical process; all reform of the law and the legal system is meant to redress some type of harm or confer some type of benefit. Therapeutic jurisprudence would merely be another name for figuring out what is best.

Alternatively, given its progenitors' reliance on social science, the concept could be limited by reference to psychological theory. So defined, *therapeutic* might mean beneficial in light of what behavioral science has to say about the effect of the law and why people behave the way they do. Once again, however, this meaning may be so broad as to eliminate any unique feature of TJ. It sounds suspiciously like warmed over legal realism, which, at least initially, touted the social sciences as the primary vehicle for meaningful law reform.[20] It comes even closer to a modern derivation of legal realism known as social science in law (or the law and society and law and psychology movements),

---

19. Wexler, supra note 8, at 765.

20. Cf. Shuman, supra note 17, at 743 ("Applied outside the sphere of traditional mental health law, the interdisciplinary, empirical focus of therapeutic jurisprudence may be dismissed as the proverbial old wine in a new bottle—reconstructed legal realism.")

which involves the explicit use of the behavioral sciences to examine the assumptions the law makes about human behavior (e.g., that juries pay attention to instructions) and the effects of rules (e.g., does the exclusionary rule deter police misconduct?).[21] If TJ is only about introducing the insights of the behavioral sciences into the law, it does not add anything of jurisprudential import, even as a "heuristic."

A third definition of the word *therapeutic* could be as follows: beneficial in the sense of improving the psychological or physical well-being of a person. After all, enhancing individual welfare is the commonly understood intent of therapy. Under this definition, therapeutic jurisprudence would become *the use of social science to study the extent to which a legal rule or practice promotes the psychological and physical well-being of the people it affects.* Although Wexler wants to avoid too many constraints, this definition seems to conform to the idea encapsulated in his statement that TJ is the study of law as a "therapeutic agent."[22]

Of the three definitions considered, this last one comes closest to presenting a unique perspective. Consider first how it differentiates TJ from social science in law. Therapeutic jurisprudence, under this third definition, could be said to adopt a preference for laws that promote well-being. Social science in law, by contrast, does not necessarily dictate *any* normative stance but rather seeks to test assumptions endorsed or proposed by the law.[23]

---

21. See generally John Monahan & Laurens Walker, Social Science in Law (3d ed. 1994).

22. At other times, however, Wexler seems to propose that TJ be aimed at achieving results that reflect understandings about human behavior, and not just at results that are therapeutic, a view much closer to traditional legal realism. See Wexler, supra note 8, at 761–62 (therapeutic jurisprudence "proposes we explore ways in which, consistent with principles of justice, the knowledge, theories, and insights of the mental health and related disciplines can help shape the development of the law"). Id.

23. As with any descriptive statement about a "jurisprudence," this one can be challenged. Gary Melton, for instance, has asserted that the social science in law movement "is based at least implicitly on reverence for the moral values that underlie the Constitution (e.g., autonomy, privacy, and equality) and respect for the law as an institution that reifies our sense of community...." Gary B. Melton, Law, Science and Humanity: The Normative Foundation of Social Science in Law, 14 L. & Hum. Behav. 315, 321 (1990). But others disagree. Haney, for instance, suggests that "we [meaning the law and psychology movement] [have] a tendency to take the paradigms handed to us by the legal systems too uncritically and to work around the edges of these issues without developing a critical perspective on their center," and hypothesizes that this tendency stems from a desire to be accepted by the legal system. Craig Haney, Psychology and Legal Change: The Impact of a Decade, 17 Law & Hum. Behav. 371, 384 (1993). Trubek and Esser identify one characteristic of the founders of the law and society movement as "untroubled reformism," a perspective which

> presumes that the product, procedures, and projects of social science should be used as instruments in the service of the legal system [and is adopted by researchers] untroubled by the purposes to which their product is put either because they accept the purposes and worth of the law or because they believe that it is not the role of a social science to define the purposes to which it will be put.

David M. Trubek & John Esser, Critical Empiricism in American Legal Studies: Paradox, Program, or Pandora's Box, 14 Law & Soc. Inquiry 3, 11 (1989). Small concludes that "[t]here is no clear, distinct normative foundation [to social science in law scholarship] be-

This difference plays itself out in two ways. First, because social science in law addresses the law on its own terms, its only challenge to legal rules is indirect and occurs only when the assumptions underlying them are not supported empirically.[24] On the other hand, a therapeutic jurisprudence approach might dictate challenge of an antitherapeutic rule even when the rule is scientifically validated. For example, assume a court opts for a narrow right (say, permitting refusal of psychiatric medication only in rare circumstances) because, in its view, the overall (financial) cost of a broader right would be prohibitive or because, to the contrary, a broadly defined right would not be exercised by an appreciably greater number of people. Although either of these views may be empirically verifiable (which would be the contribution of social science in law), they produce results that could well be unacceptable under a therapeutic jurisprudence approach, for reasons provided by Winick that were alluded to earlier in this article.

At the same time, social science in law contemplates use of social science where TJ may have nothing to say. For example, in a recent article, Shuman explored the psychology of deterrence in an effort to discern whether the tort system deters harmful behavior.[25] The article canvasses a wide array of social science—from psychoanalysis and behaviorism to cognitive psychology and social learning theory—but its sole goal is to determine whether one of the principal assumptions of an important area of law makes sense, the classic role of the social science in law movement. Although Shuman can be considered one of the leading proponents of therapeutic jurisprudence, and indeed has applied it to tort law on at least three occasions,[26] he mentions the concept only once in his piece on deterrence, and then only in passing,[27] presumably because exploring the "therapeutic" impact of deterrence would be an incoherent exercise.

---

cause there is no clear, distinct SSL jurisprudence." Mark A. Small, The Normative Foundation of Social Science in Law Revisited: A Reply to Melton, 15 Law & Hum. Behav. 325 (1991).

This is not to say that social scientists cannot adopt a normative view. Indeed, Melton's own "psychological jurisprudence," which is based on autonomy values purportedly found in the ethical principles of the psychology discipline is such an attempt. Id. at 321. The point here is merely that the "social science in law" movement is not normatively driven; the extent, if any, to which it has been identified with a "progressive" agenda is an outgrowth of its exposure of legal myths, not a conscious gameplan.

24. See supra note 23. See also Austin Sarat, Legal Effectiveness and Social Studies of Law: On the Unfortunate Persistence of a Research Tradition, 9 Legal Stud. F. 23 (1985):

> The history of social research on law is quite closely tied to the study of legal effectiveness.... Legal effectiveness research begins by identifying the goals of legal policy and moves to assess its success or failure by comparing the goals with the results produced. Where, as is almost inevitably the case, the results do not match to goals, attention is given to the factors which might explain the "gap" between law on the books and law in action. Id.

25. Daniel W. Shuman, The Psychology of Deterrence in Tort Law, 42 U. Kans. L. Rev. 115 (1993).

26. In addition to the article already noted, supra note 17, see Shuman, supra note 2, and Daniel W. Shuman, The Duty of the State to Rescue the Vulnerable in the United States, in The Duty to Rescue 131 (Michael A. Menlowe & Alexander McCall Smith eds., 1993).

27. Shuman, supra note 25, at 166 n. 303.

In short, TJ can be distinguished from social science in law, despite the reliance of both on social science research, because the latter is a technological means of answering questions posed by the law, whereas the former is a prescriptive jurisprudence that happens to rely on that technology. Linking TJ to a preference for promoting rules that enhance well-being may also distinguish it from another movement with strong social science roots—law and economics. The most prolific adherents of this approach, including Judges Richard Posner and Robert Bork, believe that the ultimate goal of the law should be efficiency, in the sense of wealth maximization.[28] Defined in this way, law and economics jurisprudence would seem to differ significantly from therapeutic jurisprudence; even in a capitalist society, the amount of assets one has is not necessarily related to psychological or physical well-being. Irrationality, altruism, and emotional and personal fulfillment may often be more satisfying (psychologically speaking) than selfish wealth maximization.[29] If so, TJ and economic jurisprudence will often be at loggerheads.

It is worth noting, however, that a more recent strand of law and economics scholarship has stressed the artificiality of the premises underlying the original Posnerian approach—in particular the premise that people rationally pursue their selfish interests—and has adopted positions more sensitive to the idea that the law should take into account other types of preferences, including nonrational and societal preferences.[30] Harrison's article on the unconscionability doctrine, alluded to at the beginning of this article, is a good example of this new scholarship. The bulk of his article is an attack on one of the bulwarks of traditional law and economics—Pareto superiority, or the idea that exchanges that make all parties feel better off are to be encouraged. Harrison disputes this doctrine's underlying premise that the avowed preferences of the parties should determine the validity of a contract, at least when one of the parties come from the poorer classes; such people, he hypothesizes, have been taught by society to expect less and thus are more willing to accept a bad deal. To help remedy this situation, he proposes expanding unconscionability doctrine to allow more *ex post* challenges of their agreements. He contends that this step will not only redress unequal bargaining power, but could also have a reverse educative effect, teaching them to expect more. In the long run, it would increase the self-esteem of downtrodden groups by empowering them to fight back.[31]

---

28. Richard A. Posner, the Economics of Justice (1981); Richard A. Posner, Utilitarianism, Economics, and Legal Theory, 8 J. Legal Stud. 103 (1979); Richard A. Posner, Legal Formalism, Legal Realism, and the Interpretation of Statutes and the Constitution, 37 Case W. Res. L. Rev. 179, 185–86 (1986); Robert Bork, Emerging Substantive Standards: Developments and Need for Change, 50 Antitrust Bull. 179 (1981–82).

29. See generally Jeffrey L. Harrison, Egoism, Altruism, and Market Illusions: The Limits of Law and Economics, 33 UCLA L. Rev. 1309 (1986).

30. For examples of the "new" law and economics scholarship, a development which some have labeled socioeconomics, see Richard H. McAdams, Relative Preferences, 102 Yale L.J. 1 (1992); Kenneth G. Dau-Schmidt, An Economic Analysis of the Criminal Law as a Preference-Shaping Policy, 1990 Duke L.J. 1; John R. McKean & Robert R. Keller, The Shaping of Tastes, Pareto Efficiency and Economic Policy, 12 J. Behav. Econ. 232 (1983).

31. Harrison, supra note 3, at 445–51, 493–500.

Does this new, more humanistic law and economics theory preempt therapeutic jurisprudence? Given the elastic boundaries of any jurisprudence, I am not sure this is even a meaningful question. However, in this regard, it is interesting to look again at Harrison's article. Perhaps because Pareto superiority and other economic concepts do not easily incorporate softer variables like self-esteem, Harrison found it useful, if not necessary, to turn to Wexler and Winick's work in developing his thesis. In other words, therapeutic jurisprudence may have provided him a perspective that law and economics did not.[32]

Finally, one needs to consider the relationship of TJ to other modern jurisprudences, such as critical legal studies, the feminist movement, and critical race theory.[33] Although social science in law is not normative, and law and economics, at least in its old version, does not seem to endorse a therapeutic approach, these latter three movements might be said to share the same goal as TJ—improving well-being—albeit with respect to specific groups (i.e., the politically oppressed, women, and African Americans) rather than everyone.[34] Indeed, TJ could be seen as an umbrella for, and therefore somewhat redundant with, any specific-group perspective.[35]

---

32. Cf. Winick, supra note 14, at 738–39 (noting that his proposal for using the power of the bet to provide incentives for treatment and other societally sought behavior "could be seen as deriving from...modern economic theory. I prefer the paradigm of psychology").

33. Of course, this list leaves out literally scores of other "jurisprudences," including major ones like positivism, formalism, and legal realism, and less well-known ones like practical legal studies, civic republicanism, and law as interpretation. See generally Bailey Kuklin & Jeffrey W. Stempel, Foundations of the Law: An Interdisciplinary and Jurisprudential Primer 131–192 (1994). For some of these—i.e., legal realism and practical legal studies—the jurisprudences discussed in the text can serve as proxies; critical legal studies, feminist theory, and critical race theory all derive in large part from legal realism, as do practical legal studies. Positivism and formalism, on the other hand, clearly do not, and for this reason are easily distinguishable from therapeutic jurisprudence. Finally, civic republicanism, which focuses on law as a consensus of the community, and the law as interpretation movement, which looks at how the meaning of law derives from its "interpretative community," seem quite different as well. Id. at 182–83, 176–78.

34. No attempt to describe these jurisprudences in more detail will be made here. See generally Kuklin & Stempel, supra note 33, at 174–82. For some examples of possible overlap between therapeutic jurisprudence and these various theories, see Charles Lawrence, The Id, the Ego, and Equal Protection: Reckoning with Unconscious Racism, 39 Stan. L. Rev. 317, 329–31 (1987) (using psychoanalytic theory to support the proposition that racism is a "public health problem"); Mari J. Matsuda, Public Response to Racist Speech: Considering the Victim's Story, 87 Mich. L. Rev. 2320, 2335–2341 & n. 84 (1989) (describing, based on social science studies, the "negative effects" of racist speech, including emotional stress, psychosis, suicide, and loss of self-esteem); Martha Fineman, Dominant Discourse, Professional Language, and Legal Change in Child Custody Decisionmaking, 101 Harv. L. Rev. 727 (1988) (looking at psychological impact of the "gender neutrality paradigm" in family law). See also Joseph A. Baldwin, African Self-Consciousness and the Mental Health of African-Americans, 15 J. Black Stud. 177 (1984).

35. Including—ironically, given TJ's mental health law origins—the movement to force legal recognition and understanding of those with mental disability, best identified with Michael Perlin and his writings on "sanism" and "pretextuality." The link between the later movement and TJ is clearest in Michael L. Perlin, Therapeutic Jurisprudence: Understanding the Sanist and Pretextual Bases of Mental Disability Law, 20 New Eng. J. Crim. & Civ. Con-

At a lower level of abstraction, however, there would seem to be some significant differences between TJ and these other movements. First, as already indicated, TJ is closely wedded to the social sciences, particularly the behavioral sciences, whereas some of those writing under the rubric of these other movements (especially those associated with critical legal studies) often ignore or are even actively hostile to such information.[36] Second, although the promotion of well-being, particularly psychological well-being, is clearly the primary goal of TJ, it often seems secondary to these other jurisprudences; the central focus of critical legal studies, feminist jurisprudence, and critical race theory may well be a push for power and understanding, rather than therapeutic results per se.[37] Third, even if a significant overlap between TJ and these other movements exists, TJ may provide a useful perspective precisely because it is not bound to a particular group. For instance, work on the benefits of choice, of the type pioneered by Winick, or on the psychological effects of a fault-based tort system, noted by Shuman, may be more likely to come from the global perspective afforded by TJ than from the narrower focus of feminist jurisprudence or critical race theory.

Does TJ's expansive nature create an identity dilemma for its adherents? It does tend to blend in with the new law and economics and other modern jurisprudences. These latter movements themselves have inchoate boundaries, however. Perhaps it is fair to say that TJ has a uniqueness to it, but more by way of emphasis than content.

---

finement 369 (1994). See also Michael L. Perlin, Pretexts and Mental Disability Law: The Case of Competency, 47 U. Miami L. Rev. 625 (1993); Michael L. Perlin, The Jurisprudence of the Insanity Defense (1994).

36. See, e.g., Mark G. Kelman, Trashing, 36 Stan L. Rev. 293 (1984) (concluding that empirical research is unlikely to aid in achieving the CLS utopia, because "the technical problems are just too great"); William H. Simon, Homo Psychologicus: Notes on a New Legal Formalism, 32 Stan. L. Rev. 487, 488–89 (1980) (decrying the formalism of psychologically inspired discourse about law); Martha L. Fineman & Anne Opie, The Uses of Social Science Data in Legal Policymaking: Custody Determinations at Divorce, 1987 Wis. L. Rev. 107, 126–39 (rejecting custody research because of its male bias).

37. For instance, one commentator has summarized the three themes of feminist jurisprudence as: (a) the difference between men and women, (b) the different voice of women's reasoning, and (c) the dominance of the male legal and social hierarchy. Cass R. Sunstein, Feminism and Legal Theory, 101 Harv. L. Rev. 826–28 (1988) (book review). These themes may overlap with, but do not coincide with, the therapeutic agenda. See also Nancy S. Ehrenreich, Pluralist Myths and Powerless Men: The Ideology of Reasonableness in Sexual Harassment Law, 99 Yale L. J. 1177 (1990) (a "fem-crit" piece focusing on the extent to which harassment subordinates women, rather than on its psychic impact on them). As another example, consider the fact that, given the class-based thesis of the piece by Harrison discussed in the text, one would think he would have turned to scholarship from the "crits," but in fact there is very little in that literature about improving the self-esteem of the disadvantaged. See generally William N. Eskridge, Jr. & Philip P. Frickey, Cases and Materials on Legislation: Statutes and the Creation of Public Policy 329–30 (1988) (stating that CLS writings focus on revising the current structure of representative government, encouraging more activist judicial interpretation of statutes, and using the law's status to transform society by moving it away from the goal of wealth maximization and toward achievement of greater rights for those with lower socioeconomic status).

II. The Definitional Dilemma

The conclusion that TJ's goal of enhancing psychological well-being gives it a vision independent of other jurisprudences solves only half the definitional problem, however. Whereas the words therapeutic and well-being may be specific enough to help differentiate TJ from other perspectives, they are still extremely vague. At least some effort must be made to identify the meaning of these terms if this jurisprudence is to be critically evaluated.

One might respond, perhaps, that the meaning of these phrases is self-evident. Consider, for instance, the four examples in the beginning of this article. Can anyone seriously dispute the therapeutic impact of ensuring insanity acquittees' adherence to treatment plans, empowering individuals through promoting choice, constructing a tort system that restores the psychological balance of plaintiffs, and increasing the self-esteem of those traditionally subject to contracts of adhesion? The answer is yes. Although I personally agree with the authors' assumptions that their suggestions will be therapeutic, I also think one can plausibly play the devil's advocate with each.

For instance, as evidenced by the articles cited above, both Wexler and Winick believe that involving patients in construction of the treatment plan and having them commit to it is therapeutic. They contend that such involvement not only enhances the person's motivation to achieve treatment goals, but is also a psychological good in its own right. Winick in particular speaks of this latter aspect, stressing that choice can be "developmentally beneficial" because it avoids "infantilizing" the person and undergirds the "basic human need" to "exercis[e] self-determination."[38]

In the abstract, conferring decision-making power would seem to enhance psychological well-being. But there is not necessarily a causal relationship between the two. Whereas Winick persuasively argues that forcing treatment on a person can be countertherapeutic, he is less sensitive to the effect of forcing people to make a choice, when they would rather delegate that decision to others. Consider in this regard Michael Shapiro's review of the informed consent research performed by Charles Lidz and several others.[39] Lidz and his colleagues found that patients are often willing to surrender decision making about medication to the doctor; consequently, the authors, like Winick, urged that doctors promote more self-direction.[40] Shapiro suggests, however, that the patients' "apparent abandonment of choice [may be] an autonomous choice to relieve oneself of burdens so that other aspects of life can be dealt with more adequately."[41] He notes, for instance, that the Lidz study itself found that the same patients who allowed doctors to be the primary decision makers about

---

38. Right to Refuse, supra note 15, at 108–109.

39. Michael H. Shapiro, Is Autonomy Broke? (book review) 12 Law & Hum. Behav. 353 (1988).

40. C. Lidz et al. Informed Consent: A Study of Decisionmaking in Psychiatry 326–34 (1984) (hereinafter Lidz). The authors conclude that "it is not unduly harsh to conclude that current informed consent policy has been a dismal failure in the settings we studied, at least when measured against the loftier goals of the doctrine" and then discuss changes in medical education and improvements in consent forms, among other proposals.

41. Shapiro, supra note 39, at 353.

treatment insisted on making their own decisions "about nonmedication-related issues...after their clinicians had made suggestions, [and] strongly resisted suggestions about how they should conduct their lives outside [the clinic]."[42] Apparently, the patients "chose" to exercise only certain choices. Accordingly, Shapiro speculates, "[e]ven if many persons have gone too far (or not far enough?) in delegating tasks, 'correcting' the situation may harm autonomy more than it helps it. Promoting autonomy is [conceivably] hazardous to it."[43]

Furthermore, empowering people to make choices implies making sure they have complete information. In fact, however, giving people multiple options may cause anxiety and perhaps even be debilitating. Examples of situations where one might beneficially eschew decision making abound—ranging from patronizing grocery stores and cable stations with too many selections to choosing from among five different treatment modalities with different risks and benefits. As the so-called "therapeutic exception" to the informed consent doctrine recognizes, it may be more therapeutic to keep certain information from the patient.[44] Perhaps, in some situations and for some people, ignorance really is bliss.

A second definitional issue raised indirectly by the Wexler and Winick articles concerns how one evaluates the therapeutic value of the treatment itself. For example, improving compliance with conditional release programs may not meet everyone's definition of therapeutic if, as is often the case,[45] the program is designed primarily to curb dangerous behavior rather than treat the whole person.[46] Similarly, facilitating a choice to enter a public mental institu-

---

42. Id. at 359 (quoting Lidz, supra note 40, at 321).

43. Id. at 354.

44. One of the leading cases on the issue is Canterbury v. Spence, 464 F.2d 772 (D.C. Cir. 1972)

> It is recognized that patients occasionally become so ill or emotionally distraught on disclosure as to foreclose a rational decision, or complicate or hinder the treatment, or perhaps even pose psychological damage to the patient....The critical inquiry is whether the physician responded to a sound medical judgment that communication of the risk information would present a threat to the patient's well-being.

See also Cobbs v. Grant, 8 Cal.3d 229, 502 P.2d 1 104 Cal. Rptr. 505 (1972); A.B.A. Model Rule of Professional Conduct Rule 1.4 Comment (4) ("a lawyer might withhold a psychiatric diagnosis of a client when the examining psychiatrist indicates that disclosure would harm the client.")

45. See J. Goldmeier et al., Community Intervention with the Mentally Ill Offender: A Residential Program, 8 Am. Acad. Psychiatry & L. Bull. 72 (1980); R. Rogers & J. L. Cavanaugh, A Treatment Program for Potentially Violent Offender Patients, 25 Int'l J. Offender Therapy and Comp. Criminology 53 (1981).

46. Indeed, an argument can be made that, to the extent they are coercive, such programs should be required to focus solely on reducing dangerousness. See Christopher Slobogin, Involuntary Community Treatment of People Who Are Violent and Mentally Ill: A Legal Analysis, 45 Hosp. & Comm. Psychiatry 685 (1994). If one accepts the latter conclusion, then a tension may develop between the most "therapeutic" approach and the approach dictated by principles of justice. This type of tension raises the "internal" balancing issue discussed later in this article. See infra text accompanying notes 88–107.

tion or accept treatment recommended by public mental health professionals may not improve psychological well-being if the primary agenda behind the hospitalization or treatment is to protect the public.[47] The definitional dilemma is captured nicely by one of the meanings assigned to the word *therapeutic* in *Webster's New Collegiate Dictionary:* "an agency designed or serving to bring about social adjustment."[48] Public mental health professionals, and probably most other people as well, would accept social adjustment as a major goal of therapy. Most, however, would probably also recognize that a socially adjusted person may not be a happy or fulfilled person, or even a productive person.[49] As John Petrila points out,[50] TJers—most of whom will be professionals, either legal or scientific—must be careful about implicitly accepting a definition of *therapeutic* that fails to take into account consumer preferences.[51]

Differing perceptions of well-being might also change one's view of Shuman's and Harrison's articles. Assuming a fault-based system for resolving automobile injury claims increases a sense of "empowerment" and "vindication" (to use Shuman's words),[52] is this outcome really therapeutic, or will it breed hatred and vindictiveness when, psychologically speaking, forgiveness (or forgetting) is more appropriate?[53] Assuming a broader unconscionability doctrine

---

47. See generally Petrila, supra note 6, at 897–904. Petrila concludes that "studies conducted to date show little correlation between professional identification of what people in treatment need and self-identified need." Id. at 899.

48. Webster's New Collegiate Dictionary 1210 (5th ed. 1977).

49. Consider, for instance, the conclusions of a psychiatrist that Sir Winston Churchill, Oliver Cromwell, George Frederick Handel, and Hart Crane suffered from mood disorders and that 38% of the leading artists and writers she treated in 1982 and 1983 sought treatment for depression or manic-depressive illness, compared to 1% of the general population. Richard Holguin, Study Supports Madness-Creativity Theory, Philadelphia Inquirer, Sept. 23, 1984, at C14. According to Kay Jamison, director of the Affective Disorders Clinic at UCLA, "[t]here are positive aspects to some of the serious psychiatric disorders, and it's important to treat the negative sides and not get rid of the positive....Clearly having a mood disorder doesn't make you creative, but creative people may be helped along by some aspects of their mood disorders." Id. Also relevant here are the images so provocatively raised by the play Equus, in which a psychiatrist agonizes over whether ridding a patient of his "undesirable" aspects might also eradicate what is "best" in him.

50. Petrila, supra note 6, at 899.

51. Of course, Wexler and Winick would not disagree with these latter observations. In the articles at issue, they do not purport to be vouching for particular treatments, but rather make proposals for assuring that, assuming a good treatment plan has been developed, patients follow it. And elsewhere they call for research to determine the most efficacious treatment modalities for those with mental and other disabilities. Wexler & Winick, supra note 1, at 25 ("Much more work is of course needed in the area of the intended and unintended consequences of forced hospitalization and other coercive treatments on mental patients, drug abusers, and alcoholics.")

52. See Shuman, supra note 17, at 756.

53. As the Bible teaches, "Ye have heard that it hath been said, An eye for an eye, and a tooth for a tooth: But I say unto you, That ye resist not evil: but whosoever shall smite thee on the right cheek, turn to him the other also." Matthew, 5:38–39 (King James). Consider also the view that no-fault divorce has reduced the hostility of divorce litigation: Herbert Jacob, Silent Revolution: The Transformation of Divorce Law in the United States 151

increases assertiveness and hope among those who are disadvantaged, will this outcome increase well-being or will it merely increase frustration and tension as unfulfillable expectations are created?[54]

Again, my own reaction to each of the four articles used here as examples is positive. The point is merely that one might sensibly question whether encouraging participation in treatment plans, cajoling people into making choices and commitments, facilitating feelings of vindication, and enhancing self-esteem are unmitigated psychological goods. Even assuming that the psychological effects the authors posit occur, we cannot be sure that these effects are therapeutic until we define the term. Perhaps TJ is about promoting autonomy, regardless of its other consequences. Perhaps instead it is about enhancing therapy in the sense of social adjustment. Maybe, as a third possibility, it is an academic term for "happiness jurisprudence." The tension between these possibilities will probably be reconcilable in most instances, but it will exist often enough to create a definitional dilemma.

Furthermore, as the adherents of the critical legal studies movement are so fond of reminding us, the choice of definition in those situations where it makes a difference will usually be ideologically driven, rather than selected according to some "neutral" criterion. In the mental health arena, for instances, the old libertarians may opt for an autonomy orientation to TJ, whereas the old paternalists may opt for a social adjustment or happiness version. Thus, to give a more specific illustration, the argument from a lawyer (Winick) for a right to refuse treatment derived from the therapeutic value of choice might be attacked as "antitherapeutic" by a mental health professional, to the extent that patients exercising such a right regress psychologically.[55] At least until the definitional dilemma is resolved, then, TJ may often merely be putting old wine in new bottles.

III. The Dilemma of Empirical Indeterminacy

Assuming an adequate definition of *therapeutic*, the next challenge is to try to measure the therapeutic effect of a given rule. Therapeutic jurisprudence re-

---

(1988); Wendell H. Goddard, A Report on California's New Divorce Law: Progress and Problems, 6 Fam. L. Q. 405, 414–15 (1972). But see Lynn D. Wardle, No-Fault Divorce and the Divorce Conundrum, 1991 B.Y.U. L. Rev. 79, 99–103 (1991).

54. Consider, for instance, the possible consequence of convincing minorities that they have "equal opportunity." Orlando Patterson states that "when the equal opportunity doctrine goes beyond the middle classes and is wholly accepted by the poor and the dispossessed, especially that segment which is black, we are no longer dealing with a harmless bourgeois faith, but with the most sinister form of ideological mystification." Inequality, Freedom, and the Equal Opportunity Doctrine, in Equality and Social Policy 15, 29 (W. Feinberg ed., 1978). See also Alan Freeman, Racism, Rights and the Quest for Equality of Opportunity: A Critical Legal Essay, 23 Harv. C.R.-C.L. L. Rev. 295, 370 (1988) ("the knowledge of equality of opportunity as a largely false hope undermined by racism may drive many nonwhites to more rage than their white counterparts").

55. Cf. Paul S. Appelbaum & Thomas G. Gutheil, Rotting With Their Rights On: Constitutional Theory and Clinical Reality in Drug Refusal by Psychiatric Patients, 7 Am. Acad. Psychiatry & L. 306 (1979).

lies on social science theory and research—in particular, mental health and behavioral work—to answer this question. Indeed, TJ *must* rely on such theory and research because, as noted earlier, that reliance is a prime aspect of its uniqueness as a jurisprudence. As a result, TJ may be more dependent on social science than any other prescriptive jurisprudence.

Unfortunately, the latter discipline may frequently be unable to provide TJ with much useful information for two reasons, one which is general in nature and one which is more specific to TJ. First, social science has often proved inadequate to the task of investigating legal assumptions. Second, even if this general concern can be overcome, the types of empirical questions TJ asks may be particularly difficult to answer. Consequently, TJ may be confronted with another dilemma: To the extent it grows dependent on social science data it may rest on shaky foundations, but to the extent it does not it loses its allure.

A. The Lack of "Science" in Social Science

That social science methods are often particularly difficult to apply in the legal context is common knowldge to those who, like the proponents of TJ, work with these methods. The best type of research is a true experiment.[56] This methodology involves random assignment of identical populations to conditions that meaningfully isolate the variable in which the researcher is interested. Unfortunately, the inherent conservatism of the law (in many ways a good thing) is a scientist's nightmare, because it significantly inhibits randomization. Furthermore, because the types of manipulation necessary to test legal assumptions often involve doing something (or refraining from doing something) to *people,* they may run up against ethical or constitutional (i.e., equal protection) prohibitions.[57]

Thus, for example, arranging experiments in which well-matched populations are randomly assigned to conditions varying the right to refuse psychoactive medication, the degree of contract unconscionability, or the type of compensation for tort injuries is likely to be a formidable task.

---

56. Monahan & Walker, supra note 21, at 57. The true experiment can be compared to the case study (typically too anecdotal), the correlational study (which has difficulty demonstrating causality and eliminating third variables), and the quasi-experiment (which does not involve randomization). Id. at 61.

57. One line of experiments of direct relevance to TJ that has been frustrated by such prohibitions are those attempting to evaluate the efficacy of community treatment programs for those with serious mental disabilities. A true experiment would randomly assign those found to meet the commitment criteria to either the hospital or the community treatment program (with perhaps a third group being left untreated). However, judges (and clinicians) are unlikely to allow the imminently dangerous to go unhospitalized. Christopher Slobogin, Treatment of the Mentally Disabled: Rethinking the Community-First Idea, 69 Neb. L. Rev. 413, 424 (1990). Note, however, that within hospitals and other institutions, many types of random assignments may be ethically and legally permissible. Cf. Bruce Winick, A Preliminary Analysis of Legal Limitations on Rehabilitative Alternatives in Corrections and Correctional Research, in New Directions in the Rehabilitation of Criminal Offenders 359 (S. Martin et al. eds., 1981) ("if the proposed research is not otherwise constitutionally impermissible, random assignment of research subjects, with limited exceptions, should not be considered to violate equal protection.")

Even more modest true experiments can flounder on methodological matters. Say, for instance, one wants to test the hypothesis underlying Wexler's proposition that health care compliance principles will work in the conditional release context. A reasonable true experiment would require two courts (one of which would adopt Wexler's proposals) to agree to the random assignment of insanity acquittees who are eligible for release and try to match these two groups according to recidivism potential, treatment needs, and other characteristics that might affect compliance. To isolate the dependent variable, the judge using Wexler's methods should be similar in all other respects to the judge who did not (perhaps it should be the same person). One would also have to ensure that the monitoring of the released acquittees was comprehensive; otherwise, the criterion variable (compliance) would not be measured adequately.[58]

To counter the problems associated with field studies of the type just described, analogue and laboratory studies, both of which permit more control over the variables, are often the experimental methods of choice. For example, an analogue version of the study mentioned above might survey two groups of insanity acquittees selected because of their similar characteristics, one of which is asked how it would react to normal release procedures and the other how it would react to Wexler's approach. A laboratory study might assess the obedience of college students to pressure from authority figures. Unfortunately, the generalizability of these latter studies to the issue in question is highly suspect. The inherent tradeoff between internal and external validity is well-documented.[59]

Furthermore, as many commentators have pointed out,[60] even sound research can be tainted by value judgments. It is interesting to note, for instance, that two of the most prominent "therapeutic jurisprudence" articles on the impact of the adversarial process in the civil commitment context reach diametrically opposed conclusions.[61] John Ensminger and Thomas Liguori, both em-

---

58. Wexler notes some additional difficulties with testing his hypothesis through a true experiment. Wexler & Winick, supra note 1, at 218 n.148 ("if...the experimental judges hold the hospital to certain standards of behavioral contracting and the like, the hospital may well begin to employ those high standards with all patients, including those falling under the jurisdiction of the control judges.").

59. See generally Vladimir J. Konecni & Ebbe B. Ebbesen, External Validity of Research in Legal Psychology, 3 Law & Hum. Behav. 39 (1979).

60. See supra note 36. See also David Faigman, To Have and Have Not: Assessing the Value of Social Science to the Law as Science and Policy, 38 Emory L. J. 1005, 1026–39 (1989) (discussing four ways in which researcher bias can affect social science: (a) the selection of problems; (b) the determination of the contents of conclusions; (c) the identification of fact; and (d) the assessment of evidence); Haney, supra note 23, at 388 (1993) (after noting the dominance of White males in the psychology discipline, Haney states "I worry that our research agendas are badly skewed and our problem definitions are extremely limited by these demographic facts."); Michael Seigel, A Pragmatic Critique of Modern Evidence Scholarship, 88 NW. U. L. Rev. 995, 1038 (1994) ("Determining whether research results are generalizable between places and over time—that is, overcoming the problem of external validity—requires the use of reasoning techniques that include analogy, imagination, common sense, experience, and induction").

61. John J. Ensminger & Thomas D. Liguori, The Therapeutic Significance of the Civil Commitment Hearing: An Unexplored Potential, 6 J. Psychiatry & L. 5 (1978); Marc Amaya & W.V. Burlingame, Judicial Review of Psychiatric Admissions: The Clinical Impact

ployees of New Jersey's legal advocacy department when they wrote their article, conclude that "the civil commitment process has considerable potential for therapeutic effect."[62] In contrast, Marc Amaya and W. V. Burlingame, both mental health professionals who have testified at children's commitment proceedings, list a number of "harmful results" that can emerge from such hearings, many of which are equally applicable to adults.[63] Whereas Ensminger and Liguori aver that the hearing represents an open acknowledgement that the patient's hospitalization is involuntary, thus avoiding the antitherapeutic "double message" conveyed by professionals who act as if they care only about the patient's well-being,[64] Amaya and Burlingame state that "the fragile relationship between youth and therapist may be ruptured by the court encounter in which the therapist opposes releases and marshals suitable but threatening 'evidence.'"[65] Ensminger and Liguori conclude that the "hearing may...provide a mechanism for educating the family as to the needs of a particular member caught in the commitment process."[66] while Amaya and Burlingame state that "the already tenuous or damaged relationship between youth and parent may be further eroded in response to the open collision and conflict in court."[67] Generally, Ensminger and Liguori see a benefit to the "airing" provided by the adversarial clash, whereas Amaya and Burlingame worry about significant psychological harm from these procedures.[68]

This divergence between the two articles may result from differing definitions of therapeutic, and thus may better illustrate the point made previously about the effect of ideology on terminology. But the two studies seem to focus on the same variables—the psychological impact of a judge, counsel, and

---

on Child and Adolescent Inpatients, 20 J. Amer. Acad. Child Psychiatry 761 (1981). Although these articles appeared before the advent of TJ, they were both reprinted in Wexler, supra note 1, at 243, 261, the first collection of TJ essays.

62. Ensminger & Liguori, supra note 61, at 7.

63. Amaya & Burlingame, supra note 61, at 281.

64. Ensminger & Liguori, supra note 61, at 13, 14, 20.

65. Amaya & Burlingame, supra note 61, at 766.

66. Ensminger & Liguori, supra note 61, at 24.

67. Amaya & Burlingame, supra note 61, at 766.

68. Compare Ensminger & Liguori, supra note 61, at 20 ("we have observed generally, that the introduction of commitment hearings leads to better documentation and earlier staffing [and] a greater tendency to release patients...in cases where the case for committability appears to be marginal") with Amaya & Burlingame, supra note 61, at 766 (adversarial proceedings may create "a considerable possibility that a seriously troubled youth may be unexpectedly and abruptly released without a plan or placement, through accident, judicial ignorance or whimsy, a technicality, or the unpreparedness or inexperience on the part of treatment personnel."). Compare also Ensminger & Liguori, supra note 61, at 21 (hearings may provide an opportunity to provide a "therapeutic community" through "crisis resolution" techniques which include "face-to-face confrontation" with those involved "under skilled neutral leadership" and "open communication without fear of reprisal") with Amaya & Burlingame, supra note 61, at 766 (hearings may cause "stress [which] may overtax the child's or adolescent's adaptive resources, precipitating a psychotic episode, regression, withdrawal, or aggressive acting out" and "severe declines in self-esteem...in response to testimony regarding diagnosis, personality, structure, or dynamics," and loss of "considerable amounts of treatment time...as the child or adolescent prepares his 'defense,' putting emotional energies into securing release rather than addressing pathology.").

cross-examination on the parties—which suggests that the dissonance between the two pieces is not a matter of characterization. Instead, it appears that the authors, who in both cases relied on their observations and experiences, simply see the commitment process differently. Influenced by their training and education, they looked at the adversarial process and its effects from vantage points that (inevitably?) led them to contrary conclusions.

I obviously do not mean to suggest that such research should not be done.[69] For the most part, it is better to have empirically based information than to do without it.[70] Again the point is a simple one: TJers' heavy reliance on such data will mean their conclusions are subject to all of the vagaries that afflict social science itself.

B. The Definitional Dilemma Revisited

Even methodologically sound, value-free research (or perhaps *especially* research that is done well and close to value free) will obtain indefinite results when the criterion variable is something as broad in scope as therapeutic impact. The typical TJ question is much more difficult to answer than, say, whether 12- or 6-member juries deliberate better, whether eyewitnesses are affected by weapons focus, or whether people predicted to be dangerous are subsequently violent,[71] all of which present difficult enough research agendas. Rather, therapeutic jurisprudence might ask something like: Does the adversarial process have an overall negative or positive impact on a prospective patient's psychological well-being? Do plaintiffs who receive compensation under a fault-based tort system feel more restored than those who are compensated under a no-fault system? Would a broad unconscionability doctrine increase self-esteem?

None of these questions is necessarily unanswerable. However, it can be anticipated that, for each, constructing a methodology that isolates the proper

---

69. I myself have engaged in the empirical enterprise, each time with the expert assistance of behavioral scientists. See, e.g., Gary B. Melton et al., Community Mental Health Centers and the Courts: An Evaluation of Community-Based Forensic Services (1985); Slobogin et al., The Feasibility of a Brief Evaluation of Mental State at the Time of the Offense, 8 Law & Hum. Behav. 305 (1984); Christopher Slobogin & Joseph E. Schumacher, Reasonable Expectations of Privacy and Autonomy in Fourth Amendment Cases: An Empirical Look at "Understandings Recognized and Permitted by Society," 42 Duke L.J. 727 (1993); Norman Finkel & Christopher Slobogin, Insanity, Justification, and Culpability: Toward a Unifying Schema, Law & Hum. Behav. (in press). Of course, my hope for each piece was that it would be a useful contribution to the relevant legal issues. I must also say, however, that these experiences with empirical research reinforce the points in the text. Despite earnest efforts, both the methodology and the neutrality of these studies fall far short of pristine "science." See, e.g., Slobogin & Schumacher, supra, at 743–51.

70. This statement assumes that the legal system knows how to evaluate the empirical information it receives, which is a major assumption. Cf. David W. Barnes and John M. Conley, Statistical Evidence in Litigation 3–4 (1986) (describing the use of social science research in constitutional decisionmaking as "cautious at best and uninformed at worst; the nonuse and misuse of statistics have been more common than its use").

71. These are all typical research questions, as a perusal of the table of contents of Law and Human Behavior and similar journals will attest.

variables and then devising outcome measures that accurately gauge concepts like "psychological well-being," "restoration," and "self-esteem" will require painstaking work. Of course, the latter concepts can be broken down into subhypotheses. In some ways, however, this approach makes matters more difficult: More studies need to be conducted, and one must decide how to combine the results. Consider the empirical questions that Wexler himself has derived from the work of Ensminger and Liguori and related articles in an effort to test the therapeutic value of adversarial procedures: Is there greater therapist knowledge about the patient in jurisdictions which authorize independent evaluations? Do commitment hearings lead to better documentation and earlier staffing? Are the therapeutic community principles endorsed by Ensminger and Liguori in conflict with other well-documented psychological theories that suggest that, at least with people diagnosed with schizophrenia, the law should avoid family confrontations? "[I]n the treatment of schizophrenics, how important is straight talk and the avoidance of mixed messages?"[72]

In summary, the indeterminacy of the empirical information on which therapeutic jurisprudence relies may be exacerbated by the definitional dilemma discussed earlier in this article. The typical uncertainty of social science, although frustrating, does not vitiate its usefulness to the law.[73] But the social science generated by TJ may be unusually uncertain. If so, TJ will be relatively more speculative, for a longer period of time.[74] In the meantime, its proposals may be hard to take seriously.

IV. The Rule of Law Dilemma

Assume that methodologically sound, relatively value-free research has been conducted on a TJ-type question. Indefinite results are still likely, not because of methodological problems (these have been assumed away), but because the studied rule or practice will probably turn out to be neither wholly therapeutic nor antitherapeutic (i.e., it will benefit some and harm some). In such instances, a fourth dilemma for TJ may arise.

To see why, consider first several illustrations of situations in which TJ research might produce mixed results. It has already been suggested that, whereas choice may improve the psychological well-being of some, it may be harmful to others; similarly, a fault-based tort system may be therapeutic for some plaintiffs but may cause anxiety for those who do not like the stress of litigation, and a broader unconscionability doctrine may teach self-esteem in

---

72. Wexler & Winick, supra note 1, at 32–33, 37. For other examples of the provocative but complex types of questions TJ might ask, see Wexler & Winick, supra note 1, at 308–309 (concerning the therapeutic impact of a right to refuse treatment); David B. Wexler & Bruce J. Winick, Therapeutic Jurisprudence and Criminal Justice Mental Health Issues, 16 Men. & Phys. Dis. L. Rep. 225, 226–27 (1992) (concerning the therapeutic impact of forcibly treating death row inmates to restore them to competency).

73. See, e.g., Faigman, supra note 60, at 1051 ("The uncertainties that will continue to attach to even the best social research should only qualify its value.... An inability to explain completely human behavior hardly undermines the value of social science to the legal process.").

74. For other examples of this phenomenon, see infra note 81.

some cases but produce a loss of self-esteem in others.[75] Other examples of potential outcome indeterminacy are easily found in the TJ literature. For instance, Shuman has speculated that, because they increase the level of stress, reports filed under mandatory child abuse reporting statutes increase the likelihood of abuse, at least from parents who fit the battering parent syndrome.[76] Yet it may also be true that the report, and the therapeutic or legal intervention that accompanies it, improves the abuser's well-being and thus reduces the abuse; indeed, the available research suggests that reporting is correlated with psychological improvement in approximately 40% of the parents who are accused.[77] Keri Gould has suggested that the current ability of prosecutors, under the federal sentencing guidelines, to force offenders to choose between a stiff sentence and "ratting" on their colleagues in crime can be demoralizing to the offender and encourage disrespect for the system, thus exacerbating antipathy toward rehabilitation and recidivism[78]; it takes little imagination, however, to think of situations in which offenders could benefit from being encouraged to help put someone behind bars.[79] Jeffrey Klotz has suggested that removal of the psychotherapist-patient privilege might create a disincentive to commit crime (and thus be therapeutic) because patients would know that any statements they made to their therapists about criminal desires could be used against them.[80] Yet, it is also possible that eliminating the privilege might discourage some from making such statements in the first place, thus reducing the therapist's ability to recognize and treat violence proneness.[81]

---

75. Cf. Patricia J. Williams, Alchemical Notes: Reconstructing Ideals from Deconstructed Rights, 22 Harv. C.R.-C.L. L. Rev. 401, 419–20 & n. 54 (1987) (wondering whether defending consumers on the theory of unconscionability is worth the loss of their self-esteem entailed by claiming they are incompetent, stupid, weak, or desperate).

76. Daniel W. Shuman, The Duty of the State to Rescue the Vulnerable in the United States, in the Duty to Rescue: The Jurisprudence of Aid (Michael A. Melowe & Alexander McCall Smith eds., 1993).

77. Holly Watson & Murray Levine, Psychotherapy and Mandated Reporting of Child Abuse, 59 Am. J. Orthopsychiatry 246, 252–53 (1989). See also Gordon Harper & Elizabeth Irvin, Alliance Formation with Parents: Limit-setting and the Effect of Mandated Reporting, 55 Am. J. Orthopsychiatry 550, 554 (1985) (mandated reports improved parent cooperation with medical treatment).

78. Keri A. Gould, Turning Rat and Doing Time for Uncharged, Dismissed, or Acquitted Crimes: Do the Federal Sentencing Guidelines Promote Respect for the Law?, 10 N.Y.L. Sch. J. Hum. Rts. 835 (1993).

79. Gould herself notes that ratting can help prevent substantial harm to society, id. at 868–69, knowledge of which could significantly enhance the self-esteem of an informer.

80. Jeffrey A. Klotz, Limiting the Psychotherapist-Patient Privilege: The Therapeutic Potential, 27 Crim. L. Bull. 416 (1991).

81. Klotz disagrees with this latter assertion, citing Shuman and Weiner's findings that the existence of the privilege is generally not needed to elicit statements useful in pursuing therapy. Id. at 423–25. See Daniel W. Shuman & Myron S. Weiner, The Privilege Study: An Empirical Examination of the Psychotherapist-Patient Privilege, 60 N.C. L. Rev. 893 (1982). If his conclusion is correct, however, note the paradox: The idea that privilege law has little effect on patient behavior undercuts the entire premise of Klotz's article, which assumes that patients do pay attention to this law and will be affected by it.

A similar paradox may occur in Shuman's work. In a vein analogous to his privilege

In short, the typical TJ article seems to be based on thought-provoking but speculative theories that are likely to be only partially supported by any good research that is carried out. One could choose to be paralyzed by this indeterminacy and simply maintain the status quo. However, this option would ignore insights that have been empirically validated for a certain segment of the population and in any event is unlikely to be attractive to a true TJer. A more activist response would attempt to mirror the empirical results: The rule should be applied to those for whom it is therapeutic but not to those for whom it is not.

As many have recognized, however, any attempt to individualize the law may undermine it.[82] More specific to an assessment of TJ, abandoning "the rule of law" may well work to the ultimate detriment of those it affects, because it places so much authority in the hands of practitioners. For instance, if it is true that some batterers get worse and some get better after an abuse report, therapists might logically be required to report only those batterers likely to improve once the report is made. Given our current state of predictive knowledge and the usual quotient of human error, however, this approach could result in a considerable number of false positives and false negatives; the overall impact of this standard may well be more antitherapeutic than a rule requiring the reporting of all abusers or none.[83] In other words, the individual-

---

study, his article on the deterrent effect of tort law, discussed earlier, suggests that tort law has little impact on behavior. See Shuman, supra note 25. Yet the tone of still another Shuman article seems to make the contrary assumption in arguing that a subjective definition of reasonableness in the tort context will encourage mentally ill people to seek treatment. Shuman, supra note 2, at 424–27.

These various articles demonstrate the point made in the previous section about empirical indeterminacy and the resulting unsubstantiated speculation TJ may encourage. Further empirical testing of the assertions made in these articles is clearly needed but will be very difficult. In the meantime, because of the empirical gaps, we have a welter of apparently conflicting propositions, some of them from the same people.

82. The classic statement of the tension between rigid "rules" and flexible "standards" is found in Duncan Kennedy, Form and Substance in Private Law Adjudication, 89 Harv. L. Rev. 1685 (1976). After making the point repeated in the text, id. at 1688 ("It has been common ground...that the two great social virtues of formally realizable rules, as opposed to standards or principles, are the restraint of official arbitrariness and certainty"), he goes on to argue that attempting to decide in the abstract, independently of political factors, whether rules or standards exert the most control over individual actors is impossible. Id. at 1705–10.

83. A generous assumption, on the basis of diagnostic reliability studies, is that therapists could accurately identify those parents who would benefit from being reported 50% of the time. See David Faust & Jay Ziskin, The Expert Witness in Psychology and Psychiatry, 241 Science 31 (1988) (reporting reliability rates of from 49% to 1% for all diagnoses). If, as reported in the text, supra note 77, the 40–60 split between those who benefit from mandatory reporting and those who do not is correct, this accuracy rate would still result in a greater overall antitherapeutic impact than if abuse reporting were simply prohibited. Note that when, as will be typical, the split between those who will benefit from a rule and those who will not is not as close (e.g., 70–30), an "individualized" rule involving diagnostic decision making is even more likely to be countertherapeutic than an all-or-nothing one.

ized approach might leave too much discretion to people who are likely, in good faith or bad, to make the wrong decision.

The dilemma for TJ is how to decide whether the greatest good to the greatest number will come from individualizing a rule or from adopting a less flexible approach. Although this dilemma afflicts any attempt at legal reform, it may be particularly excruciating for TJ, given its quantitative empiricism. The choice is likely to be more informed, but also more painful.

V. The Balancing Dilemma

One final dilemma will inevitably afflict TJ proposals even when good research clearly indicates they improve the well-being of the people they affect. Put in question form, it can be encapsulated in this way: How much weight should be given to showing that a legal rule or practice is therapeutic in light of countervailing considerations? The balancing dilemma is inevitable because therapeutic results will always be counterbalanced by factors of some sort. Some will be trivial, but many will be substantial, perhaps even of constitutional dimension.

To date, those who write from a therapeutic jurisprudence perspective have pretty much dodged the balancing question. In the introduction to their book, Wexler and Winick stated the following:

> We assume general agreement that, *other things being equal*, mental health law should be restructured to better accomplish therapeutic values. But whether other things are equal in a given context is often a matter of dispute. Therapeutic jurisprudence, although it seeks to illuminate the therapeutic implications of legal practices, does not resolve *this* dispute, which requires analysis of the impact of alternative practices on other relevant values.[84]

In later pieces, Wexler states that TJ is meant to explore ways in which the insights of mental health and related disciplines can help shape the law, "consistent with principles of justice,"[85] and that TJ "in no way suggests that therapeutic considerations should trump other considerations such as autonomy, integrity of the fact-finding process, community safety, and many more."[86] These statements provide general acknowledgment of the balancing problem. However, with one exception to be described later, TJers have not attempted to construct a more specific framework for engaging in the balancing process.

Of course, therapeutic jurisprudence would still be able to produce intriguing notions without engaging in balancing; the latter task could be left to others. But paying attention to this issue is likely to increase the impact of TJ on legislators and courts, which otherwise might react dismissively to its proposals (e.g., "That's interesting, but..."). Furthermore, both TJ and society at large will be better off if its proponents have made a good faith effort to determine whether their solutions are feasible, not just in terms of therapeutic

---

84. Wexler & Winick, supra note 1, at XII (emphasis in original).

85. David B. Wexler, Justice, Mental Health, and Therapeutic Jurisprudence, 40 Clev. St. L. Rev. 517, 518 (1992).

86. Wexler, supra note 8, at 762.

concerns, but in light of political and social variables as well.[87] Finally, consideration of other interests might lead to recognition of previously unnoticed therapeutic or countertherapeutic impacts.

To better understand the balancing dilemma inherent in TJ, it is useful to divide the balancing process into "internal" and "external" components, with the first connoting a balancing between discrete individual interests and the second describing balancing between individual and other interests.

A. "Internal" Balancing

Proponents of TJ argue, and they seem to be right, that therapeutic values and other individual interests often "converge."[88] But when such convergence is not present—that is, when a proposal that is considered therapeutic for a particular person runs afoul of some other interest of that person—the need for internal balancing is triggered. As noted above, in this situation Wexler and Winick have repeatedly emphasized that therapeutic jurisprudence does not dictate the more therapeutic outcome; the goal of therapeutic jurisprudence is to pinpoint the therapeutic impact of legal rules, not to require that therapeutic values trump other values. Wexler has further asserted that, given this agenda, therapeutic jurisprudence "in no way supports paternalism, coercion, or a therapeutic state."[89]

As a conceptual matter, setting as one's goal the identification of therapeutic considerations, subsequently to be balanced against other considerations, is a coherent and sensible position. However, it may be one that is very difficult to maintain in practice, at least where internal (as opposed to external) balancing is concerned. The empiricism of TJ and its alluring call for therapeutic results may combine to create a tendency to support proposals that, although not necessarily "bad" in an ultimate sense, are thoroughly paternalistic.

For instance, assume that empirical testing discovers, contrary to Ensminger and Liguori's assertions, that adversarial commitment procedures are antitherapeutic for people with schizophrenia; further assume that the most therapeutic procedure for such people (and one that is just as accurate) is informal review by an independent mental health professional in the absence of counsel (a process sanctioned by the U.S. Supreme Court in *Parham v. J.R.*[90] for involuntary commitment of children).[91] From this research one might well conclude

---

87. Cf., Randy E. Barnett, Foreword: Of Chickens and Eggs—The Compatibility of Moral Rights and Consequentialist Analyses, 12 Harv. J. L. & Pub. Pol'y 611, 618 (1989). Barnett makes a standard distinction between "moral rights" analysis and consequentialist (TJ-type) analysis and argues that the former can

> obviate the need for costly and potentially tragic "social experiments" that may be recommended by faulty consequentialist analyses. Even when such experiments are destructive, there is often no efficient way to terminate them. It is far better to use a moral rights analysis to look before one leaps.

88. See Wexler, supra note 85, at 518–20.

89. Wexler, supra note 8, at 762.

90. 442 U.S. 584 (1979).

91. This hypothetical is not completely speculative. The assumption that adversarial procedures may be harmful to people with schizophrenia is supported not only by Amaya and Burlingame's conclusions, supra note 61, but also by "expressed emotion" theory, which

that adversarial commitment procedures should be eliminated. Unfortunately, this conclusion would conflict with voluminous precedent which, through analogy to constitutional rulings on the criminal process, guarantees the adult subjected to civil commitment the rights to an impartial judicial decision maker, counsel, confrontation, and compulsory process.[92]

How is this conflict between therapeutic and constitutional values to be resolved? Is this a case in which, all other things being equal, the therapeutic proposal should win out? Or is one of the things that needs to be balanced the fact that the Constitution is implicated and, if so, do its commands outweigh TJ's prescription?

These questions may pose a real dilemma, not just for therapeutic jurisprudence but for society at large. Therapeutic jurisprudence requires a focus on the therapeutic value of a rule, even a rule that is constitutional. If a "principle of justice," to use Wexler's phrase, is clearly antitherapeutic, a plausible argument can be made that it should be given *no* weight in the internal balancing process (where competing individual interests are involved), even when it comes from the supreme law of the land. The reasoning is as follows: Because the Bill of Rights is meant to protect the individual from harm by the state, we do not need it when that harm is empirically proven to be nonexistent;[93] in such cases, the Constitution is an empty formalism. Thus, empirical research indicating that adversarial procedures are antitherapeutic and no more accurate than informal procedures will create a strong urge to ignore legal precedent or at least to nullify it (by saying, e.g., that adults with schizophrenia would systematically waive the rights to counsel and confrontation if they knew what was good for them).[94] The logic of TJ, in other words, may obscure any values encapsulated in the Constitution not connected with therapeutic results.

Another example of the internal balancing dilemma comes from Robert F. Schopp, who has addressed it explicitly. In an article titled *Therapeutic Jurisprudence and Conflicts Among Values in Mental Health Law*,[95] he attempts to construct a framework for balancing "principles of justice" (in particular, the concept of autonomy) against therapeutic considerations. He concludes

---

suggests that a patient's schizophrenic symptoms can be seriously exacerbated by critical comments from and emotional overinvolvement with the family. See Wexler & Winick, supra note 1, at 28. The assumption that Parham-type procedures are as accurate as adversarial procedures was of course made in Parham itself, and may also be supported by Amaya and Burlingame's work. See supra note 68.

92. See generally Ralph Reisner & Christopher Slobogin, Law and the Mental Health System: Civil and Criminal Aspects 716–30 (2D ed. 1990).

93. One might make the novel argument that the Bill of Rights protects not only the rights of individuals subjected to state intervention but also the interests of the public generally, in this case the public's need to believe the commitment process is fair. Even assuming this public interest is constitutionally protected, it is not relevant to internal balancing, but rather to external balancing, to be discussed below.

94. Although one could further justify this approach by noting that the wording of the Sixth Amendment, from which these rights derive, only speaks of "criminal prosecutions," note that the foregoing reasoning would reject application of any positivist legal principle, including one that is clearly found in the Constitution.

95. 11 Behav. Sci. & L. 31 (1993).

that, under some circumstances, the state may be able to infringe a person's sovereignty in order to give him or her the capacity to make autonomous choices, but that nondangerous people who are *already* autonomous cannot be forced to improve their well-being or their autonomy. To Schopp, personal sovereignty should be given priority over improvement of a person's well-being because, in his words, doing so is necessary to maintain the person's "status as sovereign" and to enable that person "to define his own life and embrace various aspects of well-being as his well-being."[96]

Although persuasive as a matter of traditional legal analysis, this reasoning may create the same dilemma encountered in the adversarial procedures hypothetical. As Schopp admits, he is able to prioritize sovereignty over well-being only by assuming what he calls a "nonderivative value for sovereignty,"[97] that is, a deontological value rather than a consequentialist or empirically based value. Just as one arguing in favor of adversarial procedures in the face of their antitherapeutic impact must formalistically declare that the Constitution is the law of the land, Schopp is simply positing the necessity of affirming a person's "status as sovereign" and ability to "embrace various aspects of well-being as his well-being." But what if, as an empirical matter, no such necessity exists? As noted earlier, Winick has suggested that there is a basic human need for self-determination.[98] This conclusion can be questioned, however. For example, some Asian societies value allegiance to the family and the state over individual rights; perhaps it is more therapeutic to do so.[99] If so, why should an abstract desire for autonomy trump individual well-being?

In short, depending on the empirical findings, the logic of TJ could undermine the normative premises of the legal system. Of course, assuming the conflict is recognized, a TJer could simply refuse to adopt a therapeutically indicated position when it violates the Constitution or autonomy values. Once the

---

96. Id. at 41–42.

97. Id. at 43–44. Schopp notes that utilitarians, for instance, might deny a nonderivative value and states that "[t]his paper cannot resolve fundamental questions of moral philosophy such as the relative merit of utilitarian and autonomy based theories." Id.

98. Right to Refuse, supra note 15, at 108.

99. The recent international flap over the caning of Michael Fay in Singapore led several commentators to point out the trade-off between individualism and security. See, e.g., Asians Question America's Moral Authority to Lecture on Rights, Washington Post, Apr. 22, 1994, at A33 (speaking of a "clash of cultures, which pits the American emphasis on individual rights against Confucian respect for authority and the importance of community welfare"). Consider also this excerpt from David H. Bayley, Ironies of Law Enforcement, 3 Police and L. Enforcement 20–21 (1985):

> Assertive independence rather than harmonious membership is the mark of individual maturity in the United States....Not so in Japan; not so in China. The cost that Americans pay for rampant individualism may be very high and not solely in the area of crime: They may also pay in mental health, physiological well-being, and psychic satisfactions.

See generally Duncan Kennedy, The Structure of Blackstone's Commentaries, 28 Buffalo L. Rev. 205, 205–21, 257–65, 294–98 (1979) (identifying the contradiction between liberty and security in liberal societies).

therapeutic-empirical can of worms is opened, however, it will be difficult to shut. As the above examples illustrate, deontological reasoning can be difficult to sustain in the light of hard evidence disputing its premises, especially when addressing the legislative and policymaking audiences TJ wishes to influence; simply saying that therapeutic values do not automatically prevail does not eliminate their reductionist power. Furthermore, Wexler and Winick may have (unintentionally) exacerbated matters with their constant reference to the "sterility" of "traditional" mental health law,[100] the focus of which is precisely the constitutional and deontological values that TJ's findings could undermine.

At the same time, proponents of therapeutic jurisprudence should not be dismayed if their research occasionally challenges basic beliefs by shaking allegiance to such bromides as "adversarial procedures," "autonomy," and "arm-slength" contracts (the last a concept questioned in Harrison's article). The likelihood that therapeutic jurisprudence scholarship will magnify the tension between individualism and paternalism, and thus force a closer examination of the issue, is a good thing. The danger lies in denying it will have this effect, because doing so may foster a tendency to ignore other values or create a temptation to see the convergence of therapeutic and other values where none exists.

An example of the latter tendency may come from the work of Winick himself. Consider again Winick's proposal to permit individuals of marginal competence to assent to recommended psychiatric treatments. More specifically, he proposes that when the treatment agreed to is recommended by a physician, "it is appropriate to presume, in the absence of evidence of gross incompetence, that individuals who are able to express a choice are competent."[101] As I stated earlier, Winick makes plausible arguments, largely on the basis of empirical literature, that encouraging this practice will be therapeutic both because it improves treatment success and because it enhances the patient's sense of "autonomy, dignity, and self-efficacy."[102] However, concluding that the proposal will promote the individual's *sense* of autonomy says nothing about the separate, deontological issue of whether it is consistent with respect for the *concept* of autonomy. On the latter issue, Winick's primary observation justifying his approach is that "[a]n individual able to express a choice exercises at least some autonomy."[103] In fact, a good argument can be made that people

---

100. See, e.g., Wexler & Winick, supra note 1, at 5 (stating that traditional mental health law "surely has its place [but] a nearly exclusive emphasis on this approach is both risky and, after twenty years, sterile"). See also Winnick, supra note 12, at 20–21.

101. Wexler & Winick, supra note 1, at 66.

102. Wexler & Winick, supra note 1, at 72, 112, 125. (Note that these pages are from both Winick's competency to consent to treatment piece and his competency to consent to voluntary hospitalization work, the relevant portions of which are virtually identical).

103. Id. at 65. Winick also notes that the ability to exercise a choice standard is the standard apparently applied by the courts when the choice is for recommended treatment, but see Zinermon v. Burch, 494 U.S. 113 (1990), and that mentally ill people who are not grossly psychotic should not be treated any differently than others, especially in light of the variable nature of competency. Wexler & Winick, supra note 1, at 51–63. However, neither of these reasons confront the core question of whether the ability to express a choice represents a sufficient degree of competency to satisfy the demands of the autonomy precept.

who are only able to give assent of the type Winick envisions are not capable of the kind of self-determination one might require as a normative matter.[104] If this argument is correct, Winick's proposal, although attractive therapeutically, is inimical to the deontological autonomy value. Yet, far from recognizing this possibility, Winick asserts that adoption of the evidence-of-choice standard "*prevents* excessive paternalism."[105]

Whether Winick's proposal or an approach requiring a greater degree of competency for consent to treatment is ultimately "better" is not germane here (there is much to be said for both points of view).[106] What is relevant, especially so in light of his demonstrated commitment to autonomy as a philosophical matter,[107] is the ease with which Winick justifies his proposal on deontological grounds. Although he probably would not agree with this assessment, I think his writings on the assent issue show how one can be seduced by therapeutic concerns into slighting autonomy values.

----

104. Professor Elyn Saks has constructed an elaborate and convincing argument that the appropriate balance between what she calls the "abilities" aspect of autonomy and the "unconventionality" and "irrationality" aspects of autonomy requires a higher level of competency, to wit, an understanding of all evidence relevant to the treatment decision, as well as no patently false beliefs about that evidence. Elyn R. Saks, Competency to Refuse Treatment, 69 N.C. L. Rev. 945 (1991). Although Saks focuses on refusals of treatment, her analysis applies to assents as well; indeed, her article was originally titled Competency to Make Psychiatric Treatment Decisions. Addressing a proposal similar to Winick's, she writes:

> [T]his view thoroughly undermines competency doctrine by allowing the evaluator to make an assessment that the doctrine vouchsafes to the patient himself— what is a good or bad decision—and then to limit his liberty on the basis of the expert's personal values. The view, in short, is at odds with a fundamental purpose of competency doctrine.

Id. at 996. Contrary to Winick's assertion that the courts "accept" the evidence-as-choice standard, see supra note 103, she avers that consent to "routine and obviously beneficial treatment" is automatically honored "because the overwhelming likelihood is that treatment will be approved as the most appropriate course if the patient is found incompetent; hence the finding [of incompetence] is of no practical significance." Id., at 996 n. 208.

See also Richard J. Bonnie, The Competence of Criminal Defendants: Beyond Dusky and Drope, 47 U. Miami L. Rev. 539, 545 & n. 29 (1993) (rejecting a proposal by Winick in the competency to stand trial context similar to the one described in the text because "[i]n the end...it effectively forecloses inquiry on the competence of a person to waive legal safeguards designed to protect incompetent defendants.").

105. Winick & Wexler, supra note 1, at 65 (emphasis added).

106. If autonomy values are to be considered paramount, then one might prohibit recommended treatment upon mere assent unless, along the lines suggested by Schopp, the treatment's ability to restore autonomous capacities outweighs its potential negative effects. This latter proposal does not go as far as the Supreme Court's dictum in Zinermon v. Burch, 494 U.S. 975 (1990), of which Winick is highly critical, Wexler & Winick, supra note 1, at 90–96, but gives more weight to the autonomy value than he does. On the other hand, perhaps the autonomy value should not be considered paramount. Winick not only identifies therapeutic values relevant to internal balancing, but also numerous practical problems associated with the *Zinermon* approach that are relevant to external balancing. Id. at 117–21. See also supra note 104.

107. See Bruce J. Winick, On Autonomy: Legal and Psychological Perspectives, 37 Vill. L. Rev. 1705 (1992).

B. "External" Balancing

Fortunately for TJ, the internal balancing dilemma is likely to be rarely confronted. In some situations (e.g., the effect on plaintiffs of a fault-based tort system), there may be no substantial individual interest against which to balance therapeutic concerns. In many others, as noted above, therapeutic and other values will in fact converge. For instance, although one can question whether legitimizing mere assent to (recommended) treatment is compatible with autonomy as well as therapeutic interests, Winick's related arguments that autonomy and therapeutic values converge when fully competent people make treatment decisions are more persuasive.[108] Similarly, if Ensminger and Liguori are right (contrary to the assumption made above), then the constitutional and therapeutic considerations associated with adversarial procedures reinforce one another. Wexler has identified still other examples of such convergence.[109]

Even when convergence occurs, however, the individual interests so highlighted will have to be balanced externally (i.e., against the interests of others). This balancing process is well-known to all who are familiar with constitutional litigation, where individual interests are routinely pitted against majoritarian and governmental interests.[110] The primary point made here is that proponents of TJ must not be myopic with respect to these other interests; the excitement of recognizing that a rule is therapeutic for some must not blind them toward its potentially negative impact on others. Put slightly differently, the point is that, despite the difficulty of external balancing, it must be undertaken to preserve TJ's credibility.

One example of the need for external balancing, already discussed in the section on the rule of law dilemma, is when the relevant research indicates that a given legal practice is therapeutic for only a portion of those studied (e.g., an empirical discovery that a fault-based tort system is restorative for most but not all plaintiffs). So as not to overlook the interests of those in the minority, some attempt might be made to identify them and treat them differently. As noted earlier, however, in this situation respect for the rule of law and the desire to avoid the countertherapeutic effect of discretionary decision making may require that a practice damaging to some be selected.

Unfortunately, that decision will usually not be the end of the matter. For the rule's impact on those individuals, groups and institutions *not* studied must also be considered. To explain, I return to the four examples used throughout this article. Assuming a fault-based system does better restore (most) plaintiffs

---

108. See generally Winick, supra note 14; Winick, supra note 15.

109. Wexler, supra note 85, at 518–20 (citing his health care compliance piece, supra note 9, and his and Winick's proposal that sex offenders be required to admit to the underlying offense at the plea hearing, in Wexler & Winick, supra note 72, at 229–30).

110. See generally Robert H. Bork, Neutral Principles and Some First Amendment Problems, 47 Ind. L.J. 1, 3 (1971) (describing the need in a democracy for reconciling majority and minority interests through the Supreme Court's power to interpret the Constitution); Louis Henkin, Infallibility Under Law: Constitutional Balancing, 78 Colum. L. Rev. 1022 (1978); T. Alexander Aleinikoff, Constitutional Law in the Age of Balancing, 96 Yale L.J. 943 (1987); Lawrence H. Tribe, Seven Deadly Sins of Straining the Constitution Through a Pseudo-Scientific Sieve, 36 Hastings L.J. 155 (1984).

psychologically, should such a system be favored over the no-fault approach even though the latter is a far less costly reimbursement system and is more likely to avoid inefficient practices (e.g., defensive medicine)?[111] Assuming a broad unconscionability doctrine is shown to increase the self-esteem of the disadvantaged, should it be adopted in the face of evidence that it will drive merchants out of the ghettos or undermine the sanctity of contracts?[112] Assuming giving people the right to refuse psychiatric treatment is therapeutic for patients (as well as respectful of constitutional values), should it be granted in light of the attendant costs to other patients (in terms of harm from those who refuse), staff (in terms of making their work more difficult), and the state (in terms of bureaucratic and procedural expenses)?[113] Assuming health care compliance principles improve the compliance of insanity acquittees with their treatment plans, should such a system be adopted if it would be more time consuming and if judges vehemently resist "playing social worker"?[114]

Note that balancing the types of factors listed here against the therapeutic effect of a rule may raise the "apples and oranges" dilemma familiar to many constitutional law scholars;[115] individual interests (e.g., psychological vindication of plaintiffs) must be weighed against external-societal ones (e.g., costs to medical care and to the legal system). This problem might be mitigated to the extent that the external factors themselves can be converted into the therapeutic "currency" (e.g., a study of the anxiety level experienced by doctors working in a fault-based malpractice system). Even when the same unit of analysis is used, however, the balancing will be difficult: How does one balance the restorative impact of a fault-based system on plaintiffs against the anxiety produced by such a system on putative defendants?

---

111. Cf. (1979) Designated Compensable Event System: A Feasibility Study 1–10, A.B.A. Commission on Medical Professional Liability (suggesting that a variation of a no-fault compensation system which designates the type of event and amount to be compensated, regardless of fault, would reduce transaction costs, decrease defensive medicine by improving the predictability of outcomes, and create a strong impetus to prevention efforts).

112. Harrison notes both possibilities. As to the first, he argues that if merchants leave the neighborhood because unconscionability doctrine has increased the cost of doing business there, the fact that they were shown to be involved in unfair dealing should make their loss easier for those left behind to take, although he admits that this is "an empirical question." Harrison, supra note 3, at 500. In response to the second possibility, he contends that current unconscionability doctrine is no more likely than his proposal to affirm contract principles because its narrowness, although purportedly designed to encourage people to become better educated and read the fine print, is more likely to teach the disadvantaged that they are ill-regarded by society. Id. at 497–98.

113. On these points, see Alexander D. Brooks, The Right to Refuse Antipsychotic Medication: Law and Policy, 39 Rutgers L. Rev. 339, 367–74 (1987).

114. Wexler notes the possibility that judges will resent or fail to understand the gist of his proposals given their lack of mental health training. Wexler & Winick, supra note 1, at 217. Wexler also states that, once a judge has agreed to release an acquittee, "continuity of care principles suggest" that he continue to monitor that acquittee, id. at 215 n. 133, another "social work" role judges may find unpalatable.

115. See, e.g., Aleinikoff, supra note 110, at 972.

Perhaps some framework for external balancing can be developed.[116] Regardless of whether such a framework is feasible, however, proponents of TJ must engage in the balancing process.[117] Failing to do so raises a serious risk that their efforts will be marginalized. Experience with other jurisprudences provides many illustrations of self-referential "pie in the sky" scholarship read by a small coterie of devoted groupies and no one else.[118] I for one hope TJ does not disintegrate into such "jurobabble."

VI. Conclusion

As the last comment indicates, I am sympathetic toward the therapeutic jurisprudence agenda—a "TJ-symp," as it were.[119] The occasionally critical tone

---

116. For instance, in the constitutional context, Faigman has advocated what he calls "Madisonian balancing," a framework which requires the individual asserting that the government has violated his constitutional rights to bear the burden of showing what right or rights were violated and the depth of the violation, at which point the burden shifts to the government to show, by an evidentiary standard (e.g., beyond a reasonable doubt, preponderance of the evidence) proportionate to the depth of the violation that a justification exists for interfering with the right. David L. Faigman, Madisonian Balancing: A Theory of Constitutional Adjudication, 88 NW. U. L. Rev. 641 (1994). See also David L. Faigman, Measuring Constitutionality Transactionally, 45 Hastings L.J. 753 (1994) (modifying the analysis in the previously cited piece but not in the essentials noted here). In connection with the discussion in the text, this framework is most easily applicable in those situations (like the right to refuse) where external balancing requires resolution of individual and governmental interests; in such situations, a showing that therapeutic and constitutional rights "converge" might increase the "depth" of the rights violation, thereby requiring the government to make a greater justificatory showing.

Even in private-law situations (e.g., contract and tort law), an analogous framework might be useful; for instance, a showing that unconscionability doctrine diminishes the autonomy of the disadvantaged might require a greater showing that countervailing factors (e.g., the departure of merchants from ghetto areas and consequent injury) are likely to occur. Faigman's evidentiary framework lends itself to the kind of empirical assessment that therapeutic jurisprudence encourages.

117. Both Wexler and Winick seem attuned to this need. For instance, whereas his article on voluntary hospitalization can be faulted with respect to its internal balancing, see text accompanying notes 101–107 supra. Winick is very attentive to the various other legal and practical concerns connected with his proposal. See Wexler & Winick, supra note 1, at 117–21. Similarly, Wexler has not only pointed to the possibly therapeutic effects of adversarial proceedings on those subjected to civil commitment, but has also asked which procedure complainants might find fairer. Wexler, supra note 85, at 524.

118. See Louis B. Schwartz, With Gun and Camera Through Darkest CLS-Land, 36 Stan. L. Rev. 413, 440 (1984) (speaking of the "irresponsibility" of critical legal studies scholars, given their "pronounced preference... for citing each other rather than for coming to grips with opposing views" and "willingness to advance, almost casually, the most grotesque proposals— 'solutions' to problems of government that take no account of alternatives or costs and totally ignore difficulties of implementation").

119. Indeed, I have resorted to therapeutic jurisprudence reasoning in a recent piece. See Christopher Slobogin, Dangerousness as a Legal Criterion in the Criminal Process, in Law,

of this article is meant to be constructive. To make this point clear, I summarize the various dilemmas reviewed above as positive suggestions: (a) Therapeutic jurisprudence should carve out a niche for itself by focusing its analysis on the impact of legal rules on the well-being of those they affect; this focus would differentiate it from other law-in-action disciplines and, as envisioned by Wexler, allow it to offer insights from the rich array of mental health and behavioral sciences. (b) When deciding whether a rule promotes individual well-being, proponents of TJ should be careful to define further their outcome measure (e.g., autonomy, social adjustment, psychological contentment) so their implicit value judgments will be apparent. (c) TJers should be sensitive to the shortcomings of social science methods as a way of testing the law and, when developing a hypothesis that a given practice is therapeutic, should break it down into as many subhypotheses as possible to make it more testable. (d) If, as will usually be the case, the therapeutic impact of a rule is mixed, an evaluation of the rule's value should consider not only the proportion of people who are likely to benefit from it but also the extent to which that proportion will be accurately identified by those who apply the rule. (e) The potential for TJ to support paternalistic results should be frankly recognized and not considered a bad thing; instead, therapeutic values should be carefully segregated from and balanced against other individual-centered interests and the interests of society, ideally using an identifiable analytical framework, so as to increase TJ's chances of being taken seriously.

These suggestions, or others like them, are needed to goad therapeutic jurisprudence into a critical self-consciousness. For TJ is too valuable an addition to legal analysis to let it develop in an indiscriminate fashion. Given the wealth of psychological research that has been produced and is likely to be produced (no doubt in part due to prodding by TJ scholars), therapeutic jurisprudence will generate at least as many innovative proposals as other jurisprudences that have made their appearance in recent years. Furthermore, it may help give direction to a social science movement that has been notably rudderless in the last two decades.[120] The number of articles explicitly endorsing its approach within the short time TJ has existed testifies to the hunger for a new interdisciplinary way of looking at law.[121]

Most important, that hunger is legitimate. As Edward S. Robinson wrote, "men who resolve to think about human affairs without recourse to psychol-

---

Mental Health, and Mental Disorder (Bruce Sales & Daniel Shuman eds.) (forthcoming, Brooks/Cole Publishing).

120. Many commentators have claimed to observe this phenomenon. Trubek & Esser, supra note 23, at 5–6 (speaking of fears that the law and society movement "is becoming an intellectual backwater"); Haney, supra note 23, at 378 (observing in the law and psychology movement "a sense of the waning of collective effort, a loss of common goals, and an abandoning of a sense of mission—the mission of change."); Harvey Perlman, Foreword, The Law as a Behavioral Instrument (G.B. Melton ed., 1985) (stating that social science in law has yet to have a major impact on legal discourse given its failure to develop a unifying principle, in contrast to law and economics).

121. See Bibliography of Therapeutic Jurisprudence, 10 N.Y.L. Sch. J. Hum. Rts. 915 (1993) (listing roughly 30 authors other than Wexler and Winick who have used the therapeutic jurisprudence perspective since 1990).

ogy never actually succeed in avoiding psychology; they simply make up a crude, uncritical psychology of their own."[122] Therapeutic jurisprudence, carefully pursued, will help produce a critical psychology that will force policymakers to pay more attention to the actual, rather than the assumed, impact of the law and those who implement it.

---

122. Law and Lawyers 72 (1935).

Chapter 40

The Newly Emerging
Mental Health Law

Bruce D. Sales
Daniel W. Shuman

[This selection appears as the introductory chapter in Sales and Shuman's excellent new book, *Law, Mental Health, and Mental Disorder* (Brooks Cole, 1996). References in the selection to chapters in "this volume" accordingly refer to chapters in the Sales and Shuman book, not to chapters in the present volume.]

We might begin an examination of mental health law by asking why the topic exists. For instance, why should there be law relating to and affecting the work of mental health professionals (MHPs)? Many MHPs wonder whether they and the mental health system would be better off without the imposition of law, as long as they and mental health administrators act ethically. For example, consider how adherence to four leading moral principles or shared values of the mental health community would affect the interests of patients and society. *Respect* for the client should ensure that clients are fully accorded their right to consent to or avoid services. *Beneficence and nonmalfeasance* should assure clients that therapists will do good—or at a minimum, no harm. *Justice* should ensure that both procedural justice (that is, fairness in procedures applied to persons) and distributive justice (fairness in the distribution of services) would be built into services. And *fidelity* should ensure that services are appropriately provided.

Unfortunately, however, adherence to the ethical principles of the mental health disciplines does not ensure that patient or societal interests are protected, because the ethical codes are limited in several ways. First, although ethical guidelines can provide some professional direction, they speak in generalities; therefore, significant room exists for professional divergence in their implementation. Consider an ethical guideline requiring informed consent to ensure patient autonomy. Without further specific behavioral standards or rules for implementation, decisions about the amount and type of information to provide to the patient will remain idiosyncratic. Must the therapist provide information on alternatives to the suggested treatment (and if so, which alternatives), or can the therapist present only the benefits and risks of the targeted treatment? If risks must be presented, how significant must risk factors be to require disclosure? Does the ethical guideline demand that the information presented during the consent process be understood by the recipient or only that the needed facts be included in the information presented? Because guidelines derived from ethical principles and ethical codes lack detailed behavioral standards or rules with which to interpret them, there is substantial room for disagreement about how therapists should relate to clients of mental health services. This room for disagreement limits the efficacy of professional ethics in protecting the rights of recipients of mental health services.

Second, because ethical guidelines are necessarily generic, often they do not specifically address some of the concerns or needs of clients. For example, what guidelines would guarantee that services will be available for all persons in need? What of those persons in rural areas who have to travel hundreds of miles to gain access to services and are therefore effectively precluded from services? Ethical guidelines do not address these and many other issues that are important to persons with mental disabilities and others in need of services.

Third, a related limitation of ethical principles and codes is that they are created by private professional organizations; however, many issues important to persons with mental disabilities should be responded to in public forums. Decisions about whether these persons should be free from discrimination in public services and employment should be entrusted to legislators and other elected officials (see Chapter 9), not to the mental health professions. Similarly, although MHPs should and do provide services to crime victims, it would be inappropriate for them to dictate social policy on victims' rights—even though, for example, the handling of a case by the criminal justice system may affect the mental health of the victims and cause secondary victimization (see Chapter 20). Granting victims' wishes would mean a degree of involvement in criminal law and procedure that is not feasible for MHPs.

Fourth, because the mental health disciplines create their own ethical guidelines, they are likely to be limited by professional self-interest. In drafting guidelines, professionals will probably not create standards for behavior that they cannot easily meet. Rather, they are more likely to incorporate into the guidelines that which is easy to do and likely to be done than that which should be done. In addition, if these guidelines are violated, and there are no legal avenues for redress, what sanctions will the profession impose? Professional ethics committees are much more likely to be concerned with educating practitioners than with punishing them or with compensating harmed clients. Moreover, mental health professionals can avoid ethical sanctions of private, voluntary professional associations simply by resigning from them.

Although professional ethical principles and standards are important, they are insufficient fully to meet the needs of persons with mental disabilities, clients of mental health services, and society. Thus, it should not be surprising that legislators and courts have developed a body of law relevant to the mental health professions and the clients of their services.

For better or worse, MHPs are, and will continue to be, both directly and indirectly affected by that law. Their practice is directly controlled by laws that regulate such matters as licensure and certification, third-party reimbursement, and professional incorporation (for example, Sales & Miller, 1995). The quality of their services is subject to review by courts in malpractice actions (see Chapter 5), while their collective actions are subject to antitrust scrutiny (Chapter 6). Even when not directly affected, MHPs are indirectly affected by the law because their clients are increasingly involved in legal entanglements in which mental status issues are pivotal, such as child custody disputes (Chapter 25), litigation over mental or emotional injury (Chapter 14), and involuntary civil commitment (Chapter 11).

Given the expansiveness of this law and its potential to affect mental health professionals, the clients of their services, and mental health care more generally, this chapter has many purposes: First we will consider the rationale for the initial development of mental health law. Then we will discuss the importance of empirical research for studying the consequences of mental health law and consider a new perspective for studying and improving this area of the law—therapeutic jurisprudence. We will assess the benefits and limits of this approach and discuss its implications for redefining the appropriate terrain of mental health law. Next, we will examine the other grounds for defining the newly emerging mental health law. We then consider factors that threaten the success of mental health law in attaining its goals. Finally, we conclude with a discussion of the relationship that must emerge between the legal and mental health disciplines to make mental health law therapeutic by advancing positive psychological consequences for those it affects.

Early Rationale for Mental Health Law

Mental health law, which grew out of the civil rights and consumer movements of the 1960s and the 1970s, was initially dominated by a deontological perspective that conceives of the law as advancing important values that reflect what *ought* to be done, often ensconced within normative constitutional principles that reflect what customarily *is* done. This orientation resulted in mental health lawyers seeking to achieve a litany of rights for persons who suffered from, or were alleged to suffer from, mental disorders. Indeed, during the 1960s and 1970s, society witnessed the conferral of rights as an end in itself. The vernacular of this rights-based analysis, such as the right to treatment and the right to refuse treatment (Chapter 13), as well as the right to counsel and a hearing (Chapter 2), shaped the discussion of mental health law during that era and defined its original boundaries.

To apply this mode of analysis to interactions between mental health professionals and patients, mental health law borrowed from other areas of law where "rights" were equally important and commonly accepted. For example, involuntary civil commitment of persons with mental disabilities (Chapter 11), one of the early focuses of mental health law, was sufficiently similar to criminal proceedings to justify arguing that the same due process rights should apply (such as the rights to counsel, confrontation and cross-examination of adverse witnesses, and the privilege against self-incrimination) (Chapter 2).

Not all topics considered part of mental health law, however, originated during this period. The contemporary formulation of the insanity defense, for example, was born during the 1800s (Chapter 16). Yet the insanity defense and related topics, such as competency to stand trial (Chapter 15), were comfortably included in books and courses on mental health law because they advanced a concern for the rights of persons with mental disabilities.

The civil rights and consumer movement bases for mental health law lost their strength in the late 1980s and early 1990s for a variety of reasons. First, these driving forces succeeded in accomplishing many of their goals. Many, if not most, of the rights that mental health legal advocates targeted were secured, at least on paper. For example, commitment hearings now require many of the same procedural protections as criminal proceedings, and the conditions under which persons with mental disabilities are involuntarily confined are subject to judicial scrutiny.

Second, because a new conservative national ideology was less receptive to the original goals of the mental health law movement, the U.S. Supreme Court, particularly its newer members, became far less receptive to expanding the rights of persons with mental disabilities, whether those sought-after rights related to institutionalization (Chapters 11 and 23) or to community-based services (Chapter 8). In addition, state legislatures and Congress often shared this conservatism. Thus, the battle for expansion of these rights has dramatically slowed (Chapter 8).

Third, the movement lost vitality because of a growing sense that attaining its goals did not achieve the ends it sought (Shuman, 1992). For example, an increasing number of legal and mental health scholars and practitioners came to doubt that recognizing rights for their own sake was satisfying or beneficial. Despite the legal victories, it was unclear whether the lives of people with mental disabilities had substantially improved. Further, where improvement had occurred, scholars and advocates began to question whether this was because of the legal changes—or in spite of them. For instance, judges and lawyers who played a role in securing rights for persons in civil commitment proceedings did not, for the most part, see beyond these initial goals. In the rush to guarantee a right to counsel, the courts did not ask how counsel would affect the accuracy of commitment decisions, whether the subjects of commitment petitions could cope with an adversarial process, or how those committed to inpatient facilities would respond to the treatment provided in these settings.

Empirical Questioning of Mental Health Law

The deontological perspective of law contrasts with the utilitarian view, which holds that legal rules are important to achieving some end. For example, while the deontological perspective maintains that recognition of a right to a judicial hearing preceding civil commitment should turn on whether commitment is a deprivation of liberty from the standpoint of the Fourteenth Amendment of the U.S. Constitution, the utilitarian perspective maintains that the right to a hearing should turn on the desirability of its consequences, such as improving the accuracy of commitment decisions (Tyler, 1993).

Although much of the previous generation of mental health law scholarship and decision making was deontologically oriented, a significant body of literature developed at the same time that was shaped by this utilitarian perspective, tracing its roots to the early 20th-century Legal Realist movement (Monahan & Walker, 1994). This literature was concerned with empirically testing whether laws were achieving their explicit and implicit goals. This approach to law and behavioral and social science interactions asserts that almost all laws are based on behavioral, social, and economic assumptions whose validity can be empirically determined (Sales, 1983; Sales & Hafemeister, 1985; Shuman, 1984). Thus, when a federal court ordered that persons with mental disabilities residing in state hospitals be accorded their right to privacy, utilitarian-oriented research was able to demonstrate that the subsequent changes in the institutions did not achieve the goals of this court ruling (O'Reilly & Sales, 1986, 1987).

Moreover, empirical questioning will challenge not only the fundamental basis for a law but also the accepted practice of MHPs that the law regulates. Consider, for example, reporting laws, which constitute one exception to confidentiality law. All states require MHPs to report child abuse, including child sexual abuse (Chapter 22); some states also require the reporting of abuse of adults, such as those who are incapacitated, who are particularly vulnerable. Laws such as these opt for protection of the victim over rehabilitation of the perpetrator and have created significant controversy within the mental health community. This controversy is apparent in the debate about and practice of reporting father-daughter incest perpetrators. Some MHPs argue that to divulge such otherwise confidential information, which was learned in the therapeutic relationship with a client, will decrease the likelihood that offenders will seek therapy and overcome their problems. The utilitarian perspective leads us to ask the following question: To what extent are perpetrators voluntarily seeking therapy and benefiting from it in the absence of reporting? If reporting occurred and resulted in the conviction of the offender, is therapy mandated as part of the court's disposition? If the answer is yes, is this therapy more or less successful than that provided voluntarily?

Therapeutic Jurisprudence Lens on Mental Health Law

Building on this empirical heritage, *therapeutic jurisprudence*, a new school of thought in mental health law, evolved (Wexler & Winick, 1991; Wexler, 1990). Rather than exclusively relying on deontologically driven legal rules, advocates of this new movement analyze the consequences of these legal rules and attempt to incorporate this information in legal decision making. The overarching goal of therapeutic jurisprudence is to ensure that mental health law realizes its potential to advance therapeutic outcomes, at least when it is possible to do so without violating other important principles (such as constitutional principles). Those who subscribe to this school of thought believe not that therapeutic considerations should take precedence over all others but that legal decisions should acknowledge their therapeutic and antitherapeutic consequences.

For example, consider the law's role in the delivery of mental health services in the community. In Chapter 8, Perlin explores the proposition that judicial involvement over the last two decades has had an antitherapeutic impact on the availability of these services. His analysis reveals how myths and stereotypes about persons with mental disabilities, myths to which judges are not immune, limit the therapeutic achievements of the courts.

It can be argued that therapeutic jurisprudence is old wine in a new bottle—that is, the substance of its message is what law and behavioral and social science specialists have been promoting for years—using empirical data and behavioral and social science theory to evaluate the desirability of different legal alternatives. Whether therapeutic jurisprudence is simply a new label for an ongoing major school of thought, however, is not nearly as important as other considerations. Therapeutic jurisprudence can create a climate in which mental health and legal scholars and professionals can agree that mental health law should not be made or carried out without considering its therapeutic consequences, determined empirically, to the extent possible at the time of the legal decision.

Redefining the Boundaries of Mental Health Law

The therapeutic jurisprudence perspective thus suggests the need for one fundamental reorientation of mental health law. Mental health law needs to be examined to determine how its application affects the interests of its intended beneficiaries, and whether therapeutic, or psychologically constructive, outcomes have been or will be advanced. Such work should utilize feedback from MHPs and clients, the work of mental health scholars, and empirical research.

A second fundamental shift needs to occur as well. For mental health law to be therapeutic, it must incorporate a broader vision of what an effective, truly therapeutic, system for the delivery of mental health services would entail. Without this richer view, it is understandable why MHPs have been frustrated with the law's incursions into their domain. In essence, the law has been playing at the fringe of an enormous tapestry that defines mental health care, pulling at individual threads, seemingly oblivious to the larger patterns. The next generation of mental health law and scholarship should have the law participate with MHPs in making appropriate mental health services available to consumers who seek them.

Without abandoning normative constitutional values, such efforts should include a vision of mental health services that incorporates (1) identification of those in need of services and those not being served, and the reasons for this discrepancy; (2) development of a comprehensive plan of integrated services; (3) provision of services with clear outcome goals; (4) systematic collection of accurate information on the delivery of services and the operation of systems providing those services, and the reporting of those data in a meaningful fashion; (5) use of the data to aid in decision making on mental health care; (6) provision of appropriate services to ethnic minorities; (7) provision of sufficient funding to support legally mandated entitlements (for example, National Institute of Mental Health, 1991). This shift in focus should help to reorient mental health law to the core concerns of consumers who need and want mental health services, and of MHPs who provide those services. In addition, these seven requirements support a rational planning and implementation process by legal and public policymakers/administrators responsible for interpreting and implementing legal guidelines. And they facilitate effectiveness and efficiency in the delivery of mental health services. These goals are timely and appropriate because nationally we are plagued by a mental health system that is disjointed and uncoordinated, with no clear communication links between subsystems. The system also suffers from inadequate planning and funding (Chapter 7).

A third fundamental reorientation for mental health law is also necessary. Early mental health law focused on the rights of persons with mental disabilities, primarily in criminal situations—for instance, those involving insanity defense (Chapter 16), competency to stand trial (Chapter 15), and commitment of sex offenders with mental disorders (Chapter 18)—and quasicriminal situations, including situations where the law imposes restrictions on liberty, such as in involuntary civil commitment (Chapter 11) and guardianship (Chapter 10). But early mental health law did not elaborate the other important ways in which the law relates to the mental health professions and its clients: the functions of MHPs, the responsibilities of MHPs, and the operation of systems involved with the delivery of mental health services.

Functions of MHPs

The law affects the functions of MHPs. For example, many legal situations mandate an evaluation of a person by a MHP and specify the legal standard for which the MHP must test (Chapter 17, this volume; Sales & Miller, 1995; Melton, Petrila, Poythress, & Slobogin, 1987). In competency-to-stand-trial determinations, for instance, the court is not directly interested initially in whether the defendant has a mental illness. Rather, the court is concerned with whether the person has the ability to understand the nature of the charges and the legal proceedings, and to aid in the defense. Not all findings of incompetency to stand trial result from a mental illness, and even severe mental illness (that is, psychosis) does not automatically make the person incompetent to stand trial (Chapter 15). Thus, the functions of the mental health professional are articulated in the law and logically should be part of mental health law. Not to incorporate this law as part of mental health law increases the chances that MHPs will not provide appropriate services, and thereby increases the potential of harm to the subjects of legal evaluations. This component of the reorientation requires mental health law to incorporate all topics where MHPs may or are required to testify as to a mental status issue as part of litigation. It also encompasses situations where the clinical work of MHPs will be dictated by the standard within the law or where their clinical opinion will be asked for in regard to a legal issue in the case (for example, workers' compensation, competency to contract or sign a will, guardianship, dangerousness of alleged or adjudicated offenders).

Responsibilities of MHPs

The law also imposes responsibilities on MHPs in numerous ways. Some laws focus on the requirement that MHPs become licensed or certified to perform certain functions, in addition to requiring them to adhere to certain standards in performing their duties (Simon, Sales, & Sechrest, 1992). Other laws require mental health facilities to be licensed prior to operation. A third type of law constrains the types of practice in the mental health professions, whether it be, for example, in a health maintenance organization (HMO), a preferred provider organization, or a multidisciplinary corporation (one that provides services to different professional disciplines). Although these types of law also cross over into another category (see the section titled "Operation of the System"), they can have a substantial impact on the responsibilities of MHPs and the quality of care that they deliver to their clients. Consider, for example, the explosive growth of HMOs. To the extent that the law allows the HMO to limit the number of patient visits (for instance, to ten sessions), what are the consequences to a client who continues to need care, what are the responsibilities of the therapist who has to terminate the therapy, and will this approach increase malpractice claims by patients who allege inappropriate early termination?

Some laws focus on the responsibilities of MHPs much more directly. The law relating to informed consent requires MHPs to provide certain information to prospective clients and to secure their consent to services prior to initiating treatment. Other laws focus on requiring confidential treatment of information obtained from clients during a professional relationship (Chapter 4). Or they focus on the responsibility of the MHP to release this information in very explicit circumstances (for instance, pursuant to a valid search by law enforcement authorities, or pursuant to a valid subpoena by a court). Moreover, given the impact of these laws on MHPs and their clients, and the ways services are delivered, it makes little sense to exclude them from the domain of mental health law.

Operation of the System

Finally, the law affects the operation of the mental health system, and other public or private systems, in their provision of services to persons who suffer from some type of mental disorder. There is more than one mental health system. Mental health services are required in a variety of contexts. School systems today must evaluate students for serious emotional disturbance and are obligated to provide appropriate services to students with special needs (Chapter 9). The juvenile justice system often bases dispositions on the treatment needs of the juveniles who come before the court (Chapter 24). A recurring dilemma for the criminal justice system is how to deal with incarcerated persons in jails and prisons who suffer from mental disorder (Cohen, 1995) and how to respond to battered partners (Chapter 21). Mental health law must incorporate these concerns so as to represent the full panoply of laws addressing, and issues facing, persons with mental health service needs. This is important because if law is to be therapeutic, it should be effective across the spectrum of situations where it might apply. For example, if the law allows deprivation of liberty for civil commitment of adults (Chapter 11), juveniles (Chapter 23), and delinquent juveniles (Chapter 24) with mental illness, under what deontological and utilitarian rationales should the commitment be allowed when it is shown that treatment in the prescribed facilities is not effective?

A fourth rationale for fundamentally reorienting our old conception of mental health law is based on the irony that the field is labeled *mental health* law, when it focuses on mental disorder. Where is the *health*? Indeed, there is a substantial body of law that focuses on people's mental status, where mental illness either is not present or may not be present. By focusing on mental status rather than mental illness, mental health law should be concerned with the continuum of mental status issues that perplex legal decision making. This focus allows mental health law scholars to rephrase critical questions from "Does the institutionalized person with a mental illness have the capacity to consent to services?" to "How should the law best conceptualize and interpret the legal mandate for consent to services for all persons along the continuum from 'the highly intelligent' to 'the severely retarded,' and from 'the normal' to 'the severely mentally disordered'?" Legal standards should be revisited to determine their appropriateness for the spectrum of relevant fact situations faced by the full range of people to whom the law might apply. This reconsideration will probably eventually lead to more thoughtfully defined legal constructs.

In addition, when we focus on mental status, it becomes apparent that mental health law also should be concerned with therapeutic consequences, using the word *therapy* the way mental health professionals use it—to mean positive psychological consequences. What we should be interested in are the psychological consequences of different laws that affect a person's mental health. This broadened conception of mental health law perhaps widens the therapeutic jurisprudence lens, but it is consistent with its basic tenets. By utilizing this broader perspective, topics such as child custody determinations will be incorporated into mental health law scholarship. For example, if the custody decision is based on the child's best interests (Rohman, Sales, & Lou, 1990), mental health law should ask what we know about the mental health consequences to children of various divorce arrangements (Rohman, Sales, & Lou, 1990). Mental health law can also legitimately probe the psychological impact of the legal process on divorcing parents. To be concerned with the therapeutic or antitherapeutic effects of institutionalization, but not be concerned with the potentially devastating psychological effects of other laws such as divorce, foster care, and adoption, diminishes the mental health component of mental health law.

The fifth and final basis for reinventing mental health law is being fueled by the feminist jurisprudence literature (Chapter 12). Feminist scholars point out what we all might have guessed, namely, that our laws reflect a male standard that often ignores the needs of the sizable percentage of women and ethnic minorities that comprise the institutionalized or those in need of services today. David Wexler (1971) and a number of his students reported the outrageous case of a 19-year-old Mexican American woman who was committed to the Territorial Asylum for the Insane in Phoenix in 1912 for "mental problems as being supposedly caused by bathing in cold water at menstrual period and as probably being only temporary in nature" (as quoted from court papers). The woman was still there in 1971, then 78 years of age. The law has redressed some of the problems she faced—in particular, indefinite commitment. But feminist writings are driving mental health and legal scholars to realize that unrecognized prejudice and indifference toward the special needs of women and ethnic minorities still permeate mental health law and practice (Chapter 12, this volume).

Factors Threatening the Success of the New Mental Health Law

Some factors may undermine the success of the effort to reinvent mental health law and put mental health back into it. For example, despite the apparent benefits of the therapeutic jurisprudence orientation on the part of lawyers and legal scholars, MHPs and scholars will not invariably find this approach a panacea. As already noted, therapeutic jurisprudence seeks to advance therapeutic outcomes by encouraging legal decision makers to consider therapeutic consequences; it does not dictate the selection of legal rules that advance a therapeutic outcome. Therapeutic jurisprudence clarifies the stakes involved in the decision but does not purport to resolve them; balancing values cannot be done through a simplistic formulaic analysis. For example, if empirical research reveals that recognition of a right to refuse treatment is antitherapeutic, a court or legislature may either refuse to recognize that right based on that research, or notwithstanding that research, may recognize that right based on a deontological valuation of the importance of autonomy (Schopp, 1993).

When legal decision makers choose to recognize a rule that is therapeutic or refuse to recognize a rule that is antitherapeutic, the judgments of the legal system and the mental health system are congruent. Note, however, that the congruence in the judgments of the two disciplines can either be because legal decision makers utilize a utilitarian approach that accepts the empirical outcomes as dispositive, or because legal decision makers utilize a deontological approach that coincidentally concurs with the empirical research. The absence of congruence occurs when, for deontological reasons, legal decision makers choose laws that are antitherapeutic or reject laws that are therapeutic. This absence of congruence has understandably troubled MHPs whose language and professional values do not share the legal system's deontological concerns. Indeed, MHPs should not expect from therapeutic jurisprudence and the new mental health law a change in legal values or orientation that subordinates normative constitutional values to therapeutic values.

This approach could not only lead to the rejection of therapeutic concerns in favor of normative constitutional values. Emphasizing therapeutic considerations could also lead those who see these considerations as paramount to neglect important normatively derived constitutional values. These normative constitutional values are crucial to the structure and fabric of our society and have enabled our system of government to endure for over 200 years. They have demarcated the protection of the individual from the state in a way that has transcended changes in technology and culture. Thus, they should not be dismissed as mere technicalities; they define us as Americans.

Other factors that may inhibit the ultimate success of this new conception of mental health law derive from the fundamental differences between the legal and mental health systems and between legal and mental health professionals. These differences can lead to conceptual, definitional, and pragmatic schisms and can reduce the ability of the disciplines and systems to work effectively together.

For example, the legal and mental health systems possess different vocabularies with encoded signals that affirm their worldviews but that often lead to miscommunication between the fields. The description of the common law system as an adversary system, for example, which is intended by lawyers to exalt the values of process and participation, is often taken by MHPs to exalt hostility and noncooperation. The illusion that results when lawyers and MHPs believe that they are communicating in a shared language all too often leads to problems like MHPs providing assessment services that do not address the relevant legal issue.

Even where the two groups attempt to communicate effectively, tensions can result because various normative and policy questions are inaccurately and inappropriately identified as involving scientific or technical issues. In an attempt to avoid addressing these normative and policy issues head on, legal decision makers often erroneously recast them as technical questions to be answered by "experts." Even when issues require scientific rather than normative judgments, legal reliance on mental health expertise is problematic because MHPs often do not have relevant empirically grounded knowledge and are willing to render opinions beyond their areas of expertise (Chapters 3 and 25).

Fundamental differences between the fields are also reflected in tensions and conflicts in their respective goals. For example, in dealing with forensic patients, the criminal justice and correctional systems value incapacitation and social control goals, while the mental health system values therapeutic objectives. This conflict continues to occur despite the fact that both systems are charged with the responsibility of treating dangerous persons who have a mental illness as well as protecting society.

Conflicts in goals also occur intraprofessionally, making their resolution all the more complex. Prosecutors may want maximum sentences imposed to protect society, while defense attorneys might argue for the imposition of diversion programs incorporating outpatient services. Similarly, MHPs have strong but divergent views. In considering services, some MHPs value large state hospitals in a mental health service system, while others question the rationale for their existence. It will be difficult for the legal and mental health disciplines to agree on therapeutic, and psychologically constructive, outcomes when this intraprofessional dissension undermines their discussions.

Finally, conflicts can exist between the values, interests, and needs of key participants in law and mental health interactions (that is, policymakers, institutions and organizations providing services, program administrators, providers, clients, family members, and researchers). What if a state institution wishes to deinstitutionalize a minor, but the parents do not wish to have the minor returned to the home (Frohboese & Sales, 1980)? And what if the MHP objects to being used by prison administrators for social control purposes when providing services, such as where the prison asks the MHP to do evaluations to determine dangerousness for security purposes?

But perhaps the most important factors that may limit the therapeutic success of the new mental health law will come from outside the legal or mental health fields. As Rubin notes in Chapter 7, financing drives service systems. The lack of sufficient state or federal appropriations can cripple the best-intentioned public service programs for persons with mental illness and make a sham of government entitlement programs for persons in need of mental health services. The reason is obvious. Without funding, MHPs will not be hired to work, or providers of lesser training and sometimes lesser skills will be substituted. Where funding is provided for the MHP, its level may be so meager that it allows for only a brief or minimal intervention, rather than for the care required for a successful intervention with a client. Moreover, without needed state appropriations to support mental health services, they simply will not exist, either on an inpatient or an outpatient basis. As one person with a mental illness asked in a public forum in a large metropolitan area, "why does the system provide me with drugs to allow me to function but refuse to support psychosocial therapies so that I can function decently?" With limited funding, psychosocial therapies and rehabilitation are out of favor. Indeed, one public employee in that same state reported that a public agency was using a high school graduate to provide mental health services because it could not afford to pay for trained staff. As Perlin observes in Chapter 8, this is an issue of politics, and in the political arena, the need for mental health care has traditionally received only lip service.

A New Relationship for the Legal and Mental Health Disciplines

If the newly emerging mental health law is to be successful, it must create a bridge to overcome the factors that threaten its ability to foster psychologically constructive outcomes. For instance, viewing mental health law from the patient's rights perspective inevitably placed mental health professionals in a defensive posture. A patient right, such as the right to informed consent, concomitantly creates a mental health professional duty at the same time: the duty to determine the competency of the patient to consent to services, the duty to provide all relevant information about the risks and benefits of services, and so on. So viewed, the law is negative to the MHP, and the less involvement with it the better. Changing that construct to focus on and understand the therapeutic and antitherapeutic consequences of informed consent allows the mental health disciplines to participate in the law in constructive ways that are familiar to them. Equally important, it offers MHPs a legitimate and substantial basis for working with the legal community to change the law when therapeutic outcomes are not achieved or antitherapeutic consequences are generated by it.

The time is ripe for this transition. Although the deontologically driven mental health law substantially succeeded in establishing many rights for persons with mental disabilities, as already noted, our national temperament is unlikely to support dramatic growth in this area in the immediate future (Chapter 8). That may be appropriate. More rights may not be needed to achieve appropriate services for persons with mental disabilities.

A renewed, invigorated interaction between legal and mental health professions should increase the chance of achieving this goal. While MHPs are well versed in the clinical needs of their clients, they are often ill-prepared to design a system to deliver mental health services that would be legally appropriate. Lawyers, on the other hand, are typically trained in setting up complex organizations for their clients, and thus bring a rich set of skills to the table to complement those of MHPs. Together, these professionals can exert significant influence on the shape of politically driven legislative acts and appropriations. The interaction of lawyers and MHPs is particularly needed, since mental health services are provided through a complex array of government and private entities that can easily result in systemic neglect of problems and certain unserved populations falling through the cracks. Whether lawyers will seize this opportunity and MHPs will view legal participation at this systemic level as intrusive or helpful may depend, in part, on how effective the newly emerging mental health law is in convincing the professions of the need for joint efforts.

In fact, this newly emerging mental health law and the therapeutic jurisprudence lens that can be applied to it should stimulate, for a variety of reasons, renewed discussion and debate about the therapeutic effects of laws and the psychological consequences of different legal arrangements. First, both MHPs and lawyers will find the therapeutic jurisprudence perspective beneficial because it sheds light on the tensions between law and mental health, even if it will not always resolve them. As already noted, therapeutic jurisprudence provides a lens that reminds lawyers and MHPs to examine empirically the therapeutic consequences of legal decision making and that helps make the rationale for these decisions more explicit. As MHPs know, talking openly about conflict has therapeutic value.

Second, in areas of the law where conflicts now exist between the goals of mental health law and mental health care, therapeutic jurisprudence may advance shared therapeutic goals previously frustrated by ill-conceived legal rules (for example, Wexler, 1993). Consider the matter of plea bargaining for sex offenders, in which the defendant is often allowed to avoid a trial by pleading no contest. By doing so, the defendant does not have to acknowledge that he committed the specific acts of abuse. If research reveals that not acknowledging one's guilt promotes the abuser's cognitive distortions and makes treatment less likely to succeed, changing the legal rule to require acknowledgment of the abusive acts in the plea bargain may advance the therapeutic goals of reducing abuse (Klotz, Wexler, Sales, & Becker, 1992).

Third, therapeutic jurisprudence reveals that legal rules often have explicit or implicit therapeutic agendas that sometimes get lost in the tumult of their day-to-day application. Consider guardianship laws. They were implemented to aid incapacitated persons in a variety of ways, such as by creating opportunities for these individuals to continue to live in the community and by having guardians arrange for habilitative and rehabilitative services. Unfortunately, empirical research suggests that guardians are neither trained nor prepared for their responsibilities and that courts fail to monitor guardians' performance despite the statutory obligation to do so. Under the new mental health law, mental health personnel would be encouraged to work with lawmakers and the courts to identify these types of problems and work toward needed solutions. Malpractice laws provide another good example. They are intended to improve the quality of care delivered by MHPs and aid in making whole those injured by substandard care. By understanding the impact of these laws on providers, consumers of mental health services, and mental health care, legal decision makers can better fashion rules that accomplish these goals (Shuman, 1993; Chapter 5, this volume).

Fourth, the new mental health law should invite mental health scholars and professionals to examine the psychological consequences of a broad array of rules that were previously unexamined. By encouraging such an analysis, the mental health disciplines are likely to find a paucity of empirical support for either protherapeutic or antitherapeutic claims. This result raises a fascinating opportunity for more research and ongoing interactions between the legal and mental health communities. For example, in Chapter 11, La Fond points to data suggesting that the expansion of the legal standard for involuntary hospitalization, enacted within the last decade for the therapeutic purpose of enhancing mental health care for an expanded group of persons with mental illness, has had significant antitherapeutic effects. How should this law develop in light of this finding?

Conclusion

Although the focus of this discussion has been on legal change, we are not suggesting that lawyers will necessarily have a diminished *traditional* role in the new mental health law. The mental health disciplines will continue to require legal guidance about their obligations and rights in the creation of practices and the delivery of services. In addition, persons with mental disabilities will continue to need legal representation. Despite the best intentions of the mental health professions, the interests of service providers are not always congruent with those of their clients. Whatever other goals they may share, MHPs earn money for their services. If their appointment calendars or hospital beds are not full, they suffer potentially severe financial consequences. These consequences may lead MHPs to recommend overutilization of their services. Concerns over malpractice litigation may also generate recommendations for excessive services to avoid future claims of failure to diagnose. And mental health professionals may recommend overutilization of services because they genuinely believe in the power of their services to do good without considering the empirical data to support that assumption. Finally, rather than keeping people out of the involuntary service system, mental health lawyers will also be involved in securing services for their clients. Lawyers can petition for state and federal entitlements and benefits for clients and help people navigate barriers that may challenge even individuals without disabilities (Chapters 2 and 9).

Similarly, MHPs will continue to have a traditional role in aiding in the administration of the law. They will continue to provide forensic evaluations, testimony, and treatment, as well as empirical research for services planning.

Yet we hope that the new mental health law will stimulate a far broader and richer interaction between the legal and mental health disciplines than has existed previously. The legal and mental health disciplines should see themselves as allied professions, both for the purposes of administering and implementing mental health law and for attempting to achieve therapeutic outcomes and positive psychological consequences.

References

Frohboese, R. F., & Sales, B. D. (1980). Parental opposition to deinstitutionalization: A challenge in need of attention and resolution. Law and Human Behavior, 4, 1–88.

Klotz, J. A., Wexler, D. B., Sales, B. D., & Becker, J. V. (1992). Cognitive restructuring through law: A therapeutic jurisprudence approach to sex offenders and the plea process. University of Puget Sound Law Review, 15, 579–595.

Melton, G. B., Petrila, J., Poythress, N., & Slobogin, C. (1987). Psychological evaluations for the courts: A handbook for mental health professionals and lawyers. New York: Guilford Press.

Monahan, J., & Walker, L. (1994). Social science in law: Cases and materials (3rd ed.). Westbury, NY: Foundation Press.

National Institute of Mental Health. (1991). Caring for people with severe mental disorders: A national plan of research to improve services (DHHS Publication No. ADM 91-1762). Washington, DC: U.S. Government Printing Office.

O'Reilly, J., & Sales, B. (1986). Setting physical standards for mental hospitals: To whom should the courts listen? International Journal of Law and Psychiatry, 8, 301–310.

O'Reilly, J., & Sales, B. (1987). Privacy for the institutionalized mentally ill: Are court-ordered standards effective? Law and Human Behavior, 11, 41–53.

Rohman, L., Sales, B., & Lou, M. (1990). The best interests standard in child custody decisions. In D. Weisstub (Ed.), Law and mental health: International perspectives: Vol. V (pp. 40–90). Elmsford, NY: Pergamon Press.

Sales, B. D. (1983). The legal regulation of psychology: Professional and scientific interactions. In C. J. Scheirer & B. L. Hammonds (Eds.), The master lecture series: Vol. 2. Psychology and the law (pp. 5–36). Washington, DC: American Psychological Association.

Sales, B. D. & Hafemeister, T. (1985). Law and psychology. In E. Altmaier & M. Meyer (Eds.), Applied specialties in psychology (pp. 331–373). New York: Random House.

Sales, B. D., & Miller, M. O. (1995). Law and mental health professionals. Washington, DC: American Psychological Association. (A 52-volume book series that covers the law affecting mental health professionals in each of the 50 states, the District of Columbia, and the federal jurisdictions)

Sales, B., & Shuman, D. (1994). Mental health law and mental health care. American Journal of Orthopsychiatry, 64, 172–179.

Schopp, R. F. (1993). Therapeutic jurisprudence and conflicts among values in mental health law. Behavioral Sciences and the Law, 11, 31–45.

Shuman, D. W. (1984). Decisionmaking under conditions of uncertainty. Judicature, 67, 326–335.

Shuman, D. W. (1992). Therapeutic jurisprudence and tort law: A limited subjective standard of care. Southern Methodist University Law Review, 46, 323–327.

Shuman, D. W. (1993). Making the world a better place through tort law? Through the therapeutic looking glass. New York Law School Journal of Human Rights, X, 739–758.

Simon, Sales, B., & Sechrest. (1992). Licensure of functions. In D. K. Kageiro & W. S. Lawfer (Eds.), Handbook of psychology and law (pp. 542–564). New York: Springer-Verlag.

Tyler, T. R. (1993). The psychological consequences of judicial procedures: Implications for civil commitment hearings. Southern Methodist University Law Review, 46, 433–445.

Wexler, D. B. (1971). Special project: The administration of psychiatric justice. Arizona Law Review, 13, 1–259.

Wexler, D. B. (Ed.). (1990). Therapeutic Jurisprudence: The law as a therapeutic agent. Durham, NC: Carolina Academic Press.

Wexler, D. B. (1993). Justice, mental health, and therapeutic jurisprudence. Cleveland State Law Review, 40, 517–526.

Wexler, D. B., & Winick, B. J. (Eds.). (1990). Essays in therapeutic jurisprudence. Durham, NC: Carolina Academic Press.

Chapter 41

Reflections on the Scope of Therapeutic Jurisprudence

David B. Wexler

Therapeutic jurisprudence, the study of the role of the law as a therapeutic agent,[1] is producing a considerable literature.[2] To date, most of the comments, questions, concerns, and critiques of therapeutic jurisprudence have centered on three major areas: rights-justice,[3] empirical matters,[4] and what might be

---

1. Essays in Therapeutic Jurisprudence (David B. Wexler & Bruce J. Winick eds., 1991) [hereinafter Essays]; Therapeutic Jurisprudence: The Law as a Therapeutic Agent (David B. Wexler ed., 1990); David B. Wexler, New Directions in Therapeutic Jurisprudence: Breaking the Bounds of Conventional Mental Health Law Scholarship, 10 N.Y.L. Sch. J. Hum. Rts. 759 (1993) [hereinafter New Directions].

2. 1 Psychol. Pub. Pol'y & L. (1995); Special Section, Mental Health Law and Mental Health Care, 64 Am. J. Orthopsychiatry 172 (1994); Symposium, Therapeutic Jurisprudence: Restructuring Mental Disability Law, 10 N.Y.L. Sch. J. Hum. Rts. 623 (1993); Bibliography to Symposium, Therapeutic Jurisprudence: Restructuring Mental Disability Law, 10 N.Y.L. Sch. J. Hum. Rts. 915 (1993); Symposium, 20 New Eng. J. on Crim. & Civ. Confinement 243 (1994). For an excellent assessment and thoughtful critique of therapeutic jurisprudence scholarship to date, see Christopher Slobogin, Therapeutic Jurisprudence: Five Dilemmas to Ponder, 1 Psychol. Pub. Pol'y & L., 193–219 (1995).

3. Robert F. Schopp, Therapeutic Jurisprudence and Conflicts of Values in Mental Health Law, 11 Behavioral Sci. & L. 31 (1993); Slobogin, supra note 2 (discussing the "balancing" dilemma); Mark A. Small, Legal Psychology and Therapeutic Jurisprudence, 37 St. Louis U. L.J. 675 (1993; David B. Wexler, Justice, Mental Health, & Therapeutic Jurisprudence, 40 Clev. St. L. Rev. 517 (1992); David B. Wexler & Bruce J. Winick, Patients, Professionals, and the Path of Therapeutic Jurisprudence: A Response to Petrila, 10 N.Y.L. Sch. J. Hum. Rts. 907 (1993) [hereinafter Response]; John Petrila, Paternalism & the Unrealized Promise of Essays in Therapeutic Jurisprudence, 10 N.Y.L. Sch. J. Hum. Rts. 877 (1993) (reviewing David B. Wexler & Bruce J. Winick, Essays in Therapeutic Jurisprudence (1991)).

4. Fred Cohen & Joel A. Dvoskin, Therapeutic Jurisprudence and Corrections: A Glimpse, 10 N.Y.L. Sch. J. Hum. Rts. 777 (1993); David Finkelman & Thomas Grisso, Therapeutic Jurisprudence: From Idea to Application, 20 New Eng. J. on Crim. & Civ. Confinement 243 (1994); Slobogin, supra note 2 (discussing the dilemma of "empirical indeterminacy"); Small, supra note 3; Richard L. Wiener, Social Analytic Jurisprudence & Tort Law: Social Cognition Goes to Court, 37 St. Louis U. L.J. 503 (1993). For empirical work in therapeutic jurisprudence, see Elizabeth Anderson et al., Coercive Uses of Mandatory Reporting in Therapeutic Relationships, 11 Behavioral Sci. & L. 335 (1993); Bruce Feldthusen. The Civil Action for Sexual Battery: Therapeutic Jurisprudence? 25 Ottawa L. Rev. 203 (1993); Murray Levine, A Therapeutic Jurisprudence Analysis of Mandated Reporting of Child Maltreatment by Psychotherapists, 10 N.Y.L. Sch. J. Hum. Rts. 711 (1993); Norman G. Poythress & Stanley L. Brodsky, In the Wake of a Negligent Release Law Suit: An Investigation of Professional Consequences and Institutional Impact on a State Psychiatric Hospital, 16 Law & Hum. Behav. 155 (1993); Daniel W. Shuman et al., The Health Effects of Jury

called questions of the "scope" of therapeutic jurisprudence.[5] This article deals with the concept of scope.

The scope of therapeutic jurisprudence actually involves several distinct, though somewhat related, matters. When one speaks of the law as a therapeutic agent, the following scope questions are immediately raised: What is meant by therapeutic, and how broad should that term be? Therapeutic for whom? What is meant by law, and how broad should that concept be? What substantive areas of law are or should be involved? Finally, should the unit of legal analysis be micro (e.g., a particular rule or procedure) or macro (e.g., a body of law) or both? Not surprisingly, these scope questions of therapeutic jurisprudence may be subsumed under the more general headings "therapeutic" and "jurisprudence." Let us consider the scope questions under those two principal designations.

Therapeutic

What Is *Therapeutic?*

Therapeutic jurisprudence has been criticized for not offering a clear-cut definition of the term therapeutic.[6] As a mere lens or heuristic for better seeing and understanding the law, however, I think therapeutic jurisprudence has quite rightly opted not to provide a tight definition of the term, thereby allowing commentators to roam within the intuitive and common sense contours of the concept.[7] There are actually two questions involved in "defining" the term therapeutic, one regarding researchers-scholars, the other regarding society and legal-political decision makers. Taking the second question first, what is ultimately regarded as "therapeutic"—and the law's role in promoting therapeutic aims—is a sociopolitical decision,[8] decided by legal-political decision makers,[9] with, it is hoped, important input given to consumers or recipients of the law's therapeutic aims.[10] In that connection, what is ultimately therapeutic and when therapeutic goals should prevail over other ones is an issue raised but not resolved by therapeutic jurisprudence.

There remains, however, the question of what therapeutic should mean for the purposes of researchers and academics.[11] Once again, a tight definition of

---

Service, 18 Law & Psychol. Rev. 267 (1994); Jack Susman, Resolving Hospital Conflicts: A Study on Therapeutic Jurisprudence, 22 J. Psychiatry & L. 107 (1994); Julie Magno Zito et al., Toward a Therapeutic Jurisprudence Analysis of Medication Refusal in the Court Review Model, 11 Behavioral Sci. & L. 151 (1993).

5. Gary Melton, Therapy through Law, 39 Contemp. Psychol. 215 (1994); Slobogin, supra note 2 (discussing the "identity" and "definitional" dilemmas); Small, supra note 3.

6. Melton, supra note 5.

7. New Directions, supra note 1, at 765.

8. Response, supra note 3.

9. Id.; Harry T. Edwards, The Growing Disjunction between Legal Education and the Legal Profession: A Post Script, 91 Mich. L. Rev. 2191, 2196 n.20 (1993).

10. Response, supra note 3; Petrila, supra note 3.

11. The questions are, of course, related to the extent that scholarly prescriptions are addressed to legal-political decisionmakers. See David B. Wexler, Therapeutic Jurisprudence and Changing Conceptions of Legal Scholarship, 11 Behavioral Sci. & L. 17 (1993) [here-

therapeutic should be avoided. A restrictive definition might simply be ignored by the research community or, far worse, might be taken seriously and might prematurely eclipse the issues that may be subject to research.

Of course, working within the broad intuitive boundaries of the concept, each individual researcher or academician writing about therapeutic jurisprudence must settle on a definition of therapeutic and ought to be fairly explicit about what definition is being used and why.[12] Making the definition reasonably explicit will ease the empirical measurement of dependent variables or outcome measures and will also raise the issue for normative debate in the political arena. Naturally, empirical researchers will bear the brunt of this obligation, but even articles of a more theoretical and speculative nature need to be sensitive—more sensitive than they have been—to the definitional matters. For example, is rehabilitation defined by attitudinal changes or by the absence of criminal activity (itself measured by self-reports or by official records)? Should one care about achieving rehabilitation if it is manifested only by attitudinal change? Why or why not? How is emotional stress to be measured? Should one be concerned with the law's impact on emotional stress in the short-term, in the long-term, or both? Why?

Thus, it is important for each writer, commentator, or researcher to come to grips with the therapeutic dimension so that research and debate might best proceed. Thus far scholars have dealt not only with the law's impact on psychosis[13] but also with an array of emotional issues relating to law such as the stress of serving as a juror in a traumatic criminal case,[14] the stresses of surviving sexual assault,[15] and the stresses of major life events.[16] Commentators have also touched on the cognitive distortions of sex offenders,[17] the short fuse of the battering parent,[18] the rehabilitative potential of certain sentencing

---

inafter Changing Conceptions]. It is therefore important to consider the involvement and input of consumers-recipients at the research stage. For examples, see Shuman et al., supra note 4; Zito, supra note 4.

12. This discussion is, I think, consistent with Slobogin's suggestions for dealing with the "definitional" dilemma. See Slobogin, supra note 2. See also Cohen & Dvoskin, supra note 4.

13. Bruce J. Winick, Competency to Consent to Voluntary Hospitalization: A Therapeutic Jurisprudence Analysis of Zinermon v. Burch, 14 Int'l J. L. & Psychiatry 169 (1991).

14. Shuman et al., supra note 4.

15. Feldthusen, supra note 4.

16. Daniel W. Shuman, Therapeutic Jurisprudence and Tort Law: A Limited Subjective Standard of Care, 46 SMU L. Rev. 409 (1992); Grant H. Morris, Requiring Sound Judgments of Unsound Minds: Tort Liability and the Limits of Therapeutic Jurisprudence, 47 SMU L. Rev. 1837 (1994).

17. Jeffrey A. Klotz et al., Cognitive Restructuring Through Law: A Therapeutic Jurisprudence Approach to Sex Offenders and the Plea Process, 15 U. Puget Sound L. Rev. 579 (1992); Jeffrey A. Klotz, Sex Offenders and the Law: New Directions, in Mental Health and the Law: Research, Policy, and Services (Bruce D. Sales & S. A. Shah eds., forthcoming 1995); David B. Wexler & Bruce J. Winick, Therapeutic Jurisprudence and Criminal Justice Mental Health Issues, 16 Mental & Physical Disability L. Rep. 225 (1992).

18. Daniel W. Shuman, The Duty of the State to Rescue the Vulnerable in the United States, in the Duty to Rescue: The Jurisprudence of Aid (Michael A. Menlowe & Alexander McCall Smith eds., 1993).

schemes,[19] and the secondary gain effects of physical illness and injury.[20] Other recent work looks at the successful integration in the workplace of employees with disabilities[21] and the impact of contract law on the self-esteem of lower income consumers.[22]

Although the definition of the term therapeutic thus needs to be left very flexible for purpose of promoting research, it is also probably true that, to preserve the camaraderie (and efficient work) of a common scholarly community, there ought to be some notion about the core concept and its rough bounds. In that connection it is noteworthy that the therapeutic jurisprudence literature to date has overwhelmingly conformed to areas within the ordinary mental health-health connotation of the term therapeutic: mental health-mental illness and health, illness, injury, disability, treatment, rehabilitation, and habilitation. Moreover, because therapeutic jurisprudence conceptualizes the law itself as the therapeutic agent, the focus has been on sociopsychological ways in which mental health, health, and mental illness might be promoted or inhibited by the law.

Therefore, what is meant by therapeutic far exceeds the reversal of psychosis. On the other hand, the term therapeutic has not yet become (and in my view for research purposes ought not to become) synonymous with simply achieving intended or desirable outcomes. Therapeutic jurisprudence deserves to retain its distinctiveness as a discipline relating to mental health and psychological aspects of health. Thus, certain matters central to law and psychology generally, such as the accuracy of eyewitness identification or the impact of jury size on jury decision making, would not in and of themselves be of interest to therapeutic jurisprudence. Such areas could be brought into therapeutic jurisprudence, however, if they were expanded to ask certain questions about impact on emotional life. It would be interesting to know, for example, whether in traumatic criminal cases 6-person juries suffer greater or less stress than 12-person juries.

More to the point, it will be helpful to the therapeutic jurisprudence community if a relatively discrete literature is regarded as principally relevant to the enterprise. Rather than the whole of social science, or even the whole of psychology, of special interest should be those articles, whether expressly related to law or not, that are written on cognitive-affective-behavioral topics by and for mental health professionals—psychiatrists, psychologists, social work-

---

19. Keri A. Gould, Turning Rat and Doing Time for Uncharged, Dismissed, or Acquitted Crimes: Do the Federal Sentencing Guidelines Promote Respect for the Law?, 10 N.Y.L. Sch. J. Hum. Rts. 835 (1993).

20. William E. Wilkinson, Therapeutic Jurisprudence and Workers' Compensation, Ariz Att'y, Apr. 1994, at 28. See also Bruce J. Winick, Rethinking the Health Care Delivery Crisis: The Need for a Therapeutic Jurisprudence, 7 J.L. & Health 49 (1993); Daniel W. Shuman, The Psychology of Compensation in Tort Law, 43 U. Kansas L. Review 39 (1994).

21. Rose A. Daly-Rooney, Designing Reasonable Accommodations Through Co-Worker Participation: Therapeutic Jurisprudence and the Confidentiality Provision of the Americans with Disabilities Act, 8 J.L. & Health (in press).

22. Jeffrey L. Harrison, Class, Personality, Contract, and Unconscionability, 35 Wm. & Mary L. Rev. 445 (1994).

ers, counselors, and criminal justice and correctional professionals. In that way, efficiency will be promoted, for therapeutic jurisprudence scholars will have a handle on the kind of literature they need to keep up with and examine through the legal lens of therapeutic jurisprudence.[23] Of course, therapeutic jurisprudence analysis and approaches might influence developments far beyond the rough research definition of therapeutic proposed here, and that is all to the good. If therapeutic jurisprudence is to retain a sense of identity, however, it must have a substantive focus that is meaningful and manageable. A focus on the mental health and psychological aspects of health seems to me to be the most appropriate, recognizing that even this is (and should remain) very rough around the edges. The definition suggested by Slobogin[24] best captures my sense of the appropriate scope: "the use of social science to study the extent to which a legal rule or practice promotes the psychological or physical well-being of the people it affects."

Therapeutic for Whom?

When one speaks of for whom the law might be therapeutic, again the therapeutic jurisprudence lens provides no answer and no particular limit. Growing as it did out of mental health law,[25] therapeutic jurisprudence began its exploration with the impact of the law on respondents in commitment cases and on mental patients within the legal system. However, scholarly interest soon spread to examining the law's therapeutic or antitherapeutic impact on criminal defendants,[26] victims,[27] jurors,[28] mental health professionals,[29] personal injury plaintiffs,[30] and employees with disabilities.[31] There may, of course, sometimes be a clash whereby a legal rule is therapeutic for one person or

---

23. When one looks through a therapeutic jurisprudence lens at behavioral science literature on the cognitive distortion of sex offenders, one is tempted to ask how the law might promote or inhibit cognitive distortions. Similarly, when one approaches the psychological principles of health care compliance through a therapeutic jurisprudence lens, he or she might want to ask whether those principles might somehow be imported into the legal system. See David B. Wexler, Putting Mental Health into Mental Health Law: Therapeutic Jurisprudence, 16 L. & Hum. Behav. 27 (1992) [hereinafter Putting Mental Health].

24. Slobogin, supra note 2. See also Bruce J. Winick, Psychotropic Medication in the Criminal Trial Process: The Constitutional and Therapeutic Implications of Riggins v. Nevada, 10 N.Y.L. Sch. J. Hum. Rts. 637, 638 (1993). On the difficulties of striking an appropriate balance, see Daniel W. Shuman, Making the World a Better Place Through Tort Law?: Through the Therapeutic Looking Glass, 10 N.Y.L. Sch. J. Hum. Rts. 739, 752 (1993).

25. New Directions, supra note 1.

26. Gould, supra note 19; David B. Wexler, Therapeutic Jurisprudence and the Criminal Courts, 35 Wm. & Mary L. Rev. 279 (1993).

27. Feldthusen, supra note 4.

28. Shuman et al., supra note 4.

29. Poythress & Brodsky, supra note 4.

30. Shuman, supra note 24. (Cf. Wilkinson, supra note 20.)

31. Daly-Rooney, supra note 21.

participant and antitherapeutic for another. Once again, therapeutic jurisprudence merely throws light on this issue and does not resolve the normative debate. Instead, that normative analysis can be undertaken and then addressed to the legal or political arena.[32]

Thus far, regardless of who might be involved with or affected by the law, the focus has largely been on the individual. Of course, there is no need for the focus to be so constrained; it could relate to the family,[33] the community,[34] and society in general. When one thinks of the therapeutic impact in terms of family, community, or society, one anticipates the microanalytic-macroanalytic discussion in the final section of this article.

Jurisprudence

What Is *Law?*

The most important change in legal scholarship in recent years, including the scholarship involving therapeutic jurisprudence, is the movement beyond an almost exclusive focus on the study of legal doctrine.[35] Recognizing that most "law" today is made by legislators and administrators, rather than by the appellate judiciary, legal scholars have broadened their focus and no longer concentrate their attention exclusively on trying to resolve the "next-generation issues" likely to come before the appellate courts. Therapeutic jurisprudence was obviously affected by that general change in legal scholarship as well as by a slowdown in the judicial promulgation of rights regarding those with mental disability.[36] Regardless of that slowdown, however, Melton is quite right in asserting that the doctrinal study of mental health law needed rejuvenation:

> Even if the movement for broad construction of civil rights had not waned, it is likely that mental health law would have become an increasingly less interesting area of legal doctrine. Regardless of the specific domain, the same general issues recur. Whether one is discussing insanity, civil commitment, or guardianship, there are common questions about the nature of mental disability and the justifications for using it as a foundation for greater coercion or entitlements or lower responsibility.[37]

---

32. Slobogin, supra note 2. Of course, finding a convergence of interests—for example, between defendants and victims—is the hoped-for goal, although it is understandably not always reachable. (Cf. Schopp, supra note 3.)

33. For example, Shuman's child abuse piece makes reference not only to the battering parent and to the battered child, but also to other children in the family. Shuman, supra note 18.

34. Martha Minow, Questioning Our Policies: Judge David L. Bazelon's Legacy for Mental Health Law, 82 Geo. L.J. 7, 17 (1993). See also Harrison, supra note 22.

35. Changing Conceptions, supra note 11. See generally Edward L. Rubin, The Concept of Law and the New Public Law Scholarship, 89 Mich. L. Rev. 792 (1991).

36. Michael L. Perlin, What Is Therapeutic Jurisprudence?, 10 N.Y.L. Sch. J. Hum. Rts. 623, 624 (1993); Putting Mental Health, supra note 23.

37. Melton, supra note 5, at 216.

When therapeutic jurisprudence speaks of looking at the law as a potential therapeutic agent, it refers to looking at legal (and administrative) rules and procedures and at the roles of legal actors or "players,"[38] which typically include lawyers and judges but may include many other actors, such as therapists[39] and employers.[40] Accordingly, therapeutic jurisprudence scholarship is addressed not only to the appellate judiciary[41] but also to legislators,[42] administrative agencies, and, importantly, trial courts.[43] The emphasis on roles of legal actors, especially when the actors operate in a relatively unconstrained legal field[44]—with great discretion in other words—is particularly ripe for therapeutic jurisprudence analysis. Informally, some of my students have questioned whether this is "really" law; they therefore pose a jurisprudential question regarding the appropriate scope of therapeutic jurisprudence. To me, however, the answer is clear. These various legal actors—implementers, enforcers, and administrators of the law—have great potential for influencing outcome therapeutically or antitherapeutically, as I show later. Moreover, until relatively recently, the law's almost exclusive interest in doctrine relegated the study of the roles of legal actors to a scholarly wasteland. Accordingly, there is great potential for study here and great interest to legal scholars because of important, albeit nuanced, subtle, and often completely hidden, therapeutic or antitherapeutic consequences. Moreover, whether any rule of law or legal procedure, in the traditional sense, will succeed or fail may depend as much or more on these "implementation" matters as on anything else.

Although, by including a heavy emphasis on legal roles, the definition of law is in one sense quite broad, it is important to note that, to date, therapeutic jurisprudence scholarship has generally been quite "microanalytic," focusing on particular rules, procedures, and roles rather than on a "body of law" or a "bundle or package" of appellate decisions.[45] It is possible, of course, to expand the unit of legal analysis to include and encompass that still broader conception of law and that is something that the potential "macroanalytic" study of therapeutic jurisprudence might involve, as is discussed in a later section.

---

38. Deborah A. Dorfman, Effectively Implementing Title I of the Americans with Disabilities Act for Mentally Disabled Persons: A Therapeutic Jurisprudence Analysis, 8 J.L. & Health (in press).

39. Jeffrey A. Klotz, Limiting the Psychotherapist-Patient Privilege: The Therapeutic Potential, 27 Crim L. Bull. 416 (1991).

40. Daly-Rooney, supra note 21.

41. Therapeutic Jurisprudence scholarship is addressed to the appellate judiciary through policy arguments grounded in empirical and clinical insights as well as psychological theory. Changing Conceptions, supra note 11, at 21–23.

42. Id. at 26. See also Edward L. Rubin, Public Choice in Practice and Theory, 81 Cal. L. Rev. 1657 (1993) (book review).

43. Changing Conceptions, supra note 11, at 26–27; Wexler, supra note 26.

44. Changing Conceptions, supra note 11, at 26.

45. Therapeutic jurisprudence scholarship on legal roles, at least those roles that allow for considerable discretion in their discharge, may be microanalytic "with a vengeance," because the unit of analysis in that enterprise is not even particular rules of law or particular procedures, but merely the nuanced implementation or application of existing law.

The Substantive Legal Range

Another legal scope issue concerns the nature of the substantive law involved in therapeutic jurisprudence. A related inquiry concerns how broadly therapeutic jurisprudence will illuminate legal questions.

Although therapeutic jurisprudence grew out of mental health law, it is not the case that "therapeutic jurisprudence is self-limited to a descriptive and normative theory of mental health law and does not attempt to influence areas of law outside that domain."[46] In Essays in Therapeutic Jurisprudence, for example, Bruce Winick and I noted the following:

> It seems only natural...that initial forays into therapeutic jurisprudence take place within the core content areas of mental health law. Obviously, however, therapeutic jurisprudence will also have applications in forensic psychiatry generally, in health law, in a variety of allied legal fields (criminal law, juvenile law, family law), and probably across the entire legal spectrum.[47]

Acknowledging the theoretically possible movement of therapeutic jurisprudence beyond the domain of mental health law, Mark Small nonetheless questioned its likelihood:

> The strength of therapeutic jurisprudence is that the promoted value of "therapy" is consistent with the therapeutic value long prized and implicit in mental health law. When one moves to other areas of the law, the value of therapy takes on considerably less significance, and at times becomes irrelevant. For example, there seems little benefit in empirically analyzing issues in antitrust law, secure transactions, or water law according to therapeutic outcomes. These and other areas of law were created to serve a variety of purposes, perhaps least (if at all) among them is that there is or should be a therapeutic outcome that is of consequence.[48]

Actually, Small's comment has two aspects to it. The first is that therapeutic jurisprudence will be less significant, and perhaps irrelevant, in certain substantive fields. The second is that "therapeutic jurisprudence as a template fails to cover the diversity of work being done within the field of legal psychology."[49] As to this latter aspect, Small is surely correct. Viewing therapeutic jurisprudence as a particular version of psychological jurisprudence, Small argued that the "relationship between law and psychology would be enhanced by developing a psychological jurisprudence that is more inclusive of legal psychology."[50] Even in its broadest sense, therapeutic jurisprudence, whether micro or macro, will not grapple with all issues explored by legal psychology, as demonstrated earlier in my discussion of eyewitness testimony and of jury size and decision making.

Whether Small is correct in pushing for a psychological jurisprudence that would be co-extensive with the area of legal psychology is not at all clear to me. A jurisprudence that encompasses the whole of legal psychology might

---

46. Wiener, supra note 4, at 506.
47. Essays, supra note 1 at x.
48. Small, supra note 3, at 698–99.
49. Id. at 699.
50. Id. at 676.

lose its explanatory or normative power.[51] Neither law and economics nor feminist jurisprudence seems to shed light on all conceivable legal issues, and surely therapeutic jurisprudence can make no such all-inclusive claim.

As to Small's first point—regarding the substantive law scope of therapeutic jurisprudence—it is interesting to note that therapeutic jurisprudence scholarship has already spread to many substantive legal areas beyond mental health law.[52] Therapeutic jurisprudence has moved from mental health law to other areas that involve law and mental health but that fall outside of the substantive domain of traditional mental health law.

Given the earlier discussion of the sorts of cognitive, affective, and behavioral matters that seem comfortably to fall under the rubric of what might be called therapeutic, it is no surprise to see therapeutic jurisprudence scholarship not only in mental health law but also in criminal law and procedure, sentencing and corrections law, juvenile and family law, health law, disability law, personal injury law, and workers' compensation law.[53]

The commentators who have produced this corpus of scholarship belong to a community of scholars who previously wrote in traditional mental disability law.[54] Indeed, as noted elsewhere,[55] it may be that, somewhat ironically, therapeutic jurisprudence may make its greatest impact outside of traditional mental disability law. That is because hard-core psychosis, the typical issue of mental disability law, is probably most difficult to impact (cause or correct) by a social force such as the law. On the other hand, the emotional stresses and strains that often arise in the areas of law noted earlier—health, corrections, disability, personal injury, workers' compensation, juvenile and family—may be more susceptible to therapeutic intervention by the force of law.

In addition, if we as therapeutic jurisprudence scholars concern ourselves with a broad range of emotional-behavioral difficulties, we may, with any luck, help break down the we-they distinction often drawn to isolate those with mental disabilities. To the extent that lawyers, law students, and behavioral scientists interested in law-mental health issues are exposed to this range of mental health problems throughout the curriculum, mental disorders and disabilities of various types may become less stigmatized.

Finally, mental disability law scholars, who in the past often operated in their own little corner of the academy, may now be mainstreamed into the general law school world of teaching and scholarship. They may have something to add by raising questions previously unasked in a number of different substantive areas of law.

Therapeutic jurisprudence as a field of inquiry now brings together, under a more-or-less coherent conceptual umbrella, a number of topics that have not

51. See supra note 24 and accompanying text.

52. Whereas Small criticizes therapeutic jurisprudence for its supposed failure to be of assistance outside of mental health law, Melton fears its influence beyond that area: "The problem is that Wexler and Winick aspire to do more. They purport to provide a philosophical structure and analytic approach to the law in general, although their focus thus far has been largely limited to mental health law." Melton, supra note 5, at 216.

53. New Directions, supra note 1.

54. Id. at 775–76.

55. Id. at 776.

generally been recognized as related: how the criminal justice system might traumatize sexual battery victims,[56] how workers' compensation schemes might create the moral hazard of prolonging work-related injury,[57] how the confidentiality provision of the Americans With Disabilities Act (ADA) might operate to stymie the workplace integration of an employee with a disability,[58] and how the current law of contracts might operate to reinforce the low self-esteem of disadvantaged contracting parties.[59]

So where does this leave us in terms of Small's comment about the substantive range of therapeutic jurisprudence? Surely, therapeutic jurisprudence is not limited to mental health law. Potentially, it could have bearing in any substantive legal area, although it is obviously most likely to be of immediate use and interest in the more social and health legal areas.

Furthermore, therapeutic jurisprudence scholars seem to find particularly appealing the uncovering of therapeutic and antitherapeutic legal consequences that are subtle or hidden. The irony may therefore be that therapeutic jurisprudence scholars will find greater intellectual interest in areas where the express purpose of the law is not necessarily to promote therapeutic gains than in those areas where it is![60]

Perhaps therapeutic consequences will be particularly difficult to find in areas such as antitrust law, securities law, or water law. On the other hand, if such consequences are actually found in those areas, those issues may be extremely exciting to therapeutic jurisprudence scholars. Once one starts approaching legal areas with the use of the therapeutic jurisprudence lens, who can tell what one will find? If certain legal arrangements or procedures seem to lead to high stress, anger, feuding behavior, even violence between different persons, parties, neighbors, riparian landowners, and so forth, those arrangements and procedures may indeed become ripe for therapeutic jurisprudence inquiry.

Thus, if it is true that the most exciting intellectual work seems to be in exploring less obvious therapeutic and antitherapeutic consequences, then there will be a natural expansion from mental health law—where the therapeutic focus is express[61]—to other substantive areas—like criminal, juvenile, health, disability, family, workers' compensation, torts, and even to water law, although there the connection may be so subtle and hidden one may have to dig rather deep to hit a therapeutic jurisprudence well.

Therapeutic jurisprudence may then grow tremendously in scope to embrace all, or virtually all, legal areas. Although this legal scope is "broad," however, the unit of legal analysis remains microanalytic, with a focus on particular rules, procedures, and roles of players in the legal arena. I now turn to

---

56. Feldthusen, supra note 4.

57. Wilkinson, supra note 20.

58. Daly-Rooney, supra note 21.

59. Harrison, supra note 22.

60. The true irony is that the law may actually have greater impact in those areas. See text accompanying note 55.

61. David B. Wexler and Robert F. Schopp. Therapeutic Jurisprudence: A New Approach to Mental Health Law, in Handbook of Psychology and Law (Dorothy K. Kagehiro & William S. Laufer eds., 1992).

a further elaboration (and defense) of the present microanalytic emphasis of therapeutic jurisprudence and to a short discussion of the possibility of therapeutic jurisprudence expanding its scope in a macroanalytic direction.

Unit of Legal Analysis: Microanalytic-Macroanalytic

As much of the prior discussion has indicated, the overwhelming bulk of therapeutic jurisprudence scholarship to date has been microanalytic rather than macroanalytic. Sales and Shuman said it well in the context of mental health law:

> Even though...mental health law now benefits from a therapeutic jurisprudence perspective that focuses on the consequences of the law, it still suffers from lack of a broader vision of what an effective, truly therapeutic system for the delivery of mental health services would entail....In essence the law has been playing at the fringe of the enormous tapestry that is mental health care, pulling at individual threads while apparently oblivious to the larger patterns.[62]

Sales and Shuman suggested that therapeutic jurisprudence turn its attention to ways in which the law can help create appropriate and adequate mental health services.

Kathleen Williamson, a lawyer, pro tem judge, and adjunct professor of feminist jurisprudence now doing graduate work in cultural anthropology, critiqued microanalytic therapeutic jurisprudence from a much more radical perspective. In an informal weekly reaction paper prepared for a therapeutic jurisprudence seminar,[63] Williamson discussed Shuman's analysis of the DeShaney case,[64] which held the state had no constitutional duty to rescue victims of child abuse:

> Shuman importantly questions the meaning of duty of care. What is therapeutic jurisprudence if not thinking of some duty of care? But to whom? A parent? A child? How can the treatment of one individual overcome the problems and stress of poverty? Shuman is to be applauded for raising the macro questions of class poverty [as they relate to producing child abuse]. Therapy is addressing the larger issues, housing, health care, education, decent jobs. Not manipulating and coercing people one by one through criminal/medical systems. The legislators who raise these questions are neither liberal (those who would treat the [battering] individual) nor conservative (those who would incarcerate the individual) but radical (those who would look to the society and environment for cause and cure for such rampant problems). We don't have one or two people committing child abuse. It is rampant. It is societal. It is not an individual's problem. It is unlikely that the government is going to become involved in such a strategy, and that is one reason why these types of policymakers or lawmakers are labeled as radical. They make perfectly good sense. But they are the sub-

---

62. Bruce D. Sales and Daniel W. Shuman, Mental Health Law and Mental Health Care: Introduction, 64 Am. J. Orthopsychiatry 172, 178 (1994).

63. For a discussion of reaction papers, see David B. Wexler, An Introduction to Therapeutic Jurisprudence, in Essays, supra note 1, at 17. See also Wexler, supra note 3.

64. DeShaney v. Winnebago County Department of Social Services, 489 U.S. 189 (1989), 103 L.Ed. 2d 249, 109 S. Ct. 998 (1989).

terranean voice in our capitalistic society holding values of autonomy and no duty to care as esteemed.

It is accurate to categorize the great bulk of therapeutic jurisprudence writing to date as rather "centrist" in terms of seeking to reform the law rule by rule, procedure by procedure. In this sense, therapeutic jurisprudence seems to share assumptions with the New Public Law and with the great bulk of Social Science in Law scholarship as well.[65] Thus far, therefore, the therapeutic jurisprudence microanalytic approach lacks the transformative thrust of the "outsider" jurisprudence common to feminist jurisprudence, Critical Legal Studies, and Critical Race Theory. Interestingly, however, and for the same reasons, microanalytic therapeutic jurisprudence has in no way sought to construct a Therapeutic State: Therapeutic jurisprudence has been playing at the fringe of the mental health care tapestry and has not been designing the larger pattern.[66]

There has, however, been at least some macroanalytic therapeutic jurisprudence scholarship to date. Shuman's look at poverty as a cause of child abuse, however, cannot rightly be so considered, for his solution to the problem turns out to be completely microanalytic (but perhaps workable and achievable!)—tinkering with and proposing modest adjustments of the existing law.[67] Shuman did some "macro" work, however, by scrutinizing the tort compensation system[68] and looking psychologically at whether the compensation scheme promotes healing or prolonged suffering.[69] Winick has proposed a health care system using principles derived from a therapeutic jurisprudence look at the health care crisis.[70] For example, he proposed exploiting the treatment benefits that can come from the psychological power of choice. In a very creative recent piece, Harrison has suggested that the current law of contracts may reinforce the low self-esteem of disadvantaged consumers.[71]

It appears that a macroanalytic therapeutic jurisprudence is needed and is indeed emerging. A macroanalytic therapeutic jurisprudence is likely to develop in several strands.[72] As macroanalytic approaches develop, they will surely pose a number of tricky issues. One can immediately see, however, that the three basic issues that have been raised about microanalytic therapeutic jurisprudence—rights-justice, empirical questions, and scope questions—will again surface in the macro domain.

---

65. Changing Conceptions, supra note 11, at 29.

66. Sales & Shuman, supra note 62.

67. Shuman, supra note 18, at 149.

68. Shuman, supra note 24.

69. For other macro work, see Robert F. Schopp, Sexual Predators and the Structure of the Mental Health System: Expanding the Normative Focus of Therapeutic Jurisprudence, 1 Psychol. Pub. Pol'y & L., 161–192 (1995).

70. Winick, supra note 20.

71. Harrison, supra note 22.

72. For example, there may be scholars looking at the therapeutic impact on society, or on sectors thereof, of clusters of decisions or of major legal doctrines. Scholars may critique the roots of the law and call for fundamental, transformative, societal changes. Psycholegal architects may propose the creation of new service systems.

For example, if and when society and legal scholars seek to create and make available an array of mental health services, care will need to be taken to provide safeguards so that the system is not used coercively. As Martha Minow has noted, there are "those who see social control in every form of service or treatment."[73] Surely, most people believe that society can create mental health services without creating a therapeutic state, but the therapeutic state issue is much more likely to require serious argument in the macro sphere than in the micro sphere. Empirical questions will also arise, particularly around a macro-analytic approach that focuses not on an isolated rule of law but on clusters of judicial decisions and "packages" of law. Issues will arise regarding how, if at all, one might measure the impact of such broad-based legal developments, and concerns will expectedly arise as well regarding the direction of causality—whether the cluster of decisions has really caused, or is rather the result of, certain societal attitudes. In addition, scope questions will again arise, not only in distinguishing macro from micro (a somewhat blurred distinction in many instances, as it is in economics)[74] but also in ascertaining whether the contours of the definition of therapeutic for law reform and research questions are really the same or something very different when one speaks in macro rather than micro terms.

The emerging macroanalytic issues are likely to be fascinating. In this section, however, I explain why, in my view, therapeutic jurisprudence developed originally on a microscale. In addition, I present a nonapologetic and thoroughly enthusiastic justification for why microanalytic therapeutic jurisprudence ought to proceed with all deliberate speed.[75]

For better or for worse, therapeutic jurisprudence scholars seem to find intellectual interest and excitement in ferreting out subtle, nuanced, hidden, and unintentional antitherapeutic impacts (or in spotting potential but hidden therapeutic impacts that might be exploited). The principal premise of therapeutic jurisprudence is that, know it or not, like it or not, the law often has therapeutic or antitherapeutic consequences. Therapeutic jurisprudence "proposes that we be sensitive to those consequences, rather than ignore them, and that we ask whether the law's antitherapeutic consequences can be reduced and its therapeutic consequences enhanced without subordinating due process and justice values."[76] The notion, then, is that particular legal arrangements need to be examined for their therapeutic impact. When the impact is subtle and hidden, one seems to be necessarily talking about working at the "tapestries" of the law rather than explicitly focusing on and addressing and creating therapeutic systems. The very notion of a system being expressly therapeutic

---

73. Minow, supra note 34, at 14.

74. Harrison, supra note 22, at 452.

75. Microanalytic therapeutic jurisprudence is itself not all that micro: it does not involve simply helping an individual client or consumer. By advocating the reform of law or practice, one hopes to affect all future similarly situated people. Legal services attorneys often debated the appropriateness of an "individual client service" model versus a "test case law reform" model. Microanalytic therapeutic jurisprudence actually more closely resembles the "law reform" model, for legal services law reform attorneys typically did battle to challenge—and change—a particular (and therefore micro) rule or procedure.

76. New Directions, supra note 1, at 762.

means that the principal thrust of the enterprise is not latent, hidden, or subtle at all.

Writing about sex offenders and the law,[77] Jeffrey Klotz has captured the essence of what, to date, has interested therapeutic jurisprudence legal scholars. Klotz noted that the law may affect therapeutic ends either deliberately or inadvertently. Then he noted, with respect to inadvertent impact,

> it is these less obvious connections between the law and therapeutic outcomes which have been of particular interest to therapeutic jurisprudence scholars, perhaps because identifying these relationships, which later may become the focus of empirical research, may be the most challenging and exciting aspect of therapeutic jurisprudence scholarship.[78]

Klotz explained why the interest to legal scholars revolves around the inadvertent consequences: "asking whether a particular treatment promotes therapeutic outcomes will not tell us whether the law itself promotes therapeutic outcomes."[79]

Klotz's chapter on sex offenders actually provides interesting "data" on what is of interest to therapeutic jurisprudence scholars. Although he summarized the clinical research regarding the adequacy of treatment programs, the great bulk of his chapter is an inquiry attempting to "flesh out otherwise 'hidden' empirical links between the mental health and behavior of sex offenders and various legal apparatuses."[80] Accordingly, Klotz focused on such matters as the "gatekeeping" function of sexual psychopath legislation—various "methods employed to include or exclude offenders from the treatment programs"[81]—and on the way in which the legal system promotes treatment incentives or inhibits efforts to receive treatment.[82]

Why is it that therapeutic jurisprudence legal scholars seem interested in the hidden and unintended therapeutic consequences rather than in the deliberate or expressed therapeutic consequences of laws? It seems to me that the answer lies in the general expertise of legal scholars and their interest in nuanced legal issues. Legal scholars are not particularly suited, or interested in, simply finding out "what works" and then mandating it by law.[83] An example, albeit from microanalytic therapeutic jurisprudence, can help explain this point.

---

77. Klotz, supra note 17.

78. Id. Changing these inadvertent antitherapeutic aspects may also be relatively uncontroversial. See Wilkinson, supra note 20, at 32–33:

> Therapeutic jurisprudence suggests that change is appropriate when anti-therapeutic consequences of legal arrangements can be corrected with little or no impact on justice considerations. Application of therapeutic jurisprudence principles is especially appropriate in situations where antitherapeutic arrangements are simply inadvertent.

79. Klotz, supra note 17.

80. Id.

81. Id.

82. Id.

83. There is in some cases a sharp difference between intellectual interest and importance. The mere fact that lawyers may not be particularly interested in (or good at) drafting a grand scheme of mental health services does not mean the task ought not to be undertaken. It may simply suggest that the particular strand of microanalytic therapeutic jurisprudence ought to

Legal scholars are likely to be particularly interested in a therapeutic jurisprudence problem if both the source of the antitherapeutic consequence and the solution to the problem reside in an interesting way in the law. Take the research by Shuman and Hamilton[84] regarding the health or stress effects of serving on juries in traumatic criminal cases. Those researchers have concluded that such service can indeed lead to some substantial stress, and it is actually the law itself that is responsible for producing such stress. But consider then the issue of remedy. One possible solution is to make available to such jurors—even mandating such by law—the services of a mental health professional to debrief the jury and to engage them in stress-reduction exercises.

That solution may be appropriate, highly important, and highly effective, but it is simply not terribly interesting to legal scholars. Of far more legal interest, by contrast, is one of Shuman's proposed solutions: to provide a jury instruction regarding the importance of the deliberation process.

> [A] post-trial instruction encouraging jurors not only to share their feelings during deliberations, but also to encourage jurors to discuss the case fully, to encourage those with minority viewpoints to make their views known, and to respect the views of all members of the jury is a reasonable alternative. This approach is an example of therapeutic jurisprudence. Encouraging more extensive communications between jurors benefits the deliberative process: it avoids groupthink and encourages more thoughtful deliberation. And, encouraging talking about these shared juror experiences benefits the therapeutic process: it is psychologically and physically beneficial to jurors.[85]

It is my sense, then, that legal therapeutic jurisprudence scholars are unlikely to have the expertise or interest to deal particularly well with express or deliberate therapeutic laws in macro terms of broadly creating new systems. Consider again the suggestion by Sales and Shuman that therapeutic jurisprudence be used to provide, develop, and require adequate mental health services. Much of their proposal sounds more like pure psychology or like mental health or health administration than like law (e.g., "the development of a comprehensive plan of integrated services"[86], even if the panoply of mental health services will have a legal avenue in terms of being mandated by law (e.g., "the provision of sufficient funding to support legally mandated entitlements").[87]

Might legal scholars in therapeutic jurisprudence have a role in the macro establishment of the kind of mental health services that Sales and Shuman proposed? I definitely think so, but the irony is that the interesting questions for such scholars will likely lie in the microanalytic realm.

---

be carried out by persons principally interested and trained in psychology, mental health and health administration, and related fields, rather than by persons who are primarily legal scholars.

84. Shuman et al., supra note 4.

85. Id. Of course, it is an empirical question whether Shuman's solution will work. Note that some recent research documents that juror alternates are also stressed by their role in traumatic criminal cases. Thomas L. Hafemeister, Juror Stress, 8 Violence & Victims 177, 183–84 (1993). Thus, even a jury instruction that works to reduce stress during the deliberation process would not reach those persons who are merely juror alternates.

86. Sales & Shuman, supra note 62, at 178.

87. Id.

Suppose legal or, better yet, mental health scholars ascertained just what kind of mental health services are effective and ought to be provided in a community. And assume further that the governing bodies could be persuaded to appropriate the funds and require the establishment of these services by law. Will this legal arrangement work? In that connection, the micro questions seem to be key. For example, in The Well-Being Project: Mental Health Clients Speak for Themselves,[88] Jean Campbell and Ron Schraiber found that 47% of polled mental health clients said they avoided treatment for fear of being involuntarily committed.[89] That finding, if not attended to in the micro sense of implementing the legal arrangement, may mean the entire service-providing project is doomed to failure.

Given that finding, one wonders whether certain clinics might be designated as "safe houses" where, by law, professionals may be relieved of the duty and even the right of instituting commitment proceedings, giving Tarasoff warnings, reporting instances of child abuse, and so forth. Even if the law created such safe houses, would the word sufficiently get out to the consumers, and would consumers be sufficiently trusting and relieved of fear so as to avail themselves of the services?

These, then, are interesting microanalytic questions of the subtle impact of law on therapeutic outcomes and are likely to be of great interest to legal scholars undertaking therapeutic jurisprudence projects. This does not mean, of course, that macroanalytic therapeutic jurisprudence of the type proposed by Sales and Shuman ought not or will not develop. It is simply my prediction that this particular strand of potential macroanalytic therapeutic jurisprudence will principally lie in the province of behavioral scientist therapeutic jurisprudence scholars, with help from the legal community in considering microanalytic concerns of implementation.

What of the more "radical" macroanalytic strand, looking, for example, at the extent to which child abuse has its roots in poverty? To the extent that therapeutic jurisprudence scholars can ascertain these causes and advocate for housing, education, and employment, as Shuman did in his article on child abuse, attention will of course be directed to those avenues. Once again, however, important as the matter is, the "legal" input seems not all that interesting. Should one push for and mandate better housing and more employment opportunities? Of course one should, and therapeutic jurisprudence scholars, even of the microanalytic variety, may be able to expose some of these issues. Their own solutions, however, as in Shuman's case, may be microanalytic, such as devising legal arrangements to ensure that people will avail themselves of the newly provided housing.

When one speaks of the microtask of therapeutically implementing law, one begins to see another potential application of microanalytic therapeutic jurisprudence, alluded to in an earlier section.[90] What I refer to now is the ther-

---

88. Jean Campbell & Ron Schraiber, The Well-Being Project: Mental Health Clients Speak for Themselves (1989).

89. Id. at 118.

90. See supra text accompanying notes 38–45.

apeutic "administration" or "application" of existing law. Because, in this case, the unit of analysis is the existing law, and scholars urge only a change in practice, administration, or role—not a change even in a single rule of law or legal procedure—this microtask might be viewed as microanalytic with a vengeance.[91] Indeed, as noted earlier,[92] some might argue that we are not now truly dealing with "law."

With conventional legal scholarship's doctrinal focus, this aspect of the law has not traditionally been regarded as "true law." Accordingly, research into the therapeutic or antitherapeutic consequences of various arrangements applying or administering existing law has not received very much attention. This is, however, a most promising avenue of microanalytic therapeutic jurisprudence.

There are many reasons why the study of therapeutic legal administration should be of interest and importance. First, simply on the interest front, searching for potential ways to administer existing laws in a more therapeutic fashion taps the legal scholar's interest in subtleties, nuances, and unearthing hidden possibilities. Second, on a practical level, the entire reform enterprise may seem less controversial when the only matter at issue is how to administer or apply a law. Third, all laws are fair game—the legal universe is enormous. Fourth, the process itself is so much easier than formal law reform,[93] although because these suggested administrative revisions are not self-executing,[94] they will, of course, be easier to resist as well. Thus, the task of the legal scholar in this regard will be to argue convincingly to potential legal administrators to change their behavior.[95] This ease is very important, however. Compared with formal law reform, it is far easier to experiment with a mere administrative change. If the change proves to "work," actual law reform may be unnecessary. Finally, the law is a blunt instrument, and one of the problems faced by jurisprudence is that certain laws will be therapeutic for some and not therapeutic for others. It is very difficult to try and slice up laws and apply particular laws only to situations where they will have therapeutic ends for all. With therapeutic application or administration, however, it is somewhat easier to individually tailor the application. Perhaps two examples will put the potential of this microanalytic exercise into clearer focus.

In Therapeutic Jurisprudence and Worker's Compensation,[96] William Wilkinson analyzed the worker's compensation law and its tendency to produce a "moral hazard" or "secondary gain" consequence of unintentionally prolonging injury for some workers. Instead of scrapping the law, or suggesting major surgery for it, however, Wilkinson took a therapeutic jurisprudence approach in suggesting ways in which the existing worker's compensation law might be administered somewhat differently to encourage workers to return to

---

91. See supra note 45.

92. See supra text accompanying notes 44–45.

93. David B. Wexler, Reforming the Law in Action through Empirically Grounded Civil Commitment Guidelines, 39 Hosp. & Community Psychiatry 402 (1988).

94. Paul S. Applebaum, Civil Commitment from a Systems Perspective, 16 L. & Hum. Behav. 61, 69 (1992).

95. Rubin, supra note 42.

96. Wilkinson, supra note 20.

the workplace. One of his suggestions involves "wagering" with the employee to return to work earlier, in exchange for greater short-term compensation.[97] If this sort of wagering scheme could be resorted to under existing law[98]—without the necessity of legislative reform—it would be an example of implementing an existing law in a therapeutic manner.

A powerful example of therapeutic legal administration, also involving the workplace, is provided by Rose Daly-Rooney, who analyzed the confidentiality provision of the ADA from a therapeutic jurisprudence perspective.[99]

Drawing on the psychological insight that providing people with voice in a process leads them better to accept the outcome as fair, Daly-Rooney posited that an employee with a disability might be best integrated into the workplace if the employee were to waive the confidentiality provision of the Act and divulge something about the disability to relevant coworkers. The coworkers could then help ascertain the essential functions of the job and could help design reasonable accommodations for the employee with a disability. This might decrease rumors about the new employee and decrease resentment by the coworkers, who now have had a voice in the process and have some sort of stake in the success of the designed accommodation.

Of course, whether this works or not is an empirical question, which Daly-Rooney urged be tested. The thesis could be tested without going to the legislature to change the law. If certain employers were persuaded to implement the law according to Daly-Rooney's proposal on an experimental basis, the results could be compared with other comparable companies that merely continued doing business as usual. Ultimate law reform might be accomplished by micro-analytic therapeutic jurisprudence scholars persuading certain administrators of the ADA, who in this case are employers, to urge employees with disabilities to consider the waiver of the confidentiality provision. The matter is subject to individual tailoring because, for some employees, confidentiality will outweigh the interest in coworker involvement, but for others it will not. Moreover, this change is easier to accomplish than changing the confidentiality law itself. Changing the confidentiality law itself would be tremendously controversial and would raise all sorts of justice concerns. The administrative solution, on the other hand, leads to a convergence between justice and therapeutic concerns: Confidentiality is preserved for those who deem it important to them, and yet divulgence and co-worker involvement are made available to those who wish to follow that route for hoped-for therapeutic gains.[100] Furthermore, as "micro" as this illustration seems, the suggested change might help an untold number of employees with disabilities and might, indeed, be ultimately transformative of the workplace environment. Thus, certain microchanges might well lead to macroresults, again demonstrating the blurriness and overlapping nature of the therapeutic jurisprudence scope questions.[101]

---

97. Id. at 31–32.
98. Id. at 32.
99. Daly-Rooney, supra note 21.
100. Cf. Slobogin, supra note 2 (discussing the "rule of law" dilemma).
101. See supra note 75.

Conclusion

Therapeutic jurisprudence is far broader in scope than mental health law, but it is not simply a law-psychology or even a law-mental health smorgasbord. Instead, it has a rather sharp focus on the law itself as a social force potentially enhancing or inhibiting therapeutic outcomes.

In one sense, therapeutic jurisprudence is not at all new, for many scholars, researchers, and practitioners were playing with these insights before therapeutic jurisprudence was explicated. What is new is the effort at making the perspective explicit and conceptualizing it as a field of inquiry. The perspective raises new questions, invigorates the discussion of others, and, in any event, brings together and situates under one conceptual umbrella areas that previously seemed disparate, many of which were developed in isolation, ranging from victims' rights to compensation neurosis. Therapeutic jurisprudence enables these subjects to be brought together into one area of study and practice. Therapeutic jurisprudence itself, then, provides a lens and a new scope of scholarly inquiry.

Chapter 42

Applying the Law Therapeutically

David B. Wexler

Recently, a number of academics and practitioners interested in law/psychology interactions have turned their attention to the study of therapeutic jurisprudence. Therapeutic jurisprudence (Bibliography, 1993; Finkelman & Grisso, 1994; Perlin, 1993; Slobogin, 1995; Wexler, 1995; Wexler & Winick, 1991), which focuses on the law's impact on emotional life, is a perspective that recognizes that the law *itself* can be seen to function as a kind of therapist or therapeutic agent.

The law—which consists of legal rules (Bloom & Williams, 1994), legal procedures (Tyler, 1992), and the roles of legal actors (Gould, 1995; Wexler, 1991)—is a social force that sometimes produces therapeutic or antitherapeutic consequences, and therapeutic jurisprudence involves "the use of social science to study the extent to which a legal rule or practice promotes the psychological or physical well-being of the people it affects" (Slobogin, 1995, p. 196).

The therapeutic jurisprudence perspective grew out of mental health law scholarship, and much therapeutic jurisprudence work therefore concentrates on matters such as civil commitment (Tyler, 1992), the insanity defense (Perlin, 1994), the conditional release of insanity acquittees (Bloom & Williams, 1994; Wexler, 1991), incompetency to stand trial (Gould, 1995; Winick, 1995a), the right to refuse treatment (Susman, 1994; Winick, 1994), and the like. Recent applications, however, make it clear that the potential of therapeutic jurisprudence extends far beyond traditional mental health law; therapeutic jurisprudence is actually a mental health perspective on the law in general (Sales & Shuman, in press; Slobogin, 1995; Wexler, 1993a; Wexler, 1995), and the perspective has been applied beyond mental health law (Winick, 1995b) to criminal law and procedure (Gould, 1993; Klotz et al., 1992; Wexler, 1993b; Yates, 1994), family and juvenile law (Simon, 1995), health law (Winick, 1993), disability law (Daly-Rooney, 1994), workers' compensation law (Wilkinson, 1994), personal injury and tort law (Shuman, 1994), and even to contract law (Harrison, 1994).

Broad Reach of Therapeutic Jurisprudence

A recent example of the broad reach of therapeutic jurisprudence is Kay Kavanagh's analysis of the "Don't Ask, Don't Tell" regulation regarding gays in the military (Kavanagh, 1995). Under the policy, recruits will not be asked about their sexual orientation, but a statement by a person that he or she is gay creates a rebuttable presumption that the servicemember intends to engage in homosexual acts, and such a statement can trigger separation proceedings.

Kavanagh advocates a different policy, one that might be called "Don't Ask, Tell if You Want to." She is concerned that denying a servicemember the ability voluntarily to disclose matters of sexual orientation perpetuates homophobia and, more to the point of the present article, operates to create superficial social interactions and relations with others. In essence, Kavanagh claims, the Government, by the policy, creates social isolation or anomie for gay servicemembers.

The reason for the isolation is that "this forced concealment entails concealment of other details that surround the secret—sexual identity—details that could lead to revelation of the secret" (Kavanagh, 1995, p. 143). To conceal the prohibited fact of homosexual orientation, Kavanagh notes that gay servicemembers will be chilled from revealing basic life events and facts. The policy will have a chilling effect on

> making truly unremarkable disclosures, such as *with whom* one goes grocery shopping, shares a checking account, takes a vacation; *to whom* one apologizes for failing to do the dishes (or for failing to do them properly), for squeezing the toothpaste from the top of the tube rather than from the bottom, for leaving various household supplies scattered throughout the house rather than returning them to their appointed places; *from whom* one receives a phone call, a message, or flowers on one's birthday; and *with or without whom* one goes home for the holidays. (p. 154)

Kavanagh's proposed law reform, permitting but not requiring disclosure of sexual orientation, resembles the treatment of another possible secret—disability—by the Americans with Disabilities Act (ADA). Under the ADA, employers are to focus on job requirements and applicant abilities, not on disability, and are barred from inquiring into a prospective employee's disability. If offered a position, the employee can work without disclosing the disability or, if he or she needs a "reasonable accommodation" in the workplace in order to perform (e.g., the modification of equipment or of a work schedule), the employee can reveal the disability to the employer and request an adjustment or accommodation. Even then, under the ADA's confidentiality provision, the disability would need to be disclosed only to the employer, the employee's supervisor, and perhaps to safety personnel (Daly-Rooney, 1994).

Nonetheless, like Kavanagh's analysis of the psychological benefits that might flow to many from voluntary disclosure of sexual orientation, Rose Daly-Rooney's therapeutic jurisprudence analysis of the confidentiality provision of the ADA suggests that an employee with a disability may often profit from waiving confidentiality and from voluntarily disclosing the disability to relevant co-workers. Secrecy, again, may lead to isolation and superficial social relations. Daly-Rooney gives an example of a non-disclosing employee with mild retardation who lives in a group home. If, to protect her secret, she declines a co-worker's offer of a ride home on a rainy day, she will likely appear strange or unfriendly.

Moreover, drawing on the psychological insight that providing people with voice in a process leads them better to accept the outcome as fair (see Tyler, 1992; Wexler, 1991), Daly-Rooney posits that an employee with a disability might be best integrated into the workplace if the employee waives the confidentiality provision of the Act and divulges something about the disability to relevant co-workers. The co-workers, who after all probably know more than the new employee (and perhaps even more than the employer) about the requirements of the given job, could then help ascertain the essential functions of the job and could help design reasonable accommodations for the employee with a disability. This interaction might decrease rumors about the new employee and might decrease resentment by the co-workers, who now have had a voice in the process and have some sort of stake in the success of the designed accommodation.

Note that a key difference between the Kavanagh and the Daly-Rooney pieces is that Kavanagh advocates a change in the law *itself* (see Wexler, 1993c), whereas Daly-Rooney, writing about a law that *already* embraces "Don't Ask, Tell if You Want to," advocates "law reform" through what might be called the therapeutic application of existing law (Wexler, 1995)—in this case, the voluntary waiver of the ADA's confidentiality provision, and the disclosure of the disability to relevant co-workers.

The Therapeutic Application of Existing Law

The remainder of the present article will focus on the therapeutic application of existing law as a promising path for applied psychology. Perhaps the enterprise will seem more comfortable and familiar to psychologists and other mental health professionals if we focus, for the moment, on some concrete examples that fall solidly within the "core" of traditional mental health law—topics with which mental health professionals are likely more versed than they are with the ADA or with the regulation relating to gays in the military. Let us, then, turn to two more traditional topics: the *Tarasoff* (Tarasoff v. Regents of University of California, 1976) issue, and the issue of a patient's right to refuse mental health treatment.

Tarasoff

The California *Tarasoff* case established a therapist's duty to warn or otherwise protect the potential victim of a patient's predicted violence. The decision was severely criticized by mental health professionals as constituting an antitherapeutic rule of law. Alan Stone (1976), for example, claimed the *Tarasoff* duty "will imperil the therapeutic alliance and destroy the patient's expectation of confidentiality, thereby thwarting effective treatment and ultimately reducing public safety" (p. 368).

In an article written more than 15 years ago, (Wexler, 1979), employing an approach that clearly foreshadowed the therapeutic jurisprudence perspective, I challenged Stone's view. Noting that *Tarasoff*-type threats are overwhelmingly made against potential victims who are family members or their equivalents, I wrote:

> Principally, my purpose is to assert that the enmity of Stone and others toward *Tarasoff* is bottomed largely on their adherence to an "individual pathology" model of violent behavior which, the literature suggests, is theoretically and therapeutically unwarranted. More important, what *is* apparently warranted, according to those who have seriously studied the type of interpersonal violence that is therapeutically preventable, is an approach that focuses on troubled *relationships*. Ideally, such an approach should involve both the pa-

tient and the potential victim and should therefore often take the form of "couple" or "family" therapy. Finally, it is my thesis that, if taken seriously and followed widely, the *Tarasoff* decision, despite its many obvious drawbacks, has the clear-cut potential of prompting and prodding practicing therapists to terminate their continued clinging to an outmoded "individual pathology" model of violence, and to accept the paradigm of "interactional" or "couple" violence already endorsed by the professional literature. (p. 4)

I foresaw *Tarasoff*, which is triggered when a patient threatens violence against a specified other, possibly playing out along the following lines:

1. After *Tarasoff*, a typical therapist, despite intrapsychic therapeutic inclinations, is likely to focus far more than before on the potential victim and on the extent to which harm to the victim can be averted.

2. For fear of *Tarasoff* liability in the event he or she takes no action and a threatened victim is later seriously injured or killed by a patient, the therapist will presumably be induced, even in fairly borderline cases, to seek some acceptable means of alerting the potential victim of a patient's serious or possibly serious threat.

3. Ideally, of course, the therapist would wish to act in a manner acceptable to the patient—in a manner, that is, not disruptive of their on-going therapeutic relationship.

4. Fortunately, since the typical potential victim is a family member who presumably knows the patient is in therapy and who also typically knows at least to some extent of the patient's hostility toward the victim, a skillful therapist ought often to be able to secure the patient's consent to notify the potential victim.

5. If the patient's consent to the divulgence is obtained, *Tarasoff* can of course be satisfied without sacrificing the patient's trust and without the therapist running the risk of violating ethical or legal obligations to keep a patient's confidences.

6. When the victim is contacted, the therapist may first learn, as some therapists are apparently now first learning post-*Tarasoff*, of the victim's contributory or provocative role in the patient's potential violence.

7. In addition or alternatively, the therapist may learn from the victim certain significant facts about the patient's behavior.

8. If the therapist ascertains a meaningful presence of victim precipitation, he may seek—and obtain—the patient's consent to have additional contact with the potential victim, and the potential victim, particularly if he or she is a member of the patient's family, may be very willing to cooperate.

9. Even if victim contribution is not apparent, if the potential victim provides the therapist with important information about the patient, that information may be used to enhance therapy. Often, too, the patient may have an explanation that will lead the therapist to seek additional dialogue with the potential victim, and which may then provide evidence of victim contribution.

10. In any event, if the above chain of events begins to occur with any regularity, the typical therapist treating a potentially violent patient will find him- or herself, because of the pressure of *Tarasoff*, transformed from a practitioner of "intrapsychic" psychotherapy to a practitioner of a presumably preferable "interactionist" model of treating interpersonal violence. (pp. 26–28)

What I clearly realize now (even more so than when I wrote over 15 years ago) is that if I was right in thinking, contrary to Stone, that *Tarasoff* might be a therapeutically advantageous development, it would be so only if clinicians skillfully discharged the *Tarasoff* obligation in an appropriate manner. The therapeutic application of *Tarasoff* is by no means self-executing; it is entirely in the hands of mental health professionals.

Tarasoff will surely not have therapeutic yields if mental health professionals apply it in what Perlin (1992, p. 57) calls a "passive-aggressive style of behavior." Some commentators have noted that, to escape *Tarasoff*-type legal liability, "some clinicians have become reluctant to probe into areas of their patient's lives dealing with violence, while others have altered their record-keeping (either by obscuring information that might suggest violence or by 'padding' a record with information so as to support a decision not to warn)" (Perlin, 1992, p. 58).

But the *Tarasoff* case *can* in many instances be applied in a clinically-sound manner. For example, Wulsin, Bursztajn, and Gutheil (1983) present a clinical report of a Mr. A, a 20 year old single man admitted to the Massachusetts Mental Health Center's day hospital:

> When Mr. A's hallucinations took the form of commands to kill his mother, we as part of the treatment staff became concerned about a possible duty to third parties....In keeping with the principle of maintaining the therapeutic alliance whenever possible, especially in legal matters, we elected to involve the patient maximally in the process. To this end, we proposed a draft of a letter that would inform Mr. A's mother of the danger to her and that would also serve to document our response to her son's threats. In keeping with an alliance-seeking approach, Mr. A's therapist went over the letter and the attendant rationale with him. The letter stated that the patient "feared he might harm [his mother]." Mr. A agreed with the content of the letter and insisted on talking to his mother before we mailed the letter, fearing the letter would cause his mother to wish never to speak to him again. His mother first responded to the letter by saying that he should be "locked up with the key thrown away." During the ensuing conversation, however, she stated openly, "I love you"; Mr. A responded, "I love you, too," and both began to cry.
>
> Thereafter, Mr. A abided by a temporary agreement with the therapist not to see his mother outside the treatment setting; but he continued telephoning her and the family every day. Although his mother volunteered information to us by telephone, she otherwise refused to participate actively in her son's treatment. No civil commitment or further intervention was necessary for Mr. A. (p. 602)

The original *Tarasoff* debate—between Stone and myself—was on the rule of law level: is the *Tarasoff* rule antitherapeutic, as the conventional wisdom would have it, or might it actually, in the aggregate, be therapeutic? The present discussion, however, takes *Tarasoff* as a given; regardless of whether it is overall a good or bad thing so far as therapy and therapists are concerned (after all, its principal purpose is to protect public safety, not to enhance therapy), the present discussion looks at the discretionary roles of mental health professionals and asks how mental health professionals may best—most therapeutically—be able to apply, implement, enforce the existing *Tarasoff* obligation. Surely the clinically-sensitive Wulsin, Bursztajn and Gutheil approach seems preferable to the "passive-aggressive" approach taken by some other therapists.[1]

---

1. These examples should provide a powerful reminder to lawyers, law reformers, policymakers, and legal theorists: reforming rules of law—whether through legislation, administrative regulation, or judicial doctrine—will only accomplish therapeutic ends if the new rules will be applied or enforced therapeutically. Of course, this also raises the issue of the

The Right to Refuse Mental Health Treatment

The right of a hospitalized psychiatric patient to refuse mental health treatment is another rule of law or legal doctrine that has engendered much controversy. Mental health professionals often worry that according patients such a right will lead to the refusal of needed treatment, resulting in patients rotting with their rights on (Winick, 1994, p. 99 note 1). Similarly, mental health professionals often claim that, if forced to accept mental health treatment, patients will improve and retrospectively thank their doctors for having provided the needed treatment (Winick, 1994, p. 99 note 2). Winick (1994, p. 100), on the other hand, has argued that the recognition of a right to refuse treatment might empower patients in ways that have therapeutic value.

Once again, however, it may be enlightening to change the analytical exercise: regardless of whether a right to refuse treatment is in general considered therapeutically beneficial or detrimental, if a jurisdiction for whatever reason *recognizes* a firm right to refuse treatment, how might that rule be applied or implemented by mental health professionals to maximize its therapeutic potential? If we search for the "most therapeutic application" of a legal right to refuse treatment, what might we come up with?

A therapist can, of course, simply instruct a patient to take certain medication, and if the patient declines, the therapist can allow the patient to rot, rights and all. Winick (1994), however, has suggested that mental health professionals use the right to refuse treatment to "reshape the therapist-patient relationship into a tool that is both more humane and more effective" (p. 132).

> The right to refuse treatment can increase the likelihood that therapists will respect the dignity and autonomy of their patients, and recognize their essential role in the therapeutic process. This reshaping of the therapist's role can increase the potential for a true therapeutic alliance in which therapists treat their patients as persons. The result can be more patient trust, confidence, and participation in decision-making in ways that can cause patients to internalize treatment goals. A therapeutic relationship restructured in this fashion can enhance the patient's intrinsic motivation and the likelihood that the goal-setting effect, commitment, and the reinforcing effects of cognitive dissonance will occur.
>
> A real therapist-patient (or counselor-offender) dialogue concerning treatment planning and decision-making can only bolster the patient's faith in the therapist and in his or her dedication to the patient's best interests. This faith and the expectations it generates may be essential to producing the Hawthorne effect or other interactive mechanisms that can increase the likelihood of therapeutic success. Without trust, the therapeutic opportunities provided by the therapist-patient relationship are drastically reduced. (Winick, 1994, p. 112)

It is a heavy dose of therapist-patient dialogue and of according patients considerable "voice" (Tyler, 1992) in the decision-making process that characterizes nurses' behavior with patients in Susman's (1994) study of the resolution of right to refuse medication conflicts in three Maryland psychiatric hos-

---

amount of discretion that should be accorded legal actors (Wexler, 1993), as well as the issue of the extent to which the legal environment may enhance or constrain the exercise of discretion.

pitals. Susman, a criminologist and consultant to St. Elizabeth's Hospital in the District of Columbia, found, ironically, that patients considered the informal procedures used by nurses to be fairer than the dispute resolution process provided by the legislatively mandated, supposedly rights-protective Clinical Review Panel (CRP). The CRP is established by statute to review a patient's treatment refusal and to recommend a course of action. It is headed by a psychiatrist (other than the patient's own physician), and is convened by a member of the patient's treatment team. The CRP reviews the patient's medical record and has the patient's doctor appear. The patient may be invited to appear, principally to explain why he or she is refusing medication, perhaps to determine if the patient is a "symptomatic refuser" (Susman, 1994, p. 125). The CRP's decision binds the treatment team and the patient (Susman, 1994, p. 127–128, note 3).

As noted, Susman found patients much more supportive of the informal procedure used by the nurses than they were of the procedures used by the psychiatrist-headed CRP. He postulates this fairness may have consequences beyond those examined in his study:

> It may in fact aid treatment and recovery; fairness may enhance the authority of doctors, nurses, and other staff members, as well as increase the legitimacy of psychiatric hospitals and the psychiatric profession. Furthermore, fair processes in the hospital context may increase compliance with medical decisions among patients and may improve the prospects of patients for reintegrating into the community upon release from the hospital.... (Susman, 1994, pp. 122–23)

Susman's patient interviews underscored the importance of both the quantity and the quality of staff/patient interaction in patient assessments of fairness (p. 117). He suggests the CRP proceedings could be improved by affording patients greater voice and in the CRP explaining its decision to the affected patient:

> The relatively large proportion of patients who expressed a feeling that the doctors' legal procedures were unfair may, in addition to reacting to mute processes, also be responding to the professionalism of the hospital staff. This perverse result may have occurred because the proceedings are conducted by medically trained personnel who are no doubt careful of the medical details necessary to produce a therapeutically sound outcome to their deliberations. But scrupulous attention to clinical detail may inadvertently thwart the need of patients to tell in their own terms their side of the story.
>
> The clinical review panel may often limit the opportunities for expression by patients because of time constraints and medical proprieties. They must be sensitive to the ordinary work schedules of the other members participating in the dispute resolution process and consequently may take an overly narrow approach to the medical issues at hand. These may prompt them to limit patients' opportunities to speak. The clinical review panel members are also knowledgeable about psychiatric matters and may restrict patients' opportunities to present information or tell their story when such would be medically irrelevant or inappropriate. In these situations, the panel would be acting in a medically professional and appropriate manner but unwittingly interfering with patients' sense of what a satisfying and fair procedure should be.

* * *

> Acceptance of unfavorable decisions rendered by the clinical review panel could probably be enhanced if the doctors provided patients with a rationale for the decision, especially one that indicated to them that their side of the dispute was considered when the decision was made. Further research could clarify these matters. (Susman, 1994, pp. 117–118)

The crucial point is that Susman is not recommending legislative repeal or reform of the CRP or of Maryland's qualified right to refuse treatment. He states simply that "what can be confirmed from the present body of procedural justice theory in psychiatric hospitals is that there is a developing body of knowledge, from the perspective of therapeutic jurisprudence, that could lend itself to the creation of principles of justice that should be utilized in administrative dispute resolution as well as by courts in deciding cases." (Susman, 1994, p. 123)

When Susman speaks of therapeutic jurisprudence, he is referring to that dimension of therapeutic jurisprudence emphasized in the present article: the therapeutic application of existing law. The CRP law can be applied more therapeutically than it now is:

> In the research reported here, it was found that patients could judge procedures fair even when the results were unfavorable from their standpoint. And even when the outcome of the dispute was favorable, they did not invariably also believe that the procedure was fair. But overall, more patients found the dispute resolution norms of nurses to be fairer than the doctors' process of dispute resolution, mandated and endorsed as an effective way to protect patients' autonomy and self-respect. This points to some inherent difficulty in balancing the state's interests and patients' rights. Psychiatrists using the clinical review process to override patients' objections to treatment would benefit from a short training course on procedural justice theory and other dimensions of therapeutic jurisprudence. Utilizing the theory and perspective of therapeutic jurisprudence in the conduct of clinical review panels could greatly increase patients' sense of fairness of the deliberations. (Susman, 1994, p. 121)

Relative Familiarity of the Legal Terrain

If psychologists increase their emphasis on applying the law therapeutically, as I hope they will, it is probably only natural that initial interest will concentrate on "core" mental health law areas, such as the just-discussed areas of *Tarasoff* and the right to refuse treatment. Such areas are likely to be familiar to mental health professionals, and to seem particularly relevant to them, because those legal areas impact not only on their clients, but also impact directly on the mental health professionals themselves: when a *Tarasoff* obligation is triggered, a mental health professional is required, under threat of legal liability, to take some action to protect an endangered third party; in the right to refuse treatment context, a patient's treatment refusal may frustrate a mental health professional's suggested course of action.

It is important to recognize, however, that many laws that do not directly touch mental health professionals—and that are not within the "core" of mental health law—may impact dramatically on the lives of clients. To the extent that mental health professionals deal regularly with clients affected by such laws, and to the extent that clients might be able to take some action to be able to cope more therapeutically with such laws, those laws too ought to be carefully examined from the perspective of the therapeutic application of existing law.[2]

Take as an example the very "Don't Ask, Don't Tell" military regulation discussed earlier. Kavanagh (1995) has argued forcibly that the regulation ought to be changed. But, in the meantime, what about gay and lesbian servicemembers for whom a military career is important *today*? Can mental health professionals and lawyers help improve the day-to-day lives of those servicemembers?

Remember, Kavanagh's chief concern is that the existing policy antitherapeutically promotes superficiality in social relations because it "naturally" chills the disclosure of "the day to day life events that people who work together often share with each other" (p. 154). Kavanagh notes, however, that "the new policy does not explicitly prohibit the disclosures [she identifies as] so natural and crucial. Nevertheless, the natural result of the requirement that gay men, lesbians and bisexuals not reveal their sexual orientation is to preclude disclosure of related information in an effort to conceal the prohibited fact" (p. 154, note 54).

But if we are operating under the existing policy, mental health and legal professionals might wish to advise their clients that the "natural result of the requirement" is not the *legally obligatory* result. Apparently, so long as a gay servicemember can learn to comfortably refrain from stating explicitly his or her gay identity, and can learn to deflect or comfortably refuse to answer an inquiry about sexual orientation—an inquiry made more likely by disclosure of daily life events—the day-to-day life event disclosures should be legally permissible.

Working together and with gay clients, legal and mental health practitioners might suggest various "scripts" that those gay clients interested in maximum disclosure could rehearse and role play before embarking on real-world disclosures. The development of legally acceptable and therapeutically-beneficial disclosures (Pennebaker, 1990) within the constraints of the existing law ought to be an exciting cooperative therapeutic jurisprudence venture for mental health and legal academics and professionals.

Conclusion

Psychologists and other mental health professionals can play a major role in the development of therapeutic jurisprudence. They can help therapeutic jurisprudence—and ultimately themselves and their clients—in a number of

---

2. The development of *legal* interest in therapeutic jurisprudence has followed a similar path, initially covering topics within "core" mental health law and now embracing a mental health approach to law in general. The ripple effect in legal scholarship was anticipated:

It seems only natural (at least to those of us who specialize in mental health law) that initial forays into therapeutic jurisprudence take place within the core content areas of mental health law. Obviously, however, therapeutic jurisprudence will also have application in forensic psychiatry generally, in health law, in a variety of allied legal fields (criminal law, juvenile law, family law), and probably across the entire legal spectrum. (Wexler & Winick, 1991, p. x)

ways. For example, they can carefully attend to how the law is actually operating (on themselves, their clients, or both), and can suggest reforms in the law that would serve justice and yet better promote mental health.

A recent Massachusetts statewide conference was just such a therapeutic jurisprudence exercise in law reform "from the bottom up" (Finkelman & Grisso, 1994), as opposed to the more typical law reform effort, which is spawned by armchair academics. At the conference, psychologists working in the Massachusetts mental health system were asked to use the therapeutic jurisprudence lens to examine the laws they work with and to come up with suggestions for reform (e.g., Haycock, 1994; Packer, 1994).

Often, of course, the proposed reforms will involve suggested changes in the law itself. But, as the present article demonstrates, creative thought can many times lead to suggestions for reform through a different *application* of the existing law.

The process of reform by means of a more therapeutic application of existing law is far easier, both in terms of researching the effectiveness of the reform and in terms of effectuating the desired policy change, than would be the case with legislative reform. Moreover, the process is often likely to be far less controversial than legislative reform.

The relative ease of the enterprise, as compared with legislative revision, is well illustrated by Daly-Rooney's (1994) suggestion that a waiver of confidentiality under the Americans with Disabilities Act may often facilitate the integration into the work setting of an employee with a disability. As I have noted elsewhere (Wexler, 1995), Daly-Rooney's

> thesis could be tested without going to the legislature to change the law. If certain employers were persuaded to implement the law according to Daly-Rooney's proposal on an experimental basis, the results could be compared with other comparable companies that merely continued doing business as usual. Ultimate law reform might be accomplished by therapeutic jurisprudence scholars persuading certain administrators of the ADA, who in this case are employers, to urge employees with disabilities to consider the waiver of the confidentiality provision. The matter is subject to individual tailoring because, for some employees, confidentiality will outweigh the interest in co-worker involvement, but for others it will not. Moreover, this change is easier to accomplish than changing the confidentiality law itself. Changing the confidentiality law itself would be tremendously controversial and would raise all sorts of justice concerns. The administrative solution, on the other hand, leads to a convergence between justice and therapeutic concerns: Confidentiality is preserved for those who deem it important to them, and yet divulgence and co-worker involvement are made available to those who wish to follow that route for hoped-for therapeutic gains. Furthermore,...the suggested change might help an untold number of employees with disabilities and might, indeed, be ultimately transformative of the workplace environment (p. 236).

Contemplating how the existing law might be applied in a more therapeutic manner is likely something that mental health professionals already occasionally do, at least with respect to laws that affect themselves as well as their clients. The present process of applying laws therapeutically is, however, probably performed in a highly erratic and unsystematic manner.

Psychologists and other mental health professionals should now begin to engage in the exercise expressly, routinely, and broadly (e.g., even in areas where the law impacts adversely on clients but does not directly affect psychologists). The possibility of creative and therapeutic application of existing law should regularly be considered as an alternative to formal law reform, and should be a matter explicitly discussed, researched, and written about.

The therapeutic application of existing law is an endeavor that can bring together practitioners and academics. Moreover, as the development of "scripts" for gay military personnel illustrates, the endeavor is ideally a cooperative, interdisciplinary one that can unite professionals and scholars from the mental health field with their counterparts in the field of law (Sales & Shuman, in press).

Finally, to the extent that, even without legislative action, existing law may be applied more therapeutically by altering the actions of mental health professionals or their clients, this dimension of therapeutic jurisprudence can be imported into practice *today*. The therapeutic application of existing law, then, raises the exciting possibility of an academic pursuit being able immediately to involve legal and mental health practitioners and clients/consumers in practical, cooperative, action-oriented scholarship, research, and reform.

References

Bibliography of therapeutic jurisprudence (1993). New York Law School Journal of Human Rights, 10, 915–926.

Bloom, J.D. and Williams, M.H. (1994). Management and treatment of insanity acquittees: A model for the 1990s. Washington, D.C.: American Psychiatric Press.

Daly-Rooney, R.A. (1994). Designing reasonable accommodations through co-worker participation: Therapeutic jurisprudence and the confidentiality provision of the Americans with Disabilities Act. Journal of Law and Health, 8, 89–104.

Finkelman D. and Grisso, T. (1994). Therapeutic jurisprudence: From idea to application. New England Journal on Criminal and Civil Confinement, 20, 243–257.

Gould, K.A. (1993). Turning rat and doing time for uncharged, dismissed, or acquitted crimes: Do the federal sentencing guidelines promote respect for the law? New York Law School Journal of Human Rights, 10, 835–875.

Gould, K.A. (1995). A therapeutic jurisprudence analysis of competency evaluation requests: The defense attorney's dilemma. International Journal of Law and Psychiatry, 18, 83–100.

Harrison, J.L. (1994). Class, personality, contract, and unconscionability. William and Mary Law Review, 35, 445–501.

Haycock, J. (1994). Speaking truth to power: Rights, therapeutic jurisprudence, and Massachusetts mental health law. New England Journal on Criminal and Civil Confinement, 20, 301–320.

Kavanagh, K. (1995). Don't ask, don't tell: Deception required, disclosure denied. Psychology, Public Policy, and Law, 1, 142–160.

Klotz, J.A., Wexler, D.B., Sales, B.D., and Becker, J.V. (1992). Cognitive restructuring through law: A therapeutic jurisprudence approach to sex offenders and the plea process. University of Puget Sound Law Review, 15, 579–595.

Packer, I.K. (1994). The court clinic system in Massachusetts: A therapeutic approach vs. a rights-oriented approach. New England Journal on Criminal and Civil Confinement, 20, 291–300.

Pennebaker, J.W. (1990). Opening Up: The healing power of confiding in others. New York: W. Morrow.

Perlin, M.L. (1992). Tarasoff and the dilemma of the dangerous patient: New directions for the 1990s. Law and Psychology Review, 16, 29–63.

Perlin, M.L. (1993). What is therapeutic jurisprudence? New York Law School Journal of Human Rights, 10, 623–636.

Perlin, M.L. (1994). The jurisprudence of the insanity defense. Durham, NC: Carolina Academic Press.

Sales, B.D. and Shuman, D.W. (in press). The newly emerging mental health law. In Sales, B.D. and Shuman, D.W. (Eds.), Law, Mental Health, and Mental Disorder. Pacific Grove, CA: Brookes/Cole.

Shuman, D.W. (1994). The psychology of compensation in tort law. University of Kansas Law Review, 43, 39–77.

Simon, L.M.J. (1995). A therapeutic jurisprudence approach to the legal processing of domestic violence cases. Psychology, Public Policy, and Law, 1, 43–79.

Slobogin, C. (1995). Therapeutic jurisprudence: Five dilemmas to ponder. Psychology, Public Policy, and Law, 1, 193–219.

Stone, A.A. (1976). The Tarasoff decisions: Suing psychotherapists to safeguard society. Harvard Law Review, 90, 358–378.

Susman, J. (1994). Resolving hospital conflicts: A study on therapeutic jurisprudence. Journal of Psychiatry and Law, 22, 107–133.

Tarasoff v. Regents of University of California, 17 Cal.3d 425, 551 P.2d 334, 131 Cal. Rptr. 14 (1976).

Tyler, T.R. (1992). The psychological consequences of judicial procedures: Implications for civil commitment hearings. Southern Methodist University Law Review, 46, 433–445.

Wexler, D.B. (1979). Patients, therapists, and third parties: The victimological virtues of Tarasoff. International Journal of Law and Psychiatry, 2, 1–28.

Wexler, D.B. (1991). Health care compliance principles and the insanity acquittee conditional release process. Criminal Law Bulletin, 27, 18–41.

Wexler, D.B. (1993a). New directions in therapeutic jurisprudence: Breaking the bounds of conventional mental health law scholarship. New York Law School Journal of Human Rights, 10, 759–776.

Wexler, D.B. (1993b). Therapeutic jurisprudence and the criminal courts. William and Mary Law Review, 35, 279–299.

Wexler, D.B. (1993c). Therapeutic jurisprudence and changing conceptions of legal scholarship. Behavioral Sciences and the Law, 11, 17–29.

Wexler, D.B. (1995). Reflections on the scope of therapeutic jurisprudence. Psychology, Public Policy and Law, 1, 220–236.

Wexler, D.B., and Winick, B.J. (1991). Essays in therapeutic jurisprudence. Durham, NC: Carolina Academic Press.

Wilkinson, W.E. (1994). Therapeutic jurisprudence and workers' compensation. Arizona Attorney, 30, 28–33.

Winick, B.J. (1993). Rethinking the health care delivery crisis: The need for a therapeutic jurisprudence. Journal of Law and Health, 7, 49–54.

Winick, B.J. (1994). The right to refuse mental health treatment: A therapeutic jurisprudence analysis. International Journal of Law and Psychiatry, 17, 99–117.

Winick, B.J. (1995a). Reforming incompetency to stand trial and plead guilty: A restated proposal and a response to Professor Bonnie. Journal of Criminal Law and Criminology, 85, 571–624.

Winick, B.J. (1995b). The side effects of incompetency labeling and the implications for mental health law. Psychology, Public Policy, and Law, 1, 6–42.

Wulsin, L.R., Bursztajn, H., and Gutheil, T.G. (1983). Unexpected clinical features of the Tarasoff decision: The therapeutic alliance and the duty to warn. American Journal of Psychiatry, 140, 601–606.

Yates, K.F. (1994). Therapeutic issues associated with confidentiality and informed consent in forensic evaluations. New England Journal on Criminal and Civil Confinement, 20, 345–368.

III.
Empirical
Explorations

The Civil Action for Sexual Battery: Therapeutic Jurisprudence?

Bruce Feldthusen

[This chapter, although largely theoretical, also has an important empirical dimension, consisting of classifying the available sexual battery cases in Canada into categories relating the commencement of civil litigation to what has happened—or has not happened—in the criminal courts.]

I. Introduction

Something new and provocative is happening in the law of torts. Victims of rape,[1] other sexual assaults,[2] "incest",[3] and other forms of child

---

1. The rape cases have all been what S. Estrich called in Real Rape (Cambridge, Mass.: Harvard University Press, 1987) at 4, "aggravated rape" cases (i.e. rapes involving extrinsic violence). None were stranger rapes. Civil battery actions against the perpetrators include Glendale v. Drozdzik, [1990] B.C.J. No. 1489 (S.C.) (QL) [hereinafter *Glendale*]; E.D.G. v. Drozdzik, [1993] B.C.J. No. 532 (C.A.) (QL); C. v. M. (1990), 74 D.L.R. (4th) 129, 46 C.P.C. (2d) 254 (Ont. Gen. Div.); Myers v. Haroldson, [1989] 3 W.W.R. 604, 48 C.C.L.T. 93 (Sask. Q.B.) [hereinafter *Myers*]. B.(P.) v. B.(W.), infra note 3, might be described as both an incest and a rape case. The father violently raped his daughter twice, when she was seventeen and twenty years old, after she moved into her own home. See also Q. v. Minto Management Ltd. (1986), 57 O.R. (2d) 781, 34 D.L.R. (4th) 767 (C.A.) [hereinafter *Minto*]; and W. v. Meah, [1986] 1 All E.R. 935 (Q.B.) [hereinafter *Meah*].

2. Khalsa v. Bhullar, [1992] B.C.J. No. 378 (S.C.) (QL) [hereinafter *Khalsa*]; H.R. v. F.M. (1992), 129 N.B.R. (2d) 303 (Q.B.); and P.C.P. v. DaCosta, [1992] B.C.J. No. 2303 (S.C.) (QL) [hereinafter *DaCosta*]. The perpetrators in each case were known to the victims; they were, respectively, a priest, a family friend, and an employment supervisor.

3. Incest is defined in the Criminal Code, R.S.C. 1985, c. C-46 [hereinafter *Code*], s. 155(1) on the basis of sexual intercourse with blood relations. In this context, I prefer to use the term to include all defendants who were in loco parentis with the plaintiff including as step-fathers and foster-fathers. As well, I have not limited the category to intercourse cases. Neither blood relationship, nor intercourse specifically, are likely to be significant from the plaintiff's perspective. On this point, see M.(K.) v. M.(H.), [1992] 3 S.C.R. 6, 142 N.R. 321 (upholding a jury award of $50,000); and J.(L.A.) v. J.(H.) (1993), 13 O.R. (3d) 306 (Gen. Div.). Other civil incest cases include Madelena v. Kunn (M.(M.) v. K.(K.)) (1989), 61 D.L.R. (4th) 392, 50 C.C.L.T. 190 (B.C.C.A.) [hereinafter *Madelena*]; Brandner v. Brandner (1991), 71 Man. R. (2d) 265 (Q.B.) [hereinafter *Brandner*]; G. v. R., [1991] B.C.J. No. 66 (S.C.) (QL); P.(L.) v. L.(A.), [1991] O.J. No. 1360 (Gen. Div.) (QL); B.(A.) v. J.(I.) (1991), 81 Alta. L.R. (2d) 84, [1991] 5 W.W.R. 748 (Q.B.); M.O. and D.T. v. F.A. (1991), digested in The Lawyers Weekly (8 February 1991) 19 (B.C.S.C.); Beaudry v. Hackett (S.M.A.B. v. J.N.H.), [1991] B.C.J. No. 3940 (S.C.) (QL) [hereinafter *Beaudry*]; W.J.L.M. v. R.G.R., [1992] B.C.J. No. 1014 (S.C.) (QL); R.N. v. S.L.S., [1993] N.S.J. No. 99 (S.C. T.D.) (QL); K.G. v. J.T., [1992] B.C.J. No. 1365 (S.C.) (QL) (great uncle); D.C. v. K.C., [1993] N.J. No. 144

sexual abuse[4] are using the civil justice system to sue the perpetrators in numbers[5] and in circumstances never seen before.[6] Although some courts have referred to these as "new" tort actions for "sexual assault", in fact, the action is none other than the traditional action in battery.[7] What is

---

(S.C.T.D.) (QL) (father-son); D. Brillinger, "Sex Assault Victim Wins $125,000 Award Against Father" The Lawyers Weekly (15 September 1989) 8 [hereinafter $125,000 Award] (a report on Kunz v. Kunz); "Daughter May Not Get $284,000" The Globe and Mail (3 December 1992) A1 (discussing a jury award of $284,000); and B.(P.) v. B.(W.) (1992), 11 O.R. (3d) 161 (Gen. Div.). Another case involving a successful action by a stepdaughter is referred to in D.C.G.(Re), [1992] B.C.J. No. 2506 (S.C.) (QL). See also Stubbings v. Webb, [1991] 3 All E.R. 949 (C.A.) [hereinafter *Stubbings*].

4. Lyth v. Dagg (1988), 46 C.C.L.T. 25 (B.C.S.C.) [hereinafter *Lyth*]; Harder v. Brown (1989), 50 C.C.L.T. 85 (B.C.S.C.) [hereinafter *Harder*]; N.(J.L.) v. L.(A.M.) (1988), [1989] 1 W.W.R. 438, 47 C.C.L.T. 65 (Man. Q.B.); S.M.Q. v. Hodgins, 36 R.F.L. (3d) 159 (Gen. Div.); Gray v. Reeves (1992), 89 D.L.R. (4th) 315, 64 B.C.L.R. (2d) 275 (S.C.) [hereinafter *Gray*]; G.(K.) v. T.(J.) (1992), digested in The Lawyers Weekly (28 August 1992) 27 (B.C.S.C.); Jody Lynn N. v. Le Strat (1988), digested in The Lawyers Weekly (11 November 1988) 19 (Man. Q.B.) [hereinafter *Jody Lynn N.*]; D.S. v. D.A.M. (Slinn v. Morgan), [1993] B.C.J. No. 315 (S.C.) (QL) [hereinafter *Slinn*]; T.K.S. v. E.B.S., [1992] B.C.J. No. 2452 (S.C.) (QL) (cousins); and M.(A.K.) v. B.(M.) (22 June 1990), (Ont. Gen. Div.) [unreported], referred to in C. v. M., supra note 1. See also D.M. Van Ginkel, Finally Compensating The Victim: Harder v. Brown (1990), 8 Can. J. Fam. Law 388 at 392, noting an unreported Ontario jury award of $100,000 plus $25,000 punitive damages (this was probably Kunz v. Kunz: see Brillinger, supra note 3).

5. I will discuss thirty-three sexual battery actions litigated since 1985: see infra note 9. Often these have not been reported in conventional law reports. In a few cases, I have had to rely on digests of the reasons for judgment, newspaper reports, or references to unreported decisions in other judgments.

Of these, twenty-six involve sexual batteries perpetrated against children: fourteen by persons in loco parentis, ten by other family members and friends, one by a teacher and one by an employment supervisor.

In all but five cases, the victims were women or girls. The exceptions were: a boy molested by his father in D.C. v. K.C., supra note 3; a boy molested along with his sisters in B.(A.) v. J.(I.), supra note 3; a boy molested by his uncle in *Slinn*, supra note 4; a male adolescent fondled by his employment supervisor in *DaCosta*, supra note 2; and a male adolescent enticed into a homosexual encounter with his teacher in *Lyth*, supra note 4. All the perpetrators have been adult males, except the defendant in T.K.S. v. E.B.S., supra note 4, who was an adolescent cousin of the plaintiff.

Of the thirty civil actions in which the information is clear from the record, seventeen were undefended, and thirteen defended: see infra note 63. Of the twenty-nine cases in which the information is clear from the record, sixteen followed criminal convictions and two followed criminal acquittals: see infra note 70.

6. One can only speculate as to what combination of social and legal change has fostered this development. Abolition of interfamilial tort immunity has permitted incest cases to go forward. Certainly, the influence of feminist legal academics and practitioners can not be discounted. Also, I suspect that many victims have not been aware of their civil option, but as the number of suits and attendant publicity grow, so too does public and professional awareness.

7. As to the proper cause of action being battery, see Norberg v. Wynrib, [1992] 2 S.C.R. 224, 92 D.L.R. (4th) 449 [hereinafter *Norberg*]; and M.(K.) v. M.(H.), supra note 3. I use the term "battery" in an effort to emphasize the crucial difference between the tort action and the criminal action for sexual "assault". As explained below, the civil sexual battery action covers

new is the growing tendency for sexual battery victims[8] to exercise the long available, but largely ignored, civil option.[9]

---

some actions that would probably not meet the criminal definition of sexual assault. Nevertheless, the definition of sexual assault from the criminal law provides a useful point of departure:

> [T]he test for the recognition of sexual assault does not depend solely on contact with specific areas of the human anatomy.... [Sexual assault] is committed in circumstances of a sexual nature, such that the sexual integrity of the victim is violated.

R. v. Chase, [1987] 2 S.C.R. 293 at 301 & 302, 59 C.R. (3d) 193 at 199, per McIntyre J.

8. I use the word "victim" with reservation. On the one hand, the word accurately suggests that an innocent person has been terribly injured by another: see E.M. Schneider, Particularity and Generality: Challenges of Feminist Theory and Practice in Work On Woman-Abuse (1992) 67 N.Y.U.L. Rev. 520 at 530. On the other hand, it may also suggest a certain passivity and hopelessness entirely inappropriate for many survivors of sexual battery and especially those who have been brave enough to enter the legal forum. In N. West, Rape in the Criminal Law and the Victim's Tort Alternative: A Feminist Analysis (1992) 50 U.T. Fac. L. Rev. 96 at 114, the author suggests that the civil action may be therapeutic precisely because it breaks the victimization pattern. It is never my intention to imply passivity or helplessness on the part of the women whom I describe in the text as victims.

9. Note that common law barriers to litigation between family members meant that civil incest suits were not viable until recently. There is a possibility that parallels to the present situation might be found by examining the action for seduction, especially at the turn of the century when the action became available to women themselves in some jurisdictions. As far as I know, little research has been done in this area. See C. Backhouse, The Tort of Seduction: Fathers and Daughters in Nineteenth Century Canada (1986) 10 Dalhousie L.J. 45.

That aside, there exists two generations of civil actions for sexual battery. The first generation, consisting of only a few cases, was characterized by rape cases in which the plaintiff's claims were disbelieved. See, e.g., M. v. P. (MacKenzie v. Palmer) (1921), 14 Sask. L.R. 117, 56 D.L.R. 345 (C.A.), rev'd (1922), 62 S.C.R. 517, [1922] 1 W.W.R. 880 (failing on issue of consent). When the plaintiff was believed, the damages tended to be trivial. See, e.g., Pie v. Thibert, [1976] C.S. 180 ($2,400 damage), S. v. Mundy (1969), [1970] 1 O.R. 764, 9 D.L.R. (3d) 446 (Co. Ct.) [hereinafter *Mundy*] ($1,500 exemplary damages), and Radovskis v. Tomm (1957), 9 D.L.R. (2d) 751, 21 W.W.R. 658 (Man. Q.B.) ($2,000 damages). See generally S. Batt, Our Civil Courts: Unused Classrooms For Education About Rape in Feminism Applied: Four Papers (Ottawa: Canada Research Institute for the Advancement of Women, 1984) 56, citing 8 Canadian cases before 1976. See also Compensation For Battered Women, (1984) [unpublished], a handbook prepared by law students at the University of Western Ontario; and C.A. MacKinnon, Sexual Harassment Of Working Women: A Case of Sex Discrimination (New Haven: Yale University Press, 1979).

In the second generation, damage awards are becoming substantially larger, although still much lower than the basic rules of tort damage quantification suggest they ought to be. See B. Feldthusen, Discriminatory Damage Quantification In Civil Actions For Sexual Battery [forthcoming in U.T.L.J. in 1994]. Also, at least to date, consent has tended to be less controversial than one might have expected and usually resolved with some sensitivity to the victim's position. See generally E. Sheehy, Compensation For Women Who Have Been Raped in J.V. Roberts & R.M. Mohr, eds., Confronting Sexual Assault: A Decade of Legal and Social Change (Toronto: University of Toronto Press, 1994) 205. Interesting discussions of consent are found in *Norberg,* supra note 7; *Madelena,* supra note 3; *Harder,* supra note 4; and Weisenger v. Mellor, [1989] B.C.J. No. 1393 (S.C.) (QL) [hereinafter *Mellor*]. The first Canadian case that I would identify as belonging to the new generation discussed in this article was *Minto,* supra note 1. This was a negligence action against a landlord for failing to maintain secure premises, not an action against the perpetrator. Compare Storrie v. Newman

In addition, at least two truly "new" avenues of civil relief appear to be developing in the area of sexual wrongdoing. The first deals with "sexual exploitation" in power-imbalanced relationships. The second consists of negligence claims against third parties. In the exploitation cases, the defendant, typically a male professional, employs his relative power to secure the victim's apparent "consent" to sexual conduct.[10] Courts are beginning to take the power imbalance seriously and to invalidate on that ground what traditionally might have been accepted as the plaintiff's consent. A majority in the Supreme Court of Canada decided recently to resolve such claims under the traditional action in battery. The two women justices, McLachlin and L'Heureux-Dubé JJ., preferred to deal with the action as one for breach of fiduciary duty.[11] Regardless, it is clear that the courts have recognized implicitly the differences between the exploitation cases and, for example, the paradigmatic case of sexual battery by threat of physical force.[12] It is premature to decide whether the ex-

---

(1982), 139 D.L.R. (3d) 482, 39 B.C.L.R. 376 (S.C.) [hereinafter *Storrie*]. The recent proliferation of civil sexual battery suits seems to have begun in the United States. See the cases cited in M.(K.) v. M.(H.), supra note 3, and McConnell, infra note 44. In contrast, in Britain, both the civil rape claim in Meah, supra note 1 and the civil incest claim in *Stubbings*, supra note 3 are described as the first of their kind in the respective reasons for judgment.

10. See *Norberg*, ibid. at 463, La Forest J.(doctor-patient exploitation). These are cases where, unless the court takes the power imbalance into account, the plaintiff would probably be held to have consented to the contact. There were two such cases prior to *Norberg* in which the analysis was not as explicit. See, e.g., *Mellor*, ibid. (doctor-patient exploitation); *Lyth*, supra note 4 (teacher-student exploitation). Some of the incest and other child sexual abuse cases might be included here, but the courts seem to take a much stricter view of these, denying the defense of consent as a matter of law. See, e.g., *Madelena*, supra note 3, but see also the trial judgment in *Madelena* (1987), 35 D.L.R. (4th) 222 (S.C.). *Lyth*, ibid., and *Da Costa*, supra note 2, both involved older adolescents and fall at the borderline. I adopt this categorization scheme for analytical purposes only. Whether the law ought to distinguish the exploitation cases in doctrine or remedy is a difficult question which is not considered herein. Note that in at least one case, the plaintiff has brought an action against the doctor, and also an action in negligence against the professional regulatory agency for failing to suspend the doctor after investigating a previous complaint. See "Alleged Sex-Assault Victim Sues" The Globe & Mail (17 July 1993) A3. Other negligence actions of this type are discussed in the following paragraph.

11. The issue is considered in both *Norberg*, ibid., and M.(K.) v. M.(H.), supra note 3.

12. This is clear from the attention given to the issue of consent in *Norberg*, ibid. It is even clearer from the relatively low damage awards given in these cases. In *Norberg*, for example, the majority concluded that the plaintiff had been subjected to two years of continuous non-consensual sexual relations. During that same time the defendant doctor had failed to respond to her request for help in overcoming her drug addiction. Instead, he promoted it by supplying restricted drugs in return for sexual favours. The majority concluded that the apparent consent was invalid and held the doctor liable in battery. LaForest J. stated that "[i]t is hard to imagine a greater affront to human dignity" than non-consensual sexual intercourse: ibid. at 470. In light of all this, it is difficult to comprehend how the majority could have awarded the plaintiff only $20,000 compensatory damages and $10,000 in punitive damages, an amount that would hardly have made a dent in her legal bills. This point was presumably noted by McLachlin J. in her minority judgment. She would have awarded costs on a solicitor and client basis, as had been done in *Mellor*, supra note 9. It is perhaps not coincidental that the two women justices, McLachlin and L'Heureux-Dubé JJ., would

ploitation cases are simply variations of traditional sexual battery, or whether they truly constitute a new and as yet imperfectly defined cause of action.

The new negligence claims are based on an allegation that the third party breached a legal duty to protect the victim from a sexual battery perpetrated by another. Defendants in third party negligence claims have included landlords,[13] child welfare agencies,[14] school boards,[15] and police officials.[16] Negligence actions have also been brought against mothers for failing to protect their daughters from sexually abusive fathers and stepfathers.[17]

It is too early to predict whether the trend to employ the civil action in sexual battery cases will continue.[18] If it does, it may have interesting implications for the entire law of torts. Today, tort law has little direct impact on individu-

---

have awarded $45,000 compensatory and $25,000 punitive damages. It seems certain that had the plaintiff in *Norberg* been raped at knife-point weekly over a two-year period the award would have been considerably higher. See also the comments about the adequacy of damages awarded in M.(K.) v. M.(H.), ibid., per McLachlin and L'Heureux-Dubé JJ. If the court in *Lyth*, supra note 4, truly believed that the adolescent student had been pressured into a non-consensual homosexual encounter with his teacher, how could it justify an award of only $5000 to a plaintiff still experiencing emotional problems years later? See generally Feldthusen, supra note 9.

13. *Minto*, supra note 1.

14. *Madelena*, supra note 3; Jane Doe v. Awasis Agency of Northern Manitoba (1990), 67 M.R. (2d) 260, 72 D.L.R. (4th) 738 (Q.B.); Gareau v. B.C. (Family and Child Services), [1989] B.C.J. No. 1267 (C.A.) (QL).

15. *Lyth*, supra note 4; Aleck v. Canada, [1991] B.C.J. No. 3058 (S.C.) (QL).

16. Doe v. Metropolitan Toronto (Municipality) Commissioners of Police (1990), 74 O.R. (2d) 225, 72 D.L.R. (4th) 580 (Gen. Div.) [hereinafter Doe v. Toronto Police cited to O.R.], leave to appeal den'd (1991), 1 O.R. (3d) 416 (C.A.).

17. See J.(L.A.) v. J.(H.), supra note 3, which appears to have been the first such successful action against the non-intervening mother. She was held jointly liable with the perpetrator-father for compensatory damages, and solely liable for punitive damages, the punitive claim against the father being precluded by his previous criminal conviction. In M.(K.) v. M.(H.), supra note 3, claims of mental distress and breach of fiduciary duty were also brought against the plaintiff's mother who allegedly ignored her daughter's reports of the incest. It is unclear from the case report whether the case against the mother went to trial or to the jury, but it was reported by L. Hurst, "Sex, Memory and the Courts" The Toronto Star (29 August 1993) B1, that the negligence claim was unsuccessful. The adoptive mother was also named as a defendant to the trial action of *Stubbings*, supra note 3, although she was not made a party to the appeal. See also (Feb 1993) A.B.A. J. at 16, in which two such claims, believed to be the first of this type in the United States, are discussed. Claims of this sort may be attractive because household insurance policies that exclude coverage for intentional or criminal conduct may cover parental negligence. The plaintiffs might also have therapeutic motives for seeking to hold liable the non-intervening parent. For a provocative and contextual analysis of the "bad" mother in this situation, see M. Ashe & N.R. Cahn, Child Abuse: A Problem For Feminist Theory (1993) 2 Tex. J. Women & L. 75; M. Ashe, The 'Bad Mother' in Law and Literature: A Problem of Representation (1992) 43 Hastings L.J. 1017. However rational and expedient the decision in J.(L.A.) v. J.(H.), ibid., may appear from some perspectives, one cannot help but regard the differential consequences for the mother and father-perpetrator as perverse and discriminatory from another.

18. See Section II, below, in which doubt is expressed.

als.[19] Few individuals, unless backed by a subrogating insurer, can afford to invoke the tort process. Fewer still are willing and able to bring an action against an effectively judgment-proof individual defendant. The true parties to most tort litigation are large enterprises, insurers, and governments. Most doctrinal and academic developments are premised on collectivist and instrumentalist notions such as loss allocation, risk distribution, deterrence, insurance and compensation. The vehicle through which these goals are to be achieved is inevitably the award of substantial monetary damages.

What is striking about the sexual battery actions, or at least many of them, is that they appear far more consistent with the corrective justice model than with any instrumentalist notion of tort law.[20] Most sexual battery actions are brought by individual women standing alone, and against individual defendants.[21] Moreover, damages do not always seem central to the action. Frequently, plaintiffs have litigated sexual battery actions knowing in advance that there would be virtually no prospect of collecting on the judgment.[22]

---

19. See generally B. Feldthusen, If This is Torts, Negligence Must Be Dead in K. Cooper-Stephenson & E. Gibson, eds., Tort Theory (Toronto: Captus Press, 1993) c. 7. I am speaking here about the role of the individual as instigator and manager of tort litigation. I do not mean to suggest, however, that once implicated in tort litigation, individuals do not experience psychological consequences from litigation. For example, being a named defendant in a tort suit, even if fully insured, may, and probably does, have psychological consequences. See S.C. Charles, J.R. Wibert & K.J. Franke, Sued and Nonsued Physicians' Self-Reported Reactions to Malpractice Litigation (1985) 142 Am. J. Psych. 437.

20. One group of tort theorists, represented best by Weinrib, attempt to explain tort doctrine in terms of Aristotle's notion of corrective justice. Victim and perpetrator come together in an unmediated legal interaction characterized by formal equality. The action corrects the wrong by having the defendant return to the plaintiff something of value equal to that which was wrongfully taken or inflicted. See E.J. Weinrib, Understanding Tort Law (1989) 23 Val. U. L. Rev. 485. The corrective justice approach has excellent historical and intellectual credentials, but it does not purport to be, and is not generally, useful in explaining tort law as it actually functions in modern society. See Feldthusen, ibid.

21. The Women's Legal Education and Action Fund (LEAF) actively participated in the litigation of *Norberg*, supra note 7; M.(K.) v. M.(H.), supra note 3; and Doe v. Toronto Police, supra note 16. In T. Claridge, "Lawyer Says Incest Award May Not Be Paid", The Globe and Mail (3 December 1992) A10, the lawyer indicated that he took the case on a community service basis. I suspect that other lawyers may have done the same in other cases.

22. It is not easy to discover this from the case reports. The plaintiff in *Myers*, supra note 1, admitted to the press that she had no expectation of recovery. See C. Allard, "Sask. Victim Wins $40,000 Punitive Award From Rapist" The Lawyers Weekly (28 April 1989) 2. See $125,000 Award, supra note 3. The lawyer for the plaintiffs in the apparently unreported cases of Kunz v. Kunz, and M.L.M. v. R.T., indicated that it was unlikely the clients would collect on either judgment. The plaintiff's lawyer in *Brandner*, supra note 3 said: "it wasn't the money that was the issue. She wanted to make her father answerable to her for what he had done to her.... And she felt that if she came forward, and took a step like this, then maybe others would have the courage to do so as well." The lawyer indicated they expected to collect "some" of the judgment, but was unsure exactly how much. See D. Brillinger, "Manitoba Woman Awarded $170,000 for Sex Assaults by Father During Childhood" The Lawyers Weekly (12 April 1991) 1 [hereinafter $170,000 for Sex Assaults]. The defendant's meagre assets were discussed in S.(B.J.) v. S.(F.T.), [1990] A.J. No. 1059 (Q.B.) (QL), a case in which the court refused to accept a settlement on behalf of the three minor plaintiffs. The matter went to trial in B.(A.) v. J.(I.), supra note 3, and culminated in a sub-

Instead of the prospect of financial gain, many sexual battery plaintiffs have reported therapeutic motivations for suing.[23] By therapeutic, I mean only that some aspect of the litigation—the complaint, the process, or the outcome—is expected to, or does, assist the victim along the path to recovery.[24] For some plaintiffs, the sexual battery litigation was perceived as part of the healing process.[25] Others have indicated that they brought suit to punish their as-

---

stantial, and one assumes purely symbolic, award. In P.(L.) v. L.(A.), supra note 3, counsel admitted that he would have to accept less than the full amount of the judgment. In Claridge, ibid., the lawyer who represented (without fee) an incest victim awarded $284,000 reported that the father had attempted to make himself judgment proof and that the client was aware that she would probably not collect before taking action. Hurst, supra note 17, reports that the judgment in *Marciano*, supra note 3, has not been paid. The author says: "In reality, the chance of recovering any money are (sic) slim to nil in most cases". See also infra note 63, citing a substantial number of cases in which the defendant did not appear or present a defense. These raise the inference that the judgment will not be paid. See also Sheehy, supra note 9 at 217.

A similar pattern is evident with nineteenth century seduction actions. See Backhouse, supra note 9, n. 87.

23. This probably strikes mental health care providers as less strange than it might strike lawyers. Herman identifies the "fantasy of compensation", which "usually includes components that mean more to the patient than any material gain. The compensation may represent an acknowledgement of harm, an apology, or a public humiliation of the perpetrator". See J. Herman, Trauma and Recovery (New York: Basic Books, 1992) at 190.

24. Therefore, the term is used to describe and include the somewhat different plaintiffs' motivations itemized in the text, ranging from altruism through cathartic testimony to revenge. Monetary recovery will also have therapeutic consequences, but I try to exclude these for analytical purposes when speaking of therapeutic expectations and outcomes in the text. I do not consider the therapeutic aspects of the litigation for persons other than the plaintiff, such as the defendant.

I use the term therapy with some misgivings. See M. Daly, Gyn/Ecology: The Metaethics of Radical Feminism (Boston: Beacon Press, 1978). Yet the term therapeutic works best to emphasize in this paper the potential benefits of the action for the victim rather than more traditional collectivist goals of tort law such as deterrence. "Therapeutic Jurisprudence" as an emerging school of legal analysis is interested in the role of law as a potential therapeutic agent. See D. Shuman, The Duty of the State to Rescue the Vulnerable in the United States in M. Menlowe & A. McCall Smith, eds., The Duty To Rescue: The Jurisprudence of Aid (London: Dartmouth Press, 1993) 131 & 137. The author explains therapeutic jurisprudence as follows: "whenever possible to do so without offending other important normative values, legal rules should encourage therapeutic outcomes". See generally D.B. Wexler & B.J. Winick, Therapeutic Jurisprudence As A New Approach to Mental Health Law Policy Analysis and Research (1991) 45 U. Miami L. Rev. 979. Borrowing from that, one might describe the sexual battery action as an explicitly therapeutic cause of action. For many litigants the therapeutic benefits are the main, not the incidental, aspects of the action.

25. The plaintiff in *Mellor*, supra note 9, when asked why she was bringing the action, said: "I have a right not to be molested when I walk into a physician's office. I have a right to trust. Secondly, it is a catharsis for me to be in court." See also $125,000 Award, supra note 3. The lawyer in *Kunz*, supra note 3, told the reporter that his client was looking for a "cathartic effect" and that the litigation had produced such an effect. In *Beaudry*, supra note 3, the trial judge said:

I am of the opinion that this trial will be therapeutic for Ms. B. Apart from any counselling and therapeutic help she may receive it should not ever again be necessary for her to go through the trauma of restating in graphic detail the events of the

sailant.[26] Still others claim they sought public vindication.[27] At least one plaintiff specifically hoped her suit would encourage other victims.[28] Taken together,
these constitute an unusual[29] modern manifestation of the original justifications
for tort law: corrective justice, vindication, appeasement, and even retribution.

This is not to say that this new trend in the civil justice system is without instrumental merit. On the contrary, sexual battery and third-party negligence
actions appear to be collectively beneficial on a number of fronts.[30] But if ac-

---

sexual abuse. She has done that, and I believe she has come through it very well.
In *Khalsa*, supra note 2, the judge, perhaps thinking the observation only relevant in an action by a Sikh woman against a Sikh priest, said:

> To some extent the impact on Mrs Bhullard (sic) is lessened, as her success in this
> lawsuit vindicates her and face is saved in a society where it is very important. By
> the same token, the plaintiff (sic) is discredited and has lost all respect and credibil-
> ity in his community.

See also Herman, supra note 23 at 210, quoting an incest survivor who brought a civil suit
against her father:

> I saw that it was a necessary thing. It wasn't that I needed a confession. I needed to
> do the action of holding someone accountable.

In Hurst, supra note 17, one survivor is quoted as saying she wants "the satisfaction of confronting [her abusive father] in court", and a counsellor of abused men is quoted as saying
"[m]oney isn't what it's about. It's about having the abusing parent acknowledge what he's
done and take responsibility."

26. In *Lyth*, supra note 4 at 30, the plaintiff's medical expert testified that "[h]is primary
motivating force for the civil suit would appear to be his feelings of anger and his desire to
seek revenge and further punish Mr. D". This was an action by a male student against a male
school teacher. Compare *Brandner*, supra note 3, discussed in $170,000 for Sex Assaults,
supra note 22. The client regarded the three year criminal sentence as "totally insufficient".
Sheehy, supra note 9, identifies three cases in which the police had failed to press charges:
Myers, supra note 1; *Harder*, supra note 4; and Mundy, supra note 9; and one, C. v. M.,
supra note 1, where the defendant was acquitted of the criminal charge.

27. See the discussion of *Kunz* in $125,000 Award, supra note 3 at 8, where the victim's
lawyer stated that "she was after the ability to speak out and disclose the matter publicly."
See also *Myers* and *Brandner*, discussed ibid.

28. See *Brandner*, ibid. See also Herman, supra note 23 at 210: "I'll do it for that little
girl. I'll do it for my brothers and sisters."

29. There are other instances of ordinary individual plaintiffs using the tort system to
make a point independent of recovering damages. See R.L. Binder, M.R. Trimble & D.E.
McNeil, Is Money a Cure? Follow-up of Litigants in England (1991) 19 Bull. Am. Acad. Psychiatry & L. 151 at 154. There would be many more instances had a common law tort of
discrimination been permitted to evolve in Canada, instead of requiring that these traditional
functions of tort law be performed through statutory human rights tribunals. See Seneca
College v. Bhadauria, [1981] 2 S.C.R. 181, 17 C.C.L.T. 106. See L.H. Mayhew, Institutions
Of Representation: Civil Justice and The Public (1975) 9 Law & Soc'y Rev. 401 at 413–14,
indicating that parties in discrimination lawsuits tend to "seek justice" (as opposed to an expedient outcome) overwhelmingly more often than do parties to other types of civil suits.

30. This is a topic in its own right, not considered here. I would note that what Linden
would call the ombudsman function of tort law probably figures heavily here, more heavily
in my estimation than deterrence. See A.M. Linden, Reconsidering Tort Law as Ombudsman
in F.M. Steel & S. Rodgers-Magnet, eds., Issues In Tort Law (Toronto: Carswell, 1983) at 1.
See also the discussion of Choisir, the French feminist action group that litigates these claims
for symbolic damages only, discussed in Sheehy, and in Batt, supra note 9.

tions of this sort are to continue, or even to flourish, it will be because individual plaintiffs continue to believe that the civil suit offers benefits, especially non-pecuniary benefits, that exceed their anticipated financial and psychological costs of litigation.

The main purpose of this article is to examine the ways in which the tort action might, and might not, achieve the therapeutic expectations which so many plaintiffs seem to hold. The analysis will of necessity be preliminary and incomplete. Although one can identify theoretical advantages of the tort suit, this is an area which requires empirical investigation. The sample of reported cases is far too small, and the period following litigation far too short, to enable one to draw definitive conclusions. An attempt will be made to articulate specific questions for further investigation.

In Section II, I will outline the theoretical arguments for and against the sexual battery action as therapeutic jurisprudence. This will be based on a contrast between the role of the victim as plaintiff in tort, and as complainant in criminal prosecution. I will emphasize the formal equality between plaintiff and defendant which is the foundation of civil litigation, and the relatively greater degree of control enjoyed by the plaintiff at each stage of the tort process.

In Section III, I will explore the possibility that therapeutic expectations and outcomes may differ according to the role that has previously been played, or not played, by the criminal justice system.[31] I consider four scenarios, each exhibited in the recent case law. First is the case where civil litigation is commenced after the Crown has proven unwilling or unable to press criminal charges. Second is the case where the victim herself declines to press criminal charges. Third is the case where the tort suit is brought after the defendant has been acquitted of criminal charges in respect of the same conduct. Fourth is the case where the action is brought after the defendant has been convicted of criminal charges.

II. The Speculative Case For and Against the Civil Action for Sexual Battery as Therapeutic Jurisprudence

The fundamental distinction between the criminal and civil justice systems lies in the different roles played by the defendant and victim in each. The os-

---

31. There are many other differences amongst the sexual battery cases that might prove more significant, each of which is worthy of empirical study. Possibly significant variables include: age, sex, race, and social class of the victim, both as a victim and as a plaintiff; similar characteristics of the defendant; characteristics of the relationship between the parties—strangers, family members, trusted personal or professional acquaintances; the plaintiff's expectation and recovery of damages, including punitive damages, and the quantum thereof; the cost, duration and degree of difficulty of the litigation; the role of the defendant, if any, in the litigation; the therapeutic skills of plaintiff's counsel; the circumstances of the battery—isolated attack or prolonged series of attacks, extrinsic violence, violation of trust. The significance of some of these variables to the victims themselves has been studied. See, e.g., studies cited in Feldthusen, supra note 9. There have been no studies of how these variables relate to the therapeutic expectations and outcomes in sexual battery actions.

tensible purpose of the criminal law is to promote the public interest by controlling criminal conduct. Only to the extent, often a limited extent, that the victim's interest is co-extensive with the state's definition of the public interest in a particular case does the criminal system address the interests of the victim.[32] Des Rosiers puts it this way:

> The procedural protection to the accused, guaranteed by the Canadian Charter of Rights and Freedoms, will never disappear. The harm done to the victim and the place of women are not and will not be the cornerstones of our system. The criminal system is ill-equipped to reaffirm the victim's worth....[33]

In contrast to the peripheral position of the victim, the accused criminal stands at the centre of the criminal justice system. Conviction requires proof beyond a reasonable doubt. The introduction of damaging evidence is strictly controlled. The concerns of victims, the interest of rape victims in their dignity and privacy, for example, is considered less important than the accuseds' interest in an impeccably fair trial. Sentencing tends to be centred on the characteristics of the criminal, as much or more than on the characteristics of the crime.

These features of the criminal justice system may be a good thing. Indeed, the attempt to prevent innocent persons from being wrongfully convicted of crimes may be fundamental to our entire legal culture. Nevertheless, this focus on the rights of the accused inflicts costs on society, and it inflicts particular costs on victims of crime. Guilty criminals go free. The criminal process will often be alienating, and in the case of sexual crime, offensive, harmful or destructive to victims. There is also the fear (or the fact) that the acquitted or leniently sentenced perpetrator will commit further sexual crimes against the same or other victims.[34]

One of the marvellous advantages of our legal system is that it separates the criminal and civil consequences of the same act into different legal regimes. This offers the possibility that some of the shortcomings of the criminal system can be addressed by the civil system. And all this can be accomplished without influencing directly either the substantive or symbolic principles of the criminal

---

32. A stunning example was the recent decision of an Arizona court to handcuff and hold in contempt of court an eleven-year-old girl who, under pressure from her family, refused to testify against the male relative accused of sexually molesting her. See "Arena of intimidation" Arizona Daily Star (16 May 1993) F2. Therapeutic jurisprudence would have to conclude that for the sexual assault victim, the criminal process is anti-therapeutic. Herman, supra note 23, at 72–73 says: "If one set out by design to devise a system for provoking intrusive post-traumatic symptoms, one could not do better than a court of law. Women who have sought justice in the legal system commonly compare this experience to being raped a second time." Of course, the issue here, raised but not resolved, is whether a tort suit is any better.

33. Limitation Periods and Civil Remedies for Childhood Sexual Abuse (1992) 9 Can. Fam. L.Q. 43 at 48, n. 12. See also Herman, ibid. at 72.

34. In S.(B.J.) v. S.(F.T.), supra note 22, the court stated:

> A second major effect of the abuse is that of fear. All three children, and the two girls in particular, have expressed fear that Mr. S. was "after them", i.e., that he might seek revenge for going to jail. This fear is not uncommon among sexually abused children, even though the perpetrator may not have made explicit threats to do so.

One wonders, however, whether the tort suit might provoke rather than restrain such a perpetrator.

law. Regardless of whether and how the criminal law has dealt with perpetrator and victim, the prospect of a victim-initiated civil suit remains.

The civil system is premised on the equality of the plaintiff and defendant. This is the critical difference between it and the criminal system that makes it an attractive option for victims of sexual battery. True, this is merely "formal equality".[35] Ordinarily, one would not suggest that formal equality was likely to be of much use to typical victims of sexual battery. Their civil actions are generally brought against perpetrators who have been able to victimize them by brute force or abuse of trust and power. Not only are the victims relatively less powerful, but the perpetrators may be persons of relatively high stature to whom judicial deference might be extended.[36] Nevertheless, compared to the criminal system, the formal equality of the civil system constitutes a dramatic improvement in the relative power positions of victims and perpetrators of sexual battery.

Perhaps the best example of the significance of formal equality lies in the contrast between the civil and criminal burden of proof. In cases of sexual wrongdoing, it will often be a matter of "only her word against his". This is an argument that can stifle criminal charges, let alone convictions. However, in a civil case, courts can and do take her word over his.[37] The plaintiff's version need only be more credible than the defendant's. In the civil suit it is reasonably possible for a victim standing alone to be believed. Moreover, believing the tort plaintiff entails granting judgment on her behalf. In a criminal trial, the judge or jury might well believe the victim, but nevertheless acquit over a reasonable doubt.

Nor is it necessarily the case that tort law will be ruled by formal equality alone. We have witnessed recently, particularly in the Supreme Court of Canada, a remarkable willingness to look beyond formal equality and to con-

---

35. See Weinrib, supra note 20.

36. In West, supra note 8 at 99, the author reports that a common idea in modern rape research is that rape is related to the low status of women in society. She further states that the most likely rape victims are the powerless, either by social station or by virtue of having been prior victims, and suggests that women's powerless role in criminal law reinforces this: ibid. at 110. See also the judge's comments in *Mellor*, supra note 9: "Her evidence must be viewed with scepticism because it is so accusatory of an apparently reputable physician."

37. This seems to have been the case in each of the defended actions, where in every case except R.N. v. S.L.S. (plaintiff by counterclaim unrepresented), supra note 3, the plaintiff has prevailed. See especially *Mellor*, ibid.; and C. v. M., supra note 1 where after giving "due allowance for emotionally driven exaggerations with respect to the number or frequency of the assaults", the court expressly took her word over his. Nevertheless, it must be kept in mind that empirical studies indicate that both men and women, but especially men, tend to regard men as more credible than women. See L.H. Schafran, Practising Law in a Sexist Society in L.L. Crites and W.L. Hepperle, eds., Women, The Courts and Equality (Newbury Park, Calf.: Sage Publications, 1987) at 196–98. In M. Zapf, "Collecting Awards for Sex Assault Can Be Difficult" The Lawyers Weekly (11 June 1993) 12 [hereinafter Collecting Awards], counsel Joseph Murphy suggests that the very symptoms of abuse may make the victim a less credible witness. Against that, another counsel, Megan Ellis, suggests that trial judges encounter these allegations frequently in the criminal context and may have less difficulty believing them than might a typical civil litigation lawyer. See M. Zapf, "Suing for Sexual Assault" The Lawyers Weekly (11 June 1993) 1 at 1 and 10. See also infra note 65.

sider real power imbalances in civil cases of sexual battery.[38] This is far less likely to occur in the criminal system where the power imbalance between the state and the accused is the one that dominates the agenda.[39]

Subject to the resource constraints discussed below, the plaintiff can control her own case. With one potentially crucial exception,[40] she can choose whether to sue at all. Within limits, the plaintiff may be entitled to proceed anonymously, or if she prefers, to insist that the parties be publicly identified by name.[41] She can choose what facts are brought before the courts, what expert evidence is presented and how,[42] and what legal theory of tortious wrongdoing constitutes her case.[43] The plaintiff may explain in detail the damaging consequences of the battery from her own personal point of view.[44] This is a matter that might receive little attention in the criminal trial.

It is an attractive assumption that by seizing control of the litigation, by speaking out, and bringing the perpetrator to justice, the once powerless victim can restore her self-control and self-respect. Authors have endorsed it, if somewhat tentatively.[45] Plaintiffs have expressed their own therapeutic expectations

---

38. See especially *Norberg*, supra note 7, and other cases cited supra note 10.

39. See, e.g., R. v. Seaboyer, [1991] 2 S.C.R. 577, 66 C.C.C. (3d) 321. See also supra note 33.

40. This option may be constrained somewhat by the increasing tendency for the alleged perpetrator to initiate a civil action for defamation against women who have spoken about sexual abuse to their therapists and other family members. The party claiming to have been victimized may then have little choice but to sue in sexual battery by counterclaim. The use of the defamation action in this context is potentially very troubling, and clearly anti-therapeutic for the party attempting to cope with her problems in therapy who does not wish to litigate. Thus far, the courts have dealt effectively with these actions. See especially Corney v. Corney, [1992] B.C.J. No. 2802 (S.C.) (QL), suspending the actions until alleged victims deemed able to testify by a competent therapist. See also *Khalsa*, supra note 2, where the defamation claim was dismissed and the counterclaim in sexual battery succeeded; and R.N. v. S.L.S., supra note 3, where both claims failed.

41. For a discussion of the law governing whether a plaintiff is entitled to maintain an action identifying the parties solely by their initials, see M.(S.) v. C.(J.R.) (1993), 13 O.R. (3d) 148 (Gen. Div.), where the plaintiff's motion was denied. However, there are also cases where the victim prefers to be named and to have the perpetrator named as well. See "Judge Lifts Name Ban for Assault Victim, 11" Saskatoon Star Phoenix (18 June 1993) A13.

42. See Sheehy, supra note 9 at 214–15; Feldthusen, supra note 9.

43. See infra text accompanying notes 82–89.

44. See K. Sutherland, Measuring Pain: Quantifying Damages in Civil Suits for Sexual Assault in Cooper-Stephenson & Gibson, eds., supra note 19, c. 4; Feldthusen, supra note 9; and J.E. McConnell, Incest as Conundrum: Judicial Discourse on Private Wrong and Public Harm (1992) 1 Texas J. Women & L. 143. Note that s. 735 of the Code provides for victim participation, including a description of harm or loss, at the sentencing phase of the trial. As to the importance of the victim reconstructing the trauma to her therapist, see Herman, supra note 23 at c. 9. It is unknown whether retelling the story in court will have the same therapeutic consequences.

45. In the specific context of sexual battery litigation, see West, supra note 8, at 114; Sutherland, supra note 44; Batt, supra note 9; and Sheehy, supra note 9. Sheehy is less optimistic than the others. More generally, Herman speaks of the third stage of recovery for sexual assault victims: "She is ready to take concrete steps to increase her sense of power and control" and "The first principle of recovery is the empowerment of the survivor." See supra note 23 at 197 & 133.

during and immediately after the litigation.[46] And the assumption of therapeutic benefit enjoys some support in the empirical literature that deals with different types of civil litigation.[47] There we learn that litigants' evaluation of the litigation experience is little influenced by the actual outcome in the case, by the time or money spent on the litigation, or by variables such as age, education, race or sex. Rather, what really counts is whether or not litigants perceive that they have been treated fairly. Litigants want to perceive the proceedings as unbiased. They respond favourably to how they are treated, especially to whether they are treated with dignity and respect. They prefer a procedure in which they can participate, have a voice, or control. They value this even when they expect it to have little influence on the outcome. The formal equality of tort law has a tremendous advantage over criminal law in all these respects. In addition, there is the undoubted therapeutic benefit of achieving justice and vindication by winning the suit.[48] All people have a need for "value affirmation of their status by legal authorities as competent, equal, citizens and human beings".[49] Victims of sexual abuse have a particular need in this regard, and it is a need to which the civil justice system may be uniquely suited to respond.

In Trauma and Recovery, Judith Herman identifies three stages of recovery for victims of trauma including sexual trauma:

> The central task of the first stage is the establishment of safety. The central task
> of the second stage is remembrance and mourning. The central task of the third
> stage is reconnection with ordinary life.[50]

If tort is to make any therapeutic contribution whatsoever, the civil action would only be useful as part of the third stage.[51] At this point, the victim is

---

46. See supra notes 25–28. But see B.(P.) v. B.(W.), supra note 3 at 164. The plaintiff reported that she wished to make up for the abuse by establishing a normal father-daughter relationship with her incestuous father. It is unclear how litigation was expected to contribute to this goal. Also, the judge observed that testifying in open court had been "obviously most painful for her": ibid. at 166. Perhaps her motives for suing were financial. However, in that the defendant was in prison and did not chose to defend the suit, this seems unlikely.

47. See generally T.R. Tyler, The Psychological Consequences of Judicial Procedures: Implications for Civil Commitment Hearings (1992) 46 S.M.U. L. Rev. 433 at 436–37, summarizing E. A. Lind et al., In The Eye of The Beholder: Tort Litigants, Evaluations of Their Experiences in the Civil Justice System (1990) 24 Law & Soc'y Rev. 953; and Binder, Trimble & McNeil, supra note 29. Readers should also consult L. Sas et al., Three Years After the Verdict (1993), available from the Child Witness Project, London Family Court Clinic, 254 Pall Mall St., London, Ontario, N6A 5P6. Unfortunately, this report was published too late to be taken into account herein. It summarizes many findings that may apply to this article, and contains many important references. The study raises serious concern about the therapeutic impact of child victim testimony in criminal sexual assault cases.

48. See supra note 29.

49. See Tyler, supra note 47 at 440.

50. Supra note 23 at 155. Similar stages recognized by others are summarized at 156.

51. Obviously, civil litigation is the antithesis of the first stage. Counsel ought to take steps to advise against premature litigation. The tort suit could provide a forum in which the survivor passed through the second stage, telling "the story of the trauma...in depth and in detail." Herman, ibid. at 175. However, it would appear that this is better accomplished first in the care of a competent lay or professional therapist. The witness stand is no place to

"ready to take concrete steps to increase her sense of power and control..." [and to make] a conscious choice to face danger."[52] "The first principle of recovery is the empowerment of the survivor."[53]

Addressing the role of the community specifically, Herman says:

> The response of the community has a powerful influence on the ultimate resolution of the trauma....[This] depends, first, upon public acknowledgement of the traumatic event and, second, upon some form of community action.... [T]he community must take action to assign responsibility for the harm and to repair the injury. These two responses—recognition and restitution—are necessary to rebuild the survivor's sense of order and justice.[54]

Although Herman does not appear to contemplate the civil justice system as a possible vehicle for this community response, on the surface the tort action seems ideal.

In addition, a substantial minority of trauma victims find it therapeutic to make their personal tragedy the basis for social action.[55] One advocate for battered women put it this way:

> To make this system that victimized....so many women work for us, not being mean or corrupt about it, but playing by their rules and making it work: there's a sense of power.[56]

That, then, is the general case in favour of civil sexual battery litigation as a therapeutic agent. It remains to consider what remains unproven, and what reasons there are for wondering whether the case made so far might be too good to be true.

Herman does not claim to have done empirical research about the therapeutic value of civil litigation. Nothing in her book indicates that she would endorse such a course of action for the typical sexual trauma survivor. Her most explicit discussion of the issue arises when she deals with the "fantasy of compensation". She concludes that it may be better for the victim to break completely with the perpetrator and to seek restitution in a more social, general and abstract process than to struggle for compensation from the perpetrator.[57] In other words, sexual battery litigation might prolong, not assist, the recovery process. Along the same lines, Megan Ellis, who has represented a number of sexual battery plaintiffs, says: "The nature of the litigation is that the probing of both the abuse and the effects of the abuse is deeper than many survivors have experienced in therapy, and....this will precipitate a need for further therapy."[58]

---

come to grips with repressed memories of the traumatic events. In Hurst, supra note 17 at B5, psychologist Judith Golden is quoted as saying: "If you attempt it at the wrong time in your healing process, you can get trapped in the angry revenge stage. If you're going to do it, you must do it at the end of therapy."

52. Herman, ibid. at 197.
53. Ibid. at 133.
54. Ibid. at 70 (emphasis added).
55. Ibid. at 207.
56. Ibid. at 211, quoting an interview with S. Buel.
57. Ibid. at 190.
58. "Suing for Sexual Assault", supra note 37 at 10.

Nor are the conclusions to be drawn from the empirical research about general civil litigation described above clearly relevant to this cause of action. None were based on studies of actual litigants. None tell us whether the subject might have benefited more had she not litigated, but tried to obtain vindication otherwise, or even done nothing at all. None of the litigation research to date has been conducted specifically with sexual battery victims. It is reasonable to suppose that therapeutic expectations and outcomes from litigation could differ significantly between sexual battery and other plaintiffs. Differences amongst sexual battery actions themselves, a few of which are discussed below, must also be considered before making across-the-board predictions about the therapeutic benefits of litigation. And what of the therapeutic consequences of settlement compared to litigation, especially in sexual battery actions?[59]

Pending empirical investigation, there are at least a few good reasons to suggest that civil litigation offers the potential to make matters worse, if not generally, at least in particular cases. In other contexts, cost, delay and stress usually make civil litigation the option of last resort, not something potential plaintiffs turn to for therapeutic benefit. Is the sexual battery action truly different in that regard and why?[60] Some feminists would begin with the opposite presumption; that a male-centred legal system was unlikely to offer anything of substantial benefit for women.[61]

Anecdotal remarks of plaintiffs and lawyers in the immediate aftermath of victory should be assessed with caution. We must learn how the plaintiff and others assess the experience after the euphoria wears off. What really was the therapeutic outcome? How does it compare to the plaintiff's expectations going into the litigation?

Thus far, plaintiffs have enjoyed an exceptional degree of success in their sexual battery actions.[62] But then, a great many civil battery actions have been unde-

---

59. For one victim's report of the anti-therapeutic impact of accepting a monetary settlement without securing an acknowledgement of guilt, see Hurst, supra note 17 at B5. Clients ought to be advised of this prospect by their lawyers. See generally P.C. Rosenblatt, Grief and Involvement in Wrongful Death Litigation (1983) 7 Law & Hum. Behav. 351 for some useful observations about the therapeutic impact of wrongful death litigation. It seems to me that many of Rosenblatt's hypotheses ought also to be tested in the context of sexual battery litigation. For example, he speculates about how lengthy litigation may delay the recovery process, about how itemizing damages may exaggerate them and about how termination of the litigation may provoke new therapeutic needs. One of the goals of Rosenblatt's article is to sensitize lawyers to these issues so that they may take them into account when advising their clients.

60. Sheehy, supra note 9, addresses cost, stress and delay in sexual battery actions. See also West, supra note 8 at 116. As to litigants' psychological dissatisfaction with accident litigation, see Binder, Trimble & McNeil, supra note 29 at 154.

61. See, e.g., M. Frye, Wilful Virgin (Freedom, Cal.: Crossing Press, 1992) at 97.

62. This is not meant to suggest that the civil system provides a complete set of remedies for all victims of sexual abuse. There undoubtedly exists sexual wrongdoing (stalking, or street and telephone harassment, for example) for which the common law has yet to fashion an adequate remedy. However, in the cases discussed herein in which the conduct is covered by the tort of battery, judgment was given for the plaintiff in every single case except one, R.N. v. S.L.S., supra note 3. There the alleged victims sued by way of counterclaim to a defamation action, and proceeded at trial without legal representation, to, the judge observed, their probable detriment. Compare the ninety per cent success rate in the very com-

fended.[63] It would be useful to determine whether this is a coincidence. Or, do plaintiffs prefer to litigate undefended suits, even without any prospect of obtaining damages, because these are a relatively safe means of achieving therapeutic goals? If so, is this a prudent investment on the part of the plaintiff or society?[64]

When the action is defended, there is a real risk that the plaintiff's high hopes might be shattered. A vigorous civil defence has the potential to be every bit as brutal for the victim as its better-known criminal equivalent.[65] This is unlikely to be perceived by the victim as a fair procedure directed toward

---

mon fathers' actions for seduction in late nineteenth century. See Backhouse, supra note 9 at 76–77. Whether plaintiffs who received low damage awards, such as in *Norberg*, supra note 7 or *Lyth*, supra note 4, would regard their cases as successful is another question. Herman, supra note 23 at 201 & 211 discusses the risk of a negative outcome and the necessity of accepting this in advance of the public battle.

63. Of the thirty-two cases in which the information is clear from the record, eighteen were undefended, and fourteen defended.

The undefended actions were:

—of the rape cases listed supra note 1, *Myers*.

—of the other sexual assault cases, supra note 2, H.R. v. F.M., and *Da Costa*.

—of the incest cases listed supra note 3, *Madelena*; P.(L.) v. L.(A.); B.(A.) v. J.(I.); *Brandner*; *Beaudry* (personal appearance first day only); M.O. and D.T. v. F.A.; K.G. v. J.T.; D.C. v. K.C.; and B.(P.) v. B.(W.).

—of the other child sexual abuse cases listed supra note 4, M.(A.K.) v. B.(M); N.(J.L.) v. L.(A.M.); S.M.Q v. Hodgins; G.(K.) v. T.(J.); *Jody Lynn N.*; and *Slinn*, defended on damages only.

One defended rape action was C. v. M., supra note 1, in which the defendant was acquitted previously of criminal sexual assault. See infra text at notes 100–01. Defended incest cases, supra note 3, include: *Kunz*, defended by deceased defendant's estate; M.(K.) v. M.(H.), a case in which the defendant had prevailed on a limitations issue in the lower courts; W.J.L.M. v. R.G.R., a case where the defendant had been acquitted at a prior criminal trial and was represented at least during the preliminary stages of the civil action; G. v. R. (personal defense); and L.A.J. v. H.J. where the father-perpetrator and mother were defended jointly. Defended child abuse cases, supra note 4, include: *Gray*; T.K.S. v. E.B.S.; and *Harder*, all cases in which there had been no prior criminal action. All three exploitation cases, supra note 10, were defended.

Amongst the undefended actions are some of those in which the highest damage awards have been made: see B.(P.) v. B.(W.); B.(A.) v. J.(I.); *Brandner*; and *Beaudry*; and *Kunz* all supra note 3; and *Jody Lynn N.*, supra note 4.

64. See infra text accompanying notes 119–25.

65. But see Sheehy, supra note 9 at 214–15; but see also at 206–07. Consider the emerging notion of the so-called "false memory syndrome", an unsubstantiated idea used to describe an allegation that the victim's claim is based on imagined memories, likely aroused by her therapist. Given the historical tendency to disbelieve women, especially about sexual assault, it is reasonable to expect that this idea will be received sympathetically in some courts. How will plaintiffs fare when told in a public forum that their injuries are based on "false memories"? This "false memory" notion also has a strong potential to invade the therapeutic process, again to the detriment of victims. For an example of a case in which it was held that some of the plaintiff's memories seemed to have been induced by her therapists, see T.K.S. v. E.B.S., supra note 4. For an example of a case which is being defended vigorously, see K.L.V. v. D.G.R., [1993] B.C.J. No. 1917 (S.C.) (QL), a case in which there have been numerous preliminary motions, including one which culminated in the plaintiff having to produce her private personal diaries on discovery.

value affirmation with dignity and respect. What will be the impact on vulnerable plaintiffs who, with the help of their therapists, pour out the intimate details of their damages, only to have them dismissed or discounted?[66] What will happen to plaintiffs who fail to meet even the civil burden, or who are found to have consented to the conduct of which they complain?[67]

Finally, civil litigation is an expensive proposition. Damages in the exploitation cases have not yet proven sufficient to fund the litigation.[68] Many other sexual battery actions have been brought with no expectation of full, or even partial, recovery of damages.[69] True, these have often been the relatively inexpensive undefended actions against defendants previously convicted in the criminal courts, but even these cost money.[70] The possibility that the defendant's intentional misconduct will be covered by his liability insurance policies seems remote.[71]

---

66. See Binder, Trimble & McNeil, supra note 29 at 153–54, reporting psychological impact on plaintiffs who generally perceived that their damages were too low. I wonder about this in cases like *Norberg*, supra note 7 or *Lyth*, supra note 4. See also Rosenblatt, supra note 59 and Sheehy, supra note 9 at 214 and at 219–20. Sheehy also discusses judicial insensitivity, another therapeutic risk run by the plaintiff.

67. See Binder, Trimble & McNeil, ibid. at 154, reporting negative effect of being blamed in litigation for own personal injury. I know of no Canadian case to have explicitly blamed the victim, although *Lyth*, supra note 4 and *Mellor*, supra note 9, come close. There are also comments from well-meaning judges which suggest that if the plaintiff suffers any future losses, especially economic losses, this will be her own fault. See Feldthusen, supra note 9. Sheehy, supra note 9 at 219, approaches this from the opposite perspective, speaking of the judges rewarding victims who have behaved "appropriately".

68. See Feldthusen, ibid. One counsel who has litigated cases of this sort estimated to the author that disbursements alone to cover the costs of experts on economic loss and rehabilitation therapy would fall in the range of $7,500–$15,000. These funds must usually be paid well in advance of trial or judgment.

69. See supra note 22.

70. Seven cases were identified supra note 22 as ones in which plaintiffs had indicated that they knew they would not recover, or recover much, on the judgment. I could locate the necessary information about five of them, and all were undefended except *Kunz*, which was defended by the defendant's estate.

Of the twenty-nine cases in which the information is clear from the record, sixteen followed criminal convictions. See infra note 89. In only five of those cases did the defendant bother to defend the subsequent civil suit. Those were: *Glendale,* supra note 1, in which the defendant was probably solvent because the case went to appeal on quantum; *Lyth*, supra note 4, where liability was controversial and the defendant probably solvent; G. v. R., supra note 3, where the defendant represented himself; *Slinn*, supra note 4, where liability was conceded; and J.(L.A.) v. J.(H.), supra note 1 where the mother accused of negligence and the father-perpetrator were defended jointly.

71. In the long run, the viability of the sexual battery action may depend on this. This has not been considered in detail in this article. See C. Brown, Insuring Against Family Violence and Incest [unpublished; on file with author]; Storrie, supra note 9; C. Cleary, Litigating Incest Torts Under Homeowner's Insurance Policies (1988) 18 Golden Gate U. L. Rev. 593; J. Colonari & D. Johnson, Coverage for Parents' Sexual Abuse (1992) For The Defense 2–5; D.K. Frey, Application of Intentional Acts Exclusion under Homeowner's Insurance Policies to Acts of Child Molestation (1991) 68 Denv. U. L. Rev. 429 (case note on Allstate Insurance Co. v. Troelstrup, 789 P. 2d 415 (Colo. 1990)); Collecting Awards, supra note 37 at 13; and

Who is funding this litigation? Nothing in the case reports yet suggests that sexual battery plaintiffs are typically women of substantial means, an intriguing fact in its own right.[72] If anything, many seem to have been unemployed women in precarious financial situations.[73] Do, and, if so, should Legal Aid plans fund tort litigation with no prospect of financial recovery? For how long can we continue to expect these actions to be financed by advocacy groups and charitable lawyers?[74] Eventually, will the sexual battery action exist only for the benefit of wealthy plaintiffs or to the detriment of wealthy defendants?

III. Sexual Battery Suits Compared and Contrasted According to the Presence or Absence of Prior Criminal Litigation

In this section, I consider four different sets of circumstances in which the civil action for sexual battery might be litigated. The first is the case where civil litigation is commenced after the Crown has proven unwilling or unable to press criminal charges. The second is the case where the victim herself declines to press criminal charges. The third is the case where the tort suit is

---

E.T. Lanham, Suing Parents in Tort for Child Abuse: A New Role for the Court Appointed Guardian Ad Litem? (1992) 61 U.M.K.C. L. Rev. 101 at 113–14. See also supra note 17. Also, once insurers are involved, a far more vigorous defence can be expected, along with other complications in the litigation. See Hurst, supra note 17.

72. The apparent absence of any incest or child sexual abuse litigation between members of relatively wealthy families is curious. Do the relatively wealthy avoid public civil litigation? Do they settle rather go to trial? Are relatively wealthy defendants likely to mount such a vigorous defense as to destroy likely therapeutic benefits to the plaintiff? One U.S. study found reported child physical and sexual abuse four times more frequent in families with annual incomes of less than $15,000. If accurate, this effectively limits the prospect of damage recovery in many cases. However, the data may reflect only the incidence of reported abuse, not actual abuse. See Lanham, ibid. at 113.

Concern has been expressed that the development of a viable civil action may establish a new class of poorer victims, one more likely to be raped because she can not employ the civil action to her advantage. See West, supra note 8 at 116. That prospective tort liability alone would direct rapists away from wealthy victims and towards poorer victims seems unlikely. This is rather like saying that reckless drivers choose poorer neighbourhoods to minimize their damage exposure. It should, however, be the case that relatively wealthy perpetrators are better deterred than relatively poorer ones. The deterrent value of the civil sexual battery action requires more attention.

73. I do not question Sheehy's observation that the tort process probably works best for women "relatively privileged in our current social structure by being heterosexual, able-bodied, white-skinned, and not poor". See supra note 9 at 228. I would only observe that neither have upper middle class or professional women tended to sue in civil battery. Virtually the same pattern has been identified with nineteenth century seduction actions. See Backhouse, supra note 9 at 75.

74. For an example of the lawyers' traditional and understandable preference for cases that promise a financial return see Collecting Awards, supra note 37, and Hurst, supra note 17. One Area Director of the Ontario Legal Aid Plan indicated to me that although Area Directors might differ, he would not expect certificates to be granted in cases in which it was clear that no recovery would be possible. See also supra note 21.

brought after the defendant has been acquitted of criminal charges in respect of the same conduct. The fourth is the action brought after the defendant has been convicted of criminal charges. I will situate the decided cases within these categories, and explore the possibility that therapeutic needs, expectations and outcomes may differ from one to the other.[75] Again I emphasize that the decisions are too few, and the issues too little explored to offer any definitive conclusions. I hope instead to suggest areas for further empirical research.

A. The Police or Crown Decline To Press Criminal Charges

It seems reasonable to postulate that the therapeutic benefits of tort litigation would be greatest in situations untouched by the criminal justice system. Indeed, if this were not the case, it would suggest that the criminal process itself created additional therapeutic needs for victims.[76] Furthermore, one might predict that the benefits of tort would be greatest in situations where access to the criminal justice system had been denied by state officials, rather than declined by the victim herself.[77] There are any number of reasons why officials in the criminal justice system might decide against criminal prosecution. I will consider three.

Perhaps the most common example, and also the most difficult to discover, is the case in which the police simply refuse to take and investigate the complaint seriously. A similar situation arises when the criminal sexual assault complaint is not prosecuted because officials simply do not believe the complainant. She may, perhaps accurately, strike officials as a poor, or even unreliable witness.[78] It will surely be unpleasant, if not harmful, for a willing complainant to learn that officials do not consider her case serious enough or strong enough to warrant criminal prosecution. The complainant may be vic-

---

75. There are many other differences amongst the sexual battery cases that might prove more significant, each of which is worthy of empirical study. See supra note 31.

76. This is not implausible based on the discussion in Section II, above. See especially supra note 32.

77. Sheehy, supra note 9 at 205, says: "It may be the most empowering action available to her, especially if the criminal process has derailed, as it so often does." See also West, supra note 8 at 112. The social importance of power to control entry into the legal system is also enormous, and in this context may affect dramatically what society comes to regard as typical and wrongful sexual misconduct. See generally D.J. Black, The Behavior of Law (New York: Academic Press, 1976); and G.L. Priest, Common Law Process and the Selection of Efficient Rules (1977) 6 J. Legal Stud. 65.

78. Here, I am considering adult complainants only. I leave aside the child and incest cases, because I am not confident that they could be described as cases in which "willing complainants" were denied access by state officials. The therapeutic aspects of tort suits involving children as plaintiffs require separate attention. See A.M. Boland, Civil Remedies for Victims of Child Sexual Abuse (1986) 13 Ohio N.U. L. Rev. 223 at 228. Boland notes the difficulty with the testimony of children, the fear instilled in the child by the perpetrator, and the fact that some child victims will remain dependent living in the home of the perpetrator. See also Diamond, infra note 100. Developments in child testimony in criminal cases are discussed in A.H. Young, Recent Canadian Developments in the Treatment of Children and their Evidence in Criminal Sexual Abuse Cases (1992) 1 Annals of Health L. 157; and N. Bala, Child Sexual Abuse Prosecutions in Canada: A Measure of Progress (1992) 1 Annals of Health L. 177.

timized a second time by a criminal system that has priorities and perspectives different from her own.

If a sufficiently large number of cases like this were to emerge, it would be useful to explore whether they exhibit unique therapeutic expectations and outcomes. Does it matter that criminal access is denied because of a negative assessment about the victim's credibility, rather than because of some non-personal problem with the substance of the criminal law? How do therapeutic expectations and outcomes compare to those where the matter has been previously tried in the criminal courts? How do they compare to those in the sexual exploitation cases?

Unfortunately, there have been so few such cases that the most we can safely conclude is that state refusal to prosecute does not account for the majority of civil battery actions. There have been two civil sexual battery cases where the evidence indicates a refusal by the police to pursue the complaint seriously.[79] There have also been at least three Canadian cases in which the civil action was initiated after the police declined to prosecute.[80] Only in one of these five cases, *Myers*, do we have any evidence that the civil suit was motivated by the state's refusal to prosecute. This was a violent acquaintance-rape case with racial overtones. The plaintiff pursued the civil case with explicit therapeutic motives and no prospect of financial gain.[81] This is a classic case of victim vindication in the face of state inaction, but it stands alone.

A second reason why officials might refuse to prosecute a sexual assault is because they have a relatively conservative definition of sexual assault. Within the limits of reasonable statutory interpretation, there is some flexibility about what constitutes a criminal sexual assault, consent, and so on. At the system entry level, state officials monopolize the power to make these definitions. The paradigmatic sexual assault in the male centred criminal justice system is the

---

79. See H.R. v. F.M., supra note 2 at 308:

> On October 28 the plaintiff telephoned the Fredericton City Police to report the incident. The officer with whom she spoke told her it was a very minor assault and, because of the defendant's age, she was wasting everybody's time. The officer said there was very little the police could do and suggested she see a lawyer. She later went to the City Police again and was told that, because the assault had happened outside the city, she should see the R.C.M.P. which she did. She gave them a copy of a written statement she had given her then solicitor. She called the R.C.M.P repeatedly after that with no result.

While this may have been relevant to the plaintiff's decision to sue, there is no direct evidence to confirm this. See also *Khalsa*, supra note 3:

> Following her disclosure of the assault to her husband they went to the police, who suggested that the matter be sorted out in the Sikh community.

Here, the victim only sued by way of counterclaim to a defamation action.

80. Sheehy, supra note 9 at 211, cites *Myers*, supra note 1; *Harder*, supra note 4; and *Mundy*, supra note 9. In addition, see *Kunz*, supra note 3, where the perpetrator died before the criminal action could begin. Sheehy suggests that there might have been problems in securing a criminal conviction in *Myers* and *Mundy* because the plaintiffs were intoxicated, and because in both cases the plaintiff and defendant had been involved in a prior relationship with one another.

81. Supra note 1. See also Allard, supra note 22. The attacker referred to his victim as a "squaw" while administering the beating and sexual attack.

extrinsically violent stranger rape.[82] One could hypothesize that the further away from the paradigm, the less likely are officials to believe the complaint, regard the complaint as a serious matter, or to believe (perhaps correctly) that the complaint will succeed in a criminal trial. Tort, on the other hand, offers plaintiffs the opportunity to define the wrong in the way in which they experience it. This in itself, it might be supposed, could have therapeutic benefit.[83]

We know that women are more likely to experience child sexual abuse or "non-violent" sexual assault at the hands of trusted acquaintances, than violent stranger rape.[84] One way to determine whether the tort system was being used to expand the type of sexual wrongdoing generally addressed by the criminal law would be to compare the types of cases in the two systems. One might predict, for example, that a good number of non-paradigmatic sexual assaults would be litigated in tort, certainly far more than in the criminal system.

The evidence is mixed. One striking difference between the civil and criminal cases is that there has not yet been a single civil judgment rendered against a defendant who was a stranger to the plaintiff.[85] And it is perhaps no coincidence that the two cases indicating clearly the police force's refusal to take a criminal complaint seriously were not rapes, but non-violent sexual assaults perpetrated by older acquaintances of the victim. In both cases, the victims were awarded damages in their civil actions.[86] In addition, one may speculate that in at least three other successful tort cases, criminal convictions would have been problematic. In *Harder*, it seems possible that a criminal prosecution could have failed on the issue of consent. And in two others, *Myers* and *Mundy*, a conviction might have been difficult because the complainants were intoxicated victims who knew their assailant.[87]

On the other hand, all the adult victim civil rape cases involved considerable extrinsic violence.[88] And virtually all the reported civil incest and child sexual abuse cases have dealt with conduct easily recognized as criminal. Indeed,

---

82. See J.M. Feinman, The Ideology of Legal Reasoning in the Classroom (1992) 57 Mo. L. Rev. 363 at 366; T.M. Massaro, Experts, Psychology, Credibility and Rape (1985) 69 Minn. L. Rev. 395 at 406 citing C. Bohmer, Judicial Attitudes Toward Rape Victims (1974) 57 Judicature 303 at 304, who claims that judges tend to accept a "real rape", "stranger in the alley" paradigm.

83. See West, supra note 8 at 115.

84. See Massaro, supra note 82 at 403 & 429. See also K. MacFarlane, Sexual Abuse of Children in J.R. Chapman and M. Gates, eds., The Victimization of Women (Beverly Hills, Calf.: Sage, 1978) 81 at 86, reporting that approximately 80 per cent of child sexual abuse cases are perpetrated by men the children knew and trusted.

85. See West, supra note 8 at 117 who predicts this and suggests that tort is likely to be safest and most effective in these cases. Note that in general people tend to sue strangers, not close relations. See Black, supra note 77, especially at 41–48; and D.M. Engel, The Oven Bird's Song: Insiders, Outsiders, and Personal Injuries in an American Community (1984) 18 Law & Soc'y Rev. 551. Perhaps what is different about sexual battery actions in this respect is that one of the purposes of the action is to terminate symbolically the relationship. But see supra note 46. In any event, the plaintiff's difficulty in breaking with the general pattern should not be underestimated.

86. Supra note 79.

87. See supra note 80.

88. See supra note 1.

more often than not, criminal convictions had actually been obtained before the civil actions were brought.[89]

Only the sexual exploitation cases, and of them only two, appear to have granted legal relief where it was clearly unavailable from the criminal law.[90] They both dealt with sexual relations in "power-imbalanced (doctor-patient) relationships",[91] sexual relations that would have been defined as consensual under the Code. Until recently, they probably would have been defined as consensual in tort law as well. Nevertheless, civil courts have found exploitation deserving of civil punishment through punitive damages.[92]

There are a number of reasons to predict that exploitation cases would offer high therapeutic expectations and outcomes. Tort provides the victim the unique opportunity to obtain legal recognition and sanction of patently objectionable conduct. The actions deal with a particular type of misconduct, breach of trust, which may create unique therapeutic needs.[93] In two of the three reported exploitation cases the plaintiffs themselves explicitly claimed therapeutic motives for their tort litigation.[94] Again, actual data from a much larger sample of exploitation cases is required to verify the therapeutic expectations and outcomes.

---

89. Cases in which the defendant had been previously convicted in the criminal courts for the same set of events are: of the rape cases, supra note 1, *Glendale*; of the other sexual assault cases listed supra note 2, *Da Costa*; of the incest cases listed supra note 3, *Madelena*, A.(B.) v. I.(J.), *Brandner, Beaudry*, M.O. and D.T. v. F.A., B.(P.) v. B.(W.), J.(L.A.) v. J.(H.), D.C. v. K.C., and G. v. R.; of the other child sexual abuse cases listed supra note 4, N.(J.L.) v. L.(A.M.), S.M.Q. v. Hodgins, *Slinn,* and *Jody Lynn N.*; and of the exploitation cases, *Lyth*, supra note 10.

Only three cases appear to have been initiated after a criminal acquittal: C. v. M., supra note 1; W.J.L.M. v. R.G.R., supra note 3; and the case referred to in D.C.G.(Re), supra note 3.

It is unclear from the reports whether there had been prior criminal charges in P.(L.) v. L.(A.), supra note 3, M.(A.K.) v. B.(M.), supra note 4, and G.(K.) v. T.(J.), supra note 4.

90. There was a prior conviction in *Lyth*, ibid.; the other two were *Norberg*, supra note 7; and *Mellor*, supra note 9. The closest to a criminal action for sexual exploitation is defined in s. 153 of the Code. It makes it an offense for an adult in a position of trust or authority to engage in sexual activity with a child between the ages of fourteen and eighteen. Consent is not a defence. See R. v. M.(G.) (1992), 11 O.R. (3d) 225, 11 C.R. (4th) 221 (C.A.). Consider also former s. 158(2) of the Code, now repealed. It attempted to protect relatively blameless, previously chaste female employees under the age of twenty-one from intercourse with their employers and others with power over them in the employment setting.

91. See *Norberg*, ibid. at 457–58, per LaForest J.

92. In *Mellor*, supra note 9, the Court awarded $15,000 in punitive damages; in *Norberg*, ibid., the Court awarded $10,000 in punitive damages. No punitive damages were awarded in *Lyth*, supra note 4, a case in which there had been a prior criminal conviction.

93. Exploitation cases can be compared to other breach of trust and confidence cases such as incest and many other child sexual abuse cases, cases which also constitute criminal behaviour. They can be contrasted to actions based on batteries perpetrated by strangers, and to batteries involving extrinsic violence. It would be intriguing to discover, for example, that the victims' therapeutic needs from the legal system were greatest in these exploitation cases that the law had, until recently, neglected entirely. For an analysis of the psychological significance of the breach of the professional trust relationship, see M.R. Peterson, At Personal Risk: Boundary Violations in Professional-Client Relationships (New York: Norton, 1992).

94. See supra notes 25 & 26.

What remains to be seen is whether actions of this sort will proliferate in the wake of the Supreme Court's decision in *Norberg*.[95] That may depend more on financial considerations than on therapeutic ones. On the surface, the action appears more attractive than most others from a financial point of view. The successful plaintiff has an excellent chance of obtaining an award of punitive damages. Defendants in these cases will usually be able to honour any liability that the courts are likely to impose.[96] However, exploitation litigation may be more expensive than other sexual battery cases. The parameters of the cause of action are still uncertain. These are the types of defendants from whom a vigorous defence might be expected.[97] Moreover, damage awards in the exploitation cases have been strikingly low.[98] I suspect that relatively few plaintiffs in the future will be able to incur the risks and expense of exploitation litigation to meet therapeutic expectations alone.

B. The Plaintiff Declines To Press Criminal Charges

By definition, what is unique about the cases in this category is that the civil plaintiff herself has made the decision not to press criminal charges.[99] One possibility is that the victim may not want her assailant to suffer criminal penalties. For example, a mother might not want to have the father of her child incarcerated or given a criminal record.[100] Perhaps she would see this as detrimental to the child. Perhaps she could not afford to give up a possible source of child support. A more conventional, and more compelling explanation is simply that the victim did not wish to participate in a criminal trial in which her reputation and conduct might be judged more harshly than the accused's, all with no guarantee of conviction or, from her point of view, appropriate penalty. The civil suit promises the victim a safer and better chance of securing some legal relief.

The prospect of obtaining an award of punitive damages may provide an additional, or even a separate reason why a victim would decline to press a criminal charge. The significance of a prior criminal conviction for a civil

---

95. Supra note 7.

96. I say this in part because of the general correlation between power and wealth; in part because of the relatively low awards in the cases. It may also be possible to recover under the defendant's malpractice insurance in the case of professional defendants.

97. The defendants have a financial stake in the outcome. They are also likely to have a professional stake in the outcome, particularly if there has been no prior criminal conviction. They have more resources to mount a serious defense than many other defendants. And they may seriously believe they have done nothing wrong or unlawful.

98. See Feldthusen, supra note 9; and Sheehy, supra note 9. See also supra note 12. Compare to a similar pattern with nineteenth century seduction actions discussed by Backhouse, supra note 9 at 74.

99. My assumption for the sake of analysis is that the Crown would be willing to prosecute with the cooperation of the victim.

100. See West, supra note 8 at 113; R.L. Kohler, The Battered Woman and Tort Law: A New Approach to Fighting Domestic Violence (1992) 25 Loy. L.A. L. Rev. 1025 & 1028; and V. Diamond, Does the Law Help the Sexually Abused Child? (1990) 140 New L.J. 1033 at 1033.

claim for punitive damages is somewhat uncertain in sexual battery actions. At one time, the conventional view seemed to have been that punitive damages could not be awarded against a defendant who had been convicted previously of a crime based on the same wrongful conduct. There is still judicial support for this position.[101] However, exceptions are appearing in the sexual battery cases. The civil courts have awarded punitive damages because the prior criminal convictions did not cover the full course of conduct canvassed in the civil trial.[102] Moreover, at least two courts have expressed the view, in obiter, that a criminal conviction for precisely the same event need not necessarily preclude an award of punitive damages.[103] Regardless, it is beyond doubt that if the sexual misconduct has not been the subject of a prior criminal conviction, the successful sexual battery plaintiff is virtually assured that the court will award punitive damages.[104] So, although there is no evidence in the decided cases to suggest that the pursuit of punitive damages motivated defendants to decline to press charges, this might become a consideration in future actions against solvent defendants.

Given both these rationales, one might have expected a large number of cases in which the victim chose to employ the civil suit as an alternative to criminal prosecution.[105] In fact, more civil cases have followed criminal prosecutions than seem to have substituted for them. And of the latter, there is no case in which the plaintiff would appear to have forgone a realistic chance at criminal prosecution.[106]

---

101. See, e.g., *Slinn,* supra note 4; and J.(L.A.) v. J.(H.), supra note 3.

102. See B.(A.) v. J.(I.), supra note 3; B.(P.) v. B.(W.), supra note 3; and *Da Costa,* supra note 2. In S.M.Q. v. Hodgins, supra note 4, punitive damages were awarded against a previously convicted defendant with no discussion. See generally Ontario Law Reform Commission, Report on Exemplary Damages (Toronto: Publication Services, 1991) especially at 43–46. Query whether this may affect the criminal action. For example, it could influence whether criminal defendants are willing to plead guilty to one charge in return for having the others dropped, knowing this leaves them with residual civil exposure for punitive damages.

103. See especially E.D.G. v. Drozdzik, supra note 1, per Lambert J.A., indicating a willingness to redress an inappropriately lenient sentence with a punitive damage award; and H.R. v. F.M., supra note 2. In that the civil case has different parties, different burdens, and different evidence, it is not demonstrably wrong to punish the defendant for acts which did not support a conviction in the criminal trial. See Report on Exemplary Damages, ibid.

104. Indeed, the only argument against punitive damages in such a case is that the compensatory award is sufficiently large to achieve the goal of civil punishment.

105. The role, or potential role, of legal counsel may be relevant here. It is not known whether any plaintiffs had received independent legal advice at the time the criminal charges were under consideration. Perhaps some plaintiffs were unaware at the time that they could forgo prosecution for a civil suit, let alone that such a choice might lead eventually to an award of punitive damages. What would be the implications of directing state officials to inform victims of their civil options? One possibility suggested to me by Professor Shuman is that the Crown might promote civil suits as an alternative to criminal prosecutions. See H.R. v. F.M., supra note 2, in which the police did exactly that.

106. Of the twenty-nine civil cases in which the information was available, only thirteen were not preceded by a criminal conviction. Two were initiated after a criminal acquittal: see C. v. M., supra note 1 and W.J.L.M. v. R.G.R., supra note 3. In five others, the Crown or police declined to press charges: see supra notes 79 & 80. In *Kunz,* supra note 3, the defendant died before trial. Criminal prosecution was not a realistic option in either *Norberg,* supra

If such cases ever do emerge, it would be useful to compare them to the cases in which a state official prevented a willing complainant from proceeding with a criminal prosecution. This would help us to isolate the therapeutic impact of official rejection, and the therapeutic benefit of the civil response. We might also compare these plaintiffs to those who declined to participate in either the civil or criminal justice system. But perhaps most interesting of all would be a comparison with plaintiffs who experienced both the criminal trial and the civil action. To these situations, I now turn.

C. Defendant Previously Acquitted in a Criminal Trial

There are numerous reasons why a criminal defendant might be acquitted of a charge of sexual assault or incest, even though he did in fact sexually assault the victim. This is the classic situation in which the civil action offers the possibility of affirming the victim's story, alleviating whatever harm she may have suffered from the criminal process and verdict, and possibly even punishing the assailant with punitive damages.[107]

Surprisingly, there appear to have been only two decided cases which fit this model, only one of which has gone to civil trial.[108] That was C. v. M., a case in which the defendant was actually convicted of ordinary assault and sentenced to six months in jail. What makes it fit this model, and fit it rather well, was that the defendant had also been tried on criminal charges of sexual assault, buggery, and forcible confinement, but acquitted on those. Although difficult to believe after reading the reasons for judgment in the civil trial, I suspect that the defendant may have established reasonable doubt in the criminal proceedings about whether the plaintiff, after having been brutally beaten, had "consented" to the sexual acts. The defendant argued consent again in the civil action, but the judge chose to believe the plaintiff's version. The defendant was held liable for $40,000 compensatory damages. The court did not award any punitive damages because of the prior criminal conviction, although arguably it might have done so.[109] What we do not know is whether and to what extent the plaintiff in C. v. M. was motivated to sue for therapeutic reasons as opposed to financial reasons. The defendant was one of the few defendants who contested the civil action with counsel, so the possibility of a real financial stake in the outcome can not be ignored. But even if the plaintiff's motives were largely therapeutic, we can not be certain that the prior acquittal was significant in shaping these motives. There are simply too many civil suits that follow criminal convictions to allow us to draw such an inference.

Why is it that there have not been more tort actions brought after criminal acquittals? It would be interesting to interview similarly situated victims who, although aware of the tort option, had chosen not to attempt to rectify the

---

note 7, or *Mellor*, supra note 9. The last three actions, M.(K.) v. M.(H.), supra note 3, *Gray*, supra note 4, and T.K.S. v. E.B.S., supra note 4, were all brought many years after the event.

107. See Section II, above.

108. In one of them, W.J.L.M. v. R.G.R., supra note 3, a case in which the defendant was acquitted, the case has yet to come to civil trial. The plaintiff's motives are unknown.

109. See supra note 102 and accompanying text.

criminal acquittal in the civil courts. Of course, it is premature to reach any firm conclusions, but a few are worth considering.

One is that a criminal trial that results in an acquittal, especially an acquittal based on doubts about the victim's credibility or her willing participation, must be a most unpleasant, if not seriously harmful, experience for the victim. It is entirely reasonable to suppose that the last place to which such a victim would turn for therapeutic relief would be to lawyers and courts that have already failed and injured her.

Another is that the plaintiff's case will be more difficult than it would have been had the defendant been convicted. This is especially so if we expect that acquitted defendants are more likely to vigorously defend than are defendants who have been convicted and jailed. For example, it is surely no coincidence that C. v. M. was defended, whereas so many of the actions following criminal convictions were not.[110] These are discussed next.

D. Defendant Convicted in a Prior Criminal Trial

Once the defendant has been convicted and sentenced in criminal court, it might be reasonable to expect that relatively few victims would still feel it necessary to initiate civil actions for therapeutic reasons.[111] The decided cases support exactly the opposite conclusion. Of the twenty-six cases in which the information is clear from the record, fifteen followed criminal convictions.[112] In only four of those cases did the defendant bother to defend the subsequent civil suit.[113] And, if the number of undefended suits is any indication, there was little or no prospect of financial recovery in most of them.[114]

One possible explanation for why so many civil suits follow criminal convictions is that the criminal trial itself, including all its procedures, witness ex-

---

110. Cases in which defendants who were previously convicted in the criminal courts actively defended the civil suit are few: see *Lyth*, supra note 4 and G. v. R., supra note 3. In J.(L.A.) v. J.(H.), supra note 3, the civil action was defended jointly by the parents, the father having previously been convicted.

Active civil defences were the rule whenever the defendant had not previously been prosecuted in the criminal courts. This was the case in the two criminal acquittals, C. v. M., supra note 1 and W.J.L.M. v. R.G.R., supra note 3. Vigorous defences were also presented in cases in which no charges were laid, although they might have been: see *Gray,* supra note 4; T.K.S. v. E.B.S., supra note 4; and *Harder*, supra note 4. See also *Kunz*, supra note 3 (defendant dying before trial) and M.(K.) v. M.(H.), supra note 3 (limitations problems). Also defended were *Norberg*, supra note 7 and *Mellor*, supra note 9, two exploitation cases in which criminal charges would have been highly problematic, if not impossible. The only undefended cases in which there had been no prior criminal convictions were *Myers*, supra note 1; H.R. v. F.M., supra note 2; and K.G. v. J.T., supra note 4. There were also three actions initiated by persons who were then named in counterclaims as perpetrators of sexual battery: see supra note 40.

111. These plaintiffs could also have turned to the criminal injuries compensation schemes instead of using the civil courts against presumably judgment-proof defendants. See infra notes 124 & 125.

112. Supra note 106.

113. See supra note 63.

114. See supra notes 63 & 70.

aminations, and sentencing, may have inflicted additional injury on the complainants which, they hope, can be remedied in the civil action.[115] A comparison with plaintiffs who have not experienced a criminal trial, especially those who decided against pressing charges, would enlighten us on this point. A related explanation would see the plaintiff turning to the civil system to further penalize a defendant who had received a criminal sentence perceived as inadequate. At least two plaintiffs have admitted as much.[116]

A somewhat different line of explanation, although not necessarily incompatible with others, follows from points raised in the previous discussion of the criminal acquittal cases. Civil suits that follow criminal convictions are probably the least expensive sexual battery actions to litigate. The plaintiff is virtually certain to prevail. The exercise is likely to be a relatively safe one for the plaintiff.[117] She may be able to rely largely on the transcript from the criminal trial. Undefended actions do not pose the risk of anti-therapeutic cross-examination.[118] So, even if the therapeutic needs were relatively less in cases of this sort, the prospects of achieving safe, cost effective therapeutic benefits may be relatively better.

If this is true, the question arises whether it is a prudent allocation of scarce judicial resources to employ an expensive formal trial when it is clear from the outset that no defense will be presented and no damages recovered. Even assuming that only formal legal process of some sort can meet these therapeutic needs, alternatives to undefended civil action are worth considering. The two logical possibilities are that the victims' legitimate therapeutic needs might be met by innovation in the criminal trial itself, or in the criminal injuries compensation schemes. If either approach were successful, it would be less expensive and time consuming than a civil trial, and would make the therapeutic benefits available to victims who could not afford to maintain a civil action.

Given the criminal law's focus on the perpetrator, significant innovations there may be impossible. It is, however, possible that the interests of victims might assume relatively more importance at the sentencing phase.[119] One intriguing possibility is that the law could encourage defendants to offer sincere

---

115. See supra note 32.

116. See *Lyth* and *Brandner,* discussed supra note 26. I wonder whether this rationale would apply equally to cases where the civil action is undefended and there is, however, no prospect of recovery.

117. I emphasize the word "relatively". Litigation is always stressful, and the procedures and outcomes always uncertain. Sexual battery victims always take a chance when they enter the civil justice system. See also E.D.G. v. Drozdzik, supra note 1, where the court imposed an extra cost penalty upon the defendant who forced the plaintiff to establish liability at trial, although he had been previously convicted for the same incidents.

118. It would be interesting to compare the successful plaintiffs' levels of satisfaction after defended and undefended actions.

119. For the reasons given in Section II, above, the ability of the criminal trial to respond to the needs of victims is limited. The victim may speak at the sentencing phase. See supra note 44. Another possibility is that what a judge says, and in what manner he or she says it during sentencing, could make a therapeutic difference to the criminal complainant. Also, the criminal trial is the one forum in which the defendant is certain to be present. This may in itself have therapeutic significance.

public apologies to their victims.[120] A sincere apology tendered in the criminal trial[121] might reduce the need for the plaintiff to sue an impecunious defendant in a subsequent action.[122] The parties to the civil actions have all been family members or close acquaintances, never strangers. It is from those we know best that a sincere apology is most likely to be meaningful. It is also possible that encouraging sincere apologies would assist in the rehabilitation of sexual battery defendants themselves.[123]

As matters now stand, a criminal injuries compensation claim may be even more anti-therapeutic for the victim than the criminal trial itself.[124] But unlike

---

120. The role of apology is not entirely unknown in our law. Apology plays a central remedial role in defamation law, another branch of tort law where non-pecuniary loss figures so prominently. In criminal law, defendants who are perceived as having accepted responsibility for their acts are likely to receive more lenient sentences, and vice versa. See also *Mellor*, supra note 9, where punitive damages were increased because of the defendant's perceived lack of remorse. See generally H. Wagatsuma & A. Rosett, The Implications of Apology: Law and Culture in Japan and the United States (1986) 20 Law & Soc'y Rev. 461. In order to work to anyone's benefit, the court would have to be able to ensure that the apology was sincere. Unfortunately, at least in our culture, there may be much truth to Herman's observation that "Genuine contrition in a perpetrator is a rare miracle." See supra note 23 at 190.

121. The defendant could be encouraged to tender the apology in conjunction with a guilty plea. One assumes this would suit the victim, who would not have to go through the criminal trial. It is difficult to see this having any negative repercussions for the defendant, except perhaps if he later wished to invalidate the guilty plea on appeal. It may be more problematic to encourage apologies from defendants who are convicted despite having perjured themselves to deny their guilt. Defendants who effectively admit to perjury when offering a sincere apology may risk being punished for obstructing justice more than rewarded for accepting responsibility to the victim.

It is not clear whether and how these competing interests might be balanced. In D.B. Wexler & B.J. Winick, Therapeutic Jurisprudence and Criminal Justice Mental Health Issues (1992) 16:2 Mental & Physical Disability L. Rep. 225 at 229, the authors suggest that in the interests of effectively treating the criminal defendant, the law ought to encourage defendants to accept responsibility and plead guilty, and punish those who stand trial and offer a perjurious defence. The authors do not appear to have considered the possible therapeutic benefits for the victim who receives a sincere apology, even after a perjurious denial of guilt.

122. Indeed, this option is most promising in cases in which the defendant is unable to pay damages. One would have to doubt the sincerity of an apology tendered by a solvent defendant if it were unaccompanied by an offer of financial reparation. An apology could still have an important role to play in actions against solvent defendants, but probably within the context of a tort action for damages. In that case, the incentive to offer the apology could be part of the civil process (reduction of punitive damages, for example). With the impecunious defendant, the incentives would have to be part of the criminal process.

123. See Wexler & Winick, supra note 121.

124. See Sheehy, supra note 9, who notes several possible advantages, but more anti-therapeutic aspects, to the compensation process as it presently operates. In particular, by limiting recovery to the "blameless" victim, these schemes may prove even more harmful to the sexual assault victim than the criminal process itself. Also, Newfoundland and many American states exclude claims arising from criminal acts committed by family members. See Sheehy, supra note 9 at 228 and D.B. Wexler, Victimology and Mental Health Law: an Agenda (1980) 66 Va. L. Rev. 681 at 688–96. Compare R. Langer, Battered Women and the Criminal Injuries Compensation Board: Re A.L. (1991) 55 Sask. L. Rev. 453, and Brown, supra note 71.

the criminal trial, the compensation process need not be, and indeed should not be, harmful to victims of crime. Improvements to the compensation claims process are both needed and feasible.[125] One possible development would be to have the boards mimic, so far as possible, whatever the civil court does for the benefit of the plaintiff in her suit against an absent, judgment-proof defendant.

IV. Conclusion

I remain sceptical that many victims will prove both willing and able to finance civil litigation in the long run without the prospect of substantial recovery. Even if tort litigation has important therapeutic benefits, a plausible but unproven hypothesis, I suspect that the costs, and other barriers to litigation, will put these benefits beyond the reach or desire of most potential plaintiffs.

The most one can claim is that the victim has far more power over the process in the civil system than in the criminal system. In consultation with good counsel,[126] the victim can be informed of the risks and benefits of litigation for and to her personally. She can make an informed decision whether or not to take the risk, and she can make an investment in the process designed to control the risk. If successful, the tort suit has the potential to address the wrong done to the victim—a potential which is absent, by design, from the criminal system. For the victim, all of this constitutes a dramatic improvement

---

On the other hand, a number of frontline counsellors have told me that their clients are highly satisfied with the process, and with awards typically in the $4,000 to $6,000 range. The Chairperson of Ontario's Criminal Injuries Compensation Board reports that "Sexual assault is now our biggest category, and incest cases the largest group within it", with 1,000 incest cases expected in 1993 alone. See Hurst, supra note 17.

125. Indeed, a properly designed criminal injuries compensation scheme could perform the therapeutically necessary closing of the breach between the traumatized person and the community every bit as well as the tort action. See text accompanying note 54. Moreover, by using the compensation process, the victim could avoid the risk of the "fantasy of compensation" discussed supra note 57.

126. It would be naive to overestimate the degree to which any client, let alone a legally-inexperienced victim of sexual abuse, actually controls her own lawyer, the civil process, or the court. It is more accurate to think in terms of the victim's lawyer (once she finds and engages one) as assuming a degree of control over the action. It must then be accepted that both the progress of the suit and the degree to which the process involves or empowers the victim will depend greatly on the skill and goals of the lawyer. One hopes that certain members of the bar will develop expertise in suits of this sort. Non-legal expertise and contacts with other professionals are also needed to guide the plaintiff, articulate the claim, and prove the damages.

Speaking more broadly, the role of the plaintiff's counsel as a therapeutic agent requires more examination. It might prove to be one of the more significant factors in influencing both therapeutic expectations and outcomes. Although I know of no writing directly on point, a substantial literature about feminist and other progressive styles of lawyering is developing. See, e.g., Theoretics of Practice: The Integration of Progressive Thought and Action (1992) 43:4 Hastings L.J. and within this issue see especially A.V. Alfieri, Disabled Clients, Disabling Lawyers at 769. The author discusses "victimization strategy" employed by benevolent lawyers to the detriment of their clients. See also A.V. Alfieri, Reconstructive Poverty Law Practice: Learning Lessons of Client Narrative (1991) 100 Yale L.J. 2107.

over the criminal action. It nevertheless remains a stressful and risky proposition, and one well beyond the means of the ordinary victim of sexual battery.

Looking at the pool of cases decided to date, a few preliminary observations are in order.

The overwhelming number of these civil actions involve persons attacked as children. Does this reflect accurately the incidence of sexual abuse in our society? Do these plaintiffs have unique therapeutic needs, expectations and outcomes from civil litigation? A great deal of study directed specifically at the role of tort law for child victims is urgently needed.

It is undoubtedly significant that all of the actions to date have been brought against family members, former friends, lovers and acquaintances. Are the therapeutic benefits of the sexual battery action uniquely available for these relational wrongs?

No plaintiff has yet come forward after deciding to forgo the criminal system in favour of tort. A few seem to have been prompted to sue after being denied the right to prosecute by state officials. A few others seem to have been prompted to sue after the defendant was acquitted in the criminal courts. But the great majority brought undefended actions against persons previously convicted in the criminal courts and unlikely to be able to honour the judgment. Here, it is worth considering whether these legitimate therapeutic needs might be addressed more efficiently to the benefit of more victims outside the tort system.

The most important conclusions we can reach are these: First, the prevalence of sexual battery, especially child sexual battery, is staggering and tort litigation is one way of making this public. Second, the therapeutic needs of victims are not being met by the criminal justice system. Third, no one really knows whether the tort system is capable of meeting the therapeutic needs of victims. It is time to find out.

Chapter 44

In the Wake of a Negligent Release Law Suit: An Investigation of Professional Consequences and Institutional Impact on a State Psychiatric Hospital

Norman G. Poythress
Stanley L. Brodsky

Therapeutic Jurisprudence and Juridical Psychopathology

In his recent book. *Therapeutic Jurisprudence*, Wexler[1] asserted that "mental health law would better serve society if major efforts were undertaken to study, and improve, the role of the law as a therapeutic agent."[2] Wexler's thesis is that the law—including substantive law, legal procedure, and legal roles—can and should be studied empirically to determine the relationships between legal arrangements and therapeutic outcomes. While some law may have no intended or actual impact on any therapeutic dimension, much law is created with the objective of enhancing therapeutic outcomes—for example, commitment laws that provide for involuntary treatment of the mentally ill, confidentiality laws that may encourage clients to fully explore their problems in therapy, and so forth.

Wexler advocates that "when the law seeks expressly to promote therapeutic objectives...the impact of the law should be examined carefully to see whether that goal is in fact being realized."[3] Wexler's framework for studying the law anticipates that the law may have an unintended and/or undesirable impact on therapeutic outcomes and may itself cause or contribute to psychological dysfunction. He has coined the term *juridical psychopathology* to capture the notion of law-related psychological dysfunction, and he concludes that "the role of inquiry, research, and policy in this area is to identify and, to the extent such a course of action would be compatible with objectives of justice, to minimize law-produced dysfunction."[4]

---

1. D.B. Wexler, Therapeutic Jurisprudence (1990).
2. Id. at vii.
3. Id. at 8.
4. Id. at 5.

Negligent Release Litigation: Potential Benefits and Costs

This article reports the application of Wexler's framework to a case study of negligent release litigation. For the law and psychiatric institutions alike, one particularly troublesome problem is the decision to release psychiatric patients from involuntary commitment. This decision involves weighing public protection interests on the one hand against the liberty interests of the patient, who is no longer clearly in need of inpatient treatment, on the other. Once released, the patients are less closely supervised, medication compliance is more difficult to monitor, and environmental factors contributing to aggressive acts are more difficult to control. Occasionally, expatients behave aggressively toward citizens in the community, resulting in property damage, injury, or death. When this occurs the victims or, in the case of aggression resulting in death, the victims' families, may seek legal action against the mental health professionals who were involved in the decision to release. These lawsuits are civil actions that allege malpractice, claiming that the defendant doctors were negligent and that they failed to exercise due care[5] in reaching the decision to release—thus the term *negligent release* torts.

There are at least three theoretical benefits of negligent release torts. A special category of personal injury/malpractice torts, these cases provide a legal mechanism through which victims can seek relief and compensation for their injuries or loss. In a successful suit, the plaintiffs may be awarded compensatory damages, and this money may enable them to obtain treatment to relieve their pain and suffering or otherwise cope with the sequelae of the patient's aggression. Second, punitive damages, if awarded, are intended to have a deterrent effect against the negligent defendants[6]; the financial loss is a punishment for failure to maintain professional standards of clinical practice. Ideally, such litigation also serves to enhance the level of care in the general community.[7] To the degree that a particular case articulates specific standards and that information is conveyed to other practitioners, the law serves an educational function that may enhance the level of care offered by other practitioners. In Wexler's framework these are the intended and potentially therapeutic benefits of negligent release torts.

---

5. In recent years, the legal bases for such suits have expanded owing to case law arising in the context of outpatient treatment; beyond the general obligation of doctors to provide due care, courts have articulated specific duties including the duty to warn potential victims, duty to protect the public, or the duty to predict patients' violent actions. See A. R. Felthous, The Psychotherapist's Duty to Warn or Protect (1989); Greenberg, The Evolution of Tarasoff...Recent Developments in the Psychiatrist's Duty to Warn Potential Victims, Protect the Public and Predict Dangerousness, 12 J. Psychiatry & L. 315 (1984).

6. "Although deterring substandard care is perhaps the central purpose of malpractice law, almost no systematic investigation exists on how malpractice experience affects medical quality or vice versa." Zuckerman, Koller, & Bovbjerg, Information on Malpractice: A Review of Empirical Research on Major Policy Issue, 49 Law & Contemp. Probs. 85, 87 (1986).

7. See generally, Bovbjerg, Medical Malpractice on Trial: Quality of Care Is the Important Standard, 49 Law & Contemp. Probs. 321 (1986).

Alongside these theoretical benefits of negligent release torts stands another set of potential outcomes that are not so benevolent. Whether juries find for the plaintiffs, thus achieving the first theoretical benefit, or not, some have expressed concern that the stress of prolonged litigation may be pathogenic. Studies based on the self-report of physicians sued in general medical malpractice cases have shown that defendants often experience psychological symptoms (predominately depression and pervasive anger) in conjunction with the litigation process.[8]

Doubts have also been expressed about the alleged deterrent function of torts. Damage awards may be limited by statute or reduced to the amount of the defendant's liability insurance coverage, and money is then paid by the insurance company rather than by the doctor. The defendant's out-of-pocket expense, liability insurance premiums, may be passed along to the public via higher costs for medical care, thus undermining whatever potential deterrent value the judgment may have had.

It has been argued that the form in which jury verdicts are rendered makes it difficult for defendants to determine the locus of negligence.[9] While negligence may be alleged in several actions which defendants took (or failed to take), jury verdicts are simply "for the plaintiff" and are unarticulated with respect to which of the various allegations were judged to be below the prevailing standard of care. The lack of articulation in jury verdicts, and in appellate reviews as well,[10] may undermine the theoretical educational function of negligent release verdicts.[11]

Brodsky[12] has suggested that professionals may develop an excessive fear of litigation ("litigaphobia") that adversely affects their clinical practice; clini-

---

8. See: Charles, Wilbert, & Kennedy, Physicians' Self-reports of Reactions to Malpractice Litigation, 141 Am. J. Psychiatry 563 (1984); Charles, Wilbert, & Franke, Sued and Nonsued Physicians' Self-reported Reactions to Malpractice Litigation, 142 Am. J. Psychiatry 437 (1985); Charles, Warnecke, Wilbert, & Lichtenberg. Sued and Nonsued Physicians: Satisfactions, Dissatisfactions, and Sources of Stress, 28 Psychosomatics 462 (1987). The work of Charles and her colleagues makes it clear that it is the chronic involvement with the litigation process, not trial outcome, that is associated with the occurrence of psychological symptoms; of the sued physicians in the second study cited, only 1.6% had an adverse trial verdict.

9. Poythress, Negligent Release. Paper presented at the Mid-Winter Meeting of the American Psychology-Law Society (1986); Poythress, Avoiding Negligent Release: Explicit Standards versus Legal Fictions. Paper presented at the Eleventh Annual Symposium on Mental Health and the Law (1988) sponsored by the Institute of Law, Psychiatry & Public Policy, University of Virginia School of Law.

10. "To the extent that uncertainty is the problem, the best solution is legislative clarification of the practices that will satisfy the practitioner's legal obligations.... [M]ost courts tend to prefer open-textured standards for jury resolution." Bonnie, Professional Liability and the Quality of Mental Health Care, 16 Law. Med. & Health Care 229, 237 (1988).

11. The function of educating the community of practitioners at large is also undermined by the fact that "...the judicial process is not well geared to provide efficient notice to the relevant audience, even when specific legal requirements are articulated." *Id.* at 237.

12. Brodsky, Fear of Litigation in Mental Health Professionals, 15 Crim. Just. & Behav. 492 (1988).

cians' attitudes about their work and their patients may suffer, and clinicians may come to practice defensively.[13] Wexler and Schopp[14] have noted the form that defensive practices might take with respect to negligent release fears:

> Releasing authorities...[may adopt] highly restrictive discharge practices, resulting in a marked increase in false positive determinations of dangerousness and in the unwarranted deprivation of patient liberty. In therapeutic jurisprudence terms, such an alteration in discharge practice would constitute law-caused unnecessary hospitalization.[15]

Though we have found no systematic studies of the actual impact of negligent release judgments, the effect that Wexler and Schopp hypothesize has been demonstrated experimentally in laboratory analogue research[16] and in case law.[17]

Beyond impinging on the freedom interests of patients, to the degree that litigation fear subverts the release decision-making process it also reduces the quality of mental health care system-wide. Patients kept in the hospital beyond the period warranted by a candid appraisal of their clinical condition and violence potential suffer the increased risk of institutionalization. Simultaneously, hospital census remains unnecessarily high, reducing the staff-to-patient ratio and thus diluting the services to patients. Hospitals may develop "waiting lists" for acutely ill persons in the community who may be warehoused in set-

---

13. This concern about defensive practice has been confirmed to some degree by the self-report of previously sued physicians. See studies cited at note 8 supra.

14. Wexler & Schopp, How and When to Correct for Juror Hindsight Bias in Mental Health Malpractice Litigation: Some Preliminary Observations, Behav. Sci. & L. 485 (1989).

15. Id. at 486.

16. Ninety-six clinicians were provided case vignettes that varied on dimensions of social class and criminal history for persons about whom violence was to be predicted. The clinicians were asked to indicate the appropriate level of custody for these persons. The experimenter manipulated consequences to the clinician making the predictions; in the "high" consequences condition, the risk of litigation was an explicit factor. A significant main effect for consequences to the clinician was obtained; clinicians in this condition made more conservative judgments about patients' violence potential and asserted the need for more secure custody placements. Beidleman, The Effects of Perceived Consequences, Social Class, and Criminal History on Perceptions of Dangerousness, unpublished doctoral dissertation. The University of Alabama (1982).

17. The reluctance of the staff at one state hospital to release a patient appeared to the appellate court to be strongly related to their receipt of a letter from an attorney which read as follows:

> I am aware of the fact that some doctor or doctors have to certify in writing that they feel as though someone like Dudley Carlisle is capable of being placed back into society, and I would by this letter demand to know the name of the doctor or doctors who have so indicated in writing that they feel he is able to be placed back into society.
>
> I want to make it extremely clear to your hospital and to the doctors that I have every intention of bringing action against them in the event that Dudley Carlisle harms or threatens to harm in any way, shape or fashion my client or any other person, because I clearly think that the hospital and the doctors involved are negligent at the outset in placing him back into society at this early date.

Carlisle v. State, 512 So. 2d 150, 151–152 (1987).

tings such as jails where little or no mental health services may be available. In these ways, clinicians' and administrators' fears of litigation may cause a rippling effect that has a broad and essentially negative impact on the delivery of services to the mentally ill.

The Present Study

The purpose of the present study was to examine the effects on both individual hospital staff members and hospital procedure of a negligent release case that resulted in a substantial judgment for the plaintiffs. Within the guidelines of Wexler's therapeutic jurisprudence framework, the primary objective was to assess the consequences of the lawsuit in terms of both the theoretical benefits of negligent release torts and the potential unintended and undesirable outcomes.

This research was undertaken at an 1,100-bed state psychiatric hospital in a southern state. In January, 1985, a negligent release suit was filed against several staff members, alleging that they had been professionally negligent in releasing a patient from the hospital's substance abuse treatment unit. Approximately 2½ months after release, the patient killed a member of the plaintiff's family. In January, 1987, the negligent release case went to trial and in February, the jury returned a verdict for the plaintiffs, awarding damages totalling $11.75 million.[18]

Nearly a year after the verdict, the state supreme court overturned the judgment and ruled that hospital staff are entitled to qualified immunity for their involvement in hospital release decisions. In 1989, this study was initiated to assess the impact of this case on hospital staff as individuals and on hospital procedures.

Method

Participants

A total of 16 hospital staff members took part in a structured interview[19] that lasted approximately 1 hour and 15 minutes. Eleven of the subjects were psychiatrists, psychologists, and social workers presently assigned to clinical responsibilities; the remaining 5 participants included four mental health professionals and one attorney assigned to primarily administrative duties.

Only staff members who had been employed at the hospital for the duration of the lawsuit were selected for the study; 18 staff members met these criteria, and 16 of the 18 agreed to be interviewed. Four of the participants had been named as defendants (named defendants) in the suit, although two had been

---

18. Each of three hospital staff members named as defendants in the suit were held liable in the amount of $2.25 million. The remaining $5 million was judgment against the former patient, who was also named as a defendant in the suit. Before the tort case went to trial in January, 1987, the former patient had been tried and found guilty of murder in a state criminal court.

19. A copy of the structured interview is available from the authors.

dropped from the suit prior to trial. The remaining 12 participants (nondefendants) were senior-level staff who might be involved in release decision making in the course of their own work and thus vulnerable to this type of lawsuit.

Measures

The Stress of Litigation

We were interested in the staff's attitude toward litigation, particularly the degree to which their experience with litigation was stressful for them. Thus, prior to asking about this particular negligent release lawsuit, a portion of the interview requested that participants identify up to five *uplifts* (routine positive events) and up to five *hassles* (routine negative annoyances) about their jobs that they associated with *any* prior litigation experience. This component of the study drew on the theory of Richard Lazarus[20] that routine, daily events compose a key part of the experience of stressors.[21] Questions were framed such that the staff could focus on the effects of any previous lawsuits; their responses were presumed to reflect their "longer view" of litigation as a change mechanism in the mental health system.

A second portion of the structured interview solicited personal reactions to their particular negligent release lawsuit. Participants were asked to "Please describe and discuss for us the effects or impacts, either positive or negative, that [name of the lawsuit] had on you as an individual." After recording the responses to this open-ended question, a series of probes focused on the effect or impact of the suit in a number of specific areas: (1) personal morale, (2) attitude about working at the hospital, (3) attitude toward the department of mental health, (4) attitude toward patients, (5) actual clinical practices, (6) feelings about yourself and your profession, (7) increase/decrease in litigation fear, and (8) willingness to participate in release decisions.

A final measure of potential stress was a self-report questionnaire that had been used in Charles's earlier research.[22] Using a 4-point scale (*none, mild, moderate, severe*), participants rated the degree to which they had experienced various symptoms, feelings, and thoughts in conjunction with the negligent release litigation.

The Instructional Value of the Litigation

A section of the structured interview asked participants to indicate whether the case "was instructive in some positive sense such that the professional staff at the hospital learned about changes that would improve patient care and re-

---

20. R. Lazarus, Patterns of Adjustment and Human Effectiveness, (1969).

21. See, e.g., Flannery, Major Life Events and Daily Hassles in Predicting Health Status: Methodological Inquiry, 42 J. Clin. Psychology 485 (1986).

22. The questionnaire includes 25 symptoms culled from various diagnoses in the Diagnostic and Statistical Manual of Mental Disorders, Third Edition (e.g., depressed mood, social withdrawal, drug abuse) as well as feelings (e.g., low self-esteem; shame; loss of nerve in clinical situations) and cognitions (e.g., the plaintiff's case is unjustified; resentment of counsel's efforts to settle) that may have been experienced in the context of litigation. See Table 1 from Charles, Wilbert, & Franke, supra note 83.

lease decision making." After recording their answer to the open-ended question, a series of probes inquired whether the case had been instructive about (a) how to better assess a patient's potential for violence, (b) the need for new or different therapies, (c) the need for new or different aftercare strategies, or (d) the need for new or different institutional programs.

Another portion of the interview went at this same issue somewhat differently. Participants were asked whether they had observed "any formal changes in hospital practice and procedure that resulted from issues raised in [name of the lawsuit]." "Formal" changes were defined as those mandated in new or revised hospital policies and procedures (e.g., promulgated by the clinical director or the medical staff) drafted to correct deficiencies that had been uncovered in the lawsuit. Again, a series of specific probes followed elicitation of the response to the open-ended inquiry: (a) change in formal criteria for discharge, (b) change in procedure for assessing patients' violence potential, (c) change in documentation procedures regarding inpatient violence, (d) change in the release decision process (e.g., more levels of review), (e) change in staff training requirements on issues of release and risk assessment, (f) new groups or programs for prerelease patients, (g) changes in therapy requirements (e.g., more sessions), (h) changes in prerelease (transitional) activities, (i) change in aftercare services or monitoring, and (j) change in liaison with aftercare agencies.

The Impact on Hospital Release Practices

Two archival measures were used to assess the impact of the negligent release case on hospital release practices. First, trends in hospital release practices over the course of the study (6 months prefiling through 6 months postverdict) were assessed by reviewing records of monthly discharges prepared by the hospital's medical records department. The dependent measure was the number of patients discharged to community placements in a given month divided by the hospital census at the beginning of that month (expressed as a percent).[23]

At this particular hospital most patients were committed through the civil probate courts and could subsequently be released on the authority of the attending psychiatrist. However, the hospital also had a Hospital Review Board

---

23. A methodological note is that careful reviewing and sorting of the discharge data was necessary to compute the appropriate percentages. Because this study focused only on release decisions which placed the hospital staff at potential risk for liability due to patients' subsequent violence in the community, not every patient identified as a "discharge" on the monthly hospital reports qualified as a "community release" for purposes of this study. Some patients counted by the hospital as "discharged" were transferred to other agencies (e.g., VA Hospitals or nursing homes). On the other hand, some patients kept on the books as in the hospital were actually on extended home visits (up to 6 months) and were not noted on the monthly records as discharged until successful completion of the home visit; these patients were counted as released to the community for purposes of this study. For these reasons, extensive reviewing and sorting of the data in the monthly discharge records was necessary in order to gather valid estimates of the monthly percent of patients placed in community settings. The authors gratefully acknowledge the help of our research assistants, Kimberly Svec and Dena Kirton, who gathered the archival data for this study.

(HRB) to which the attending psychiatrist could refer cases for a second opinion prior to release. The second archival measure of hospital release practices was the percent of patients approved for release by the HRB. Data were gathered on HRB activities for two time periods: the 8 months prior to trial (pretrial) and 13 months including trial and 12-month follow-up (posttrial).

Procedures

Each participant was contacted by one of the authors and invited to participate in an interview. Participation was voluntary, but those who agreed to be interviewed were told at the conclusion of the interview that they would receive a token payment of $20 for assisting in the research. One participant who had resigned from the hospital staff was interviewed at the first author's private office; another had resigned from the hospital staff and was interviewed at his own private office; the remaining 14 participants were interviewed in their own offices at the hospital. The interviews were conducted 2 years after the case had gone to trial.

With the permission and cooperation of the hospital director's office, archival data regarding monthly discharges were gathered in the medical records department. Records of HRB deliberations and decisions were extracted from written minutes that were maintained in the hospital director's office.

Results

Subjects' Experience of Litigation

The staff's experience of litigation generally was assessed through their responses to inquiries about uplifts and hassles which they associated with some aspect of the hospital's litigation history. Each participant was invited to report up to five of each type event.

The 16 participants reported a total of 64 uplifts. Many of these responses reflected awareness by the staff of major improvements in staffing levels, quality of staff, quality of treatment, physical plant, and fiscal resources that had resulted from major right-to-treatment litigation. Other responses reflected awareness of state cases that had led to increased legal protections for patients (e.g., enhanced due process requirements for involuntary admission or readmission to state psychiatric hospitals). In contrast, participants reported a total of only 49 hassles that they associated with litigation experience.[24] Approximately one fourth of these ($n = 12$) were spontaneous references to ongoing fear of future litigation, whereas others reflected an attitude of excessive caution in dealing with involuntarily committed patients, paperwork that was perceived as unnecessary, or lack of understanding in the community of the mission and limits in the hospital.

Table 1 summarizes the staff's responses to inquiries about how this particular negligent release lawsuit had affected them. While this open-ended ques-

---

24. The differences between the number of uplifts and hassles reported was not significantly different ($x2 = 1.73$, n.s.).

Table 1 Frequency of Reports of Positive or Negative Impact of Negligent Release Litigation on Sixteen Hospital Staff

Aspect of professional experience affected	Qualitative rating of impact		
	Positive	None	Negative
A. Morale	0	2	13
B. Attitude toward working at hospital	0	9	6
C. Attitude toward Mental Health Depart.	1	4	10
D. Attitude toward patients	0	14	0
E. Attitude toward self and profession	1	8	5
F. Your own fear of litigation	0	0	16
G. Attitude toward taking part in future release decisions	1	13	1

Note. Narrative responses were jointly coded by authors as Positive (e.g., "This case renewed my confidence in the Central Office staff of the Department"), Negative (e.g., "My morale was really down because of this case"), or None (e.g., "It didn't change my attitude toward my patients one way or the other." Rows add to less than 16 because some responses were coded as not responsive to the question, or some items were not applicable to the staff member.

tion encouraged subjects to report both positive and negative impact, the data in Table 1 reveal that where impact was felt, it was almost uniformly negative. An increase in fear of litigation was reported by all 16 participants, while 13 reported lower morale and 10 reported more negative attitudes toward the state Department of Mental Health as a result of the litigation. Despite these negative impacts, the professional staff reported that attitudes toward patients or willingness to participate in future release decisions were not adversely affected. None of the participants reported a change in attitude toward patients, and 13 indicated no change in their willingness to take part in release decisions. Separate chi-square analyses for the items in Table 1 were significant at $p < .05$ for all items except E: Attitude toward self and profession.

The emotional impact as reflected in answers to the open-ended inquiry was powerful, wide ranging, and profound on most staff. The negative impacts reported ranged from anger and despair to loss of confidence in clinical decision making, to contemplation or implementation of early retirement, and to increased tension in family and other social situations. The two participants who were named defendants at trial reported the strongest and most negative personal reactions, followed closely by the named-but-deleted defendants. This pattern appeared throughout the study: the more central the staff member to the litigation, the more intense the emotional reaction. The qualitative nature of these responses may be seen in Table 2. Descriptors used by the staff to describe the impact of the case on them include "outraged," "hopelessly vulnerable," and "sobering." As one of the comments indicates, one staff member (who was a named-but-deleted defendant) voiced a clear intention to take an early retirement as soon as a specific number of years of service had been completed. Another named defendant participant had already retired earlier than planned and informed the authors that this law suit was unequivocally the reason for his early retirement.

Table 2   Emotional Impact of the Legal Action: In the Staff's Own Words

"I felt outraged that they would bring such a case. I felt despair that the department couldn't protect us better....I had the feeling it could happen to me."

"Being friends with the parties, I felt a great deal of empathy with them....increased defensiveness I felt in predicting patients' behaviors after they leave."

"This case will be the cause for early retirement...It's not as pleasant here as it used to be. I'm skittish all the time. Overall I'm more bitter toward the legal system and toward medicine...very much disenchanted. I went through three years of something I don't ever want to do again. I don't know if my stomach problems are due to this, but I've had more troubles since this case."

"Before the appeal, I felt hopelessly vulnerable. I could be held responsible for things I couldn't control. Increased anxiety. I felt less safe."

"It was a tremendous embarrassment. Raised questions about my competency as a clinician. I felt isolation, guilt, and embarrassment."

"Real negative feelings...wonder about myself, how could I be such a vile and bad person...Tension was high; with my anxiety, more arguments with my wife. I got good support at work and outside the hospital....It was agony for two years."

"I got pissed off like everyone else, at the legal people leaving our people out on a limb."

"A vigorous appeal won a reversal. It renewed my faith somewhat."

"We do more window dressing type questions with patients, i.e., 'Are you going to go out and kill somebody?' I make more detailed progress notes."

"I'm more cautious about medications, which may not be a bad thing. I'm concerned about tardive dyskinesia cases."

"Frightening and sobering how much the courts hold us responsible for."

"We slowed down the discharge process. We all stopped dead in our tracks and took a closer look at patients."

"I used to look over my shoulder for assaultive patients; now I look to see if I'm going to be sued."

The third measure of the impact of the lawsuit on staff members as individuals was the self-report measure regarding 25 symptoms experienced in conjunction with the litigation. Symptoms experienced were rated as mild, moderate, or severe. As one would expect, named defendants endorsed more symptoms ($M = 9.5$) than did nondefendant staff. However, nondefendant staff were not spared the psychological distress associated with the litigation; the 12 nondefendants endorsed an average of 5.0 symptoms.

The symptoms endorsed by 3-4 of the named defendants included anger, inner tension, depressed mood, frustration, irritability, insomnia, social withdrawal, and excessive use of alcohol. Half ($n = 2$) of the named defendants also reported having experienced difficulty concentrating and decreased sex drive. Symptoms endorsed by nondefendants included anger (83%), inner tension (100%), depressed mood (50%), frustration (92%), irritability (66%), and indecision (41%). A variety of other symptoms (e.g., fatigue, exacerbation of physical illness) were endorsed by a smaller percentage in either group. The cluster of symptoms common to both groups (anger, inner tension, irritability, etc.) is consistent with one of the two most common clusters reported by Charles and her colleagues in their study of sued physicians.[25]

Negative feelings endorsed by half or more of the named defendants included being misunderstood, being defeated, decreased self-confidence, loss of nerve in clinical situations, low self-esteem, and guilt. Among nondefendants, half or more reported feeling misunderstood, being defeated, and decreased self-confidence.

In summary, when questioned about their experiences of litigation generally, through inquiries about daily uplifts and hassles associated with prior legal outcomes, the participants identified more uplifts than hassles (64 vs. 49) and were able to articulate a number of specific and important ways in which the hospital and its staff and patients had benefited from previous law suits. When questioned about their experiences of this particular case, however, their personal reactions were almost uniformly negative. Increase in litigation fear was universal and morale was negatively impacted. All participants endorsed some negative feelings or symptoms of psychological dysfunction in conjunction with the negligent release litigation, with named defendants being more adversely affected. Self-reports of these participants indicate that the experience of this law suit will ultimately contribute to earlier-than-planned retirement from mental health service for two of the four named defendants.

The Educational Value of the Law Suit

In response to interview questions about the instructive value of the law suit, the modal response ($n = 7$) was that no constructive lessons were learned. Four participants mentioned the need to improve documentation in patients' charts, an observation which accurately reflected criticisms raised by expert witnesses for the plaintiffs at trial. Two others suggested that more comprehensive psychological testing procedures had resulted from the case, although follow-up inquiries failed to reveal that this had occurred. In one case, the informant's response was obviously speculative, as he spontaneously volunteered, "I think that was a result of the case; I hope I'm not just making this up." In the other instance, we checked with the responsible psychologist on the program in question, who reported that recent changes in testing procedure were properly attributable to efforts to meet JCAHO[26] standards rather than to the negligent release litigation. Two other participants mentioned "the need to get more second opinions," comments that may reflect a desire to have the responsibility for release decision spread more broadly.

The staff reported changes in clinical practice in terms of increased scrutiny and documentation of release decisions. However, they did not identify specific clinical material that the law suit indicated should be added to records. The staff responses indicated a lack of specific, corrective feedback. The staff did busy themselves seeking to make clinical judgments and release decisions "more carefully," but without knowing exactly what improvements in procedure would enhance their efforts.

---

25. See references at note 8 supra, and note 22 supra.
26. Joint Commission on the Accreditation of Healthcare Organizations.

A second approach to assessing the instructional value of the law suit was to inquire about formal changes in procedure that might have been mandated by the clinical director, the hospital staff, or other administrative body. Again, the modal response ($n = 9$) was that no changes in procedures for release decisions had been mandated from above. Three participants reported a change in admission procedures apparently intended to shelter the particular unit (Substance Abuse Treatment) from legal vulnerability accompanying treating involuntary patients. The change required all involuntarily committed patients to be admitted to and housed on an acute admissions unit. Persons with substance abuse problems could not be housed[27] on the Substance Abuse Treatment Unit unless they were first discharged from that involuntary admission and then voluntarily readmitted themselves to the hospital's Substance Abuse Treatment unit.

A few participants mentioned hospital procedures for recording occasions of inpatient aggression or for notifying citizens previously threatened by a patient of that patient's pending discharge as changes stemming from this negligent release case. Again, follow-up inquiry revealed that these changes had been brought about after a previous law suit[28] rather than the one that was the focus of this study. The interviews failed to confirm any changes in formal criteria for discharge, therapy requirements, programs or groups for prerelease patients, or in other areas specifically probed.[29] At most, the staff noted a brief burst of training on risk management and negligent release issues, somewhat increased documentation practices at time of release, and the occasional use of more levels of review before release was ordered.

In summary, interviews with 16 staff members from this hospital failed to reveal evidence that the negligent release law suit had been instructional in any systematic way.

Hospital Release Practices

Figure 1 displays the monthly discharge rates for the 36-month period of the study. During the 6 months prior to the filing of the suit (baseline), the average monthly discharge rate was 10.9%. During the 23-month pretrial period, the average monthly discharge rate was 10.6%; during the third period, which included the month of trial (January, 1987) and 6-month follow-up, the average monthly release rate was 6.7%.

The monthly release rates for the three phases of litigation were analyzed using a one-way analysis of variance (ANOVA).[30] Because of the longitudinal nature of these data, a test for autocorrelation between consecutive error terms

27. These patients could still participate in substance abuse treatment, however, by walking across campus for prescribed activities.

28. In 1983 a previous negligent release law suit against staff members of this hospital had resulted in a judgment against the defendants in the amount of $25 million. The case was eventually settled while on appeal, unofficially for less than $1 million.

29. The reports of the staff interviewees were checked with the Clinical Director and the Hospital Director, from whose offices any formal changes in policies or procedures would have been promulgated.

30. The invaluable advice and assistance of William Kearns, Paul Greenbaum, and Mary Murrin in conducting the data analysis are gratefully acknowledged.

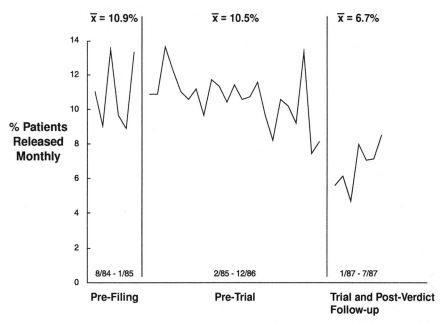

Fig. 1. Percentage of patients discharded monthly to community placements during three periods of negligent release litigation.

was conducted first.[31] The residual errors from a Lag (*xt, xt − 1*) correlation were analyzed using Geary's procedure[32]; the results of this analysis indicated that residual error terms in these data are not autocorrelated (*r* = 20, n.s.).[33] The results of the one-way ANOVA were significant, $F(2.33) = 18.24$, $p < .05$. Planned contrasts revealed that release rates during the trial and follow-up period were significantly lower than during the prefiling and pretrial phases. $t(33$, *n*'s = 29,7) = 5.86$, $p < .05$; release rates were not significantly different between the prefiling and pretrial periods, $t(33$, *n*'s = 6,23) = .395$, n.s.[34]

---

31. C. W. Ostrom, Time Series Analysis: Regression Techniques (1978).

32. Geary, Relative Efficiency of Count of Sign Changes for Assessing Residual Autoregression in Least Squares Regression, 57 Biometrika 123 (1970).

33. Habibagahi & Pratschke, A Comparison of the Power of the Von Neumann Ratio, Durbin-Watson and Geary Tests, 54 Rev. Econ. & Statistics 179 (1972), Table 1.

34. Alternative analyses suggested by our consultants and by an anonymous reviewer of an earlier draft yielded essentially the same results. The dependent measure values were percentages and, already restricted in range to 0%–100%, the observed values appeared to fall in a further restricted range (5%–14%, Figure 1). Thus, it was recommended that the analyses be performed on a natural log transformation of the data in case the observed data violated the assumption of an underlying normal distribution. However, inspection of the raw score histogram and indices of normality (e.g., skewness and kurtosis) using SPSSPC/Frequencies indicated that the raw score distribution did not violate the assumption of normality. (Using the in [x] transformation, both the test for autocorrelation of error terms and the ANOVA yielded the same results as reported in the text.) Another suggestion was to conduct an analysis of covariance (ANCOVA) on the release data using hospital census as a covariate. In the ANCOVA, the overall F was significant and contrasts on the adjusted means revealed a significant difference in the predicted direction between the trial & follow-up phase

Data regarding the actions by the HRB to approve or disapprove community placement of patients referred to the board by the attending psychiatrists indicated a reduction in approval for community placement following the negligent release case. During the 8-month pretrial period, the HRB reviewed 20 patients provisionally recommended by their treatment teams for community placement and approved release to the community in 19 cases (95%). However, during the 13-month posttrial period, 33 patients were referred for HRB review and release was approved in 25 cases (76%), indicating a greater reluctance by the HRB to approve community releases following the negligent release verdict. This difference in release attitude by the HRB approached statistical significance (Fishers Exact Test, $p = .07$). There was not a significant increase in the rate of referrals to the HRB following the negligent release verdict; the average monthly referral rate during both periods was approximately 2.5 cases.

Discussion

The analyses of the self-report measures indicated that this negligent release suit adversely affected hospital staff in a number of ways. It does not appear reasonable to attribute the effects reported to a generally negative attitude by the hospital staff toward litigation. Participants were able to identify more uplifts than hassles associated with the hospital's long-term litigation history. It was only in response to direct inquiries about this specific case that the uniformly negative reports emerged.

Both named defendant and nondefendant participants reported experiencing symptoms of psychopathology in association with the litigation. All subjects confessed to an increased fear of litigation in conjunction with this case. There was also unanimous agreement among participants that their colleagues either explicitly or implicitly weighed their own liability risk when making subsequent release decisions. One staff member captured the essence of these comments: "Everybody has been sort of scared. The entire medical staff is scared about releasing patients with a history of violence. Their attitude is, they don't want to release."

The archival data regarding hospital discharge rates were consistent with the staff's subjective impression that fear of litigation may have led to a decrease in community releases. The average monthly discharge rate fell by more than one third,[35] and the rate at which patients were approved for release by the HRB fell by one fifth.[36]

Theoretically, in a case in which negligence is affirmed through a finding for the plaintiff, defendant doctors have the opportunity to learn the errors of their ways and to modify future practices accordingly. In this case, however,

---

and the prefiling and pretrial phases. The contrast between adjusted means for the prefiling and pretrial phases was also statistically significant, though not in the predicted direction; the adjusted mean for the period after the law suit was filed (pretrial) was higher than the adjusted mean for the prefiling (baseline) phase.

35. Followup Rate/Pretrial Rate = 6.7%/10.6% = .63.

36. Followup Rate/Pretrial Rate = 76%/95% = .80.

the participants' responses regarding the instructive value of the lawsuit did little to instill confidence that the decrease in patient releases was related to release procedures that had been improved in any systematic way by feedback from the litigation. Participants reported that no significant learning took place in terms of clarifying the appropriate procedures and standards for release decision making. Though they noted some general observations about the need for thorough documentation, the staff did not report any specific change in release procedures that resulted from feedback obtained through the litigation. Consistent with these data regarding individual learning, the staff did not report any systematic changes in hospital-wide policies and procedures. In addition to these self-report findings regarding the absence of meaningful instruction, a review of the minutes of the HRB for the eight cases referred to the HRB during the trial and follow-up period in which community placement was disapproved revealed no mention of the treatment staff's failure to follow a procedure explicated by the negligent release case.

The failure to learn from the negligent release litigation is a finding that merits further comment. One possible explanation, favored by a number of the participants in this study, is that the verdict for the plaintiffs was simply emotional, made independently of any finding of real negligence. The plaintiffs had suffered an undeniable loss in the death of their son, and the monetary damages would likely be paid by the clinicians' insurance companies or by the state's general fund. The participants thought that the jurors reached a judgment for the plaintiffs which could compensate the family without creating any "real" financial burden on the defendants.

A less cynical explanation may be derived by analyzing negligent release sanctions in terms of the principles of operant learning. By providing an unarticulated verdict—"for the plaintiff" without specifying the locus of negligence—and a liability damage award, the tort system relies more on punishment that on corrective information to effect change in behavior. Modifying a scheme developed by Cavender[37] to analyze legal deterrence via learning principles, Table 3 arrays eight criteria for the effective use of punishment as a learning device along with descriptions of how these learning principles operate in negligent release litigation. A description of a typical negligent release case will indicate that few of the criteria are met in practice.

Legislators have not created statutes that make explicit the criteria for hospital release decisions. Hospitals are free to develop their own policies and procedures, which routinely go unscrutinized by the legal system. Occasionally a released patient will harm someone in the community and a negligence suit will be filed. The filing of the suit is typically weeks or months after the release decision was made, and disposition is commonly months or years after the filing. Because there is no scrutiny of the myriad of release decisions that did not eventuate in a bad result, clinicians will escape punishment (Table 3, Item 1) most of the time that allegedly negligent procedures were used[38] and, clearly, punish-

---

37. Cavender, Special Deterrence: An Operant Learning Evaluation, 3 Law & Human Behav. 203 (1979).

38. Under present tort law, clinicians could not be punished simply for using substandard procedures; it is also required that harm be proved, as well as a causal link between the neg-

Table 3. A Failure to Instruct or Deter: An Operant Learning Analysis of Negligent Release Litigation

Criteria for effective punishment	The application of punishment in negligent release litigation
1. Escape from punishment is impossible.	Escape from punishment is typical; tort action is triggered not by discovery of bad procedure, but by an unfortunate result.
2. Punishment should be intense.	Trial judgments may be severe (one case resulted in a $25 million award) but the amount may be reduced by the trial judge or appellate court. The money is usually paid by defendant's insurance company or state general fund and thus is not intensely felt by defendant.
3. Frequency of punishment: 1:1 ratio is desirable.	1:1 ratio is not possible; adequacy of procedures goes unscrutinized and unchallenged in most releases.
4. Punishment should be delivered immediately after the behavior.	Considerable time lag between the release decision and the sanction; litigation process is slow.
5. Punishment should be a signal for extinction.	Feedback from litigation process may not specify which aspects of the release procedure are to be changed. Punishment may be premised on sympathy for the victim rather than on clinical negligence.
6. Reduce motivation to do undesired act.	Motivation to make releases negligently is reduced; motivation to make releases generally continues. Lack of discrimination learning may make it difficult to distinguish the two.
7. Provide reinforceable alternatives to the undesired act.	Feedback through the trial process is not clear. Plaintiff's criticisms of the release procedure are rebutted by defendant's experts; the jury's final judgment does not make the locus of negligence explicit, nor does it articulate a standard of care.
8. Access to different situation providing similar reinforcement.	The hospital situation typically remains unchanged. Continued use of inadequate release procedures may not be punished because legal scrutiny is triggered only by the infrequent occurrence of patient violence.

ment will not approximate the 1:1 ratio (Item 3). The length of the litigation prohibits the application of the punishment in a timely manner (Item 4).

Punishment should be a signal for extinction of the undesired behavior (Item 5), but the manner in which civil trials are adjudicated makes it difficult for defendants to learn which particular aspects of their release practices were found wanting. Through the testimony of plaintiffs' expert witnesses, jurors may hear criticisms of any number of behaviors associated with the release decision—how the patient was assessed, what treatment was provided, how the

ligence and the harm. For an alternative theory of liability, see Schroeder, Corrective Justice and Liability Increasing Risks, 37 U.C.L.A. L.Rev. 439 (1990).

transition to the community was planned, and so forth. However, they will also hear rebuttal testimony on these points from the defendants' experts. Because the process does not demand that jurors sort out these conflicting claims and explicate the locus of negligence, no effective signal of the behavior to be extinguished is communicated (Item 5), nor is there clarification of alternative behaviors that would be deemed appropriate clinical practice (Item 7). The defendant clinicians may be left wondering which, if any, of their procedures were found inadequate or whether, as the hospital staff in this case suspected, the jury had reached a verdict on emotional grounds.

A final point of discussion is to note parallel findings in other areas of social research that may provide a useful framework for viewing our results regarding the impact on individual staff members. The literature on sudden, traumatic life events offers some useful perspectives. When individuals experience events that they see as unpredictable, outside their control, seriously distressing, and threatening to their well-being, common patterns of emotional strain appear. At the extreme are natural disasters, such as earthquakes and floods,[39] in which sleep disturbances, substance abuse, and residual affective disorders occur. Closer on the continuum to the present legal action are less sudden, traumatic life events, such as the occupational distresses of severe harassment on the job[40] and mass unemployment.[41] In both instances, the affected individuals experienced substantial personal distress as long as the job-related disruption was in place. The unemployed workers became hypochondriacal and fell into a stunned immobility, while subjects of the job harassment, depending on psychological vulnerability, experienced residuals of the harassment for years after its occurrence. Our results similarly suggest a half-life of the emotional impact that extends into years. Though our interview data were gathered more that 2 years after the case went to trial and more than a year after the judgment was reversed by the state's supreme court, the staff remained very much in touch with the fear, stress, and anxiety associated with the litigation process.

Negligent Release and Juridical Psychopathology

In light of Wexler's therapeutic jurisprudence framework, this negligent release case achieved few if any of the intended and theoretically beneficial objectives of malpractice torts. The plaintiffs did not receive any compensation for the pain and suffering associated with the death of their son; although the jury found for the plaintiff and announced a sizable damage award, the judgment was ultimately overturned by the state supreme court.[42] The results also

---

39. See G. Gleser, B. Green, C. Winget. Prolonged Psychosocial Effects of Disaster: A Study of Buffalo Creek (1981).

40. C. M. Brodsky, The Harassed Worker (1976).

41. T. F. Buss & F. S. Redburn, Mass Unemployment: Plant Closings and Community Mental Health (1983).

42. Barnes v. Dale, 530 So. 2d 770 (A1, 1988). Reportedly the plaintiff did receive some compensation through a companion "dram shop" suit filed against the hotel lounge at which the former patient and the victim had been drinking prior to the shooting. With respect to the present case, $5 million of the total $11.25 million judgment was assessed against the former patient himself. The patient, who was indigent, had been living with his parents at

suggest that the case did not serve as an effective learning device either for the defendants or for the other members of the hospital staff that would be involved in subsequent release decisions. More disturbing is the implication that this particular theoretical benefit of negligent release litigation may not be achieved even when the case is "successful" from the plaintiff's perspective. If there is not sufficient discrimination learning in the process to teach clinicians which behaviors meet the standard of care and which do not, then it is unlikely that finding for the plaintiff will enhance the standard of practice for release decision making or serve as an effective deterrent.

On the other side of the ledger, many unintended and undesirable outcomes were obtained. Self-report measures indicate that the litigation was experienced by defendants and other hospital staff as fear inducing, pathogenic, and stressful; in the absence of evidence that the case was meaningfully instructive, the archival data suggest that the staff resorted to defensive clinical practice by indiscriminately reducing hospital discharges. The implications of these findings for patients' liberty interests and for the quality of care system-wide have been noted[43]; there may have been other adverse consequences as well.[44]

Directions for Future Research

Although the present study raises serious questions about the value of negligent release torts as a remedy for the unfortunate consequences of some hospital release decisions, it does not provide sufficient data for generalized judgments. Other negligent release cases may follow any of a number of scenarios: dismissal subsequent to filing, settlement prior to trial, verdict (upheld) for plaintiffs, verdict for defendants, and so forth. With each type of outcome there will be a different costs—benefits matrix. Only by studying a large sample containing representative cases for the various types of outcomes can adequate costs—benefits information be gathered. The present study, however, does suggest a methodology for empirical work in an area thus far largely ignored.

An epidemiological study is badly needed. Little is known about how frequently these cases arise and how they are resolved. If different case scenarios do in fact produce different costs—benefits profiles, it will be meaningful to know the relative frequency of the different types of scenarios.

Future research might also explore a broader list of dependent measures for assessing the costs and benefits of negligent release litigation. In the present study, for example, we did not explore the financial costs of the litigation or resources consumed in terms of clinicians' time involved in the litigation process (e.g., meeting with counsel, time in depositions). Other archival evidence of sys-

---

the time of the shooting. The plaintiff pursued the $5 million judgment against the patient via a law suit against the insurance company with which the patient's parents had a general home owners insurance policy. In that law suit the jury found for the defendant insurance company.

43. See note 15, supra, and accompanying text.

44. Other information provided by our subjects suggests that this case may have impaired the staff's efforts to get malpractice insurance as well as making applicants for professional staff positions wary of accepting positions at the hospital.

tem impact may reside in hospitals' records of waiting lists for admission or calculations of average length of stay during varying stages of litigation.

There is a long tradition in this country for citizens to seek redress from life's misfortunes through litigation. Negligence torts are the primary mechanism presently available for persons injured by mental patients. It is not the case, however, that this action is the only mechanism for relief that might be employed. In many work settings, for example, workmen's compensation programs have replaced individual negligence claims against employers as a mechanism for providing relief to injured workers. Many states have a state-funded victims' compensation program through which persons injured by the criminal actions of others may seek financial relief. Other countries, such as New Zealand,[45] have developed a juridical and scientific panel approach to resolving personal injury disputes, an approach some have strongly advocated for use in the United States.[46]

Adaptations of programs such as these provide potential alternative legal remedies for persons injured by former mental patients. The tradition of litigation, however, provides considerable inertia on the side of negligent release actions. Research such as the type reported and recommended here can provide important information to policymakers about the relative merits of litigation as a legal remedy and provide an empirical basis for a reasoned choice among available alternatives.

---

45. Gellhorn, Medical Malpractice Litigation (U.S.)—Medical Mishap Compensation (N.Z.), 73 Cornell L.R. 170 (1988).

46. Sugarman, The Need to Reform Personal Injury Law Leaving Scientific Disputes to Scientists, 248 Science 823 (1990).

Chapter 45

Coercive Uses of Mandatory Reporting in Therapeutic Relationships

Elizabeth Anderson
Murray Levine
Anupama Sharma
Louise Ferretti
Karen Steinberg
Leah Wallach

The identification of the battered child syndrome in the mid-1960s created renewed interest and attention to issues of child welfare and child protection (Levine & Levine, 1992). Seminal work by Kempe and his associates, (Kempe, Silverman, Steele, Drogemueller, & Silver, 1962; Kempe & Helfer, 1974) led to an amazingly quick acceptance at a policy level of the necessity to protect children by making physicians responsible for reporting suspected child abuse. Reforms were quickly adopted in all states to mandate the reporting of child maltreatments by designated professionals to child protection authorities. Few legislative enactments have had as much impact on the mental health profession as the mandated reporting law. At present, there are approximately 2,500,000 reports a year. The reporting rate is 30.6 per 1000 children (American Humane Association, 1987) and mandated reporters account for half or more of all reports (National Center on Child Abuse and Neglect, 1982; Eckenrode, Powers, Doris, Mansch, & Balgi, 1988).

Policymakers focused on protecting children from harm, but many working professionals responded unfavorably to reporting statutes because of infringements on their professional prerogatives. Previous research has indicated that although some mental health professionals have, on occasion, deliberately refused to report, most probably make mandated reports most of the time (Brosig & Kalichman, 1992). Though this is the case, we have had little examination of the impact of reporting laws on psychotherapeutic relationships.

Wexler (1990), and Wexler and Winick (1991), have proposed a concept of "therapeutic jurisprudence." They argue that, in addition to the implications for individual rights, laws ought to be evaluated with respect to their "therapeutic" and "antitherapeutic" effects on other relationships. A lot of this work has examined therapeutic effects of involuntary hospitalization laws and procedures. Some of it has been extended to speculation about how plea bargaining may effect cognitive distortions of sex offenders (Klotz, Wexler, Sales, & Becker, 1992; Wexler & Winick, 1992). It is axiomatic that laws may have unintended and unanticipated consequences (Faller, 1982). The child abuse reporting laws were designed to facilitate the therapeutic purpose of protecting children. What other effects do they have?

The law may become a resource in the treatment relationship that can be used for several purposes. For example, therapists attempt to achieve a therapeutic alliance with their clients (Horvath & Greenberg, 1986; Marmar, Horowitz, Weiss, & Maziali, 1986). Within this framework, they expect resistance in treatment and are prepared to work with the client to overcome resistance. Although therapists may feel great responsibility for a client or for a family, they may be stymied by a client's resistance attitudes. In addition, an unresponsive client may not validate the therapist's sense of professional competence. Because of these emotional considerations, the mandate to report and the therapist's ability to invoke the coercive power of the state may enable therapists to use mandated reporting in a manipulative manner that may serve the therapist's ends. There is already a significant power imbalance between therapists and clients (Perlin, 1991), and the mandate to report may add to that imbalance. The legal mandate to report may become a resource in enhancing the therapist's sense of potency in a frustrating role and a frustrating situation.

In this study, many of the therapists worked in public agencies with clients who were considered at high risk for child maltreatment. Many of these clients were already enmeshed in the welfare, child protection, or criminal justice systems. They may have been referred by the department of social services, or strongly urged to enter treatment by school authorities. These clients may already feel coerced and are distrustful. Because therapists working with such clients may feel a great responsibility to protect children, the use of the reporting power may be welcome as a therapeutic tool to set limits with clients (Harper & Irvin, 1985). The coercive use of the reporting power to serve therapeutic purposes or to set limits may facilitate certain therapeutic aims, but may impede others.

The term coercion has pejorative connotations. To the extent that therapists view mandatory reporting as a source of police power, or as a tool for social control, it will be used, and may be abused, within the context of a therapeutic relationship. At this point, however, we prefer to consider the term descriptively and to withold judgment about whether this use of coercion facilitates or impedes therapeutic ends.

Method

This report is based on a thematic analysis of semi-structured interviews with thirty psychotherapists who, in the previous 12 months, had made a report of child maltreatment on a child or family already in treatment with them. The therapists were recruited from six agencies in two counties. They volunteered in response to a notice. They were predominantly white (97%), female (75%), social workers (80%), and ranged in experience from new workers on internship to those with more than ten years of experience. We completed similar semi-structured open-ended interviews with 25 experienced child protective service (CPS) workers who had investigated mandated reports from mental health sources. They were also recruited from CPS departments in two counties. We shall use excerpts from the interviews with CPS workers when they illustrate the phenomena from a different perspective (i.e., to provide a form of corroboration for the observations we report from interviews with the therapists).

We do not have systematic samples of therapists nor of CPS workers. Our aim, rather, is to produce representations of experience that "ring true" and that will be useful to others in understanding the world of therapy as affected by mandated reporting.

Results

The Law and Therapists' Feelings

The therapists we interviewed typically accepted the necessity of reporting legislation, characterizing it as a "necessary evil" or a "problematic good." Although the therapists accepted reporting as a professional obligation, they had mixed feelings about the obligation. They experienced the mandate as a personal responsibility, a source of potential legal liability, and a source of considerable personal stress when the occasion to report arose. Moreover, many had serious doubts about whether a report actually helped the child or the family. (A more complete description of these matters can be found in Levine *et al.*, 1992).

The power to make a mandated report places the therapist in conflict, but it may also elicit anger in therapists. Some experience mandated reporting as "unnecessary bureaucratic intrusion on the professional's autonomy," as an "indictment of competence" (Pollak & Levy, 1989, p. 516) or as an infringement of the therapist's independence. The therapist may experience the underlying "policing" (see *People v. New York Society for the Protection of Cruelty to Children*, 1900) aspect of the role:

> Oh I hate it...I feel like a social policeman. I don't want to be a social policeman. I don't want children to be at risk. I truly don't, but...I really hate that part of my job. I mean I do it. I know I have to do it. And I agonize for hours afterwards. Then I say, "I'm going to quit."...It is necessary, but I never like myself after I do it.

The context surrounding mandatory reporting (i.e., working with abusive, difficult, resistant or victimized clients) may contribute to the arousal of anger. As one therapist stated:

> I get angry. I get angry about having to be put in this position of reporting, angry about having to stay on the phone for long periods of time, angry I have to do an extra amount of paperwork, angry about having to do all the time consuming things, and I'm angry, really, at the client for putting me in that position.

CPS investigators observed that the reporting power may be used by therapists in an angry fashion even though concern for children is also present:

> Sometimes there's another agenda in terms of...in this particular case I'm not sure their agenda is not getting dad [anger at him], and Jane, I'll show you that you [client] are all wrong about this man [boy friend]. But I think in general

their hearts are in the right place. I don't have a lot of concern about inappropriate referrals.

Another CPS worker said:

> I am thinking about another case that I am dealing with. I get pretty angry about this, and it's just that these particular professionals that I feel had kind of lost perspective on a particular situation and no matter what this father does, [they are] constantly calling in a referral because he hasn't done this right and that right. I feel in that particular situation, it's just people that have lost a sense of perspective on where this man is coming from. But again, I can't say it's not because they [therapists] don't have concern for these kids.

Thus, seen from both the therapist's perspective and confirmed by observations from CPS workers, the therapist may "blame" the client for the therapist's predicament. As the CPS worker indicated above, therapists may lose perspective about a client resulting in inappropriate reports being made. The potential for acting out anger through use of the coercive element of the reporting process may be a consideration in some cases. The therapist may become overly identified with the policing and social control aspects of the role. This in turn may lead to an apparent abusive use of power. While therapists usually believed that what they were doing was in the best interests of their clients, or children they felt were in danger, sometimes their desire to help was manifested in ways that appeared coercive.

Therapists noted that mandatory reporting offered them a form of power that could be used to serve several purposes and potentially have therapeutic effects. The following sections will detail the different uses of reporting described by therapists, with some observations corroborated by CPS workers.

To Prompt Change in the Family System

While the therapists recognized and were sensitive to the negative impact reporting had on families (Levine *et al.*, 1992; R. Wexler, 1990), some also felt that the circumstances and stress created by reporting might prompt change for the better in dysfunctional family systems. Many therapists welcome the "muscle" the law gave them. They used the mandated report, or the threat of a report, to affect the client. The following statements illustrate this use of reporting:

> I can see a family for two years and not affect them, but if I call something in, it may just jolt the system enough that something changes...I really use reporting as the power and authority that I have, knowing that I need help from outside to effect change.
>
> Reporting is a way to acknowledge to parents that your behavior has a very serious impact on how your kids will behave, and there are some things that you have to start taking in a responsible way...In terms of family functioning, they are going to have to acknowledge a problem and deal with it instead of denying it.
>
> What I really wanted was a crisis. I really wanted a crisis to blow everything up.

Other statements made by the therapists indicate the report was made:

> To show the client [the therapists] were serious;

Almost as coercion;

[To get] down to some real work that needed to be done. When I think about it, that was sort of the last crisis. Actually, we have been able to deal a lot around her own sexual abuse when she was a child and that [the report] was sort of a turning point;

To scare the client into recognition that their behavior was endangering their children, or at least the recognition that others would not tolerate it.

CPS investigators reported observing similar events in cases they received from mental health sources:

It seemed that she [therapist] really wanted to have mom face the issue of abuse or her abusive past...I don't know if she felt that this is something the parent just had to openly deal with...she thought like this would be therapeutic for the mom to have a report, you know report the incident, have us come out and mom would deal with this, and it just didn't work out the way the therapist thought it would work out because the mother didn't go back to treatment.[2]

One therapist clearly identified how much more controlling he felt the reporting incident had made him be:

I had to be more directive. There was no argument. There was no "let's explore this together." It was "You will do this." As a therapist and a clinician, in a relationship with this patient, it bothered me because it made me feel like I was just manipulating him...this was simply a matter of coercion.

Child protection workers investigating reports from mental health sources made similar observations. In one case, the CPS worker believed the therapist used the reporting power to bring about an action the client had refused to take:

I know that they [therapists] feel obligated because the law says they have this duty, but sometimes when they call it in, I can't tell if they don't know the law or if they are misinterpreting it. I remember this one case that a therapist called in. The father had abused the children in the past, over two years ago, and was currently visiting in the home and the mother refused to get a restraining order so the therapist called it in.

The incident suggests that the therapist substituted her judgment for that of the client in whether the relationship was a good one for the client. The therapist might have been correct in that judgment, but should the therapist have used the mandated reporting law to override the client's wishes? If the father was violent in the past, arguably he could be violent again. However, the alleged abuse was old. There was no evidence of ongoing abuse nor of any imminent danger to the child. Unless something else was happening in the home, the CPS worker would not be able to do much. In the CPS worker's view, the report was inappropriate.

To Enforce Engagement in Therapy

Some therapists said they might delay making a report while the client was working well in treatment or if they felt that they had not yet established a

---

2. Watson and Levine (1989) reported that about 25% of clients who were the subjects of mandated reports failed to continue treatment.

good therapeutic alliance. On the other hand, some therapists also indicated a degree of willingness to use reporting as a threat to prompt clients to become more engaged in treatment and also to keep resistant clients in treatment.

> I have a case now where I just told the parents that if they continue not to comply and come in with the child who has tried to commit suicide, that I will call them in for neglect. It is a form of abuse.
>
> I think it was made pretty clear to the father, because he was the reluctant one, that he had no choice but to follow through.

In a case where the therapist made a second report due to the child and mother failing to attend therapy sessions, the therapist illustrated how reporting can be used to coerce engagement in treatment and how this may backfire as well.

> When Protection went out and investigated, the boy showed up again at my office on his own and said that he was back because he felt he'd be kicked out of the home if he didn't come back to see me...I called the mother to say that I was glad he was back but I would really need her involvement because it was a complicated case...She asked if I made the report...but I didn't see them again, she never came back and he never came back.

A number of CPS investigators told us they had investigated reports that were stimulated by the therapist's desire to keep a client in treatment. From the CPS investigator's viewpoint, sometimes these reports contained an element of anger:

> In cases where the family has terminated services themselves or there's been a problem between the therapist and the family, where you almost get the feeling they are calling it in out of spite—of gee, you junked me, I'll call child protection and then you'll see where your problem gets you.
>
> Child Protective cannot mandate that someone accept services and that if [the therapist had] been unable to engage someone into voluntary services, we are probably going to have the same difficulty. That's usually when you hear, "Well, Child Protective is more of a threat and maybe people will take it more seriously"...this kind of situation is not a Child Protective issue and we can't mandate that these voluntary services be accepted.

In some cases, the reporting power may be used as a therapeutic instrument to help the client address issues that had previously been avoided. In these instances the reports are not made primarily to protect the child, although that is the pretext for the report.[3] In one case, a therapist who was seeing a mother with a history of abuse and had called in a report described the process:

> I tried to draw parallels between her experiences and the experiences this child might have as a result of this (abuse),...I felt over the course of the next few weeks she understood how important this was.

---

3. Therapists sometimes make reports to achieve a therapeutic purpose, and not necessarily to protect a child. Our therapists mentioned such cases. The following is an excerpt from an interview with a CPS investigator:

I think he just made it to help the mother. It was her idea that he make the report...he considered it part of the therapy. It was a little different because usually they make it because they are concerned. But I think he felt she was having a tough time dealing with what went on or supposedly went on and he was trying to help her either relieve some of her guilt or help her...just to resolve it in her own mind, you know whether or not it did happen.

Some clients may also use the mandate to report to manipulate the therapist into making a report on a third party not in treatment (Deed, in press; *Roe v. Superior Court*, 1991). Watson and Levine (1989) found that when a report alleged a third party not in treatment was the perpetrator, clinical notes sometimes showed clients improved or were relieved of distress. However, they did not obtain evidence that such third party reports were necessarily false or maliciously intended.

Mandated Therapy

Whether a client is mandated to treatment appears to be an important determinant of the impact of the report on the therapeutic relationship. The coercive nature of mandated therapy may severely impair the development of the alliance and preclude productive therapeutic work.

> I think the problem surrounding these cases, and this may be specific to preventive services, is that people supposedly come voluntarily to therapy, but they feel the pressure of a mandate, because if they do not agree to therapy the children are going to be taken away. Psychologically, these people feel that they are being pressed, so engagement with these clients is difficult.

CPS investigators feel sympathy with families in this position:

> I think sometimes they [clients] feel like they are victims. They've had so many people in their lives telling them what to do, this is just one more time.

Although the context is psychotherapy, when families enter treatment after a mandated report has been made, the therapeutic task often becomes one of monitoring the family. The reporting power is a means of enlisting CPS to enhance the monitoring function:

> So our primary role at [the agency] was to service the intact family in the home to assure that no harm or neglect came to those children still in the home...We were providing family therapy on a weekly basis to really get a sense of what was going on from the children's point of view, the parents' point of view, and trying to get the parents to admit the environment was not the best in terms of assuring that the children were safe and not neglected and working on how that could be remedied.

It is worth noting that despite the coercive context which often resulted in passive resistance in the clients, some therapists reported favorable therapeutic outcomes with some clients. Some clients were able to overcome the feelings of resentment or mistrust following a report and continued to work in treatment. These instances suggest that the exercise of coercive power does not inevitably lead to an unfavorable therapeutic outcome (Harper & Irvin, 1985).

Discussion

There is a fundamental dilemma when therapists are faced with fulfilling the helping role therapists have and the "punishing" or "policing nature" of mandatory reporting. This dilemma reflects the creation of child protection services under the police power of the state. The New York Court of Appeals held that the state board for charities had no authority to regulate the New

York Society for the Protection of Cruelty to Children because the Society was chartered not as a charity, but under a statute giving it police powers (*People v. New York Society for the Protection of Cruelty to Children*, 1900). Perhaps it is not surprising that therapists use mandated reporting in ways not intended by the original statute. For one, the legal mandate to report changes the therapeutic context and adds the potential for the coercive use of reporting.

It is certainly morally defensible to use coercion under some circumstances. Whether one of those circumstances is the use of coercion to promote better engagement of clients in treatment is open to debate. Harper and Irvin's (1985) view that reporting is a form of limit setting to protect children is an argument in favor of using reporting "coercively."

It is quite another matter if coercion is used to promote a therapist's interests. We had a number of examples of the use of reporting as a vehicle for venting therapist anger at a resistant client or a client who didn't accept the therapist's judgment about the client's situation. This use is troublesome because it is difficult to control. It can be considered an "antitherapeutic" effect of the law, although the frequency of such occurrences, the precise conditions under which such effects might arise, and their therapeutic consequences are difficult to specify. It may require more careful supervisory monitoring of the decision to report to limit any "countertransference" use of the reporting power. Such use presents a moral and ethical problem for the field. It also result in unnecessary reports which add to the workload of CPS investigators, and may take away from time necessary to investigate more serious allegations (Levine *et al.*, 1992).

Working with children and families at risk for maltreatment arouses strong feelings in therapists. Therapists receive some training in the duty to report, but receive little information about how to handle issues in reporting, or what to expect, or how to cope with the sequelae of reporting. More attention during training and during inservice training toward these issues is important and has been neglected.

The mandate to report creates special problems when working with clients who have been ordered into treatment. Under some circumstances the Fifth Amendment right against self incrimination may also be implicated. A person who is mandated to treatment but refuses to acknowledge responsibility for sexually abusing acts may be under pressure to admit sexual offenses under threat of a severe loss (e.g., continuation of probation, see *Montana v. Imlay*, 1992; or loss of custody, or of parental rights, see Levine & Doherty, 1991). The client's fate may depend on the therapist's judgment that he or she is improving. The judgment that the person is improving is often contingent upon the admission of an abusive act. However, if the client does admit, the therapist may have a duty to report and subject the client to further prosecution. Our therapists reported they received referrals from CPS investigators who didn't have enough evidence of abuse, but hoped the therapist would obtain a disclosure that would assist in further investigation or would support a petition to Family Court. This use of the reporting power can be quite coercive and puts the therapist in a god-like position vis-à-vis the client.

Is it coercive for a therapist to withhold information as to the limits of confidentiality, especially with high risk clients, in order to increase the probability of a disclosure so that a child might be protected? The mandate to report presents difficult issues with regard to informed consent (Racusin & Felsman, 1985). What should a prospective client be told about the limits of confidentiality and what effect would that have on client willingness to disclose (Berlin, Malin, & Dean, 1991; Faustman & Miller, 1987)? Furthermore, what effect does making a mandated report have on legal privilege in other contexts, and what duties does a therapist have to apprise the client of foreseeable events that have a low probability of occurrence (Deed, 1992)?

Research on this problem of the use of coercion is difficult to carry out. We have employed an interview method; one of our group (Karen Steinberg) is currently conducting a mail survey to examine some of these issues. However, we are not certain that the subtleties can be captured in a closed ended survey. We believe that the phenomena need to be examined *in vivo*. In our own work, we use a method of triangulation, and seek to identify the phenomena by examining them from the perspective of therapists, and CPS investigators. We hope to be able to examine clients' viewpoints as well. When the viewpoints converge, we can have some confidence that we are reliably identifying something substantial.

There is no simple answer to the therapeutic jurisprudence inquiry in the case of mandated reporting and psychotherapy. The problems of ensuring the safety and well being of a child when the parents, presumably the child's natural protectors, pose harm to the child is difficult in any event. The problem is compounded when the mandated reporting law brings the conflict between parents and children's interests into the therapeutic relationship (Anderson *et al.*, 1992). Any legal mandate affecting therapy introduces potential conflicts and complexities into the professional role. How we can control and limit these problems is unclear. Some problems may be solved by more careful supervisory oversight of the reporting process. Other problems may be inherent in the way the reporting mandate modifies the therapeutic role and thus the therapeutic relationship.

Modifications of reporting laws may be required for the system to work more efficiently and cooperatively than it now does, and ultimately to better protect children. These modifications might serve to reduce the "policing" aspect of the role and the potential coercive use of reporting. For one, when a client is already in treatment, less serious allegations could be left to the discretion of therapists and supervisors, with some provision for careful monitoring of the situation. As it stands now, a report must be made immediately (see New York Social Services Law Sec. 415) when a mandated reporter "has reasonable cause to suspect" child maltreatment. In addition, the law should be rewritten to consider a higher standard for reporting when a client is already in treatment, perhaps simply requiring contact with CPS, but no full blown investigation (Besharov, 1988; Meriwether, 1986; Smith & Meyer, 1984) until more evidence develops. Another important step would be to establish a "statute of limitations" for reports of past episodes when there is little imminent danger of repetition of the maltreatment. These modifications could reduce unnecessary reports, limit the use of reporting to more serious situations, and lessen the burden of investigation of the social service system. We recognize that any provision that enhances discretion also enhances the potential for the abuse of discretion. We therefore believe that alerting the field to the problems might enhance the use of a consultative or supervisory process to limit reports to those situations in which palpable harm to a child might be prevented.

In the final analysis, we may expect that the reporting instrument will be used as a resource in a situation of uncertainty. We hope that our research and that of others might help to clarify when the coercive use of reporting is destructive of therapeutic aims, and when it may be considered a meaningful form of limit setting that protects children.

References

American Humane Association (1987). Highlights of official child neglect and abuse reporting 1985. Denver, CO: American Humane Association.

Anderson, E., Ferretti, L., Levine, M., Sharma, A., Steinberg, K., & Wallach, L. (1992). Consequences and dilemmas in therapeutic relationships resulting from mandatory reporting legislation. Law & Policy, 14, 241–256.

Berlin, F.S., Malin, H.M., & Dean, S. (1991). Effects of statutes requiring psychiatrists to report suspected sexual abuse of children. American Journal of Psychiatry, 148, 449–453.

Besharov, D.J. (1988). The need to narrow the grounds for state interventions. In D.J. Besharov (Ed.), Protecting children from abuse and neglect: Policy and practice, (pp. 47–90). Springfield, IL: Charles C. Thomas.

Brosig, C.L., & Kalichman, S.C. (1992). Clinicians' reporting of suspected child abuse: A review of the empirical literature. Clinical Psychology Review, 12, 155–168.

Deed, M.L. (1992). Mandated reporting revisited: Roe v. Superior Court. Law Policy, 14, 219–239.

Eckenrode, J., Powers, J., Doris, J., Mansch, J., & Bali, N. (1988). Substantiation of child abuse and neglect reports. Journal of Consulting and Clinical Psychology, 56, 63–69.

Faller, K.C. (1982). Unanticipated problems in the United States child protection system. Child Abuse and Neglect, 5, 9–16.

Faustman, W.O., & Miller, D.J. (1987). Considerations in prewarning clients of the limitations of confidentiality. Psychological Reports, 60, 195–198.

Harper, G., & Irvin, E. (1985). Alliance formation with parents: Limit-setting and the effect of mandated reporting. American Journal of Orthopsychiatry, 55, 550–560.

Horvath, A.O., & Greenberg, L. (1986). The development of the working alliance inventory. In L. Greenberg & W. Pinsof (Eds.), The psychotherapeutic process: A research handbook, (pp. 529–556). New York: Guilford Press.

Kempe, C.H., & Helfer, R.E. (Eds.). (1974). The battered child. (2nd ed.). Chicago: University of Chicago Press.

Kempe, C.H., Silverman, F., Steele, B., Droegemueller, W., & Silver, H. (1962). The battered child syndrome. Journal of the American Medical Association, 181, 17–24.

Klotz, J.A., Wexler, D.B., Sales, B.D., & Becker, J.V. (1992). Cognitive restructuring through law: A therapeutic jurisprudence approach to sex offenders and the plea process. University of Puget Sound Law Review, 15, 579–595.

Levine, M., Anderson, E., Chavez, F., Sharma, A., Steinberg, K., Doueck, H.J., Deisz, R., & Goerge, N. (1992). Child protection service workers' views of mandated reports of child maltreatment made by psychotherapists. Paper presented at Baldy Center for Law and Social Policy Colloquium, September, 1992, SUNY Buffalo.

Levine, M., Anderson, E., Ferretti, L., Steinberg, K., Sharma, A., & Wallach, L. (1991). Mandated reporting and the therapeutic alliance in the context of the child protection system. Baldy Center Working Paper Series. Buffalo, NY: Baldy Center for Law and Social Policy.

Levine, M., & Doherty, E. (1991). Professional issues. The Fifth Amendment and therapeutic requirements to admit abuse. Criminal Justice and Behavior, 18, 98–112.

Levine, M., & Levine, A. (1992). Helping children: A social history. New York: Oxford University Press.

Marmar, C.R., Horowitz, M.J., Weiss, D.S., & Maziali, E. (1986). The development of the therapeutic alliance rating system. In L. Greenberg & W. Pinsof (Eds.), The psychotherapeutic process: A research handbook, (pp. 367–390). New York: Guilford Press.

Meriwether, M.H. (1986). Child abuse reporting laws: Time for a change. Family Law Quarterly, 20, 141–171.

Montana v. Imlay, 61 U.S.L.W. 4001 (1992).

National Center on Child Abuse and Neglect (1982). National study of the incidence and severity of child abuse and neglect. DHHS Publication No. OHDS 81–30329. Washington, DC: U.S. Government Printing Office.

Perlin, M.L. (1991). Power imbalance in therapeutic and forensic relationships. Behavioral Sciences and the Law, 9, 111–128.

People of the State of New York *ex rel* the State Board of Charities v. The New York Society for the Prevention of Cruelty to Children, 161 N.Y. 233 (1900).

Pollak, J., & Levy, S. (1989). Countertransference and failure to report child abuse and neglect. Child Abuse and Neglect, 13, 515–522.

Racusin, R.J., & Felsman, J.K. (1985). Reporting child abuse: The ethical obligation to inform parents. Journal of the American Academy of Child Psychiatry, 25, 485–489.

Roe v. Superior Court, 280 Cal. Rptr. 380 (1991).

Smith, S.R., & Meyer, R.G. (1984). Child abuse reporting laws and psychotherapy: A time for reconsideration. International Journal of Law and Psychiatry, 7, 351–366.

Watson, H., & Levine, M. (1989). Psychotherapy and mandated reporting of child abuse. American Journal of Orthopsychiatry, 59, 246–256.

Wexler, D.B. (1990). Therapeutic jurisprudence. The law as a therapeutic agent. Durham, NC: Carolina Academic Press.

Wexler, D.B., & Winick, B.J. (1991). Essays in therapeutic jurisprudence. Durham, NC: Carolina Academic Press.

Wexler, D.B., & Winick, B.J. (1992). Therapeutic jurisprudence and criminal justice mental health issues. Mental and Physical Disability Law Reporter, 16, 225–231.

Wexler, R. (1990). Wounded innocents: The real victims of the war against child abuse. Buffalo: Prometheus Books.

Chapter 46

Resolving Hospital Conflicts:
A Study on Therapeutic Jurisprudence

Jack Susman

This article, based on empirical research[1] conducted in three Maryland institutions for mentally ill patients, undertakes to examine the contrasting methods of dispute resolution over medication and to measure resistant patients' levels of satisfaction with these contrasting modes.[2] The results raise serious questions as to (1) the meaningfulness of formal, legally mandated dispute resolution procedures, usually clinical or treatment review panels, in the psychiatric hospital context;[3] (2) whether the "right" to resist treatment and

---

1. Wexler DB, Winick BJ: Essays in Therapeutic Jurisprudence. Durham: Carolina Academic Press, 1991, lays out an ambitious agenda for a new paradigm that bridges law and social science, teaching and research.

2. The study reported here utilizes a theory of procedural justice as developed by Thibaut and Walker. See Thibaut J, Walker L: Procedural Justice: A Psychological Analysis. Hillsdale, NJ: Earlbaum, 1975; Thibaut J, Walker L: A theory of procedure. California Law Review 66:541–566, 1978. In the latter they define procedural justice as the belief that the techniques used to resolve a dispute are fair and satisfying in themselves. The theory suggests that to the extent that disputants are allowed an active participatory role in contributing information to the decision maker or in vetoing any preliminary decision mode, the more likely the disputant is to be satisfied with the final decision regardless of whether or not it coincides with the original position or desires of the disputant. In Procedural Justice, they make the point that "the use of a fair procedure can increase the satisfaction of all concerned without any increase in the real outcomes available for distribution." Id. at 29.

3. Studies of more formal systems and their processes for intervening in and managing disputes and grievances over treatment in mental hospitals have been limited in their scope. Bloom JD, Faulkner LR, Holm VM, Rawlinson, RA: An empirical view of patients exercising their right to refuse treatment. International Journal of Law and Psychiatry 7:315–328, 1984; Zito JM, Lentz SL, Routt WW, Olson GW: The treatment review panel: A solution to treatment refusal? Bulletin of the American Academy of Psychiatry and Law 12: 349–358, 1984; Hassenfeld IN, Grumet, B: A study of the right to refuse treatment. Bulletin of the American Academy of Psychiatry and Law 12:65–74, 1984.

Studies of the formal methods and procedures utilized in Oregon and Minnesota to manage grievances and disputes tell us some things, but not all that we would like, that are important to know about the management of treatment disputes. For one thing, the focus is almost entirely upon measures of efficiency, the number of cases processed. By the same token, the studies do not tell us much about other ways of handling disputes, such as informal resolution by the staff using threats, bribes, and persuasion. See, for example, Appelbaum PS, Gutheil TG: Drug refusal: A study of psychiatric inpatients. American Journal of Psychiatry 137: 340–346, 1980.

In Maryland, the clinical review panel (CRP) is convened by some member of the refusing patient's treatment team, usually with the knowledge and concurrence of the other treatment team members. The membership of the CRP by statute excludes the physician or other treat-

due process procedures to protect that right in fact protect the feelings and interests of patients confined in institutions; (3) the therapeutic effects of procedures used to resolve treatment disputes.

The legal profession, using the rhetoric of reform, has claimed dispute resolution territory in hospitals, displacing to some extent disputing norms indigenous to hospital culture. The extent to which the law dominates current discussions of psychiatric disputes hides the reality that the fair and ethical treatment of psychiatric patients has not improved.

To understand how these conclusions were reached, it is necessary to examine some aspects of hospital culture and how it interacts with law in shaping the resolution of disputes with, and the ethical treatment of, patients in psychiatric hospitals. Hospital culture contains its own norms for resolving disputes; nurses' disputing norms and doctors' disputing norms. The U.S. Supreme Court has permitted the preemption of doctors' norms for resolving disputes by virtue of its recent decisions,[4] which in the case of *Harper* endorsed state law and in the case of *Cruzan* laid down some minimal principles that states should follow as they fashion their own system, in effect mandating some form of dispute resolution process.

The Court could have, but did not, view the patient as a full-fledged citizen with all the autonomy and freedom that this implies. Thus the Court did not find it necessary to provide a procedure with full legal representation and other due process protections that support the decisions and choices of an autonomous person who resists and refuses treatment and whose wishes could be disregarded only if he/she were found to be legally incompetent. Because the Supreme Court treated the rights of psychiatric patients so tentatively, the slo-

---

ment team members who are directly involved in treatment of the resisting patient. In terms of procedural justice theory, the CRP has process control; this usually takes the form of reviewing the patient's medical record and having his or her doctor appear before the CRP. The patient may be invited to appear, but principally to explain why he or she is resisting medication; the resistant patient has no other input. Decision control is also in the hands of the CRP. The decision reached by the CRP is binding on the treatment team and the patient. Although the statute is silent regarding post-CRP actions, it appears the patient may appeal to the hospital superintendent and may also take the matter to court. It appears that the CRP is convened when the more informal give-and-take between patient and staff have reached a stalemate and/or the patient's condition has deteriorated but has not yet reached emergency proportions.

The conflict, if not resolved to the staff's satisfaction, tends to escalate into a confrontation between the patient and a formal clinical review panel made up of hospital staff and headed by a physician. The CRP, exercising its process control, may ask the patient to provide some limited input. But the CRP has decision control and reaches a decision that usually resolves the dispute.

The dependent variables in these procedural contexts are the patient's satisfaction with, and belief in the fairness of, the processes by which the outcome was reached and the dispute resolved. In the literature of procedural justice, fairness of and satisfaction with the procedures are notable procedural justice effects of procedures that give the patient some process control. In terms of therapeutic jurisprudence, these effects are desired, because they imply that the procedures are serving therapeutic ends.

4. Washington v. Harper, 110 S. Ct. 1028 (1990); Cruzan v. Missouri, 110 S. Ct. 2841 (1990).

gan adopted by the Court of balancing the patients' rights against the needs of the state[5] should be examined critically. It focuses attention on the ambiguous relationship between patient and hospital and suggests that the patient is seen as a creation of law with a specific and narrow patient identity, a bundle of limited legal rights. By this means the Court also situates the patient, perhaps inadvertently, in the hospital culture, at least to the extent that the hospital represents the state's interests.

As a result of the contrast and conflict between nurses' disputing norms and clinical or treatment review dispute resolution, two different results would be possible. Because the clinical review system created by legislation in Maryland and other states was designed ostensibly to protect patients' right to resist medication,[6] patients should find these procedures, used by doctors, to be fairer than any procedures based on preexisting hospital disputing norms. On the other hand, patients may believe the fairest procedures for resolving their disputes with the hospital are those that are indigenous to hospital culture and have not been displaced by statute or court decisions—namely, negotiation or bargaining procedures used by nurses.[7]

Background

Examining this intersection of law and psychiatry, it is argued (as others have argued) that the law is virtually superfluous, because decision-making procedures in law are at odds with medical decision-making practices in hospitals. In addition, it is argued that legal procedures fail to achieve the goals announced by the Court because hospital staff do not share these goals. Doctors essentially make a technical decision: to do whatever is possible and nec-

---

5. See Washington v. Harper, 110 S. Ct. at 1038–1039. The Court examined Washington's policy according to "standards which recognize both the prisoner's medical interests and the State's interest...."

6. The Annotated Code of Maryland, Health-General Article section 10-708, Refusal of medication; clinical review panel. "An individual in a facility may elect to refuse medication used for treatment of a mental disorder except:...".

7. Thibaut and Walker, supra note 2, use the term "procedural justice" to refer to social psychological consequences of procedural variation, with emphasis on procedural effects on judgments of fairness. Subsequently, they defined procedural justice as the belief that the techniques used to resolve a dispute are fair and satisfying in themselves. Walker L, Lind EA, Thibaut J: Relation between procedural and distributive justice. Virginia Law Review 65:1401–1420, 1979. This approach is to be contrasted with the commonly held belief that the outcome of a dispute is the single most important consideration in people's minds when they evaluate a process. See Lind EA, Tyler TR: The Social Psychology of Procedural Justice. New York: Plenum Press, 1986.

Nader L, Todd HF: The Disputing Process in Ten Societies. New York: Columbia University Press, 1978. Nader and Todd have argued that in societies in which people's circle of social interaction is limited and interpersonal relationships are stable and ongoing, methods of dispute resolution, such as mediation and negotiation, that allow compromising outcome decisions are preferred. It has also been argued that in interdependent situations, negotiation is preferred over adjudication. See also Gulliver PH: Disputes and Negotiations, New York: Academic Press, 1979.

essary in terms of treatment.[8] It is instructive to begin with the *Cruzan* case. In this case, the Court expressed respect for the resistant patient as a person and concern for the patient's dignity and autonomy, which would be manifested by honoring a patient's choice regarding treatment. In *Cruzan*, this referred to the withdrawal of life-support treatment.

This report on an empirical study of patients' satisfaction with legally mandated dispute resolution processes strongly suggests that these procedures, supporting neither patients' dignity nor respect compared with procedures indigenous to hospital culture, are not therapeutic.[9] As things now stand, psychiatric patients find nurses to be fairer than doctors.

Recognition of and support for autonomy for institutionalized patients derives principally from the function autonomy can perform in reinforcing some rather specific behaviors and attitudes imposed by the hospital and the staff on patients. Otherwise the patient is left with minimal autonomy and compromised self-respect, which does not prepare him or her to deal adequately with the sick-role requirements and their enforcement within the hospital, to say nothing of the complex and demanding behavior required for satisfactory living outside of an institution.[10]

My primary concern is with the relative desirability of administrative resolution and nursing resolution of disputes over treatment. However, as this article sets forth, the solution to the undeniable problems associated with paternalistic medicine is *not* simply to turn the decision-making system into an administrative law-dominated system. Recognizing that the behavior of psychiatrists in dealing with patients has at times been outrageous,[11] this article nonetheless intends to defend the psychiatric profession. Indeed, the adoption of the perspective of therapeutic jurisprudence and the ethical test proposed here for decision making and resolving treatment disputes, based on the psy-

---

8. See *Cruzan*, 110 S. Ct. at 2850.

9. This is one of the tests proposed to judge the therapeutic benefits of legal procedures in Wexler and Winick, supra note 1.

10. Hospitalization in a psychiatric institution can often create a master identity for the patient that amounts to an ascriptive identity. Through customary practices, ingrained attitudes, and usual expectations, the master identity of the psychiatric patient makes it very difficult to convince ex-patients that they are free to act. Despite the disadvantages of inferior social status, the role of former psychiatric patient can seem to be an advantageous one. For one thing, the ex-patient is relieved of the strain of financial responsibility and social obligation. Therefore, successful return to the community must begin even as the patient first enters the hospital. This beginning must occur in the minds of the doctors and nurses and extend to their behavior toward the patient. The law seems blind to these matters, but hospital culture does not ignore them.

11. See, for example, Zinermon v. Burch, 110 S. Ct. 975 (1990). Burch, hallucinating and confused, signed forms giving his consent to admission and treatment and was confined for three days in a community mental health center, where he was diagnosed as paranoid schizophrenic and was given psychotropic medication. From the center he was referred to a state psychiatric hospital. He was admitted and signed additional forms, although at admission a doctor noted in his medical record that he was distressed and confused. He remained at the hospital for five months, during which time no hearing was held regarding his hospitalization and treatment.

chology of procedural justice,[12] is directed in part to minimizing such abuses without excessive resort to the hammer of the law.

Evaluating Two Dispute-Resolution Processes: The Research Study

Methodology

Maryland statutory law[13] has displaced common law doctrine under which the patient had an unrestricted right to treatment self-determination:[14] only through a judicial determination of incompetency could this common law right be ignored. The statute provides a procedure for convening a clinical review panel to review the patient's rejection of treatment and recommend a course of action.[15]

The research issue in procedural justice is the relationship between user satisfaction and sense of justice and the procedures used to manage disputes. The study reported here examines two procedures utilized in Maryland public mental hospitals to resolve or manage some of the conflict engendered by the resistance and refusal of patients to take medication, and the satisfaction of patients with the procedures and the outcome of the dispute.[16] It is assumed

---

12. Wexler and Winick, supra note 1, appear to expressly adopt the methodology and theory of procedural justice as a tool for research in therapeutic jurisprudence.

13. Health-General Article section 10-708.

14. Williams v. Wilzack, 319 Md. 485, 573 A.2d 809 (1990).

15. The highest court in Maryland has since reviewed the statute and found it unconstitutional. See Williams v. Wilzack, supra note 14. The Maryland Department of Health and Mental Hygiene continued to deal with treatment-resisting patients under the terms of the statute until the statute could be amended by the legislature. In 1993 the statute was amended so as to make it conform to the standards found in the administrative policy of Washington, which had withstood U.S. Supreme Court scrutiny in *Harper.*

16. A major methodological issue concerns the way in which subjects are selected; this influences the generalizability of the findings and conclusions. There is no list of patients who belong to the population of interest. As a result, it is not possible to define a sampling frame in which each refusing patient in the population has a known probability of being selected. For these reasons I interviewed all patients whose refusal resulted in a nontrivial conflict with the staff.

At a certain but not fixed point in time, a patient's resistance or objection to medication limits the value of the medication or makes it valueless, as far as the hospital staff is concerned. Although patients may often be ambivalent about many aspects of treatment, a nontrivial rejection means a consistent refusal that represents the patient's dominant view regarding participation in the treatment regimen developed for him or her by the treatment team. A nontrivial dispute over medication begins with a request by the staff that a patient take the drug, in either a solid or a liquid form. The original refusal to do so is followed by further refusals, which continue over a period of time. The original refusal may be simple nonappearance at the medication cart. Continued nonappearance, verbal rejection and physical rejection all constitute a refusal. Patients who covertly palmed or tongued medication could not be categorized as resistant or as refusers until and unless they were discovered or had overtly refused. The resistance continues until the patient resumes some or all new or

that some refusals lead to public conflict with the staff, and the conflict generates processes to contain, manage, or resolve it.[17] The concern here is not with the reasons why patients resist treatment; an explanation of refusals is not being attempted. It appears that some patients see forced medication as an act of terrorism, an invasion of the body. The body becomes, with regard to the patient rejecting drug regimens, a location for the exercise of a clash of wills.[18]

The empirical foundations of the theory of procedural fairness have most often been based upon disputants who are independent, autonomous individuals, sharing a universe of discourse and a consensually derived frame of reference. Hospitalized psychiatric patients do not fit this description. The inequality of power between involuntary patient and staff in public psychiatric hospitals is obvious. In addition, patients are a dependent population cut off from the world outside the hospital except for such contact as law, policy, and the staff allow. Patients are often at odds with their families before as well as during their hospitalization, further limiting their resources. Patient advocacy and other legal efforts to protect the patient are probably effective insofar as egregious abuse is concerned. But patients and staff live together on a daily basis, and it is likely that most of the time staff actions count for more than periodic contact by patient advocates, legal aid, and other concerned persons. The patient is not powerless, but his/her residual power is seldom exercised.

Significant results of the study of procedural justice

Four significant results are discussed: whether psychiatric patients are concerned about procedural fairness; whether nurses' disputing norms are fairer than doctor-dominated clinical review panels; whether "voice" procedures are fairer from the patients' point of view than "mute" procedures; and whether the outcomes of the disputes influence the patients' sense of the fairness.

One important and basic issue addressed by the study reported here is whether the procedures used in Maryland[19] for psychiatric hospitals to follow

---

original medication; or in the rare case perhaps is discharged. Excluded from the study were those patients whose refusal was limited in time, such as one or two days; these short-duration objections or refusals are generally known but are ignored by the staff and do not produce conflict.

17. On the transformation of disputes, see Felstiner WLF, Abel RL, Sarat A: The emergence and transformation of disputes: Naming, blaming, and claiming. Law and Society Review 15:631–654, 1981. They suggest that a dispute is a process of naming, blaming and claiming. The essential step in the creation of a dispute is what the authors refer to as "a perceived injurious experience." We assume that for some patients this perception is focused on medication, and refusal is their reaction to their perception. The perceived injurious experience is transformed into a grievance. The authors take the perspective of the grievant in developing their model. The grievant attributes the injurious experience to the fault of another individual or entity. The third transformation occurs when someone with a grievance voices it to another person believed to be responsible and asks for some remedy; this is claiming. A claim is transformed into a dispute when it is rejected in whole or in part.

18. Turner BS: Body and Society. London: Basil Blackwell, 1984.

19. Williams v. Wilzack, 319 Md. 485, 573 A.2d 809 (1990). The highest court in Maryland, applying federal law, held unconstitutional a statute allowing forcible, nonemergency medication of an involuntarily committed psychiatric patient because it failed to provide

in order to override patients' refusal of treatment are just and fair—i.e., do patients perceive these legislatively mandated procedures to be fair?

The broader question is whether hospitalized psychiatric patients are similar to or different from nonpsychiatric patients with regard to issues of procedural fairness. Although statistical data are lacking, the qualitative preliminary study indicates that psychiatric patients are sensitive to and able to distinguish procedural as well as distributive justice issues concerning the resolution of their disputes with staff over drug treatment. Patients in psychiatric hospitals are very concerned with receiving fair process in the resolution of these disputes.

The implication drawn from this is that procedural fairness may be important to psychiatric patients not only in terms of dispute resolution but also in many other interpersonal situations they experience in their daily lives in the hospital but that were not a specific part of my study. There is a need for further research to clarify *when* procedural justice is relevant to patients. In addition, criteria other than fairness may be used by patients in assessing the value of conflict resolution processes. Further research is also needed in this area.

Another significant issue that was dealt with explicitly in the research is the extent to which procedural or process "control" explains, among hospitalized psychiatric patients, preferences for procedures that are used in the hospital to resolve their dispute with staff over drug treatment. That is, did the patients favor the procedural norms, manifest in bargaining with nurses, that give them

---

necessary procedural due process protections. See The Annotated Code of Maryland, 1993 Cumulative Supplement, Health-General Article section 10-708.

Williams refused to take a drug prescribed for him by his treating psychiatrist, claiming it would alter his thought processes and would interfere with the exercise of his religion as well as with his ability to rationally assist his attorney at a subsequent release hearing. Under the existing statute, a clinical review panel met to review Williams's refusal. The panel gave Williams only five minutes' notice of the hearing and allowed him to be present long enough to explain why he refused to take the drug. The panel did not give Williams or his lawyer the opportunity to present evidence or to cross-examine witnesses. Williams v. Wilzack, supra note 14. The panel unanimously determined that Williams should be required to take the medication, and he was forcibly medicated for two and one-half weeks. When he told the hospital that he was going to court to obtain an *ex parte* injunction against the forcible medication, the State agreed to discontinue it and to review his case a second time. A second clinical review panel unanimously recommended that he be medicated over his objection. Williams responded by filing suit in the circuit court against the State, alleging that the medication under the procedures of section 10-708 violated his state and federal constitutional rights to privacy, due process, freedom of speech, thought, and religion, and equal protection under the law. He also claimed that under the Maryland and United States constitutions, due process requires a judicial proceeding to determine one's competence before a hospital may forcibly administer antipsychotic drugs. He lost the suit and appealed to the court of appeals. The high court held that section 10-708, on its face and as applied in this case, did not afford the required procedural due process protections that the state and federal constitutions guarantee, and it therefore could not be enforced against him. Specifically, the court found, citing Washington v. Harper, 110 S. Ct. 1028 (1990), that the absence of provisions for advance notice to the patient of the proceedings, and for an opportunity to present evidence and cross-examine witnesses, rendered the statute procedurally unconstitutional under federal law.

Table 1   Fairness of procedures*

| | Procedures | | |
Fairness	All (n = 42)	Doctors' CRP (n = 14)	Nurses' Bargaining (n = 28)
Fair	45.2% (19)	28.5% (4)	53.6% (15)
Neither fair nor unfair	19.0% (8)	35.7% (5)	10.7% (3)
Unfair	35.7% (15)	35.7% (5)	35.7% (10)

* Question 27: Do you believe that the procedure, the way the situation was handled, was fair, neither fair nor unfair, unfair?

greater control over the bargaining process than the legal procedures[20] used in the doctors' clinical review panel? The latter greatly limits patients' control over the process. It was hypothesized that a greater percentage of patients would perceive the nurses' procedures of bargaining on the ward as fairer than perceived as fair the autocratic procedures of the psychiatrists' clinical review panel.

The evidence relating to this question, found in Table 1, indicates that of the 28 patients whose disputes were resolved by bargaining with nurses, 15 (54%) felt it was fair and 10 (36%) found it unfair. In this latter category was one patient who told me, "I'm waiting 'till the doctors meet. Then I'll do what they tell me."

Of the 14 patients whose refusal led to the intervention of a physician-dominated clinical review panel, four (28%) expressed the feeling that it was a fair process and five (35.7%) felt it was unfair. The patients in the sample found doctors' legally mandated disputing procedures to be less fair than nurses' bargaining norms for resolving disputes. This result, predicted by the theory of procedural justice, may be related to the greater degree of process control available through nurses' norms than through doctors' processes. This result was to be expected in terms of procedural justice theory. But the theory does not explain why nurses, who actually administer drugs to patients on the ward, seemed fairer than doctors to rejecting patients. This issue will be explored in a subsequent report.

A third issue addressed by the study focuses on the extent to which unfavorable outcomes of the dispute resolution process are ameliorated and made more acceptable by evidence that decision makers gave consideration to patients' opinions, as suggested by procedural justice theory. In other words, did a greater percentage of psychiatric patients who had an opportunity to provide input ("voice") to the decision-making process perceive the procedures used to manage their dispute as fair than those who were not given an opportunity to provide input ("mute")?

Patients were asked whether the staff gave them a chance to explain why they refused medication: "Did the (doctor) (nurse) listen to your argument and

---

20. Thibaut and Walker characterize this as autocratic or inquisitorial. See Thibaut J, Walker L, supra note 2.

give it serious consideration?" If the patient responded affirmatively, the process allowed "voice"; if negatively, it was a "mute" procedure. One patient explained his negative experience this way: "The only thing that happened was that the doctor came into my room holding a needle in one hand and pills in the other."

Table 2 presents these data. Thirty-three patients answered this question; 18 patients (55%) indicated a voice procedure was followed and 15 patients (45%) a mute one. Of the 18 voice proceedings patients, 14 (78%) perceived it as fair and 2 (11.1%) as unfair. Of the 15 mute proceeding subjects, eight (53%) indicated it was unfair and three (20%) fair. The overall impression that the data present is that voice proceedings are fairer than mute proceedings. How does this play out when doctors and nurses are compared?

Looking at the 10 subjects who faced doctors' clinical review panels, six (60%) had a voice procedure and four (40%) a mute one. Of the six with an autocratic voice proceeding, three patients (50%) found it fair and two (33%) unfair. Of the four with mute clinical review proceedings, 50% reported them as unfair. Even when confronted with autocratic procedures, patients believed voice proceedings to be fairer than mute proceedings by a 2 to 1 ratio, as predicted by procedural justice theory.

Among the 23 patients whose disputes were resolved by nurses, 12 (52%) reported "voice"; 11 (48%) had mute procedures. Of the 12 voice patients, 92% reported their procedures were fair, and none reported them as unfair—a remarkable result even with the small sample size. Of the 11 mute disputing norm patients, six (55%) found the process unfair. Three patients (27%) reported the mute proceedings were fair. The nurses' disputing norm procedures, if accompanied by voice processes, were favored by patients by a ratio of more than 2½ to 1. Regardless of whether the procedures used to resolve their dispute with staff over medication involved nursing norms of bargaining with nurses or legally mandated clinical review procedures utilized by doctors, patients believed that voice processes were fairer than mute processes. This supports a basic tenet of procedural justice theory.

Something more than simply being given the opportunity to state one's case provides an increase in a sense of fairness of the procedures used to resolve the dispute. The quality of the interaction between staff and patients is clearly very important. These are matters that were never considered by legislators or courts.

On the theoretical level, these data on voice in procedures also lend some support to one of two theories about the importance of process control. Tyler[21] refers to them as expressive and instrumental theories. The expressive theory presumes that control over the outcome of a dispute resolution process is too limited or too indirect to be a real factor. This approach sees voice as a purely expressive act with little consequential meaning. The instrumental theory directs our attention to the presumed importance of voice as an exercise in disputant control, albeit limited and indirect control, over the outcome.

The results of the study do not offer support for the instrumental voice theory. For the most part, patients who refuse treatment have treatment forced on

21. Tyler TR: Procedural justice research. Social Justice Research 1:41–65, 1987.

Table 2   Process fairness* and voice and mute procedures**

Process Fairness	Voice Procedures			Mute Procedures		
	All (n = 1%)	Doctors' CRP (n = 6)	Nurses' bargaining (n = 12)	All (n = 15)	Doctors' CRP (n = 4)	Nurses' Bargaining (n = 11)
Fair	77.7% (14)	50.0% (3)	91.6% (11)	20.0% (3)	(0)	27.2% (3)
Neither fair nor unfair	11.1% (2)	16.6% (1)	8.3% (1)	26.6% (4)	50.0% (2)	18.1% (2)
Unfair	11.1% (2)	33.3% (2)	(0)	53.3% (8)	50.0% (2)	54.5% (6)

* Question 27: Do you believe that the procedure, the way the situation was handled, was fair, neither fair nor unfair, unfair?
** Question 17: Did the doctor/nurse listen to your argument and give it serious consideration? Yes=voice procedures; dispute resolution processes where patients felt that staff listened to their explanation of why they were refusing drug medication and considered it in reaching the decision. No=mute procedures; dispute resolution processes where patients felt that staff did not listen to them or give them a chance to explain their reasons for refusing.

Table 3   Fairness of procedures* and outcomes**

	Fair Procedure	Neither Fair nor Unfair Procedure	Unfair Procedure
Fair Outcome	78.9% (15)	37.5% (3)	13.3% (2)
Neither Fair nor Unfair Outcome	10.5% (2)	25.0% (2)	13.3% (2)
Unfair Outcome	10.5% (2)	37.5% (3)	73.3% (11)

* Question 27: Do you believe that the procedure, the way the situation was handled, was fair, neither fair nor unfair, unfair?
** Question 28: Do you believe that the decision, the outcome of your dispute, was fair, neither fair nor unfair, unfair?
Chi-square = 17.3, p=.001.

them; the outcome of the dispute goes against them. Voice is important to them, then, not because it changes the outcome, but for its symbolic and expressive value. The expressive value for rejecting patients is tied to the apparent willingness of the decision maker, the other party to the dispute, to recognize they are autonomous individuals.

There is another reason why the study does not support an instrumental view of voice proceedings. The relatively large proportion of patients who expressed a feeling that the doctors' legal procedures were unfair may, in addition to reacting to mute processes, also be responding to the professionalism of the hospital staff. This perverse result may have occurred because the proceedings are conducted by medically trained personnel who are no doubt careful of the medical details necessary to produce a therapeutically sound outcome to their deliberations. But scrupulous attention to clinical detail may inadvertently thwart the need of patients to tell in their own terms their side of the story.

The clinical review panel may often limit the opportunities for expression by patients because of time constraints and medical proprieties. They must be sensitive to the ordinary work schedules of the other members participating in the dispute resolution process and consequently may take an overly narrow approach to the medical issues at hand. These may prompt them to limit patients' opportunities to speak. The clinical review panel members are also knowledgeable about psychiatric matters and may restrict patients' opportunities to present information or tell their story when such would be medically irrelevant or inappropriate. In these situations, the panel would be acting in a medically professional and appropriate manner but unwittingly interfering with patients' sense of what a satisfying and fair procedure should be.

In addition, lack of support for instrumental voice theory may be the result of the failure of the doctors to consistently give patients a justification for unfavorable decisions.[22] Acceptance of unfavorable decisions rendered by the clinical review panel could probably be enhanced if the doctors provided patients with a rationale for the decision, especially one that indicated to them that their side of the dispute was considered when the decision was made. Further research could clarify these matters.

The level of support given to what Tyler[23] refers to as instrumental theory may in addition stem from other interpersonal aspects of patients' hospitalization. Patients in psychiatric hospitals may be acutely sensitive to how they are treated by authorities and others with whom they must deal in the hospital. Dishonesty and rudeness, as well as politeness and respect, may emerge as important nonprocedural matters that influence patients' response to the resolution of their dispute.

---

22. A recent Harris Survey of general medical patients who had switched doctors reported that 40% said the doctor "didn't answer questions honestly and completely," and 30% said the doctor "didn't explain problems understandably." *Washington Post*, August 23, 1992, pp. C1, C4.

23. Tyler, *supra* note 21.

The research also looked at what, for hospitalized psychiatric patients, the connection is between outcomes and procedures. Do patients believe that a fair procedure, whether based on norms or on law, produces a fair outcome? Are process fairness judgments linked to judgments of the fairness of outcomes the procedures produce? Do patients' views of the fairness of procedures differ when the outcome is desirable compared with undesirable? More specifically, without regard for the type of procedure used, when patients' sense of fairness of the procedures is high, will their sense of fairness of the outcomes be high? One patient who thought her treatment refusal was handled fairly also felt that the outcome—that she was forced to take medication—was unfair. Along with expressing her feelings of unfairness, she noted that "...it's not my medicine they want me to take, it's their medicine."

The data in Table 3 are a Chi-Square analysis of outcome fairness and unfairness and process fairness and unfairness. Since this is the total population, unbiased estimates of sample parameters or estimates of statistical variances are not relevant. The purpose of the cross-tabulation is merely to suggest that the relationship is not due to chance. Forty-two responses were cross-tabulated; four subjects (fewer than 10% of the sample) completely rejected a connection between outcome and procedure. In 62% of the cases (26 subjects) there was concordance between process and outcome.

These data tend to support what may be referred to as a halo effect. That is, fair procedures are apparently related to fair outcomes, and unfair procedures are related to unfair outcomes, in the minds of our subjects. It is impossible, however, to tell whether fairness in procedure is influencing judgment about fairness of outcome, and vice versa. Given the small sample size, it is concluded only that the data lend support to a halo effect.

Implications of the study

In the research reported here, it was found that patients could judge procedures fair even when the results were unfavorable from their standpoint. And even when the outcome of the dispute was favorable, they did not invariably also believe that the procedure was fair. But overall, more patients found the dispute resolution norms of nurses to be fairer than the doctors' process of dispute resolution, mandated and endorsed as an effective way to protect patients' autonomy and self-respect. This points to some inherent difficulty in balancing the state's interests and patients' rights. Psychiatrists using the clinical review process to override patients' objections to treatment would benefit from a short training course on procedural justice theory and other dimensions of therapeutic jurisprudence. Utilizing the theory and perspective of therapeutic jurisprudence in the conduct of clinical review panels could greatly increase patients' sense of fairness of the deliberations.

Procedural fairness in resolving treatment disputes between staff and patients may have an impact beyond enhancing patient autonomy and supporting patient dignity with regard to medications. Fair and satisfying processes of decision making may be as relevant to patients' treatment as drugs and therapy. The aim of treatment is, after all, the ultimate return of the patient to the community outside the hospital and to participation in community life. Patients should expect the authorities with whom they deal, both within the hospital and outside, to treat them in the humane and respectful fashion that one should treat all neighbors.[24] From this perspective our study has an optimistic message. The majority of psychiatric patients who have been involved in non-trivial disputes over treatment have perceived the dispute resolution process as fair when this experience provided them with the opportunity to tell their story, and especially when they felt that what they said also affected the outcome of their case. These experiences and their reactions to them may in turn strengthen their perception of the legitimacy and authority of elites and social institutions and contribute to and stabilize their recovery.

At their best, psychiatric hospitals can create ward communities where relationships between patients and staff function therapeutically and can help to transform the patient. In such situations, dignity and care, citizenship and participation, as well as other ideals and values, are played out. At their worst, psychiatric hospital wards are intensely conflictual environments.[25] Glass is very sensitive to the power disparity in the hospital between patient and staff. But he also acknowledges that "While...professional intervention [is]...an exercise of power (domination), the patient may demand it in the frantic search for relief from pain and for acknowledgement that the pain is real and terrifying."[26]

The Glass study also raises another matter concerning the patients in their sick role. The sick role may actually decrease a person's concern with fairness while increasing concern with treatment. For some patients, their principal concerns and preoccupations may lead them in other directions, such as relief from the pain of illness, relief from the effects of drugs, transfer to a different ward, or release from the hospital. The procedures used to resolve the immediate dispute over medication may, for them, simply not be salient. But this does not seem to be the case for most patients in the present study most of the time.

This study indicates that for most patients, fair procedures are relevant. Fairness in resolving disputes may have far-reaching consequences, beyond those examined directly in this study. It may in fact aid treatment and recovery; fairness may enhance the authority of doctors, nurses, and other staff members, as well as increase the legitimacy of psychiatric hospitals and the psychiatric profession. Furthermore, fair processes in the hospital context may increase compliance with medical decisions among patients and may improve the prospects of patients for reintegrating into the community upon release from the hospital, although these relationships have not been subject to empirical examination here. Any and all of these consequences support the therapeutic function of fair dispute resolution procedures.

Last, what can be confirmed from the present study of procedural justice theory in psychiatric hospitals is that there is a developing body of knowledge, from the perspective of therapeutic jurisprudence, that could lend itself to the creation of principles of justice that should be utilized in administrative dis-

---

24. Supra note 22. These are referred to as the humanistic values of compassion, respect, and integrity.

25. Glass JM: Private Terror/Public Life: Psychosis and the Politics of Community. Ithaca: Cornell University Press, 1989.

26. Ibid. at 206.

pute resolution as well as by courts in deciding cases. These principles of justice will strengthen and support the legitimacy and authority of elites by providing firmer, empirical foundations for just decisions. Just decisions take account of the human needs of the individuals who are parties to cases and controversies, and not simply the doctrinal and judicial needs of the system.

Conclusions

There is a longstanding conflict between mental health professionals and patients' rights advocates over the right of involuntarily confined psychiatric patients to refuse treatment when that treatment would, according to the former, clearly improve their condition, make them less dangerous to others and themselves while in confinement, and perhaps lead to their earlier release from the hospital. The controversy is rooted in two distinct and conflicting mind sets, which Milner characterizes as two models of rationality.[27]

From the perspective of these models, it is possible to understand the development of informed consent, and especially the legal right to refuse treatment. "Such a right stresses individual autonomy, especially the degree to which people are free from governmental interference....the right to refuse decisions assumes that individual assertiveness is the most important characteristic that rightholders have."[28] Milner seems to believe that from the point of view of the courts, the patient has the right to be uncooperative. Whether or not this is the case is not clear. Maryland's highest court, relying on the Maryland and federal constitutions and U.S. Supreme Court decisions, moved cautiously into this arena. Although it invalidated a Maryland statute that recognized committed patients' right to refuse treatment, it pulled back from ordering that a judicial hearing on competency was necessary to overrule the rejecting patient's wishes.[29]

Milner reviewed textbooks in psychiatry to determine how the profession viewed and dealt with the uncooperative patient. The textbooks stressed the need to gain the patient's cooperation in treatment and to avoid coercion. But, he concluded, there is a tradition of ignoring the problem of coercion. When uncooperative-patient cases were discussed in the textbooks, it turned out that the patient was refusing to go along with a *reduction* in drug dosage. This was interpreted as the patient's craving for continued nurturance. Furthermore, there was a reluctance on the part of the writers of psychiatry textbooks to recognize the possibility that uncooperative behavior was rational.

An example of this feeling can be found in a recent study of medication-refusing patients. The authors, both psychiatrists, made the point that resisting medication was symptomatic of the mental illness of a small number of patients they studied. In reference to this group, they concluded, "...if the legal system fails to recognize that their refusal is a manifestation of their illness and not a conscious exercise of their civil rights...then constitutional arguments

---

27. Milner N: Models of rationality and mental health rights. International Journal of Law and Psychiatry 4:35–52, 1981.
28. Ibid. at 39.
29. Williams v. Wilzack, supra note 14.

only serve to justify deprivation of care."[30] The legal theory of treatment refusal does not distinguish among patients in terms of empirically defined categories or patients' motivations and rationales for rejecting drug therapy; as things now stand, the right to refuse treatment, limited as it may be, applies equally to the episodic, short-term refuser and the periodic, long-term refuser, other things being equal. If Appelbaum and Gutheil's remark is interpreted broadly, it represents a criticism of the legal system's approach to patients' rights. Some members of the judiciary have also expressed an awareness of this potential problem; in a recent case[31] it was noted with approval "that the goal of restoration of a patient's health and the patient's civil rights may conflict."[32]

This conflict between two mind sets suggests strongly that the goals of recognition of patients' rights and autonomy and patients' satisfaction with the procedures and decision making that support the rights utilized to resolve their conflict with the staff over treatment will not be met.[33] Yet if therapeutic jurisprudence is to have any efficacy, it will require a willingness to change and come together on the part of both the psychiatric and the legal professions.[34]

The research indicates that these procedures, provided by law to override a patient's objections to treatment, are not in harmony with decision making on the hospital ward. The clinical review panel is not viewed by the hospital staff as analogous to a court of last resort, as the law seems to imply. Rather, the panel may ratify the decision of the treatment team with minimal attention to the intent of the law. Only on occasion is the refusing patient invited to come before the panel. When this does occur, the patient's input is limited to an explanation of why he or she refuses to take the prescribed drug, perhaps in an attempt to determine whether the patient is what has been referred to as a "symptomatic refuser."

The legal process of recognizing and protecting patients' rights pits the legal profession against hospital culture. The law's conception of medical decision making is implicitly based on an assumption that is invalid in a substantial number of situations.[35] This is the assumption that medical practice is linear

---

30. See Appelbaum and Gutheil, supra note 3 at 345; see also Appelbaum PS, Gutheil TG: "Rotting with their rights on": Constitutional theory and clinical realities in drug refusal by psychiatric patients. Bulletin of the American Academy of Psychiatry and Law 7:306–315, 1979.

31. Rogers v. Commissioner of Mental Health, 458 N.E.2d 308 (Mass. 1983).

32. Ibid. 317.

33. While there are many important differences between psychiatry and general medicine, they share many important dimensions of the culture of medicine. A significant one for our purposes is the absence of a tradition of seeking patients' consent in medical practice. See Faden RR, Beauchamp TL: A History and Theory of Informed Consent. New York: Oxford University Press, 1986. Even today, seeking patients' input seems to cause anxiety and resistance among many physicians. By extension, rejection of treatment by patients is often taken as a personal rejection of, if not an attack on, the doctor.

34. Such an argument seems somewhat utopian, given the recent pessimistic review of "hidden agendas." Miller RD: Hidden agendas at the law-psychiatry interface. Journal of Psychiatry & Law 20:35–58, 1992.

35. Zussman R: Intensive Care: Medical Ethics and the Medical Profession. Chicago: University of Chicago Press, 1992; see also Fox RC: The Sociology of Medicine. New York: Prentice-Hall, 1989.

and discrete—that is, broken into distinct parts, or decision units. According to law, informed consent by the patient to each of these individual parts can be obtained, and refusing treatment is an easily identifiable matter of the patient's saying No. However, patients seem to learn various bits of information, some relevant to decision making and some not, from doctors' and nurses' efforts to obtain compliance and from situational etiquette. Decisions are not made by patients. Doctors make recommendations to patients. Usually there is acquiescence, or what is known as compliance, sometimes the absence of an objection; occasionally there is a veto or refusal of, or noncompliance with, the recommendation or recommendations. When refusal actually begins is not a clear-cut matter. In psychiatric hospitals, the medication nurse is often aware of a patient's manifest and obvious refusal but usually does nothing immediately. If refusal persists, she will usually talk to the patient and try to convince him or her to comply. As the conflict escalates, her efforts become more focused, and the consequences to the patient become more coercive. If the attending physician learns of the dispute regarding medication at all, it is only when early efforts by the nursing staff fail to resolve the dispute and gain the patient's compliance.

It should be emphasized that the perspective of therapeutic jurisprudence, by way of the application of the theory of procedural justice and its subjective psychological approach to effectiveness of court decisions and legislative actions aimed at institutional changes, is not just a theoretical exercise without any practical payoff. Wexler and Winick[36] have argued forcefully that the empirical study of therapeutic effects of procedures are important practical tools for law revision and legal change. Potentially at least, procedural justice theory offers to provide an ethical and informed empirical basis for understanding the ways in which legal and medical systems actually interact in modern society. It can thus help to develop principles of therapeutic justice along with more realistic expectations and objectives for public policy and more appropriate strategies for putting policies into effect. But the incorporation and implementation of this knowledge remains a difficult and long-term goal.

---

36. Wexler and Winick, supra note.

Chapter 47

Therapeutic Jurisprudence and Patients' Perceptions of Procedural Due Process of Civil Commitment Hearings

Alexander Greer
Mary O'Regan
Amy Traverso

Introduction

Regarding proposals to modify either the substantive criteria or procedural rules of civil commitment, David Wexler has urged that "before we are overrun by a counter-revolutionary bandwagon, we give some serious thought to the question whether the 'tension between the benevolent and libertarian impulses in our society' necessarily means a mutual exclusivity between 'rights' and 'therapy'" (Wexler, 1991). With Bruce Winick, he has devised and developed a framework for consideration of these sorts of questions: therapeutic jurisprudence. "Therapeutic jurisprudence is the study of the role of the law as a therapeutic agent" (Wexler, 1991). The research reported here is the first step in a study of the therapeutic effect of the procedures of the law of involuntary hospitalization; it employs the techniques and findings of a body of psychological research into citizens' perceptions of the fairness of dispute resolution procedures.

Since the civil liberties revolution of the 1960s and 1970s, the legal procedures for the involuntary hospitalization (civil commitment) of the mentally ill have been the focus of intense debate between civil libertarian advocates and those who provide treatment for the mentally ill (Ensminger & Ligouri, 1976). Civil libertarians argue (and the courts have generally agreed) that stringent substantive and procedural due process protections are necessary to prevent the abuses of the mentally ill that occurred in the past as a result of unfettered decision-making by psychiatrists (Morse, 1982). Mental health professionals, psychiatrists in the main, argue that "substantive and procedural guarantees [are] destructive of patients' treatment needs, misguided, one-sided interference with the treatment of persons with debilitating mental disorders" (Haycock, et al ,1994). "Throughout the debate each side contended, either implicitly or explicitly, that mental patients viewed civil commitment as it did" (Edelsohn & Hiday, 1990, p 66). Initially, there was little empirical support for those claims, however. There is now a growing body of empirical research about patients' attitudes about civil commitment (Edelsohn & Hiday, 1990; Hiday, 1988; Kalman, 1983; Kane, et al, 1983; Toews, et al, 1986; Toews, et al, 1981; Weinstein, 1979). That research, however, has focused on patients' perceptions of the *outcome* of civil commitment hearings (Edelsohn & Hiday, 1990); to date, there are no studies of patients' perceptions of the legal *procedures* of the hearing (Tyler, 1992, emphasis added). Such studies are needed because there is an extensive body of psychological research that has found that "people are *not* primarily influenced by the outcome of their experience" (Tyler, 1992) with legal authorities, but are influenced by their "assessment of the fairness of the case disposition process" (Tyler, 1992). This finding is of critical importance to our understanding of the therapeutic impact of the procedures of civil commitment: procedures that are perceived by patients to be unfair may interfere with treatment, while procedures that are perceived as just and fair may encourage treatment compliance.

The research reported here is the first phase of a project to ascertain patients' perceptions of their own civil commitment hearings and the therapeutic impact of those perceptions. This paper will describe that research and plans for future research in this area.

Civil Commitment

Prior to the civil liberties revolution of the 1970s in the United States, the substantive criteria and procedural rules for the commitment of the mentally ill were significantly less stringent than those in force today. Mentally ill people were hospitalized based on the state's *parens patriae* power to care for those who could not care for themselves; the power of psychiatrists and treatment staff to commit or retain a person in a state hospital was essentially unfettered by due process procedures.

Hearings for the involuntary hospitalization of mentally ill people in the United States now have many of the same procedural features as criminal trials. In *Lessard v. Schmidt*, for example, a federal district court ordered the institution of a full range of due process procedures for civil commitment, including timely notice to the subject of the hearing, right to a jury trial, a probable cause hearing for detentions longer than 48 hours, the right to representation, the exclusion of hearsay evidence, and the right against self-incrimination. To be sure, not every state requires that level of due process protections, but, in general, civil commitment hearings in the United States have many of the same procedural protections as criminal trials.

The rigorousness of these procedural rules, together with stringent substantive requirements, has, in the view of psychiatrists, prevented the treatment of seriously mentally ill people or aggravated the therapeutic relationship between patient and psychiatrist so as to delay needed treatment (Treffert, 1973; Lamb & Mills, 1986; Hermann, 1986). The potential antitherapeutic effects of these rules include psychological distress or damage to the patient from the psychiatrist's disclosure of the patient's illness and prognosis in a public setting, the creation of an adversarial relationship between the patient and the members of the treatment team, the reinforcement of the passivity of the patient and the undermining of the development of the patient's sense of responsibility for his or her own treatment, increased anxiety for the patient and the members of the treatment team concerning the hearing, and the focusing of the treatment around issues of dangerousness and the sufficiency of the evidence for commitment rather than on the treatment needs of the patient (Haycock, et al, 1994).

Another set of criticisms of the present procedures of civil commitment arise from consistent empirical findings that the practice of civil commitment fails to meet the standards set by the courts and legislatures (Turkhiemer & Parry, 1992); attorneys do not zealously advocate for their clients (Leavitt & Maykuth, 1989; Poythress, 1978), independent expert witnesses are rarely employed, judges most often ratify the decisions reached by clinicians, and hearings are extraordinarily brief, often lasting only minutes (Turkheimer & Parry, 1992). The "yawning gap" between practice and policy engenders, it is argued, feelings of worthlessness and a loss of dignity on the part of the patient (Haycock, et al, 1994). The existence of the gap is the result of the conflict—felt by mental health professionals and lawyers—between the stringent and adversarial nature of the mandated procedures and the paternalistic nature of the substance in issue—the potential patient's need for treatment in hospital (Haycock, et al, 1994).

In this perspective, when the procedural rules are scrupulously observed, an antitherapeutic effect ensues; when the rules are routinely ignored, an antitherapeutic effect ensues. The rules, the argument continues, should be modified. Much of that argument is, however, based on anecdotal evidence provided by clinicians or on supposition.

Outcome Studies

One method for verifying or disproving the claims of the antitherapeutic nature of the procedures of, and substantive criteria for, involuntary hospitalization is to ask former patients about their attitudes towards their commitment. In one such study, Edelsohn and Hiday (1990) surveyed individuals who had been involuntarily hospitalized in South Carolina between 1984 and 1985. They measured ex-patients' attitudes on five scales: perceived need for commitment, perceived personal consequences, view of medication while hospitalized, view of primary physician, and overall view of hospital experience. They conclude that the ex-patients have a "mixed view of their experiences" (p. 74). While many patients had a positive view of the personal consequences of hospitalization, the hospital physician, and the experience itself, "a substantial minority of excandidates view their experiences negatively, seeing their relationships harmed, their physicians and medications as not helpful, and their hospitalization as unnecessary, degrading, and depressing" (p. 75). These results support the findings of other similar, but less extensive, studies (See Hiday, 1988 for a review).

Interpreting these results for their therapeutic meaning is difficult because they confound the *process* of commitment with the outcome of the hearing, the treatment accorded during the period of hospitalization, and the outcome of the treatment. That is, we cannot separate patients' perceptions of the fairness of their civil commitment hearings from their perceptions of the impact of the commitment itself. It is critical that we do so because "people respond to *how* decisions are made—a response that is not simply linked to *what* decisions are" (Tyler, 1992, p. 443).

Perceptions of Procedural Due Process

Research on the role of perceptions of procedural due process in litigant satisfaction began with the work of Thibaut and Walker in 1975 (Thibaut & Walker, 1975); since that time, a number of studies have investigated their thesis that the procedure of dispute resolution was connected to the satisfaction of the parties to the dispute. Casper, Tyler, and Fisher (1988) summarize the findings of the research:

> Subsequent work has confirmed the hypothesis that legal procedures influence litigant satisfaction and that such effects generalize to evaluations of legal authorities. Such effects occur not only when litigants have experienced formal courtroom procedures but also disputant reactions to alternative dispute resolution procedures. Finally, fair process effects have been found outside the legal arena in allocation and dispute resolution within work organization and interpersonal relations.

Since Casper, et al wrote in 1988, research in procedural due process has focused on "*what* it is about a legal procedure that leads those involved to consider it to be fair" (Tyler, 1988, p. 104; emphasis in original). Tyler identified three factors that are "important determinants of people's judgments about procedural fairness" (Tyler, 1992, p. 439): participation, dignity, and trust.

Participation includes the opportunity to present evidence on one's behalf and to voice one's view of the dispute ('voice'), the opportunity to influence the outcome of the dispute resolution (decision control), or both (Tyler, 1992). "Voice" appears to be so central to disputants' sense of the fairness of the process that even when their statement or evidence will not affect the outcome of the decision, they value the chance to be heard (Tyler, 1992).

Dignity refers to disputants' sense that they are being treated with "respect, politeness, and dignity, and whether their rights as citizens are acknowledged" (Tyler, 1992 p. 440). People treated with dignity by legal authorities have their status as "competent, equal, citizens and human beings" confirmed (Tyler, 1992, p. 440). People who perceive that the dispute resolution procedure does not afford them a requisite amount of dignity feel devalued as a member of society.

Trust speaks to the disputant's perception that the actors (judges, lawyers) "are concerned with their welfare and want to treat them fairly" (Tyler, 1992, p. 441). Trust of the legal actors is related to the degree to which the disputant is given an opportunity to participate and the dignity afforded the disputant, but it also requires the disputant to attribute a positive, or at least benign, motivation to the legal actor.

The importance of participation, dignity, and trust for disputants' perceptions of the fairness of legal proceedings should not be underestimated; "[e]ach of these three factors has more influence on judgments of procedural justice than do either evaluations of neutrality or evaluations of the favorableness of the outcome of the hearing" (Tyler, 1992, p. 442).

These three factors play a role in disputants' perception of the fairness of their hearing (as compared to the significance of the outcome on those perceptions) because of "the important role that legal and political authorities play in defining peoples' feelings of self-esteem, self-worth, and their sense of personal responsibility" (Tyler, 1992, p. 442). Self-respect and value as a member of society are particularly critical to the mentally ill, who already have been marginalized and stigmatized by informal social mechanisms (Perlin, 1992). Moreover, as Tyler (1992) notes, "perhaps no type of hearing more directly threatens a person's belief that they are an equal member of society than a mental commitment hearing" (p. 444). Thus, one would expect that respondents in civil commitment hearings would be particularly sensitive to issues of participation, dignity, and trust.

The Present Research

In order to investigate the claims of the therapeutic impact of the present procedures of civil commitment, we sought first to ascertain mentally ill persons' perceptions of the procedures employed in their civil commitment hearings.

Method

The research was conducted at the Psychiatric Treatment Center (hereafter, PTC) operated by the University of Massachusetts Medical Center's Department of Psychiatry at Worcester State Hospital in Worcester, Massachusetts. The substantive criteria for civil commitment in Massachusetts mirror the 'dangerousness' standard employed in many states. Massachusetts permits the involuntary hospitalization of a person if (1) the person is suffering from a mental illness, (2) the failure to hospitalize the person would result in a likelihood of serious harm by reason of the mental illness, and (3) there is no less restrictive alternative for the patient (104 Consolidated Massachusetts Regulations 3.07). A likelihood of serious harm is defined as (1) a substantial risk of physical harm to the patient, (2) a substantial risk or serious harm to others, or (3) a very substantial risk of physical impairment or injury to the patient (Massachusetts General Laws, chapter 123, section. 1). Mental illness is defined as "a substantial disorder of thought, mood, perception, orientation, or memory that grossly impairs judgment, behavior, capacity to recognize reality, or ability to meet the ordinary demands of life" (104 C.M.R. 3.01). Massachusetts permits the "emergency" involuntary hospitalization of a mentally ill person for a ten day period based on an application by a physician or psychologist. Prior to the expiration of the ten day period, the superintendent of the hospital must release the person, admit the person as a voluntary patient, or petition the court for the person's involuntary admission (M.G.L. c. 123, sec 11). The initial "non-emergency" commitment of a patient is for a period of six months; all subsequent commitments are for a period of one year (M.G.L. c. 123, sec. 8(d)). A court hearing on a commitment petition must be held within fourteen days of the filing of the petition. Massachusetts, unlike most other states, requires proof beyond a reasonable doubt in all civil commitment proceedings. The procedures required in civil commitment hearings include the right to counsel[1], the right to acquire (at state expense if indigent) and present

---

1. In Massachusetts most patients are indigent and legal services are provided by lawyers from the Committee for Public Counsel Services. That organization now requires specialized

the evidence of independent mental health experts, the right to notice of, and the allegations contained in, the petition of commitment, the right to address the court, and a right to appeal an adverse judgment to a higher court. Patients examined by state-employed experts, including treatment staff, must receive and understand a warning that in the event a petition for commitment is filed, their statements will be used as evidence at the hearing (*Commonwealth* v. *Lamb*, 1972). All commitment hearings are held before a judge of the District Court—the trial level court for both criminal and civil cases in Massachusetts.

Civil commitment hearings are held on alternate Wednesdays at Worcester State Hospital for patients from the PTC; the lawyer representing the PTC at civil commitment hearings usually has significant advance notice of the hearing dates and the names of the patients who are the subject of impending re-commitment hearings. During the week prior to the week in which a hearing is scheduled, one of the researchers (M.O. or A.T.) obtained the names of the patients scheduled for a hearing in the coming week. Patients who have been adjudged incompetent to make ordinary decisions were excluded from the research at this point. Prior to the hearing, one of the researchers (M.O.) identified and contacted the patient's treating physician for permission to interview the patient. The researchers (M.O. or A.T.). attended each commitment hearing; following the hearing, each patient for whom permission was obtained from the treating physician was approached on the treatment unit for informed consent to be interviewed. Patients who did not speak English were excluded from the research at this point. Interviews were conducted by one researcher (M.O.) and observed by another (A.T.) as soon as possible following the hearing, either on the treatment unit or, if that was inappropriate or impossible, at another location in the hospital that afforded privacy. Basic demographic information, diagnosis, and present medication were gathered by a researcher (A.T.) from the patient's medical record after the interview.

The questionnaire used in this study was a modified version of one used by Tyler (1990) to conduct his survey of citizens of Chicago regarding their perception of their encounters with legal authorities. Questions and responses were read to the subject by one researcher and recorded by both researchers.

Results

The results reported here are of a pilot study to determine if mentally ill patients were able to understand and respond to a questionnaire regarding their perceptions of their civil commitment hearings. This research is the first phase of a larger study to determine the therapeutic effect of patients' perceptions of the procedures of civil commitment hearings. The results of the pilot study are both encouraging and instructive for the potential of this type of research.

During the six-month period in which the study was conducted, 57 individuals were scheduled for a commitment hearing; 54% (N=31) had a hearing and 16 hearings were continued without a finding. Of the remaining 31 individuals, 74% (23) attended their hearings. Treating physicians would not give permission to interview the patient in 17% (4) of the cases (most often citing

---

training in the diagnosis and treatment of mental disorders for attorneys who seek certification to represent mentally ill people in commitment and treatment refusal hearings.

significant patient distress as reason for the denial). Of the seventeen remaining cases, 41% (7) of the patients refused to participate and 17% (4) were either unable to complete the interview because of their illness or withdrew from the interview before completion. On average, the interview took 45 minutes to conduct (range 25 to 70 minutes).

All of the patients (N=9) knew that they had been involved in a civil commitment hearing on that day and all of them were able to provide an objectively rational description of the purpose of the hearing. One patient described it as "A petition to keep me in the hospital, me against the doctor" (Pt # 10). When asked whose idea the hearing was, six patients indicated that it was the doctor, one thought it was his lawyer, one patient identified "criminals in the neighborhood" (Pt #9), and one patient was unsure. Seven of the nine patients knew and could describe the outcome of the hearing; one patient responded that the result was "intentional infliction of permanent irreversible brain and body damage" (Pt. #9) and another patient responded that the outcome meant "that he had to be a little more careful" (Pt. # 3). All nine of the patients were able to correctly identify the participants in the hearing and were often able to name their lawyer and the testifying physician.

The ability to trust the participants in the legal action is one of the most important contributors to overall satisfaction with legal proceedings. We asked each patient six questions about each of the participants in the hearing: their lawyer, the PTC lawyer, the judge, and the testifying psychiatrist. Seven of the nine patients responded that they trusted their lawyer and none of them were angry with their lawyer. Only three of the patients interviewed trusted the PTC lawyer, but only one reported being angry with that attorney. Six patients indicated that they trusted the judge, but six also responded that they were frustrated with the judge, although only one person indicated that the judge embarrassed him during the hearing.

These findings indicate that patients have general level of trust of their lawyer and the judge, but are somewhat distrustful of the hospital lawyer. The lack of trust in the treating physician, however, stands in stark contrast to that finding; only one patient responded that he trusted his doctor. Five out of eight patients (one patient refused to respond to the series of questions about the psychiatrist; this may be fairly read as an indication of the patient's anger towards the clinician) were angry at their doctor; six out of eight patients were frustrated with the doctor and four of seven (two patients refused to respond) reported that the doctor embarrassed them at the hearing. Overall, only one patient described his feelings toward his doctor as positive.

The patients' perception of the dignity or respect accorded to them in the hearing was measured by six questions about each of the participants in the hearing. In general, patients believed that their lawyer treated them with respect and dignity, and most patients reported that this was very or quite important to them. A striking exception to this finding is that five patients reported that their lawyer did not listen to "what they had to say." One patient reported of his lawyer that "she didn't let me say anything" (Pt.# 7). The PTC's lawyer and the judge were perceived as being less respectful of the patients' dignity than were their lawyers. Patients reported that the PTC lawyer did not show concern for their rights and that the lawyer did not listen to what the patient had to say. One-half of the patients reported that the judge did not show respect for the patients' rights and only three of the patients reported that the judge listened to what they had to say. One patient asked the interviewer to skip the questions in this area because "the judge didn't have nothing to do with the hearing" (Pt. #5). Treating physicians were perceived by the patients as being disrespectful, impolite, and dishonest. Further, the patients believed the physicians failed to listen to them and showed a lack of concern for their rights. Five of the patients indicated that it was very important to them how well they were treated at the hearing by their physician. These findings indicate the patients perceive that they are treated with a lack of dignity and respect by the legal actors in civil commitment hearings; treating physicians are perceived as least respectful, followed by the hospital's lawyer and the judge. We would expect that the patients' own lawyers should be perceived as treating them with regard and respect; the patients surveyed here generally endorsed that expectation, but significantly felt that the lawyers were uninterested in their story.

Perceived participation (voice) in the proceedings was measured by five questions. Patients felt that they had little or no voice in the proceedings; all but one patient reported that they did not have an opportunity to say what they wanted. Five of the patients reported that information that they wished had remained private was revealed in court and five reported being embarrassed by information that was disclosed in court. Five patients perceived the methods used by the judge to resolve the dispute favored the PTC over their side. Only one patient reported that he had a great deal of influence in the outcome of the hearing.

As all of the patients were involuntarily hospitalized, it is not surprising that only one person reported being very satisfied with the outcome of the hearing. All but one of the patients reported that it was very important to them if they won or lost the hearing and seven of the patients were surprised that they did not win release from the hospital. At the end of the hearing the patients, in general, felt angry, sad, displeased, and confused. Eight of the patients felt that they had been coerced by the process.

It bears repeating that this was a pilot study of the feasibility of collecting patients' perceptions of the fairness of their civil commitment hearings. As such, the results are provisional and should be considered with extreme wariness. Nonetheless, this study has shown that patients are sufficiently aware of the procedural aspects of their hearings and of the actions of the actors in those hearings and can report those perceptions through a structured interview administered by an experienced mental health professional. Additionally, the results of this interview *suggest* that patients' perception of the procedural due process of commitment hearings may affect the course and conduct of their treatment in the hospital: patients' perceptions of their lawyer, the hospital lawyer and the judge can be fairly summarized as mixed; patients trusted their lawyer, the hospital lawyer, and the judge, but perceived them as somewhat disrespectful and uninterested in their story. Their perceptions of the treating clinician's role in the hearings, however, can only be characterized as strongly negative in every regard. We can conjecture that patients' perceptions of the procedural fairness of civil commitment hearings do not "encourage the continuation of productive exchange between individuals" (Thibaut & Walker, 1995, p. 67) and, thus, do not advance the therapeutic progress of the patients.

Future Research

The next phase of this project is to refine the questionnaire; a process we have already begun. A critical problem in the administration of the interview is that patients found the questions redundant; our review of the questions revealed no literally redundant questions. We surmise that patients had some difficulty in differentiating between questions that have subtle differences in wording and may be bored by the somewhat repetitive nature of the questions. Another problem that we faced was the inability of some patients to concentrate on the questions and the interview, in general. Both problems suggest that the questionnaire has to be shortened and the language made simpler.

The full scale study will be conducted in two jurisdictions, Massachusetts and Ontario, Canada. Civil commitment hearings in Ontario employ many of the same procedures—e.g., rights to counsel, notice, and appeal—as do many American jurisdictions, but hearings are conducted by a board consisting of five members—two psychiatrists, two lawyers, and one lay person. Informal observation of these hearings suggest that hearings in Ontario are conducted with greater regard for patients' dignity and that board members are more interested in patients' stories. This methodology will provide an opportunity to compare patients' perceptions of the procedural fairness of the two types of hearings.[2]

The full scale study will also measure patients' *pre-hearing* perceptions of the fairness of civil commitment hearings. Many of the patients we surveyed in the pilot study had been previously involuntarily hospitalized and, therefore, have pre-existing perceptions and expectations of the fairness of the hearings. Moreover, some of the patients may have had contact with other legal authorities (police, for example) and experienced other legal proceedings (criminal trials). In order to isolate the patients' view of the fairness of the present hearing and measure the therapeutic effect of that perception, it is critical to measure those existing expectations and perceptions. Similarly, treating /testifying psychiatrists will be surveyed about their prior experiences with civil commitment hearings, other legal authorities, and their general perceptions of the fairness of legal proceedings.

Wexler (1991b) has noted that there are two obstacles to determining the therapeutic consequences of a law or legal process; the first is to determine an appropriate measure of therapeutic outcome and the second is to establish an appropriate time frame for the measurement of therapeutic outcome. The full scale study must surmount both those obstacles. The measurement of therapeutic outcome is complicated by the involuntary nature of the patient/therapist relationship; patients have already expressed their displeasure with some aspects of the treatment they are receiving in the hospital; some may believe that they do not have a mental disorder and thus are not in need of treatment.

---

2. In the present study we viewed the treating/testifying psychiatrist as a legal actor in civil commitment hearings; our observations of the hearings, the results of the present pilot study, and the review of the relevant literature has led us to revise that position. The treating/testifying psychiatrist is more properly seen both as a legal actor and as a party to the dispute—a litigant. The full scale study will therefore also focus on the treating psychiatrist's perceptions of the process, and their effect on the therapeutic relationship.

The selection of an appropriate time frame is similarly confounded by empirical evidence that patients' views of civil commitment become more positive over time (Towes, et al, 1986). The patients we surveyed were angry and confused immediately following their re-commitment hearing; measurement of the therapeutic consequences at that point would reflect that anger, but one might ask whether it would it be a true measure of the therapeutic relationship. One of us (A.G.) is presently developing a survey instrument to measure the therapeutic impact in this area.

The therapeutic effect of the patients' perceptions of the fairness of civil commitment hearings cannot be measured without understanding the *pre-hearing therapeutic state*. We propose to question patients about their perceptions of the treatment they are receiving, their willingness to comply with the recommendations of the treating physician, and, generally, their allegiance to the treatment regime. We also intend to survey treatment staff, particularly treating psychiatrists, about their perception of the present state of the treatment relationship. These two measures can then be compared and combined to describe the pre-hearing therapeutic state against which we can compare the post-hearing state.

In the full-scale study, a researcher will observe and collect data on each civil commitment hearing in which a subject is a respondent. The researcher will record the length of each hearing, the degree to which the patient participates in the hearing, and, using a survey instrument (now in development), the degree to which the procedures of the hearing conform to statutory or court mandated requirements.

Finally, the next phase of the project will include interviews with the treating psychiatrist, the other members of the treatment team, and the patient regarding changes in the patient's course of treatment, compliance with treatment, and their perception of the effect of the procedures of the civil commitment hearing on the therapeutic relationship.

Conclusion

The results of the research presented here is encouraging for several reasons. First, it "brings patients back in" to the debate about the adequacy and necessity of stringent procedural rules for civil commitment hearings. Society and clinicians have an interest in those rules, but patients are, after all, the people most affected. Surely, we ought to consult with them as we propose changes in those rules. Second, the research has shown that patients are aware of the process of commitment and can relate those perceptions. Third, this research is a first step in determining the therapeutic impact of the process of civil commitment. The full scale study described here will go a long way in deciding if, and how, the process should be altered. For example, can testifying physicians alter their manner or tone of testifying so as to raise patients' perceptions of fairness (Wexler, in press)? If not, what impact—on patient perceptions of fairness and on treatment outcome—might result from changing the process so that the testifying physician is not the *treating* physician of the given patient-respondent, but is instead merely (vis-a-vis that particular patient) one who *evaluates* and *testifies*? Future research and thinking might be directed at such representative issues.

References

Casper, J.D., Tyler, T., & Fisher, B. (1988) Procedural justice in felony cases. Law and Society Review, 22, 483–507.

Commonwealth v. Lamb, 365 Mass. 265, 303 N.E.2d 122 (1974).

Edelsohn, G.A., & Hiday, V.A. (1990). Civil commitment: A range of patient attitudes. Bulletin of the American Academy of Psychiatry and Law, 18, 65–77.

Ensminger, J.J., & Ligouri, T.D. (1978). The therapeutic significance of the civil commitment hearing: An unexplored potential. Journal of Psychiatry and Law, 6, 5–44.

Haycock, J., Finkelman, D., & Presskreischer, H. (1994). Speaking truth to power: Rights, therapeutic jurisprudence, and Massachusetts mental health law. New England Journal on Criminal and Civil Confinement, 20, 310–320.

Hermann, D.H.J. (1986). Barriers to providing effective treatment: A critique of revisions in procedural, substantive, and dispositional criteria in involuntary civil commitment. Vanderbilt Law Review, 1, 86–103.

Hiday, V.A. (1988). Civil commitment: A review of the empirical research. Behavioral Sciences and the Law, 6, 15–43.

Kalman, T.P. (1983). An overview of patient satisfaction with psychiatric treatment. Hospital and Community Psychiatry, 38, 48–54.

Kane, J.M., Quitkin, F., & Rifkin, A. (1983). Attitudinal changes of involuntarily committed patients following treatment. Archives of General Psychiatry, 40, 374–377.

Lamb, H.R., & Mills, M.S. (1986). Needed changes in law and procedure for the chronically mentally ill. Hospital and Community Psychiatry, 37, 475–480.

Leavitt, N., & Maykuth, P. (1989). Conformance to attorney performance standards: Attorney advocacy behavior in a maximum security hospital. Law and Human Behavior, 13, 217–230.

Lessard v. Schimdt, 349 F.Supp. 1078 (E.D.Wisc. 1972).

Perlin, M. (1992). On "sanism." Southern Methodist University Law Review, 45, 373–407.

Poythress, N.G. (1978). Psychiatric expertise in civil commitment: Training attorneys to cope with expert testimony. Law and Human Behavior, 2, 1–23.

Thibaut, J., & Walker, L. (1978). A theory of procedure. California Law Review, 66, 541–566.

Toews, J., el-Guebaly, N., & Leckie, A. (1981). Patients' reactions to their civil commitment. Canadian Journal of Psychiatry, 26, 251–254.

Toews, J., el-Guebaly, N., & Leckie, A. (1986). Change with time of patients' reactions to committal. Canadian Journal of Psychiatry, 31, 413–415.

Treffert, D. (1973). Dying with their rights on. American Journal of Psychiatry, 130, 1041.

Turkheimer, E., & Parry, C. D. H. (1992). Why the gap? Practice and policy in civil commitment hearings. American Psychologist, 47, 646–655.

Tyler, T. (1992) The psychological consequences of judicial procedures: Implications for civil commitment hearings. Southern Methodist Law Review, 46, 433–445.

Tyler, T. (1988) Why people obey the law.

Weinstein, R.M. (1979). Patient attitudes toward civil commitment: A review of quantitative research. Journal of Health Sociology & Behavior, 20, 237–258.

Wexler, D.B. (1991). Putting mental health into mental health law: Therapeutic jurisprudence. In D.B. Wexler and B.J. Winick (eds). Essays In Therapeutic Jurisprudence (pp. 3–15). Durham, NC: Carolina Academic Press.

Wexler, D.B. (1991b) Therapeutic jurisprudence as a new research tool. In D.B. Wexler and B.J. Winick (eds). Essays in Therapeutic Jurisprudence (pp. 303–320).

Wexler, D.B. (1990). Grave disability and family therapy: The therapeutic potential of civil libertarian commitment codes. In D.B. Wexler (ed.) Therapeutic Jurisprudence: The Law as a Therapeutic Agent (pp. 165–187). Durham, NC: Carolina Academic Press.

Wexler, D.B. (in press), Applying the Law Therapeutically. Applied and Preventive Psychology.

Chapter 48

Toward a Therapeutic Jurisprudence Analysis of Medication Refusal in the Court Review Model

Julie Magno Zito
Jozsef Vitrai
Thomas J. Craig

The right to refuse psychotropic drug therapy for involuntarily hospitalized mentally ill persons has been developing in psychiatric practice for nearly 20 years. After an initially heated debate between extreme positions at each end of the spectrum, states have quietly settled into various procedures which give tacit assurance that a limited right to refuse treatment exists. These procedures have been grouped into two broad categories (Appelbaum, 1988), one reflecting a judicial (so-called rights-driven) model with a primary goal of achieving due process for the individual and the other reflecting a medical or clinical (treatment-driven) model because of an emphasis on the person's clinical needs as perceived by the treating psychiatrist. Regardless of how the approaches are labelled, they are different in practice and produce different experiences for patients and clinicians. Whether these approaches produce differing clinical outcomes is the heart of the controversy.

In both approaches to resolving treatment refusal, the procedures usually involve an assessment of the individual's competency. In one case, the court is the primary authority to make the determination, and in the other case a clinician, usually a psychiatrist, makes this determination. Competency or capacity, in this context, refers to the individual's ability to reach a treatment decision (McKinnon, Cournos, & Stanley, 1992). The emphasis on competence in the case law on treatment refusal is illustrated in the *Rivers v. Katz* (1986) decision. Here the court enunciated two criteria to be met before medicating an individual over objection in non-emergency circumstances: to show the incompetence of the individual to make the treatment decision, and to show that the proposed medication regimen is tailored to meet the treatment needs of the individual. When the two criteria are considered together, the review might be described as pharmacologic due process.

To the near exclusion of the second criterion, the judicial approach *in practice* has focused on the issue of competence. Once it has been shown that court referred patients are incompetent, the issue rarely moves courts to monitor the effectiveness of forced medication or to call for trials of alternative treatments. Experience well illustrates this point. In New York, the Office of Mental Health defined three major criteria for psychiatrists who are assessing treatment competence for *Rivers'* hearings. These criteria are factual understanding, rational use of information, and appreciation or understanding of the issue. In a study of the role of these criteria in determining medication refusal competency (McKinnon *et al.*, 1992), according to the psychiatrists' written assessments for *Rivers'* proceedings, most clinicians gave *general* comments about rational use of information (62% of cases) or about appreciation of the issue (79% of cases) as indications of incompetence, while only 6% of the assessments were *specific* to the treatment being refused. Recently (Binder & McNiel, 1991), the term "fluctuating competence" was used to emphasize short-term refusal which has been described in previous studies of stereotypic refusal (Appelbaum & Gutheil, 1980), or "least symptomatic" refusal (Zito, Routt, Mitchell, & Roerig, 1985). Collectively, the findings support the notion that competency is evolving from a general, one-time, irreversible determination to a specific, issue-oriented, time-dependent one (Appelbaum, Lidz, & Meisel, 1987) but with, as yet, inadequate attention by practitioners to illustrate how individuals meet specific drug refusal incompetency.

The judicial model is carried out by a court review usually separate from the commitment hearing. In states like Massachusetts and New York, it represents a costly (Schouten & Gutheil, 1990) and administratively cumbersome (Zito, Craig, & Wanderling, 1991) approach. Empirical findings from both settings suggest limited achievement of the due process goals articulated by the case law responsible for the new procedures. They also suggest that these goals have been achieved at the expense of a loss of effectiveness of the underlying clinical process. To illustrate this point, if we measure the relative procedural efficiency of court review, we may imply a positive outcome from a due process viewpoint because patients are not "rotting with their rights on" (Appelbaum & Gutheil, 1979). But, this interpretation ignores or subverts the larger, long-term goals of encouraging negotiated agreements and fostering patient-doctor relationships. In this broader context, procedural efficiency appears to be counter-therapeutic because it promotes a quick administrative solution to a long-term, individualized problem and thwarts the opportunity for a dialogue on the benefits and risks of long-term maintenance medications for frequently hospitalized, chronically psychotic individuals.

Additional examples emanate from judicial model data which are used to paint a clinical profile of the refusing patient. Retrospective data (Zito *et al.*, 1991) showing that court adjudicated refusing patients are more likely to be middle aged, with a crime-related legal status on admission and to have an intermediate length of hospital stay compared with the non-refusing patient can be interpreted in several ways. In addition, it is unclear whether the early discharge seen for the case with an application that is withdrawn before court review is a sign of better clinical response or an indication of an unsuccessful and potentially anti-therapeutic treatment termination (Zito *et al.*, 1991). Prospective study findings from Massachusetts (Hoge *et al.*, 1990) and a more recent California study (Levin, Brekke, & Thomas, 1991) suggest a different clinical profile of the refusing patient that involves acute, symptomatic individuals often with grave disability, history of refusals, and little insight to the nature of their illness. They are reported to be more troublesome during treatment, with psychotic reasons for refusal and a longer time to discharge than for non-refusers. Collectively, these later empirical portraits confirm some earlier findings (Appelbaum & Gutheil, 1980; Bloom, Faulkner, Holm, & Rawlinson, 1984; Marder *et al.*, 1983) and, in conjunction with the nearly unanimous agreement by the courts to medicate over objection, have led many within the clinical community to conclude that court review is an unnecessary duplication of the treating psychiatrist's opinion. A contrasting profile was derived from the early Minnesota multidisciplinary clinical model which had outside, independent advocacy for patients in the context of a weekly, in-hospital, clinical review and, by several measures, showed more favorable outcomes (Zito, Hendel, Mitchell, & Routt, 1986). Unfortunately, the model proved subject to abuse by clinical administrators and has been overshadowed by the adoption of the judicial model (*Jarvis v. Levine,* 1988) in Minnesota and elsewhere (Binder & McNiel, 1991).

Two underlying premises for the drug refusal research model seem necessary: First, that many social as well as clinical factors simultaneously impinge on the life course and treatment outcome of those with severe mental disorders. Second, that the settings in which refusal takes place can structure the possible outcomes. With these assumptions in mind, do the research data, narrowly framed, tend to oversimplify and obfuscate the right to refuse treatment? Perhaps, the research findings require a wider context for more vigorous debate. Without such a context the data may inadvertently stall the search for alternatives and improvements in our methods for assuring pharmacologic due process. To explore this hypothesis, recent data will be presented and a therapeutic jurisprudence analysis (Wexler & Winick, 1992) of the judicial model for resolving treatment refusal will be attempted.

The role of law in defining the appropriateness of treatment is viewed by some as completely inappropriate. Notwithstanding this extreme position, one may legitimately ask about the effects of the law's incursion into what was previously largely the realm of clinicians. Therapeutic jurisprudence is a concept intended to meet this need. Wexler and Winick (Wexler & Winick, 1991) defined the concept as the extent to which substantive rules, legal procedures, and the roles of lawyers and judges produce therapeutic or anti-therapeutic consequences. In their view, the task of therapeutic jurisprudence is "to identify—and ultimately to examine empirically—relationships between legal arrangements and therapeutic outcomes." The empirical approach of the researcher is fundamental to their aim of looking at the law as a therapeutic agent. Their goals mandate a multidisciplinary endeavor and, while they emphasize therapeutically-relevant psychology, both clinical sciences and other social sciences are clearly important. This approach points to the need for a dialogue that respects the organizing principles, training, and technical language of many disciplines. Going beyond the research and academic agenda, however, therapeutic jurisprudence seeks to tease apart the practical consequences of legal rules, procedures and roles in terms of their therapeutic efficacy or neutrality. Ultimately, this approach may provide a much needed, broader context for a review of the right to refuse treatment.

This paper will use the therapeutic jurisprudence framework to analyze the legal and administrative aspects of court review procedures from the initial phase of a 1 year prospective study of drug refusal. Characteristics of the review process, and selected clinical factors of court-referred refusing patients are examined in an effort to apply a therapeutic jurisprudence analysis.

Method

Setting

The court review program initiated by the New York State Office of Mental Health was begun in July 1986 shortly after the New York Court of Appeals upheld the right to refuse treatment (*Rivers v. Katz*, 1986). A description of the details of the procedure has been reported previously (Zito, Haimowitz, Wanderling, & Mehta, 1989). For the present study, three psychiatric facilities located in an urban, suburban or mixed suburban/rural area of New York were selected for a prospective, clinical evaluation of the impact of drug refusal and *Rivers'* proceedings on the course of treatment and outcome. The patient population is a mix of acute and chronic patients and, in recent years, there have been steep reductions in the bed capacity of these facilities. Increasingly, the patient census of these facilities on any given day represents two distinct subgroups, one consisting of rapid turnover beds for acute short stay patients (median length of stay of 58 days) and a larger pool of severely dysfunctional patients who fail to be managed in the community, and have hospital stays ranging from 1 year to more than a decade (Unpublished report, Rockland Psychiatric Center, June 30, 1992).

Design

The study was designed to evaluate the medication experience of refusers who are referred by the treating psychiatrist for court review of their refusal of psychotropic drug treatment. After approval by the Institutional Review Board, a one year study consisting of multiple patient interviews and a review of records was launched in April 1990.

Study Sample

The study sample consisted of 61 patients who met entry criteria of having an application submitted to the court for review of treatment over objection and gave written consent to participate in the research project. The sample represented 63% of a total of 97 eligible court-referred patients identified at the three study sites over a 14-month period. The 36 eligible patients who did not participate were either non-consenters to the research protocol ($N = 23$) or had incomplete information due to administrative errors ($N = 13$). The study patients were referred for a court hearing to override their treatment refusal, presumably by reason of lack of competence, and do not include patients who refused treatment but were not referred to court. Characteristics of those eligible patients completing the study differed from the non-participants only regarding gender, with more women in the non-participant group (67% versus 41%, $\chi^2 = 4.52$, $df = 1$, $p < .03$) for a 12 month cohort ($N = 87$). There were no significant differences between the groups in mean age, median time to refusal (i.e., from admission to refusal), DSM-IIIR Axis I diagnosis made by the treating psychiatrist at the time of application (68% of non-participants and 73% of completers had a diagnosis of schizophrenia) or proportion of applications withdrawn before court review (11.1% for non-participants versus

19.6% for completers). There was a trend regarding the time to resolution of the refusal application in that the time from application to the court decision or withdrawal was slightly longer for non-participants (median = 17.5 versus 14 days, 2 sample Median Test, Z = 1.75, p < .08). Among 61 study patients, 29 psychiatrists were responsible for the applications for treatment over objection. Fifty-eight court review applications, 49 final orders made by the reviewing judge, 29 psychiatrist interviews, and 61 patient interviews were available for the present report.

Procedures

A trained interviewer blind to the hypotheses of the study interviewed each refusing patient on two occasions: (1) shortly after the application for court review was filed, and (2) after the application was acted upon. In addition, the interviewer returned to the hospital to interview the patients' treating psychiatrists at the latter point.

Several patient characteristics are likely to influence one's expectations about the role of court adjudication for determining a patient's right to refuse treatment. These factors include age, gender, Axis I of the DSM-IIIR diagnosis according to the treating psychiatrist at the time of refusal, legal status at refusal, and time to refusal, i.e., the length of time in the hospital before refusal occurred. Review procedure characteristics for the 61 refusing patients are presented in terms of legal outcome, time to resolution, (from application date to court decision date), time to withdrawal (from application to withdrawal from the court calendar), and the nature of the medication requests. In addition, the attitudes of the 29 treating psychiatrists who participated in court review proceedings are presented. Finally, a number of descriptive aspects of refusal were derived from patient interviews. Following previous approaches (Hoge *et al.*, 1990; McEvoy, Aland, Wilson, Guy, & Hawkins, 1981), we assessed patients' attitudes about mental illness by a series of questions regarding the presence of symptoms of mental illness, appropriateness of their hospitalization, the role of medication during treatment and the reasons for refusal and satisfaction with the court review. Descriptive statistics consisted of chi-square for noncontinuous variables, *t*-tests for normally distributed continuous variables, and median tests for continuous variables with skewed distributions.

Results

Patient Characteristics

The study cohort ranged in age from 23 to 59 with a mean age of 40 ± 8.3 years. The majority were male (61%, N = 37) and the DSM-IIIR Axis I diagnosis was schizophrenia in 75% (N = 46) of the cohort. Bipolar disorder was applied to 12% (N = 7) and other diagnoses (e.g., atypical psychosis and depression) applied to the remaining cases. The time to refusal (from admission to the application for court review) varied from a low of 14 days to a high of 5969 days for a case subsequently dropped from later analyses; however, the median time to refusal was 55 days. At admission, 20% (N = 12) had an admission associated with a crime but half of these were converted to civil or pending status at the time of refusal.

Review Procedure Characteristics

Legal outcome

Among the 61 study cases, 20% of the court applications ($N = 12$) were withdrawn before a court review could take place. The most frequent reason, cited in 10 cases, was that the patient had agreed to take the medicine, including one patient who also negotiated a transfer from the state facility to a Veterans Administration Hospital. The other two cases presented different issues. In one, the patient left the hospital AMA before the court date occurred. In the other case, the application was withdrawn from court review because the patient agreed to a trial of clozapine, the newly marketed antipsychotic for treatment-resistant schizophrenia. The average time from initiation to withdrawal of the application was (22.9 ± 17.7 days) for these 12 patients, with a range of 5–57 days. Among the 49 study cases reviewed by the court, the treating psychiatrists' request for medication over objection was approved in 90% ($N = 44$) of the cases and denied in five cases.

Resolution Time

For the 49 study cases reaching court review, the average time from the filing of the application to the date of court review was 18.1 ± 15.7 days (range of 5–88 days). The court review occurred within three weeks in 75% of cases. The two longest delays occurred in cases with an independent consultant psychiatrist.

Medications Requested

The most striking similarity in the medications requested by the treating psychiatrists concerned the type of antipsychotic requested. In nearly all cases (47/49) the request was for a long-acting antipsychotic agent in the form of the decanoate ester injection of fluphenazine or haloperidol. Most requests involved dosages within the recommended state guidelines (Zito, 1990). While 6 requests exceeded the guidelines, there was only one instance in which the final order of the court was changed to reflect the guidelines' recommended maximum dose. Overall, the requests were similar and showed little individualization. Only two requests specified medications that had been successful for the individual in the past. In one instance, the judge augmented the request with a directive for a neurological examination.

Psychiatrists' Satisfaction

Court decisions were reported by the treating psychiatrist as satisfactory for those cases with decisions upholding the request (44/49). Dissatisfaction due to the denied applications was expressed variously. Of these five cases, one physician was perplexed and did not understand the reason the court denied the application, while two decisions were disputed by the respondents as showing the judge's naivete. In the latter two situations the judges did not perceive the patients as paranoid and symptomatic as reported by the psychiatrists. The other two denials were acknowledged by the treating psychiatrists as reasonable differences of opinion. Ironically, one of the latter was brought to court because the hospital administration feared future litigation if the case of the patient who was terminally ill with HIV-related illness was later subjected to review for failure to render treatment. The respondents also reported changes in the medication orders in three of these five cases: one of the decisions denied the request for an antipsychotic but allowed brief treatment with a benzodiazepine pending approval of this medication by the patient's mother. Although this case reflects a role for family in the court review, this was the lone exception of this kind, a point that was later raised by one of the interviewed psychiatrists who lamented the general absence of a role for families in these proceedings.

In the majority of court reviewed applications (61%, N = 30) the psychiatrist did not find court review helpful to their resolution of the patient's refusal. The chief reason expressed (N = 7) was the delay in accomplishing the review for which they faulted both the internal hospital procedure and the external court procedure. Only two respondent psychiatrists expressed a positive view: one respondent thought the experience of a court review was useful as a one time experience for heuristic purposes. The other respondent felt that the time off medication was an opportunity to more clearly demonstrate the patient's degree of disorganization and need for treatment. In 88% of the upheld decisions the respondents believed that the judge approved the applications based on the information given by the respondent.

Psychiatrists' Ranking of Administrative Procedures

Five options for handling drug treatment refusal were ranked by 28 of the 29 responding psychiatrists as follows:

(1) In-hospital clinical review by a group of professionals (e.g., psychiatrist, medical doctor, clinical psychologist, quality assurance nurse, clinical pharmacist, mental health lawyer, and patient advocate): 61% (N = 17) rated this as their first choice.
(2) Independent consultant psychiatrist from outside the state system: 21% (N = 6) rated this as their first choice.
(3) Pre-*Rivers* era New York state regional review program involving a clinical review by a designated state psychiatrist for each of five geographic regions: 10% (N = 3) ranked this option first.
(4) Court adjudication mandated by *Rivers* decision: only one rated this as first choice while 55% (N = 16) of the respondents selected this as their fourth or fifth choice.
(5) No review process was the least preferred: 93% (N = 26) listed it as the last choice.

Patients' Attitudes Toward Mental Illness at the Time of Refusal

To better appreciate the refusing patient's understanding of the circumstances surrounding the use of medication, patients were asked *at the time of refusal* whether they agreed or disagreed with statements about their suffering from mental illness and their need for treatment both at the time they were admitted and at the time of the interview. In some cases (N = 8), their answers indicated that they did not understand the question. Thirty percent (N = 18) of the respondents agreed that they had mental symptoms at the time of admission to the hospital while 66% disagreed. The need for a place to reside was given as the reason for the hospitalization by three respondents. At the time of the interview, 28% (N = 17) agreed that mental symptoms were present currently while the remainder disagreed; the proportion who agreed that continued hospitalization was still necessary was 12% (N = 7). A future recurrence of mental symptoms was reported as possible by 20% (N = 12), and denied by 71% (N = 43) while five commented that their future mental health would depend on their living arrangements. Thirty-nine percent (N = 24) agreed that they might need a psychiatrist or mental health clinic after discharge with three citing the need for medication as the purpose of the contact. Among those denying the need for follow-up care (51%, N = 31), two reported that previous clinic use was ineffective. An attitude of hopelessness regarding discharge was expressed by several of the remaining respondents. There were 20% (N = 12) who agreed that medication had been necessary at admission and 21% (N = 13) agreed to the need for it at the time of refusal—with one assenting because it was viewed as necessary for discharge, while the remainder disagreed. Few agreed to the future need for medication (16%, N = 10), the majority denied it (71%, N = 43) while the remainder gave indirect comments such as lack of belief that discharge would occur or the hope that a therapist alone would be sufficient.

Patients' Reasons for Refusal

Multiple reasons for refusal were given. Side effects of medication was the most frequently reported reason (72%, N = 44) while the belief that medication was not needed at the time of refusal was next (44%, N = 27). The third most common reason concerned the ineffectiveness of the medication for their symptoms (34%, N = 21). Other reasons were recorded 11 times, including religious beliefs (unsubstantiated by further inquiry), interference with the spiritual life, fear of heart problems, weakening of the immune system, fear of experimentation, and the assertion by one individual that he was an alcoholic and, therefore, not in need of treatment for mental illness, while a clear paranoid basis for refusal was expressed by one respondent.

Patients' Satisfaction with the Review Process

When asked about the effect of the refusal process on their hospital experience, of 53 respondents, 51% felt better about themselves, but at the same time 53% thought the staff treated them worse than if they had accepted medication. Only one respondent stated that the relationship with the psychiatrist was better than before they refused medication while 42% said it was worse. Overall, dissatisfaction with the court decision was expressed by 65% (N = 28) of the 43 court-reviewed respondents. Poor representation in court was cited by one patient, and, in at least one instance, the patient unequivocally denied that a court review had taken place.

Discussion

Before undertaking a discussion of the possible therapeutic or anti-therapeutic influence of court adjudication that can be inferred from the study findings, several issues of validity deserve comment. Although our initial entry rate was 72% of eligible patients, losses during the study resulted in a final inclusion of 63%. This rate is acceptable given the extreme lability and distrust among refusers who are referred for court adjudication. Regarding potential consent and non-participation bias as an influence on the responses obtained, those who participated differed from non-participants only by gender among those characteristics examined. However, the possibility that systematic differences existed between these groups is an open question which is common to all studies requiring written informed consent (Edlund, Craig, & Richardson, 1985). The observed gender difference in study participants may have been due to the lower responsiveness of women to a woman interviewer but this is speculative. The sociodemographic and clinical profile of these refusers, like that of previously reported court adjudication refusers, suggests that they are typical, chronically psychotic patients of a public system. Interview information was incomplete in approximately 13% of the respondents, thought to be due to impatience or lack of interest or understanding by the patient. Interview data on attitudes of patients regarding their need for hospitalization and treatment at the time of admission is subject to recall bias and is a limitation of the interview method. Bearing in mind these limitations, the findings can be assessed in terms of their effect on the course of treatment.

Anti-therapeutic effects may be inferred from broad, structural issues, such as the fact that the court program is inherently adversarial and structured in a way that demands both time and the involvement of the public mental health bureaucracy. Critical to this discussion is whether empirical findings support this position.

The findings offer several indices of anti-therapeutic effects. Since it is widely believed that many more patients are dissatisfied and partially refusing medication than are resolved by court review (Hoge *et al.*, 1990; Zito *et al.*, 1986), the court review procedure may produce a selection bias that leads to the least debatable cases being reviewed (Schouten & Gutheil, 1990) with the outcome virtually assured. Assured outcome was observed in this study (90% approval) and confirms previous findings (Hoge *et al.*, 1990; Levin *et al.*, 1991; Zito, Craig, & Wanderling, 1991). The evaluation data on court review may be interpreted as having an anti-therapeutic effect if the same end were to be accomplished in a shorter time by a less adversarial, and more pharmacologically sophisticated procedure. Previously, we suggested that the multidisciplinary Minnesota Treatment Review Panel which was composed of a range of mental health professionals as well as a lawyer with mental health expertise as an advocate for the patient (Zito, Lentz, Routt, & Olson, 1984) might provide a model for a less adversarial, patient-oriented review. In the present study, the amount of time needed to resolve applications (mean = 18 days) is symbolic of the polarized nature of the assessment of judicial review processes. Viewed from the perspective of the bureaucracy (both mental health and legal), this is seen as a remarkably efficient process. However, to the patient awaiting a decision and being forced to be kept in a clinical holding pattern, it can be seen as an inordinately long and perhaps abusive process, especially if the patient's welfare is in jeopardy during this interval prior to treatment. The final orders of the court did not show significant changes in the requested treatment orders, did not review past medication experience in a meaningful way, and did not request specific therapeutic monitoring nor challenge the treating psychiatrist's recommendations. Requests for decanoate medications offered the assurance of guaranteed compliance with fewer times of administration, without necessarily engaging the patient in any long-term motivation to accept medication. Similar to previous findings on competency (McKinnon *et al.*, 1992), the present court applications emphasized lack of competency on a general rather than a specific, medication-related basis. The absence of individualization of the final orders points to decisions which did not incorporate the patients' perspective into the review or subsequent treatment program and did not address clinical appropriateness or effectiveness of the proposed treatment. For these reasons, efficiency, in the absence of tailoring final orders to reflect individual patients, suggests an anti-therapeutic outcome. Thus, from an empirical perspective, in contrast to the more ideal perspective of the *Rivers'* opinion, the process may be viewed as anti-therapeutic.

Several themes emerged from the psychiatrists' interviews. The first was pragmatism and was reflected in their general satisfaction with the process because the system has become familiar to the survey respondents and because the resulting decisions usually uphold the request to medicate over objection. Many remarked that a clinical review would accomplish this with less time and bureaucracy although it was not specified how due process would be assured in alternative approaches. The second notion reflected dissatisfaction with the adversarial nature of the proceedings. They complained of time wasted in debate with lawyers, their belief that decisions frequently were based on non-drug factors such as dangerousness, and a loss of the possibility for a therapeutic alliance with the patient. In this regard, a suggestion was made to separate the role of the physician who attends the court hearing from the treating psychiatrist in order to avoid this dilemma. There was one positive opinion of the court review in regard to the doctor-patient relationship. This exception involved a patient given an Axis II diagnosis of borderline personality. The psychiatrist stated that the proceedings relieved the staff of blame for forcing medication and stopped the patient's "splitting", because it was the court that was setting limits on her. The third theme expressed in the interviews focused on the naivete of the court to discern the quality and appropriateness of psychopharmacologic drug therapy for the individual patient being reviewed. It was clear that most psychiatrists have come to accept the notion of a patient's right to refuse drug therapy since so few ranked "no review process" as a preference.

The contrast between psychiatrists' satisfaction and patients' dissatisfaction speaks to the gap created by a procedure that does not take a longitudinal view of the treatment process. To close this gap, the procedure for reviewing the merits of treatment refusal should produce a closed-loop model in which decisions are subject to re-review and the effects of forced medication are reported back so that the patient, treating psychiatrist, and impartial reviewer(s) can appreciate treatment goals and the role of medication in accomplishing these goals.

Patients' attitudes toward symptoms of mental illness, need for hospitalization and pharmacological treatments were overwhelmingly negative and are similar to those from previous reports for individuals with chronic schizophrenia (McEvoy *et al.*, 1981). But the findings should be integrated with their reasons for refusing medication and their past experience with medication to obtain a more complete picture of the reasonableness of refusal. Regarding reasons for refusal, the most frequently reported reason was medication side effects, a finding that calls for greater integration of longitudinal monitoring of symptoms and side effects to find a reasonable drug regimen that patients may better tolerate. The frequency of citing lack of need for medication as a basis for refusal is a more difficult, probably psychotic, basis for refusing and, along with lack of effectiveness, raises questions about the futility of cross-sectional approaches for the review process and states the need for a longitudinal model for reviewing refusal. To foster therapeutic outcome, the review process would need to strengthen opportunities for a psychoeducational approach to assess patients' problems, evaluate alternative dosage schedules, and measure long-term effectiveness and side effects.

Patients' experience with psychotropic side effects revealed large proportions with common side effects, and some patients associated specific antipsychotics with particular effects, e.g., haloperidol and fluphenazine with restlessness and strange thoughts of a psychotic nature. This situation crystallizes a dilemma in understanding patients' problems with medications known as behavioral toxicity (Van Putten & Marder, 1987). It refers to medication-induced adverse effects which cannot be readily distinguished from the behavioral symptoms of the underlying disorder. Thus, if patients attribute their symptoms to the medication, they view their problems as worsened by medication while the clinician perceives the situation as related to the illness and requiring more medication. Such confusion may explain the contrasting views of some patients and their clinicians. While research efforts (Van Putten, Marder, Mintz, & Poland, 1988) have begun to address this issue, the problem remains a challenge to psychopharmacologic research. If a court review process is to serve therapeutic outcomes, decisions should encompass longitudinal monitoring aimed at resolving this dilemma in individuals.

In the context of therapeutic jurisprudence, the present data suggest several conclusions. First, the presence of a judicial process which, in this study, focused virtually exclusively on the issue of competency to refuse treatment, resulted in a *pro forma* exercise in which a determination of incompetency occurred in 90 percent of cases. In addition, the absence of any judicial or independent clinical oversight of the proposed treatment leaves the patient at the mercy of the treatment team's discretion in a situation where the formation of a therapeutic alliance is less likely than before the adversarial application process began.

In the present study, court review led to maximum convenience for the treatment staff by requesting long-acting depot neuroleptics with virtually no individualization based on the clinical circumstances of each case. An additional, potentially anti-therapeutic ramification of this system that is not addressed by the present study is the fate of those patients whose lack of competence to refuse treatment is more questionable and, thus, are not brought to the court application procedure. Are such patients prematurely discharged or deprived of necessary treatment because their clinicians are reluctant to present any but the most disabled patients for court review? In addition, since competence to refuse treatment is directly linked in many patients to their clinical status, what is the effect of this process on the ongoing course of treatment after medication has been administered over objection and the patient's mental status has improved? Clinical outcome is the subject of the next phase of the present study.

In attempting a therapeutic jurisprudence analysis of the judicial model for medication refusal, we found the process to be essentially anti-therapeutic by the legal and administrative measures we examined. Patient advocates and experts in law and psychiatry who are dissatisfied with the existing system should advocate for alternative approaches to the determination of competency to refuse treatment. Ideally, a clinically-oriented selection and monitoring of psychiatric treatments administered over patient objection should be conducted by knowledgeable individuals who can foster negotiated agreements between refusing patients and their treating psychiatrists. When dissatisfaction occurs, the judicial review can be a court of last, rather than first, resort.

References

Appelbaum, P. S. (1988). The right to refuse treatment with antipsychotic medications: Retrospect and prospect. American Journal of Psychiatry, 145, 413–419.

Appelbaum, P. S., & Gutheil, T. G. (1979). "Rotting with their rights on": Constitutional theory and clinical reality in drug refusal by psychiatric patients. Bulletin of the American Academy of Psychiatry and the Law, 7, 306–315.

Appelbaum, P. S., & Gutheil, T. G. (1980). Drug refusal: A study of psychiatric inpatients. American Journal of Psychiatry, 137, 340–346.

Appelbaum, P. S., Lidz, C. W., & Meisel, A. (1987). Informed consent: Legal theory and clinical practice. New York: Oxford University Press.

Binder, R. L., & McNiel, D.E. (1991). Involuntary patients' right to refuse medication: Impact of the *Riese* decision on a California inpatient unit. Bulletin of the American Academy of Psychiatry and the Law, 19, 351–357.

Bloom, J. D., Faulkner, L. R., Holm, V. M., & Rawlinson, R. A. (1984). An empirical view of patients exercising their right to refuse treatment. International Journal of Law and Psychiatry, 7, 315–328.

Edlund, M. J., Craig, T. J., & Richardson, M. A. (1985). Informed consent as a form of volunteer bias. American Journal of Psychiatry, 142, 624–627.

Hoge, S. K., Appelbaum, P. S., Lawlor, T., Beck, J. C., Litman, R., Greer, A., Gutheil, T. G., & Kaplan, E. (1990). A prospective, multicenter study of patients refusal of antipsychotic medication. Archives of General Psychiatry, 47, 949–956.

Jarvis v. Levine, 418 N.W. 2d 139 (Minn. Sup. Ct. 1988).

Levin, S., Brekke, J. S., & Thomas, P. (1991). A controlled comparison of involuntarily hospitalized medication refusers and acceptors. Bulletin of the American Academy of Psychiatry and the Law, 19, 161–171.

Marder, S. R., Mebane, A., Chien, C. P., Winslade, W. J., Swann, E., & Van Putten, T. (1983). A comparison of patients who refuse and consent to neuroleptic treatment. American Journal of Psychiatry, 140, 470–472.

McEvoy, J. P., Aland, J., Jr., Wilson, W. H., Guy, W., & Hawkins, L. (1981). Measuring chronic schizophrenic patients' attitudes toward their illness and treatment. Hospital and Community Psychiatry, 32, 856–858.

McKinnon, K., Cournos, F., & Stanley, B. (1992). *Rivers* in practice: Clinicians' assessments of patients' decision-making capacity. Hospital and Community Psychiatry, 40, 1159–1162.

Rivers v. Katz, 495 N.E. 2d 337, 504 N.Y.S. 2d 74 (Ct. App. 1986).

Schouten, R., & Gutheil, T. G. (1990). Aftermath of the *Rogers* decision: Assessing the costs. American Journal of Psychiatry, 147, 1348–1352.

Van Putten, T., & Marder, S. R. (1987). Behavioral toxicity of antipsychotic drugs. Journal of Clinical Psychiatry, 48 Suppl. 13–19.

Van Putten, T., Marder, S. R., Mintz, J., & Poland, R. E. (1988). Haloperidol plasma levels and clinical response: A therapeutic window relationship. Psychopharmacology Bulletin, 24, 172–175.

Wexler, D. B., & Winick, B. J. (1991). Essays in therapeutic jurisprudence. Durham: Carolina Academic Press.

Wexler, D. B., & Winick, B. J. (1992). Therapeutic jurisprudence and criminal justice mental health issues. Mental and Physical Disability Law Reporter, 16, 225–231.

Zito, J. M. (ed.) (1990). NYS psychotherapeutic drug manual. Albany, NY: New York State Office of Mental Health.

Zito, J. M., Craig, T. J., & Wanderling, J. (1991). New York under the Rivers decision: An epidemiologic study of drug treatment refusal. American Journal of Psychiatry, 148, 904–909.

Zito, J. M., Haimowitz, S., Wanderling, J., & Mehtas, R. M. (1989). One year under Rivers: Drug refusal in a New York State psychiatric facility. International Journal of Law and Psychiatry, 12, 295–306.

Zito, J. M., Hendel, D. D., Mitchell, J. E., & Routt, W. W. (1986). Drug treatment refusal, diagnosis, and length of hospitalization in involuntary psychiatric patients. Behavioral Sciences and the Law, 4, 327–337.

Zito, J. M., Lentz, S. L., Routt, W. W., & Olson, G. W. (1984). The treatment review panel: A solution to treatment refusal? Bulletin of the American Academy of Psychiatry and the Law, 12, 349–358.

Zito, J. M., Routt, W. W., Mitchell, J. E., & Roerig, J. L. (1985). Clinical characteristics of hospitalized psychotic patients who refuse antipsychotic drug therapy. American Journal of Psychiatry, 142, 822–826.

Chapter 49

The Health Effects of Jury Service

Daniel W. Shuman
Jean A. Hamilton
Cynthia E. Daley

I. Introduction

The right to trial by jury is a fundamental and unique characteristic of the American judicial system.[1] The judicial system benefits from the use of juries in at least three ways. First, jury trials may enhance the objective accuracy of the judicial system.[2] Second, jury trials may legitimate the trial process.[3] Third, jury trials may educate jurors and inform their perceptions of the fairness of the judicial system.[4]

Jurors may benefit from jury service through a sense of empowerment by participating in the decisionmaking process.[5] They may also experience a sense of pride and accomplishment which may result from fulfilling a civic duty.[6] The question posed by this Article is: Are the benefits of jury trials reciprocal? Jurors may benefit the trial process, but does the trial process benefit jurors?

Despite the potential benefits of jury service, recent studies and anecdotal reports suggest that jury service may have an adverse effect on juror health.[7] These studies and reports suggest that jurors may experience stress from being removed from their families and jobs, from being shown especially graphic evidence, or from the trial process itself.

---

1. See, e.g., Duncan v. Louisiana, 391 U.S. 145 (1968). "(I)n the American States, as in the federal judicial system, a general grant of jury trial for serious offenses is a fundamental right." Id. at 157–58. The right to trial by jury in criminal cases is guaranteed by the Sixth Amendment. U.S. Const. amend. VI. See also U.S. Const. amend. VII (right to jury trial in civil cases). This study focuses on jury participation in criminal trials rather than in civil trials. While participation in civil trials may affect juror health, the anecdotal reports, discussed below, suggest that criminal trials are more likely to adversely affect juror health than civil trials.

2. Glenn Newman, Note, The Summary Jury Trial as a Method of Dispute Resolution in the Federal Courts, 1990 U. Ill. L. Rev. 177, 182 (1990).

3. Alexis de Tocqueville, Democracy in America 290 (Henry Reeve trans., 1900).

4. Daniel W. Shuman et al., Jury Service—It May Change Your Mind: Perceptions of Fairness of Jurors and Nonjurors, 46 SMU L. Rev. 449, 470 (1992).

5. Id. at 458–60.

6. Id.

7. E.g., Thomas L. Hafemeister & W. Larry Ventis, What Burden Have We Placed on Our Juries?, 3 St. Ct. J., Fall 1992, at 35. Stanley M. Kaplan & Carolyn Winget, The Occupational Hazards of Jury Duty, 20 Bull. Am. Acad. Psychiatry L. 325 (1992).

There are anecdotal reports and limited studies suggesting that jurors may experience psychophysical symptoms and overt illness as a result of jury service.[8] However, these studies report reactions of jurors in highly traumatic trials involving graphic evidence of multiple violent deaths and dismemberment and fail to compare the experiences of jurors serving in other cases.

To discover what negative health effects, if any, arise after serving as a juror in traumatic and nontraumatic criminal trials, 312 individuals who had served on twenty-six Dallas County Criminal District Court juries within the preceding four to six months were sent questionnaires. Half of these jurors were exposed to traumatic criminal trials and half were exposed to nontraumatic criminal trials. This Article examines our hypothesis that jurors experience negative health effects as a result of jury service, such as symptoms of depression or Post-traumatic Stress Disorder (PTSD), and that these negative health effects will differ depending on whether the trial is traumatic or nontraumatic.

II. *Relevant Research*

A. Juror Trauma Research

Numerous anecdotal reports suggest that jury participation may have negative health effects for jurors.[9] A brief review of the anecdotal evidence reveals the need for a more rigorous examination of the relationship between health and jury service to control for other variables. For example, the highly publicized trial of Jeffrey Dahmer provides anecdotal evidence of negative health effects resulting from jury service.[10] Jurors participating in the Dahmer trial were exposed to gruesome evidence of necrophilia and cannibalism. Some of the jurors exposed to this evidence experienced discomfort, mood swings, and sleepless nights. One juror who could stand no more, ran from the courtroom.[11]

Similarly, in the trial of a man who killed his wife by stabbing her in the throat, a juror stated "nothing is done to help with how upset you can feel."[12] The juror also reported that, "even months after the trial she found herself becoming suddenly distrustful and wary among strangers, swept by anxiety" and tears, particularly when she would see something on television that reminded her of the case.[13] One juror who helped sentence Richard Farley to death for the murder of seven coworkers said "she vomited after several court sessions, and experienced nightmares and unexplained crying."[14]

---

8. Id.

9. E.g., Katherine Bishop, When a Jury Hears Details too Gruesome to Bear, N.Y. Times, Jan. 31, 1992, at B7; Richard Holland, Juror's Fears Can Cause Trauma, Newsweek, Jan. 27, 1992, at 45.

10. Kate Rauch, After the Verdict; Healing Jurors who Have Been Traumatized by Violent Testimony, Wash. Post, Apr. 14, 1992, at Z10.

11. Id.

12. Daniel Goleman, For Many Jurors, Trial Begins After the Verdict, N.Y. Times, May 14, 1991, at C1.

13. Id.

14. Bishop, supra note 9, at 87.

Gruesome trials are not the only type of trials having negative effects on jurors. Jurors who served in the trial of John Gotti, a reputed mobster, experienced disturbing dreams and troubling thoughts.[15] The sequestration bothered them as well. The jurors said they asked themselves, "Are our employers going to carry us through this time?" and "Will our families understand why we can't see them for such a long period of time?"[16]

In response to these reports of jurors exhibiting negative health effects from jury service, several studies have examined the relationship between jury service and health.[17] These studies have sought to determine whether the anecdotal reports of negative health effects from jury service are anomalies.

Judge James E. Kelley polled 500 former jurors in Davenport, Iowa, to determine whether they suffered any adverse psychological effects from their service. More than 65% of the respondents indicated stress levels greater than the general population.[18] Although the findings reveal that jurors may feel higher levels of stress due to jury service, the report does not indicate what elements of the trial process induce stress in jurors or whether certain jurors are more susceptible to higher levels of stress from jury service than others.

A study by Stanley M. Kaplan and Carolyn Winget explored the physical and psychological consequences that may result from stressful jury service.[19] They interviewed jurors who had served in one of four criminal trials: a child abuse trial, an obscenity trial, and two murder trials. The degree of stress they experienced varied with the nature of the testimony and evidence presented, the length of sequestration, the difficulty of establishing the defendant's guilt or innocence, the juror's interpersonal relationships, the public's attitude of the trial, and the background of the individual juror.[20] Twenty-seven of the forty jurors questioned reported one or more physical and/or psychological symptoms attributable to jury duty.[21] Seven jurors experienced psychophysiological disturbances that caused them to become ill, and three jurors required medical attention.[22]

Kaplan and Winget found that jurors experienced two different types of symptoms of illness. The first type of symptoms were psychophysiological symptoms such as sleeplessness, anorexia, depression, heart palpitations, faintness, numbness, phobic reactions, and sexual inhibitions. The second type of symptoms were overt illnesses such as peptic ulcers, hives, visual scotomata, and hypertension. Further, four jurors met the DSM-III-R criteria for Posttraumatic Stress Disorder.[23]

Although the Kaplan and Winget study provides useful insight into the relationship between jury service and health, its methodology limits the inferences

---

15. See Holland, supra note 9.

16. Id.

17. Victoria Slind-Flor, Counties Begin to Help Jurors Cope Afterwards; In Grisly Trials, Nat'l L.J., Jan. 20, 1992, at 3; Kaplan & Winget, supra note 7, at 326.

18. Slind-Flor, supra note 17, at 3.

19. Kaplan & Winget, supra note 7, at 325.

20. Id.

21. Id. at 327.

22. Id. at 328–32.

23. See infra note 32 and accompanying text.

one can draw from it.[24] Kaplan and Winget note that the conclusions they revealed were limited because of the absence of certain important structural elements. There was no control group with which to compare the jurors who participated in the study. In addition, it did not account for other independent variables, such as the stress inherent in day-to-day life outside the courtroom.

Another recent study, conducted by the National Center for State Courts (NSCS)), focuses on two trials: the Westley Alan Dodd trial, involving the mutilation, molestation, and murder of three boys, and the Kentucky school bus trial, in which twenty-seven passengers in a church bus were killed by a drunk driver.[25] The researchers report that:

> the jury in these cases may be isolated, exposed to offensive and gruesome details, subjected to close media scrutiny or outside influence and intimidation, involved in a lengthy and complex process they have never experienced before, required to undergo an extensive disruption to their personal lives, and expected to make decisions that will affect other individuals for years to come.[26]

The NSCS researchers conclude that "notorious trials place 'different and magnified strains on the jury.'"[27] As in Kaplan and Winget's research, however, there is no control group to which a base comparison can be made, or an accounting for other independent variables, including jurors' lives outside the courtroom and its influence on the amount of stress jurors experience.

Another study conducted by Roger Bell and Theodore Feldmann reports juror reactions to the Kentucky school bus trial and a Kentucky trial of a teacher charged with decapitating his wife.[28] All of the jurors in the school bus trial report suffering intrusive thoughts of the trial, as well as agitation, restlessness, disturbing dreams, and sleeping problems.[29] Further, the jurors in both trials were shocked and severely agitated by the more graphic evidence and unprepared for the experience of serving on a jury.[30] This study suggests that juror stress may transcend socio-cultural boundaries because the reactions of both juries were similar although the juries were demographically different.[31]

Bell and Feldman also suggest that instructions to jurors not to discuss the case with anyone during the trial may contribute to the jurors' negative reactions to participating in the trials; these instructions prevent the jurors from discussing their feelings about the trial as a means of maintaining emotional

---

24. One social scientist states that it is "futile to argue whether or not a certain design is 'scientific'...(because) (i)t is not a case of scientific or not scientific, but rather one of good or less good design." Edward A. Suchman, General Considerations of Research Design in Delbert C. Miller, Handbook of Research Design and Social Measurement 50 (4th ed. 1983).

25. Hafemeister, supra note 7, at 37.

26. Id. at 39.

27. Id.

28. Theodore B. Feldman & Roger A. Bell, Crisis Debriefing of a Jury After a Murder Trial, 42 Hosp. & Community Psychiatry 79 (1991); Roger A. Bell & Theodore Feldman, Managing Stress in the Jury Box, Newsday, Jan. 22, 1992, at 74.

29. Feldman & Bell, Crisis Debriefing, supra note 28, at 80.1

30. Id.; Bell & Feldman, Managing Stress, supra note 28.

31. Id.

equilibrium. As in Kaplan and Winget's research and the NSCS study, there is no control group for comparison and no way to account for other independent variables, including the stress associated with living in modern society.

This Article builds on the anecdotal reports and studies discussed above as it explores the association between jury service on traumatic trials and adverse health effects, including symptoms of depression and Post-traumatic Stress Disorder.

B. Depression and Anxiety Disorders

Depression can refer to negative mood symptoms, or to clinical syndromes.[32] One type of depression is defined as a Major Depressive Episode:[33] "The essential feature of a Major Depressive episode is either depressed mood or the loss of interest or pleasure in all, or almost all, activities, and associated symptoms, for a period of at least two weeks."[34] Symptoms are not attributable to a Major Depressive Episode if they are the result of an established organic disorder or normal reaction to the death of a loved one, or delusions or hallucinations in the absence of prominent mood symptoms.

The average age of those developing Major Depressive Episode is the late twenties.[35] While its onset varies, the symptoms typically develop over days or weeks. Duration also varies across cases. Untreated, an episode usually lasts six months or longer.

Research suggests a variety of factors which contribute to the likelihood that a given individual will experience a Major Depressive Episode.[36] Stress is a major risk factor in the development of depressive symptoms.[37] In general, depressed patients experience more stressful life events in the six months before they are diagnosed than the general population.[38] A common finding by analysts is that stressors precede an episode of depression.[39] Even "microstressors," or "minor daily unpleasant events" are associated with depression.[40] If jury service on a traumatic trial qualifies as a stressor or a microstressor, jurors who participate in traumatic criminal trials may be at higher risk for depression than the general population.

---

32. Joyce T. Bromberger & Elizabeth J. Costello, Epidemiology of Depression for Clinicians, 37 Soc. Work 120 (1992).

33. American Psychiatric Association, Diagnostic and Statistical Manual of Mental Disorders 218 (3d ed. rev. 1987).

34. Id.

35. Id. at 220.

36. Peter M. Lewinsohn et al., Prospective Study of Risk Factors for Unipolar Depression, 97 J. Abnormal Psych. 251, 252–53 (1988).

37. Paul Robbins et al., Stress, Coping Techniques, and Depressed Affect: Explorations Within a Normal Sample, 70 Psychol. Rep. 147 (1992). The five most important include: sociodemographic characteristics (e.g. females, persons aged 20–40, divorced or separated persons, etc.), stressors, amount and quality of social contacts, level of engagement and enjoyment of pleasant activities, cognitive style, and prior history of depression.

38. George W. Brown et al., Life Events and Illness (1989).

39. Id.

40. Id.

C. Post-Traumatic Stress Disorder

Post-traumatic Stress Disorder (PTSD) is an anxiety disorder identified by "the development of characteristic symptoms following a psychologically distressing event that is outside the range of usual human experience...."[41] Although PTSD was only formally recognized in the American Psychiatric Association Diagnostic and Statistical Manual of Mental Disorders in 1980, the concept has existed under various labels for at least 100 years. For example, after World War I, what we now recognize as PTSD was referred to as "shell shock."[42] Later, it was called "gross stress reaction."[43]

There are two categorical requirements for PTSD.[44] The first is that a stressor occur in the individual's life. A stressor is an event that causes psychological distress due to its unusual and unique nature. The second requirement is that the individual experience symptoms characteristic of PTSD victims for more than a month in duration.[45] If either of these two categorical requirements are missing, the diagnostic criteria are not met.[46]

1. The Requirement of a Stressor.—The stressor necessary to trigger PTSD must be a sudden traumatic stimulus[47] "outside the range of usual human experience,"[48] and which is "markedly distressing to almost anyone."[49] PTSD is more likely to develop from bizarre occurrences than from everyday stres-

---

41. American Psychiatric Ass'n, supra note 33, at 247.

42. B. Kathleen Jordan et al., Lifetime and Current Prevalence of Specific Psychiatric Disorders Among Vietnam Veterans & Controls, 48 Archives Gen. Psychiatry 207, 210 (1991).

43. Herbert C. Modlin, Is There An Assault Syndrome?, 13 Bull. Am. Acad. Psychiatry & L. 139 (1985).

44. American Psychiatric Ass'n, supra note 33, at 247–51.

45. Id.

46. Id. at 247.

47. Anthony Feinstein & Ray Dolan, Predictors of Post-Traumatic Stress Disorder Following Physical Trauma: An Examination of the Stressor Criterion, 21 Pyschol. Med. 85 (1991); Elizabeth A. Brett et al., DSM-III-R Criteria for Posttraumatic Stress Disorder, 145 Am. J. Psychiatry 1232 (1988).

48. American Psychiatric Ass'n Task Force, DSM-IV Options Book H: 16–17 (forthcoming 1991). Three alternatives have been proposed to the stressor requirement for PTSD in the DSM-IV:

> Option A1: The person has experienced, witnessed, or been confronted with an event or events that involve actual or threatened death or injury, or a threat to the physical integrity of oneself or others.
> Option A2: The person has been exposed to a traumatic event in which both of the following have been present:
> (1) the person has experienced, witnesses, or been confronted with an event or events that involve actual or threatened death or injury, or a threat to the physical integrity of oneself or others
> (2) the person's response involved intense fear, helplessness, or horror
> Option A3: Exposure to an exceptional mental or physical stressor, either brief or prolonged.

Id.

The option selected will have a significant impact on the diagnosis of PTSD based upon jury service as a stressor.

49. American Psychiatric Ass'n, supra note 33, at 247.

sors.[50] Case studies consistently illustrate[51] that extreme trauma differs significantly from everyday stressors in such a way that extreme trauma is a strong predictor of PTSD.[52] Everyday stressors, unlike extreme trauma, are stable and repetitive occurrences, because individuals develop a mechanism for coping with them.[53] PTSD occurs in response to specific and particular events,[54] including the possible loss of life, violence, traumatic loss, and witnessing or hearing about death.[55]

For PTSD to result from jury service, jury service must meet the definition of a stressor. Accordingly, one would expect jury service to cause PTSD only if the juror's experience in the courtroom is an extremely traumatic event outside the range of usual human experience.

2. Symptomatology.—Once the requirement of a stressor is satisfied, several characteristic symptoms must exist for a diagnosis of PTSD to be made.[56] The DSM-III-R symptom criteria require (1) re-experiencing the stressor, (2) avoidance of the stressor, and (3) arousal. Re-experiencing the stressor refers to persistently re-experiencing the traumatic event and can involve "intrusive recollections of the event," or "recurrent distressing dreams of the event." Avoidance of the stressor occurs when an individual avoids the "stimuli associated with the trauma" or when there is a "numbing of general responsiveness" not present before the trauma. Finally, the arousal phase may include "difficulty falling or staying asleep," "irritability or outbursts of anger," and "difficulty concentrating." The required number of symptoms in each category must be present to diagnose PTSD. To ascertain the presence of these diagnostic criteria, the questionnaire includes a series of items in which respondents were asked whether they had experienced symptoms characteristic of depression and PTSD.

D. Cognitive/Social Psychology Research

Psychological and sociological research on jurors rarely focuses on the effects of jury service on the jurors themselves. Rather, it concentrates on two areas: the influences on jury verdicts and the dynamics of jury decisionmaking.[57] The research concerning the influences on jury verdicts examines the ex-

---

50. Andrew Baum et al., Stress and the Environment 37 J. Soc. Issues 4 (1981).

51. Jacob D. Lindy et al., Commentary—The Stressor Criterion and Posttraumatic Stress Disorder, 175 J. Nervous & Mental Disease 269 (1987).

52. Brett et al., supra note 47, at 1233.

53. Baum, supra note 50, at 13.

54. Baum, supra note 50, at 14; American Psychiatric Ass'n, supra note 33; Naomi Breslau, Stressors: Continuous and Discontinuous, 20 J. Applied Soc. Psychol. 1666, 1669 (1990).

55. American Psychiatric Ass'n Task Force, supra note 48.

56. American Psychiatric Ass'n, supra note 33, at 250.

57. While there is no single predictor of a jury's verdict, several extralegal factors have been identified that can affect the outcome of a jury's decision. The background characteristics of jurors such as race, sex and age have been associated with certain verdict preferences. See, e.g., Dale W. Broeder, The University of Chicago Jury Project, 38 Neb. L. Rev. 744 (1959); Denis Chimaeze E. Ugwuegbu, Racial and Evidential Factors in Juror Attribution of Legal Responsibility, 15 J. Experimental Soc. Psychol. 133 (1979).

tralegal factors that can affect a jury's decision, but has shed little light on the health effects of jury service. The research on the dynamics of decisionmaking promises greater insight into this question.

Because interaction among jurors may affect the likelihood of an individual juror experiencing adverse health effects, it is important to examine the prominent psychological and sociological theories of group dynamics. The informational influence theory and the normative influence theory are two prominent theories that help explain how group dynamics affect individual judgment.[58] Informational influence refers to the changing of opinion as a result of the exchange of information in a group.[59] Normative influence refers to the changing of an opinion as a result of conforming to the desires of other group members.[60] According to both theories, jurors holding a minority view will generally follow the majority.[61]

Another relevant and important theory is groupthink. Groupthink is a process of "concurrence-seeking that interferes with adequate consideration of decision alternatives, and leads to poor decisions."[62] The antecedent conditions thought to increase the likelihood of groupthink are indigenous to juries. The first antecedent factor is cohesion, "members' positive valuation of the group and their motivation to continue to belong to it."[63] A jury has inherent motivation because it is required to reach a decision. Cohesion increases in groups which have homogeneity in ideology and social background, which are common characteristics of many juries. The second antecedent factor is isola-

---

However, other conclusions have indicated that demographics have only a small effect on a jury's verdict. R.J. Simon, Comments on Jury Selection and Jury Behavior Papers, in Communication Strategies in the Practice of Lawyering 274–77 (Ronald J. Matlon & Richard J. Crawford eds., 1983).

The influence of counsel's behavior on the outcome of trials is currently being examined. One study concludes that jurors' opinions of the prosecuting or defense attorneys, including their style, appearance, manner and dress, affected the way the jurors interpreted the case. Ann B. Pettus, The Verdict is in: A Study of Decisionmaking Factors, Moment of Personal Decision, and Jury Deliberations—From the Jurors' Point of View, 1990 Comm. Q. 83, 93. Others studies have focused on usefulness and effectiveness of covert psychological persuasion techniques used by attorneys. Victor Gold, Covert Advocacy: Reflections on the Use of Psychological Persuasion Techniques in the Courtroom, 65 N.C. L. Rev. 481 (1987).

Judicial behavior may also have an effect on the outcome of a trial. Peter D. Blanck et al., The Appearance of Justice: Judges' Verbal and Nonverbal Behavior in Criminal Jury Trials, 38 Stan. L. Rev. 89 (1985). Jurors place great weight on judges' instructions on the law and suggestion of bias in the case. Id. at 90. In addition, judges' unintentional and subtle nonverbal behavior can sometimes affect trial outcomes. Peter D. Blanck, What Empirical Research Tells Us: Studying Judges' and Juries' Behavior, 40 Am. U. L. Rev. 775 (1991).

58. See Morton Deutch and Harold B. Gerard, A Study of Normative and Informational Social Influences upon Individual Judgment, 51 J. Abnormal & Soc. Psychol. 629 (1955).

59. Id.

60. Id.

61. Id.

62. Clark McCauley, The Nature of Social Influence in Groupthink: Compliance and Internalization, 57 J. Pers. and Soc. Psychol. 250, 251 (1989) (citations omitted).

63. Irving L. Janis, Groupthink: Psychological Studies of Policy Decisions and Fiascoes 4 (2d ed. 1983).

tion and insulation of the decisionmaker.[64] This occurs during jury deliberation since no additional information is communicated to the jurors, and they are not allowed to discuss the case with those outside the jury. Sequestered juries may experience exacerbated versions of these conditions.

A third factor predisposing juries to groupthink is the lack of prescribed procedures for appraisal of alternatives.[65] No formal mechanisms govern jury determinations of witness credibility or evidence. Therefore, individual juror personalities can have a great effect on the outcome.

Finally, high stress combined with little opportunity to find a solution better than the one which the leader favors also contributes to groupthink.[66] Members of the group fail to give careful scrutiny to majority proposals. "When groupthink dominates, suppression of deviant thoughts takes the form of each person's deciding that his misgivings are not relevant, and that the benefit of any doubt should be given to the group's consensus."[67]

Though a jury should seek concurrence, groupthink often leads to premature consensus-seeking, usually involving internalization, ("private acceptance of the group hypothesis") or compliance ("public without private agreement").[68] Compliance and internalization are expected of juries; to reach a unanimous decision, jurors not sharing the same opinion as the majority will either comply or internalize.

Under the theories of informational influence, normative influence, and groupthink, individual and group dynamics affect the decisionmaking process and outcome of a trial. Further, under these theories, members of the jury holding a minority view will often conform to the majority view, thereby allowing the majority view to prevail. While consensus may benefit judicial efficiency, jurors who profess agreement with a verdict, but who harbor private misgivings, may suffer stress from that compliance.[69] Dissonance may influence minority members of the group.[70] The reward for outward agreement is often coupled with internalized misgivings about the outcome of the case. While a juror can return to work and end the time-consuming obligation of jury duty, the feelings resulting from such internalization and dissonance can cause additional stress.

The stress that jurors experience from groupthink may be correlated with negative health effects. According to one theory of inhibition, discussing or confronting a traumatic experience is "psychologically and physically benefi-

---

64. Id. at 242.

65. Id. at 249.

66. Id. at 250–54.

67. Id. at 247.

68. McCauley, supra note 62.

69. Leon Festinger, A Theory Cognitive Dissonance 89 (1957).

70. Dissonance almost always exists after a decision has been made between two or more alternatives (when decisions are influenced) by offering rewards or threatening punishment to elicit behavior that is at variance with private opinion. If the overt behavior is successfully elicited, the person's private opinion is dissonant with his knowledge concerning his behavior. The knowledge that some other person...holds one opinion is dissonant with holding a contrary opinion. Id. at 261.

cial," while suppressing a traumatic experience is associated with physiological work and, over time, stress-related disease.[71]

Jurors may develop increased health problems because of jury duty where they find an experience traumatic and fail to disclose their feelings to others. When a juror engages in self-censorship to conform to group pressure, that juror often experiences stress from compliance.[72] This self-induced inhibition can exacerbate negative health effects, particularly where jurors are sequestered.

E. Rules and Regulations Governing Juries

The Sixth and Seventh Amendments to the United States Constitution address the use of juries in resolving disputes.[73] As noted earlier, juries serve several important functions in our legal system. First, by placing the verdict in the hands of impartial individuals who have no stake in the outcome and who have diverse world views and experiences, the jury system enhances the objective accuracy of trial outcomes.[74] Second, through the inclusion of members of the community who are independent of the formal judicial structure, juries legitimize the judicial process and increase compliance with its decisions.[75] Third, jury trials help serve an educative function for jurors and thereby inform public perceptions of the fairness of the judicial system.[76]

However, if jury service is associated with negative health effects, this may dissuade people from jury service and debilitate the functioning of the judicial system. Given the importance of juries, and the potentially harmful consequences for our judicial system if juror health is jeopardized, the potential effects of judicial rules on juror health cannot be ignored. Thus, two important issues must be addressed: whether the rules governing trials consider the interests of jurors as separate from the litigants and whether the rules that govern trials play a role in producing negative health effects.

The Federal Rules of Evidence, which serve as a model for many state evidence codes, are a logical starting point for determining to what extent, if any, the rules that govern trials consider the interests of jurors as separate from those of the litigants or witnesses. The Federal Rules of Evidence are intended to advance the determination of truth,[77] and, in general, they favor admission of evidence.[78] Despite the bias in favor of admission of relevant evidence under the Federal Rules, there are significant limitations. The rules recognize that relevant evidence may nonetheless have a powerful impact on the jury that may

---

71. James W. Pennebaker & Joan R. Susman, Disclosure of Traumas and Psychosomatic Processes, 26 Soc. Sci. Med. 327 (1988).

72. See McCauley, supra note 62, at 250, 251.

73. U.S. Const. amends. VI & VII.

74. Newman, supra note 2, at 184.

75. See Herbert Jacob, Justice in America: Courts, Lawyers and the Judicial Process 125–36 (3d ed. 1978).

76. Shuman, supra note 4, at 468.

77. Fed. R. Evid. 102.

78. Id.; Fed. R. Evid. (401 advisory committee's notes).

frustrate the search for truth. Rule 403 recognizes that the probative value of relevant evidence may be outweighed by its prejudicial effect.[79] However, the negative consequences that jurors may suffer as a result of perceiving certain evidence is not an explicit consideration of Rule 403.[80]

The absence of juror trauma as an explicit criterion to be considered in Rule 403 raises two issues: Whether Rule 403 or other rules governing the admission of evidence should be read to permit a consideration of juror trauma, and, if not, whether Rule 403 should be amended to make juror trauma a factor.

The factors to be considered under Rule 403 can be divided into two categories: Dangers to the trial process and efficiency considerations. The dangers to the trial process include unfair prejudice, confusion of the issues, and misleading the jury. The efficiency considerations include undue delay, waste of time, and needless presentation of cumulative evidence.[81]

The category consisting of dangers to the trial process addresses the concern that the admission of certain evidence, though relevant, may cause the jury's verdict to be based on improper grounds or may distort the decisionmaking process.[82] Exclusion of evidence for these reasons prevents the jury from reaching a verdict irrationally, which could jeopardize the search for truth.[83]

The first factor listed as a danger under Rule 403 is unfair prejudice. "Unfair prejudice means an undue tendency to suggest decision on an improper basis, commonly though not necessarily an emotional one."[84] Certain evidence may cause a jury to decide against a party because such evidence stirs sympathies, incites horror, or arouses an instinct to punish.[85] Under Rule 403, the court must determine whether, on balance, the quest for truth will be assisted or obstructed by the admission of emotionally charged evidence.[86]

However, evidence may not be excluded simply because it is unpleasant.[87] When gruesome photographs are, because of their nature, excluded from evidence, it is because they will "inflame the minds of the jury or...impair their objectivity."[88] The focus is on the needs of the litigants and not on the needs of the jurors. Of course, if evidence could be excluded solely due to its grisly na-

---

79. Fed. R. Evid. 403. "Although relevant, evidence may be excluded if its probative value is substantially outweighed by the danger of unfair prejudice, confusion of the issues, or misleading the jury, or by consideration of undue delay, waste of time, or needless presentation of cumulative evidence."

80. Id.

81. An argument can be made that by promoting judicial efficiency and preventing the waste of time, jurors, as well as the judicial system, benefits. However, while jurors may benefit from the exclusion of evidence so as to promote judicial efficiency, for example by lessening the amount of time jurors must spend at trial, any such benefit would be only incidental.

82. Fed. R. Evid. 403.

83. Jack B. Weinstein & Margaret A. Berger, Weinstein Evidence: A Commentary on Rules of Evidence for the United States Courts & Magistrates ¶ 403(03), at 403-41.

84. Fed. R. Evid. 403 (advisory committee's note).

85. United States v. Qamar, 671 F.2d 732, 737 (2d Cir. 1982).

86. Weinstein & Berger, supra note 83, at 403(01), 401-13.

87. Id.

88. State v. Chapple, 660 P.2d 1208, 1217 (Ariz. 1983).

ture, then the more gruesome the crime, the harder it would be for plaintiff or prosecutor to prove his case.[89]

The second and third dangers listed in Rule 403, confusion of the issues and misleading the jury, are also not concerned with protecting the jurors' interests, but seek to assure that the jury's decisionmaking process is not distorted by confusing or misleading evidence.[90] The concern underlying these factors is that the admission of evidence, although relevant, may hinder rather than advance the jury's search for the truth. Unfortunately, the sensibilities of jurors are not addressed by either of these factors.

Although the Federal Rules of Evidence are generally concerned with protecting the rights of the litigants, at least one Federal Rule of Evidence seeks to protect the interests of witnesses.[91] Rule 611(a) provides that:

> The court shall exercise reasonable control over the mode and order of interrogating witnesses and presenting evidence so as to (1) make the interrogation and presentation effective for the ascertainment of the truth, (2) avoid needless consumption of time, and (3) protect witnesses from harassment or undue embarrassment.[92]

The concern of 611(a)(3) is to protect witnesses from "interrogation tactics (which) entail harassment or undue embarrassment."[93] The protection of 611(a)(3) is intended to protect the vulnerable witness from questions merely meant to harass, humiliate, or annoy.[94] On its face, Rule 611(a)(3) appears concerned with the emotional well-being of the witness. After all, a witness, who is present to assist the judicial system and whose participation is encouraged, should not be subject to potentially devastating abuse. Similarly, a juror, who is present to assist the judicial system and whose participation is also encouraged, should be protected from the potentially negative health effects of the trial process.

Although under the Federal Rules of Evidence the interest in juror health is not a factor considered when determining the admissibility of evidence, there are rules and regulations that do seek to protect jurors. For instance, one stage of the trial process where rights of jurors are sometimes statutorily protected is jury selection.[95] The desirability of avoiding embarrassment to jurors during the voir dire process has been recognized under Massachusetts law.[96] "When the question of a juror's embarrassment is involved under this section it is suggested that the judge question the prospective juror in the absence of the jury

---

89. Weinstein & Berger, supra note 83, at 403(03), 403-44; Papp v. Jago, 656 F.2d 221 (6th Cir. 1981), cert. denied, 454 U.S. 1035 (1981). In *Papp,* a rape case, color autopsy photos of the dissected intimate parts of a young girl's anatomy were allowed in evidence. Although the court stated that the prosecution should be wary of offering such evidence due to its prejudicial nature, they allowed the photos due to their strong probative value.

90. Fed. R. Evid. 403; Weinstein & Berger, supra note 83, at 403(04), 403-50.

91. Fed. R. Evid. 611.

92. Fed. R. Evid. 611(a).

93. Fed. R. Evid. 611(a)(3) (advisory committee note).

94. Fed. R. Evid. 611(a)(3) (advisory committee note citing Alford v. United States, 282 U.S. 687 (1931)).

95. E.g., Mass. Gen. Laws Ann. § 234-1 (1989).

96. See Commonwealth v. Martin, 257 N.E.2d 444, 446 (Mass. 1970).

and make a statement of the findings or other basis for his (or her) decision to excuse or not to excuse the prospective juror."[97]

The American Bar Association Model Rules of Professional Conduct provide another source of juror protection:

> In representing a client, a lawyer shall not use means that have no substantial purpose other than to embarrass, delay, or burden a third person, or use methods of obtaining evidence that violate the legal rights of such a person.[98]

However, there is no prohibition against using means that are embarrassing, delaying, or burdensome to a third person, presumably including a juror, as long as this is not the "substantial purpose" of employing the particular means. Thus, the protection afforded jurors from negative consequences of jury service is at best minimal. In addition, these rights are apparently secondary in importance to numerous other factors.

The American Bar Association Model Code of Professional Responsibility does recognize a juror's right to be free from harassing or embarrassing questions following a jury trial.[99] Under DR 7-108, "(a)fter discharge of the jury from further consideration of a case with which the lawyer was connected, the lawyer shall not ask questions or make comments to a member of that jury that are calculated merely to harass or embarrass the juror or to influence his (or her) actions in future jury service."[100] Individual states, in their Codes of Professional Responsibility, have recognized jurors' rights to freedom from harassment or embarrassment following jury trials.[101] This protection is intended to apply, however, only after jury service is complete. The rules afford no protection to jurors from any negative consequences of the trial process itself.

While the rules do not completely overlook the interests of jurors, juror health is not a prominent concern in our judicial system.[102] As a result, the question remains: is juror trauma an appropriate factor to be considered by the rules which govern the judicial system? The answer to this question depends, in the first instance, on whether juror health is adversely affected by jury service.

III. Methodology

The Article documents the results of our study which was designed to assess the health effects on jurors of service on criminal juries. Questionnaires were

---

97. Commonwealth v. Morgan, 339 N.E.2d 723 (Mass. 1974), cert. denied, 427 U.S. 905 (1976).

98. Model Rules of Professional Conduct Rule 4.4 (1983).

99. Model Code of Professional Responsibility DR 7-108 (1981).

100. Id.

101. E.g., New York Code of Professional Responsibility DR 7-108(D) (1990).
    After discharge of the jury from further consideration of a case with which the lawyer was connected, the lawyer shall not ask questions of or make comments to a member of that jury that are calculated merely to harass or embarrass the juror or to influence the juror's actions in future jury service.

102. See State v. Moore, 100 P. 629, 630 (Kan. 1909).

Table 1. Comparison of the demographic characteristics of the sample from Dallas State Court Survey† and the present study
(results in percentages which were rounded.

		Dallas State Courts	Entire Sample
Sex	Male	53	47
	Female	47	53
Age	18–39	43	43
	40–71	57	57
Marital Status	Married	70	74
	Never Married/Cohabitating	14	16
	Divorced	11	9
	Separated	3	1
	Widowed	2	1
Race	Caucasian	77	83
	African American	19	10
	Hispanic	•	5
	Native American	•	1
	Asian/Pacific Islander	•	0
	Other	4	1
Education*	Less than 4 years of High School	5	1
	4 years of High School	24	12
	1–3 years of College	27	34
	4 years of College or more	44	53
Family Income*	under $49,999	57	44
	over $50,000	43	56
Job Status	Employed Full-time	77	75
	Employed Part-time	4	8
	Self-Employed	8	10
	Homemaker	4	6
	Retired	4	1
	Student	1	0
	Other/seeking Employment	2	0
Occupation*	Managerial	19	24
	Professional	21	28
	Technical/Sales	22	26
	Service	5	14
	Agriculture	1	0
	Mechanic/Craftsman	5	5
	Labor/Transportation	5	3
	Other	22	0

† Dallas State Court Survey conducted by the National Center for State Courts in The Relationship of Juror Fees and Terms of Service to Jury Service Performance, March 1991, Appendix C.
* = Chi-square sifniŀcant for frequency differences between the two groups; see the text.
• (dot) = percentage is less than 1%

sent in September of 1992 to 312 individuals who served on 26 criminal juries, hearing either traumatic or non-traumatic cases, five to six months earlier.

This preliminary division into traumatic and nontraumatic cases was made to insure participation in the study by jurors who served on trials with a broad spectrum of offenses.[103] The cases identified as traumatic involved charges of

---

103. The basis for categorizing a case as traumatic as opposed to nontraumatic included: the nature of the offense and the types of evidence that was likely to be introduced during

murder, aggravated kidnapping, aggravated sexual assault, aggravated assault, and child abuse. The cases identified as nontraumatic involved charges of burglary, robbery, delivery of a controlled substance, credit card abuse, possession of a controlled substance, and unauthorized use of a motor vehicle. The final sample of 152 respondents consisted of 79 jurors who served on traumatic juries and 73 jurors who served on nontraumatic juries. After a 37 day interval, the overall response rate was 49%, which is generally acceptable for this type of survey study.[104]

The trauma and nontrauma groups in the sample were demographically similar with the exception of age, as assessed by the chi-square statistic for frequency data.[105] To determine if the respondents were representative of typical Dallas jurors, the data was collapsed and the entire sample compared to a previous survey of Dallas jurors.[106]

The National Center for State Courts[107] conducted research addressing an unrelated issue but summarized demographic characteristics of Dallas juries (N=891).[108] The present study sample appears to be somewhat representative of jurors in Dallas State District Courts. The two samples are similar for sex (chi-square approximation=1.4, degrees of freedom, d.f.=1, criteria at p>.05, i.e., samples are not significantly different), age (chi-square=0, d.f.=1, p>. 05), marital status (chi-square=2.5, d.f.=4, p>.05), and occupation (chi-square=10.8, d.f.=6, p>.05), as assessed by frequency analysis.

However, the samples differ on several other demographic variables: race, education, family income, and occupation. In particular, this sample included a significantly greater proportion of Caucasians (chi-square=7, d.f.=2, p<.05), a greater proportion of jurors with more education (chi-square=12.9, d.f.=3, p<.01), a greater proportion of jurors with higher incomes (chi-square=6.9, d.f.=1, p<.025), and a greater proportion of jurors in management and professional occupations (chi-square=44.4, d.f.=7, p<.001).

---

the course of the trial. Offenses against the person were categorized as traumatic while offenses against property were categorized as nontraumatic. Cases which would probably involve the introduction of graphic evidence were categorized as traumatic.

104. See Thomas A. Heberlein & Robert Bauragartner, Factors Affecting Response Rate to Mailed Questionnaires, 43 Amer. Soc. Rev. 451 (1978) (response rates from 183 social science studies, using mailed questionnaires, averaged 48%).

105. Lyman Ott, An Introduction To Statistical Methods and Data Analysis 218–221 (1982). Hypotheses were tested using a chi-square goodness-of-fit procedure to determine if the demographic characteristics' cell probabilities were equal for the trauma and non-trauma groups. Cell probabilities were calculated. If the cell probabilities for a demographic characteristic appear to be the same, it may be assumed that the present sample is representative.

106. See Table 7.

107. This survey of the Dallas State Courts was reported in The Relationship of Juror Fees and Terms of Service to Jury System Performance, Mar. 1991, Appendix C. Demographics of respondents are reported as percentages; however, these do not sum to 100% due to procedures used for rounding data. As approximations, percentages reported in Table 1 have been adjusted to total 100%. Also, the study did not separately assess Hispanic origin, so that race/ethnicity comparisons to other samples are problematic. It is likely, for example, that some individuals who would be classified as Hispanic in other surveys are here classified as Caucasians.

108. See Table 1.

The representativeness of this sample has been examined further by assessing possible response biases to the questionnaires. The demographics of those who received questionnaires were compared to the demographics of those returning them to determine whether the populations varied in any systematic way. Since information on individuals summoned for jury duty does not—by law—include race,[109] the questionnaire asked each respondent to recall the racial composition of his or her jury. The responses were then averaged by jury to obtain an accurate racial composition for each jury. This average was then compared to the frequency count of the races reported by the responding jurors. The results indicate that African Americans had a substantially lower response rate (28%) than Caucasians (53%), Hispanics (40%), and Native Americans (67%). These results appear to illustrate a response bias.

Of the 152 returned surveys, 47% of the respondents were male and 53% percent female. They ranged in age from 23–74, with both a median and mean age of 43.[110] Almost 75% of the group were married, 15% were single or cohabitating, 9% were divorced, and less than 10% were separated or widowed.[111]

An overwhelming 83% of the respondents were Caucasian. The rest were African American (10%), Hispanic (5%), and Native American (1%). Most of the respondents were well-educated; the majority had four years of college or more.

More than half of the jurors surveyed had a family income of over $50,000 (56%). Seventy-five percent of them were employed full time, 8% part-time, and only 1% retired. The remainder were either self-employed (10%), or worked in the home (6%).

The types of careers that predominated the survey were professional (i.e. teachers, doctors) (28%). These were closely followed by those in technical/sales positions (26%) and those in managerial positions (24%). While no jurors were employed in agriculture, 14% were employed in the service industry, 5% in the mechanics/craftsmen industry, and 3% in the labor/transportation industry.

Although the data collected concerning religion and political preference was not conducive to analysis, it is interesting that more than half of the sample group was Protestant (63%), with the next two largest groups being Catholic (14%) or "Other" (13%). The remaining categories for religious preference included Buddhist (1%), Hindu (1%), Muslim (1%), and "None" (7%). The political preferences of the jurors ranged from 46% Republican to 28% Democrat, with 24% Independent and 2% Other.

The survey questionnaire was specifically designed for this project.[112] Readability and clarity pretesting was conducted on a nonrandom group of 22 subjects, none of whom were included in the final sample of respondents. The questionnaire consisted of several sections: the first gathered demographic in-

---

109. See 28 U.S.C. § 1861 (1993).

110. Although the median age was 43, a median age of 40 was used for the analysis in order to compare it to the Dallas State Courts Survey.

111. See Table 1.

112. Questionnaire on file with Law and Psychology Review.

formation, while the other sections solicited responses about jurors' overall health, as well as potential stress and trauma experienced before, during, and after the trial.

The first twelve questions addressed demographics. They pertained to the respondent's gender, age, marital status, family size, race, religious preference, political preference, educational level, household income, occupation, and job status. The next set of questions asked specifically about the type of trial in which the juror served, the duration of the trial (including possible sequestration), the amount of publicity the trial received, and the verdict rendered.

Specific questions measured the types of witness testimony and exhibits the parties presented. These questions were used to determine whether such evidence was disturbing or offensive, or important to the juror's decision of innocence or guilt. The next six questions inquired about the makeup of the jury (number of males and females on the jury and racial distribution) and how jury members related to each other. A Likert scale was used to measure the resulting degree of stress and intimidation associated with juror relations.[113] Then each juror was asked at which point in the trial he or she reached a decision.

The next set of questions dealt with specific symptoms jurors might have experienced during the trial proceedings, during the jury deliberations, and after the trial's conclusion. The list of symptoms included those necessary to determine if the diagnostic criteria was met for Major Depression and Post-traumatic Stress Disorder from DSM III-R.[114] Other symptoms were selected based on those reported in the current literature associated with the topic.

The next questions were designed to measure jurors' feelings toward the defendant and the victim (i.e., whether they identified with either the defendant or the victim). Jurors were also asked about their experience during the trial, such as whether they shared personal information with other jurors, and whether the degree of trauma they actually experienced exceeded their expected degree of trauma.

In addition, seven health-related measures were included: medication taken before, during, and after the trial; self-reported health; and the number of doctors visits before, during, and after trial. Jurors were also asked to respond to a list of possible life changes prior to and following the trial (e.g., divorce, loss of job, death in family), and questions about their typical reaction to stressful situations.

Additionally, factors not related to the trial that contributed to any prior stress or trauma were included in the survey. These questions included participation in military combat, criminal victimization, and prior counseling. Finally, the jurors were questioned regarding their overall jury experience, such as whether they enjoyed service and would willingly serve again.

---

113. Rensis Likert, A Technique for the Measurement of Attitudes 140 Arch. Psychol. 11 (1932). Five point scales were studied as possible ways of measuring attitudes and opinions in large samples of subjects. It was found that use of this methodology was more simple, less biased, and required fewer items to yield comparable reliability.

114. American Psychiatric Ass'n, supra note 33, at 247.

Table 2.   Trauma and Stress Factors

Trauma-related Factors	Mean	Standard Deviation
Objective Factors Related to Trial		
Crime Category; Charts, Photos	3.85	2.08
Defendant Testimony; Sound/Video	1.84	1.24
Subjective Factors Related to Trial		
Rating Evidence Offensiveness	1.23	0.42
Self-reported Trauma Rating	2.68	1.65
Other Factors Not Related to Trial		
Crime Victim; Military Combat	2.77	0.67
Stress-Related Factors		
Objective Factors Related to Trial		
Deliberation Length; Period of Sequestration	2.47	0.87
Trial Publicity; Served as Jury Foreperson	3.87	0.36
Subjective Factors Related to Trial		
Rating Stress in Trial; Stress and Intimidation in Deliberations	9.28	4.10
Self-reported Participaton and Confrontation in Deliberations	12.41	2.05
Other Factors Not Related to Trial		
Life Events Before Trial	0.66	0.91
Life Events After Trial	0.55	0.75

IV. Survey Results and Discussion

From the questionnaires, six trauma-related factors were identified for analysis. The first factor was the degree of trauma associated with each type of case. Jurors were arbitrarily identified as receiving high or low trial-related trauma exposure, based on our impression of trauma likelihood for the alleged crime (e.g., homicide is high and credit card abuse is low). The next two factors involved the types of evidence presented at trial. The authors identified two factor-analytically derived measures[115] related to the objective characteristics of the evidence presented at trial, one consisting of a rating of the crime along with characteristics of photographs or charts used (e.g., color, enlargement, or containing graphic material); and the other consisting of whether the defendant testified and whether other media was used (e.g., sound or video). The remaining factors consisted of a subjective rating by the juror of offensiveness of the evidence presented at trial; a subjective rating by the juror of trauma related to the trial; and a rating of exposure to trauma not related to the trial (e.g., military combat or victim of a crime).[116]

---

115. Anne Anastasi, Psychological Testing, 154–55, 374–90 (1982). Factor analysis is a statistical procedure that reduces the number of variables being examined. It is accomplished by first computing the intercorrelations for a set of data. Then mathematical techniques are used which generate several higher-order factors. These new factors account for clusters of variance in the data set. It is the psychometrician's job to name these new clustered variables according to their respective domains.

116. See Table 2.

Table 3.   Health Outcome Measures
(Percentage Meeting Diagnostic Criteria)

Symptoms	Baseline	Trial	Deliberations	After	Population Base-rate
>= 5 Depressive	—	7.3	4.0	0.7	4–5
Non-Traumatic Trial	—	2.6	1.3	8.0	—
Traumatic Trial	—	12.3	7.0	1.4	—
>= 6 PTSD	—	0.0	0.7	0.0	5–10
Non-Traumatic Trial	—	1.3	1.3	0.0	—
Traumatic Trial	—	0.0	0.0	0.0	—

The authors also identified six stress-related factors. Two of these consisted of factor-analytically derived measures related to objective aspects of the trial. The first consisted of the duration of the deliberations and whether the jury was sequestered; the second consisted of the degree of publicity the trial received and whether the juror served as the foreperson. Two factor-analytically derived measures related to subjective aspects of the trial. Jury deliberations were also identified: One consisted of ratings of stress during the trial and deliberation along with intimidation during deliberations; and the second consisted of the degrees of participation and confrontation during deliberations. The final two stress-related factors were based on measures of life events experienced in the year before and after the trial (although 88% of the respondents were assessed within six months after the trial).[117]

From the demographic information collected, the following factors were selected for use in the regression analyses: gender, age, education, income, and racial or ethnic status. The remaining demographic information was not suitable for the regression analyses.[118]

The questionnaire included a symptom checklist derived from the diagnostic criteria for depression and PTSD. A few of the jurors reported at least some of the symptoms that must be met for the clinical diagnosis of depression or PTSD.[119] However, virtually none of the jurors displayed enough of the particular symptoms needed to meet the diagnosis of PTSD.[120]

A. Main Effects of Trauma and Stress Factors

To identify the trauma and stress factors that have health-related effects, we estimated separate regression models using four different health measures as outcomes. Three of our health outcome models are based on the sum of symptoms reported by the jurors during the trial, during deliberations, and after the trial. The other health outcome model is based on the change (post-trial minus pretrial) in visits to the doctor. First, separate regression models were esti-

---

117. Id.

118. Multiple regression analysis is a technique for assessing the effects of multiple variables on a dependent variable.

119. American Psychiatric Ass'n, supra note 33, at 250.

120. See Table 3.

mated with each of the nine health measures as outcomes, and the six trauma-related factors[121] entered simultaneously as predictors. Next, we estimated regression models for each of the nine health outcomes with the six stress-related factors[122] entered simultaneously as predictors. Then, to control for the relationship between demographic factors and health related effects, we estimated regression models for each of the nine health outcomes using the five demographic factors as predictors.[123]

1. Sum of Symptoms Reported During the Trial.—The first measure of juror health is the sum of the symptoms reported during the trial. Respondents were asked to identify from the symptom checklist any symptoms they experienced because of the trial during the trial proceedings.[124] Of the jurors who reported experiencing symptoms during the trial, more jurors in the trauma group reported experiencing those symptoms than did jurors in the non-trauma group (53.47% vs. 46.53%; chi-square=8.0250, d.f.=1, p<.05). Further, jurors in the trauma group reported experiencing nearly three times as many symptoms during the trial as did the jurors in the nontrauma group.[125] Using the sum of the symptoms reported during the trial as the measure of health outcome, two trauma-related factors (Self-rated Trauma Exposure[126] and Objective Evidence[127], no stress-related factors, and three demographic factors (Sex,[128] Age and Race[129]) emerged as important.[130] Together these factors account for about 45% of the variability in symptoms reported during the trial. However, while the overall model was significant (p<.0001), only Self-rated Trauma Exposure and Sex were independently significant factors.[131]

Self-rated Trauma Exposure alone accounted for nearly 22% of the variability in this model. One might, however, question the inclusion of Self-rated Trauma Exposure in each of the health outcome models that are based on the respondent's report of symptoms.[132] This might indicate that people who report trauma also report symptoms. To determine if our findings were an artifact, we estimated a regression model with the sum of the symptoms reported during the trial as the measure of health outcome without the subjective Self-

---

121. Due to the low response rate the rating of exposure to trauma not related to the trial was eliminated from the estimations.

122. Due to the low response rate concerning life events before and after the trial, these factors were dropped from the estimations.

123. A stepwise regression was conducted on each of the three models with alpha-to-enter and alpha-to-remove = 15. to confirm which of these factors entered into the models.

124. See survey question 14r.

125. See Table 7.

126. A subjective rating of trauma related to the trial. See survey question 14z.

127. A factor-analytically derived measure consisting of the rating of the crime together with characteristics of photographs or charts used during the trial.

128. 1=male, 2=female.

129. Race was determined to be either minority or nonminority (nonminority=2, minority=1).

130. This model had a R^2 =.45 and p<.0001.

131. See Table 4.

132. See Table 4.

Table 4.   Sum of Reported Symptoms as Health Measure

Factors	At Trial		In Deliberations		After Trial	
	B[a]	SE[b]	B[a]	SE[b]	B[a]	SE[b]
Self-Reported Trauma Rating	0.95***	0.15	0.39**	0.14	0.21**	0.07
Crime Category; Charts, Photos	0.24	0.13	—	—	—	—
Self-Rated Stress Exposure	—	—	0.21***	0.06	0.05	0.03
Sex	1.52**	0.49	1.08**	0.39	-0.34	0.21
Age	0.03	0.02	-0.05**	0.02	-0.02	0.01
Race	1.07	0.70	—	—	—	—
R^2	0.45		0.34		0.20	
N	108		139		137	

a. Unstandardized regression coefficient
b. Standard error of the regression coefficients
* includes stress with jury deliberations
** p < .01
*** p < .001

rated Trauma Exposure variable.[133] While the predictive value of the model was reduced (R^2 =.23), the finding was still significant (p<. 0001).

The next factor that emerged as important is Sex, which also appears in each of the other health outcome models that are based on the report of symptoms. Sex is positively correlated with the sum of the symptoms during the trial. The literature suggests that given exposure to traumatic events, women are more likely to report PTSD symptoms than men.[134] This may account for the positive correlation of sex in this model.

The next factor that emerged as important is Objective Evidence. Objective Evidence refers to photographs and other graphic evidence presented at trial; therefore, we would expect this factor to affect the incidence of symptoms arising during the trial. Further, because this factor is not correlated with reports of symptoms during deliberations or after the trial, it would appear that jurors are distinguishing the trial from the deliberations. The inclusion of Objective Evidence as an important factor in this model supports the theory that the use of photographs and other graphic materials does contribute negatively to juror health.

Age, the next factor in this health outcome model, is the most problematic variable in our survey. Since our trauma group is statistically younger than our nontrauma group,[135] the fact that age is positively correlated with symptoms reported during the trial may indicate that older people have more symptoms even though they served on less traumatic trials. This possibility may help to account for many of the symptoms reported during the trial by the jurors ex-

---

133. A similar estimation was performed with health outcome measured by the change in medication taken during deliberations with similar results.

134. Bonnie L. Green et al., Post-traumatic Stress Disorder: Toward DSM-IV, 173 Nerv. Ment. Dis. 406, 407 (1985).

135. See Table 6.

Table 5. Change in Doctor Visits as the Health Outcome Measure

Factors	B[a]	SE[b]
Crime category; charts, photos	−0.21**	0.06
School	−0.35*	0.14
Income	0.26**	0.08
R^2	0.20	
N	103	

a. unstandardized regression coefficient
b. standard error of the regression co-efficient
* $p<.01$
** $p<.001$

posed to nontraumatic cases. That is, these symptoms may in fact be unrelated to the trial. However, age is negatively correlated with symptoms during deliberations and after the trial. This would indicate that older people globally suffer fewer symptoms. During deliberations, this can be accounted for by the fact that there are more older people in the nontraumatic group, but after the trial we would expect to see a positive correlation.

The final factor in this model is Race. This was the only health outcome model in which race emerged as an important factor and even in this model it was not independently significant. Nevertheless, race emerged as a factor when the step-wise regression analysis was performed. While the racial makeup of the high and low trauma groups was not statistically different, there appears to be a trend toward a higher percentage of Caucasians in the low trauma group.[136] Since race displays a positive correlation to symptoms during the trial, and there is a trend toward more Caucasians in the low trauma group, low trauma may be associated with fewer reported symptoms.[137] Another possibility is that something offensive may have occurred during the trial, perhaps jury selection or a comment from a witness or an attorney, which made the trial traumatic or stressful to particular minority jurors.

2. Sum of Symptoms Reported During the Deliberations.—The second measure of juror health is the sum of the symptoms reported during the deliberations. Respondents were asked to identify, from a list, any symptoms that they experienced because of the trial during the jury deliberations. Again, more of the jurors in the trauma group reported experiencing symptoms during deliberations than did jurors in the nontrauma group (55.07% vs. 44.93%; chi-square=4.9562, d.f.=1, p<.05). Jurors in the trauma group reported experiencing nearly three times as many symptoms during the deliberations as did jurors in the non-trauma group.[138] Finally, with the sum of the symptoms reported during the deliberations as the measure of health outcome, one trauma-related factor (Self-rated Trauma Exposure), one stress-related factor (Self-rated Stress

---

136. See Table 6.

137. Again this may be due to the overall lower response rate to the questionnaire of African-Americans. See discussion supra.

138. See Table 7.

Exposure[139], and two demographic factors (Sex and Age) emerged as important predictors with each independently significant.[140] These variables account for approximately 34% of the variability in symptoms reported during the deliberations.

The factors that emerged for this measure of health outcome are substantially similar to, or the same as, those emerging during the trial. These health models differed only by their inclusion or exclusion of three factors: Objective Evidence; Self-rated Stress Exposure; and Race. Objective Evidence is related to the trial experience. It appears in the model based on the sum of the symptoms during trial, but is absent from the model based on the sum of the symptoms during deliberations. Jurors are exposed to photographs and other graphic evidence during the trial. For this reason, we expected the effects of that exposure, as evidenced by the report of symptoms, to occur during the trial rather than during deliberations. Self-rated Stress Exposure, which is composed of the rating of stress during the trial and the stress and amount of intimidation during the deliberations, is also more closely associated with the deliberations.[141]

3. *Sum of Symptoms Reported After the Trial.*—In the final measure of juror health (based on a self-report of symptoms), respondents were asked to identify from a list any symptoms they experienced since the trial ended because of the trial. Once again, of the jurors who reported experiencing symptoms after the trial, more of the jurors in the trauma group reported symptoms than did jurors in the nontrauma group (62.86% vs. 37.14%; chi-square=4.8225, d.f.=1, p <.05). Using the sum of symptoms reported after the trial as the measure of health outcome, the important predictors were the following: one trauma-related factor (Self-rated Trauma Exposure), one stress-related factor (Self-rated Stress Exposure), and two demographic factors (Sex and Age), with only Self-rated Trauma Exposure emerging as independently significant.[142] These factors account for around 20% of the variability in symptoms reported after the trial.

The predictive factors that surfaced for the sum of the symptoms after the trial were the same as those during deliberations, and differed only in order of importance as determined by the step-wise regression analysis. This may indicate that while evidence produced during the trial has a short term effect on a juror's health, the factors which arise during deliberations may contribute to more long term effects.

The most interesting aspect of this model is that sex is negatively correlated with reporting symptoms after the trial,[143] with more men reporting symptoms

---

139. A factor-analytically derived measure consisting of subjective ratings of stress during the trial and deliberations along with intimidation during deliberations.

140. This model had a R^2 =.34 and p<.0001.

141. This finding would support the concept of groupthink. However, if symptoms were based predominantly on the stress associated with groupthink, more symptoms would be reported during the deliberations than during the trial.

142. This model had a R^2 =.20 and p<.0001.

143. See Table 4.

Table 6. Chi-square Analysis of Groups Based on a priori Global Trauma

Factors	Trauma Exposure	
	High	Low
Sex		
Male	49	51
Female	48	52
Age		
18–39	58	42
40–71	41	59
Education		
Some High School	50	50
High School Degree	39	61
Some College	51	49
College Degree	51	49
Graduate School	45	55
Income		
Up to 49,999	43	57
50,000 and above	52	48
Race		
Caucasian	44	56
Minority	49	51

after the trial than women. This differs from the report of symptoms during the trial and deliberations. It may have something to do with the way men are affected by trauma and stress, or perhaps in how they report it.[144]

4. *Change in Visits to the Doctor.*—The last measure of juror health is the change in visits to the doctor. Respondents were asked how many times they visited the doctor in the six months before the trial and in the six months after the trial. The number of visits before the trial were then subtracted from the number of visits after the trial to get the change in visits to the doctor. This health model is surprising in that jurors in the trauma group went to the doctor less after the trial than before the trial.[145] There are several plausible explanations for this finding. First, the trauma group is statistically younger. Since young people tend to make fewer trips to the doctor, this may be an artifact due to age. Second, most of the trials took place in late winter and early spring when people are more likely to get sick and go to the doctor (e.g., mild upper respiratory viral illness) than at other times of the year. Third, it may be work-related. Jurors who were forced to take time off for jury duty may not have been able to take any additional days off to see a doctor.

Using the change in visits to the doctor as the measure of health outcome, one trauma-related factor (Objective Evidence), no stress-related factors, and two demographic factors (Income and Education) emerged as important and independently significant predictors.[146] These factors together account for about 20% of the variability in change in visits to the doctor.

---

144. Women may talk more about their problems than men. According to Pennebaker's theory, the more people talk about traumatic events the less likely they suffer long term symptoms. Pennebaker, supra note 71.

145. See Table 7.

146. This health outcome model had a $R^2 = .20$ and p<.0001.

The first factor is objective evidence presented at the trial. This factor, which is negatively correlated to the change in visits to the doctor, appears to dispute our hypothesis that a more traumatic trial will result in more visits to the doctor after the trial than before the trial. Since this factor was positively correlated to symptoms reported during the trial, it may be that people associated those symptoms with the trial and did not bother to see a doctor about them after the trial.[147]

The factor that is the most easily explained in this model is Income. Income is positively correlated with change in visits to the doctor.[148] People with a higher income can afford to go to the doctor more often. People with less money might be less inclined to go to the doctor. Since many Americans are uninsured or underinsured,[149] people with lower incomes might not be able to afford an ordinary visit to the doctor.

The third and final factor was Education, which was negatively correlated with changes in visits to the doctor.[150] Those who were less educated went to the doctor more following a traumatic experience. This may indicate that people with less education had more trouble with the traumatic nature of the trial and, therefore, went to the doctor more.[151]

B. Specific Health Effects of Serving on a Jury in a Traumatic Trial

While it appears that jurors who serve on traumatic trials generally suffer more adverse health effects than jurors who serve on nontraumatic trials, the findings with regard to more specific health problems are mixed.

1. Depression.[152]—During the trial, jurors serving on traumatic trials were almost six times more likely to develop a sufficient number and type of symptoms to meet the DSM-III-R symptom criteria for depression than jurors serving on nontraumatic trials (12.3% vs. 2.6%). While diminishing over time, this difference persists during deliberations (7% vs. 1.3%), and remains after the trial (1.4% vs. 0%). It is perhaps more important that the percentage of jurors serving on traumatic cases who met the minimum screening criteria for depression exceeded the population base rate of 4–5%[153] both during the trial and deliberations.[154]

---

147. Jurors were asked how many visits they took to the doctor before and after the trial, but not during the trial.

148. See Table 7.

149. See M. Eugene Moyer, A Revised Look at the Number of Uninsured Americans, 8 Health Aff. 102 (1989); see also Bureau of the Census, Health Insurance Coverage, 1986–1988 (1990) (approximately 31.5 million Americans under 65 were uninsured in 1988).

150. The respondents had a high overall degree of education. See Table 1.

151. See Table 7.

152. See Table 3.

153. See Table 3; Max Hamilton, A Rating Scale for Depression, 23 J. Neuro. Neurosurg. Psychiatry 56, 62 (1960).

154. See Table 3.

Table 7. Health-Related Scores by Main Trial-Related Predictors

Factors	Sum of Symptoms				Change in Doctor Visits	
	Trial		Deliberations			
	Mean	SD	Mean	SD	Mean	SD
Trauma Exposure						
High	2.9	3.4	1.94	3.11	−0.33	1.34
Low	1.3	2.18	0.97	2.09	0.10	1.20
Change %	120		100		−430	
Self-Rating of Trauma						
High	2.81	3.24	1.95	3.06	−0.10	1.26
Low	0.67	1.40	0.27	0.54	−0.12	1.35
Change %	320		620		17	
Objective Trial-Related Stress						
High	3.60	3.98	2.58	3.91	−0.52	1.37
Low	1.30	1.70	0.78	1.13	0.14	1.17
Change %	180		230		−470	
Subjective Trial-Related Stress						
High	2.92	3.53	2.13	3.25	−0.15	1.19
Low	1.11	1.46	0.51	1.01	−0.05	1.41
Change %	160		320		−15	

2. Post-traumatic Stress Disorder.[155]—The results of this study do not support the hypothesis that jurors are more likely than the general population to experience PTSD; nor do the results support the hypothesis that jurors serving on traumatic trials are more likely than jurors serving on nontraumatic trials to experience PTSD. While many of the jurors did report some of the symptoms associated with PTSD, only one of the jurors reported symptoms consistent with a PTSD diagnosis. There are two possible explanations for this finding. The first is that jury service, regardless of the nature of the trial, does not qualify as a stressor of sufficient magnitude to trigger PTSD. The second explanation, and the one supported by the anecdotal evidence discussed above, is that most trials of violent crimes are not sufficiently stressors to trigger PTSD; and that it is only the rare trial that is sufficiently traumatic to trigger PTSD.

V. Conclusion

The genesis of this study was a concern that traumatic trials have serious negative health effects for jurors. The data support the hypothesis that jury service on traumatic trials does have a negative health effect for jurors. However, there is less cause for concern than was anticipated. The data do not show that jurors on a traumatic trial are at a higher risk for PTSD. Only one juror in this study reported symptoms consistent with a PTSD diagnosis, and that juror did not serve on a traumatic trial.

While this study has not shown that PTSD is a concern for most jurors serving on run-of-the-mill traumatic trials, the findings relating to depression are cause for greater concern. Twelve percent of jurors serving on traumatic trials developed a sufficient number and type of symptoms to meet the DSM-III-R

---

155. See Table 3.

symptom criteria for depression, compared with the base rate of 4% to 5% of the general population.[156] Jurors serving on traumatic trials were almost six times more likely to meet the DSM-III-R symptom criteria for depression than jurors serving on nontraumatic trials.

In light of these findings, the responsibility of the judicial system to protect jurors from the negative health effects of service on traumatic trials is not only a fair recompense for jury service, but also advances the interests of the judicial system that relies on these jurors. There are two directions that might be taken to address this problem. First, the negative health effects jurors feel could be addressed by systemic changes that limit juror exposure to traumatic trials. Second, the negative health effects could be addressed by administrative changes that respond to the way in which jurors experience traumatic trials.

Two possible ways for systemic change to limit juror exposure to traumatic trials are to limit the evidence presented at trial, and to modify the selection of jurors. The rules of evidence could be amended to include the interests of jurors as an additional consideration in admitting evidence. This approach, however, places the policy interests of protecting jurors from traumatic evidence on a collision course with the litigants' interests in presenting relevant evidence. The externalities raised by this alternative are enigmatic and it is beyond the scope of this study to examine the adjudicative considerations raised by this alternative.

Excluding individuals from jury service who are more susceptible to depression from traumatic trials is equally problematic. Because numerous factors may predispose an individual to depression, significant segments of society could be excluded from jury duty. Women might be excluded at disproportionately higher rates because they are at higher risk for depression.[157] Racial minorities with lower incomes might be excluded at disproportionately higher rates because the risk of depression has been linked to lower income.[158] Aside from the administrative burden of finding replacement jurors, this alternative raises troubling questions about the legitimacy and constitutionality of the judicial process.

The systemic approaches threaten both adjudicative and legitimizing considerations. In the absence of compelling data that most jurors are traumatized by criminal trials, which our data do not support, it is reasonable to look to less drastic solutions to the problems of the negative health effects of jury service. The administrative approaches to dealing with the effects of traumatic trials offer solutions that do not threaten these adjudicative and legitimizing considerations and may therefore be more palatable.

There are a number of possible administrative approaches to the problem of jurors experiencing negative health effects. One alternative is to provide a professional counselor to jurors before, during, and after the trial. This option, seemingly the most effective for the protection of juror health, is not only the most expensive, but may be unnecessary. Because this study found that only 12.3% of jurors exhibit symptoms of depression or approximately one juror

---

156. Hamilton, supra note 153.
157. Green, supra note 134.
158. Id.

per panel of twelve, a more cost effective option seems appropriate for most cases.

Another alternative is debriefing of the jury by the judge after the trial.[159] This alternative is attractive because it is relatively inexpensive. Moreover, since debriefing would occur after the trial, it would be unlikely to prejudice the interests of the litigants. However, because debriefing takes place after the trial's conclusion, this alternative may not be effective in preventing the negative health effects of jury service. This study indicates that by the time the trial ends some jurors have already begun to experience symptoms of depression. And, judges are not trained to engage in mental health counseling.

A related alternative is to allow the judge to monitor juror mental health during the trial and provide counseling when necessary.[160] The advantages of this alternative are its relative low cost and its low probability of prejudicing the litigants. However, this alternative is not very practical; judges are neither trained in mental health counseling, nor are they likely to have the time or opportunity to monitor the jury adequately during a typical trial.

Another administrative alternative is an instruction to jurors providing them with information that may help lessen any negative health effects of jury service. This research reveals that negative health effects, including depression, begin before the trial ends. Thus, from the perspective of juror health, it is preferable to inform jurors before the trial begins about strategies they might use to minimize the negative health effects of the trial. For example, they could be instructed that they should feel free to talk about their feelings about the case, although not the facts of the case itself, during the trial. It might be beneficial if a juror in a rape case could tell fellow jurors that he or she felt more vulnerable to physical attack since the trial began. But, it would clearly be inappropriate for him or her to say that the defendant scares him or her, and in unsupervised discussions, it might be unreasonable to expect jurors to heed that line. Thus, while preferable for jurors, this approach might be unacceptable to judges and lawyers.

As a second alternative, a post-trial instruction encouraging jurors to share their feelings during deliberations and discuss the case fully, to encourage those with minority viewpoints to make their views known, and to respect the views of all members of the jury might be reasonable. This approach is an example of therapeutic jurisprudence.[161] Encouraging more extensive communications between jurors benefits the deliberative process: it avoids groupthink and encourages more thoughtful deliberations.[162] And, encouraging discussion about shared juror experiences benefits the therapeutic process: it is psychologically and physically beneficial to jurors.[163] Moreover, it does not call upon judges to be mental health counselors. It can be standardized to avoid signaling that a particular trial will be traumatic for jurors. There are no out of pocket costs involved.

---

159. Hafemeister, supra note 7, at 40.

160. See, e.g., Marjorie O. Dabbs, Jury Traumatization in High Profile Criminal Trials: A Case for Crisis Debriefing, 16 Law & Psychol. Rev. 201 (1992).

161. David B. Wexler & Bruce J. Winick, Essays in Therapeutic Jurisprudence (1991).

162. See text accompanying note 63, supra.

163. See discussion in text accompanying note 71, supra.

However, there are problems with this approach. More open discussions among jurors may result in lengthier deliberations or greater inability to reach a verdict. This tension between managerial and adjudicative concerns is not, however, unique to this problem.[164]

Reasonable people may disagree as to which approach is preferable. However, it is clear that jurors are at an increased risk of suffering from depression resulting from their participation on traumatic trials. It is also clear that the judicial system has a responsibility for the harm it causes jurors.

---

164. Maureen Armour, Challenging the Managerial Bias of Rule 11: Judicial Discretion as a Self-Limiting Concept and the Close Case as a Regulatory Bright Line (unpublished manuscript on file with the author).

Chapter 50

Ex Post ≠ Ex Ante: Determining Liability in Hindsight

Kim A. Kamin
Jeffrey J. Rachlinski

[In an article cited in this chapter, Wexler and Schopp note that psychiatric patients may be confined for periods longer than is clinically warranted because the releasing authorities may fear litigation and liability in the event a released patient happens to injure a third person after release. The releasing authorities may be especially fearful, and particularly conservative, because they know that if such an injury occurs, and litigation ensues, the reasonableness of their behavior may be judged by a jury using 20/20 hindsight. Operating with the knowledge that an injury occurred, and with the benefit of hindsight, the jury may find the patients to have been dangerous, and the releasing authorities correspondingly negligent in authorizing release. The releasing authorities, however, can rely only on foresight, and to judge their actions by hindsight is unfair to them and to the many patients who, because of hindsight in the legal system, are subjected to law-caused unnecessary hospitalization. In their article, Wexler and Schopp discuss various "debiasing" schemes for possibly eliminating the hindsight bias, among them a type of jury instruction. The present chapter examines empirically the effect on the hindsight bias of a particular jury instruction in an area of the law outside the negligent release context.]

Life involves risk and danger. The potential for accidental harm looms in every environment and situation. When careless conduct causes an accident, injuring people or damaging property, the American tort system obliges a party who has negligently caused damage to pay for it. The tort system recognizes that not every accident is the product of negligence. To obtain compensation, a plaintiff suing for negligence must prove four things: (1) The defendant owed a duty of care to the plaintiff; (2) the duty was breached; (3) the breach caused (4) damage to the plaintiff (American Law Institute [ALI], 1965, p. 4). Negligence law requires that judgment of the second element, whether the defendant's conduct breached a duty of care, be based on the defendant's knowledge *before* the plaintiff's injury (ALI, 1965, p. 68). Yet, the legal system necessarily judges a defendant's conduct *after* the harm has occurred. Research on human judgment suggests that people cannot ignore a known outcome when assessing an event's likelihood—a phenomenon known as "the hindsight bias" (Fischhoff, 1975). In this article, we address the possibility that the hindsight bias may make precautions that seem reasonable in foresight look inadequate in hindsight.

In most negligence suits, defendants are liable only for consequences arising from their failure to exercise "reasonable care" in avoiding injury to the plaintiff. Legal scholars have described reasonable care in terms of a cost-benefit analysis (ALI, 1965, pp. 54–57). As articulated by Judge Learned Hand, "if the probability [of an injury] be called P; the injury, L; and the burden [of precautions] B; liability depends upon whether B is less than L multiplied by P" (*United States v. Carroll Towing Co.*, 1947, p. 173). In effect, if an accident's cost multiplied by the probability of its occurrence outweighs the cost of untaken precautions, a defendant may be found liable for breaching the duty of reasonable care (Grady, 1989). Judge Hand's formula has attracted widespread support and is "the negligence standard most often cited in legal discussions of the problem" (Brown, 1973, p. 194). In fact, it remains the fundamental description of reasonable care in tort law treatises (Keeton, 1984, p. 173), and is embodied in jury instructions (Devitt, Blackmar, & Wolf, 1987, p. 138). It has even been applied to the causation element of negligence (Grady, 1983; Landes & Posner, 1983).

In the application of the Hand formula to a defendant's conduct, a judge or jury must assess the costs and benefits of precautions based upon what the defendant should have known when making the judgment, regardless of what has been learned after the fact (ALI, 1965, p. 68). This requires making a post hoc evaluation of "what particular precautions the defendant could have taken, but did not" (Grady, 1989, p. 140). To correctly apply Hand's formula and determine liability, legal decision makers must make *ex post* (after the fact) judgments of the *ex ante* (before the fact) probabilities. In effect, a proper adjudication of reasonable care requires a judge or jury to disregard the obvious fact that the precautions failed to prevent an accident (Devitt et al., 1987, p. 138).

The Hindsight Bias

Ignoring a known outcome while recreating a decision is a difficult cognitive task. In making such judgments, people overestimate both the probability of the known outcome and the ability of decision makers to foresee the outcome (Fischhoff, 1975). When trying to reconstruct what a foresightful state of mind would have perceived, people remain anchored in the hindsightful perspective. This leaves the reported outcome looking much more likely than it would look to the reasonable person without the benefit of hindsight (Fischhoff, 1982a, p. 343).

Research on the hindsight bias has demonstrated the effect in a diverse range of subject populations across varied laboratory and applied settings. Detmer, Fryback, and Gassner (1978) reported a hindsight bias in surgeons appraising surgical cases. Arkes, Wortmann, Saville, and Harkness (1981) found it among physicians assessing a medical diagnosis. Pennington, Rutter, McKenna, and Morely (1980) found it in women reacting to the results of a pregnancy test. The bias has also been found in voters' election predictions (Leary, 1982), in nurses' employee evaluations (Mitchell & Kalb, 1982), and may contribute to the phenomenon of blaming a rape victim for her misfortune (Carli & Leonard, 1989). These studies suggest the robustness of the bias across a variety of subjects, situations, and tasks.

The Hindsight Bias and Legal Decision Making

The hindsight bias' potential relevance to law has not escaped the notice of legal and psychological scholars. In discussing a demonstration of the hindsight bias in medical diagnosis, Arkes (1989) claimed that the bias could affect liability judgments in misdiagnosis cases. Since a failure to diagnose a disorder will look much more culpable after discovering the true nature of an illness, doctors may be subject to liability even for reasonable diagnostic procedures that turn out badly. Wexler and Schopp (1989) expressed similar concerns about doctors sued for "negligently" releasing psychiatric patients who later commit violent acts.

Researchers have conducted several empirical demonstrations of the hindsight bias in legal settings. In a study by Bodenhausen (1990), undergraduates read case summaries containing the results of jury deliberations. The study revealed that the jury's conclusion heavily influenced subject evaluations of the defendant's culpability. Casper, Benedict, and Perry (1989) had students and adults called for jury service assess opening and closing arguments in a hypothetical suit against police officers who allegedly had conducted illegal searches. Although the legality of a search does not depend on its outcome, both types of participants were more sympathetic to the plaintiff when the search uncovered nothing than when it uncovered damning evidence against him. Kagehiro, Taylor, Laufer, and Harland (1991) extended Casper's findings, concentrating on the hindsight bias' influence on judicial review of third-party consent to warrantless searches. In their study, undergraduates read vignettes describing a warrantless police search and then responded to a questionnaire. Results indicated that search outcome heavily influenced judgments of the search's legality.

Because decision making in a legal context differs from nonlegal demonstrations of hindsight, in both complexity and the influence that previously held attitudes have on its outcome (e.g., Thompson, Cowan, Ellsworth, & Harrington, 1984), one might suppose it to be immune from the bias' influence. These studies suggest otherwise. As these studies show, neither the attitudinal variables nor the complexity of legal decisions appears to mitigate the bias' effect.

Tort law itself lacks a generic empirical demonstration of the hindsight bias. Although Wexler and Schopp (1989) provide a fairly detailed discussion of the effects the bias might have on psychiatric malpractice cases, they collected no data. Furthermore, Wexler and Schopp (1989) limit their discussion to psychiatric malpractice. In recognition of the generality of the effect, however, they include a comment by professor Robert Rabin that "negligent release cases appear simply to be a variant on the general structure of accident law" (Wexler & Schopp, 1989, p. 489). As this comment indicates, the hindsight bias problem probably extends beyond psychiatric malpractice. Indeed, Saks (1986) has suggested that foreseeability issues in tort law could occupy a lifetime of research.

Debiasing Techniques

Demonstration of pervasive bias in a significant area of law begs the question of a remedy. Unfortunately, the hindsight bias has proven resistant to most debiasing techniques (Fischhoff, 1982b). Attempts to undo the hindsight effect with strategies that rely on motivation, such as suggesting to people that they try harder (Davies, 1987; Fischhoff, 1977), increasing personal relevance of the task (Connolly & Bukszar, 1990), and rewarding people for unbiased responses (Heil, Gigerenzer, Gauggel, Mall, & Muller, 1988), have proven ineffective. Furthermore, alerting people to the bias' influence does not mitigate the effect (Fischhoff, 1977; Kurtz & Garfield, 1978; Wood, 1978). Some researchers have obtained limited debiasing by significantly restructuring the decision-making task (Fischhoff, Slovic, & Lichtenstein, 1978), or by having participants consider alternative outcomes (Arkes, Faust, Guilmette, & Hart, 1988; Einhorn & Hogarth, 1986). Although these cognitive strategies have reduced the influence of the bias, no known technique completely eliminates the effect.

Wexler and Schopp (1989) considered debiasing strategies suitable for the courtroom. They suggested bifurcating trials to avoid prejudice from knowing outcomes while judging negligence. Bifurcation of trials, in fact, may decrease the liability juries attribute to defendants (Horowitz & Bordens, 1990; Zeisel & Callahan, 1967). However, as Wexler and Schopp admit, bifurcation is an imperfect solution. It is unlikely that the jury determining negligence could be kept completely ignorant of the fact that an accident has occurred. Furthermore, although bifurcation of liability and damage issues is common, bifurcation to avoid outcome knowledge is unprecedented. Wexler and Schopp's proposal may be the only method for completely eradicating the bias, but it presents enormous practical difficulties.

A less intrusive courtroom technique would be to incorporate the successful cognitive debiasing techniques into jury instructions. As Wexler and Schopp (1989) explain, these instructions must do more than merely admonish jurors to disregard outcome information. Rather, they should employ successful debiasing techniques, such as imagining alternative outcomes. If written in plain language, reviewed before revealing the evidence, and then repeated at the end of the trial, these instructions might impact the decision-making process. Alternatively, expert testimony could serve the same function, much as it does in cases involving eyewitness identification (Loftus, 1993). In addition, the defense attorney could make efforts to restructure the case to avoid the bias, or induce other decision making heuristics favorable to a defendant such as counterfactual reasoning—the mental "undoing" of an adverse event (e.g., Miller & McFarland, 1986; Wells, Taylor, & Turtle, 1986).

The Present Experiment

The present experiment tested the influence of the hindsight bias in a negligence suit and the effectiveness of jury instructions as a debiasing method. The study compared participants' evaluations in an administrative hearing (choosing precautions for a potential accident) to those in a mock trial (in which an accident had already occurred). A second hindsight-trial condition was identical to the first except for the addition of debiasing instructions designed to reduce probability estimates and findings of liability.

The stimuli in the present experiment depicted a situation similar to that of a famous tort case, *Petition of Kinsman Transit Co.* (1964). In the foresight condition, participants learned that a city had constructed a drawbridge and needed to determine whether the risk of a flood warranted maintaining a bridge operator during the winter when the bridge was not in use. Hiring the operator would serve as a precaution. The operator would monitor weather conditions and raise the bridge if the river threatened to flood. The foresight condition asked participants without outcome knowledge to decide whether a flood was sufficiently probable for the city to appropriate funds for the operator.

The hindsight manipulations contained the same background facts. The story continued, however, stating that the city had decided not to hire the operator. During the first winter of the bridge's existence, debris lodged under it. This resulted in a flood that could have been prevented had an operator been hired. The flood damaged a neighboring bakery, whose owner then sued the city. Participants in the hindsight condition were instructed to hold the city liable if the flood was sufficiently probable that the city should have hired the operator to prevent it. The second hindsight condition added a debiasing manipulation in which the judge instructed participants to recognize the influential effects of hindsight and to consider alternative outcomes as had the city in foresight. All three conditions required participants to base their decisions on a critical percentage derived from the application of Judge Hand's reasonable care formulation.

The stimuli consisted of an audio-tape with an accompanying slide-show. Each subject heard one of the three versions of the stimuli (foresight, hindsight, or debiasing). Dependent variables were the participants' ratings of probability and their ultimate decision to hire the operator or hold the city responsible for failing to hire an operator. Other measures (whether the city should pay damages, how well the two opposing sides had done, how realistic the simulations were, and how difficult it was to decide the accident's probability) served as manipulation checks.

The primary hypothesis was that participants in the foresight condition would be less inclined to take the precaution than participants in the hindsight condition would think they should have been. We expected these decisions to correspond with higher probability estimates generated by participants in the hindsight conditions. We also expected that hindsight participants would tend to think the city should pay for flood damages more than foresight participants would. For the manipulation checks, we predicted that hindsight would influence the case alone and would not affect evaluations of the attorneys or the simulation itself. Finally, participants in the debiasing condition should give lower probability estimates and be less likely to hold the city liable than those in the hindsight condition. Since other studies show that this debiasing strategy tends to reduce the bias, but not eliminate it, we expected a similar effect in this study.

Method

Participants

Seventy-six undergraduates at Stanford University, 37 women and 39 men, received either $5 in cash or course credit in an introductory psychology class for their voluntary participation in the study.

Experimental Materials

Separate transcripts for each of the three conditions (foresight, hindsight, and debiasing) were read onto audio-tape by actors. The tapes each lasted approximately 30 minutes. The foresight tape depicted an administrative hearing of "The Duluth Urban Planning Committee," while the two hindsight tapes presented the same information in the form of a civil trial, *Continental Bakeries, Inc., v. City of Duluth.* Each role in the foresight condition had an analogous part in the trial conditions, and the same actors performed in all three versions. In the administrative hearing, one member of the committee board advocated taking the precaution and played a role analogous to the plaintiff's attorney in the trial versions. Similarly, another administrator opposed the precaution, thereby assuming the defense attorney's position. The secretary of the committee mirrored the bailiff in the trial. A neutral chairman mirrored the judge. Six witnesses appeared in the same order in both the administrative hearing and the trial versions of the story. Where appropriate, multiple conditions contained recordings of identical materials. In all conditions, two exhibits discussed in the audio-tape were made available to the participants during the presentation.

The presentational format was standardized as a slide-show with the accompanying audio-tape. The slides presented different models posing as each of the characters. The background for the witnesses was a stark paneled wall; two witnesses were standing in front of a wooden door, while all the others were sitting in what looked like a wooden witness stand. Each condition used the same slides in the same order. The only exception was that the slides for the judge and the bailiff differed from those for the corresponding chairman and the secretary of the planning committee. These differences were necessary to show the judge in robes and the bailiff in uniform. Transcripts and all other materials are available from the authors on request.

Opening Instructions

The opening instructions in each of the conditions contained only those differences necessary to create the setting for the manipulations. The foresight tape began with the committee chairman describing the administrative setting. The hindsight tapes opened with the judge describing the trial setting. Below are the actual instructions (with the hindsight text indicated in italics):

> First, [*both parties have agreed to*] let me give you an abbreviated version of the [situation/*facts which are not in dispute*]. [Last May/*During May* 1988], the City of Duluth completed construction of a drawbridge across the mouth of the Miniwapa river. The Miniwapa river sees a considerable amount of commercial traffic during the summer and early fall from many upstream businesses. During the months of December through April, the river is usually frozen. Hence, there is no commerce on the waterway in the winter. During the active months, the city maintains a bridge operator 24 hours a day, seven days a week, so that the bridge can be lowered or raised at any time. The city [presently is deciding whether or not to employ a bridge operator during the winter months/*decided not to employ a bridge operator during the winter months. It is this decision that is in contention here today*].

The foresight tape then explained:

> The City Disaster Preparedness Commission has alerted us to the fact that some possibility of winter and spring flooding exists as a result of the new bridge. A flood could be caused by a premature thaw or else by ice and debris

getting caught under the bridge so as to create a dam. A flood would be a terrible event, potentially causing severe damage to property along the bank of the river. Employing a bridge operator during the winter and spring would alleviate this threat, but is fairly costly. The decision as to whether or not the city should hire an operator is the decision that is in question here today. I am torn between the two options. But two other members of our committee, Ms. Sugal and Mr. Markwell, have chosen sides and we will hear from a series of visitors to help you make your decision. My ambivalence arises from the uncertainty associated with the probability of a flood occurring. I would like you to review the available testimony to determine how likely it is that a flood will occur during the winter months.

The hindsight tapes explained instead:

During the middle of March 1989, the weather turned unexpectedly warm, and the normally frozen Miniwapa river began to thaw. When it thawed, the river approached flood stages and turned into a violent torrent, filled with ice floes. On the night of March 17, 1989, the river crested at eighteen feet high, only two feet below the bottom of the new bridge. While this occurred, a barge broke loose upstream. This barge lodged under the bridge, and along with numerous large chunks of ice, created a temporary dam, blocking the flow of water under the bridge. This backlog resulted in the river flooding upstream before the bridge could be raised. Had the bridge been raised, it would have freed the barge and the ice and prevented the river from flooding. The flood only affected Continental Bakeries' property and a public park owned by the city.

Finally, the debiasing tape included these additional instructions:

Deciding this case will eventually require you to make a determination abount the probability that a flood like the described one will occur in any given year. Making such an assessment may be difficult since the accident has already occurred. When listening to the evidence, you should consider how the events which led up to the accident could have turned out differently.

Testimony

Following the opening instructions, the six witnesses were questioned by the committee members/attorneys. The opposing characters first made opening statements and then called the witnesses.

The first witness, a meteorologist discussing yearly water levels, testified that in the past 60 years the river had crested to dangerous levels on 14 occasions in five different years. He also introduced a memorandum describing each of these instances. On none of these occasions did the river rise to the level of the new drawbridge. The next witness, a civil engineer for the City Disaster Preparedness Commission, discussed the possibility that a flood could occur if ice, debris, or loose boats lodge under the bridge, forming a dam. This witness introduced a memorandum written by the City Disaster Preparedness Commission. The memorandum described several hazards posed by the new bridge, including automobile accidents, boat collisions, and flooding. It explained that enough ice or debris caught under the bridge could create a backlog and cause a flood. It also recommended that the city consider employing a bridge operator throughout the winter to monitor the bridge. The third witness was the accounting officer of the Planning Committee. She stated that the flood precaution (i.e., hiring an operator for the winter) would cost the city

$100,000 annually, while the cost of the potential damages from a flood was approximately $1,000,000 per occurrence—ten times the cost of prevention on an annual basis.

Next, the chairman of the City Disaster Preparedness Commission testified on behalf of the opponent/defendant. He attacked the credibility of the "over-zealous" civil engineer who had testified for the proponent/plaintiff. The second witness for the opponent/defendant was the current dock inspector. He stated that in his ten years of experience no boats had broken loose on the river during the winter. The final witness, a retired dock inspector, rebutted this testimony. He claimed that in his 40 years of service boats had broken loose four or five times, although under cross examination he could not specifically recall the occasions when this occurred.

Closing Arguments

Following the testimony, the opposing sides each made closing arguments to highlight the facts supporting their respective points. The proponent/plaintiff claimed that the flood was a likely event that should be/have been prevented. The opponent/defendant claimed that the flood was too unlikely to warrant the costs of prevention. In the debiasing condition, the defense attorney also asked the participants to imagine the possibility that the flood had not occurred, and to consider the waste of hiring a bridge operator "who would sit in a booth every hour of every day in the winter to watch for floods."

Closing Instructions

The tapes' closing instructions were as follows (the hindsight text is in italics):

> The law also gives you a clear definition as to which precautions are reasonable, and which are not. In deciding whether the employment of a bridge operator throughout the winter (is/*was*) a reasonable precaution, you must consider the economics of the decision. If the precaution [will prevent/*would have prevented*] more harm than its cost, then the city is responsible for not taking the precaution. If, however, the precaution costs more than the harm it would have prevented, then the city is not responsible. When making this determination, you must take into account the probability [of an accident occurring/*that the accident was going to occur. This evaluation must be one of the probability that the flood would have occurred given the information available at the time the decision not to hire was made, not as of now*].
>
> The law makes the task fairly simple here. [We know that the damage from a flood would cost/*The parties have stipulated to the amount of damages at*] $1,000,000 [*and the defense has stipulated that this is the amount of damage they predicted*]. [The annual cost of eliminating the risk of the flood by employing the operator is/*Also, both parties have stipulated to the cost of precautions*]: $100,000. The only number missing from our calculation is the probability [of a flood/*that the flood was going to occur*]. It is your job to supply that number. Therefore, if you find that the probability of a preventable flood each year exceeds 10% then you must [agree with Ms. Sugal that the city should hire an operator/*side with the plaintiff*]. If you find that the probability of a flood is less than 10%, then [you must side with Mr. Markwell that an accident is too unlikely to be worth the cost of hiring an operator/*the city is not responsible for the flood since the precaution was not reasonable under the circumstances*].

The [committee/*court*] has provided a special verdict form which includes these instructions. You are to fill out this form when deciding the case. [The committee thanks you for your participation as an auxiliary member/*Thank you for your attention.*]

In the debiasing tape the judge added a final admonishment:

Making a fair determination of probability may be difficult. As we all know, hindsight vision is always 20/20. Therefore it is extremely important that before you determine the probability of the outcome that did occur, you fully explore all other possible alternative outcomes which could have occurred. Please take a moment to think of all the ways in which the event in question may have happened differently or not at all.

The Questionnaire

After watching the simulated meeting or trial, participants received a three-page questionnaire. The questionnaire was entitled "Final Determination Form" in the foresight condition, and "Final Verdict Form" in the hindsight conditions. The first page asked participants to provide estimates for "the probability of a preventable flood in any year." It then asked them to give their opinion as to whether the city "should hire an operator" or "was responsible for the flood damage." On the next page, the questionnaire asked participants to provide a written explanation for their decisions.

The final page asked participants to agree or disagree with five short statements using 7-point Likert scales. These statements were: "(1) The [proponent/*plaintiff's attorney*] did a good job arguing her position; (2) The [opponent/*defense attorney*] did a good job arguing his position; (3) The City of Duluth should be made to pay for damages [if a flood were to occur because of the absent bridge operator]; (4) The [meeting/*trial*] simulation was realistic; and (5) It was difficult to decide the correct probability."

Procedure

Participants were run alone or in pairs. They entered the room and were greeted by a female experimenter who instructed them to serve as committee members or jurors in a decision-making task. They were told to pay careful attention to the slide and audio presentation that would describe the decision-making task. At appropriate times during the presentation, participants were given written copies of the exhibits being discussed. At these times the experimenter said: "You will now receive a copy of Exhibit [A/B] to look over briefly and then refer to as it is discussed." Participants were instructed not to take notes.

Upon completion of the slide and audio presentation, the experimenter turned on the lights and gave participants the "Final Determination/Verdict Form" and written copies of the closing statements and instructions. Participants run in pairs were instructed to work individually and to avoid discussing their answers. All participants were alloted ten minutes in which to complete the questionnaire. The participants were then debriefed about the background and hypothesis behind the experiment. At this time they were informed about all three conditions, told of the experimental predictions, and given the opportunity to discuss the experiment.

Results

Preliminary analyses revealed no significant effects involving sex of subject and whether or not they were paid. Therefore, the results are reported collapsed across these variables.

Of the participants in the foresight condition, only 24% (6 out of 25) chose to hire the operator, whereas 56.9% (29 out of 51) of those in the two combined hindsight conditions believed that the defendant should have hired the operator: a statistically significant difference, $x2$ (1, $n = 76$) = 7.3, $p < .01$. A similar analysis comparing the hindsight cell to the debiasing cell showed no significant differences; 57.7% in the hindsight condition (15 out of 26) found the defendant liable versus 56.0% in the debiasing condition (14 out of 25) found the defendant liable. χ^2 (1, $n = 51$) = .01, $p > .5$.

Two problems with the distributions of the probability estimates led us to use a nonparametric analysis on this variable. First, the distributions were positively skewed. Second, a smaller number of the estimates were extremely popular among the participants (e.g., 14 participants chose 5% and 11 chose 15%). This made a transformation somewhat meaningless and generally muted the level of variance in the data. Consequently, the data were analyzed using the Mann-Whitney Rank Test. Comparing the foresight condition with the two hindsight conditions revealed that participants in hindsight made significantly higher estimates of the probability that the accident would occur in any given year, $U = 436$, $p < .025$. Participants in the debiasing condition did not differ from the ordinary hindsight condition, $U = 301$, $p > .5$.

Further analyzing only participants who chose to hire the operator (or to hold the city liable) indicated that the hindsight participants' likelihood estimates were only slightly, and not significantly, higher than the foresight ones, $U = 86$, $p > .5$. The mean probabilities were 15.85 for the foresight participants and 17.78 for the hindsight participants. Similarly, among participants who chose not to hire the operator (or to exonerate the city) probability estimates did not differ significantly (foresight = 7.03, hindsight = 6.53, $U = 183.5$, $p > .1$). This suggests that participants could have first decided whether the flood was more likely than 10%, and then chosen a particular probability anchored on the 10% cutoff.

The remaining data from the 7-point Likert scales (measuring the simulation's realism, the difficulty in deciding the probability, the effectiveness of the opposing advocate characters, and whether or not the city should pay damages) were analyzed using a 2 × 3 ANOVA, with main effects of choice (hire/hold liable vs. don't hire/don't hold liable) and condition (foresight, hindsight, and debiasing). Participants who chose to hire/hold liable agreed with the statement that the city should pay for accident damages significantly more than participants who chose not to hire or hold the city liable, $F(1.70) = 15.7$, $p < .001$. This rating did not differ by condition, $F(2.70) = 2.0$, $p > .1$. Nor did the interaction between choice and condition affect the rating, $F(2.70) = 0.2$, $p > .5$. Analysis of the participants' ratings of the simulation's realism and of the task difficulty revealed no significant main effects or interactions, F's < 2.8, p's $> .05$.

Participants' ratings of the effectiveness of the proponent/plaintiff's attorney did not differ by condition, choice or their interaction, F's < 2.3, p's $> .1$. The ratings of opponent/defense attorney did not differ by choice, $F(1.70) = .05$, p

> .5, but the effect of condition was significant, $F(2.70) = 4.4$, $p < .01$. (Means are 4.12, 3.00, 3.60, for foresight, hindsight, and debiasing, respectively, with higher numbers indicating a worse rating.) Post hoc analysis using the Tukey[Honestly Significant Differences test revealed that this effect was driven primarily by the low rating given by the hindsight participants in contrast to the foresight participants. No other contrasts were significant. The interaction between choice and condition did not significantly affect ratings of the defense attorney's effectiveness, $F(2.70) = .67$, $p > .5$.

Discussion

These results demonstrate that the hindsight bias influences judgments of liability. In this study, outcome knowledge deeply affected participants' interpretations of a complex story. A majority of participants randomly assigned to the hindsight condition judged the choice made by over three quarters of the foresight participants to be negligent. As the study shows, a good faith effort to determine a reasonable level of precautions in foresight may receive harsh judgment when viewed in hindsight.

The data did not support the secondary hypothesis; the judicial debiasing instructions failed to reduce the hindsight bias. There are several possible explanations for the ineffectiveness of the debiasing instructions. The instructions may simply have been missed or ignored in the context of the full trial. Research on jury instructions shows that they often do not produce their desired effects (Diamond, 1993; Sue, Smith, & Caldwell, 1973), or that they may even have a counterproductive influence (Thompson, Fong, & Rosenhan, 1981.

Alternatively, participants may not have actively followed the instructions to "consider how the events that led up to the accident could have turned out differently." Unlike this experiment, the successful debiasing studies all required their participants to actually state reasons why other outcomes may have occurred (Arkes et al., 1988) or to list supporting facts for various potential outcomes (Davies, 1987). Confined by the context of a court hearing, the present study indicates that merely encouraging participants to "imagine alternative outcomes" may not be adequate for reducing the bias. Although this study tested a technique easily suitable for the courtroom, its failure suggests that more intrusive procedures might be necessary to counteract the bias' influence.

The data support the hypothesis that the hindsight bias would affect judgments of the events and not the characters involved. Participants' evaluations of the opposing characters' abilities and of the simulation in general did not differ between conditions, except that hindsight participants rated the opponent/defense attorney's performance significantly higher than did the foresight participants. This finding is difficult to explain, and the effect is in the opposite direction from what the hindsight bias might predict. Hindsight participants felt that the defense attorney did a better job, despite expressing more disagreement with his position. The meaning of this effect is unclear.

There may be other limitations within the study, as well. Participants in the trial conditions were not given instructions on the plaintiff's burden of proof. This was to ensure that the two conditions were parallel, but it did result in a deviation from normal trial procedures. Since hindsight's influence was so large (57% versus 24%), the effect should have occurred anyway, but this variance from normal procedures may have exacerbated the effect size.

Additionally, the study tested individual judgments rather than those of a jury. The sample is unrepresentative of a typical jury pool, and no group deliberation occurred. However, researchers (e.g., Casper et al., 1989) have found college student samples to display the hindsight bias in patterns similar to adults called for jury service. Furthermore, at present the effects of group deliberation on the hindsight bias are unknown. In reality, juries decide few civil suits. Bench trials have become increasingly popular (Hans & Vidmar, 1986), and more importantly, the vast majority of cases settle before trial (Lempert & Saunders, 1986). Hence, the outcome of civil suits is determined primarily by attorneys and clients reviewing the merits of their case, or by arbitrators and mediators. This means that liability judgments are often decided by individuals rather than by groups. One might argue that data from undergraduates do not apply to the decision making of attorneys or arbitrators, but the robust nature of the hindsight bias across differing populations suggests otherwise.

The differences in the instructions and testimony or even the basic differences in format (meeting vs. trial) could also be said to account for the results. Yet differences in the instructions and testimony probably cannot account for the effect because there were so few. The instructions necessarily differed, as described in the methods section, but required the participants to make the same assessment. The substance of each witness' testimony did not vary, and the text itself was practically identical.

The basic format may have had some effect. While an administrative hearing demands an honest assessment of accident likelihood, trials tend to focus more on the assignment of blame. The possibility exists that these may be fundamentally different chores. In this study, however, participants in each condition were instructed to base their decisions on their probability judgments. Furthermore, not only were hindsight participants more likely to judge the city liable, but they also estimated higher annual flood likelihood. This suggests that the hindsight bias, rather than a difference in tasks, drove the effect. Finally, even if the basic format made a difference, then the implications for law would be the same. Potential defendants who take what appear to be reasonable precautions in foresight might find their choices indefensible once being sued.

One aspect of analysis indicates that something other than the hindsight bias may have driven the effect. After accounting for the decision to hire/hold liable, hindsight participants' probability estimates are only slightly, and not significantly, higher than those of the foresight participants. Thus, arguably the data cannot distinguish participants who decided liability first and then determined probability, from participants who decided the probability was greater or less than 10% first, and then anchored their judgment on this point. Since anchoring is a well-known phenomenon (Tversky & Kahneman, 1982), finding it in a study with a salient probability should be expected. We suggest that although anchoring distorted the distribution of the probability estimates, there is no reason to believe it affected the way in which the hindsight bias drove the decision to find the defendant liable.

In referring to the problem as a hindsight bias, however, we do not mean to suggest that supposedly reasonable minds in foresight do not err in assessing probabilities. It is possible that people underestimate the likelihood of that which has not yet occurred. Instead of "what did happen had to happen" (Fischhoff, 1975), "what has not happened will not happen." This would be a foresight bias. In either case, the tort system promises to only hold defendants liable for the level of precautions that appeared reasonable to them before an accident occurred. Thus under any interpretation, the bias ensures that some reasonable defendants will feel ambushed by adverse liability judgments after an accident has occurred.

Implications

Finding the hindsight bias in a generic case such as this one indicates the bias' potential influence in any negligence case. Since all tort litigation necessarily involves such *ex post* judgments, any untaken precaution may later give rise to liability, even if that precaution could not reasonably have been justified *ex ante*. The data may be interpreted as describing a pervasive flaw in the deterrence model of torts. Under the deterrence theory, requiring negligent defendants to compensate plaintiffs forces them to internalize the full social costs of their activities (Posner, 1992, pp. 163–167). The theory holds that potential injurers forced to bear the full costs of their activities will make socially correct choices about the costs and benefits of precaution, spending neither too much nor too little on safety. The deterrence theory has always assumed that errors in such estimates are random (Grady, 1983). To the extent that attorneys, judges, and juries reach estimates of *ex ante* probabilities that deviate systematically from the actual *ex ante* estimates, potential injurers will respond by spending more on safety precautions than cost-benefit analysis would justify.

Beyond the tort system, the hindsight bias may affect other areas of law, since foreseeability limitations pervade legal thinking. A computer search of the California Code reveals that the words "foresight," "foreseeable," "unforeseeable," and their variations appear in 193 different statutes. These range from statutes governing such diverse areas as attorney's fees (California Business and Professions Code, Sec. 6146), endangered species (California Fish and Game Code, Sec. 2067), pesticides (California Food and Agricultural Code, Sec. 12978), and earthquake education (California Public Resources Code, Sec. 2806). The United States Code contains 179 such references and the laws of other states also include significant use of the terms (Illinois, 68 statutes; New York, 89; Texas, 80). Furthermore, the application of the Hand formula is enormously popular. The difficulty of fairly determining foreseeability in hindsight seems to have escaped the notice of the legislators and judges.

Conclusions

Given the present research, this article cannot offer a solution to the hindsight problem. As we have demonstrated, mere judicial instructions are apparently unable to activate the cognitive processes necessary to reduce the bias. Perhaps more effective instructions could nevertheless be drafted. Other solutions for bias reduction could include elaborate special verdict forms or Wexler and Schopp's (1989) suggestion on bifurcating trials. A special verdict form would contain a detailed set of instructions to the jury as to how they should decide the case. It could direct them to consider alternative outcomes and could even require them to write out such alternatives. Since Wiggins and Breckler (1990) have shown that special verdict forms improve comprehension of jury instructions in civil trials, perhaps such forms could improve the cognitive processes of jurors as well.

Legal scholars have suspected for some time that the current standard of deciding negligence in hindsight may be inadequate (Green, 1977). The bias is likely to be influencing other legal judgments as well. The ubiquity of foreseeability judgments in law suggests the need for developing effective debiasing techniques.

References

American Law Institute. (1965). Restatement of torts, second (Vol. 2). St. Paul: American Law Institute.

Arkes, H.R. (1989). Principles in judgment/decision making research pertinent to legal proceedings. Behavioral Sciences & the Law, 7, 429–456.

Arkes, H.R., Faust, D., Guilmette, T.J., & Hart, K. (1988). Eliminating the hindsight bias. Journal of Applied Psychology, 73, 305–307.

Arkes, H.R., Wortmann, R.C., Saville, P.D., & Harkness, A.R. (1981). The hindsight bias among physicians weighing the likelihood of diagnoses. Journal of Applied Psychology, 66, 252–254.

Bodenhausen, G.V. (1990). Second-guessing the jury: Stereotyping and hindsight biases in perceptions of court cases. Journal of Applied Social Psychology, 20, 1112–1121.

Brown, J.P. (1973). Toward an economic theory of liability. In M. Kuperberg & C. Beitz (Eds.), Law, economics, and philosophy (pp. 185–205). Totowa, New Jersey: Rowman and Allanheld.

California Business and Professional Code, Sec. 6146 (1993).

California Fish and Game Code, Sec. 2067 (1993).

California Food and Agricultural Code, Sec. 12978 (1993).

California Public Resources Code, Sec. 2806 (1993).

Carli, L.L., & Leonard, J.B. (1989). The effect of hindsight on victim derogation. Journal of Social and Clinical Psychology, 8, 331–343.

Casper, J.D., Benedict, K., & Perry, J.L. (1989). Juror decision making, attitudes, and the hindsight bias. Law and Human Behavior, 13, 291–310.

Connolly, T., & Bukszar, E.W. (1990). Hindsight bias: Self flattery or cognitive error? Journal of Behavior Decision Making, 40, 50–68.

Davies, M.F. (1987). Reduction of the hindsight bias by restoration of foresight perspective: Effectiveness of foresight encoding and hindsight-retrieval strategies. Organizational Behavior and Human Decision Making, 3, 205–211.

Detmer, D.E., Fryback, D.G., & Gassner, K. (1978). Heuristics and biases in medical decision making. Journal of Medical Education, 53, 682–683.

Devitt, E.J., Blackmar, C.B., & Wolf, M.A. (1987). Federal jury practice and instructions: Civil (4th ed.). St. Paul: West.

Diamond, S.S. (1993). Instructing on death: Psychologists, juries, judges. American Psychologist, 48, 423–434.

Einhorn, H.J., & Hogarth, R.M. (1986). Judging probable cause. Psychological Bulletin, 99, 3–19.

Fischhoff, B. (1975). Hindsight ≠ foresight: The effect of outcome knowledge on judgment under uncertainty. Journal of Experimental Psychology: Human Perception and Performance, 1, 288–299.

Fischhoff, B. (1977). Perceived informativeness of facts. Journal of Experimental Psychology: Human Perception and Performance, 3, 349–358.

Fischhoff, B., Slovic, P., & Lichtenstein, S. (1978). Fault trees: Sensitivity of estimated failure probabilities to problem representation. Journal of Experimental Psychology: Human Perception and Performance, 4, 330–344.

Fischhoff, B. (1982a). For those condemned to study the past: Heuristics and biases in hindsight. In D. Kahneman, P. Slovic, & A. Tversky (Eds.), Judgment under uncertainty: Heuristics and biases (pp. 335–351). New York: Cambridge University Press.

Fischhoff, B. (1982b). Debiasing. In D. Kahneman, P. Slovic, & A. Tversky (Eds.), Judgment under uncertainty: Heuristics and biases (pp. 422–445). New York: Cambridge University Press.

Grady, M.F. (1983). A new positive economic theory of negligence. Yale Law Journal, 92, 799–829.

Grady, M.F. (1989). Untaken precautions. Journal of Legal Studies, 18, 139–153.

Green, L. (1977). Foreseeability in negligence law. In L. Green (Ed.), The litigation process in tort law: No place to stop in the development of tort law (2nd ed.) (pp. 283–302). Indianapolis: Bobbs-Merril.

Hans, V.P., & Vidmar, N. (1986). Judging the jury. New York: Plenum.

Heil, W., Gigerenzer, G., Gauggel, S., Mall, M., & Muller, M. (1988). Hindsight bias: An interaction of automatic and motivational factors? Memory & Cognition, 16, 533–538.

Horowitz, I.A., & Bordens, K.S. (1990). An experimental investigation of procedural issues in complex tort trials. Law and Human Behavior, 14, 3, 269–285.

Kageniro, D.K., Taylor, R.B., Lauter, W.S., & Harland, A.T. (1991). Hindsight bias and third-party consents to warrantless police searches. Law and Human Behavior, 15, 305–314.

Keeton, W.P. (1984). Prosser and Keeton on the law of torts (5th ed.). St. Paul: West.

Kurtz, R.M., & Garfield, S.L. (1978). Illusory correlation: A further exploration of Chapman's paradigm. Journal of Consulting and Clinical Psychology, 46, 1009–1015.

Landes, W.M., & Posner, R.A. (1983). Causation in tort law: An economic approach. Journal of Legal Studies, 12, 109–134.

Leary, M.R. (1982). Hindsight bias and the 1980 presidential election. Personality and Social Psychology Bulletin, 8, 257–263.

Lempert, R., & Saunders, J. (1986). An invitation to law and social science. Philadelphia: University of Pennsylvania Press.

Loftus, E.F. (1993). Psychologists in the eyewitness world. American Psychologist, 48, 550–552.

Miller, D.T., & McFarland, C. (1986). Counterfactual thinking and victim compensation: A test of norm theory. Personality and Social Psychology Bulletin, 12, 513–519.

Mitchell, T.R., & Kalb, L.S. (1982). Effects of job experience on supervisor attributions for a subordinate's poor performance. Journal of Applied Psychology, 67, 181–188.

Pennington, D.C., Rutter, D.R., McKenna, K., & Morely, I.E. (1980). Estimating the outcome of a pregnancy test: Women's judgment in foresight and hindsight. British Journal of Social and Clinical Psychology, 20, 89–96.

Petition of Kinsman Transit Co., 338 F.2d 708 (2d Cir. 1964).

Posner, R.A. (1992). Economic analysis of law (4th ed.), Boston: Little Brown.

Saks, M.J. (1986). The law does not live by eyewitness testimony alone. Law and Human Behavior, 10, 279–280.

Sue, S., Smith, R.E., & Caldwell, C. (1973). Effects of inadmissible evidence on the decisions of simulated jurors: a moral dilemma. Journal of Applied Social Psychology, 3, 345–353.

Thompson, W.C., Cowan, C.L., Ellsworth, P.C., & Harrington, J.C. (1984). Death penalty attitudes and conviction proneness: The translation of attitudes into verdicts. Law and Human Behavior, 8, 95–113.

Thompson, W.C., Fong, G.T., & Rosennan, D.L. (1981). Inadmissible evidence and juror verdicts. Journal of Personality and Social Psychology, 40, 453–463.

Tversky, A., & Kahneman, D. (1982). Judgment under uncertainty: Heuristics and biases. In D. Kahneman, P. Slovic, & A. Tversky (Eds.), Judgment under uncertainty: Heuristics and biases (pp. 335–351). New York: Cambridge University Press.

United States v. Carroll Towing, Co., 159 F.2d 169 (2d Cir. 1947).

Wells, G.L., Taylor, B.R., & Turtle, J.W. (1987). The undoing of scenarios. Journal of Personality and Social Psychology, 53, 421–430.

Wexler, D.B., & Schopp, R.F. (1989). How and when to correct for juror hindsight bias in mental health malpractice litigation: Some preliminary observations. Behavioral Sciences and the Law, 7, 485–504.

Wiggins, E.C., & Breckler, S.J. (1990). Specials verdicts as guides to jury decision making. Law & Psychology Review, 14, 1–36.

Wood, G. (1978). The knew-it-all-along effect. Journal of Experimental Psychology: Human Perception and Performance, 4, 345–353.

Zeisel, H., & Callahan, T. (1967). Split trials and time savings: A statistical analysis. Harvard Law Review, 76, 1606–1629.

About the Editors

DAVID B. WEXLER is John D. Lyons Professor of Law and Professor of Psychology at the University of Arizona in Tucson, Arizona. He also lives part of the year in San Juan, Puerto Rico, where he is affiliated with the University of Puerto Rico School of Law and with the Caribbean Center for Advanced Studies in Psychology. His other books include *Essays in Therapeutic Jurisprudence* (with Bruce J. Winick, Carolina Academic Press, 1991), *Therapeutic Jurisprudence: The Law as a Therapeutic Agent* (Carolina Academic Press, 1990), and *Mental Health Law: Major Issues* (Plenum Press, 1981). He received the American Psychiatric Association's Manfred S. Guttmacher Forensic Psychiatry Award; chaired the American Bar Association's Commission on Mental Disability and the Law; chaired the Association of American Law Schools Section on Law and Mental Disability; chairs the Advisory Board of the National Center for State Courts' Institute on Mental Disability and the Law; was a member of the National Commission on the Insanity Defense; was a member of the Panel on Legal Issues of the President's Commission on Mental Health; served as Vice President of the International Academy of Law and Mental Health; received the New York University School of Law Distinguished Alumnus Legal Scholarship/Teaching Award; and serves as a member of the MacArthur Foundation Research Network on Mental Health and the Law.

BRUCE J. WINICK is Professor of Law and Scholar in Residence at the University of Miami School of Law in Coral Gables, Florida. His other books include *The Right to Refuse Mental Health Treatment* (American Psychological Association Press, forthcoming 1997), *Therapeutic Jurisprudence Applied: Essays on Mental Health Law* (Carolina Academic Press, forthcoming 1996), *Essays in Therapeutic Jurisprudence* (with David B. Wexler, Carolina Academic Press, 1991), and *Current Issues in Mental Disability Law* (co-edited with Alexander D. Brooks, 1987). He is co-editor of the American Psychological Association Press book series, *Law and Public Policy/Psychology and the Social Sciences*. He also serves on the editorial boards of *Law and Human Behavior* and of *Psychology, Public Policy & Law*, and is a reviewer for the *American Journal of Psychiatry*. He has served as legal consultant to the American Psychiatric Association Task Force on Consent to Voluntary Hospitalization, and has chaired the Association of American Law Schools Section on Law and Medicine. Prior to joining the faculty of the University of Miami in 1974, Professor Winick served as New York City's Director of Court Mental Health Services and as General Counsel of the New York City Department of Mental Health and Mental Retardation Services. He received his law degree from the New York University School of Law.

Bibliography of Therapeutic Jurisprudence

Books

Perlin, Michael L. *The Jurisprudence of the Insanity Defense*. Durham: Carolina Academic Press, (1994).

Sales, Bruce D., and Daniel W. Shuman, editors. *Law, Mental Health, and Mental Disorder*. Pacific Grove: Brooks/Cole Publishing Company (1996).

Wexler, David B., editor. *Therapeutic Jurisprudence: The Law as a Therapeutic Agent*. Durham: Carolina Academic Press (1990).

Wexler, David B., and Bruce J. Winick. *Essays in Therapeutic Jurisprudence*. Durham: Carolina Academic Press (1991).

Wexler, David B., and Bruce J. Winick, editors. *Law in a Therapeutic Key: Developments in Therapeutic Jurisprudence*. Durham: Carolina Academic Press (1996).

Winick, Bruce J. *The Right to Refuse Mental Health Treatment*. American Psychological Association Books, (forthcoming, 1997).

———. *Therapeutic Jurisprudence Applied: Essays on Mental Health Law*. Durham: Carolina Academic Press (forthcoming, 1996).

Symposia

American Journal of Orthopsychiatry: "Mental Health Law and Mental Health Care," Volume 64, pp. 172–251 (1994).

New England Journal on Criminal and Civil Confinement: "Therapeutic Jurisprudence: Bridging the Gap From Theory to Practice," Volume 20, pp. 243–383 (1994).

New York Law School Journal of Human Rights: "Therapeutic Jurisprudence: Restructuring Mental Disability Law," Volume 10, pp. 623–926 (1993).

Psychology, Public Policy, and Law: "Therapeutic Jurisprudence," Volume 1, pp. 6–236 (1995).

Articles, Chapters, etc.

Abisch, Janet B. "Mediational Lawyering in the Civil Commitment Context: A Therapeutic Jurisprudence Solution to the Counsel Role Dilemma." *Psychology, Public Policy, and Law*, Volume 1, pp 120–141 (1995).

Abrams, Roger I., Frances E. Abrams, and Dennis R. Nolan. "Arbitral Therapy." *Rutgers Law Review*, Volume 46, pp. 1751–1785 (1994).

Acker, James R. Review of *Essays in Therapeutic Jurisprudence*, by David B. Wexler and Bruce J. Winick. *Journal of Psychiatry and Law*, Volume 20, pp. 272–278 (1992)

Anderson, Elizabeth, Murray Levine, Anupama Sharma, Louise Ferretti, Karen Steinberg, and Leah Wallach. "Coercive Uses of Mandatory Reporting in Therapeutic Relationships." *Behavioral Sciences and the Law*, Volume 11, pp. 335–345 (1993).

Barnum, Richard, and Thomas Grisso. "Competence to Stand Trial in Juvenile Court in Massachusetts: Issues of Therapeutic Jurisprudence." *New England Journal on Criminal and Civil Confinement*, Volume 20, pp. 321–344 (1994).

Bloom, Joseph D. and Mary H. Williams. "Conditional Release as a National Standard for the Treatment of Insanity Acquittees." In *Management and Treatment of Insanity Acquittees: A Model for the 1990's*, by Joseph D. Bloom and Mary H. Williams, pp. 203–217. Washington, D.C.: American Psychiatric Press, Inc. (1994).

Carson, David. "Therapeutic Jurisprudence for the United Kingdom?" *The Journal of Forensic Psychiatry*, Volume 6, pp. 463–466 (1995).

Carson, David, and David B. Wexler. "New Approaches to Mental Health Law: Will the UK Follow the US Lead, Again?" *The Journal of Social Welfare and Family Law*, Number 1, pp. 79–96 (1994).

Cohen, Fred. "Liability for Custodial Suicide: The Information Base Requirements." *Jail Suicide Update*, Volume 4, pp. 1–11 (1992).

Cohen, Fred, and Joel A. Dvoskin. "Therapeutic Jurisprudence and Corrections: A Glimpse." *New York Law School Journal of Human Rights*, Volume 10, pp. 777–804 (1993).

Costello, Jan C. "Why Would I Need a Lawyer? Legal Counsel and Advocacy for People with Mental Disabilities." In *Law, Mental Health, and Mental Disorders*, edited by B. Sales and D. Shuman, pp. 15–39. Pacific Grove: Brooks/Cole Publishing Company (1996).

Coyle, Genevieve Sansoucy. Review of *Essays in Therapeutic Jurisprudence*, by David B. Wexler and Bruce J. Winick. *Social Work in Health Care*, pp. 135 (1992).

Daly-Rooney, Rose. "Designing Reasonable Accommodations Through Co-Worker Participation: Therapeutic Jurisprudence and the Confidentiality Provision of the Americans with Disabilities Act." *Journal of Law and Health*, Volume 8, pp. 89–104 (1994).

Dorfman, Deborah A. "Through a Therapeutic Jurisprudence Filter: Fear and Pretextuality in Mental Disability Law." *New York Law School Journal of Human Rights*, Volume 10, pp. 805–824 (1993).

———. "Effectively Implementing Title I of the Americans With Disabilities Act For Mentally Disabled Persons: A Therapeutic Jurisprudence Analysis." *Journal of Law and Health*, Volume 8, pp. 105–121 (1993–1994).

Drinan, Robert F. Review of *Essays in Therapeutic Jurisprudence*, by David B. Wexler and Bruce J. Winick. *Martindale-Hubbell Legal Publishing Review*, pp. 187 (June 1992).

Elwork, Amiram. "Psycholegal Treatment and Intervention: The Next Challenge." *Law and Human Behavior*, Volume 16, pp. 175–183 (1992).

Elwork, Amiram, and G. Andrew H. Benjamin. "Lawyers in Distress." *Journal of Psychiatry and Law*, Volume 23, pp. 205–229 (1995).

Feldthusen, Bruce. "The Civil Action for Sexual Battery: Therapeutic Jurisprudence?" *Ottawa Law Review*, Volume 25, pp. 205–234 (1993).

Finkelman, David, and Thomas Grisso. "Therapeutic Jurisprudence: From Idea to Application." *New England Journal on Criminal and Civil Confinement*, Volume 20, pp. 243–257 (1994).

Foley, M. A. Review of *Essays in Therapeutic Jurisprudence*, by David B. Wexler and Bruce J. Winick. *Choice*, pp. 613 (June 1992).

Goldstein, Elizabeth J. "Asking the Impossible: The Negilgence Liability of the Mentally Ill." *Journal of Contemporary Health Law and Policy*, Volume 12, pp. 67–92 (1995).

Gould, Keri A. "Turning Rat and Doing Time for Uncharged, Dismissed, or Acquitted Crimes: Do the Federal Sentencing Guidelines Promote Respect for the Law?" *New York Law School Journal of Human Rights*, Volume 10, pp. 835–875 (1993).

———. "A Therapeutic Jurisprudence Analysis of Competency Evaluation Requests: The Defense Attorney's Dilemma." *International Journal of Law and Psychiatry*, Volume 18, pp. 83–100 (1995).

Greer, Alexander. Review of *Essays in Therapeutic Jurisprudence*, by David B. Wexler and Bruce J. Winick. *Hospital and Community Psychiatry*, Volume 43, pp. 1151–(1992).

Greer, Alexander, Mary O'Regan, and Amy Traverso. "Therapeutic Jurisprudence and Patients' Perceptions of Procedural Due Process of Civil Commitment Hearings." *Law in a Therapeutic Key*, edited by David B. Wexler and Bruce J. Winick. Durham: Carolina Academic Press (1996).

Harrison, Jeffrey L. "Class, Personality, Contract, and Unconscionability." *William & Mary Law Review*, Volume 35, pp. 445–501 (1994).

Haycock, Joel. "Speaking Truth to Power: Rights, Therapeutic Jurisprudence, and Massachusetts Mental Health law." *New England Journal on Criminal and Civil Confinement*, Volume 20, pp. 301–320 (1994).

Haycock, Joel, David Finkelman, and Helene Presskreischer. "Mediating the Gap: Thinking About Alternatives to the Current Practice of Civil Commitment." *New England Journal on Criminal and Civil Confinement*, Volume 20, pp. 265–289 (1994).

Joseph, Philip. Review of *Therapeutic Jurisprudence: The Law as a Therapeutic Agent*, by David B. Wexler. *Criminal Behavior and Mental Health*, Volume 1, pp. 107 (1991).

Kamin, Kim A., and Jeffrey J. Rachlinski. "Ex Post ≠ Ex Ante: Determining Liability in Hindsight." *Law and Human Behavior*, Volume 19, pp. 89–103 (1995).

Kane, Robert J. "A Sentencing Model for the 21st Century." *Federal Probation, A Journal of Correctional Philosophy and Practice*, pp. 10–15. Published by the Administrative Office of the United States Courts, Washington DC 20544 (September, 1995).

Kapp, Marshall B. "Treatment and Refusal Rights in Mental Health: Therapeutic Justice and Clinical Accommodation." *American Journal of Orthopsychiatry*, Volume 64, pp. 223–234 (1994).

Kavanagh, Kay. "Don't Ask, Don't Tell: Deception Required, Disclosure Denied." *Psychology, Public Policy, and Law*, Volume 1, pp. 142–160 (1995).

Kelly, Kathryn. Review of *Essays in Therapeutic Jurisprudence*, by David B. Wexler and Bruce J. Winick. *Journal of Contemporary Health Law and Policy*, Volume 9, pp. 623–627 (1993).

Klotz, Jeffrey A. "Limiting the Psychotherapist-Patient Privilege: The Therapeutic Potential." *Criminal Law Bulletin*, Volume 27, pp. 416–432 (1991).

———. "Sex Offenders and the Law: New Directions." In *Mental Health and Law: Research, Policy, and Services*, edited by Bruce D. Sales and Saleem A. Shah, pp. 257–282. Durham: Carolina Academic Press (1996).

Klotz, Jeffrey A., David B. Wexler, Bruce D. Sales, and Judith V. Becker. "Cognitive Restructuring Through Law: A Therapeutic Jurisprudence Approach to Sex Offenders and the Plea Process." *University of Puget Sound Law Review*, Volume 15, pp. 579–595 (1992).

La Fond, John Q. "Law and the Delivery of Involuntary Mental Health Services." *American Journal of Orthopsychiatry*, Volume 64, pp. 209–222 (1994).

Laufer, William S. Review of *The Jurisprudence of the Insanity Defense*, by Michael L. Perlin. *Journal of Legal Medicine*, Volume 16, pp. 453 (1995).

Levine, Murray. "Law and Psychiatry or Law Versus Psychiatry?" Review of *Therapeutic Jurisprudence: The Law as a Therapeutic Agent*, by David B. Wexler. *Contemporary Psychology*, Volume 36, pp. 931–932 (1991).

———. "A Therapeutic Jurisprudence Analysis of Mandated Reporting of Child Maltreatment by Psychotherapists." *New York Law School Journal of Human Rights*, Volume 10, pp. 711–738 (1993).

McDaniel, Ellen G. Review of *Therapeutic Jurisprudence: The Law as a Therapeutic Agent*, by David B. Wexler. *The Journal of Psychiatry and Law*, Volume 20, pp. 103–106 (1992).

Melton, Gary. Review of *Essays in Therapeutic Jurisprudence*, by David B. Wexler and Bruce J. Winick. *Contemporary Psychology*, Volume 39 (February 1994).

Menninger II, Karl. Review of *Therapeutic Jurisprudence: The Law as a Therapeutic Agent*, by David B. Wexler. *Journal of Psychiatry and Law*, Volume, pp.103 (1992)

Morris, Grant H. "Requiring Sound Judgments of Unsound Minds: Tort Liability and the Limits of Therapeutic Jurisprudence." *Southern Methodist University Law Review*, Volume 47, pp. 1837–1860 (1994).

Mossman, Douglas. "Veterans Affairs Disability Compensation: A Case Study in Countertherapeutic Jurisprudence." *Bulletin of the American Academy of Psychiatry and Law*, Volume 24, p. 27 (1996).

Packer, Ira K. "The Court Clinic System in Massachusetts: A Therapeutic Approach vs. a Rights-Oriented Approach." *New England Journal on Criminal and Civil Confinement*, Volume 20, pp. 291–300 (1994).

Parry, John W. "Psychiatric Treatment and Justice at Odds." Review of *Therapeutic Jurisprudence: The Law as a Therapeutic Agent*, by David B. Wexler. *Mental and Physical Disability Law Reporter*, Volume 15, pp. 119–123 (1991).

Perlin, Michael L. "Reading the Supreme Court's Tea Leaves: Predicting Judicial Behavior in Civil and Criminal Right to Refuse Treatment Cases." *American Journal of Forensic Psychiatry*, Volume 12, pp. 37–67 (1991).

———. "Fatal Assumption: A Critical Evaluation of the Role of Counsel in Mental Disability Cases." *Law and Human Behavior*, Volume 16, pp. 39–59 (1992).

———. "Tarasoff and the Dilemma of the Dangerous Patient: New Directions for the 1990's." *Law and Psychology Review*, Volume 16, pp. 29–63 (1992).

———. "Pretexts and Mental Disability Law: The Case of Competency." *University of Miami Law Review*, Volume 47, pp. 625–688 (1993).

———. "What is Therapeutic Jurisprudence?" *New York Law School Journal of Human Rights*, Volume 10, pp. 623–636 (1993).

———. "Hospitalized Patients and the Right to Sexual Interaction: Beyond the Last Frontier." *New York University Review of Law and Social Change*, Volume 20, pp. 517–547 (1993–1994).

———. "The ADA and Persons with Mental Disabilities: Can Sanist Attitudes Be Undone?" *Journal of Law and Health*, Volume 8, pp. 15–45 (1993–1994).

———. "Law and the Delivery of Mental Health Services in the Community." *American Journal of Orthopsychiatry*, Volume 64, pp. 194–208 (1994).

———. " Therapeutic Jurisprudence: Understanding the Sanist and Pretextual Bases of Mental Disability Law." *New England Journal on Criminal and Civil Confinement*, Volume 20, pp. 369–383 (1994).

———. "Therapeutic Jurisprudence." *Law and Mental Disability*, Section 5.01, pp. 661–663, Charlottesville: Michie Co. (1994).

———. "Therapeutic Jurisprudence: A Multi-Professional Perspective." In *Mental Health Law and Practice Through the Life Cycle*, edited by S. Verdun-Jones, pp. 76 (1994).

———. "New Academic Approach: Therapeutic Jurisprudence." *Mental Disability Law: Civil and Criminal*, Charlottesville: Michie Co. (1989), Section 1.05A (1995 Supp.).

———. "The Voluntary Delivery of Mental Health Services in the Community." In *Law, Mental Health, and Mental Disorder*, edited by Bruce D. Sales and Daniel W. Shuman, pp. 150–177. Pacific Grove: Brooks/Cole Publishing Company (1996).

———. "Myths, Realities, and the Political World: The Anthropology of Insanity Defense Attitudes." *Bulletin of the American Academy of Psychiatry and Law* (forthcoming 1996).

Perlin, Michael L., and Deborah A. Dorfman. "Sanism, Social Science, and the Development of Mental Disability Law Jurisprudence." *Behavioral Sciences and the Law*, Volume 11, pp. 47–66 (1993).

———. "Is It More Than 'Dodging Lions and Wastin' Time? Adequacy of Counsel, Questions of Competence, and the Judicial Process In Individual Right to Refuse Treatment Cases." *Psychology, Public Policy, and Law*, (in press, 1996).

Perlin, Michael L., and Keri K. Gould. "Rashomon and the Criminal Law: Mental Disability and the Federal Sentencing Guidelines." *American Journal of Criminal Law*, Volume 22, pp. 431–459 (1995).

Perlin, Michael L., Keri K. Gould, and Deborah Dorfman. "Therapeutic Jurisprudence and the Civil Rights of Institutionalized Mentally Disabled Persons: Hopeless Oxymoron or Path to Redemption?" *Psychology, Public Policy, and Law*, Volume 1, pp. 80–119 (1995).

Petrila, John. "Paternalism and the Unrealized Promise of Essays in Therapeutic Jurisprudence." Review of *Essays in Therapeutic Jurisprudence*, by David B. Wexler and Bruce J. Winick. *New York Law School Journal of Human Rights*, Volume 10, pp. 877–905 (1993).

Pincus, William Hoffman. "Civil Commitment and the 'Great Confinement' Revisited: Straightjacketing Individual Rights, Stifling Culture." *William and Mary Law Review*, Volume 36, pp. 1769–1817 (1995).

Poythress, Norman G., and Stanley L. Brodsky. "In the Wake of a Negligent Release Law Suit: An Investigation of Professional Consequences and Institutional Impact on a State Psychiatric Hospital." *Law and Human Behavior*, Volume 16, pp. 155–173 (1992).

Quattrocchi, Michael R., and Robert F. Schopp. "The Normative and Conceptual Foundations of a Clinical Duty to Protect." *Behavioral Sciences and the Law*, Volume 11, pp. 165–180 (1993).

Sadoff, Robert L. "When is Law Therapeutic?" Review of Therapeutic Jurisprudence: The Law as a Therapeutic Agent, by David B. Wexler. *Contemporary Psychiatry*, Volume 9, pp. 245–246 (1990).

———. "Therapeutic Jurisprudence: A View From a Forensic Psychiatrist." *New York Law School Journal of Human Rights*, Volume 10, pp. 825–833 (1993).

Sales, Bruce D., and Daniel W. Shuman. "The Newly Emerging Mental Health Law." In *Law, Mental Health, and Mental Disorder*, edited by B. Sales and D. Shuman, pp. 2–14. Pacific Grove: Brooks/Cole Publishing Company (1996).

———. "Mental Health Law and Mental Health Care: Introduction." *American Journal of Orthopsychiatry*, Volume 64, pp. 172–179 (1994).

Samuels, Alec. Review of *Therapeutic Jurisprudence: The Law as a Therapeutic Agent*, by David B. Wexler. *Medicine, Science, and the Law*, Volume 30, p. 275 (1992).

———. Review of *Essays in Therapeutic Jurisprudence*, by David B. Wexler and Bruce J. Winick. *Medicine, Science, and the Law*, Volume 32, p. 358 (1992).

Satin, Mark I. "Law and Psychology: A Movement Whose Time Has Come." *1994 Annual Survey of American Law*, p. 581 (1995).

Schopp, Robert F. "The Psychotherapist's Duty to Protect the Public: The Appropriate Standard and the Foundation in Legal Theory and Empirical Premises." *Nebraska Law Review*, Volume 70, pp. 327–360 (1991).

———. "Therapeutic Jurisprudence and Conflicts Among Values in Mental Health Law." *Behavioral Sciences and the Law*, Volume 11, pp. 31–45 (1993).

———. "Sexual Predators and the Structure of the Mental Health System: Expanding the Normative Focus of Therapeutic Jurisprudence." *Psychology, Public Policy, and Law*, Volume 1, pp. 161–192 (1995).

Schopp, Robert F., and Michael R. Quattrocchi. "Predicting the Present: Expert Testimony and Civil Commitment." *Behavioral Sciences and the Law*, Volume 13, pp. 159–181 (1995).

Schopp, Robert F., and David B. Wexler. "Shooting Yourself in the Foot with Due Care: Psychotherapists and Crystallized Standards of Tort Liability." *The Journal of Psychiatry and Law*, Volume 17, pp. 163–203 (1989).

Shiff, Allison R., and David B. Wexler. "Teen Court: A Therapeutic Jurisprudence Perspective." *Criminal Law Bulletin*, Volume 32, pp. 342–357 (1996).

Shuman, Daniel W. "Overview." *Southern Methodist University Law Review*, Volume 46, pp. 323–327 (1992).

———. "Therapeutic Jurisprudence and Tort Law: A Limited Subjective Standard of Care." *Southern Methodist University Law Review*, Volume 46, pp. 409–432 (1992).

———. "Making the World a Better Place Through Tort Law?: Through the Therapeutic Looking Glass." *New York Law School Journal of Human Rights*, Volume 10, pp. 739–758 (1993).

———. "The Duty of the State to Rescue the Vulnerable in the United States." In *The Duty to Rescue: The Jurisprudence of Aid*, edited by Michael A. Menlowe and Alexander McCall Smith. Brookfield: Dartmouth (1993).

———. "The Psychology of Compensation in Tort Law." *University of Kansas Law Review*, Volume 43, pp. 39–77 (1994).

———. Review of *Almost a Revolution: Mental Health Law and the Limits of Change*, by Paul Appelbaum. *Journal of Health Politics, Policy, and Law*, Volume 20, pp. 1068 (1995).

Shuman, Daniel W., and Cynthia E. Daley. "Compensation for Mental and Emotional Distress." In *Law, Mental Health, and Mental Disorder*, edited by B. Sales and D. Shuman, pp. 294–308. Pacific Grove: Brooks/Cole Publishing Company (1996).

Shuman, Daniel W., Jean A. Hamilton, and Cynthia E. Daley. "The Health Effects of Jury Service." *Law and Psychology Review*, Volume 18, pp. 267–307 (1994).

Simon, Leonore M. J. "A Therapeutic Jurisprudence Approach to the Legal Processing of Domestic Violence Cases." *Psychology, Public Policy, and Law*, Volume 1, pp. 43–79 (1995).

Slobogin, Christopher. "Therapeutic Jurisprudence: Five Dilemmas to Ponder." *Psychology, Public Policy, and Law*, Volume 1, pp. 193–219 (1995).

———. "Dangerousness as a Criterion in the Criminal Process." In *Law, Mental Health, and Mental Disorder*, edited by B. Sales and D. Shuman, pp. 360–383. Pacific Grove: Brooks/Cole Publishing Company (1996).

Small, Mark A. "Advancing Psychological Jurisprudence." *Behavioral Sciences and the Law*, Volume 11, pp. 3–16 (1993).

———. "Legal Psychology and Therapeutic Jurisprudence." *St. Louis University Law Journal*, Volume 37, pp. 675–700 (1993).

Smith, Jeanette. Review of *Essays in Therapeutic Jurisprudence*, by David B. Wexler and Bruce J. Winick. *Expert Evidence*, Volume 2, pp. 43 (1993).

Smith, Steven R. "The Justice Mission and Mental Health Law." *Cleveland State Law Review*, Volume 40, pp. 527–531 (1992).

———. "Liability and Mental Health Services." *American Journal of Orthopsychiatry*, Volume 64, pp. 235–251 (1994).

Smith-Bell, Michele, and William J. Winslade. "Privacy, Confidentiality, and Privilege in Psychotherapeutic Relationships." *American Journal of Orthopsychiatry*, Volume 64, pp. 180–193 (1994).

Stirling, James L., Jr. "'Litigaphobia' in Alabama's State Mental Hospitals: Can Qualified Immunity put the King's Men Back Together Again?" *Law and Psychology Review*, Volume 15, pp. 185–209) (1991).

Stransky, Douglas S., "Civil Commitment and the Right to Refuse Treatment: Resolving Disputes from a Due Process Perspective." *University of Miami Law Review*, Volume 50, pp. 413–443 (1996).

Susman, Jack. "Resolving Hospital Conflicts: A Study on Therapeutic Jurisprudence." *Journal of Psychology and Law*, Volume 22, pp. 107–133 (1994).

Tyler, Tom R. "The Psychological Consequences of Judicial Procedures: Implications For Civil Commitment Hearings." *Southern Methodist University Law Review*, Volume 46, pp. 433–445 (1992).

Wexler, David B. "Inducing Therapeutic Compliance Through the Criminal Law." *Law and Psychology Review*, Volume 14, pp. 43–57 (1990).

———. "Training in Law and Behavioral Sciences: Issues From a Legal Educator's Perspective." *Behavioral Sciences and the Law*, Volume 8, pp. 197–204 (1990).

———. "Health Care Compliance Principles and the Insanity Acquittee Conditional Release Process." *Criminal Law Bulletin*, Volume 27, pp. 18–41 (1991).

———. "Justice, Mental Health, and Therapeutic Jurisprudence." *Cleveland State Law Review*, Volume 40, pp. 517–526 (1992).

———. "Putting Mental Health into Mental Health Law: Therapeutic Jurisprudence." *Law and Human Behavior*, Volume 16, pp. 27–38 (1992).

———. "New Directions in Therapeutic Jurisprudence: Breaking the Bounds of Conventional Mental Health Law Scholarship." *New York Law School Journal of Human Rights*, Volume 10, pp. 759–776 (1993).

———. "Therapeutic Jurisprudence and Changing Conceptions of Legal Scholarship." *Behavioral Sciences and the Law*, Volume 11, pp. 17–29 (1993).

―――. "Therapeutic Jurisprudence and the Criminal Courts." *William and Mary Law Review*, Volume 35, pp. 279–299 (1993).

―――. "An Orientation to Therapeutic Jurisprudence." *New England Journal on Criminal and Civil Confinement*, Volume 20, pp. 243–257 (1994).

―――. "Reflections on the Scope of Therapeutic Jurisprudence." *Psychology, Public Policy, and Law*, Volume 1, pp. 220–236 (1995).

―――. "Applying the Law Therapeutically." *Applied and Preventive Psychology*, Volume 5 (1996).

―――. "Some Therapeutic Jurisprudence Implications of the Outpatient Civil Commitment of Pregnant Substance Abusers." *Politics and the Life Sciences*, Volume 15, pp. 73–75 (1996).

―――. "Some Thoughts and Observations on the Teaching of Therapeutic Jurisprudence." *Revista de Derecho Puertorriqueño*, Volume 35, number 2 (forthcoming 1996).

―――. "Therapeutic Jurisprudence in Clinical Practice." *American Journal of Psychiatry*, Volume 153, pp. 453–455 (1996).

Wexler, David B., and Robert F. Schopp. "How and When to Correct for Juror Hindsight Bias in Mental Health Malpractice Litigation: Some Preliminary Observations." *Behavioral Sciences and the Law*, Volume 7, pp. 485–504 (1989).

―――. "Therapeutic Jurisprudence: A New Approach to Mental Health Law." In *Handbook of Psychology and Law*, edited by Dorothy K. Kagehiro and William S. Laufer. New York: Spinger-Verlag (1992).

Wexler, David B., and Bruce J. Winick. "Therapeutic Jurisprudence as a New Approach to Mental Health Law Policy Analysis and Research." *University of Miami Law Review*, Volume 45, pp. 979–1004 (1991).

―――. "The Potential of Therapeutic Jurisprudence: A New Approach to Psychology and the Law." In *Law and Psychology: The Broadening of the Discipline*, edited by James R. P. Ogloff. Durham: Carolina Academic Press (1992).

―――. "Therapeutic Jurisprudence and Criminal Justice Mental Health Issues." *Mental and Physical Disability Law Reporter*, Volume 16, pp. 225–231 (1992).

―――. "Patients, Professionals, and the Path of Therapeutic Jurisprudence: A Response to Petrilla." *New York Law School Journal of Human Rights*, Volume 10, pp. 907–914 (1993).

Whitley, Ann B. "Therapeutic Jurisprudence: A New Approach to the Criminal Law." Review of *Essays in Therapeutic Jurisprudence*, by David B. Wexler and Bruce J. Winick. *American Journal of Criminal Law*, Volume 20, pp. 303–306 (1993).

Wiebe, Richard P. "The Mental Health Implications of Crime Victims' Rights." In *Law, Mental Health, and Mental Disorder*, edited by B. Sales and D. Shuman, pp. 414–438. Pacific Grove: Brooks/Cole Publishing Company (1996).

Wiener, Richard L. "Social Analytic Jurisprudence and Tort Law: Social Cognition Goes to Court." *St. Louis University Law Journal*, Volume 37, pp. 503–551 (1993).

Wilkinson, William E. "Therapeutic Jurisprudence and Workers' Compensation." *Arizona Attorney*, Volume 30, pp. 28–33 (1994).

*Winick, Bruce J. "Competency to Consent to Treatment: The Distinction Between Assent and Objection." *Houston Law Review*, Volume 28, pp. 15–61 (1991).

―――. "Competency to Consent to Voluntary Hospitalization: A Therapeutic Jurisprudence Analysis of *Zinermon v. Burch*." *International Journal of Law and Psychiatry*, Volume 14, pp. 169–214 (1991).

―――. "Harnessing the Power of the Bet: Wagering with the Government as a Mechanism for Social and Individual Change." *University of Miami Law Review*, Volume 45, pp. 737–816 (1991).

---

* Articles co-authored by Professor Bruce J Winick and David B. Wexler are listed only under David B. Wexler and Bruce J. Winick.

———. "Voluntary Hospitalization after *Zinermon v. Burch*: Possible Antitherapeutic Consequences Following a Supreme Court Ruling." *Psychiatric Annals*, Volume 21, pp. 584–589 (1991).

———. "Competency to be Executed: A Therapeutic Jurisprudence Perspective." *Behavioral Sciences and the Law*, Volume 10, pp. 317–337 (1992).

———. "On Autonomy: Legal and Psychological Perspectives." *Villanova Law Review*, Volume 37, pp. 1705–1777 (1992).

———. "New Directions in the Right to Refuse Mental Health Treatment: The Implications of *Riggins v. Nevada*." *William and Mary Bill of Rights Journal*, Volume 2, pp. 205–238 (1993).

———. "Presumptions and Burdens of Proof in Determining Competency to Stand Trial: An Analysis of *Medina v. California* and the Supreme Court's New Due Process Methodology in Criminal Cases." *University of Miami Law Review*, Volume 47, pp. 817–866 (1993).

———. "Psychotropic Medication in the Criminal Trial Process: The Constitutional and Therapeutic Implications of *Riggins v. Nevada*." *New York Law School Journal of Human Rights*, Volume 10, pp. 637–709 (1993).

———. "Rethinking the Health Care Delivery Crisis: The Need for a Therapeutic Jurisprudence." *Journal of Law and Health*, Volume 7, pp. 49–54 (1993).

———. "How to Handle Voluntary Hospitalization After *Zinermon v. Burch*." *Administration and Policy in Mental Health*, Volume 21, pp. 395–406 (1994).

———. "The Right to Refuse Mental Health Treatment: A Therapeutic Jurisprudence Analysis." *International Journal of Law and Psychiatry*, Volume 17, pp. 99–118 (1994).

———. "Ambiguities in the Legal Meaning and Significance of Mental Illness." *Psychology, Public Policy, and Law*, Volume 1, pp. 534–611 (1995).

———. "Reforming Incompetency to Stand Trial and Plead Guilty: A Restated Proposal and a Response to Professor Bonnie." *Journal of Criminal Law and Criminology*, Volume 85, pp. 571–624 (1995).

———. "The Side Effects of Incompetency Labeling and the Implications for Mental Health Law." *Psychology, Public Policy, and Law*, Volume 1, pp. 6–42 (1995).

———. "Incompetency to Proceed in the Criminal Process: Past, Present, and Future." In *Law, Mental Health, and Mental Disorder*, edited by Bruce D. Sales and Daniel W. Shuman, pp. 310–340. Pacific Grove: Brooks/Cole Publishing Company (1996).

———. "The MacArthur Treatment Competence Study: Legal and Therapeutic Implications." *Psychology, Public Policy, and Law*, Volume 2, (forthcoming, 1996).

———. "The Psychotherapist-Patient Privilege: A Therapeutic Jurisprudence View." *University of Miami Law Review*, Volume 50, pp. 249–265 (1996).

———. "When Treatment is Punishment: Eighth Amendment Limits on Mental Health and Correctional Therapy." *Criminal Law Bulletin*, Volume 32, pp. 211–243 (1996).

———. "The Jurisprudence of Therapeutic Jurisprudence." *Psychology, Public Policy, and Law*, Volume 2 (forthcoming 1996).

———. "Advance Directive Instruments for Those with Mental Illness." *University of Miami Law Review*, Volume 51, p. 1 (forthcoming 1996).

Winick, Bruce J., and Francine Cournos, et al. *Consent to Voluntary Hospitalization.* American Psychiatric Association Task Force Report No. 34.

Wisnom, Patricia Monroe. "Probate Law and Mediation: A Therapeutic Perspective." *Arizona Law Review*, Volume 37, pp. 1345–1363 (1995).

Yates, Kathy Faulkner. "Therapeutic Issues Associated with Confidentiality and Informed Consent in Forensic Evaluations." *New England Journal on Civil and Criminal Confinement*, Volume 20, pp. 345–368 (1994).

Zito, Julie Magno, Jozsef Vitrai, and Thomas J. Craig. "Toward a Therapeutic Jurisprudence Analysis of Medication Refusal in the Court Review Model." *Behavioral Sciences and the Law*, Volume 11, pp. 151–163 (1993).

Index